HANDBOOK OF YOUTH MENTORING

THE SAGE PROGRAM ON
APPLIED DEVELOPMENTAL SCIENCE

Consulting Editor

RICHARD M. LERNER

The field of Applied Developmental Science has advanced the use of cutting-edge developmental systems models of human development, fostered strength-based approaches to understanding and promoting positive development across the life span, and served as a frame for collaborations among researchers and practitioners, including policymakers, seeking to enhance the life chances of diverse young people, their families, and communities. The **SAGE Program on Applied Developmental Science** both integrates and extends this scholarship by publishing innovative and cutting-edge contributions.

HANDBOOK OF
YOUTH
MENTORING

EDITED BY

David L. DuBois
University of Illinois at Chicago

Michael J. Karcher
University of Texas at San Antonio

SAGE Publications
Thousand Oaks ▪ London ▪ New Delhi

For information:

 Sage Publications, Inc.
2455 Teller Road
Thousand Oaks, California 91320
E-mail: order@sagepub.com

Sage Publications Ltd.
1 Oliver's Yard
55 City Road
London EC1Y 1SP
United Kingdom

Sage Publications India Pvt. Ltd.
B-42, Panchsheel Enclave
Post Box 4109
New Delhi 110 017 India

Printed in the United States of America.

Library of Congress Cataloging-in-Publication Data

Handbook of youth mentoring / edited by David L. DuBois, Michael J. Karcher.
    p. cm. — (The Sage program on applied developmental science)
Includes bibliographical references and indexes.
ISBN 0-7619-2977-0 (cloth)
    1. Youth—Counseling of—United States. 2. Mentoring—United States.
3. Youth development—United States. 4. Social work with youth—United States.
I. DuBois, David L. II. Karcher, Michael J. III. Series.
HV1431.H3 2005
362.7′083—dc22

                                         2004024566

This book is printed on acid-free paper.

05 06 07 08 09 10 9 8 7 6 5 4 3 2 1

Acquisitions Editor:	Jim Brace-Thompson
Editorial Assistant:	Karen Ehrmann
Production Editor:	Tracy Alpern
Copy Editor:	Carla Freeman
Typesetter:	C&M Digitals (P) Ltd.
Indexer:	Molly Hall
Cover Designer:	Michelle Kenny

CONTENTS

FOREWORD

In 2002, a young man named Ean Garrett told his personal story about the role mentors had played in shaping the first 16 years of his life. He also delivered a powerful call to action, telling a packed room of corporate chieftains and influential policymakers this:

> From the start I was expected to lose. Everything I have right now is mostly because I defied what the world concluded about me before I could even speak a word in my defense. And my defense is that I am just as capable as any person to do great things. Like you, I think about all the things this world could achieve if only every child was given the right tools. Mentoring is the right tool and it is the way to the American Dream.

Since its founding in 1990 by Geoff Boisi and Ray Chambers, the leaders of MENTOR have been strong and unequivocal advocates for mentoring as an essential tool for leveraging positive youth development. We have been equally strong and unequivocal in our support for taking a critical approach to the task of ensuring that the practice of mentoring is guided by the best available theory and research. But the challenge therein was this: The body of research that existed was neither as plentiful nor as substantive as the research that undergirds many other comparable fields of practice. In addition, the high-quality research that did exist was not easily accessible to a young and markedly fluid group of practitioners nor to an emerging cadre of policy analysts and policymakers.

With the publication of *Handbook of Youth Mentoring,* David DuBois and Michael Karcher have thoughtfully and thoroughly addressed this challenge. They, along with the exceptional scholars and thinkers they have gathered, offer readers both an aerial and a close-up view of virtually every dimension of mentoring in the 21st century.

The aerial view quickly emerges from reviewing the table of contents, which reveals the scope of the issues covered, ranging from the theoretical underpinnings of mentoring to the nature of both formal and informal mentoring relationships to the contexts or settings in which mentoring occurs. Most important, a perusal of the table of contents underscores the dominant and vitally important theme of the book: why good research is central to good programming and good policy making.

The close-up view is delivered in a series of 36 authoritative chapters. Collectively, these chapters highlight promising theoretical models that can enrich our understanding of the mentoring process, synthesize and critically evaluate extant research, and offer insightful discussions of crucial issues and areas of debate in practice. Importantly, the contributors to this volume also advance specific recommendations regarding many issues that could benefit markedly from either further study or more energetic advocacy.

For example, they underscore repeatedly that we have much to learn about the value of natural mentoring relationships versus those that are established through formalized programs. Although we know a fair amount about how to support formal relationships, we need to know far more about how to help cultivate informal relationships, as well as how to make the mentoring that occurs within such relationships (between a teacher and student, or youth worker and participant in a Boys & Girls Club program, for example) more intentional and, therefore, more effective.

In contrast, the research available on the central role of several fundamental features of mentoring relationships (for example, the existence of a close emotional bond) in facilitating outcomes is extensive and convincing. Yet the all-important issue of translating this knowledge into practice is in a much earlier stage of development. Pressing needs include widely available and easily applied instruments for evaluating relationships' duration, quality, and impact as well as the means for engineering program practices that ensure that high-quality relationships are the norm regardless of the youth population, host setting, or outcomes of interest. In this instance, as in other areas you will read about, we don't need to know more, we need to act more forcefully on the knowledge base that scholars have already developed.

As the pages that follow make clear, mentoring is an ancient form of social intervention with a wide array of very modern applications. The applications that matter most to scholars are those built on a foundation formed by strong theory and exacting research. The applications that matter most to mentoring practitioners and policymakers alike are those that genuinely benefit the young people of this nation and those in countries throughout the world—young people who deserve the very best that we can deliver on their behalf.

Serious researchers, dedicated practitioners, and thoughtful policymakers will all find the rich contents of the *Handbook of Youth Mentoring* to be at once informative, stimulating, and, sometimes, downright provoking. I have no doubt that this remarkable compendium will measurably and decisively help these three distinct groups achieve their complementary aims. So read on, for this is just the kind of book that our evolving field needs to ensure that high-quality youth mentoring—in all its many forms—is not only what we aspire to but also what we *consistently* and *expansively* deliver.

Gail Manza
MENTOR/National Mentoring Partnership

PREFACE

T his volume represents the culmination of several years of planning, writing, and editing in an effort to develop a resource for the field of youth mentoring that would be scholarly yet applied, and that would address the need for a comprehensive and integrative accounting of both the field's progress to date and its most promising future directions. This vision was present from the start, but evolved and took its full shape over the course of the project. Most notably, this process involved the cultivation of a shared commitment with our contributors to create a scholarly account of youth mentoring with all of its limits and potential, without bias or inflated estimates of impact, but with conviction in the merits of its study.

As editors, we embarked on this journey by first charting out what we regarded as the most salient overarching domains or areas within the field of youth mentoring from the perspectives of both science and practice. We next identified the specific topics to which chapters would be devoted within each of these general areas. It is unfortunate, but perhaps an unavoidable circumstance for any newly emerging field, that several potential chapter topics did not "make the cut" at this stage of our planning because in our judgment they currently lack a critical mass of attention from scholars even when applying a somewhat liberal criterion. These topics include some of the newest modalities of mentoring (e.g., group mentoring), mentoring of certain specialized populations (e.g., gay, lesbian, and bisexual youth), and treatments of specific program practices (e.g., mentor supervision). Accordingly, to the extent that we have succeeded in our quest to be comprehensive, it is with the caveat that this has been accomplished by working within the field's existing scholarly base rather than addressing the full scope of concerns that may be important from the broader perspectives of theory and practice. We hope to see this gap narrow as the field matures and grows and thus be notably less evident in future editions of this volume.

We next turned to identifying and recruiting our contributors. For topics benefiting from relatively more investigation, we sought out well-established scholars who have worked within these areas of the youth mentoring literature. In the remaining instances, we broadened our approach to enlist prominent scholars from relevant literatures outside of the mentoring field. In doing so, we hoped to have the volume highlight opportunities for diverse literatures to inform research in newly emerging areas of the field. We were extremely fortunate to enjoy a high rate of acceptance for all of our invitations. The resulting list of contributors is, by any measure, an all-star lineup of individuals with exceptional credentials and records of accomplishment.

Our charge to authors was to provide a thorough, critical, and forward-minded account of theory, research, and practice within the areas of youth mentoring that were the subjects of their chapters. Further guidelines conveyed our desire as editors for a focus on youth mentoring to be maintained throughout the volume. A considerable body of scholarship exists on the mentoring of adults, particularly in the workplace and in educational contexts. Due to the obvious developmental differences involved and the more limited range of purposes associated with programs directed toward adults, we encouraged authors to draw only sparingly on these literatures and to avoid doing so in ways that might become overgeneralized to youth. We also asked authors to take care to distinguish between youth mentoring research and research with youth on related, but distinct, topics so as not to inadvertently create the impression that the knowledge base for the field is more advanced than it really is at present. This, we hoped, would help highlight the work that remains to be done.

Each contribution to this volume benefited from multiple stages of revision and review. As editors, we found the stimulating discussions of theory, research, and practice crafted by our contributors to be rich fodder for reflection and feedback. Believing strongly in the payoffs of these exchanges, we read and provided feedback to each chapter at least three times. We are grateful to all of our contributors for enduring this arduous process, for so graciously tolerating our editorial excesses and eccentricities along the way, and for their more-than-generous commitments of time and energy to their chapters amidst many other competing and important demands.

Other acknowledgments are due as well. We are indebted to Jim Brace-Thompson, Senior Editor at Sage Publications, for his highly able and always patient and understanding stewardship of this project from inception to completion, and to Karen Ehrmann, Tracy Alpern, and Carla Freeman for shepherding us so capably through the submission and production process. We also had the great fortune of working together, a collaboration punctuated by lively and informative exchanges and strengthened by one another's good counsel throughout the many stages of this project. Further thanks are due to the academic programs and institutions with which we have the good fortune to be affiliated, the School of Public Health and Institute for Health Research and Policy at the University of Illinois at Chicago and the College of Education and Human Development at the University of Texas at San Antonio, and to the William T. Grant Foundation and the National Institute of Mental Health for their generous support of our programs of research on youth mentoring. Finally, each of our families deserves our heartfelt appreciation for their patience and understanding during what turned out to be a far more demanding undertaking than either of us had anticipated. To our spouses, Natalie and Sara, we offer special thanks for so tirelessly supporting our labors in both spirit and deed.

David L. DuBois

Michael J. Karcher

Sage Publications wishes to acknowledge the following reviewers:

Sharon G. Portwood
Department of Psychology
University of Missouri–Kansas City

Michael Nakkula
Risk and Prevention Program
Harvard Graduate School of Education

Marc Zimmerman
School of Public Health
University of Michigan

Hardin Coleman
Department of Counseling Psychology
University of Wisconsin–Madison

Craig A. Mason
Child LINK
University of Maine

We dedicate this handbook to the older and wiser ones in our lives.

To my parents, J. Howard and Gwyneth, with a deep debt of gratitude for their guidance, love, and support, and to Bill Friedman, Bart Hirsch, Robert Felner, and Lizette Peterson, mentors par excellence of my professional development one and all.

—D. L. D.

To my uncle Alberto Mijangos who saw and nurtured the artist in my brother Kenneth Karcher, and to Mike Nakkula, Chuck Woehler, and Hardin Coleman who continue to influence my personal, spiritual, and professional life in countless and immeasurable ways.

—M. J. K.

PART I

INTRODUCTION

1

YOUTH MENTORING

Theory, Research, and Practice

DAVID L. DUBOIS AND MICHAEL J. KARCHER

INTRODUCTION

The concept of mentoring youth can be traced back nearly three millennia to its namesake character, "Mentor," in Homer's *Odyssey*. Despite this extensive history, its remarkable surge in popularity during the past decade is clearly unprecedented. More than 4,500 agencies and programs in the United States now provide mentoring services for youth (Rhodes, 2002). Similar programs and initiatives are increasingly appearing in other countries as well, thus offering a growing global dimension to the youth mentoring movement. Undergirding these trends is the widely held belief by the public that supportive relationships between young people and nonparental adults, whether established via programs or through more informal connections, represent assets vital for positive youth development (Scales, 2003).

Historically, the mentoring movement in this country was sparked by localized grassroots initiatives. More recently, however, its base of support has expanded to include the involvement of a growing array of not-for-profit organizations, corporations, and legislative initiatives at state and national levels. Organizations such as MENTOR/National Mentoring Partnership and the National Mentoring Center offer a wealth of resources to individuals and organizations interested in mentoring and serve as advocates for the field's expansion. Over the past 10 years, MENTOR/National Mentoring Partnership (2004b) also has established state and local Mentoring Partnerships in 23 states and 15 urban centers. Corporations increasingly are sponsors of large-scale mentoring initiatives involving their employees or having direct ties to their services. Illustratively, the "Digital Heroes Campaign" was launched in 2002 with the support of *People* magazine, AOL, and the Waitt Family Foundation (headed by the founder of Gateway Computers) to use the Internet as a vehicle for noteworthy Americans to provide mentoring to underserved youth nationwide (Digital Heroes Campaign, 2002). In the meantime, governmental support for mentoring has risen to record levels. This growth was punctuated by President George W. Bush's announcement during his State of the Union address in 2003 of a plan for a massive $450 million expansion of mentoring programs for youth. The first installment of this plan was passed in fiscal year 2004, with $50 million allotted for school-based mentoring programs through the Department of Education and another $50 million for the Department of Health and Human Services Mentoring for Children of Prisoners program

(MENTOR/National Mentoring Partnership, 2004a).

As the practice of youth mentoring gains momentum, it is critical that the field's further growth and development be informed by theory and research (Rhodes & DuBois, 2004). Studies of resilience among youth from at-risk backgrounds first alerted scholars to the protective functions that can be fulfilled by relationships with nonparental adults (Werner, 1995). These findings were coupled with convincing demonstrations of the benefits that nonprofessional and para-professional helping relationships can provide, often rivaling those associated with services provided by therapists and other professionals with advanced training (Orford, 1992). It is only in recent years, however, that youth mentoring has begun to receive sustained interest from scholars working in fields such as psychology, sociology, education, human development, social work, public health, and medicine. The multidisciplinary nature of this work is in many ways a boon for the field's knowledge base. At the same time, the dispersion of scholarship across literatures from numerous disciplines poses significant challenges for both researchers and practitioners. For researchers whose disciplinary boundaries limit regular exposure to one another's work, opportunities for synergy within and across different areas of inquiry can be difficult to identify and thus in many instances may go undetected and unexplored. For practitioners, "one-stop shopping" for definitive accounts of existing scholarship and its applied implications has been difficult to come by, thus compromising the capacity for intervention and policy efforts to profit from available theory and research.

These concerns underscore the need for a single source of cross-disciplinary, integrative, and comprehensive accounts of theory, research, and practice in the field of youth mentoring. *Handbook of Youth Mentoring* was undertaken with the aim of addressing this need. The *Handbook* is divided into seven sections. The first section includes a historical overview by Baker and Maguire, followed by several foundational chapters pertaining to theory, research, and practice. Subsequent sections focus on mentoring relationships, developmental and cultural perspectives on mentoring, and formal mentoring programs. Separate sections also are devoted to mentoring within different contexts of youth development as well as mentoring for specific populations of youth. The *Handbook* concludes with a collection of chapters that address topics of importance to public policy and youth mentoring.

There are several common organizational features across chapters in the *Handbook*. With only a few exceptions, the main body of each chapter is organized around separate sections addressing theory, research, and practice issues. All chapters, furthermore, conclude with a brief synthesis and separate sets of recommendations for research and practice.

In the remainder of this introductory chapter, we first briefly consider definitions of mentoring as well as the prevalence and scope of current forms of youth mentoring that are addressed in the *Handbook*. We then discuss the significance of theory, research, and practice and their interrelationship to the field, drawing on contributions to the *Handbook* as illustrations. We conclude by highlighting the need for scholarship to keep pace with the fast-expanding and evolving practice of youth mentoring.

DEFINITIONS, PREVALENCE, AND SCOPE

Definitions

A shared understanding of what is meant by the terms *mentoring* and *mentor* is clearly important for purposes of this *Handbook* and for development of the field of youth mentoring more generally. Even a brief perusal of the literature reveals no shortage of proposed definitions for either construct. A representative, but by no means exhaustive, sampling of such descriptions is provided in Table 1.1. Recurring themes in these and other conceptualizations that have appeared in the literature suggest a consensus regarding at least three core elements of mentoring (cf. Freedman, 1992). First, the mentor is someone with greater *experience* or wisdom than the mentee. Second, the mentor offers *guidance* or instruction that is intended to facilitate the growth and development of the mentee. Third, there is an *emotional bond* between mentor and mentee, a hallmark of which is a sense of trust.

Table 1.1   Definitions of Mentoring and Mentor

Mentoring

"Mentoring is a structured and trusting relationship that brings young people together with caring individuals who offer guidance, support, and encouragement aimed at developing the competence and character of the mentee." (MENTOR/National Mentoring Partnership, 2003a)

". . . a relationship between an older, more experienced adult and an unrelated, younger protégé—a relationship in which the adult provides ongoing guidance, instruction, and encouragement aimed at developing the competence and character of the protégé." (Rhodes, 2002, p. 3)

". . . a powerful emotional interaction between an older and younger person, a relationship in which the older member is trusted, loving, and experienced in the guidance of the younger. The mentor helps shape the growth and development of the protégé." (Merriam, 1983, p. 162)

Mentor

"A wise and trusted counselor or teacher." (*American Heritage Dictionary of the English Language,* 1976)

"A mentor is an older, more experienced person who seeks to further the development of character and competence in a younger person by guiding the latter in acquiring mastery of progressively more complex skills and tasks in which the mentor is already proficient. The guidance is accomplished through demonstration, instruction, challenge, and encouragement on a more or less regular basis over an extended period of time. In the course of this process, the mentor and the young person develop a special bond of mutual commitment. In addition, the young person's relationship to the mentor takes on an emotional character of respect, loyalty, and identification." (U. Bronfenbrenner, personal communication, September 1988; cited in Hamilton & Hamilton, 2004)

"The mentor is ordinarily several years older, a person of greater experience and seniority in the world the young mentee is entering. This person acts as teacher, sponsor, counselor, developer of skills and intellect, host, guide, exemplar and one who supports and facilitates the realization of the young mentee's dream." (University of South Florida, 2003; adapted from Levinson, Darrow, Klein, Levinson, & McKee, 1978)

Beyond these foundational concepts, there are a multitude of areas in which the conceptual boundaries of mentoring are decidedly fuzzier and less well articulated. For example, must the mentor be older than the mentee? If so, by how many years? Can mentors be paid? Must relationships be sustained for some minimum period of time to constitute mentoring? If so, for how long? And with specific relevance to mentoring youth, what range of ages or developmental stages of young persons does this concept encompass? What degree of relation, if any, can exist between mentors and youth? Indeed, with the exception of Rhodes (2002), none of the definitions in Table 1.1 explicitly includes parents as mentors, although this appears to be an assumption held by most scholars and practitioners in the field.

From our perspective, these unresolved issues are indicative of the youth mentoring literature's early stage of development. Only with the articulation of more detailed and elaborated theories of mentoring and empirical investigation of the processes and outcomes that are posited in those theories will progress be able to made in refining our conceptualizations of the construct. We are reminded in this regard of Cronbach and Meehl's proposition in their classic paper on construct validity: "A construct is defined implicitly as a network of associations or propositions in which it occurs. Constructs employed at different stages of research vary in definiteness" (see Meehl, 1973, p. 30). Applied to youth mentoring, it thus becomes understandable that at this stage of the literature's development, definitions of the construct lack a high degree of specificity or precision. As researchers continue to articulate and test theories in ways that reflect differing assumptions about what mentoring does and does not encompass, greater clarity will be forthcoming. Thus, if predictions that are made about the processes and outcomes that occur when mentoring youth prove tenable under only certain conditions but not others (e.g., mentors are volunteers, but not when they are paid), then the construct may be appropriately narrowed in scope. Conversely, when support for theoretical predictions about what occurs while mentoring youth is found across a wide spectrum of conditions (e.g., regardless of whether mentors are or are not family members), our construct definition would be broadened accordingly. These considerations foreshadow our principal conclusion that the field of youth mentoring is ripe for a strong injection of the types of theory and research that are described throughout this *Handbook*.

Prevalence and Scope

As noted at the outset of this chapter, thousands of agencies and programs now identify themselves as providing mentoring to youth. Big Brothers Big Sisters of America (Big Brothers Big Sisters, 2004) alone currently includes approximately 500 agencies serving more than 5,000 communities across the country. Added to this number are more than 4,000 individual mentoring programs that operate outside of this organization (Manza, 2003). The organizational, corporate, and governmental initiatives described previously promise continued expansion of the field in the foreseeable future.

Findings from recent surveys of nationally representative samples of adults and youth also provide insight into the prevalence of mentoring relationships. In a survey of a sample of 2,000 adults in the United States conducted by the AOL Time Warner Foundation (2002), approximately 1 in 3 respondents (34%) indicated that they had provided mentoring to a young person during the past year. Similar results were obtained in another national survey of adults conducted by the Commonwealth Fund (McLearn, Colasanto, & Schoen, 1998). In this survey, 31% of respondents reported having been a mentor to a child or young person at some point in his or her life, and 1 in 7 (14%) reported

currently being involved in a mentoring relationship. From the perspective of youth, analyses of data from 3,187 participants aged 18 to 26 in the national Add Health study revealed that 7 of 10 respondents viewed themselves as having benefited from a significant relationship with a nonparental adult (DuBois & Silverthorn, in press-b). The average relationship was between 9 and 10 years in duration, thus encompassing a substantial portion of the young person's development.

All told, program and relationship data suggest that considerable progress is being made toward reaching the goal initially articulated by leaders of MENTOR/National Mentoring Partnership at the country's first national conference on mentoring in 1990, and later amplified by General Colin Powell's America's Promise Campaign: that the lives of all youth in our country (and, we would argue, others countries as well) should be strengthened and enriched by an ongoing relationship with at least one mentor or other caring adult (America's Promise: The Alliance for Youth, 1999; G. Manza, personal communication, August 31, 2004). The scope of programs and relationships that comprise the current landscape of mentoring, however, is equally important to consider. As the growth in mentoring's popularity unfolds, the traditional one-on-one community-based model of mentoring embodied in programs such as Big Brothers Big Sisters is giving way to a proliferation of alternative approaches that make use of varying configurations of persons (e.g., group mentoring, team mentoring, cross-age peer mentoring), sites (e.g., schools, workplace, faith-based organizations), and modes of communication (e.g., Internet). Indeed, the most recent estimates indicate that programs employing a community-based model are now only slightly more common (54%) than those in which mentoring activities are site based (Manza, 2003). Indeed, Big Brothers Big Sisters of America recently expanded their services to include site-based mentoring in schools and to support older peer as well as adult mentors (Hansen, 2003).

Similar diversity in the sources and types of mentoring relationships that adults and youth report is readily apparent in the findings of the national surveys referred to previously. In the AOL Time Warner Foundation (2002) survey, only approximately one third of those who indicated that they had provided mentoring to a young person (11% of the overall sample) reported having done so in affiliation with an organization or program. The other two thirds of this group (23% of the overall sample) reported mentoring through less structured avenues, often referred to as "natural mentoring relationships" (see Zimmerman, Bingenheimer, & Behrendt, this volume). Furthermore, among those who did report mentoring in association with an organization, only a minority (1.2% of the overall sample) reported having done so on a one-to-one basis through a formal, structured program such as Big Brothers Big Sisters. Reports of mentoring youth in a group situation and in the context of programs with more broadly defined purposes were both commonplace. Thus, whereas findings from this survey were extrapolated to estimate that 2.5 million youth are currently involved in one-to-one formal/structured mentoring relationships, the same process yields an estimate of 68.7 million youth in other types of mentoring relationships (most likely, both of these estimates are inflated by the reality that many individual youth receive mentoring from multiple adults, but the comparison between them should not be unduly biased by this circumstance).

Findings from the two other national surveys are consistent with these trends. In the Commonwealth Fund survey (McLearn et al., 1998), respondents were much more likely to report that their mentoring relationships with youth were established through informal contacts with young persons through neighborhood, family, or other connections (83% of the sample) than through formal, structured programs (17%). The overwhelming majority of the mentors reported by participants in the Add Health study similarly were either members of their extended families or persons with whom they likely came into contact through the natural course of their daily activities in arenas such as school, work, extracurricular programs, or informal socializing with friends and neighbors (DuBois & Silverthorn, in press-a).

In sum, a wide range of programs and relationships are encompassed by current estimates of the prevalence of youth mentoring. As editors, we regard this diversity as a positive indication of the broad potential relevance of mentoring to youth development and, as noted previously, a realistic sign that the field is still in the process of defining its boundaries. More specifically, available data underscore the importance of recognizing the potential for youth mentoring to occur not only within relationships that are established through formal programs but also through naturally occurring ties that involve existing members of the youth's social network. We would argue on similar grounds for the value of conceptualizations that are flexible enough to accommodate not only adults of varying ages but also older peers as mentors, as well as the wide range of potential variations in mentoring that may be observed as a function of factors such as location or setting, the number of persons involved, predominant activities and goals, and relationship duration.

The *Handbook*'s contents reflect this broad and inclusive conceptualization of youth mentoring. A chapter by Zimmerman and colleagues, for example, is dedicated to an in-depth examination of natural mentoring relationships (i.e., those not arranged through formal programs). Numerous other chapters address newly emerging program models, such as e-mentoring (Miller & Griffiths), cross-age peer mentoring (Karcher), and intergenerational mentoring (Taylor, LoSciuto, & Porcellini), as well as mentoring relationships and programs that are tied to particular contexts, such as educational settings (Portwood & Ayers), after-school programs (Hirsch & Wong), work and service-learning (Hamilton & Hamilton), and faith-based organizations (Maton, Sto. Domingo, & King). The remaining contributions, furthermore, consistently address a wide range of facets and dimensions of mentoring that are relevant to their topics. It is our hope that through the earnest application of theory and research in the directions highlighted within the *Handbook,* the diversity currently encompassed by the concept of youth mentoring will be further elaborated and clarified in ways that extend understanding of the construct beyond the three core elements we referred to previously.

THEORY, RESEARCH, AND PRACTICE

Theory

To date, there have been only limited efforts to articulate theoretical models of youth mentoring. The most noteworthy model has been proposed by Rhodes (2002). As Rhodes describes in one of the *Handbook*'s foundational chapters, this model posits several general categories of processes that may be important in mediating and moderating the effects of mentoring relationships on youth outcomes. The model is used by chapter authors throughout the *Handbook* to inform theoretical discussions of mentoring. These efforts are complemented by the consideration of a wide range of theoretical viewpoints from outside of the mentoring literature. The latter perspectives serve to direct attention to processes and outcomes of mentoring that may be uniquely important when focusing on particular types of programs, contexts, and populations of youth.

By drawing on such literatures, contributors are able to formulate more fine-grained hypotheses. In several instances, these hypotheses are further integrated into a conceptual framework or model specific to the program, context, or population involved. Examples of such frameworks can be found in chapters that address mentoring in the contexts of faith-based organizations (Maton, Sto. Domingo, & King) and after-school programs (Hirsch & Wong); integration of mentoring with other programs and other services (Kuperminc et al.); and the mentoring of academically at-risk youth (Larose & Tarabulsy) and juvenile offenders (Blechman & Bopp).

Research

The importance of establishing a strong knowledge base for the field of youth mentoring through programmatic research is emphasized throughout the *Handbook*. A key requirement in this regard is adherence to rigorous standards of inquiry. A foundational chapter by DuBois and Silverthorn provides a set of general principles and guidelines for methodological rigor in research on youth mentoring. Methodological issues relating to the topics of relationship assessment (Nakkula & Harris), program evaluation (Grossman), and cost-benefit analysis (Yates) also receive in-depth treatment in separate chapters. Throughout the *Handbook,* research findings that fall within the scope of individual chapters are critically evaluated and synthesized. These reviews serve to highlight numerous emerging areas of knowledge and understanding within the field. Of equal note, however, each review inevitably reveals an array of limitations and gaps in extant research and thus highlights important issues in need of further investigation.

Practice

Practice and policy issues receive thoughtful attention throughout the *Handbook* as well. A foundational chapter by Sipe provides an overview of efforts to develop reliable and valid typologies of mentoring programs as well as the different types of mentoring relationships commonly observed by practitioners. Further chapters are dedicated to issues involved in developing a mentoring program (Weinberger), strategies for recruiting and sustaining volunteer mentors (Stukas & Tanti), and a social policy analysis of youth mentoring (Walker). As noted, with few exceptions, all chapters in the *Handbook* include a section dedicated to practice issues. These discussions provide informative and critical overviews of prevailing trends in mentoring practice that are germane to the topics addressed by each chapter. Noteworthy innovations are highlighted and illustrated through descriptions of practices within specific programs and organizations. The recommendations for practice at the conclusion of each chapter build on these discussions by proposing concrete actions that can be taken by those in program administration and policy roles to promote effective mentoring of youth.

Interrelationship of Theory, Research, and Practice

Theory, research, and practice within the field of youth mentoring are revealed throughout the *Handbook* to be mutually informing

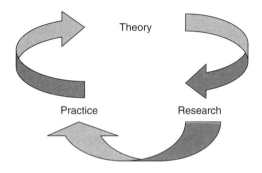

Figure 1.1   Interrelationship of Theory,
Research, and Practice in Youth
Mentoring

and facilitative. Ideally, this interdependence assumes the form of a cycle similar to that depicted in Figure 1.1, in which the primary linkages are from theory to research and from research to practice. The former reflects the pivotal role of theory in facilitating more conceptually sophisticated and informative research on youth mentoring. The latter represents the essential contribution of a rigorous, evidence-based orientation to ensuring safe and effective practice throughout all stages of program development, evaluation, and dissemination (see DuBois & Silverthorn, this volume). These linkages are essential for the successful advancement of the field's knowledge base and, ultimately, for ensuring that beneficial forms of mentoring are made widely available to youth.

At present, interrelationships between theory, research, and practice are lacking in many important respects and thus in need of greater cultivation. Collectively, the different chapters in this *Handbook* make significant inroads toward addressing this limitation. The theoretical perspectives and models that are introduced in each chapter offer a rich interpretive lens for reviewing empirical findings as well as a template for bringing into relief important gaps in the extant literature. Results of available investigations, in turn, are utilized to guide critical evaluation of existing programs and procedures and to generate evidence-based guidelines for future practice. Completing the cycle, innovative

trends in practice highlight promising new avenues for theory and research.

From Theory to Research

Throughout the *Handbook,* authors draw creatively from diverse theoretical perspectives and disciplines to highlight promising directions for research on youth mentoring. Spencer and Rhodes, for example, draw attention to the comparative wealth of theory (and supporting research) within the counseling and psychotherapy literatures and its potential to inform the investigation of topics that are of shared concern for youth mentoring, such as mechanisms of change in relationships and effects of training and supervision. Keller similarly draws upon theories of close relationships and their dynamics over time to articulate an agenda for research on the developmental stages of youth mentoring relationships. Sánchez and Colón utilize theories that address the role of culture in development and interpersonal relationships to argue for more in-depth and process-oriented research on race and ethnicity within youth mentoring. Barrera and Bonds articulate a range of untapped potential applications of social support theory within youth mentoring research. Cavell and Smith effectively mine the areas of prevention science and developmental psychopathology to illustrate their potential to inform investigations of how mentoring may benefit preadolescent children. In a companion chapter, Darling applies both developmental and ecological theories to identify a range of important issues meriting investigation in the mentoring of adolescents.

Collectively, these contributions represent an important advance in forging the strong conceptual foundations that are needed to guide future empirical investigations within different areas of the field. In nearly all instances, it is too early to evaluate which specific avenues are most likely to prove fruitful in terms of yielding increased knowledge and understanding of youth mentoring. Although many of the theories discussed have received empirical support in other contexts, their applicability to youth mentoring will require careful and thoughtful investigation.

From Research to Practice

Those in practice and policy roles depend on credible scientific evidence regarding youth mentoring to guide their decision making. Bringing the practice of mentoring into alignment with a solid research base is critically important not only for maximizing the potential good that mentors and mentoring interventions can do, but also for ensuring that they *do no harm*. Indeed, whereas much fanfare has been made of the potential benefits of youth mentoring, comparatively little attention has been paid to its potential risks (Rhodes, 2002). Several chapters in the *Handbook* provide authoritative overviews of procedures and tools that are available to facilitate a strong linkage between research and practice. Grossman, for example, provides a wealth of practical recommendations for navigating the wide range of issues relating to study design, measurement, and data analysis that must be taken into account in evaluation research to obtain accurate and defensible estimates of program impact. Yates, likewise, details guidelines for addressing the many challenges and complexities that are involved in attempting to generate reliable estimates of program cost and then incorporate these into cost-benefit and cost-effectiveness analyses. Finally, Coyne, Duffy, and Wandersman describe how recently developed evidence-based accountability tools may be used as comprehensive resources for informing the planning, design, and evaluation of mentoring interventions.

Another recurring theme throughout the *Handbook* is the manner in which available research directs attention to opportunities and challenges involved with mentoring youth that are specific to particular types of programs, relationships, contexts, and populations. Those associated with mentoring of specialized populations of youth are illustrative in this regard. Because traditional models of mentoring may not extend directly to these groups and because they may be especially susceptible to negative impacts of poor-quality relationships or programs, research that helps illuminate approaches that have the promise of being safe and effective for such populations is critically important. Contributions

to the *Handbook* detail, for example, how research is being used to inform the development of mentoring programs that are tailored to the unique needs of pregnant and parenting teens (Pike) as well as those of abused and neglected youth (Britner & Kraimer-Rickaby). McDonald, Balcazar, and Keys similarly draw on their systematic review of research on the mentoring of youth with disabilities to inform their discussion of the use of mentoring to promote skill development for this population in areas such as communication and independent living. Callahan and Kyburg utilize available research on the mentoring of talented and gifted youth to similar advantage. These and other contributors to the *Handbook* demonstrate the potential that exists to derive informed judgments about mentoring practice based on careful consideration of even the limited amounts of empirical investigation that are characteristic of many areas of the literature.

Ultimately, well-controlled studies of program efficacy, in combination with analyses of cost-effectiveness and cost-benefit, will be required to establish a strong empirical foundation for practice within different areas of the field. This foundation, however, remains in a very early stage of development. It is not clear, for example, that any mentoring program for youth can be regarded as having established efficacy or effectiveness according to criteria recently adopted by the broader field of prevention (DuBois & Silverthorn). Similar limitations apply to initial efforts to derive estimates of cost-benefit and cost-effectiveness (Yates).

From Practice to Theory

Opportunities for practice to inform theory are readily apparent throughout the *Handbook* as well. Bogat and Liang, for example, discuss how interest in gender-specific approaches to mentoring has yielded a number of innovative programs and practices that could help guide theory development in this area. Similarly, the international perspective afforded by chapters that focus on the practice of youth mentoring in the United Kingdom and Europe (Liabø, Lucas, & Roberts) as well as in Australia and

New Zealand (Evans, Jory, & Dawson) cast a light on gaps in the U.S. theoretical literature that heretofore have gone unaddressed.

CONCLUSIONS

The trends described in this chapter convey an imbalance between research and practice in the field of youth mentoring, in which developments in practice have outstripped the research community's ability to keep pace and provide sufficient guidance. This imbalance can be traced to the explosive growth in youth mentoring programs of all kinds and across diverse contexts in recent years, contrasted with the much more slowly evolving status of corresponding scholarly work. Despite noteworthy efforts to make useful guides for practice available to those pursuing mentoring initiatives in schools, communities, and youth-serving agencies, these resources are based largely on commonsense and trial-and-error experiences in the field rather than on sound empirical evidence. Aside from curtailing opportunities to realize the full scope of the potential benefits of mentoring, the present circumstances amplify the risk for both unintended and undetected adverse outcomes, as referred to previously.

Although clearly formidable, the challenge of bringing research into alignment with practice can be tackled strategically on several fronts. First, areas in most pressing need of scholarly attention can be identified and prioritized for investigation. The remainder of the *Handbook* addresses this need by bringing limitations in the field's knowledge base into sharp relief and by articulating promising directions for future research to address these gaps. Further guidance is available in the form of a recently proposed National Research Agenda for Youth Mentoring (Rhodes & DuBois, 2004), an outgrowth of the 2003 National Research Summit on Mentoring (MENTOR/National Mentoring Partnership, 2003b). Second, there can be a concerted effort made for research and evaluation efforts to ascend to new levels of methodological rigor and theoretical sophistication. The primers on state-of-the-art methodology and the cutting-edge conceptualizations that

are featured in the *Handbook* provide a valuable set of blueprints for progress in this area. Third, researchers can help ensure the applied relevance of their work by forging strong collaborations with those in practice and policy roles. The mutually informing linkages between theory, research, and practice that are highlighted in the *Handbook* provide strong impetus for all involved to commit their time and energies to forging these types of arrangements.

Finally, there can be a coordinated effort to increase the availability of funding for research on youth mentoring. To date, investigations have been supported primarily on an ad hoc basis through general-purpose funding mechanisms of governmental agencies and private foundations. Funding earmarked for youth mentoring, such as the initiatives described at the start of this chapter, with only rare exceptions has been directed toward expanding the practice base of the field rather than programmatic research or rigorous evaluation. To the extent that this trend continues, growth in the practice of youth mentoring that is disproportionate to its supporting research base can be expected to continue, and result in a widening of the gulf between them. In an effort to remedy this situation, the national research agenda referred to previously recommends that governmental and private sources be used to establish dedicated streams of funding to support rigorous scholarship on youth mentoring (Rhodes & DuBois, 2004). Priority areas for funding include a multisite consortium study of youth mentoring program effectiveness, a national longitudinal study of youth mentoring relationships, and development of a standardized system to increase the quality of program accountability and evaluation efforts throughout the field. In many ways, this *Handbook* can be regarded as a prospectus for investment in research on youth mentoring that is linked to the concerns and needs of the practice community. All of us stand to share in the dividends that will result from having a stronger scientific foundation to inform our mentoring of this and future generations of youth.

REFERENCES

The American Heritage Dictionary of the English Language (New College Ed.). (1976). Boston: Houghton Mifflin.

America's Promise: The Alliance for Youth. (1999). *Report to the nation: 1999.* Alexandria, VA: Author.

AOL Time Warner Foundation. (2002). *Mentoring in America 2002.* New York: Author. Retrieved July 20, 2004, from http://mentoring.web.aol.com/common/one_report/national_poll_report_final.pdf

Big Brothers Big Sisters. (2004). *Frequently asked questions.* Retrieved July 21, 2004, from http://www.bbbsa.org/site/pp.asp?c=iuJ3JgO2F&b=14603

Digital Heroes. (2002). *The Digital Heroes campaign.* Retrieved July 18, 2004, from http://www.digitalheroes.org/dhc/

DuBois, D. L., & Silverthorn, N. (in press-a). Characteristics of natural mentoring relationships and adolescent adjustment: Evidence from a national study. *Journal of Primary Prevention.*

DuBois, D. L., & Silverthorn, N. (in press-b). Natural mentoring relationships and adolescent health: Evidence from a national study. *American Journal of Public Health.*

Freedman, M. (1992). *The kindness of strangers: Reflections on the mentoring movement.* Philadelphia: Public/Private Ventures.

Hamilton, S. F., & Hamilton, M. A. (2004). Contexts for mentoring: Adolescent-adult relationships in workplaces and communities. In R. M. Lerner & L. Steinberg (Eds.), *Handbook of adolescent psychology* (pp. 395–428). New York: Wiley.

Hansen, K. (2003). *Big Brothers Big Sisters High School Bigs Evaluation for School Year 2002–2003.* Philadelphia: Big Brothers Big Sisters of America.

Levinson, D. J., Darrow, D., Klein, E. B., Levinson, M. H., & McKee, J. B. (1978). *The seasons of a man's life.* New York: Knopf.

Manza, G. (2003, October). *The state of mentoring 2003.* Paper presented at 2003 National Research Summit on Mentoring, Kansas City, MO.

McLearn, K. T., Colasanto, D., & Schoen, C. (1998). *Mentoring makes a difference: Findings From the Commonwealth Fund 1998 Survey of Adults Mentoring Young People.* New York: The Commonwealth Fund. Retrieved July 18, 2004, from http://www.cmwf.org/programs/child/mclea277.asp

Meehl, P. E. (1973). *Psychodiagnosis: Selected papers.* New York: Norton.

MENTOR/National Mentoring Partnership. (2003a). *Elements of effective practice* (2nd ed.). Alexandria, VA: Author.

MENTOR/National Mentoring Partnership. (2003b). *National Research Summit on Mentoring.* Retrieved August 1, 2004, from http://www.mentoring.org/summit/wg.htm

MENTOR/National Mentoring Partnership. (2004a). *$450 million dollars for mentoring: Issue brief.* Retrieved July 18, 2004, from http://www.mentoring.org/take_action/hot_issues/president/index.adp

MENTOR/National Mentoring Partnership. (2004b). *State mentoring partnerships.* Retrieved July 21, 2004, from http://www.mentoring.org/state_partnerships/state_local_profiles.adp?Entry=home

Merriam, S. (1983). Mentors and protégés: A critical review of the literature. *Adult Education Quarterly, 33,* 161–173.

Orford, J. (1992). *Community psychology: Theory and practice.* Chichester, UK: Wiley.

Rhodes, J. E. (2002). *Stand by me: The risks and rewards of mentoring today's youth.* Cambridge, MA: Harvard University Press.

Rhodes, J., & DuBois, D. (2004). *National research agenda for youth mentoring.* Alexandria, VA: MENTOR/National Mentoring Partnership. Retrieved July 14, 2004, from http://www.mentoring.org/research_corner/researchagenda.pdf

Scales, P. C. (2003). *Other people's kids: Social expectations and American adults' involvement with children and adolescents.* New York: Kluwer Academic/Plenum.

University of South Florida. (2003). *Mentoring.* Retrieved August 1, 2004, from http://www.aa.ufl.edu/aa/affact/ummp/mentoring.htm

Werner, E. E. (1995). Resilience in development. *Current Directions in Psychological Science, 4,* 81–85.

PART II

CONCEPTS, FRAMEWORKS, AND FOUNDATIONS

2

MENTORING IN HISTORICAL PERSPECTIVE

DAVID B. BAKER AND COLLEEN P. MAGUIRE

INTRODUCTION

Ask just about anyone whether they have heard of mentoring and they are likely to answer yes. Chances are also good that their impression of mentoring is a positive one. Mentoring invokes an image of an older, wiser adult providing thoughtful and caring guidance to a young person, usually a child or adolescent. It is an image that is fairly accurate. Less accurate, however, is the public perception of the efficacy of mentoring programs (e.g., reducing risk for delinquency and substance use, improving self-esteem, or increasing academic achievement). In fact, most studies on the efficacy of mentoring provide limited support (DuBois, Holloway, Valentine, & Cooper, 2002; Rhodes, 2002). How is it that the public has such faith in a largely unproven intervention? The answer to this question is found in part through an examination of the history of mentoring in America. Although various types of formal and informal mentorship (e.g., apprenticeships) were salient at early points in world history, much of the public's current perception of mentoring can be traced to developments occurring primarily in the 20th century throughout America. In this chapter, mentoring in America is examined through four historical stages of development:

emergence, establishment, divergence, and focus (see Table 2.1). Drawing from this historical perspective, implications for future research and practice are offered.

EMERGENCE

The term *mentor* has a long history dating back to 800 B.C. It was derived from the character "Mentor" in Homer's epic tale *The Odyssey*. Mentor was a trusted friend of Odysseus, the king of Ithaca. When Odysseus went to fight in the Trojan War, Mentor served as friend and council to Odysseus's son Telemachus. The image of the benign helper has been enduring. Indeed, wherever and whenever an older and more mature guide provides direction to a younger charge, it is likely in today's times to be described as mentoring. Rhodes (2002) elaborated on this basic conceptualization to provide the following description of mentoring from a contemporary perspective:

> The term has generally been used in the human services field to describe a relationship between an older, more experienced adult and an unrelated, younger protégé—a relationship in which the adult provides ongoing guidance, instruction, and

Table 2.1   Stages of the Mentoring Movement in America

Stage	Theme
Emergence	Industrialization and urbanization became related to problems of child conduct. Concerned members of society began to recognize the need to intervene with children and young adults in order to prevent and treat delinquency.
Establishment	Formalization and implementation of charitable youth services designed to aid youth through the provision of a caring adult relationship, including the country's first formal mentoring programs (e.g., Big Brothers Big Sisters).
Divergence	Movement of mentoring initiatives away from public charity and toward a science of delinquency and its prevention.
Focus	Better understanding and identification of variables involved in the mentoring process through increased research on mentoring relationships and programs combined with growth in support for mentoring practice through national organizations and policy initiatives.

encouragement aimed at developing the competence and character of the protégé. Over the course of their time together, the mentor and protégé often develop a special bond of mutual commitment, respect, identification, and loyalty which facilitates the youth's transition into adulthood. (p. 3)

It is important for purposes of the present analysis, furthermore, to note that these conceptualizations encompass both mentoring relationships that are formal in the sense of being arranged by programs (e.g., Big Brothers Big Sisters) and those that are informal (e.g., coaches, teachers). In the case of formal mentoring programs, mentors receive training, supervision, and support designed to allow them to fulfill the demands of their role (for more about this, see Rhodes, 2002, and Weinberger, this volume). Informal mentoring, often referred to as "natural mentoring," can be understood as a relationship with a caring nonparental adult that develops spontaneously and fulfills important functions such as guidance, encouragement, and emotional support (see Zimmerman, Bingenheimer, & Behrendt, this volume).

It is noteworthy as well in terms of background for the present analysis to recognize that throughout history, mentoring has been used as an instrument of social learning in which the mentored are inculcated into a particular set of values and practices. These values may be religious, military, political, or vocational. Therefore, the practice of mentoring has been contextually driven, meeting the needs and mirroring the values of the time and place in which it occurs.

Mentoring in America

In America, formal mentoring is largely a 20th-century development, intertwined with the rise of an industrial economy and urban order that was unlike anything ever seen or known before. It is hard to imagine the magnitude of change that took place in America at the beginning of the 20th century. Consider that in 1900, automobiles, airplanes, electricity, and indoor plumbing were new to most people.

The explosion in technology was matched by the explosion of urban centers. America was being defined by burgeoning industrial cities such as Chicago, New York, Boston, and Philadelphia. These city centers drew people from all over the world in search of a better, more prosperous life (Zinn, 1999). Changes in demographics, culture, and capital were believed to be signs of progress, progress that depended on human and mechanical machinery. Mass production appeared as a major achievement of human ingenuity and technological sophistication. However, mass production was useless unless it was efficient. Progress, precision, and efficiency quickly became the central tenants of the new social order that was the Progressive Movement (Johnson, 1997). Those identified as progressives expressed faith in science and technology, tempered by an equal measure of public concern for others. Progressives wanted the government to ensure that societal institutions responded to the needs of all its members. The changing social order provided much fodder for the progressive cause, and followers lobbied for such things as women's suffrage and government regulation of industry. Indeed, the changes in American society raised many concerns.

These concerns were partly a product of the poor social conditions experienced by many immigrants. Those who migrated to America's urban centers often were poor and uneducated. Immigrants from other nations did not know the language or the culture. Exploitation was always a concern, but the new city inhabitants were more often focused on other immediate needs such as employment, food, and shelter. The most susceptible members of this already vulnerable group were children. America, a young nation itself, took a significant interest in its youngest citizens. The result was the child-saving movement, a national commitment to protect children from the ravages of poverty, exploitation, and neglect (Baker, 2002; Davidson & Benjamin, 1987). The impulse toward child saving rallied many individuals and institutions to the protection and defense of children. Children's aid societies flourished, child labor laws were enacted, educational reforms were instituted, and the vocational guidance movement was born (Baker, 2002). Most important for this chapter, this was the setting for the beginning of the juvenile court system and the emergence of the modern mentoring movement in America.

Troubled Youth

If we could travel back in time, we would see that many children suffered great injury and injustice in early-20th-century America. To be a poor child in the city was a tremendous disadvantage that offered multiple hazards. Factory work could easily lead to injury and death; schools seldom noticed or cared whether children dropped out (which many did by sixth grade); and there were few, if any, safeguards in place to protect against the physical, sexual, or emotional abuse of children and adolescents. Add overcrowding, stress, and severe poverty to this picture and there were enough risk factors to create all manner of problems (Levine & Levine, 1992).

One difficulty that became a focal point for social reformers was delinquency. Throughout the 20th century, juvenile delinquency has been used to describe behavior of youth that is deemed socially unacceptable. However, like all such diagnostic terms, it must be considered within the context in which it appears and unfolds.

In 19th-century America, children in trouble with the law could expect incarceration, trial, and sentencing as an adult. Consider the case of 15-year-old Charley Miller (aka "Kansas Charley"). An orphan and transient, Charley shot two teenagers in 1890. Turning himself in to authorities, he was tried, found guilty, sentenced to death, and hanged in 1892. At the time, the American public was divided. There were those who viewed the hanging of Charley as a horrific brutality visited upon a child, and there were those who found it a fair act of justice (Brumberg, 2003).

The crimes and offenses of most poor city youth at the start of the 20th century were far less lethal and noxious. Stealing, smoking, truancy, and related offenses were crimes for which juveniles were routinely brought into the legal system. The number of offenders was high, and the courts were largely ineffective in reducing recidivism. Juvenile delinquency was seen as symptomatic of a larger ill—an early and slow ascent into a vicious cycle of poverty, moral decay, and social decline. It was a vision of wretchedness that had appeal to child savers of all persuasions (Levine & Levine, 1992).

The Juvenile Court

Fears of a cultural and social malaise brought on by the new urban industrial age filtered perceptions about the causes of many social ills, including delinquency. Children who ran afoul of the law most often were seen as victims of circumstance. Their annoying and recalcitrant behavior was considered a by-product of a calamitous and toxic environment not of their making. Ernest Coulter (1871–1952), an icon of the early youth mentoring initiatives, expressed it this way:

> In the Children's Courts appear most clearly all the wrongs and inequalities whereby organized society, selfish and therefore ignorant, warps, thwarts and denies the future citizen. If the child is not to grow up to become a public charge, to fill the charitable institutions, the hospitals, the prisons, he must have light and air and space. Every crowded, ill-ventilated tenement is a tax upon the future. Each too, is a breeding place of parental as well as juvenile delinquency; for each the community is responsible. It has the right, the privilege, the power to correct these evils, but it has not been attending to the conduct of its own affairs. These matters, the massing of the population, the regulation of immigration, the hygienic conditions of the tenements, rents and wages have been left in the hands of those, who profiting by congestion and extortion, have been blind to the rights of our neighbor and his child. Our Children's Courts will do much to help the new awakening. (Coulter, 1913, p. xvi)

The first juvenile court in America was established in Chicago in 1899. A group of socially minded women, including Lucy Flower, Julia Lathrop, and Jane Addams, provided the impetus for the founding of this court. Flower and Lathrup were members of the Chicago Women's Club, a philanthropic organization of affluent women who took an active role in social reform. Jane Addams (1860–1935) was the founder of the settlement home, Hull House. A unique form of social science experiment, settlement homes were residences located in impoverished working-class neighborhoods in cities such as Chicago, Boston, New York, and Philadelphia. Funded by charitable and religious groups and staffed by artists, clergy, professors, and college students, the settlement homes provided for the social, economic, cultural, artistic, and intellectual interests and needs of the communities they served. A centerpiece of the progressive cause, settlement homes enjoyed widespread popularity and support. Indeed, Jane Addams and Hull House became world famous. Addams was

keenly interested in the problems of youth and was particularly angered and outraged by the many cases of destitute young women forced into prostitution (Addams, 1914). She worked tirelessly on behalf of the working poor, and in 1931, she became the first American woman to earn the Nobel Peace Prize.

Addams and other women addressing the juvenile court system set upon the problem of delinquency with great fervor and mission. They personally attended the court and served as guardians and advocates for the court's young charges. Realizing that the need was greater than their numbers, they raised the necessary funds to hire the court's first probation officers. In many ways, these probation officers were among the first mentors of disadvantaged youth in America. They sought to provide caring, guidance, and nurturing to their young charges. Mrs. Joseph T. Bowen, the second president of the Juvenile Court Committee, recalled:

> I think the first probation officer was Mrs. Alzina Stevens, perhaps the best example of what a probation officer should be. Her great desire was to be of use to her fellow-men. Her love of children was great; her singleness of purpose and strength of character so remarkable that she exerted a great influence over the children committed to her charge. I find among some old papers the following concerning the duties of probation officers: "They must be men and women of many sides, endowed with the strength of Samson and the delicacy of an Ariel. They must be tactful, skillful, firm and patient. They must know how to proceed with wisdom and intelligence and must be endowed with that rare virtue—common-sense." These qualities would seem to be needed just as much today as they were twenty-five years ago. (Bowen, 1925, pp. 299–300)

Soon the number of privately supported probation workers grew to more than 20, and they formed the Juvenile Protective Association. These were not trained professionals; rather, they were socially minded individuals who shared a common belief that delinquency resulted from abhorrent circumstances in need of remedy. Describing their efforts, Levine and Levine (1992) reported:

The Juvenile Protection Association thought in preventative terms, identifying conditions in the city that adversely affected the lives of children and young people and acting to correct these conditions. The association worked with the Druggists' Association to induce its members to stop selling indecent postcards; with the Saloon Keepers' Association to stop selling liquor to minors; with the Grocers' Association to stop tobacco sales to minors; with watchmen in the railroad yards to persuade them to report boys to the association instead of arresting them for trespassing; with theatre owners to provide wholesome entertainment; and with film makers to develop educational materials that presented information about health and morals in an entertaining and instructive manner. The association worked to have social centers opened, to turn unused buildings into recreation centers, to turn vacant lots into gardens, to organize hiking parties, to develop bathing beaches, and to open public schools for social purposes. (pp. 101–102)

The work of the association made clear the value and importance of probation officers in helping these youth to overcome their limited environments, pointing to the role of advocacy in facilitating their development. Within a short time, the city of Chicago placed probation officers on the city payroll. According to Levine and Levine (1992), the move from voluntary to civic service was the "kiss of death for the juvenile court in Chicago" (p. 98). In essence, the probation officers became city workers, subject to the whims and fancies of city hall rather than the philanthropic needs and values upon which their work was founded. Then, as now, probation officers quickly became underpaid and overworked, and advocacy initiatives became more of a rarity in the work of mentors.

Chicago was not unlike many other industrial cities of the early 1900s. Industry and the human resources needed to keep them running created the same scenario no matter where one was. New York, Denver, Philadelphia, and Cincinnati housed sizable populations of working poor, all struggling under a similar set of disadvantages and discouragements. Each also had a philanthropic community. Similar to contentions about modern mentoring programs (see Freedman, 1999), some would argue that the

philanthropy of the era was about class control—the wealthy forcing, through charity, the inculcation of middle-class values and ideals onto the poor (Jones, 1999). No doubt, there were myriad motivations that powered the actions of child savers and progressives in the early 20th century; however, their efforts to create the juvenile courts contributed directly to the establishment of the mentoring movement in America.

ESTABLISHMENT

The plight of the working class was a popular topic not only with progressives and child savers but also with observers of contemporary culture. In Chicago during the early 1900s, there was a popular cartoon series titled *When a Feller Needs a Friend.* The notion that those down on their luck could benefit from a hand up from a caring friend resonated with the American public. This idea was linked to the positive sentiment of natural mentorships. The phrase "When a feller needs a friend" found its way into advertisements for pipe tobacco and dog-grooming products, and it served as the title for a 1932 movie starring Jackie Cooper, who played a young boy victimized by others because of a physical disability. More important, it was a notion that supported the formation and institutionalization of the mentoring movement in America.

Big Brothers and Big Sisters

The mission of the Big Brothers Big Sisters of America (BBBSA) is widely known. It has become the major mentoring program in America, serving over 100,000 children and youth in more than 500 agencies throughout the United States (Big Brothers Big Sisters, 2004).

The founding of the BBBSA was located in the same time and place as the juvenile court movement, and like that movement, it appeared simultaneously in cities across the United States. For example, in 1902, the Ladies of Charity of New York City organized a program of support for children appearing before the New York City juvenile court (later, they became the Catholic Big Sisters of New York).

In that same year, the *New York Times* carried a report on the efforts of juvenile court judge, Julius M. Mayer, to secure 90 influential men to befriend a child brought before the court. It was an act of kindness and concern that inspired court clerk Ernest Coulter. A journalist by trade, Coulter felt passionately about the plight of children in New York City. Leaving journalism to serve as a clerk in Mayer's court, Coulter continued the call for volunteers to serve the city's disenfranchised youth. Coulter's commitment and verve caught the attention of a fellow reporter and social reformer, Jacob Riis. Writing in the foreword of Coulter's 1913 book, *The Children in the Shadow,* Riis described the formation of the nascent Big Brothers movement and Coulter's commitment to the cause:

> Mr. Coulter does more than give warning of disaster; he knows the way out and he points to it. Long years ago, at a gathering of serious men, when he had told of the sights he saw daily and the shamed question struggled to the surface: "Can nothing be done?" he was ready with the answer. "Yes, be the neighbor! You are forty sitting here. If each of you were to be neighbor, brother, to one of these little ones and see him through, forty would be saved from shipwreck. It is not law the lad needs, but justice, the kind of justice which only the brother can give—the love, the friendship, for which his life has been starving. All the rest will come on the trail of that." And that night forty entered the lists for the boy. The forty have swelled into hundreds, and the Big Brother and the Little Brother have made the world a better place to live in. For they have helped us understand that "neighbor" is the pass-word that gets us over the hard places, and that nothing else will; not laws nor reforms, nor political platforms and propagandas. They are all ways of helping, but *the* way with the lad is neighborly friendship. A hand laid on his shoulder that shrunk just now from the copper's vengeful grip is more potent for his conversion than a term in the best reformatory that was ever planned, if there is one deserving of the name. (pp. xv–xvi)

At about the same time Coulter was calling for volunteers, a similar scene was unfolding in Cincinnati. The story is told that one day in 1903, a Cincinnati businessman, Irvin Westheimer, looked out of his office window to see a young boy rummaging through the garbage in search of food. Moved by what he saw, Westheimer befriended the boy and his family and soon was encouraging others to do the same. Later, in 1910, the Big Brothers of Cincinnati was formed. The source of some debate, Westheimer is credited with the concept of the Big Brothers, while Coulter is acknowledged as the founder of the formal organization (Beiswinger, 1985).

Just as fast as Big Brothers took root, a Big Sisters organization surfaced to initiate the mentoring of girls. The secular efforts of groups like the Chicago Women's Club and the members of Hull House had many counterparts in the religious community. In New York, for example, refuge could be found in the Ladies of Charity, the New York Jesuit Big Sisters, and the Protestant Big Sisters. With names like "Vanderbilt" attached to the cause, there was widespread support both in terms of human and financial capital. Such resources enabled the provision of a host of services to young women in trouble. Big Brothers and Big Sisters, similar in so many ways, maintained separate identities until 1978, when they merged to become Big Brothers Big Sisters of America (for more detailed information, see Beiswinger, 1985).

Mentoring was work that few had any argument with, and the growth was explosive. By 1917, mentoring programs could be found in as many as 98 cities in America (Beiswinger, 1985). For the many thousands of children the program reached, BBBSA was, like so much of America, largely a White organization serving White children and families. This raises the important question of what kind of mentoring African Americans and other minority youth were receiving throughout this time of severe racial segregation.

Natural Mentors

During this time period, it seems that minority youth were more likely involved in natural mentoring relationships with members of their own communities, such as extended kin and concerned neighbors (Edelman, 1999). As Dortch (2000) stated:

In the African American community, there is a long tradition of passing on our successes, our beliefs, and our values from one generation to the next. It is a tradition of "lifting as we climb," in the words of the motto of the National Council of Negro Women. (p. 134)

Marian Wright Edelman (1999) reflected on her own experience growing up in a racially segregated America and the positive influences she felt from mentors who helped guide her way:

All of my mentors, men and women of different faiths and colors, in their own way personified excellence and courage, shared and instilled a vision and hope of what could be, not what was, in our racially, gender, class, and caste constricted country; kept America's promise of becoming a country free of discrimination, poverty, and ignorance ever before me; put the foundations of education, discipline, hard work, and perseverance needed to help build it beneath me; and instilled a sense of the here and now and forever faithful presence of God inside me. (p. xvii)

Informal mentoring relationships seemed most often to be locally determined, a trend that continues today. As Edelman (1999) stated:

My parents did not have to raise me and my sister and brothers alone. The whole community helped them and me just as they helped other people raise their children. Every place I went, there were eyes watching me and people reporting on me when I strayed into places or company or engaged in behavior they knew or thought my parents would not approve. (p. 13)

To summarize, the mentoring movement in America was given animation and vitality through the efforts of the early pioneers of the Progressive Movement. It was a movement whose time was right, and the public embraced the volunteer spirit of caring for vulnerable youth. The rapid expansion of formal initiatives to support mentoring, although not extending equally to all segments of society, was proof of its value and need. Acceptance of mentoring as a public service provided solid footing for the movement in the minds of the American public. However, the benefits attached to mentoring were largely in the minds of the public and not necessarily in the data on its effectiveness.

DIVERGENCE

Even with mentoring programs, recidivism was a growing problem. It was a situation that was particularly vexing to Chicago's progressive child savers, who hoped their good intentions and activities would be a palliative cure for the problem of delinquency. An important part of the Progressive Movement was acceptance of science and the scientific method. In the early 20th century, science had contributed technologies that made life easier, more efficient, and in many ways, more pleasant. The newly emerging science of mind, psychology, offered similar promise for mental life. A science of psychology was a relatively recent undertaking, emerging in late-19th-century Germany from a blending of experimental physiology and mental philosophy. In America, the new science took a decidedly applied turn, with psychological scientists seeking to apply the lessons of the lab to industry, education, government, and social service (Benjamin & Baker, 2003).

Child Science

With a PhD in experimental psychology from the University of Leipzig in Germany, Lightner Witmer (1867–1956) opened the first psychological clinic in America at the University of Pennsylvania in 1896. Historical documentation reports that Witmer was asked by a local school teacher to help a 14-year-old boy who had learning problems. Witmer (1907) reasoned "that if psychology was worth anything to me or to others it should be able to assist the efforts of a teacher in a retarded case of this kind" (p. 4). Using a combination of physiological, psychological, and medical measures, Witmer diagnosed the boy with a visual problem, which was treated with eyeglasses and tutoring. The clinic grew rapidly, and Witmer soon became a national expert on the assessment and treatment of children with what was termed "mental and moral retardation." Reflecting the zeitgeist of the times, Witmer saw delinquency as an environmentally induced phenomenon and therefore amenable to rehabilitation. Commenting on this, Witmer (1911) noted:

> Who can improve a man's inheritance? And what man's environment can not be bettered? In place of the hopeless fatalism of those who constantly emphasize our impotence in the presence of the heredity factor, we prefer the hopeful optimism of those who point out the destructive activity of the environment. To ascribe a condition to the environment, is a challenge to do something for its amelioration or cure; to ascribe it to heredity often means that we fold we our hands and do nothing. (p. 232)

Witmer pioneered methods of assessment that have become standards in the practice of school and clinical psychology. His efforts gave credence to the view that children could be evaluated and the results used in service of treatment and rehabilitation, a point that was not lost on the women of Chicago who had been working with so much energy on behalf of delinquent youth. Seeking to take advantage of the new science of mind and behavior, a committee was formed by Chicago Juvenile Court Judge Merritt W. Pinckney. It included two well-known progressives, Julia Lathrop and Ethel Sturges Dummer, and a young physician named William Healy (1881–1962). Trained at Harvard and Rush Medical School, Healy was sympathetic to the progressive cause and had an ongoing interest in the causes of delinquency. The group recommended the formation of a special institute to assist in the physical and psychological examination of children brought before the court. Ethel Dummer would finance the operation, and William Healy would head it; in 1909, the Juvenile Psychopathic Institute (JPI) was founded. There were high hopes for the JPI, and Healy himself looked forward to the opportunity to gather data on the nature of delinquency, its causes, and cures. He enjoyed widespread support from the medical, psychological, and social service community and soon was identified as one of the nation's leading authorities on delinquency (Jones, 1999; Levine & Levine, 1992).

The establishment of the JPI signaled some fundamental changes in the way that at-risk youth were to be viewed and treated. The term *psychopathic* was an example of the change. No longer was delinquency a social ill, begotten from the streets; rather, it was a malady best understood through examination by the psychologist and physician. From this perspective, delinquency was less an ill for social reformers to cure than a problem for social scientists to solve. Healy's methods and data walked a line between the views of his progressive sponsors and his service to science. For example, he found that delinquent youth, as a group, were not mentally abnormal or deficient. To emphasize the point, the JPI changed its name in 1914 to the Institute of Juvenile Research (Jones, 1999). Healy believed that environment was but one of many factors that contributed to delinquency. In his writings, he described some 20 factors that contributed to the development and maintenance of delinquent behavior (Healy & Bronner, 1936).

For Healy, assessment was an intensive process of individual study that relied on medical, psychological, social, and behavioral data. After careful consideration of all available information, a diagnosis could be made and a treatment plan rendered. Treatment, like assessment, was not limited to one method. In this new and increasingly popular medical/psychological model, mentoring would receive less attention. Psychosocial treatments, such as individual counseling and guidance, were the domain of the professional, be it a psychiatrist, psychologist, or social worker. In essence, the work of Healy was serving as the template for the emergence of professional child guidance (Jones, 1999).

Mentoring Obscured

Increasingly, mentoring relationships were relegated to social service roles staffed by willing volunteers. Organizations such as the Big Brothers and Big Sisters, the Young Men's and Young Women's Christian Association (YMCA and YWCA), and the Benevolent and Protective Order of Elks continued to serve at-risk youth and provide mentoring programs, while Healy and his colleagues constructed a view of delinquency based on the authority of social science. Commenting on these developments, Jones (1999) noted:

Healy also began to establish an independent perspective on the cause of delinquency, one that emphasized the individuality of each child, the multifaceted causes of delinquency, and the emotional content of the child's mind. Ultimately there would be little room in this new, professionally driven, psychological explanation of juvenile crime for the delinquency prevention work, the environmentalist interpretations of conduct, or the advocacy of broad-scale legislative programs so familiar to Healy's sponsors. (p. 44)

By 1917, the juvenile court of Chicago was financed and controlled by Cook County. Apparently, Healy did not find his new sponsor to his liking. Along with staff psychologist Augusta Bronner, he moved to Boston to direct a similar program at the newly created Judge Baker Foundation. Bronner, a doctoral student studying juvenile delinquency, met Healy when he was teaching a summer course at Harvard in 1913. Psychologist Grace Fernald had just left Healy's Chicago institute, and he offered the position to Bronner. It was the beginning of a long collaboration, one that was both professional and personal (Savickas & Baker, in press).

In the Northeast, Healy and Bronner were celebrated experts whose work and opinions were immensely important to everyone in the field of juvenile delinquency, including Richard Clarke Cabot (1868–1939). A Harvard-trained physician with impressive credentials and a strong social conscience, Cabot was eager to bring the scientific method to the identification of factors that would ameliorate juvenile delinquency. In 1936, Cabot launched the Cambridge-Somerville Youth Study (CSYS). Named after the two communities from which participants were drawn, the study was an ambitious and well-designed effort to study the development of delinquency. More accurately, the study sought to find ways of preventing delinquency and improve adjustment. Lasting 6 years, the study identified a community sample of more than 500 children, who were carefully matched on a host of variables (e.g., age, intelligence, family histories) at the outset of the study. After each pair of boys were matched, a coin was tossed to determine which boy would receive the treatment and which boy would be in the control group. Children in the treatment group received a wide range of social, educational, and health services. Most services were coordinated through counselors assigned to each child in the treatment group. These counselors were paid employees who were generally recent college graduates, most having had training in social work (Powers & Witmer, 1951).

Cabot, like Healy, attributed delinquency to adverse personal and environmental factors that could be combated through a supportive and responsive environment. Like the progressive child savers of decades past, Cabot believed a good mentor could cure many ills. He hoped that the actions of counselors in the CSYS would be testament to this belief. In a sense, the first scientific study of mentoring was under way.

Cabot died before the study ended in 1945. He would not have been pleased with the results. Improvements for children in the treatment group were marginal, a finding that was a disappointment to many associated with the study, including Harvard psychologist Gordon Allport. A colleague and close personal friend of Cabot, Allport took on the leadership of the study upon Cabot's death. Writing in the foreword of the 1951 publication of the study, Allport urged caution in abandoning efforts to prevent delinquency through the judicial application of personal caring and support (Powers & Witmer, 1951).

Indeed, results of the CSYS not only failed to show benefits of the counseling treatment but also indicated that the efforts to help may have done more harm than good. Thirty years after the study, researchers began to question the inherent "goodness" of socially conscious programs and to highlight the importance of reporting both positive and negative outcomes. In an effort to determine the long-term effects of the counseling treatment condition of the CSYS, McCord (1978) set out to collect outcome information from the original participants, who then were entering middle adulthood. Data collection ensued from 1975 through 1981 and consisted of gathering participant testimonials, court records, mental hospital records, records from facilities treating alcoholism, and death records. Although personal testimonials suggested positive outcomes for those who received treatment, further study yielded opposing interpretations. Specifically, McCord (1992) found that in comparison to control participants, individuals who had received treatment were significantly more likely to have been convicted for serious street crimes, died an average of 5 years younger, and were more likely to have been diagnosed with alcoholism, schizophrenia, or manic depression. In fact, McCord (2003) reported that evidence of negative treatment effects increased as the duration and intensity of treatment increased. Overall, McCord suggested that the treatment condition of the CSYS had been harmful to youth who participated in it. Although mentoring was but one of several services provided to youth in the study—making it difficult to identify which specific services may have been harmful and which were not—this study opened the door to the possibility that mentoring might not be the panacea for delinquency it was hoped to be.

The results of the CSYS, which continues to be a topic of discussion and debate, did not provide any needed enthusiasm for mentoring in America. Mentoring remained a civic-minded activity buoyed largely by the efforts of the organizations we have already mentioned (e.g., Big Brothers and Big Sisters). However, the efficacy of mentoring was not substantiated by scientific study. The Progressive Era was over, and the nation was facing a new postwar environment. The suburbs were growing, and the cities were shrinking. The sense of activism that fortified social reformers was gone.

Focus

The growth of social science brought with it more and better tools for designing studies and evaluating data. Studies like the CSYS had yielded myriad analyses and interpretations. To Cabot, a supportive and caring relationship was an essential element in delinquency prevention; to researchers, it was just another variable in a sea of hypotheses, interventions, and outcomes. The counselor assigned to each child in the CSYS served many roles, as much social worker as mentor, and data-reporting practices varied among counselors (M. Simmel, personal communication, December 12, 2003). Taken together, it was difficult to quantitatively isolate the effects

of the intervention, let alone make any definitive statements about mentoring.

The Community Psychology Movement

More focused programs of research pertinent to youth mentoring came into being in the 1960s. An important development was the emergence of community mental health. In 1963, President John F. Kennedy signed into law the Community Mental Health Centers Act. The act would provide the needed funds to build and staff community mental health centers that would serve the mental health needs of the communities where they were located. In a sense, the act lent legitimacy to the efforts of those like Jane Addams, Lightner Witmer, William Healy, and Augusta Bronner, who had worked so tirelessly to establish clinics, institutes, and homes to serve troubled youth. This new concern for the well-being of all Americans was further enhanced by President Lyndon Johnson, who, in 1964, presented to America his vision of the Great Society. Johnson followed with significant federal support for programs aimed at reducing poverty and alleviating suffering through improved health care and education. It was within this context that the community psychology movement grew and flourished (Meritt, Greene, Jopp, & Kelly, 1999).

Reminiscent of the Progressive Era, community psychology concerned itself with the impact of larger social and cultural forces on the mental health of individuals. Locating pathology in the environment rather than in the individual also suggested that nonprofessionals could play a role in treatment. Traditionally trained mental health professionals were not in great number, and the cost of their services was prohibitive for many. These developments helped promote acceptance of nonprofessionals as mental health service providers. Of these, mentors were a group that had a long history of social service. Studies like that of Goodman (1972) brought a clear and sharp focus to the experimental study of mentoring.

The Measure of a Mentor

Goodman's (1972) work employed nonprofessionals (mainly college students) to implement a newly developed therapy, companionship therapy. Goodman saw an opportunity to develop and evaluate a training program based on the principles of mentoring. Companionship therapy sought to help troubled school-aged boys by creating dyads with one adult and one child. In collaboration with both the Berkeley (California) Big Brothers program and a local YMCA, Goodman trained nonprofessionals using a Rogerian client-centered perspective. Overall, 160 preadolescent boys participated in the study. Of these, 88 participants were assigned randomly to the treatment condition (with companion), while 74 served as no-treatment controls (without companion). The study lasted 4 years, from 1962 to 1966. The results were mixed, with generally only small and often non-significant differences between children who received a companion and those who did not. However, this study helped place mentoring in the experimental spotlight, offered a rationale and method for assessing its efficacy, and helped mentoring gain more footing in the research literature and lexicon. In the decades that followed, researchers began to consider characteristics of mentors, their training and needs, and the context in which mentoring programs occur.

Contemporary Research

As we begin a new century, the information we have about mentoring is improving, both in terms of quality and quantity. A significant force contributing to this progress is the work of Public/Private Ventures (P/PV), a nonprofit organization that supports programs for youth. P/PV has a strong reputation for conducting research examining the effects of mentoring and for their dedication to linking this research to mentoring practices by providing easily accessible publications to community practitioners. In the 1990s, P/PV conducted a landmark experimental evaluation of the impact of participation in Big Brothers Big Sisters programs. In 1992 and 1993, 1,138 youth (aged 10–16) applying for mentoring through Big Brothers Big Sisters programs located in several different U.S. cities were assigned randomly to either a treatment group, which would

immediately receive mentors, or to a control group, which would be wait-listed for a mentor for 18 months. Based on interviews completed by youth at baseline and 18-month follow-up assessments, the mentored participants, in comparison to those in the control group, were less likely to initiate alcohol and drug use; were less likely to hit someone; skipped school less often; felt more academic competence; and had more positive parent and peer relationships (Tierney, Grossman, & Resch, 1995). The results of this study received widespread media attention upon their release and, in effect, provided legitimacy to the mentoring movement. The study's findings and conclusions continue to be used frequently by practice and advocacy groups to justify calls for a significant role of mentoring in efforts to forge more effective social policy for at-risk youth.

Subsequent analyses of the data from the P/PV study have served to moderate the enthusiasm for its findings. First, Rhodes (2002) pointed to the fact that *both* treatment and control groups in the 1995 P/PV study increased in academic, social-emotional, behavioral, and relationship problems (youth with mentors just increased at a slower rate). Second, DuBois and colleagues (2002) found that findings of this study translated into only small effect sizes when assessed using a conventional metric in their meta-analysis of the youth mentoring literature. Unlike common perceptions of mentoring, these studies seem to indicate that mentoring is unlikely to be a "cure-all" for at-risk youth. In fact, echoing the results of the CSYS research referred to previously, one recent reanalysis of the P/PV study data found evidence that some of the mentoring relationships seemed to have a negative impact. Grossman and Rhodes (2002) analyzed the study data for effects of relationship duration and found that relationships that lasted less than 3 months were associated with significantly larger drops in self-worth and perceived academic competence for youth in the treatment group than those evident for youth in the control group. Finally, other authors (Lucas & Liabø, 2003) have raised concerns about the exclusive reliance of the P/PV study on self-report data. For example, the indicated reductions in substance use, truancy, and aggressive behavior were not verified with more objective measures (e.g., school records). Lucas and Liabø suggested in this regard that participants in the treatment condition may have been especially motivated to endorse socially desirable behaviors at follow-up (e.g., for fear of "letting down" their mentors), thus potentially accounting at least in part for the apparent favorable effects of mentoring.

In another significant development, DuBois and colleagues (2002) undertook a meta-analytic study to summarize and review the literature, from 1970 through 1998, pertaining to a variety of mentoring programs for youth. Their study included an investigation of 55 evaluations of one-on-one youth mentoring programs. Findings indicated only a small positive effect for the average youth participating in a mentoring program. Nonetheless, other findings from this research highlight the advances that have been made in understanding the factors that contribute to good mentors, good outcomes for mentees, and best practices for mentoring programs. Of particular note, DuBois and colleagues (2002) demonstrated that positive program effects systematically increased as programs made use of a greater number of recommended practices, including mentor screening and supervision, initial and ongoing mentor training, structured mentoring activities to facilitate relationship development, expectations for frequency of contact, parental support and involvement, and monitoring of the overall program implementation.

Parallel to research on formal mentoring programs, studies examining informal, naturally occurring mentoring relationships also have been conducted. Indeed, findings from the youth resilience literature, such as Emmy Werner's longitudinal study of high-risk youth growing up on the Hawaiian Island of Kauai, proved influential in fueling contemporary support for mentoring initiatives by providing evidence that a strong relationship with a nonparental adult can be an important protective factor in the life of at-risk youth (Werner, 1995). Subsequent studies focused on natural mentors have served to document evidence of associations between these types of ties and a wide range of positive youth outcomes (see Zimmerman, Bingenheimer, & Behrendt, this volume).

Contemporary Trends in Practice and Policy

Several developments in mentoring practice and policy have further facilitated an increased focus on youth mentoring in our contemporary times (for details, see Walker, this volume). These include the volunteer movement that has emerged in America at the turn of the 21st century, stimulated by events such as the Volunteer Summit held in Philadelphia in 1997, in which General Colin Powell urged and set goals for greater volunteer involvement in the lives of the nation's youth. Within the mentoring field, too, there have been noteworthy developments to both support and inform the practice of youth mentoring. Organizations such as the National Mentoring Partnership (n.d.) and centers and clearinghouses such as the National Mentoring Center (n.d.) have been established and now provide ready access to a wealth of resources to individuals and organizations interested in mentoring. Governmental support for mentoring also has blossomed in recent years, as indicated most notably by President George W. Bush's announcement in 2003 of a plan for a massive $450 million expansion of mentoring programs for youth. Finally, the traditional one-on-one community-based model of mentoring embodied in programs such as Big Brothers Big Sisters has given way to a proliferation of alternative models that make use of varying configurations of persons (e.g., group mentoring, team mentoring, cross-age peer mentoring), specific sites (e.g., schools, workplace, faith-based organizations), and the Internet (see Sipe, this volume). Each of these emergent models in one way or another reflects a strategic response of the field to changes in the lives of youth and adult volunteers as well as to broader shifts in society as a whole.

At the same time, other societal developments have not augured as well for natural mentoring relationships. The significance of these relationships in helping young people make successful transitions from childhood to adulthood is often acknowledged, and their prevalence appears to far outnumber those established through formal programs (McLearn, Colasanto, & Schoen, 1998). There is growing concern, however, that once-strong community ties are diminishing the prospects for youth to profit from links to natural mentors (Scales, 2003). In this regard, a range of cultural assumptions and social norms (e.g., increased individualistic values, norms discouraging adults' involvement with others' children) seem to be leading to a decrease in the occurrence of naturally occurring mentoring relationships (Scales, 2003).

FUTURE DIRECTIONS

Synthesis

The impulse toward mentoring appears to be a natural one, perhaps related to an instinctual need to protect our vulnerable young. As we have seen, mentoring in America has unfolded through a series of stages that we have described as emergence, establishment, divergence, and focus. Mentoring in America was born out of a strong sense of social justice and a concern and caring for the plight of youth, who through no fault of their own were often at the mercy of an environment that offered many more opportunities for ruin rather than riches. The first who came to the aid of such children created the mentoring movement that we simultaneously value and carefully examine today.

Those drawn to the call of social justice did not share any particular affiliation. They were men and women, rich and poor, young and old. By and large, they were volunteers unified by a common cause of caring. As a social science emerged in the 20th century, it eschewed the significance of the volunteer, preferring the authority of the professional. The events and conditions that fortified the volunteer spirit of the first generation of mentors also were drawn into the sphere of professional authority. Social scientists cast their nets far and wide, developing detailed models of juvenile delinquency that implicated individual, social, and environmental variables, all in need of examination and measurement. Against this backdrop, mentoring had a place, but it was a place shared with many other concepts, constructs, and practices. Mentors too lost their standing. Social scientists now promoted child guidance, a movement complete with a cadre of professionals who had their own specialized education and training, be they social worker, psychiatrist, or psychologist. Outside of the academy, the call to mentoring was always answered, and volunteer organizations such as Big Brothers and Big Sisters flourished.

Advances in social science research methodologies allowed social scientists to test their models of the causes and cures for delinquency. Investigation of community-based counseling interventions for youth, mostly vaguely defined and poorly operationalized, shed some of the first scientific light on the potential impact of mentoring. The early results were not encouraging; the good intentions and social ideals of the child savers did not appear to be salve enough for the wounds of troubled youth. Indeed, for most of the 20th century, despite high hopes, deep conviction, and strong belief, mentoring in America remained a largely unproven intervention. Such a declaration, however, does not indicate that progress has not been made. Indeed, as this volume is testament to, mentoring theory, practice, and research are in a state of rapid acceleration. It is work that shows progress and points to promise.

Today, civic-minded volunteers and data-minded social scientists are forming unions that allow for the testing of well-designed and-executed mentoring interventions. Such efforts highlight the best that both have to offer, and the results are data that have a meaningful impact on both theory and practice. We are beginning to know more about mentors, mentees, and mentoring programs. However, there is still a great deal to learn about mentoring practices.

Future research can further inform practice by clarifying how to select and train good mentors, develop programs that are effective, and measure outcomes that have real-world implications. As it stands, the present historical analysis of mentoring can offer the basis for further recommendations for this research and practice.

Recommendations for Research

1. *Continued research on both formal/ program-initiated and informal/naturally occurring mentoring relationships.* As noted in this chapter, both formal/program-initiated and informal/naturally occurring types of mentoring have important historical foundations. These foundations and more contemporary trends

indicating benefits of both types of relationships for youth highlight the need for more research on similarities and differences between them and the circumstances under which each may be especially likely to promote positive outcomes.

2. *Research focused on not only potentially beneficial but also harmful effects of mentoring is needed.* Previous research has often taken for granted and assumed positive effects of mentoring. The danger of this assumption is illustrated by a historical thread from the negative findings of early studies (Cambridge-Somerville Youth Study) to more contemporary findings that suggest negative outcomes for short-term relationships (Grossman & Rhodes, 2002). Future research would do well to heed these results and make careful investigation of unintended adverse effects of mentoring relationships and programs a routine part of investigations.

3. *Scholarly inquiry by historians, demographers, and others regarding the influences of sociohistorical context on different aspects of mentoring should be pursued.* As demonstrated in this chapter, variables that are introduced due to the zeitgeist of the times inevitably affect mentoring practices. For example, the Progressive Era played an influential role in the birth of contemporary mentoring programs, and the role of race relations in this country served to shape the demographics of youth and mentors who participated in early programs. Currently, the modern volunteer movement may facilitate mentoring practices due to the positive influences of volunteer recruitment and program funding. However, the increased transiency and mobility of Americans may be interfering with the development of natural mentoring relationships due to a variety of societal trends referred to previously (Scales, 2003). Historical analyses and scholarship from multiple other disciplines (e.g., demography, sociology) should be consulted when investigating the origins, nature, and consequences of these types of sociohistorical influences on mentoring.

4. *More-sophisticated research is needed to promote stronger links between mentoring practices and mentoring research.* The need for a strong bridge between the research and practice domains in the mentoring field is underscored by the historical analysis of this chapter, including the negative consequences of the unfortunate gap between them that arose during the past century and has begun to close somewhat in more recent times. More researchers would be wise in this regard to follow the model of P/PV's work, which attempts to carefully link mentoring research and practice and to investigate the efficacy of recently developed tools that may be useful for facilitating this aim (see Coyne, Duffy, & Wandersman, this volume).

Recommendations for Practice

1. *Sociopolitical influences should be taken advantage of for the purposes of supporting and implementing mentoring programs and/or promoting natural mentoring.* Just as the founders of the initial mentoring initiatives were able to capitalize on the Progressive Movement, current possibilities exist to take advantage of contemporary sociopolitical influences. For example, advocates could take advantage of the current bipartisan political enthusiasm for mentoring, which could serve to expand the range of funding opportunities and to increase volunteer recruitment pools. Strategic efforts to exploit such facets of the contemporary zeitgeist may be instrumental to further growth and support for mentoring initiatives, and those should be a priority.

2. *Research-based knowledge should be consulted when developing mentoring programs and initiatives.* The need for using research-based knowledge as a foundation for the development of mentoring programs and initiatives is indicated by the ways in which the mentoring movement fell outside the margins of mainstream social science early in the 20th century, which was to its detriment both in being able to improve scientific knowledge of mentoring and in lending the field scientific credibility. Today, practitioners could move in this direction to improve the efficacy of their programs by utilizing research-based elements of effective practice in program design and implementation (e.g., DuBois et al., 2002) and by accessing the resources of national organizations that have become important repositories of research-based knowledge on youth mentoring.

3. *Mentoring practices should be directed to the needs of the current societal context as defined by trends in demography, historical events, and evolving communities.* As noted in this chapter, the enduring success of the mentoring movement for nearly a century in this country is significantly attributable to the manner in which the mentoring concept and practices have been adapted to meet the changing needs and circumstances of people in our society. Accordingly, those in the policy and practice communities will do well to continue to adapt mentoring programs and initiatives to contemporary societal needs and opportunities.

REFERENCES

Addams, J. (1914). *A new conscience and an ancient evil.* New York: Macmillan.

Baker, D. B. (2002). Child saving and the emergence of vocational psychology. *Journal of Vocational Behavior, 60,* 374–381.

Beiswinger, G. L. (1985). *One to one: The story of the Big Brothers Big Sisters movement in America.* Philadelphia: Big Brothers Big Sisters of America.

Benjamin, L. T., & Baker, D. B. (2003). *From séance to science: A history of the profession of psychology in America.* Belmont, CA: Wadsworth.

Big Brothers Big Sisters. (2004). *Frequently asked questions.* Retrieved July 21, 2004, from http://www.bbbsa.org/site/pp.asp?c=iuJ3JgO2F&b=14603

Bowen, J. T. (1925). The early days of the juvenile court. In J. Addams (Ed.), *The child, the clinic, and the court* (pp. 298–309). New York: New Republic.

Brumberg, J. J. (2003). *Kansas Charley: The story of a nineteenth-century boy murderer.* New York: Viking.

Coulter, E. (1913). *The children in the shadow.* New York: McBride, Nast.

Davidson, E., & Benjamin, L. T., Jr. (1987). A history of the child study movement in America. In J. A. Glover & R. R. Ronning (Eds.), *Historical foundations of educational psychology* (pp. 187–208). New York: Plenum Press.

Dortch, T. W., Jr., and the 100 Black Men of America, Inc. (2000). *The miracles of mentoring: The joy of investing in our future.* New York: Doubleday.

DuBois, D. L., Holloway, B. E., Valentine, J. C., & Cooper, H. (2002). Effectiveness of mentoring programs for youth: A meta-analytical review. *American Journal of Community Psychology, 30,* 157–197.

Edelman, M. W. (1999). *Lanterns: A memoir of mentors.* Boston: Beacon Press.

Freedman, M. (1999). *The kindness of strangers: Adult mentors, urban youth, and the new voluntarism.* Cambridge, UK: Cambridge University Press.

Goodman, G. (1972). *Companionship therapy: Studies in structured intimacy.* San Francisco: Jossey-Bass.

Grossman, J. B., & Rhodes, J. E. (2002). The test of time: Predictors and effects of duration in youth mentoring relationships. *American Journal of Community Psychology, 30,* 199–219.

Healy, W., & Bronner, A. F. (1936). *New light on delinquency and its treatment: Results of a Research Conducted for the Institute of Human Relations, Yale University.* New Haven, CT: Institute of Human Relations, Yale University Press.

Johnson, P. (1997). *A history of the American people.* New York: HarperCollins.

Jones, K. (1999). *Taming the troublesome child: American families, child guidance, and the limits of psychiatric authority.* Cambridge, MA: Harvard University Press.

Levine, M., & Levine, A. (1992). *Helping children: A social history.* New York: Oxford University Press.

Lucas, P., & Liabø, K. (2003, April). One-to-one, non-directive mentoring programmes have not been shown to improve behavior in young people involved in offending or anti-social activities. *What Works for Children Group Evidence Nugget.* Retrieved July 20, 2004, from http://www.whatworksforchildren.org.uk/docs/Nuggets/pdfs/Mentoring230703.pdf

McCord, J. (1978). A thirty-year follow-up of treatment effects. *American Psychologist, 33,* 284–289.

McCord, J. (1992). The Cambridge-Somerville Study: A pioneering longitudinal-experimental study of delinquency prevention. In J. McCord & R. E. Tremblay (Eds.), *Preventing antisocial behavior: Interventions from birth through adolescence* (pp. 196–208). New York: Guilford Press.

McCord, J. (2003). Cures that harm: Unanticipated outcomes of crime prevention programs. *Annals of the American Academy of Political and Social Sciences, 587,* 16–30.

McLearn, K. T., Colasanto, D., & Schoen, C. (1998). *Mentoring makes a difference: Findings From the Commonwealth Fund 1998 Survey of Adults Mentoring Young People.* New York: The Commonwealth Fund. Available at http://www .ecs.org/html/Document.asp?chouseid=2843

Meritt, D. M., Greene, G. J., Jopp, D. A., & Kelly, J. G. (1999). A history of Division 27 (Society for Community Research and Action). In D. A. Dewsbury (Ed.), *Unification through division: Histories of the divisions of the American Psychological Association* (Vol. 3, pp. 73–98). Washington, DC: American Psychological Association.

National Mentoring Center. (n.d.). Retrieved January 22, 2004, from http://www.nwrel.org/mentoring/

National Mentoring Partnership. (n.d.). Retrieved June 3, 2004, from http://www.mentoring.org/

Powers, E., & Witmer, H. (1951). *An experiment in the prevention of delinquency: The Cambridge-Somerville Youth Study.* New York: Columbia University Press.

Rhodes, J. E. (2002). *Stand by me: The risks and rewards of mentoring today's youth.* Cambridge, MA: Harvard University Press.

Savickas, M., & Baker, D. B. (in press). The history of vocational psychology: Antecedents, origin, and early development. In B. Walsh & M. Savickas (Eds.), *Handbook of vocational psychology.* New York: Erlbaum.

Scales, P. C. (2003). *Other people's kids: Social expectations and American adults' involvement with children and adolescents.* New York: Kluwer Academic/Plenum.

Tierney, J. P., Grossman, J. B., & Resch, N. L. (1995). *Making a difference: An impact study of Big Brothers/Big Sisters.* Philadelphia: Public/ Private Ventures.

Werner, E. E. (1995). Resilience in development. *Current Directions in Psychological Science, 4,* 81–85.

Witmer, L. (1907). Clinical psychology. *The Psychological Clinic, 1,* 1–9.

Witmer, L. (1911). Criminals in the making. *The Psychological Clinic, 4,* 221–239.

Zinn, H. (1999). *A people's history of the United States: 1492–present.* New York: Harper Collins.

3

A MODEL OF YOUTH MENTORING

JEAN E. RHODES

INTRODUCTION

Most of us know of instances in which a mentoring relationship has enabled a child or adolescent to overcome even the most difficult life circumstances. Anecdotal reports of mentors' protective qualities are corroborated by a growing body of research that indicates the potential positive influence of mentors on a range of outcomes (for reviews, see DuBois, Holloway, Valentine, & Cooper, 2002; Rhodes, 2002). What is missing, however, is research on the processes that account for mentors' influence. How is it that certain youth can be seemingly so profoundly affected by mentoring relationships, whereas others appear to benefit little or even be harmed? More generally, *how does mentoring work?* This fundamental question has been largely overshadowed by more prosaic programmatic concerns. Yet developing and testing answers to it—in essence, getting to the heart and soul of the change process in mentoring—is critical to advancing a more theoretically informed and practically applicable understanding of youth mentoring. This chapter presents a model of the mentoring process along with some preliminary findings supporting the pathways of influence. Implications of the model for future research and practice in the field also are considered. The chapter begins with a brief overview of theoretical and empirical literature that underscores the need for a

deeper understanding of the processes in mentoring relationships that may account for variability in youth outcomes.

Research interest in formal mentoring relationships is relatively new, and most program evaluations have yielded relatively modest effects (DuBois, Holloway, et al., 2002; Roberts, Liabø, Lucas, DuBois, & Sheldon, 2004). Nonetheless, interest in and financial support of mentoring programs remain strong. Currently, more than 4,000 agencies and programs offer mentoring services for young people, and new federal and state initiatives continue to fuel expansion. This mismatch between evidence and action has arisen in part from our intuitive beliefs and observations concerning the healing power of social ties, as well as a long history of research on the benefits of naturally occurring helping relationships. Thirty years ago, Caplan (1964) discussed the potential importance of "extrafamilial helping figures . . . such as older people with a reputation for wisdom" (p. 49), arguing that they are much closer to individuals in need both "geographically and sociologically" than professional caregivers. Along similar lines, sociologists have stressed the importance of mentors in the lives of youth (e.g., Lefkowitz, 1986; Williams & Kornblum, 1985). In his ethnographic research, Anderson (1999) has described the vital, yet diminishing, role of respected authority figures in urban communities who act as "a kind of guidance counselor and moral cheerleader" (p. 35). Resiliency researchers also have observed robust associations between a strong supportive relationship with a caring adult and the tran scendence of difficult life circumstances by youth (Masten & Coatsworth, 1998).

Despite this convergence of observational evidence, many questions remain concerning the direction and context of mentors' influence on developmental outcomes. For example, rather than being a causal factor, mentor relationships might simply correlate with good outcomes. Youth who are physically attractive, engaging, intelligent, and better able to regulate their emotions (all of which are protective factors in their own right) may be more likely to attract the positive attention of caring adults. Researchers have found, for example, that resilient youth are more adept than nonresilient youth at controlling their emotions and sustaining attention: skills that suit them well in garnering support from adults (Buckner, Mezzacappa, & Beardslee, 2003; Eisenberg et al., 2004).

Also unresolved are issues pertaining to the role of parents, including how they might respond to or mediate mentors' influence. Ainsworth (1989) viewed mentors as "parent surrogates to whom they [children] become attached and who play an important role in their lives, especially in the case of children who find in such relationships the security they could not attain with their own parent" (p. 714). Others have noted that mentor relationships might instead supplement children's extant healthy relationships. Youth who have enjoyed positive relationships with their parents, for example, may have greater confidence and trust in adults as well as the skills for seeking out mentoring relationships with them (see Zimmerman, Bingenheimer, & Behrendt, this volume). Particularly during adolescence, as they attempt to gain some emotional and cognitive autonomy from their families, such youth might be drawn to other adults as confidants and role models. In this regard, Allen and Land (1999) have argued that attachment security may be necessary for such exploration, providing the mental and emotional latitude needed for adolescents to begin to realistically assess the limits of their parental relationships.

Findings such as these underscore the importance of considering children's and adolescents' mentoring relationships in the context of their ongoing relationships and broader social environments. As we move toward gaining a more nuanced understanding of the dynamics of mentoring, it will be important to take into account not only differences among youth but also the family, community, and cultural circumstances that may foster and shape mentoring relationships.

TOWARD A MODEL OF YOUTH MENTORING

The model of youth mentoring processes presented in this chapter represents the further elaboration of a model proposed previously in Rhodes (2002). The model assumes that mentoring relationships can promote positive outcomes for youth through a range of processes, specifically those that foster social-emotional, cognitive, and identity development (see Figure 3.1).

Mentors whose influence extends into more than one of these three arenas are assumed to have the greatest impact on youth outcomes. Pathways relating to each arena of development are considered in the sections that follow. However, it bears emphasizing at the outset that this model assumes, at a more fundamental level, that beneficial effects of a mentoring relationship can be expected only to the extent that the mentor and mentee manage to forge a strong connection with each other. For each portion of the model, both theoretical concerns and findings of relevant research are considered separately.

Mentoring Relationship: Mutuality, Trust, and Empathy

Theory

The model assumes that the dynamics through which mentoring relationships can promote positive developmental outcomes are unlikely to unfold without a strong interpersonal connection, specifically one characterized by mutuality, trust, and empathy (see Figure 3.1, Component a). As Levinson (1979) observed,

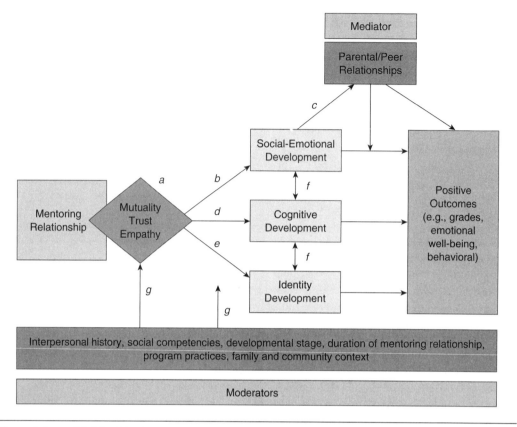

Figure 3.1   Model of Youth Mentoring

"Mentoring is not a simple, all-or-none matter" (p. 100), and if a bond does not form, youth and mentors may disengage from the match before the relationship lasts long enough to have a positive impact on youth.

Theoretically, a meaningful connection becomes possible only to the extent that the mentee is willing to share his or her feelings and self-perceptions and is actively engaged in the relationship (Csiksizentmihalyi & Rathunde, 1998). Dworkin, Larson, and Hansen (2003) have described this process in terms of both motivation and concentration—wherein the youth is "involved in actively constructing personal change" (p. 17). This focus on empathy and engagement does not imply that every moment needs to be packed with profundity and personal growth. It seems more likely that successful mentoring of youth is more often characterized by a series of small wins that emerge sporadically over time. Yet these mundane moments, which might be laced with boredom,

humor, and even frustration, can help forge a connection from which the mentee may draw strength in moments of vulnerability or share triumph in moments of accomplishment.

Research

Research has indicated the benefits of attunement in adult-youth relationships (Pianta, 1999). Allen et al. (2003), for example, found that more empathic and supportive parenting was predictive of attachment security among adolescents—such parents appeared to be better able to provide the sort of safe haven that youth need to take on challenges and cope with emotional stress. By the same token, mentors who are attuned with their mentees are likely to be in a better position to handle discussions around vulnerable topics without undermining the youngsters' sense of self-confidence. After examining survey data on more than 600 mentoring pairs in community- and school-based programs, Herrera, Sipe, and McClanahan (2000) concluded that "at the crux of the mentoring relationship is the bond that forms between the youth and mentor" (p. 72). Similarly, Rhodes, Reddy, Roffman, and Grossman (in press), found that levels of trust and closeness in Big Brothers Big Sisters (BBBS) mentoring relationships predicted positive academic and behavioral outcomes above and beyond the effects of relationship length.

Social and Emotional Development

Theory

As noted, one primary pathway of mentor influence on positive outcomes may be through intermediate improvements in youth social and emotional development that result from a close relationship (see Figure 3.1, Path b). Theoretically, by modeling caring and providing support, mentors can challenge negative views that youth may hold of themselves or of relationships with adults and demonstrate that positive relationships with adults are possible. The mentoring relationship thus may become a "corrective experience" for youth who may have experienced unsatisfactory relationships with their parents (Olds, Kitzman, Cole, & Robinson, 1997). As Kohut (1984) has argued, close relationships can be therapeutic in and of themselves, helping individuals realize "that the sustaining echo of empathic resonance is indeed available in the world" (p. 78).

The basis for expecting that positive mentoring relationships can modify perceptions by youth of other relationships is derived largely from attachment theory (Bowlby, 1988). According to attachment theorists, children construct cognitive representations of relationships through their early experiences with primary care givers (Bretherton & Waters, 1985). These experience-based expectations, or working models, are believed to be incorporated into the personality structure and to influence behavior in interpersonal relationships throughout and beyond childhood (Ainsworth, 1989; Bowlby, 1988). Working models are considered to be relatively stable over time yet flexible to modification in response to changing life circumstances, such as engagement in unconditionally supportive

relationships (Belsky & Cassidy, 1994; Carlson & Sroufe, 1995).

By serving as a sounding board and providing a model of effective adult communication, mentors also may help children and adolescents better understand, express, and regulate both their positive and negative emotions (Pianta, 1999). Gottman (2001) has referred to "emotion coaching," in which adults model and teach strategies for managing feelings. Mentors who openly display positive emotions, particularly under difficult circumstances, actively model the process of using positive emotions constructively (Denham & Kochanoff, 2002). In doing so, mentors can help mentees to broaden and build their personal resources and learn to approach negative experiences as opportunities for intimacy and learning.

In some cases, connections with mentors also may function as alternative or secondary attachment figures, providing a secure base from which youth can achieve crucial social and cognitive competencies. In other cases, the relationship might have a positive impact by simply alleviating some of the relationship tensions and conflicts that arise throughout adolescence.

Closely related to the above discussion is the assumption that positive experiences with mentors can generalize, enabling youth to interact with others more effectively (see Figure 3.1, Path c). When there has been a history of unsatisfactory ties, mentors can precipitate fundamental shifts in children's and adolescents' abilities to form and sustain beneficial connections to others. Among youth with generally healthy relationships, mentoring relationships may ease difficulties in everyday interactions by promoting improved communication and emotional regulation.

Research

Preliminary research support has emerged for the potential of positive relationships with mentors to strengthen or modify the social-emotional development of youth. Mentoring relationships formed through community- and school-based programs have been linked to improvements in children's and adolescents' perceptions of their parental relationships, including levels of intimacy, communication, and trust (Karcher, Davis, & Powell, 2002; Rhodes, Grossman, & Resch, 2000). These improvements, in turn, have been found to be associated with positive changes in a wide array of areas, such as overall feelings of self-worth, perceived scholastic competence, and grades (Rhodes et al., 2000); spelling achievement (Karcher et al., 2002); and substance use (Rhodes, Reddy, & Grossman, in press). Other studies have found evidence of mentoring ties contributing to improvements in perceptions by youth of support from peer relationships (Rhodes, Haight, & Briggs, 1999) and from significant adults in their social networks (DuBois, Neville, Parra, & Pugh-Lilley, 2002).

Cognitive Development

Theory

Mentoring relationships also may affect a range of cognitive developmental processes (see Figure 3.1, Path d). As children develop, they experience improvements in basic cognitive processes, such as information processing, abstract and relativistic thinking, and self-monitoring. It has been widely posited by developmental theorists that social interaction plays a major role in facilitating these cognitive changes. Vygotsky (1978) described a "zone of proximal development" in which learning takes place: beyond what a child or adolescent can attain when problem solving independently but within the range of what he or she can do while working under adult guidance or with more capable peers. When children's or adolescents' interactions with caring adults stretch them into this zone, this is assumed to facilitate cognitive and intellectual growth. Along similar lines, Rogoff (1990) has described how children "appropriate" from shared activities with more sophisticated thinkers. These considerations suggest that a relationship with a mentor may help provide the scaffolding for children and adolescents to acquire and refine new thinking skills. Meaningful, youth-relevant conversations between mentors and mentees may be one important mechanism through which such benefits accrue (DuBois, Neville, et al., 2002; Hamilton & Darling, 1996). In this way, mentoring relationships may provide a safe haven

for youth to air sensitive issues and for mentors to transmit adult values, advice, and perspectives (Rhodes, 2002).

Research

Research on the role of social support in fostering cognitive development underscores the social nature of learning and, specifically, the potential contributions of adults in mentoring roles. Feelings of closeness with teachers, for example, have been associated with more positive academic adjustment for children and adolescents (e.g., Connell & Wellborn, 1991). In particular, consistent associations have been documented between perceptions of teacher-student relationships and increases in student motivation, academic competence and achievement, school engagement, school value, and behavioral adjustment (Reddy, Rhodes, & Mulhall, 2003; Roeser & Eccles, 1998; Ryan & Grolnick, 1986). Several studies also have revealed improvements in academic outcomes for youth in the context of close and enduring ties with natural and assigned mentors (Klaw, Fitzgerald, & Rhodes, 2003; Lee & Cramond, 1999; Slicker & Palmer, 1993).

Identity Development

Theory

As noted, mentoring relationships also may facilitate identity development of youth (see Figure 3.1, Path e). Freud (1914) described an identification process in which people internalize the attitudes, behaviors, and traits of individuals they wish to emulate. Similarly, Kohut (1984) theorized that children and adolescents attach themselves to an idealized parental "imago" whose qualities they incorporate into their own personalities. As they identify with their mentors and view them as role models, children's and adolescents' early internalizations may begin to change, causing shifts in their sense of identity and social roles.

This process is related to what Cooley (1902) described as the "looking-glass self"—wherein significant people in children's and adolescents' lives can become social mirrors into which the young people look to form opinions of themselves. The opinions that they see reflected back at them then become integrated into their sense of self. Mead (1934) similarly posited that individuals can incorporate the "reflected appraisal" of others' views of them—imagining how they are perceived by significant people in their lives. As the mentor's perceived positive appraisal becomes incorporated into the mentee's sense of self, it may modify the way the youth thinks that parents, peers, teachers, and others see him or her.

Through this process of reflected appraisals, mentors may help shift children's and adolescents' conceptions of both their current and future identities.

Along similar lines, Marcus and Nurius (1986) also have referred to "possible selves": individuals' ideas of what they might become, what they would like to become, and what they fear becoming. Such possibilities, which often emerge as youth observe and compare the adults they know, can inform current decisions and behavior. Indeed, many lower-income youth have limited contact with positive role models outside the immediate family and believe that their opportunities for success are restricted (Anderson, 1999). Even among middle-income youth, adult occupations and skills can seem obscure and out of reach (Larson, 2000). Still other youth have unrealistic expectations and little knowledge about the levels of education that are needed for their chosen professions.

More generally, relationships with adults can provide both social and cultural capital in the form of knowledge (Dubas & Snider, 1993), helping youth to make use of community resources and recreation programs and opening doors to educational or occupational opportunities. Participation in such new opportunities also can facilitate identity development by providing experiences on which children and adolescents can draw to construct their sense of self (Erikson, 1964; Yates & Youniss, 1996). Indeed, Waterman (1982) has proposed that activities provide opportunities for discovering special talents and abilities and are thus a primary source through which identity is formed. Beyond this function, participation in prosocial activities and settings may expose youth to more socially desirable or high-achieving peer groups with whom they can identify.

Research

Research evidence supports the possibility that mentors can affect change in youth behaviors relating to their identity development. Children and adolescents with natural and volunteer mentors have been found to be less likely to take part in delinquent problem behaviors (Aseltine, Dupre, & Lamlein, 2000; Davidson & Redner, 1988; Grossman & Tierney, 1998) and more likely to graduate from high school (Klaw et al., 2003), both of which suggest the presence of a more positive future orientation in the identities of mentored youth. In a study of future perceptions, Hellenga, Aber, and Rhodes (2002) empirically distinguished between adolescents with and without discrepancies between their vocational aspirations and expectations for the future. Having a career mentor was associated with a match (as opposed to a gap) between adolescents' aspirations and expectations (Hellenga et al., 2002). However, it should be noted the direction of the preceding types of linkages is not yet fully established. It also is plausible in this regard, for example, that being prosocial, academically successful, and future oriented increases the likelihood that natural mentors will emerge in the lives of such youth.

Bidirectional Pathways

The social-emotional, cognitive, and identity processes described in the preceding sections are assumed to work in concert with one another over time (see Figure 3.1, f arrows). For example, the use of a mentor as a role model and the ability to entertain multiple possible selves may be fostered by the ability of youth to make more nuanced comparisons across relationships and a growing capacity to understand the world from the perspective of others (Keating, 1990). Growth in these cognitive abilities, in turn, can enhance the capacity of youth to regulate complicated emotions (Diamond & Aspinwall, 2003) and to select institutions and relationships that best match their goals, values, and abilities (Clausen, 1991). Likewise, adolescents' striving for autonomy and their intensifying desire for connection to others and involvement in the larger social context provide opportunities for the revision of working models of attachment

(Allen & Land, 1999; Main, Kaplan, & Cassidy, 1985) as well as openings for role models and other forms of social capital.

Moderating Processes

As noted, the proposed model further assumes that both the strength of the mentoring relationship's foundation in trust, empathy, and mutuality and the pathways linking model components to youth outcomes are conditioned by a range of individual, family, and contextual influences as well as the length of the relationship (see Figure 3.1, g arrows).

Child's Interpersonal History

Children and adolescents who have enjoyed healthy relationships with their parents may more easily be drawn to adults as role models and confidants. In such cases, the relationship may focus more on the acquisition of skills and the advancement of critical thinking than on emotional issues (Hamilton & Darling, 1996). Indeed, Rhodes, Contreras, and Mangelsdorf (1994) found that compared with those who did not report having a natural mentor, adolescents with natural mentors recalled early relationships with their mothers as more accepting. More recently, Soucy and Larose (2000) found evidence that the positive effects of mentors were stronger among youth who reported having higher levels of security in their relationships with their mothers. This suggests that mentors may not entirely compensate for insecure family bonds—instead, they may be beneficial as long as there is already a minimum level of support from at least one parent.

On the other hand, those who have experienced unsatisfactory or difficult parental ties may initially resist the overtures of a caring adult, but over time develop more intense bonds with their mentors that help satisfy their social and emotional needs. Mentoring relationships also may serve to compensate for absent relationships. Immigrant youth, for example, many of whom have suffered long separations from their parents, may gravitate to mentors for compensatory emotional support. Mentors may provide these youth with a safe haven for learning new cultural norms and practices, as well as

with information that is vital to success in school (Roffman, Suarez-Orozco, & Rhodes, in press; Stanton-Salazar & Spina, 2003). The same holds true for youth in foster homes, many of whom have suffered child abuse and neglect. Rhodes et al. (1999) found that foster youth derived greater interpersonal benefits (i.e., improvements in peer relationships, heightened trust and comfort in interactions with others) than nonfoster youth.

Social Competencies

As mentioned earlier, youth who are better able to regulate their emotions and who have positive temperaments and/or other engaging attributes may be primed for higher levels of involvement with adults than are peers who lack these attributes. Werner and Smith (1982), for example, observed that youth who had thrived despite adversity tended to have hobbies or other interests and a capacity to connect with adults through those activities. More generally, youth with higher levels of social competence tend to be held in higher regard by their peers and teachers (Morison & Masten, 1991). The research on mentoring bears this out: Adolescents who are overwhelmed by social or behavioral problems tend to be less likely to benefit from mentoring (DuBois, Holloway, et al., 2002; Grossman & Johnson, 1998). Grossman and Rhodes (2002), for example, found that mentoring relationships with adolescents who had been referred for psychological treatment or who had sustained emotional, sexual, or physical abuse were less likely to remain intact. Such youth appear to have more difficulties trusting adults and may have little experience with behaviors that establish and maintain closeness and support (Lynch & Cicchetti, 1997).

Developmental Stage

The mentee's age may also affect the nature and course of a mentoring relationship. For example, whereas early adolescents who are beginning to struggle with identity issues may wish to engage in abstract conversations with their mentors, children whose levels of cognitive sophistication are less advanced may benefit more from structured activities (Keating, 1990). In addition, adolescents on the brink of adulthood may be less interested in establishing emotional ties with mentors, instead gravitating to peers and vocational skill-building activities. Older adolescents tend to be more peer oriented than their younger counterparts and less likely to sustain their involvement in structured mentoring programs. Indeed, researchers have found that relationships with older adolescents are characterized by lower levels of closeness (Herrera et al., 2000), heightened risk for termination during any given month (Grossman & Rhodes, 2002), and shorter duration than those with younger youth (Bauldry & Hartmann, 2004).

Relationship Duration

The benefits of mentoring appear to accrue over a relatively long period of time. Grossman and Rhodes (2002) found that the associations of mentor relationships with outcomes varied as a function of their duration. Relative to controls, youth whose relationships terminated within a year appeared to derive the fewest benefits, and those in short matches (i.e., terminating within the first 3 to 6 months) actually suffered declines in reported levels of feelings of self-worth and perceived scholastic competence. For youth who were in matches that lasted more than a year, however, positive effects were evident on levels of self-worth, perceived social acceptance and scholastic competence, parental relationship quality, school value, and levels of both drug and alcohol use. These findings are consistent with other studies (Lee & Cramond, 1999) as well as a meta-analysis of mentoring program evaluations (DuBois, Holloway, et al., 2002).

Program Practices

Programs that offer adequate infrastructure increase the likelihood that relationships can endure difficult periods (DuBois, Holloway, et al., 2002; Rhodes, 2002). In fact, program practices that support the mentor and relationship (i.e., training for mentors, offering structured activities for mentors and youth, having high expectations for frequency of contact, and monitoring of overall program implementation) produce stronger positive effects (DuBois,

Holloway, et al., 2002). These practices, which speak to a program's ability to not only match mentors and youth but also sustain those matches, converge with the beneficial practices identified by other researchers (Herrera et al., 2000). Unfortunately, moving youth off long wait lists can sometimes take priority over creating high-quality matches. Even among the growing number of programs with careful recruitment, screening, and matching, a relatively smaller proportion devote themselves to in-depth training of volunteers or ongoing support to the mentors (DuBois, Holloway, et al., 2002; Rhodes, 2002; Sipe & Roder, 1999). Cost, combined with a general reluctance to make demands on volunteers, is the primary obstacle to providing more sustained involvement and infrastructure beyond the initial match (DuBois, Holloway, et al., 2002).

Family Context

The likelihood of a child or adolescent forming strong ties with mentors may be affected by a range of processes in the family, including the encouragement and opportunities that parents provide for the development of such ties. Families characterized by sensitivity to others' ideas and needs and open expression of views are more likely to encourage adolescents to become involved in positive relationships outside the family (Cooper, Grotevant, & Condon, 1983). With specific relevance to mentoring, children and adolescents with more supportive parental relationships and higher levels of shared family decision making have been found to be more likely to report natural mentors (Zimmerman, Bingenheimer, & Notaro, 2002). Parents who actively cultivate connections and channel their children to community-based recreational and social programs also may increase the likelihood that their children will form beneficial relationships with adults beyond the nuclear family (Zimmerman et al., 2002). Mentoring programs that reach out to parents tend to have greater success in shaping youth outcomes. Other factors, including family stability, mobility, and the extent to which mentoring programs reach out to parents, can affect the establishment and maintenance of strong ties (DuBois, Holloway, et al., 2002; Rhodes, 2002).

Neighborhood Ecology

Researchers have observed that extracurricular activities and supportive relationships with adults tend to be more beneficial to adolescents raised in urban poverty than to lower-risk youth, who encounter more supportive adults in their everyday lives (DuBois, Holloway, et al., 2002; Grossman & Johnson, 1998). Indeed, neighborhood characteristics and norms can affect the availability of caring, informal adult ties as well as the willingness of volunteers to genuinely connect with children and adolescents. Changing family and marital patterns, crowded schools, and less cohesive communities have dramatically reduced the availability of caring adults in the lives of youth (Putnam, 2000). Even when they are available, however, fewer American adults are willing to offer support and guidance to unrelated youth. Parents have come to be considered solely responsible for their children, so the involvement of other adults is often met with suspicion and discomfort (Scales, 2003). Indeed, words like *clergy, uncles,* and even *neighbors* no longer simply conjure images of front-porch warmth and goodwill; they also evoke parental anxiety and confusion about the boundaries of trust and safety. Similarly, as mentoring programs increasingly accommodate volunteers' busy schedules, they have eased requirements for relationship commitment and intensity. The result in some cases has been the formation of perfunctory ties that resemble, but share little in common with, the long-term community-based relationships from which they have evolved (Rhodes, 2002). In essence, changing family and neighborhood configurations, busy schedules, and shifting norms regarding adult involvement in the lives of youth have limited the likelihood that youth will engage in the sorts of caring relationships with mentors that can lead to developmental change.

FUTURE DIRECTIONS

Synthesis

This chapter has presented a model in which a close mentoring relationship characterized by mutuality, trust, and empathy is the catalyst for several intertwined developmental processes pertaining to the social-emotional, cognitive, and identity development of youth. These developmental gains, in turn, contribute to positive outcomes for youth, mediated at least in part by their contributions to positive growth in other significant relationships in their lives. The extent to which foundational qualities (e.g., trust) are established, as well as how and in what sequence the various model pathways are activated, is presumed to be governed, at least in part, by the length of the relationship, as well as the youth, family, and contextual characteristics. Research to date provides support for the model's key assumptions. However, this research is limited in scope and has not addressed the nature and extent of several of the specific processes that are posited in the model.

The practical implications of many of the assumptions set forth in this chapter remain unclear, and further research is urgently needed. For example, despite an emerging consensus regarding the fundamental importance of a close mentor-mentee relationship, the road to establishing such closeness remains the subject of considerable debate. Some researchers suggest that irrespective of attachment histories, close relationships are most likely to emerge when the focus of their interaction is on skills. Darling, Hamilton, and Niego (1994), for example, have found that mentors who engage with youth in challenging, goal-directed activities are more likely to be successful than those whose primary focus is to get to know the adolescent. They noted that emotional relationships appeared to grow out of adults' validation of the efforts and abilities of youth. "Ironically, relationships were built when building a relationship was not the main purpose of getting together" (Darling et al., 1994, p. 220). Similarly, relative to controls and other relationship types, youth in BBBS relationships that were characterized by moderate levels of both activity and structure were found to derive the largest number of benefits from the relationships (Langhout, Rhodes, & Osborne, 2004). Others have highlighted the value of a more emotion-focused approach (Spencer, 2003). McClanahan (1998), for example, found that youth who were engaged in more emotionally based activities reported more positive perceptions of their relationships than those whose relationships focused primarily on working toward goals. Liang, Tracy, Taylor, and Williams (2002) have argued that mentors' traditionally more instrumental functions (e.g., advice, skill building) might be less relevant to females.

Recommendations for Research

1. *Further investigation and refinement of the proposed model.* The model described in this chapter should be further tested and refined through additional research. For example, it will be important to examine the ways in which mentor relationships operate within and depart from the emotional frameworks developed through parent-child relationships. Longitudinal investigations should be conducted whenever possible to help clarify directions of effect and long-term magnitude of impact of different types of model effects. Further investigation of moderation processes in the model should receive priority as well. This includes a need to explore how mentoring relationship processes in the model may differ in their effects on youth from diverse backgrounds as well as on those who have struggled with difficult interpersonal histories or show deficits in social competencies. By the same token, we know little about how different aspects of the model apply to youth who differ by gender, sexual orientation, age, and ethnicity. A better understanding of relationship processes, from both the mentors' and mentees' perspectives, could contribute to a deeper understanding of the processes in the proposed model.

2. *Examine processes across different types of relationships and programmatic contexts.* There is a need for systematic comparisons of the relationships that are forged in natural versus assigned relationships and in programs that vary in type, intensity, supervision, training, matching, and length. The relative effectiveness and cost of approaches such as group mentoring, peer mentoring, and e-mentoring need to be gauged carefully, using, if possible, randomized, controlled studies. In essence, relationships, programs, and practices need to be evaluated for their ability to produce enduring, positive outcomes that generalize across multiple areas of functioning.

Recommendations for Practice

1. *Explore the use of multiple program strategies to target pathways to change in mentoring relationships.* Once a close mentoring relationship is forged, the pathways to developmental change appear to vary on the bases of both individual and contextual influences. Given this diversity, it is promising that mentoring programs are in the process of expanding into a wide array of program strategies, including mentoring in groups, at schools and work settings, and even over the Internet. At the same time, it would be shortsighted to assume that all of these newer types of relationships will offer the same benefits as the well-run, community-based, one-to-one mentoring programs that have been studied most intensively. Pending this type of research, one promising strategy for practitioners is to critically examine the extent to which different mentoring program strategies are likely to address the mediating processes emphasized in the model proposed in this chapter.

2. *Create strong program infrastructures.* As described in this chapter, a strong program infrastructure that promotes the development and maturation of close positive relationships between youth and their mentors is likely to be critical to the formation of close relationships and, ultimately, the effectiveness of the newer forms of mentoring. For example, given the evidence of an important moderating effect of relationship duration in the formation of close relationships, efforts should be made to recruit and retain mentors who are willing to stick with their mentees through thick or thin. Recruitment efforts should thus describe both the benefits a volunteer can expect and the commitment that is required. Once recruited, volunteers should be screened by program staff who are sensitive to any circumstances and characteristics that might put volunteers at risk for early termination.

3. *Tap into pools of volunteers at lower risk for termination.* In addition to screening out or perhaps enhancing support to volunteers who may have difficulty making the necessary commitment, it might also be helpful to tap into pools of volunteers who are at lower risk for termination. Some programs have recognized the

enormous volunteer potential that exists among retired adults. Older adults have more time to devote to this pursuit and are ideally positioned to provide the level of personal attention and emotional support that many youth need (Taylor & Bressler, 2001). At the same time, efforts should be made to facilitate the volunteer efforts of working parents and other adults. It also should not be overlooked that these pools of volunteers may include individuals whose backgrounds and abilities make them well prepared to enhance processes (e.g., role modeling, advocacy) that are discussed in this chapter as mediating positive effects of relationships on outcomes.

4. *Involve and engage parents.* Another assumption of the model with direct practical application is that the positive effects of mentoring relationships can reverberate back, ultimately drawing adolescents and their parents closer together. Although mentoring programs have not always involved parents and families in a comfortable or coherent manner, program personnel should remain aware of the ways that successful mentoring relationships can improve family dynamics, and they should take steps to capitalize on that possibility. If parents feel involved in—as opposed to shut out by—the process that brings other adults into their children's lives, they may be more likely to reinforce mentors' positive influences (DuBois, Holloway, et al., 2002).

As mentoring programs assume an increasingly important role in our society, we need to improve our understanding of the conditions and processes by which they work—and don't work. With a deeper understanding of the mentoring process described in this model, programs can more effectively capitalize on the potential for positively influencing a range of developmental outcomes.

References

Ainsworth, M. (1989). Attachments beyond infancy. *American Psychologist, 44,* 709–716.

Allen, J. P., & Land, D. (1999). Attachment in adolescence. In J. Cassidy, P. R. Shaver, et al. (Eds.), *Handbook of attachment: Theory, research, and clinical applications* (pp. 319–335). New York: Guilford Press.

Allen, J. P., McElhaney, K. B., Land, D. J., Kuperminc, G. P., Moore, C. W., O'Beirne-Kelly, H., et al. (2003). A secure base in adolescence: Markers of attachment security in mother-adolescent relationship. *Child Development, 74,* 292–307.

Anderson, E. (1999). *Code of the street: Decency, violence, and the moral life of the inner city.* New York: Norton.

Aseltine, R. H., Jr., Dupre, M., & Lamlein, P. (2000). Mentoring as a drug prevention strategy: An evaluation of across ages. *Adolescent & Family Health, 1,* 11–20.

Bauldry, S., & Hartmann, T. A. (2004). *The promise and challenge of mentoring high-risk youth. Findings from the national faith-based initiative.* Philadelphia: Public/Private Ventures.

Belsky, J., & Cassidy, J. (1994). Attachment: Theory and evidence. In M. Rutter & D. F. Hay (Eds.), *Development through life: A handbook for clinicians* (pp. 373–402). Oxford, UK: Blackwell Science.

Bowlby, J. (1988). *A secure base: Parent-child attachment and healthy human development.* New York: Basic Books.

Bretherton, I., & Waters, E. (Eds.). (1985). Growing points of attachment theory and research. *Monograph of the Society for Research in Child Development 50*(1–2, Serial No. 209), pp. 66–104.

Buckner, J. C., Mezzacappa, E., & Beardslee, W. R. (2003). Characteristics of resilient youths living in poverty: The role of self-regulatory processes. *Development and Psychopathology, 15,* 139–162.

Caplan, G. (1964). *Principles of preventive psychiatry.* New York: Basic Books.

Carlson, E. A., & Sroufe, L. A. (1995). Contribution of attachment theory to developmental psychopathology. In D. Cicchetti & D. Cohen (Eds.), *Developmental psychopathology, Vol. 1: Theory and methods* (pp. 581–617). New York: Wiley.

Clausen, J. A. (1991). Adolescent competence and the life course, or why one social psychologist needed a concept of personality. *Social Psychology Quarterly, 54,* 4–14.

Connell, J. P., & Wellborn, J. G. (1991). Competence, autonomy, and relatedness: A motivational analysis of self-system processes. In M. R. Gunnar & L. A. Sroufe (Eds.), *Minnesota Symposium on Child Psychology: Vol. 23. Self-processes in development* (pp. 43–77). Hillsdale, NJ: Erlbaum.

Cooley, C. H. (1902). *Human nature and the social order.* New York: Scribner.

Cooper, C. R., Grotevant, H. D., & Condon, S. M. (1983). Individuality and connectedness both foster adolescent identity formation and role taking skills. In H. D Grotevant & C. R. Cooper (Eds.), *Adolescent development in the family* (*New Directions for Child Development: Theory, Research, and Practice, No. 22,* pp. 43–59). San Francisco: Jossey-Bass.

Csiksizentmihalyi, M., & Rathunde, K. (1998). The development of person: An experiential perspective on the ontogenesis of psychological complexity. In W. Damon (Series Ed.) & R. M. Lerner (Vol. Ed.), *Handbook of child psychology: Vol. 1. Theoretical models of human development* (5th ed., pp. 635–684). New York: Wiley.

Darling, N., Hamilton, S. F., & Niego, S. (1994). Adolescents' relations with adults outside the family. In R. Montemeyor & G. R. Adams (Eds.), *Personal relationships during adolescence, advances in adolescent development: An annual book series* (pp. 216–235). Thousand Oaks, CA: Sage.

Davidson, W. S., & Redner, R. (1988). The prevention of juvenile delinquency: Diversion from the juvenile justice system. In R. H. Price, E. L. Cowen, R. P. Lorion, & E. J. Ramos-McKay (Eds.), *Fourteen ounces of prevention: Theory, research, and prevention* (pp. 123–137). New York: Pergamon Press.

Denham, S., & Kochanoff, A. T. (2002). Parental contributions to preschoolers' understanding of emotion. *Marriage & Family Review, 34,* 311–343.

Diamond, L. M., & Aspinwall, L. G. (2003). Emotion regulation across the life span: An integrative perspective emphasizing self-regulation, positive affect, and dyadic processes. *Motivation and Emotion, 27,* 125–156.

Dubas, J. S., & Snider, B. A. (1993). The role of community-based youth groups in enhancing learning and achievement through non-formal education. In R. M. Lerner (Ed.), *Early adolescence: Perspectives on research, policy, and intervention* (pp. 150–174). Hillsdale, NJ: Erlbaum.

DuBois, D. L., Holloway, B. E, Valentine, J. C., & Cooper, H. (2002). Effectiveness of mentoring programs for youth: A meta-analytic review. *American Journal of Community Psychology, 30,* 157–197.

DuBois, D. L., Neville, H. A., Parra, G. R., & Pugh-Lilly, A. O. (2002). Testing a new model of mentoring. In G. G. Noam (Ed. in chief) & J. E. Rhodes (Ed.), *A critical view of youth mentoring* (*New Directions for Youth Development: Theory, Research, and Practice, No. 93*), pp. 21–57. San Francisco: Jossey-Bass.

Dworkin, J. B., Larson, R., & Hansen, D. (2003). Adolescents' accounts of growth experiences in youth activities. *Journal of Youth and Adolescence, 32,* 17–26.

Eisenberg, N., Spinrad, T. L., Fabes, R. A., Reiser, M., Cumberland, A., Shepard, S. A., et al. (2004). The relations of effortful control and impulsivity to children's resiliency and adjustment. *Child Development, 75,* 25–46.

Erikson, E. H. (1964). *Identity and the life cycle.* New York: Norton.

Freud, S. (1914). On narcissism: An introduction. In J. Strachey (Ed.), *Standard edition of the complete psychological works of Sigmund Freud, 14,* 73–102.

Gottman, J. M. (2001). Meta-emotion, children's emotional intelligence, and buffering children from marital conflict. In C. D. Ryff & B. H. Singer (Eds.), *Emotion, social relationships, and health* (pp. 23–39). New York: Oxford University Press.

Grossman, J. B., & Johnson, A. (1998). Assessing the effectiveness of mentoring programs. In J. B. Grossman (Ed.), *Contemporary issues in mentoring* (pp. 25–47). Philadelphia: Public/Private Ventures.

Grossman, J. B., & Rhodes, J. E. (2002). The test of time: Predictors and effects of duration in youth mentoring programs. *American Journal of Community Psychology, 30,* 199–219.

Grossman, J. B., & Tierney, J. P. (1998). Does mentoring work? An impact study of the Big Brothers Big Sisters program. *Evaluation Review, 22,* 403–426.

Hamilton, S. F., & Darling, N. (1996). Mentors in adolescents' lives. In K. Hurrelmann & S. F. Hamilton (Eds.), *Social problems and social contexts in adolescence: Perspectives across boundaries* (pp. 199–215). New York: Pergamon Press.

Hellenga, K., Aber, M. S., & Rhodes, J. E. (2002). African American adolescent mothers' vocational aspiration-expectation gap: Individual, social and environmental influences. *Psychology of Women Quarterly, 26,* 200–212.

Herrera, C., Sipe, C. L., & McClanahan, W. S. (2000). *Mentoring school-age children: Relationship development in community-based and school-based programs.* Philadelphia: Public/Private Ventures. (Published in collaboration with MENTOR/National Mentoring Partnership, Alexandria, VA)

Karcher, M. J., Davis, C., & Powell, B. (2002). The effects of developmental mentoring on connectedness and academic achievement. *The School Community Journal, 12*(2), 35–50.

Keating, D. P. (1990). Adolescent thinking. In S. S. Feldman & G. R. Elliott (Eds.), *At the threshold: The developing adolescent* (pp. 54–89). Cambridge, MA: Harvard University Press.

Klaw, E. L., Fitzgerald, L. F., & Rhodes, J. E. (2003). Natural mentors in the lives of African American adolescent mothers: Tracking relationships over time. *Journal of Youth and Adolescence, 32,* 322–232.

Kohut, H. (1984). *How does analysis cure?* Chicago: University of Chicago Press.

Langhout, R. D., Rhodes, J. E., & Osborne, L. (2004). An exploratory study of youth mentoring in an urban context: Adolescents' perceptions of relationship styles. *Journal of Youth and Adolescence, 33,* 293–306.

Larson, W. (2000). Toward a psychology of positive youth development. *American Psychologist, 55,* 170–183.

Lee, J., & Cramond, B. (1999). The positive effects of mentoring economically disadvantaged students. *Professional School Counseling, 2,* 172–178.

Lefkowitz, B. (1986). *Tough change: Growing up on your own in America.* New York: Free Press.

Levinson, D. J. (1979). *The seasons of a man's life.* New York: Ballantine Books.

Liang, B., Tracy, A. J., Taylor, C. A., & Williams, L. M. (2002). Mentoring college-age women: A relational approach. *American Journal of Community Psychology, 30,* 271–288.

Lynch, M., & Cicchetti, D. (1997). Children's relationships with adults and peers: An examination of elementary and junior high school students. *Journal of School Psychology, 35,* 81–100.

Main, M., Kaplan, N., & Cassidy, J. (1985). Security in infancy, childhood, and adulthood: A move to the level of representation. In I. Bretherton, & E. Waters (Eds.), *Growing points of attachment theory and research. Monographs of the Society for Research in Child Development, 50*(1–2, Serial No. 209), 66–104.

Marcus, H., & Nurius, P. (1986). Possible selves. *American Psychologist, 41,* 954–969.

Masten, A. S., & Coatsworth, J. D. (1998). The development of competence in favorable and unfavorable environments: Lessons from research on successful children. *American Psychologist, 53,* 205–220.

McClanahan, W. S. (1998). *Relationships in a career mentoring programs: Lessons learned from the hospital youth mentoring program.* Philadelphia: Public/Private Ventures.

Mead, G. H. (1934). *Mind, self, and society from the standpoint of a social behaviorist.* Chicago: University of Chicago Press.

Morison, P., & Masten, A. S. (1991). Peer reputation in middle childhood as a predictor of adaptation in adolescence. A seven-year follow-up. *Child Development, 62,* 991–1007.

Olds, D., Kitzman, H., Cole, R., & Robinson, J. (1997). Theoretical formulations of a program of home visitation for pregnant women and parents of young children. *Journal of Community Psychology, 25,* 9–26.

Pianta, R. C. (1999). *Enhancing relationships between children and teachers.* Washington, DC: American Psychological Association.

Putnam, R. D. (2000). *Bowling alone: The collapse and revival of American community.* New York: Simon & Schuster.

Reddy, R., Rhodes, J., & Mulhall, P. (2003). The influence of teacher support on student adjustment in the middle school years: A latent growth curve study. *Development and Psychopathology, 15,* 119–138.

Rhodes, J., Reddy, R., & Grossman, J. (in press). The protective influence of mentoring on adolescents' substance use: Direct and indirect pathways. *Applied Developmental Science.*

Rhodes, J. Reddy, J., Roffman, J., & Grossman, J. (in press). Promoting successful youth relationships: A preliminary screening questionnaire. *Journal of Primary Prevention.*

Rhodes, J. E. (2002). *Stand by me: The risks and rewards of mentoring today's youth.* Cambridge, MA: Harvard University Press.

Rhodes, J. E., Contreras, J. M., & Mangelsdorf, S. C. (1994). Natural mentor relationships among Latina adolescent mothers: Psychological adjustment, moderating processes, and the role of early parental acceptance. *American Journal of Community Psychology, 22,* 211–228.

Rhodes, J. E., Grossman, J. B., & Resch, N. R. (2000). Agents of change: Pathways through which mentoring relationships influence adolescents' academic adjustment. *Child Development, 71,* 1662–1671.

Rhodes, J. E., Haight, W. L., & Briggs, E. (1999). The influence of mentoring on the peer relationships of foster youth in relative and nonrelative care. *Journal of Research on Adolescence, 9,* 185–201.

Roberts, H., Liabø, K., Lucas, P., DuBois, D., & Sheldon, T. A. (2004). Mentoring to reduce antisocial behaviour in childhood. *British Medical Journal, 328,* 512–514.

Roeser, R. W., & Eccles, J. S. (1998). Adolescents' perceptions of middle school: Relation to longitudinal changes in academic and psychological adjustment. *Journal of Research on Adolescence, 8,* 123–158.

Roffman, J. G., Suarez-Orozco, C., & Rhodes, J. E. (in press). Facilitating positive development in immigrant youth: The role of mentors and community organizers. In D. F. Perkins, L. M. Borden, J. G. Keith, & F. A. Villarruel (Eds.), *Positive youth development: Creating a positive tomorrow.* New York: Kluwer Academic Press.

Rogoff, B. (1990). *Apprenticeship in thinking: Cognitive development in social context.* New York: Oxford University Press.

Ryan, R. M., & Grolnick, W. S. (1986). Origins and pawns in the classroom: Self-report and projective assessments of individual differences in children's perceptions. *Journal of Personality and Social Psychology, 50,* 550–558.

Scales, P. C. (2003). *Other people's kids: Social expectation and American adults' involvement with children and adolescents.* New York: Kluwer Academic Press.

Sipe, C. L., & Roder, A. E. (1999). *Mentoring school-age children: A classification of programs.* Philadelphia: Public/Private Ventures. (Published in collaboration with MENTOR/National Mentoring Partnership, Alexandria, VA)

Slicker, E. K., & Palmer, D. J. (1993). Mentoring at-risk high school students: Evaluation of a school-based program. *The School Counselor, 40,* 327–333.

Soucy, N., & Larose, S. (2000). Attachment and control in family and mentoring contexts as determinants of adolescent adjustment at college. *Journal of Family Psychology, 14,* 125–143.

Spencer, R. (2003). *Getting to the heart of the mentoring process: An in-depth interview study with adolescents and their adult mentors.* Manuscript submitted for publication.

Stanton-Salazar, R. D., & Spina, S. U. (2003). Informal mentors and role models in the lives of urban Mexican-origin adolescents. *Anthropology & Education Quarterly, 34,* 231–254.

Taylor, A. S., & Bressler, J. (2001). *Mentoring across generations: Partnerships for positive youth development.* New York: Kluwer Academic Press.

Vygotsky, S. (1978). *Mind in society.* Cambridge, MA: Harvard University Press.

Waterman, A. S. (1982). Identity development from adolescence to adulthood: An extension of theory and a review of research. *Developmental Psychology, 18,* 341–358.

Werner, E. E., & Smith, E. S. (1982). *Vulnerable but invincible: A study of resilient children.* New York: McGraw-Hill.

Williams, T. M., & Kornblum, W. (1985). *Growing up poor.* Lexington, MA: Lexington Books.

Yates, M., & Youniss, J. (1966). Community service and political-moral identity in adolescents. *Journal of Research on Adolescence, 6,* 271–284.

Zimmerman, M. A., Bingenheimer, J. B., & Notaro, P. C. (2002). Natural mentors and adolescent resiliency: A study with urban youth. *American Journal of Community Psychology, 30,* 221–243.

4

RESEARCH METHODOLOGY

DAVID L. DuBOIS AND NAIDA SILVERTHORN

INTRODUCTION

What are the defining features or dimensions of mentoring relationships for youth? How do these change or evolve across different stages of relationships? Across different types of youth, mentors, or contexts? What are the effects of mentoring relationships on youth? On mentors? What processes are responsible for these effects?

What is the impact of mentoring programs on youth? How do these effects vary across modes of mentoring (e.g., one-on-one, group), program sites (e.g., community, school, workplace), populations of youth, and types of outcomes? What are "best practices" for different types of mentoring programs? What is the cost-effectiveness of different types of practices and programs?

Mentoring of youth, as illustrated by these questions, is a complex and multifaceted phenomenon. Methods used to investigate youth mentoring need to be sensitive to this complexity and thus capable of providing valid answers to the full range of questions that may be posed regarding both relationships and programs. As this understanding highlights, rigorous research methodology is required for advancement of the scientific knowledge base of the field. From an applied perspective, sound research methods represent an invaluable tool for informing the development, evaluation, ongoing refinement, and dissemination of effective mentoring interventions for youth. In the absence of evidence generated by such methods, we run the risk of having practice in the field of mentoring driven by a pseudo–knowledge base in which opinion and anecdote (or perhaps worse, "bad" science) serve as the primary guide for action (Roberts, Liabø, Lucas, DuBois, & Sheldon, 2004). Potential costs associated with this scenario include not only falling well short in our efforts to maximize the transformative power and reach of youth mentoring relationships but also a failure to identify and avert their unintended negative consequences. Finally, research that meets criteria for scientific rigor may be instrumental to encouraging investment in youth mentoring by individuals, youth-serving organizations, and funding sources. Public/Private Ventures landmark experimental study of the effectiveness of Big Brothers Big Sisters (BBBS) programs is illustrative in this regard (Tierney, Grossman, & Resch, 1995). The widely perceived scientific legitimacy of this study has enabled its findings and conclusions to propel mentoring to firm footing on the social policy landscape nationally

The writing of this chapter was supported in part by a grant to David L. DuBois from the National Institute of Mental Health (1 R21 MH069564–01).

(see Walker, this volume) and at the local level, to become a ubiquitous part of efforts to recruit new volunteers to programs (see Stukas & Tanti, this volume).

These upsides notwithstanding, there are some potential downsides of adhering to high standards in research methodology. The investment of time, effort, and other resources for researchers, study participants, and supporting organizations can be substantial. Funders too can be expected to need to invest significant resources to support high-quality investigations of mentoring (Rhodes & DuBois, 2004). Simply put, good science "costs" more than bad science and is not cheap in either human or financial terms. This understanding underscores the importance of identifying ways in which state-of-the-art research methodology can be utilized in studies of youth mentoring to make the most efficient use of available resources and yield maximal returns.

Adherence to stringent methodological standards also has a potential downside for mentoring advocacy efforts. Those working in this capacity may be confronted with research that although high in scientific credibility, threatens to undercut their efforts to secure further resources and support for youth mentoring. In many instances, this may occur because of limitations in how findings are presented and interpreted. This possibility highlights the need for rigorous standards not only in conducting but also in reporting research on youth mentoring.

With these considerations as background, the present chapter reviews methodological issues in research on youth mentoring relationships and programs. First, separate sections are devoted to the issues of sampling, study design, measurement, data analysis, and reporting and interpretation of findings for individual investigations. Within each of these areas, a general principle is described, followed by a critical examination of existing studies of youth mentoring relationships and programs vis-à-vis this principle. Methodological recommendations are then provided, along with discussion of challenges to implementing them that are specific to the field of youth mentoring. Next, methodological issues relating to the need for integration across different studies are discussed using a similar framework. Finally, recommendations for

those in the research and practice communities are presented. The reader also is directed to Table 4.1, which provides a summary of the recommendations that are made throughout the chapter, along with relevant resources.

INDIVIDUAL STUDIES

Sampling

General Principle

Studies need to be based on samples that are both representative of populations of interest and large enough to have sensitivity to processes and effects of interest.

Sample representativeness bears directly on the issue of external validity, the degree to which study findings can be generalized to other individuals or situations (Heiman, 2001). Issues of sample size have direct relevance to statistical power, which refers to the likelihood that a statistically significant result will be obtained when testing an association or effect that is actually present in the larger population (Cohen, 1992; Lipsey, 1990). A Type II error is when an incorrect inference is made because a significant result is not obtained despite the existence of the association or effect being tested (i.e., Type II error rate corresponds to 1 minus power). These considerations highlight the potential for sample limitations in studies of mentoring to result in incorrect and nonrepresentative conclusions about both relationships and programs.

Studies of Relationships

Numerous studies of youth mentoring relationships have been based on samples of participants drawn from BBBS programs. As the investigators conducting these studies themselves have noted (e.g., Morrow & Styles, 1995), findings thus may not generalize either to populations of youth who differ in age, risk status, or other characteristics from those served by BBBS or to relationships established through programs that have different goals or practices in areas such as matching, training, or supervision. Similar concerns regarding representativeness apply to samples drawn from other individual programs. In the case of naturally occurring

Table 4.1   Summary of Recommendations and Resources

Recommendations	*Resources*
Sampling	
S1. Utilize samples in studies of youth mentoring relationships and programs that are representative of the populations of interest.	For an overview of choices in sampling and their research implications, see Henry (1998).
S2. Plan sample size to ensure adequate sensitivity to anticipated size of effects in studies of youth mentoring relationships and programs.	For a discussion of sample size estimation and guidelines for conducting statistical power analyses, see Cohen (1992) and Lipsey (1990); for a discussion of statistical power in structural equation modeling (SEM), see Kaplan (1995); for a list of online power analysis resources, see Pezzullo (n.d.)
Design	
D1. Utilize longitudinal designs to investigate youth mentoring relationships and programs.	For an overview of longitudinal designs in basic research, see Menard (2002); for intervention studies, see Shadish et al. (2002).
D2. Utilize experimental[a] or well-conceived quasi-experimental[b] designs to investigate effects of mentoring programs and practices.	For an overview, see Shadish et al. (2002); for a discussion specific to mentoring, see Grossman, this volume.
Assessment	
A1. Assess mentoring relationships using data from multiple informants, including both mentors and youth, as well as additional sources such as direct observation.	For assessment of closeness and intimacy in relationships, see Mashek and Aron (2004); for assessment of mentoring relationship quality, see Nakkula and Harris, this volume.
A2. Incorporate comprehensive assessment of youth outcomes,[c] mediating and moderating influences, dosage and fidelity, costs, and the mentoring relationships of youth in comparison or control groups in evaluations of mentoring programs.	For assessment of youth outcomes, see Grossman, this volume; for theory regarding potential mediators and moderators, see chapters by Rhodes and others, this volume; for assessment of dosage and fidelity, see Tebes (2003); for assessment of costs, see Yates, this volume.
Data Analysis	
DA1. Utilize the most advanced data analytic procedures possible to investigate youth mentoring relationships and programs.	For SEM, see Byrne (1994, 1998, 2001); for hierarchical linear modeling, see Singer and Willett (2003); for analyses of dyadic relationship data see Malloy and Albright (2001).
DA2. Expand analyses of the overall impact of youth mentoring programs to include examination of mediating and moderating processes, variation in outcomes as a function of dosage and fidelity, and cost-effectiveness.	For mediating and moderating processes, see Kenny (2003); for dosage and fidelity, see Tebes (2003); for cost-effectiveness, see Yates, this volume.

Recommendations	*Resources*
Reporting and Interpretation of Findings	**Reporting and Interpretation of Findings**
R1. Provide appropriate qualification when describing causal effects that may be reflected in the findings of investigations of youth mentoring relationships and programs and discuss potential alternative (e.g., noncausal) explanations for the findings.	For an overview of issues in causal interpretation, see Davis (1985); for recommendations regarding communication of SEM findings, see Hoyle and Panter (1995) and McDonald and Ringo Ho (2002).
R2. Provide information relating to risk for Type II error, effect size (including practical significance), and external validity (including, if appropriate, a well-delineated efficacy or effectiveness statement) when reporting findings from studies of mentoring relationships and programs.	For guidelines regarding reporting of effect size and practical significance, see Thompson (2002); for guidelines on efficacy and effectiveness statements, see SPR (n.d.) *Standards of Evidence*.
Programmatic Research	
PR1. Mentoring programs should be developed, evaluated, and disseminated in accordance with the principles and recommended stages of research-driven frameworks that are described in the broader intervention literature.	For descriptions of phases of research frameworks, see Flay (1986), IOM (1994), and National Advisory Mental Health Council Workgroup on Mental Disorders Prevention Research (2001); for criteria and guidelines for efficacy and effectiveness studies, see SPR (n.d.) *Standards of Evidence*.
Research Synthesis	
RS1. State-of-the-art methods of research synthesis should be utilized periodically to review and integrate empirical evidence on different topics and questions of interest concerning youth mentoring relationships and programs.	For a guide to synthesizing research using literature reviews, see Cooper (1998); for a guide to meta-analysis, see Lipsey and Wilson (2001).

a. Experimental designs also may be valuable for other purposes, such as laboratory research in which participants in actual or simulated mentoring relationships respond to different stimuli or situations (for examples, see Sánchez & Colón, this volume).

b. Other alternatives to experimental designs include interrupted time-series designs and regression discontinuity designs (see Shadish et al., 2002).

c. Assessment of youth outcomes using data from multiple sources, including objective indicators, is highly desirable (for details, see Grossman, this volume).

mentoring relationships, youth typically have been sampled from specific populations of interest to investigators such as teen mothers (e.g., Klaw, Rhodes, & Fitzgerald, 2003), adolescents utilizing pediatric care facilities (Beier, Rosenfeld, Spitalny, Zansky, & Bontempo, 2000), and college students who grew up in homes with alcoholic parents (Cavell, Meehan, Heffer, & Holladay, 2002). Although clearly worthwhile, the results of such studies do not allow for confident generalization to the broader population of young people experiencing naturally occurring mentoring relationships.

Most studies of youth mentoring relationships also have been based on relatively small samples. Investigations thus have not necessarily possessed adequate statistical power to detect subtle but important processes in relationships. Those associations detected with small samples, furthermore, are subject to greater uncertainty and thus may be less likely to replicate across studies. Such limitations are especially salient for studies that have utilized advanced data analytic procedures such as structural equation modeling (e.g., Parra, DuBois, Neville, Pugh-Lilly, & Povinelli, 2002), for which there typically are more demanding sample size requirements.

The recent literature on youth mentoring relationships includes some noteworthy exceptions to the preceding trends regarding sample size and representativeness. Herrera, Sipe, and McClanahan (2000), for example, conducted a study of youth mentoring relationships based on data obtained from mentors within a cross section of 44 different school- and community-based programs. There also has been a survey of a nationally representative sample of adults regarding their mentoring relationships with youth (McLearn, Colasanto, & Schoen, 1998), as well as research utilizing data obtained from a nationally representative sample of young people participating in the Add Health study (DuBois & Silverthorn, in press-a, in press-b).

Studies of Programs

Most studies of youth mentoring programs have focused on a single program implemented at one site. The findings of these types of investigations cannot be considered representative of either mentoring programs in general or even the particular program involved given the potential for substantial variation in quality of implementation across sites. The rapid expansion of different modes and sites of mentoring programs poses a further noteworthy threat to external validity. Thus, whereas evaluation studies have focused primarily on traditional, one-on-one community-based

programs, their findings cannot safely be assumed to be representative of the much larger landscape of current programs (Rhodes & DuBois, 2004).

Evaluations of mentoring programs also frequently have been based on relatively small samples of youth. In their meta-analysis of youth mentoring program evaluations, DuBois, Holloway, Valentine, and Cooper (2002) reported a sample size (n) of 65 or smaller in 30 of the 59 independent samples included in the review. Power for a sample size of 65, assuming a two-group design with equal ns per condition and a two-tailed $p < .05$ level of significance, is only approximately .12 and .09 for detecting effects of small magnitude as defined by criteria suggested by Cohen (1992) of $d = .20$ and Lipsey (1990) of $d = .15$, respectively. Or, put somewhat differently, such studies run the risk of Type II error rates as high as 88% and 91%! As this exercise illustrates, it is clear that in many if not most instances, evaluations have lacked sufficient sensitivity to the types of effects found to be most characteristic of mentoring programs. (DuBois, Holloway, et al., 2002).

Recommendation S1

Utilize samples in studies of youth mentoring relationships and programs that are representative of the populations of interest.

Significant resources are likely to be required to obtain representative samples in studies of youth mentoring relationships and programs. It may be impractical for individual investigators or funding sources to support these types of investigations, especially given the needs that may exist for both data collection and program implementation across multiple sites. In other fields, consortium studies (i.e., collaborative investigations involving multiple teams of investigators and funding sources) have been used to collect data from nationally representative samples on topics of interest in youth development (e.g., adolescent sexuality) as well as to examine the effectiveness of particular types of intervention (e.g., early childhood education) across a representative range of program models. The data obtained from such studies then can be made available to the field as a whole for primary or secondary analyses. Rhodes and DuBois (2004) recommended this type of approach be used to support both a national longitudinal study of youth mentoring and a study of mentoring program effectiveness across multiple sites and program models.

Recommendation S2

Plan sample size to ensure adequate sensitivity to anticipated size of effects in studies of youth mentoring relationships and programs.

Mentoring research poses several special challenges related to planning of sample size. First, in many instances, only effects of small magnitude may be reasonably anticipated. The DuBois, Holloway, et al. (2002) meta-analysis of youth mentoring program evaluations found an average estimated effect size of $d = .18$. Although a comparable estimate is not available for effects involving youth relationships, available findings suggest that these too are likely to be small rather than large in magnitude (e.g., DuBois & Silverthorn, in press-a). A relatively large sample (and hence expenditure of resources) therefore often is likely to be required to ensure sensitivity to effects of mentoring programs or relationships. Second, many studies of mentoring involve youth nested within different units of analysis such as program sites or schools. Under these circumstances, power estimates must take into account whatever degree of nonindependence is expected for observations within units as assessed by the intraclass correlation (Raudenbush, 1997). The higher the degree of nonindependence, the greater the required sample size, holding anticipated effect size constant. A final issue pertains to the estimation of sample size required for adequate power and robustness in conjunction with use of advanced data analytic procedures (see "Data Analysis" section later in this chapter). Estimates of power may be derived under these circumstances when reasonable assumptions can be made regarding anticipated values of model parameters. Findings from prior research may be useful to consult for guidance in this regard. However, at present, most areas of the mentoring literature lack the depth necessary to support this approach. Instead, researchers likely will need to rely on less precise but still useful general guidelines or "rules of thumb" to determine sample size requirements associated with the use of advanced data analytic procedures. For structural equation modeling, for example, Bollen (1989) recommends a ratio of at least 10 observations to each estimated model parameter.

Design

General Principle

Studies should utilize designs that are well suited to answering primary questions of interest.

A major concern in this regard is internal validity, which generally can be thought of as the accuracy of inferences that are made about causal relationships among variables included in a study. In the context of intervention research, internal validity refers to the validity of inferences about whether findings reflect a causal relationship between treatment status and outcome measures (Shadish, Cook, & Campbell, 2002).

Studies of Relationships

Studies of youth mentoring relationships have been based nearly exclusively on cross-sectional designs. This type of design hinders efforts to investigate potential antecedents or consequences of relationships or how characteristics of relationships themselves change and influence each other over time. In several studies, for example, youth reporting natural mentoring relationships have been found to exhibit more favorable adjustment (see Zimmerman, Bingenheimer, & Behrendt, this volume). These studies, however, are primarily cross-sectional in design. Associations interpreted as evidence of beneficial effects of natural mentoring ties on youth outcomes therefore also could reflect a greater capacity among well-adjusted youth to seek out and develop mentoring relationships. One approach to addressing such concerns would be to utilize a prospective design (Newcomb & Bentler, 1988). In this type of design, assessments of mentoring relationships would be examined as predictors of later adjustment, controlling statistically for baseline levels of functioning. Reciprocal effects in the direction of initial youth adjustment influencing their likelihood of subsequently forming natural mentoring relationships could be investigated as well. Although a few recent studies of youth mentoring relationships have made use of longitudinal data (DuBois & Silverthorn, in press-a, in press-b; Klaw et al., 2003), none has yet incorporated all of the features of a prospective design.

Studies of Programs

Several efforts to evaluate youth mentoring programs have been limited to obtaining data about program participants at the end of program participation (i.e., a single-group, posttest-only design). This type of design may yield data that are useful for a variety of purposes, such as monitoring the experiences of program participants and informing program accountability efforts (see Coyne, Duffy, & Wandersman, this volume). It is not a suitable design, however, for drawing reliable inferences about the potential impact of programs on youth (or mentor) outcomes (DuBois, Holloway, et al., 2002; Rhodes, 2002; see also Grossman, this volume). Retrospective reports from youth or others regarding possible changes in their adjustment, not to mention whether any such changes are attributable to the program, are simply too inherently unreliable and subject to bias to support their use in gauging program impact.

A further concern is that when pre- and posttest assessments have been obtained, it has not been unusual for studies to lack a comparison group (DuBois, Holloway, et al., 2002). The findings produced with this type of design are subject to many threats to internal validity, such as simple maturation of participants, historical events, and test-retest effects, all of which also could lead to changes on outcome measures (Shadish et al., 2002; see also Grossman, this volume). When a comparison group has been included, only a minority of studies have utilized random assignment to treatment and control conditions (DuBois, Holloway, et al., 2002). With notable exceptions such as the Public/Private Ventures evaluation of BBBS referred to previously (Tierney et al., 1995), most evaluations of youth mentoring programs therefore have lacked the type of design that is most likely to yield unbiased conclusions about intervention impact (Grossman, this volume).

Recommendation D1

Utilize longitudinal designs to investigate youth mentoring relationships and programs.

It is important in longitudinal research to determine the optimal timing and number of assessments that should be carried out within the constraints of available resources. If the primary goal is to investigate processes of change in relationships (or programs) that are likely to unfold over relatively brief intervals, frequent assessments concentrated on a short period of time may be essential for detecting dynamics of interest. Several investigations have reported difficulty obtaining this type of data from participants via either questionnaires returned by mail or telephone interviews (Parra et al., 2002). A more successful strategy might be to provide mentors and youth with Web-based access to measures, thus reducing the need for direct researcher-participant contact and providing participants with greater flexibility in how data are provided.

On the other hand, if processes of greatest interest are likely to unfold over longer periods of time, a smaller number of more widely spaced assessments may be most efficient and productive. This might be the case when attempting to investigate the full life course development of mentoring relationships, or the long-term effects of mentoring relationships or programs on youth outcomes. With relevance to this latter concern, the *Standards of Evidence* recently proposed by the Society for Prevention Research ([SPR], n.d.), for establishing the efficacy or effectiveness of a program include the criterion that for outcomes that may decay over time, there must be a report of significant effects for at least one long-term follow-up at an appropriate interval beyond the end of the intervention (e.g., at least 6 months). The few evaluations in the mentoring literature that have included follow-up assessments demonstrate the potential for significant decay in outcomes over time (e.g., Aseltine, Dupre, & Lamlein, 2000) and thus underscore the importance of designing studies to test directly for maintenance of program effects whenever these are of interest.

Recommendation D2

Utilize experimental or well-conceived quasi-experimental designs to investigate effects of mentoring programs and practices.

Experimental studies are the ideal or "gold standard" because they offer the most powerful tool available to ensuring the equivalence of treatment and control conditions on all relevant factors other than group status (see Grossman, this volume). A challenge often encountered in efforts to use this type of design in evaluations of mentoring programs is that most programs are developed and implemented by community-based agencies and organizations. Researchers thus may not be able to negotiate experimental control over which youth participate in a program or which youth are exposed to different practices within programs. In these situations, researchers should strive to utilize the strongest possible quasi-experimental design. Designs without comparison groups technically may be considered quasi-experimental (Shadish et al., 2002). This would include the studies noted previously in which youth in a mentoring program are assessed at the beginning and end of the program (i.e., single-group, pre-post design).

A notably stronger quasi-experimental design, however, is one in which a similar group of youth not receiving mentoring also are assessed. Indeed, in the SPR *Standards of Evidence* (n.d.), one of the criteria for efficacy and effectiveness is that the evaluation design must include at least one comparison condition that does not receive the tested intervention. The merits of this type of design depend largely on the extent to which youth in the comparison group can be assumed to be equivalent to those in the treatment group on any attributes that could influence outcome measures (Grossman, this volume). One concern for mentoring programs is the potential for non-equivalence to be introduced by the self-selection of youth into programs (self-selection in the context of mentoring programs includes parental decisions to enroll youth in programs as well as selective referrals of children to programs by persons such as counselors or teachers). The issue of selection bias is so difficult to overcome with confidence that the SPR *Standards of Evidence* (n.d.) include the caveat that matched

control designs may constitute acceptable evidence of efficacy or effectiveness only when assignment to conditions is by some means other than self-selection (e.g., geography).

Grossman (this volume) describes a variety of procedures for helping minimize the potential for bias arising from nonequivalence of treatment and control groups in quasi-experimental evaluations of mentoring programs. The interested reader also should consult Shadish et al. (2002) for an extended discussion of several variations on both single-group and two-group quasi-experimental designs. Many of these variations (e.g., use of multiple pretests) involve the addition of design elements that may significantly increase internal validity.

Assessment

General Principle

Studies should assess constructs of interest using reliable and valid measures.

A key concept in this regard is construct validity, the degree to which a measure reflects the hypothetical constructs of interest (Heiman, 2001).

Studies of Relationships

Measures of youth mentoring relationships are in an early stage of development (see Nakkula & Harris, this volume). Currently, the field lacks any measure with well-established psychometric support for use across a wide range of different populations or programmatic contexts. Most measures have been developed on an idiosyncratic basis for use within individual studies. This has made it difficult to compare findings across investigations. Furthermore, because instruments with well-established norms are not yet available, it has not been possible to gauge with any precision the extent to which the characteristics of relationships found to exist for a given sample are typical or atypical in a broader sense.

Most studies have had mentors or youth, but not both complete relationship measures. Other types of assessments, furthermore, such as direct observation, have been used only rarely.

The general omission of multi-informant and multisource data on relationships is problematic for both substantative and methodological reasons. Substantively, perspectives of both mentors and youth (as well as those offered by other sources of data) may be required to glean a full understanding of relationship processes and dynamics. Methodologically, multimethod data are critically important for establishing the convergent and discriminant validity of measures, both of which are necessary for construct validity. Multimethod data also can be highly desirable when using advanced data analytic techniques such as structural equation modeling.

In most studies, measures of potential influences on or outcomes of mentoring relationships have been obtained from the same informant who reports on the relationships (e.g., youth report on both mentoring relationships and outcomes). Shared source variance across measures thus may lead to bias in findings of these investigations. Illustratively, in a recent study of participants in the Add Health study who reported having mentors (DuBois & Silverthorn, in press-a), it was found that those who reported greater feelings of closeness to their mentors were more likely to report favorable outcomes such as high self-esteem and lack of illicit drug use. It is possible, however, that motivation to provide socially desirable responses could have led some youth to provide favorable reports of both their relationships with mentors and their individual adjustment, thus artificially inflating associations between the two types of measures.

Studies of Programs

Evaluations of mentoring programs have focused on assessment of potential youth outcomes resulting from program participation (for a discussion of outcome assessment in mentoring programs, see Grossman, this volume). Notably less attention has been paid to including measures of either (a) intervening processes that may account for effects on outcomes (*mediators*) or (b) factors that may influence the strength or direction of effects (*moderators*). Evaluations often have assessed indicators of the intensity of mentoring relationships established in programs, such as their frequency of

contact and overall duration. There have been relatively few efforts, however, to assess the extent and quality of overall program implementation in areas such as mentor screening, mentor-youth matching, training, or supervision. The former typically would be referred to as indicators of *dosage* (as would indices of the exposure of individual youth to other program elements, such as a lessons in a curriculum), whereas the latter would represent indices of *fidelity* because they address whether a program was implemented as planned (Tebes, 2003). Without assessing both dosage and fidelity, only an incomplete understanding of factors influencing observed impacts of the program on youth may be obtained. Assessment of program costs has been lacking as well, despite their necessity for being able to gauge the cost-effectiveness of programs (see Yates, this volume). Mentoring relationships that youth in the comparison or control group experience through other sources also are an important consideration in analyses of program impact (see Grossman, this volume). Relatively few evaluations, however, have assessed the presence of these types of relationships.

Recommendation A1

Assess mentoring relationships using data from multiple informants, including both mentors and youth, as well as additional sources such as direct observation.

Although desirable in principle, there may be significant challenges to collecting data on youth mentoring relationships from multiple sources. Observational data on mentoring relationships, for example, have the potential to be highly informative. However, in traditional community-based mentoring programs, mentors and youth typically are given wide latitude to choose when and where they will spend time together. This presents a formidable barrier to direct observation of mentor-youth interactions. Several approaches nevertheless may be useful in obtaining observational data on mentoring relationships in community-based programs. These include planned observations of youth-mentor interactions at agency-sponsored events as well as in research laboratory settings. Participatory methods in which researchers occupy the dual role of both mentor and observer are a further possibility (DuBois, 2002).

Recommendation A2

Incorporate comprehensive assessment of youth outcomes, mediating and moderating influences, dosage and fidelity, costs, and the mentoring relationships of youth in comparison or control groups in evaluations of mentoring programs.

In accordance with the literature's early stage of development, there are few, if any, well-established mediators or moderators of the impact of mentoring programs on youth. The field is comparatively rich, however, in theoretical models or perspectives that can be used to inform assessment decisions in this area. The general model of mentoring proposed by Rhodes, in this volume, for example, includes several classes of mediating and moderating influences on the outcomes of mentoring relationships for youth. Numerous other chapters discuss potential mediating and moderating processes for particular types of programs, contexts, or populations.

Data Analysis

General Principle

Data analytic procedures should provide optimal sensitivity and accuracy for addressing questions or hypotheses of interest.

Studies of Relationships

Too often, studies of youth mentoring relationships have been limited to the analysis of bivariate associations among measures. This approach fails to control for potential confounding influences and does not allow for tests of mediating or moderating mechanisms that may link relationship processes to one another or to outcomes. These limitations have been addressed in several recent studies through the use of relatively straightforward data analytic procedures such as multiple regression (e.g., Greenberger, Chen, & Beam, 1998; Zimmerman, Bingenheimer, & Notaro, 2002). More advanced multivariate procedures, however, also present

a wealth of opportunities for the analysis of data on youth mentoring relationships. These include the use of confirmatory factor analysis for testing hypotheses regarding the structure or dimensionality of relationships, latent growth curve modeling and related techniques for tracking trajectories of change in relationships over time, and structural equation modeling for testing and refining theoretical models of relationship processes and outcomes. To date, only a handful of studies have made use of these kinds of procedures.

Qualitative analyses of data on mentoring relationships also clearly have great potential value and have appeared with some frequency in the literature (e.g., Morrow & Styles, 1995). To date, however, efforts in this area have not reflected attention to certain key methodological concerns. These include the need for detailed specification of the procedures used to identify proposed relationship themes or categories from qualitative data as well as the importance of establishing the reliability of procedures used to code the status of individual relationships within frameworks.

Studies of Programs

Data analyses in evaluations of youth mentoring programs typically have reflected a relatively simplistic "input-output model" in which investigators test whether program participation is linked directly to improvements in youth adjustment (DuBois, Neville, Parra, & Pugh-Lilly, 2002). With notable exceptions (e.g., Rhodes, Grossman, & Resch, 2000), mediating or intervening processes through which program effects might accrue seldom have been examined. Aside from limitations in understanding engendered by the lack of these types of analyses, a further consequence is that evidence of program impact may be overlooked. In one recent evaluation of a BBBS program (DuBois, Neville, et al., 2002), for example, a positive impact on youth outcomes (e.g., behavior problems) became apparent only when considering a hypothesized chain of intervening processes that involved social support and self-esteem.

Evaluations typically also have not tested systematically for moderators of program impact. These types of analyses may identify subgroups of youth for whom program effects are notably different in magnitude and even direction from the remainder of the sample. With relevance to this concern, the SPR *Standards of Evidence* (n.d.) include the following recommendation:

> It is desirable that subgroup analyses demonstrate efficacy for subgroups within the sample (e.g., gender, ethnicity/race, risk levels). A small main effect may involve a large effect for a particular (e.g., high-risk) group and small or no effects for other subgroups. (p. 4)

Examination of how outcomes vary in association with indices of dosage and fidelity similarly represents a valuable opportunity to help identify particularly influential facets of relationships and program practice. Even when relevant data are available, very few evaluations report these types of analyses (for a noteworthy exception, see Grossman & Rhodes, 2002). The same is true of data regarding program costs that could be used to advantage in cost-effectiveness analyses.

Recommendation DA1

Utilize the most advanced data analytic procedures possible to investigate youth mentoring relationships and programs.

Numerous resources are available that provide guidance on the use of the types of advanced data analytic procedures described previously (see Table 4.1). It should be noted, however, that situations in which data on relationships are available from both mentors and youth present special issues. In these circumstances, it may be most appropriate to utilize data analytic techniques developed specifically for the analysis of dyadic relationship data (Malloy & Allbright, 2001). The use of these procedures may be required on statistical grounds as a means of taking into account the nonindependence of data obtained from mentors and youth. Substantively, procedures for analyzing dyadic data provide a valuable opportunity to investigate a range of questions that may be of theoretical interest. These include, for example, examination of interpersonal constructs (e.g., closeness) at the level of relationship itself, as opposed to only from the separate perspectives of mentors and youth; investigation of the extent to which the experiences of mentors in relationships influence those of youth and vice versa (termed "partner effects"; see Malloy & Albright, 2001; and analysis of trajectories of change in dyadic phenomena in mentoring relationships over time.

Recommendation DA2

Expand analyses of the overall impact of youth mentoring programs to include examination of mediating and moderating processes, variation in outcomes as a function of dosage and fidelity, and cost-effectiveness.

As noted, studies in which either a specific mentoring program or differing types of programs are implemented at multiple sites may be particularly useful in advancing the knowledge base of the field. From the standpoint of data analysis, these types of evaluations present a special challenge. Specifically, analyses of program impact will be accurate only to the extent that they take into account nonindependence of data within implementation sites—that is, the extent to which participants within sites are more similar to one another than to participants at other sites (Raudenbush, 1997). Multilevel modeling procedures (e.g., hierarchical linear modeling) can be used to implement this type of control (for relevant resources, see Table 4.1). These procedures also provide an important opportunity to investigate potential site-level influences on program impacts such as implementation fidelity, characteristics of youth and mentors participating in programs, and differences in program goals and practices. Analyses of this nature typically require a large number of different higher-order units (in this case, program implementation sites), a rough rule of thumb being at least 10 units per predictor (Bryk & Raudenbush, 1992). One strategy to making this type of data available within the mentoring field would be to conduct large-scale consortium studies of the type referred to previously. Another possibility would be to encourage utilization of common sets of measures across separate evaluations (Rhodes & DuBois, 2004).

Reporting and Interpretation of Findings

General Principle

Findings should be reported and interpreted accurately and in ways that are well suited to informing practice and policy.

Studies of Relationships

Causality is one important issue that must be addressed when reporting and interpreting findings from research on youth mentoring. This issue is a salient concern in studies of both relationships and programs. It is noteworthy in this regard that studies of youth mentoring relationships have been exclusively correlational (i.e., nonexperimental) in design. Indeed, by their nature, many of the features of mentoring relationships of greatest interest are likely to be difficult, if not impossible, to subject to direct experimental control. These include, for example, the existence of naturally occurring mentoring relationships as well as the prevailing characteristics of relationships established through formal mentoring programs. This should not preclude investigators from noting when correlational findings are or are not consistent with potential causal linkages (e.g., "Findings are consistent with the hypothesis that a youth-oriented mentoring style promotes longer-term relationships"). Investigators in many instances, however, have gone well beyond this type of presentation to report and interpret observed associations between measures as being reflective of causal effects (e.g., "The presence of a mentoring relationship had a positive effect on school performance"; "Longer-term mentoring relationships had more favorable consequences for youth outcomes"). Relatedly, even when framed appropriately, causal explanations favored by investigators have not consistently been balanced by discussion of plausible alternative explanations. These include methodological considerations (e.g., shared source variance) as well as the potential for differing directions of effect. Unless informed by these types of discussions, those attempting to translate findings into implications for practice may do so without an adequate understanding of the limitations of the research involved.

Studies of Programs

Further important issues that pertain to how findings are reported and interpreted include Type II error, effect size, and external validity. Each of these issues again is relevant to studies of both relationships and programs, although this discussion considers implications only for the latter. As discussed previously, there is ample potential for Type II error in evaluations of youth mentoring programs (i.e., a failure to detect differences that do, in fact, exist between intervention and comparison groups on outcome measures) due both to small sample sizes and the challenge of attempting to detect effects of limited magnitude. In view of these considerations, it would be useful when reporting findings to indicate the level of power that exists for detecting effects of a given magnitude with the sample size available (software packages such as SPSS now include the option for observed power to be reported as part of the output from different types of analyses, although it should be noted that these estimates will depend on the specific level of effect observed in the sample). Readers then could be cautioned against assuming that a lack of statistically significant findings implies the absence of program effects. This type of admonition could be integrated with discussion of other factors that have the potential to obscure evidence of program effects, such as limitations in the reliability or validity of outcome measures and sample attrition. To date, these issues pertaining to statistical power have received only limited attention when reporting and interpreting findings of mentoring program evaluations.

A related concern is the magnitude or size of those program effects that are evident. Few evaluations of mentoring programs have reported standardized estimates of effect size. This has made it difficult to gauge the magnitude of estimated effects relative to those obtained elsewhere in the mentoring literature or in evaluations of other types of interventions. The SPR *Standards of Evidence* (n.d.) also include the criterion that in order for an intervention to qualify as efficacious or effective, "It is necessary to demonstrate *practical significance* in terms of public health impact" (p. 5). To help gauge this type of impact, it may be useful for estimated effects to be expressed in the original or raw (i.e., unstandardized) units of outcome measures. These units often will be more directly relevant to the concerns of those in policy and advocacy roles.

In an effort to provide this latter type of information, the Public/Private Ventures evaluation of BBBS reported estimates of the percentage change in outcomes due to program participation. For example, it was estimated that program participation led to a 46% reduction in the numbers of youth who initiated drug use during the course of the study (Tierney et al., 1995). The easily interpretable nature of this information undoubtedly contributed to the study's impressive impact on policymakers (see Walker, this volume). Such estimates, however, do not always coincide with estimates of effect size that are expressed in standardized form. Indeed, DuBois, Holloway, et al. (2002) found that despite the substantial size of program impacts suggested by the Public/Private Ventures estimates, standardized estimates of effect size for this study were actually small in magnitude by conventional criteria. A similar potential for standardized estimates to suggest only a small effect even though differences observed in actual outcomes appear to be of practical significance has been noted elsewhere in the intervention literature (Bloom & Lipsey, 2004).

Taking these various considerations into account, it seems advisable for evaluations of mentoring programs to report and interpret information about program impact both as standardized effect sizes and in the original units of the outcome measure. A further goal should be to present such information within the context of the estimated cost of achieving the outcomes in question, as well as their monetary or societal value. Clearly, findings of cost-effectiveness and cost-benefit analyses when available would be useful to report for these purposes (SPR, n.d.).

With regard to external validity, the SPR *Standards of Evidence* (n.d.) emphasize the need for specificity in statements that are made concerning a program's efficacy (or effectiveness):

> Because outcome research results are specific to the samples (or populations from which they were

drawn) and the outcomes measured, it is essential that conclusions from the research be clear as to the population(s) and outcomes for which efficacy is claimed. Therefore, a statement of efficacy should be of the form that *"Program X is efficacious for producing Y outcomes for Z population."* (p. 1)

In addition to emphasizing the need for specificity regarding outcomes and populations, this recommendation makes clear the need to limit conclusions to particular programs. This runs counter to the tendency observed in the literature to make broad inferences about the efficacy or effectiveness of mentoring as an intervention when reporting and interpreting results in program evaluation studies. Nor would inferences regarding general classes of programs defined by parameters such as the mode or site of mentoring be supported (e.g., one-on-one or community-based) given the wide variation likely to exist within those types of groupings (see Sipe, this volume).

Recommendation R1

Provide appropriate qualification when describing causal effects that may be reflected in the findings of investigations of youth mentoring relationships and programs, and discuss potential alternative (e.g., noncausal) explanations for the findings.

It may be tempting to ascribe causal status to findings pertaining to different characteristics of mentoring relationships when these are generated within the context of well-controlled evaluations of mentoring programs, especially those that make use of an experimental design. There is a general consensus, after all, that the relationships formed between the volunteers and youth constitute the active ingredient of such interventions. Yet it is not relationships that typically are subject to experimental control, but rather the assignment of youth to mentoring and nonmentoring conditions. Consequently, although examination of how outcomes vary in association with characteristics of relationships (e.g., duration, frequency of contact) clearly has the potential to be informative, it should be kept in mind that results obtained in such analyses are correlational in nature and thus subject to the same limitations in terms of inferences of causality as other types of correlational findings (see Grossman, this volume). It also should be kept in mind that even those findings of experimentally designed evaluations that focus on program impact do not necessarily provide definitive proof of causation. When outcome measures are obtained only from program participants or others who are aware of which youth are assigned to the mentoring program, for example, demand characteristics may represent a plausible alternative explanation for findings (cf. SPR, n.d.).

Recommendation R2

Provide information relating to risk for Type II error, effect size (including practical significance), and external validity (including, if appropriate, a well-delineated efficacy or effectiveness statement) when reporting findings from studies of mentoring relationships and programs.

Along with the need to address issues of external validity when reporting findings, there may be the added challenge of determining whether an investigation and its results should be regarded as falling within the scope of the youth mentoring literature at all. At present, the boundaries for what does or does not constitute research on mentoring relationships or on mentoring as an intervention strategy are not fully defined. Consensus is lacking, for example, with regard to whether investigations that focus on relationships between youth and older peers or those that evaluate interventions involving the use of paid paraprofessionals should be incorporated as part of the field. The determination of whether research falls within the scope of the youth mentoring literature may have limited significance in the context of reporting and interpreting the findings of individual studies. However, the process of establishing what studies to include as relevant becomes a more salient issue when the goal is to synthesize findings from one or more areas of the literature. This observation leads us naturally into our discussion of methodological issues that bear on the integration of findings across different studies.

INTEGRATION ACROSS STUDIES

Programmatic Research

General Principle

Interventions should be developed through a series of steps or phases that progress from basic research to program development to investigations of program efficacy and effectiveness and, ultimately, to dissemination.

The progression referred to in this principle is reflected consistently in widely adopted frameworks for programmatic intervention research (see, e.g., Flay, 1986; Institute of Medicine [IOM], 1994; National Advisory Mental Health Council Workgroup on Mental Disorders Prevention Research, 2001).

Studies of Mentoring

As applied to mentoring, basic or "preintervention" research could be used to increase knowledge about mentoring relationships and the processes through which they influence youth outcomes. This foundation then would be used to inform the development of mentoring programs that, after being refined through preliminary evaluation research, would be rigorously evaluated in an efficacy trial. An efficacy trial investigates "the extent to which an intervention (technology, treatment, procedure, service, or program) does more good than harm when delivered under optimal conditions" (SPR, n.d., p. 1). "Optimal" typically is taken to refer to situations in which special precautions are taken to ensure that the intervention is implemented with a high level of fidelity. These efforts may entail researchers delivering the intervention themselves or providing financial or technical support to those responsible for implementation. If found to be efficacious, a mentoring program then would be evaluated for effectiveness. "Effectiveness trials test whether interventions are effective under 'real world' conditions or in 'natural' settings" (SRP, n.d., p. 7). In these types of studies, intervention developers may no longer be involved. Finally, if found to be effective, the mentoring program would be disseminated on a larger-scale through system- and policy-level initiatives. At this stage, research would be conducted to identify the most successful approaches to ensuring that the program is adopted, implemented, and sustained within host settings. This cycle would be recursive as the knowledge that is acquired through these latter stages of intervention research is used to strengthen the knowledge base of the field (IOM, 1994).

In reality, very few mentoring programs have been developed, evaluated, and then disseminated in a manner resembling this type of progression. One reason for this may be the "grassroots" nature of the mentoring movement, in which the establishment and widespread adoption of programs such as BBBS has been fueled primarily by societal concern and activism rather than through the efforts of science (see Baker & Maguire, this volume). There are significant potential costs to this trend. First, programs developed in this way do not have the opportunity to benefit from insights gleaned from either basic research or formative evaluation studies. Second, once established, efforts to refine and improve programs are unable to profit from the type of guidance that can be provided by the findings of rigorous evaluations of efficacy. The net result of these omissions is that programs may fall well short of realizing their potential benefits for youth. They also may be more likely to do harm, perhaps in ways not even anticipated. A further consideration is that when programs developed outside of the supportive context of research are evaluated, the conditions involved are likely to most resemble those of effectiveness trials. As such, there may be formidable obstacles to achieving a high level of fidelity in program implementation (e.g., resource limitations, lack of availability of technical assistance). To the extent that this occurs, the potential benefits of programs may be systematically underestimated given that effectiveness trials typically are expected to yield weaker effects than efficacy trials conducted under more optimal conditions (SPR, n.d.). Finally, we would note that to the extent that non-research-driven program development and dissemination efforts remain commonplace, it may encourage an "ethic" in the field that foregoing this process is acceptable despite its significant potential downsides.

There are noteworthy exceptions to this trend in which mentoring programs for youth have been developed and evaluated within research-driven frameworks (see, e.g., Cavell & Hughes, 2000; Karcher, 2005; Taylor, LoSciuto, Fox, Hilbert, & Sonkowsky, 1999). These types of efforts are few in number, however, and have not yet progressed to the stage of involving large-scale effectiveness trials or systemwide dissemination efforts. It is thus too early to assess their potential to have significant impact on the quality of practice within the field of youth mentoring.

Recommendation PR1

Mentoring programs should be developed, evaluated, and disseminated in accordance with the principles and recommended stages of research-driven frameworks that are described in the broader intervention literature.

Prevention programs developed within research-driven frameworks and found to be efficacious may experience difficulty demonstrating effectiveness because of obstacles to successful implementation under real-world conditions (IOM, 1994). Programs, furthermore, even if found to be effective, may achieve only limited diffusion within the broader practice community because of institutional and other barriers to their systemwide adoption. These challenges may be especially great within the field of youth mentoring, in which many agencies have limited resources to support implementation of new programs and in which there already are a large number of "competing" programs that enjoy widespread support among practitioners and policymakers.

One approach for addressing these challenges is for researchers to establish collaborative arrangements with mentoring agencies. This strategy may increase the potential for programs that are developed to be implemented successfully within the constraints of real-world agencies and to be disseminated throughout larger systems within the practice community. It is noteworthy, furthermore, that existing agency programs, although lacking rigorous evaluation, may be well suited to serve as a foundation for research-driven intervention development efforts. These possibilities are illustrated by a collaborative project that the authors of this chapter are engaged in with Big Brothers Big Sisters of Metropolitan Chicago. The immediate goals of this project are to further develop and evaluate an innovative agency program for girls in which traditional one-on-one mentoring is combined with the joint participation of youth and their mentors in an extended series of psychoeducational workshops. If ultimately found to be effective, the resulting program will have the built-in potential for dissemination to the hundreds of BBBS affiliate agencies that exist nationwide.

Research Synthesis

General Principle

The available empirical evidence on topics and questions of interest should be reviewed and integrated periodically using recommended methodological procedures for research synthesis (Cooper, 1998).

Underlying this principle is the understanding that as the knowledge base in a given area such as youth mentoring expands, it becomes valuable to systematically review and synthesize findings obtained across different studies that address topics of interest to the field. Carefully conducted reviews have the potential to identify patterns in findings that otherwise would go undetected or be left to the subject of debate based on idiosyncratic consideration of selected aspects of available evidence. Systematic reviews also typically serve to highlight substantive gaps in the existing literature on a given topic as well as methodological limitations of available studies. Systematic reviews thus may be instrumental both in advancing the knowledge base in a given area and in charting the course for the next generation of research (Cooper, 1998).

It is important to note that the principle of adhering to well-defined methodological procedures in conducting research syntheses holds when conducting either narrative (nonquantitative) or meta-analytic (quantitative) reviews. In either case, it is essential that literature search procedures are well defined and that well-operationalized criteria are applied to determine the types of studies and evidence that are included. Increasingly, however, the social and behavioral sciences, as well as other disciplines (e.g., medicine), have come to favor quantitative methods of review as the most reliable and

authoritative basis for synthesizing research evidence, especially with regard to questions of intervention effectiveness. This trend is reflected in guidelines for reviews that are utilized by organizations established in recent years to help prepare, maintain, and disseminate systematic reviews of studies of interventions in the social, behavioral, and educational arenas. These organizations include the international Campbell Collaboration (n.d.) as well as the What Works Clearinghouse (n.d.) established by the U.S. Department of Education Institute of Education Sciences.

Status of Research in Youth Mentoring

There have been numerous narrative reviews of research in the youth mentoring literature, each reflecting a varying degree of attention to recommended methodological procedures for conducting these types of reviews (Cooper, 1998). As noted previously, DuBois, Holloway, et al. (2002) conducted a meta-analytic review of youth mentoring program evaluations. In line with the potential benefits of systematic reviews discussed above, this synthesis proved useful in terms of (a) demonstrating noteworthy trends in findings across studies (e.g., increased estimates of effect size for programs that utilized recommended "best practices"); (b) gaps in the existing knowledge base (e.g., a dearth of studies addressing the effectiveness of older adults as mentors for young people); and (c) methodological limitations (e.g., limited use of experimental designs and lack of consistent follow-up assessments). A limitation of the review, however, is that it did not benefit from the involvement and support of an organization specializing in research synthesis of intervention studies. For example, whereas the review included evaluations lacking a comparison group, these likely would have been excluded based on criteria suggested by the Campbell Collaboration and What Works Clearinghouse. This would have provided enhanced consistency between the evidence base used in the review and the SPR criteria established for individual studies of program efficacy and effectiveness that are discussed in this chapter. It is also noteworthy that a quantitative synthesis of research on youth mentoring relationships has not yet been conducted, although it would appear that sufficient research has accumulated to merit a review with this focus.

Recommendation RS1

State-of-the-art methods of research synthesis should be utilized periodically to review and integrate empirical evidence on different topics and questions of interest concerning youth mentoring relationships and programs.

Several excellent resources exist to guide interested researchers in conducting systematic reviews (see Table 4.1). Identification and retrieval of relevant studies is a significant challenge to synthesis of research from the field of the mentoring. Because of multidisciplinary and applied interest, reports on any given topic are likely to be scattered across diverse literatures and in many instances may have been published privately by foundations or other organizations (DuBois, Holloway, et al., 2002). DuBois, Holloway, et al. (2002) recommended that the field establish a central registry of research as one strategy for addressing this challenge. Enhanced channels of communication also are likely to be helpful. Illustratively, in 2003, MENTOR convened a National Research Summit on Mentoring to facilitate exchange and collaboration among leading researchers in the field (Rhodes & DuBois, 2004). It is noteworthy too that the field currently lacks a flagship journal.

FUTURE DIRECTIONS

Synthesis

The use of state-of-the-art methodology in research on youth mentoring is important for ensuring continued growth in the field's knowledge base, the development of safe and effective mentoring programs, and informed decisions from policymakers. It is of concern, therefore, that few existing studies of either mentoring relationships or programs would qualify as methodologically rigorous in the sense of comprehensive adherence to the guidelines and recommendations set forth in this chapter. Sustained programs of research that reflect systematic progression of investigations across the

multiple phases of intervention development, evaluation, and dissemination are vitally important as well to ensure a strong linkage between science and practice in the field. To date, however, these are a rarity. At the same time, there is an encouraging trend in the literature for studies of youth mentoring relationships and programs to incorporate greater attention to the methodological issues that are highlighted in this chapter. Likewise, there are a few noteworthy examples of programmatic research being initiated, as well as efforts to conduct systematic reviews of existing evidence.

As this chapter highlights, there are formidable challenges to embracing standards for methodological rigor when conducting research on youth mentoring. These challenges, along with the relatively recent emergence of sustained scientific interest in youth mentoring, undoubtedly help account for the uneven methodological quality of research to date. Yet if the field's empirical foundation is truly to become solidified and realize its promise of informing effective practice, it will need to redouble its efforts to overcome obstacles to the use of state-of-the-art methodology. Both researchers and practitioners have a vital role to assume in this process. Accordingly, we conclude with recommendations for steps that each can take to strengthen the methodological underpinnings of the field's knowledge base.

Recommendations for Research

1. *Conduct methodologically rigorous studies of youth mentoring relationships and programs.* Investigations of youth mentoring need to be conducted that reflect comprehensive adherence to both the general methodological principles and specific recommendations stemming from these principles described in this chapter. The identified resources accompanying these guidelines should be utilized, furthermore, to facilitate informed decision making regarding the specific methodological procedures that are most appropriate for any given research question or investigation and to ensure that selected procedures then are implemented appropriately.

2. *Programmatic research should be used to guide the development, evaluation, and*

dissemination of youth mentoring programs. Frameworks for programmatic intervention research that have become widely accepted within the field of prevention science should be utilized to guide the development, evaluation, and dissemination of youth mentoring programs. A scientifically driven approach promises to yield safer and more effective mentoring programs than the current trend, in which most programs are developed and disseminated (in several cases, widely) without the benefit of systematic guidance from research. It should be a priority in this regard to demonstrate efficacy and, subsequently, effectiveness for specific youth mentoring programs. To date, it does not appear that any program yet meets the criteria for efficacy proposed by SPR (n.d.). In seeking to remedy such limitations, researchers should keep in mind the potential highlighted in this chapter to engage in productive collaborations with community-based mentoring agencies and organizations in which existing program models are used as a foundation for scientifically driven intervention research and development activities.

3. *Systematic reviews should be conducted of youth mentoring literature using state-of-the-art methodologies for research synthesis.* As the youth mentoring literature continues to grow, it will be important to periodically synthesize available evidence in different areas using state-of-the-art procedures (e.g., meta-analysis). As noted, systematic reviews may serve an integral role not only by solidifying and advancing the existing base of knowledge in the field but also by highlighting methodological issues in need of greater attention in future research. Currently, it appears that an updated review of the expanding literature on mentoring program effectiveness as well as a synthesis of research on youth mentoring relationships could be beneficial. Priority should be given to reviews that are conducted with the support and endorsement of established organizations within the burgeoning field of research synthesis.

4. *Establish improved channels of communication and sharing among those conducting research on youth mentoring.* Communication among those engaged in research on youth mentoring provides an opportunity for

methodological standards and procedures to be adopted more consistently throughout the field. Communication of this nature should be encouraged through mechanisms such as regular conferences, establishing a flagship journal for the field, and creating a listserv dedicated to mentoring research.

Recommendations for Practice

1. *Practitioners and policymakers should be discriminating consumers of research on youth mentoring.* Those in practice and policy roles should aspire to become familiar with the basic principles and standards of high-quality research in the field of youth mentoring. Acquiring a measure of sophistication in this regard may allow practitioners and policymakers to be more judicious in which programs are selected for implementation or funding support. Awareness of guidelines for methodological quality also may allow practitioners to enter into more beneficial collaborations with researchers (see Recommendation 2 below). In the public policy realm, it may facilitate greater attention to methodological rigor when developing guidelines for funding streams directed toward research or evaluation (see Recommendation 3). More generally, from a supply-and-demand perspective, through their own appreciation of the need for attention to issues of quality in youth mentoring research, practitioners and policymakers can encourage researchers to provide the field with more methodologically rigorous investigations.

2. *Practitioners should collaborate with researchers to conduct high-quality research on the programs that they develop, implement, and disseminate.* It is unrealistic to expect that the typical mentoring agency or organization will be able on its own to conduct research that conforms to the methodological guidelines described in this chapter. A more promising alternative is for practitioners to establish collaborative ties with researchers. These types of arrangements can provide community-based agencies and organizations with the resources and technical support necessary to conduct methodologically rigorous research on the development, implementation, and dissemination

of their programs that otherwise would not be possible. For many agencies and organizations, local area universities and colleges provide a potentially rich source of collaborators on mentoring research.

3. *Policymakers should prioritize funding for research on youth mentoring that adheres to the highest methodological standards.* To date, governmental and privately funded initiatives to support youth mentoring have paid only passing attention to the importance of research and evaluation. Even less consideration has been given to the criteria for methodological rigor highlighted in this chapter. For future policy efforts to bring about desired results, we believe that it is essential for funders to make a much more serious investment in supporting high-quality research on youth mentoring. It is important in our view that this investment take the form of both (a) appropriate levels of support for rigorous program evaluation within practice-oriented policy initiatives and (b) independent streams of funding dedicated solely to research on youth mentoring programs and relationships (Rhodes & DuBois, 2004). With appropriate emphasis on methodological quality, these investments promise to yield dividends for current and future generations of youth alike.

REFERENCES

Aseltine, R. H., Dupre, M., & Lamlein, P. (2000). Mentoring as a drug prevention strategy: An evaluation of Across Ages. *Adolescent and Family Health, 1,* 11–20.

Beier, S. R., Rosenfeld, W. D., Spitalny, K. C., Zansky, S. M., & Bontempo, A. N. (2000). The potential role of an adult mentor in influencing high-risk behaviors in adolescents. *Archives of Pediatrics and Adolescent Medicine, 154,* 327–331.

Bloom, H. S., & Lipsey, M. W. (2004). *Some food for thought about effect size.* Unpublished methodological note, MDRC, New York. Retrieved July 22, 2004, from http://www.wtgrantfoundation.org/newsletter3039/newsletter_show.htm?doc_id=215108

Bollen, K. A. (1989). *Structural equations with latent variables.* New York: Wiley.

Bryk, S., & Raudenbush, S. W. (1992). *Hierarchical linear models: Applications and data analysis methods.* Newbury Park, CA: Sage.

Byrne, B. M. (1994). *Structural equation modeling with EQS and EQS/Windows: Basic concepts, applications, and programming.* Thousand Oaks, CA: Sage.

Byrne, B. M. (1998). *Structural equation modeling with LISREL, PRELIS, and SIMPLIS: Basic concepts, applications, and programming.* Mahwah, NJ: Erlbaum.

Byrne, B. M. (2001). *Structural equation modeling with AMOS: Basic concepts, applications, and programming.* Mahwah, NJ: Erlbaum.

Campbell Collaboration. (n.d.). Retrieved September 12, 2004, from http://www.campbellcollaboration.org/

Cavell, T. A., & Hughes, J. N. (2000). Secondary prevention as context for assessing change processes in aggressive children. *Journal of School Psychology, 38,* 199–235.

Cavell, T. A., Meehan, B., Heffer, R. W., & Holladay, J. (2002). Natural mentors of adolescent COAs: Characteristics and correlates. *The Journal of Primary Prevention, 23,* 23–42.

Cohen, J. (1992). *Statistical power analysis for the behavioral sciences* (2nd ed.). Hillsdale, NJ: Erlbaum.

Cooper, H. (1998). *Synthesizing research: A guide for literature reviews* (3rd ed.). Newbury Park, CA: Sage.

Davis, J. A. (1985). *The logic of causal order.* Newbury Park, CA: Sage.

DuBois, D. L. (2002). Life imitates (and informs) meta-analysis: A participatory approach to increasing understanding of effective youth mentoring practices. *Journal of Prevention & Intervention in the Community, 24*(2), 3–15.

DuBois, D. L., Holloway, B. E., Valentine, J. C., & Cooper, H. (2002). Effectiveness of mentoring programs for youth: A meta-analytic review. *American Journal of Community Psychology, 30,* 157–197.

DuBois, D. L., Neville, H. A., Parra, G. R., & Pugh-Lilly, A. O. (2002). Testing a new model of mentoring. In G. G. Noam (Ed. in chief) & J. E. Rhodes (Ed.), *A critical view of youth mentoring* (*New Directions for Youth Development: Theory, Research, and Practice, No. 93*), pp. 21–57. San Francisco: Jossey-Bass.

DuBois, D. L., & Silverthorn, N. (in press-a). Characteristics of natural mentoring relationships and adolescent adjustment: Evidence from a national study. *Journal of Primary Prevention.*

DuBois, D. L., & Silverthorn, N. (in press-b). Natural mentoring relationships and adolescent health: Evidence from a national study. *American Journal of Public Health.*

Flay, B. R. (1986). Efficacy and effectiveness trials (and other phases of research) in the development of health promotion programs. *Preventive Medicine, 15,* 451–474.

Greenberger, E., Chen, C., & Beam, M. R. (1998). The role of "very important" nonparental adults in adolescent development. *Journal of Youth and Adolescence, 27,* 321–343.

Grossman, J. B., & Rhodes, J. E. (2002). The test of time: Predictors and effects of duration in youth mentoring programs. *American Journal of Community Psychology, 30,* 199–219.

Heiman, G. W. (2001). *Understanding research methods and statistics* (2nd ed.). Boston: Houghton Mifflin.

Henry, G. T. (1998). Practical sampling. In L. Bickman & D. J. Rog (Eds.), *Handbook of applied social research methods* (pp. 101–126). Thousand Oaks, CA: Sage.

Herrera, C., Sipe, C. L., & McClanahan, W. S. (2000). *Mentoring school-age children: Relationship development in community-based and school-based programs.* Philadelphia: Public/Private Ventures.

Hoyle, R. H., & Panter, A. T. (1995). Writing about structural equation models. In R. H. Hoyle (Ed.), *Structural equation modeling: Concepts, issues, and applications* (pp. 158–176). Thousand Oaks, CA: Sage.

Institute of Medicine (IOM). (1994). *Reducing risks for mental disorders.* Washington, DC: National Academy Press.

Kaplan, D. (1995). Statistical power in structural equation modeling. In R. H. Hoyle (Ed.), *Structural equation modeling: Concepts, issues, and applications* (pp. 100–117). Thousand Oaks, CA: Sage.

Karcher, M. J. (2005). The effects of school-based developmental mentoring and mentors' attendance on mentees' self-esteem, behavior, and connectedness. *Psychology in the Schools, 42,* 65–78.

Kenny, D. A. (2003). *Mediation.* Retrieved July 15, 2004, from http://users.rcn.com/dakenny/mediate.htm

Klaw, E. L., Rhodes, J. E., & Fitzgerald, L. F. (2003). Natural mentors in the lives of African American adolescent mothers: Tracking relationships over time. *Journal of Youth & Adolescence, 32,* 223–232.

Lipsey, M. W. (1990). *Design sensitivity: Statistical power for experimental research.* Thousand Oaks, CA: Sage.

Lipsey, M. W., & Wilson, D. B. (2001). *Practical meta-analysis,* Thousand Oaks, CA: Sage.

Malloy, T. E., & Albright, L. A. (2001). Multiple and single interaction dyadic research designs: Conceptual and analytic issues. *Basic and Applied Social Psychology, 23,* 1–19.

Mashek, D. J., & Aron, A. (Eds.). (2004). *Handbook of closeness and intimacy.* Mahwah, NJ: Erlbaum.

McDonald, R. P., & Ringo Ho, M. H. (2002). Principles and practice in reporting structural equation analyses. *Psychological Methods, 7,* 64–82.

McLearn, K. T., Colasanto, D., & Schoen, C. (1998). *Mentoring makes a difference: Findings From the Commonwealth Fund 1998 Survey of Adults Mentoring Young People.* New York: The Commonwealth Fund. Available at http://www.ecs.org/html/Document.asp?chouseid=2843

Menard, S. (2002). *Longitudinal research* (2nd ed.). Thousand Oaks, CA: Sage.

Morrow, K. V., & Styles, M. B. (1995). *Building relationships with youth in program settings: A study of Big Brothers/Big Sisters.* Philadelphia: Public/Private Ventures.

National Advisory Mental Health Council Workgroup on Mental Disorders Prevention Research. (2001). Priorities for prevention research at NIMH. *Prevention & Treatment, 4,* Article 17. Retrieved July 14, 2004, from http://www.journals.apa.org/prevention/volume4/pre0040017a.html

Newcomb, M. D., & Bentler, P. M. (1988). Impact of adolescent drug use and social support on problems of young adults: A longitudinal study. *Journal of Abnormal Psychology, 97,* 64–75.

Parra, G. R., DuBois, D. L., Neville, H. A., Pugh-Lilly, A. O., & Povinelli, N. (2002). Mentoring relationships for youth: Investigation of a process-oriented model. *Journal of Community Psychology, 30,* 367–388.

Pezzullo, J. C. (n.d.). *Interactive statistical calculation pages: Power, sample size and experimental design calculations.* Retrieved July 16, 2004, from http://members.aol.com/johnp71/javastat.html#Power

Raudenbush, S. W. (1997). Statistical analysis and optimal design for cluster randomized trials. *Psychological Methods, 2,* 173–185.

Rhodes, J. (2002, December). *Research Corner: Gauging the effectiveness of youth mentoring.* Retrieved September 12, 2004, from http://www.mentoring.org/research_corner/dec_background.adp

Rhodes, J., & DuBois, D. (2004). *National research agenda for youth mentoring.* Alexandria, VA: MENTOR/National Mentoring Partnership. Retrieved July 14, 2004, from http://www.mentoring.org/research_corner/researchagenda.pdf

Rhodes, J. E., Grossman, J. B., & Resch, N. R. (2000). Agents of change: Pathways through which mentoring relationships influence adolescents' academic adjustment. *Child Development, 71,* 1662–1671.

Roberts, H., Liabø, K., Lucas, P., DuBois, D., & Sheldon, T. A. (2004). Mentoring to reduce antisocial behaviour in childhood. *British Medical Journal, 328,* 512–514.

Shadish, W. R., Cook, T. D., & Campbell, D. T. (2002). *Experimental and quasi-experimental designs for generalized causal inference.* Boston: Houghton Mifflin.

Singer, J. D., & Willett, J. B. (2003). *Applied longitudinal data analysis: Modeling change and event occurrence.* New York: Oxford University Press.

Society for Prevention Research. (n.d.). *Standards of evidence: Criteria for efficacy, effectiveness, and dissemination.* Retrieved July 14, 2004, from http://www.preventionresearch.org/StandardsofEvidencebook.pdf

Taylor, A. S., LoSciuto, L., Fox, M., Hilbert, S. M., & Sonkowsky, M. (1999). The mentoring factor: Evaluation of the Across Ages' intergenerational approach to drug abuse prevention. *Child & Youth Services, 20,* 77–99.

Tebes, J. K. (2003, October). *Program implementation.* Paper presented at 2003 National Research Summit on Mentoring, Kansas City, MO.

Thompson, B. (2002). "Statistical," "practical," and "clinical": How many kinds of significance do counselors need to consider? *Journal of Counseling and Development, 80,* 64–71.

Tierney, J. P., Grossman, J. B., & Resch, N. L. (1995). *Making a difference. An impact study of Big Brothers/Big Sisters.* Philadelphia: Public/Private Ventures.

What Works Clearinghouse. (n.d.). Retrieved September 12, 2004, from http://www.w-w-c.org/

Zimmerman, M. A., Bingenheimer, J. B., & Notaro, P. C. (2002). Natural mentors and adolescent resiliency: A study with urban youth. *American Journal of Community Psychology, 30,* 221–243.

5

Toward a Typology of Mentoring

Cynthia L. Sipe

Introduction

Historically, prevailing conceptions of mentoring relationships and programs have referred to one-to-one relationships between an adult "mentor" and a youth "mentee" (see Baker & Maguire, this volume). Until recently, the vast majority of formal mentoring programs matched one youth with one adult mentor, who met (face to face) on a regular basis—at a time and place of their own choosing—to engage in activities that the pair decided on with little input from program staff. A constellation of factors, both financial and practical during the last decade, have led the program landscape to diversify dramatically through the emergence of a wide range of alternatives to the traditional mentoring model. These include, but are not limited to, group mentoring (in which one adult mentors several youth); team mentoring (in which a team of adults mentor one or several youth); peer mentoring (in which youth mentor other youth); and online or e-mentoring (in which the mentor and youth communicate via the Internet rather than face to face).

A growing body of research has underscored the substantial variability in the characteristics of mentoring relationships, whether formed programmatically or naturally outside of programs,

and the potential for these differences to have important consequences for youth outcomes (see, for example, chapters by Rhodes; Keller; and Zimmerman, Bingenheimer, & Behrendt, this volume). Available research suggests, furthermore, the potential for noteworthy interdependencies between mentoring program models, type of mentoring relationships, and youth outcomes (e.g., Herrera, Sipe, & McClanahan, 2000).

As the construct of mentoring and the field's understanding of it have become more complex, researchers and practitioners have felt some pressure to develop ways to organize or classify the different forms of mentoring programs and relationships. There are, in fact, several reasons that a classification system or typology may be useful to the mentoring field. A typology has the potential to be useful, first, simply as a way to organize and make sense of both the variety of current models of mentoring and identified variations in mentoring relationships, to provide a coherent description of the field and its boundaries (i.e., what types of programs and relationships should be viewed as constituting mentoring and which as falling outside of the field's domain). A second important consideration is the manner in which development of a classification system may facilitate communication among both researchers who are studying mentoring and practitioners who are implementing programs.

Finally, a typology may be useful for both predicting and increasing our understanding of the benefits of different types of mentoring programs and relationships for youth. Most research to date has focused on face-to-face, one-to-one mentoring, including both naturally occurring mentoring relationships and programmatically created matches. Much less attention has been paid to understanding the benefits of other forms of mentoring. To the extent that different mentoring types can be clearly delineated, this can be expected to facilitate and encourage investigation of the impact of a broader range of different forms of mentoring. Two phenomena that could be better understood if there were a typology of mentoring upon which to base investigations include (a) variation in the practices that may be necessary to maximize outcomes within different forms of mentoring and (b) how benefits may vary in relation to factors such as youth and mentor characteristics and the specific outcomes being considered. The development of such a knowledge base, furthermore, clearly can be expected to be useful to practitioners and funders as they make decisions about which mentoring models to implement and what populations of youth and mentors to target, depending on the specific goals of a given organization. Similarly, to the extent that we increase our understanding of differing types of mentoring relationships and their implications for youth outcomes, programs will be in a better position to direct training and support of mentors (and matches) toward encouraging the development of particular types of relationships.

This chapter focuses on various ways the mentoring field might approach the development of a typology (or typologies) of mentoring. First, however, issues related to the process of typology development are discussed, drawing on the experience of other, more developed fields. Following this discussion, existing efforts to develop typologies of mentoring relationships and programs, respectively, are considered. The chapter concludes by offering suggestions for future directions in the development and utilization of typologies for both researchers and practitioners.

CREATING A CLASSIFICATION SYSTEM

The American Heritage College Dictionary defines *typology* as "the study or systematic classification of types." The literature on classification interchangeably employs the term *taxonomy*, which is defined as "the classification of organisms in an ordered system that indicates natural relationships." Achenbach (2001) defines taxonomy as a process of "grouping cases according to their distinguishing features" (p. 264).

Most fields of science go through a classification phase, usually during the early stages of their development (Goodwin, 1999). This classification phase provides a way to bring order to the field and to provide uniform descriptions of entities within that field. As noted, however, creating a typology (or typologies) of mentoring may be useful not only as a descriptive tool but also for guiding future research on mentoring and its benefits as well as for guiding practitioners who develop and implement youth mentoring programs.

Other fields have encountered a number of issues in their efforts to develop typologies that now guide research and practice in those areas. Three key questions provide a framework for this discussion: (a) What will be classified? (b) How should the classification be produced? (c) Is the classification reliable and valid?

What Will Be Classified?

Within the mentoring field, there is a need to classify multiple "entities." In particular, it seems likely to be useful to develop separate typologies for mentoring relationships and mentoring programs. Virtually all of the research examining the benefits of mentoring suggests that youth involved in "stronger" relationships, however defined, accrue more benefits from their involvement with a mentor (or mentors). However, to understand, better predict, and support the development of effective relationships, we need to better define which dimensions of mentoring relationships are important. Whereas most research to date has focused on different features of relationships in relative isolation from one another, a typological approach offers a strategy for identifying more broadly defined categories of relationships, each of which may encompass a constellation of many interrelated characteristics. Likewise, as noted, there has been a proliferation of different types of mentoring programs in recent years. Clearly distinguishing among different approaches will be essential for increasing our understanding of differences in relative effectiveness and costs across program approaches, as well as the specific practices, goals, and youth populations that are best suited to each approach.

How Should the Classification Be Developed?

For guidance on how to approach the development of a typology, we can gain some insight by exploring the processes followed in other fields. As Achenbach (2001) discusses, both theory and empirical evidence may contribute to the development of a typology, each of which has both advantages and disadvantages. A theory-driven, or (in Achenbach's terms) nosological, approach to classification may be useful for generating agreement among various experts within a field. However, the potential exists for bias in various forms, such as the omission of newly emerging or controversial categories that may be important, but not yet widely recognized or accepted by experts. The criticisms directed over the years at the *DSM (Diagnostic and Statistical Manual),* used in the mental health field and developed originally using a "top-down" theoretical approach, are illustrative of these types of potential difficulties (Achenbach, 2001).

In contrast, an empirically driven approach works from a "bottom-up" perspective, drawing upon data collected on relatively large samples of the "things" being classified to help determine the appropriate categories. Using the psychopathology field again as an example, researchers working within an empirical paradigm began by collecting data on "problems" for large samples of individuals (Achenbach, 2001). They began to make sense of these data by attempting to identify "sets" of characteristics or behaviors that tended to appear together as "syndromes." These syndromes served as operational definitions of the taxonomic constructs within the overall system. The resulting typology includes some syndromes that have counterparts within the original *DSM,* but this method also identified syndromes that are distinct categories within the empirically based typology, but which were combined within a single category of the original *DSM.*

Even though an empirical approach may be more useful for researchers, it is not without its potential disadvantages. An empirically based approach to classification depends on the appropriateness of the statistical procedures used to identify types (Beauchaine, 2003). Typically, researchers rely on cluster analysis techniques when creating classification systems. (Beauchaine, 2003, describes alternative statistical procedures that may be more appropriate for taxometric classification; however, a presentation of these methods is beyond the scope of the current discussion.) Cluster analysis divides the cases in any given sample into groups by either maximizing between-group variance or minimizing within-group variance on a specified set of measures. Only constructs or attributes that are "measured" can be used to define the classification, but the technique always produces partitions in the sample based on the factors included in the analysis. It is up to the researcher to interpret the resulting partitions and decide whether the groups identified represent real differences in types or simply statistical artifacts.

Further difficulties may arise, regardless of the specific statistical procedures employed, if the sample on which data are collected is not fully representative of the underlying population, the key attributes needed for accurate classification are not assessed, or these attributes are measured with error. These situations may lead some categories to be overlooked in developing the final classification and for others to be included that do not represent "true" types.

Is Classification Reliable and Valid?

The final issue that needs to be considered in the development of any typology is the extent to which the resulting system is both reliable and valid. The concepts of reliability and validity (of various types) are generally associated with the development of measurement instruments. The application of these concepts to a classification system, however, also is important (Volkmar, Schwab-Stone, & First, 2002). With respect to reliability, our primary concern is with the extent to which any proposed typology of mentoring relationships or programs is replicable across different samples of relationships or programs (as well as, ideally, across different sets of measures used to assess program or relationship attributes and across different types of statistical procedures used for classification). Achieving reliability in classification depends, in turn, on the availability of standardized and reliable measurement tools for assessing both mentoring relationships and programs. Presently, several promising instruments are available for assessing characteristics of mentoring relationships (see Nakkula & Harris, this volume). In contrast, only limited work has addressed the need for the development and validation of instruments for assessing program characteristics.

Classifications developed using a theoretical approach may have face validity, based on a general agreement of the definition of categories within the typology. However, from the perspective of predictive validity, it is important to establish that the categories distinguished in the typology are associated with meaningful differences in factors external to the classification system itself (Volkmar et al., 2002). In mentoring, this would include differences in the impact that varying types of relationships or programs are found to have on youth outcomes or for differing populations of youth. Other considerations, such as differences in the types of program practices needed to support varying types of relationships and differences in the "best practices" that are found to comprise effective programming across varying types of programs, also may be critical for establishing validity.

TYPOLOGY OF MENTORING RELATIONSHIPS

Not all mentoring relationships look the same. Even a cursory examination of programmatically created mentoring relationships reveals differences in the nature and strength of these relationships. Most of the work on the classification of mentoring relationships has been empirically based rather than theoretical. We begin this section with a consideration of several ways in which mentoring relationships have been categorized on objective characteristics of the relationship. We then consider typologies based on differences in mentor style, followed by those that focus primarily on the function that relationships assume in the youth's life.

Objective Characteristics

Several studies have distinguished different categories of mentoring relationships on the basis of objective criteria such as whether the mentor and youth are matched in terms of gender or ethnicity (Rhodes, Reddy, Grossman, & Lee, 2002), the frequency of contact between mentor and youth (Howitt, Moore, & Gaulier, 1998), the length of the relationship (Grossman & Rhodes, 2002), and, in the case of naturally occurring mentoring relationships, the role of the adult in the youth's life (DuBois & Silverthorn, in press). In many instances, these distinctions have yielded significant associations with outcomes. Grossman and Rhodes (2002), for example, found that relationships in Big Brothers Big Sisters programs lasting 12 months or longer produced greater benefits for youth than those that lasted shorter periods of time. In a study of naturally occurring mentoring relationships, DuBois and Silverthorn (in press) have discriminated between relationships in which the adult was a family member, had an informal role (e.g., neighbor), or was a professional (e.g., teacher, counselor). Significant differences in outcomes were found across these categories, although the pattern was complex and did not consistently favor one role over another.

The preceding types of distinctions, however, are limited from the standpoint of building a typology of mentoring relationships for several reasons. First, typically only one characteristic of relationships has been used as a basis for categorization. Second, more subtle or subjective interactional aspects of relationships have not been considered. Finally, categories generally have been determined on the basis of the preexisting conceptualizations of researchers and thus have not benefited from empirical methodologies for classification.

Mentor Style

Styles and Morrow (1992) interviewed youth and mentors from four Linking Lifetimes programs within the first 6 months of the match and again when the matches had existed for 10 to 15 months. Linking Lifetimes targeted young offenders and adolescents who were at risk of dropping out of school and matched them with older adult (age 55 and older) mentors. Based on a content analysis of 26 matches, the researchers classified relationships into *satisfied* (17) and *dissatisfied* (9) matches, identifying characteristics of the matches that distinguished between the two types. The inductive content analysis involved extracting evidence from interview transcripts regarding behavior, perceptions of the relationship and each other, role of the mentor, and context of the relationship in the participants' lives (see Styles & Morrow, Appendix B, for a full description of the analysis strategy). Contrary to what might have been expected, activities of the pairs were reported not to differ across types; rather, the style of interaction defined as "how the adult and youth carry out their interactions" (Styles & Morrow, p. 14) was reported to be the key factor distinguishing satisfied and dissatisfied matches.

In a subsequent study (Morrow & Styles, 1995), these same researchers interviewed members of 82 matches drawn from eight Big Brothers Big Sisters agencies. Matches involving youth aged 10 to 15 that had been meeting for at least 4 months but not more than 18 months were selected randomly and interviewed; a second round of interviews was conducted approximately 9 months later. Despite the earlier work that resulted in the satisfied/dissatisfied categorization of relationships, the researchers again approached their analysis of the data inductively. (See Morrow & Styles, 1995, pp. 15–19, for a full description of the analysis strategy.) What emerged from the content analysis was again a two-type categorization of relationships in which the mentor's interaction style appeared to be the most critical distinguishing feature. The labels assigned to these relationship types reflect the differences in the mentor's approach to the relationship. In *developmental* relationships (54 of the 82 pairs), mentors "focused on providing youth with a comfort zone in which to address a broad range of developmental tasks—such as building emotional well-being, developing social skills, or gaining straightforward exposure to a range of recreational and cultural activities" (Morrow & Styles, p. 19). In contrast, mentors in *prescriptive* relationships (28 pairs) "demonstrated consistent reluctance or difficulty in adjusting their already formulated notions about their youth and the potential of the mentoring intervention to yield rapid, readily discernible and long-term changes in their youth's lives" (Morrow & Styles, p. 19).

Interestingly, the authors reported that at the time of the first interview, the two relationship types generally were not distinguishable in terms of the partners' levels of satisfaction; over time, however, the two groups were reported to diverge. For example, over time, youth in developmental relationships exhibited greater satisfaction with the relationships and began to voluntarily divulge difficulties in their lives. In contrast, youth in prescriptive relationships were typically dissatisfied with the relationships and tended to avoid discussions about problems they were having. This finding underscores the importance of viewing relationships as growing and changing as opposed to static entities (see Keller, this volume) and suggests the value of assessing the validity of typologies within a longitudinal framework. Furthermore, with respect to reliability, a similar classification scheme for relationships (based on youth satisfaction) emerged from two separate samples of mentors and youth participating in different types of programs.

It is also important to note that contrary to some interpretations of the preceding classification, both developmental and prescriptive relationships were often goal oriented and included the provision of instrumental as well as emotional support. The key difference between the two relationship types described by Morrow and Styles lies in the flexibility of mentors in developmental relationships to adjust to the needs and desires of mentees at any given moment, in contrast to the more narrow focus on preidentified goals or issues found in prescriptive relationships. Similar to their earlier work, however, Morrow and Styles did not address the issue of differential benefits related to relationship type within this study.

Based on interviews with 31 mentors participating in the Linking Up program (in which seventh- and eighth-grade youth with varying degrees of academic and psychosocial risk were matched with adult mentors), Hamilton and Hamilton (1990) proposed a typology of relationships based on the mentors' reports of the primary type of support they provided youth. Analysis of mentor interviews involved several stages, including an inductive generation of categories to define mentoring purposes and indexing relationships across variables such as youth risk level, number of meetings, and match termination. Hamilton and Hamilton described two primary types of mentoring relationships: *social* (8 matches) and *instrumental* (23 matches). In the former, mentors are respectful, concerned, and encouraging, but the primary goal is relationship development. In contrast, instrumental relationships are ones in which the mentor helps the youth to accomplish a task or goal by providing advice, guidance, and explanations. Although the researchers were not able to examine benefits for youth participating in each relationship type, they did note that during the course of the study, 75% of matches classified as social had terminated, compared with only 17% of matches classified as instrumental.

It is important to note that in contrast to Morrow and Styles's classification, which focused primarily on youth perceptions of mentor style, the Hamilton and Hamilton classification is based on mentors' goals for the relationship. Relationship types across these two typologies are not equivalent; having instrumental goals for the mentoring relationships does not preclude mentors' taking a developmental approach to the relationships.

Roberts's (1999) distinction between mentors' expressive and instrumental roles (based on data collected from 60 individuals who served as mentors for younger staff at schools and colleges in the United Kingdom) seems somewhat similar to the Hamilton and Hamilton classification. He concluded, however, that rather than comprising distinct roles, mentors generally were called upon to offer both types of support, depending on the specific situation in which they found themselves. Ford's (1998, cited in Hall, 2003) description of mentoring styles, based on

qualitative research conducted on the Mentoring Action Project in the United Kingdom, similarly concluded that mentors took on a variety of roles, which he described as *good parent, learning facilitator, career guidance provider,* and *social worker.* Ford's conceptualization also suggested that mentoring roles were fluid, with mentors moving between roles depending on the situation. Such fluidity, to the extent that it is found to be a predominant characteristic of mentoring relationships for youth, may render classifications focusing on support functions somewhat less useful as a way to categorize relationships. Ultimately, however, regardless of our ability to definitively classify relationships into distinct categories, the usefulness, and validity, of any proposed typology may be established to the extent that it can be applied productively to tasks such as predicting variation in youth outcomes.

Research conducted by Langhout, Rhodes, and Osborne (in press) is one of the few efforts to explicitly measure and classify mentoring relationships into types and then relate those types to youth outcomes. Relative to the preceding classifications, this research identified a more complex typology of relationship types that distinguished among several mentoring styles. As part of the Public/Private Ventures study of Big Brothers Big Sisters programs, more than 500 adolescents were interviewed approximately 12 months after being matched (18 months after the initial interview). (Similar interviews were conducted with a randomly assigned comparison group of youth who were not matched with mentors.) In addition to collecting data on outcomes that allowed the researchers to examine the impact of being in a mentoring relationship, these interviews included an extensive battery of questions designed to describe the nature of the mentoring relationship (e.g., frequency and type of activities, the youth's feelings toward and impressions of the mentor). Exploratory factor analysis of these items yielded 15 mentoring relationship scales. Further analyses reduced these 15 scales to three latent categories: (a) *support,* described as the youth's satisfaction with the relationship and their perception of the mentor's provision of unconditional support; (b) *structure,* described as the extent to which discussions of the relationship, goals and/or problems characterized the youth's experience of the relationship; and (c) *activity,* defined as the extent to which the youth reported the pair participated in a variety of activities (Langhout, Rhodes, & Osborne, in press).

Based on a cluster analysis of measures of these three dimensions of relationships, Langhout et al. identified four types of mentoring relationships: *moderate* (112 matches), *unconditionally supportive* (69 matches), *active* (104 matches), and *low-key* (42 matches). Youth in relationships characterized as "supportive" reported high levels of support coupled with moderate levels of structure and activity. "Moderate" relationships were characterized by reports of moderate levels of structure and activity, but lower-reported levels of support than other types. Relationships described as "active" reported the most participation in a variety of activities, but low levels of structure. Finally, "low-key" relationships were characterized by youth reports of high support, moderate structure, and few activities.

Having identified these four relationship types, the researchers used multivariate analysis of variance (MANOVA) to examine the extent to which the groups of youth classified into the clusters representing the different types of relationships benefited across a range of outcomes relative to the comparison group. (No comparisons across the relationship types without reference to the control group were reported.) Controlling for Time 1 outcome measures, these analyses indicated that youth who were in "moderate" relationships appeared to have better psychological, parent, peer, and school outcomes. Relative to those in the comparison group, these youth reported an improved sense of self-worth and school competence, decreased alienation from parents, and decreased conflict and inequality with friends. Youth in "active" relationships reported better school and peer relationship outcomes (e.g., improved peer emotional support and intimacy and increased school competence), whereas youth in "low-key" relationships reported experiencing less peer conflict relative to controls. The researchers found no benefits for youth in the unconditional support group relative to control youth; in fact, youth in this group reported increased parental alienation relative to controls.

As the authors discussed, these results may have implications for the selection and training of volunteer mentors. Rather than acting as "good friends" who provide youth with unconditional support, mentors may be more successful in affecting the lives of youth when they provide some level of support along with expectations for their mentees.

Each of the typologies of relationships discussed thus far was developed based on an examination of "traditional" one-to-one mentoring relationships, usually within the context of a mentoring program. Philip and Hendry (1996), however, developed a typology of naturally occurring mentoring relationships that takes into account not only the mentor's role but also the configuration of the mentoring relationship. Specifically, they included group as well as one-to-one relationships and peer as well as adult-youth mentoring in their classification. The researchers conducted individual and group interviews with 150 young people (recruited through voluntary and mandatory organizations, youth agencies, and self-help groups), ranging in age from 13 to 18. Using a multistage content analysis of the interview transcripts, Philip and Hendry (1996) identified five forms of mentoring (the percentage of youth reporting each type of mentoring was not reported): *classic* mentoring, described as one-to-one relationships between a youth and an adult; *individual-team* mentoring, which involves one or more adults providing support to a group of youth; *friend-to-friend* mentoring, described as "best friends" providing each other with mutual support; *peer-group* mentoring, which involves a group of youth supporting each other; and long-term mentoring provided by *risk-taking* adults, which is similar to classic mentoring in form, but in which the adult mentor may not conform to a society's definition of a good role model. Philip and Hendry (1996) argued that each of these mentoring forms varies with respect to gender, context, and life events that draw youth to particular forms of mentoring and the qualities youth expect from their mentors. These conclusions were based on the authors' interpretation of descriptions by youth of the mentoring they had experienced rather than statistical tests of differences across types.

Nature and Status of
Relationships in the Lives of Youth

Whereas the preceding typologies tend to focus on the interactional style and role of the mentor, other research suggests the importance of distinguishing among relationships according to the nature and status of the function that mentors assume in the lives of youth. Based on a qualitative study of 47 matches in several small intergenerational mentoring programs, Freedman (1988) argued that significant (i.e., mentoring) relationships fell into one of two types: primary (16 matches) and secondary (21 matches). The remaining 10 matches examined were defined as "nonsignificant." As reported by Freedman, both types of significant relationships were characterized by "personal closeness, attachment, trust, enjoyment and importance," but primary relationships displayed these characteristics in "highly developed form" (p. 17). Freedman went on to characterize primary relationships as closely resembling kinship attachments, with the mentor becoming one of the most important people in the youth's life. The attachments in these relationships were described as unconditional; the mentor reinforced the youth's positive feelings and behaviors as well as dealt with negative aspects of the youth's life.

In contrast, secondary relationships were reported to be more limited in their nature (Freedman, 1988). Mentors in these relationships might be thought of more as "good neighbors" than close relatives. The focus in these relationships was more on supporting and reinforcing the youth's positive behavior, with less emphasis on actively dealing with negative aspects of the youth's life and environment. Relative to primary relationships, these relationships appeared to be characterized by less intimacy in the form of sharing of personal thoughts and feelings.

Freedman (1988) used his classification to attempt to explain differences in benefits that youth appeared to derive from the mentoring relationships. He argued (based on interviews with youth and observations by program staff) that youth in primary relationships accrued more benefits than those in secondary relationships, who, in turn, benefited more than youth who did not develop significant relationships with their mentors. In line with this finding, DuBois and colleagues (DuBois, Neville, Parra, & Pugh-Lilly, 2002) recently reported findings suggesting that whether or not the youth identified his or her mentor as a "significant person" in his or her life, using an open-ended nomination procedure mediated the effects of participation in a Big Brothers Big Sisters program on emotional and behavioral adjustment.

Limitations

There are several noteworthy limitations of efforts to empirically derive a typology of mentoring relationships. First, these efforts predominantly have been based on relatively small, qualitative studies of programmatic mentoring relationships. The extent to which typologies would be supported by quantitative classification procedures (e.g., cluster analysis) as well as the degree to which findings can be generalized, especially to naturally occurring mentoring relationships, is unclear. Second, studies have for the most part focused on simply delineating relationship types rather than also examining the linkages that may exist between relationship types and outcomes. Thus, issues of validity for proposed typologies remain largely unexplored. Furthermore, most of these classifications have described mentoring relationships in relatively static terms rather than incorporating changes in relationships over time (see Keller, this volume, for a discussion of change in mentoring relationships over time). Finally, to a large extent, researchers have worked independently, developing a new classification system with each piece of research completed. This serves to impede not only the ability of the field to gauge the reliability of proposed typologies but also the capacity of the field as a whole to progress toward a more unified typology (or set of typologies) for mentoring relationships.

TYPOLOGY OF MENTORING PROGRAMS

Efforts to classify mentoring programs have been both theoretically driven and empirically informed. Proposed classification systems using each of these two approaches are considered separately in this section.

Theoretical Approaches

The Mentoring Center (Jacks, 2000), a mentoring organization located in Oakland, California, developed a typology of youth mentoring program models based on a theory of change that focuses primarily on the extent of the needs of youth. In this typology, the severity of need exhibited by the youth determines the type of mentoring required, with implications for the appropriate selection and training of mentors and the types of activities in which matches will be asked to engage. The typology identifies two types of *assistance mentoring:* low/moderate or moderate (for youth exhibiting low to moderate levels of risk). In both types of assistance mentoring, appropriate activities are expected to include basic companionship, academic tutoring, career guidance, and activities designed to improve self-esteem (Jacks, 2000).

Youth with greater needs are viewed as better served by one of two types of *transformative mentoring:* intensive or very intensive. Intensive mentoring is intended for youth with high levels of risk—those who are lacking in adult guidance, are poor students, or are influenced by negative surroundings. Youth with the highest levels of risk are viewed as requiring very intensive mentoring: These youth include those who are rebellious and highly influenced by negative peer groups and those who have been institutionalized for long periods of time (Jacks, 2000). Although a transformative mentoring program is likely to include all of the activities found in assistance mentoring, the greater needs of the youth are expected to call for additional activities, including those directed toward development of skills for conflict resolution, parenting, and helping youth to develop respect for self, private property, and authority.

In contrast to the Mentoring Center's focus on youth needs, the Center for Substance Abuse Prevention (CSAP, 2002) presented a classification of programs based primarily on where the mentoring activity takes place and the configuration of the match. CSAP proposed three primary types of programmatic mentoring: one-to-one, group, and team. Crosscutting match configuration in this typology is the location of mentoring activities, which can be classified as either *community-based* (i.e., the location of mentoring activities is left unspecified by the program) or *site-based* (i.e., the majority of mentoring activities take place at a location specified by the program). In this classification, site-based programs are further differentiated by the specific place where activities take place (school, workplace, youth agency, housing complex, or faith institution).

In addition to the potential shortcomings of a theoretical approach to classification discussed previously (including lack of independent empirical verification), these typologies have other limitations that may influence their usefulness in terms of informing research or practice. In the Mentoring Center's classification, for example, key constructs used in determining differing types of programming, such as the youth's level of risk, tend not to be well specified, thus making it difficult potentially to either evaluate this typology in a research context or to apply it in a practice context. Relatedly, although not a limitation of the typology itself, guidance regarding how to structure a mentoring program is not provided. Similarly, although CSAP's classification may be useful for descriptive purposes, guidance for determining which model is most appropriate for specific youth and/or mentors is lacking. These latter limitations are perhaps indicative of the overall lack of attention given to these issues in research to date as well as a tendency for theory-based typologies to be less likely to receive this type of consideration than those that are empirically derived within a research framework.

Empirical Approaches

One of the first empirically informed typologies of mentoring programs was developed by Saito and Blythe (1992) at the Search Institute. As a precursor to an evaluation of the Buddy System (a group of mentoring agencies overseen by the Minneapolis Youth Trust), these researchers created a typology for categorizing this group of programs. Derived through a combination of literature review and interviews with staff at several programs, Saito and Blythe categorized programs into five types: *traditional; long-term, focused activities; short-term, focused activities; team;* and *group.* Program features that distinguish among types included configuration of the relationship (i.e., one-to-one or group); the location and nature of mentoring activities (i.e., specified or unspecified); and the length and intensity of the required mentor commitment. The researchers did not provide information regarding the distribution of program types across the Buddy System agencies.

Traditional mentoring programs were characterized by one-to-one matches of relatively high intensity and duration (at least once a week meetings for at least 6 months). Meetings between mentors and youth were not directly supervised by program staff (i.e., program staff were not present during mentoring meetings); what pairs did together and where meetings took place were not specified by the program.

In contrast to traditional mentoring, both types of focused-activity programs specified where and when matches would meet, generally in a common location that was actively supervised by program staff. Both involved frequent meetings of one-to-one matches; only the duration of the match distinguished the two types. Short-term programs were defined as 2 to 5 months in duration, whereas long-term programs lasted at least 6 months.

Finally, team and group mentoring programs were distinguished from the other types by their deviation from the traditional one-to-one match configuration. *Team mentoring* was defined as a "team, couple, or family" mentoring one youth. Matches were relatively unsupervised (i.e., program staff were not present during mentoring meetings), intensive and of long duration, with the nature and location of activities not specified by the program. In group mentoring, one adult was matched with a group of youth who met in a specified location and who engaged in activities largely determined and supervised by program staff.

Saito and Blythe (1992) also discussed potential implications of program type for program practices. For example, these researchers argued for the importance of screening, matching, and systematic communication for programs in which match activities are not directly supervised. The relationship between program type and the utilization of such practices, however, was not addressed in the context of this proposed typology, nor was there examination of the linkage between different types of

programs and youth outcomes. Furthermore, although the typology was empirically informed based on analysis of interviews with program staff, it was not empirically derived, in the sense that a statistical classification procedure was not applied to data collected about programs.

The most extensive typology of mentoring programs to date, developed by researchers at Public/Private Ventures for MENTOR/National Mentoring Partnership (Sipe & Roder, 1999), addresses this latter limitation. This typology was derived based on data from a survey of mentoring program directors. The researchers employed "snowball" techniques to identify potential programs to participate in the survey. Attempts were made to collect data from more than 2,000 programs that were nominated for inclusion; ultimately, staff from 722 programs completed the questionnaire.

Although the primary goal of this research was descriptive, factors that were assessed on the questionnaire and that went into the analysis as potential distinguishing characteristics were selected based on hypotheses regarding what factors are important for maximizing the development of strong, positive relationships between youth and mentors participating in mentoring programs (and ultimately, for maximizing benefits for youth). These factors included, for example, configuration of the mentoring matches and program practices related to screening, training, and ongoing support. Based on a cluster analysis of the survey data, the researchers developed a typology of mentoring programs containing 11 different program types (see Figure 5.1). The most fundamental distinction in the typology is in terms of the match configuration: either one-to-one or group matches. Within each type of match configuration, programs were further distinguished based on the location of program activities: either community-based or site-based. Group mentoring programs were not further differentiated. However, one-to-one programs were further differentiated based on the expected duration and/or intensity of the match.

Programs classified as *long-term,* whether site-based or community-based, included those requiring mentors and youth to commit to the match for at least 12 months, whereas *short-term* programs required less than a full year's

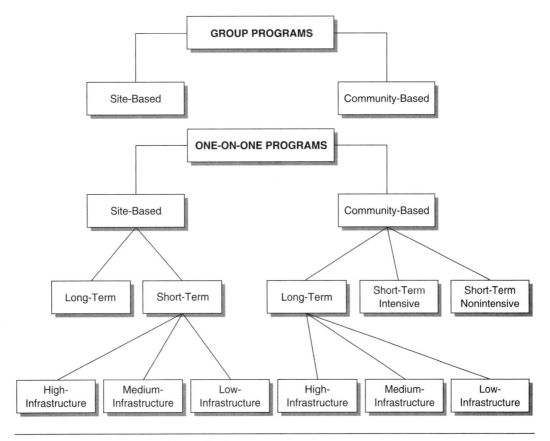

Figure 5.1   Classification of Mentoring Programs

SOURCE: Adapted from Sipe and Roder (1999).

commitment. For community-based programs, those classified as short-term were further differentiated as intensive or nonintensive programs depending on whether they required at least weekly (intensive) or less frequent (nonintensive) meetings between youth and mentors.

Finally, short-term site-based programs and long-term community-based programs were classified into three separate types depending on the level of infrastructure provided by the program. *High-infrastructure* programs were characterized by reported extensive screening and prematch training of mentors as well as the reported provision of intensive support to mentors throughout the life of the match (either through monthly contact with program staff and/or through mentor support groups). Programs classified as having *medium infrastructure* reported conducting some screening and providing some prematch training to mentors, but

these practices were not as extensive as those in high-infrastructure programs, and the programs varied with respect to the reported amount of ongoing support provided to mentors. Programs characterized by *low infrastructure* reported conducting little or no screening of mentors and providing little or no training and ongoing support to mentors.

Theoretically, further investigation could support the extension of this typology. For example, both site-based long-term and short-term community-based programs are likely to include varying levels of infrastructure. Site-based programs might be further differentiated by the specific location (e.g., school, workplace, agency) where match activities take place (CSAP, 2000). As in any empirically based typology, the specific set of categories derived was limited based on the sample of programs available for analysis. One might anticipate that additional categories would emerge were this analysis replicated using a different sample of programs.

Limitations

Most of the program typologies described here focus primarily on structural characteristics of programs (e.g., match configuration, location of mentoring activities, duration and intensity of the match). The Sipe and Roder typology is somewhat unique with the addition of program infrastructure factors (i.e., screening, training and support) into the mix, but these are still structural features of all mentoring programs. With the exception of the Mentoring Center's typology, none of the proposed classifications take youth characteristics into account (e.g., age or developmental stage, gender, or ethnicity/ culture). Similarly, none of these classification systems takes into account characteristics of the mentors. The importance of considering these factors is illustrated by the manner in which mentor age has served as the primary basis for identifying both intergenerational mentoring (in which youth are matched with older adults) and peer mentoring (in which youth are matched with other, typically older, youth as mentors) as distinct program types (Karcher, Kuperminc, Portwood, Sipe, & Taylor, 2004; see also chapters by Taylor, LoSciuto, & Porcellini; and by Karcher, this volume).

The omission of program types based on the age of mentor in the Sipe and Roder (1999) typology illustrates the challenges of empiri- cally derived approaches to classification of mentoring programs. In this research, of the 714 programs for which data were available on the age of the mentor, only 7% used youth exclu- sively as mentors, and only 5% used only older adults as mentors. With such small percentages of programs, it was difficult to justify classify- ing either peer mentoring or intergenerational mentoring as distinct program types, particu- larly given that these programs varied with regard to other program characteristics already included in the typology (such as match config- uration and location of activities).

Similarly, the majority of the programs sur- veyed could not be distinguished based on other youth or mentor characteristics. For example,

more than half the programs in the Sipe and Roder (1999) analysis (51%) served youth across the entire age range examined (i.e., kindergarten through 12th grade). And the majority of pro- grams (82%) served youth from a range of dif- ferent racial or ethnic groups. Thus, these types of characteristics were not useful from an empir- ical perspective for distinguishing types of men- toring programs. To the extent that additional program types based on participant characteris- tics could have been incorporated in their typol- ogy, the lack of validity evidence to guide such decisions is also noteworthy.

A further limitation is that most of the typologies were completed several years ago and thus do not necessarily reflect the most recently emerging types of programs in the field of youth mentoring. The growing prominence of a diverse array of site-based program models, for example, is not fully reflected in most of the typologies that have been developed. Further- more, an entirely new "location" for mentoring activities has emerged that is not reflected in any of the typologies to date: the Internet. As recently as the time programs were surveyed for Sipe and Roder's research, mentoring was con- ceived of nearly exclusively as a "face-to-face" relationship. Recently, however, an increasing number of programs have emerged that rely on e-mail as the only means of communication between mentors and youth (see Griffiths & Miller, this volume). One might hypothesize that their typology thus could be extended to incorporate e-mentoring as an additional pro- gram type under both group and one-to-one match configurations.

The typology developed by Sipe and Roder (1999) is the only proposed typology to date that is empirically derived in the sense of being based on application of a statistical classifica- tion procedure to program data. Neither the reliability nor the validity of this typology, how- ever, has been evaluated. The typology was derived based on data from a relatively large sample of programs, yet we know that Big Brothers Big Sisters agencies comprised a large portion of the sample and that some types of programs (e.g., faith-based models, peer men- toring programs) were underrepresented.

Finally, very little work has been done to relate the program types to outcomes in this or other proposed typologies. Indeed, beyond the research that addresses the impact of one-to-one, community-based programs, we know very little about the benefits youth derive from participating in the wide range of other types of programs that have been included in typologies and, importantly, whether such effects differ across program types in ways that would support their differentiation within a classification system.

FUTURE DIRECTIONS

Synthesis

The mentoring field has made some inroads into developing typologies of both relationships and programs. Clearly, however, much work remains to be done. Classifications of mentoring relationships primarily have been derived empirically, although based on relatively small samples of mentoring relationships and relying primarily on qualitative methodology. Some theoretical work has been directed toward classification of mentoring programs, but these appear to be relatively isolated pieces of work. Empirically derived typologies of programs have evolved over time, with a fairly extensive classification described by Sipe and Roder (1999), based on analysis of a relatively large sample of mentoring programs. For the most part, these typologies have focused on structural features of programs, rather than characteristics of the participants, to distinguish among the various types. There have been only limited efforts to investigate the reliability or validity of proposed typologies of either relationships or programs. Consequently, neither the extent to which they generalize across different samples or use of varying classification procedures nor the extent to which they have implications for understanding and predicting youth outcomes is well understood. Of further note is that research conducted on classifying mentoring relationships and that focused on classifying programs has proceeded more or less independently. Only recently have attempts been made to relate characteristics of different program types to the development of mentoring relationships (Herrera et al., 2000). Given the consistent

evidence of the importance of relationship characteristics for youth outcomes, the lack of systematic investigation of the connections between different types of programs and relationships within typologies that have been proposed to date seems a particularly noteworthy omission.

Recommendations for Research

1. *Further investigate existing typologies of mentoring relationships.* One priority for future research should be the further investigation of existing proposed typologies of mentoring relationships. These should include Morrow and Styles's distinction between *developmental* and *prescriptive* relationships. Although this distinction has been more or less embraced by the field, it merits additional investigation for several reasons. First, this typology was derived from an analysis of relationships in Big Brothers Big Sisters agencies. We need to verify that this classification is equally valid across other program settings. Morrow and Styles's classification and the proposed relative advantages of developmental relationships within their typology, furthermore, often has been perceived to be at odds with Hamilton and Hamilton's conceptualization of mentoring relationships as either *social* or *instrumental,* in which instrumental ties are suggested to be more desirable. The latter classification, however, is based on the "goals" of the relationship, whereas Morrow and Styles's conceptualization is based on the mentor's "style" or approach to the relationship (see Keller, this volume, for further discussion). It seems likely that a more complex and theoretically more useful classification for the field might emerge by combining these two classification schemes. One could envision developmental mentors who focus on social goals as well as those who focus on instrumental goals within the relationship. Similarly, mentors whose style is prescriptive also might be found both in relationships with social goals and those with instrumental goals. Future research might examine whether this combination of style and goal yields distinct relationship types and, if so, what their implications are for youth outcomes. Ideally, this type of research should be conducted using objective

empirical methods to assess the viability of different typological possibilities, in a manner similar to the work of Langhout et al. (in press).

2. *Develop updated typology of mentoring programs.* Given the continued development and expansion of the mentoring field, additional work to update the Sipe and Roder (1999) typology of mentoring programs is needed. Although it can be hypothesized that further differentiation of some of the program types included in their classification would be useful, this remains to be verified empirically. Further research also would help determine whether new forms of mentoring, such as e-mentoring, should be viewed as a distinct program type or simply as variations of more traditional mentoring forms.

3. *Investigate the reliability and validity of proposed typologies.* For both typologies of relationships and of mentoring programs, much work remains to be done to establish their reliability and validity. Future research needs to better establish the extent to which proposed typologies are relatively stable across differing samples of relationships and programs, measurement approaches, and classification methodologies.

Studies then need to address a range of concerns pertinent to the substantive implications of such typologies. These include fundamental questions such as the extent to which specific types of mentoring relationships and program models vary in their implications for youth outcomes, as well as more complex issues such as those pertaining to associations between types of mentoring relationships and programs. As part of this work, research should also be directed toward helping the field identify programs that do not merit inclusion as "mentoring." Such exclusion might be based, at least in part, on weak or nonexistent ties with youth outcomes.

Recommendations for Practice

1. *Develop an understanding of program models and their implications for practice.*

Practitioners should become familiar with the various program models that exist and be clear and explicit about the specific type of mentoring program they are implementing. As research becomes available that addresses the effectiveness of various types of mentoring programs—particularly to the extent that benefits are found to vary across particular groups of youth or outcome domains—program operators also need to be aware of the implications of this research for their programs. For example, if research suggests that benefits of school-based one-to-one mentoring were limited to improving academic outcomes, such a program model would not be appropriate if the population of youth being served did not need assistance in this area or the goal was to provide benefits that extend to nonacademic outcome domains. In general, practitioners cannot assume that results obtained for "traditional" one-to-one mentoring models apply to other program configurations (Rhodes, 2002).

2. *Develop an understanding of relationship types and their connection with youth outcomes.* Similarly, practitioners should be aware of variation in the types of mentoring relationships that may be developed even within the same program. Current classifications of mentoring relationships are based to a large extent on differences in the individual mentor's style or approach to the relationship. To the extent that practitioners want to foster "developmental" mentoring relationships (Morrow & Styles, 1995), for example, they need to look for evidence that prospective mentors are capable of taking that approach and/or to stress in prematch and ongoing training the importance of taking a particular approach to the match.

Program operators, furthermore, need to be aware of the potential implications of different types of relationships for outcomes. Research such as that conducted by Langhout et al. (in press) suggests that youth outcomes vary depending on the types of relationships formed with their mentors. Thus, practitioners may want to select mentors and develop training materials and other program supports that are designed to foster specific relationship forms depending on the outcome goals of the program.

REFERENCES

Achenbach, T. M. (2001). Challenges and benefits of assessment, diagnosis, and taxonomy for clinical practice and research. *Australian and New Zealand Journal of Psychiatry, 35,* 263–271.

The American Heritage College Dictionary (4th ed.). (2002). Boston: Houghton Mifflin.

Beauchaine, T. P. (2003). Taxometrics and developmental psychopathology. *Development and Psychopathology, 15,* 501–527.

Center for Substance Abuse Prevention. (2002). *Mentoring initiatives: An overview of youth mentoring* (A Center for Substance Abuse Prevention Conference and Meeting Document). Washington, DC: Author.

DuBois, D. L., Neville, H. A., Parra, G. R., & Pugh-Lilly, A. O. (2002). Testing a new model of mentoring. In G. G. Noam (Ed. in chief) & J. E. Rhodes (Ed.), *A critical view of youth mentoring* (*New Directions for Youth Development: Theory, Research, and Practice, No. 93,* pp. 21–57). San Francisco: Jossey-Bass.

DuBois, D. L., & Silverthorn, N. (in press). Characteristics of natural mentoring relationships and adolescent health: Evidence from a national study. *Journal of Primary Prevention.*

Ford, G. (1998). *Career guidance mentoring for disengaged young people* (NICEC/ICG Briefing). Stourbridge, UK: Institute of Careers Guidance.

Freedman, M. (1988). *Partners in growth: Elder mentors and at-risk youth.* Philadelphia: Public/Private Ventures.

Goodwin, C. N. (1999). Improving future fluvial classification systems. *Stream notes.* Article Oct99a1. Retrieved December 14, 2003, from http://www.stream.fs.fed.us/news/streamnt/oct99

Grossman, J. B., & Rhodes, J. E. (2002). The test of time: Predictors and effects of duration in youth mentoring relationships. *American Journal of Community Psychology, 30,* 199-219.

Hall, J. C. (2003). *Mentoring and young people: A literature review.* Glasgow, UK: University of Glasgow, The SCRE Centre.

Hamilton, M. A., & Hamilton, S. H. (1990). *Linking up: Final report of a mentoring program for youth.* Ithaca, NY: Cornell University, College of Human Ecology, Department of Human Development and Family Studies.

Herrera, C., Sipe, C. L., & McClanahan, W. S. (2000). *Mentoring school-age children: Relationship development in community-based and school-based programs.* Philadelphia: Public/Private Ventures. (Published in collaboration with MENTOR/National Mentoring Partnership, Alexandria, VA)

Howitt, P. S., Moore, E. A., & Gaulier, B. (1998). Winning the battles and the wars: An evaluation of comprehensive, community-based delinquency prevention programming. *Juvenile and Family Court Journal, 49*(1), 39–49.

Jacks, M. (2000). *The Mentoring Center's philosophy and opinions.* Oakland, CA: The Mentoring Center.

Karcher, M. J., Kuperminc, G. P., Portwood, S. G., Sipe, C. L., & Taylor, A. S. (2004). *Mentoring programs: A typology to inform program development, research and evaluation.* Manuscript submitted for publication.

Langhout, R. D., Rhodes, J. E., & Osborne, L. N. (in press). An exploratory study of youth mentoring: Toward a typology of relationships. *Journal of Youth and Adolescence.*

Morrow, K. V., & Styles, M. B. (1995). *Building relationships with youth in program settings: A study of Big Brothers/Big Sisters.* Philadelphia: Public/Private Ventures.

Philip, K., & Hendry, L. B. (1996). Young people and mentoring—towards a typology? *Journal of Adolescence, 19,* 189–201.

Rhodes, J. E. (2002). *Stand by me: The risks and rewards of mentoring today's youth.* Cambridge, MA: Harvard University Press.

Rhodes, J. E., Reddy, R., Grossman, J. B., & Lee, J. (2002). Volunteer mentoring relationships with minority youth: An analysis of same- versus cross-race matches. *Journal of Applied Social Psychology, 32,* 2114–2133.

Roberts, A. (1999). Androgyny and the mentoring role: An empirical study to examine for prominent mentor expectations. *Mentoring & Tutoring, 7,* 145–162.

Saito, R. N., & Blythe, D. A. (1992). *Understanding mentoring relationships.* Minneapolis, MN: Search Institute.

Sipe, C. L., & Roder, A. E. (1999). *Mentoring school-age children: A classification of programs.*

Philadelphia: Public/Private Ventures. (Published in collaboration with MENTOR/National Mentoring Partnership, Alexandria, VA)

Styles, M. B., & Morrow, K. V. (1992). *Understanding how youth and elders form relationships: A study of four Linking Lifetimes programs.* Philadelphia: Public/Private Ventures.

Volkmar, F. R., Schwab-Stone, M., & First, M. (2002). Classification in child and adolescent psychiatry: Principles and issues. In M. Lewis (Ed.), *Child and adolescent psychiatry: A comprehensive textbook* (pp. 499–505). New York: Lippincott Williams & Wilkins.

PART III

MENTORING RELATIONSHIPS

6

THE STAGES AND DEVELOPMENT OF MENTORING RELATIONSHIPS

THOMAS E. KELLER

INTRODUCTION

The defining feature of youth mentoring is the personal relationship established between a young person and a caring, competent individual who offers companionship, support, and guidance. Conceptual models proposing how individuals might benefit from mentoring necessarily begin with the assumption that some type of relationship exists between the youth and mentor (Rhodes, 2002). Nevertheless, the development of the mentoring relationship itself rarely has been the object of study. A better understanding of the processes involved in the formation, maintenance, and conclusion of mentoring relationships holds promise for more effective intervention. With knowledge of the typical course in mentoring relationships, programs could anticipate challenges and provide supportive services at crucial junctures in the relationship. Promoting the sustained development of positive relationships is a primary goal because longer-lasting relationships tend to yield greater benefits for youth, while short-term relationships may have unintended

negative consequences (Grossman & Rhodes, 2002).

Every mentoring relationship has a life of its own, and the aim of this chapter is to examine the natural progression of these relationships over time. Like individual lives, relationships have beginnings, follow diverse trajectories, and ultimately reach their endings (Hinde, 1997). As in research on development over the life span, the study of mentoring relationships requires attention to normative patterns in development, individual differences in development, and variability or flexibility within a single relationship (Baltes, Lindenberger, & Staudinger, 1998). Accordingly, the chapter begins by highlighting theoretical perspectives on the development of relationships by addressing three fundamental questions: What features of relationships are subject to change? How do relationships change? Why do relationships change? Next, a heuristic model proposing normative phases in the development of youth mentoring relationships is presented. Then, this stage model is used to organize both a review of empirical research on the development of mentoring

The writing of this chapter was supported in part by a grant from the National Institute of Mental Health (1RO3MH067129–1A1).

relationships and a discussion of program practices that may foster relationship development. The chapter concludes with a discussion of future directions for research and practice.

THEORY

What Features of Relationships Are Subject to Change?

A concept of close relationships is prerequisite for examining what changes over the course of their development. Any definition or description of human relationships must necessarily be incomplete given their inherent complexity and the variability they demonstrate across time and contexts (Hinde, 1997). Nevertheless, a few core principles provide a basis for understanding the features of significant relationships. A close relationship involves a pattern of social interaction over an extended time in which each individual influences the subsequent behavior of the other individual (Reis, Collins, & Berscheid, 2000). Participants exchange information, express emotions, negotiate goals, and regulate their own behavior and that of the other person. To distinguish relationships from a series of casual or routine contacts, meanings must be attributed to these interdependent, enduring, and reciprocal interactions (Laursen & Bukowski, 1997). Experiences with the other person are interpreted and organized into mental representations of the particular thoughts, emotions, and actions that characterize the relationship (Hartup & Laursen, 1999). Expectations derived from the interactive history of the relationship affect current exchanges, and current exchanges, in turn, influence future relations (Reis et al., 2000).

Despite sharing some core features, relationships come in many varieties. The relationships of children and adolescents may be distinguished by the type of interactive partner, such as parent, teacher, coach, neighbor, counselor, or friend (Blyth, Hill, & Thiel, 1982). Likewise, relationships may be differentiated by their main functions, such as protection, nurturance, play, education, and emotional support. Function and partner often have a specific correspondence (Furman & Buhrmester, 1985). For example, attachment behaviors are activated in times of distress to elicit protection and comfort from a parent or caregiver, whereas affiliative behaviors operate in the presence of peers to promote social engagement and friendship (Cassidy, 1999).

Relationships also may be contrasted on dimensions such as permanence (e.g., voluntary, kinship, committed), social power (e.g., resources, experience, rank), and gender (e.g., gender roles, same- vs. opposite-sex pairs) (Laursen & Bukowski, 1997). In parent-child relationships, the obligations of kinship promote permanence, and the greater capacities of the parent create a power differential. The emphasis is on maintaining the relationship despite unequal exchanges in which resources generally flow from parent to child. In peer friendships, which are voluntary and potentially temporary, the emphasis is on an egalitarian reciprocity in which each individual benefits from continuing the relationship. The parent-child relationship is a prototypic *vertical* relationship, while friendship is a prototypic *horizontal* relationship (Hartup, 1989).

Given these distinctions, how should mentoring relationships be conceptualized? Various types of mentoring may differ in permanence (e.g., natural mentors vs. mentors with program obligations) and social power (e.g., older and wiser mentors vs. peer mentors). Mentoring programs may promote particular roles (e.g., friend or coach) and corresponding functions (e.g., fun or education). In many instances, the mentor is more experienced and capable than the mentee, but the mentor is encouraged to act like a friend to the mentee. Thus, mentoring may represent a hybrid relationship, incorporating features of both vertical and horizontal models. A potential advantage of mentoring is that the mentor need not be constrained to a particular role and may respond as appropriate in several different domains of the child's life. Hamilton and Hamilton (1992) observe: "A mentor might act as a tutor one day (helping with math homework), a sponsor the next day (helping find a job), and a confidant the third day (offering emotional support following a family crisis)" (p. 546).

Even relationships that fall into the same category according to form and function may vary in the nature and quality of interpersonal interaction that characterizes the dyad. For example, relationships might be assessed on a number of dimensions: content and diversity of activities; qualities of verbal and nonverbal communication; frequency and pattern of interaction; nature and degree of conflict; use of power and control; amount and significance of self-disclosure; level of satisfaction; and strength of commitment (Hinde, 1997). With regard to youth mentoring relationships, some authors have pointed to the importance of factors such as trust, satisfaction, disappointment, and coping assistance (Rhodes, Reddy, Roffman, & Grossman, in press). Others have emphasized attributes such as empathy, engagement, authenticity, and empowerment (Liang, Tracy, Taylor, & Williams, 2002). In summary, over time, mentoring relationships may exhibit change and development on several aspects of form, function, and mode of interaction.

How Do Relationships Change?

Just as there are many aspects of a relationship subject to change with the passage of time, there are many ways in which change in relationships may occur. Despite consistencies in behavior and meaning over time, relationships are multidetermined and dynamic (Hinde, 1997). Thus, a major challenge is accounting simultaneously for relationship continuities and discontinuities (Collins, 1997). Applying concepts from general systems theory (Cox & Paley, 1997), interactions between individuals in a relationship must have pattern and structure (e.g., rules, codes) for the relationship to survive. On one hand, relationships have self-stabilizing, homeostatic features that compensate for changing conditions in the environment. On the other hand, change and evolution are inherent in open, living systems. Challenges to existing patterns can result in reorganization of the system, frequently in a more complex and differentiated form.

Over an extended time, these developmental phenomena define the life course of a relationship, with adjustments to changing circumstances and significant events altering its developmental pathway. Because mentoring responds to the individualized needs and circumstances of youth, every relationship follows a distinctive trajectory marked by turning points, transitions, and transformations. Reflecting the complexity of developmental pathways, Sroufe (1997) outlines five propositions:

1. Adaptation to current challenges forecasts the capacity to adapt to future challenges.

2. Change is possible at many points in time.

3. Change is constrained by prior adaptation as patterns of behavior solidify with time.

4. Multiple pathways can lead to similar outcomes (equifinality).

5. Similar initial pathways can lead to different outcomes (multifinality).

In the context of a mentoring relationship, the resolution of each ambiguous situation, whether deciding on an outing or dealing with a family crisis, provides a point of reference for how the relationship will cope when faced with similar conditions in the future. In addition, the accumulation of shared experiences generates routines—what they do, what they say, how they say it—that give the relationship form, familiarity, and substance. Inevitably, however, the mentor and youth negotiate new and different circumstances that require ingenuity and flexibility. These moments present possibilities for the developmental pathway of the relationship to be deflected. At such times, the adaptive capacity and sustainability of the relationship may depend not only on the behaviors of the mentor and youth but also on contextual factors. In formal mentoring programs, for example, these factors may include the structural components of the program (e.g., policies, guidelines) as well as the support and corrective action of parents and program staff (Keller, in press). Given the particular combination of personal and situational factors, some mentoring relationships may develop quickly into a strong bond; some may experience a series of setbacks and breakthroughs; and others may struggle along without being able to establish a meaningful connection.

A relationship's trajectory may be revealed by tracing particular dimensions of the relationship. Taking self-disclosure as an example, the course of development might be charted according to changes in frequency, in variety of topics addressed, in nature or significance of revelations, and in reciprocity of exchanges (cf. Hays, 1985). A relationship characteristic measured on a continuum may not change (e.g., constant function), may show steady growth or decline (e.g., monotonic function), may fluctuate up and down (e.g., cyclical function), or may demonstrate sudden, dramatic shifts (e.g., step function). Alternatively, change may occur as a qualitative transition or transformation from one mode of functioning to another.

Changes in relationships also need to be analyzed with regard to distinctions between behavior and meaning. The outward nature of interactions in the relationship might change although a coherence of function is maintained over time (Sroufe & Waters, 1977). For example, Hartup and Stevens (1997) propose a distinction in relationships between *deep structure,* the fundamental and stable qualities defining the essence of the relationship, and *surface structure,* the actual content of social exchange that changes with age and circumstance. Applied to youth mentoring relationships, the mentor may remain a consistent companion and role model despite evolution of the specific activities and conversations in which the mentor and youth participate.

Why Do Relationships Change?

Change in relationships may occur for at least three reasons. First, relationship processes are influenced by the individual development of members of the dyad. The course of a mentoring relationship will be inextricably linked with the child's biological, cognitive, and social development (Hartup, 1989; Laursen & Bukowski, 1997). As contexts for development, relationships foster children's psychosocial growth and teach important lessons about social interaction (Hartup & Laursen, 1999). In turn, relationships evolve as children expand their capabilities as interactive partners and exhibit advances in their understanding of the world, their complex reasoning, their social skills, their level of responsibility, and their competencies in other domains (Collins & Repinski, 1994). Interpersonal adaptations to individual development also can be spurred by milestones like moving from one level of schooling to the next, the onset of puberty, and the initiation of dating (Collins, 1997). Although perhaps not as rapid or obvious, the maturation of the mentor also may prompt changes in the dynamics of the relationship.

Second, interpersonal exchanges within the dyad may be a source of change and development in relationships. For example, in the context of mentoring, self-disclosure may be both an indicator of the depth of the relationship and also a part of the process that either strengthens or weakens the relationship. The management of conflict also may influence the course of the relationship. Conflict resolved in a constructive and nonthreatening manner can promote growth and understanding that strengthens the relationship, whereas conflict perceived as hostile can lead to defensiveness and intransigence with negative consequences (Collins & Laursen, 1992). Similarly, other strains and ruptures in the relationship can weaken the bond or provide opportunities for the mentor and youth to learn to address matters directly, explore their emotional content, and validate self-assertion within the relationship (cf. Safran, Muran, & Samstag, 1994). Thus, many interactive episodes can represent critical junctures that determine whether a mentoring relationship is maintained, strengthened, or damaged.

Finally, like all relationships, mentoring relationships may change and develop in response to events and circumstances in the lives of the participants. For example, the ease of maintaining contact may increase or decrease as a result of residential moves or changes in jobs or schools. Likewise, the relationship may be altered if either partner experiences an accident, illness, or other significant life event. The effect of such events on the mentoring relationship may depend on several factors, such as whether the mentor and youth can anticipate them and prepare for adjustments. Another factor in the context of formal mentoring programs is assistance provided by program professionals in negotiating the implications of the changes for the relationship.

Organizing Framework for Stages of Mentoring Relationships

Although the development of relationships is clearly complex and highly variable, they do

Table 6.1 Proposed Stages of Development of Youth Mentoring Relationships

Stage	Conceptual Features	Factors Addressed in Research	Program Practices
Contemplation	Anticipating and preparing for relationship	Mentor motivations, expectations, and goals	Recruiting, screening, training
Initiation	Beginning relationship and becoming acquainted	Mentor patience, similarity of mentor and youth interests	Matching, making introductions
Growth and maintenance	Meeting regularly and establishing patterns of interaction	Frequency and nature of activities, mentor style	Supervising and supporting, ongoing training
Decline and dissolution	Addressing challenges to relationship or ending relationship	Mentor and youth characteristics, mentor style	Supervising and supporting, facilitating closure
Redefinition	Negotiating terms of future contact or rejuvenating relationship	Not available	Facilitating closure, rematching

progress through a temporal sequence that generally includes a beginning, middle, and end. A heuristic model that divides mentoring relationships into chronological stages thus may aid in the understanding of both normative processes and individual differences in their development. Although awareness of continual fluctuations in relationships instills caution about such models, distinguishing different phases in mentoring relationships provides a coherent organizing framework. The model suggested in this chapter is based on Hinde's (1997) discussion of the periods of change in the course of a relationship and Fehr's (2000) overview of the life cycle of friendship. It is noteworthy, furthermore, that the proposed stages share similarities with those in Kram's (1983) stage-based model for natural mentoring relationships that arise between adults in the workplace to foster career development. The model presented here and summarized in Table 6.1 covers five potential periods in the developmental course of mentoring relationships: contemplation, initiation, growth and maintenance, decline and dissolution, and redefinition.

Although relationships may be marked by defining moments, such as the initial meeting or the final good-bye, the model is not meant to imply that mentoring relationships pass through clearly demarcated stages. Nor is it suggested that the timing and sequence of the stages necessarily follow a universal or invariant progression. Furthermore, although the model focuses on the interpersonal behaviors of mentor and youth due to space constraints, it should be recognized that mentoring is embedded within a network of other relationships, a physical setting, and cultural and societal contexts. Transactions with these different levels of environmental organization may profoundly influence the relationship processes described in the model.

Contemplation

Depending on the type of mentoring, there may be a period of anticipation and preparation before the relationship actually commences. In contrast to voluntary friendships or romances that begin spontaneously, many relationships involve a preceding obligation or commitment, as with parents expecting a baby or teachers beginning with new students. The contemplation phase would be applicable to program mentoring, where individuals choose to participate in a new relationship and have preconceived ideas about what it will entail. Natural mentoring relationships also may be established with intentionality and forethought, or they may evolve into significant relationships without much attention to the goal of mentoring.

Salient processes in the contemplation phase would include obtaining information about mentoring, planning for future activities, and forming expectations about the relationship. These preparations may be influenced by the motivations, attitudes, values, goals, and needs that lead each person to enter a mentoring relationship. In the case of formal mentoring, expectations may be shaped by stated goals and guidelines and the training practices of the program. The contemplation phase sets the stage for initial behavior in the relationship.

Initiation

The initiation phase involves the process of becoming acquainted. In a new relationship, the mentor and youth are likely to be motivated to learn about each other. They each may assess what the other partner brings to the relationship, monitor how their behavior affects the other, make comparisons against their expectations for the relationship, and evaluate their potential together (Hinde, 1997). In addition, the mentor and youth may exchange views and determine their similarity and compatibility in multiple domains, such as interests, attitudes, and activity preferences. Working to the advantage of a new mentoring relationship is the fact that individuals are more likely to have an initial positive response and engage in reciprocal sharing when they perceive that the other person is inclined to have a relationship with them and when they expect ongoing contact with the other person (Fehr, 2000).

Growth and Maintenance

The growth and maintenance phase can encompass almost the full duration of the mentoring relationship. Growth can be viewed as a reduction of uncertainty about the existence of the relationship and an increase in agreement about the nature of the relationship (Duck, 1995). In co-constructing the relationship over time, the mentor and youth may establish idiosyncratic patterns of communication, conventions for turn-taking, and routines of behavior. They negotiate understandings on a range of issues, including what topics will be excluded from conversation, what types of support will be provided, and how conflict will be managed (Hinde, 1997). Self-disclosure may increase in breadth and depth. A growing sense of predictability, reliability, and familiarity may foster trust and encourage commitment to continuing the relationship. The relationship may be maintained both implicitly through the everyday activities that make up the relationship (e.g., conversation, dining together) and explicitly through behaviors expressing the importance of the relationship (e.g., affection, discussing the relationship itself, cards, and gifts) (Duck, 1994). Providing social and emotional support may be another important factor in maintaining the mentoring relationship. In addition, the growth and maintenance of the relationship may be enhanced by simple experiences of fun and enjoyment together. Joking, laughter, informal language, and relaxed attitude are associated with relationship satisfaction and closeness in other types of relationships (Planalp & Benson, 1992).

Decline and Dissolution

Decline refers to a reduction in the importance or level of closeness in the mentoring relationship, whereas dissolution indicates the termination of the relationship. Dissolution may or may not be recognized, negotiated, or acknowledged. It may be punctuated by a clear event ending the relationship, or the mentor and youth may passively "drift apart" until the relationship is over by default. Relationship decline and dissolution may result if the maintenance activities outlined above are neglected or prove unsuccessful. Relationships also may deteriorate due to conflict, betrayal, or the discovery of unattractive personal characteristics in the partner (Fehr, 2000). Alternatively, mentoring may have accomplished its purpose or outlived its usefulness as the needs, expectations, interests, and life circumstances of the participants change (Hinde, 1997). Situational factors also may be influential, especially those that diminish opportunities for contact between mentor and youth (e.g., residential moves, work or school commitments). Finally, many mentoring programs, particularly those operating during a school year, designate an expected duration for matches. Anticipated match endings naturally follow a different course than those disrupted by relationship difficulties or life events.

Redefinition

A mentoring relationship in decline may not always be destined for complete or permanent dissolution. One alternative may be an agreement to have the relationship continue in an altered form, with expectations regarding the amount of contact and the nature of interactions redefined to fit new circumstances. Another possibility is that a broken relationship can be restored or rejuvenated by an apology, a change in problematic behavior, or a talk to resolve differences or set new ground rules (Wilmot, 1994). Also, relationships that "fade away" passively often leave open the possibility of being resumed sometime in the future (Fehr, 2000). Even if the mentoring relationship is known to be over, the mentor or youth may reflect on and reinterpret experiences in the relationship. This process may provide new insights, reveal new lessons, and reinforce the influence of the relationship on the person's life. Because the benefits of mentoring may become apparent only years later, the protégé may wish to express appreciation long after the match. Similarly, the mentor's curiosity about what has become of the youth may motivate a renewal of the relationship after many years.

RESEARCH

Very little research traces the developmental course of youth mentoring relationships. A few studies have generated descriptions of stages in relationship development for informal mentoring between adults in the workplace (Pollock,

1995). Although nothing directly comparable is found in the literature on youth mentoring, several studies report findings relevant to considering different stages of development in youth mentoring relationships. The following review of this research is organized according to the five phases of relationship development outlined above.

Contemplation

Findings from several studies are consistent with the view that mentor expectations and motivations play a role in the development of relationships in formal programs. In a path model using prospective data from Big Brothers Big Sisters (BBBS) matches, Parra and colleagues (Parra, DuBois, Neville, Pugh-Lilly, & Povinelli, 2002) found that mentor-perceived self-efficacy at the beginning of the match was associated with greater mentor-youth contact, greater involvement in program-relevant activities, and fewer mentor-reported obstacles to relationship development. These factors were associated, in turn, with higher ratings of relationship closeness and with relationships of longer duration. With regard to factors important in the contemplation phase, mentor-perceived self-efficacy was associated positively with mentor ratings of the quality of training received prior to matching. Similarly, in a cross-sectional survey of 669 school- and community-based mentors, greater participation in prematch orientation and training was associated with closer and more supportive relationships, and analyses suggested a mediating process: Mentors reporting more training also reported spending more time with their mentees and engaging in more social activities with them (Herrera, Sipe, & McClanahan, 2000).

Research employing in-depth qualitative interviews to learn the experiences of mentors and youth provides further insights about the significance of the contemplation phase. Examining 26 relationships in a program matching elders with at-risk youth, Styles and Morrow (1992) classified satisfied and dissatisfied pairs according to feelings of liking and attachment, indications of appreciation and support, and commitment to continuing the relationship. Mentors in satisfied matches expected from the outset that the relationship would be one-directional; focused on benefits for the youth. These mentors were realistic about changes that might result from the match, and they considered even slow progress in forming the relationship an accomplishment. In comparison, mentors who began matches expecting to transform their protégés and to receive recognition for their efforts were typically disappointed.

In a similar study on relationship formation with a sample of 82 BBBS matches, Morrow and Styles (1995) again identified two major types of relationships with different patterns of interaction, which they labeled *developmental* and *prescriptive*. The prescriptive classification, however, had two subcategories, as described below. Mentors in each type of relationship commenced their matches with distinctly different expectations regarding the needs of the youth, the goals of the match, and their purpose as a mentor. Mentors in developmental relationships ($n = 54$) more often conceived of their role as a friend to the youth. These mentors believed they should meet the needs of the youth by being flexible and supportive, incorporating the youth's preferences, and building a solid relationship. In contrast, mentors in the larger subcategory of prescriptive relationships ($n = 17$) typically viewed their role as being an authority figure, with some responsibility for regulating the youth's behavior. These mentors initiated their matches with goals for transforming the youth and began their attempts to address difficulties in the youth's life early in the relationship. In the smaller subcategory of prescriptive matches ($n = 11$), the mentors expected that their protégés, despite their young age and inexperience in friendships with adults, would take an equal responsibility for maintaining the relationship by initiating contacts and planning activities. Compared with prescriptive matches, developmental matches tended to last longer and were more likely to be described in positive terms by both mentors and youth. Morrow and Styles (1995) interpreted their findings as emphasizing the importance of the mentor's initial approach to the program: "The attitudes, expectations, and styles of the volunteers were the most salient factors in determining how, and into what types, relationships evolved" (p. 19).

Reporting on a university-initiated mentoring program, Hamilton and Hamilton (1992) also noted a connection between mentors' understanding of their purposes and the nature of their relationships with protégés. Mentors were classified into four levels based on comments about their aims for their matches: Level 1 mentors focused primarily on developing a relationship; Level 2 mentors spoke of introducing opportunities; Level 3 mentors stressed developing character; and Level 4 mentors saw their task as developing the youth's competence. Importantly, the four levels were hierarchical. Mentors at higher levels talked about the importance of lower-level purposes as well, but lower-level mentors did not mention higher-level purposes. Level 1 mentors were the least likely to persist in their matches, whereas the higher-level mentors spent more time with their protégés and had more functional relationships. These findings are discussed in relation to those of Morrow and Styles later in the chapter.

Information regarding the expectations and motivations of youth who enter mentoring relationships is sparse. Spencer (2002) conducted retrospective interviews with adolescents in strong mentoring relationships and reported that most had expected the mentoring program to be fun. Some had yearned for an adult who would give them individualized attention.

Initiation

Mentors in qualitative studies frequently note an initial period in the relationship, sometimes 6 months to a year in length, when youth are uncommunicative, are reluctant to trust, and may fail to keep appointments or return phone calls (Spencer, 2002; Styles & Morrow, 1992). Mentors credit patience and perseverance during this time of testing with the eventual development of a solid relationship. Their accounts of relationship formation suggest the process of getting acquainted cannot be rushed (Morrow & Styles, 1995; Spencer, 2002). Mentors in satisfied relationships reported waiting for their protégés to decide whether and when to confide in them, assuming that time would be needed to establish trust in the relationship. Mentors who tried to develop their relationships by pressing youth to disclose personal information or to discuss difficult issues in their lives typically were met with resistance (Styles & Morrow, 1992).

Recognizing shared interests was found to be an important factor associated with close and supportive relationships in the survey of school- and community-based mentors by Herrera et al. (2000). Likewise, teens in a workplace intern- ship program who perceived greater similarity with their mentors in terms of views, values, and approaches to problems were more likely to indicate satisfaction with their relationships and report intentions to continue them (Ensher & Murphy, 1997). These findings from cross- sectional studies of existing relationships sug- gest that early identification of interpersonal similarity and compatibility may be associated with positive mentoring experiences, but prospective studies that examine how this process unfolds are lacking.

Growth and Maintenance

Frequent and consistent contact appears to be an important ingredient in the creation of strong mentoring relationships (DuBois, Neville, Parra, & Pugh-Lilly, 2002; Herrera et al., 2000). Research findings also suggest the nature of activities mentors and youth do together may be significant in the growth and maintenance of relationships (DuBois et al., 2002; Herrera et al., 2000; Morrow & Styles, 1995). DuBois et al. (2002), for example, reported that rela- tionships in which youth consistently nominated their mentors as significant adults in their lives were distinguished by youth reports of greater frequency of contact, increasing discussion of the mentee's personal relationships and of social issues (e.g., current events), and increasing par- ticipation in sports and athletic activities. Using survey data reported by mentors, Herrera et al. (2000) examined a regression model containing multiple demographic, program, and activity- related variables (including social, academic, and job-related activities) and discovered that engaging in social activities (e.g., hanging out, going to events, having lunch) was the factor most strongly associated with every indicator of relationship closeness used in the study. Reflecting these results and the theoretical pro- position that fun and enjoyment are important in

relationship growth and maintenance, Morrow and Styles (1995) found that youth in develop- mental relationships were more likely than those in prescriptive relationships to report that their mentors took them to places they really wanted to go (97% vs. 65% prescriptive) and proposed activities that were really fun (84% vs. 38% prescriptive).

In their research, Styles and Morrow (1992) also observed differences in the patterns of interaction described by participants in satisfied and dissatisfied matches. In satisfied matches, mentors appeared to follow a "youth-driven" approach, in which the mentor attempted to identify the needs and interests of the youth and address them in such a way that the protégé would be receptive to help. In these matches, the mentor typically included the youth in determin- ing both the activities they would do together and the areas in which the mentor would offer assistance. In a similar vein, Morrow and Styles (1995) noted that mentors in developmental relationships were more likely to include their protégés in making decisions about their time together and negotiating the selection of mutu- ally enjoyable activities. When youth were ini- tially slow to express their preferences, the mentors listened closely for indications of their interests and "learned through trial and error what the youth's interests were by observing how they responded to various activities that the mentors chose" (Styles & Morrow, 1992, p. v). This process accords with the example of a Level 4 mentor described by Hamilton and Hamilton (1992). Because the youth to whom he was matched did not offer suggestions for outings, the mentor generated various ideas for activities that would teach new skills, provide new experiences and challenges, and inspire new pursuits for the youth. Throughout this process of experimentation, the mentor was devoted to learning more about the youth's interests and identifying activities the youth would enjoy.

The findings of the studies by Styles and Morrow (Morrow & Styles, 1995; Styles & Morrow, 1992) are similar in their identifica- tion of other patterns of interaction that distin- guished more successful from less successful relationships. Mentors in matches characterized as developmental were more likely to offer consistent reassurance and kindness to their protégés, to respond to requests for help in a nonjudgmental manner, to offer suggestions and alternatives, to avoid criticizing and lecturing, and to employ practical, problem-solving approaches to address issues. In the beginning of these matches, the mentor typically emphasized establishing trust and building a strong foundation for the relationship so that the youth would develop confidence in the mentor as a reliable source of support in times of need (Morrow & Styles, 1995). As developmental relationships solidified, youth began to voluntarily disclose their difficulties at home or school, allowing the mentor to provide advice and guidance. Similarly, as developmental relationships strengthened, mentors started to address objectives beyond relationship building, such as helping the youth to improve in school or to become more responsible. According to Morrow and Styles, developmental mentors often expressed interest in influencing grades and youth behavior in contexts outside the match, but they balanced these aims with maintaining open, trusting, and supportive relationships.

It is noteworthy that both the mentors in developmental relationships described by Morrow and Styles (1995) and the Level 3 and 4 mentors featured in the research of Hamilton and Hamilton (1992) were similar in devoting attention to the dual goals of ensuring a solid relationship and developing competence and positive attributes in the youth to whom they were matched. Furthermore, both types of mentors approached these goals by attempting to discern the interests of their protégés and introducing learning opportunities built around those interests. However, consistent with theory suggesting there are multiple pathways to a positive mentoring experience, the two frameworks diverge somewhat in the relative primacy accorded to relationship-building and competence-building efforts in developing mentoring relationships. Based on their findings, Morrow and Styles (1995) proposed that a focus on youth-driven relationship building was an important precursor to youth transformation efforts. Hamilton and Hamilton (1992) concluded that challenging and rewarding activities with instrumental goals to enhance competence were an ideal

vehicle for developing a warm interpersonal relationship.

Resolution of this debate may come with further investigation of possible moderating factors such as the structure and goals of the mentoring programs, the reasons youth seek a mentor, and the developmental age of the youth. For instance, Darling and colleagues (Darling, Hamilton, & Niego, 1994) noted older adolescents' relationships with nonparental adults are more likely to revolve around instrumental support that helps them to learn specific skills and gain a sense of accomplishment. It is also possible, however, that the importance of sequence may be less than implied by the two perspectives. Relationship development and the promotion of youth competencies can occur simultaneously, and very likely one will reinforce the other. Furthermore, both perspectives seem compatible with a view that flexible and creative mentors can find opportunities throughout the relationship to promote youth development in activities that are enjoyable, challenging and engaging, and aligned with youth interests. The key, it seems, is for the mentor to find a balance between vertical and horizontal models of relationships by providing adult structure and scaffolding to support youth development while encouraging the youth's voluntary continuation in the relationship.

Decline and Dissolution

Research by Grossman and Rhodes (2002) highlights the importance of examining the circumstances surrounding the decline and dissolution of mentoring relationships. Findings from their experimental evaluation of BBBS programs indicated that beneficial effects from program participation, assessed relative to a randomly assigned control group, were more clearly evident when the mentoring relationship lasted at least 12 months, whereas matches ending after a very short period (i.e., less than 3 months) could have detrimental effects. A recent national survey of mentoring programs found that 76% had a minimum time commitment over 6 months but only 15% had an expectation of more than 12 months (MENTOR/National Mentoring Partnership, 2003). BBBS programs generally ask new participants to make a 1-year commitment, although long-lasting relationships are the goal. A cross-sectional study of 821 existing BBBS matches from eight different programs found the average length to be 28 months, with the longest reporting 13 years together (Furano, Roaf, Styles, & Branch, 1993). Following 378 BBBS matches prospectively, Grossman and Rhodes (2002) observed that the risk of match termination each month was relatively low and stable (i.e., 2%–4% of matches) but peaked around the 1-year anniversary (about 10% of matches). Based on the average hazard rate, they projected an expected match length of approximately 17 months.

The study by Grossman and Rhodes (2002) also tested multiple youth and mentor characteristics for their association with relationship duration. Earlier termination was more likely for youth who were between the ages of 13 and 16, who had been referred for services with identified difficulties at home or school, or who had a history of abuse. Married mentors between the ages of 26 and 30 and mentors with lower incomes tended to have shorter matches. In addition, relationship termination was associated with youth reports that mentors did not take their interests into consideration and youth reports that they felt let down or disappointed by mentors.

Processes that appeared to increase the probability for the deterioration of mentoring relationships were identified in the qualitative studies discussed above. Among mentors focused primarily on building a relationship, Hamilton and Hamilton (1992) noted the potential for difficulties included (a) the mentor worrying whether the youth liked him or her, (b) the mentor worrying about selecting the right activities, (c) the mentor being disappointed if the youth did not share personal information after a few meetings, and (d) the mentor feeling inadequate as a counselor when the youth actually asked for advice on serious personal matters. Morrow and Styles (1995) described similar patterns for the subcategory of prescriptive relationships in which mentors expected an equal relationship. When youth did not initiate contact or show sufficient appreciation, the mentors often interpreted this as disinterest or laziness, and then the mentors became disappointed and failed to persevere in these relationships.

Morrow and Styles (1995) reported a different cycle of increasing frustration and disappointment that apparently contributed to the demise of relationships in the other prescriptive subcategory. As noted previously, mentors approached these relationships with predetermined agendas for transforming the youth in a relatively short period of time. From the outset, these mentors tended to set the goals, determine the pace, select the activities, and establish the ground rules for the relationship with little regard for the youth's preferences or abilities. As depicted by Morrow and Styles (1995), for example, a common approach of a prescriptive volunteer was to point out the youth's mistakes, state expectations for change, and express displeasure if they were not met. The relationship suffered as the youth resisted the mentor's efforts to focus on problem areas in the child's life, often by avoiding contact with the mentor and withdrawing from the relationship. Because prescriptive mentors were reluctant to adjust their high expectations and were disappointed in the failure of their protégés to respond, tensions and frustrations increased on both sides, and these matches were typically short-lived (Morrow & Styles, 1995; Styles & Morrow, 1992). To briefly summarize, mentors who adopted predominantly horizontal (e.g., equality) or predominantly vertical (e.g., authority) relationship models seemed to experience difficulties.

Redefinition

The research literature does not furnish information about how mentors and youth part ways when relationships end. Likewise, researchers have not followed former mentors and mentees past their program involvement, so what form their interaction might take at a later point in time is unknown. The possibility that participants, particularly youth, are better able to realize with the benefit of hindsight how a mentoring relationship affected them also remains unexplored.

PRACTICE

The practice of mentoring occurs within the mentor-youth relationship as the mentor takes a personal interest in the youth's life and attempts to foster the youth's development. The growth and maintenance of the relationship rests heavily on the wisdom, skill, and dedication of the mentor. However, as noted previously, a mentoring relationship exists within a social context, and thus other individuals may influence its developmental course. In a program setting, the mentoring intervention can be conceptualized as a coordinated system involving not only the child and mentor but also the parent and agency professional (Keller, in press). Interactions among mentor, child, parent, and professional staff are guided by program policies and procedures. The structure and function of program practices frequently correspond to the stages posited for the development of mentoring relationships, and the following discussion of relevant program practices is organized according to this model. The discussion draws from recent recommendations regarding "best practices" for mentoring disseminated in a set of guidelines from MENTOR/National Mentoring Partnership and a series of technical assistance packets prepared by Public/Private Ventures (P/PV) based on their research findings (Sipe, 1995). Illustrative examples are based on traditional BBBS community-based mentoring, which has a highly developed program infrastructure with national practice standards (Furano et al., 1993).

Contemplation

Program procedures for recruiting, screening, and training may provide opportunities to assess and to influence individual motivations, attitudes, and expectations as participants prepare to embark on new relationships. By addressing issues in the contemplation stage highlighted by theory and research, these practices ideally would establish mutual understanding about the purpose of the program, clarify the roles and responsibilities of each person involved in the match, and promote a sense of efficacy in facing the challenges of mentoring.

Recruitment materials may instill enduring impressions about the program as prospective participants learn about the recommended frequency of contact, the usual types of activities, and the objectives of the relationship. For example, recruitment messages typically indicate that youth in the program could benefit from the attentive support of a caring adult as they face the challenges of growing up. These initial communications should aim to avoid the perception common among prescriptive mentors that they need to take responsibility for a youth's academic success or rescue a troubled youth from a life of disadvantage.

Screening practices based on specific eligibility criteria can determine the skills, resources, and needs that participants bring to the match. Drawing on theory and research presented above, intensive screening of potential mentors could enhance the prospects for positive relationship development by attempting to identify mentors who demonstrate adaptability and flexibility in interpersonal situations, who express understanding of the developmental needs of youth, who appreciate the role of fun and social activities in relationships, and who are amenable to feedback and cooperative decision making. Given the research of Morrow and Styles (1995) and Hamilton and Hamilton (1992), for example, it may be important to discourage volunteers who pursue mentoring primarily as means to make a new friendship and who desire mutual exchange and equal reciprocity as signs that they are liked and valued.

As noted previously, training prior to matching is associated with positive indicators of relationship development. Prematch training provides opportunities to communicate program guidelines and expectations, to prepare participants for situations that may arise, and to teach skills for facilitating relationship development. Based on available evidence, trainings should advise that relationship development is enhanced when mentors elicit youth interests and preferences, include them in making decisions, offer them consistent and sensitive support, and engage in enjoyable activities that promote competence and provide a sense of accomplishment. Above all, it may be important to help mentors understand their dual role, balancing the responsibility of vertical relationships with the mutuality of horizontal relationships.

In practice, and in the literature, screening and training tends to focus on mentors rather than youth or parents. Nevertheless, knowledge of the child's history, needs, interests, and family circumstances seems highly relevant for making a suitable match and providing appropriate program support. In addition, child and parent training like that for mentors—discussing roles and responsibilities and practicing communication skills—would likely foster the development of the mentoring relationship.

Initiation

A program's matching procedures have potentially important implications for the initiation phase of mentoring relationships. Within a program context, the first step in creating a relationship is determining which mentor and youth will be paired. Consistent with theory and research, numerous factors may be useful to weigh in the matchmaking decision, such as the child's needs, the mentor's capabilities, the similarity of their attitudes, and the overlap of shared interests (Furano et al., 1993). In addition, many programs allow mentors and parents to indicate preferences on characteristics such as age, race, religion, and geographic proximity.

Procedures for introducing program participants to each other may influence first impressions and facilitate the process of getting acquainted. For example, a supervised prematch meeting between mentor and parent can provide an opportunity for each to discuss their respective expectations for the relationship and to assess their compatibility before actually deciding to accept or reject a proposed match. Such preliminary steps may give participants a sense of ownership, establish forthright communication, and convey useful information about what to anticipate. Similarly, the initial meeting between mentor and youth may be structured to include activities that serve as "icebreakers," exercises for planning activities and setting goals, and reminders of program guidelines.

Growth and Maintenance

Because the growth and maintenance of mentoring relationships is inherently complex and variable, individual matches established within the same program may follow different developmental pathways. Reflecting this proposition, the research conducted to date has identified distinctive patterns of mentor-youth

interaction with apparent implications for relationship success and longevity. Furthermore, even within the broad relationship categories that have been portrayed (e.g., developmental, prescriptive), there is further diversity in individual relationship experiences. Programs that provide ongoing professional supervision via regular contacts with mentors, youth, and parents have the potential to assess the patterns of interaction being established within each relationship, to provide individualized support to address relationship challenges, and to reinforce agency guidelines and interpersonal strategies that promote positive relationship development. Such supervision may be especially valuable early in a match, when the relationship is still tentative and patterns of interaction are taking shape.

Reflecting theory and research presented above, professional support to the relationship may take several forms. Caseworkers may encourage collaborative decision making about match activities and suggest ideas for activities that simultaneously build the relationship and youth competence. Another important role for the caseworker is to manage the participants' expectations regarding the mentoring relationship and what it is intended to accomplish. For example, caseworkers may help mentors to maintain a reasonable perspective on the extent of their influence and help them find the balance between underinvolvement and overinvolvement. In this respect, guidance from caseworkers may be particularly useful when participants need to define boundaries regarding matters that involve parental responsibility (e.g., academics, youth behavior). In addition, caseworkers may intervene to promote the resolution of disagreements and conflicts that arise in the relationship. Maintaining a case record that documents these ongoing contacts with match participants may provide an invaluable history of the relationship's development that can be used for clarifying agreements, assessing progress toward goals, recalling effective strategies, and placing the overall life of the relationship in perspective.

Although caseworker support was not a central focus of their research, Morrow and Styles (1995) reported that volunteers appreciated ideas for activities, advice about how to deal with the youth's family, recommendations for how to include the youth in decision making, and reminders that relationships may develop slowly. Of note, developmental volunteers commonly solicited the support of caseworkers, particularly in the formative stages of their relationships. In contrast, despite the difficulties that tended to arise in their relationships, prescriptive mentors rarely sought casework assistance and sometimes discounted the advice they received.

Another way programs may support the growth and maintenance of mentoring relationships is through a continuing series of training sessions (Herrera et al., 2000). Conceptually, follow-up training permits the application of program guidelines and professional advice to the concrete issues facing participants in their relationships. In addition, ongoing trainings can focus on selected topics relevant to specific groups of participants, such as those in relationships involving adolescents or those approaching later phases in the life course of the relationship.

Decline and Dissolution

To potentially forestall unnecessary decline and dissolution, consistent program supervision may prove valuable as a means of detecting indications of relationship difficulties and facilitating their constructive resolution. Based on the research of Grossman and Rhodes (2002), it may be especially valuable to give extra attention and support to relationships in which youth have been referred due to preexisting difficulties. As noted before, the ability to overcome challenges and successfully repair ruptures may make the relationship still stronger and more enduring.

Nevertheless, a mentoring relationship is destined to end, and careful management of the match termination process offers the possibility of a positive, if painful, learning experience. Unfortunately, the process of ending mentoring relationships has received little attention in research or practice relative to its potential importance. However, theoretical considerations discussed previously suggest several promising directions for how programs may address the dissolution of mentoring relationships in a constructive manner. In a time-limited program

with a predetermined closing date, the mentor can openly acknowledge well in advance that the relationship will be ending. To prepare for saying good-bye, the mentor and youth can discuss their feelings about the relationship and its conclusion, review their accomplishments and enjoyable times together, and plan a special way of marking the occasion. Final meetings might focus on projects to preserve memories of the match, such as taking photographs, exchanging letters or pictures, or creating a scrapbook.

The ending of a relationship in an open-ended mentoring program is likely to be more challenging. Nevertheless, the goal can be a process similar to the one just described. As observed previously, mentoring relationships end for a variety of reasons, and specific circumstances present different opportunities to provide program structure and support. For successful, long-lasting relationships, a date to close the match and celebrate its achievements may be chosen to correspond with another milestone event, such as the youth's graduation. Matches ending due to a residential move or other anticipated change in circumstances also may permit a planned process around a certain date. When a relationship is ending due to lack of contact, loss of interest, frustration, or unresolved conflict, the involvement of a program professional may be valuable for addressing feelings of guilt, anger, or sadness. In private conversations with each individual, a case manager might give a clear appraisal of the reason for ending the match, review both the positive and negative aspects of the relationship, and assess the potential for a final meeting in which everybody can reach closure in an amicable fashion.

Redefinition

A formal procedure to officially end the match presents a valuable opportunity to clarify the terms of the relationship between mentor and child. Depending on the history of the match and the circumstances for its closure, the program may recommend against any future contact. In other cases, the relationship may continue with occasional activities, phone calls and letters, or holiday cards. Alternatively, the mentor may invite the youth to initiate later contacts, perhaps to report a special accomplishment, to seek advice, or to request a reference. To avoid disappointments, both mentor and child should be conservative when making these commitments.

Often, a mentor or youth remains eligible for the program after a match ends. Some programs may attempt to match a child to a new volunteer rapidly to ease feelings of loss, but the value of this approach should be assessed according to the circumstances of each case. Theory reviewed previously suggests that each mentoring relationship, like all close relationships, should be regarded as distinctive, and thus mentors should not be seen as interchangeable. Furthermore, ideas and impressions formed in the first relationship are likely to shape expectations for the new match. Program professionals can prepare individuals for a rematch by helping them to reflect on the previous relationship for lessons about how to repeat successes and avoid difficulties.

FUTURE DIRECTIONS

Synthesis

Theory and related research on the nature and development of close relationships imply an important temporal dimension in mentoring relationships for youth. Extrapolating from this literature, it was proposed in this chapter that mentoring relationships, in the normal course of their development, are likely to navigate a series of challenges and opportunities as they trace an arc from contemplation and initiation through growth and maintenance to decline, dissolution, and redefinition. Theoretically, every relationship can be expected to chart a distinctive pathway through these stages depending upon the developmental needs, interpersonal capabilities, and social contexts of the mentor and child.

In general, research on the developmental course of youth mentoring relationships is lacking. However, findings relevant to particular stages in the model suggest that mentors are influential in setting the tone and course of relationship development. In particular, mentors employing youth-centered approaches appear to have longer and more productive relationships.

Based on descriptions derived primarily from qualitative research, these mentors seem to enter their relationships with a clear vision that their purpose is to support the development of the youth with broad aims such as building the relationship, introducing opportunities, and developing competencies. Once the relationship begins, they are flexible and proceed according to the needs, interests, and circumstances of the youth. In addition, these mentors attempt to incorporate opportunities for learning and developing skills into projects that youth find interesting and engaging. Notably, however, prospective studies employing more objective measures have yet to establish whether this style of mentoring or any other particular patterns of mentor-youth interaction correspond to better outcomes for relationships or for youth. Nor is it known whether similar or different approaches are likely to facilitate the growth and maintenance of mentoring relationships in contexts other than community-based programs such as BBBS.

Finally, from a practice perspective, theory and available research suggest many ways in which mentoring programs may be able to support relationships in each phase of their development. Although program practices have rarely been the focus of investigation, greater attention to the salient issues of each developmental stage may highlight their specific contributions to effective mentoring.

Recommendations for Research

1. *Investigate normative trends over the course of mentoring relationships.* Studies investigating the developmental pathways followed by mentoring relationships for youth are needed. Ideally, studies would be prospective in design and include multiple and frequent assessments of the relationship. Longitudinal data of this type would permit growth curve analyses of relationship trajectories or latent transition analyses evaluating a stage model of relationship development such as the one proposed in this chapter. Long-term studies are important because the full life cycle of relationships cannot be observed for matches that are intact when a study ends, and the experience of these longer relationships may be very different from those

that begin and end within the study period. In addition, it may be informative to follow individuals even after relationships end to investigate the potential for a continuing influence of the relationship long after actual interaction has ceased.

2. *Investigate factors that account for individual differences in developmental pathways of mentoring relationships.* A corresponding task is to investigate sources of variability in the development of mentoring relationships. Theoretically important factors from several domains should be considered: individual factors (e.g., age, attitudes, needs), dyadic factors (e.g., similarity), program support factors (e.g., training, casework), cultural factors (e.g., community norms), and historical factors (e.g., publicity campaigns). As knowledge in this area increases, efforts should be directed toward the development and testing of models that combine key factors from different domains to represent their holistic and interactive functioning.

3. *Explore processes involved in relationship change and development.* Much more can be learned about the interpersonal dynamics that contribute to developmental patterns of change and stability in mentoring relationships. This research might investigate more closely how particular types of interactions may lead relationship development to advance quickly or stall. This research also might explore how relationships adapt to changing circumstances, maturational demands, and life events. Studies that employ direct observation of relationships and those that apply data analytic strategies for time-series data, such as nonlinear dynamic modeling, could prove particularly valuable for understanding developmental processes that unfold within particular episodes or over a series of occasions within relationships.

Recommendations for Practice

1. *Provide comprehensive support for all stages in the development of relationships.* Program procedures for screening, training, and matching program participants are essential, but they address just the beginning phases of relationship development. Programs also should

provide ongoing supervision and training to mentoring relationships throughout their life course, with practices specifically designed to address the needs of each developmental stage. To illustrate, a continuing series of training sessions first could recommend strategies for communicating in ways that facilitate the growth of relationships, then address strategies for identifying and responding to indications of relationship decline, and, finally, cover strategies for appropriately ending or redefining the terms of relationships.

2. *Pursue innovative approaches for promoting relationship development.* The literature reviewed for this chapter was notable for its lack of attention to three areas with potentially important implications for the development of mentoring relationships: (a) screening of youth and parents, (b) training of youth and parents, and (c) closing of matches and discussion of arrangements regarding any subsequent contact. Development of more sophisticated means for assessing child needs and family circumstances could enhance the matching process, thereby facilitating the earliest stages of relationship development. In addition, such knowledge could improve responsive service provision in later phases of relationship development. Training of youth and parents could clarify their roles and responsibilities in the match and help them develop relationship-building skills. Finally, clear expectations and procedures for ending or redefining mentoring relationships could promote constructive resolution of the mentoring experience and consolidate the accomplishments achieved during each stage of the relationship's development.

References

Baltes, P. B., Lindenberger, U., & Staudinger, U. M. (1998). Life-span theory in developmental psychology. In W. Damon (Series Ed.) & R. M. Lerner (Vol. Ed.), *Handbook of child psychology: Vol. 1. Theoretical models of human development* (5th ed., pp. 1029–1143). New York: Wiley.

Blyth, D. A., Hill, J. P., & Thiel, K. (1982). Early adolescents' significant others: Grade and gender differences in perceived relationships with familial and nonfamilial adults and young people. *Journal of Youth and Adolescence, 11,* 425–450.

Cassidy, J. (1999). The nature of the child's ties. In J. Cassidy & P. R. Shaver (Eds.), *Handbook of attachment: Theory, research, and clinical applications* (pp. 3–20). New York: Guilford Press.

Collins, W. A. (1997). Relationships and development during adolescence: Interpersonal adaptation to individual change. *Personal Relationships, 4,* 1–14.

Collins, W. A., & Laursen, B. (1992). Conflict and relationships during adolescence. In C. U. Shantz & W. W. Hartup (Eds.), *Conflict in child and adolescent development* (pp. 216–241). New York: Cambridge University Press.

Collins, W. A., & Repinski, D. J. (1994). Relationships during adolescence: Continuity and change in interpersonal perspective. In R. Montemayor, G. R. Adams, & T. P. Gullotta (Eds.), *Personal relationships during adolescence* (Vol. 6, pp. 7–36). Thousand Oaks, CA: Sage.

Cox, M. J., & Paley, B. (1997). Families as systems. *Annual Review of Psychology, 48,* 243–267.

Darling, N., Hamilton, S. F., & Niego, S. (1994). Adolescents' relations with adults outside the family. In R. Montemayor, G. R. Adams, & T. P. Gullotta (Eds.), *Personal relationships during adolescence* (Vol. 6, pp. 216–235). Thousand Oaks, CA: Sage.

DuBois, D. L., Neville, H. A., Parra, G. R., & Pugh-Lilly, A. O. (2002). Testing a new model of mentoring. In G. G. Noam (Ed. in chief) & J. E. Rhodes (Ed.), *A critical view of youth mentoring (New Directions for Youth Development: Theory, Research, and Practice, No. 93,* pp. 21–57). San Francisco: Jossey-Bass.

Duck, S. (1994). Steady as (s)he goes: Relational maintenance as a shared meaning system. In D. J. Canary & L. Stafford (Eds.), *Communication and relational maintenance* (pp. 45–60). San Diego, CA: Academic Press.

Duck, S. (1995). Talking relationships into being. *Journal of Social and Personal Relationships, 12,* 535–540.

Ensher, E. A., & Murphy, S. E. (1997). Effects of race, gender, perceived similarity and contact on mentor relationships. *Journal of Vocational Behavior, 50,* 460–481.

Fehr, B. (2000). The life cycle of friendship. In C. Hendrick & S. S. Hendrick (Eds.), *Close relationships: A sourcebook* (pp. 71–82). Thousand Oaks, CA: Sage.

Furano, K., Roaf, P. A., Styles, M. B., & Branch, A. Y. (1993). *Big Brothers/Big Sisters: A study of program practices.* Philadelphia: Public/Private Ventures.

Furman, W., & Buhrmester, D. (1985). Children's perceptions of the personal relationships in their social networks. *Developmental Psychology, 21,* 1016–1024.

Grossman, J. B., & Rhodes, J. E. (2002). The test of time: Predictors and effects of duration in youth mentoring relationships. *American Journal of Community Psychology, 30,* 199–219.

Hamilton, S. F., & Hamilton, M. A. (1992). Mentoring programs: Promise and paradox. *Phi Delta Kappan, 73,* 546–550.

Hartup, W. W. (1989). Social relationships and their developmental significance. *American Psychologist, 44,* 120–126.

Hartup, W. W., & Laursen, B. (1999). Relationships as developmental contexts: Retrospective themes and contemporary issues. In W. A. Collins & B. Laursen (Eds.), *Relationships as developmental contexts* (Vol. 30, pp. 13–35). Mahwah, NJ: Erlbaum.

Hartup, W. W., & Stevens, N. (1997). Friendships and adaptation in the life course. *Psychological Bulletin, 121,* 355–370.

Hays, R. B. (1985). A longitudinal study of friendship development. *Journal of Personality and Social Psychology, 48,* 909–924.

Herrera, C., Sipe, C. L., & McClanahan, W. S. (2000). *Mentoring school age children: Relationship development in community-based and school-based programs.* Philadelphia: Public/Private Ventures. (Published in collaboration with MENTOR/National Mentoring Partnership, Alexandria, VA)

Hinde, R. A. (1997). *Relationships: A dialectical perspective.* Hove, UK: Psychology Press.

Keller, T. E. (in press). A systemic model of the youth mentoring intervention. *Journal of Primary Prevention.*

Kram, K. E. (1983). Phases of the mentor relationship. *Academy of Management Journal, 26,* 608–625.

Laursen, B., & Bukowski, W. M. (1997). A developmental guide to the organization of close relationships. *International Journal of Behavioral Development, 21,* 747–770.

Liang, B., Tracy, A. J., Taylor, C. A., & Williams, L. M. (2002). Mentoring college age women: A relational approach. *American Journal of Community Psychology, 30,* 271–288.

MENTOR/National Mentoring Partnership. (2003). *2002 state and local prevalence of mentoring survey.* Alexandria, VA: Author.

Morrow, K. V., & Styles, M. B. (1995). *Building relationships with youth in program settings.* Philadelphia: Public/Private Ventures.

Parra, G. R., DuBois, D. L., Neville, H. A., Pugh-Lilly, A. O., & Povinelli, N. (2002). Mentoring relationships for youth: Investigation of a process-oriented model. *Journal of Community Psychology, 30,* 367–388.

Planalp, S., & Benson, A. (1992). Friends' and acquaintances' conversations: I. Perceived differences. *Journal of Social and Personal Relationships, 9,* 483–506.

Pollock, R. (1995). A test of conceptual models depicting the developmental course of informal mentor-protégé relationships in the workplace. *Journal of Vocational Behavior, 46,* 144–162.

Reis, H. T., Collins, W. A., & Berscheid, E. (2000). The relationship context of human behavior and development. *Psychological Bulletin, 126,* 844–872.

Rhodes, J. E. (2002). *Stand by me: The risks and rewards of mentoring today's youth.* Cambridge, MA: Harvard University Press.

Rhodes, J., Reddy, R., Roffman, J., & Grossman, J. (in press). Promoting successful youth mentoring relationships: A preliminary screening questionnaire. *Journal of Primary Prevention.*

Safran, J. D., Muran, J. C., & Samstag, L. (1994). Resolving therapeutic alliance ruptures: A task analytic investigation. In A. O. Horvath & L. S. Greenberg (Eds.), *The working alliance: Theory, research and practice* (pp. 225–255). New York: Wiley.

Sipe, C. L. (1995). *Mentoring: A synthesis of P/PV's research, 1988–1995.* Philadelphia, PA: Public/Private Ventures.

Spencer, R. A. (2002). *Hanging out and growing strong: A qualitative study of relationships with adults that foster resilience in adolescence.* Unpublished dissertation, Harvard University, Cambridge, MA.

Sroufe, L. A. (1997). Psychopathology as an outcome of development. *Development & Psychopathology, 9,* 251–268.

Sroufe, L. A., & Waters, E. (1977). Attachment as an organizational construct. *Child Development, 48,* 1184–1199.

Styles, M. B., & Morrow, K. V. (1992). *Understanding how youth and elders form relationships: A study of four Linking Lifetimes programs.* Philadelphia: Public/Private Ventures.

Wilmot, W. W. (1994). Relationship rejuvenation. In D. J. Canary & L. Stafford (Eds.), *Communication and relational maintenance* (pp. 255–273). San Diego, CA: Academic Press.

7

Assessment of Mentoring Relationships

Michael J. Nakkula and John T. Harris

Introduction

Recent research on mentoring has moved beyond the question of whether mentoring works to more specific investigations of how it works, under what conditions, and toward the attainment of what outcomes. At the center of these more focal questions is the concept of *mentoring relationship quality* (MRQ). The conception and assessment of MRQ varies according to theoretical orientation and practical purposes. Nonetheless, our review of theoretical conceptions of relationship quality within and beyond the mentoring literature suggests that *relationship closeness* and *perceived support* are at the core of most definitions.

In the research section of this chapter, we review instruments that focus explicitly on the assessment of MRQ in adult-youth matches, with *youth* defined as college age or younger. Our definition of youth is intentionally broad enough to capture the important assessment work done on the mentoring of older adolescents and young adults. We exclude the larger field of adult-adult mentoring because it is highly focused on career development and thus is of limited help in understanding the developmental issues inherent to adult-youth mentoring relationships. Though qualitative approaches to

assessing MRQ may be particularly helpful in exploring the nature and depth of constructs such as relational closeness, we have focused on quantitative assessment in order to limit the scope and maximize the practical utility of the chapter.

The formal assessment of MRQ is in an early stage of development. The instruments that have achieved some semblance of validity evidence have been the focus of research only recently published or accepted for publication. Nonetheless, there is a fairly robust theoretical foundation to support this emerging research and a strong practical need for it.

In this chapter, we discuss the state of MRQ assessment. Toward that end, we summarize the theoretical literature on relationship development that mentoring researchers have used to conceptualize their approaches to assessing relationship quality. We then critically review instruments used to assess relationship quality. In the practice section of the chapter, we discuss how mentoring programs might go about selecting and using instruments based on programmatic needs and interests. We close with recommendations for future directions in the assessment of relationship quality that we have gleaned from the literature and from our experience in the field.

THEORY

In this section, we delineate theoretical contributions to understanding MRQ. Based on our review of the literature on the assessment of relationship quality within the adult-youth mentoring field, and to a lesser extent within related bodies of literature such as counseling and interpersonal development, we have organized our presentation of the theory and research sections around key theoretical constructs. Table 7.1 provides a heuristic for these constructs, while Table 7.2 shows which of them are captured by the assessment instruments we reviewed.

As Table 7.1 indicates, *Internal* versus *External* indicators of relationship quality mark our first level of categorization. Internal constructs represent what is occurring within a relationship or characteristics of the relationship itself. They capture the *subjective perspectives* of the mentors and mentees, as well as *objective descriptions* of match characteristics. The internal category is further divided into two subcategories that designate fundamental approaches to and distinctions within conceptions of mentoring and mentoring relationships. The *Relational/Experiential* subcategory encompasses constructs that focus strictly on the relationship itself, without necessarily connecting the relationship and its quality with identifiable goals or secondary benefits. The "experiential" aspect of the subcategory captures the emphasis on assessing the experience of the relationship, as opposed to its structure, goals, accomplishments, or other related factors. The *Instrumental/Goal-Oriented* subcategory encompasses constructs that pertain to the presence of a strategic goal orientation in relationships. Such constructs may include recognition of the value of the relationship itself, but focus especially on the relationship as a means to particular ends, such as improved social functioning or better academic achievement.

Although it might be argued that MRQ should focus strictly on the nature and experience of the match itself, we view relationship quality as intrinsically embedded within and partially defined by the immediately surrounding context. Therefore, we have included an external subcategory within our theoretical conception of MRQ; however, we have limited it to only those factors that have been found to be most fundamental to an understanding of mentoring relationship quality.

Relational/Experiential Factors

Closeness is an organizing construct for conceptions of relationship quality throughout the mentoring literature (Rhodes, 2002). Table 7.1 lists five subjective experiences in the *Relational/Experiential* column, the ordering of which represents a progressive building toward closeness as the primary organizer for the relational/experiential approach to MRQ assessment.

Relational/Experiential Compatibility. Studies have suggested that it is important that both the adult and youth feel they share some things in common, whether personal traits, such as being energetic or empathic, or simply common interests that serve to focus the match (Herrera, Sipe, & McClanahan, 2000). Whether the commonalities exist prior to the relationship or develop within it, the experience of compatibility around some combination of *traits* and *focuses* is important to building a close mentoring relationship.

Mentor's Approach. Given a basic sense of compatibility, a core set of mentee perceptions of the mentor's approach may be important to the continued building of a close relationship. *Youth-centeredness* captures the mentee perception that he or she and his or her concerns are the focal point of the match. Derived in part from literature in the client-centered counseling tradition, youth-centeredness stands in contrast to more agenda-centered approaches that can leave the mentee feeling as if he or she has little control over the relationship's direction (Morrow & Styles, 1995). Theoretically, it is important for youth to feel a *sense of control* or agency in the relationship. Feeling positively valued (*positive regard*) on a consistent basis, rather than judged for one's shortcomings or mistakes, also may be important given evidence for a mediating role of gains in self-esteem in processes contributing to positive outcomes in mentoring relationships (DuBois, Neville, Parra, & Pugh-Lilly, 2002).

Table 7.1   Mentoring Relationship Quality: Overview of Constructs*

Internal		External
Relational/Experiential	*Instrumental/Goal-Oriented*	*Environmental*
Subjective	Subjective	Both subjective & objective
♦ Relational/experiential compatibility	♦ Instrumental compatibility	♦ Programmatic support
o Traits	o Nature of goals/focuses	o Supervision
o Focuses	o Preferred intensity of pursuing goals/focuses	o Training
♦ Mentor's approach	♦ Mentor's instrumental orientation	o Provides structured activities
o Youth-centeredness	o Mentor seen as role model	♦ Parents' or guardians' engagement
o Youth feels sense of control	o Mentor seen as supporting goal/growth orientation	♦ Support networks
o Positive regard	o Mentor validates achievement	
♦ Youth's engagement	o Mentor seen as source of inspiration	
o Youth's desire to participate	♦ Mentee's instrumental orientation	
o Youth actively engages	o Initiates goal-oriented activity	
o Youth's behavior interferes with engagement	o Youth seeks support	
♦ Precursors to closeness	♦ Perceived support	
o Empathy	o Youth's satisfaction with relationship's instrumentality	
o Trust	o Mentor's perceived efficacy in relation to instrumentality	
o Respect	Objective	
♦ Closeness	♦ Received support	
o Feeling connected	o Engaged, goal-directed activity	
• Mentee feelings of being cared for	o Topics discussed	
• Mentee has sense of belonging to reciprocal network	o Advocacy	
o Intimacy		
• Genuine conversation/sharing		
• Mutuality		
• Intensity		
o Satisfaction with relationship		
Objective		
♦ Current meeting frequency		
♦ Historic meeting frequency		
♦ Current meeting intensity		
♦ Historic meeting intensity		
♦ Longevity of the relationship		
♦ Durability/resilience		

*These constructs are generally presented in a positive valence, but research suggests in some cases it is most useful to measure negative valence.

Youth Engagement. Just as youth perceptions of the mentor's approach to the match are theoretically important to MRQ, so too are mentors' perceptions of their mentees' responses to their efforts. At the most basic level, it may be important for mentors to feel that their mentees have a sincere *desire to participate* in the match. Perceived apathy or chronic resistance may lead mentors to feel that the match is floundering and that their time is not being well used (Karcher, Nakkula, & Harris, in press). *Youth active engagement* follows the desire to participate. Such engagement tends to energize mentors and enhances the likelihood that they too will stay actively involved (Rhodes, 2002). Finally, in some cases, mentors report that the *youth's behavior interferes with engagement* in the match. Accordingly, when mentors view the mentee's risk status as particularly severe, their experience of relationship quality may be compromised (Blocker, 1993; Slicker & Palmer, 1993).

Precursors to Closeness. *Trust, empathy,* and *respect* have been found to be essential to the establishment of relational closeness (Roberts & Strayer, 1996; Selman & Schultz, 1990). Complex relational experiences such as trust and empathy can take time to develop within matches, which, according to Rhodes (2002), is precisely why match sustainability is so important. Although some researchers (Morrow & Styles, 1995) view empathy and trust as part of closeness itself, we have conceptualized these factors, along with respect, as key precursors to closeness because although close relationships often include these factors, the factors themselves can exist apart from closeness.

Closeness. At the core of relational closeness is the experience of *feeling connected* to the person or group with which one is involved (Jordan, 1991). In the case of mentoring and other forms of youth programming, such experiences of connectedness involve *feeling cared for* by the mentor or other significant adults involved and feeling a *sense of belonging to a reciprocal network* (Morrow & Styles, 1995; Rhodes, 2002). Theoretically, to achieve a high level of relationship quality, it may be important for mentees not only to feel cared for by their mentors but also to experience themselves as providing care and commitment to the mentors. Furthermore, the notion of a reciprocal network argues that the relationship should not exist in a vacuum; rather, it should be embedded within a network of other caring relationships in the participants' lives, deepening the mentoring relationship by incorporating into it the fuller context of the participants' social connections.

Intimacy refers to the quality and degree of closeness experienced in the relationship. Intimate relationships commonly include honest discussion, which researchers have conceptualized as authentic or *genuine conversation* (Brown & Gilligan, 1992; Rhodes, 2002). By definition, genuine conversation includes *mutuality,* or meaningful reciprocal sharing, which may be essential to healthy mentoring relationships (Morrow & Styles, 1995). Through such reciprocal exchanges, youth may learn the skills for connecting within and beyond the immediate relationship (Rogoff, 1990). *Intensity* relates to the degree of intimacy involved in close relationships. DuBois, Neville, et al. (2002) described relationship intensity as characterized by several observable, concrete indicators, such as *regularity and frequency of contact, longevity* of the relationship, types of *activities engaged* in, and *topics discussed.* While these objective indicators may be helpful for gauging relationship intensity, subjective experience (the degree to which the relationship is perceived as deep, meaningful, and honest) also warrants consideration.

In many respects, *satisfaction with the relationship* may be seen as an artifact of connectedness and intimacy (DuBois, Holloway, Valentine, & Cooper, 2002). However, it should be assessed separately given its theoretical importance to match quality (Roffman, Ranjini, Rhodes, & Grossman, in press). Because satisfaction with the match is a subjectively idiosyncratic concept, we should not infer that all participants want the same degree of connection and intimacy. Satisfaction certainly is linked with other subjective constructs, such as compatibility and feeling respected, but we include it as an indicator of closeness because of its strong association with that construct.

Objective Indicators. Objective relationship characteristics also are theoretically relevant to MRQ from a relational/experiential perspective. *Meeting frequency* (Sipe, 1998), *meeting intensity* (e.g., length of meetings; DuBois, Neville, et al., 2002), and relationship *longevity* (Grossman & Rhodes, 2002; Hamilton & Hamilton, 1992) are all important to building close, satisfying matches. Within our heuristic, we have presented two forms of match frequency and meeting intensity: *current* and *historic*. In formal mentoring programs, it generally is recommended that matches meet at least once every other week for a period of at least 2 hours (for community-based matches) or more frequently but for less time (especially for school-based matches). Matches that currently meet at such rates might warrant a positive assessment on current meeting frequency, but the assessment of frequency could be enhanced if consideration is given to whether the match has maintained a high meeting frequency over an extended period of time (historic meeting frequency). The same holds with meeting intensity: Matches that currently meet more frequently, for long periods of time, include discussions of topics that might be objectively coded as more intense (e.g., family dynamics, personal concerns), or are rich in relationship-building activities would be objectively assessed as highly intense, but it may be important to assess whether the pattern has held over time.

Longevity, which has been found to be critical to the development of high-quality mentoring relationships (Grossman & Rhodes, 2002; Hamilton & Hamilton, 1992), is objectively assessed by simply documenting the length of the match. We have added *durability/resilience* as a special form of longevity, based on Foster and Nakkula's (1999) qualitative study of youth mentoring, which found that the ability to persevere through challenges in the match was a critical marker of relational health.

Instrumental/Goal-Oriented Factors

Whereas the subjective assessment of relationship quality culminates in closeness within the relational/experiential domain, it culminates in perceived support within the instrumental/goal-oriented domain. From an instrumental perspective, a high-quality mentoring relationship is marked by the mentee's perception that he or she is being supported in accomplishing particular goals and by the mentor's perception that he or she is being helpful in this effort (Hamilton & Hamilton, 1992; see also Hamilton & Hamilton, this volume).

Instrumental Compatibility. Compatibility takes a goal-oriented focus within the instrumental domain. How does the pair feel, jointly, about the *nature of the goals/focuses* set forth? Do they share a similar *intensity of interest* in pursuing the targeted goals? If they are incompatible on either of these levels, match quality is likely to be compromised. Highly intense instrumental mentors, for example, are at risk for imposing their agendas on the direction of the match, making it more prescriptive than constructively developmental (Morrow & Styles, 1995).

Mentor's Instrumental Orientation. Theoretically, it is important that mentees' perceive their mentors to be supportive and capable allies rather than unilaterally directive instructors. Accordingly, it may be helpful if the mentor is viewed as a *role model* who uses his or her social status within the match to *support the mentees' goal-oriented efforts* and to *validate achievements* associated with those efforts. Such mentors commonly may be viewed as a *source of inspiration* for their mentees by virtue of their own achievements and because of the qualities displayed within the relationship (Blechman, 1992; Rhodes, 2002).

Mentee's Instrumental Orientation. When mentors work from an instrumental orientation, they themselves may be more engaged in this part of the mentoring process when they perceive their mentees to be invested in instrumentality as well. Therefore, mentees' *initiation of goal-oriented activity* may be helpful to promoting MRQ for a variety of reasons, such as enhancing mentor feelings of efficacy. Karcher et al. (in press) found that mentees' efforts to *seek support* from their mentors inspired positive feelings about the match in the mentors. Support seeking has been found in the resilience (Garmezy, 1985) and social support literature (Sarason, Sarason, & Pierce, 1990) to be pivotal in facilitating positive developmental outcomes for youth.

Perceived Support. As noted above, perceived support defines the heart of MRQ within our conceptualization of the instrumental/goal-oriented domain. For mentees, perceived support would include their satisfaction with the nature and intensity of the relationship's instrumentality. If they feel undersupported, pushed too hard, or steered in a direction in which they are not interested, they are likely to experience dissatisfaction with instrumental aspects of the relationship, thus compromising overall MRQ. For mentors, perceived support reflects the degree to which they feel instrumentally supportive. When mentors feel they are playing an important role in supporting their mentees' growth, they may be more likely to experience the match relationship as healthy and more likely to remain active in the match over an extended period of time (Blocker, 1993).

Objective Indicators. Objective levels of *received support* also are a theoretically important component of instrumental aspects of MRQ. Therefore, along with assessing whether mentees feel supported and mentors feel effective in providing support, it may be important to systematically document the nature and extent of *engaged, goal-directed activities* in which the relationship partners have been involved (Hamilton & Darling, 1989). Documenting *topics discussed* is another objective means of capturing some aspects of instrumental relationship quality (DuBois, Neville, et al., 2002). Finally, *advocacy* is another activity that can be objectively documented. When mentors advocate with parents, teachers, or other institutions on behalf of their mentees, it may build trust and the experience of feeling cared for (Hamilton & Darling, 1989; Rhodes, 2002). Advocacy marks an effort to support the match not only by connecting within it but also by working within the contexts in which the relationship is embedded.

Environmental Factors Fundamental to MRQ

A mentoring relationship does not exist within a vacuum; rather, the relationship is embedded within varying degrees of contextual or environmental support. Although the majority of theory and research on MRQ focuses on the workings and experiences within the relationship, it is important to recognize and assess those factors external to the relationship that may be fundamental to its current functioning and longer-term sustainability. We believe that MRQ is inextricably linked to these factors.

Programmatic Support. Because mentors are often lay people with no training in child or youth development, it may be beneficial for relationships to be supported by adequate *supervision* and *training* (see Weinberger, this volume). Supervision refers to the availability of professional support from mentoring program staff. Such support is used to address mentors' questions and to provide guidance with day-to-day issues such as activities selected and topics discussed. Training is tailored to group presentations on topics such as approaches to use within the match and communication strategies for engaging with parents and teachers. Mentoring programs can *provide structured activities* that may be important for building strong relationships, particularly within new or instrumentally oriented matches (DuBois, Neville, et al., 2002).

Parents' or Guardians' Engagement. As with programmatic support, the nature of parent or guardian engagement may be a pivotal influence on the long-term health of relationships. Parents who disapprove of a mentor or the mentor's approach, for example, have the power to discontinue the relationship even though the participants feel positively about their relationship. On the other hand, Rhodes (2002) reported findings suggesting that participation in a mentoring program may improve parent-child relationships, which can, in turn, support the longer-term health of the match.

Support Networks. Ideally, healthy relationships help youth become more engaged in supportive contexts outside of the match, including school, clubs, or constructive peer groups. As relationships mature, many are marked by connections made to other potentially supportive organizations and social contexts (Hamilton & Darling, 1989). As mentor and mentee connect together across a range of supportive environments, their relationship may become defined more fluidly and become less limited to their one-on-one interactions.

RESEARCH

In this section, we review instruments that primarily assess participants' perceptions of the MRQ. We focus on mentoring-specific instruments in order to attend closely to the state of assessment of this unique type of relationship. No existing instrument specifically designed to measure MRQ has been scrutinized to an extent that it may be considered thoroughly validated. However, we found six measures that show promise for assessing the subjective elements of mentoring relationships. To identify these instruments, we searched published materials and consulted with researchers and organizations that have been most active in the measurement of relationship quality. We found that only five of the instruments developed expressly to assess mentoring relationships with school-aged youth/young adults have had validation methodology published either in peer-reviewed journals or in an edited scholarly book. The validity evidence for each of these instruments is mixed. Nonetheless, they represent important steps in the evolution of research on MRQ.

Youth-Mentor Relationship Questionnaire (YMRQ)

The Public/Private Ventures (P/PV) landmark study of mentoring (Grossman & Tierney, 1998) provided one of the earliest and most definitive demonstrations that mentoring can provide significant benefits to youth. Included among the items administered to youth participating in that study were dozens of questions intended to measure objective and subjective indications of match quality. Two instruments based on this initial study's compilation of items have been published; both are reviewed here, though only one is presented in a formal validation study in a peer-reviewed journal (Roffman et al., in press).

Roffman et al.'s Youth-Mentor Relationship Questionnaire (YMRQ) comprises empirically derived subscales from the larger pool of items used in the P/PV study. Among instruments with validity evidence published in a peer-reviewed journal, the YMRQ is the only measure of MRQ specifically designed to be completed by elementary and secondary school students (aged 9–16).

The YMRQ was derived through exploratory and confirmatory factor analyses from a sample of 74 items. All the final items load well on their factors, and the internal consistency of those factors is strong; however, it should be noted that three of the items load on multiple factors. The YMRQ assesses internal, subjective constructs that attend to both positive and negative perspectives on relational/experiential and instrumental indicators; it does not measure external or objective factors. For a summary of constructs measured by this and the other reviewed instruments, please see Table 7.2.

The validation evidence supporting the YMRQ is noteworthy for several reasons. The instrument was administered as part of a landmark study using an experimental design that incorporated a large sample of mentored and control group participants and concurrently used other instruments to assess construct validity evidence. Correlations were found between the YMRQ and both length of match (longevity) and youth reports of their academic performance. In this sense, the study's findings suggest that the YMRQ effectively assesses important facets of youth-adult mentoring relationships. The instrument also offers an important strength beyond the rigor of its empirical development: The negative focus adopted by many of the prompts seems likely to call attention to potentially problematic matches and thus may be well suited to directing practitioners' attention to matches particularly in need of help.

However, the YMRQ is somewhat limited in its scope—and potentially in its application. Two of the subscales ("Not Dissatisfied," "Not Unhappy") appear to address very similar constructs and are substantially correlated ($r = .77$). Whereas only 3 of the 15 items included in the measure assess positive experiences of the match, most theory on mentoring matches emphasizes the positive qualities that predict outcomes (see Rhodes, this volume). These characteristics were empirically derived; however, the degree of negativity in the items comprising the instrument (e.g., "When I am with my mentor I feel bored.") and the narrowness of the focus raise the question of whether its usefulness may be limited to identifying matches at risk for failure, as opposed to differentiating quality across relatively healthy matches. The

Table 7.2 Characteristics of Instruments for Assessing Mentoring Relationship Quality

Reviewed Scale/Author(s)*	Intended Respondents	Named Factors Measured (Number of Items)	Internal Consistency	Constructs Assessed (Corresponding With Table 7.1)	Scope of Subscales (Corresponding With Table 7.1)†
Youth-Mentor Relationship Questionnaire (Roffman et al., 2003)	Mentees in primary and secondary school	Overall scale (15)** Not dissatisfied (3) Helped to cope (3) Not unhappy (6) Trust not broken (6)	N/A .74 .81 .85 .81	Relational/experiential Instrumental/goal-oriented Subjective Internal	Precursors to closeness Closeness Perceived support
Youth Survey (Public/Private Ventures, 2002)	Mentees in primary and secondary school	Overall scale (19) Youth-centered relationship (5) Emotional engagement (8) Dissatisfaction (6)	N/A	Relational/experiential Subjective Internal	Mentor's approach Precursors to closeness Closeness
Match Characteristics Questionnaire v2.0 (Harris & Nakkula, 2003)***	Mentors of youth in primary and secondary school	Overall scale (58 plus 4 written questions) Strength of connection (5) Compatibility (10) Child is open (5) Satisfaction (4) Child seeks relational support (3) Child seeks instrumental support (4) Mentor focus, fun, & sharing (8) Mentor focus, character/mind/outlook (12) Programmatic support (4) Parental involvement (3) Most frequent activities engaged (listed) Special activities engaged (listed) Main teaching focuses (listed) Overall match focuses (listed)	.94 .87 .86 .73 .87 .78 .77 .81 .88 .79 .70 N/A N/A N/A N/A	Relational/experiential Instrumental/goal-oriented Objective Subjective Internal External	Relational/experiential compatibility Youth's engagement Precursors to closeness Closeness Durability/resilience Instrumental compatibility Youth's instrumental orientation Programmatic support Parent's/guardian's engagement Received support

(Continued)

Table 7.2 (Continued)

Reviewed Scale/Author(s)*	Intended Respondents	Named Factors Measured (Number of Items)	Internal Consistency	Constructs Assessed (Corresponding With Table 7.1)	Scope of Subscales (Corresponding With Table 7.1)†
Youth Mentoring Survey (Harris & Nakkula, 2003)	Mentees in primary and secondary school	Overall scale (33 plus 3 written questions) Easy connection/intimacy (8) Instrumentality (6) Focus on fun (5) Focus on sharing & intimacy (6) Focus on instrumentality/outlook (8) Activities engaged (listed) Motivation for participation (listed) Problems in match (listed)	.90 .68 .76 .61 .84 .75 N/A N/A N/A	Relational/experiential Instrumental/goal-oriented Subjective Internal	Relational/experiential compatibility Mentor's approach Closeness Mentor's instrumental orientation Perceived support Received support
Relational Health Indices (RHI-M) (Liang et al., 2002)	Female college-age mentees	Mentoring subscale of RHI (11) Engagement (3) Empowerment/zest (4) Authenticity (4)	.86 .72 .72 .77	Relational/experiential Instrumental/goal-oriented Subjective Internal	Mentor's approach Precursors to closeness Closeness Mentor's instrumental orientation Perceived support
Mentoring Scale (Darling et al., 2002)	College-age mentees	Overall scale (24, USA; 25, JPN) Mentoring scale (4)	*USA JPN* .69 .72	Instrumental/goal-oriented Subjective Internal	Mentor's instrumental orientation Perceived support

† Theoretical constructs in the reviewed surveys are coded according to categories presented in Table 7.1.

* Each instrument uses a Likert scale except where noted.

** Three items load on two factors.

*** Only the most recent version of the MCQ is presented here, as there is substantial overlap between items and subscales between the MCQ v1.0 and v2.0.

validation study also had several limitations that the authors note: There was no complementary measure to assess perspectives other than those of the youth; the data were entirely retrospective (collected only at posttest, when many relationships already had ended), which could be problematic given the question of how accurately youth aged 9 to 16 can be expected to recall experiences and perceptions over their preceding 18 months); and the data were collected at only one point in time, thereby preventing the possibility of evaluating the measure's ability to assess growth.

The Youth Survey: Measuring the Quality of Mentor-Youth Relationships

The "Youth Survey" (P/PV, 2002) is derived from the same sample of items as the YMRQ, those collected in the landmark P/PV study of Big Brothers Big Sisters programming. In fact, the two surveys share nine items in common. The items in this instrument were substantially adapted from a study by Grossman and Johnson (1999), who found mentoring relationship quality to be related to differences in outcomes for mentored students, especially in relation to self-reported data on academic achievement and substance abuse.

Because they are derived from the same set of items and outcome data as the YMRQ, both instruments share the landmark P/PV study's strong research design elements. Unlike other available measures of MRQ, this instrument comes closest to offering standardized norms. The Youth Survey is accessible with an administrative guide that includes normative data on ranges and average scores for the hundreds of youth in the original study. This information facilitates comparisons among scores for youth in programs using the instrument and those in the original study from which these norms were developed.

However, the instrument shares most of the limitations of the YMRQ and two important additional ones. First, there is no published information about validation efforts or about the reliability of the subscales. Second, the scale measures positive and negative aspects of internal, subjective, and relational/experiential dimensions of the match but does not assess external, objective, or instrumental dimensions (see Table 7.2).

The Match Characteristics Questionnaire (v1.1 & v2.0) and the Youth Mentoring Survey

The Match Characteristics Questionnaire (MCQ) (Harris & Nakkula, 1999, 2003a) is the only measure of adult-youth MRQ that is designed to be completed by adults and is supported by published validity evidence (Karcher et al., in press). The instrument's development was informed broadly by the literature described in the theory section of this chapter and by in-depth interviews conducted by the authors with mentors, mentees, and parents in a community-based mentoring program. Prompts for the MCQ (v1.1) were selected through an exploratory factor analysis of 65 items that produced six coherent and distinct subscales. All retained items loaded well on their factors, and the internal consistency of those factors was strong. The principal strength of the instrument's design is that it assesses the adult's perspective on internal, external, relational/experiential, and instrumental indicators. Only the most recent version of the MCQ (v2.0) is reflected in Table 7.2.

Karcher et al.'s (in press) study yielded evidence of predictive and concurrent validity. Specifically, subscales reflecting MRQ 2 months into the matches predicted mentors' experiences of their matches 6 months later. Concurrent validity was assessed through a comparison of MRQ from mentee and mentor reports about the relationship, the only instance of such a comparison among the instruments reviewed in this chapter. A statistically significant relationship was found between mentors' reports of perceived self-efficacy as a mentor and two mentee-reported scales when the match was 2 months old: experience of empathy, praise, and attention from the mentor ($r = .45$) and mentees' feelings that they mattered to their mentors early in the relationship ($r = .52$). There was a moderate but nonsignificant relationship between mentors' ratings of relationship quality and mentees' reports of how much they experienced empathy, praise, and attention from the mentor when the match was 6 months old ($r = .28$).

However, the instrument and its validity study have several limitations. The MCQ does not assess negative aspects of relationship quality, perhaps making it less useful for detecting troubled matches, and it does not assess objective dimensions of MRQ. In the study assessing validity evidence, predictive validity for developmental outcomes of youth was not assessed. In addition, the mentoring model with which the MCQ was used focused on high school students mentoring younger at-risk youth, rendering results potentially less generalizable to adult-youth matches. In addition, the sample was relatively small (63 matches) and restricted in scope, with the matches coming from one school and the mentors being all White and predominantly female.

More recent, unpublished adaptations of the MCQ have yielded complementary adult and youth instruments (MCQ v2.0 and the Youth Mentoring Survey [YMS]; Harris & Nakkula, 2003b). Although these are unpublished measures, they warrant mention here because they are adapted from the original MCQ. Furthermore, they focus more directly on the dimensions of MRQ found in the mentoring literature to be highly relevant to mentoring relationships, and they differentiate more theoretically distinct aspects of those dimensions (see Table 7.1). For example, items designed to assess support seeking were broken down into distinct sets intended to capture both relational and instrumental support. Also, greater attention was paid to the strength of the connection, openness of the mentee, match compatibility, and types of activities engaged. The YMS and MCQ v2.0 are designed to complement each other and to be used in concert with more concrete data provided by case managers (e.g., demographics, match history). Each of these instruments measures internal subjective (rated) and objective (listed) indicators, as well as relational/experiential and instrumental/ goal-oriented indicators. However, only the MCQ measures external indicators, and only the YMS measures negative perceptions about MRQ. Preliminary analyses of data from 159 relationships show high internal consistencies for the overall surveys and most subscales (see Table 7.2). Also, moderate correlations between youth and

adult instruments completed for individual matches were obtained.

Relational Health Indices (RHI)

The Relational Health Indices (RHI) (Liang et al., 2002) were developed to study growth-fostering relationships with peers, mentors, and in communities among female college students. The instrument is grounded in theory specific to women's psychological development, stemming primarily from the relational model (Jordan, 1991; Miller & Stiver, 1997). Reflecting this theoretical perspective and the age of its respondents, the mentor scale (RHI-M) is intended to assess dimensions of relationship quality that are slightly different from the constructs measured by the youth report instruments, and with individual items assessing more complex concepts. We will focus here solely on the 11-item mentor index (RHI-M), because the RHI's peer and community indices extend beyond the purview of this chapter. The three subscales of the mentor index (see Table 7.2) offer a theoretically unique perspective on subjective, internal, and relational/ experiential dimensions of MRQ. The measure also includes some items related to instrumentality. However, it does not address external or objective factors affecting the relationship and does not assess negative perspectives on MRQ (see Table 7.2).

In contrast to the instruments described above, students complete the RHI-M in relation to the "most important" (informal) mentors in their lives, an important contribution in that unlike previous instruments discussed, it was developed with the aim of providing an assessment of natural mentoring relationships. Development of the RHI-M included exploratory and confirmatory factor analyses, which originally reduced a larger pool of theoretically derived items to 25, which, in turn, was empirically reduced to the final 11-item, 3-factor scale (see Table 7.2). In addition to the rigorous instrument development procedures used, the validation study is particularly strong in two other ways. The RHI-M was positively correlated with non-mentoring-specific measures of depth and support in relationships (construct validity), and the findings are based on a relatively large sample (303 participants who identified natural mentors).

The main limitation of the instrument and the study is that it will be difficult to generalize findings from the RHI-M without validation studies involving more diverse populations than the sample of first- and fourth-year female students at a liberal arts women's college. This limitation currently is being addressed through the development of a related instrument that will be appropriate for use with a diverse sample of high school students (B. Liang, personal communication, June 5, 2004).

Mentoring Scale

Darling, Hamilton, Toyokawa, and Matsuda (2002) developed two closely related surveys to compare social roles and functions among natural mentors in the United States and Japan. These instruments and subscales are unnamed with the exception of a central scale of common items within one factor that the authors call the "mentoring scale." The authors developed this scale by asking a sample of college students from each country to nominate the 10 associates they deemed most important in their lives, based on their functioning as natural mentors. They then rated each of the nominees according to a theoretically derived list of items related to natural mentoring. Through exploratory and confirmatory factor analyses, the authors derived a six-item factor from the Japanese data and an eight-item factor from the U.S. data to assess natural mentoring relationships. The final mentoring scale comprises four items common to these two factors and found to be reliable in both cultures.

An important contribution of the validation study's cross-cultural design is that the final mentoring scale yielded similar responses across diverse cultures. In fact, cultural differences explained less than 3% of the variance in reported levels of mentoring. Another strength of the study is its approach to assessing natural mentoring; students were asked to rate their 10 most significant relationships and then to rate the degree to which these were mentoring relationships. The resulting four-item scale for assessing such relationships is parsimonious and has cross-cultural validity evidence, thus increasing its potential usefulness.

There are several limitations to the instrument's utility, however. First, the study provides no indication of the mentoring scale's correlation with developmental outcomes. Second, the participants' ratings were retrospective (asking about mentorship prior to their entry to college), which raises questions about their validity. Third, the scale's use of dichotomous (yes or no) ratings reduces the capacity for the instrument to capture subtler variations in response. Fourth, the scale focuses solely on internal, subjective ratings of instrumentality and does not measure external, relational/experiential, or objective dimensions of natural mentoring relationships. The broader survey from which the mentoring scale was derived does include additional subscales that address relational/experiential elements of MRQ, but no related validity evidence is presented to support them.

Summary

The instruments for assessing mentoring relationship quality reviewed in this chapter are empirically and theoretically promising, each offering at least one unique strength in relation to the others. The Youth-Mentor Relationship Questionnaire is the only measure with substantial evidence of validity that is designed to be completed by youth. The Youth Survey offers the closest approximation to standardized norms. The Mentor Characteristics Questionnaire measures mentors' perspectives on adult-youth relationships. The Relational Health Indices Mentoring Scale is designed to assess mentoring, with particular sensitivity to women's experiences of relationships. Darling et al.'s (2002) mentoring scale identifies common elements of mentorship across cultural boundaries. The latter two instruments also are noteworthy in that they call upon respondents to rate *any* mentors in their lives, including natural ones.

Each of the instruments, however, has substantial limitations related to the scope or the design of the study providing validity evidence (and moreover, the lack of programmatic validation research across multiple studies typically needed to provide strong evidence of validity). None assesses the full range of theoretical factors we discuss here as relevant to MRQ. Only one (the MCQ) has concurrent validity evidence incorporating youth and adult perspectives on MRQ. And all of the surveys designed to assess MRQ in formal mentoring programs have been studied in the context of only one organization, rendering it difficult to assess their validity for use in assessing relationships formed in other types of programs or those established outside of programs altogether (i.e., natural mentoring relationships).

Some empirically derived factors in these instruments seem to comprise multiple theoretical constructs that could be investigated as fully developed, individual subscales. There appears to be a dialectical tension here between empirical parsimony and theoretical comprehensiveness that can be explored further as this area of research matures. From a psychometric perspective, in-depth examination of convergent and discriminant validity of proposed subscales on measures using analytic tools, such as a multitrait-multimethod matrix, has not yet been reported for any of the instruments. Likewise, although associations with outcomes have provided evidence of concurrent and predictive validity, it is not clear to what extent the multiple subscales included on measures make distinctive contributions to prediction of outcomes independent of their overlap with one another.

Only recently have authors such as DuBois, Neville, et al. (2002) and Rhodes (2002) presented integrated mentoring theories that may facilitate more precise analysis of mentoring-specific relational dynamics. Informed by the development of such theories, ongoing rigorous investigations may be more likely to be free of the foregoing limitations. However, we recommend that findings generated by instruments assessing MRQ be considered tentative until these issues can be addressed to a more satisfactory extent.

Instruments other than those reviewed above could be applied to MRQ assessment, but they lack sufficient validity evidence to support their widespread use. For instance, Information Technology International (Mertinko, Novotney, Baker, & Lang, 2000) and Big Brothers Big Sisters of America (Lyons & Curtis, 1998) have developed brief youth and adult instruments that assess elements of relationship quality but are not supported by reliability and validity evidence.

A handful of researchers have developed qualitative designs to augment or complement their quantitative work. DuBois, Neville, et al. (2002) have discussed the utility of logs and visit reports (summary of processes and activities) to assess MRQ. They also propose the assessment of relationships through interview data that consider (a) frequency of contact, (b) perceived closeness, (c) obstacles to relationship development, (d) helpfulness of agency staff, and (e) activities engaged in and topics discussed. In another ongoing study, Keller, Pryce, and Neugebauer (2003) have presented an observational method to support an empirically grounded theory that can describe dynamics within school-based mentoring relationships. This promising research is using a mixed-methods design that incorporates interviews, structured naturalistic observation, and surveys. The study's main goals include the identification of mentoring processes that contribute most strongly to MRQ and the development of a typology that facilitates the association of mentoring relationship patterns with academic outcomes.

PRACTICE

The assessment of MRQ is fundamentally important to mentoring programs. In addition to helping determine the efficacy of services, assessments of MRQ can assist programs in identifying "best practices" for the youth they serve and the mentors they support. For example, an instrument with sufficient validity evidence as well as useful norms or criterion indicators could inform supervision of matches and ongoing mentor training. Timely assessment can detect match problems such as a dissatisfied mentee or a mentor who feels ineffective. Conversely, youth-reported assessments that reveal positive relationship dynamics may be shared with mentors as encouraging evidence of their usefulness and their match's positive development, which is important given mentors' common failure to recognize the value of their efforts. Using assessments to help identify successful relationship processes and to help identify particular needs for intervention and support may facilitate the development and maintenance of more durable and high-quality matches.

If a program opts for a quantitative approach to assessing MRQ, which instrument should it choose? In general, the instrument should return meaningful data that are aligned with the program's goals. Such data can best be obtained by using instruments that have shown a range of validity evidence based on studies such as those reported in this chapter and by matching instrument selection with both the program's goals (e.g., academically focused, career focused, or purely relationship focused) and the characteristics of its participants (e.g., age, gender, and academic issues). Other important criteria for choosing instruments include their use of clear and age-appropriate language and the amount of time needed to administer them, including the frequency with which they must be administered to be useful.

Given the free and easily accessible nature of the instruments described in this chapter, it may not be necessary to use all of the subscales of specific instruments or even to use only one instrument. When practitioners need broader assessment than that provided by a single instrument, a feasible strategy might be to use one instrument in its entirety and to augment it with subscales from another. However, it is important to remember that while longer instruments that assess more constructs can generate greater insight on different aspects of relationship quality, this comprehensiveness comes at a cost. Both youth and adults can become bored or frustrated by longer scales, particularly if they require administration at multiple points in time or appear to contain undue overlap between items in the subscales. Finally, because the utility of MRQ assessments may be greatest when incorporated into regular programming infrastructure, it is important to encourage participants' buy-in. In such cases, participants should be made aware at the outset that they will be asked to complete surveys regularly and should be helped to understand why this process is important to the functioning of the program.

Survey instruments such as those described here require the summation and interpretation of scores, which will be enhanced by the involvement of trained researchers/evaluators. Such external support for analysis ensures accuracy and lends credibility to interpretations of the data. However, professional evaluation support can be difficult for programs to afford. This is especially true when longer, more complex instruments are used and more intensive analyses are required. Still, partnership with external evaluators is vital, especially given the absence of norms and benchmarks associated with instruments developed to date. Without professional support, the meaning of scores may be vague, and their value may be limited to within-group comparison (between matches within only one program).

A final consideration is how to use the selected instrument. Although baseline data are prized in program evaluation, it does not make sense to assess match quality before a relationship has had a chance to develop. We believe it is more advantageous to administer MRQ assessments after the match has been meeting regularly for at least 3 months, to allow the match to progress beyond the initial awkwardness and/or a "honeymoon" stage. The interval between the initial and follow-up assessments should likewise allow sufficient time for the relationship to evolve, likely about 3 to 6 months. Assessments of MRQ made in conjunction with other pre- and postassessments of outcomes, such as self-esteem or grades, can help determine whether changes in MRQ predict changes in outcomes. Finally, MRQ assessment can inform match supervision. For instance, it would be useful to assess match quality after the first 9 to 12 months given the importance of building and sustaining long-term relationships.

FUTURE DIRECTIONS

Synthesis

The assessment of mentoring relationships is an important but, to this point, underdeveloped area of study. Researchers have drawn primarily from social, resilience, and relational theories in developing instruments, though only recently have they begun to integrate these perspectives coherently in the assessment of MRQ. Emerging models for the study of mentoring processes represent an important departure from preexisting work that focused on outcomes only. These new models offer approaches to understanding *how* mentoring relationships contribute to targeted outcomes, rather than simply determining which outcomes have been attained and whether they can be attributed to mentoring.

Because the study of MRQ is so new, programs have relatively fewer choices when deciding which instruments to use. In fact, many mentoring programs still are assessing match relationships with instruments that are atheoretical and have not been tested adequately for reliability and validity evidence. Based on our review of the literature, programs that serve primary and secondary school students have only two youth and one adult instrument with published validity and reliability evidence from which to choose; there are only two such instruments for college-aged students. The strength of these measures is that each has a fairly strong theoretical and empirical foundation, and it is useful that they offer a range of perspectives on a core set of constructs organized around the global themes of relational closeness and instrumental support. However, even as a group, the instruments do not offer the means to measure the full range of constructs discussed in this chapter as highly relevant to MRQ.

MRQ is a rich and complex dynamic, with dimensions that warrant broader and more precise investigation. Some of the instruments reviewed in this chapter are already being revised to address these issues. In addition, promising qualitative research has been undertaken and is beginning to inform the field. However, more work is needed to identify discrete mentoring-specific constructs that both expand the scope of and sharpen insight on MRQ. As yet, the disconnection between theoretically and empirically derived constructs is great enough that it may be important to consider findings tentative even when generated by the relatively validated instruments reviewed in this chapter. In the future, it will be necessary to develop (a) a range of age-appropriate instruments, (b) instruments that are refined to differentiate relationship processes between various mentoring models, and (c) instruments that are sufficiently resistant to being influenced unduly by the week-to-week ebb and flow of the mentoring relationship.

We conclude by outlining broad directions for future research and practice in the area of mentoring relationship quality.

Recommendations for Research

1. *Strengthen methodology for developing MRQ assessment instruments.* To inform the development of instruments with increased validity evidence, researchers must employ more rigorous empirical standards. Future studies should incorporate larger and more diverse samples, measures of MRQ obtained from multiple informants and sources, and use longitudinal experimental/quasi-experimental designs (perhaps including comparison groups rating informal relationships) to establish clearer evidence of the links between MRQ and related variables.

2. *Further synthesize and develop existing MRQ measurement theory.* The development of integrative models is a promising new trend in the field that must be developed in order to thoroughly explicate the processes for assessing MRQ. This work will facilitate the development of more advanced models for understanding MRQ and its relationship to targeted outcomes.

3. *Differentiate patterns of MRQ across programs and populations.* Future studies should explore the nature of MRQ across a broader range of programs, models, and populations. They should expand beyond the predominant focus on BBBSA and its basic models (school- and community-based one-to-one models) to render findings most relevant to the broader mentoring community. Likewise, comparisons of MRQ assessments across programmatic and natural mentoring relationships are needed. Furthermore, studies must account for the more subtle ways that age, gender, and culture may influence the experience of closeness and instrumental support in mentoring relationships.

4. *Define and assess MRQ specific to mentoring typologies.* Because relationship-building approaches may vary according to the purposes and goals of the match, it seems misguided to assess MRQ the same way across all matches. Variations between relationships

within individual programs point toward the usefulness of a typology-specific exploration of MRQ, one that assesses MRQ in relation to particular types of goals, focuses, or approaches across matches. Creation of more differentiated typologies may facilitate clearer understanding of how MRQ develops, and should be assessed within particular match types.

5. *Clarify differences between MRQ states and traits.* Instrumentation should distinguish between temporary states and more durable traits of MRQ and assess whether perceived or reported traits are experienced currently. For instance, perceptions of MRQ can be substantially influenced by recent experiences in the match (present states), and conversely, participants sometimes hold enduring perceptions (traits) of MRQ even after the circumstances that generated those perceptions have changed dramatically.

6. *Pursue rigorous qualitative assessments of MRQ.* Further qualitative research is needed to broaden and deepen insight on MRQ and to inform the development and revision of survey instruments. Through interviews and observation, broad constructs such as closeness and instrumentality may be more carefully articulated.

Recommendations for Practice

1. *Incorporate MRQ assessment into program infrastructures.* To better understand and improve MRQ within their programs, directors should incorporate the assessment of MRQ into existing infrastructures. Collection of subjective data on MRQ should be instilled as part of normal practice, and administrators should commit to the accurate tracking of objective data, such as meeting frequency and duration, match and closure dates, and demographic information.

2. *Match instrument selection with program needs and purposes.* Programs should use instruments with strong validity evidence that are most appropriate to their models, focuses, and populations served. This will require staying abreast of developments in instrumentation as new and revised instruments become available

in the context of expanding research on MRQ. This pursuit can be facilitated by organizations such as the MENTOR/National Mentoring Partnership or the National Mentoring Center, which post updates and guidance for practitioners on Web sites.

3. *MRQ assessment should help shape program practices.* To effectively utilize the results of MRQ assessment, programs should implement explicit strategies for promoting high relationship quality within their matches. This may entail the use of assessment results within supervision and training, or in workshops dedicated to "best practices" in this area. Finally, in the absence of national standards for MRQ, programs can partner with qualified researchers to establish their own baseline and program norms for the instruments they use.

REFERENCES

Blechman, E. A. (1992). Mentors for high-risk minority youth: From effective communication to bicultural competence. *Journal of Clinical Child Psychology, 21,* 160–169.

Blocker, K. M. (1993). Factors in sustaining adult voluntary mentoring relationships with at-risk youth. *Dissertation Abstracts International, 54*(6-A).

Brown, L. M., & Gilligan, C. (1992). *Meeting at the crossroads: Women's psychology and girls' development.* Cambridge, MA: Harvard University Press.

Darling, N., Hamilton, S., Toyokawa, T., & Matsuda, S. (2002). Naturally occurring mentoring in Japan and the United States: Roles and correlates. *American Journal of Community Psychology, 30,* 245–270.

DuBois, D. L., Holloway, B. E., Valentine, J. C., & Cooper, H. (2002). Effectiveness of mentoring programs for youth: A meta-analytic review. *American Journal of Community Psychology, 30*(2), 157–197.

DuBois, D. L., Neville, H. A., Parra, G. R., & Pugh-Lilly, A. O. (2002). Testing a new model of mentoring. In G. G. Noam (Ed. in chief) & J. E. Rhodes (Ed.), *A critical view of youth mentoring* (*New Directions for Youth Development: Theory, Research, and Practice, No. 93,* pp. 21–57). San Francisco: Jossey-Bass.

Foster, K., & Nakkula, M. (1999). *Mentors and minotaurs: An intercultural approach to community-based mentoring for youth.* Unpublished manuscript, Harvard Graduate School of Education, Cambridge, MA.

Garmezy, N. (1985). Stress resistant children: The search for protective factors. In J. E. Stevenson (Ed.), *Recent research in developmental psychopathology* (pp. 213–233). Oxford, UK: Pergamon Press.

Grossman, J. B., & Johnson, A. (1999). Assessing the effectiveness of mentoring programs. In J. B. Grossman (Ed.), *Contemporary issues in mentoring* (pp. 24–47). Philadelphia: Public/Private Ventures.

Grossman, J. B., & Rhodes, J. E. (2002). The test of time: Predictors and effects of duration in youth mentoring relationships. *American Journal of Community Psychology, 30,* 199–219.

Grossman, J. B., & Tierney, J. P. (1998). Does mentoring work? An impact study of the Big Brothers Big Sisters Program. *Evaluation Review, 22,* 403–426.

Hamilton, S. F., & Darling, N. (1989). Mentors in adolescents' lives. In K. Hurrelmann & U. Engel (Eds.), *The social world of adolescents: International perspectives* (pp. 121–140). New York: Walter de Gruyter.

Hamilton, S. F., & Hamilton, M. A. (1992). Mentoring programs: Promise and paradox. *Phi Delta Kappan, 73,* 546–550.

Harris, J. T., & Nakkula, M. J. (1999). *Match Characteristics Questionnaire (MCQ).* Unpublished measure, Harvard Graduate School of Education, Cambridge, MA.

Harris, J. T., & Nakkula, M. J. (2003a). *Match Characteristics Questionnaire v 2.0.* Unpublished measure, Harvard Graduate School of Education, Cambridge, MA.

Harris, J. T., & Nakkula, M. J. (2003b). *Youth Mentoring Survey.* Unpublished measure, Harvard Graduate School of Education, Cambridge, MA.

Herrera, C., Sipe, C., & McClanahan, W. (2000). *Mentoring school-aged children: Relationship development in community-based and school-based programs.* Philadelphia: Public/Private Ventures. (Published in collaboration with MENTOR/National Mentoring Partnership, Alexandria, VA)

Jordan, J. V. (1991). The meaning of mutuality. In J. V. Jordan, A. G. Kaplan, J. B. Miller, I. P. Stiver, & J. L. Surrey (Eds.), *Women's growth in connection: Writings from the Stone Center* (pp. 81–96). New York: Guilford Press.

Karcher, M. J., Nakkula, M. J., & Harris, J. T. (in press). Developmental mentoring match characteristics: The effects of mentors' efficacy and mentees' emotional support seeking on the perceived quality of mentoring relationships. *Journal of Primary Prevention.*

Keller, T. E., Pryce, J. M., & Neugebauer, A. (2003). *Observational methods for assessing the nature and course of mentor-child interactions.* Unpublished manual, University of Chicago.

Liang, B., Tracy, A., Taylor, C. A., Williams, L. M., Jordan, J. V., & Miller, J. B. (2002). The relational health indices: A study of women's relationships. *Psychology of Women Quarterly, 26,* 25–35.

Lyons, M., & Curtis, T. (1998). *Program outcome-based evaluation (POE).* Philadelphia: BBBSA.

Mertinko, E., Novotney, L., Baker, T., & Lang, J. (2000). *Evaluating your program: A beginner's self-evaluation workbook for mentoring programs.* Washington, DC: Office of Juvenile Justice and Delinquency Prevention.

Miller, J. B., & Stiver, I. P. (1997). *The healing connection: How women form relationships in therapy and in life.* Boston: Beacon Press.

Morrow, K., & Styles, M. (1995). *Building relationships with youth in program settings: A study of Big Brothers/Big Sisters.* Philadelphia: Public/Private Ventures.

Public/Private Ventures. (2002). *Technical assistance packet #8: Measuring the quality of mentor-youth relationships: A tool for mentoring programs.* Portland, OR: Northwest Regional Educational Laboratory. Retrieved on April 23, 2003, from http://www.nwrel.org/mentoring/packets.html

Rhodes, J. E. (Ed.). (2002). *A critical view of youth mentoring (New Directions for Youth Development: Theory, Research, and Practice, No. 93,* G. G. Noam, Ed. in chief). San Francisco: Jossey-Bass.

Roberts, W., & Strayer, J. (1996). Empathy, emotional expressiveness, and prosocial behavior. *Child Development, 67,* 449–470.

Roffman, J., Ranjini, R., Rhodes, J., & Grossman, J. B. (in press). Promoting successful youth mentoring relationships: A preliminary screening questionnaire. *Journal of Primary Prevention.*

Rogoff, B. (1990). *Apprenticeship in thinking.* New York: Oxford University Press.

Sarason, B. R., Sarason, I. G., & Pierce, G. R. (Eds.). (1990). *Social support: An interactional view.* New York: Wiley.

Selman, R. L., & Schultz, L. H. (1990). *Fostering friendship: Developmental theory and pair therapy.* Chicago: University of Chicago Press.

Sipe, C. L. (1998). Mentoring adolescents: What have we learned? In J. B. Grossman (Ed.), *Contemporary issues in mentoring* (pp. 10–23). Philadelphia: Public/Private Ventures.

Slicker, E. K., & Palmer, D. J. (1993). Mentoring at-risk high school students: Evaluation of a school-based program. *The School Counselor, 40,* 327–334.

8

A COUNSELING AND PSYCHOTHERAPY PERSPECTIVE ON MENTORING RELATIONSHIPS

RENÉE SPENCER AND JEAN E. RHODES

INTRODUCTION

At the heart of both psychotherapy and mentoring is a human connection, the explicit goal of which is to foster the positive development of one of the partners (Rhodes, 2002). A bit of mystery will likely always surround efforts to understand why two people hit it off, whether as therapist and client or as mentor and protégé. However, in the psychotherapy literature, some significant headway has begun to be made into determining why some therapeutic relationships "work" and others do not. This literature, with its rich theoretical and empirical knowledge base examining the role that relationships and relational processes play in the change process, potentially has much to offer in the way of helping us deepen our knowledge of mentoring relationships, whether formed naturally or through programs. Still, the comparisons to be made between mentoring and psychotherapy relationships are not tidy ones, as there are and should be differences between these two distinct types of relationships.

In this chapter, we consider theory and research addressing some of the fundamental components of psychotherapy relationships and discuss the implications of these for mentoring relationships. We examine the contributions to client outcomes both of what have been called common or relationship factors and of approaches and techniques that are specific to particular theoretical orientations. In addition, the structural supports of psychotherapy, such as training and supervision, are discussed, given that parallel efforts have been viewed as important for mentoring programs. Then, we turn our attention to the findings of relevant research on mentoring, noting where our existing knowledge falls short, and follow this with a discussion of related current mentoring program practices. Finally, we provide recommendations for future research and for present practice, in light of the existing knowledge base offered by both the mentoring and the psychotherapy literatures.

THEORY

In psychotherapy, as in mentoring, there are many and often opposing ideas about what makes such relationships "work" and even what the outcome of such endeavors should be. Both are interventions delivered in and through a relationship established between one person who is more expert or experienced in some way and another who is seeking or has been identified as needing assistance. Although there is clear agreement that the relationship between therapist and client is important, there are differing ideas about the role that the relationship itself plays in the change process and what the nature and focus of these kinds of interactions ought to be.

Common Factors

The search for evidence promoting the efficacy of one type of psychotherapeutic treatment over another has yielded few consistent differences among theoretical approaches (Ahn & Wampold, 2001). Differences have tended to appear more so within theoretical approaches, with, for example, more skillful therapists getting consistently better results with their clients than do their less skilled counterparts using the same approach (Ogles, Anderson, & Lunnen, 1999). Such findings have fueled the search for common factors in effective therapies. The relationship factors that have received the greatest attention and empirical support are those originally delineated by Rogers (1959) in his person-centered (now often called client-centered) approach: (a) empathic understanding, (b) warmth and positive regard, and (c) congruence or authenticity (Lambert & Barley, 2002). It is important to note, and potentially instructive for the study of mentoring, that it is the clients' perception of these factors, rather than observer measurements, that are more consistently predictive of client outcomes (Lambert & Barley, 2002; Wampold, 2001). In addition, research has indicated that the therapeutic alliance is a significant component of the change process, regardless of the theoretical approach or specific techniques employed. This alliance is comprised of (a) the therapist's use of the above three "facilitative conditions," (b) the ability to effectively deal with ruptures in the relationship, and (c) mutual agreement on the goals or focus of the therapy (Lambert & Barley, 2002, p. 24).

Jerome Frank (Frank & Frank, 1991) also developed a common factors model based on his clinical experience, a synthesis of the psychotherapy literature, and a consideration of other forms of healing. In this model, psychotherapy is examined alongside other approaches to alleviating human suffering, such as spiritual healing, to identify a set of distinct features shared by these diverse forms of healing. These features are (a) "an emotionally-charged confiding relationship with a helping person," (b) "a healing setting," (c) "a rationale, conceptual scheme, or myth that provides a plausible explanation for the client's symptoms and prescribes a ritual or procedure for resolving them," and (d) "a ritual or procedure that requires the active participation of both client and therapist and that is believed by both to be the means of restoring the client's health" (Frank & Frank, 1991, pp. 40–43). Each of these four elements, present in every form of relationship-based healing approach, also may reflect important elements of mentoring, not all of which have been examined in prior research or highlighted in best practice suggestions for mentoring.

There may be other "common factors" not identified in the psychotherapy literature that are important for mentoring relationships. For example, having fun together, or enjoying one another's company, may be one such factor. Unlike psychotherapy, mentors and protégés engage in social activities, and for some youth, such activities may be not only an important part of building a strong relationship but also a welcome respite from difficult circumstances with which they are faced (Sipe, 1999). The research on social support has also begun to highlight engaging in mutually pleasurable social activities as a distinct aspect of important relationships, labeling it companionship and distinguishing it from other forms of social support that are sought out during times of distress (Sarason & Sarason, 2001).

To summarize, whatever the specific framework used, the research on psychotherapy clearly points to the importance of attending to certain common dimensions of helping or change-oriented relationships. Efforts to identify such common dimensions in mentoring could help distinguish more effective relationships from those that are only marginally helpful or even harmful. These factors may be closely aligned with those identified in the psychotherapy research, or they may prove to be somewhat different. It stands to reason that warmth, empathy, and genuineness are all likely to be central components of mentoring relationships that make a difference. However, given that mentoring is not necessarily a treatment or remedial approach, the importance of goal consensus, for example, may vary depending upon the nature of the mentoring relationship. Goal consensus could prove critical in a short-term program whose purpose is to foster the protégé's development of a specific set of prescribed skills, whereas a broad and general agreement about expectations of the nature of the relationship may be more fitting for an ongoing community-based or a natural mentoring relationship. Finally, given the highly social nature of many mentoring relationships, a distinct common factor may be the pleasure and support derived through experiences of companionship.

Therapeutic Strategies

Other psychotherapy research has focused on the contributions that the specific theory-based approaches to treatment and their accompanying techniques make to the change process. With estimates that there are more than 200 theoretical frameworks and an even larger number of accompanying sets of specific techniques in the literature on counseling and psychotherapy today (Hubble, Duncan, & Miller, 1999), it can be daunting to consider which approaches might be most fruitfully applied to the mentoring process. Many of the more long-standing approaches, each grounded in its own set of assumptions about change and growth and all of which have been applied in some way to the practice of mentoring, can be grouped into three major categories: interpersonal, cognitive-behavioral, and systems theories.

Interpersonal approaches, which incorporate many client-centered ideas and techniques, recognize that mental health concerns have numerous roots causes, but emphasize that they typically occur within an interpersonal context (Weissman, Markowitz, & Klerman, 2000). Focusing on the current interpersonal dynamics

within the therapy relationship itself is thought to offer as much, if not more, insight into how to assist the client with his or her concerns than does inquiring in detail about the past. The interpersonal therapist is to offer warmth and unconditional positive regard, along with gentle confrontation, in order to facilitate the client's development of more effective and satisfying ways of relating with others. The emphasis is on helping clients to identify and understand the connections between their symptoms and what is happening in their lives and in their primary relationships and to develop more adaptive ways of dealing with interpersonal problems. Importantly, the therapeutic relationship itself is viewed as a mechanism of change in this approach (Gelso & Hayes, 1998; Greenberg & Rice, 1997). Solving those problems in the therapy relationship that parallel interpersonal problems the client experiences in other important relationships can provide a model for and generate improvements in the client's functioning in these other relationships (Weissman et al., 2000). The potential impact of mentoring relationships can also be viewed through this interpersonal lens. For example, Rhodes (2002) has suggested that positive mentoring relationships can provide a place for youth to further develop their capacities for making and maintaining strong connections with others, and for youth with more troubled interpersonal histories, may challenge negative views of themselves or of relationships with adults and provide opportunities to develop more positive and prosocial ways of relating with others.

Cognitive-behavioral therapy (CBT) approaches, which are based on social learning and behavior theories, have received a great deal of attention in the research on psychotherapy outcomes, partly due to their clearly defined focus on identifying problems, setting clear goals, and employing particular sets of strategies in the change process (Gelso & Hayes, 1998; Hollon & Beck, 1994). These strategies include behavioral contracting, developing problem-solving skills, and changing internal cognitive patterns and self-statements. From a cognitive-behavioral perspective, learning is the key mechanism of change. A client's difficulties are believed to be rooted in maladaptive thought and behavior patterns, and the therapist assists the client with changing these through goal setting, education, modeling, and conditioning. With the potential that mentoring relationships hold for the development of a variety of new skills and ways of viewing oneself and the world, mentoring researchers and practitioners may benefit from lessons learned from CBT research and practice.

Another set of approaches with a long history and avid supporters, but less empirical study of effectiveness, is based on systems theory. Although most often associated with family therapy, systems theory in its many forms also can be applied when working with individuals and groups. Generally speaking, a systems approach takes into account the interdependent nature of human life. That is, we are continuously engaged in interactions with multiple interpersonal, institutional, and societal forces, all of which may be contributing in some way to the difficulties an individual may be experiencing (Bor, Legg, & Scher, 1996; Kurtz, 1996). No one person is considered to be the locus of a problem, and therefore all participants in a system and even the system itself may at any time become the focus of treatment. When using a systems approach in family therapy, for example, the therapist looks to the interactional patterns within the family and the forces outside the family when considering the appropriate intervention, which may be with the child or adolescent, the parents, a sibling, and/or the family as a whole. Given that mentoring relationships do not exist in a vacuum, rather they are formed and developed within specific interpersonal and cultural contexts, systems theory likely has much to offer the field of mentoring, both for researchers interested in understanding and accounting for change processes and for practitioners assisting mentors with navigating the larger relational terrain within which mentoring relationships reside.

Proponents of each of the major groups of theoretical approaches can point to some research that supports its efficacy. The growth in psychotherapy outcomes research has contributed to strong movements to encourage counselors to engage only in what have been called evidence-based or empirically supported treatment approaches (Deegear & Lawson, 2003). Yet consistently, meta-analyses culling and comparing studies that examine specific manualized treatment techniques have failed to find strong support for differences in efficacy among treatments. A repeated conclusion is that some form of psychotherapy is better than none but that the specific approach applied has not been as useful as hoped in predicting outcomes. More useful in explaining differential outcomes from psychotherapy have been differences within an approach as well as between approaches in the strength of the relationship or the therapeutic alliance. In view of the available findings, some have urged that research on the relative efficacy of approaches anchored to differing theoretical orientations to therapy be abandoned in favor of the continued pursuit of deepening our understanding of the common factors that appear across approaches (Hubble et al., 1999; Norcross, 2002; Wampold, 2001).

Another view is offered, however, when examining the research comparing the efficacy of different specific treatment approaches with an eye toward therapeutic allegiance, or the degree to which the therapist believes in the efficacy of the treatment approach rather than adherence to the specific interventions and techniques prescribed by a manual. One important common factor in the psychotherapy context, suggested by the work of Frank and Frank (1991), noted earlier, appears to be therapeutic allegiance, or the degree to which the therapist believes in the efficacy of the treatment approach and works from it consistently. Therapist allegiance to a treatment approach, any approach, has been found to be a greater determinant of client outcomes than the effectiveness of any one set of specific techniques. Indeed, the degree to which the therapist works consistently from a theoretical approach has been found to explain nearly 10% of variance in outcomes from therapy (Wampold, 2001).

In therapy, as in mentoring, helping professionals often may vary from directly prescribed tasks to meet what they perceive as the immediate needs of the client, their relationship, and the presenting problem. That is, from a common factors perspective, when the relationship is viewed as the means to healing, flexible application of techniques and theory may be more the rule than the exception in effective helping relationships. Norcross (2002) has suggested that psychotherapists pursue "empirically-supported relationships" rather than "empirically-supported treatments" (p. v), emphasizing that treatment approaches and therapy relationships cannot be coherently separated from one another.

Indeed, some studies have found that adhering too closely to a manualized treatment may interfere with the treatment relationship and have a negative impact on the client (Wampold, 2001). For this reason, many have advocated for technical eclecticism or integrative approaches (Arkowitz, 1992; Lampropoulos, 2000). Therapists who utilize this approach select from among a variety of techniques and apply those they think will work best given the individual client and presenting problem. Therapists may maintain some allegiance to a primary guiding theoretical framework while also drawing freely from others to tailor the therapy to the needs of the client (Lampropoulos, 2000). Such approaches have the potential to encompass and account for both the general factors in effective treatment and the role that specific techniques may play, while also being mindful of other aspects of the relationship, such as therapist factors like competence and allegiance; client factors, which include motivation and interest in the change process; and the match between therapist and client.

Given the community-based lay volunteer roots of mentoring, the field has been relatively free from debates about the relative effectiveness of different approaches. What little debate exists has tended to resemble the general factors versus specific ingredients debate discussed above, with some researchers emphasizing the importance of focusing on the development and maintenance of the relationship itself (Rhodes, Reddy, Roffman, & Grossman, in press) and others suggesting that a focus on the more instrumental aspects of the relationship and encouragement of specific kinds of changes or skill development are apt to be most fruitful (Darling, Hamilton, & Niego, 1994). Mentoring is likely to work differently with different youth. Youth who have enjoyed good relationships with their parents, for example, may be drawn to adults as role models and guides. In such cases, the relationship may focus more on the acquisition of skills and the advancement of critical thinking than on emotional issues (Darling,

Hamilton & Hames, 2003). On the other hand, youth who have experienced unsatisfactory or difficult parental ties may develop more intense bonds with their mentors to satisfy their social and emotional needs (Rhodes, Spencer, Keller, Liang, & Noam, 2004).

Structural Supports for Psychotherapy Relationships

Training in psychotherapy is broadly conceived as consisting of two major and essential components: didactic classroom teaching and supervision of students' application of learning in their fieldwork with clients (Matarazzo & Garner, 1992). Classroom teaching provides students with an initial general knowledge base and set of skills with which to begin, whereas supervision offers guidance around the issues particular to a given case, providing the developing therapist with opportunities to obtain alternative perspectives on what is happening in the psychotherapy relationship and to consider possible interventions, which can be particularly important during times of confusion (Watkins, 2003). In recent years, an additional key component of training and supervision has been the development of knowledge and skills needed to work effectively with diverse clients, particularly important for professionals who work with clients with racial, ethnic, cultural, and class backgrounds different from their own (Sue & Sue, 2003). There is little research that directly examines the contribution of therapist training and supervision to client outcomes (Beutler & Kendall, 1995; Watkins, 1998). Still, evidence has accumulated that training focused on developing specific relationship skills contributes to an increase in the proficiency of trainees (Stein & Lambert, 1995). Research has also indicated that supervision focused on the systematic development of specific skills can be particularly effective (Lambert & Ogles, 1997).

Although the literally thousands of hours required for professional education and training are not feasibly replicated by mentoring programs, a considerable investment up front and some support over the course of the relationship may significantly increase the effectiveness of youth mentoring relationships. Research on the training of paraprofessionals as counselors is instructive. Paraprofessionals selected, trained, and supervised by professional therapists have been found to be as effective as practicing professionals (Lambert & Bergin, 1994). In one meta-analysis (Hattie, Sharpley, & Rogers, 1984) examining comparisons of paraprofessionals with and without training, those who participated in an orientation followed by a minimum of 15 hours of training tended to be more effective than those without such training. It is important to note that there are many limitations to the existing knowledge base on the effectiveness of paraprofessionals, such as the lack of comparisons across the full range of mental health problems (Christensen & Jacobson, 1994).

Still, this research points to the potential importance of training for mentors, in the form of both up-front instruction and ongoing skill development, whether didactic or more supervisory in nature. Training and supervision that focuses on enhancing mentors' relationship-building skills and helping them navigate the complicated situations that may arise over time could be particularly beneficial. Opportunities for mentors to become involved and even incorporated into the day-to-day lives of their protégés, one of the strengths of mentoring versus psychotherapy, can add significant complexity to the role of mentor. Mentors may find themselves in the middle of situations that they feel uncomfortable being in or even ill equipped to handle, such as a family conflict, and may need guidance in how to respond to their protégés in ways that do not jeopardize the protégés' or parents' trust and thereby the mentoring relationship itself. Mentoring program staff should be readily available to provide opportunities for mentors, protégés, and family members to seek advice, guidance, and direct assistance when challenging situations arise.

RESEARCH

Research on mentoring relationships converges with the psychotherapy literature in terms of indicating that the relationship—in this instance, between mentor and protégé—is a primary catalyst for meaningful experiences and growth. In this section, we examine some of the research on mentoring relationships in light of the theory and research on psychotherapy relationships presented in the previous section, identifying the potentially instructive lessons and new questions the psychotherapy literature offers to the study of mentoring.

Common Factors

The presence of a strong emotional connection has been found repeatedly to be a distinguishing feature of mentoring relationships that are associated with better outcomes (DuBois & Neville, 1997; Grossman & Rhodes, 2002; LoSciuto, Rajala, Townsend, & Taylor, 1996). Indeed, recent research has suggested that the perceived benefits of mentoring relationships flow through relationship closeness for mentors and protégés, rather than being directly linked with variables such as amount of contact and types of shared activities (Parra, DuBois, Neville, & Pugh-Lilly, 2002). Such findings beg the question of whether some of the same general or relationship factors considered important for effective psychotherapy relationships are also at work in more effective mentoring relationships.

A recent study of natural mentoring relationships among college-aged women (Liang, Tracy, Taylor, & Williams, 2002) suggests that this may be the case. In this study, higher-quality mentoring relationships—distinguished by a higher composite score on measures of perceived authenticity, engagement, and empowerment—were associated with lower reported levels of loneliness and higher reported levels of self-esteem among participants. Confirmatory factor analyses indicated that these three facets were distinct but they were also highly interrelated. Together, these relational dimensions of mentoring were better predictors of outcomes than were some structural aspects of relationships, such as frequency of contact and length of relationship. The preceding study is limited for the present purposes by its focus on college-aged individuals, whose experiences in mentoring relationships may be different than those of younger, noncollege youth targeted by most mentoring programs. In an in-depth qualitative study of enduring mentoring relationships, authenticity, empathy, and companionship were found to be predominant themes (Spencer, 2004). Among this group of 24 matched pairs of male and female adolescents (aged 12–17) and adults, authenticity on the part of both mentor and protégé and the empathic response of the mentor facilitated the deepening of the relationship, and as these pairs' knowledge of one another grew and the relationships deepened, some youth became increasingly open to a wider range of assistance from their mentors, in some instances reporting accepting help in areas where they had previously refused any adult assistance.

An important difference between mentoring and psychotherapy is that the support, assistance, and guidance that mentoring can offer often occurs within the context of a more socially based relationship. Other possible common factors of effective mentoring relationships may be related to this more social dimension. Some research has indicated that pairs who engage in recreational activities (such as going out to eat) and in discussions across a range of topic areas, including the youth's relationships, also tended to report that the mentoring relationship was more effective (DuBois & Neville, 1997; DuBois, Neville, Parra, Pugh-Lilly, 2002). Another study concluded that for both community- and school-based mentoring programs, adult-youth pairs who engaged in social activities and shared in the decision-making process around what they would do together tended to have closer relationships (Herrera, Sipe, & McClanahan, 2000). A qualitative study (Morrow & Styles, 1995) emphasized the importance of the adult being open and responsive to the youth's particular interests and attending to the youth's need for fun in building and maintaining strong relationships. For mentoring relationships to grow closer and to last, it is likely that the pair must find some common ground so that their time together is pleasurable and satisfying to both in some ways.

Therapeutic Strategies

Little attention has yet been paid to the contribution of specific theoretical approaches to the effectiveness of mentoring relationships. Evidence for the potential importance of a systems approach is offered by two studies.

Rhodes, Grossman, and Resch (2000) found that improvements in self-worth and academic functioning derived from mentoring relationships were partially mediated through improvements in the protégés' relationships with their parents. This finding offers support for the idea that mentor relationships may contribute to improvements in the adolescents' other important relationships, which, in turn, enhance self-worth and academic performance. In addition, a metaanalysis of mentoring program evaluations found evidence of greater effectiveness for programs that involved the parents in some way than those that did not (DuBois, Holloway, Valentine, & Cooper, 2002).

Studies that compare the efficacy of different types of theory-based mentoring approaches are rare. Fo and O'Donnell (1974) compared three different approaches among a group of 42 youth invited to participate in a mentoring program called the Buddy System over the course of about 12 weeks. The goal of this program was to increase school attendance, and the researchers were interested in whether a relationship-based approach could be enhanced by social and behavioral reinforcements. Mentors were given one of the following three sets of instructions: (a) Focus on building a warm and positive mentoring relationship (noncontingent relationship), (b) offer a warm, positive relationship when the desired behavior on the part of the youth is present (social approval), or (c) offer both a warm, positive relationship and a material reward when the desired behavior on the part of the youth is present (social and material reinforcement). Youth were randomly assigned to one of the three treatment groups or to a control group (not matched with a mentor). There were no changes in school attendance among youth assigned to the noncontingent relationship group or to the control group of youth. However, school attendance improved for youth in both the social approval and the social and material reinforcement groups.

Davidson and Redner (1988; Davidson, Redner, Amdur, & Mitchell, 1990) paired 213 adolescents in the juvenile justice system with college-student volunteers. The adolescents were randomly assigned to work with volunteers trained in one of four following approaches: (a) a combination of relationship-building, behavioral-contracting and child advocacy techniques, (b) adding family-focused behavioral interventions to the first set of approaches, (c) an interpersonal approach in which volunteers were to focus on empathy, unconditional positive regard, good communication, and genuineness, and (d) a nonspecific attention group in which volunteers were given background information about delinquency and encouraged to apply their natural skills in their relationships with the adolescents. As in the research comparing different approaches to psychotherapy, youth paired with volunteers who received training and supervision in and implemented some coherent approach, whether it was more interpersonal or behavioral in nature, demonstrated less recidivism than did youth who were paired with volunteers who received some general information about delinquency and general suggestions about what they might do in their meetings with the adolescents.

Cavell and Hughes (2000) randomly assigned 62 children identified as aggressive by their teachers to one of two types of mentoring: (a) therapeutic mentoring in which mentors were provided background information about aggression in children, training in relationship-building and problem-solving skills, and weekly group supervision and (b) standard mentoring in which mentors received a 1-hour orientation and no supervision, although they were informed that they could contact program staff with any questions. The therapeutic mentoring was part of a larger set of interventions that participants in this group also received. There were no differences between these two groups with regard to changes in aggressive behaviors; however, youth in the therapeutic mentoring, on average, rated the quality of the mentoring relationship more highly.

Rather than supporting one specific approach over another, these findings suggest that having an approach is what may prove most helpful. Building a warm and empathic relationship may be a necessary but not sufficient ingredient for effective mentoring. Relying on mentors' natural skills may be missing an opportunity for mentoring programs to have a greater effect. Providing mentors with training in some of the behavior change and adaptive coping techniques offered in the counseling and psychotherapy literature may augment their efforts in critical ways.

Structural Supports for Mentoring Relationships

Assertions about the importance of mentor training for strong, positive relationships between mentors and youth matches are abundant (e.g., Grossman & Furano, 2002; Sipe, 1996), but the empirical evidence, although supportive to date, remains sparse. In one study of 98 community- and school-based programs in which 669 mentors were surveyed by telephone, mentors who received less than 2 hours of prematch training tended to report the lowest levels of closeness with their protégés, whereas those receiving at least 6 hours tended to report the highest, as did mentors who received some form of training or support after the match had begun (Herrera et al., 2000). In the study by Davidson and colleagues (Davidson & Redner, 1988; Davidson et al., 1990), described above in the section on specific strategies, the mentors in the more effective treatment groups received a total of 80 hours of training and supervision over the course of 26 weeks, whereas the mentors in the least effective group received considerably less training—only 6 hours prematch—and this training consisted solely of background information and general guidelines. In the Cavell and Hughes (2000) study examining an intervention program for aggressive youth, the protégés of mentors who received 18 hours of prematch training and participated in a weekly supervision group rated the quality of their relationships more highly on average than did the protégés of mentors who received only 1 hour of prematch training and no regular ongoing supervision. In the meta-analysis of mentoring program evaluations by DuBois and colleagues (DuBois, Holloway, et al., 2002), there was evidence of greater effectiveness for programs that provided ongoing training for the mentors as well as for those that provided structured activities for the matches. Program use of supervision and mentor support groups did not turn out to be significant predictors of effectiveness. However, these practices did contribute to an overall index of theory-based practices, on which higher scores were associated with stronger program effects.

The amount and intensity of prematch and ongoing training mentors should receive has yet to be carefully considered. Although we would not expect mentors to undertake the kind of rigorous training that someone who is entering the counseling profession engages in, the existing empirical evidence does suggest that an up-front investment and some type of continued training may increase the effectiveness of the mentoring relationship. To our knowledge, there are currently no studies systematically examining whether specific amounts and types of training and supervision translate into better youth outcomes, a question that is only minimally addressed in the psychotherapy literature. However, as discussed previously, there is some evidence that training and supervision specifically focused on the development of relationship skills can pay off in psychotherapy training (Lambert & Ogles, 1997; Stein & Lambert, 1995). The possible benefits of such training for mentoring programs warrant serious future attention.

PRACTICE

The psychotherapy theory and research literature, like that on mentoring, is practice driven in that these knowledge-building efforts are focused on informing and improving the services delivered to clients. In this section, we examine current mentoring program practices from within the frame offered by the psychotherapy theory and research discussed thus far, to consider what new light this body of knowledge may shed on mentoring.

Common Factors

Building a strong relationship has long been a concern of many mentoring programs, and in recent years, greater effort has been directed toward providing specific guidance for mentors to help them accomplish this goal. Training and resource guides for new mentors have been made widely available through the Internet (Jucovy, 2001a, 2001b; National Mentoring Partnership's Learn to Mentor Training, n.d.). Typically, these guides include general tips about what to expect and how to build relationships and communicate effectively with youth. Yet most materials largely skim the surface of what is involved in forming and sustaining close connections, employing a commonsense approach and relying heavily on anecdotes. The psychotherapy literature remains largely an untapped resource for more detailed, complex, and sophisticated approaches to working with mentors to cultivate their relationship skills. To address this need, programs and strategies developed for training and supervising both professional therapists and paraprofessional counselors that have been effective could potentially be modified and applied to mentoring.

Therapeutic Strategies

Although many programs do stress the importance of building a strong relationship, few mentoring programs are explicitly applying a coherent theoretical approach to the mentoring process. One mentoring program, Across Ages (Taylor, LoSciuto, Fox, Hilbert, & Sonkowsky, 1999), provides an example of a program that is successfully utilizing what could be considered an eclectic or integrative approach from a counseling or psychotherapy perspective. This program matches youth with older adults as a part of a multicomponent intervention program in schools. It requires volunteer mentors to participate in a 2-day training session prior to being matched with a child. This training includes general information about youth development as well as (a) how to work with youth to set goals (a cognitive-behavioral approach), (b) building relationships with the youth's family members and key school personnel (a strategy based on principles of systems theory), and (c) strategies for how to build relationships with youth and enhance the mentor's own listening and communication skills (arguably an interpersonal approach). In the 4 hours a week they are asked to spend with their protégés, mentors are encouraged to focus on building trust and effective communication as they engage in a variety of activities, such as working on class projects or attending school sporting events. By joining attention to fostering mentors' relationship-building skills with training and guidance in how to use more focused change-directed approaches, this program illustrates the potential for effectively integrating a common factors approach with the use of specific theoretically and empirically informed techniques.

Prematch Training and Ongoing Support for Mentoring Relationships

There is a general consensus in the practice community that mentoring programs should offer some form of training and support. The revised and updated *Elements of Effective Practice* (2003), published by MENTOR, a national mentoring partnership, emphasizes the need for the orientation, training, and ongoing supervision of mentors as well as the ongoing monitoring of mentoring relationships. In one survey of almost 800 mentoring programs, approximately 80% of the programs reported that they do require mentors to attend an orientation and complete some type of prematch training, although the total amount of time spent in these activities varied greatly (Sipe & Roder, 1999). In another survey of 1,762 programs (Manza, 2003), 76% of programs reported providing orientation and training, and 94% offered some type of continuing support to matches. However, programs vary considerably in the amount of training and support offered to the paired mentors and protégés. Caseworker involvement in the monitoring of matches can vary from weekly contact to less than one phone call per month (Rhodes, 2002). Good mentoring, like good psychotherapy, may require application of a cluster of skills similar to those that have been identified as important for psychotherapy, including relationship building and maintenance, the capacity to contextualize individual problems, strong teaching and problem-solving skills, and the ability to engage with youth around strong emotions. Although programs seem well aware of the importance of many of these skills, few are aggressively putting the kinds of supports in place that are likely to encourage the development of the full depth and range of these skills.

Future Directions

Synthesis

The counseling and psychotherapy literatures provide important insights into the contribution that building strong working relationships may make to effective mentoring relationships. The debate about the relative contribution of relationship factors and specific approaches and techniques in the psychotherapy literature, and the research that has addressed this concern, offers a potentially valuable lesson for the study of similar issues as they pertain to youth mentoring. Specifically, it seems that both of these dimensions of helping relationships may be important, albeit perhaps in different ways depending on the needs and interests of the person seeking guidance or assistance. Furthermore, the supervision model developed to support psychotherapy relationships clearly seems relevant to the practice of youth mentoring, as it offers the potential for continuous training and assistance with the rocky moments that may inevitably crop up over time in the course of relationships. Yet to date, empirical examination of support for these assumptions regarding the applicability of concepts and findings from the psychotherapy literature has been limited. Thus, although initial findings are in many ways encouraging, they do not offer the in-depth and systematic investigation that is needed. The ways in which different concepts and strategies borrowed from psychotherapy may need to be refined or expanded to translate effectively to mentoring is a salient concern in this regard. The intriguing evidence that unlike psychotherapy, good mentoring also may require being able to be a good social partner or companion for a young person is illustrative of the importance of not ignoring the need for careful study of the translation process no matter how compelling or intuitive the links may seem to be.

Recommendations for Research

Examining theory and research from the counseling and psychotherapy literature, in combination with the related literature on youth mentoring, highlights three major areas for further study.

1. *Investigate which common factors promote the development of effective mentoring relationships.* We need to build on our knowledge of the elements that contribute to the formation of close mentoring relationships, such as

regular contact over time, by also focusing on identifying some of the specific process-level factors that may be critical for good mentoring relationships, both formal and natural. The psychotherapy literature would suggest that we examine the role that empathic understanding, authenticity, warmth, and positive regard may play, and this is supported by recent studies examining the relational dimensions of mentoring. Measures of these dimensions in therapy relationships could likely be adopted and adapted for the study of mentoring (see, e.g., Cavell & Hughes, 2000).

Still, it would be unwise to limit ourselves to only those common factors identified in the psychotherapy literature. Rather, we should remain open to the possibility that there may be other factors, perhaps both unique to and common across mentoring relationships, whether formal or natural. Qualitative studies that focus on the intricacies of mentoring relationships, what youth identify as mattering the most to them, and what mentors do and how they think about what they do in their relationships with youth could help identify new common factors to examine in relation to mentoring. Furthermore, sources of data should be selected that are tailored specifically to mentoring, in which the perspectives of not only mentor and protégé but also others such as caregivers and program staff may be essential. Using methods such as structural equation modeling would allow for the inclusion of measures from multiple sources (e.g., mentor, protégé, family members, program staff) in the effort to identify and examine the relative contributions of different relational processes. Longitudinal studies are particularly needed in order to deepen our understanding of factors that may be common to close and effective mentoring relationships and how these develop, are sustained, and change over time.

2. *Identify the factors distinguishing particularly effective mentors.* Another priority for future research should be to further identify what distinguishes effective mentors. We should heed the cautionary tale offered by the psychotherapy literature and not engage in our own theory wars, but rather seek to understand what is happening when mentoring is going well. Phenomenological studies offering in-depth

qualitative examinations of the mentoring process and what particularly good mentors do could prove particularly informative.

It seems likely that mentors who attend to building and maintaining their relationships with their protégés and who offer helpful, appropriately timed, and effective advice and guidance will prove more effective. We need to go beyond such basic understandings, however, to identify what specific strategies, gleaned from the full range of approaches outlined in the counseling and psychotherapy literature, are most helpful to mentors in their efforts to build close and growth-promoting relationships with youth. The psychotherapy research would suggest that some common factors across many different types of mentoring programs are likely to emerge and that we also might expect to see evidence of benefits of specific strategies depending on the goals of the mentoring program, youth served, and mentors recruited. Psychotherapy research has tended to focus on either the treatment approach or the therapist, with each tending to occlude the contributions of the other (Elkin, 1999). Research in programs where mentors are matched with more than one protégé would offer opportunities to focus both on the potential contribution of the specific approach taken and on the skills and personal characteristics of the mentors.

3. *Identify what specific types and amounts of mentor training and match supports contribute to the formation and maintenance of effective mentoring relationships in which contexts.* The psychotherapy literature indicates that training and supervision can increase the skills of professionals and paraprofessionals alike. Similar evaluations of existing efforts toward training mentors and providing support to mentoring relationships are much needed. There is evidence to suggest these efforts contribute to the effectiveness of mentoring programs, but greater specificity about (a) how much and what types of training and support make the greatest difference in which types of mentoring programs and (b) whether and how much such efforts contribute positive outcomes for youth have yet to be delineated. The psychotherapy literature would suggest that both prematch and ongoing didactic training as well as supervision,

whether in the form of individual contact with program case managers or in structured group settings, are all good candidates for investigation. That said, this literature offers little guidance in terms of how much training and supervision would be appropriate to consider. The existing research on training in the mentoring literature suggests that more may be better, with the limited research indicating that fewer than 6 hours of training may not be as helpful—but how much more is unclear, as is what combination of up-front, early in the match, or ongoing training and support is likely to prove most effective, making these all important areas for further investigation.

Recommendations for Practice

1. *Promoting the development of a strong and close relationship.* Mentoring programs would be wise to heed the overwhelming evidence from the research on counseling and psychotherapy that demonstrates the importance of a strong relationship to the change process. Research specific to mentoring is beginning to yield convergent findings, with closer and more enduring relationships associated with greater positive outcomes for youth involved in them. Whatever the focus of the mentoring relationship, whether short-term tutoring or long-term emotional support, some attention should be given to building a working relationship with the protégé. Furthermore, the research on psychotherapy indicates that the basic relationship skills can be taught, with some limited evidence that such training is associated with better client outcomes (Stein & Lambert, 1995). Devoting time up front to training mentors in basic relationship-building skills may help prevent early terminations, which can be devastating for already vulnerable youth. That said, it is also important to consider the length of the mentoring relationship, and if it is to be of a relatively short-term nature, the relationship structure should match this intention, with the protégé knowing when and how the relationship is to end, to prevent the building up of expectations that will not be met. Basic guides for beginning counselors (e.g., Patterson & Welfel, 2000) could serve as valuable resources for topics to be considered, and approaches such as

microcounseling (Daniels, Rigazio-Digilio, & Ivey, 1997) could be drawn from and modified to inform training procedures.

2. *Consider the use of appropriate theory-based and empirically supported approaches to change offered by the counseling and psychotherapy literature.* There is as yet little guidance as to which specific change-directed approaches may be most effective. Furthermore, there is strong evidence in the psychotherapy literature to caution us against advocating for one particular approach over another, and this is further bolstered by the current dearth of comparative study of specific approaches within the field of mentoring. Still, mentoring programs should examine the relevant clinical literature that focuses more specifically on the kinds of problems or concerns that youth being served present with, to determine which specific approaches have the potential to add to the effectiveness of the program.

3. *Offer prematch and ongoing training and supervision to mentors.* Mentor relationships, like all relationships, can be hard work, and disruptions and even impasses may be part of the process. Although the research in this area is in its nascence, intensive, preferably multisession, prematch training that provides not only an orientation to the program but also information and guidance around forging and maintaining a strong and productive relationship with a young person is likely to be a worthwhile investment. Including content on diversity issues, particularly around understanding and effectively dealing with racial, ethnic, cultural, and class differences, may be particularly important for some programs. In addition, for programs serving youth with specific concerns (i.e., aggression, having a parent who is incarcerated), providing mentors with background information about issues such as what is known about the particular stresses or relational styles of youth in these groups would augment more general approaches to training. In addition to training prior to the match, providing structured, ongoing support or supervision to mentors and protégés, and to the families of youth, such as monthly telephone check-ins or mentor supervision groups, particularly in the early stages

when the relationship is forming, could prove critical to increasing the chances that the relationship will take hold and endure.

REFERENCES

Ahn, H., & Wampold, B. E. (2001). Where oh where are the specific ingredients? A meta-analysis of component studies in counseling and psychotherapy. *Journal of Counseling Psychology, 48,* 251–257.

Arkowitz, H. (1992). Integrative theories of therapy. In D. K. Freedheim (Ed.), *History of psychotherapy: A century of change* (pp. 261–303). Washington, DC: American Psychological Association.

Beutler, L. E., & Kendall, P. C. (1995). Introduction to the special section: The case for training in the provision of psychological therapy. *Journal of Consulting and Clinical Psychology, 63,* 179–181.

Bor, R., Legg, C., & Scher, I. (1996). The systems paradigm. In R. Woolfe & W. Dryden (Eds.), *Handbook of counselling psychology* (pp. 240–257). London: Sage.

Cavell, T. A., & Hughes, J. N. (2000). Secondary prevention as context for assessing change processes in aggressive children. *Journal of School Psychology, 38,* 199–235.

Christensen, A., & Jacobson, N. S. (1994). Who (or what) can do psychotherapy: The status and challenge of the nonprofessional therapies. *Psychological Science, 5,* 8–14.

Daniels, T. G., Rigazio-Digilio, S. A., & Ivey, A. E. (1997). Microcounseling: A training and supervision paradigm for the helping professions. In C. E. Watkins (Ed.), *Handbook of psychotherapy supervision* (pp. 277–295). New York: Wiley.

Darling, N., Hamilton, S. F., & Hames, K. (2003). Relationships outside the family: Unrelated adults. In G. R. Adams & M. D. Berzonsky (Eds.), *Blackwell handbook of adolescence* (pp. 349–370). Oxford, UK: Blackwell.

Darling, N., Hamilton, S. F., & Niego, S. (1994). Adolescents' relations with adults outside the family. In R. Montemayor, G. R. Adams, & T. P. Gullotta (Eds.), *Personal relationships during adolescence* (pp. 216–235). Thousand Oaks, CA: Sage.

Davidson, W. S., & Redner, R. (1988). The prevention of juvenile delinquency: Diversion from the juvenile justice system. In R. S. Price, E. L. Cowen, R. P. Lorion, & J. Ramos-McKay (Eds.), *14 ounces of prevention: A casebook for practitioners.* Washington, DC: American Psychological Association.

Davidson, W. S., Redner, R., Amdur, R., & Mitchell, C. M. (1990). *Alternative treatments for troubled youth: The case of diversion from the justice system.* New York: Plenum Press.

Deegear, J., & Lawson, D. M. (2003). The utility of empirically supported treatments. *Professional Psychology: Research and Practice, 34,* 271–277.

DuBois, D. L., Holloway, B. E., Valentine, J. C., & Cooper, H. (2002). Effectiveness of mentoring programs for youth: A meta-analytic review. *American Journal of Community Psychology, 30,* 157–197.

DuBois, D. L., & Neville, H. A. (1997). Youth mentoring: Investigation of relationship characteristics and perceived benefits. *Journal of Community Psychology, 25,* 227–234.

DuBois, D. L., Neville, H. A., Parra, G. R., & Pugh-Lilly, A. O. (2002). Testing a new model of mentoring. In G. G. Noam (Ed. in chief) & J. E. Rhodes (Ed.), *A critical view of youth mentoring (New Directions for Youth Development: Theory, Research, and Practice, No. 93,* pp. 21–57). San Francisco: Jossey-Bass.

Elkin, I. (1999). A major dilemma in psychotherapy outcome research: Disentangling therapists from therapies. *Clinical Psychology: Science and Practice, 61,* 10–32.

Fo, W. S., & O'Donnell, C. R. (1974). The Buddy System: Relationship and contingency conditions in a community intervention program for youth with nonprofessionals as behavior change agents. *Journal of Consulting and Clinical Psychology, 42,* 163–169.

Frank, J. D., & Frank, J. B. (1991). *Persuasion and healing: A comparative study of psychotherapy.* Baltimore: Johns Hopkins University Press.

Gelso, C. J., & Hayes, J. A. (Eds.). (1998). *The psychotherapy relationship: Theory, research, and practice.* New York: Wiley.

Greenberg, L. S., & Rice, L. N. (1997). Humanistic approaches to psychotherapy. In P. L. Wachtel & S. B. Messner (Eds.), *Theories of psychotherapy: Origins and evolution* (pp. 97–139). Washington, DC: American Psychological Association.

Grossman, J. B., & Furano, K. (2002). *Making the most of volunteers.* Philadelphia: Public/Private Ventures.

Grossman, J. B., & Rhodes, J. E. (2002). The test of time: Predictors and effects of duration in youth mentoring programs. *American Journal of Community Psychology, 30,* 199–219.

Hattie, J. A., Sharpley, C. F., & Rogers, H. J. (1984). Comparative effectiveness of professional and paraprofessional helpers. *Psychological Bulletin, 95,* 534–541.

Herrera, C., Sipe, C. L., & McClanahan, W. S. (2000). *Mentoring school-age children: Relationship development in community-based and school-based programs.* Philadelphia: Public/Private Ventures. (Published in collaboration with MENTOR/National Mentoring Partnership, Alexandria, VA)

Hollon, S. D., & Beck, A. T. (1994). Cognitive and cognitive-behavioral therapies. In A. E. Bergin & S. L. Garfield (Eds.), *Handbook of psychotherapy and behavior change* (pp. 428–466). New York: Wiley.

Hubble, M. A., Duncan, B. L., & Miller, S. D. (Eds.). (1999). *The heart and soul of change: What works in therapy.* Washington, DC: American Psychological Association.

Jucovy, L. (2001a). *Building relationships: A guide for new mentors.* Philadelphia: Public/Private Ventures.

Jucovy, L. (2001b). *Training new mentors.* Philadelphia: Public/Private Ventures.

Kurtz, R. R. (1996). Family systems theory: A brief review for the clinician. *Journal of Psychological Practice, 2*(2), 21–28.

Lambert, M. J., & Barley, D. E. (2002). Research summary on the therapeutic relationship and psychotherapy outcome. In J. C. Norcross (Ed.), *Psychotherapy relationships that work: Therapist contributions to responsiveness to patients* (pp. 17–32). New York: Oxford University Press.

Lambert, M. J., & Bergin, A. E. (1994). The effectiveness of psychotherapy. In A. E. Bergin & S. L. Garfield (Eds.), *Handbook of psychotherapy and behavior change* (pp. 143–189). New York: Wiley.

Lambert, M. J., & Ogles, B. M. (1997). The effectiveness of psychotherapy supervision. In C. E. Watkins (Ed.), *Handbook of psychotherapy supervision* (pp. 421–446). New York: Wiley.

Lampropoulos, G. K. (2000). Evolving psychotherapy integration: Eclectic selection and prescriptive applications of common factors in therapy. *Psychotherapy, 37,* 285–297.

Liang, B., Tracy, A. J., Taylor, C. A., & Williams, L. M. (2002). Mentoring college-age women: A relational approach. *American Journal of Community Psychology, 30,* 271–288.

LoSciuto, L., Rajala, A. K., Townsend, T. N., & Taylor, A. S. (1996). An outcome evaluation of Across Ages: An intergenerational mentoring approach to drug prevention. *Journal of Adolescent Research, 11,* 116–129.

Manza, G. (2003, October). *The state of mentoring 2003.* Paper presented at the National Research Summit on Mentoring, Kansas City, MO.

Matarazzo, R. G., & Garner, A. M. (1992). Research on training for psychotherapy. In D. K. Freedheim (Ed.), *History of psychotherapy: A century of change* (pp. 850–877). Washington, DC: American Psychological Association.

MENTOR/National Mentoring Partnership. (2003). *Elements of effective practice* (2nd ed.). Alexandria, VA: Author.

Morrow, K. V., & Styles, M. B. (1995). *Building relationships with youth in program settings: A study of Big Brothers/Big Sisters.* Philadelphia: Public/Private Ventures.

National Mentoring Partnership's Learn to Mentor Training. (n.d.). Retrieved October 31, 2003, from http://www.mentoring.org/training/TMT/index.adp

Norcross, J. C. (Ed.). (2002). *Psychotherapy relationships that work.* New York: Oxford University Press.

Ogles, B. M., Anderson, T., & Lunnen, K. M. (1999). The contribution of models and techniques to therapeutic efficacy: Contradictions between professional trends and clinical research. In M. A. Hubble, B. L. Duncan, & S. D. Miller (Eds.), *The heart and soul of change: What works in therapy* (pp. 201–225). Washington, DC: American Psychological Association.

Parra, G. R., DuBois, D. L., Neville, H. A., Pugh-Lilly, A. O., & Povinelli, N. (2002). Mentoring relationships for youth: Investigation of a process-oriented model. *Journal of Community Psychology, 30,* 367–388.

Patterson, L. E., & Welfel, E. R. (2000). *The counseling process.* Belmont, CA: Wadsworth.

Rhodes, J. E. (2002). *Stand by me: The risks and rewards of mentoring today's youth.* Cambridge, MA: Harvard University Press.

Rhodes, J. E., Grossman, J. B., & Resch, N. R. (2000). Agents of change: Pathways through which mentoring relationships influence adolescents' academic adjustment. *Child Development, 71,* 1662–1671.

Rhodes, J. E., Spencer, R., Keller, T. E., Liang, B., & Noam, G. (2004). *A model for the influence of mentoring relationships on youth development.* Manuscript submitted for publication.

Rhodes, J. Reddy, R., Roffman, J., & Grossman, J. (in press). Promoting successful youth mentoring relationships: A preliminary screening questionnaire. *Journal of Primary Prevention.*

Rogers, C. R. (1959). A theory of therapy, personality and interpersonal relationships. In S. Koch (Ed.), *Psychology: A study of a science* (pp. 184–256). New York: McGraw-Hill.

Sarason, B. R., & Sarason, I. G. (2001). Ongoing aspects of relationships and health outcomes: Social support, social control, companionship, and relationship meaning. In J. Harvey & A. Wenzel (Eds.), *Close romantic relationships: Maintenance and enhancement* (pp. 277–298). Mahwah, NJ: Erlbaum.

Sipe, C. L. (1996). *Mentoring: A synthesis of the P/PV's research: 1988–1995.* Philadelphia: Public/Private Ventures.

Sipe, C. L. (1999). Mentoring adolescents: What have we learned? In J. B. Grossman (Ed.), *Contemporary issues in mentoring* (pp. 10–23). Philadelphia: Public/Private Ventures.

Sipe, C. L., & Roder, A. E. (1999). *Mentoring school-age children: A classification of programs.* Philadelphia: Public/Private Ventures. (Published in collaboration with MENTOR/National Mentoring Partnership, Alexandria, VA)

Spencer, R. (2004). *Getting to the heart of the mentoring process: An in-depth interview study with adolescents and their adult mentors.* Manuscript submitted for publication.

Stein, D. M., & Lambert, M. J. (1995). Graduate training in psychotherapy: Are therapy outcomes enhanced? *Journal of Consulting and Clinical Psychology, 63,* 182–196.

Sue, D. W., & Sue, D. (2003). *Counseling the culturally diverse: Theory and practice* (4th ed.). New York: Wiley.

Taylor, A. S., LoSciuto, L., Fox, M., Hilbert, S. M., & Sonkowsky, M. (1999). The mentoring factor: Evaluation of the Across Ages' intergenerational approach to drug abuse prevention. *Child and Youth Services, 20*(1–2), 77–99.

Wampold, B. (2001). *The great psychotherapy debate: Models, methods, and findings.* Mahwah, NJ: Erlbaum.

Watkins, C. E. (1998). Psychotherapy supervision in the 21st century: Some pressing needs and impressing possibilities. *Journal of Psychotherapy Practice and Research, 7,* 93–101.

Watkins, C. E. (2003). Defining psychotherapy supervision and understanding supervisor functioning. In C. E. Watkins (Ed.), *Handbook of psychotherapy supervision* (pp. 3–10). New York: Wiley.

Weissman, M. M., Markowitz, J. C., & Klerman, G. L. (2000). *Comprehensive guide to interpersonal psychotherapy.* New York: Basic Books.

9

MENTORING RELATIONSHIPS AND SOCIAL SUPPORT

MANUEL BARRERA, JR., AND DARYA D. BONDS

INTRODUCTION

There are intimate connections between the concepts of social support and mentoring. When Rhodes (2002) defined a mentoring relationship as one in which "the adult provides ongoing *guidance, instruction, and encouragement* aimed at developing the competence and character of the protégé" (p. 3, italics added), she described, in essence, the central components of social support. During the course of a mentoring relationship, mentors and mentees participate in a variety of activities that often include recreation and discussions about the mundane as well as emotionally charged topics. Mentors might teach skills or serve as companions for attending movies and concerts. In our attempt to understand the process and outcomes of mentoring, we believe that social support concepts provide a useful framework for describing what occurs in mentoring and how it might affect youth development. It also is true that mentoring programs are interventions for creating meaningful changes in the social support that youth receive. In reviews of intervention strategies that make effective use of social support concepts, mentoring programs are

identified as prominent examples (Barrera & Prelow, 2000; Eckenrode & Hamilton, 2000).

The purpose of this chapter is to consider how theory and research findings on social support could inform our understanding of youth mentoring. Relevant research and practices on mentoring are reviewed that are pertinent to the topic of social support. Finally, recommendations are made for future research and practice.

CONCEPTS AND TERMINOLOGY

Volumes have been written about the fundamentals and intricacies of social support (e.g., Belle, 1989; Cohen, Underwood, & Gottlieb, 2000; Vaux, 1988). Of particular value to the field of mentoring are typologies that attempt to capture the overt behavioral manifestations of support. Barrera and Ainlay (1983) proposed a behavioral typology that included (a) material aid—provisions of material objects, (b) physical assistance—sharing tasks, (c) nondirective support—listening, expressions of caring, being with a person during a time of need, (d) directive guidance—giving advice, guidance,

The second author was funded by a postdoctoral fellowship through the National Institute of Mental Health grant (T32-MH18387).

information, instruction, and (e) social participation—sharing fun and relaxing activities. This typology has attractive features for mentoring research and practice. First, it includes the category of social participation and thus an explicit acknowledgment of shared leisure activities as legitimate supportive acts that are beneficial in their own right and that often set the stage for building close relationships. Second, this typology and others like it could facilitate research that describes what mentors do (cf. Rhodes, Ebert, & Fischer, 1992) and the supportive mentoring behaviors that are most effective. Such research, in turn, could inform the training of mentors and the development of intervention manuals that specify mentor behaviors that promote positive child development. Third, the typology provides terminology (e.g., nondirective support, directive guidance) that can be used to describe the supportive behaviors that are studied in mentoring research and that are incorporated in mentoring interventions. This terminology is used throughout this chapter.

THEORY

Theories of social support could play a vital role in mentoring research and practice. There is not a single, unified formal theory of social support that could explain the full range of mechanisms underlying mentoring. There are, however, several theoretical perspectives that could advance our understanding of mentoring. In the following section, we will consider two theoretical perspectives.

Provisions of Social Relationships

Weiss (1973) articulated a theory of social relationships that had three components: (a) a specification of the functions of social relationships, (b) the deficits that result when these functions are not part of one's social life, and (c) specificity in the functions that are provided by certain types of relationships, such as spouses or same-sex friends. He identified five functions of social relationships: (a) emotional integration (emotions are expressed and stabilized in the relationship), (b) social integration

(companionship and exchanges around mutual interests are made), (c) opportunity for nurturance, (d) reassurance of worth, and (e) provision of assistance. He also speculated that the absence of certain functions leads to specific deficits or forms of distress. Weiss (1973) wrote,

> We conjecture that deficits and symptoms are associated in this way: The absence of emotional integration results in loneliness; of social integration in boredom; of opportunity for nurturance in a sense of emptiness or pointlessness; of reassurance of worth in a sense of worthlessness; and of assistance in a sense of vulnerability or of having been abandoned. (p. 110)

Weiss (1973) reported research findings from qualitative studies that were consistent with the idea that particular types of relationships might serve specific functions that are unlikely to be served by other types of social ties. Based on research conducted with women who participated in the organization Parents Without Partners, Weiss concluded that friendships for those women, no matter how close, did not compensate for the loss of a husband. Conversely, in studying families that had relocated to new communities from distant states, he noted that husbands in good marriages did not compensate for their wives' loss of close women friends. Weiss speculated that husbands provided emotional integration, but not social integration. In contrast, he thought that friends provided social integration, but not emotional integration.

There are potential contributions of this theory for understanding mentoring relationships. First, Weiss's specification of functions informs us of the range of possible social functions that mentors might provide to mentees. Emotional integration, social integration, reassurance of worth, and provision of assistance are functions that could be supplied by mentors to their mentees. Weiss's perspective even identified a function of social relationships, "opportunity for nurturance," that captures an important benefit that many mentors might derive from their social relationships with mentees. That function might motivate adults to become mentors and sustain their long-term commitments to their mentees. Perhaps the most provocative feature of Weiss's perspective is his assertion about specificity in the functions of social relationships and its implications for mentoring. If we extend his observation about the specificity of relationships with spouses and friends, we might wonder whether support from mentors can compensate for the absence of certain types of relationships, such as parents or peers.

Attachment and Internal Models of Social Behavior

Bowlby (1969) referred to attachment to explain the affective bond that develops between an attachment figure and a child that facilitates the development of internal working models of the self and others. Internal working models are representations of the self and others based on beliefs and expectations derived from experiences with one's primary attachment figure (Bretherton, 1985). According to this theory, when the attachment figure is consistently warm and appropriately responsive to the child's signals, the child tends to develop positive internal working models of the self and others.

One hypothesis that emerges from this theory is that a child's positive experience with early attachment figures increases his or her receptivity to natural mentoring relationships later in life. This theory also leads to the prediction that a positive early attachment relationship will increase the chances that a youth will be receptive to a volunteer mentoring intervention. Therefore, attachment status might moderate the effects of mentoring such that mentoring programs could be more effective for youth with secure attachments than they could be for youth with insecure attachments.

RESEARCH

We organize our review of research on social support and mentoring around four topics: (a) the types of support that are provided in mentoring relationships, (b) the effects of social support on the formation of mentoring relationships, (c) the role of social support in mediating

the beneficial effects of mentoring relationships for youth, and (d) the role of social support in moderating the effects of mentoring.

Types of Support Provided in Mentoring Relationships

Support Types Described in Definitions of Natural Mentors

In the literature, there is a basic distinction between natural mentors (who exist within normal relationships between youth and family, friends, neighbors, and professionals) and volunteer mentors (who come into the lives of youth through community-based programs). Investigations of natural mentors routinely include the actual instructions that were used to help youth identify such individuals in their lives. For example, Rhodes, Contreras, and Mangelsdorf (1994) defined a mentor as an adult who met the following criteria:

> 1) That you could count on this person to be there for you, 2) that he or she believes in and cares deeply about you, 3) that he or she inspires you to do your best, and 4) that knowing him or her has really influenced what you do and the choices you make. (p. 216)

In another study, a natural mentor was defined as a person "you can go to for support and guidance or if you need to make an important decision, or who inspires you to do your best" (Zimmerman, Bingenheimer, & Notaro, 2002, p. 226). Implied in both of these definitions are tangible assistance, nondirective support, and directive guidance (terms that were introduced at the beginning of this chapter). These three support functions also were identified through factor analytic research on supportive behaviors (Barrera & Ainlay, 1983; Finch et al., 1997). It was somewhat surprising that a fourth support function, positive social interaction, has not been incorporated explicitly into definitions of natural mentors because that category includes things such as shared recreation and leisure activities, activities that are prominent in volunteer mentoring programs (Parra, DuBois, Neville, Pugh-Lilly, & Povinelli, 2002). It is clear, however, that the provision of basic support functions is what researchers use for the most part to define a natural mentor.

Support Types Provided by Mentors

Several studies used procedures that, first, had research participants identify natural mentors and then asked participants to rate the support functions that natural mentors provided to them (Beam, Chen, & Greenberger, 2002; Cavell, Meehan, Heffer, & Holladay 2002; Rhodes et al., 1992; Rhodes et al., 1994; Sanchez & Reyes, 1999). Rhodes et al. (1992) studied the social support of 129 young African American mothers. Mentors were viewed as active providers of emotional support (72.4%), cognitive guidance (79.3%), positive feedback (82.8%), and tangible assistance (87.9%). Somewhat smaller, although still substantial, percentages of mentors were rated as providers of child care assistance (65.5%) and social participation (44.8%). Similarly, in a study of 54 Latina adolescent mothers (Rhodes et al., 1994), high percentages of mentors were reported to provide emotional support (78.9%), cognitive guidance (84.2%), positive feedback (94.7%), and parenting support (84.2%). Relatively less often, mentors were identified as sources of tangible assistance (57.9%), child care assistance (42.1%), and social participation (31.6%). Similar to the results of those studies with African American and Latina young mothers, research with 11th-grade students also found that more than 80% of those who had mentors reported that their mentors showed respect, provided emotional support, were available for talking, and supported various activities in which the mentees were engaged (Beam et al., 2002).

It appears that the natural mentors of adolescents in these studies typically engage in all the support behaviors identified by Barrera and Ainlay (1983) with the possible exception of social participation (activities for relaxation and recreation). However, these relatively modest reports of social participation with mentors of older adolescents might be a function of mentee age. In childhood recollections of natural mentor activities, social participation (recreation, 68%) was the second most frequent mentoring activity after general conversation and correspondence (84%) (Cavell et al., 2002).

The nature of social support provisions reported in studies of natural mentors parallels the results of studies on volunteer mentors. The Commonwealth Fund 1998 Survey of Adults Mentoring Young People (McLearn, Colasanto, & Schoen, 1998) was based on telephone interviews with 1,504 adults who reported being either natural or formal (program-assigned) mentors of youth. Respondents reported their participation in 15 mentoring activities, which included talking with the mentee about personal problems (89%), teaching social skills (83%), standing up for the mentee when he or she was in trouble (75%), and teaching job-related skills (54%). Findings revealed a positive association between the range of supportive mentoring activities reported and respondents' perceptions of success as mentors. One third of those respondents who reported a relatively wide variety of mentoring activities (12 of 15 activities) perceived themselves to be successful with mentees. In contrast, only 20% of mentors who reported relatively fewer mentoring activities (8 or fewer activities) perceived themselves to be successful mentors. It remains to be determined whether the diversity of mentoring support predicts actual youth outcomes assessed with objective measures.

The Influence of Social Support on the Development of Mentoring Relationships

The chapter by Zimmerman, Bingenheimer, and Behrendt in this volume addresses the influence of social support on the formation of natural mentoring relationships, so that literature is only briefly summarized here. In their longitudinal study of more than 700 urban adolescents, Zimmerman and his colleagues found that the absence of parents did not increase the likelihood that adolescents would develop natural mentoring relationships. Other studies have also not found an association between adolescents' perceptions of the quality of their relationships with parents and adolescents' cultivation of natural mentoring relationships (Beam et al., 2002; Rhodes et al., 1994). One possible conclusion from those studies is that youth do not compensate for the absence of parents or deficits in parental support by forming a natural mentoring relationship during adolescence.

In contrast to those null findings, Zimmerman et al. (this volume) reported a positive association between mother, father, friend support, and presence of a mentor in their longitudinal study of urban adolescents. Another investigation found that having a natural mentor was correlated with adolescents' perceptions of maternal acceptance during childhood (Rhodes et al., 1994). Acceptance is a construct with some conceptual overlap with social support. In summary, there was little evidence that natural mentoring relationships develop because of deficits in parental support or parental absence. Instead, there is some evidence that parental acceptance during childhood and parental support during adolescence could promote development of natural mentors among youth.

Social Support as a Mediator of the Effects of Mentoring

Do mentoring interventions exert their beneficial effects by improving the supportive relationships that adolescents have with family members and friends? One study posited that improved parental relationships mediated the effects of mentoring on adolescents' academic adjustment (Rhodes, Grossman, & Resch, 2000). Data were derived from the randomized control trial of nearly 1,000 youth who had applied to Big Brothers Big Sisters programs. The measure of parental relationships was the same self-report measure of secure attachment used by Soucy and Larose (2000) and therefore assessed concepts that overlapped with social support, such as trust and positive communication. Results showed that mentoring affected mentees' academic adjustment by improving the quality of their relationships with parents. An evaluation of another mentoring program also found that the intervention strengthened mentees' sense of connectedness with parents and that sense of parental connectedness predicted academic gains (Karcher, Davis, & Powell, 2002).

Two other studies by Rhodes and her colleagues were concerned with social support as a possible mediator of the effects of natural mentors (Rhodes et al., 1992; Rhodes et al., 1994). Their research with Latina adolescent mothers found that those who could identify natural

mentors were less depressed and anxious than those without mentors, but there was no evidence that social support mediated this effect (Rhodes et al., 1994). In a separate study with young African American mothers, there was evidence that those who had natural mentors were less depressed than those who could not identify mentors in their lives (Rhodes et al., 1992). Subsequent analyses, however, failed to show that support from mentors or others were viable mediators of mentorship's effect on depression.

The clearest test that social support mediates the effects of mentoring interventions was provided in a study of Big Brothers Big Sisters participants and a comparison group of demographically similar youth (DuBois, Neville, Parra, & Pugh-Lilly, 2002). This study proposed a model in which enhancements in social support from extrafamilial adults mediated the effects of mentoring program participation on youth competencies and psychological well-being and, more distally, on susceptibility to emotional and behavioral problems. In general, the data fit a model in which mentoring program participation resulted in greater perceived social support from nonparental significant adults. Ratings of this type of social support were linked subsequently in the model to reports of more positive self-esteem, which, in turn, were predictive of improvements in emotional and behavioral problems as rated by youth, teachers, and parents. This study illustrated the kind of design, assessments, and analyses that are required to establish that mentoring achieves its effects at least in part by increasing social support, which can have subsequent effects on other constructs (e.g., self-esteem) that affect youth outcomes.

Social Support as a Moderator of the Effects of Mentoring

Moderating effects of social support are demonstrated when the effectiveness of mentoring is influenced by the level of social support that youth report. Mentoring interventions are sometimes established on the premise that they would be particularly effective for youth who have deficits in social support or who have key vacancies in their social lives. The largest formal mentoring program in the United States,

Big Brothers Big Sisters, was designed for children from single-parent homes. However, in their meta-analysis of evaluations of youth mentoring programs, DuBois, Holloway, Valentine, and Cooper (2002) did not find evidence that number of parents in the home moderated program effects. This same review cited evidence from one study that children who lacked family support benefited more from a mentoring intervention than those who had supportive family relationships (Johnson, 1997, cited in DuBois, Holloway, et al., 2002). Although a crude variable such as number of parents in the household might not affect youth responsiveness to mentoring programs, a variable that reflects the supportive family milieu might capture a quality that influences the effectives of mentoring interventions. That is a research question that merits additional attention.

Somewhat in contrast to the results of the research by Johnson (1997), one study of at-risk college students suggested that mentoring effects might be moderated by students' ratings of attachment to their mothers (Soucy & Larose, 2000). Mentors were volunteer teachers who received training in providing key social support functions of "acceptance, encouragement, guidance, and information" (p. 129). The researchers did not assess social support per se, but did assess attachment, a construct that was conceptualized as incorporating the related concepts of trust, positive communication, and feelings of alienation. Results showed that mentees who perceived a secure attachment with their volunteer mentors reported greater emotional adjustment, academic adjustment, and attachment to the institution at the end of the first semester. Those associations remained even after accounting for a measure of students' adjustment at the beginning of the semester. However, there was a significant interaction between students' secure attachment with their mothers and secure attachment with their mentors. That interaction revealed a stronger association between secure attachment with mentors and end-of-semester outcomes among students who reported greater attachment to their mothers.

It is difficult to reach any firm conclusion about the role of social support as a moderator of mentoring effects. There have not been a sufficient number of well-designed studies with conventional measures of social support to establish any strong evidence for social support moderating effects. There are viable rationales for conflicting hypotheses: that mentoring is most effective for youth with impaired family support (cf. Johnson, 1997) and that mentoring is most effective for youth with highly supportive families (cf. Soucy & Larose, 2000). At present, there is inadequate evidence for either one of the hypotheses.

PRACTICE

In this section, we consider implications of theory and research reviewed in the previous sections of this chapter for practice issues in youth mentoring. Evidence suggests that mentoring programs with structured activities for youth and mentors to participate in together have a greater impact on youth outcomes (DuBois, Holloway, et al., 2002). It is possible that structured mentoring activities might have more beneficial outcomes when they are theoretically and empirically based tools for increasing the supportiveness of mentor-youth relationships. First, we will discuss the implications of Weiss's theory for the provision of social support through structured mentor-youth activities. Next, we will use several examples to illustrate how research with natural mentors may inform the design of structured mentoring activities.

Weiss's provision of social relationships is a theoretical representation of mentor-youth interactions during structured activities that could also be used as a basis for designing structured mentoring activities. For instance, the Healthy Kids Mentoring Program includes a "Relationship Building" component to promote the provision of social support through journal sharing (King, Vidourek, Davis, & McClellan, 2002). Journal sharing is a good example of a structured activity that may evoke important support behaviors by providing a context for emotional integration, social integration, nurturance, reassurance of worth, and provision of assistance. In the Healthy Kids Mentoring Program, mentors responded to dialogue questions (e.g., What is the hardest thing about growing up?) in their journals each week and shared their responses with the youth. The mentees were encouraged to respond to the same question and generate additional questions for their mentors. Results indicated that the youth participating in the mentoring program had a greater sense of family and school connectedness at posttest compared with the pretest evaluation and significantly higher levels of family and school connectedness at posttest compared with nonmentored youth in the same school.

Empirical research on natural mentors may inform practice in mentoring programs by revealing the most essential forms of support to target through structured mentoring activities. According to mentored youth in two studies, nondirective support (i.e., emotional support) and directive guidance (i.e., cognitive guidance) were the most frequent types of support provided by natural mentors (Rhodes et al., 1992; Rhodes et al., 1994). A number of innovative mentoring programs have designed structured activities that promote these types of support. The Developmental Mentoring Program included the development of structured mentoring activities to facilitate academic achievement through the provision of directive guidance behaviors (Karcher et al., 2002). Mentors and youth participated in structured recreational and academic activities, were exposed to diverse cultures, and engaged in social skills development activities. Every Saturday of the summer, the mentors and mentees also engaged in recreational activities with parents. Results of a randomized trial indicated that mentored youth exhibited significantly higher gains in spelling achievement than did comparison youth. Analyses indicated that the effect of the mentoring program on gains in spelling achievement was mediated by gains in parent connectedness. This program is a promising model for using structured activities to facilitate the provision of directive guidance behaviors and to strengthen parent-child connectedness.

The National Mentoring Partnership developed the *Learn to Mentor Toolkit,* an easily accessible online handbook of structured activities that encourage supportive behaviors mentoring relationships. The toolkit includes descriptions of structured activities to promote nondirective support in mentoring relationships, such as discussion-based activities that encourage mentors and youth to talk about their strengths, weaknesses, relationships, and personal values. Also included are descriptions of structured activities focusing on directive guidance, such as assisting youth with homework, talking about balancing a checkbook, working on a résumé, and visiting a community college. The *Learn to Mentor Toolkit* appears to be a useful resource for mentors, but future research will be necessary to determine its effectiveness. Mentoring practitioners make essential contributions by translating theory and research on social support into explicit actions that mentors can take when they interact with mentees.

FUTURE DIRECTIONS

Synthesis

Social support has direct relevance to the developing literature on the mentoring of youth. The theoretical perspectives addressing support functions of social relationships and internal models of social relationships that were considered earlier in this chapter illustrate the range of processes relating to social support that are relevant to consider as well as the opportunities that exist to deepen our understanding of youth mentoring processes and outcomes. There is evidence that natural and volunteer mentors tend to provide a range of socially supportive behaviors. Evidence is lacking to indicate that support from natural mentors is sought out by youth to compensate for the lack of support from parents or peers. Research suggests that mentoring might promote positive outcomes for youth by improving their relationships with parents. There are some examples of promising programs and practices that seek to capitalize on a role for social support in promoting beneficial effects of mentoring relationships for youth, but the empirical foundation needed to inform these efforts is lacking.

Recommendations for Research

1. *Design research to determine whether mentors' social support contributes to the*

positive effects of mentoring interventions. Experimental and quasi-experimental trials of mentoring interventions provide opportunities to test the hypothesis that mentors' social support influences positive outcomes for mentees. However, research on social support interventions, including mentoring interventions, often has missed opportunities to test this hypothesis because explicit measures of social support were not included to determine whether (a) interventions were successful in altering support and (b) changes in social support accounted for (mediated) changes in other youth outcomes (Barrera & Prelow, 2000). Testing social support mechanisms would be best achieved through controlled trials of mentoring interventions in which mentoring support is manipulated explicitly.

2. *Explore how natural support might affect mentoring interventions.* There is value in understanding how preexisting supportive ties and a child's history of supportive relationships might influence the effectiveness of mentoring interventions. There are two divergent hypotheses that could be tested. One hypothesis, the support facilitation hypothesis, is that the rich get richer; mentees who have supportive network relationships and a history of using supportive resources benefit most from mentoring interventions. A second and contrasting hypothesis, the support-need hypothesis, is that those who have the greatest need for support, either because key relationships are missing or because of deficits in existing provisions of support, will benefit the most from mentoring interventions. At present, there is insufficient support for either hypothesis.

3. *Examine the effects of mentoring interventions on natural social support.* Mentoring interventions might be influenced by preestablished supportive relationships, but mentoring interventions also might have an impact on preestablished social ties, for better or worse. Studies to evaluate the effects of mentoring on supportive relations with members of mentees' natural support networks should be pursued, particularly within the context of controlled trials.

4. *Obtain both mentor and mentee perspectives on social support.* With few exceptions, studies on the interface between social support and mentoring almost always collect data from either mentors or mentees, but not both reporters. Because support involves transactions between people, findings based on reports of both mentors and mentees would strengthen our confidence in research results and conclusions. In studies of social support, interrater agreement tends to be low to moderate (e.g., Barrera, Baca, Christiansen, & Stohl, 1985; Barrera & Stice, 1998). We would expect mentors and mentees to share some perceptions of mentoring support, but the differences in perceptions might result in different conclusions concerning the effects of mentoring support.

Recommendations for Practice

1. *Provide a diversity of support activities.* Mentoring activities should be broadly construed to include the full spectrum of support types: emotional support, advice and guidance, tangible assistance, and social participation. Existing theory and research suggest that youth can derive benefits not only from mentor activities that provide emotional support and guidance but also from social participation in activities that offer opportunities for children to experience joy and competency. There is good justification for formal mentoring programs that train and encourage mentors to engage in a broad array of supportive activities.

2. *Secure parent figure's support for a youth's participation in mentoring.* Mentoring interventions appear to be most effective when there is a positive connection between the mentor and a youth's parenting figure. Even parents who are in conflicted relationships with their children should be enlisted to provide support by encouraging their children's participation in mentoring. Formal efforts to strengthen relationships between parents and mentors also might pay dividends in the overall effectiveness of mentoring interventions.

REFERENCES

Barrera, M., Jr., & Ainlay, S. L. (1983). The structure of social support: A conceptual and empirical analysis. *Journal of Community Psychology, 11,* 133–143.

Barrera, M., Jr., Baca, L. M., Christiansen, J., & Stohl, M. (1985). Informant corroboration of social support network data. *Connections, 8,* 9–13.

Barrera, M., Jr., & Prelow, H. (2000). Interventions to promote social support in children and adolescents. In D. Cicchetti, J. Rappaport, I. N. Sandler, & R. P. Weissberg (Eds.), The *promotion of wellness in children and adolescents* (pp. 309–339). Washington, DC: CWLA Press.

Barrera, M., Jr., & Stice, E. M. (1998). Parent-adolescent conflict in the context of parental support: Families with alcoholic and non-alcoholic fathers. *Journal of Family Psychology, 12,* 195–208.

Beam, M. R., Chen, C., & Greenberger, E. (2002). The nature of adolescents' relationships with their "very important" nonparental adults. *American Journal of Community Psychology, 30,* 305–325.

Belle, D. (Ed.). (1989). *Children's social networks and social supports.* New York: Wiley.

Bowlby, J. (1969). Disruption of affectional bonds and its effects on behavior. *Canada's Mental Health Supplement, 59*(12).

Bretherton, I. (1985). Attachment theory: Retrospect and prospect. In I. Bretherton & E. Waters (Eds.), *Growing points in attachment theory and research. Monographs of the Society for Research in Child Development, 50*(1–2, Serial No. 109), 3–35.

Cavell, T. A., Meehan, B. T., Heffer, R. W., & Holladay, J. J. (2002). The natural mentors of adolescent children of alcoholics (COAs): Implications for preventive practices. *Journal of Primary Prevention, 23,* 23–42.

Cohen, S., Underwood, L. G., & Gottlieb, B. H. (2000). *Social support measurement and intervention: A guide for health and social scientists.* New York: Oxford University Press.

DuBois, D. L., Holloway, B. E., Valentine, J. C., & Cooper, H. (2002). Effectiveness of mentoring programs for youth: A meta-analytic review. *American Journal of Community Psychology, 30,* 157–197.

DuBois, D. L., Neville, H. A., Parra, G. R., & Pugh-Lilly, A. O. (2002). Testing a new model of mentoring. In G. G. Noam (Ed. in chief) & J. E. Rhodes (Ed.), *A critical view of youth mentoring (New Directions for Youth Development: Theory,*

Research, and Practice, No. 93, pp. 21–57). San Francisco: Jossey-Bass.

Eckenrode, J., & Hamilton, S. (2000). One-to-one support interventions: Home visitation and mentoring. In S. Cohen, L. G. Underwood, & B. H. Gottlieb (Eds.), *Social support measurement and intervention: A guide for health and social scientists* (pp. 246–277). New York: Oxford University Press.

Finch, J. F., Barrera, M., Jr., Okun, M. A., Bryant, W. H. M., Pool, G. J., & Snow-Turek, A. L. (1997). Factor structure of received social support: Dimensionality and the prediction of depression and life satisfaction. *Journal of Social and Clinical Psychology, 16,* 323–342.

Johnson, A. W. (1997). Mentoring at-risk youth: A research review and evaluation of the impacts of the Sponsor-A-Scholar Program on student performance. Doctoral dissertation, University of Pennsylvania. *Dissertation Abstracts International, 58*(03), 813A.

Karcher, M. J., Davis, C., & Powell, B. (2002). The effects of developmental mentoring on connectedness and academic achievement. *The School Community Journal, 12*(2), 35–50.

King, K. A., Vidourek, R. A., Davis, B., & McClellan, W. (2002). Increasing self-esteem and school connectedness through a multidimensional mentoring program. *Journal of School Health, 72,* 294–299.

McLearn, K. T., Colasanto, D., & Schoen, C. (1998). *Mentoring makes a difference: Findings From the Commonwealth Fund 1998 Survey of Adults Mentoring Young People.* New York: The Commonwealth Fund. Available at http://www.ecs.org/html/Document.asp?chouseid=2843

Parra, G. R., DuBois, D. L., Neville, H. A., Pugh-Lilly, A. O., & Povinelli, N. (2002). Mentoring relationships for youth: Investigation of a process-oriented model. *Journal of Community Psychology, 30,* 367–388.

Rhodes, J. E. (2002). *Stand by me: The risks and rewards of mentoring today's youth.* Cambridge, MA: Harvard University Press.

Rhodes, J. E., Contreras, J. M., & Mangelsdorf, S. C. (1994). Natural mentor relationships among Latina adolescent mothers: Psychological adjustment, moderating processes, and the role of early parental acceptance. *American Journal of Community Psychology, 22,* 211–228.

Rhodes, J. E., Ebert, L., & Fischer, K. (1992). Natural mentors: An overlooked resource in the social networks of African-American adolescent mothers. *American Journal of Community Psychology, 20,* 445–462.

Rhodes, J. E., Grossman, J. B., & Resch, N. L. (2000). Agents of change: Pathways through which mentoring relationships influence adolescents' academic adjustment. *Child Development, 71,* 1662–1671.

Sanchez, B., & Reyes, O. (1999). Descriptive profile of the mentorship relationships of Latino adolescents. *Journal of Community Psychology, 27,* 299–302.

Soucy, N., & Larose, S. (2000). Attachment and control in family and mentoring contexts as determinants of adolescent adjustment to college. *Journal of Family Psychology, 14,* 125–143.

Vaux, A. (1988). *Social support: Theory, research, and intervention.* New York: Praeger.

Weiss, R. S. (1973). Materials for a theory of social relationships. In W. G. Bennis (Ed.), *Interpersonal dynamics: Essays and readings on human interaction* (pp. 103–110). Homewood, IL: Dorsey.

Zimmerman, M. A., Bingenheimer, J. B., & Notaro, P. C. (2002). Natural mentors and adolescent resiliency: A study with urban youth. *American Journal of Community Psychology, 30,* 221–243.

10

NATURAL MENTORING RELATIONSHIPS

MARC A. ZIMMERMAN, JEFFREY B. BINGENHEIMER, AND DIANA E. BEHRENDT

INTRODUCTION

The focus of this chapter is naturally occurring mentoring relationships. Natural mentors are nonparental adults, such as extended family members, teachers, or neighbors, from whom a young person receives support and guidance as a result of a relationship developed without the help of a program specifically designed to connect youth and adults to form such a relationship (i.e., program mentors). Thus, natural mentors are distinct from adults assigned to work with individual youth through formal mentoring programs such as Big Brothers Big Sisters. In an AOL Time Warner Survey (2002), 34% of adults reported mentoring a youth in the last 12 months. The survey also indicated that among adults who mentored, only 31% did so formally (i.e., through employers, community organizations, places of worship), whereas 68% mentored informally (i.e., were actively sought out, but not connected to any specific program). Similarly, 31% of the adults in the Commonwealth Survey reported mentoring in the last 5 years, of which 83% mentored informally and 17% formally (McLearn, Colasanto, & Schoen, 1998). In a study of a larger nationally representative sample of respondents ages 18 to 26, nearly three quarters (72.9%) reported having had a mentor since the age of 14 outside of any reference to a formal sponsoring mentoring program (DuBois & Silverthorn, in press-b).

In addition to their apparently high prevalence, other considerations make it important to consider natural mentoring relationships. One issue for formal programs that assign mentors and youth to one another is that many of these relationships may be terminated after only a short period of time due to factors such as lack of commitment and follow-through by either or both the mentor and youth (Rhodes, 2002). In comparison, the unique personal bond formed in a natural mentoring relationship may be more long lasting due to the fact that it is developed

The writing of this chapter was supported by grants from the National Institute on Drug Abuse (DA07484), the Centers for Disease Control (CDC) funded Prevention Research Center of Michigan (FO0804), and the CDC-funded Youth Violence Prevention Center (CCR518605). This chapter does not necessarily represent the views of the National Institute on Drug Abuse or the Centers for Disease Control.

through a more organic (i.e., natural) connection among the partners. Youth who form these bonds, furthermore, may have the confidence and capability to engage with nonparental adults and benefit from such relationships. Conversely, youth assigned mentors in a mentoring program may lack the self-confidence and social skills necessary to develop such relationships on their own. In fact, one could argue that the need for such a program may be one reason they have not developed relationships with nonparental adults. The personality characteristics and behaviors of youth who successfully form natural mentoring relationships with adults may help inform strategies to foster sustained mentoring relationships in formal programs.

Natural mentoring relationships have been an important component of youth development throughout history (see Baker and Maguire, this volume). Scholarly interest in natural mentoring relationships is a more recent phenomenon that partly grew out of findings suggesting that nonparental adults may help youth overcome adversity (Werner, 1993; Werner & Smith, 1992). In their classic study of Hawaiian youth, Werner and Smith (1992) found that many of the high-risk youth in their sample who grew into healthy adaptive adults had natural mentors such as teachers or concerned relatives. They noted that the role of natural mentors might be a key resource that helps youth be resilient against risks they face. Research on naturally occurring mentoring relationships is in an early stage of development, and therefore empirical information, is somewhat limited.

In this chapter, we examine both the antecedents and the consequences of natural mentoring relationships. Attachment theory, social support, and resiliency theory are discussed as conceptual frameworks that may help us better understand why some youth form these bonds, while others, perhaps those youth who could benefit the most from such relationships, may not readily form these close ties with adults. Although research on natural mentors is limited, we critically analyze the empirical literature on natural mentors and present results of a study that identifies predictors of youth who form natural mentoring relationships. Practice issues that pertain to natural mentoring relationships then are examined in the context of

available theory and research. Finally, promising directions for future research and practice are discussed.

THEORY

Several theoretical frameworks may be useful for understanding the social and psychological factors that influence which youth will develop natural mentoring relationships (i.e., antecedents). These theories also may help explain how natural mentors may influence developmental outcomes (i.e., consequences). We focus on three theoretical frameworks to help us understand the antecedents and developmental consequences of natural mentors. These are (a) attachment theory, (b) social support, and (c) resiliency theory.

Attachment Theory

Focusing on the bonds formed with parents (or guardians) at the earliest stages of development, attachment theory suggests that these bonds provide the psychosocial basis (e.g. working model of self, self in relation to others) upon which future relationships are made and experienced (Bowlby, 1969). The attachments made as a child, therefore, help define the way future relationships are developed, the characteristics of the relationships, and the level of trust and closeness formed in them. Yates, Egeland, and Sroufe (2003) concluded based on available research that secure attachment in infancy is related to the increased capacity of children to improve adaptation after a period of difficulty.

Antecedents

Attachment theory may be particularly useful for understanding why some youth form natural mentoring relationships and others do not. In particular, it follows from attachment theory that youth with close attachments to parents will have the confidence, experience, and openness to develop the kind of relationships with nonparental adults that can provide youth with natural mentoring resources. The secure-base concept from attachment theory (Bowlby, 1988) provides a conceptual link between children's and adolescents' attachment to others and the likelihood of forming a relationship with a natural mentor. According to attachment theory, a primary function of the attachment figure (usually the mother) is to provide the child with a reliable source of support and felt security (Sroufe & Waters, 1977). This secure base is then thought to enable the child to put attachment concerns aside and focus on exploring the physical and social world, which, in turn, promotes development. Relevant to this possibility, Rhodes, Contreras, and Mangelsdorf (1994) suggested that a positive association between perceptions of parental social support and the probability of having a natural mentor among adolescents could be understood in terms of the social attachments youth formed as infants and children. They argued that the secure base from these early attachments may help youth have the social and emotional confidence to form intergenerational relationships. A secure base from parental support, furthermore, may allow youth to trust other nonfamilial adults to form relationships, an essential step for the growth of a natural mentoring relationship.

Consequences

Attachment theory also may provide a basis for predicting that youth with natural mentors may have more healthy developmental outcomes than youth without natural mentors. A secure base may enable youth with natural mentors to develop more conventional social norms and behaviors they learn from their mentors. Under these circumstances, youth may be more likely to be able to develop the trust and commitment necessary for the mentoring relationship to work most effectively. In essence, they are more psychologically prepared to reap the benefits that a natural mentor may offer.

Social Support

Attachment to parents in the early years of development may evolve into social support during the latter stages of childhood and during adolescence. Social support consists of many different types of support, including emotional support (empathy, love, trust, and caring); instrumental support (tangible aid and service);

informational support or cognitive guidance (advice, suggestions, and information); and appraisal support (information that is useful for self-evaluation). Social support is delivered through social networks, where relationships are defined by their characteristics of reciprocity, intensity, complexity, and density (Heaney & Israel, 2002). Family members, teachers, coaches, clergy, peers, neighbors, and other members of the community are all potential sources of social support outside of the family. Although traditional adolescent development theories (e.g., Blos, 1962; Erikson, 1968) have defined emotional autonomy from parents as a crucial hallmark of individuation and maturity, more recently, research findings have indicated the importance of ongoing supportive relationships with parents (e.g., Franz & White, 1985; Gilligan, 1982; Grotevant, 1989; Hill & Holmbeck, 1986; Josselson, 1988). In accordance with these findings, theories of adolescent identity development and individuation view supportive and increasingly symmetric relationships with parents as the foundation for the emergence of role-taking skills and psychosocial competence during the teenage years (e.g., Grotevant & Cooper, 1986).

Antecedents

Parental support in particular may be a vital antecedent for the development of natural mentoring relationships among youth because parents can give guidance and material support that can help create opportunities for their children to develop mentoring relationships. Material (instrumental) support may come from rides to teen centers and programs where adults are involved, monetary support to join sports teams or other programs with financial requirements, or simply connections made through work experiences that may enhance their children's social capital. Cognitive guidance also may be part of parental support that provides youth with ideas about the benefits of connecting with other adults, as well as suggestions for how to get the most from these relationships. Finally, emotional support, as noted previously, may provide youth with the secure base and confidence to form mentoring relationships with adults. Barrera and Bonds (this volume) provide a more in-depth analysis of the connections between social support and mentoring relationships in the lives of youth.

Theoretically, it also is possible that the association between parent support and the likelihood of having a natural mentor is not linear. That is, youth with the highest levels of parent support (a secure base) may be more likely to develop a natural mentoring relationship, while those with very low levels of parent support also may have a tendency to seek natural mentors (to compensate). Youth with moderate amounts of parent support may be least likely to form relationships with natural mentors because they have neither enough of the support (secure base) that would help them develop these relationships nor the motivation to seek the support of other adults because parental support is not lacking. The result might be a U-shaped relationship between parental support and the probability of having a natural mentor.

Consequences

With respect to how and why natural mentoring relationships may be beneficial for youth, it is noteworthy that these relationships may provide youth with many different forms of support. They may provide cognitive guidance (informational support) for decision making, such as what courses to take for which job interests or what post–high school choices to make for which career goals. Mentors may provide emotional support for a variety of stressors youth face, including death of a loved one, romantic breakups, or schoolwork. They also may provide material support in the form of invitations to sports and entertainment events, cultural activities, or job and career opportunities.

Resiliency Theory

Many youth faced with adversity do not necessarily exhibit the negative outcome predicted by risk factor models (Garmezy, 1991; Garmezy & Masten, 1991; Masten 1994; Rutter, 1987; Werner, 1993; Zimmerman & Arunkumar, 1994). Other factors in the lives of youth (i.e., assets or resources) may protect them from the negative consequences of a given risk factor. Two models of resiliency are particularly

relevant concerning natural mentoring relationships: the compensatory and protective factor models (Garmezy, Masten, & Tellegen, 1984; Zimmerman & Arunkumar, 1994; Zimmerman, Steinman, & Rowe, 1998).

The compensatory model of resiliency suggests that positive factors in a youth's life may counteract the potentially negative consequences of risk factors. Having peers who use alcohol, for example, may increase the likelihood that a youth will use alcohol. This negative influence, however, may be counteracted by a positive influence such as parental support. The protective factor model suggests that resources may reduce the association between a risk and an outcome (risk-protective) or enhance the effects of another asset (protective-protective) (Brook, Brook, Gordon, & Whiteman, 1990). Zimmerman et al. (1998) described a risk-protective mechanism in their study of adolescent violence. They found that the association between having violent friends (risk factor) and adolescent males' violent behavior (negative outcome) was lower for youth who reported high levels of mother support (protective factor). The protective-protective effect is the notion that resources can mutually facilitate one another. An example of a protective-protective mechanism was evident in the finding reported by Zimmerman, Ramirez, Washienko, Walter, and Dyer (1995) that a strong cultural identity was associated with enhanced power for self-esteem as a predictor of lower alcohol use among Native American youth.

Antecedents

Resiliency theory suggests that resources in the lives of youth may help them develop natural mentoring relationships. Thus, the resources suggested in attachment theory (i.e., secure base) and social support theory (e.g., parental support) can be framed in resiliency theory as assets for the development of natural mentoring relationships. Expanded networks for social resources and social capital, for example, may contribute to the development of natural mentoring relationships. Assets or resources that may promote the development of natural mentoring relationships include positive social support, self-confidence, emotional maturity, and social and communication skills.

Consequences

Resiliency theory also suggests that natural mentors can be vital resources to help youth overcome risks they face (i.e., assets that help youth to be resilient to adversity). Theoretically, natural mentors may provide youth who are burdened by high levels of risk with the guidance, social capital, support, and adult supervision that is necessary to overcome these obstacles and achieve positive developmental outcomes. They may, for example, help youth avoid the negative influence of friends involved in problem behavior. Natural mentors, furthermore, may function as resources that enhance the influences of other assets. Illustratively, they may enhance the salutary effects of parental support by providing complementary forms of assistance or by reinforcing or supporting parental messages.

RESEARCH

In this section, we first review findings on what is known about the prevalence, sources, and prevailing characteristics of natural mentoring relationships. We then consider empirical findings regarding both the antecedents and consequences of natural mentoring relationships.

Prevalence, Sources, and Characteristics

In a study by DuBois and Silverthorn (in press-a), 60% of natural mentors were categorized as nonfamilial. Of the entire sample, one third of the respondents reported professional natural mentors, one quarter reported informal mentoring relationships, and the remaining 40% reported familial natural mentors. DuBois and Silverthorn (in press-a) also found that characteristics of natural mentoring relationships found to predict differences in consequences among youth with natural mentors include the role of the mentor in the youth's life, frequency of contact, emotional closeness, and duration of relationship. Research that goes beyond analysis of the presence or absence of mentoring linked to outcomes is vital to understand the variability in natural mentoring ties among youth.

Although the length of natural mentoring relationships varies, long-term commitment on behalf of the mentor may be one of the most important characteristics of a successful mentor. Youth who reported having natural mentoring relationships that lasted over 2 years were 3.5 times more likely to be in school or to have graduated than those who did not report having natural mentors (Klaw, Rhodes, & Fitzgerald, 2003). Similarly, formal mentoring relationships lasting at least 1 year appear to have the most positive influence on youth, whereas relationships terminating quickly may be less influential or have negative effects (Grossman & Rhodes, 2002).

Antecedents

Research Literature

Research on the antecedents (predictors) of natural mentoring among youth is limited. Darling, Hamilton, Toyokawa, and Matsuda (2002) studied 56 male and 70 female college juniors from the United States and 119 male and 120 female college freshmen from Japan. They examined how natural mentoring relationships develop in each country (e.g., older relatives, siblings, teachers, peers). In both countries, adolescents were more likely to attribute the role of mentor to adults than to peers, to relatives than to nonrelatives, and to people of the same gender than opposite gender. Similar results from both countries suggest that mentoring relationships may be relatively universal in industrial societies.

Hamilton and Darling (1996) and Rhodes et al. (1994) each examined antecedents of natural mentoring among adolescents. Hamilton and Darling (1996) studied 126 third-year undergraduates at Cornell University. They found that males whose parents performed mentorlike functions were more, rather than less, likely to report having natural mentors than were males whose parents did not perform such functions. No such association was found for females. Rhodes et al. (1994) studied 54 inner-city Latina adolescent mothers. They found that adolescents with natural mentors reported greater levels of intangible support (including emotional support, positive feedback, and guidance) from their mothers and greater perceived maternal acceptance during early childhood. The findings of these studies contradict the notion that natural mentors serve as substitutes for unsupportive parents. Instead, they suggest that parental support somehow may enable adolescents to form relationships with natural mentors. This interpretation is consistent with predictions derived from attachment theory described previously.

The fact that an association between parental support and the probability of having a natural mentor was found in these small samples with limited statistical power suggests that the effects of parental support may be substantial. Moreover, although each sample was relatively homogeneous, they were quite different from one another, suggesting that the association may be robust across different adolescent populations. Nevertheless, replication of the results in a larger and more diverse sample would be useful.

We describe below an empirical analysis of 726 urban adolescents to build upon the scant research literature examining antecedents of natural mentor relationships. This analysis expands on previous work in three critical ways. First, it includes a larger sample than past work. Second, it includes a more diverse sample than previous research. Third, we examine both linear and nonlinear effects among several predictors. We used multivariate logistical regression, adjusted for race and sex, in several stages to predict the likelihood of having a natural mentor.

Empirical Analysis

Participants included 726 adolescents who participated in the second (1995, 10th grade) and fourth (1997, 12th grade) waves of a 4-year panel study of high school dropout and drug use in a large Midwestern city (Zimmerman & Schmeelk-Cone, 2003). Only African American and White participants were included in the study. Students with an 8th-grade GPA of higher than 3.0 and those diagnosed by the school system as being either emotionally impaired or developmentally disabled were excluded. The sample was mostly African American (82%) and consisted of 52% female participants. The 726 youth included in the present analyses represent 88% of those participating in the first wave of the interview study.

In the fourth wave of the study (when the respondents were high school seniors), an item about mentors was included that was similar to the one used by Rhodes and her colleagues (Rhodes et al., 1994; Rhodes, Ebert, & Fischer 1992). Participants were asked, "Is there an adult 25 years or older who you consider to be your mentor? That is, someone you can go to for support and guidance or if you need to make an important decision, or who inspires you to do your best?" Participants who responded "yes" then were asked, "What is his/her relationship to you?" If the respondent named a family member, he or she then was asked a second set of questions that were similar to the first but that specified "other than a family member (or the person who raised you)." Those who named someone other than an immediate family member or a boyfriend or girlfriend on either question were defined as having a natural mentor. Participants who said they had no mentor or who named only a boyfriend, girlfriend, or an immediate family member (e.g., biological parent, sibling, stepparent) were defined as having no natural mentor. Thus, we created a dichotomous variable indicating presence or absence a natural mentor. Overall, 389 respondents (53.6%) reported having a natural mentor. Almost 42% of the total sample reported extended family members (aunts, uncles, cousins, grandparents). A smaller number of respondents from the sample (11.6%) reported having a teacher, coach, counselor, or minister as their natural mentor.

A shortened version of Procidano and Heller's (1983) social support instrument was used to assess mother, father, and friend support. Respondents who reported that their mothers or fathers were deceased or who reported that they had no contact with them were given a score of zero on the respective measure. The mean for mother support was 19.63 ($SD = 5.27$), and the Cronbach alpha was 0.90. Mother absence and father absence were assessed by asking respondents to list all the people living in their households in the first year of the study (1994) and to report any changes in their household composition in subsequent years. Overall, 87% ($n = 634$) of respondents were living with a maternal figure, but only a minority of respondents (46%, n = 331) were living with a paternal figure. The family decision-making subscale from the Family Environment Scale (Moos & Moos, 1981) also was used.

Results indicated that females and males were equally likely to report a natural mentor, with 55% of females and 52% of males reporting such a relationship ($\chi^2(1) = .456$, *ns*). African American respondents, however, were substantially more likely than White respondents to report a natural mentor ($\chi^2(1) = 11.068$, $p < .001$). Fifty-seven percent of African American youth but only 40.4% of White youth reported having a mentor. Mother support, father support, shared family decision making, and friend support were all associated with an increased likelihood of reporting a natural mentor. When all variables were entered into the equation, the estimated odds ratios for these five predictors were each approximately 1.2, which suggests that an increase of one standard deviation in any of these predictors is associated with a 20% increase in the odds that an adolescent will report a natural mentor. Neither mother absence nor father absence from the adolescent's household was associated with reporting a natural mentor.

In a second set of logistic models, we compared the predictive power of mother support with that of father support, and the predictive power of mother and father support with that of friend support. We entered each pair of predictors simultaneously into a model already containing race and sex, thus generating three new models. Mother and father support did not differ in predicting having a natural mentor ($t (721) = .097$, *ns*). Similarly, mother support was equal to that of friend support ($t (720) = .034$, *ns*), and father support was equal to that of friend support ($t (720) = -.096$, *ns*) for predicting having a natural mentor. This provides support for the role of attachment theory as a safe base from which youth may develop mentoring relationships. It also indicates that social support plays a critical role in the development of these relationships.

Finally, we examined the potential for curvilinear associations of mother and father support with the likelihood of reporting a natural mentor by entering a squared mother (or father) support

term into a logistic model already containing sex, race, and mother (or father) support. We found no evidence that the relationship between mother support and the likelihood of reporting a natural mentor was curvilinear (-2 log likelihood $= .303$, *ns*). The test of the quadratic term for father support fell just beyond the .05 significance level (-2 log likelihood $= 3.387, p = .07$). Although we found only marginal significance for parental support having a curvilinear relationship with having a natural mentor, inspection of the quadratic trend for this finding indicated that youth reporting the highest and lowest levels of parental support (U-shaped curve) were most likely to develop a natural mentor. This provides additional evidence that attachment and social support theories are useful frameworks for understanding antecedents of youth mentoring relationships. On the one hand, youth with low support may try to make up for it through relationships with other adults, but on the other hand, youth with high levels of support may have the secure base necessary to develop such relationships.

Consequences

Several studies have examined the association between natural mentors and differing aspects of youth adjustment and functioning. Rhodes et al. (1992) studied 129 young African American mothers and found that those reporting natural mentors reported lower levels of depression, more benefit from social support, and being less affected by relationship problems compared with those not reporting mentors. Reported levels of life stress, parental stress, economic strain, social functioning, and support resources were similar across groups. Their definition of natural mentors was similar to the study described above but also included wording that it be a person they can count on, who believes in and cares about them, and who inspires them to do their best and that knowing him or her has really affected what they do and the choices they make. Mentors that were less than 8 years older than the participants were excluded.

Rhodes et al. (1994) obtained similar results in a study of 54 inner-city Latina adolescent mothers. Youth indicating that they had natural mentors reported lower levels of anxiety and depression, greater satisfaction with the social support they received, and fewer negative psychological effects of relationship and support network problems. Mentors were defined as they were in Rhodes et al. (1992), with the exception that an 8-year age differential was not required. They also did not find differences for life stress, economic strain, support, or relationship problems between those with or without mentors.

Zimmerman, Bingenheimer, and Notaro (2002) used resiliency theory to guide their analytic approach in the same sample of urban African American adolescents (described previously). They found that adolescents who indicated having natural mentors reported more positive school attitudes and less problem behaviors, such as alcohol use, marijuana use, and nonviolent delinquency, compared with those without natural mentors. Furthermore, they found evidence that natural mentors may help protect youth from the negative effects of friends' influence. Youth with natural mentors maintained relatively positive attitudes toward school even when their friends' attitudes were negative. Those without natural mentors were more vulnerable to these negative peer influences.

Beier, Rosenfeld, Spitalny, Zansky, and Bontempo (2000) studied 294 adolescents between the ages of 12 and 23 years. They were predominantly female, mixed race/ethnicity, and from diverse socioeconomic backgrounds. Their sample was somewhat limited, however, because it consisted of individuals receiving routine outpatient health care at an adolescent health service center within a suburban, community-based teaching hospital. Respondents were asked whether they had any adults in their lives who they could usually turn to for help and advice. They found that adolescents with mentors were less likely to report carrying a weapon, illicit drug use in the past 30 days, smoking more than five cigarettes per day, and having sex with more than one partner in the past 6 months. Adolescents reporting either a parental mentor or a nonparental mentor were less likely to report two or more risk behaviors than adolescents who reported no mentor. DuBois and Silverthorn (in press-a), however, found that nonfamilial natural mentoring

relationships were more likely than familial natural mentoring relationships to be associated with positive outcomes in education and physical health in youth.

Farruggia and colleagues (2003) studied the association between reporting a very important nonparental adult (VIP) and academic achievement and school connectedness among an ethnically diverse sample of 1,190 12th graders. They found that reporting a VIP predicted greater school connectedness and modestly greater academic success, as assessed by a four-item, five-point scale, and self-reported grades, respectively, compared with those who did not report one. Beam, Gil-Rivas, Greenberger, and Chen (2002) found evidence that perceived VIP disapproval of problem behaviors reduced the influence of high peer risk for them (crosscontextual). Similarly, those who perceived VIPs participating in problem behaviors were more likely to report engaging in problem behaviors. It should be noted, however, that these investigations did not explicitly study natural mentors. Rather, they examined VIPs, which may differ from a focus on natural mentors because youth are not asked explicitly about the types of support or guidance received from these persons. VIPs, thus, could include adults who do not provide mentoring, but who are important to youth in different ways. Coaches who are listed, for example, may not be doing anything beyond their jobs as coaches. A coach may not, for example, provide cognitive guidance, material support, or other mentorlike behaviors. Rather, their work with a particular youth may focus on team spirit, motivation, and skill building pertaining to the sport. While this may be a VIP to a youth, it may not be a natural mentor, because they do not fulfill other support outside of the sport activity.

Cavell, Meehan, Heffer, and Holladay (2002) studied the association of natural mentors with outcomes for children of alcoholics (COAs). This was a retrospective study of 95 mostly White 18-year-olds. They found that those with mentors tended to be less well-adjusted than those without. These findings contradict almost all the past research done on natural mentors. One possible explanation for this is that the mentors, who were mostly friends of the COA's parents, may have aggravated the situation because of their desire to support their friends. An interpretation based on attachment theory is that COAs with natural mentors were more likely to have insecure and preoccupied (anxious-ambivalent) attachment styles because the mentors were actually just mirroring the attitudes and behavior of the parents. Thus, the mentors did not provide relief from problematic parental relationships, but actually reinforced them. Individuals with this style of attachment tend to report more psychiatric symptoms and have a positive view of others, while having a negative view of self. Adolescents with insecure and preoccupied attachment styles, for example, tend to exaggerate emotional distress more than other adolescents (Bartholomew & Horowitz, 1991), and the help of a natural mentor may not be sufficient to overcome their distress. This might help account for the average of a 4-year gap between the time COAs reported meeting their mentors and the time the relationship became significant.

Klaw et al. (2003) studied 11- to 19-year-old African American adolescent mothers ($n = 198$) for 2-years postpartum (in two waves), all of whom were unmarried and enrolled in an alternative school. Adolescent mothers whose mentoring relationships were reported to last for 2 years were 3.5 times more likely to have graduated or remained in school than those who did not identify a mentor at either point in time. Characterized by reports of weekly to daily interaction, long-term mentoring relationships were described by mothers as providing a wide range of support and as being very important to them. In addition, those reporting long-term mentors reported more satisfaction and a more important relationship with their mentors compared with the support they received from their mothers. The findings of this study provide additional support for the positive effects of natural mentors on adolescent development, but it is somewhat limited by the selective sample.

DuBois and Silverthorn (in press-b) used nationally representative data to analyze longitudinally, in two waves, 6 years apart, how natural mentoring relationships relate to health and problem behaviors. Respondents were 18 to 26 years old at the second wave ($N = 3,187$). Presence of a mentor was measured by the following question in Wave III of the Add Health

study (Udry, 2003, cited in DuBois & Silverthorn, in press-b): "Other than your parents, has an adult made an important positive difference in your life at any time since you were 14 years old?" Measures of initial levels of functioning and indicators of exposure to individual and environmental risk were controlled in their analysis. Reporting a mentor was associated with a broad range of favorable outcomes, including significantly decreased likelihood of being in a gang, hurting someone in a fight in the last year, and risk taking; relatively high levels of self-esteem and life satisfaction; and high levels of physical activity and regular birth control use. Although beneficial effects were not indicated for all measured outcomes, the positive effects may indicate a potential for natural mentoring relationships to offset the effects of risk factors for healthy outcomes.

Limitations

The research literature on natural mentoring relationships has several limitations. The number of studies on natural mentoring relationships is sparse. Most of the research on the antecedents and consequences of natural mentoring is cross-sectional in design. Although this research provides a beginning, longitudinal prospective studies are needed to further understand how natural mentoring relationships develop, whether their effects are sustained or diminished over time, and how they may change youth trajectories for school, career, and behavior.

Researchers also currently lack a common definition of natural mentors and ways to define these relationships. Some researchers, for example, have included family members, whereas others have not. The age of the mentor also varies across studies. Must mentors be older than their mentees? How much older do they need to be to qualify as a mentor? Researchers have also focused on identification of a single mentor, but youth may have multiple natural mentors whose cumulative effect may be protective-protective. Research that examines how many mentors youth have and how they contribute to healthy development would be useful.

We know very little about the qualities of natural mentoring relationships, specifically the amount and the kinds of interaction within them. Are mentoring relationships limited to mainly cognitive guidance, similar to those characterized by multiple activities? Is the amount of time spent with mentors associated with more positive developmental outcomes?

Research on natural mentors also has suffered from the lack of a clearly articulated theoretical base. As a result, existing research has focused on a narrow range of potential predictors of the formation of natural mentoring relationships and on relatively simplistic, main effects of these relationships on outcomes. Cultural differences also have been not been examined in detail. New immigrant youth, for example, may benefit more from natural mentors because they need assistance to figure out and adapt to their new environment. The content or style of mentoring that is most effective, furthermore, may differ across ethnic groups. Scales and colleagues (2003) examined research on societal and cultural factors that affect adults' inclination to mentor. Yet research that examines ecological and contextual factors that influence the likelihood of having a natural mentor is lacking. Beam et al. (2002) examined contextual influences, but they focused only on parents, peers, and VIPs. Finally, more critical analysis of natural mentoring is needed. It is possible that some natural mentoring relationships actually increase youth risk for negative outcomes. The assumption in the literature is that natural mentors provide positive guidance, but what if a supportive nonparental adult helps guide the youth into criminal activity or serves as model for certain types of problematic health behaviors, such as smoking? With notable exceptions (Beam et al., 2002), these types of possibilities have not received significant attention.

PRACTICE

Practitioners may want to be cautious when considering recommendations on how to build and sustain natural mentoring relationships. A mentoring relationship requires time, effort, and commitment from both mentor and youth to be successful. Although many youth programs are designed to encourage or establish mentoring relationships by pairing mentors and mentees,

critical factors for success may be that (a) these relationships are mutually defined, so that the amount of time and commitment is prearranged, and (b) both the mentor and youth nurture the relationship within the agreed framework. Practitioners may benefit from promoting strategies designed to strengthen the antecedents of natural mentoring relationships in ways that foster the creating of the social contexts for these relationships to develop on their own.

Practitioners may need to support parents and caretakers by promoting the formation of support and bonds with their children that allow youth to feel socially secure enough to explore relationships with adults. Attachment theory suggests that these parenting practices may be most effective the earlier they start. Churches, community centers, and other organizations may be vital resources to help mothers and fathers improve their parenting skills. Furthermore, community organizations and churches may provide settings and opportunities for intergenerational contact and a social climate conducive to the formation of natural mentoring relationships. Practitioners may help youth develop mentoring relationships by helping these organizations create programs for adults and youth to interact in safe, supervised, and fun activities.

The Fathers and Sons Project of the Prevention Research Center of Michigan is an example of a structured program that helps fathers and sons interact in positive ways (Caldwell, Zimmerman, Bernat, Sellers, & Notaro, 2002). Practitioners teach communication skills to adults and youth. Fathers learn strategies and are coached to help them talk about risky behaviors with their sons. This program teaches fathers vital parenting skills and helps them form secure bonds with their sons. Programs that also include mothers and daughters provide other examples of helping youth develop the family support that may provide the foundation necessary for youth to develop natural mentoring relationships (Lee & Jeter, 2000; Morton-Young, 1995; Wasserman, Miller, & Corther, 2000).

Programs in schools and community centers also are a potentially important source of support for teachers, coaches, and other key adults whom youth look up to and may see as role models. These types of programs may provide a critical opportunity to help such adults develop an understanding of their role in fostering the development of youth with whom they have regular contact. Smith and Smoll (2002) developed a training program for coaches (Coach Effectiveness Training) to help them be more effective in interacting with youth. Practitioners can develop similar programs for other adults working with youth in different roles. Offered both in person and online, programs could help give potential mentors the knowledge, strategies, tools, and confidence needed to be effective mentors.

It also may be helpful to provide opportunities for mentor-youth pairs to engage in discussion and activities with adults and youth who have not yet formed such relationships. These could take place in a variety of settings, ranging from schools to community programs to work sites. Although we are not aware of the existence of such groups, they seemingly could help nurture natural mentoring relationships by sharing ideas and stories relevant to the development of these ties and by engaging in fun activities, like attending a sports event together or volunteering at a local community organization. Groups of this nature would provide existing mentor/youth pairs with the opportunity to learn from each other and to further enhance their bonds, commitment, and mutual interests. Discussion groups and peer education, furthermore, may provide a forum for programs to provide training for initiating mentoring relationships that incorporate an honest exploration of potential challenges and the commitment that is necessary. Similarly, experiences shared by natural mentor/youth pairs could provide youth program coordinators with a vital resource for helping make formal mentoring programs more effective.

Finally, the extent to which adults are reticent to get involved with unrelated youth may be a barrier practitioners need to address. Scales and colleagues (2003) suggested a variety of practices to encourage most adults to participate in the lives of youth. Practitioners can encourage capable adults to start with small steps of interaction. Communities and neighborhoods also may be able to agree on a social contract of reasonable responsibility for the area youth.

To this extent, parents also may want to give explicit permission to other adults to engage with their youth. Adults should be informed that most parents want their children to engage with other adults, many adults already engage with youth, and there are many personal rewards related to forming relationships with youth.

FUTURE DIRECTIONS

Synthesis

Natural mentoring relationships may provide a key component in healthy development for many youth. The limited research on natural mentoring has indicated that social support is a critical antecedent for youth to develop natural mentoring relationships. It also has consistently indicated that these relationships may promote healthy behavior and outcomes. Attachment, social support, and resiliency theories are frameworks that may help us better understand the antecedents and consequences of natural mentoring relationships. Yet, to date, most research has lacked a strong foundation in these or other theoretical perspectives. Although practice has been focused mainly on providing program-assigned mentors to youth who are identified as in need, strategies designed to cultivate antecedents of natural mentoring relationships may be a useful complement to these efforts. The formation of natural mentoring relationships may be facilitated (a) by efforts to promote strong parent-child bonds in early developmental years that foster youth skills and confidence for forming ties with other adults and (b) by program practices that promote adult behaviors and interactions with youth that are conducive to mentoring.

Recommendations for Research

1. *Need for greater understanding of how parental support may help promote the development of natural mentoring relationships.* With a deeper and more refined understanding of the factors that contribute to the development of natural mentoring relationships, practitioners can develop programs to enhance these factors as a way to build adult and youth mentoring

relationships. Existing research on antecedents suggests the importance of parental support, but it has not teased apart what aspects of that support (e.g., emotional, cognitive guidance, tangible assistance) may be more critical than others. It is also not clear how mother and father support, respectively, may influence the likelihood of a youth forming natural mentoring relationships. The findings from the analyses in this chapter provide initial evidence that they are equally predictive, but the sample was somewhat narrow; different types of support were not measured; and a single study is not enough to make definitive conclusions. As suggested by the preceding results, it also may be important to attend to possible curvilinear relationships in this area.

2. *Research on natural mentoring relationships that is informed by resiliency theory should be conducted.* Greater investigation of natural mentors as an asset within the context of resiliency theory is needed to increase understanding of whether these types of bonds help compensate for or protect against risks youth face. The few relevant studies suggest that natural mentors can play a significant role in helping youth to overcome negative influences in their lives. A priority for future research should be to examine this issue in relation to a broader range of risks and outcomes. Many outcomes such as psychological well-being (e.g., depression, self-esteem); problem behaviors (e.g., delinquency, alcohol and drug use); school performance and attitudes; and involvement in prosocial activities (e.g., extracurricular, youth programs) have not been well studied. Risks in need of study pertaining to these outcomes include negative friend influences, stress exposure, poverty, and family violence. In addition, research on the characteristics of a mentoring relationship and their association with youth resiliency would also be useful. DuBois and Silverthorn (in press-a) have provided a foundation to develop studies that integrate mentoring research.

3. *Prospective longitudinal studies should be conducted to further our understanding of the developmental significance of natural mentors.* Several studies provide specific cross-sectional

evidence that natural mentors benefit at-risk youth. Longitudinal investigations are needed, however, to clarify the implications of natural mentoring relationships for developmental outcomes. These types of investigations also would provide a valuable opportunity to study how natural mentoring relationships change over time and how that change may be influenced by differing stages of the youth's development. The study of adolescents making the transition to young adulthood, for example, may benefit from longitudinal analyses, due to the fundamental developmental changes during this period.

4. *Studies that provide a more in-depth understanding of the types, characteristics, and numbers of natural mentoring relationships and their implications for youth outcomes are needed.* Future research needs to devote greater attention to increasing understanding of the important features of natural mentoring relationships. Few researchers, for example, have studied characteristics of the natural mentors and youth and their association with success of the relationship. Factors such as age differential, gender match (or not), mentor profession, and youth behavior problems (or lack thereof) may be related to both the quality and the longevity of the mentoring relationship and hence have significant implications for the relationship's ultimate effects on outcomes. Studies of the overall networks of natural mentoring ties that youth experience and their implications for developmental outcomes would be informative because most research has focused on the presence or absence of a natural mentoring relationship. Research that provides a more in-depth analysis of the interactions that occur in natural mentoring relationships and how these evolve and change over time is needed as well. The findings of the preceding types of research could help inform applied efforts to cultivate natural mentoring relationships as well as help formal mentor programs develop strategies to sustain the mentoring relationships they intend to create.

Recommendations for Practice

1. *Practitioners may find it useful to encourage supportive relationships with parents and*

create opportunities for them to develop effective parenting skills. Programs designed to create adult-youth mentoring relationships may be more effective if they focus on creating contexts for intergenerational interaction and allowing such relationships to form naturally. It also may be useful for programs to foster the social context in the family necessary to nourish mentoring possibilities. Thus, programs that focus on parental support and family cohesion may have the useful side effect of helping natural mentor relationships to develop.

2. *Programs that support and train adults who are in roles that require interaction with youth also may be helpful.* Programs for teachers, clergy, coaches, and other members of the community who interact with youth can provide additional support and guidance for them, such as the Coach Effectiveness Training program developed by Smith and Smoll (2002). Positive youth development requires caring, supportive, and engaging adults (National Research Council and Institute of Medicine, 2002). Encouraging capable adults to start with small steps toward interacting with youth can spark greater personal and social interest in adult-youth relationships (Scales et al., 2003). Programs that help them develop the necessary skills for interfacing with youth may be beneficial even if they do not develop into mentoring relationships.

REFERENCES

AOL Time Warner Foundation. (2002). *Mentoring in America 2002*. New York: Author.

Bartholomew, K., & Horowitz, L. M. (1991). Attachment styles among young adults: A test of a four-category model. *Journal of Personality and Social Psychology, 61,* 226–244.

Beam, M. R., Gil-Rivas, V., Greenberger, E., & Chen, C. (2002). Adolescent problem behavior and depressed mood: Risk and protection within and across social contexts. *Journal of Youth and Adolescence, 31,* 343–357.

Beier, S. R., Rosenfeld, W. D., Spitalny, K. C., Zansky, S. M., & Bontempo, A. N. (2000). The potential role of an adult mentor in influencing high-risk behaviors in adolescents. *Archives of Pediatrics and Adolescent Medicine, 154,* 327–331.

Blos, P. (1962). *On adolescence.* New York: Free Press.

Bowlby, J. (1969). *Attachment and loss: Vol. 1. Attachment.* New York: Basic Books.

Bowlby, J. (1988). *A secure base: Parent-child attachment and healthy human development.* New York: Basic Books.

Brook, J. S., Brook, D. W., Gordon, A. S., & Whiteman, M. (1990). The psychosocial etiology of adolescent drug use: A family interactional approach. *Genetic, Social, and General Psychology Monographs, 116,* 111–267.

Caldwell, C. H., Zimmerman, M. A., Bernat, D. H., Sellers, R. M., & Notaro, P. (2002). Racial identity, maternal support and psychological distress among African American adolescents. *Child Development, 73,* 1322–1336.

Cavell, T. A., Meehan, B. T., Heffer, R. W., Holladay, J. J. (2002). The natural mentors of adolescent children of alcoholics (COAs): Implications for preventive practice. *The Journal of Primary Prevention, 23,* 23–42.

Darling, N., Hamilton, S., Toyokawa, T., & Matsuda, S. (2002). Naturally occurring mentoring in Japan and the United States: Roles and Correlates. *American Journal of Community Psychology, 30,* 245–270.

DuBois, D. L., & Silverthorn, N. (in press-a). Characteristics of natural mentoring relationships and adolescent adjustment: Evidence from a national study. *Journal of Primary Prevention.*

DuBois, D. L., & Silverthorn, N. (in press-b). Natural mentoring relationships and adolescent health: Evidence from a national study. *American Journal of Public Health.*

Erikson, E. H. (1968). *Identity, youth, and crisis.* New York: Norton.

Farruggia, S. P., Chang, E., Gil-Trejo, L., Heckhausen, J., Greenberger, E., & Chen, C. (2003, April). *The role of very important nonparental adults in adolescent school connectedness, academic achievement, and educational aspirations and expectations.* Paper presented at the Meeting of the Society for Research in Child Development, Tampa, FL.

Franz, C. E., & White, K. M. (1985). Individuation and attachment in personality development: Extending Erikson's theory. *Journal of Personality, 53,* 224–256.

Garmezy, N. (1991). Resilience and vulnerability to adverse developmental outcomes associated with poverty. *American Behavioral Scientist, 34,* 416–430.

Garmezy, N., & Masten, A. S. (1991). The protective role of competence indicators in children at risk. In E. M. Cummings, A. L. Green, & K. H. Karraker (Eds.), *Life-span developmental psychology: Perspectives on stress and coping* (pp. 151–174). Mahwah, NJ: Erlbaum.

Garmezy, N., Masten, A. S., & Tellegen, A. (1984). The study of stress and competence in children: A building block of developmental psychopathology. *Child Development, 55,* 97–111.

Gilligan, C. (1982). *In a different voice: Psychological theory and women's development.* Cambridge, MA: Harvard University Press.

Grossman, J. B., & Rhodes, J. E. (2002). The test of time: Predictors and effects of duration in youth mentoring relationships. *American Journal of Community Psychology, 30,* 199–219.

Grotevant, H. D. (1989). Child development within the family context. In W. Damon (Ed.), *Child development today and tomorrow* (pp. 34–51). San Francisco: Jossey-Bass.

Grotevant, H. D., & Cooper, C. R. (1986). Individuation in family relationships: A perspective on individual differences in the development of identity and role-taking skill in adolescence. *Human Development, 29,* 82–100.

Hamilton, S. F., & Darling, N. (1996). Mentors in adolescents' lives. In K. Hurrelmann & S. F. Hamilton (Eds.), *Social problems and social contexts in adolescence* (pp. 121–139). Hawthorne, NY: Aldine de Gruyter.

Heaney, C. A., & Israel, B. A. (2002). Social networks and social support. In K. Glanz, B. K. Rimer, & F. M. Lewis (Eds.), *Health behavior and health education* (pp. 185–209). San Francisco: Jossey-Bass.

Hill, J. P., & Holmbeck, G. N. (1986). Attachment and autonomy during adolescence. *Annals of Child Development, 3,* 145–189.

Josselson, R. (1988). The embedded self: I and thou revisited. In D. K. Lapsley & F. Clark-Power (Eds.), *Self, ego, and identity: Integrative approaches* (pp. 91–106). New York: Springer-Verlag.

Klaw, E. L., Rhodes, J. E., & Fitzgerald, L. F. (2003). Natural mentors in the lives of African-American adolescent mothers: Tracking relationships over time. *Journal of Youth and Adolescence, 32,* 223–232.

Lee, P. M., & Jeter, D. Z. (2000). *Helping your child learn responsible behavior: Discussion leader guide.* Washington, DC: U.S. Department of Education, Office of Educational Research and Improvement.

Masten, A. S. (1994). Resilience in individual development: Successful adaptation despite risk and adversity. In M. Wang & E. W. Gordon (Eds.), *Educational resilience in inner-city America* (pp. 3–25). Mahwah, NJ: Erlbaum.

McLearn, K. T., Colasanto, D., & Schoen, C. (1998). *Mentoring makes a difference: Findings From the Commonwealth Fund 1998 Survey of Adults Mentoring Young People.* New York: The Commonwealth Fund. Available at http://www.ecs.org/html/Document.asp?chouseid=2843

Moos, R. H., & Moos, D. S. (1981). *Family Environment Scale manual.* Palo Alto, CA: Consulting Psychologists.

Morton-Young, T. (1995). *After-school and parent education programs for at-risk youth and their families.* Springfield, IL: Charles C Thomas.

National Research Council and Institute of Medicine. (2002). (J. Eccles & J. Appleton Gootman, Eds.), *Community programs to promote youth development.* Committee on Community-Level Programs for Youth. Washington, DC: National Academy Press.

Procidano, M. E., & Heller, K. (1983). Measures of perceived social support from friends and from family: Three validation studies. *American Journal of Community Psychology, 11,* 1–24.

Rhodes, J. E. (2002). *Stand by me: The risks and rewards of mentoring today's youth.* Cambridge, MA: Harvard University Press.

Rhodes, J. E., Contreras, J. M., & Mangelsdorf, S. C. (1994). Natural mentors' relationships among Latino adolescent mothers: Psychological adjustment, moderating processes, and the role of early parental acceptance. *American Journal of Community Psychology, 22,* 211–228.

Rhodes, J. E., Ebert, L., & Fischer, K. (1992). Natural mentors: an overlooked resource in the social networks of youth, African American mothers. *American Journal of Community Psychology, 20,* 445–462.

Rutter, M. (1987). Psychosocial resilience and protective mechanisms. *American Journal of Orthopsychiatry, 57,* 316–331.

Scales, P. C., Benson, P. L., Mannes, M., Hintz, N. R., Roehlkeartain, E. C., & Sullivan, T. K. (2003). *Other people's kids: Social expectations and American adults' involvement with children and adolescents.* New York: Kluwer Academic/Plenum.

Smith, R. E., & Smoll, F. L. (2002). Youth sports as a behavior setting for psychosocial interventions. In J. L. Van Raalte & B. W. Brewer (Eds.), *Exploring sport and exercise psychology* (2nd ed., pp. 341–371). Washington, DC: American Psychological Association.

Sroufe, L. A., & Waters, E. (1977). Attachment as an organizational construct. *Child Development, 48,* 1184–1199.

Wasserman, G. A., Miller, L. S., & Corther, L. (2000, April). Prevention of serious and violent juvenile offending. *Juvenile Justice Bulletin.* Retrieved September 19, 2004, from http://www.ncjrs.org/html/ojjdp/jjbul2000_04_1/contents.html

Werner, E. E. (1993). Risk, resilience, and recovery: Perspectives from the Kauai Longitudinal Study. *Development and Psychopathology, 5,* 503–515.

Werner, E. E., & Smith, R. S. (1992). *Overcoming the odds: High risk children from birth to adulthood.* Ithaca, NY: Cornell University Paperbacks.

Yates, T. M., Egeland, L. B., & Sroufe, A. (2003). Rethinking resilience: A developmental process perspective. In S. S. Luthar (Ed.), *Resilience and vulnerability: Adaptation in the context of childhood adversities* (pp. 243–266). Cambridge, UK: Cambridge University Press.

Zimmerman, M. A., & Arunkumar, R. (1994). Resiliency research: Implications for schools and policy. *Social Policy Report, 8*(4), 1–18.

Zimmerman, M. A., Bingenheimer, J. B., & Notaro, P. C. (2002). Natural mentors and adolescent resiliency: A study with urban youth. *American Journal of Community Psychology, 30,* 221–243.

Zimmerman, M. A., Ramirez, J., Washienko, K. M., Walter, B., & Dyer, S. (1995). Enculturation hypothesis: Exploring direct and protective effects among Native American youth. In H. I. McCubbin, E. A. Thompson, & A. I. Thompson (Eds.), *Resiliency in ethnic minority families: Vol. I. Native and immigrant American families* (pp. 199–220). Madison: University of Wisconsin.

Zimmerman, M. A., & Schmeelk-Cone, K. H. (2003). A longitudinal analysis of adolescent substance use and school motivation in African American youth. *Journal of Research on Adolescence, 13,* 185–210.

Zimmerman, M. A., Steinman, K. J., & Rowe, K. J. (1998). Violence among urban African American adolescents: The protective effects of parental support. In X. B. Arriaga & S. Oskamp (Eds.), *Addressing community problems: Psychological research and interventions* (pp. 78–103). Thousand Oaks, CA: Sage.

PART IV

DEVELOPMENTAL AND CULTURAL PERSPECTIVES

11

MENTORING CHILDREN

TIMOTHY A. CAVELL AND ANNE-MARIE SMITH

INTRODUCTION

In this chapter, we give an up-to-date accounting of what is known and not known about the mentoring of children. We consider the following questions: (a) Are children generally helped by mentoring? (b) Can it be harmful? (c) How much do we know about the mechanisms by which mentoring helps children? (d) Are some children more likely to be helped than others? We also describe recent trends in the practice of child mentoring and address issues that arise when designing a formal mentoring program for children. We end with specific recommendations for those helping shape the future of child mentoring, whether as researchers or as practitioners.

We focus primarily on the mentoring of children in the elementary school grades. Our upper developmental boundary is middle school or junior high school rather than a particular age or developmental stage (e.g., puberty). Entering the middle/junior high school context signals a significant shift in the life space and task demands of the developing individual. As such, this boundary represents a useful way to distinguish our chapter from Nancy Darling's chapter, this volume, on mentoring adolescents. We also emphasize so-called formal or assigned mentoring, although much of what we discuss also applies to informal or natural mentoring relationships. Finally, unless otherwise indicated,

our discussion is restricted to one-on-one, adult-to-child mentoring.

We should note that our bias is toward the mentoring of children who face known risk factors. A recent survey revealed that 80% of adults who had been mentors believed their mentees faced at least one of a dozen different child-related problems (e.g., low self-esteem, poor grades) and that nearly 25% faced five or more problems (McLearn, Colasanto, Schoen, & Shapiro, 1999). These findings, coupled with the challenge of finding and retaining sufficient numbers of mentors, suggest that mentoring programs are best reserved for children who face clearly substantiated and empirically based risk factors. We use the terms *risk* and *risk factor* to mean any variable that, if present, is known to statistically increase the likelihood of children's maladjustment. Understanding risk variables should enable mentor programmers to strike a balance between children who face minimal risk of future maladjustment and children whose risk levels exceed what can be helped through mentoring. For example, Big Brothers Big Sisters of America (BBBSA) previously limited their mentoring program to children living in homes headed by a single adult. (Currently, their only criterion is an adult's belief that the child could benefit from an additional caring adult.) Children living in such homes might face many challenges, but it is an empirical question whether this one demographic adequately identifies children for whom mentoring is both effective and necessary. Conversely, one could question the widely recommended practice of mentoring adjudicated youth. Delinquent youth are clearly at risk for later problems, but they may be less likely to benefit from mentoring (Smith, 2002; see Blechman & Bopp, this volume). In short, knowledge about risk factors and children's development should drive the study and practice of child mentoring.

Mentoring programs that serve children versus adolescents are apt to find the younger age group has its advantages and disadvantages. What are the challenges and unique opportunities that come with child mentoring? Mentoring children has the potential advantage of providing greater preventive impact than mentoring adolescents. Children have had fewer opportunities to experience serious risks, significant trauma, and maladaptive models of behavior, whereas adolescent development is marked by greater crystallization of internal representations and behavioral tendencies. This tendency toward canalization and integration could diminish the impact that mentoring has on adolescents, relative to children. Child-focused mentoring programs also may be better able to help young children navigate key transition points before severe problems arise. For example, mentoring could be used to help young preschoolers with their entry into formal schooling or school-aged children with their transition to middle school. All things being equal, one also would expect mentors to view school-aged children as easier to manage than adolescents. Children are less involved in extracurricular activities and less embedded in peer networks that compete for adolescents' time and attention. In general, children should also be less resistant than adolescents to mentors' planned activities and less likely to engage in disruptive or antisocial behavior during or between mentoring visits.

Mentoring children also poses significant challenges. Children's cognitive and verbal abilities could limit their capacity to benefit from mentoring experiences. Compared with adolescents, children are less able to articulate specific needs or desires, whether the desire is for an ice cream cone or for a parent's recovery from drug addiction. Similarly, mentors' information sharing may have less impact if couched in nuance, symbolism, irony, or some other kind of subtlety that is more difficult for younger children to comprehend. Finally, children's cognitive and verbal abilities could make them less likely to use mentoring as an opportunity to work on identity issues, viewing mentors as potential role models and themselves as apprentices.

We have three goals in writing this chapter. The first is to assist with efforts to advance youth mentoring beyond political appeal and social faddism (Mosle, 2000). Mentoring programs currently enjoy wide public support as a remedy to the problems of at-risk youth (e.g., Armstrong, 2000; Dortch, 2000); however, sound research in support of this practice is surprisingly sparse (Blechman, 1992; DuBois, Holloway, Valentine, & Cooper 2002; Rhodes, 1994; Smith, 2002). If child mentoring is to be more than a passing fancy, it needs a firm research base. As researchers, we need to determine when it works, for whom it works, and for how long it works. We also need to understand why it works. Indeed, discerning the mechanisms by which mentoring actually leads to change is perhaps our greatest challenge. A second goal is to encourage greater appreciation for the social and developmental contexts in which child mentoring occurs. Outcome data that do exist clearly obligate researchers and practitioners to understand both the promise and the peril of mentoring programs geared specifically for children (DuBois, Holloway, et al., 2002; Rhodes, 1994). No longer can we assume that pairing children with an unfamiliar mentor is beneficial or, at worst, neutral, especially if the children suffer from serious and multiple risk factors. Our final goal is to encourage researchers to focus more directly on the processes and outcomes associated with child mentoring. A chapter devoted specifically to child mentoring is limited by an extant literature in which there is a decided lack of empirical data and explicit theory. It is not that children are rarely mentored or that children have been excluded from studies of mentoring; rather, it is that research on youth mentoring—as the phrase suggests—has focused primarily on adolescents and not children per se. Until such work is done, we cannot be sure whether child mentoring is a practice to be strongly encouraged, actively discouraged, or simply tolerated.

THEORY

Mentoring and Developmental Theory

A generation ago, developmental psychologists focused much of their attention on age-related trends and normative shifts in children's abilities (e.g., perceptual, motor, language, and reasoning skills), often making reference to developmental milestones, age-specific tasks, qualitatively distinct stages, and critical periods. Less attention was given to understanding the developmental pathways of individual children, especially those who failed to meet normative expectations. The contributions of both nature and nurture were recognized, but in a way that underappreciated the role of genetic endowment and that underspecified the complex interplay of genes and environment (Collins, Maccoby, Steinberg, Hetherington, & Bornstein, 2001). Theories of socialization overemphasized parental influence, underestimated forces outside the family (e.g., peers, teachers, media), and failed to appreciate that children substantially shape their environmental experiences (Harris, 1995; Scarr, 1992). Such was the state of developmental science in the decades before "youth mentoring" became a household term and a political catch phrase.

Today, developmental science is characterized by a sophisticated array of investigative tools and a large body of knowledge about factors that contribute to human development (e.g., Bergman, Cairns, Nilsson, & Nystedt, 2000). Theories of atypical or disrupted development and person-centered analyses are now considered useful means for gaining knowledge about normative developmental processes; models of socialization now treat as givens the role of child effects, extrafamilial factors, and gene X environment interactions; and long-term, multilevel designs are now the standard for investigators seeking to explain developmental continuity and discontinuity (Collins et al., 2001; Harris, 1995; Kuczynski, 2002; Scarr,

1992). Thus, researchers who rely on current developmental theory, methods, and findings are better able to gauge the influence of adult mentors in the lives of children and adolescents. Indeed, recent estimates that youth mentoring programs yield modest effect sizes (DuBois, Holloway, et al., 2002) are not surprising in light of what is known today about continuity and discontinuity in children's development, especially among children exposed to chronic and multiple risks (Cairns & Cairns, 1994; Cicchetti & Hinshaw, 2002).

Developmental Theory and Prevention Science

Research and practice in the field of mentoring assumes that mentoring is helpful to children. The nature of this help has not been clearly articulated. Borrowing from Sandler (2001), we can imagine at least three ways in which mentoring could be a benefit: (a) as a strategy for *preventing* children from starting down a negative developmental course, (b) as a mechanism for *protecting* children who are already on a risk trajectory, or (c) as a means of directly *promoting* children's competencies and capacities to meet their basic developmental needs. Mentoring relationships are but one potential source of influence in children's lives, and simple notions about children being shaped in a top-down, unilateral fashion by significant adults are no longer viable (Kuczynski, 2002). As a prevention tool, mentoring is better served by an organizational-developmental model of risk and protection (Cicchetti & Hinshaw, 2002). This framework considers the transactional nature of children's interactions with the environment and identifies the processes that promote or disrupt children's developmental organization across multiple systems (e.g., biological, cognitive, social, familial). An organizational-developmental model also recognizes that children coconstruct their experiences and that dispositional (e.g., difficult temperament) and environmental (e.g., harsh parenting) variables operate in mutually reciprocal and complex ways over time. This blurring of cause and consequence makes our task as researchers more difficult and presents significant challenges to mentoring programmers. At the same time, the complex interplay between child effects and environmental effects helps explain why some children profit greatly from their mentoring experiences (Rhodes, 2002).

Developmentally Informed and Theory-Driven Studies of Child Mentoring

Designing and implementing effective prevention programs requires two kinds of models: The first is an accurate rendering of the problem(s) to be prevented, and the second is a practical model for implementing effective prevention, protection, or promotion strategies (Coie et al., 1993; Hughes, 2000; Sandler, 2001). Though related, the two models are not simply opposite sides of the same coin. Researchers hoping to build a science of youth mentoring will need to consider both types of models when developing and evaluating future mentoring programs.

Model of the Problem

Well-designed mentoring programs should begin with an empirically sound and clearly articulated description of the conditions that give rise to the problems to be prevented (Coie et al., 1993). An explicit model of the problem is especially critical for children who face chronic and serious risk factors. Failure to adequately capture the factors that maintain developmental continuity and impede therapeutic discontinuity could lead either to programs that are weak and ineffective or, worse, to the misuse of child mentoring. The costs of misuse are not limited to time, money, and effort spent on ineffective programs; mentoring has the potential to harm the very children it was intended to help (Karcher, 2005; McCord, 1978; Rhodes, 1994, 2002).

Model of Change

Prevention researchers have the additional task of developing models of change that are effective, practical, and sustainable. Developing a successful model of change requires specifying and assessing the mechanisms by which change

will occur. Some risk and protective factors are unlikely to change, and not all changes will lead to significant and benign shifts in children's development. Applied to mentoring, models of change must go beyond vague statements about children benefiting from supportive relationships or positive role models.

The Example of Children of Divorced Parents

To illustrate the task of fitting mentor programming to a specific population of at-risk children, we use the example of children whose parents are divorced. Before we consider whether mentoring would be helpful to these children, it is important to ask whether children of divorced parents actually need help. Extensive research on this population of children (e.g., Hetherington, 1999) cast doubt on the presumption that all children of divorced parents need extraordinary assistance. However, this same body of research indicates that children of divorced parents are at greater risk for social, emotional, behavioral, and academic difficulties when compared with children whose biological parents are happily married. Still needed is a clear picture of why these children are at risk and what specific processes and outcomes are likely to be improved via mentoring. For example, children of divorced parents have been shown to suffer when there is a significant loss of family income and when parents engage in recurring, unresolved conflict (Hetherington, 1999; Johnston, Gonzalez, & Campbell, 1987). We suspect few mentors would solve a family's financial worries or successfully mediate between warring ex-spouses, but a mentor could theoretically reduce the impact of these stressors. Regular visits from a supportive mentor could provide children of divorced parents with a certain degree of emotional comfort and relationship security. Mentors could also help by removing children from highly stressful settings or providing them with a sense of hope during a particularly trying period. Even with such provisions, mentoring could still lack the potency or duration needed to offset the potential damage caused by ongoing parental conflict or a family's financial woes.

Would mentoring be equally effective for children of divorce regardless of the child's age, sex, or cultural background? For example, should we expect daughters and sons of divorced parents to benefit equally from mentoring? Relevant here is Hetherington's (1999) research on divorced parents who had remarried. Girls whose mothers had remarried tended to fare worse than girls whose mothers had not remarried; bringing a stepfather into the family seemed to disrupt or threaten the previously close relationship daughters had with their divorced mothers. Would an unfamiliar mentor be seen in a similarly negative light? Keep in mind that most data on youth mentoring were drawn from BBBSA programs geared for youth living with a single or unmarried caregiver. Grossman and Rhodes (2002) found that girls rated their Big Sisters less positively than boys rated their Big Brothers; similarly, DuBois, Neville, Parra, and Pugh-Lilly (2002) found that girls were less likely to nominate mentors as significant in their lives.

It should be clear from this discussion that designing and evaluating child mentoring programs is greatly facilitated when empirical questions are grounded in previous research and explicit theory. By couching mentoring within developmental theory and prevention science, researchers not only learn about the outcomes of youth mentoring, they also add to the larger body of knowledge on children's development (Cavell & Hughes, 2000).

Potential Mechanisms of Action in Child Mentoring

Because mentoring can involve a range of activities and interactions across multiple settings, practitioners and researchers must be mindful of the potential forces at work. Unfortunately, there are very few mentoring studies that have tested specific models of change (cf. Cavell & Hughes, 2000; DuBois, Neville, et al., 2002; Grossman & Rhodes, 2002; Karcher, 2005; Rhodes, Grossman, & Resch, 2000). The greater tendency among researchers is to overlook questions about the change process and hope that mentoring will, somehow, lead to significant and lasting benefits. But even in programs in which mentors are extensively trained and mentees meet uniform selection criteria, there can be tremendous

variability in the quality of the relationships and the activities pursued (e.g., Alfonso, Cavell, & Hughes, 2004; Cavell & Hughes, 2000). In an effort to promote mentoring research that is theory driven and developmentally informed, we offer a list of possible mechanisms by which mentoring could produce positive outcomes. These mechanisms were drawn from recently articulated models of mentoring (DuBois, Neville, et al., 2002; Rhodes, 2002; Rhodes, this volume) as well as from the broader research literature on child-focused, psychosocial interventions. Our goal is to push investigators to think creatively but precisely about the processes operating when adult mentors interact over time with at-risk children.

Changes in Behavioral Contingencies

The first mechanism we discuss involves changes in the external contingencies that govern the performance of children's behavior. Practitioners and researchers who consider interpersonal dynamics or children's internal representations as key mechanisms of action could easily overlook this more parsimonious view of child mentoring. Critical to understanding the role of behavioral contingencies in child mentoring is an appreciation for the Matching Law and its application to the study of child behavior (McDowell, 1982; Snyder & Patterson, 1995). The Matching Law states that the probability of a child performing a given behavior will match the probability of the child being reinforced for that behavior relative to all other behaviors. For example, children whose coercive behavior produces more reliable payoffs than prosocial behavior are likely to adopt coercion as a dominant influence strategy (Snyder & Patterson, 1995). Mentoring could be a way to ensure that children are being reinforced for positive behaviors that are seldom rewarded in other settings. A positive mentoring experience also could have an indirect effect on external contingencies and children's behavior. The Matching Law would predict that an increase in the *total* level of noncontingent reinforcement available would reduce the *relative* utility of previously relied upon behaviors (McDowell, 1982). If true, then children who enjoy a supportive mentoring relationship might be less likely to use aversive behavior (e.g., whining, pestering) to gain parents' attention and influence others (Cavell, 2000). This would explain why mentoring would have beneficial effects on parents' relationships with youth (Rhodes et al., 2000). A supportive mentoring relationship could be especially beneficial to children who live in environments where the reinforcement schedule for positive behavior is rather lean. The finding that youth living with environmental (versus individual) risk factors are more likely to benefit from mentoring could be seen as supporting such an argument (DuBois, Holloway, et al., 2002).

Acquisition of Knowledge, Skills, or Scripts

Λ second potential mechanism of change is children's acquisition of useful knowledge, adaptive skills, or behavioral scripts. Because mentoring is often used as a way to improve children's academic performance or psychosocial functioning, it would make sense that mentoring serves to expand children's fund of knowledge or repertoire of skills. Whether the skill is long division, taking turns when playing, or managing one's anger, mentoring has the potential to imbue children with a range of adaptive skills and useful information. Mentoring could also help children acquire behavioral scripts to use in unfamiliar situations (e.g., sporting events, restaurants, museums, concerts). Mentoring programs that include a specific, structured curriculum are counting on the acquisition of knowledge, skills, and scripts as a mechanism of change (e.g., Karcher, 2005). But even unstructured mentoring programs can provide opportunities for gaining useful information and skills (Rhodes, 2002). For example, children who spend a great deal of time playing games or sports with their mentors could be developing skills that lead to greater peer acceptance (Lindsey & Mize, 2000).

Enhanced Social Cognitions

A third possible change mechanism involves positive shifts in children's social cognitions (Rhodes, 2002). *Social cognition* is a broad term that refers to a number of internal structures and processes, including children's beliefs, expectancies, goals, perceptions, and interpretations about themselves and others with whom they interact. Mentoring could yield a number of social cognitive benefits: (a) enhanced self-worth, (b) increased efficacy about a specific skill (e.g., reading, math), (c) more adaptive interpersonal goals, (d) greater tendency to reflect on difficult social problems, (e) more accurate attributions about the causes of important events, (f) less rumination about being hurt by others, (g) greater willingness to trust others and seek help, and (h) a stronger and more enduring sense of optimism about the future. Some changes might generalize over time and across settings, but others are likely to be short-lived or evident in specific situations or a single domain of functioning. It is also important to recognize the reciprocal relation among social cognitive variables. Changes in children's beliefs or expectations can significantly alter the processing of new social information (Crick & Dodge, 1994). Thus, mentoring designed to enhance social cognitions in one social domain (e.g., with the mentor) could change the way children perceive and interpret interactions in other social domains (e.g., with teachers or with parents).

Improved Affect

Negative affectivity is not only a source of distress for children, it is also a potential disruptor of their ability to think clearly, to use good judgment, and to perform routine skills (Albano, Chorpita, & Barlow, 1996; Hammen & Rudolph, 1996). Conversely, positive emotions can reinvigorate children who feel helpless or oppressed and provide them with the energy they need to take calculated risks and perform demanding tasks. Currently, we know very little about the impact of mentoring on children's moods and emotions.

Changes in or Removal From Harmful Ecosystems

For some children, poverty, substance abuse, and threats of violence are chronic fixtures in their homes or neighborhoods, leaving many feeling lost and confused, if not severely traumatized. Other children live in more benign settings but still experience overly harsh parenting or the daily brunt of peer victimization. Mentoring could be helpful to such children if it reliably reduced their exposure to stressful circumstances or traumatic events. Physically removing children is one way that mentors can reduce children's exposure to harmful ecosystems, but it need not be the only strategy. Mentors could also affect significant change simply by being present on a regular basis. For example, a positive and admired mentor in the life of a child could lead others to reexamine how they view the child (Heider, 1958). We found surprising benefits when college student mentors made regular visits to aggressive, high-risk children during school lunch (Hughes, Cavell, Meehan, Zhang, & Collie, 2004). This "Lunch Buddy" program was meant to be an attention control condition; we expected few relationship-building opportunities in a crowded, noisy school lunchroom. And like other researchers (e.g., DuBois, Neville, et al., 2002; Rhodes, 2002), we had assumed that the quality of the mentoring relationship was a critical determinant in successful mentoring. We may have been mistaken, however, about the need for high-quality, affectively rich mentoring relationships. Children in our Lunch Buddy program showed significant improvements in teacher-rated aggressive behavior and peer-rated social preference scores. Anecdotal reports indicated that classmates often made positive comments and other social bids to target children and their mentors.

Instrumental Aid

Other researchers have written about the fact that mentors occasionally assist mentees through the provision of food, money, transportation, or other material goods. Is this helpful, or does it distort the "larger" goals of the mentoring relationship? Without empirical findings to draw from, we can only speculate about the answer. Our view is that instrumental aid is likely to be most helpful when provided to children during times of crisis or transition. Some children or their family members encounter serious, even life-threatening crises; others are burdened by a cascade of smaller crises. At these times, mentors' availability,

reliability, and material resources could prove more helpful than their emotional support. Material support from mentors would also be needed to support a disadvantaged child's participation in structured peer activities (e.g., sports teams, school bands) that require money, equipment, or transportation. From a positive youth development perspective (Larson, 2000), mentoring would not be the primary mechanism of change in such activities, but it could be a prerequisite to enacting change (Cavell & Hughes, 2004).

RESEARCH

The science of youth mentoring lags years behind research on other types of psychosocial interventions for children and adolescents. Until the mid-1990s, studies of youth mentoring were mainly descriptive reports outlining the practices of a particular mentoring program and qualitative reviews of the benefits observed. This deficiency is only made more salient when one considers the dearth of studies specific to child mentoring. There are a few exceptions (e.g., Barron-McKeagney, Woody, & D'Souza, 2001), but studies of child mentoring programs are rare. Another concern is that child-focused mentoring programs are often combined with other intervention components, thereby clouding the inferences one can draw about the impact of mentoring per se (see Kuperminc et al., this volume). If early intervention holds greater promise for prevention (Coie et al., 1993; Werner, 1990), the lack of child mentoring studies is a serious impediment to realizing that promise.

Previous studies of child mentoring suffer from numerous threats to internal and external validity. Sorely lacking are empirical trials in which children are assigned randomly to mentoring or comparison conditions (see Grossman, this volume). Other problems include (a) inconsistent operational definitions of mentoring, (b) poor program infrastructure, (c) little attention to program fidelity, (d) overreliance on nonstandardized self-report measures, (e) a failure to assess mentor or child characteristics affecting the relationship, and (f) a reluctance to consider potential iatrogenic effects (see reviews by

Blechman, 1992; DuBois, Holloway, et al., 2002; Freedman, 1992; Rhodes, 1994; Rhodes, Haight, & Briggs, 1999; Smith, 2002; Stein, 1987). Another serious limitation has been the failure to use designs that are sensitive to the potential long-term impact of mentoring. Studies of formal mentoring programs for children rarely report follow-up assessments, despite the assumption that mentoring will have lasting effects.

Another concern is the quality of assessment. Lacking are studies that rely on sound measures, multiple informants, and multiple methods. Standardized ratings by parents, teachers, and peers, phone interviews, direct observations of mentor-mentee interactions, and even beeper-initiated journaling are possible strategies to consider. All too common is the use of a single assessment method or a single informant—typically the mentor or the mentee—yet the relative utility of these two data sources has not been adequately addressed (see below and DuBois, this volume). Also needed are detailed conceptualizations of the proximal changes that mentoring is designed to produce. Research should begin with clearly stated hypotheses indicating how targeted changes will impact children's immediate and long-term adjustment. Previous investigators have rarely tested such hypotheses. Doing so would require assessing the proximal targets of change as well as key outcomes. Earlier, we described several potential mechanisms of action, including behavioral contingencies, acquired skills, social cognitions, improved affect, reduced exposure to stress, and instrumental aid. Each of these can be reliably and validly assessed, though some will entail greater costs and effort than others. For example, changes in children's affective responses could be assessed via self-report instruments, ratings by significant others, observational coding systems (e.g., facial expressions), or even physiological recordings or biochemical assays.

As with any type of intervention, it is also essential to consider the possibility that mentoring is inadvertently causing harm. Consider the well-known Cambridge-Somerville Youth study in which high-risk, antisocial boys in the intervention group fared worse in adulthood than children in the no-treatment control group (McCord, 1978). As part of the intervention, boys were paired with mentor/counselors who also gathered them together each summer for various recreational activities. At the time of this study, there was little appreciation for the powerful role that peers have on the growth trajectory of antisocial behavior (Dishion, McCord, & Poulin, 1999). A more recent analysis revealed that bringing together these high-risk youth may have led to unintended negative effects—effects that were proportionate to the involvement of youth in the summer gatherings (Dishion et al., 1999).

Key Studies

Despite these many concerns about research on child mentoring, there are some studies that deserve our attention and include a proportion of child subjects. Perhaps the most widely cited mentoring study is the evaluation of BBBSA programs undertaken by Public/Private Ventures (Grossman & Tierney, 1998; Tierney, Grossman, & Resch, 1995). Problematic for our purposes is that we do not know whether mentored children in this study fared differently than mentored teens. A second study was Stein's (1987) meta-analysis examining the effects of "companionship therapy" for at-risk children. Across 19 studies, Stein found an average effect size of .22 in the areas of anxiety, general adjustment, and school performance. Stein did, however, find several factors that were associated with more positive outcomes: longer relationships, adults' outgoing nature, and the use of older adults (vs. high school or college students).

DuBois, Holloway, et al. (2002) published the first meta-analysis to follow Stein's, and their findings were similar. They found that mentoring yielded, on average, only modest benefits (overall ds ranged from .14–.23). Nearly identical results were obtained by Smith (2002) in her meta-analysis of 43 mentoring studies involving at-risk youth. Effect sizes ranged from .14 to .27, with smaller effects in the area of aggression/delinquency and larger effects in the area of academic/career variables. As mentioned earlier, one might expect larger effect sizes for child versus adolescent mentees, but there is only partial support for this notion (DuBois, Holloway, et al., 2002; Smith, 2002).

DuBois and colleagues found evidence that children and younger adolescents benefited more than older adolescents (ds of .21 and .10, respectively; see Footnote 7, p. 181), but this difference was lost when controlling for number of best practices used. Smith found that at-risk elementary and high school students benefited more from mentoring than middle/junior high school students.

Mediators and Moderators

There are a handful of studies that examine youth mentoring from the lens of an explicit theoretical model (Cavell & Hughes, 2000; DuBois, Neville, et al., 2002; Grossman & Rhodes, 2002; Karcher, 2005; Karcher, Davis, & Powell, 2002; Parra, DuBois, Neville, & Pugh-Lilly, 2002; Rhodes et al., 2000). Most used samples that combined child and adolescent mentees. In two of the studies, the benefits of mentoring were predicted by improvements in the parent-youth relationship (Karcher et al., 2002; Rhodes et al., 2000). In another, Parra et al. (2002) found support for a process-oriented model of youth mentoring in which feelings of closeness mediated the effects of other relationship factors on the benefits and continuation of mentoring. Grossman and Rhodes (2002) found significant gains in the academic, psychosocial, and behavioral outcomes of youth when mentoring lasted for a year or more; however, relationships that ended prematurely resulted in lower self-worth and perceived academic competence.

Two recent studies focused on children below Grade 6 (Cavell & Hughes, 2000; Karcher, 2005), and both represent a useful guide for future investigations into child mentoring. Karcher (2005) drew from multiple theoretical models (Bronfenbrenner, 1979; Hirschi, 1969; Kohut & Wolf, 1978) to design a structured, school-based mentoring program for children in Grades 4 and 5. Mentors were older students (Grades 8–12), and mentoring took place in the context of a group-based "connectedness curriculum." Three hypotheses were tested: (a) that mentoring would lead indirectly to greater connectedness to family and school; (b) that mentoring would lead directly to self-development as measured by gains in social

skills, self-esteem, and self-management skills; and (c) that gains in self-development would mediate the relation between mentor involvement and child connectedness. Karcher (2005) also tested the alternative hypothesis that gains in connectedness would be predicted by mentees' levels of exposure to the connectedness curriculum. Participating were 77 children, 33 of whom were selected randomly to meet with a mentor after school twice a week for 6 months. Karcher found support for the two hypotheses linking mentoring to gains in connectedness and self-development. He also found clear indication that children's self-views, especially their self-rated physical attractiveness, changed for the worse when mentors failed to attend regularly. He found no support for the alternative hypothesis.

Cavell and Hughes (2000) developed a mentoring program for aggressive children based on an integrated model of risk and resilience. Their approach to understanding the needs of aggressive, high-risk children blended aspects of both social learning and attachment theory. The notion was proposed that aggressive children's overreliance on coercion was partly a function of their mental representations of earlier relationship experiences. To counter this tendency, these investigators designed a prevention program known as "PrimeTime," which blended skill-based interventions based on social learning theory with relationship-based interventions derived largely from attachment theory. In PrimeTime, mentoring was combined with consultation for parents and teachers and social problem solving skills-training groups (PSST) for children. PrimeTime mentors received extensive training and supervision in child-directed play skills. Cavell and Hughes randomly assigned 62 children to the PrimeTime mentoring program or to a stand-alone "Standard Mentoring" condition in which mentors were minimally trained and unsupervised. Children in both conditions showed significant improvement in ratings of aggression at posttreatment, but teacher-rated gains were lost at the 1-year follow-up.

Cavell and Hughes (2000) had tested a number of hypotheses about factors predicting or moderating treatment outcome. For example, they hypothesized that the quality of children's mentoring relationships would predict changes in aggression. For children in the PrimeTime group, self-rated relationship quality was predictive of both parent and teacher rated aggression posttreatment. However, only mentors' perceptions of the relationship predicted teacher-rated aggression at follow-up, underscoring the differential utility of mentee and mentor assessments. Cavell and Hughes also proposed that supportive mentoring relationships might serve to "prime" children for PSST by relaxing and improving maladaptive internal models of self, others, and relationships. In line with this hypothesis, PSST was delayed until children had been mentored for at least 6 months. As expected, mentees' perceptions of the quality of children's mentoring relationships (assessed prior to the start of PSST) predicted their posttreatment scores on measures of social cognition.

Cavell and Hughes (2000) also tested the notion that children who were less open to others' support and feedback would be more responsive to the PrimeTime mentoring program. Prime-Time was a more comprehensive program, and PrimeTime mentors had been trained specifically to deal with children whose behavior was challenging and whose self-views were often inflated (Hughes, Cavell, & Grossman, 1997). As predicted, aggressive children nominated by peers as narcissistic (i.e., "stuck up or think they are better than others") were more responsive to the PrimeTime program than to the standard mentoring condition: Teachers rated them as less aggressive at posttreatment, and peers saw them as more accepted at follow-up. Similar (nonsignificant) patterns were also evident at follow-up for teacher ratings of acceptance and aggression. Cavell and Hughes (2000) offered the following interpretation:

> By providing relationally at-risk children with a new relationship that was successfully begun, successfully maintained, and successfully ended, we may have been able to provide some degree of help for a group of children that clearly did not benefit from standard mentoring. (p. 230)

Cavell and Hughes (2000) also found, unexpectedly, that aggressive children low in peer-rated narcissism responded well to standard mentoring. If replicated, this finding would suggest that weekly contact with an untrained but supportive mentor is a cost-effective intervention for aggressive children who are open to such experiences but that additional training may be necessary if the mentees are both aggressive and narcissistic.

The studies by Karcher (2005) and by Cavell and Hughes (2000) illustrate the rich findings that accrue from mentoring research that is developmentally informed and theory driven. Both investigations tested specific hypotheses derived from extant research and relevant theory. And both studies went beyond outcome evaluations to examine important process issues.

Natural Mentoring

Our focus has been on formal or assigned mentoring; however, it appears that the preponderance of youth mentoring relationships in this country develop naturally (McLearn et al., 1999). Researchers have begun to empirically examine the correlates of natural mentoring relationships (Rhodes, 1994; Rhodes, Ebert, & Fischer, 1992; Zimmerman, Bingenheimer, & Behrendt, this volume; Zimmerman, Bingenheimer, & Notaro, 2002). Generally, natural mentoring relationships are associated with positive youth outcomes (Cowen & Work, 1988; Freedman, 1992; Rhodes, 1994; Werner, 1990), although this is not a uniform finding (e.g., Cavell, Meehan, Heffer, & Holladay, 2002). It also appears that most natural mentoring relationships begin in childhood (Cavell et al., 2002), but the impact on children's functioning has received little attention. Prospective studies that examine the long-term benefits of natural mentoring initiated during childhood would be a valuable contribution to the mentoring literature.

PRACTICE

The dearth of research specific to child mentoring is paralleled by a noticeable lack of information about the practice of mentoring children. Thus, in describing the practice of child mentoring, we borrow somewhat from programs that target both children and adolescents.

Mentoring Children Versus Adolescents

Activities and Skills

The kinds of interactions that lead children to trust and learn from their mentors are likely to differ from those used with adolescents. Adolescents tend to discuss a wide range of topics with their mentors (DuBois & Neville, 1997; DuBois, Neville, et al., 2002), and these discussions create opportunities to enter the world of the adolescent. Adults who mentor children cannot depend on extended verbal exchanges to gather information about or build relationships with their mentees. Most of what will be learned about their mentees will be obtained from other adults, gleaned from occasional conversations, or inferred from recurring patterns of behavior. The verbal give-and-take that characterizes adolescent-adult interactions will have to be supplanted by activities that are significant and meaningful (e.g., trips to the park, playing sports and games, making arts and crafts). Small wonder that DuBois and Neville (1997) found involvement in recreational activities predicted perceived benefits for younger mentees (M age = 11.57 years) but not for older mentees (M age = 15.37 years).

The difference between child and adolescent mentoring is not unlike the difference between child and adolescent psychotherapy. The younger the clients, the more likely the need for activity-based interventions, such as child-directed play therapy. Axline (1969) described child-directed play therapy as a downward extension of the verbal skills Rogerian therapists used to provide clients with warmth, genuineness, and unconditional positive regard. Child-directed play skills can also be used in child-oriented mentoring programs (Cowen, 1985). For example, Cavell and Hughes (2000) trained college student mentors of aggressive children to use child-directed play skills. Mentors were trained to follow the children's lead during play, to restate or summarize any comments made, to describe ongoing play activities, to identify and label expressed emotions, and to summarize the overall pattern of behavior both within and across visits. Of course, even trained mentors will vary in how well they use these skills, but without this training, mentors could rely too heavily on asking questions, giving help or advice, or focusing on the activity more than the children. Other mentors might feel bored and doubtful that childish play activities can help build a meaningful relationship. Over time, as children begin to express needs for relationship security, emotional closeness, or physical affection, these same mentors might see the relationship as too intense and overly close.

Risk of Harm

Recent findings indicate that mentoring can be harmful as well as helpful to children (Karcher, 2005; Rhodes, 1994, 2002). One type of harm is mentoring that ends prematurely, although the specifics of this harm (e.g., feeling abandoned or rejected) have not been explicated. But there are other potential sources of harm. Indeed, for young children, the greater risk could be from mentoring that lasts too long. If we can assume that children are less capable of ending a problematic mentoring relationship (i.e., by refusing to participate, by making visits intolerable), then they are more vulnerable to mentors who act with malice. Research clearly demonstrates that the younger and more dependent the child, the greater the risk of being victimized (Finkelhor & Dzuiba-Leatherman, 1994). Child mentees are perhaps less likely to communicate harmful experiences to parents or other caring adults and more susceptible to the kinds of "grooming" strategies (e.g., false praise, bribes) used by adults who sexually victimize young children (Berliner & Conte, 1990). These scenarios might seem rather far-fetched in light of the good intentions of many volunteer mentors and the common practice of conducting criminal background checks, but those who oversee mentoring programs should recognize that their first priority is to do no harm.

Mentor Programming and the Delivery of Change

As challenging as it is for researchers to specify the precise mechanisms by which mentoring leads to change, more challenging is making certain that mentoring actually produces those changes. Mentoring researchers can hypothesize and measure putative change processes more easily than mentoring programmers can control them. Tightly managing mentoring relationships is a reasonable goal for researchers seeking treatment fidelity, but it is somewhat antithetical to the notion that mentoring is, first and foremost, an interpersonal relationship. Thus, a daunting task facing mentor programmers is how to ensure that mentoring is producing change through activities and interactions that are reliable, uniform, and safe.

For example, if children are to learn specific, targeted skills from mentors, what kind of structure, format, and schedule would work best? What type of mentor or mentoring activity is capable of increasing and sustaining a child's overall level of positive reinforcement? Can mentor training effectively promote mentor-child interactions that leave children feeling optimistic about their futures and trusting of helpful adults? How long before mentoring relationships provide children with sustained improvements in mood and reductions in worry and concern? What logistical obstacles must be overcome if mentors are to succeed in removing children from stressful ecologies or support them instrumentally during periods of crisis? How should mentors end their relationships so that children are not harmed in the process? Such questions defy simple answers. For one thing, mentoring is unlikely to involve a single type of change mechanism. Newly acquired academic or interpersonal skills are often accompanied by a sense of mastery, improved mood, and a greater likelihood of receiving reinforcement from others. Even mentors who do not plan to teach a structured curriculum may nevertheless model for children an array of adaptive behaviors.

One way to achieve reliability and uniformity across mentoring relationships is to identify relationship parameters to which all mentors adhere. A common seen parameter is the general role that mentors are to adopt. Examples include coach, teacher, tutor, counselor, confidant, friend, caseworker, advocate, benefactor, behavior modifier, surrogate parent, and role model (Cavell et al., 2002). Of course, mentors are likely to differ among themselves in how they interpret an assigned role, and the role a mentor adopts could differ from the child's view of that role. Other relationship parameters include the

settings in which mentoring occurs, the frequency and length of each visit, and the duration of the relationship itself. Hughes et al. (2004) gave rather strict guidelines to their Lunch Buddy mentors. As noted earlier, these mentors were part of a school-based prevention program for aggressive elementary age children. Lunch Buddies visited their mentees twice each week during the school lunch period and limited their visits to this one setting. Also, Lunch Buddies could mentor a given child for only a single academic semester. Mentors were free to vary other aspects, but these guidelines helped ensure a fair degree of uniformity and reliability among the mentors. Other relationship parameters that one could use include specific duties that mentors are to perform, structured curricula to follow, and explicit goals to achieve (e.g., Karcher, 2005). By adopting such guidelines, practitioners increase treatment fidelity and the likelihood that specific change processes are adequately targeted.

Recent Innovations

There are several recent innovations in the mentoring field, some of which involve children. One is the rapid increase in site-based mentoring programs (Herrera, Sipe, & McClanahan, 2000). The majority of these programs (approximately 70%) are based in schools (Sipe & Roder, 1999), and most youth participating are elementary school students (Herrera, 1999). Herrera et al. (2000) found that site-based mentors rated relationships with elementary school children as closer and as more supportive than those with middle- or high school students. Herrera (1999) proposed that school-based mentoring is less costly, more convenient, and creates opportunities to interact with school staff. Whether these advantages lead to greater benefits for children awaits further study.

Another trend is the use of group mentoring, especially when mentors are lacking. Unknown at this point is whether group mentoring would be more advantageous for children or adolescents, given the risks of aggregating deviant, at-risk youth (Dishion et al., 1999). Another intriguing venture is the use of paid mentors. In the Friends of the Children program, mentors are paid a salary commensurate with that of beginning schoolteachers. Mentoring begins in kindergarten and concludes at the end of the 12th grade. Because this is a full-time job, mentors are more involved with parents, schools, and communities. The program has shown promise, despite its costs (Friends of the Children, 2003). One last innovation is the fostering of natural mentor relationships. This is currently more theoretical than practical (see Zimmerman et al., this volume). Schools, youth centers, after-school programs, sports leagues, and places of worship are all sites for promoting informal matches. Is it possible to increase the base rate of natural matches, creating what Freedman (1992) called "mentor-rich environments"? Currently, little is known about what promotional campaigns or incentive programs can make natural mentoring a more salient and attractive option for caring adults.

FUTURE DIRECTIONS

Synthesis

More than a decade ago, Blechman (1992) concluded that studies of mentoring lacked clear articulation of the underlying principles and theoretical models upon which decisions about mentoring were made. That assessment is true today, especially for child-focused mentoring. If policymakers were to examine the evidence in support of mentoring children, they might conclude that the benefits had been overstated and the risks underplayed. Thus, it is critical that we identify the parameters of effective mentoring: When does it work for children, and when is it harmful? We also need to know how it works and for which children is it most effective. Such questions are not part of the history and culture of youth mentoring. Instead of adding to our catalogue of effect sizes, researchers are encouraged to consider the developmental and social contexts within which mentoring occurs. For those who study and promote mentoring, it is no longer sufficient to "do good"; we must also strive to "do good science."

Recommendations for Research

1. *Build a research base specific to child mentoring.* We began this chapter noting the lack of research and theory devoted specifically to child mentoring. This is an uncomfortable position for those who would call for investing greater money and human capital into mentor programs for children. Early studies using mixed samples of children and adolescents made important contributions, but our first recommendation is to challenge researchers to conduct child mentoring studies that are separate from the larger domain of youth mentoring.

2. *Conduct research that is developmentally informed and theory driven.* Albert Einstein once remarked, "There is nothing quite so practical as a good theory." If true, then we should be concerned about the practice of child mentoring. The field has long been void of explicit theory and empirical evidence to guide what mentors do and support how well they are doing it. Mentor programmers and mentoring researchers who do not incorporate developmental theory and empirical knowledge into their work will soon be left out of the rapidly maturing field of prevention science. Effective and sustainable mentor programs require an accurate model of the problem to be prevented and a clear understanding of how mentoring will lead to proximal change and future adjustment.

3. *Increase the methodological rigor and sophistication of mentoring research.* Earlier, we noted the litany of methodological limitations that characterize previous research on the mentoring of children. Most problematic are the lack of randomly controlled trials; an overreliance on single-agent, self-report assessments to assess outcomes; and a failure to measure the long-term impact of mentoring children. Also lacking is the use of newer, more powerful data analytic strategies (e.g., linear growth curve modeling; see DuBois, this volume). So-called person-centered strategies that enable investigators to identify and track the development of children with and without natural or formal mentors also are warranted.

4. *Examine change processes in child mentoring.* We need to document the processes as well as the outcomes of child mentoring. Doing so will mean being open-minded and

developmentally informed about the potential processes at work. For example, there is support for the notion that the relationship is the final common pathway through which children are influenced when mentored (e.g., Karcher, 2005; DuBois, Neville, et al., 2002). However, it would be important not to foreclose prematurely on the possibility that other factors carry as much or more weight.

5. *Identify which children are likely to bene-fit from mentoring.* Mentoring is often viewed as a one-size-fits-all approach to preventing later difficulties in children. But current developmental theory casts doubt on finding large, ubiquitous main effects for the impact of child mentoring. More likely are interaction effects showing that some children benefit and others do not (e.g., Cavell & Hughes, 2000; DuBois, Holloway, et al., 2002). Rather than pairing mentors with children who do not benefit or who actively reject the mentoring experience, it seems more prudent to identify children who are willing and able to participate in and profit from mentoring.

Recommendations for Practice

1. *Structure programs to address child safety issues.* Mentoring is at times more harmful than helpful. It is not clear, however, whether children are more likely to be harmed by mentoring than by other kinds of psychosocial interventions (e.g., group therapy, inpatient hospitalization). Still, the potential iatrogenic nature of mentoring cannot be ignored. Therefore, potential risks associated with child mentoring (e.g., prematurely terminated relationships, poorly trained or impaired mentors, accidents) should be reflected in the policies and practices of all child mentoring programs. Parents and guardians should be informed of these risks and limitations before enrolling their children.

2. *Reduce the number of poorly run child mentoring programs.* Companies that insure mentoring programs, schools and agencies that house such programs, and professionals who develop and coordinate mentoring programs must understand that best practices are their best safeguard against harmful programs. This is especially true for harm caused by early termination and poorly trained or impaired mentors.

3. *Pay close attention to termination issues.* Parents, children, mentors, and program staff must have a clear and shared understanding about the ending of mentor relationships. All relationships come to an end—even the most supportive and productive mentoring relationships. Mentoring researchers would be wise to study how and when these endings should occur. Until then, practices (e.g., use of incentives) that protect against early terminations should be in place.

REFERENCES

Albano, A. M., Chorpita, B. F., & Barlow, D. H. (1996). Childhood anxiety disorders. In E. J. Mash & R. A. Barkley (Eds.), *Child psychopathology* (pp. 196–241). New York: Guilford Press.

Alfonso, L. M., Cavell, T. A., & Hughes, J. N. (2004). *Conflict and satisfaction in mentors' relationships with aggressive children: The role of attachment-related variables.* Manuscript submitted for publication.

Armstrong, J. (2000). I got it: Mentoring isn't for the mentor. *Newsweek, 135,* 10.

Axline, V. (1969). *Play therapy.* New York: Ballantine Books.

Barron-McKeagney, T., Woody, J. D., & D'Souza, H. J. (2001). Mentoring at-risk Latino children and their parents: Impact on social skills and problem behaviors. *Child & Adolescent Social Work Journal, 18,* 119–136.

Bergman, L. R., Cairns, R. B., Nilsson, L. G., & Nystedt, L. (2000). *Developmental science and the holistic approach.* Mahwah, NJ: Erlbaum.

Berliner, L., & Conte, J. R. (1990). The process of victimization: The victims' perspective. *Child Abuse & Neglect, 14,* 29–40.

Blechman, E. A. (1992). Mentors for high-risk youth: From effective communication to bicultural competence. *Journal of Clinical Child Psychology, 2,* 160–169.

Bronfenbrenner, U. (1979). *The ecology of human development: Experiments by nature and design.* Cambridge, MA: Harvard University Press.

Cairns, R. B., & Cairns, B. D. (1994). *Lifelines and risks: Pathways of youth in our time.* New York: Cambridge University Press.

Cavell, T. A. (2000). *Working with parents of aggressive children: A practitioner's guide.* Washington, DC: American Psychological Association.

Cavell, T. A., & Hughes, J. N. (2000). Secondary prevention as context for assessing change processes in aggressive children. *Journal of School Psychology, 38,* 199–235.

Cavell, T. A., & Hughes, J. N. (2004). *Preventing substance abuse in antisocial 6th graders.* Unpublished manuscript, University of Arkansas, Fayetteville.

Cavell, T. A., Meehan, B., Heffer, R. W., & Holladay, J. (2002). Natural mentors of adolescent COAs: Characteristics and correlates. *The Journal of Primary Prevention, 23,* 23–42.

Cicchetti, D., & Hinshaw, S.P. (2002). Prevention and intervention science: Contributions to developmental theory. *Development & Psychopathology, 14,* 667–671.

Coie, J. D., Watt, N. F., West, S. G., Hawkins, D. J., Asarnow, J. R., Markman, H. J., et al. (1993). The science of prevention: A conceptual framework and some directions of a National Research Program. *American Psychologist, 48,* 1013–1022.

Collins, W. A., Maccoby, E. E., Steinberg, L., Hetherington, E. M., & Bornstein, M. H. (2001). Toward nature WITH nurture. *American Psychologist, 56,* 171–173.

Cowen, E. L. (1985). Person-centered approaches to primary prevention in mental health: Situation-focused and competence-enhancement. *American Journal of Community Psychology, 13,* 31–48.

Cowen, E. L., & Work, E. (1988). Resilient children, psychological wellness and primary prevention. *American Journal of Community Psychology, 16,* 591–607.

Crick, N. R., & Dodge, K. A. (1994). A review and reformulation of social information-processing mechanisms in children's social adjustment. *Psychological Bulletin, 115,* 74–101.

Dishion, T. J., McCord, J., & Poulin, F. (1999). When interventions harm: Peer groups and problem behavior. *American Psychologist, 54,* 755–764.

Dortch, T. (2000). *The miracles of mentoring: The joy of investing in our future.* New York: Doubleday.

DuBois, D. L., Holloway, B. E., Valentine, J. C., & Cooper, H. (2002). Effectiveness of mentoring programs for youth: A meta-analytic review. *American Journal of Community Psychology, 30,* 157–197.

DuBois, D. L., & Neville, H. A. (1997). Youth mentoring: Investigation of relationship characteristics and perceived benefits. *Journal of Community Psychology, 25,* 227–234.

DuBois, D. L., Neville, H. A., Parra, G. R., & Pugh-Lilly, A. O. (2002). Testing a new model of mentoring. In G. G. Noam (Ed. in chief) & J. E. Rhodes (Ed.), *A critical view of youth mentoring (New Directions for Youth Development: Theory, Research, and Practice, No. 93,* pp. 21–57). San Francisco: Jossey-Bass.

Finkelhor, D., & Dzuiba-Leatherman, J. (1994). Victimization of children. *American Psychologist, 49,* 173–183.

Freedman, M. (1992). *The kindness of strangers: Reflections on the mentoring movement.* Philadelphia: Public/Private Ventures.

Friends of the Children. (2003). *Northwest Professional Consortium (NPC) 2002–2003 annual evaluation report on Friends of the Children–Portland.* Portland, OR: Author.

Grossman, J. B., & Rhodes, J. E. (2002). The test of time: Predictors and effects of duration in youth mentoring programs. *American Journal of Community Psychology, 30,* 199–219.

Grossman, J. B., & Tierney, J. P. (1998). Does mentoring work? An impact of the Big Brothers/Big Sisters program. *Evaluation Review, 22,* 403–426.

Hammen, C., & Rudolph, K. D. (1996). Childhood depression. In E. J. Mash & R. A. Barkley (Eds.), *Child psychopathology* (pp. 153–195). New York: Guilford Press.

Harris, J. R. (1995). Where is the child's environment? A group socialization theory of development. *Psychological Review, 102,* 458–489.

Heider, F. (1958). *The psychology of interpersonal relations.* New York: Wiley.

Herrera, C. (1999). *School-based mentoring: A first look into its potential.* Philadelphia: Public/Private Ventures.

Herrera, C., Sipe, C. L., & McClanahan, W. S. (2000). *Mentoring school-age children: Relationship development in community-based and school-based programs.* Philadelphia: Public/Private Ventures. (Published in collaboration with MENTOR/National Mentoring Partnership, Alexandria, VA)

Hetherington, E. M. (1999). *Coping with divorce, single parenting, and remarriage: A risk and resiliency perspective.* Mahwah, NJ: Erlbaum.

Hirschi, R. T. (1969). *Causes of delinquency.* Berkeley: University of California Press.

Hughes, J. N. (2000). The essential role of theory in the science of teaching children: Beyond empirically supported treatments. *Journal of School Psychology, 38,* 301–330.

Hughes, J. N., Cavell, T. A., & Grossman, P. B. (1997). A positive view of self: Risk or protection for aggressive children? *Development and Psychopathology, 9,* 75–94.

Hughes, J. N., Cavell, T. A., & Meehan, B., Zhang, D., & Collie, C. (2004). *Adverse school context moderates the outcomes of two selective intervention programs for aggressive children.* Manuscript submitted for publication.

Johnston, J. R., Gonzalez, R., & Campbell, L. E. G. (1987). Ongoing postdivorce conflict and child disturbance. *Journal of Abnormal Child Psychology, 15,* 493–509.

Karcher, M. J. (2005). The effects of school-based developmental mentoring and mentors' attendance on mentees' self-esteem, behavior, and connectedness. *Psychology in the Schools, 42,* 65–78.

Karcher, M. J., Davis, C., & Powell, B. (2002). The effects of developmental mentoring on connectedness and academic achievement. *The School Community Journal, 12*(2), 35–50.

Kohut, H., & Wolf, E. S. (1978). The disorders of the self and their treatment: An outline. *International Journal of Psycho-Analysis 59,* 413–425.

Kuczynski, L. (2002). *Handbook of dynamics in parent-child relations.* Thousand Oaks, CA: Sage.

Larson, R. W. (2000). Toward a psychology of positive youth development. *American Psychologist, 55,* 170–183.

Lindsey, E. W., & Mize, J. (2000). Parent-child physical and pretense play: Links to children's social competence. *Merrill-Palmer Quarterly, 46,* 565–591.

McCord, J. (1978). A thirty-year follow-up of treatment effects. *American Psychologist, 33,* 284–289.

McDowell, J. J. (1982). The importance of Herrnstein's mathematical statement of the law of effect for behavior therapy. *American Psychologist, 37,* 771–779.

McLearn, K. T., Colasanto, D., Schoen, C., & Shapiro, M. Y. (1999). Mentoring matters: A national survey of adults mentoring young people. In J. B. Grossman (Ed.), *Contemporary issues in mentoring* (pp. 66–83). Philadelphia: Public/Private Ventures.

Mosle, S. (2000, July 2). The vanity of volunteerism: Mentoring children from New York's inner city. *New York Times Magazine,* pp. 22–27, 40, 52–54.

Parra, G. R., DuBois, D. L., Neville, H. A., Pugh-Lilly, A. O., & Povinelli, N. (2002). Mentoring relationships for youth: Investigation of a process-oriented model. *Journal of Community Psychology, 30,* 367–388.

Rhodes, J. E. (1994). Older and wiser: Mentoring relationships in childhood and adolescence. *The Journal of Primary Prevention, 14,* 187–196.

Rhodes, J. E. (2002). *Stand by me: The risks and rewards of mentoring today's youth.* Cambridge, MA: Harvard University Press.

Rhodes, J. E., Ebert, L., & Fischer, K. (1992). Natural mentors: An overlooked resource in the social networks of young, African American mothers. *American Journal of Community Psychology, 20,* 445–461.

Rhodes, J. E., Grossman, J. B., & Resch, N. L. (2000). Agents of change: Pathways through which mentoring relationships influence adolescents' academic adjustment. *Child Development, 71,* 1662–1671.

Rhodes, J. E., Haight, W. L., & Briggs, E. C. (1999). The influence of mentoring on the peer relationships of foster youth in relative and nonrelative care. *Journal of Research on Adolescence, 9,* 185–201.

Sandler, I. (2001). Quality and ecology of adversity as common mechanisms of risk and resilience. *American Journal of Community Psychology, 29,* 19–61.

Scarr, S. (1992). Developmental theories for the 1990s: Development and individual differences. *Child Development, 63,* 1–19.

Sipe, C. L., & Roder, A. E. (1999). *Mentoring school-age children: A classification of programs.* Philadelphia: Public/Private Ventures. (Published in collaboration with MENTOR/National Mentoring Partnership, Alexandria, VA)

Smith, A. M. (2002). *Does mentoring really work? A meta-analysis of mentoring programs for at-risk youth.* Unpublished doctoral dissertation, Texas A&M University, College Station.

Snyder, J. J., & Patterson, G.R. (1995). Individual differences in social aggression: A test of a reinforcement model of socialization in the natural environment. *Behavior Therapy, 26,* 371–391.

Stein, D. M. (1987). Companionship factors and treatment effects in children. *Journal of Clinical Child Psychology, 16,* 141–146.

Tierney, J. P., Grossman, J. B., & Resch, N. L. (1995). *Making a difference: An impact study of Big Brothers/Big Sisters.* Philadelphia: Public/Private Ventures.

Werner, E. E. (1990). Protective factors and individual resilience. In S. J. Meiseils & J. P. Shonkoff (Eds.), *Handbook of early childhood intervention* (pp. 97–116). New York: Cambridge University Press.

Zimmerman, M. A., Bingenheimer, J. B., & Notaro, P. C. (2002). Natural mentors and adolescent resiliency: A study with urban youth. *American Journal of Community Psychology, 30,* 221–243.

12

MENTORING ADOLESCENTS

NANCY DARLING

INTRODUCTION

Mentoring is, by its very nature, a developmental phenomenon. MENTOR/National Mentoring Partnership (2003) defines mentoring as occurring within relationships that bring "young people together with caring individuals who offer guidance, support, and encouragement aimed at developing the competence and character of the mentee" (p. 9). Such relationships seem intimately linked with the time of life we call adolescence. As youth move from early to late adolescence, they experience a normative expansion in their social networks, more actively shape their social environments, and develop self-concepts that include awareness of both their current and potential adult selves. Adolescents also experience a shift in relations with parents at the same time that relations with peers take on new qualities of reciprocity and intimacy (for review, see Steinberg & Morris, 2001). In addition, adolescents typically adopt two key social roles during this period that will define much of the remainder of their lives: that of romantic partner and that of worker. In other words, adolescence can be described as an intense time in the life course, characterized by intrapersonal and social demands that the individual learn both how to do and how to be. The rapid and simultaneous changes and the adaptation of new roles seem to make it a period ripe for both the instrumental and affective supports mentoring is thought to provide.

Despite the fact that the nature of adolescence appears to make it an ideal time for mentoring, research on natural and programmatic mentoring has been discouraging. Naturalistic studies of relationships with unrelated adults indicate that such relationships are both less frequent and less emotionally salient than relationships with parents, peers, or extended family members (for review, see Darling, Hamilton, & Shaver, 2003). Matches between assigned mentors and protégés are less likely to last if the protégé is an adolescent rather than a child, and adolescent protégés and their mentors have been found to be less satisfied with their relationships than are younger protégés and their mentors (Grossman & Rhodes, 2002). The goal of this chapter is to review the adolescent mentoring literature from a developmental perspective with an eye toward the "fit" between adolescents' needs and characteristics, the social institutions in which adolescents live their lives, and mentoring relationships in order to gain insight into the gap between mentoring's promise and the results of current research.

THE DEVELOPMENTAL CHARACTERISTICS OF ADOLESCENTS

Four changes seem particularly relevant to understanding the fit between mentoring and the needs of adolescents: changes in the parent-adolescent relationship, changes in the peer context (including romantic relationships), adolescents' entrance into the workplace, and the move from elementary to middle and high school. Although there is little research to support the stereotype of early adolescents wanting little more from their parents than someone to rebel against (Holmbeck, 1996), parent-child relationships do change markedly during the transition to adolescence. Although adolescents remain close to their parents, they spend more time unsupervised and less time at home and are less likely to disclose information to parents (Csikszentmihalyi & Larson, 1984). At the same time, adolescents face increased exposure to peers involved in problematic behaviors such as drinking, sexual experimentation, and substance use. Peer relationships change as well, becoming increasingly focused on intimate self-disclosure and social support, particularly for girls, and somewhat less focused on shared activities (Brown & Klute, 2003). Children play. Adolescents hang out. Romantic relationships also become common during high school, involving approximately 20% of the population at any given time (Bouchy & Furman, 2003). Although early adolescent romantic relationships tend to be short-lived, they are often emotionally intense and take a great deal of time. During middle adolescence, romantic relationships come to be viewed as a context for intimacy and romantic partners as a primary source of social support (Brown, Feiring, & Furman, 1999).

Work provides another new context for adolescents. Over 90% of students have held paid jobs in the formal workplace prior to graduation (Steinberg & Morris, 2001). Although the work environment theoretically offers the opportunity for youth to become involved with adults in meaningful ways, the reality is quite different. Most teens' jobs are supervised by youth only slightly older than themselves, making work another peer context rather than an opportunity to develop close bonds with adults outside the family and school (Greenberger & Steinberg, 1986).

These changes in close relationships and social contexts are accompanied by changes in another key institution that shapes the lives of youth: schools. The move from elementary to middle school often is accompanied by increasing distance between teachers and students,

greater emphasis on social comparison and performance expectations, and fewer opportunities for creativity and abstract thinking (Eccles, Lord, & Buchanan, 1996). On a positive note, middle and high schools tend to offer a greater variety of extracurricular activities and thus more opportunities to form close relationships with school personnel outside the confines of a classroom. School-based extracurricular activities are associated with many positive outcomes (e.g., greater school bonding, lower levels of dropout, and higher achievement even when controlling for prior adjustment; see Darling, Caldwell, & Smith, in press), and some of these benefits may be mediated by supportive relationships youth have with activity leaders (Mahoney, Schweder, & Stattin, 2002).

Taken together, each of these changes moves adolescents toward a social environment that is relatively more dominated by peers, less populated by caring adults, and more tightly controlled and scheduled. In addition, they tend to make adolescents' schedules markedly fuller than those of children, often encompassing family and peer commitments, romantic relationships, work, and school-based extracurricular activities. These changes are highly relevant to thinking about how mentoring relationships and programs may best fit the needs of the adolescent age group. On the one hand, new role demands and loss of close, natural contact with unrelated adults may make mentors particularly salient. On the other hand, program-introduced mentors of adolescents are competing with many more time demands than are the mentors of children.

THEORY

Ecological Systems Theory as a Framework for Understanding Mentoring

Ecological systems theory (Bronfenbrenner & Morris, 1998) is a model of human development characterized by (a) an emphasis on an active person who influences and interprets, as well as is influenced by, the environment; (b) a focus on understanding the processes underlying development; and (c) attention to the interrelationships among multiple contexts in which the developing person interacts. The expansion of social contexts and more active role adolescents play in shaping their environments makes it particularly applicable to understanding mentoring during this developmental period. This theory is used most often to draw attention to variation in the processes operating for individuals who differ in their characteristics or their life circumstances (e.g., examining the differential effects of parental control on youth living in high- and low-risk neighborhoods). A central but often neglected aspect of ecological systems theory, however, is its emphasis on engagement in progressively more complex reciprocal activities as the driving force underlying development—what Bronfenbrenner calls "developmentally instigative activities." This emphasis draws from Vygotskian theory and can be seen in Bronfenbrenner's definition of a mentor:

> A mentor is an older, more experienced person who seeks to further the development of character and competence in a younger person by guiding the latter in acquiring mastery of progressively more complex skills and tasks in which the mentor is already proficient. The guidance is accomplished through demonstration, instruction, challenge, and encouragement on a more or less regular basis over an extended period of time. In the course of this process, the mentor and the young person develop a special bond of mutual commitment. In addition, the young person's relationship to the mentor takes on an emotional character of respect, loyalty, and identification. (U. Bronfenbrenner, personal communication, September 1998)

Ecological systems theory offers several important insights into the study and the practice of mentoring. First, it focuses attention on the roles of both the mentor and the protégé in shaping the interaction and developmental processes that drive mentoring. Second, it places the primary attention of the researcher on the functional role of mentoring and the processes that underlie it, rather than on the social roles of mentor or protégé. Third, implicit in ecological systems theory is the idea that development is optimized by adolescents'

involvement in developmentally instigative activities (i.e., activities that have the potential to become progressively more complex and therefore facilitate development). From this perspective, mentoring effectiveness should vary depending upon the extent to which mentors foster protégé involvement in developmentally instigative activities and provide sensitive and appropriate scaffolding. Finally, ecological systems theory focuses attention on how mentor-protégé relationships fit into the broader context of social relationships and social networks the protégé and mentor experience. The latter point is key in understanding mentoring in the complex social world of adolescence.

Theories of Individual Differences That Influence Mentoring

Risk and Resilience

The utility of ecological systems theory in studying mentoring and evaluating mentoring programs can be illustrated by examining four potential populations of adolescents whom mentoring might serve: youth who have shown evidence of emotional or behavioral problems, vulnerable youth who are "at risk" for developmental difficulty, youth of average ability at no particular risk, and gifted youth. In the context of an already existing problem, mentoring needs to function as an intervention and change an existing developmental trajectory by altering existing dysfunctional processes and substituting new ones. The ability of mentoring to cause this change in trajectory depends on the ability of mentors to interrupt the processes that led to the problem and sustain its continuation. The effectiveness of mentoring for at-risk youth needs to be evaluated in terms of the reduction of negative outcomes as well as the increase in positive developmental outcomes. Adolescence is a particularly difficult time to detect such changes in trajectories because rapid normative changes in most outcomes of interest make it difficult to document the effects of a process such as mentoring (see Darling & Cumsille, 2003, for an extensive treatment of this topic).

On the other hand, the benefits of mentoring for adolescents who are at risk for developmental problems but do not yet manifest them should operate through a different set of processes. In this context, mentors are assets that can (a) directly reduce risk or (b) buffer youth against risk. For example, mentors who provide tutoring and other forms of support may decrease the likelihood that adolescents with poor academic skills drop out of school. This example follows a *compensatory model* of resilience insofar as the presence of a mentor has a main effect on youth functioning that mitigates some of the negative effects of poor academic skills (Zimmerman, Bingenheimer, & Notaro, 2002). Alternatively, in a *risk protective model,* mentors can buffer adolescents against risk by increasing their resistance to its effects. In this way, mentors who provide social support to adolescents or teach them effective coping strategies may not reduce the stress that adolescents are exposed to, but they may make youth less vulnerable to its negative effects (DuBois, Neville, Parra, & Pugh-Lilly, 2002). Mentors can also increase the power of other protective factors, as when emotional support by the mentor increases the protective power of optimism through reinforcement of positive beliefs. Research suggests that mentoring programs are more effective at preventing problem behaviors among youth who are at risk for developmental problems due to environmental or personal factors than at turning around youth who are already manifesting such problems (DuBois, Holloway, Valentine, & Cooper, 2002). It is thus possible that early adolescents who are at risk may be more sensitive to intervention by mentors than later adolescents who are already manifesting problems.

In the first two examples, where mentoring functions as either an intervention or as prevention, mentoring disrupts negative processes or promotes positive processes, such as social support, that would otherwise be absent. In contrast, the mentoring of average or gifted adolescents is a promotive process whereby it is hoped that mentors will optimize development or provide avenues of development that could not otherwise be pursued, by providing new activities or fostering better performance in existing ones (e.g., Hamilton, 1999). It may be that mentors and role models are important in the lives of average and gifted youth because they affirm the ideal self-image of youth aspiring to high levels of achievement, provide specific support in the face of challenge, and provide practical information on how to reach their desired goals. These are all key processes in normative adolescent development. However, the idiosyncratic needs of gifted adolescents, combined with ceiling effects for achievement, may make it difficult to quantitatively document the effects of such relationships.

In terms of ecological systems theory, the preceding discussion illustrates how attending to individual differences in adolescent characteristics and the processes underlying mentoring has important implications for the design and assessment of mentoring programs during adolescence. In addition, the kinds of activities, supports, and relationship qualities that will help build and sustain mentor-protégé relationships may be different for adolescents at risk and those who are already well functioning and who have well-functioning social networks.

Attachment

Another promising model with which to examine individual differences in mentors and protégés and the effects these differences may have on mentoring processes is attachment theory. The attachment model has been widely used to describe individual differences in how adolescents interact with significant others, including parents, peers, and romantic partners. Attachment styles describe individual differences in representations of the availability and quality of support, beliefs about the extent to which the self is worthy of love and support, and perceptions regarding appropriate responses to the distress of others (Collins & Read, 1994). Secure adolescents are low in anxiety and avoidance; preoccupied adolescents are high in anxiety but low in avoidance; dismissing-avoidant adolescents are low in anxiety but high in avoidance; and fearful-avoidant adolescents are high in both anxiety and avoidance (Collins & Feeney, 2000).

Ecological systems theory underscores how attachment theory and other frameworks for understanding how adolescents and mentors approach close relationships might provide insight into the processes that differentiate successful and unsuccessful pairings and approaches. The next section focuses on the four major insights ecological systems theory provides on mentoring of adolescents: the active roles of mentor and protégé, a focus on process, the role of activities, and the fit between mentoring programs and social context.

RESEARCH

The Active Roles of Mentor and Protégé

One impetus for the creation of formal mentoring programs is the perception that parents are less available to teens than they once were and that youth increasingly are separated from relatives and casual social contact with unrelated adults (Rhodes, 2002). It is difficult to estimate the prevalence and importance of relationships with unrelated adults and even more difficult to estimate how many adults act in ways consonant with the functional role of mentor (Darling et al., 2003). Although unrelated adults make up only a small proportion of the people adolescents name as significant others (one widely cited statistic is approximately 10%; Blyth, Hill, & Thiel, 1982), most adolescents name at least one unrelated adult among their significant others (Blyth et al., 1982; Darling, Hamilton, Toyokawa, & Matsuda, 2002). Nonetheless, it seems apparent that some youth are more likely to have nonparental adults in their lives than others are. Why?

Past research suggests that demographic characteristics, such as the gender and ethnicity, tell us little about the processes or success of mentoring (Grossman & Tierney, 1998), either directly or when they are examined as a means of mentor-protégé matching (DuBois, Holloway, et al., 2002). Focusing on the mentoring process, however, leads to five potential avenues through which protégé characteristics are critical in the effectiveness of mentoring programs: (a) formation of natural mentoring relationships, (b) variations in the mentor-protégé bond, (c) protégés' interpretation of the behavior of their mentors, (d) protégés' willingness and ability to engage in the processes through which mentoring relationships effect developmental change, and (e) characteristics of the larger social and cultural milieu in which the mentor-protégé relationship operates.

Consistent with the theoretical role of attachment discussed previously, there is evidence that attachment style influences the ability of adolescents to successfully attract mentors and maintain relationships with them. Research on the transition to college suggests that attachment orientation influences adolescents' use of social support resources during the transition to college, including their effective use of professors as help providers (Larose, Bernier, Soucy, & Duchesne, 1999). Because attachment behaviors are most likely to be elicited by high levels of stress and insecurity (Bowlby, 1988), conflict in mentor-protégé relationships or serious problems on the part of protégés are most likely to evoke negative responses from individuals with insecure attachment patterns, whether they be adolescents or mentors. Generalizing from the literature on how college-aged youth respond to stress in romantic relationships, preoccupied adolescents may cling to their mentors in times of stress, may be ineffective help seekers, and may become frustrated with the help that mentors offer (Collins & Feeney, 2000). In contrast, avoidant youth may reject help when stressed or may feel threatened by mentoring relationships when they become intimate. Such responses may make it difficult for mentors. In qualitative research with a small sample of young adolescents, Hamilton and Hamilton (1993) found that assigned mentors often were discouraged by the failure of their early adolescent protégés to respond positively to support offers and that this was a frequent reason for relationship discontinuation. On the other hand, a demanding adolescent mentee may put off volunteers who have limited resources in terms of time. Fearful-avoidant youth who are at once emotionally needy and difficult to satisfy may be particularly likely to evoke exactly the kind of abandonment that they fear. It seems likely that youth with the most troubled family relationships will be least likely to be able to find or accept help from mentors.

Individuals also differ in how they respond to negative affect. For example, youth who are sensitive to rejection react strongly to negative feedback and are likely to interpret neutral responses as rejection or hostility (Levy, Ayduk,

& Downey, 2001). Thus, objective feedback or scheduling difficulties may be interpreted as signs of rejection and decrease the likelihood that the youth will seek out the mentor in the future. Rejection sensitivity may also influence how mentors react to the sometimes daunting schedules of adolescents and may lead to premature termination of an otherwise promising relationship (De Anda, 2001; Hamilton & Hamilton, 1993). Mentors have reported that many youth with troubled histories test them, and if the relationship fails, the failure confirms the youth's initial lack of trust (Noam & Hermann, 2002).

Like attachment, rejection sensitivity highlights how differences in adolescents' interpretations of mentors' behaviors may influence their responses. Other beliefs may also be important. For example, one experimental laboratory study found that negatively stereotyped youth, such as African Americans, may attribute negative performance feedback to stereotyped beliefs held by the evaluator and thus fail to respond effectively to criticism or incorporate feedback into their behavior (Cohen, 1999). However, when mentors provided identical negative feedback combined with statements of both high standards and their faith that the protégé could meet those standards, feedback was more likely to be accepted and acted upon. This experimental study concluded that the linking of criticism, high standards, and expressed confidence was more effective than any specific component alone or than buffering criticism with praise. Together with research on attachment and rejection sensitivity, this study underscores the importance of understanding how the beliefs of youth and mentors shape mentoring processes.

Mentoring Processes

There is clear consensus within the literature that merely taking part in a mentoring program provides adolescents with few objective benefits in terms of outcomes such as improved academic achievement, higher self-esteem, or reduced use of drugs or alcohol (DuBois, Holloway, et al., 2002; DuBois & Neville, 1997; Rhodes, 2002). This is true despite the satisfaction many mentors and protégés express in such programs

and the commonly held belief that participation in mentoring programs helps troubled youth (De Anda, 2001; Grossman & Tierney, 1998; Kahne et al., 2001; Tierney, Grossman, & Resch, 2000). Process-oriented studies, however, have shown more promising results. For example, DuBois, Neville, et al. (2002) tested models of involvement in mentoring programs predicting outcomes from relationship processes among 7- to 15-year-olds. In this study, participation in a formal mentoring program (Big Brothers Big Sisters) at Time 1 predicted increased likelihood that the mentor would be viewed as a significant adult in the early adolescent's life at 6 months after youth-mentor matching (Time 2), which was, in turn, associated with higher self-esteem. High self-esteem at Time 2 was associated with both lower levels of problem behavior and higher emotional well-being. Viewing the mentor as a significant adult at Time 2 also predicted higher levels of social support from nonparental significant adults at Time 2 (DuBois, Neville, et al., 2002). Thus, although there was no direct relationship between program participation and outcomes, participation in Big Brothers Big Sisters contributed to higher self-esteem and increased social support, which were associated with positive development. Two points are noteworthy in this example. First, it was only by modeling theoretically important processes that the effectiveness of the program could be demonstrated. Second, it shows the subtlety with which mentoring works. Mentoring may be more like the slow accumulation of pebbles that sets off an avalanche than the baseball bat that propels a ball from the stadium.

As indicated in the previous study, one key process is the formation of a strong relationship (Rhodes, 2002), as indicated by the nomination of the mentor as a significant other. Process-focused studies suggest that youth who consistently nominate program staff as mentors over three time points are more likely to be male, meet more frequently with their mentors, and feel emotionally close to mentors. In addition, these stable relationships were characterized by discussions of issues, increasing involvement over time in sports and discussion of relationships and social issues (DuBois, Neville, et al., 2002). Mentors who reported higher mentoring efficacy were more likely to be consistently nominated by youth (DuBois, Neville, et al., 2002). Evaluations of formal mentoring programs suggest that there is little association between early and late relationship quality, and for this reason, mentors should be encouraged to "stick it out" even in the face of a slow start (DuBois, Neville, et al., 2002). Potential difficulties should be addressed in early training and may be one reason that ongoing support of mentors is so effective (DuBois, Holloway, et al., 2002; Hamilton & Hamilton, 1993).

Although several authors have argued that emotional support and felt closeness may be at the core of effective mentoring (e.g., Rhodes, 2002), particularly for females (Liang, Tracy, Taylor, & Williams, 2002; Sullivan, 1996), others disagree. Based on reviews of naturally occurring relationships, Darling, Hamilton, and their colleagues have argued that one reason that associations between relationships with teachers and other unrelated adults and adolescent outcomes have been relatively weak is that researchers have focused primarily on the emotional quality of such relationships rather than on their instrumental qualities (Darling, Hamilton, & Niego, 1994; Darling et al., 2003; Darling et al., 2002). Naturally occurring relationships with unrelated adults differ from relationships with parents and peers in being characterized by relatively higher levels of challenge and teaching and lower levels of emotional support. In addition, affect—both positive and negative—was relatively independent of perceived mentoring provided by unrelated adults (Darling et al., 2002). Their argument may be particularly salient during adolescence, when support may be available from both peers and romantic partners, adolescents are cognitively capable of making finer distinctions between different aspects of relationships, and new role demands require the acquisition of new skills.

The relative importance of affective versus instrumental qualities may depend on how mentoring in conceived. If the process through which mentors influence their protégés is one of imparting knowledge, the ability of the mentor to facilitate the protégé's performance is dependent on (a) mentors' knowledge and (b) the skill with which they teach it. In contrast, if the process through which mentors influence their protégés is providing support, the determining factor is the experience of the person mentored. At this point in time, there is little research available that would allow us to differentiate between these two models.

Shared Activities

In studying the developmental influence of significant others, researchers in the United States have placed a stronger emphasis on affective relationship qualities than on shared activities (Silbereisen & Eyferth, 1986). Adolescent leisure has been similarly understudied, although many outcomes of interest to adolescent researchers (substance use and sexual activity, for example) are forms of leisure and take place in leisure settings. Unlike school, leisure is a context in which adolescents are encouraged to exert personal control and act autonomously. Leisure also provides opportunities for identity exploration and skill building, as well as both social differentiation and integration (Kleiber, 1999).

Some mentoring programs, such as those offered through the YMCA or scouting, are explicitly leisure- and activity-based. Shared activities may be one of the glues that holds successful mentoring relationships together as the relationship moves from the meeting of strangers toward intimacy. Activities shared by mentor and protégé also allow youth to explore aspects of their identities, a key process during adolescence. Waterman (1984) suggests that identity is discovered through participation in activities that allow one to recognize one's true self, rather than through introspection. It is also possible that the cognitive and social skills required by activity participation carry over to other areas of adolescents' lives. Learning a skill or developing a hobby can become the basis of a lifelong pursuit. In addition, activities are often associated with particular contexts and crowds at a high school. Because activities can influence youths' choice of settings, including coursework, school-based extracurricular activities (Brown & Klute, 2003), and careers, the influence of activities shared with a mentor may extend far beyond the length of the relationship (Darling et al., 1994).

Mentoring and Contextual Fit

Normative changes that occur from middle childhood to late adolescence mean that adolescents typically have relatively more sources of intimacy and social support available to them and increasingly busy lives. This creates a challenge for mentoring programs. Meaningful relationships take time to develop. What can mentors offer adolescents that makes these relationships worth the time they take from already jammed schedules? Adolescents who have incomplete or dysfunctional social networks have a clear need for the support of mentors. However, the finding that boys are more likely than girls to name their assigned mentor as important to them (DuBois, Neville, et al., 2002; Parra, DuBois, Neville, Pugh-Lilly, & Povinelli, 2002) may be a function of the relative lack of intimacy characteristic of boys' relationships, especially those who do not experience close relationships with parents and whose peer and romantic relationships are relatively immature. Activity-focused mentoring, on the other hand, especially activities that tie into adolescent needs, such as identity exploration and job skills, may fill a unique function in adolescents' lives that may help anchor mentor-protégé relationships and give them time to develop.

Summary and Critique

It has been difficult to document strong associations between either participation in mentoring programs (Rhodes, 2002) or close, naturally occurring relationships with unrelated adults (Darling et al., 2003) and adolescent outcomes. Perhaps these results are not surprising. First, establishing a warm, supportive emotional relationship is the primary task with which most mentors are charged. Such support may be quite distally related to objective assessments of adolescent outcomes, especially in light of the kind of sensitive measures needed to document changes in developmental trajectory for adolescents at risk (see DuBois, Neville, et al., 2002, for discussion of a similar point). Second, mentoring is an idiosyncratic process that is difficult to document using traditional statistical methods. For example, mentors enter adolescents'

lives at different times. One mentor may help a young person mend her relationships with her mother. Another may help a young person get a job. Another may help his protégé into substance use treatment. Each of these mentors has been effective, but a main effects model predicting parent-adolescent relationships or employment or substance use may show that nothing has happened. This may be particularly true as the expanding contexts, roles, and needs of adolescents may increase the variability of ways in which mentors may contribute to their development.

The scarcity of methodologically strong evaluation studies that include youth outcomes is unfortunate. Evaluation of mentoring programs is critical because it provides programs, funders, and participants with realistic expectations, allows programs to build on elements that work and eliminate or change aspects that do not, and allows practitioners to target youth that existing programs work for and develop new programs to serve youth for whom they do not work. Program evaluation is challenging, and discussion of the many techniques available to meet this challenge is beyond the scope of this chapter. Evaluations of programs serving adolescents are especially difficult, because rapid normative changes in many outcomes of interest (substance use, school engagement, sexual behavior, self-esteem, etc.) make it difficult to detect even strong effects. However, one key element of successful evaluations is that the measures and research design accurately reflect key elements of the program. With regard to mentoring, key questions that need to be addressed include: What predicts relationship success? How do relationship characteristics predict intermediary goals and outcomes, such as self-esteem, values, activities, and other social relationships? How are these intermediary goals related to more distal outcomes such as substance use, violence, pregnancy, or school success? Does the association of intermediate goals and distal outcomes vary as a function of relationship characteristics? Although these questions seem to imply the need for complex path or structural equation models, the sample sizes required by these statistical techniques are beyond those available to most small programs. This does not, however, mean that each separate question cannot be addressed through thoughtful application of simpler models and careful use of matched controls and longitudinal designs.

Newer statistical techniques such as hierarchical linear models (HLM) also can substantially increase statistical power and the ability to detect differences in smaller samples (Bryk & Raudenbush, 1992). For example, one might hypothesize that involvement in a good-quality mentoring relationship will be associated with positive outcomes in general (better academic performance and peer relationships, lower substance use, etc.) but that outcomes would be especially positive in those areas that the mentor and protégé actively focus on. In this case, variability in outcomes will depend upon (a) individual differences among youth prior to entering the mentoring program, (b) overall quality of the mentor-protégé relationship, and (c) whether or not the area was focused on within the mentor-protégé relationship. HLM allows researchers to model all three sources of variability. It thus allows researchers to answer, (a) What predicts *between- youth* differences in outcomes? (e.g., felt support from the mentor, length of the relationship, frequency of meetings), (b) What predicts *within-youth* differences in outcomes? (e.g., discussions or activities specific to the area), and (c) Do between-youth differences moderate within-youth processes? (e.g., does greater emotional support increase the benefit of talking about the importance of school with the mentor?). Because the specificity of the HLM model parses variance into between- and within- person components, it increases statistical power and facilitates detection of effects in small samples.

PRACTICE

Research suggests that formal mentoring programs are most effective when they adopt and carry out key elements of best practices (DuBois, Holloway, et al., 2002). Successful programs that include formal mentoring are varied. They share, however, elements of strong programmatic planning that are theoretically linked to the larger literature of developmental research and organizational resources dedicated to building and nurturing mentor-protégé relationships.

Three specific programs are described below that differ in their focus, but each are promising as mentoring programs for adolescents. They provide an illustration of the variety of ways in which mentoring can be used to meet the developmental needs of adolescents.

One Adult Who Is Crazy About You: Big Brothers Big Sisters

Bronfenbrenner argued that the single most important thing that children need to grow into healthy adults is the presence of one person who is irrationally attached to them (Bronfenbrenner & Morris, 1998). Big Brothers Big Sisters (BBBS), the oldest, largest, and best-documented organization dedicated to mentoring, is built upon that model (see, for example, Grossman & Tierney, 1998; Rhodes, Haight, & Briggs, 1999; Tierney et al., 1995). Although there is no evidence that the effects of BBBS are greater than those of other, similarly well-run programs (DuBois, Holloway, et al., 2002), it is the touchstone for high-quality, one-on-one mentoring programs serving youth at risk. Volunteer mentors in BBBS programs are carefully screened and matched with protégés, and there are strong expectations that mentors and protégés will meet frequently and make a minimum 1-year commitment. The stability of mentoring relationships seems to be particularly important to the success of the program, as research has suggested that the greatest gains from the program are experienced by protégés whose relationships last a year or longer, and early termination of relationships is associated with negative youth outcomes (Grossman & Rhodes, 2002). BBBS programs are most successful in establishing and maintaining relationships in dyads involving children under the age of 10 and those with fewer initial problems (Grossman & Tierney, 1998). Although it might be thought that younger mentors (26–30) and those who shared the disadvantaged backgrounds of their protégés would be more successful as mentors, the demands on their time make these pairings more prone to early termination. Although the model has not yet been tested, findings that it is easier to establish successful relationships with at-risk youth at a young age (the program begins serving youth as young as 8) suggest that one strategy for successfully delivering mentoring to adolescents is establishing the relationship early and maintaining it through the transition to middle school.

It Takes a Village: RALLY

RALLY is a comprehensive, developmentally sensitive prevention program focusing on youth making the transition to middle school (Noam & Hermann, 2002). The program focuses on coordinating different developmental contexts and shaping them to support adolescent development at a developmental period in which the confluence of biological, cognitive, social, and contextual changes put many youth at risk, and it appears to be strongly influenced by ecological systems theory (Bronfenbrenner & Morris, 1998). The developers of the program are critical of traditional mentoring programs, such as Big Brothers Big Sisters, because they fail to take into account the complex and often disjointed social institutions and supports (e.g., traditional classrooms, special education services, after-school care, family) that adolescents must negotiate. By focusing on providing emotional support, Noam argues that traditional mentoring programs attempt to change the adolescent to fit the system rather than change the system to fit the adolescent.

In RALLY, mentors serve as a bridge between adolescents' family, school, and after-school environments. The role of mentors is not to help individual adolescents to cope better by providing emotional support, but to structure the environment in which the adolescents function so that it is fundamentally less stressful. RALLY is a schoolwide program in which professional mentors (who are often training to be in helping professions such as clinical psychology) are assigned to youth falling into three categories: those at high risk, those currently in crises, and other youth. Within schools, mentors work within classrooms to reduce discipline problems, foster academics, and coordinate "pull-out" services, such as special education. Mentors also are involved in after-school programs to build social and academic skills and work closely with families. Because all students in the school are involved, one goal of the program is to promote an overall change in the social environment and to reduce risk associated with negative peer influence. One-on-one mentoring is tailored to promote specific areas of potential growth, such as academic improvement or improvement in parent-adolescent relationships. A central conceptual element of this model is that crisis and problems are seen as potential triggers for effecting positive developmental change rather than as markers of failure.

Learning Through Work: The Cornell Youth and Work Program

The Cornell Youth Apprenticeship Demonstration Project places youth in work settings related to their areas of interest (Hamilton, 1999; Hamilton & Hamilton, 1999). This activity-focused program for high school youth differs from RALLY and BBBS in its focus on expanding adolescents' understanding of and preparation for the workplace and in its commitment to rotating them through a series of mentoring relationships in order to give them a fuller appreciation of the total work setting. Two types of mentors are assigned to each youth: (a) coordinators who supervise the adolescents' placements throughout the company and (b) mentors who work closely with adolescents in specific settings. A major focus of many mentors' activities is to help introduce adolescents into the social demands of work, such as teamwork, responsibility, and positive work attitudes. Although the program is specifically aimed at easing the adolescent's transition to work, both mentors and protégés report that their relationships often move beyond the bounds of the task to include advice about school and a broader vision of the adolescent's future (Hamilton, 1999; Hamilton & Hamilton, 2002).

FUTURE DIRECTIONS

Synthesis

The word *mentor* is used to describe many different types of relationships with individuals, filling many different social roles. Mentoring programs are similarly varied, ranging from one-on-one relationships to traditional sports or leisure programs to ambitious interventions aimed at changing entire communities. This raises the question of the usefulness of mentoring as a construct. There is a large literature on significant relationships and their role in the lives of adolescents. In thinking about mentoring programs, therefore, it might be useful to return to the roots of the construct and ask some basic questions. What can we do to facilitate the involvement of adolescents in developmentally instigative activities? How can we create contexts in which adults and adolescents have opportunities to get together and become involved in the kinds of relationships and activities that we know are good for adolescents? Combining our understanding of what makes programs work with what we know about adolescent development more generally may provide us with new ways to think about and facilitate processes that support youth.

Recommendations for Research

1. *Model process.* Main effects models provide little insight into what makes mentoring work (or not work) and for whom. Key questions to be addressed include: What predicts relationship success? How do relationship characteristics predict intermediary goals and outcomes, such as self-esteem, values, activities, and other social relationships? How are these intermediary goals related to more distal outcomes? Does the association of intermediate goals and distal outcomes vary as a function of relationship characteristics?

2. *Study what mentors and protégés do, not just what they feel.* Shared activities are an understudied component of mentoring. Research suggests that they can provide a bridge to strong emotional bonds as well as a continuing source of positive influence on the protégé after the mentor-protégé relationship has ended. New models of activity involvement need to be drawn from relevant literatures in developmental psychology and leisure studies.

3. *Put mentoring relationships in context.* Little research has been done to examine how mentoring relationships fit into adolescents' already established social networks (see Barrera

& Bonds, this volume). Examining this question may provide important insight into factors differentiating successful and unsuccessful mentor pairings.

4. *Make use of within-dyad variability.* Within-dyad variability in goals and focus can be modeled using techniques such as HLM, instead of being relegated to the between-dyad error term, as it is in standard regression techniques. This can lead to a substantial increase in power.

Recommendations for Practice

1. *Educate mentors about adolescents.* One clear message from the literature is that programs need to follow recommended best program practices, including supervision, support, and training (e.g., MENTOR/National Mentoring Partnership, 2003). Mentors need to understand adolescent development and the social contexts in which they live. For example, healthy adolescents make clear distinctions between how they act in intimate relationships and in relationships with acquaintances, and their lives tend to be much busier than those of children. Training can provide mentors with realistic expectations about their relationships with protégés, especially during the early phases.

2. *Encourage mentors to stick it out.* It should be made clear to volunteers that premature termination of mentor-protégé relationships may be harmful to youth. Scheduling difficulties, canceled appointments because of dates or social events, or the constrained emotional expressiveness of adolescents, compared with children, may be interpreted by mentors as lack of interest. Relationship quality at the early and later phases is not strongly correlated. Shared structured activities may provide a bridge during the formation of new mentor-protégé relationships that will make it easier for mentors to overcome relationship obstacles. Adding a new and meaningful relationship to one's life takes time and requires adjustment, which scheduled activities may help facilitate. Programs serving high-risk youth with whom it is difficult to maintain relationships may want to combine

explicit expectations for frequency of meetings and duration of commitment.

3. *Consider individual differences and related needs in training.* Differences in relationship style should be explicitly dealt with through pretraining and ongoing support. Understanding of attachment and rejection sensitivity may be particularly useful frameworks for mentors to understand the behavior of their adolescent protégés.

4. *Use knowledge about personality to make matches.* Explicit recognition should be given to individual differences in relationship styles. Compatibility of attachment styles might be one potential dimension for matching mentors and protégés. For example, it is clear that preoccupied youth, who tend to be emotionally needy, would be poorly matched with volunteers who are anxious-avoidant, and uncomfortable with dependence.

5. *Screen out mentors at risk for premature relationship termination.* It may be helpful to screen out or provide extra support for rejection-sensitive volunteers because of the potential damage severed relationships may have for clients. Caution should also be used with transient volunteer populations, such as college students. Mentoring programs are not designed to provide learning experiences for mentors, but rather helping relationships for protégés. Although the shortage of volunteers makes it tempting to accept all comers, recognition that failed relationships are not neutral but potentially harmful to youth argues for greater conservatism.

REFERENCES

Blyth, D. A., Hill, J. P., & Thiel, K. S. (1982). Early adolescents' significant others: Grade and gender differences in perceived relationships with familial and nonfamilial adults and young people. *Journal of Youth & Adolescence, 11,* 425–450.

Bouchy, H. A., & Furman, W. (2003). Dating and romantic experiences in adolescence. In G. R. Adams & M. D. Berzonsky (Eds.), *Blackwell handbook of adolescence* (pp. 313–330). Oxford, UK: Blackwell.

Bowlby, J. (1988). *A secure base.* New York: Basic Books.

Bronfenbrenner, U., & Morris, P. (1998). The ecology of developmental processes. In W. Damon (Series Ed.) & R. M. Lerner (Vol. Ed.), *Handbook of child psychology: Vol. 1. Theoretical models of human development* (5th ed., pp. 993–1028). New York: Wiley.

Brown, B. B., Feiring, C., & Furman, W. (1999). Missing the Love Boat: Why researchers have shied away from adolescent romance. In W. Furman, B. B. Brown, & C. Feiring (Eds.), *The development of romantic relationships in adolescence* (pp. 1–16). New York: Cambridge University Press.

Brown, B. B., & Klute, C. (2003). Friendship, cliques, and crowds. In G. R. Adams & M. D. Berzonsky (Eds.), *Blackwell handbook of adolescence* (pp. 330–348). Oxford, UK: Blackwell.

Bryk, A. S., & Raudenbush, S. W. (1992). *Hierarchical linear models: Applications and data analysis methods.* Newbury Park, CA: Sage.

Cohen, G. L. (1999). *The mentor's dilemma: Providing critical feedback across the racial and gender divides.* Doctoral dissertation, Stanford University, Stanford, CA.

Collins, N. L., & Feeney, B. C. (2000). A safe haven: An attachment theory perspective on support seeking and caregiving in intimate relationships. *Journal of Personality and Social Psychology, 78,* 1053–1073.

Collins, W. A., & Read, S. J. (1994). Cognitive representations of attachment: The structure and function of working models. In D. Perlman & W. Jones (Eds.), *Advances in personal relationships: Attachment processes in adulthood* (Vol. 4, pp. 29–70). London: Jessica Kingsley.

Csikszentmihalyi, M., & Larson, R. (1984). *Being adolescent.* New York: Basic Books.

Darling, N., Caldwell, L., & Smith, R. C., Jr. (in press). Participation in school-based extracurricular activities and adolescent adjustment. *Journal of Leisure Research.*

Darling, N., & Cumsille, P. (2003). Theory, measurement, and methods in the study of family influences on adolescent smoking. *Addiction, 98*(Suppl. 1), 21–36.

Darling, N., Hamilton, S. F., & Niego, S. (1994). Adolescents' relations with adults outside the family. In R. Montemayor & G. R. Adams (Eds.), *Personal relationships during adolescence* (pp. 216–235). Thousand Oaks, CA: Sage.

Darling, N., Hamilton, S. F., & Shaver, K. H. (2003) Relationships outside the family: Unrelated adults. In G. R. Adams & M. D. Berzonsky (Eds.), *Blackwell handbook of adolescence* (pp. 349–370). Oxford, UK: Blackwell.

Darling, N., Hamilton, S. F., Toyokawa, T., & Matsuda, S. (2002). Naturally-occurring mentoring in Japan and the United States: Social roles and correlates. *American Journal of Community Psychology, 30,* 245–270.

De Anda, D. (2001). A qualitative evaluation of a mentor program for at-risk youth: The participant's perspective. *Child and Adolescent Social Work Journal, 18,* 97–117.

DuBois, D. L., Holloway, B. E., Valentine, J. C., & Cooper, H. (2002). Effectiveness of mentoring programs for youth: A meta-analytic review. *American Journal of Community Psychology, 30,* 157–197.

DuBois, D. L., & Neville, H. A. (1997). Youth mentoring: Investigation of relationship characteristics and perceived benefits. *Journal of Community Psychology, 25,* 227–234.

DuBois, D. L., Neville, H. A., Parra, G. R., & Pugh-Lilly, A. O. (2002). Testing a new model of mentoring. In G. G. Noam (Ed. in chief) & J. E. Rhodes (Ed.), *A critical view of youth mentoring (New Directions for Youth Development: Theory, Research, and Practice, No. 93,* pp. 21–57). San Francisco: Jossey-Bass.

Eccles, J. S., Lord, S., & Buchanan, C. M. (1996). School transitions in early adolescence: What are we doing to our young people? In J. A. Graber & J. Brooks-Gunn (Eds.), *Transitions through adolescence: Interpersonal domains and context* (pp. 251–284). Mahwah, NJ: Erlbaum.

Greenberger, E., & Steinberg, L. (1986). *When teenagers work: The psychological and social costs of adolescent employment.* New York: Basic Books.

Grossman, J. B., & Rhodes, J. E. (2002). The test of time: Predictors and effects of duration in youth mentoring relationships. *American Journal of Community Psychology, 30,* 199–219.

Grossman, J. B., & Tierney, J. P. (1998). Does mentoring work? An impact study of the Big Brothers Big Sisters program. *Evaluation Review, 22,* 403–426.

Hamilton, M. A. (1999). *Learning well at work: Choices for quality.* Ithaca, NY: Cornell University Press.

Hamilton, M. A., & Hamilton, S. F. (1993) *Toward a youth apprenticeship system: A progress report from the Youth Apprenticeship Demonstration Project in Broome County, New York.* Ithaca, NY: Cornell University Press.

Hamilton, M. A., & Hamilton, S. F. (2002). Why mentoring in the workplace works. In G. G. Noam (Ed. in chief) & J. E. Rhodes (Ed.), *A critical view of youth mentoring (New Directions for Youth Development: Theory, Research, and Practice, No. 93*), pp. 59–89). San Francisco: Jossey-Bass.

Hamilton, S. F., & Hamilton, M. A. (1999). *Building strong school-to-work systems: Illustrations of key components.* Ithaca, NY: Cornell University Press.

Holmbeck, G. N. (1996). A model of family relational transformations during the transition to adolescence: Parent-adolescent conflict and adaptation. In J. A. Graber & J. Brooks-Gunn (Eds.), *Transitions through adolescence: Interpersonal domains and context* (pp. 167–199). Mahwah, NJ: Erlbaum.

Kahne, J., Nagaoka, J., Brown, A., O'Brien, J., Quinn, T., & Thiede, K. (2001). Assessing after-school programs as contexts for youth development. *Youth and Society, 32,* 421–446.

Kleiber, D. A. (1999). *Leisure experiences and human development: A dialectical interpretation.* New York: Basic Books.

Larose, S., Bernier, A., Soucy, N., & Duchesne, S. (1999). Attachment style dimensions, network orientation and the process of seeking help from college teachers. *Journal of Social & Personal Relationships, 16,* 225–247.

Levy, S. R., Ayduk, O., & Downey, G. (2001). The role of rejection sensitivity in people's relationships with significant others and valued social groups. In M. R. Leary (Ed.), *Interpersonal rejection* (pp. 251–289). New York: Oxford University Press.

Liang, B., Tracy, A. J., Taylor, C. A., & Williams, L. M. (2002). Mentoring college-age women: A relational approach. *American Journal of Community Psychology, 30,* 271–288.

Mahoney, J. L., Schweder, A. E., & Stattin, H. (2002). Structured after-school activities as a moderator of depressed mood for adolescents with detached relations to their parents. *Journal of Community Psychology, 30,* 69–86.

MENTOR/National Mentoring Partnership. (2003). *Elements of effective practice* (2nd ed.). Alexandria, VA: Author.

Noam, G. G. M., & Hermann, C. A. (2002). Where education and mental health meet: Developmental prevention and early intervention in schools. *Development & Psychopathology, 14,* 861–875.

Parra, G. R., DuBois, D. L., Neville, H. A., Pugh-Lilly, A. O., & Povinelli, N. (2002). Mentoring relationships for youth: An investigation of a process-oriented model. *Journal of Community Psychology, 30,* 367–388.

Rhodes, J. E. (2002). *Stand by me: The risks and rewards of mentoring today's youth.* Cambridge, MA: Harvard University Press.

Rhodes, J. E., Haight, W. L., & Briggs, E. C. (1999). The influence of mentoring on the peer relationships of foster youth in relative and nonrelative care. *Journal of Research on Adolescence, 9,* 185–201.

Silbereisen, R. K., & Eyferth, K. (1986). Development as action in context. In R. K. Silbereisen, K. Eyferth, & G. Rudinger (Eds.), *Development as action in context: Problem behavior and normal youth development* (pp. 3–16). Berlin, Germany: Springer-Verlag.

Steinberg, L., & Morris, A. S. (2001). Adolescent development. *Annual Review of Psychology, 52,* 83–110.

Sullivan, A. M. (1996). From mentor to muse: Recasting the role of women in relationship with urban adolescent girls. In B. J. R. Leadbeater & N. Way (Eds.), *Urban girls: Resisting stereotypes, creating identities* (pp. 226–249). New York: New York University Press.

Tierney, J. P., Grossman, J. B., & Resch, N. L. (1995). *Making a difference: An impact study of Big Brothers/Big Sisters.* Philadelphia: Public/Private Ventures.

Waterman, A. (1984). Identity formation: Discovery or creation? *Journal of Early Adolescence, 4,* 329–341.

Zimmerman, R., Bingenheimer, J. B., & Notaro, P. C. (2002). Natural mentors and adolescent resiliency: A study with urban youth. *American Journal of Community Psychology, 30,* 221–243.

13

RACE, ETHNICITY, AND CULTURE IN MENTORING RELATIONSHIPS

BERNADETTE SÁNCHEZ AND YARÍ COLÓN

INTRODUCTION

Issues of race, ethnicity, and culture are salient in youth mentoring programs. In many instances, programs serve primarily minority youth, and it is commonplace to pair them with White mentors (Grossman & Tierney, 1998; Sipe, 1996). At the same time, however, these same programs typically place special emphasis on attempting to pair minority youth with minority mentors whenever feasible. In some instances, programs are restricted entirely to same-race relationships (e.g., Royse, 1998). The preceding practices highlight the importance of understanding the roles of race, ethnicity, and culture in youth mentoring relationships. Despite these considerations, there has been only limited systematic examination of the roles of these factors in mentoring. This chapter aims to fill this gap in the literature. We first consider theoretical perspectives on the roles of race, ethnicity, and culture in mentoring relationships. Second, we review research findings that explicate the roles of race, ethnicity, and culture in youth mentoring. Third, programs that incorporate race, ethnicity, or cultural factors are described. Finally, we suggest future directions for researchers and practitioners to consider.

Before delving into the roles of race, ethnicity, and culture in youth mentoring, it is important to understand the difference between these terms, which often are used interchangeably. *Race* refers to the biological, genetic heritage of a group (Robinson & Howard-Hamilton, 2000). Although phenotypic variables, such as skin color and hair type, do not necessarily determine one's race, they are often used as the basis for assigning people to a racial group (Robinson & Howard-Hamilton, 2000). *Ethnicity* refers to groups of individuals who have a common culture, nationality, history, or religion (Robinson & Howard-Hamilton, 2000). There is no agreed upon definition of *culture,* but overall, culture refers to the shared patterns of a society (e.g., values, communication styles) that are transmitted over time through generations (Betancourt & Lopez, 1993). Ethnic group members' interactions with one another are ways in which culture is transmitted. Hence, ethnic group can determine culture. On the other hand, cultural background can determine ethnic group (Betancourt & Lopez, 1993).

It is important to understand the definitions of race, ethnicity, and culture because individuals often assume that people of the same race are also of the same ethnicity or culture. Awareness of the distinction between race and ethnicity and ethnic or cultural differences is a relevant consideration with respect to both mentors and youth within relationships and those administering mentoring programs. At the relationship level, a mentor and mentee can be of the same race, such as Black, but have different ethnicities, such as Jamaican, African American, or Dominican. Individuals in each of these ethnic groups have a common language, nationality, or history. The mentor might make assumptions about the cultural values of his or her mentee just because they share the same race, which could have a negative impact on the quality of their communication. At the program level, it is important for staff to be aware of the nuances of race, ethnicity, and culture, which would help them in making better matches and better training mentors on youths' needs. However, most of the mentoring literature has not examined the roles of race, ethnicity, and culture, and even attention to the influence of racial similarity or difference within the mentor-mentee relationship has only recently begun to receive attention.

THEORY

In this section, we consider four theories that may be helpful in understanding how race, ethnicity, and culture contribute to effective mentoring relationships with youth. Each of these theories addresses processes that have been proposed by Rhodes (2002; this volume) and others to be important influences on the outcomes of mentoring relationships for youth. The similarity-attraction paradigm, the first theoretical perspective that we consider, proposes that individuals are attracted to those similar to themselves (Byrne, 1971). Rhodes posits in her model that mentors are more effective when they have a vested interest in the development of their mentees. Yet this paradigm suggests that some individuals may feel less of an interest in others who appear different based on race/ethnicity. The second theory is Ogbu's framework (1990) regarding minority youth in the United States. Ogbu argues that racial minority youth are best matched with mentors of the same race who have experience in combating racism in the United States. In her model, Rhodes (2002) proposes that role modeling and

advocacy are key processes through which mentors can enhance youth development. Ogbu argues that mentors who themselves belong to racial minority groups are in the best position to role model and teach youth from these groups how to cope with discrimination. The third theory is stereotype threat, which refers to the threat that others' judgments or one's actions will cause a person to be negatively stereotyped (Steele, 1997). Effective mentoring relationships are likely to be based on a foundation of trust, respect, and understanding (Rhodes, 2002). Yet racial/ethnic minority youth mentored by adults from different racial/ethnic backgrounds might experience greater stereotype threat as a function of a cross-race match, which could influence their trust in their mentors. Finally, cultural values are considered, such as familism (Fuligni, Tseng, & Lam, 1999) and collectivism (Vandello & Cohen, 1999), to better conceptualize the role of race, ethnicity, and culture in mentoring. With relevance to mentoring relationships, programs typically pair the youth with a single individual who is not part of the youth's existing social network of familial or nonfamilial ties. Yet cultural values may influence the receptivity of youth to viewing nonrelatives as significant adults in their lives. Having a mentor who is outside one's social network may make it difficult to develop the trust that is necessary for effective mentoring relationships.

Racial, Ethnic, and Cultural Similarity or Dissimilarity

Two theories that guide our understanding of racial, ethnic, and cultural similarity in mentoring relationships are the similarity-attraction paradigm (Byrne, 1971) and Ogbu's (1990) framework. The similarity-attraction paradigm, as stated earlier, implies that mentors and mentees of similar racial, ethnic, or cultural backgrounds, who likely have more in common, would experience more successful relationships than those of different backgrounds. However, this idea has not received consistent support from the studies conducted to date. There are those who advocate for same-race matches as well as others who argue for the necessity and effectiveness of cross-race matches. Proponents of same-race matching contend that minority youth internalize the racist attitudes of the larger society and, as such, are vulnerable to low self-esteem (Ogbu, 1990). Through role modeling and advocacy (Rhodes, 2002), minority mentors who understand the social and psychological conflicts that these youth experience can teach youth how to cope effectively. Similarly, Bowman, Kite, Branscombe, and Williams (1999) argued for the importance of Black students at predominantly White universities to be mentored by Black faculty with whom they share their "stigmatizing condition," which they argue may promote the emotional well-being of these students and alleviate their feelings of isolation.

Other researchers argue that cross-race matches in youth mentoring can work equally well. Supporters of cross-race mentoring argue that the mentor's skills, experience, interests, and openness to culture are more important than race (Flaxman, 1992). An important further consideration is that the similarity-attraction paradigm suggests that similarity in experiences and interests may be an equally or even more important matching criteria. Thus, it might be that cross-race relationships are less of an influence if mentors and mentees have similar interests and experiences. Another argument for cross-race matches is that they are a necessity, have become the norm, and, as such, are reflective of the samples in studies from which much of the positive effects of mentoring have been found. Many racial/ethnic minority youth could be on waiting lists for long periods of time if mentoring program staff attempt to match solely by race (Rhodes, Reddy, Grossman, & Lee, 2002) because programs often have a lower proportion of minority mentors compared with minority mentees (Rhodes, 2002). Rhodes et al. (2002) argue that it is more important to offer mentors to youth than to have them wait. The idea is not necessarily that cross-race mentoring is as effective as same-race mentoring, but that they can still be effective relationships given the positive findings in the literature regarding cross-race relationships. It might be more effective for more youth to be reached than not reached at all.

Stereotype Threat

Stereotype threat theory has been the impetus for research examining the role of cultural factors in the cross-race mentoring relationships of minority college students (e.g., Cohen, Steele, & Ross, 1999). Stereotype threat refers to the psychological state that an individual experiences when some property of the environment reminds him or her of stereotypes held by society (Steele, 1997). Members of the group that are the target of the stereotype then become more likely to succumb to that expectation than if they had not been cued or reminded of the stereotype (Steele, 1997). For example, it has been found in experimentally designed laboratory studies that, controlling for verbal standardized test scores, African American college students tend not to perform as well as their White peers on standardized exams only when cues, such as the words *exam* or *comparison,* are provided (Steele, 1997). However, when such cues were not presented, both groups performed equally on the same exam. Thus, when minority students take such tests, the threat that they will perform poorly on the exams is presumed to be triggered, which, as a result, negatively affects their performance.

In the context of mentoring relationships with White mentors, it has been noted that the processes proposed by stereotype threat theory may influence how minority youth perceive White mentors and how discussions and interactions within these relationships may affect mentees' performance. It has been argued that unwittingly, White mentors might do or say things that lead their mentees to experience stereotype threat (Cohen et al., 1999; Grant-Thompson & Atkinson, 1997). For instance, if a White mentor simply provides suggestions and points out weaknesses to a minority mentee, the mentee may believe that the mentor holds negative racial biases or prejudices and be less motivated to succeed in the future. This could have detrimental effects on the mentoring relationship, but it also might adversely affect other areas of the mentee's life, such as his or her academic aspirations and self-esteem, if stereotype threat is evoked.

Stereotype threat also may undermine the trust youth have in their mentors, particularly cultural mistrust. Cultural mistrust is a pervasive attitude that racial minority individuals have toward European Americans as a result of historical discrimination and oppression in the

United States (Grant-Thompson & Atkinson, 1997). Due to racism, some minority youth in academic contexts think that White individuals with power tend to doubt their ability and belonging in those environments (Steele, 1997). Cultural mistrust could play an important role in mentees' attraction to mentors and in the development of their relationships. Cultural mistrust may make it more difficult to develop a trusting and supportive mentoring relationship.

Cultural Values

A concept that may help advance our understanding of the role of race, ethnicity, and culture in mentoring is reflected in the contrasting cultural values of individualism and collectivism (Vandello & Cohen, 1999). The usefulness of these values is suggested by the tendency for individualism to be more highly valued in mainstream, White, middle-class culture in the United States, in contrast to the tendency for collectivism to be valued more strongly by African, indigenous, Asian, and Latino cultural groups (Vandello & Cohen, 1999). However, Triandis, Bontempo, Villareal, Asai, and Lucca (1988) suggested that although these values are characteristic of certain cultures, few individuals within a culture are purely collectivists or individualistic. Because of the within-group differences in how much individuals uphold a particular cultural value, it is better to actually measure the cultural values of individuals than to assume the cultural values of individuals based on group membership.

Collectivism is a culturally held value that underscores the needs, objectives, and perspectives of the in-group over the individual (Marin & Marin, 1991; Triandis, McCusker, & Hui, 1990). Cross-cultural research on individuals in the United States, Latin America, and Asia has illustrated that collectivism is related to high levels of personal interdependence, the ability to be influenced by others, conformity, and a willingness to trust and make sacrifices for the welfare of other in-group members (Marin & Triandis, 1985). Cultures that value collectivism also tend to emphasize family members' responsibilities and obligations to one another (Fuligni et al., 1999). This emphasis on one's immediate and extended family is called *familism.*

Contrasting collectivism is *individualism,* the dominant value in the United States. Cross-cultural research has revealed that individualistic cultures tend to emphasize self-reliance among individuals and prioritize the goals of the individual over those of the group (Triandis et al., 1988; Triandis et al., 1990). In individualistic cultures, people are more likely to end their relationships with in-groups when these relationships become too demanding compared with those in collectivist cultures (Triandis et al., 1988).

These cultural values may increase the likelihood of cross-cultural differences when racial minority youth are mentored by White mentors. Theoretically, collectivism and individualism have the potential to directly influence the quality and, hence, effectiveness of mentoring relationships experienced by ethnic minority youth. This includes the level of trust in the mentoring relationship, the responsiveness of the youth to mentor guidance, and mentors' ability to be satisfactory role models for mentees holding different value systems. Consider, for instance, an individualistic mentor who is paired with a mentee from a collectivist culture. This mentee might be expected by his parents to attend the local college because he is expected to remain close to the family and emphasize its goals over any individual's. However, the mentor might advise the mentee to leave home to go away to college, thereby suggesting, in contrast to these family values, that his future is most important. This contradictory advice might make it difficult for the youth to trust the mentor because of concern that following his recommendations could lead to conflict with family members.

Individualism and collectivism may also impact prevailing conceptualizations of mentoring that are emphasized by programs. With few exceptions, most programs such as Big Brothers Big Sisters have reflected a view of mentoring as a one-on-one relationship between a youth and an unrelated adult volunteer. This conceptualization can be viewed as a Western idea based on an individualistic framework. In collectivist cultures, multiple individuals are seen as responsible for the well-being of each child but most particularly the immediate and extended family. For example, in African American families, the extended family plays a large role in the upbringing of a child, as demonstrated by the flexible roles that various adults play (Boyd-Franklin, 1989). These considerations suggest that prevailing models of mentoring programming may be limited in their potential effectiveness because they fail to reflect values of collectivism and familism that may be important for youth from racial minority backgrounds. Theoretically, for example, programs that seek to actively support mentoring received from multiple individuals in the youth's existing network, including immediate and extended family members, could prove more effective when values of collectivism and familism are salient for youth.

RESEARCH

In this section, we review research that addresses the role of race, ethnicity, and culture in youth mentoring relationships. We organize this literature according to its relevance to the three overarching sets of theoretical considerations raised in the preceding section. With regard to the role of racial, ethnic, and cultural similarity, we consider findings relating to same- versus cross-race mentoring relationships. With regard to stereotype threat theory, studies of college students' perceptions of potential mentoring relationships that have been conducted within this paradigm are reviewed. Finally, research examining the role of important relationships that youth have with familial and nonfamilial adults in their lives is considered with respect to its implications for the role of cultural values in mentoring relationships for youth.

Racial Similarity or Dissimilarity

The similarity-attraction theory suggests that given the opportunity to choose their own mentors, youth more often would select mentors of the same race, ethnicity, or culture. In accordance with this prediction, investigations of naturally occurring mentoring relationships among urban, Latino, and African American youth have found that most youth report mentors of the same race/ethnicity (Klaw & Rhodes, 1995; Rhodes, Contreras, & Mangelsdorf, 1994; Rhodes, Ebert, & Fischer, 1992; Sánchez & Reyes, 1999). A study

of mostly late-adolescent White college students also found that the majority of participants reported natural mentors of the same race (Cavell, Meehan, Heffer, & Holladay, 2002). Similarly, Jackson, Kite, and Branscombe's study (1996, as cited as in Bowman et al., 1999) of Black undergraduate women in a predominantly White university revealed that most of their reported role models were Black and from outside the university. Furthermore, those who reported placing more importance on their racial identities were more likely to report having Black role models than those who placed less importance on their racial identities. This latter finding suggests that racial or ethnic identity may influence preferences for same-race mentors.

In contrast to the evidence of the proclivity of youth toward same-race mentors, racial minority youth are typically matched with White mentors in mentoring programs. Many programs report difficulty recruiting sufficient racial/ethnic minority mentors, particularly men (Rhodes, 2002; Sipe, 1996). However, in a study sponsored by AOL Time Warner Foundation (2002), telephone interviews of 2,000 adults revealed that people of color and Whites were equally likely to report being mentors. However, ethnic minority adults reported mentoring youth in diverse settings, such as schools, work environments, and religious institutions, which suggests that they may function more often as natural mentors than volunteer mentors. Another study found, however, that school-based programs tended to attract more minority mentors than do community-based programs (Herrera, Sipe, & McClanahan, 2000). Thus, perhaps the site of the program influences the type of mentor recruited.

In an effort to understand the impact of matching by race in formal mentoring programs, Rhodes et al. (2002) analyzed data regarding 190 mentored African American, Latino, American Indian, and Asian/Pacific Islander youth who participated in a national evaluation of Big Brothers Big Sisters programs. Participants included 125 youth in cross-race matches (mentors were White) and 65 in same-race matches. Matches were made by agency staff based on mentees' and mentors' shared interests, geographic proximity, and parents' and participants' same-race preferences.

No differences were found in the frequency of meetings or relationship duration between the two mentored groups. Contrary to Ogbu's argument, differences were found that favored cross-race matches. Youth in same-race matches were more likely to report initiation of alcohol use and that their mentors provided less unconditional support than those in race-dissimilar relationships. Parents of youth in cross-race matches, furthermore, reported more positive impressions of mentors and were more likely to report that the relationship improved aspects of their children's lives in comparison to parents of youth in same-race matches. The authors speculated that the positive findings toward cross-race relationships reflected White mentors' efforts to surpass racial obstacles. However, it should be kept in mind that no differences between cross-race and same-race matches were found on the vast majority of outcome measures examined, such as grades, value of school, peer relationships, and aggressive behavior. Furthermore, although effect sizes were not reported for significant findings, the relatively large sample size would allow even relatively small differences between the groups to be detected.

It is also of note that Rhodes et al. (2002) found evidence of greater benefits for same-race relationships when gender was taken into consideration as a moderator. Specifically, for boys in same-race matches, changes on measures of scholastic competence and feelings of self-worth were more favorable than for boys in cross-race matches. There were similar findings for school value and feelings of self-worth among girls. These results are consistent with Ogbu's (1990) argument that pairing racial minority youth with mentors of similar racial backgrounds may contribute beneficially to self-esteem. However, it is unclear what explains the favorable findings regarding cross-race matches. It might simply be that cross-race relationships impact different outcomes than same-race matches.

Separate analyses of all 1,138 youth in the national study of Big Brothers Big Sisters provided mixed support for same- versus cross-race matches (Grossman & Rhodes, 2002). It was found that cross-race matches (mentor was White, and mentee was a racial minority) terminated more often than same-race matches (the mentee and mentor were White). However, there was no difference in length of relationship between cross- and same-race relationships when controlling for other factors, including whether the interests of mentees and mentors was a primary matching criterion. It also was found that same-race minority matches ended marginally more often than same-race White matches. This difference did not hold, however, with respect to minority matches in which race was the explicit matching criterion. It is important to keep in mind that because Big Brothers Big Sisters programs tend to have mostly White mentors, the preceding studies addressed only cross-race matches involving White mentors and racial minority youth. Studies have not examined racial minority mentors who are paired with White mentees, nor has research examined the role of cross-race relationships in which both the mentors and mentees are of minority backgrounds (e.g., Latino mentor paired with Asian mentee).

Whereas the previously described studies found differences between cross- and same-race relationships, albeit somewhat conflicting in pattern, other research has not. In a study of 50 youth in a Big Brothers Big Sisters program, racially similar (mentor and youth both White or both Black) and dissimilar (mentor White, and youth Black) matches were not found to differ on either measures of relationship processes, such as frequency of contact and feelings of closeness, or in the duration of relationships and their perceived benefits for youth (Parra, DuBois, Neville, & Pugh-Lilly, 2002). Also, a meta-analysis of 55 evaluations of mentoring programs found that neither matching youth and mentors by race nor the race of the mentor (as assessed by percentage of mentors in study samples who were White) was associated with a significant difference in effect size for mentee outcomes (DuBois, Holloway, Valentine, & Cooper, 2002).

Overall, research that compares cross-versus same-race mentoring relationships reveals mixed findings. Several methodological limitations of this work are noteworthy and may contribute to this pattern of results. First, existing studies comparing cross- versus same-race relationships have been quasi-experimental insofar as mentor/mentee pairs were matched by a variety of factors, including shared interests and same-race match preference of parents or youth. It is therefore possible that differences across groups biased the results, a concern that is compounded by the failure of studies to incorporate measures of relevant factors (e.g., parental preference) as statistical controls in analyses (see Grossman, this volume). Most studies to date also have examined the role of race similarity somewhat superficially. Few researchers, for example, have examined factors that might contribute to the differences in cross- and same-race relationships (i.e., mediators) or that might influence the pattern and magnitude of such differences (i.e., moderators)

Stereotype Threat

Researchers interested in stereotype threat theory have focused on cross-race mentoring relationships of racial minority college students paired with White mentors. Researchers have found that the cultural mistrust of the mentee (Grant-Thompson & Atkinson, 1997), the cultural sensitivity of the mentor, and feedback provided to mentees (Cohen et al., 1999) influence match quality. Cultural mistrust may make it more difficult to develop a trusting and supportive mentoring relationship. A study of 74 Black male college students examined their levels of cultural mistrust, as assessed by two subscales of the Cultural Mistrust Inventory (Terrell & Terrell, 1981). It was found that cultural mistrust was related to students' perceptions of mentors' credibility (expertness, attractiveness, trustworthiness, counselor effectiveness) and cultural competency (Grant-Thompson & Atkinson, 1997). Students were randomly assigned to one of four conditions and listened to an audiotape of a mock mentor/ mentee interaction. The four conditions were (a) African American culturally responsive mentor, (b) African American culturally unresponsive mentor, (c) European American culturally responsive mentor, and (d) European American culturally unresponsive mentor. Students rated African American mentors as more culturally competent than European American mentors. This effect was greatest among students who reported high levels of cultural mistrust, which

suggests that the race of a mentor could be particularly important for minority youth who mistrust White individuals.

With further relevance to processes relating to stereotype threat, Cohen et al. (1999) examined 48 White and 45 Black college students' perceptions of a White evaluator when they received different types of feedback after writing a letter of recommendation. Students were assigned to one of three experimental conditions in which feedback type was manipulated: (a) critical feedback (suggestions and weaknesses) with no further comment, (b) critical feedback plus comments about the high standards that were used to evaluate the letter and an assurance that the student could meet those standards with revisions, or (c) critical feedback plus general praise about the letter. Findings revealed that Black students rated the evaluator as more biased and were less motivated to revise the letter than White students when they received critical feedback with no further comment. However, differences between students disappeared when they received the critical feedback plus the high standards and assurance (Condition b). This finding suggests the importance of the type of feedback provided to minority mentees in mentoring relationships with White mentors. If the stereotype threat is evoked by the feedback, then there will be negative effects on the mentoring relationship and possibly on the mentee.

The preceding studies related to stereotype threat provide promising evidence of how cultural processes influence cross-race relationships. A mentee's cultural mistrust might influence his or her perception of a mentor's feedback, which would influence the bond in the mentoring relationship. The type of bond, in turn, influences mentee outcomes. Thus, these factors seem to mediate the relationship between the presence of a mentor and the outcomes in a mentee. The generalizability of findings, however, is unclear given the focus on college student samples and on simulated mentoring relationships.

Cultural Values

The research most relevant to the role of cultural values in relation to mentoring relationships for youth has been conducted on natural mentoring. The cultural values of collectivism and familism suggest there will be cultural differences in the choice of familial versus nonfamilial mentors among minority youth. Cavell et al. (2002) found that within a sample of 107 predominantly White college students, relatives were just as likely to be natural mentors as nonrelatives. Yet in studies with mostly Latino and/or African American samples (Rhodes et al., 1992; Rhodes et al., 1994; Sánchez & Reyes, 1999), natural mentors were more likely to be immediate and extended family members than nonrelatives. African American adolescents have also been found to mostly identify role models from their families (Bryant & Zimmerman, 2003). Hirsch, Mickus, and Boerger (2002) similarly found that Black youth reported more grandparent involvement in teen-parent and peer relationship concerns than did White youth even when controlling for class. It is important to note that few studies have examined the role of race and socioeconomic status (SES) in mentoring relationships. Thus, when comparing different racial groups on mentoring or cross-race relationships, a potential confound might be SES.

These findings on natural mentoring relationships are consistent with the value of familism in Latino cultures and the value of extended family in African American communities (Boyd-Franklin, 1989; Fuligni et al., 1999). This suggests that for minority youth, it is important to consider the role that family can play in mentoring programs, especially considering that most programs match youth with unrelated adults. Perhaps volunteer mentors need to develop stronger relationships with adult family members.

Cross-cultural research has yielded mixed findings. A study of adolescents found that youth from Italy, where the culture tends to be collectivist, reported more frequent encounters with extended family members than did youth from Canada, Belgium, and France, where cultures tend to be individualistic (Claes, Lacourse, Bouchard, & Luckow, 2001). Darling, Hamilton, Toyokawa, and Matsuda (2002) conducted a cross-cultural study of United States and Japanese adolescents in which the mentoring functions of nominated individuals were

compared. Although each culture presumably held different cultural values, with the Japanese tending to hold collectivist values, the authors found that the reported characteristics of the examined relationships did not differ significantly. Specifically, adolescents in both cultures were more likely to credit mentoring functions to adults than to peers, to relatives than nonrelatives, and to same-gender than to different-gender associates. Another cross-cultural study examined the role of important nonparental adults (VIPs) in adolescents' lives in the United States and China (Chen, Greenberger, Farruggia, Bush, & Dong, 2003). Chinese adolescents did not identify more family members as VIPs than U.S. adolescents, contrary to what was hypothesized. However, it is possible that no differences were detected because the U.S. sample was diverse, including African American, Latino, and Asian participants, who might have held cultural values similar to the Chinese sample. As noted by Triandis and his colleagues (1990), there may be significant variation across individuals in their extent of collectivist or individualistic value orientation even within cultures or countries for which either orientation is predominant.

Overall, available research suggests that cultural values play a role in the kinds of natural mentoring relationships that youth are most likely to develop. It seems that family has a more important role in the lives youth from collectivist cultures (particularly as indicated by their racial or ethnic group membership) than those from individualistic cultures. It also might be that cultural values affect specific aspects of mentoring relationships, such as the type of support provided by mentors, but this issue apparently has not received study. Also lacking attention is the question of whether youth from collectivist and individualistic cultural backgrounds tend to benefit differentially from mentoring relationships with familial and nonfamilial adults.

PRACTICE

The *Elements of Effective Practice* (MENTOR/National Mentoring Partnership, 2003) does not indicate how race, ethnicity, and culture should be considered in mentoring programs.

However, the extent to which many programs consider this factor is by matching mentors and mentees by race. It has been found that community-based programs tend to include race as part of their matching criteria (e.g., Holland, 1996; Royse, 1998; Thile & Matt, 1995), while school-based programs are more likely to emphasize shared skills or interests as the matching criteria, particularly when mentoring may take a more academic focus. In a study of 98 school- and community-based programs, it was found that community-based programs were more likely to match mentor-mentee pairs by race/ethnicity (74%) compared with school-based programs (66%) (Herrera et al., 2000). Race/ethnicity was one of many considerations in the mentor-mentee match. Herrera et al. noted that staff members of school-based programs considered the ability of a mentor and a youngster's school-related needs more important than the similarities of the pair.

Although many programs that consider race do so by matching on this criterion, there are examples of programs in which there is more in-depth consideration of the role of racial and ethnic similarity in the matching process. In the Ethnic Mentor Undergraduate (EMU) Program (Thile & Matt, 1995), racial/ethnic minority first-year and transfer undergraduates were paired with successful senior-level or graduate students of similar racial/ethnic backgrounds and academic majors. Program developers expected that the mentee's ethnic and personal pride and academic achievement would be enhanced by being paired with a mentor of a similar background and by engaging in academic support activities with other mentees. Relative to the university-wide population of first-year students, mentees' grade point averages were significantly higher. In addition, the percentage of EMU students who returned for their second year at the university was higher than the university-wide rates. Additional steps could be taken to further address cultural factors in this program. For example, mentors could be trained on cultural competency, and more support could be provided to cross-race matches to address cultural mistrust.

Another program, the Cross-Cultural Mentoring Project, illustrates efforts to train mentors to be culturally competent. In this program, mostly

Euro-American graduate students mentored Native American youth aged 11 to 15 (Salzman, 2000). The goals of the program were to support the positive growth and development of mentees who were at risk for academic, social, or behavioral problems and to increase the cultural competence of mentors. This program included Native American cultural consultants who taught mentors about Native American culture and history. Mentors were expected to research the tribal histories and cultures of mentees, to attend local cultural events with mentees, and to examine their own cultural biases. Mentors also engaged in activities with mentees' families throughout the mentoring program. Mentor interviews suggested that they became more culturally sensitive over time. For example, rather than attribute silence on the part of mentees to the lack of success in the mentoring relationship, mentors developed the understanding that silence is a cultural tendency among Native Americans when people do not know one another well. Having this cultural knowledge may have helped mentors improve their communication skills and strengthen the development of their mentoring relationships. Very few existing programs provide such in-depth cultural training to mentors.

Similar to the Cross-Cultural Mentoring Project, another program targeting mostly Latino and African American youth encouraged parental involvement in events with mentees and mentors in order to aid communication between parents and mentors (Karcher, Davis, & Powell, 2002). This might have enabled parents and mentors to develop relationships. Including family members in the process is consistent with the target groups' cultural values of familism and extended family, which can make a mentoring program more effective.

A final program incorporated cultural values as part of its framework. The therapeutic group mentoring model was developed specifically for African American males in foster care (Utsey, Howard, & Williams, 2003) and integrated values consistent with African American culture. The program used a group mentoring approach rather than a one-on-one approach, for example, to foster a sense of community in which participants had a responsibility toward the group over their own needs. Five principles—*group above self, respect for self and others, responsibility for self and community, reciprocity,* and *authenticity*—guided all interactions within the group. Activities that focused on African American history and culture also were included in the program. Qualitative data obtained from mentors and youth included reports of positive changes in adolescents' attitudes and behaviors.

Overall, little has been published about mentoring programs that consider the racial, ethnic, and cultural needs of youth. Most programs interested in this topic match by race. However, as the literature illustrates, matching by race is insufficient. Other practices, as described above, should be considered for inclusion by all program planners in order to better meet the diverse needs of youth. Some programs have gone to great lengths to help mentors in racially dissimilar relationships become more culturally competent, which could lessen any cultural mistrust or stereotype threat a minority mentee might experience. Considering the cultural values of youth seems to have also been helpful in mentoring programs.

FUTURE DIRECTIONS

Synthesis

Overall, the available research on youth mentoring is limited, but sheds light on the roles that race, ethnicity, and culture may play in the development and quality of these relationships. Theoretically, there is a basis for expecting that same-race relationships could be more beneficial, especially for youth from ethnic minority groups. Findings relevant to this concern, however, are mixed and suggest it is a complex phenomenon. Stereotype threat theory suggests the importance of factors such as cultural mistrust and cultural sensitivity as influences on the quality of cross-race relationships, with encouraging, albeit preliminary, support from studies of simulated mentoring relationships of college samples. Similarly, in accordance with theory suggesting a potential role of individualism and collectivism in mentoring relationships, there is evidence that familial mentoring ties are more salient in the lives of ethnic and racial minority youth. Regarding practice, there are few published accounts of programs that have incorporated practices oriented toward race, ethnicity, or cultural values beyond simple matching of mentors and youth by race. We conclude with recommendations in the areas of research and practice to facilitate future efforts to examine and address the role of race, ethnicity, and culture.

Recommendations for Research

1. *Examine culture.* Much of the research that examines the roles of race, ethnicity, and culture in youth mentoring simply compares groups, and researchers assume that identified differences are due to cultural variables or membership. This ignores the complexity of race, ethnicity, and culture and the heterogeneity within groups (Betancourt & López, 1993). Researchers should specifically examine cultural factors, such as individualism and collectivism, and test their relationship to mentoring processes and outcomes. This could help broaden mentoring theory so that it is applicable to different cultural groups.

2. *Conduct within-group research.* Within-group studies should be conducted to better understand the nature and significance of cultural variations (e.g., value orientations) within groups. Although researchers may think that by comparing different racial/ethnic groups, they have sufficiently accounted for group differences, more complex research designs are necessary to understand and account for within-group variation.

3. *Consider the possible racial, ethnic, and cultural compositions of mentoring relationships.* Research on cross- and same-race relationships has examined minority youth paired with same-race mentors, minority youth paired with White mentors, and White youth paired with White mentors. Researchers have not examined White mentees paired with minority group mentors or minority mentees paired with different-race minority mentors. Certainly, this is due to the types of mentoring relationships that currently exist. However, researchers should examine the roles of race, ethnicity, and culture in a variety of cross-race matches.

4. *Examine a broader range of racial, ethnic, and cultural factors.* Theory and available research suggest a relatively broad range of racial, ethnic, and cultural factors that may be important as mediating or moderating processes in mentoring relationships and programs, including cultural sensitivity, feedback, and ethnic/racial identity. Researchers should measure these variables in future investigations and examine their influence on mentoring relationship processes and outcomes. Particular emphasis should be given to broadening the range of factors examined thus far to include other theoretically relevant constructs, such as cultural mistrust, replicating investigations of cultural issues in simulated mentoring relationships with actual relationships. Relevant methodological controls should also be incorporated in research, such as accounting for variation in SES.

5. *Examine effects of cross-cultural training and culturally sensitive program practices.* Very little is currently known about the implications of different program practices that focus on racial, ethnic, or cultural issues. This should include the design and rigorous evaluation of both cultural competency training and culturally specific program practices. Presumably, it would be beneficial to mentoring relationships if mentors were more culturally equipped, even mentors of the same race as mentees, given the potential for mentors' ethnic backgrounds and experiences to differ and contribute to misunderstandings and other limitations. Furthermore, researchers should examine other nontraditional mentoring approaches, such as the group mentoring approach employed by Utsey et al. (2003). It would be beneficial to examine whether the group approach is more effective than the one-one-one relationship for mentees with collectivist values.

Recommendations for Practice

1. *Consider the role of race/ethnicity/culture in national guidelines.* Nationally based practice guidelines should be expanded to include specific attention to practices that promote appropriate attention to race, ethnicity, and culture in programs and relationships.

2. *Do not match pairs on race/ethnicity only.* The combination of factors that contribute to successful mentoring relationships is complex and transcends racial/ethnic characteristics. Simply matching by race/ethnicity appears to be insufficient. Practitioners also should consider the interests of mentees/mentors and, with specific relevance to issues considered in this chapter, factors such as mentors' cultural sensitivity and mentees' levels of cultural mistrust and identity.

3. *Use assessments of cultural factors to target support.* Factors such as cultural mistrust, cultural values, and racial/ethnic identity can be assessed and used to target and direct support for mentoring relationships within programs. Illustratively, for youth in cross-race relationships who exhibit high levels of cultural mistrust, it may be beneficial to provide extra support to the matches to promote more effective mentoring and prevent premature termination. Similar considerations apply to cultural values. Measuring such factors at screening may be particularly useful. In this way, program staff can better match mentors and mentees and provide training to mentors that specifically addresses the cultural contexts and values of youth.

4. *Provide cultural-competency training to mentors.* Research highlights the manner in which feedback is provided in mentoring relationships as an important consideration from a cultural perspective. Simply providing suggestions and weaknesses may lead ethnic minority mentees to feel that they have been judged because of racial bias. Mentors should be trained on how to adequately provide feedback that will contribute to the well-being of mentees and the establishment of trust in the relationship. Specifically, when critical feedback is provided to minority mentees, it should always be buffered with high standards and assurance.

Mentors also should learn about mentees' cultures in order to understand their experiences and foster trusting relationships. Practitioners should consider providing cultural competence training to mentors (e.g., Cross-Cultural Mentoring Project; Salzman, 2000). It may also be useful to refer to recommendations for multicultural counseling competencies (Sue, Arredondo, &

McDavis, 1992), as these can be applied to mentor training. This kind of training may be beneficial not only in cross-race relationships but even in same-race relationships, such as in the EMU program, because "same-race" does not necessarily mean cultural understanding.

5. *Utilize natural support systems for youth.* In general, extended family members appear to have an important role as mentors for Latino and African American youth. To maximize the positive mentoring experiences of these youth, programs should explore ways of utilizing and supporting these ties. Volunteer mentors, for example, could work with natural mentors to strengthen social support networks for youth (Barrera & Bonds, this volume). Consistent with our other recommendations, developing an understanding of the cultural values of mentees may also help program staff understand how to capitalize on natural support systems for youth. During cultural competency training, volunteer mentors could be trained to work with mentees' family members, especially when working with youth who highly value familism.

6. *Consider developing culturally specific mentoring programs.* Mentoring programs should attempt to be culturally consistent in their design and activities with the lives of targeted youth. In some instances, this may merit the design of programs that are geared specifically toward the needs of a given cultural or ethnic group (e.g., Utsey et al., 2003). Programs that reflect an integrated and comprehensive attention to the cultural backgrounds of a given population of youth in this manner may yield dividends in both youth outcomes and acceptance and in support of programs within the surrounding community.

In conclusion, the mentoring literature is only in the beginning stages of revealing the roles of race, ethnicity, and culture. The research on this topic provides a basis for identifying future directions in mentoring practice and research. Given the diverse populations that mentoring programs serve across the United States, advancing our knowledge about the roles of race, ethnicity, and culture should benefit numerous programs and youth.

REFERENCES

AOL Time Warner Foundation. (2002). *Mentoring in America.* New York: Author.

Betancourt, H., & López, S. R. (1993). The study of culture, ethnicity, and race in American psychology. *American Psychologist, 48,* 629–637.

Bowman, S. R., Kite, M. E., Branscombe, N. R., & Williams, S. (1999). Developmental relationships of Black Americans in the academy. In A. J. Murrell, F. J. Crosby, & R. J. Ely (Eds.), *Mentoring dilemmas: Developmental relationships within multicultural organizations* (pp. 21–46). London: Erlbaum.

Boyd-Franklin, N. (1989). *Black families in therapy: A multisystemic approach.* New York: Guilford Press.

Bryant, A. L., & Zimmerman, M. A. (2003). Role models and psychosocial outcomes among African American adolescents. *Journal of Adolescent Research, 18,* 36–67.

Byrne, D. (1971). *The attraction paradigm.* New York: Academic Press.

Cavell, T. A., Meehan, B. T., Heffer, R. W., & Holladay, J. J. (2002). The natural mentors of adolescent children of alcoholics (COAs): Implications for preventive practices. *The Journal of Primary Prevention, 23,* 23–42.

Chen, C., Greenberger, E., Farruggia, S., Bush, K., & Dong, Q. (2003). Beyond parents and peers: The role of important non-parental adults (VIPS) in adolescent development in China and the United States. *Psychology in the Schools, 40,* 35–50.

Claes, M., Lacourse, E., Bouchard, C., & Luckow, D. (2001). Adolescents' relationships with members of the extended family and non-related adults in four countries: Canada, France, Belgium, and Italy. *International Journal of Adolescence and Youth, 9,* 207–225.

Cohen, G. L., Steele, C. M., & Ross, L. D. (1999). The mentor's dilemma: Providing critical feedback across the racial divide. *Personality & Social Psychology Bulletin, 25,* 1302–1318.

Darling, N., Hamilton, S., Toyokawa, T., & Matsuda, S. (2002). Naturally occurring mentoring in Japan and the United States: Social roles and correlates. *American Journal of Community Psychology, 30,* 245–270.

DuBois, D. L., Holloway, B. E., Valentine, J. C., & Cooper, H. (2002). Effectiveness of mentoring programs for youth: A meta-analytic review.

American Journal of Community Psychology,
30, 157–197.

Flaxman, E. (1992). *Evaluating mentoring programs.*
New York: Institute for Urban and Minority
Education Briefs, Teachers College, Columbia
University.

Fuligni, A. J., Tseng, V., & Lam, M. (1999). Attitudes
toward family obligations among American
adolescents with Asian, Latin American, and
European backgrounds. *Child Development,*
70, 1030–1044.

Grant-Thompson, S. K., & Atkinson, D. R. (1997).
Cross-cultural mentor effectiveness and African
American male students. *Journal of Black Psy-*
chology, 23, 120–134.

Grossman, J. B., & Rhodes, J. E. (2002). The test of
time: Predictors and effects of duration in youth
mentoring relationships. *American Journal of*
Community Psychology, 30, 199–219.

Grossman, J. B., & Tierney, J. (1998). Does mentoring work? An impact study of the Big Brothers
Big Sisters program. *Evaluation Review, 22,*
403–426.

Herrera, C., Sipe, C. L., & McClanahan, W. S.
(2000). *Mentoring school-age children: Rela-*
tionship development in community-based and
school-based programs. Philadelphia: Public
Private Ventures. (Published in collaboration
with MENTOR/National Mentoring Partnership,
Alexandria, VA)

Hirsch, B. J., Mickus, M., & Boerger, R. (2002). Ties
to influential adults among Black and White
adolescents: Culture, social class, and family
networks. *American Journal of Community*
Psychology, 30, 289–303.

Holland, S. H. (1996). Project 2000: An educational
mentoring and academic support model for
inner-city African American boys. *Journal of Negro*
Education, 65, 315–321.

Karcher, M. J., Davis, C., & Powell, B. (2002). The
effects of developmental mentoring on connectedness and academic achievement. *The School*
Community Journal, 12(2), 35–50.

Klaw, E. L., & Rhodes, J. E. (1995). Mentor
relationships and the career development of
pregnant and parenting African American
teenagers. *Psychology of Women Quarterly, 19,*
551–562.

Marin, G., & Marin, B. V. (1991). *Research with*
Hispanic populations. Newbury Park, CA:
Sage.

Marin, G., & Triandis, H. C. (1985). Allocentrism
as an important characteristic of the behavior
of Latin Americans and Hispanics. In R. Diaz-
Guerrero (Ed.), *Cross-cultural and national*
studies in social psychology. Amsterdam, the
Netherlands: Elsevier Science.

MENTOR/National Mentoring Partnership. (2003).
Elements of effective practice (2nd ed.). Alexandria,
VA: Author.

Ogbu, J. U. (1990). *Mentoring minority youth: A*
framework. New York: Columbia University,
Teachers College, Institute for Urban and
Minority Education.

Parra, G. R., DuBois, D. L., Neville, H. A., & Pugh-
Lilly, A. O. (2002). Mentoring relationships for
youth: Investigation of a process-oriented model.
Journal of Community Psychology, 30, 367–388.

Rhodes, J. E. (2002). *Stand by me: The risks and*
rewards of mentoring today's youth. Cambridge,
MA: Harvard University Press.

Rhodes, J. E., Contreras, J. M., & Mangelsdorf, S. C.
(1994). Natural mentor relationships among
Latina adolescent mothers: Psychological adjustment, moderating processes, and the role of early
parental acceptance. *American Journal of Com-*
munity Psychology, 22, 211–227.

Rhodes, J. E., Ebert, L., & Fischer, K. (1992). Natural
mentors: An overlooked resource in the social
networks of young, African American mothers.
American Journal of Community Psychology,
20, 445–461.

Rhodes, J. E., Reddy, R., Grossman, J. B., & Lee,
J. M. (2002). Volunteer mentoring relationships
with minority youth: An analysis of same- versus
cross-race matches. *Journal of Applied Social*
Psychology, 32, 2114–2133.

Robinson, T. L., & Howard-Hamilton, M. F. (2000).
The convergence of race, ethnicity, and gender:
Multiple identities in counseling. Upper Saddle
River, NJ: Prentice Hall.

Royse, D. (1998). Mentoring high-risk youth:
Evaluation of the Brothers Project. *Adolescence,*
33, 147–158.

Salzman, M. (2000). Promoting multicultural competence: A cross-cultural mentorship project.
Journal of Multicultural Counseling and Develop-
ment, 28, 119–125.

Sánchez, B., & Reyes, O. (1999). A descriptive
profile of the mentorship relationships of urban
Latino adolescents. *Journal of Community*
Psychology, 27, 299–302.

Sipe, C. L. (1996). *Mentoring: A synthesis of P/PV's research: 1988–1995.* Philadelphia: Public/Private Ventures.

Steele, C. M. (1997). A threat in the air: How stereotypes shape the intellectual identities and performance of women and African Americans. *American Psychologist, 52,* 613–629.

Sue, D. W., Arredondo, P., & McDavis, R. J. (1992). Multicultural counseling competencies and standards: A call to the profession. *Journal of Multicultural Counseling and Development, 70,* 477–483.

Terrell, E., & Terrell, S. (1981). An inventory to measure cultural mistrust level, and premature termination from counseling among Black clients. *Journal of Counseling Psychology, 31,* 371–375.

Thile, E. L., & Matt, G. E. (1995). The Ethnic Mentor Undergraduate Program: A brief description and preliminary findings. *Journal of Multicultural Counseling and Development, 23,* 116–126.

Triandis, H. C., Bontempo, R., Villareal, M. J., Asai, M., & Lucca, N. (1988). Individualism and collectivism: Cross-cultural perspectives on self-ingroup relationships. *Journal of Personality and Social Psychology, 54,* 323–338.

Triandis, H. C., McCusker, C., & Hui, H. (1990). Multimethod probes of individualism and collectivism. *Journal of Personality & Social Psychology, 59,* 1006–1020.

Utsey, S. O., Howard, A., & Williams, O., III. (2003). Therapeutic group mentoring with African American male adolescents. *Journal of Mental Health Counseling, 25,* 126–139.

Vandello, J. A., & Cohen, D. (1999). Patterns of individualism and collectivism across the United States. *Journal of Personality and Social Psychology, 77,* 279–292.

14

Gender in Mentoring Relationships

G. Anne Bogat and Belle Liang

Introduction

Several gender differences among both mentors and mentees have been widely noted in the literature. First, males and females are referred to mentoring programs for different reasons. Males are often referred because they are perceived as needing a male role model, females because of problems in trust, communication, and intimacy with their mothers (Rhodes, 2002). Second, mentors tend to be females, but mentees tend to be males (Herrera, 1999; Herrera, Sipe, & McClanahan, 2000; Roaf, Tierney, & Hunte, 1994). By the end of a year, however, most males and females were matched and served in approximately equal numbers. This was accomplished by matching some male mentees with female mentors. Given the differential numbers of male and female mentors and mentees as well as the divergent developmental pathways and outcomes in male and female relationships that we will discuss below, how the gender of mentors and mentees relates to participant outcomes is crucial for understanding the effectiveness of mentoring programs.

In this chapter, we examine several key questions related to gender and mentoring: Do boys and girls have different needs in mentoring relationships? Do male and female mentors differ in their effectiveness? Do same-gender and cross-gender relationships vary in their impact on youth? First, we briefly review developmental theories and research on gender differences and explore their implications for youth mentoring relationships and programs. Next, we review research addressing effects of gender on both the characteristics and outcomes of mentoring relationships, along with its limitations. We then consider implications of the theory and research reviewed for practices relating to youth mentoring, and, finally, we offer recommendations for future research and practice.

Theory

To date, theoretical perspectives attempting to explain how mentoring works (e.g., resiliency or attachment theory) have not advanced our understanding of why mentoring may work differently for boys and girls. To address the need for frameworks that facilitate understanding of these differences and their potential implications for youth outcomes, several extant theories and associated research pertaining to gender differences in identity and relationship development from the social, clinical, and developmental psychology literatures are discussed in this section.

Identity Development

Identity development theory was initially based on Erik Erikson's idea that once identity has been established, the capacity for intimate relationships develops (Erikson, 1950, 1968). Detachment from parents, sometime in adolescence, was seen as a necessary prerequisite for identity formation. More recent conceptualizations, however, emphasize adolescents' needs for emotional connection with parents as well as the importance of their establishing a sense of autonomy.

The "gender-intensification hypothesis" (Hill & Lynch, 1983) posits that the adoption of gender-specific beliefs and behaviors increases during adolescence. Furthermore, attitudinal, psychological, and behavioral differences across gender result from socialization pressures to conform to traditional feminine and masculine sex roles that boys and girls increasingly experience with age (Galambos, Almeida, & Petersen, 1990). This perspective suggests that girls might exhibit less striving than boys for autonomy during adolescence.

Relatedly, although traditional developmental theory has characterized adolescence as a time of separation, individuation, inevitable rebellion, and increasing autonomy, feminist scholars (e.g., Chodorow, 1987; Gilligan, Lyons, & Hammer, 1990; Jordan, Kaplan, Miller, Stiver, & Surrey, 1991) have suggested a different trajectory for girls. For girls, the importance of strong relationships, including those with their parents, are theorized to continue to be important into adulthood. Thus, for girls, identity is thought to develop more from relationships than is the case for males, and independence and dependence are seen as compatible. Similarly, a number of feminist scholars have posited that love and belonging are especially important developmental concerns for females (Brown & Gilligan, 1992; Harvey & Retter, 2002) and that psychological crises in girls' and women's lives appear to stem from disconnections in relationships more so than is the case for boys (Hagerty, Williams, Coyne, & Early, 1996).

Relational Theory

Following from these considerations, relational theory argues that the core component of girls' and women's identities is their orientation to interpersonal relationships (Chodorow, 1987; Jordan et al., 1991). This theory emphasizes the importance of mutuality and authenticity in relationships for women. There is some evidence that the importance of relational bonds for females transcends American culture. Karcher and Lee's (2002) research on connectedness among boys and girls found that in both the United States and Taiwan, girls reported more caring for and close contact with others. Girls also reported significantly greater connectedness across all of their relationships.

Gilligan et al. (1990) proposed that during adolescence, girls reach an impasse in which, to preserve relationships, they must either silence their own thoughts and feelings (a concept termed "loss of voice") or lose relationships. There is some evidence to support this proposition. Adolescents, for example, can describe a true and false self (identity) that they present to the world (Harter, Marold, Whitesell, & Cobbs, 1996), and in late adolescence, girls are more upset than are boys by conflicting self-attributions (Harter, Bresnick, Bouchey, & Whitesell, 1997). Relatedly, in terms of sex role orientation, higher levels of femininity, as contrasted with androgyny or masculinity, are associated with lower levels of voice in girls (Harter, Waters, Whitesell, & Kastelic, 1998). Such a loss of voice also has been associated with higher levels of depression later in life (Jack, 1991). All girls, however, may not be equally susceptible to loss of voice. Some research indicates that it is less likely to occur in girls from low socioeconomic status (SES) backgrounds and among girls of color (Clark, 1999; Way, 1995).

Friendship Development

Girls and boys seem to have different types of friendships. Girls report more intimacy in friendships compared with boys (Buhrmester, 1990), and girls are more attuned to differences in friendships (Grazyk & Henry, 2001). The quality of a friendship appears more likely to influence girls' adjustment (Berndt & Keefe, 1995), and girls expect higher levels of intimacy, self-disclosure, and empathy in their friendships than do boys (Clark & Ayers, 1993).

Way (1998) also found that boys and girls expressed different levels of resilience in their friendships. For example, the experience of a friend's betrayal affected girls differently than boys, insofar as boys were less likely to form a close friendship after a betrayal.

Most studies on friendship development have been conducted with middle-class European Americans. Friendship patterns differ when children and adolescents of color from more diverse social classes are studied. For example, DuBois and Hirsch (1990) found that peer support differed by gender (girls had more support) among European American but not among African American youth. In another study, White and Black girls from middle-class backgrounds were more likely to self-disclose to peers compared with those from low-income backgrounds (Way & Pahl, 2001). In a study of low-income adolescents, Way and Chen (2000) found that Latino girls had more general friendship support than did boys, a finding that was not true of African Americans and Asian Americans. In addition, girls in all three ethnic groups had higher levels of close friendships than did the boys in these groups. Available findings thus indicate complicated relationships between gender, ethnicity, and social class in the area of peer relationships.

Help-Seeking

There is a small literature on help-seeking among children and adolescents. In general, adolescents choose friends to talk with about personal problems; they choose parents to talk with about other matters, such as school problems (e.g., Sullivan, Marshall, & Schonert-Reichl, 2002; Youniss & Smollar, 1985). However, a number of studies have found gender differences in help-seeking. Boys reported more negative views of help-seeking than did girls (Garland & Zigler, 1994). Moreover, girls were more likely than boys to choose a friend to help solve a problem with another friend (Sullivan et al., 2002).

Girls and boys also may differ in the manner in which they seek help when under stress. Greenberger and McLaughlin (1998) found that girls reported seeking emotional support more often when under stress. Boys and girls did not differ in instrumental support-seeking or problem-solving coping.

There may be some theoretical "downsides" of girls and boys getting "what they want." For example, recent research suggests that girls engage in more "co-rumination" (excessive talk about problems in the absence of active coping) than do boys and that this is related to both closer friendships and less healthy emotional adjustment (Rose, 2002).

Implications of Theory for Youth Mentoring

The implications from the literature summarized above are that girls and boys may need different types of mentoring, may form different types of relationships with their mentors, and may have a different developmental trajectory in developing a relationship with their mentors. Issues of autonomy and connectedness in the mentoring relationship may be similar for males and females during childhood. However, based on theoretical ideas described above, in adolescence, mentoring that focuses on creating feelings of autonomy could be especially well received by male mentees, whereas an emphasis on issues of intimacy in the relationship could be more appealing to female mentees.

This latter possibility is consistent with the implications of relational theory and friendship research indicating that connectedness within the context of a mentoring relationship may be particularly important for female mentees. It is also consistent with a typology of mentoring that distinguishes between instrumental mentoring (problem focused) and psychosocial mentoring (process focused) that is discussed in the next section of this chapter. Although most mentoring relationships probably contain aspects of both instrumental and psychosocial mentoring, the theory previously discussed suggests that an emphasis on psychosocial mentoring could be more appropriate for females. The literature on help-seeking also suggests the importance of psychosocial mentoring for females. For example, mentors of female mentees may need to provide emotional support when the mentee is experiencing stress, whereas this may not be as welcomed by male mentees.

Rhodes (2002) argued in her model of mentoring that "meaningful conversation" is a key variable that mediates outcomes. However, such relationships may be more appropriate for girls as they need such activities to develop close bonds. If boys prefer not to engage in direct forms of help-seeking (Rickwood & Braithwaite, 1994), more verbally based interactions may not be helpful or lead to closer mentor/mentee relationships.

Because of space limitations, we have focused this theory section on the role of the youth's gender, rather than the mentor's. It should be noted, however, that the issues discussed (e.g., relational orientation of females) have potential relevance for the type of mentoring that men and women may feel most comfortable implementing. For example, in cross-sex mentoring pairs, a female mentor may not adequately meet the male mentee's desire for a more instrumental type of mentoring; a male mentor may not meet the female mentee's need for psychosocial mentoring. These mismatched emphases in the relationship might be a reason for lower compatibility and possible early dissolution of the mentoring pair.

Importantly, however, many of the theoretical implications discussed thus far may be less relevant to minority youth for whom gender differences in level of voice and emphasis on close relationships have been equivocal. Indeed, it is possible that males of color may be no less likely than females in primarily middle-class, Euro-American studies to resonate to nurturing, intimate mentoring relationships focused on their psychosocial needs.

Research

Gender Differences in Types of Mentoring

Two different types of mentoring were differentiated in the early literature on youth mentoring: instrumental and psychosocial (Flaxman, Ascher, & Harrington, 1988). Instrumental mentoring tends to be problem focused; the mentor helps the mentee solve problems so that the mentee can achieve his or her goals. Psychosocial mentoring is process- rather than problem-based; it relies heavily on the interpersonal relationship between the mentor and mentee and, ultimately, attempts to influence the personal characteristics of the mentee. Research on corporate mentoring suggests that instrumental mentoring is more common in matches with male mentors, whereas psychosocial mentoring is more common with female mentors (e.g., Allen & Eby, 2004; Struthers, 1995). Also, in corporate settings, Sosik and Godshalk (2000) found that female-female mentoring relationships offered a greater level of friendship, counseling, personal support, and sponsorship than did other gender combinations of mentors and mentees.

In research with youth, Morrows and Styles (1995) reported that among a sample of 82 matches in eight Big Brothers Big Sisters (BBBS) programs, male matches were more likely than female matches to have developmental relationships (those in which mentors' expectations of relationships varied over time and focused on mentees' needs). The authors offered several possible explanations for this finding that had less to do with females not wanting or needing developmental relationships and more to do with the nature of the participants (e.g., girls who were referred to BBBS had more behavioral problems than did boys) and program structure (e.g., BBBS programs in general emphasize activities over talk and thus may foster more mutually satisfying relationships among males than females). However, another explanation may be relevant. When young females' relationships with female mentors are characterized by empathy, authenticity, and intimacy, they are more highly valued and the mentees' outcomes (e.g., self-esteem, reduced depression) are more positive than when the relationships do not have these strong psychosocial components (e.g., Liang, Tracy, Taylor, & Williams, 2002; Sullivan, 1996).

Relative Effectiveness of Mentoring for Male and Female Mentees

In DuBois, Holloway, Valentine, and Cooper's (2002) meta-analysis, gender of the mentee was unrelated to the effectiveness of the mentoring program. In the national evaluation of the BBBS program, in which only same-sex matches are made, tests for differences in program impact by gender (and gender × race) indicated complicated findings for various outcomes (Tierney, Grossman, & Resch, 1995). However, any interpretation of gender differences attributable to the program must be tentative for two reasons. First, the posttest occurred at 18 months, a time at which only 60% of the matches were still meeting (the average match lasted only 12 months). Thus, whether changes can be ascribed to the program or to developmental changes is difficult to ascertain. Second, and relatedly, further analysis of the data from this study indicated that premature termination of the match (a predictor of less positive adjustment outcomes) is marginally more likely among female compared with male matches (Grossman & Rhodes, 2002). Thus, it is uncertain as to whether the overall gender differences attributed to the program that were reported in the earlier, larger study, hold up to closer scrutiny.

The national BBBS evaluation also found that over the course of a year, male and female mentees of color who were in same-race matches (and by program practice, all had same-gender matches) had less deterioration in scholastic indicators and self-worth than did males and females of color in cross-race matches (Rhodes, Reddy, Grossman, & Lee, 2002). Thus, when female-female relationships persist, equally positive outcomes from mentoring can result when the match is also same race. Of course, given the nature of the methodology (set by program practices), it is not possible to say whether the effects are related to the gender of mentor, gender of mentee, or gender match.

Consistent with the findings of Grossman and Rhodes (2002), DuBois, Neville, Parra, and Pugh-Lilly (2002), in a 1-year study of a BBBS program with repeated measurements of outcomes, found that boys were more likely than girls to fall within the category of youth who "consistently nominated" their Big Brothers Big Sisters as significant adults in their lives (73.3% vs. 26.7% of this group, respectively). Girls were more likely to fall within the category of youth who did not nominate a program mentor as a significant adult at either of two time points (66.7% vs. 33.3% of this group, respectively). This type of nomination was involved in

mediating linkages between BBBS program participation and positive emotional and behavioral outcomes as assessed by comparisons with a demographically matched nonmentoring group.

Research on natural mentors and gender is sparse as well. Zimmerman, Bingenheimer, and Notaro (2002) did not find an association between gender and psychological distress. However, examining only females, Rhodes, Ebert, and Fischer (1992) found that young African American mothers with natural mentors reported less depression than those without natural mentors.

Same Versus Cross-Gender Matches

The majority of mentoring programs that are described in the literature match youth with mentors of the same gender (DuBois, Holloway, et al., 2002; Herrera et al., 2000). Herrera et al. found this was true of 77% of 35 school-based programs and 88% of 29 community-based programs. These trends correspond to the information we have about natural mentoring. Among American boys and girls who identify a natural mentor in their lives, most identify a same-sex mentor. For example, Sánchez and Reyes (1999) reported that the majority of the Latino-American youth in their study identified a same-sex mentor (68% of boys and 70% of girls). Similarly, in a cross-cultural study of American and Chinese youth, Chen, Greenberger, Farruggia, Bush, and Dong (2003) reported that 65% of American males and 73% of American females had a natural mentor of the same gender. Gender similarity was less pronounced, however, among the Chinese sample (57% of males and 59% of females).

In a study of same-gender natural mentoring relationships for adolescent mothers, those reporting more enduring relationships were significantly more likely to graduate and/or stay in school than were females reporting less enduring ties with mentors (Klaw, Rhodes, & Fitzgerald, 2003). Relatively little information exists to elucidate whether same-gender and cross-gender mentor relationships are more or less effective. Findings to date are mixed. Evidence for no difference in outcomes based on gender matching has come from two articles that integrate data from evaluations of multiple programs. DuBois, Holloway, et al.'s (2002) meta-analysis found that matching on gender was not a moderator of program effect size. In their survey of mentors from community-based (346 mentors from 29 programs) and school-based mentoring programs (323 mentors from 35 programs), Herrera et al. (2000) found that "same-gender matches did not differ from cross-gender matches in [ratings of] closeness and supportiveness" (p. 33). In this study, however, the percentage of cross-gender matches was small in both the community- and the school-based programs (11% and 23%, respectively), and male mentor/female mentee matches in each type of program were rare (1% and 3%, respectively).

Findings from one report, however, suggest some potential benefit associated with gender matching for male mentees. In their summary of evaluations of youth mentoring programs funded through JUMP (Juvenile Mentoring Program), Novotney, Mertinko, Lange, and Baker (2000) examined differences in male mentor/male mentee and female mentor/male mentee relationships. The authors were able to identify a subsample (463 of the 5,425 youth enrolled in the programs) of participants for whom identification of the gender of mentee and mentor was available (265 female and 198 male youth). The number of male mentor/female mentee matches was too small to analyze, and the authors did not report the exact number of matches in the other three categories. However, ratings from male mentees indicated that in both same- and cross-sex relationships, mentors were equally liked, and the boys felt equally understood. There was some indication that same-sex male matches resulted in greater benefits to the boys. Both mentors and mentees rated whether the mentoring relationship helped the mentee nine areas: better grades, better class attendance, abstinence from alcohol, abstinence from drugs, avoiding fights, avoiding gangs, avoiding poor peer influences, not using lethal weapons (i.e., knives and guns), and improved family relationships. Male mentors in same-sex mentoring relationships, compared with female mentors in cross-sex mentoring relationships, were more likely to report that mentoring relationships had helped their male mentees to avoid drugs, alcohol, fights, gangs, weapons, and poor

peer influences. However, because statistical tests and significance levels were not reported, it is difficult to draw strong conclusions from this study.

Relative Efficacy of Male Versus Female Mentors

Few youth mentoring outcome studies have examined whether the gender of the mentor has an effect on the outcomes of the mentee. DuBois, Holloway, et al. (2002) tested for these effects in their meta-analysis and failed to find a significant difference. Although they found a larger effect size for female mentors, there was insufficient power to detect whether it was reliable, as a limited number of studies reported data on gender of mentors. In addition, the analyses for gender of mentor were based on the percentage of male mentors in a given program. This was not a particularly strong test of gender effects, and the analysis confounds two distinct types of matches: cross-versus same-gender.

Summary and Limitations

Evidence from the corporate mentoring literature suggests that male and female mentors may provide different types of relationships (instrumental vs. psychosocial). There has been only limited and inconclusive research with youth, however, to indicate what differences may exist in the mentoring relationships that are experienced by girls and boys. Research, furthermore, has not yet provided compelling evidence that gender of mentor, gender of mentee, or gender matching has a differential influence on youth outcomes.

Several methodological limitations have precluded the development of a more definitive and in-depth understanding of the role of gender in youth mentoring relationships. First, the extant literature examining gender is a small percentage of all the available studies on mentoring. As such, findings are restricted in number and may be unrepresentative of programs and relationships investigated in the broader literature. Second, existing research consists mainly of cross-sectional, correlational studies, and, relatedly, investigations also often have lacked adequate statistical controls. For example, in Morrow and Styles's (1995) study, it is not clear whether girls were less likely to have developmental relationships than boys due to a true gender difference or due to a third variable, such as selection bias by gender, in the types of girls and boys who tended to be referred to programs. Third, research on youth mentoring has been limited by the paucity of instruments assessing gender-specific aspects of mentoring relationships. Measures of specific relationship characteristics (much less those that reflect gendered aspects of mentoring) have rarely been included in controlled evaluations of mentoring programs (DuBois, Holloway, et al., 2002).

A final methodological concern is that study designs and analyses have not been able to adequately disentangle effects due to gender of youth, gender of mentor, and the combination of these two factors (i.e., gender matching). In the Novotney et al. study (2000), described previously, for example, the differences that favored same-gender relationships among boys relative to cross-gender relationships among girls may reflect not only a positive gender matching effect but also differences in the general effectiveness of male and female mentors, independent of gender of mentee. One antidote for this problem of confounding across potential sources of effect involving gender is a balanced design with observations in all four "cells": female mentor/female mentee, female mentor/male mentee, male mentor/female mentee, and male mentor/male mentee. The lack of male mentor/female relationships in formal mentoring programs, however, precludes this type of design. Natural mentoring relationships might more readily offer such data. No studies, thus far, have examined gender effects so systematically. The Rhodes et al. (2002) study described above also leads to caution in designs that attend only to gender and not to the race match of the mentor/mentee pairs.

Along with the preceding methodological problems, most studies addressing the role of gender in mentoring relationship processes and outcomes have not been theoretically driven. As a result, it is impossible to determine whether the most relevant process and outcome questions are being asked about girls' and boys' experiences of mentoring. This limitation is particularly salient in the area of measurement. Atheoretical measures run the risk of constraining findings by either underrepresenting important aspects of girls' and boys' mentoring relationships or by including irrelevant aspects. Measures often have been restricted to shared activities or general feelings of closeness, for example, and thus have not provided information regarding more subtle aspects of mentoring relationships that could be especially important to either girls (e.g., intimacy, conflict, authenticity) or boys (e.g., support for autonomy) based on the theory reviewed previously in this chapter. Clearly, a range of both methodological and substantive issues have yet to be systematically addressed in efforts to examine the role of gender in youth mentoring relationships.

PRACTICE

Several recent evaluations of youth interventions, other than mentoring, have demonstrated benefits for males, but not females (e.g., Amaro, Blake, Schwartz, & Flinchbaugh, 2001; Farrell & Meyer, 1997; Flay, Graumlich, Segawa, Burns, & Holliday, 2004). The implications from this literature and the theoretical literature relevant to mentoring presented earlier are that boys and girls may require different types of mentoring programs and different types of mentoring relationships.

Regardless of the paucity of empirical data on gender and mentoring, there is a movement afoot among program implementers to develop gender-specific mentoring programs. Some newer programs, such as Girls on the Run (http://www.girlsontherun.org), and more traditional ones, such as Girl Scouts of America, are focused on building relationships between adolescent girls and adult women through group, rather than individual, activities. Male-focused programs have also been developed.

For example, The Brothers Project (Royse, 1998) paired at-risk, African American males between the ages of 14 and 16 with volunteer male mentors. The program involved individual mentee/mentor meetings as well as group meetings with organized activities for all participants. Unfortunately, other than noting that the purpose of the mentoring was to provide a good role model for the youth, little description of the process of the mentoring was provided. The median match lasted 15 months. Adolescents were assigned randomly to control or mentoring groups; results indicated that the program had no significant positive effects vis-à-vis the control group.

A program aimed specifically for girls is Girl World Builders (GWB), developed by Big Brothers Big Sisters of Metropolitan Chicago (BBBSMC) in collaboration with Alternatives, Inc. This is an all-female-run and -implemented program. It capitalizes on the relational strengths of adolescent girls by engaging them in one-on-one mentoring with women volunteers and by embedding these relationships in a supportive group context through participation of mentor pairs in regular workshops. The GWB program also emphasizes enhancing feelings of self-worth and self-efficacy, thus addressing the need for strategies that reduce internalized risk sources for girls (Davis, Paxton, & Robinson, 1997). Currently, DuBois and colleagues (D. DuBois, personal communication, July 27, 2004) are working with BBBSMC to develop and evaluate a mentoring program for girls that incorporates an increased focus on enhancing self-esteem by engaging them and their mentors in activities that are directly relevant to shaping feelings of self-worth (e.g., workshop activities with a direct focus on multidimensional facets of adolescent girls' self-esteem, gender identity, and body image). In this way, mentors may gain the confidence and skills necessary to use specific strategies that are helpful in promoting self-esteem and addressing dysfunctional beliefs.

Programs such as those described above may be especially important and relevant for either girls or boys; however, program staff should be trained in sex equity so that they do not inadvertently deliver cues consistent with sex stereotypes. Nicholson (1991) argued that differential treatment in youth development programs may serve to perpetuate sex differences in interests and skills. Thus, program staff must be aware of the potential risks inherent in single-sex programs for thwarting gender equity and perpetuating gender differences (see Hughes, 2000; O'Neill, Horton, & Crosby, 1999).

Synthesis

In this chapter, based on theory and research in literatures outside of mentoring, we have proposed that gender might affect (a) the types of relationships males and females form with their mentors and (b) the type of mentoring that males and females provide to mentees. We also have suggested that same- and cross-gender matches may be more or less helpful for male and female youth. Research on gender and mentoring is in its infancy and, as noted, is characterized by both a range of methodological limitations and an absence of theory-driven investigation. Available findings, moreover, do not readily conform to predictions based on theory. Thus, whereas girls' relational orientation suggests a distinctive capacity to form and benefit from strong mentoring ties, the existing data suggest that girls, more so than boys, may be less likely to form enduring and rewarding ties with mentors in formal programs such as BBBS (DuBois, Neville, et al., 2002; Grossman & Rhodes, 2002). Because failures are so rarely reported in the literature, it is impossible to know in how many other programs girls and boys have these differential experiences.

Relatedly, despite the theoretical promise of gender-specific and gender-sensitive approaches to mentoring, these are only beginning to be implemented. The gender-based trends in mentoring relationships and outcomes that have been indicated thus far in the literature may not generalize to the experiences of male and female youth in programs that are designed to attend more closely to gender-related concerns. These considerations highlight for us the importance of examining the role of gender in mentoring more closely and of developing practices in programs that reflect a more in-depth consideration of gender-related issues.

Recommendations for Research

1. *Investigate gender differences in theoretical models of youth mentoring.* Complex, conceptual models of youth mentoring have been proposed and received preliminary support in empirical investigations (DuBois, Neville, et al.,

2002; Parra, DuBois, Neville, Pugh-Lilly, & Povinelli, 2002; Rhodes, Grossman, & Resch, 2000). These models provide a promising foundation for further examination of potential gender differences in youth mentoring processes and outcomes. Studies should examine whether the models apply equally well to males and females, as well as explore the merits of incorporating additional, gender-relevant pathways of influence into these frameworks. Processes suggested by the literatures on identity development, relational theory, friendships, and help-seeking seem especially promising avenues for elaboration of models to provide more sensitivity to gender-related processes in mentoring. Studies also should explore how gender relates to other cultural or demographic factors, such as race/ethnicity.

2. *Investigate gender-specific or gender-sensitive mentoring programs and practices.* Evaluations need to ask whether mentoring programs are more effective for boys or girls. Relatedly, do the characteristics of female-female and male-male youth mentoring relationships differ, and are same-gender and cross-gender mentor relationships equally (or more or less) effective?

These questions might best be answered through person-oriented approaches to data analysis. Current approaches to mentoring program evaluations are variable centered rather than person centered and, as such, cannot elucidate differences that might exist between the outcomes of male and female participants or the relative effectiveness of same- versus cross-sex matches. That is, to date, program evaluations have determined effectiveness based on an averaging of participants' scores on specific outcome measures. The problem with this approach is that there are often subpopulations whose dimensional structures related to the outcome variables differ from the aggregated sample (see von Eye & Bergman, 2003). Summarizing effects across these types of subpopulations may lead to various erroneous conclusions.

3. *Develop and use measures for process and outcome evaluations that can inform theoretical conceptualizations of gender and mentoring.* For example, the Relational Health Index of Mentoring has been developed with gender and cultural issues in mind (Liang et al., 2002). The measure is based on relational-cultural theory from the Stone Center and reflects concepts that are thought to be relevant to the psychological health and development of females across cultures. This measure is currently being adapted for use with boys and girls; youth are helping bridge theory with actual experiences by describing mentor relationships in their own words through separate boys' and girls' focus groups.

4. *Focus on the process of mentoring, not just the outcomes.* Research should differentiate the stages of mentoring and the qualities of relationships that are formed over the developmental course of relationships (see Keller, this volume). It is important to ascertain whether there are male and female differences in the development of mentoring relationships. Ongoing monitoring of mentors' adherence to program practices would be particularly beneficial in this regard. In conjunction with this, research is needed that relates process variables to outcomes, especially in the context of whether there are male/female differences. The research also needs to go beyond comparisons of males and females toward assessing (a) different levels of conformity to masculine and feminine norms and sex roles and (b) whether this affects individual outcomes.

Recommendations for Practice

1. *Recruit more male mentors.* As discussed earlier, most organized programs have difficulty attracting male mentors. McLearn, Colasanto, and Schoen (1998), in a representative national survey, found no differences between men and women in their reported rates of involvement as mentors. The survey's finding most likely reflects males' relatively high levels of involvement in informal mentoring relationships (which this study included in its definition). This discrepancy between the survey and program experience suggests the possibility that organized mentoring programs are ineffective at recruiting male mentors or that the programs themselves are not as attractive to potential male as to female mentors. Regarding the latter point, several BBBS programs have started "sports

buddy" programs, with the only expectation being that the adult males engage in sports activities with the male youth. Programs should continue to explore questions of whether recruitment strategies or program attractiveness suppress the number of males who volunteer to become mentors.

2. *Clearly specify program goals.* Often, the stated goals of programs are broad (e.g., to help at-risk youth). Such broad goals make it difficult to ascertain whether boys and girls are equally well served by the same program. If, in fact, girls thrive best with relationship-based mentoring and boys with activity-based mentoring, the goals of the mentoring program for girls and boys could, in practice, be different.

3. *Develop differential training for mentors.* Related to the preceding recommendation, program training of male and female mentors might be different depending on whether they are matched with boy or girl mentees. For example, it seems likely that if, as the help-seeking literature indicates, boys have more negative views of help-seeking than do girls, mentors working with boys would want to be trained to underemphasize the "helper" role and emphasize other aspects of the relationship (e.g., friend, shared activities).

REFERENCES

Allen, T., & Eby, L. (2004). Factors related to mentor reports of mentoring functions provided: Gender and relational characteristics. *Sex Roles, 50,* 129–139.

Amaro, H., Blake, S. M., Schwartz, P. M., & Flinchbaugh, L. J. (2001). Developing theory-based substance abuse prevention programs for young adolescent girls. *Journal of Early Adolescence, 21,* 256–293.

Berndt, T. J., & Keefe, K. (1995). Friends' influence on adolescents' adjustment to school. *Child Development, 66,* 1312–1329.

Brown, L. M., & Gilligan, C. (1992). *Meeting at the crossroads: Women's psychology and girls' development.* Cambridge, MA: Harvard University Press.

Buhrmester, D. (1990). Intimacy of friendship, interpersonal competence, and adjustment during preadolescence and adolescence. *Child Development, 61,* 1101–1111.

Chen, C., Greenberger, E., Farruggia, S., Bush, K., & Dong, Q. (2003). Beyond parents and peers: The role of important non-parental adults (VIPS) in adolescent development in China and the United States. *Psychology in the Schools, 40,* 35–50.

Chodorow, N. (1987). Feminism and difference: Gender, relation, and difference in psychoanalytic perspective. In M. R. Walsh (Ed.), *The psychology of women: Ongoing debates* (pp. 246–264). New Haven, CT: Yale University Press.

Clark, M. (1999). Adding the voices of Jewish girls to developmental theory. *Women & Therapy, 22,* 55–68.

Clark, M. L., & Ayers, M. (1993). Friendship expectations and friendship evaluations: Reciprocity and gender effects. *Youth & Society, 24,* 299–313.

Davis, T., Paxton, K. C., & Robinson, L. (1997). *After school action programs: Girl World Builders summary report.* Unpublished manuscript, Department of Psychology, DePaul University, Chicago, IL.

DuBois, D. L., & Hirsch, B. J. (1990). School and neighborhood friendship patterns of Blacks and Whites in early adolescence. *Child Development, 61,* 524–536.

DuBois, D. L., Holloway, B. E., Valentine, J. C., & Cooper, H. (2002). Effectiveness of mentoring programs for youth: A meta-analytic review. *American Journal of Community Psychology, 30,* 157–197.

DuBois, D. L., Neville, H. A., Parra, G. R., & Pugh-Lilly, A. O. (2002). Testing a new model of mentoring. In G. G. Noam (Ed. in chief) & J. E. Rhodes (Ed.), *A critical view of youth mentoring (New Directions for Youth Development: Theory, Research, and Practice, No. 93,* pp. 21–57). San Francisco: Jossey-Bass.

Erikson, E. H. (1950). *Childhood and society.* New York: Norton.

Erikson, E. H. (1968). *Identity, youth, and crisis.* New York: Norton.

Farrell A., & Meyer, A. (1997). The effectiveness of a school-based curriculum for reducing violence among urban sixth-grade students. *American Journal of Public Health, 87,* 979–984.

Flaxman, E., Ascher, C., & Harrington, C. (1988). *Youth mentoring: Programs and practices.*

New York: ERIC Clearinghouse on Urban Education, Institute for Urban and Minority Education, Teachers College, Columbia University.

Flay, B. R., Graumlich, S., Segawa, E., Burns, J. L., & Holliday, M. Y. (2004). Effects of 2 prevention programs on high-risk behaviors among African-American youth: A randomized trial. *Archives of Pediatric and Adolescent Medicine, 158,* 377–384.

Galambos, N. L., Almeida, D. M., & Petersen, A. C. (1990). Masculinity, femininity, and sex role attitudes in early adolescence: Exploring gender intensification. *Child Development, 61,* 1905–1914.

Garland, A., & Zigler, E. (1994). Psychological correlates of help-seeking attitudes among children and adolescents. *American Journal of Orthopsychiatry, 64,* 586–593.

Gilligan, C., Lyons, N. P., & Hammer, T. J. (1990). *Making connections: The relational worlds of adolescent girls at Emma Willard School.* Cambridge, MA: Harvard University Press.

Grazyk, P.A., & Henry, D. B. (2001, April). *A developmental perspective on the qualitative aspects of adolescent best friendships.* Paper presented at the Biennial meeting of the Society for Research in Child Development, Minneapolis, MN.

Greenberger, E., & McLaughlin, C. S. (1998). Attachment, coping, and explanatory style in late adolescence. *Journal of Youth and Adolescence, 27,* 121–140.

Grossman, J. B., & Rhodes, J. E. (2002). The test of time: Predictors and effects of duration in youth mentoring relationships. *American Journal of Community Psychology, 30,* 199–219.

Hagerty, B. M., Williams, R. A., Coyne, J. C., & Early, M. R. (1996). Sense of belonging and indicators of social and psychological functioning. *Archives of Psychiatric Nursing, 10,* 235–244.

Harter, S., Bresnick, S., Bouchey, H. A., & Whitesell, N. R. (1997). The development of multiple role-related selves during adolescence. *Development and Psychopathology, 9,* 835–853.

Harter, S., Marold, D. B., Whitesell, N. R., & Cobbs, G. (1996). A model of the effects of perceived parent and peer support on adolescent false self behavior. *Child Development, 67,* 360–374.

Harter, S., Waters, P. L., Whitesell, N. R., & Kastelic, D. (1998). Level of voice among female and male high school students: Relational context, support, and gender orientation. *Developmental Psychology, 34,* 892–901.

Harvey, V. S., Retter, K. (2002). Variations by gender between children and adolescents on the four basic psychological needs. *International Journal of Reality Therapy, 21,* 33–36.

Herrera, C. (1999). *School-based mentoring: A first look into its potential.* Philadelphia: Public/Private Ventures.

Herrera, C., Sipe, C. L., & McClanahan (2000). *Mentoring school-age children: Relationship development in community-based and school-based programs.* Philadelphia: Public/Private Ventures. (Published in collaboration with MENTOR/National Mentoring Partnership, Alexandria, VA)

Hill, J. P., & Lynch, M. E. (1983). The intensification of gender-related role expectations during early adolescence. In J. Brooks-Gunn & A. C. Petersen (Eds.), *Girls at puberty: Biological and psychological perspectives* (pp. 201–228). New York: Plenum Press.

Hughes, K. L. (2000). Gender and youth mentoring. *Advances in Gender Research, 4,* 189–225.

Jack, D. C. (1991). *Silencing the self: Women and depression.* Cambridge, MA: Harvard University Press.

Jordan, J. V., Kaplan, A. G., Miller, J. B., Stiver, I. P., & Surrey, J. L. (1991). *Women's growth in connection: Writings from the Stone Center.* New York: Guilford Press.

Karcher, M. J., & Lee, Y. (2002). Connectedness among Taiwanese middle school students: A validation study of the Hemingway Measure of Adolescent Connectedness. *Asia Pacific Education Review, 3,* 95–114.

Klaw, E. L., Rhodes, J. E., & Fitzgerald, L. F. (2003). Natural mentors in the lives of African American adolescent mothers: Tracking relationships over time. *Journal of Youth and Adolescence, 23,* 223–232.

Liang, B., Tracy, A. J., Taylor, C. A., & Williams, L. M. (2002). Mentoring college-age women: A relational approach. *American Journal of Community Psychology, 30,* 271–288.

McLearn, K. T., Colasanto, D., & Schoen, C. (1998). *Mentoring makes a difference: Findings From the Commonwealth Fund 1998 Survey of Adults Mentoring Young People.* New York: The Commonwealth Fund. Available at http://www.ecs.org/html/Document.asp?chouseid=2843

Morrow, K. V., & Styles, M. B. (1995). *Building relationships with youth in program settings: A study of Big Brothers/Big Sisters.* Philadelphia: Public/Private Ventures.

Nicholson, H. J. (1991). *Gender issues in youth development programs.* New York: Carnegie Council on Adolescent Development.

Novotney, L. C., Mertinko, E., Lange, J., & Baker, T. K. (2000). *Juvenile Mentoring Program: A progress review.* Washington, DC: U.S. Department of Justice, Office of Justice Programs, Office of Juvenile Justice and Delinquency Prevention. Available at http://www.ojjdp.ncjrs.org/jump/

O'Neill, R. M., Horton, S., & Crosby, F. J. (1999). Gender issues in developmental relationships. In A. J. Murrell, F. J. Crosby, et al. (Eds.), *Mentoring dilemmas: Developmental relationships within multicultural organizations. Applied social research* (pp. 63–80). Mahwah, NJ: Erlbaum.

Parra, G. R., DuBois, D. L., Neville, H. A., Pugh-Lilly, A. O., & Povinelli, N. (2002). Mentoring relationships for youth: Investigation of a process-oriented model. *Journal of Community Psychology, 30,* 367–388.

Rhodes, J. E. (2002). *Stand by me: The risks and rewards of mentoring today's youth.* Cambridge, MA: Harvard University Press.

Rhodes, J. E., Ebert, L., & Fischer, K. (1992). Natural mentors: An overlooked resource in the social networks of young, African American mothers. *American Journal of Community Psychology, 20,* 445–461.

Rhodes, J. E., Grossman, J. B., & Resch, N. R. (2000). Agents of change: Pathways through which mentoring relationships influence adolescents' academic adjustment. *Child Development, 71,* 1662–1671.

Rhodes, J. E., Reddy, R., Grossman, J., & Lee, J. (2002). Volunteer mentoring relationships with minority youth: An analysis of same- versus cross-race matches. *Journal of Applied Social Psychology, 32,* 2114–2133.

Rickwood, D. J., & Braithwaite, V. A. (1994). Social-psychological factors affecting helpseeking for emotional problems. *Social Science Medicine, 39,* 563–572.

Roaf, P. A., Tierney, J. P., & Hunte, D. E. I. (1994). *Big Brothers/Big Sisters of America: A study of volunteer recruitment and screening.* Philadelphia: Public/Private Ventures.

Rose, A. (2002). Co-rumination in the friendships of girls and boys. *Child Development, 73,* 1830–1843.

Royse, D. (1998). Mentoring high-risk minority youth: Evaluation of the Brothers Project. *Adolescence, 33,* 145–158.

Sánchez, B., & Reyes, O. (1999). Descriptive profile of the mentorship relationships of Latino adolescents. *Journal of Community Psychology, 27,* 299–302.

Sosik, J. J., & Godshalk, V. M. (2000). The role of gender in mentoring: Diversified and homogenous mentoring relationships. *Journal of Vocational Behavior, 57,* 102–122.

Struthers, N. J. (1995). Differences in mentoring: A function of gender or organizational rank? *Journal of Social Behavior & Personality, 10,* 265–272.

Sullivan, A. M. (1996). From mentor to muse: Recasting the role of women in relationship with urban adolescent girls. In B. J. R. Leadbeater & N. Way (Eds.), *Urban girls: Resisting stereotypes, creating identities* (pp. 226–249). New York: New York University Press.

Sullivan, K., Marshall, S. K., & Schonert-Reichl, K. A. (2002). Do expectancies influence choice of help-giver? Adolescents' criteria for selecting an informal helper. *Journal of Adolescent Research, 17,* 509–531.

Tierney, J. P., Grossman, J. B., & Resch, N. L. (1995). *Making a difference: An impact study of Big Brothers/Big Sisters.* Philadelphia: Public/Private Ventures.

von Eye, A., & Bergman, L. R. (2003). Research strategies in developmental psychopathology: Dimensional identity and the person-oriented approach. *Development and Psychopathology, 15,* 553–580.

Way, N. (1995). "Can't you see the courage, the strength that I have?" Listening to urban adolescent girls speak about their relationships. *Psychology of Women Quarterly, 19,* 107–128.

Way, N. (1998). *Everyday courage: The lives and stories of urban teenagers.* New York: New York University Press.

Way, N., & Chen, L. (2000). Close and general friendships among African American, Latino, and Asian American adolescents from low-income families. *Journal of Adolescent Research, 15,* 274–301.

Way, N., & Pahl, K. (2001). Individual and contextual predictors of perceived friendship quality among ethnic minority, low-income adolescents. *Journal of Research on Adolescence, 11,* 325–349.

Youniss, J., & Smollar, J. (1985). *Adolescent relations with mothers, fathers, and friends.* Chicago: University of Chicago Press.

Zimmerman, M. A., Bingenheimer, J. B., & Notaro, P. C. (2002). Natural mentors and adolescent resiliency: A study with urban youth. *American Journal of Community Psychology, 30,* 221–243.

PART V

FORMAL MENTORING PROGRAMS

15

DEVELOPING A MENTORING PROGRAM

SUSAN G. WEINBERGER

INTRODUCTION

Developing a formal mentoring program requires thoughtful planning and preparation. Setting aside sufficient time to develop a program properly is worth the effort and can be expected to facilitate higher quality and more effective mentoring. The focus of this chapter is on the procedures used in establishing and maintaining a mentoring program.

The chapter is organized into three sections. The aim of each section is to provide practitioners with resources to assist them in their program development efforts. The first section gives a brief historical perspective of how "best practices," which have served as guidelines for the development of effective formal mentoring programs, were created. This section also highlights the importance of a needs assessment in order to determine the current availability of formal and informal mentoring in a community and thereby identify the kinds of formal programs that may need to be established.

The second section of the chapter examines issues of program focus and structure and poses a number of questions that program practitioners should consider when establishing the parameters for their programs. These questions focus on program goals, the population to be served (that is, the selection of youth for the initiative), and who will be recruited as mentors. They also address screening and training practices for mentors, the location of mentoring sessions, program duration, focus of mentoring sessions, and the expected outcomes for the mentors, the mentees, and the organization, all of which may be critical components in designing an effective mentoring program.

The third section, which overviews program management, looks at the important management functions of a mentoring program. Issues addressed include managing and staffing a program, devising a plan to measure program success, and disseminating evaluation findings. The discussion also considers how to create an advisory council and how to develop sound financial and communications plans as well as a system to monitor the program. The chapter concludes with a synthesis of the chapter as well as recommendations for research and for practice.

DEVELOPING A MENTORING PROGRAM

Elements of Effective Practice: A Historical Perspective

In 1989, One to One (now known as MENTOR/ National Mentoring Partnership) and United Way of America convened a group of individuals with expertise in mentoring from national and community-based nonprofit organizations. Over the course of a year, the members shared their experiences, discussed barriers to successful mentoring, reviewed the research available at the time, and examined current programs. The experts created what came to be known as *Elements of Effective Practice,* which proposed a set of guidelines, principles, or "best practices" in the development of mentoring programs (MENTOR/ National Mentoring Partnership, 1990). For more than a decade, these "Elements" have guided the thinking and planning of those developing and implementing programs in the mentoring field.

The same time period witnessed a tremendous growth in the importance and popularity of mentoring. New kinds of programs began to emerge, serving the needs of many different kinds of youth, as evidenced by the "Special Populations" section of this handbook (see Baker & Maguire, this volume, for further historical background). The diversity and number of new mentoring programs prompted the original authors of *Elements of Effective Practice* to reconvene another group of mentoring authorities in 2003. Participants included three members of the original committee, along with 16 additional experts in the field of mentoring. They reexamined and reassessed the existing "Elements" and incorporated new ideas and practices to better reflect the more current mentoring policies, programming, experiences, and research, which resulted in a second edition of *Elements of Effective Practice* (MENTOR/National Mentoring Partnership, 2003). Table 15.1 provides a summary of the guidelines in *Elements of Effective Practice.*

This chapter relies primarily on the revised *Elements of Effective Practice* as the basis for suggesting guidelines to develop and implement mentoring programs. It is worth emphasizing that the stakes in doing so may be high. Available research suggests not only that adherence to the types of practices included in the "Elements" is important for realizing the potential benefits of mentoring programs but also that when such practices are lacking in implementation, there is increased potential for harmful effects of program involvement on youth.

DuBois, Holloway, Valentine, and Cooper (2002) reported that some programs have actually had harmful effects on youth. This finding is consistent with a growing number of reports and published research revealing the potentially adverse consequences of often well-meaning but poorly run programs. A wise practitioner will heed the warning that mentoring programs must be done right or not done at all!

Conducting a Needs Assessment

Prior to considering initiating a formal mentoring program, planners can use various tools to conduct a thorough assessment of the local needs of youth and the community at large. It is conceivable that youth mentoring programs already exist in the community. Such an assessment could identify the presence of similar programs and help avoid overlapping services. This process also enables developers to determine any potential gaps in serving youth, identify specific youth in need of support services, and provide vital information to assist in identifying priorities. This is important because organizations and their staff need to be invested in a program, both financially and emotionally, if it is to become successful. Ideally, a needs assessment should be conducted as one of the first steps in an ongoing process of program planning and accountability. Coyne, Duffy, and Wandersman, this volume, describe the use of these types of systems in detail.

Assessment information can be gathered by conducting focus groups, personal interviews, or surveys with youth and adults in the community or by reading community reports and information available from existing youth-serving agencies. Important information about the need for mentors in a community can be secured from local school districts by interviewing individual teachers and guidance counselors as well as by talking to law enforcement agencies and reading published reports about a community. For example, school-based mentoring programs may be able to rely heavily on recommendations from teachers to determine groups of youth within the school population who could benefit the most from mentoring. Table 15.2 provides examples of questions that can be posed to individuals being interviewed as part of a needs

Table 15.1   Elements of Effective Practice: A Summary

Program Design and Planning

   Youth population to be served
   Types of individuals who will be recruited as mentors
   Type of mentoring, one-to-one, group, team, peer, or e-mentoring
   Nature and focus of mentoring sessions
   Program accomplishments and outcomes
   When mentoring will take place
   Frequency of meetings between mentors and mentees
   Location for meetings
   How to promote the program
   How to evaluate success
   Case management protocol
   Selection of management team
   Development of financial plan

Program Management

   Formation of advisory council
   Comprehensive system for managing program information
   Fund development plan
   System to monitor the program
   Creation of professional staff development plan
   Advocacy for promentoring public policies and funding
   Public relations/communications effort

Program Operations

   Recruitment of mentors, mentees, and other volunteers
   Screening of potential mentors and mentees
   Orientation and training of mentors, mentees, and parents/caregivers
   Matching of mentors and mentees
   Location and focus of mentoring sessions
   Ongoing support, supervision, and monitoring of mentoring relationships
   Recognition of contributions of all program participants
   Assistance with mentor and mentee closure

Program Evaluation

   Plan to measure program process
   Plan to measure expected program outcomes

SOURCE: *Elements of Effective Practice, 2nd Edition.* MENTOR/National Mentoring Partnership, Alexandria, Virginia, 2004.

assessment in order to determine the need for a mentoring program.

   Local United Ways are an example of a community organization that can be asked to assist in acquiring needed information about a community during the planning phase of a program. Others include local youth-serving agencies and task forces directed by a governmental agency or the Chamber of Commerce. These organizations already may have the needed information to proceed with the mentoring initiative and may be interested in partnering to pool resources and efforts in the development and maintenance of a mentoring program.

Table 15.2   Questions to Ask Community Members When Conducting a Needs Assessment

1. What are the greatest needs facing youth in your community today?

2. Why do you think these needs exist?

3. What programs are you aware of in your community that may be addressing the need you described?

4. Are these programs successful? How do you know?

5. What suggestions do you have to meet the needs facing youth in your community?

6. What is the definition of mentoring?

7. Do you know what a mentoring program looks like? (Guide the interview by providing a description of a mentoring program at this point.)

8. To the best of your knowledge, does your community have a mentoring program?

9. If a mentoring program is developed, how do you think that it would benefit the needs facing youth in your community?

10. Do you think that it would be easy or difficult to recruit volunteers to be mentors?

11. What local youth-serving agencies should be called upon to collaborate as partners in a mentoring program?

PROGRAM STRUCTURE AND FOCUS

Setting Program Goals

Establishing goals and objectives allows a program to set a clear direction and enables it to specify measurable outcomes (see Grossman, this volume). This is a critical first step in program development. Some programs will want to focus on reducing or preventing dropouts and ensuring that youth remain in school through to high school graduation. Others may want to decrease teen pregnancy, drug use, or delinquent behaviors through mentoring. Still other programs may want to eliminate illiteracy or improve the self-esteem of identified youth. Programs matching young people with mentors may want to improve peer relationships among youth, their school attendance, or perceived social support. Sometimes the goal is as simple as providing an advocate for a young person, although "advocacy" may be one of the most difficult outcomes to measure.

Having established desired outcomes, it may be useful as a further step to build a logic model of the program (United Way of America, 1996). This exercise will require a clear specification of program activities, ranging from training and supervision conducted by staff to expectations for the frequency and duration of relationships between mentors and youth, and a realistic assessment of whether these activities are sufficient to plausibly support the attainment of desired outcomes. It also requires that resources be identified that will be sufficient to ensure that desired activities are able to occur in the amounts and at the levels of quality desired. The process of constructing a logic model thus may serve to identify needs for additional activities and services to impact targeted outcomes as well as further resources to support implementation of the program. The resulting model, furthermore, can serve as a valuable aid in focusing and directing future program evaluation efforts.

Population of Youth to Be Served

The appropriate age of the youth in the mentoring program must be determined. Illustratively, the needs assessment may reveal that the greatest need for mentoring in a community is among youth who fall in the age range of 5 to 11 or that youth who would be best served by mentoring are between 12 and 18 years old. It is conceivable that youth needing mentors could fall into more than one age category. Grossman and Rhodes (2002) found that matches involving 13- to 16-year-olds were 65% more likely to terminate in any given month than were matches with 10- to 12-year-olds, suggesting programs serving younger youth may require fewer resources. This author has designed and developed more than 400 site-based mentoring programs for two decades and has experienced that school-based programs that match mentors with youth in the elementary years are very popular. This is not surprising given that younger students may be more excited about having a new friend, have fewer obligations to occupy their time at school or after school, and may be more open to an adult who comes to visit and have fun with them. Yet older youth, when engaged, may provide more immediately rewarding experiences for adult mentors. Older youth, for example, may be more interested in exploring their future directions and career options. As these considerations illustrate, the age of youth served should be thought through carefully and in relation to issues such as the location and structure of the program and the desired outcomes for participating youth.

The family structure, as well as the socioeconomic class and ethnic background of the youth to be served, is another important consideration. Some programs focus on youth who come from single-parent, low-income, or ethnic minority families. Other initiatives direct their efforts to youth that are from two-parent, middle-class, and ethnic majority families. However, recruiting a diverse group of youth from various backgrounds for mentoring has the advantage of reducing a potential stigma attached to targeting only certain groups who are viewed as having the greatest potential to benefit from a mentoring relationship.

In the author's experience, professional staff of school- and community-based programs often select youth who may have fewer resources available to them. This is consistent with the findings of DuBois, Holloway, et al.'s meta-analytic review (2002), which indicate greater benefits for youth from backgrounds of individual and environmental risk. Eligibility criteria pertaining to the lack of and need for positive adult role models among youth may be especially relevant to consider in this regard. However, it also is useful to consider how a mentoring program may benefit youth who do not have experiences or opportunities such as exposure to music, art, sports, or computers or who may be lacking in knowledge of careers or educational opportunities. These considerations may be particularly relevant for programs that are targeting gifted youth, especially those who are female, ethnic minority, and/or from low-income families (see Callahan & Kyburg, this volume).

Types of Mentoring

Elements of Effective Practice distinguishes among several different types of mentoring programs for youth: traditional mentoring (one adult to one young person), group mentoring (one adult to up to four young people), team mentoring (several adults working with small groups of young people, in which some have argued the adult-to-youth ratio should be no greater than 1:4), peer mentoring (caring youth mentoring other youth), and e-mentoring (mentoring via e-mail and the Internet). Planners should carefully select the type of mentoring that best fits their program's goals and the needs of youth in a given community and should consult relevant resources, such as the chapters in this volume that focus on peer mentoring and e-mentoring, to inform their decision making.

Mentoring programs can be structured as a stand-alone initiative or part of an existing program (see Kuperminc et al., this volume). Big Brothers Big Sisters (BBBS) agencies offer a number of different mentoring programs to serve the needs of their communities, and mentoring is the primary focus of these agencies. Other youth-serving organizations such as Boys & Girls Clubs, however, may develop a mentoring initiative within an existing program that delivers other services to youth as well. Schools often create mentoring programs as part of their school business and community partnerships program. The decision to offer a stand-alone program or to incorporate it into an existing program should be determined based on the organization's resources and, of course, the needs of the youth. One key consideration should be the financial implications of hiring or locating the new staff required for a stand-alone program, as opposed to the possibility and benefits of having existing staff take on the mentoring initiative as an additional responsibility.

Locations of Mentoring

Elements of Effective Practice differentiates the array of settings in which mentoring occurs. The three primary locations for programs are at a site, in the community, or in the virtual community where e-mentoring takes place. Site-based programs occur at designated locations, such as the workplace; a school; a faith-based organization; residentially based locations, such as juvenile corrections facilities, prisons, and youth shelters; or agencies, such as a community center, YMCA, and Boys & Girls Clubs.

Time commitments expected of mentors in site-based programs typically are limited, often to as little as 1 hour per week. The fixed location and time commitment may be attractive to mentors who are employed during the day and who do not feel able to devote more extensive time to a program. Herrera (2000) found that mentors liked meeting with youth in a school setting, in part because they did not need to get involved with the families of youth. Some mentors also may like the opportunity to meet with their mentees at a site because it is an environment in which the mentor can serve as the youth's advocate.

Site-based programs may be relatively less costly because often school and agency staff can assume responsibility for program oversight in addition to their other job assignments. The facilities where the mentoring takes place along with materials and telephones may be offered as an in-kind contribution by the host agency or school.

The most prominent example of a community-based program is Big Brothers Big Sisters of America and its affiliate agencies across the United States. The location, timing, and focus of mentoring activities in such community-based programs typically are determined by the mentor and youth themselves. They can decide together what they are going to do each week, for how many hours they will meet, and where the meetings will take place. In most community-based programs, there is a requirement of spending at least 3 to 4 hours a week together (e.g., BBBS). Many mentors may prefer this kind of mentoring program in order to spend more time with youth in less controlled environments.

Because of their more unstructured nature, community-based programs may require greater supervision from case managers to monitor the matches and to offer guidance and help with problem solving when questions or challenges arise. This, and the fact that the mentoring agency must cover its own costs for salaries and supplies, may make community programs relatively more costly.

E-mentoring takes place with chats between mentors and mentees via the Internet. Virtual mentoring may be a less costly approach to mentoring than site-based or community-based mentoring because it does not require space for meetings and supplies. Some mentors also may prefer this option so that they do not have to leave their homes or the workplace in order to serve in the role of mentor. E-mentoring is covered in greater detail by Miller and Griffiths in this volume.

Focus of Mentoring Sessions

As suggested previously when discussing the creation of a program logic model, desired program outcomes should determine the nature and focus of the mentoring sessions. For example, in a program that is designed to improve academic performance, mentors concentrate their efforts on helping with schoolwork. However, in a program where youth are identified as needing career direction, mentors focus on employability skills and career opportunities. If the desired program outcome is youth who gain socialization skills as a result of mentoring, then mentors in these programs play with youth, offer friendship, and have fun.

An important part of mentoring should be ensuring that mentors feel that what they are doing with and for the youth during their sessions together is having an impact. Program practitioners frequently have told this author that some mentors feel they are wasting their time and the time of the mentees when they just hang out and have fun together. Program developers might consider that the strongest factor contributing to strong relationships that Herrera, Sipe, and McClanahan (2000) studied was the extent to which the youth and mentors engaged in social activities (for example, having lunch, just hanging out together). DuBois, Neville, Parra, and Pugh-Lilly (2002) also found that the use of social discussion in matches predicted greater likelihood that mentees would report that their mentors were significant adults in their lives.

Duration of Mentoring

The duration of mentoring relationships has been a debated topic among researchers and practitioners in the field for many years. Programs determine how often the mentors and mentees will meet as well as how long the match should endure. Available research (Grossman & Rhodes, 2002) suggests that at a minimum, developers of community-based programs should plan that the pairs meet regularly for at least a year. Other site-based programs such as those at churches, Boys & Girls Clubs, community centers, and the faith community programs may require, permit, or encourage additional hours. In some community-based programs, mentors and mentees are encouraged to meet a minimum of 4 to 5 hours each week.

School-based mentoring presents special challenges because these programs typically are circumscribed by the calendar for the school year, which is typically 9 or 10 months. School-based programs also tend to take time to start up, thus shortening the available window of time for actual mentoring contacts. In school-based programs, youth typically meet 1 hour each week for the school year. Schools, by their nature and scheduling constraints, may not be able to allow youth and mentors to spend longer periods of time together or have more frequent contacts.

Recruitment of Mentors

Recruitment of mentors frequently poses a serious challenge to the successful implementation of programs. Program developers must determine the pool from which they will recruit mentors, and each pool of mentors may require concomitant structural supports. For example, depending on the makeup of the community, mentors may come from the ranks of business and municipalities. However, ideally, there should be organizational support for becoming involved in mentoring, such as when corporations endorse a mentoring program at the CEO level and a municipality at the mayor or first selectman level. These commitments can help sustain matches, such as by offering release time for their employees during the work day to become mentors and by assigning a member of their staff to coordinate the mentoring effort.

Mentoring program practitioners have become creative in the ways in which they attract and recruit mentors. In this author's experience, some of the most successful efforts include (a) the presentation of stories highlighting mentors and mentees in the local media, (b) featuring the program and its participants in annual reports of corporations that are involved in mentoring, and (c) paid or pro bono advertisements on billboards and in newspapers. Many programs set up a table in the local library or supermarket during January, which is National Mentoring Month, and disseminate information to interested individuals who stop to learn about mentoring. Another approach to recruiting mentors that may prove useful is to have current mentors recruit mentors for the program from among friends, relatives, or colleagues at work. Additional strategies are discussed by Stukas and Tanti, this volume.

Mentor Selection and Screening

Sipe (1996) reviewed the literature and found that three features are essential to the success of any mentoring program. They are (a) screening, (b) orientation and training, and (c) support and supervision. She concluded that programs that omitted one or more of these three features had greater difficulty sustaining relationships.

Proper screening of mentors helps ensure protection for the youth, mentors, and the organizations delivering mentoring programs. Planners should examine staff capability to carry out screening properly. Some programs partner with others in the community who already do a good job of screening. Regardless of whether screening is done in partnership with others or is the organization's responsibility, the screening should include, at a minimum, a written application, a personal interview, a check of employment history, federal and state criminal background checks, character references, and a review of the child abuse registry. Many community-based programs may require additional screening, such as a review of driving records. Most schools today already conduct background checks on their staff and other volunteers, thus making it easy to include mentor screening as part of their already existing effort.

Mentor Training

Program developers should ensure that professional staff are prepared to properly train mentors. Developers can receive assistance through state and national organizations that hold seminars, workshops, and conferences and provide training material for this purpose. Several such organizations can be contacted through convenient Web sites (see Appendix at the end of this chapter) from which many training materials can be downloaded at no cost. Mentoring program practitioners do not need to reinvent the wheel in terms of training materials to prepare mentors for their experience. The most popular materials to assist in the process include those listed in the Appendix. Three of these organizations, Public/Private Ventures, National Mentoring Center, and MENTOR/National Mentoring Partnership, lead the way in making available high-quality training and program development materials and distributing these resources free online. Mentor Consulting Group offers a series of training guides and activity books for mentors at low cost.

Training should begin with a session before mentors are matched with youth. This provides the opportunity to discuss program policies and procedures with mentors, as well as recommended strategies for each session. But training should be ongoing. Over the life of the matches between mentors and mentees, ongoing training may increase the likelihood of longer-lasting relationships and has been found to predict more

positive youth outcomes (DuBois, Holloway, et al., 2002). In a survey of 700 nationally representative mentoring programs, however, fewer than half provided volunteers with 2 or more hours of training, and a distressing 22% of programs offered mentors no training whatsoever (Sipe & Roder, 1999).

A number of topics are essential for mentors to learn about in the initial training. At a minimum, these include program policies and procedures. Additional topics should include techniques to help mentors communicate with youth and resolve conflicts that may arise in the match. Training also should cover policies regarding gift giving (which generally in this author's experience is a bad idea), maintaining appropriate emotional and physical boundaries in the relationship, and procedures for reporting suspicion of any suspected sexual, physical, or child abuse. Mentors should be trained in the importance of maintaining confidentiality at all times and should be given information regarding practical strategies for working successfully with youth in mentoring relationships.

Program Support

Ongoing support of mentors and mentees is critical to any program's success. Mentors cannot work in a vacuum, and they need to know that professional staff will assist them when they have issues, concerns, or do not feel that they are making progress in the relationship. Among the specific program support practices for which there is empirical support are monitoring of program implementation, ongoing training, and provision of structured activities for mentors and youth to participate in together (DuBois, Holloway, et al., 2002).

Staff should be available to mentors to (a) answer questions that arise, (b) troubleshoot when there are issues and concerns in the match, and (c) recommend alternative strategies for what can be done in the mentor and mentee relationship. Case managers serve this role in most community-based programs, offering support to the matches. In site-based programs, these individuals are called program coordinators or school liaisons and serve in the same capacity. The staff should be taught the importance of contacting the pairs within the first 2 weeks of the match and of monthly follow-up checks during the first year of the relationship, to determine how the sessions are progressing. Table 15.3 presents a series of open-ended questions program coordinators might ask mentors on a regular basis as part of their work to support mentors' relationships with their mentees. These questions are designed to pull information from mentors that could signal difficulties or unclear boundaries in the relationship.

Role of the Family

Research (DuBois, Holloway, et al., 2002; Grossman & Rhodes, 2002) suggests efforts by programs to involve parents of youth can strengthen program effects. Illustrative in this regard is the Families and Mentors Involved In Learning With Youth (F.A.M.I.L.Y.) model developed by the author (Weinberger, 2001). In this model, family members meet with mentees and mentors at a site such as a school, community center, or YMCA in the evening three times a year. The purpose of the meetings is to enhance communication between mentors and families of mentees. Part of the evening meeting is social, and another part is educational. In the author's experience, these events work best when families are offered food, transportation to and from the events, and babysitting for younger children.

PROGRAM MANAGEMENT

Professional Staff Development

Most mentoring programs are run by non-profit organizations, and the staff turnover is frequent. Program developers need to put a plan in place to ensure that new staff receives adequate training to coordinate a mentoring initiative. At a minimum, mentoring program's staff should receive training in how to complete written records about the progress of each mentor and mentee match and how to document and resolve problems that may arise between the pairs. Staff also should be trained on a series of program management and mentor support tasks, and many sources are available to support these efforts (see Appendix).

Forming an Advisory Council

An important part of program management is the formation of an advisory council that can provide advice and oversight of the program. Members should be invited to join at the initial, development stage of building a mentoring program and should include individuals who have a strong interest in youth and who believe in the goals of the mentoring program. They should be recruited so that the council represents an array of points of view from a diverse set of

---

Table 15.3 Questions Staff Can Ask Mentors for the Purposes of Supervision and Evaluation

1. How often are you and your mentee meeting?

2. Does the youth seem resistant to your meetings?

3. Are you satisfied with activities that you are carrying out with your mentee?

4. How is communication between you and your mentee?

5. Are there any special problems you would like to mention?

6. Are you able to make the regular commitment to your mentee? (Does the mentor seem overwhelmed?)

7. Are there any "red flags" that say there may be trouble?

8. What are the positives about your relationship with your mentee?

9. How can the program help improve the relationship?

backgrounds. Ideally, members should include an attorney, educator, member of the clergy, banker, and accountant. The council also may benefit from inclusion of individuals from other professions, such as foundation director, computer expert, marketing and public relations professional, youth-serving agency representative, researcher, grant writer, and school superintendent. It can be advantageous to include a youth representative as well. Collectively, the preceding types of individuals can offer the assistance and expertise necessary to negotiate the full range of tasks required for development, implementation, and evaluation of a mentoring program.

Managing Program Information

Every program must develop and maintain a comprehensive system for managing program information. This information includes program finances and a detailed accounting of all funds that have been received from grants, individuals, organizations, and other sources. These records should be available for public examination at any time. The program should maintain personnel records on all employees of the mentoring program, such as those documenting when employees were hired, screened, and trained to work with mentors and youth. The data-tracking system should maintain information on all mentors, including (a) the dates from the day they began in the program to the date on which they closed their relationships, (b) demographic information on all volunteers and youth, (c) records pertaining to the matches, and (d) volunteer hours. Programs should keep records on the attendance of mentors in order to determine how consistent they are in meeting with youth. The time invested in data collection and management will be worth the time and energy it takes, in part because it keeps the program accountable to all who have invested time and money in the program.

Developing a Financial Plan

Part of creating a mentoring program is developing a program budget that is realistic and can be carried out. Most nonprofit agencies suffer from lack of funds, and this may have a profound influence on the prospects for success or failure of a mentoring initiative. Programs

need to determine the amount of funding that is necessary to start and sustain a program over time. Multiple sources of funding are highly desirable. In the author's experience, programs that rely on only one source of funding for 30% or more of the survival of their initiatives may invite a crisis before they even begin their mentoring programs.

Program developers should map out a plan to seek in-kind gifts from local businesses, advisory council members, and their contacts. With the assistance of a grant writer, preferably one that serves on the advisory council, program developers can seek out foundation and government grants. Developers must plan special events to raise both awareness of the need for mentoring as well as secure funding for the program. Individual and corporate donors should be identified that are willing to make a financial commitment to the program.

Over the past decade, increased funding has become available to support and sustain mentoring programs through federal, state, and foundation grants. Major funding has been provided by the Office of Juvenile Justice and Delinquency Prevention (OJJDP), through its Juvenile Mentoring Program (JUMP); the Mentoring for Success Act (2001), an amendment to the Elementary and Secondary Education Act, through the Department of Education; and Mentoring of Children of Prisoners, through the Department of Health and Human Services. These are just three federal grants that are awarded directly to local communities to carry out mentoring programs. Regularly, MENTOR/National Mentoring Partnership posts on its Web site current information on government entities that issue Requests for Proposals for mentoring program funding and other legislative initiatives.

In general, to sustain a program, it may be critical to develop a strategy to diversify fund raising in at least six major categories. These include a plan to secure (a) government grants, (b) individual and philanthropic donations, (c) foundation grants, (d) annual giving programs, (e) special events and cause-related marketing, and (f) third-party events—that is, when another organization runs a fund-raising event and the mentoring program does nothing more than become the beneficiary of the revenues.

Public Relations/Communications Plan

Program developers should draft a marketing plan to promote the mentoring program successfully (Weinberger, 2004). The plan should include "who, what, where, when, and how" information about the program and identify the internal and external publics that must be served by the plan. The resources available to carry out the plan may determine the location and nature of the marketing effort. Some mentoring initiatives are part of an organization's existing marketing plan, such as being part of the efforts of a school district's marketing plan developed by their public relations department. Other mentoring initiatives may need additional resources, both personnel and financial, to accomplish this task. It may mean developing partnerships with other organizations in order to share expertise and costs.

Programs should conduct a market analysis or needs assessment as a way to know how and to whom to market the program. Results may determine that the program should market its program via articles in newspapers, ads on radio and television, or through billboards. Sometimes recruitment and awareness information can be put in the internal newsletters of local organizations or businesses.

One of the author's preferred ways of recruiting mentors for a program is by providing current mentors with table tents in the shape of a paper or plastic placard, which are placed on their desks at work. These tents usually have a message on them that states that the person behind that desk is a mentor in a local program. It is a great way to raise awareness about those who currently are serving as mentors, and it invites the opportunity to talk to potential mentors about the need and benefits of mentoring programs in the community. Others have given mentors a table tent that reads, "Gone mentoring. Back in an hour." The tent is placed on the desk of mentors when they are out of the office mentoring youth.

Recognition Programs

An important part of many successful mentoring programs are planned efforts to recognize mentors, mentees, funders, and organizations that sponsor the mentoring program. In the case of school-based programs, recognition also should be directed to the staff of schools who work diligently to carry out the program. They include school principals who endorse the mentoring programs in their schools, and teachers who take the time to meet with mentors to discuss concerns or questions they have about their mentees and who make extra effort to help youth make up classwork when mentoring is conducted outside the classroom. Those who are thanked by developers typically appreciate the recognition and subsequently may be more inclined to continue playing a role in the mentoring program in future years. Finally, it is important that programs thank their funders, both as a courtesy and as a way to help ensure their continued support.

In 2002, MENTOR/National Mentoring Partnership, in conjunction with the Harvard Mentoring Project, designated and organized the first annual National Mentoring Month. Since that time, these two organizations have provided materials, press kits, and assistance to local communities trying to get the word out about the value of mentoring. January has now been accepted nationally as the month to concentrate on the message of the importance of mentoring and mentors. During this month, local and national television and radio stations as well as print media have become increasingly willing to participate in and promote the event.

Program Monitoring

Establishing a system of constant program monitoring is essential to success (DuBois, Holloway, et al., 2002). Staff should review policies, procedures, and operations on a regular basis and ask themselves how they are doing. The mentors and mentees should be regarded as the customers of mentoring programs, and information should be collected from them regularly to determine how well the program is accomplishing its goals. Staff also should be helped to anticipate problems that might arise and to respond quickly to these issues and concerns. Even in the best of mentoring relationships, there will be times when mentors, in particular, experience frustration, exasperation, impatience, anger, and in some cases even regret that they entered in the relationship in the first place. Constant monitoring will help identify problems and help staff address issues immediately and solve problems that may be addressed by providing additional training and support for mentors' needs.

Program Evaluation

Part of mentoring development is preparing a plan to measure program success and disseminate findings of research (see Coyne and colleagues, this volume). Based on the goals and objectives selected for a program, evaluators should select valid and reliable tools to measure relevant outcomes. Most nonprofit organizations are ill equipped to conduct rigorous outcome evaluations to determine the effects of their programs. Many local universities may have academic departments with faculty who may be able to assist programs with program evaluations. However, there are several nontechnical resources available to guide mentoring programs in planning, implementing, and reporting findings of evaluations, such as the United Way's guide to conducting evaluations. The types of program activities and outcomes included in the program's logic model can be used to focus evaluations conducted with these types of resources. The procedures required for more complex evaluations are explained more fully by Grossman (this volume).

Program directors should plan ahead to ensure they collect the types of data they will need to draft useful reports of program activities and outcomes. Funders, organizers, and members of mentoring advisory councils usually want to know how a mentoring program is progressing toward measurable outcomes. It also is important to set out a plan to disseminate the findings from a program on a regular basis. These reports on findings may include an annual report, periodic updates on the program provided through the program's internal newsletters, reports made to boards of education by program directors, or articles in brochures and local media. Assessing information relevant to these stakeholders and ensuring that stakeholders are kept aware of the program's progress may increase the likelihood of their continued support.

FUTURE DIRECTIONS

Synthesis

This chapter has addressed the most important components in designing an effective mentoring program. One of the most critical considerations in developing a mentoring program is ensuring maximum protection for all participants. Mentoring program developers and practitioners are encouraged to follow the guidelines proposed in *Elements of Effective Practice,* by MENTOR/National Mentoring Partnership, which also has produced an accompanying *Toolkit* (2005) to assist programs. Furthermore, developers can utilize training and technical assistance resources currently available from several national organizations (see Appendix) available at no cost.

Recommendations for Research

Research is available to support and inform many of the decisions faced by program planners. There remain many important questions for which little or no evidence is available to guide decision making.

1. *Identify the most appropriate types of mentoring program for different populations of youth and outcomes.* Mentoring programs currently being offered are one-to-one, group, team, peer, or e-mentoring. Often, developers decide what kind of program will be designed and developed based on the program's financial, staff, and volunteer resources. Very little is known, however, about the relative benefits that different types of program models offer to youth for different outcomes. Programmatic research should focus on strengthening the knowledge base that is available to program planners in this crucial area.

2. *Increase understanding of the nature and focus of effective mentoring within different types of program models.* Mentoring programs typically can accommodate the use of a variety of strategies by mentors when they are working with youth. These range from providing simple companionship to more directed efforts focused on goals such as improvement of a mentee's social skills, offering career direction, providing academic support, and training youth in

employable skills. Currently, decisions regarding which specific processes to emphasize in the training and supervision of mentors for their work with youth are dependent largely on the impressionistic judgments of program planners. To provide a stronger foundation for program planning relevant to this concern, priority should be given to conducting research that investigates the relative merits of different approaches and goals within mentoring relationships for achieving youth outcomes of interest. The effectiveness of different program practices (e.g., training models) that may be used to facilitate particular approaches to mentoring should be studied carefully as well.

3. *Determine most effective matching criteria and procedures.* At present, there is also remarkably limited data available to guide mentoring programs in determining what criteria for matching mentors and mentees are most likely to yield enduring and high-quality relationships. Little is known, for example, about the benefits and potential negative consequences of same- versus different-race matches or about the relative importance of similarity in different aspects of mentor and youth personality and interests. Likewise, although programs use a range of differing approaches in obtaining the information needed to implement matching, some of them innovative (e.g., mentor-youth mixers), their relative effectiveness has not been systematically investigated. Research thus is needed to increase understanding of both the ingredients that make for positive chemistry between mentors and mentees and the practices that are most useful for ensuring that relevant criteria factor appropriately into match decisions within the actual operations of programs.

Recommendations for Practice

1. *Encourage parental involvement in mentoring.* Some mentoring program practitioners engage the families of their mentees in activities as part of the mentoring initiative. Other programs do not include a family or parent component. What presently is known about the involvement of families in mentoring and its influence on important potential outcomes suggests the inclusion of parents is critically important, and energy should be placed into developing novel strategies for including parents in the mentoring process.

2. *Develop new ways to market mentoring programs.* Programs should develop an effective marketing plan for the purpose of recruiting mentors and mentees, recognizing program participants, and honoring funders and organizations that sponsor a mentoring program. Efforts should be directed toward the creation and dissemination of ideas for how best to market mentoring programs.

References

DuBois, D. L., Holloway, B. E., Valentine, J. C., & Cooper, H. (2002). Effectiveness of mentoring programs for youth: A meta-analytic review. *American Journal of Community Psychology, 30,* 157–197.

DuBois, D. L., Neville, H. A., Parra, G. R., & Pugh-Lilly, A. O. (2002). Testing a new model of mentoring. In G. G. Noam (Ed. in chief) & J. E. Rhodes (Ed.), *A critical view of youth mentoring* (*New Directions for Youth Development: Theory, Research, and Practice, No. 93,* pp. 21–57). San Francisco: Jossey-Bass.

Grossman, J. B., & Rhodes, J. E. (2002). The test of time: Predictors and effects of duration in youth mentoring programs. *American Journal of Community Psychology, 30,* 199–219.

Herrera, C. (2000). *School-based mentoring. A first look into its potential.* Philadelphia: Public/ Private Ventures.

Herrera, C., Sipe, C. L., & McClanahan, W. S. (2000). *Mentoring school-age children: Relationship development in community-based and school-based programs.* Philadelphia: Public/Private Ventures. (Published in collaboration with MENTOR/National Mentoring Partnership, Alexandria, VA)

Mentoring for Success Act, H.R. 1497, 147 Cong. (2001).

MENTOR/National Mentoring Partnership. (1990). *Elements of effective practice.* Alexandria, VA: Author.

MENTOR/National Mentoring Partnership. (2003). *Elements of effective practice* (2nd ed.). Alexandria, VA: Author.

MENTOR/National Mentoring Partnership. (2005). *Toolkit.* Alexandria, VA: Author.

Sipe, C. L. (1996). *Mentoring: A synthesis of Public/ Private Venture's research: 1988–1995.* Philadelphia: Public/Private Ventures.

Sipe, C. L., & Roder, A. E. (1999). *Mentoring school- age children: A classification of programs.* Philadelphia: Public/Private Ventures. (Published in collaboration with MENTOR/National Mentoring Partnership, Alexandria, VA)

United Way of America. (1996). *Measuring program outcomes: A practical approach.* Alexandria, VA: Author.

Weinberger, S. G. (2001). *Guidebook to mentoring.* Norwalk, CT: Mentor Consulting Group.

Weinberger, S. G. (2004). Mentoring, marketing, and the media. *National Mentoring Center Bulletin, 2*(1). Portland, OR: Northwest Regional Educational Laboratory.

APPENDIX

Training Materials	Organization/Source
Volunteer Education and Development Manual	Big Brothers Big Sisters of America 230 North 13th Street Philadelphia, PA 19107 http://www.bbbsa.org
Train the Trainer Manual; Manual for Mentors	Mentor Consulting Group 3 Inwood Road Norwalk, CT 06850-1017 http://www.mentorconsultinggroup.com
Technical Assistance Packets Series	National Mentoring Center Northwest Regional Educational Laboratory 101 S.W. Main Street, Suite 500 Portland, OR 97204 http://www.nwrel.org
Mentor Training Curriculum	MENTOR/National Mentoring Partnership 1600 Duke Street, Suite 300 Alexandria, VA 22314 http://www.mentoring.org
Measuring Program Outcomes: A Practical Approach	United Way of America 701 North Fairfax Street Alexandria, VA 22314-2045 http://national.unitedway.org
Self-Evaluation Workbook	Information Technology International 10000 Falls Road, Suite 214 Potomac, MD 20854 http://www.itiincorporated.com
Additional Resources	Public/Private Ventures 2000 Market Street, Suite 600 Philadelphia, PA 19103 http://www.ppv.org
	Center for Applied Research Solutions (CARS) Mentoring Technical Assistance Project 391 South Lexington Drive, Suite 110 Folsom, CA 95630 http://www.emt.org/mentoring.html

16

RECRUITING AND SUSTAINING VOLUNTEER MENTORS

ARTHUR A. STUKAS AND CHRIS TANTI

INTRODUCTION

Around the world, volunteers give of their time and themselves to avert, attenuate, or assuage social and human problems. In this chapter, we focus on individuals who volunteer to serve as mentors in formal mentoring programs for youth. Results from investigations of the effects of youth mentoring on the psychosocial and academic outcomes of youth are promising (for reviews, see DuBois, Holloway, Valentine, & Cooper, 2002; Rhodes, 2002). Yet organizations that match volunteer mentors with youth in need often have trouble recruiting sufficient numbers of mentors and sustaining their involvement over time (Roaf, Tierney, & Hunte, 1994).

Indeed, a recent AOL Time Warner Foundation survey (O'Connor, 2002) found that there are many more adults who think mentoring is a good idea than who actually sign up to be mentors; whereas 11% of respondents reported volunteering in a formal youth mentoring program, a substantial additional proportion of respondents, 42% of those not currently mentoring, reported that they would be amenable to becoming a mentor. Snyder (1993) has referred to this tendency for prosocial attitudes to surpass prosocial behavior as the "problem of inaction." The trick is to turn intentions into actions.

The most obvious way to recruit potential volunteers may be simply to ask them; social pressure can have a strong impact on the decision to volunteer (e.g., Independent Sector, 2001; Penner, 2002). But the problem of inaction will not be solved by asking individuals one by one—this is not cost-effective. Instead, we need to know who to ask. Volunteer recruitment may be aided by identifying those who might be more receptive to requests (although volunteer retention may be enhanced only by also paying careful attention to the characteristics of volunteers that predict sustained involvement; Grossman & Furano, 2002). Mentoring, furthermore, differs from many other forms of volunteerism in that there are strict exclusion criteria that must be applied to potential volunteers through a rigorous screening process (e.g., Roaf et al., 1994), making the process of recruiting volunteer mentors even more difficult.

Even if organizations manage to overcome the problem of inaction, those that manage to recruit and subsequently rely on volunteers often have another problem: retaining the volunteers they have managed to attract. Failure to maintain a pool of volunteers is devastating for many organizations. For those whose mandate involves youth mentoring, this failure could be even more critical, because early termination of mentor-mentee relationships may have a negative impact on youth (e.g., Grossman & Rhodes, 2002; McLearn, Colasanto, & Schoen, 1998).

In this chapter, we highlight theoretical approaches to recruiting and sustaining volunteer mentors, review the empirical studies that look at these processes, reveal the state of current practice among organizations, and, finally, make suggestions about important future directions for research and practice in promoting effective mentor recruitment and retention.

THEORY

Social psychologists often approach the study of behavior by taking an "interactionist" perspective, that is, by assuming that most behavior results from interactions between person-centered factors (such as personality traits, attitudes, or demographic characteristics) and situation-centered factors (such as setting- or task-based norms, rules, or cues for behavior). A good example of this approach is provided by Penner (2002), who proposed a conceptual model to suggest that sustained volunteerism may be predicted by an assortment of dispositional and organizational variables working in concert. Accordingly, we have divided our discussion of theories related to volunteering and mentoring into those that focus on features of the person and those that focus on features of the situation, recognizing that it is likely to be a combination of features that ultimately predicts successful recruitment and retention of mentors.

Features of the Person

As Grossman and Furano (2002) have pointed out, not every volunteer is right for every task. They recommend that organizations try to provide a number of different mentoring approaches to which different volunteers can be assigned. New mentoring approaches include school-based mentoring, group mentoring, and e-mentoring (Rhodes, Grossman, & Roffman, 2002). This type of matching of mentors to approaches requires an adequate understanding of how and why different volunteers may be more likely to commit to, and be appropriate for, some approaches and responsibilities than

others. Although the literature has been sparse, recent theories link demographic characteristics, personality, and motives with volunteer behavior.

Demographic Characteristics

In a recent review of sociological theories, Wilson (2000) reported that volunteerism tends to peak at middle age and may be linked to the level of social integration people attain at this period in their lives, particularly if they are part of the workforce. Social ties and networks (referred to as "social capital") are presumed to generate trust between people (Putnam, 2000), which, in turn, may make volunteerism more likely (e.g., Brady, Schlozman, & Verba, 1999; though the mechanisms through which this happens have yet to be clearly elucidated). Wilson (2000) also reported that higher levels of education and income are generally related to higher rates of volunteerism, but these relationships vary across studies, depending on the type of activity and the measurement of constructs. Individual attributes, such as income and education, can be considered to be resources (referred to as "human capital") that help offset the demands entailed by volunteerism (Wilson, 2000). However, increases in human capital also may be associated with higher "opportunity costs" (the price paid for using one's time by mentoring rather than by engaging in paid work or other personally fruitful activities). High opportunity costs could reduce likelihood of volunteering (Wilson, 2000).

Racial and ethnic differences in rates of volunteerism, which suggest Whites volunteer more often than Blacks in the United States, have been hypothesized to be due to group-level differences in human capital (Wilson, 2000). That is, Blacks may be less able to volunteer because of time and resource limitations stemming from lower levels of education, income, and occupational status; in support of this interpretation, when such features of the individual are statistically controlled, racial differences in volunteerism rates are negligible (Wilson, 2000). Community-based social capital, furthermore, may lead Blacks to volunteer more often for activities that directly affect the Black community, in settings for which the needs of that community are salient (Portney & Berry, 1997). Therefore, linking the benefits of youth mentoring to the goals and needs of particular communities during recruitment may attract more mentors from those communities.

Theoretical accounts of gender differences in helping behavior typically have focused on the type of helping performed. For example, Eagly and Crowley (1986) contend that gender norms dictate that men should engage in the types of helping that require strength and heroism, whereas women should engage in helping that involves shows of sympathy and support. Male and female mentors, then, may gravitate toward different styles of relationships with youth, with men focusing more on activities and females more on self-disclosure (Morrow & Styles, 1995). Thus, programs that are activity based, such as Big Brothers Big Sisters (BBBS), potentially could attract more men if they emphasized the activities of their programs when recruiting.

Personality Differences

Although it seems inherently plausible, psychologists have had trouble identifying the ways in which personality traits relate to helping behavior. This may be because different types of helping may be more attractive to individuals with different personalities—that is, there may be an interaction between dispositional characteristics and task features in predicting the decision to volunteer. Still, Penner and his colleagues have found evidence for a "prosocial personality" (see Penner, 2002), a constellation of traits and attitudes that may lead some individuals to be more likely to help in general than others. The Prosocial Personality Battery contains two correlated factors: (a) other-oriented empathy, which involves prosocial thoughts and feelings, and (b) helpfulness, which involves a history of prior prosocial behavior. Both factors have been shown to have small but significant relationships with length of service as a "buddy" to a person with AIDS (Penner & Finkelstein, 1998), which may involve a "relationship-building" goal similar to that of youth mentoring. However, Omoto and Snyder (1995) did not find that personality (i.e., nurturance, empathic concern, and social responsibility) predicted length of service as a buddy. Perhaps, then, a

prosocial personality may lead people to seek out volunteer opportunities (e.g., Penner, 2002), but other factors, such as satisfaction with the relationship (e.g., Omoto & Snyder, 1995), may influence duration of service.

Role Characteristics

Sociological research by Piliavin and her colleagues has examined how occupants of the role of volunteer become consistent in their behavior over time. A primary tenet of their theory is that the perceived expectations of significant others can lead people to "try out an activity—and continue in it—so as not to receive social sanctions" (Grube & Piliavin, 2000, p. 1109). Once the activity is under way, continued experience (and continued social expectations) may encourage the development of a "role identity," in which the role becomes an important feature of the person's self-concept. For example, Piliavin and Callero (1991) suggested that blood donors may develop a role identity over time. They provided data to show that the more often someone donates blood, the more likely they are to donate blood in the future. Grube and Piliavin (2000) extended this theory to examine both general role identity (as a volunteer) and specific role identity (as an American Red Cross volunteer) and found that specific role identity predicted service for a specific organization, whereas general role identity predicted overall commitment to service (across organizations). Organizations that facilitate mentors' relationships with youth might do well to encourage the development of a role identity in mentors, perhaps by using mentor support groups to reinforce the role through the creation of a new social network with shared expectations.

Motivational Differences

Recent research on the motivations underlying volunteerism has taken a functional approach and asked, "What functions does volunteerism serve for an individual?" (e.g., Snyder, Clary, & Stukas, 2000). This strategy has resulted in a theoretically derived list of motivations for volunteerism in general (Clary et al., 1998) and for AIDS volunteerism more specifically (Omoto & Snyder, 1995). The functional approach to volunteerism suggests that volunteers may engage in the same activities for very different reasons and sometimes for more than one reason (e.g., Snyder et al., 2000). Clary et al.'s (1998) Volunteer Functions Inventory (VFI) asks potential or current volunteers to rate the importance of 30 reasons for volunteering, organized into six functions or goals:

- *Values:* to express humanitarian and prosocial values through action
- *Career:* to explore career options and increase the likelihood that a particular career path can be pursued
- *Understanding:* to gain greater understanding of the world, the diverse people in it, and, ultimately, oneself
- *Enhancement:* to boost self-esteem, to feel important and needed by others, and to form new friendships
- *Protective:* to distract oneself from personal problems or to work through problems in the context of service
- *Social:* to satisfy the expectations of friends and close others

Omoto and Snyder's (1995) inventory was written to assess the reasons why people volunteer to be "buddies" for people with AIDS. Their scale contains similar, though more specifically focused, scales to the VFI, but notably adds:

- *Community concern:* to demonstrate one's interest in and commitment to the community.

Youth mentoring may offer varying opportunities to fulfill these motives for volunteering. For example, in a national U.S. survey, Clary, Snyder, and Stukas (1996) found that volunteering to work in the broad area of youth development involved higher understanding motives and somewhat lower enhancement motives than other types of volunteerism.

Potential youth mentors could also hold other motives or goals. In their qualitative study of 30 mentors in Scotland, Philip and Hendry (2000) identified the following goals for mentoring: (a) to help mentors make sense of their own experiences; (b) to gain insight into youth experiences; (c) to develop alternative kinds of relationships, such as across ages; and (d) to

develop skills that will make them "exceptional adults." Hall (2003) concluded based on a review of a number of studies (from the U.S. and the U.K.) that mentors may benefit through increased self-esteem, social insight, and social and interpersonal skills.

Another potentially important motive is generativity. *Generativity* refers to the need for one generation to pass along wisdom and knowledge to the next (Snyder & Clary, 2004) and was initially proposed by Erikson (1963) as one of the final stages of adult development. McAdams and de St. Aubin (1992) have demonstrated that generativity concerns (as assessed by the Loyola Generativity Scale) correlate with self-reported "generative" behaviors, including a moderate correlation with having "served as a role model for a young person" in the past 2 months.

Although motives are clearly person-centered variables, functional approaches do not rely on simple "main effect" predictions about which motives result in better behavioral outcomes (e.g., sustained volunteerism). Instead, functional approaches theorize that any important motive can result in good outcomes, if, and only if, the situation (e.g., task) allows for the motive to be fulfilled (Snyder et al., 2000). Clary et al. (1998) supported this interactive "matching hypothesis" by demonstrating that volunteers who reported that they received benefits relevant to their most important motives were both more satisfied and had higher intentions to volunteer in the future than volunteers who did not receive relevant benefits or volunteers who received irrelevant benefits (i.e., those related to unimportant motives). Identifying the important goals and motives of youth mentors is therefore only the first step that organizations need to take; an equally important step for recruitment and retention of mentors is to make sure that features of the situation allow for goals to be met, an issue to which we now turn.

Features of the Situation

Organizations such as BBBS are charged with the recruitment, placement, and retention of youth mentors. In this way, they have the power to shape the situational features that mentors face "on the job," even though the actual meetings between mentors and mentees may occur far from the offices of the organization. Through orientation and training materials, as well as through ongoing contact with mentors, organizations may be able to influence how mentors view their interactions and activities with youth and monitor (and perhaps enhance) the benefits and satisfaction that mentors receive.

Task-Based Affordances

The functional approach to volunteerism suggests that different volunteer tasks or environments may offer opportunities, or "affordances," to meet different motivational goals (Snyder et al., 2000). The benefits that may be afforded by volunteering as a youth mentor are numerous; however, these benefits may not always be salient to mentors, or in some cases, organizations may need to ensure that those benefits sought by mentors are indeed available. Careful attention to matching affordances and opportunities to goals and motives seems necessary for successful recruitment, placement, and retention of mentors, just as it is for volunteers more generally (Clary et al., 1998).

One common strategy for recruiting volunteers is through carefully targeted advertising. As Clary, Snyder, Ridge, Miene, and Haugen (1994) have demonstrated with video advertisements, ads that match individuals' primary reasons for volunteering (whether they have previously volunteered or not) are more persuasive and appealing than ads that do not match (Clary & Snyder, 1993). Mentoring organizations might do well to target the predominant motives of their potential mentor sample, advertising relevant benefits that could be obtained. Subsequent matching of volunteers to tasks that allow them to fulfill their primary motives may ensure successful retention (e.g., Clary et al., 1998). Different types of mentoring (for example, site-based mentoring, e-mentoring, or group mentoring) may offer different benefits that may be most appropriate for mentors with different motives. However, research has yet to examine the characteristics of volunteer tasks that most fruitfully allow for volunteer functions to be met.

Just as different volunteers or mentors may seek to meet different goals with their activities, so too it is not out of the question for motives to change over time (e.g., Snyder et al., 2000). Certain motives may become satiated in a particular task (for example, need for understanding) but could be reinvigorated by a change to a different task. Alternately, needs and goals of a volunteer may change permanently: Career goals may be satisfied early, with continued volunteerism offering only limited or no returns in this area. Organizations would be wise to keep careful track of the waxing and waning motives of their volunteers and potentially transfer mentors to new activities or approaches that may meet unfulfilled or new motives.

Volunteer Experiences and Relationship Factors

Omoto and Snyder's (1995) volunteer process model reviewed antecedents, experiences, and consequences of volunteerism, suggesting that actual experiences in volunteer activity will influence later consequences such as volunteer retention. Thus, positive or negative experiences, leading to volunteer satisfaction or dissatisfaction, may influence volunteers' decisions to stay or to leave. In Omoto and Snyder's (1995) study of volunteers serving as buddies to people with AIDS, satisfaction was a direct predictor of sustained volunteerism. As a key element in the volunteer experience, relationships (with both program staff and recipients) may influence satisfaction, longevity, and other outcomes. For example, in a review of the literature, Stukas, Clary, and Snyder (1999) highlighted collegiality of relationships with supervisors and clients as a key factor in producing positive outcomes from service-learning (volunteer work performed by students in an academic course, sometimes including mentoring). Omoto, Gunn, and Crain (1998) detailed the complex interactions between the initial expectations of volunteers who serve as buddies to people with AIDS, the developing closeness of their relationships, and the ultimate satisfaction and stress of helping. This focus on relationship characteristics, including quality or closeness, may be especially important for sustaining the commitment made by youth mentors, given that the formation of a healthy relationship is itself the goal of the activity (e.g., DuBois & Neville, 1997).

Theories about interpersonal relationships may offer insights to those who seek to ensure that mentor-youth relationships are satisfying and sustained. For example, Wieselquist, Rusbult, Foster, and Agnew (1999) provided a model to demonstrate how prorelationship behaviors (such as willingness to accommodate rather than retaliate when a partner behaves badly or to forego one's own desires for the sake of the relationship) can lead to interpersonal trust, which leads to commitment to the relationship. Although developed to explain the interdependence fostered in romantic relationships, this model could hold for the development of trust and commitment in more asymmetrical mentor-mentee relationships, potentially predicting mentor retention. Indeed, Rhodes (2002) has theorized that the establishment of mutuality, trust, and empathy are a necessary first development in a successful mentoring relationship.

RESEARCH

Although there clearly has been a groundswell in research on youth mentoring, the literature is still in its incipient stage (Rhodes, 2002). Research on the recruitment and retention of youth mentors is virtually nonexistent. We will review the relevant research that has been conducted and try to knit together the accumulating evidence about the factors that influence individuals to volunteer as youth mentors and to continue for a significant time once they have taken this step. We again divide our review to examine features of persons and features of situations separately.

Studies of mentoring recruitment and retention tend to be correlational by design, often for practical and ethical reasons. Therefore, none of the studies reviewed below meet experimental standards of internal validity (the ability to draw cause-and-effect conclusions), though most demonstrate adequate external validity (the ability to generalize from the study's findings to other examples of the phenomenon), given that they were generally conducted in actual program settings. The best research of this type manages to separate measurement of potential influences on behavior from measurement of the targeted behavior from measurement of the

consequences of behavior by including two or more time points in the study's design. As Parra, DuBois, Neville, Pugh-Lilly, and Povinelli (2002) pointed out, however, studies that use longitudinal designs or that add to validity by obtaining multisource or multirater data remain infrequent in the literature.

Mentoring Research on Features of the Person

Demographic Characteristics

The nationwide AOL Time Warner survey (O'Connor, 2002) found that respondents indicating willingness to become mentors tended to (a) be between 18 and 44 years old, (b) have household incomes above $50,000—although respondents who were already mentors reported only $25,000 or higher, (c) have some college education or more, (d) have Internet access, and (e) have a child in the household. Increasing age was associated with less willingness to mentor (except in faith-based organizations), perhaps because of retirement's negative effects on social integration. Actual mentors tended to be employed either full- or part-time. Similarly, the Commonwealth Fund survey (McLearn et al., 1998) found that college education and higher family income, two indicators of human capital, were related to mentoring. Together, these survey findings are consistent with the hypothesis that people who have more human capital and/or more social capital may be more likely to volunteer (Wilson, 2000). But contrary to Wilson's reports about ethnicity and volunteerism, the AOL Time Warner survey found that more people of color reported being willing to mentor than did Whites, although there was not a significant difference in reported rates of actual mentoring. Roaf et al. (1994) further revealed that more women than men typically volunteered to be mentors (see also Hall, 2003).

The Commonwealth Fund survey reported that 50% of self-identified mentors also participated in other community volunteer activities, leading the authors of this report to recommend looking for mentors among the population of those adults who already volunteer (McLearn et al., 1998). This is consistent with Grube and Piliavin's (2000) hypothesis that the more the volunteer role becomes a part of a person's identity, the more he or she may be receptive to engaging in further role-congruent acts. Such role identities are often embedded in a network involving shared social expectations for behavior (Grube & Piliavin, 2000). In line with this notion, Karcher and Lindwall (2003) suggested that high school students who volunteer to become mentors to younger children may be higher in social connectedness. McLearn et al. (1998) added that having had a mentor (most likely an informal or natural mentor) as a youth also was associated with increased likelihood of reported mentoring, implying the internalization of a shared expectation about the value of mentoring.

Findings like these tell us about who mentors but not about their length of service. Grossman and Rhodes (2002) reported that mentors in BBBS programs with higher incomes sustained longer relationships than did mentors with lower incomes. Married volunteers aged 26 to 30 years were more likely than 18- to 25-year-old volunteers to have relationships that terminated during any given month in the study (however, this association was attenuated when relationship quality was controlled); unmarried volunteers aged 26 to 30 were less likely to have relationships that terminated than 18- to 25-year-olds. Such findings again may attest to the manner in which resources (time and money) available to individuals at different stages and strata of society may make mentoring more or less difficult to continue (e.g., Wilson, 2000).

Personality Differences

Recently, Allen (2003) surveyed 249 formal and natural workplace mentors and 142 nonmentors in accounting and engineering societies and found that the scales of the Prosocial Personality Battery (Penner, 2002) predicted (a) whether respondents were mentors or nonmentors, using logistic regression analyses in which the helpfulness subscale was a significant predictor, and (b) respondents' willingness to mentor, using hierarchical linear regression analyses in which the other-oriented empathy subscale was a significant predictor after demographic variables were controlled. People with prosocial personalities similarly may be attracted to youth

mentoring as a way to demonstrate both empathy and helpfulness. Karcher and Lindwall (2003) also found that high school student mentors who reported higher social interest (a dispositional characteristic) persisted longer at mentoring.

Motivational Differences

Research on motivational differences in mentoring has tended to contrast altruistic goals with egoistic goals, seeking to show that one type of motive leads to more beneficial outcomes than the other. For example, Karcher, Nakkula, and Harris (in press), in a study of 63 adolescent mentors, found that mentors were less likely to perceive their relationships positively if they were motivated by self-interested reasons (as assessed by the VFI enhancement scale; Clary et al., 1998). Similarly, in a qualitative investigation of caseworker notes and interview data from 90 mentors in a BBBS program, Rubin and Thorelli (1984) found that the number of egoistic motives indicated by volunteers was related inversely to their longevity of participation. In contrast, Starke and DuBois (1997), using an adapted version of the VFI with 38 BBBS mentors, found that initial ratings of egoistic motivation, but not altruistic motivation, predicted later ratings of positive impact on youth at a 6-month follow-up assessment. Neither type of motivation was associated with relationship longevity. Research examining volunteers who serve as buddies to people with HIV or AIDS has found similar contradictions: Penner and Finkelstein (1998) found that altruistic motives were correlated with longer service, but Omoto and Snyder (1995) found that egoistic motivation positively predicted volunteer longevity. Given the lack of data on situational affordances in any of these studies, it is possible that altruistic and egoistic motives may both lead to longer and better mentoring relationships—but only to the extent that actual opportunities allow these motives to be fulfilled (see Snyder et al., 2000), which may have varied across these studies.

Alternately, different motives may predict success in different types of mentoring activities. Using her own index of mentors' motivations with a sample of workplace mentors and nonmentors (previously described), Allen (2003) found that a subscale assessing the motive "to benefit others" predicted self-reported engagement in both career and psychosocial mentoring, even after controlling for demographic variables and prosocial personality differences. However, a subscale assessing a "self-enhancement" motive predicted reports of career mentoring but not psychosocial mentoring, whereas a subscale designed to tap an "intrinsic satisfaction" motive predicted reports of psychosocial mentoring but not career mentoring. Such findings suggest at the very least that potential youth mentors with different motives may be inclined toward different mentoring activities. The AOL Time Warner survey (O'Connor, 2002) also found that potential mentors varied in the types of mentoring activities they would prefer, suggesting that a choice among mentoring options, depending on schedule and interests, might be desirable. Research that assesses both the motives that lead volunteers to engage in youth mentoring and the situational affordances available in different types of mentoring activities is sorely needed.

Mentoring Research on Features of the Situation

Recruitment Messages

A majority of the respondents to the AOL Time Warner survey reported becoming involved as mentors, both formally and informally, because they were asked or because of a connection with an organization; a smaller percentage reported seeking out the activity themselves or responding to an advertisement (O'Connor, 2002). These findings mesh with survey research on volunteering more broadly, which suggests that being asked is a key initiator of activity, with 35.5% of adults indicating that they said yes to a request to help (Independent Sector, 2001). The Commonwealth Fund survey further found that 91% of current mentors (both formal and informal) saw themselves as likely to recommend mentoring to a friend (McLearn et al., 1998), suggesting that formal programs could use current mentors as "ambassadors" for recruiting new mentors.

Another way of attracting potential mentors might be to advertise the benefits that mentors may receive from the activity (e.g., Clary et al., 1994). For example, Jackson (2002) found that university psychology students enrolled in a service-learning course reported educational benefits from youth mentoring; see Philip and Hendry (2000) for a qualitative examination of other benefits for mentors. However, Styles and Morrow (1992) reported, in a qualitative study of 26 intergenerational pairs of elders and at-risk youth, that mentors who formed satisfied relationships with youth (as judged by both members of the pair) were more likely to see the relationship as one-directional, expecting to receive few benefits themselves (at least initially) aside from the pleasure of helping someone (which may be no small thing).

Of course, some benefits to mentors—and to mentees—may accrue slowly over time and despite numerous difficulties (see Grossman & Rhodes, 2002). In keeping with this notion, Rhodes (2002) suggested:

> Providing potential volunteers with more accurate information [including about potential difficulties] about mentoring could have two positive effects: it could lower the bar to include people with a more humble self-image, while enabling volunteers—including those with a grandiose vision of their ability to make a difference—to make better informed decisions about the necessary commitment, the challenges, and the possible disappointments. (p. 80)

Thus, to avoid potential disenchantment, any advertisement of benefits might be counterbalanced with an honest report of potential challenges (see Snyder, 1993); however, data on this or any other recruitment technique for youth mentors have not yet been collected. In light of potential difficulties involved in youth mentoring, potential mentors may be receptive to information about program supports that will help them to meet such challenges. Findings from the AOL Time Warner survey (O'Connor, 2002) indicated that the factors that would encourage potential mentors to volunteer included access to expert help and orientation and training before mentoring. Potential mentors would also be willing to read an article or a book, talk to someone, use a Web site or a toll-free telephone number, or even exchange e-mail with a mentor to learn more.

Findings from the Commonwealth Fund survey suggest that another route into mentoring is through the workplace. In this survey, 27% of respondents involved in formal mentoring indicated that the program was sponsored by their employers (McLearn et al., 1998). The AOL Time Warner survey (O'Connor, 2002) reported similarly that potential mentors might be more likely to begin if employers provided time or encouragement or if youth came to the workplace. Such initiatives may make it easier, and therefore more likely, for mentors to get involved.

Training and Supervision

Adequate preparation of mentors for their task may be key to their long-term survival in formal programs. The Commonwealth Fund survey indicated that most mentors believe that orientation and training are important (including most of those who did not receive any). Fortunately, 85% of mentors involved in formal programs felt that they received the right amount of support, and only 14% would have liked more (McLearn et al., 1998). Nevertheless, Herrera, Sipe, and McClanahan (2000) reported that mentors in a sample of school- and community-based programs who underwent fewer than 2 hours of orientation subsequently reported less satisfaction with their matches, whereas mentors who had more than 6 hours of orientation reported greater satisfaction. McClanahan (1998) examined three types of mentor training provided to 266 mentors across 15 hospitals participating in the Hospital Youth Mentoring Program: formal training, mentor support groups, and discussions with program staff. The number of hours of formal training and the number of meetings with other mentors (as reported by mentors) were correlated positively with the length of the mentoring relationship. Mentors who took more advantage of support groups and had more training also reported offering more career mentoring and engaging in more social activities with youth (McClanahan, 1998). Furano, Roaf, Styles, and Branch (1993) reported that BBBS agencies that

provided regular supervision of matches by caseworkers (who contacted mentors, youth, and parents) also had matches that met more frequently than agencies that provided less supervision. However, DuBois and Neville (1997), in a small study of both BBBS and a service-learning program, reported that contacts with agency staff were negatively related to relationship closeness and length, speculating that this might have been due to a tendency to seek out staff when things go badly.

In their meta-analytic review of 55 evaluation studies, DuBois et al. (2002) found that "ongoing training for mentors, structured activities for mentors and youth as well as expectations for frequency of contact, mechanisms for support and involvement of parents, and monitoring of overall program implementation" (pp. 187–188) were associated with greater positive effects for youth in formal programs. Many of these program characteristics also could facilitate mentor retention. For example, Parra et al. (2002) found, in their study of a community-based BBBS program, that mentors' perceptions of the quality of their training predicted the length of their mentoring relationships, with this association mediated in a path model by intervening links to mentors' perceived self-efficacy and youth reports of relationship closeness.

Relationship Quality

Indeed, the closeness and supportiveness of the mentor-mentee relationship is beginning to attract research attention and may be a key factor in ensuring both mentor retention and youth benefits. In the preceding study, Parra et al. (2002) also found that youth reports of relationship closeness were predicted by the extent of the program-relevant activities engaged in by the pair. Although at first glance, the nature of programs themselves might be seen to dictate the most relevant and constructive activities for mentor-mentee pairs, Herrera et al. (2000) found in their research, using reports from mentors, that the extent of the social activities engaged in by pairs predicted relationship closeness (even when compared with academic activities in school-based programs). They also found that mentor reports of similar interests with youth predicted greater mentor perceptions of relationship closeness and supportiveness. Cumulatively, these results suggest that matching mentors to mentees on interests, particularly interests related to social activities, may set the stage for close and potentially long-lasting relationships to develop.

Taking another approach, Morrow and Styles (1995) classified 82 mentor-youth relationships (between 4 and 18 months old) in eight BBBS programs into developmental and prescriptive types using qualitative methods (based on earlier work by Styles & Morrow, 1992). Developmental relationships were described as youth driven, built on realistic expectations, and likely to focus on "relationship building" and the provision of support, whereas prescriptive relationships were described as mentor driven and often built on unrealistic expectations that focused on "transforming the youth" (e.g., by improving school performance or behavior). Nine months after assessing relationship type, Morrow and Styles (1995) found that 68% of prescriptive relationships had dissolved, whereas only 9% of developmental relationships had dissolved. Surviving developmental relationships also had been more likely to meet regularly than had surviving prescriptive relationships (90% vs. 30%). Thus, if a developmental relationship orientation can be taught successfully to new mentors, retention may be enhanced. Indeed, developmental volunteers were more likely to have had training and to take advantage of caseworkers than were prescriptive volunteers (Morrow & Styles, 1995).

McClanahan (1998) similarly reported that mentors in a hospital-based program often used a developmental strategy with older youth, allowed them greater input, and were supportive (according to youth reports). Although formal training was not related to use of a developmental style in mentors, the number of support group meetings that mentors attended was associated with greater use of this style. It should be kept in mind, however, that a developmental mentoring style has not been examined across the full range of mentoring program models.

Actual Experiences

Mentors (whether formal or informal) in the Commonwealth Fund survey overwhelmingly found mentoring to be personally satisfying and would do it again (McLearn et al., 1998). They reported receiving benefits that included feeling like a better person, increased patience, friendship, feelings of effectiveness, and skill development (in areas such as listening and working with people). Most mentors also reported that they believed that they had helped solve at least one problem for their youth (McLearn et al., 1998). DuBois and Neville (1997) also indicated that most mentors in their study felt that youth had benefited moderately or more. In keeping with the Volunteer Process Model (Omoto & Snyder, 1995), the experience of satisfaction and perceived youth benefit might help sustain mentors.

However, just as positive experiences may lead to retention of youth mentors, negative or difficult experiences may cut short mentoring relationships. Grossman and Rhodes (2002) reported, in a reanalysis of data from the Public/Private Ventures impact study of BBBS programs, that matches with youth aged 13 to 16 years were more likely to terminate in any given month than matches with youth aged 10 to 12 years. Matches with youth who had been referred for psychological treatment or educational remediation or who were victims of sexual, emotional, or physical abuse were also more likely to fail. Such youth may overwhelm mentors, though close supervision by program staff might allow problems to be detected early (Rhodes, 2002). Challenging mentees may also harm retention of younger peer mentors, although perceived self-efficacy, if developed, may alleviate this problem (Karcher et al., in press).

PRACTICE

Youth mentoring occurs in a variety of programs, including those offering school-based, group, and peer mentoring, as well as traditional community-based mentoring. The wide range of mentoring programs is reflected in varied practices for recruiting and sustaining mentors. In this section, we overview prevailing trends for recruiting mentors and sustaining their involvement in programs, and relate these practices to theory and research.

Recruiting Mentors

Successful recruitment of youth mentors requires appropriate strategies to target and select volunteers who are likely to establish and maintain effective relationships with youth. In line with our interactionist perspective, we suggest such strategies need to take into account both the features of potential mentors and the features of specific mentoring programs.

Volunteer Recruitment Strategies

Getting the word out is the primary goal of most mentor recruitment strategies. In a survey of more than 700 formal programs, 71% cited word of mouth in the community as their most common recruitment strategy (Sipe & Roder, 1999). Recruiting new volunteers also occurs through public service announcements and commercials, print advertisements, and organized presentations by program coordinators and current mentors (Roaf et al., 1994). Recruitment efforts commonly target corporations, government agencies, churches, community and civic groups (including service clubs), universities, and high schools. Some BBBS programs conduct an annual competition, or "Recruitment Challenge," where case managers, board members, mentors, and parents of mentees personally recruit new mentors from among family, friends, and colleagues. Roaf et al.'s (1994) survey of BBBS programs reported that word of mouth and television coverage were seen as the most successful of these strategies. Many of these practices are consistent with theory and research that suggest that the best way to turn intentions into action may be to ask potential mentors directly (Independent Sector, 2001; Penner, 2002), especially when the request comes from within an existing social network where shared expectations may be leveraged to increase volunteer rates (Grube & Piliavin, 2000).

However, merely getting the word out may not be enough to overcome the problem of inaction for all audiences (Snyder, 1993). Recently, programs have begun to focus their efforts on particular groups of potential mentors who may not be attracted by traditional recruitment or advertising strategies (e.g., minority groups and younger or older adults). BBBS programs have developed guidelines specifically for targeting minority volunteers (Roaf et al., 1994), although conclusive evidence on the effectiveness of such strategies is lacking. Consistent with the importance of community-based social networks for attracting volunteers, Furano et al. (1993) found the greatest proportion of minority volunteers in agencies where minority staff members were directly involved in recruitment. Recruitment guidelines from Public/Private Ventures (Jucovy, 2001) provide special considerations for recruiting college students and older adults, highlighting the need to forge links with organizations to which these groups belong. In line with theory and research supporting a functional approach (Clary et al., 1998; Snyder et al., 2000), these guidelines also focus on identifying and addressing the unique motivations of potential mentors from specific groups, as well as any potential barriers to volunteering.

Despite these varied efforts, few programs manage to recruit sufficient volunteers, as indicated by lengthy waiting lists of youth in many areas (Rhodes, 2002; Roaf et al., 1994). Across the eight BBBS programs in Roaf et al.'s (1994) study, only about half of the potential mentors who made initial inquiries went on to submit applications to become mentors. The program that had the best rate of follow-through from inquiry to application conducted informal orientations at recruitment events, where potential applicants were presented with general program information and expectations for mentors (including an outline of screening procedures and the time frame involved). In keeping with suggestions from Rhodes (2002), being upfront about both the benefits of mentoring and the difficulties and challenges that may be encountered appears to be a simple strategy for ensuring that mentors who sign up have carefully weighed the pros and cons of the activity for themselves, thus warding off later disenchantment (see also Omoto et al., 1998). As the AOL Time Warner survey (O'Connor, 2002) suggested, potential mentors may see available program supports as a helpful resource for overcoming any problems (which suggests that recruitment sessions should also highlight such supports).

Volunteer Intake Practices

Most programs place considerable impor-tance on screening potential mentors—and the process is generally rigorous and often lengthy. Thus, it is not surprising that Roaf et al. (1994) estimated that despite long waiting lists, only 37.3% of applicants were matched with youth in an 8-month period. Whereas comprehensive screening of volunteers to work with vulnerable youth is vital, overly strict processes may hinder the smooth transition from application to match-ing, and programs may do well to consider ways to streamline the process in order to avoid discouraging potential mentors. For example, where possible, data should be collected to determine the relationship of exclusion criteria to mentor outcomes, and only evidence-based criteria should be utilized.

Current screening practices tend to focus on screening for safety (detecting potential child abusers) rather than screening for suitability (finding volunteers who can form and sustain effective relationships with youth). However, Jucovy (2000) recommended that programs also identify suitability criteria that are directly related to program goals and youth characteris-tics. Such an interactionist perspective considers both features of potential mentors and features of programs and youth, and it sits well with a growing body of research and theory in social psychology (e.g., Penner, 2002). Of course, determining particular suitability criteria rests with the staff of specific programs. For example, school-based programs, such as Across Ages (Taylor & Bressler, 2000), are thought to be more suitable for older adults who may prefer structured activities or have concerns about physical safety. Activity-based programs, such as the Sports Buddies program offered by many BBBS agencies, may be more appealing to men than women (e.g., Morrow & Styles, 1995). Furthermore, in line with the functional approach's matching hypothesis (Snyder et al., 2000), Jucovy (2000) recommended that people who are screened out should be offered other oppor-tunities to serve within programs or should be referred to other types of volunteer programs that might better suit their abilities and goals.

Careful matching of volunteers and young people is crucial to promote the development of an effective and sustained mentoring relationship. According to Sipe and Roder's (1999) survey, the majority of programs used the interests of youth and mentors, typically collected through surveys or interviews, to help determine matches. This is consistent with research suggesting that matching mentors and mentees on the basis of similar interests and social activities may set the stage for effective relationships (Herrera et al., 2000; Parra et al., 2002). However, 12% of programs surveyed matched through a ran-dom process or through self-selection, which is potentially a concern. One innovative practice offered by newer programs involves an orienta-tion session for youth and potential mentors to meet, to assist matching on interests and inter-personal dynamics. For example, the Plan IT Youth project (Dusseldorp Skills Forum, 2000), a school-based program in Australia, arranges an orientation/matching day, including "getting to know you" games for mentors and youth, a BBQ lunch, and a student-led tour of the school.

Sustaining Mentors

The goal of sustaining mentors can be aided by program practices that focus on the actual experience of mentoring (as suggested by Omoto and Snyder's, 1995, volunteer process model). Practices that foster mentor satisfaction and support the development of effective men-toring relationships, as well as those that pro-vide support, feedback, and recognition, may help retain existing youth mentors. These goals can be incorporated into standard practices for orienting and training new mentors and for pro-viding ongoing support and supervision.

Orientation and Training Practices

Whereas most programs have careful recruit-ment, screening, and matching procedures, only a smaller proportion provide in-depth training to mentors. Although 95% of the 722 mentoring programs reviewed by Sipe and Roder (1999) offered some orientation, less than half provided mentors with 2 or more hours of training, and 22% offered no training at all. This stands in stark contrast to research that suggests that providing more orientation and ongoing training to mentors promotes strong mentoring relationships, mentor satisfaction, and sustained matches (DuBois et al., 2002; Herrera et al., 2000). Still, some programs excel in this area. For example, in the Plan IT Youth project (Dusseldorp Skills Forum, 2000), new mentors complete a 27-hour mentor training course (over a 2-month period) through a local technical college.

Support and Supervision Practices

After orientation and initial training, levels of support to mentors often decline. Sipe and Roder (1999) found that only one third of programs reported contacting mentors more than once a month, and less than 25% of the 55 programs reviewed in the DuBois et al. (2002) meta-analysis reported providing ongoing training for mentors. Although the Commonwealth Fund survey suggested that mentors feel that current levels of support are sufficient (McLearn et al., 1998), in other studies, greater program support has been associated with greater mentor satisfaction and longevity of relationships (Herrera et al., 2000; McClanahan, 1998). Specifically, ongoing supervision and training may provide mentors with understanding and skills to successfully develop effective mentoring relationships, feedback about their performance (e.g., any benefits to the mentee), and recognition of their efforts, all of which could enhance mentor satisfaction.

Another way that organizations can promote mentor satisfaction and retention may be to ensure that mentors are meeting their own goals for the activity (Snyder et al., 2000). Regular ongoing supervision provides organizations with opportunities to assess mentors' goals and motives, to remind mentors of the relevant benefits they receive, to monitor changing motives, and to modify task affordances as necessary. Instrumental supports, such as specifying regular meeting times and places, suggesting or scheduling activities, and providing mentors with small stipends to offset the expenses involved in activities, may also boost retention (Sipe, 1998).

Support groups for mentors may serve an important function in sustaining mentors by reinforcing the role identity of mentors through the creation of a social network with shared expectations of mentoring (e.g., Grube & Piliavin, 2000). In addition, support groups afford opportunities for meeting particular volunteering motives, such as understanding, enhancement, and social goals (Clary et al., 1998). Sipe and Roder (1999) found that 52% of programs offered a support group, yet among these programs, only 39% met monthly or more often. As McClanahan (1998) found that the number of meetings with other mentors was correlated with length of matches, programs might wish to place more emphasis on facilitating support groups for mentors as a means of sustaining mentoring relationships.

Overall, retention may be high when programs continually monitor satisfaction and effectiveness of matches and remain responsive to the changing needs of mentors. An exemplary approach of such responsiveness is illustrated in Australia by the Panyappi Indigenous Youth Mentoring Project (Crime Prevention Unit, 2002). In response to concerns from mentors about isolation and inadequate supervision, Panyappi implemented a variety of support and supervision mechanisms, including fortnightly team meetings with mentors, individual supervision, and ongoing training (leading to an accredited Certificate in Youth Work through the local university). Panyappi is now developing a two-tier mentoring system in which more experienced mentors will support new mentors (Crime Prevention Unit, 2003).

FUTURE DIRECTIONS

Synthesis

Recruiting and sustaining sufficient numbers of volunteer mentors and ensuring that those involved have the appropriate qualities and preparation to be successful have been vexing problems for the field of youth mentoring. Drawing on theory and research from the broader literature on volunteerism highlights features of persons, such as their personalities, role identities, motives, and human or social capital, as well as features of situations, such as task-based affordances, relationship factors, and actual mentoring experiences, that may interact to make prospective volunteers more receptive to serving as mentors and to sustaining their commitments over time. At present, only a limited amount of research addresses issues of mentor recruitment and retention directly. These investigations, furthermore, have seldom benefited from methodological advantages such as longitudinal or experimental designs. Nonetheless, the findings from this work, as well as from other mentoring studies that bear indirectly on recruitment and retention, parallel those reported in the broader volunteerism literature. Fortunately, there are already examples of recruitment strategies (e.g., those that tie into existing social networks or organizations) and program practices aimed at retaining mentors (e.g., those that offer ongoing supervision and support) that are supported by existing theory or research. However, there are still programs that may be failing to adopt evidence-based practices that could ensure better recruitment and retention of youth mentors.

Recommendations for Research

1. *Develop and test an inventory of motivations for youth mentoring.* Experimental research is needed that makes use of such a tool to examine recruitment messages that appeal to motives, placement of mentors into activities offering affordances to meet motives, and retention of mentors by assessing change in motives over time and transferring mentors accordingly.

2. *Conduct research to examine how actual mentor experiences relate to retention.* Longitudinal research that examines actual experiences in the mentor relationship, using behavioral observations of mentor-mentee interactions or more "objective" self-reports, can provide a link between features of persons or situations and outcomes like mentor retention.

3. *Identify the features of training and support initiatives that best predict retention.* Experimental or quasi-experimental studies that compare different types of training and supervision would help clarify the methods most likely to sustain mentors.

Recommendations for Practice

1. *Use members of existing social network to deliver recruitment messages.* Attract new mentors by using members of community groups or organizations to deliver recruitment messages; current mentors or family members of mentees may be willing.

2. *Tailor recruitment messages to the primary motivations of potential mentors.* Advertising mentoring with reference to the benefits it offers to mentors may work best. Mentioning potential difficulties and the supports offered to overcome them may help avoid later disenchantment.

3. *Provide in-depth training and orientation for mentors at the start of their service and ongoing training and supervision throughout.* Theory and research are consistent in suggesting that efforts to promote mentor retention should include an orientation to the program as well as training in mentoring skills and strategies. Maintaining contact with mentors and supporting mentor-to-mentor contact may increase satisfaction and ensure retention.

REFERENCES

Allen, T. D. (2003). Mentoring others: A dispositional and motivational approach. *Journal of Vocational Behavior, 62,* 134–154.

Brady, H., Schlozman, K. L., & Verba, S. (1999). Prospecting for participants: Rational expectations and the recruitment of political activists. *American Political Science Review, 93,* 153–169.

Clary, E. G., & Snyder, M. (1993). Persuasive communications strategies for recruiting volunteers. In D. R. Young, R. M. Hollister, & V. A. Hodgkinson (Eds.), *Governing, leading and managing nonprofit organizations* (pp. 121–137). San Francisco: Jossey-Bass.

Clary, E. G., Snyder, M., Ridge, R. D., Copeland, J., Stukas, A. A., Haugen, J., et al. (1998). Understanding and assessing the motivations of volunteers: A functional approach. *Journal of Personality and Social Psychology, 74,* 1516–1530.

Clary, E. G., Snyder, M., Ridge, R. D., Miene, P., & Haugen, J. (1994). Matching messages to motives in persuasion: A functional approach to promoting volunteerism. *Journal of Applied Social Psychology, 24*, 1129–1149.

Clary, E. G., Snyder, M., & Stukas, A. A. (1996). Volunteers' motivations: Findings from a national survey. *Nonprofit and Voluntary Sector Quarterly, 25*, 485–505.

Crime Prevention Unit, SA Attorney-General's Department. (2002). *Panyappi Indigenous Youth Mentoring Project, Progress report, July 2002.* South Australia: Author.

Crime Prevention Unit, SA Attorney-General's Department. (2003). *Panyappi Indigenous Youth Mentoring Project, Stage three report, June 2003.* South Australia: Author.

DuBois, D. L., Holloway, B. E., Valentine, J. C., & Cooper, H. (2002). Effectiveness of mentoring programs for youth: A meta-analytic review. *American Journal of Community Psychology, 30*, 157–197.

DuBois, D. L., & Neville, H. A. (1997). Youth mentoring: Investigation of relationship characteristics and perceived benefits. *Journal of Community Psychology, 25*, 227–234.

Dusseldorp Skills Forum. (2000). *Plan IT Youth Project.* Retrieved October 9, 2003, from http://www.dsf.org.au/projects.php

Eagly, A. H., & Crowley, M. (1986). Gender and helping behavior: A meta-analytic review of the social psychological literature. *Psychological Bulletin, 100*, 283–308.

Erickson, E. (1963). *Childhood and society* (2nd ed.). New York: Norton.

Furano, K., Roaf, P. A., Styles, M. B., & Branch, A. Y. (1993). *Big Brothers/Big Sisters: A study of program practices.* Philadelphia: Public/Private Ventures.

Grossman, J. B., & Furano, K. (2002). *Making the most of volunteers.* Philadelphia: Public/Private Ventures.

Grossman, J. B., & Rhodes, J. E. (2002). The test of time: Predictors and effects of duration in youth mentoring relationships. *American Journal of Community Psychology, 30*, 199–219.

Grube, J. A., & Piliavin, J. A. (2000). Role identity, organizational experiences, and volunteer performance. *Personality and Social Psychology Bulletin, 26*, 1108–1120.

Hall, J. C. (2003). *Mentoring and young people: A literature review.* Glasgow, UK: SCRE Centre.

Herrera, C., Sipe, C. L., & McClanahan, W. S. (2000). *Mentoring school-age children: Relationship development in community-based and school-based programs.* Philadelphia: Public/Private Ventures. (Published in collaboration with MENTOR/National Mentoring Partnership, Alexandria, VA)

Independent Sector. (2001). *Giving and volunteering in the United States.* Washington, DC: Author.

Jackson, Y. (2002). Mentoring for delinquent children: An outcome study with young adolescent children. *Journal of Youth and Adolescence, 31*, 115–122.

Jucovy, L. (2000). *The ABC's of school-based mentoring.* Philadelphia: Public/Private Ventures.

Jucovy, L. (2001). *Recruiting mentors: A guide to finding volunteers to work with youth.* Philadelphia: Public/Private Ventures.

Karcher, M. J., & Lindwall, J. (2003). Social interest, connectedness, and challenging experiences: What makes high school mentors persist? *Journal of Individual Psychology, 59*, 293–315.

Karcher, M. J., Nakkula, M. J., & Harris, J. (in press). Developmental mentoring match characteristics: Correspondence between mentors' and mentees' assessments of relationship quality. *Journal of Primary Prevention.*

McAdams, D. P., & de St. Aubin, E. (1992). A theory of generativity and its assessment through self-report, behavioral acts, and narrative themes in autobiography. *Journal of Personality and Social Psychology, 62*, 1003–1015.

McClanahan, W. S. (1998). *Relationships in a career mentoring program: Lessons learned from the Hospital Youth Mentoring Program.* Philadelphia: Public/Private Ventures.

McLearn, K. T., Colasanto, D., & Schoen, C. (1998). *Mentoring makes a difference: Findings from the Commonwealth Fund 1998 survey of adults mentoring young people.* New York: The Commonwealth Fund. Available at http://www.ecs.org/html/Document.asp?chouseid=2843

Morrow, K. V., & Styles, M. B. (1995). *Building relationships with youth in program settings: A study of Big Brothers/Big Sisters.* Philadelphia: Public/Private Ventures.

O'Connor, R. (2002). *Mentoring in America 2002: Research sponsored by AOL Time Warner Foundation.* Pathfinder Research & MarketFacts for

MENTOR/National Mentoring Partnership. Retrieved June 13, 2003, from http://mentoring .web.aol.com/common/one_report/national_poll_ report_final.pdf

Omoto, A. M., Gunn, D. O., & Crain, A. L. (1998). Helping in hard times: Relationship closeness and the AIDS volunteer experience. In V. J. Derlega & A. P. Barbee (Eds.), HIV & social interaction (pp. 106–128). Thousand Oaks, CA: Sage.

Omoto, A. M., & Snyder, M. (1995). Sustained helping without obligation: Motivation, longevity of service, and perceived attitude change among AIDS volunteers. Journal of Personality and Social Psychology, 68, 671–686.

Parra, G. R., DuBois, D. L., Neville, H. A., Pugh-Lilly, A. O., & Povinelli, N. (2002). Mentoring relationships for youth: Investigation of a process-oriented model. Journal of Community Psychology, 30, 367–388.

Penner, L. A. (2002). Dispositional and organizational influences on sustained volunteerism: An interactionist perspective. Journal of Social Issues, 58, 447–467.

Penner, L. A., & Finkelstein, M. A. (1998). Dispositional and structural determinants of volunteerism. Journal of Personality and Social Psychology, 74, 525–537.

Philip, K., & Hendry, L. B. (2000). Making sense of mentoring or mentoring making sense? Reflections on the mentoring process by adult mentors with young people. Journal of Community & Applied Social Psychology, 10, 211–223.

Piliavin, J. A., & Callero, P. L. (1991). Giving blood: The development of an altruistic identity. Baltimore: Johns Hopkins University Press.

Portney, K., & Berry, J. (1997). Mobilizing minority communities: Social capital and participation in urban neighborhoods. American Behavioral Scientist, 40, 632–644.

Putnam, R. D. (2000). Bowling alone: The collapse and revival of American community. New York: Simon & Schuster.

Rhodes, J. E. (2002). Stand by me: The risks and rewards of mentoring today's youth. Cambridge, MA: Harvard University Press.

Rhodes, J. E., Grossman, J. B., & Roffman, J. (2002). The rhetoric and reality of youth mentoring. In G. G. Noam (Ed. in chief) & J. E. Rhodes (Ed.), A critical view of youth mentoring (New Directions for Youth Development: Theory, Research, and Practice, No. 93, pp. 9–20). San Francisco: Jossey-Bass.

Roaf, P. A., Tierney, J. P., & Hunte, D. E. I. (1994). Big Brothers/Big Sisters of America: A study of volunteer recruitment and screening. Philadelphia: Public/Private Ventures.

Rubin, A., & Thorelli, I. M. (1984). Egoistic motives and longevity of participation by social service volunteers. The Journal of Applied Behavioral Science, 20, 223–235.

Sipe, C. L. (1998). Mentoring adolescents: What we have learned. In J. B. Grossman (Ed.), Contemporary issues in mentoring (pp. 10–23). Philadelphia: Public/Private Ventures.

Sipe, C. L., & Roder, A. E. (1999). Mentoring school-age children: A classification of programs. Philadelphia: Public/Private Ventures. (Published in collaboration with MENTOR/National Mentoring Partnership, Alexandria, VA)

Snyder, M. (1993). Basic research and practical problems: The promise of a "functional" personality and social psychology. Personality and Social Psychology Bulletin, 19, 251–264.

Snyder, M., & Clary, E. G. (2004). Volunteerism and the generative society. In E. de St. Aubin & D. P. McAdams (Eds.), The generative society: Caring for future generations (pp. 221–237). Washington, DC: American Psychological Association.

Snyder, M., Clary, E. G., & Stukas, A. A. (2000). The functional approach to volunteerism. In G. R. Maio & J. M. Olson (Eds.), Why we evaluate: Functions of attitudes (pp. 365–393). Hillsdale, NJ: Erlbaum.

Starke, M. L., & DuBois, D. L. (1997, Fall). Characteristics of mentors with successful relationships. The MU McNair Journal, 9–14.

Stukas, A. A., Clary, E. G., & Snyder, M. (1999). Service learning: Who benefits and why. Social Policy Report, 13(4), 1–19.

Styles, M., & Morrow, K. (1992). Understanding how youth and elders form relationships: A study of four Linking Lifetimes programs. Philadelphia: Public/Private Ventures.

Taylor, A. S., & Bressler, J. (2000). Mentoring across generations: Partnerships for positive youth development. New York: Plenum Press.

Wieselquist, J., Rusbult, C. E., Foster, C. A., & Agnew, C. R. (1999). Commitment, pro-relationship behavior, and trust in close relationships. Journal of Personality and Social Psychology, 77, 942–966.

Wilson, J. (2000). Volunteering. Annual Review of Sociology, 26, 215–240.

17

EVALUATING MENTORING PROGRAMS

JEAN BALDWIN GROSSMAN

INTRODUCTION

Questions about mentoring abound. Mentoring programs around the country are being asked by their funders and boards, "Does *this* mentoring program work?" Policymakers ask, "Does this particular type of mentoring—be it school based or group or e-mail—work?" These are questions about program impacts. Researchers and operators also want to know about the program's processes: What about mentoring makes it work? How long should a match last to be effective? How frequently should matches meet? Does the level of training, support, or supervision of the match matter? Does parental involvement or communication matter? What types of interactions between youth and mentors lead to positive changes in the child? Then, there are questions about who is most affected: Are mentors with specific characteristics, such as being older or more educated, more effective than other mentors or more effective with particular subgroups of youth? Are particular types of youth more affected by mentoring than others? Last, researchers in particular are interested in the theoretical underpinning of mentoring. These are the types of mediating processes Jean Rhodes addresses in Chapter 3 of this volume.

For example, to what degree does mentoring work by changing children's beliefs about themselves (such as self-esteem or self-efficacy), by shaping their values (such as about education and the future), or by improving their social and/or cognitive skills?

This chapter presents discussions of many issues that arise in answering both implementation or process questions and impact questions. Process questions are important to address even if a researcher is interested only in impacts, because one should not ask "Does it work?" unless "it" actually occurred. The first section covers how one chooses appropriate process and impact measures. The following section discusses several impact design issues, including the inadequacies of simple pre-post designs, the importance of a good comparison group, and several ways to construct comparison groups. The last section discusses common mistakes made when analyzing evaluation data and presents ways avoid them. For a more complete discussion of evaluation in general, readers are referred to Rossi, Freeman, and Lipsey (1999); Shadish, Cook, and Campbell (2002); or Weiss (1998). Due to space constraints, issues entailed in answering mediational questions are not addressed here.

Measurement Issues

A useful guide in deciding what to measure is a program's logic model or theory of change: the set of hypothesized links between the program's action, participants' response, and the desired outcomes. As Weiss (1998) states, with such a theory in hand, "The evaluation can trace the unfolding of the assumptions" (p. 58). Rhodes (this volume), presents one possible theory of change for mentoring. Process measures describe the program's actions. Outcome measures describe what effects the program has.

Process Measures

The first question to answer when examining a program is: What exactly is the program as experienced by participants? The effect the program will have on participants depends on the realities of the program, not on its official description. All too frequently in mentoring programs, relatively few strong relationships form, and the pair stops meeting. Process questions can be answered, however, at several levels. Most basically, one wants to know: Did the program recruit appropriate youth and adults? Did adults and youth meet as planned? Did all the components of program happen? Were mentors trained and supervised as expected?

To address these questions, one examines the characteristics and experiences of the participants, mentors, and the match and compares them with the program's expectations. For example, a program targeted at mentoring youth involved in criminal or violent activity tracked the number of arrests of new participants to determine whether they were serving their desired target populations (Branch, 2002). A high school mentoring program for struggling students could track the GPAs of enrolling youth (Grossman & Johnson, 1999). Two match characteristics commonly examined are the average completed length of the relationship and the average frequency of interaction. Like all good process measures, they relate to the program's theory. To be affected, a participant must experience a sufficient dosage of it. Some mentoring programs have more detailed ideas, such as wanting participants to experience certain types of experiences (academic support, for example, or peer interaction). If these are critical elements of the program theory, they too make good candidates for process measures.

A second level of process question concerns the quality of the components. How good are the relationships? Is the training and supervision useful? These are more difficult dimensions to measure. Client satisfaction measures, such as how much youth like their mentors or how useful the mentors feel the training is, are one gauge on quality. However, clients' assessment of quality may not be accurate; as many teachers say, the most enjoyable class may not be the class that promotes the most learning. Testing mentors before and after training is an alternative quality measure of the training. Assessing the quality of mentoring relationships is a relatively unexplored area. Grossman and Johnson (1999), and Rhodes, Reddy, Roffman, and Grossman (in press) propose some measures (see also Nakkula & Harris, this volume).

From a program operator's or funder's perspective, how many process data are "enough" depends on striking a balance between knowing exactly what is happening in the program versus recognizing the service the staff could have provided in lieu of collecting data. For researchers, before spending the time and money to collect data on outcomes, they should assess the quality of the implementation to be sure the program is actually delivering the services it purports to offer at a level and quality consistent with having a detectable impact. Even if no impact is expected, in order to understand one's findings, it is essential to know exactly what did or did not happen to the participants. Thus, researchers may want to collect more process data than typically would be collected by operators to improve both the quality of their generalizations and their ability to link impacts to variation in participants' experiences of core elements of the program.

Lesson: Tracking process variables is important to program managers but essential for evaluators. Before embarking on an evaluation of impacts, be sure the program is delivering its services at a quality and intensity that would lead one to expect impacts.

Outcome Measures

An early task for an impact evaluator is to refine the "Does it work?" question into a set of testable evaluation questions. These questions need to specify a set of outcome variables that will be examined during the evaluation. There are two criteria for a good outcome measure (Rossi et al., 1999). First, the outcome can be realistically expected to change during the study period given the expected intensity of the intervention. Second, the outcome is measurable and the chosen measure sensitive enough to detect the likely change.

Evaluation questions are not program goals. Many programs rightly have lofty inspirational goals, such as enabling all participants to excel academically or to become self-sufficient, responsible citizens. However, a good evaluation outcome must be concrete, measurable, and likely to change enough during the study period to be detected. Thus, for example, achieving a goal like "helping youth academically excel" could be gauged by examining students' grades or test scores.

Second, when choosing the specific set of outcomes that will indicate a goal such as "academically excelling," one must consider which of the possible variables are likely to change within the evaluation period given the likely program dosage that the participants will receive. For example, researchers often have found that reading and math achievement test scores change less quickly than do reading or math grades, which, in turn, change less quickly than does school effort. Thus, if you are evaluating the school year (i.e., 9 months) impact of a school-based mentoring program, you are likely to want to examine effort and grades, rather than test scores, or at least in addition to test scores. Considerable care and thought needs to go into deciding what outcomes should be collected, and when. Examining impacts on outcomes that are unlikely to change over the evaluation period can give the false impression that the program is a failure when, in fact, the impacts on the chosen variables may not yet have emerged.

A good technique for selecting variables is to choose a range of proximal to more distal expected impacts based on the program's theory of change, which also represents a set of impacts ranging from modestly to impressively effective (Weiss, 1998). Unfortunately, one cannot know a priori how long matches will last or how often the individuals will meet. Thus, it is wise to include some outcomes that are likely to change even with rather limited exposure to the intervention and some outcomes that would change with greater exposure, thus setting multiple "bars" of effectiveness. The most basic effectiveness goal is an outcome that everyone agrees should be achievable. From there, one can develop more ambitious outcomes.

Grossman and Tierney's (1998) evaluation of Big Brothers Big Sisters (BBBS) provides a good example of this process. Researchers conducted a thorough review of BBBS's manual of standards and practices to understand the program's logic model and, then, by working closely with staff from the national office and with the local agencies, generated multiple outcome bars. The national manual lists four "common" goals for a Little Brother or Little Sister: providing social, cultural, and recreational enrichment; improving peer relationships; improving self-concept; and improving motivation, attitude, and achievement related to schoolwork. Conversations with BBBS staff also suggested that having a Big Brother or Big Sister could reduce the incidence of antisocial behaviors, such as drug and alcohol use, and could improve a Little Brother's or Little Sister's relationship with parent(s). Using previous research, the hypothesized impacts were ordered from proximal to distal as follows: increased opportunities for social and cultural enrichment, improved self-concept, better relationships with family and friends, improved academic outcomes, and reduced antisocial behavior. At a minimum, the mentoring experience was expected to enrich the cultural and social life of youth, even though many more impacts were expected. Because motivational psychology research shows that attitudes often change before behaviors, the next set of outcomes reflected attitudinal changes toward themselves and others. The "harder" academic and antisocial outcomes then were specified. Within these outcomes, researchers also hypothesized a range of impacts, starting with attitudinal variables, such as the child's perceived sense of academic efficacy and value placed on education; to some intermediate behavioral changes, such as school attendance and being sent to the principal's office; to changes in grades, drug and alcohol use, and fighting.

Once outcomes are identified, the next question is how to measure them. Two of the most important criteria for choosing a measure are whether the measure captures the exact facet of the outcome that the program expected to affect and whether it is sensitive enough to pick up small changes. For example, an academically focused mentoring program that claims to increase the self-esteem of youth may help youth feel more academically competent but not improve their general feelings of self-worth. Thus, one would want to use a scale more targeted at academic self-worth or competence than a global self-worth scale or one that can measure both. The second consideration is the measure's degree of sensitivity. Some measures are extremely good at sorting a population or identifying a subgroup in need of help but are poor in detecting the small changes that typically result from programs. For example, in this author's experience, the Rosenberg self-esteem scale (1997) is useful at distinguishing adolescents with high and low self-esteem but often is not sensitive enough to detect the small changes in self-esteem induced by most youth programs. On the other hand, measures of academic or social competency beliefs (Eccles, Midgley, & Adler, 1984) can detect relatively small changes in the beliefs of youth.

Lesson: Choose outcomes that are integrally linked to the program's theory of change, that set multiple "effectiveness bars," that are gauged with sensitive measures, and that can be achieved within the evaluation's time frame and in the context of the program's implementation.

Choosing Informants

Another issue to be resolved for either process or outcome measures is from whom to collect information. For mentoring programs, the candidates are usually the youth, the mentor, the parent, teachers, and school records.

Information from each type of informant has advantages and disadvantages. For example, for some variables, such as attitudes or beliefs, the youth may be the only individual who can provide valid information. Youth, for example, arguably are uniquely qualified to report on constructs such as their self-esteem (outcome measures) or considerations such as how much they like their mentors or whether they think their mentors support and care for them (i.e., process measures). Theoretically, what may be important is not what support the mentor actually gives, but how supportive the youth perceives the mentor to be (DuBois, Neville, Parra, & Pugh-Lilly, 2002). However, on the other hand, youth-reported data may be biased. First, youth may be more likely to give socially desirable answers—recounting higher grades or less antisocial behavior. If this bias is different for mentored versus unmentored youth, as suggested by Lucas and Liabø (2003), impact estimates based on these variables could be biased. Second, the feelings of youth toward their mentors may taint their reporting. For example, if the youth does not like the mentor's style, he or she may selectively report or overreport certain negative experiences, such as the mentor missing meetings, and underreport others of a more positive nature, such as the amount of time the mentor spends providing help with schoolwork. Similarly, the youth may overstate a mentor's performance to make the mentor look good. Last, the younger the child is, the less reliable or subtle the self-report. For this reason, when participants are quite young (8 or 9 years old), it is advisable to collect information from their parents and/or teachers.

The mentor often can be a good source of information about what the mentoring experience is like (what they do and talk about; i.e., process measures) and also may be useful as a reporter on the child's behaviors (at least at posttest; i.e., outcome measures). The main problem with mentor reporting is that mentors have an incentive to report positively on their relationships with youth and to see effects even if there are none—justifying why they are spending all this time with the child. Although there may be a positive bias, this does not preclude mentors being accurate in reporting relative impacts. This is because most mentors do not report that their mentees have improved equally in all areas. The pattern of difference in these reports, especially if consistent with those obtained from other sources (for example, school records), thus may provide useful information about the true impacts.

Parents also can be useful as reporters. They may notice that the child is trying harder in school, for example, even though the child might not notice the change. However, like the mentor, parents may project changes that they wish were happening or be unaware of certain behaviors (e.g., substance use). Finally, teachers may be good reporters on the behaviors of their students during the school day. Teachers who are familiar with age-appropriate behavior, for example, may spot a problem when a parent or mentor does not. However, teachers are extraordinarily busy, and it can be difficult for them to find the time to fill out evaluation forms on the participants. In addition, teachers too are not immune to seeing what they want to see, but as with mentors and parents, the same caveat about relative impacts applies here.

Information also can be collected from records. Data about the occurrence of specific events—fights, cut classes, principal visits—are less susceptible to bias, unless, of course, the sources of these data (e.g., school administrators making discipline decisions) differentially judge or report events for mentored youth versus other youth.

Lesson: Each respondent has a unique point of view, but all are susceptible to reporting what they wish had happened. Thus, if time and money allow, it is advantageous to examine multiple perspectives on an outcome and triangulate on the impacts. What is important is to see a consistent pattern of impacts (not uniform consistency among the respondents). The more consistency there is, the more certain one is that a particular impact occurred. For example, if the youth, parent, and teacher data all indicate school improvement and test scores also increase, this would be particularly strong evidence of academic gains. Conversely, if only one of these measures exhibits change (e.g., parent reports), it could be just a spurious finding.

DESIGN ISSUES

Answering the questions "Does mentoring work?" and "For whom?" may seem to be relatively straightforward—achievable simply by observing the changes in mentees' outcomes. But these ostensibly simple questions are harder to answer than one might assume.

The Fallacy of Pre-Post Comparisons

The changes we observe in the attitudes, behaviors, or skills of youth while they are being mentored are not equivalent to program impacts. How can that be? The answer has to do with what statisticians call *internal validity.* Consider, again, the previously described BBBS evaluation. If one looks only at changes in outcomes for treatment youth (Grossman & Johnson, 1999), one finds that 18 months after they applied to the program, 7% had reported starting to use drugs. On the face of it, it appears that the program was ineffective; however, over the same period, 11% of the controls had reported starting to use drugs. Thus, rather than being ineffective, this statistically significant difference indicates that BBBS was able to stem some of the naturally occurring increases in drug use.

The critical distinction here is the difference between outcomes and impacts. In evaluation, an *outcome* is the value of any variable measured after the intervention, such as grades. An *impact* is the difference between the outcome observed and what it would have been in the absence of the program (Rossi et al., 1999); in other words, it is the change in the outcome that was *caused* by the program. Simple changes in outcomes in part may reflect the program's impact but also might reflect other factors, such as changes due to maturation.

Lesson: A program's impact can be gauged accurately (i.e., be internally valid) only if one knows what would have happened to the participants had they not been in the program. This hypothetical state is called the "counterfactual." Because one cannot observe what the mentees would have done in the absence of the program, one must identify another group of youth, namely a comparison group, whose behavior will represent what the participants' behavior would have been in the absence of the program. Choosing a group whose behavior accurately depicts this hypothetical no-treatment (or counterfactual) state is the crux to getting the right answer to the effectiveness question, because a program's impacts are ascertained by comparing the behavior of the treatment or participant group with that of the selected comparison group.

Matched Comparison or Control Group Construction

There are two principal types of comparison groups: control groups generated through random assignment and matched comparison groups selected judgmentally by the researcher.

Experimental Control Groups

Random assignment is the best way to create two groups that would change comparably over time. In this type of evaluation, eligible individuals are assigned randomly, either to the *control* group, and not allowed into the program, or to the *treatment* group, whose members are offered the program. (Note: "Treatments" and "controls" refer to randomly selected groups of individuals. Not all treatments may choose to participate. The term *participants* is used to refer to individuals who actually receive the program.) The principal advantage of random assignment is that given large enough groups, on average, the two groups are statistically equivalent with respect to all characteristics, observed and unobserved, at the time the two groups are formed. If nothing were done to either group, their behaviors, on average, would continue to be statistically equivalent at any point into future. Thus, if after the intervention, the average behavior of the two groups differ, the difference can be confidently and causally linked to the program, which was the only systematic difference between the two groups. Orr (1999) discusses how large each group should be.

Although random assignment affords the most scientifically reliable way of creating two comparable groups, there are many issues that should be considered before using it. Two of the most difficult are, "Can random assignment be inserted into the program's normal process without qualitatively changing the program?" and "Is it ethical to deny certain youth a mentor?" The reader is referred to Dennis (1994) for a discussion of the ethical issues.

With respect to the first issue, consider first how the insertion of random assignment into the intake process affects the program. One of the misconceptions about random assignment among mentoring staff is that random assignment means randomly pairing youth with adult. This is not the case. Random pairing would fundamentally change the program. Any evaluation of this mutated program would not provide information on the effect of the actual program. A valid use of random assignment would entail randomly dividing eligible applicants between the treatment and control group, then processing the treatment group youth just as they normally would be handled and matched. Under this design, random assignment affects only which youth files come across the staff's desk for matching, not what happens to youth once they are there. Another valid test would have staff identify two youth for every volunteer, then randomly assign one child to the treatment group and one to the control group. For the BBBS evaluation, we used the former method because it was significantly less burdensome and emotionally more acceptable for the staff. However, the chosen design meant that not all treatment youth actually received a mentor. As will be discussed later, only about three quarters of the youth who were randomized into the treatment group and offered the program actually received mentors. (See Orr, 1999, for a rich discussion of all aspects of random assignment.)

Matched (or Quasi-Experimental) Comparison Groups

Random assignment is not always possible. For example, programs may be too small, or staff may refuse to participate in such an evaluation. When this is the case, researchers must identify a group of nonparticipant youth whose outcomes credibly represent what would have happened to the participants in the absence of the program. The weakness of the methodology is that the outcomes of the two groups can differ not only because one group got a mentor and the other did not but also because of other differences between the groups. To generate internally valid estimates of the program's impacts, one must control for the "other differences," either through statistical procedures like regression analysis, and/or through careful matching.

The researcher selects a comparison group of youth who are as similar as possible to the participant group across all the important characteristics that may influence outcomes in the counterfactual state (the hypothetical no-treatment state). Some key characteristics are relatively easy to identify and match for (e.g., age, race, gender, or family structure). However, to improve the credibility of a matched comparison group, one needs to think deeply about other potential differences that could affect the outcome differential, such as whether one group of youth comes from families that care enough and are competent enough to search out services for their youth, or how comfortable the youth are with adults. These critical yet hard-to-measure variables are factors that are likely to systematically differ between participant and comparison group youth and are likely to substantially affect one or more of the outcomes being examined. The more readers of an evaluation can think of such variables that have not been accounted for, the less they will believe the resulting program impact estimates.

Consider, for example, an e-mail mentoring program. Not only would one want the comparison group to match the participant group on demographic characteristics—age (say, 12, 13, 14, or 15 years old), gender (male, female), race (White, Hispanic, Black) and income (poor, nonpoor)—but one might also want to match the two groups on their preprogram use of the computer, such as the average number of hours using e-mail or playing computer games. To match on this variable, however, one would have to collect computer use data on many nonparticipant students in order to find those most comparable to the participants.

When one has more than a few matching variables, the number of cells becomes too numerous. In the above example, we would have 4 age × 2 gender × 3 race × 2 income, or 48 cells, even before splitting by computer use. A method that is used with increasing frequency to address this issue is *propensity score matching* (PSM).

A propensity score is the probability of being a participant given a set of known factors. In simple random assignment evaluations, the propensity score of every sample member is 50%, irrespective of their characteristics. In the real world without random assignment, the probability of being a participant depends on the individual's characteristics, such as their comfort with computers in the example above. Thus, participants and nonparticipants naturally differ on many characteristics. PSM can help researchers select which nonparticipants best match the participant group with respect to a weighted average of all these characteristics (where the weights reflect how important the factors are in making the individual a participant).

To calculate these weights, the researcher estimates, across both the participant and nonparticipant samples, a logistic model of the probability of being a participant (P_i) as a function of the matching variables and all other factors that are hypothesized to be related to participation (Rosenbaum & Rubin, 1983; Rubin, 1997). For example, if one were evaluating a school-based mentoring program, the equation might include age, gender, race, household status (*HH*), reduce-priced lunch status (*RL*), as well as past academic (*GPA*) and behavior (*BEH*) assessments, as is shown in Equation 1 below. Obtaining teacher rating of the youth's interpersonal skills (*SOC*) also would help match on the youth's ability to form a relationship.

(1) $P_i = f(age, gender, race, HH, RL, GPA, BEH, SOC)$

The next step of PSM is to compute for each potential member of the sample the probability of participation based on the matching characteristics in the regression. Predicted probabilities are calculated for both participants and all potential nonparticipants. Each participant then is matched with one or more nonparticipant youth based on these predicted propensity scores. For example, for each participant, the nonparticipant with the closest predicted participation probability can be selected into the comparison group (see Shadish et al., 2002, pp. 161–165, for further discussion of PSM, and Dynarski et al., 2003, for an application in a school-based setting).

An implication of this technique is that one needs data for the propensity score logit from both the participant group and a large pool of non-participant youth who will be considered for inclusion in the comparison group. The larger the considered nonparticipant pool is, the more likely it is that one can find a close propensity score match for each participant. This data requirement often pushes researchers to select matching factors that are readily available through records, rather than incur the expense of collecting new data.

One weakness of this method is that although the propensity to participate will be quite similar for the participant and comparison groups, the percentage with a particular characteristic (such as male) may not be, because PSM matches on a linear combination of characteristics, not each characteristic one by one. To overcome this weakness, most studies match propensity scores within a few demographically defined cells (such as race/gender cells).

PSM also balances the two groups only on the factors that went into the propensity score regression. For example, the PSM in Dynarski et al. (2003) was based on data gathered from 21,000 students, to generate a comparison group for their approximate 2,500 participants. However, when data were collected later on parents, it turned out that comparison group students were from higher income families. No matter how carefully a comparison group is constructed, one can never know for sure how similar the comparison group youth are to the participant group on unmeasured characteristics, such as their ability to respond to adult guidance.

Lesson: How much a reader trusts the internal validity of an evaluation depends on how much he or she trusts that the comparison group truly is similar to the participant group on all important dimensions. This level of trust or confidence is quantifiable in random assignment designs (e.g., one is 95% confident that the two groups are statistically equivalent), whereas with a quasi-experimental design, this level of trust is uncertain and unquantifiable.

ANALYSIS

This section covers how impact estimates are derived, from the simplest techniques to more statistically sophisticated ones. Several commonly committed errors and techniques used to overcome these problems are presented.

The Basics of Impact Estimates

Impact estimates for both experimental and quasi-experimental evaluation are basically determined by contrasting the outcomes of the participant or treatment group to that of the control or comparison group. If one has data from a random assignment design, the simplest unbiased impact estimate is the difference in mean follow-up (or posttest) outcomes for the treatment and control groups, as in Equation 2,

$$(2) \qquad b = \text{Mean}(Y_{fu,T}) - \text{Mean}(Y_{fu,C})$$

where b is the estimated impact of the program, $Y_{fu,T}$ is the value of outcome Y at posttest or follow-up for the treatment group youth, and $Y_{fu,C}$ is the value of outcome Y at posttest or follow-up for the control group youth. One can increase the precision of the impact estimate by calculating the change-score or difference-in-difference estimator as in Equation 3,

$$(3) \qquad b = \text{Mean}(Y_{fu,T} - Y_{bl,T}) \\ - \text{Mean}(Y_{fu,C} - Y_{bl,C})$$

where $Y_{bl,T}$ is the value of outcome Y at baseline for the treatment group youth and $Y_{bl,C}$ is the value of outcome Y at baseline for the control group youth.

Even more precision can be gained if the researcher controls for other covariate factors that affect the outcome through the use of analysis of covariance (ANCOVA) or, equivalently, through regression, as in Equation 4,

$$(4) \qquad Y_{fu} = a + bT + cY_{bl} + dX + u$$

where b is the estimated impact of the program, T is a dummy variable equal to 1 for treatments and 0 for controls, and X is a vector of *baseline* covariates that affect Y. Another way to think of b is that it is basically the difference in the mean Ys, adjusting for differences in Xs.

When data are from a quasi-experimental evaluation, it is always best to estimate impacts using regression or analysis of covariance; not' only do you get more precise estimates, but you can control for any differences that do arise between the participant and the comparison groups. Regression allows you to simulate what outcomes youth who were exactly like participants on all the included characteristics (the Xs) would have been had they not received a mentor, assuming that all factors that jointly affect participation and outcomes are in the regression. Regressions are also useful in randomized experiments for estimating impacts more precisely.

Suspicious Comparisons

The coefficient b from Equation 3 is an unbiased estimate of the program's impact (i.e., the estimate differs from the true impact only by a random error with mean zero), as long as the two groups are identical on all characteristics (both included and excluded variables). The key to obtaining an unbiased estimate of the impact is ensuring that you are comparing groups of youth that are as similar as possible in all the important observable and unobservable characteristics that influence the outcomes normally. Although many researchers understand the need for comparability and indeed think a lot about it when constructing a matched comparison group, this profound insight is often forgotten in the analysis phase, when the final comparisons are made. Most notably, if one omits youth from either group—the randomly selected treatment (or self-selected participant) group or the randomly selected control (or matched comparison) group—the resulting impact estimate is potentially biased. Following is a list of commonly seen yet flawed comparisons related to this concern.

Suspect Comparison 1: Comparing groups of youth based on their match status, such as comparing those who received a mentor or youth whose matches lasted at least 1 month with the control or comparison group. Suppose, as occurred in the Public/Private Ventures BBBS evaluation, only 75% of the treatment group actually received mentors (Grossman & Tierney, 1998). Can one compare the outcomes of the 75% who were mentees with the controls to get an unbiased estimated of the program's

impact? No. All the impact estimates must be based on comparisons between the entire treatment group and the entire control group to maintain the complete comparability of the two groups. (This estimate often is referred to as the impact of the "intent to treat.")

There are undoubtedly factors that are systematically different between youth who form mentoring relationships and those who do not. The latter youth may be more difficult temperamentally, or their families may have decided they really did not want mentors and withdrew from the program. If researchers remove these unmatched youth from the treatment group but do nothing with the control group, they could be comparing the "better" treatment youth with the "average" control group child, biasing the impact estimates. Randomization ensures that the treatment and control groups are equivalent (i.e., there are just as many "better" youth in the control group as the treatment group). After the intervention, matched youth are readily identified. Researchers, however, cannot identify the control group youth who would have been matched successfully had they been given the opportunity. Thus, if one discarded the unmatched treatment youth, implicitly one is comparing successfully matched youth to a mixed group—those for whom a match would have been found (had they been offered participation) and those for whom matches would not be found (who are perhaps harder to serve). An impact estimate based on such a comparison has the potential to bias the estimate in favor of the program's effectiveness. (The selection bias embedded in matching is the reason researchers might choose to compare the outcomes of a matched comparison group with the outcomes of mentoring program applicants, rather than participants.) On the other hand, the estimate based on all treatments and all controls, called the "intent-to-treat effect," is unaffected by this bias.

Because, the intent-to-treat estimate is based on all treatments whether or not they received the program, it may underestimate the "impact on the treated" (i.e., the effect of actually receiving the treatment). A common way to calculate the "impact on the treated" is to divide the intent-to-treat estimate by the proportion of youth actually receiving the program (Bloom, 1984). The intent-to-treat estimate is a weighted average of the impact on the treated youth (a_p)

and the impact on the untreated youth (a_{np}), as shown in Equation 5,

$$(5) \qquad \mathrm{Mean}(T) - \mathrm{Mean}\ (C)$$
$$= a = p\ a_p + (1 - p)\ a_{np,}$$

where p = proportion treated.

If the effect of group assignment on the non-treated youth (a_{np}) is zero (i.e., untreated treatment individuals are neither hurt nor helped), then a_p is to equal a/p. Let's again take the example of the BBBS evaluation. Recall that 18 months after random assignment, 7% of the treatment group youth (the treated and untreated) had started using drugs compared with 11% of the control group youth, a 4-percentage-point reduction. Using the knowledge that only 75% of the youth actually received mentors, the "impact on the treated" of starting to use drugs would increase from a 4-percentage-point reduction to a 5.3-percentage-point reduction (= 4/.75).

Similar bias occurs if one removes control group members from the comparison for any reason. Reconsider the school-based mentoring example described above, where treatment youth are offered mentors and control youth are denied mentors for 1 year. Suppose that, although most youth participate for only a year, some continue their matches into a second school year. To gauge the impact of this longer intervention, the evaluator might (incorrectly) consider comparing youth who had mentors for 2 years with control youth who were not matched after their 1-year denial period. This comparison has several problems. Youth who were able to sustain their relationships into a second year, for example, would likely to be better able to relate to adults and perhaps more malleable to a mentoring intervention than the "average" originally matched comparison group member. An unbiased way to examine these program impacts would be to compare groups that were assigned randomly or chosen judgmentally at the beginning of the evaluation: one group being offered the possibility of a 2-year match, and the other being denied the program for 2 years. To investigate both 1- and 2-year versions of the program, one would need two treatment groups and two control groups.

Lesson: The only absolutely unbiased estimate from a random assignment evaluation of a mentoring program is based on the comparison of all treatments and all controls, not just the matched treatments.

Suspect Comparison 2: Comparing the effects of youth based on relationships characteristics, such as short matches with longer matches or closer relationships with less close relationships. Grossman and Rhodes (2002) examined the effects of different lengths of matches using the BBBS evaluation data. In the first part of the paper, the researchers reported the straightforward comparisons between outcomes of those matched less than 6 months, 6 to 12 months, and more than 12 months with the control group's outcomes. Although interesting, these simple comparisons ignore the potential differences among youth who are able to sustain their mentoring relationships for different periods of time. If the different match lengths were induced randomly across pairs or the reasons for a breakup were unrelated to the outcomes being examined, then there would be no problem with the simple set of comparisons. However, if, for example, youth who cannot form relationships that last more than 5 months are less able to get the adult attention and resources they need and consequently would do worse than the long-matched youth even without the intervention, then the first set of comparisons would produce biased estimates of impact. Indeed, when the researchers statistically controlled for this potential bias (using two-staged least squares, as discussed below), they saw evidence of the strong association of short matches with negative outcomes disappear, while the indications of positive effects of longer matches remained.

A similar problem occurs when comparing those with close relationships to those with weaker relationships. For the straightforward comparison to be valid, one is implicitly assuming that youth who ended up with close relationships with their mentors would have, in the absence of being in a mentoring program, fared equally well or poorly as youth who did not end up with close relationships. If those with closer relationships would have, in the absence of the program, been better able to secure adult attention than the other youth and done better because of it, for example, then a comparison of the close-relationship youth with either youth in less close relationships or with the control/matched comparison group could be flawed.

Lesson: Any examination of groups defined by a program variable—such as having a mentor, the length of the relationship, having a cross-race match—is potentially plagued by selection bias regardless of the evaluation design employed. Valid subgroup estimates can be calculated only for subgroups defined on preprogram characteristics, such as gender or race or preprogram achievement levels or grades. In these cases, we can precisely identify and make comparisons to a comparable subgroup within the control group (against which the treatment subgroup may be compared).

Suspect Comparison 3: Comparing the outcomes of mentored youth with a control or matched comparison group when the sample attrition at the follow-up assessment is substantial or, worse yet, when there is a differential attrition between the two groups. Once again, unless those who were assessed at posttest were just like the youth for whom one does not have posttest data, the impact estimates may be biased. Suppose youth from the most mobile, unstable households are the ones who could not be located. Comparing the "found" treatment and controls tells you only about the impact of the program on youth from stable homes, not all youth. This is an issue of generalizability (i.e., external validity; see Shadish et al., 2002). Differential attrition between the treatment and the control (or participant and comparison) group is important because it also poses a threat to internal validity. Frequently, researchers are able to reassess a much higher fraction of program participants—many of whom may still be meeting with their mentors—than of the control or comparison group youth (whom no one has necessarily tracked on a regular basis). For example, if the control or comparison group youth demonstrate increased behavioral or academic problems over the sample period, parents may move their children to attend other schools and thus make data collection more difficult. Alternatively, some treatment families may have decided not to move out of the area because the children had good mentors. Under any of these scenarios, comparing the reassessed comparison group youth with reassessed mentees could be a comparison of unlike individuals.

Lesson: Comparisons of treatment (or participant) groups and control (or comparison) groups are completely valid only if the youth not included in the comparison are simply a random sample of those included in the total sample. This assumption is easier to believe if the nonincluded individuals represent a small proportion of the total sample and if the proportions excluded are the same for the treatment and control groups.

Statistical Corrections for Biases

What do you do if you want to examine program impacts under these compromised situations? For example, you have differential attrition, or you wish to examine the impact of mentoring on youth whose matches have lasted more than a year. There are a variety of statistical methods to handle these biases. As long as the assumptions underlying the statistical methods hold, then those adjusted impact estimates should be unbiased.

Let's start by restating the basic hypothesized model:

$$(6) \qquad Y_{fu} = a + b\,M + c Y_{bl} + u$$

The level of outcome Y at follow-up is determined by the level of that variable at baseline, whether the child got mentoring (M), and unmeasured factors (u). Suppose you have information on a group of mentees and a comparison group of youth matched on age, gender, and school. Now suppose, however, the youth who actually get mentors differ from the comparison youth in that they are more likely to be firstborn. If firstborn youth do better on outcome Y (even controlling for the baseline level of Y) and you fail to control for this difference, the estimated impact coefficient, b, will be biased upward, picking up not only the effect of mentoring on Y but also the "first-born-ness" of the mentees. The problem here is that M and u are correlated.

If you hypothesize that the only way the participating youth differ from the average non-participating child is on measurable characteristics (X)—for example, they are more likely to be firstborn, or they are more likely to be Hispanic—then including these characteristics in the impact regression model, Equation 7, will fully remove the correlation between M and u, because M conditional on (i.e., controlling for) X is not correlated with u. Thus, Equation 7 will produce an unbiased estimate of the impact (b):

$$(7) \qquad Y_{fu} = a + bM + cY_{bl} + dX + u$$

Including such extra covariates is a common technique. However if, as is usually the case, one suspects (or even could plausibly argue) that the mentored group is different in other ways that are correlated with outcomes and for which you do not have measures, such as being more socially competent or from better-parented families, then the estimate coefficient still will be potentially biased.

Two-Staged Least Squares (TSLS)

Two-staged least squares regression (TSLS; also called "instrumental variables") is a statistical way to obtain unbiased (or consistent) impact estimates in this more complicated position (see Stock & Watson, 2003, chap. 10). Intuitively, this technique tries to find a variable (an "instrument") that is highly correlated with M but is not correlated with u. Consider the factors influencing M,

$$(8) \qquad M = k + mZ + nQ + v$$

where M is whether the child is a mentee, Z are variables related to M that are unrelated to Y, Q are variables related to M that are related to Y, and v is the random error. If we could somehow purge out of M that element that is correlated with u, we could get an unbiased estimate of the impact. TSLS is the instrumental variable technique that does this.

The first and most difficult step in TSLS is to identify variables (Z) that (a) are related to why a child is in the group being examined, such as being a mentee or a long-matched child, and (b) are not related to the outcome Y. These are very hard to think of and inevitably need to be thought about before data collection starts. Grossman and Rhodes (2002) used match characteristics such as the mentor and child having

similar interests and living close together. These variables were related to the match "working" (i.e., having longer duration) but not related theoretically to the child's grades or behaviors. Then, one decomposes M into a part that is and is not correlated to u by estimating,

$$(9) \qquad M = k + mZ + nX + cY_{bl} + w$$

where w is a random error. All of the variables that will be included in the final impact Equation 7, X and Y_{bl}, are included in the first-stage regression along with the instruments Z. A predicted value of M, $M' = k + mZ + nX + cY_{bl}$ then is computed for each sample member. The properties of regression ensure that M' will be uncorrelated with the part of Y_{fu} not accounted for by Y_{bl} or X (i.e., u). M' then is used in Equation 7 rather than M. The second stage of TSLS estimates Equation 7 and the corrected standard errors (see Stock & Watson, 2003, for details). This technique works only if you have good predictive instruments. As a rule of thumb, the F-test for the Stage 1 regression should have a value of at least 10 if the instrument is to be considered valid.

Baseline Predictions

Suspect Comparison 2 illustrates how any examination of groups defined by a program variable, such as having a long relationship or a cross-race match, is potentially plagued by selection bias we have been discussing. Schochet, Burghardt, and Glazerman (2001) employed a remarkably clever nonstatistical technique for estimating the unbiased impact of a program in such a case. The researchers knew that they wanted to compare the impacts of participants who would choose different versions of a program. However, because one could not know who among the control group would have chosen each program version, it appeared that one could not make a valid comparison. To get around this problem, they asked the intake workers who interviewed all applicants before random assignment (both treatments and controls) to predict which version of the program each youth would end up in if all were offered the program. The researchers then estimated the impact of Version A (and similarly B) by comparing the outcomes of treatment and control group members deemed to be "A-likely" by the intake workers. Note that they were not comparing the treatment youth who actually did Version A to the A-likely control youth, but rather comparing the A-likely treatments to the A-likely controls. Because the intake workers were quite accurate in their predictions, this technique is convincing. For mentoring programs, staff could similarly predict which youth would likely end up receiving mentors or which would likely experience long-term matches based on the information they gathered during the intake process and their knowledge of the program. This baseline (preprogram) characteristic then could be used to identify a valid comparison.

Future Directions

Synthesis

Good evaluations gauge a program's impacts on a range of more to less ambitious outcomes that realistically could change over the period of observation given the likely program dosage; they assess outcomes using measures that are sensitive enough to detect the expected or policy relevant change; and they use multiple measures and perspectives to assess an impact.

The crux to obtaining internally valid impact estimates is knowing what would have happened to the members of the treatment group had they not received mentors. Simple pre-post designs assume the participant would not have changed—that the postprogram behavior would have been exactly what the preprogram behavior was without the program. This is a particularly poor assumption for youth. Experimental and quasi-experimental evaluations are more valid because they use the behavior of the comparison group to represent what would have happened.

The internal validity of an evaluation depends critically on the comparability of the treatment (or participant) and the control (or comparison) groups. If one can make a plausible case that the two groups differ on a factor that also affects the outcomes, the estimated impact may be biased by this factor. Because random assignment (with sufficiently large samples)

creates two groups that are statistically equivalent in all observable and unobservable characteristics, evaluations with this design are, in principle, superior to matched comparison group designs; matched comparison groups can, at best, assure comparability only on the important observable characteristics. Evaluators using matched comparison groups must always worry about potential selection bias problems; in practice, researchers conducting random assignment evaluations often run into selection bias problems too by making comparisons that undermine the balanced nature of treatment and control groups. Numerous statistical techniques, such as the use of instrumental variables, have been developed to help researchers estimate unbiased program impacts. However, their use requires forethought at the data collection stage to ensure that one has the data needed to make the required statistical adjustments.

Recommendations for Research

Given the aforementioned issues discussed, researchers evaluating mentoring programs should consider the following suggestions:

1. *Design for disaster.* Assume things will go wrong. Random assignment will be undermined. There will be differential attrition. The comparison group will not be perfectly matched. To guard against these problems, researchers should think deeply about how the two groups might differ if any of these problems were to arise, then collect data at baseline that could be used for matching or making statistical adjustments. It also is useful to give forethought to which program subgroups will be examined and to collect variables that could help you predict these program statuses, such as the length of a match.

2. *Gather implementation or process information.* This information is necessary in order to understand one's impact results—why the program had no effect or what type of program had the effects that were estimated. These data and data on program quality also can enable one to explore what about the program led to the change.

3. *Use random assignment or match on motivational factors.* Random assignment

should be a researcher's first choice, but if quasi-experimental methods must be used, researchers should try to match participant and comparison youth on some of the less obvious factors. The more one can convince readers that the groups are equivalent on all the relevant variables, including some of the hard-to-measure factors, such as motivation or comfort with adults, the more credible the impact estimates will be.

Recommendations for Practice

Given the complexities of estimating valid impact estimates, what should a program do to measure effectiveness?

1. *Monitor key process variables or benchmarks.* Walker and Grossman (1999) argued that not every program should conduct a rigorous impact study. It is a poor use of resources, given the cost of research and the relative skills of staff. However, programs should use data to improve their programming (see United Way of America's *Measuring Program Outcomes,* 1996, or the W. K. Kellogg Foundation *Evaluation Handbook,* 2000). Grossman and Johnson (1999) recommended that mentoring programs track three key dimensions: youth and volunteer characteristics, match length, and quality benchmarks. More specifically, programs could track basic information about youth and volunteers: what types and numbers apply, and what types and number are matched. They could track information about how long matches last, for example, the proportion making it to various benchmarks. Last, they could measure and track benchmarks, such as the quality of the relationship (Reddy et al., in press). This approach allows programs to measure factors that (a) can be tracked easily and (b) can provide insight about their possible impacts without collecting data on the counterfactual state. Pre-post changes can be a benchmark (but not an impact estimate), and one must be careful that the types of youth served and the general environment are stable. If the pre-post changes for cohorts of youth improve over time, for example, but the program now is serving less needy youth, the change in this pre-post benchmark tells you little about the effectiveness of the program

(the counterfactual states for the early and later cohorts differ).

2. *Collaborate with local researchers to conduct impact studies periodically.* When program staff feel it is time to conduct a more rigorous impact study, they should consider collaborating with local researchers. Given the time, skills, and complexity entailed in conducting impact research, trained researchers can complete the task much more efficiently. An outside evaluation also may be believed more readily. Researchers, furthermore, can become a resource for improving the program's ongoing monitoring system.

REFERENCES

Bloom, H. S. (1984). Accounting for no-shows in experimental evaluation designs. *Evaluation Review, 8,* 225–246.

Branch, A. Y. (2002). *Faith and action: Implementation of the national faith-based initiative for high risk youth.* Philadelphia: Branch Associates and Public/Private Ventures.

Dennis, M. L. (1994). Ethical and practical randomized field experiments. In J. S. Wholey, H. P. Hatry, & K. E. Newcomer (Eds.), *Handbook of practical program evaluation* (pp. 155–197). San Francisco: Jossey-Bass.

DuBois, D. L., Holloway, B. E., Valentine, J. C., & Cooper, H. (2002). Effectiveness of mentoring programs for youth: A meta-analytic review. *American Journal of Community Psychology, 30,* 157–197.

DuBois, D. L., Neville, H. A., Parra, G. R., & Pugh-Lilly, A. O. (2002). Testing a new model of mentoring. In G. G. Noam (Ed. in chief) & J. E. Rhodes (Ed.), *A critical view of youth mentoring (New Directions for Youth Development: Theory, Research, and Practice, No. 93,* pp. 21–57). San Francisco: Jossey-Bass.

Dynarski, M., Pistorino, C., Moore, M., Silva, T., Mullens, J., Deke, J., et al. (2003). *When schools stay open late: The national evaluation of the 21st Century Community Learning Centers Program.* Washington, DC: U.S. Department of Education.

Eccles, J. S., Midgley, C., & Adler, T. F. (1984). Grade-related changes in school environment:

Effects on achievement motivation. In J. G. Nicholls (Ed.), *The development of achievement motivation* (pp. 285–331). Greenwich, CT: JAI Press.

Grossman, J. B., & Johnson, A. (1999). Judging the effectiveness of mentoring programs. In J. B. Grossman (Ed.), *Contemporary issues in mentoring* (pp. 24–47). Philadelphia: Public/Private Ventures.

Grossman, J. B., & Rhodes, J. E. (2002). The test of time: Predictors and effects of duration in youth mentoring programs. *American Journal of Community Psychology, 30,* 199–206.

Grossman, J. B., & Tierney, J. P. (1998). Does mentoring work? An impact study of the Big Brothers Big Sisters program. *Evaluation Review, 22,* 403–426.

Lucas, P., & Liabø, K. (2003, April). One-to-one, non-directive mentoring programmes have not been shown to improve behavior in young people involved in offending or anti-social activities. *What Works for Children Group Evidence Nugget.* Retrieved July 20, 2004, from http://www.whatworksforchildren.org.uk/docs/Nuggets/pdfs/Mentoring230703.pdf

Orr, L. L. (1999). *Social experiments: Evaluating public programs with experimental methods.* Thousand Oaks, CA: Sage.

Rhodes, J. Reddy, R., Roffman, J., & Grossman, J. (in press). Promoting successful youth mentoring relationships: A preliminary screening questionnaire. *Journal of Primary Prevention.*

Rosenbaum, P. R., & Rubin, D. B. (1983). The central role of the propensity score in observational studies for causal effects. *Biometrika, 70,* 41–55.

Rosenberg, M. (1979). Rosenberg self-esteem scale. In K. Corcoran & J. Fischer (2000). *Measures for clinical practice: A sourcebook* (3rd ed., pp. 610–611). New York: Free Press.

Rossi, P. H., Freeman, H. E., & Lipsey, M. W. (1999). *Evaluation: A systematic approach* (6th ed.). Thousand Oaks, CA: Sage.

Rubin, D. B. (1997). Estimating causal effects from large data sets using propensity scores. *Annals of Internal Medicine, 127,* 757–763.

Schochet, P., Burghardt, J., & Glazerman, S. (2001). *National Job Corps Study: The impacts of Job Corps on participants' employment and related outcomes.* Princeton, NJ: Mathematica Policy Research.

Shadish, W. R., Cook, T. D., & Campbell, D. T. (2002). *Experimental and quasi-experimental designs for generalized causal inference.* Boston: Houghton Mifflin.

Stock, J. H., & Watson, M. W. (2003). *Introduction to econometrics.* Boston: Addison Wesley.

Tierney, J. P., & Grossman, J. B., & Resch, N. L. (1995). *Making a difference: An impact study of Big Brothers/Big Sisters.* Philadelphia: Public/Private Ventures.

United Way of America. (1996). *Measuring program outcomes.* Arlington, VA: Author.

Walker, G., & Grossman J. B. (1999). Philanthropy and outcomes: Dilemmas in the quest for accountability. In C. T. Clotfelter & T. Ehrlich (Eds.), *Philanthropy and the nonprofit sector in a changing America* (pp. 449–460). Bloomington: Indiana University Press.

Weiss, C. H. (1998). *Evaluation.* Upper Saddle River, NJ: Prentice Hall.

W. K. Kellogg Foundation. (2000). *Evaluation handbook.* Battle Creek, MI: Author.

18

CROSS-AGE PEER MENTORING

MICHAEL J. KARCHER

INTRODUCTION

Centuries ago, before compulsory public education and when both parents' work demands left little time for them to supervise their children during the day, older siblings and peers commonly were assigned the duty of supervising younger children and in many ways serving as mentors. Those days are gone. The typical arrangement today, whether in day care or in a public school setting, is for youth of the same age to interact with one another either in unsupervised settings or under the supervision of an adult. These days, unless children have the good fortune to have the support of an older sibling, they are unlikely to have many opportunities to interact with their older and wiser peers.

For most people, the words "mentor to youth" likely conjure the image of an adult providing wisdom and guidance to a younger person. Indeed, in virtually every other chapter in this handbook, the mentors are adults. Generally, adults are viewed as the primary and most important socializing agents in children's lives, but that commonly held belief recently has come under question by researchers arguing that peers are the primary socializing agents of youth (Harris, 1998). In fact, researchers have suggested that there are systematic processes by which peers socialize peers (Kindermann, 1993) and that, when left to their own devices, this

socialization can result in adverse consequences (Dishion, McCord, & Poulin, 1999).

But peer influences need not be negative. Although the current zeitgeist regarding peer influence is that of negative peer pressure, there is a growing literature indicating positive effects of peer interactions, particularly when adults carefully structure such interaction. For example, there is a burgeoning literature on same-age peers helping their peers, either as counselors, mediators, or tutors, and the benefits of cross-age tutoring are fairly well established at this point (King, Staffeiri, & Adelgais, 1998; Morey & Miller, 1993; Powell, 1997; Topping & Ehly, 1998). However, almost nonexistent is information on the effects of older youth, typically adolescents, mentoring younger youth, typically children—that is, cross-age peer mentoring. This chapter presents an overview of what is known about peer mentoring, both in terms of research and practice as well as what theories may be most instructive for guiding future efforts at designing, coordinating, and evaluating peer mentoring programs. Indeed, given the importance and yet the paucity of theory-driven research in mentoring, in general, and peer mentoring, in particular, I attempt to introduce and then stay close to several theoretical models as I review extant research and discuss practice issues. First, however, I begin by providing a definition of peer mentoring to narrow the focus of this chapter.

Cross-Age Peer Mentoring: A Definition

Peer mentoring involves an interpersonal relationship between two youth of different ages that reflects a greater degree of hierarchical power imbalance than is typical of a friendship and in which the goal is for the older youth to promote one or more aspects of the younger youth's development. Peer mentoring refers to a sustained (long-term), usually formalized (i.e., program-based), developmental relationship. The relationship is "developmental" in that the older peer's goal is to help guide the younger mentee's development in domains such as interpersonal skills, self-esteem, and conventional connectedness and attitudes (e.g., future motivation, hopefulness). This definition of peer mentoring distinguishes it from other peer interventions in terms of age parameters, curricular or activity content, and program goals.

A first important parameter is the age difference between mentees and mentors. To be consistent with common definitions of mentoring, the mentor needs to be an "older and wiser" peer. Ideally, the mentor is someone the mentee can look up to, admire, and even idealize. This may be greatly facilitated when the mentor is a few years older than the mentee. Thus, both terms, *peer* and *cross-age,* are important. Including "peer" with cross-age mentoring is important because it conveys that the dyad consists of two peers within the same generation. "Cross-age mentoring" alone does not distinguish peer from intergenerational mentoring (see Taylor, LoSciuto, & Porcellini, this volume). Using the term *cross-age peer mentoring,* rather than *peer mentoring* or *cross-age mentoring,* also helps establish a distinction between cross-age peer mentoring and other peer interventions.

The term peer mentoring often is used rather loosely to refer to a situation in which one youth helps a same-age peer. Unlike cross-age peer mentoring, the terms peer mentoring, peer helping, and peer counseling are used (often interchangeably) to indicate a same-age peer relationship in which one peer helps another with personal problems or academic deficits. Quite commonly, peer mentoring has been used as a synonym for peer counseling, peer tutoring, or peer helping programs. However, peer counseling and helping (like peer mediation) connote and involve a greater emphasis on assessing and remediating interpersonal, psychological, or academic deficits than is typical of a mentoring relationship (Morey & Miller, 1993). Peer tutoring and mentoring commonly also have been used interchangeably, which is unfortunate because rarely is peer tutoring of sufficient duration or emotional intensity to qualify as a mentoring relationship. In contrast, the characteristic content of cross-age peer mentoring is less prescriptive, remedial, or task-focused than in these other peer interventions, and while cross-age peer mentoring can be structured, the interactions should not be purely didactic or overly instrumental.

In summary, the first step in the establishment of peer mentoring as an intervention that is distinct from other peer approaches is establishing a clear definition. The definition of cross-age peer mentoring provided here makes clear that cross-age peer mentors and mentees differ in age and that the mentor's focus is not on interpersonal or academic deficiencies (as in peer helping, counseling, and tutoring), but rather on facilitating youth development more generally.

Prevalence of Cross-Age Peer Mentoring Programs

It is difficult to determine which peer approaches are used the most. Unquestionably, peer tutoring has been the most thoroughly researched, with both outcome and process studies reported in the literature since the 1970s. There also are several well-known peer tutoring programs, such as the Coca-Cola Valued Youth Program, which claims to have worked with "more than 129,000 children, families, and educators" (Coca-Cola Youth Partnership, 2002). Another is the Chicago-based Time Dollar Tutoring program, which reportedly has provided 480,000 hours of instructional time in the Chicago schools through their program (Washington-Steward, 2000) and is now operated in seven other states and in Washington, DC. There also are large-scale peer helping organizations, such as Peer Assistance and Leadership (PAL, 2004), which reflect variants of peer tutoring (Topping & Ehly, 1998).

Learning Helpers (National Helpers Network, 1998) is a similar peer helping program that has 37 state organizations and 14 international affiliates (National Peer Helpers Association [NPHA], 2004). Inconsistent with our definition of cross-age peer mentoring, these programs include one or more of the following: short-term relationships, primary emphasis on problem or academic skill remediation, and/or involvement of same-age peers.

The prevalence of cross-age peer mentoring is even more difficult to determine. Many cross-age peer mentoring programs are coordinated by school counselors or teachers and not connected to agencies that report on their activities. Those programs that are described in the literature often are not clearly differentiated from other peer interventions. For example, "The peer programs that the National Peer Helpers Associations support have various names such as peer helping, peer counseling, peer ministry, peer education, peer leadership, peer health education, peer mediators, peer tutoring, peer mentoring and other names" (NPHA, 2004, para. 4). Similarly, the General Accounting Office (2004) recently reported on 122 student mentoring programs that were federally funded by the Department of Education between 2002 and 2004. Of the 122 programs, 46 included "school age" mentors, but only 3 enlisted solely "school age" mentors, and of the 46 programs, it is unclear whether these were same- or cross-age peer mentoring programs.

Big Brothers Big Sisters (BBBS) recently has begun a program called High School Bigs, which may provide the best example of a nationally known cross-age peer mentoring program. The High School Bigs are neither focused solely on improving specific academic skills (e.g., via tutoring or classroom "helping" presentations) nor on addressing specific problems, which makes this a true "mentoring" program. In 2003, BBBS provided mentors to approximately 95,000 youth in schools in the United States. Of these, 39,000 student mentees worked with BBBS adolescent mentors, who are called the "High School Bigs" (K. Hansen, personal communication, July 18, 2004). If the rising number of BBBS school-based, child-with-adolescent-mentor programs is any predictor, cross-age peer mentoring may emerge as a one of the most widespread mentoring approaches in the near future.

The purpose of the rest of this chapter is to overview theory, research, and practice that bear specifically on cross-age peer mentoring. In the "Theory" section that follows, theories are introduced that may illuminate the effects, both positive and potentially negative, of cross-age peer mentoring programs on mentees *and* mentors. In the subsequent "Research" section, the limited available research on cross-age peer mentoring is reviewed in terms of the previously introduced theories. Some findings from peer tutoring and peer helping research regarding potential moderators and mediators that cross-age peer mentoring researchers could explore are presented as well. The "Practice" section includes practice points borrowed from adult mentoring, other peer intervention, and extant cross-age peer mentoring research. The concluding section provides a synthesis and a set of recommendations for future research and practice.

THEORY

Unlike most other forms of mentoring discussed in this handbook, in cross-age peer mentoring, there is as much interest in the program effects on the mentors as on the mentees. For this reason, theories are needed that not only explain the likely outcomes for mentees, but for the mentors as well. Because the outcomes of peer mentoring for both mentees and mentors may be tied to what these youth bring to mentoring by way of inherent motivations, prior experience, and disposition, both theories of development and socialization are introduced.

Developmental Theories

Damon (1984) revealed the potential for Vygotsky's, Piaget's, and Sullivan's developmental theories to guide research on peer interventions. These three theories share an emphasis on how social context interacts with cognitive development and how important social perspective-taking capabilities may shape and be shaped by social interaction. Each of these theories also highlights three of the key elements of Rhodes's (this volume) theory about the factors that influence the effectiveness of mentoring relationships for youth: cognitive development, empathy, and role modeling.

One of the arguments against using youth as mentors is that they may not be emotionally or cognitively mature enough to provide empathy and understanding to a younger peer. However, research has suggested that older siblings regularly serve as natural mentors and make considerable contributions to their younger siblings' social and cognitive development by providing supportive contexts for their younger siblings to discuss family and extrafamilial issues (Brody, Kim, Murry, & Brown, 2003; Tucker, McHale, & Crouter, 2001). By modeling empathy and perspective taking, older siblings provide their younger siblings opportunities to develop their own empathic and perspective-taking skills (Howe & Ross, 1990).

According to Selman's (1980) neo-Piagetian theory of social perspective taking, there is a developmental progression in the complexity with which youth are able to take the perspectives of others into account. In a mentoring relationship, mentees and mentors who differ significantly in age are likely to view the world differently and differ in their empathy skills. Selman's theory also reveals the interrelationships between cognitive perspective-taking ability and interpersonal behavior (see Selman, 2003)—that is, how the complexity of youth's thinking guides their behaviors and thereby influences the course of their relationships with others. Elementary-aged children tend to act impulsively because they have only a limited awareness that their wants differ from others. During the later elementary years, children become better able to articulate their own points of view. By the end of elementary school, most youth are able to hold in their mind another's point of view—that is, fully understand another's wants, needs, and feelings. By the high school years, most youth become able to see their needs and wants from a perspective embedded within their relationships. This last cognitive-developmental advance ushers in the possibility

of developing a "chumship" (Sullivan, 1953). Typically, the chumship is the first relationship in which a middle or high school age youth fully discloses his or her inner life to a peer and trusts that this chum will honor shared secrets and not betray the youth. Out of this chumship can develop an appreciation for "the relationship" as well as a greater sense of caring for and trust in one's peers. In the absence of an older sibling to provide such opportunities for the development of perspective taking, empathy, and a prosocial orientation (Van Lange, Otten, De Bruin, & Joireman, 1997), cross-age mentors are in a unique position to fill this role for younger children.

A potential advantage of cross-age peer mentoring over same-age peer programs is that program effectiveness is less constrained by the level of the helper's cognitive maturity (Gibbs, Potter, Barriga, & Liau, 1996). The older mentor/younger mentee structure may simply provide better leverage for promoting competence, similar to the benefits younger children receive from supportive older siblings. Vygotsky's (1978) *zone of proximal development* refers to this phenomenon, whereby children are able to access or perform more complex skills (i.e., thoughts, emotions, behaviors) when "under the guidance or in collaboration with more capable peers" (p. 86). Although almost always, and perhaps inappropriately, this term is used by educators to illustrate to the ways that adults can facilitate children's development, Vygotsky was clearly referring to the ways in which older peers foster younger children's development by encouraging, modeling, and supporting the practice of new skills.

Theories of Peer Influence: (Peer) Group Socialization Theory

Consistent with Vygotsky's view, some researchers argue that children's peers are one another's primary socializers and cultural ambassadors. One of these, Harris (1998) summarizes her "group socialization theory" as "the theory that children identify with a group consisting of their peers, that they tailor their behavior to the norms of their group, and that groups contrast themselves with other groups and adopt different norms" (p. 264). She attributes a range of diverse developmental outcomes, such as delinquent behavior and academic success, to children's choice of and subsequent identification with specific peer groups. At best, Harris argues, adults provide contexts or opportunities for such identification to occur, but they have less influence than peers because from the child's point of view, the goal of development is "wanting to have higher status—wanting to be like a bigger kid. . . . It is in [children's] equating of maturity with status that makes little children want to behave, speak, and dress like bigger ones" (p. 267). According to Harris, older peers are enormously powerful influencing agents.

Children naturally sort themselves into peer groups, for better or worse. Adults also sort children into groups, often programmatically (e.g., through interventions and classroom assignments), also for better and for worse. Kindermann (1993) found children's attitudes and engagement in school (i.e., connectedness to school) were highly predictive of the peer groups they selected, and when children moved in and out of well-defined peer groups, each move resulted in the children identifying with the newly chosen group's attitude toward school. Conversely, even when interventions are intended to be helpful and facilitate prosocial behavior and attitudes, when antisocial or delinquent youth are aggregated, their goal of modeling one another's behaviors and attitudes can trump the well-intended efforts of adults (Patterson, Dishion, & Yoerger, 2000). Therefore, the attitudes that children bring to school or to an intervention program may lead to birds of a feather flocking together unless the context can be shaped (preferably by peers) to reward children, especially underachieving or delinquent children, for their academic successes and socially skilled (e.g., caring, empathic) behavior.

Theories of Adolescent Mentors' Motivations

Given that older peers are powerful socializing agents, the motivations and preexisting dispositions of adolescent mentors may weigh heavily on the outcomes of cross-age peer mentoring for their mentees (as well as for the mentors). Theories about youth motivations for mentoring are intimately linked to the ways in which mentors expect to benefit from mentoring.

Functional Theory of Volunteerism

The functional theory of volunteerism (Clary et al., 1998; Stukas & Tanti, this volume) posits a variety of functions that may be served by mentoring as a form of volunteerism. These functions include satisfying the desire (a) to gain career-related experience (career function), (b) to reduce one's own negative feelings (protective function), (c) to strengthen one's connections with others or to expand one's social network (social function), (d) to grow and develop personally from the experience (enhancement function), (e) to learn more about others and the world (understanding function), or (f) to act on personally held values, such as helping others or supporting a cause in which one believes (values function).

There also may be developmental factors that contribute to youth mentors' motivations. Given that socialization and identity development (Erikson, 1968) are developmental prerogatives for most adolescents and are achieved through personal and social exploration, adolescent mentors may be most motivated to mentor as a way of meeting social or enhancement needs and less motivated to mentor as a way of achieving some career function. Despite their more complex perspective-taking skills in general, adolescents' self-preoccupation or "adolescent egocentrism" (i.e., "navel staring") also may increase the likelihood that they volunteer to distract themselves from their own problems (protective function). Indeed, adolescents' inchoate perspective-taking skills and tendency to be preoccupied with their social roles within smaller social circles may limit their ability to step back and see larger social issues. This may make them less likely to mentor as a way to learn more about the world (understanding function). Gender may moderate the impact of these motivations. For example, both the tendency for girls to seek greater degrees of connectedness and the socialization of girls to become caregivers (Chodorow, 1978) may increase the likelihood that girls mentor for social reasons, role- or career-related reasons, or as an extension of the socialized value to help others. This may help explain why children who are more prosocial have been found to have more female older siblings (Van Lange et al., 1997).

Social Interest

Many of the functions described above can reflect temporal motivations—such as curiosity about careers options, need for psychological relief, or desire for greater connectedness. More enduring personality traits, such as empathy, altruism, or social interest, also may contribute to cross-age peer mentors' competence or readiness. Social interest reflects one's ability to be empathic and to identify with others (Adler, 1964). Because empathy and identification reflect cognitive functions requiring the ability to step outside one's own perspective, it is unlikely that all adolescents will have the same depth or degree of social interest.

In terms of its contribution to mentors' persistence, those who report high levels of social interest should be more likely to endure the challenges and frustrations of being a mentor than mentors with less social interest. In addition, mentors' perspective-taking abilities may mediate the relationship between age and social interest and thus may provide a better benchmark of an adolescent's readiness to serve as a mentor. Confirming this hypothesis could provide two theoretical constructs (perspective taking and social interest) for differentiating those adolescent mentors who are more likely to stay the course and be satisfied with their experience from those whose motivations are more self-centered and who may serve primarily to help themselves.

Theories Explaining the Relationship Between Children and Their Adolescent Mentors

Chance Encounters

In a rarely referenced article titled "The Psychology of Chance Encounters and Life Paths," Bandura (1982) explained the importance of

chance encounters in the life paths of individuals and recommended that psychologists attempt to explain the factors that make chance encounters influential for individuals. A chance encounter is an unintended meeting of persons unfamiliar with each other (Bandura, 1982, p. 748). Mentoring, seen from a life span perspective, also can be considered a chance encounter.

According to Bandura's (1982) hypotheses, cross-age peer mentoring should influence mentors' and mentees' "life paths through the reciprocal influence of personal and social factors" (p. 750). Bandura described three properties of reciprocal influence that may help explain the impact of cross-age peer mentoring as a chance encounter. The first is the match between mentors and mentees in terms of shared attributes and interests. "If persons are to affiliate with those whom they have had the good or bad fortune to meet, they must posses some of the personal resources needed to gain sufficient acceptance to sustain continued involvement with them" (p. 750). Having shared interests and the ability to convey them is the first predictor Bandura put forward to explain the likelihood of a positive chance encounter.

A second quality that may explain the impact of a chance encounter is interpersonal attraction between the two individuals. "Interpersonal attraction seals chance encounters into lasting bonds" (Bandura, 1982, p. 750). We do not know, however, what attributes of adolescent mentors make them most appealing to their mentees either at the start or later in the relationship. Whatever those traits turn out to be, mentees are most likely to be attracted to mentors who evoke in them feelings of esteem, importance, and attractiveness; conversely, the opposite feelings are likely to occur in response to mentors whose actions convey disinterest in the mentee, such as mentors' inconsistency, rejecting behaviors, and critical statements.

A third set of reciprocal processes that Bandura (1982) factored into the effects of chance encounters are (a) individuals' self-evaluations of the degree to which they can connect with others; (b) their need for affiliation, closeness, and someone with whom to identify; and (c) the degree to which they have already established a value set (and one that matches the person encountered). Bandura suggested "individuals contribute to their own destiny by developing potentialities that afford access to particular milieus" (p. 750), which is consistent with Harris's (1998) description of the Mathew phenomenon (i.e., "the rich get richer"), whereby mature children tend to seek out older peers and learn new skills, while immature children more often seek out same-age or younger peers who are less likely to draw them into their zone of proximal development. Therefore, children lacking social skills, who chronically misbehave, or who tend to be rejecting or rejected may be the least likely to naturally seek and subsequently form strong bonds with mentors. Such youth also may be those with whom mentors least enjoy working.

Regardless of the mentees' attributes or attractiveness in general, mentees with prior experiences of interpersonal failure (such as an abuse history) who feel they do not need others for support or identification and who are more identified with delinquent or rebellious peer groups that are negative toward school, adults, and authority should be less likely to naturally establish prosocial relationships through chance encounters. They may be the most likely to undermine the efforts and motivation of both natural and program-based mentors.

Process-Oriented Models of Mentoring

Bandura's (1982) three hypotheses are fairly consistent with two prevailing mentoring models. The first model was put forth by Parra, DuBois, Neville, Pugh-Lilly, and Povinelli (2002), who emphasize the distal and proximal influences on mentors' self-efficacy and illustrate how self-efficacy beliefs shape the nature (activities, discussions, and obstacles) of the mentoring relationship and the degree of closeness that emerges in the mentoring dyad. While they do not specify the mentees' unique contribution to the nature of the relationship and resulting close-ness as well as Rhodes's model (this volume), Parra et al. highlight the importance of structured interactions, training, and support for strengthening mentors' self-efficacy. Indeed, these may be the practices that are most important for cross-age peer mentoring because of the greater chance of authority-undermining behaviors

emerging with adolescent mentors than with adult mentors (Dishion et al., 1999; Patterson et al., 2000).

The second model emphasizing what Bandura described as the importance of a mentee's desire for connectedness, willingness to identify, and receptivity to a mentor's value set is the self psychology model of psychosocial development (Kohut & Wolf, 1978). Self psychology provides a theory to test the way in which mentoring, as a transforming relational experience, can effect changes in self-esteem, connectedness, and academic success. Effective mentoring (i.e., transformative mentoring inter-actions) from the perspective of self psychology should provide two sets of experiences to the mentee. First, mentors who provide empathy, praise, and attention should promote a positive change in mentees' perceptions of social support that results in increased feelings that the mentees matter to their mentors. This is consistent with the work of DuBois, Neville, et al. (2002), who found expanded perceptions of social support among mentees who saw their mentors as significant individuals in their lives. Changes in social support then contributed to increases in self-esteem and positive behavioral conduct. Second, mentors who are consistent, structure positive activities and conversations, and present mentees with realistic goals and expectations should find that their mentees come to value or idealize them. This idealization should result in increased connectedness with other authority figures (e.g., parents and teachers), improved social skills (through role modeling), and, consequently, increased self-esteem and academic success for the mentees.

This self psychology model may be particularly well suited to explain variation in the outcomes of cross-age peer mentoring. The two core experiences that contribute to self-development, according to Kohut and Wolf (1978), are that the mentee (a) experiences empathy, praise, and attention and subsequently (b) identifies with the mentor as an idealized other. Both Adler's (1964) and Selman's (1980) theories suggest that not all adolescents will be able to exercise high social interest and complex perspective-taking skills. Similarly, Rhodes (this volume) states that outcomes from mentoring may depend on the mentor's cognitive development. Given natural variation in empathy, perspective taking, and social interest among adolescents, it may be that less mature youth are not capable of fostering the first essential experience. Second, Harris (1998) has suggested that children may be more able to identify with and "idealize" older peers than adults:

> Kids do not look to grownups for guidelines on how to behave, speak, or dress because kids and grownups belong to different social categories that have different rules. Wanting to have higher status—wanting to be like a bigger kid—goes on *within* the group, within the social category "kids." Grownups are a different kettle of fish. To a kid, grownups are not a superior version of *us:* grownups are *them.* (p. 267)

This idealization of older peers by younger peers, coupled with the more mature peers' enhanced ability to be empathic (as a function of greater perspective-taking skills), may make older peers uniquely situated to facilitate their younger peers' development.

The Importance of Conventional Beliefs, Values, and Behaviors in Socializing Youth

The bulk of the theory presented in this section has highlighted a phenomenon called *conventionality.* Jessor and Jessor (1977) and Hirschi's (1969) social control theory highlight the role of conventional and unconventional beliefs, attachments, and behaviors in their theories of delinquency and risk-taking behavior. Ecologies that are governed and structured by adults tend reward conventional, adult-sanctioned behaviors. Individuals in these ecologies promote conventional beliefs and attachments to future-oriented, adult-dominated contexts, such as the school. However, when children are left to structure their own behaviors, they often do so in opposition to the conventional dictates of the adult world. One of the unique opportunities that cross-age peer mentors have is to help children start to bridge these two worlds by rewarding prosocial behaviors and academic attitudes, achievements, and inclinations.

Youth mentors who report low conventional connectedness may be less effective at modeling and reinforcing this conventional orientation with their mentees than are those adolescent mentors who report greater connectedness to school, family, and the future. A recent extension of these social control theories is the social development model. Advocates of this model emphasize helping children bond with school and prosocial peers by creating interventions that promote high levels of opportunity for involvement in school, skill development, and positive peer recognition (Abbott et al., 1998).

RESEARCH

There have been only a handful of empirical studies of cross-age peer mentoring to date. Unfortunately, the most commonly referenced peer-reviewed reports of cross-age peer mentoring have been descriptive and lacking empirical support (Burrell, Wood, Pikes, & Holliday, 2001; Noll, 1997; Wright & Borland, 1992). Of the few available evaluations of cross-age peer mentoring, most either (a) provided no data to support the findings (e.g., Hritz & Gabow, 1997; Noll, 1997), (b) were nonexperimental (i.e., included no control/comparison group), (c) only reported participant satisfaction levels (e.g., Bettencourt, Hodgins, Huba, & Pickett, 1998; Hansen, 2003; Sawyer, 2001), (d) reported non-significant findings (Dennison, 2000), (e) had insufficient statistical power (Karcher, Davis, & Powell, 2002; Westerman, 2002), or (f) did not distinguish between adult and adolescent mentors, group and one-on-one mentoring, or mentoring and teaching (O'Donnell & Michalak, 1997; Sheehan, DiCara, LeBailly, & Christoffel, 1999). However, extant experimental studies and empirical data do suggest the promise of using theory to enhance and increase our understanding of the effects of cross-age peer mentoring on both mentors and the mentees.

Before embarking on a review of extant empirical literature from the perspective of the theories described above, it is important to consider what evidence exists of the effects of cross-age peer mentoring in general. Selecting only studies of cross-age peer mentoring as defined in this chapter and restricting evidence of "empirical support" to those studies including at least a suitable comparison group, I searched the PsychINFO, ERIC, Dissertations Abstract International, and ProQuest databases and found four such studies. Only three of these utilized experimental designs with a randomly assigned control group (Karcher, 2005; Karcher et al., 2002; Westerman, 2002). The other study used a quasi-experimental design with a comparison group determined not through random assignment, but by selecting children from a local housing project and those on a wait list (Sheehan et al., 1999).

The outcomes examined in each of these studies differed with the exception that in all three of the experimentally designed studies, a positive effect of mentoring on connectedness to school, teachers, or parents was found (Karcher, 2005; Karcher et al., 2002; Westerman, 2002). In the quasi-experimental study, connectedness was not examined as an outcome. These findings suggest that positive changes in connectedness among mentees after cross-age peer mentoring is the outcome with the greatest empirical support. One study revealed evidence of positive program effects on academic achievement (Karcher et al., 2002), but no other studies examined achievement as an outcome. Similarly, the quasi-experimental study found evidence of a positive program effect on mentees' classroom behaviors as rated by teachers and on self-reported attitudes toward violence (Sheehan et al., 1999), but the other three studies did not examine these outcomes. Unfortunately, both of these studies are limited as a result of attrition by the size of the treatment and comparison groups ($n < 14$ per group) included in the analyses. To date, there have been no experimental or quasi-experimental studies of the effects of cross-age peer mentoring on the mentors, although there are several anecdotal, post hoc mentor reports of how older peer mentors felt it benefited them to be mentors. In sum, excluding evidence drawn from research on cross-age peer tutoring, peer counseling, and peer helping, as well as research that does not differentiate between peer tutoring and mentoring, there is very limited research available to evaluate the effects of cross-age peer mentoring.

Developmental Theories

Few studies in the cross-age peer mentoring literature have presented research from the perspective of any of the developmental theories described by Damon (1984). However, developmental concepts have been reported in other peer intervention literatures. Both in the peer mediation and the peer counseling literature, as well as in service-learning programs, encouraging youth to reflect on what has occurred or what they have learned from the intervention has been seen as way to facilitate academic skill development and positive attitudes (Stukas, Clary, & Snyder, 1999). Perspective-taking abilities also have been found to increase in association with serving as a peer mediator (Lane-Garon, 1998), but that study used an attitudinal questionnaire rather than a cognitive developmental assessment of perspective taking, leaving unclear the construct validity of the assessment. In sum, no one has experimentally tested the effects of including developmentally based activities in peer interventions.

Theories of Peer Influence: Group Socialization Theory

Harris's (1998) theory of group socialization is aligned with the hypothesis that peer mentors will be more influential than adult mentors (a) in contexts, such as in school, in which peers have considerable influence and (b) regarding outcomes that tend to be socialized by peers, such as beliefs, values, attitudes, and risk-taking behaviors. The fact that all of the peer-led Substance Abuse and Mental Health Services Administration (SAMHSA, 2004) "Model Programs" for substance use prevention are highly structured and the "Promising Programs" are not provides some support for Harris's theory and for the assertion that structured interventions involving peers will have the greatest impact on risk taking.

Theories of Adolescent Mentors' Motivations

Functional Theory of Volunteerism

To date, no research on cross-age peer mentoring has systematically looked at the role of mentors' motivations on either the outcomes for mentors or for their mentees. However, in one study of cross-age peer mentoring (Karcher,

Nakkula, & Harris, in press), the "self-enhancement" motivation on the Volunteer Function Inventory (Clary et al., 1998) predicted mentors' perceptions of relationship quality. That is, the mentors' desires to develop and grow psychologically by serving as mentors predicted how successful they viewed their matches to be. However, the actual effects of viewing the match with such rose-colored glasses are not known.

Hypotheses about age and gender differences in motivations—namely, the hypothesis that girls will be motivated more by altruistic and other-focused motivations or traditionally feminine career aspirations and that boys might be more individualistic in their motivations—could be tested through quasi-experimental research by including measures of mentors' motivations in outcome studies of cross-age peer mentoring, yet such motivations may interact with social interest or perspective taking, both of which reflect developmental maturity.

A main effect of gender in outcomes for mentees and mentors also needs to be explored in future research. In one study of 15 elementary school peer tutoring programs (only 3 programs of which were cross-age tutoring), tutored males working with female tutors benefited the least ($n = 372$; Topping & Whiteley, 1993). Overall, Topping and Whiteley found that when tutored in reading, boys did better on reading test score gains when tutored by boys than by girls ($d = .46$); girls did better when tutored by girls than when tutored by boys ($d = .38$); and the tutors in all conditions benefited more than did the students who were tutored. This poses a concern and important research question for peer mentoring because, in most studies, more girls than boys have volunteered to mentor, yet more boys than girls were referred for mentoring. This suggests there is an increased likelihood that boys will be paired with female peer mentors.

Social Interest

Social interest may prove to be a useful variable in understanding mentor motivations. In one study of 33 peer mentors, the peer mentors who reported higher initial social interest were more likely to continue or persist as mentors for a second academic year ($\eta^2 = .46$;

Karcher & Lindwall, 2003). Mentors higher in social interest also were more likely to select or choose to work with mentees who were more difficult interpersonally challenging or academically underachieving. In contrast, peer mentors who reported lower social interest were less likely to continue as mentors for a second year, and their dropout rate increased when they mentored more challenging mentees. Thus, a social interest assessment may prove useful in helping identify the peer mentors who are most likely to persist when working with challenging children.

Process-Oriented Models of Mentoring

The Role of Perceived Self-Efficacy and Perceptions of Relationship Quality

Parra et al. (2002) argued that mentors' perceived self-efficacy is a central mediator of the impact of mentoring on mentees. The importance of peer mentor's efficacy on outcomes was highlighted in a study (Karcher et al., in press) that found that peer mentors' perceptions of the quality of the mentoring relationship (at 6 weeks into the match) were predicted in part by the mentors' self-efficacy beliefs. In hierarchical regression analyses predicting relationship quality, other variables (including the mentee's risk status, parents' involvement, and overall program quality) were not significant predictors of relationship quality once mentor efficacy was accounted for. Only the mentors' motivation to have a good experience (Omoto & Snyder's, 1995, enhancement scale) and the degree to which the mentees actively sought out the mentors' support explained additional variance (beyond that explained by mentors' efficacy) in mentors' initial perceptions of relationship quality. By the end of the academic year, after approximately 5 months of mentoring, only mentors' perceived self-efficacy and mentees' support seeking predicted perceptions of relationship quality. This research is limited by the absence of objective outcome indicators (e.g., mentees' grades or self-reported attitudes). These findings suggest, however, that peer mentors' faith in their ability to mentor may be an important variable to address in mentor training and supervision.

Self-Esteem, Social Skills,
and Idealization as Mediators

The importance of identifying theory-driven mediators of outcomes (DuBois & Silverthorn, this volume) is as important in peer mentoring as in adult mentoring. The self psychology theoretical model (described earlier in the chapter), in which gains in self-esteem and social skills are hypothesized to facilitate the mentee "idealizing" or identifying with the mentor and thereby increase connectedness to school, adults, and school-related activities, was recently tested in a cross-age peer mentoring study that included 73 Caucasian middle school mentees and high school mentors. Karcher (2005) tested a hypothesized mediator model in which pre-post gains in connectedness to school, parents, friends, and reading would be greater for the mentees than for the comparison group and would be explained as a function of changes in social skills, self-esteem, and behavioral self-regulation skills resulting from receiving mentoring. The results indicated that overall changes in connectedness to school and to parents were greater for the mentees ($\eta^2 = .20$, .18), yet there was insufficient power (.26, .05) to detect the main effect of mentoring on connectedness to friends and to reading. Although the mediator model was not supported by the data (in part because of insufficient statistical power), the direction of the bivariate correlations between variables (all in the range of $r = .15$ to .36) and small but positive standardized regression coefficients (all about $ß = .10$) provided some support for the self psychology hypothesis that consistent, empathic relationships with adolescent mentors can influence changes in self-esteem, social skills, and connectedness.

Conventional Beliefs, Values, and Behaviors in Socializing Youth

The social development model (Abbott et al., 1998), the research on iatrogenic effects of peer interventions, and the connectedness research presented above suggest that peer interventions should actively promote greater conventional connectedness, such as bonding to school, with prosocial peers, and with adults (teachers and parents). How the mentors' own levels of connectedness mediate the outcomes of such peer programs is not known. In one study of 120 youth (88 girls and 32 boys), the 57 adolescents who chose to become peer mentors were higher on conventional connectedness to school, reading, family, and their future than were their peers ($\eta^2 = .42$; Karcher & Lindwall, 2003), thus suggesting that cross-age peer mentoring programs may be less interesting to adolescents who feel less connected to school or who already engage in authority-undermining behaviors (e.g., Dishion et al., 1999). It also is possible that challenging experiences may negatively affect adolescent mentors' connectedness. Karcher and Lindwall found that their mentees' academic risk status predicted their mentors' declines on connectedness to school and to reading (which was the primary joint activity they engaged in). It is possible that stressed or frustrated mentors may be adversely affected by challenging mentees.

In a study of the Buddy Program (Westerman, 2002), in which older children mentor younger children, 66 mostly Caucasian and African American fourth graders, 36 of whom were designated at risk due to family economic status, were assigned to one of four conditions. The 66 fourth graders were randomly assigned to four groups: (a) those who only received up to 16 hours of weekly mentoring from college students, (b) those who received mentoring but also served as mentors to kindergarteners, (c) those who only mentored kindergarteners, and (d) those who received no treatment. The groups of fourth graders who either were mentored or who served as mentors fared better than those who did both or were in the control condition. School-aged children who both mentored and were mentors reported declines in connectedness, bonding, and attendance compared with the children who did not perform both roles simultaneously. However, several limitations clouded the interpretation of these findings. The average number of mentoring meetings was only eight (half of the meetings were missed). The sample size, when separated into whether each fourth grader was a mentee, a mentor, or at risk (yes/no) resulted in subgroups smaller than 10. Finally, several subgroups had vastly different pre- and posttest scores on some variables, but no covariates were included to adjust for these differences.

The importance of conventional connectedness may be as an outcome and also as a mediator or facilitator of change. Consistent with the findings of Rhodes, Grossman, and Resch (2000), who found that improvements in parent-youth relations mediated the effect of mentoring on academic outcomes, in one study of cross-age peer mentoring, improvements in reading achievement among mentees were mediated by increased connectedness to parents ($\Delta R^2 = .19$; $\beta = .49$; Karcher et al., 2002). However, this sample also was very small ($n = 30$), and a main effect was found for only one of two achievement scores. Yet this finding is consistent with DuBois, Neville, et al. (2002), whose empirically supported model suggests that it is by expanding mentees' perceptions of social support from important adults that mentoring has its effects on behavioral and attitudinal outcomes.

Unique Opportunities for Research on Cross-Age Peer Mentoring

Impact on Mentors

The effect of being a youth mentor has been touted by most advocates of peer mentoring, but studied in just a few empirical investigations (Karcher, 2005; Karcher & Lindwall, 2003). Given that one of the aims of cross-age peer mentoring is to facilitate the development of the mentors as well as mentees, studies of the impact on mentors as well as of their experience, training, and levels of commitment will be important in the future.

Differential Effectiveness of Mentor and Mentee Types

There has been no research on the differential effects on high- and low-risk youth, on marginalized (e.g., disabled) versus mainstream youth, different sexes or ages, or on youth who differ in social group membership.

Mentees Reporting the Absence of Normative Declines: Is This Improvement?

Consistent with the landmark BBBS study findings, two studies found that cross-age peer mentoring helped mentees to avoid declines in conventional attitudes that may be normative,

albeit counterintuitive (Karcher et al., 2002; Sheehan et al., 1999). Future research on the strength and duration of this protective effect may reveal the potential for cross-age mentoring as a preventative intervention.

Importance of Training

While there is no research on the role of training on outcomes in cross-age peer mentoring, there is evidence from other peer interventions that high-quality training and supervision may be more important with youth than with adult mentors. A study of peer helping programs in Washington state suggests that in schools where the programs were not supervised by counselors or other trained professionals (but rather by teachers or administrators), the school reported a significantly higher student suicide rate (Lewis & Lewis, 1996). However, no effect sizes (nor sufficient information to calculate effect sizes) were reported, and the analyses were correlational (not experimental). Additional confounds include the large number of *t*-tests conducted, the low levels of statistical significance, and that no covariates were used to equate the schools on any number of variables that might covary with suicide rates.

The Role of Structure

Answering questions regarding the amount and type of structure is essential to determining the usefulness of cross-age peer mentoring. Answers to basic but interrelated questions about the effect of structure versus no structure and of instrumental activities versus developmental activities may help determine whether there are any unique benefits of cross-age peer mentoring. One of the main points of this chapter is that activities within peer mentoring cannot be the same as those in peer tutoring if it is to stand alone as a unique intervention. But this may not be true. It may be that developmentally oriented—that is, less instrumental, academic, and task-focused—mentoring interactions do not effect different or greater changes in behavioral, developmental, or academic outcomes than do other peer programs. If the outcomes of cross-age peer mentoring are the same as for other peer approaches, then the costs and efficiency of each peer approach may determine cost-effectiveness and merit.

For other peer interventions, some evidence suggests that the greater the amount of structure provided, the more effective the adolescents are and the more they get out of it (King et al., 1998). Cross-age peer mentors also may benefit from using specific structured activities with their mentees, but this is not known. What kinds of activities are most effective is an important question. Are youth mentors who spend much of their time in tutoring activities more effective than youth mentors who focus on social issues or the mentee's personal life and, if so, on what outcomes? Currently, there are no studies comparing the relative effects of different kinds of activities on academic or psychosocial outcomes, nor have there been studies that compare the effects of cross-age peer mentoring to other approaches in general. Both will be necessary for cross-age peer mentoring to become a distinct and more reputable intervention.

PRACTICE

To date, the two main practice questions, (a) what adolescent mentors should do with mentees and (b) how best to train and supervise adolescent mentors, have not received enough attention for a firm set of practices to be vigorously advocated. This section does not attempt to synthesize the variety of approaches to setting up, coordinating, or recruiting for cross-age peer mentoring programs that have been reported elsewhere (e.g., Burrell et al., 2001; Dennison, 2000; Lewis & Henney, 2003; Pyatt, 2002; Sawyer, 2001), but rather explores the implications for practice that can be drawn from the theory and research reviewed thus far.

Theoretically, what distinguishes cross-age mentoring programs from other peer approaches is its developmental orientation. Based on this perspective, cross-age peer mentoring, although predominantly implemented in school settings, should not focus solely on academic remediation or academic skill development, but include broader developmental aims such as instilling positive attitudes toward school. Similarly, cross-age peer mentoring should not be limited to a focus on treating identified problems, but rather

should provide a relational context in which youth might discuss their problems more informally. Cross-age peer mentoring furthermore should not focus solely on teaching information or skills, but it may use prevention curricula, reading materials, or other academically or problem-oriented activities as a vehicle to facilitate trust and reciprocal caring between mentors and mentees. Therefore, the content of cross-age mentoring programs, which are intimately linked to outcomes, should be relational-developmental in nature, and cognitive-developmental theories can help guide such programs.

Developmental Theories

One way to capitalize on cognitive-developmental theory is to consider structuring interactions or selecting activities that encourage perspective taking. Simply using activities that allow mentors and mentees to ask each other questions in an attempt to better understand one another, their unique experiences, and their respective goals and interests may help facilitate perspective taking and serve to strengthen the mentor-mentee bond. Prevention curricula that include such "perspective-taking activities" are Second Step (violence prevention), Project Northland (substance use prevention), and Botvin's Life Skills Training (see SAMHSA, 2004). What makes cross-age mentoring distinct from peer helping, tutoring, and counseling is its emphasis on the development of a mutually supportive, close relationship over an extended period of time. Care should be taken, therefore, to emphasize the use of any curricula to that end rather than as a means of learning specific skills. From a developmental point of view, most fruitful may be efforts that engage children in developmentally appropriate ways, such as through activities that emphasize engaging in physical activity, sharing opinions or learning information (requiring only a first-person perspective), and using those perspectives "learned" or shared to work cooperatively with a peer or with the mentor on a joint activity.

Group Socialization Theory

Harris (1998) has argued that if unsupervised, youth will work to distinguish themselves from adults. Therefore, supervision, in general, and structure, more specifically, should be key elements of effective peer programs. Structured peer approaches seem to be the most preventative against early forms of risk taking (see "Model" and "Effective" programs, such as Second Step and Project Northland, SAMHSA, 2004). Therefore, efforts to structure the meetings of the mentors and mentees may pay greater dividends than unstructured interactions.

Adolescent Mentors' Motivations

Functional Theory of Volunteerism

Program supervisors need to keep in mind the reasons that mentors volunteer to participate in cross-age mentoring programs and should never lose sight that these adolescents are their clients, too. Not only should the experience be developmental and enjoyable for the mentees, but mentors also need to benefit. There are ways that mentors may be trained to be more efficacious (see below) and thereby be "better" mentors and perhaps more skilled in the process. Program coordinators also need to pay attention to what motivates their mentors (e.g., career goals, desire for socialization, to feel better) and make efforts to ensure that the mentors are satisfied with the experience. For instance, coordinators could use the Volunteer Function Inventory (VFI) as one method of monitoring mentors' satisfaction (Omoto & Snyder, 1995). The VFI has two parts: (a) questions completed initially about why one wants to volunteer, that is, their motivations, and (b) questions to be answered during or after the experience regarding how much each of the different volunteering functions was met by participating in the program. If a sizable number of mentors, for example, want to mentor to expand their social networks, then program coordinators would be wise to make participation rewarding in that way, because doing so (a) increases the likelihood the mentors are happy and will persist and (b) helps avoid having a program in which the coordinators' and mentors' goals are at odds.

Social Interest

Screening potential mentors to better identify who will be most likely to persist is an important practice. Including an assessment of social interest in the mentor application is one method of screening (see Bass, Curlette, Kern, & McWilliams, 2002; Crandall, 1991). But program coordinators also should keep their eyes open for the characteristics that are common among the best mentors in their respective programs. I once assumed outgoing, socially engaging mentors would be superior until I learned that those adolescents also get involved in other activities that lessen their ability to be consistent mentors (Karcher, in press).

Program Practices and Activities

How can program coordinators enhance the likelihood that cross-age peer mentoring, as one type of chance encounter, positively influences the life paths of youth involved? First, coordinators can work to avoid coercive, inflexible program practices that may lead older peer mentors to create "closed social systems wielding strong coercive and rewarding power" (Bandura, 1982, p. 750) in several ways, including (a) emphasizing the importance of an empathic, supportive relationship over an emphasis on task completion; (b) training the adolescent mentors to use effective discipline and encouragement practices that minimize the likelihood that mentors will use coercive, manipulating behaviors to get mentees to behave or participate; and (c) actively monitoring and publicly acknowledging the mentors' use of assertive (rather than aggressive) and empathic communication.

Bandura (1982) made three sets of recommendations that may help coordinators create cross-age mentoring relationships that "affect life paths through the reciprocal influence of personal and social factors" (p. 750). The first is to match youth who have experiences and interests in common. Such interest lists can be found in materials available from Public/Private Ventures and MENTOR.

Second, coordinators can capitalize on the interpersonal attraction between the two individuals. One way to do this is to use a matching process in which a group of mentors and potential mentees interact through game play, discussion, and other activities as a way to get acquainted, and then to let them both indicate with whom they would most like to be matched.

In one study (Karcher, 2005), 80% of the mentees and mentors chose each other as a first or second choice after only a few hours interacting with each other. Given the research finding that when adolescent mentors were inconsistent and regularly absent, their mentees were more likely to feel less attractive over time, and that "interpersonal attraction seals chance encounters into lasting bonds" (Bandura, 1982, p. 750), program coordinators should closely supervise mentor and mentee attendance in order to avoid either person feeling rejected. When mentors begin to miss mentoring meetings or events, they should be reminded about the impact of absenteeism on mentees' self-esteem, and if the problem is not corrected, then a formal termination ritual should be conducted to impress upon the child that he or she is not at fault for the failing relationship (see Lakes & Karcher, 2002). Of course, mentors should be trained in the importance of evoking in their mentees' feelings of esteem, importance, and attractiveness.

Third, Bandura emphasized the central role of individuals' prior experiences and capacity to relate to others. Mentors may benefit from being taught that children differ in their receptivity to caring from others and that often children who have experienced rejection in the past may appear the least interested in engaging in a close, mutually supportive relationship. Mentors should be encouraged to reflect on their own as well as their mentees' (a) capacity for connecting with others; (b) need for affiliation, closeness, and someone with whom to identify; and (c) compatibility in terms of values (e.g., Is one strongly conventional while the other antagonistic toward authority or school?). In sum, adolescent mentors may need help to cognitively understand that their mentees' observable actions may not truly convey their feelings, that some children will be more or less open to a caring, supportive relationship, and that they too may wrestle with issues of trust, intimacy, or sensitivity to rejection that complicate their own experiences of the mentoring relationship.

Guidelines for Effective and Ethical Practice

When cross-age peer mentoring program coordinators begin to consider which practices to emphasize in their programs, in addition to the recommendations based on theory and research made above, four specific sources may be of particular interest. Two are drawn from the larger mentoring literature. These are the *Elements of Effective Practice,* which are available on the Web site of the National Mentoring Partnership, and the best practices identified through DuBois, Holloway, et al.'s (2002) meta-analytic review of theoretically and empirically derived practices. These will not be reviewed here. However, many of the practices may be even more important for cross-age mentors given their general level of maturity. Fortunately, one of the advantages of having adolescent mentors on-site, such as in school-based settings, is that it affords program coordinators more control over program practices, recruiting, selecting, training, and supervision.

Although not specifically focused on cross-age mentoring, cross-age peer helping and peer tutoring materials may provide useful ideas about training and supervision. On the Web site of the National Peer Helpers Association are their *Standards and Ethics* and *Programmatic Standards Checklist*. Also useful is the research and training literature on peer tutoring (e.g., Topping & Ehly, 1998) and peer helping (National Helpers Network, 1998). However, I recommend that readers focus on the *cross-age* peer helping and tutoring literature. Same-age helping, tutoring, and counseling programs present a unique set of developmental and peer dynamics that may not be appropriate for or generalize to cross-age relationships.

FUTURE DIRECTIONS

Synthesis

Older peers helping nurture their younger peers' growth is not a new practice. Yet it is becoming less and less common, especially for children without older siblings. Cross-age peer mentoring may serve the functions previously met by those natural peer mentoring relationships, but it has a long way to go to fully differentiate itself from peer tutoring, peer helping, and peer counseling. This demarcation may be achieved by emphasizing its uniquely developmental focus. Most recently structured peer interventions have focused either on tutoring academic skills or remediating social or behavioral problems. Cross-age peer mentoring, as a longer-term, relationship-focused intervention, can complement these other peer interventions, providing an intervention uniquely well suited to facilitate developmental outcomes such as connectedness to school, prosocial bonding, social skills, and self-esteem. However, cross-age peer mentoring lags behind its sibling interventions in terms of supporting research and tested practices. Therefore, until a sufficient empirical base exists to recommend specific practices and approaches, program coordinators and researchers alike would do well to rely on developmental theory as a guide and look to other cross-age interventions for ideas about how best to facilitate reciprocally satisfying mentoring relationships between older and younger youth.

Recommendations for Research

1. *Conduct rigorous efficacy trials.* Given the neophyte status of the research base on cross-age peer mentoring, a critical first step is to attempt to conduct efficacy trails that reflect the criteria described by DuBois and Silverthorn (this volume). Once general efficacy is better understood, further research may examine variations in formats and populations served.

2. *Examine effects on peer networks.* Sometimes cross-age peer mentoring is conducted one-on-one away from other youth. More often, perhaps especially when conducted in schools, cross-age peer mentoring may be conducted in a group format. To understand the effects of such programs on the larger peer networks at a school, it may be useful to study whether cross-age peer mentoring effects changes in mentors and mentees' peer networks. There may be an effect of program format such as that the outcomes of one-on-one cross-age mentoring differ depending on whether it is conducted in the context of other peers (a group format). Harris (1998) might predict a negative effect of such a group format. Cross-age mentors may become distracted by their peers (and less attentive to their mentees), bothered by their peers in the program (resulting in mentor attrition), or instigated by deviant peers (who then undermine the conventional structure of the program). Conversely, considering the normative social and cognitive-developmental needs of the mentors, it may be that having their own, same-age peers involved as fellow mentors and mentees changes the interpersonal dynamics (e.g., making peers into friends) in positive ways that affect the overall climate of a school. Such change might occur through an expansion of social network, changes in membership, or shifts in attitudes held by peer networks linked to the mentoring program. A group format also may increase or satisfy mentors' specific motivations, thereby facilitating longer matches that may mediate outcomes for both mentees and mentors.

3. *Investigate the developmental benefits of cross-age peer mentoring for subgroups of adolescent mentors.* The benefits of facilitating relationship development within a positive peer culture may be significantly greater for some mentees and mentors than others. For example, youth who are less frequently nominated as liked by their peers may benefit most from structured opportunities to interact with peers from whom they might otherwise feel rejected. For example, the Social Type Rating Scale procedure described by Brown and Lohr (1987) might be used to identify subgroups of youth (e.g., more or less popular, conventional, or academically oriented) and test group status as a moderator of program effects. Other moderators of outcomes may include personality traits, such as extroversion versus introversion, or shared experience/experiences (Bandura's hypothesis). For example, research could examine whether cross-age peer mentoring is more useful for youth experiencing similar challenges (e.g., Bettencourt et al., 1998) and test the observation-based conclusion of Karcher and Lindwall (2003) that extroverted mentors appeared more likely than their introverted peers to overcommit to other extracurricular activities, leading them to be absent more often and thereby negatively affecting mentee outcomes. Other important moderators remain untested as well. How might age, sex, and age span differences between mentors and mentees contribute to program effectiveness or

to the satisfaction of mentees and mentors in cross-age peer mentoring?

4. *Examine interactions between format and youth characteristics.* Often, program effects are revealed through interactions. It could be instructive to examine the interaction between the effects of program format (e.g., group or isolated dyads) and the effects of either (a) serving as or (b) having a cross-age peer mentor for different kinds of youth. For instance, introverted youth mentors and mentees may prefer and benefit more from one-on-one programs. Conversely, extroverted and outgoing youth may prefer but not benefit as much from the group format.

5. *Examine the effects of training and supervision.* Little is known about the training that youth mentors receive, let alone the effects of such training on mentors' persistence, mentees' experience, or program outcomes. Critical to know is whether, as argued above, ongoing mentor training and supervision are more important for cross-age peer mentors than for adult mentors (DuBois, Holloway, et al., 2002). If so, schools might want to consider providing course credit to ensure that mentors receive ongoing training and support. Despite the burgeoning interest in the civic development of youth, the instatement of mentor classes for credit is not likely to occur in an era of high-stakes testing unless it can be shown that both mentors and mentees benefit in some significant and lasting way from receiving ongoing training and support.

6. *Examine what effective matches do.* "Activities or no activities?" This is the question. Some evidence suggests that the greater the amount of structure provided to peer tutors, the more effective they are and the more the tutors themselves get out of the process (King et al., 1998). Research on cross-age peer mentoring should examine two basic questions: (a) Are program effects larger when mentors use structured activities with their mentees? For example, are mentors who also provide academic help or encouragement more effective than youth mentors who focus only on the mentee's personal life? (b) If so, what kinds of activities are most effective?

Recommendations for Practice

1. *Structure programs to meet the developmental needs of mentees and mentors.* Young children, often unaware of their own desires and wants until pressed to articulate them, enjoy fun, physical, rule-based play activities. Adolescents more often seek interaction with their peers, opportunities to explore and learn about what makes themselves unique, and contexts in which they can receive attention and praise. Programs that do not include opportunities for both of these developmentally appropriate expressions of perspective-taking skills may be more likely to frustrate mentors, mentees, or both. This may lessen the likelihood that a positive bond develops between the mentee and the mentor, the program, or its staff. Viewing cross-age peer mentoring as a developmental intervention may be vital to its success (see Selman, 2003).

2. *Screen for mentors who are most likely to persist.* Three constructs and related measures were introduced in this chapter as potential tools for screening mentors: social interest (Crandall, 1991), connectedness (Karcher, 2005), and the functions of volunteering (Omoto & Snyder, 1995). In addition, identifying a local, program-specific set of variables that predict mentors' persistence and effectiveness also may require interviewing or observing mentors across multiple years. Because each program will differ in program structure and population served, it is difficult to make general statements about what elements of programs motivate and satisfy mentors who will differ in age, cultural background, or geographic locale.

3. *Supervise, train, evaluate, and recognize.* There are the four pillars upon which effective (and safe) cross-age peer mentoring programs are most firmly built. *Supervision:* Peer programs supervised by nontrained professionals may put children at risk. *Training:* Some ways of training peer mentors may be better than others. *Evaluation:* Without evaluation, coordinators won't know what they are doing right or for whom. For example, an evaluation may reveal that a program is most effective for youth who are at lower risk for behavioral or academic problems and for youth who want mentors. It would be a travesty to continue to recruit

uninterested, high-risk youth when they get little out of it and end up frustrating the other half of your clients—the mentors. Only ongoing evaluation can reveal such effects. *Recognition:* Adolescent mentors may reap greater benefits from recognition events than do adult mentors. For youth, such events may increase self-esteem, self-efficacy, and social status and facilitate the development of their identities or self-images as helping, caring individuals.

4. *Minimize opportunities for engaging in authority-undermining behaviors.* Peers can be powerful influencing agents. In the absence of supervision, guidance, and consequences for unconventional or anti-authority behaviors or attitudes, peer programs run the risk of instilling the exact beliefs and promoting the kinds of behaviors they are intended to prevent. It is recommended that program coordinators discourage authority-undermining statements and behaviors by actively structuring opportunities and rewarding behaviors that are consistent with developmentally crucial social skills (empathy, cooperation, self-control) and positive connections to adults (e.g., parents and teachers), school, and school-related activities.

REFERENCES

Abbott, R. D., O'Donnell, J., Hawkins, J. D., Hill, K. G., Kosterman, R., & Catalano, R. F. (1998). Changing teaching practices to promote achievement and bonding to school. *American Journal of Orthopsychiatry, 68,* 542–552.

Adler, A. (1964). *Superiority and social interest.* New York: Norton.

Bandura, A. (1982). The psychology of chance encounters and life paths. *American Psychologist, 37,* 747–755.

Bass, M. L., Curlette, W. M., Kern, R. M., & McWilliams, A. E. (2002). Social interest: A meta-analysis of a multidimensional construct. *Journal of Individual Psychology, 58*(1), 4–34.

Bettencourt, T., Hodges, A., Humba, G. J., & Pickett, G. (1998). Bay Area Positives: A model of a youth based approach to HIV/AIDS services. *Journal of Adolescent Health, 23,* 28–36.

Brody, G. H., Kim, S., Murry, V. M., & Brown, A. C. (2003). Longitudinal direct and indirect pathways linking older sibling competence to the development of younger sibling competence. *Developmental Psychology, 39,* 618–628.

Brown, B. B., & Lohr, M. J. (1987). Peer-group affiliation and adolescent self-esteem: An integration of ego-identity and symbolic-interaction theories. *Journal of Personality and Social Psychology, 52,* 47–55.

Burrell, B., Wood, S. J., Pikes, T., & Holliday, C. (2001). Student mentors and protégés learning together. *Teaching Exceptional Children, 3*(3), 24–29.

Chodorow, E. (1978). *The reproduction of mothering.* Berkeley: University of California Press.

Clary, E. G., Snyder, M., Ridge, R. D., Copeland, J., Stukas, A. A., Haugen, J., et al. (1998). Understanding and assessing the motivations of volunteers: A functional approach. *Journal of Personality and Social Psychology, 4,* 1516–1530.

Coca-Cola Youth Partnership. (2002). Coca-Cola Valued Youth (para. 4). Retrieved May 14, 2003, from http://www.youthdevelopment.coca-cola.com/ach_ccvy.html

Crandall, J. E. (1991). A scale for social interest. *Individual Psychology, 47,* 108–114.

Damon, W. (1984). Peer education: The untapped potential. *Journal of Applied Developmental Psychology, 5,* 331–343.

Dennison, S. (2000). A win-win peer mentoring and tutoring program: A collaborative model. *The Journal of Primary Prevention, 20,* 161–174.

Dishion, T. J., McCord, J., & Poulin, F. (1999). When interventions harm: Peer groups and problem behavior. *American Psychologist, 54,* 755–764.

DuBois, D. L., Holloway, B. E., Valentine, J. C., & Cooper, H. (2002). Effectiveness of mentoring programs for youth: A meta-analytic review. *American Journal of Community Psychology, 30,* 157–197.

DuBois, D. L., Neville, H. A., Parra, G. R., & Pugh-Lilly, A. O. (2002). Testing a new model of mentoring. In G. G. Noam (Ed. in chief) & J. E. Rhodes (Ed.), *A critical view of youth mentoring (New Directions for Youth Development: Theory, Research, and Practice, No. 93,* pp. 21–57). San Francisco: Jossey-Bass.

Erikson, E. H. (1968). *Identity: Youth and crisis.* New York: Norton.

General Accounting Office. (2004, June). *Student mentoring programs: Education's monitoring and information sharing could be improved*

(Report to Congressional Requesters). Washington, DC: Author.

Gibbs, J. C., Potter, G. B., Barriga, A. Q., & Liau, A. K. (1996). Developing the helping skills and prosocial motivation of aggressive adolescents in peer group programs. *Aggression & Violent Behavior, 1*, 283–305.

Grossman, J. B., & Rhodes, J. E. (2002). The test of time: Predictors and effects of duration in youth mentoring programs. *American Journal of Community Psychology, 30*, 199–219.

Hansen, K. (2003). *Big Brothers Big Sisters High School Bigs evaluation for school year 2002–2003.* Philadelphia: Big Brothers Big Sisters of America.

Harris, J. (1998). *The nurture assumption.* New York: Free Press.

Hirschi, T. (1969). *Causes of delinquency.* Berkeley: University of California Press.

Howe, N., & Ross, H. S. (1990). Socialization, perspective-taking, and the sibling relationship. *Developmental Psychology, 26*, 160–165.

Hritz, S. A., & Gabow, P. A. (1997). A peer approach to high risk youth. *Journal of Adolescent Health, 20*, 259–260.

Jessor, R., & Jessor, S. L. (1977). *Problem behavior and psychological development: A longitudinal study of youth.* New York: Academic Press.

Karcher, M. J. (2005). The effects of school-based developmental mentoring and mentors' attendance on mentees' self-esteem, behavior, and connectedness. *Psychology in the Schools, 42*, 65–78.

Karcher, M. J. (in press). What happens when high school mentors don't show up? In L. Golden & P. Henderson (Eds.), *Case studies in school counseling.* Alexandria, VA: ACA Press.

Karcher, M. J., Davis, C., & Powell, B. (2002). Developmental mentoring in the schools: Testing connectedness as a mediating variable in the promotion of academic achievement. *The School Community Journal, 12*(2), 36–52.

Karcher, M. J., & Lindwall, J. (2003). Social interest, connectedness, and challenging experiences. What makes high school mentors persist? *Journal of Individual Psychology, 59*, 293–315.

Karcher, M. J., Nakkula, M. J., & Harris, J. (in press). Developmental mentoring match characteristics: The effects of mentors' efficacy and mentees' emotional support seeking on the perceived quality of mentoring relationships. *Journal of Primary Prevention.*

Kindermann, T. A. (1993). Natural peer groups as contexts for individual development: The case of children's motivation in school. *Developmental Psychology, 29*, 970–977.

King, A., Staffeiri, A., & Adelgais, A. (1998). Mutual peer tutoring: Effects of structuring tutorial interaction to scaffold peer learning. *Journal of Educational Psychology, 90*, 134–152.

Kohut, H., & Wolf, E. S. (1978). The disorders of the self and their treatment: An outline. *International Journal of Psycho-Analysis, 59*(4), 413–425.

Lakes, K., & Karcher, M. J. (2002). *Mentee-mentor termination ritual in developmental mentoring: The Children with Adolescent Mentors Program (CAMP).* Unpublished manuscript, University of Texas at San Antonio.

Lane-Garon, P. (1998). Developmental considerations: Encouraging perspective taking in student mediators. *Mediation Quarterly, 16*, 201–217.

Lewis, C., & Henney, S. (2003). *Teen Mentoring Initiative: Semi-annual report Spring 2003.* Unpublished manuscript, University of Texas at Austin.

Lewis, M. W., & Lewis, A. C. (1996). Peer helping programs: Helper role, supervisor training, and suicidal behavior. *Journal of Counseling & Development, 74*, 307–313.

Morey, R. E., & Miller, C. D. (1993). High school peer counseling: The relationship between student satisfaction and peer counselors' style of helping. *Professional Counselor, 40*, 293–301.

National Helpers Network. (1998). *Learning helpers: A guide to training and reflection.* New York: National Helpers Network.

National Peer Helpers Association. (2004). National Peer Helpers Association. Retrieved June 21, 2004, from http://www2.peerhelping.org/about/

Noll, V. (1997). Cross-age mentoring program for social skills development. *The School Counselor, 44*, 239–242.

O'Donnell, J., & Michalak, E. A. (1997). Inner-city youths helping children: After school programs to promote bonding and reduce risk. *Social Work in Education, 19*, 231–242.

Omoto, A. M., & Snyder, M. (1995). Sustained helping without obligation: Motivation, longevity of service, and perceived attitude change among AIDS volunteers. *Journal of Personality and Social Psychology, 68*, 671–686.

Parra, G. R., DuBois, D. L., Neville, H. A., Pugh-Lilly, A. O., & Povinelli, N. (2002). Mentoring relationships for youth: Investigation of a process-oriented model. *Journal of Community Psychology, 30,* 367–388.

Patterson, G. R., Dishion, T. J., & Yoerger, K. (2000). Adolescent growth in new forms of problem behavior: Macro- and micro-peer dynamics. *Prevention Science, 1,* 3–13.

Peer Assistance and Leadership. (2004). PAL Peer Assistance and Leadership. Retrieved June 12, 2004, from http://www.pantexas.org/index.html

Powell, M. A. (1997). Peer tutoring and mentoring services for disadvantaged secondary school students. *California Research Bureau Note, 4*(2), 1–10.

Pyatt, G. (2002). Cross-school mentoring: Training and implementing a peer mentoring strategy. *Mentoring & Tutoring, 10,* 171–177.

Rhodes, J. E., Grossman, J. B., & Resch, N. L. (2000). Agents of change: Pathways through which mentoring relationships influence adolescents' academic achievement. *Child Development, 71,* 1662–1671.

Sawyer, R. D. (2001). Mentoring but not being mentored: Improving student-to-student mentoring programs to attract urban youth to teaching. *Urban Education, 36,* 39–59.

Selman, R. L. (1980). *The growth of interpersonal understanding: Developmental and clinical analyses.* New York: Academic Press.

Selman, R. L. (2003). *The promotion of social awareness: Powerful lessons from the partnership of developmental theory and classroom practice.* New York: Russell Sage Foundation.

Sheehan, K., DiCara, J. A., LeBailly, S., & Christoffel, K. K. (1999). Adapting the gang model: Peer mentoring for violence prevention. *Pediatrics, 104,* 50–54.

Stukas, A. A., Clary, G. E., & Snyder, M. (1999). Service learning: Who benefits and why. *Social Policy Report: Society for Research in Child Development, 13*(4), 1–20.

Substance Abuse and Mental Health Services Administration. (2004). SAMHSA Model Programs. Retrieved July 20, 2004, from http://modelprograms.samhsa.gov

Sullivan, H. S. (1953). *The interpersonal theory of psychiatry.* New York: Norton.

Topping, K., & Ehly, S. W. (1998). *Peer-assisted learning.* Mahwah, NJ: Erlbaum.

Topping, K., & Whiteley, M. (1993). Sex differences in the effectiveness of peer tutoring. *School Psychology International, 14,* 57–67.

Tucker, C. J., McHale, S. M., & Crouter, A. C. (2001). Conditions of sibling support in adolescence. *Journal of Family Psychology, 15,* 254–271.

Van Lange, P. A. M., Otten, W., De Bruin, E. M. N., & Joireman, J. A. (1997). Development of prosocial, individualistic, and competitive orientations: Theory and preliminary evidence. *Journal of Personality and Social Psychology, 73,* 733–746.

Vygotsky, L. S. (1978). *Mind in society.* Cambridge, MA: Harvard University Press.

Washington-Steward, E. (2000). *10,000 Tutors Partnership Program evaluation.* Retrieved February 28, 2003, from http://www.timedollar tutoring.org/

Westerman, J. J. (2002). *Mentoring and cross-age mentoring: Improving academic achievement through a unique partnership.* Unpublished dissertation, University of Kentucky, Lexington.

Wright, L., & Borland, J. H. (1992). A special friend: Adolescent mentors for young, economically disadvantaged, potentially gifted students. *Roeper Review, 14,* 124–129.

19

INTERGENERATIONAL MENTORING

ANDREA S. TAYLOR, LEONARD LOSCIUTO,
AND LORRAINE PORCELLINI

INTRODUCTION

The United States is in the midst of a demographic transformation, which has tremendous potential to enhance the lives of individuals and strengthen communities across the country. Currently, the fastest-growing segment of the population is older adults (age 65-plus), who are also the healthiest, most active, and best educated in our history. At the same time we are experiencing an explosion of potential human resources at one end of the age spectrum, we are also witnessing a drain of potential human resources at the other end—a loss unparalleled at any time in our history. More than 14 million young people in the United States are growing up in adverse circumstances, often living in poverty, with the potential for school failure, engaging in delinquent behavior, substance abuse and early, risky sexual activity (Center on an Aging Society, 2003).

Mentoring is a strategy for meeting the needs of high-risk youth that is gaining increased attention from practitioners, policymakers, and funding agencies. The challenges are many, but one very obvious challenge revolves around identifying a sufficient number of qualified individuals who can mentor the millions of young people in need of positive adult support. At a time when children, youth, and families need more

help, research suggests that civic engagement, defined as involvement in the community, appears to be declining (Putnam, 2000). One reason is that greater numbers of women in the workforce and increased work hours of employed individuals have contributed to a decrease in the number of people available to volunteer. Another reason appears to be the weakening of the "social compact," the reciprocal ties that hold families, governance, and society together over time (Cornman & Kingson, 1999). Communities are torn apart by violence, crime, and interracial tension; families are strained by poverty, disorganization, and disruption of the caregiving role; and the economic disparity between the wealthy and the poor is growing (Reich, 1999). All of these factors contribute to a societal mistrust and apathy that seems to inhibit the sense of community and connectedness required for a strong and enduring social fabric (Scales, 2003).

Involvement in mentoring is one way to expand volunteer opportunities and thereby enhance civic engagement. The ever-increasing number of older adults are in an ideal position to act as mentors. They have time available, a lifetime of experience in work and caring for family, and are also striving for an enhanced sense of generativity as they age (Erikson, Erikson, & Kivnick, 1986). Historically, in many cultures, grandparents and other older adults naturally have played a key role in mentoring young people, especially in the African American, Latino, and American Indian communities. Older people were the "keepers of the meaning" (Vaillant, 2002) and passed on cultural and family traditions. Even among European American families, multigeneration households were not uncommon, and informal mentoring occurred through this network of relationships.

Programmatic intergenerational mentoring, however, is a recent phenomenon. The concept of mobilizing older adults as volunteers in significant numbers was the dream of President John Kennedy, whose vision was to "add life to the years" of older adults by providing meaningful opportunities for service. Today, the Corporation for National Service, a federal agency created in 1993, oversees a number of national programs that have demonstrated the valuable role that older adults can play in the lives of children, youth, and families (Freedman, 1999). The formal youth mentoring movement can also benefit from the increasing numbers of committed older adults.

This chapter will begin by reviewing the theoretical constructs that suggest why older adults may be especially well suited to be mentors and that reveal the age-related dynamics that can positively affect the bond an older adult has with a protégé. A review of the existing research on intergenerational mentoring will be presented that includes a discussion of how future research might be more theoretical than has characterized past research in this area. The chapter will also identify the ways in which research has informed intergenerational mentoring practice and the important considerations it raises for implementation of effective models.

THEORY

Although there is an ever-increasing number of intergenerational programs worldwide, there are still very few well-researched conceptual and theoretical models supporting them (Kuehne, 2003), which makes understanding the unique aspects of the intergenerational mentoring relationship a complex task. A theoretical framework for intergenerational mentoring can be delineated in terms of the developmental needs of older adults and youth and both the common and unique aspects of their ages and experience, especially cultural issues, that might be relevant to an understanding of intergenerational relationships. The five theoretical perspectives presented in this section may help us better understand the connection between youth and elders.

Generativity

In 1950, the psychologist Erik Erikson introduced the concept of generativity as the seventh of eight stages of human development and the life cycle. *Generativity* refers to the capacity of adults to care for family, community, and institutions; to preserve and pass on cultural traditions; and to produce products, outcomes, and ideas that will survive the self and become a legacy for future generations. As described by Erikson (1968), generativity is the "concern for establishing and guiding the next generation." Generativity is also captured by the phrase "I am what survives of me" (Erikson et al., 1986). Previous authors have suggested that the need to be "generative" as people age is a key factor in motivating older adults to get involved in the lives of youth who are not necessarily related to them (Freedman, 1988, 1999; Rhodes, 2002; Taylor & Bressler, 2000). Failure to be generative in later life, they argue, results in "stagnation," characterized by self-absorption, isolation, and disappointing personal relationships, which ultimately affects the resolution of the eighth stage in Erikson's life span model, in which the task is to develop a sense of integrity and wisdom strong enough to withstand the physical declines and challenges of old age (Erikson et al., 1986). Although generativity usually begins as early as one's 30s and is often, although not exclusively, associated with child rearing, it appears from research on generative behavior throughout the adult life span to be strongest for midlife and older adults (McAdams & de St. Aubin, 1998).

Mentoring, therefore, theoretically can provide an opportunity for an older adult to share skills and knowledge with a young person and, in so doing, validate his or her life experience, which research suggests is necessary for self-acceptance and the successful achievement of "integrity." Research suggests that nurturing, giving, and serving others—all hallmarks of effective mentoring relationships—contribute to greater ego integrity, personal happiness, and overall well-being (Sheldon & Kasser, 2001). It may be, therefore, that older adults in the mentoring role are fulfilling their own developmental needs while contributing to others' development (Kuehne, 2003; VanderVen, 1999). There currently exists a significant body of research on the generative actions of midlife and older adults suggesting that people who are engaged in volunteering in the community, for example, tend to be happier, and feel better about themselves and more positively toward others (McAdams & de St. Aubin, 1998). There is nothing, however, that specifically addresses the content of generative participation and the satisfaction that people feel doing one type of activity versus another.

Developmental Tasks of Older Adults and Youth

Effective mentoring relationships theoretically also depend on reciprocity (Philip, Shucksmith, & King, 2004). It might be useful, therefore, to extrapolate from Erikson's unidirectional notion of generativity and think in terms of reciprocal and shared needs. Newman, Ward, Smith, Wilson, and McCrea (1997) suggested that the developmental stages of children and youth parallel those of older adults, which makes youth and older adults well suited as partners in intergenerational initiatives. The question of "Who am I in this life?" that preoccupies adolescents, for example, mirrors the question of "What have I done with my life?" that predominates the later years of adulthood. This type of similarity may help facilitate the relationship between an older adult and a teen based on their mutual developmental needs.

Shared Social Status

Mutuality of experience also may contribute to unique dynamics within intergenerational mentor-protégé pairs. In Rhodes's (2002) model of youth mentoring, interpersonal history is a moderator that can influence the development of the relationship. It has been suggested that youth and elders experience the same marginalized status in society, one that encourages empathy and understanding between them and helps promote a bond that leads to effective relationships (Freedman, 1988; Newman, Ward, Smith, Wilson, & McCrea, 1997).

Contextually based social learning theory (e.g., Blechman, 1992) might provide further insight in the essential elements within the intergenerational mentor-protégé bond. This theory emphasizes the importance of mentors being "biculturally competent," that is, competent in the culture of the individual family and that of the larger community. For a youth from a low-income family with multiple risk factors, a mentor with bicultural skills can be invaluable in helping a protégé navigate successfully in his or her immediate environment while also being able to take advantage of what the larger world has to offer (Rhodes, 2002). Older adults who have learned to manage in both worlds may therefore make the most effective mentors for high-risk youth (Freedman, 1988). It would appear that experiences of marginalization might be a moderator of the effectiveness of intergenerational mentor-youth relationships.

Cultural Factors

Intergenerational mentoring relationships also may be moderated by cultural factors, including those related to race and ethnicity. For example, the grandparent role is more salient in ethnic minority groups than in the dominant culture (Barresi, 1987). In African American and Latino communities, extended family and even neighbors and friends traditionally have played an important role in raising children and providing support (Burton & Dilworth-Anderson, 1991; Hirsch, Mickus, & Boerger, 2002). These prior relationships could be helpful in establishing the legitimacy of an older adult as a mentor among youth from these groups.

The relationship between age and cultural values, however, may be group specific. Traditionally, older adults in American Indian societies have been revered and respected. However, due to substance abuse and serious chronic illness, American Indian elders over the age of 65 make up only 5.6% of the total Indian population, as opposed to 12% in the general U.S. population (Jones-Saumty, 2002). Therefore, in many American Indian communities, the term *elder* refers not to chronological age, but to someone who has taken on a leadership role. Cultural factors also might contribute to parents' acceptance of an older adult. As noted, in African American, Latino, and American Indian communities, older adults are more likely to play a central role and earn a degree of respect not enjoyed by older people in many European American communities. Grandparents and extended kin also play an important role in many Asian cultures, but care for family members stays within the family or clan and is often not well received from "strangers" outside the family unit (Weinstein-Shr & Henkin, 1991).

Social Networks

Another theory relevant to efforts to understand factors affecting the efficacy of mentoring and also relevant to intergenerational relationships is social network theory (e.g., Zippay, 1995). This theory emphasizes the benefits of social networks in helping youth gain access to the individuals, activities, and resources they need to constructively move forward in their development. By sharing their own networks of friends and colleagues, exposing youth to new ideas, and helping them set goals, mentors can help protégés discover a wider world. Because older mentors may be likely to have relatively extensive and more developed social networks, effects mediated through networking processes could be particularly salient within intergenerational mentoring and potentially enhance its effectiveness relative to mentoring provided by younger persons.

RESEARCH

To date, only modest evidence of the positive effects of intergenerational mentoring has been reported, but there appear to be several reasons for this. First, despite the proliferation of

mentoring programs across the country, very few target older adults as mentors. Therefore, there is not a huge body of work from which to draw, and the methodologies used to study those that do exist are not without problems. DuBois, Holloway, Valentine, and Cooper (2002) came to the same conclusion in their meta-analysis of 55 evaluations of mentoring programs. Inconsistent and null findings from the extant literature on intergenerational mentoring may be attributed in part to the newness of the mentoring field and the methodological flaws that have not been sufficiently addressed and in part to the issue of program longevity. To be successful, the mentor-protégé relationship should be in place at least 6 months, preferably 12 months or more, with frequent contact (Grossman, 1999). In general, most studies are funded for too short a time to see positive effects, and this is true for many intergenerational mentoring programs as well that appear to be relatively small and short-lived (Greim, 1992). The small number of intergenerational mentoring programs might be attributed to negative stereotypes and attitudes toward older adults held by practitioners and a general lack of awareness about the numbers of older people and their potential contributions to the community. In addition, recruitment of adults older than 55 years of age is challenging and requires resources and creative strategies (Taylor & Bressler, 2000). Given these constraints on effective research on intergenerational mentoring, much of what has been written in the literature has been presented in the form of qualitative and anecdotal evidence. Even though most mentoring relationships until very recently developed through informal, naturally occurring connections with youth (McLearn, Colasanto, & Schoen, 1998), few formal evaluations of naturally occurring intergenerational mentoring have been conducted, and none compare naturally occurring intergenerational mentoring with programmatic intergenerational mentoring.

Qualitative Studies

The first appearance in the literature of older adult mentors was Freedman's (1988) qualitative examination of five intergenerational mentoring programs. In his study, the most effective mentors appeared to be older adults who themselves had endured strained family relationships, battled personal problems, and struggled to overcome many major challenges in their lives. The qualitative findings of this study therefore are consistent with the theoretical potential noted previously for mutuality of experience (shared history and developmental needs) and shared marginalization to be among the moderators of effective intergenerational mentor-protégé relationships (see "Theory" section above).

In another qualitative study, Public/Private Ventures (Styles & Morrow, 1992) examined the relationships formed between elders (55 or older) and at-risk youth (12–17) at four Linking Lifetimes intergenerational mentoring demonstration sites developed by Temple University's Center for Intergenerational Learning. In-person, semistructured interviews were conducted with 26 pairs of mentor/youth 3.5 months after being matched, and again approximately 9 months later. The intent of this project was not to measure outcomes, but instead to identify well-functioning mentoring relationships, defined as those in which both members were satisfied, thus suggesting that a strong bond had been formed. Relationships best meeting these criteria were those that appeared to be youth driven in timing, content, and activity selection. Mentors in relationships identified as well functioning were those who appeared to be active listeners and who tailored the interaction to what they learned from youth. It appeared that these mentors tended not to be critical of youth, but instead offered problem-solving strategies that youth found useful.

Quantitative Studies

Four quantitative studies of intergenerational mentoring in high-risk youth programs have provided some insight into the efficacy of intergenerational mentoring and the challenges with regard to research designs and methods. Given the difficulty of implementing evaluation designs in the field, it is not surprising that each of the studies is flawed to some extent, nor is it surprising that all encountered some of the same difficulties in design or execution. In each case, the choice of schools or other primary units was necessarily dictated by pragmatic considerations, such as available contacts or willingness to participate. The negative effects or potential bias of purposive sampling, however, may be mitigated to the extent that the programs chosen are "typical" of the intended universe, but this, of course, is a judgment call. Other common difficulties, such as attrition and "program dosage" varied in extent and severity across the studies and are discussed below as they affected each.

Across Ages, developed by Temple University's Center for Intergenerational Learning, is a multidimensional program that combines mentoring, social competence training, and community service and is one of the few programs that utilize only older adults (55 and older) as mentors. The initial evaluation of the program, conducted by the Institute for Survey Research (ISR) from 1991 to 1995 (LoSciuto, Rajala, Townsend, & Taylor, 1996), employed a randomized pretest-posttest control group design (Campbell & Stanley, 1996). In this study, 562 participants from three middle schools in the inner city of Philadelphia were assigned randomly to one of three groups: (a) Program & Mentoring, those who participated in the full program including mentoring; (b) Program Only, those who participated in the full program excluding mentoring; and (c) Control Group, no intervention. Compared with Program Only and Control youth, the mentees in the Program & Mentoring group showed statistically significant positive outcomes on attitudes toward school and the future and on attitudes toward older adults. In addition to these measures, mentees showed more positive outcomes than the Control Group on measures of alcohol, tobacco, and drugs (ATOD) knowledge, self-perception, community service, and knowledge about older people. Although mentees fared better than the Control Group on the latter scale, Program Only youth scored more positively than mentees. Compared with both the Control Group and the Program Only youth, mentees showed improved school attendance and decreases in school suspension. Compared with those whose mentors were less involved, youth whose mentors were highly involved (i.e., spent 6 or more hours with them per week) showed significant positive differences on 5 of the 11 outcome measures (absenteeism; attitudes toward school, future, and elders; attitudes toward older people; reactions to situations involving drug use; and knowledge about substance abuse). In addition, the process data revealed that relationships lasting a year or more, in which the pairs met consistently and youth achieved certain benchmarks established together with their mentors, were those in which there was the most parental involvement in the program, as indicated by participation in program activities and communication with staff and mentors. Parents appeared to be receptive to an older adult in the mentoring role because they viewed this person as "another grandparent" who was perceived to be a source of support rather than someone who would replace them or usurp their authority.

Although random assignment of students was implemented to rule out threats to internal validity and the outcome results were generally quite positive, the study was not without problem areas. First, as noted above, although the students were assigned randomly to each of the three groups, the findings may not be generalizable because the three middle schools were selected based on an estimated degree of risk for drug use of students and also on willingness of school officials to participate fully in the study. Detailed process logs were taken to check for possible effects of differential history (i.e., significant events that might differentially affect schools or classes). No such effects were uncovered. Because experimental and control groups were drawn from the same schools, contamination also was possible, such that program effects were transferred from the experimental subjects to the controls. Although there was no evidence for this as measured through process logs or student interviews, it still may have occurred. From a measurement perspective, perhaps the biggest constraint on the data was restriction of score range. Most students reported very positive (prosocial) attitudes and intentions on the pretest as well as very low drug use, so there was little room for positive change. In addition, during analysis, the significance testing described above might have been augmented by statistical power calculations in order to indicate relative magnitudes of the demonstrated effects.

As is usually the case, some students who completed the pretest did not take the posttest

for a variety of reasons, including transfers, dropouts, and illnesses. However, the attrition rate (23%) was not particularly high for such a study and, most important, was about the same for both the experimental and control groups. The study included a pretest at the beginning and a posttest at the end of the school year. It was not possible to take additional follow-up measures beyond this, although such testing is desirable to examine possible latency or decay of program effects.

The Across Ages model has been adopted by many agencies and organizations throughout the United States and therefore has been evaluated in other sites as well. An evaluation of an Across Ages program (Aseltine, Dupre, & Lamlein, 2000) in Springfield, Massachusetts, over a 3-year period included approximately 400 students in 10 middle schools. Ten sixth-grade classrooms were assigned randomly to one of the following three conditions: (a) Program Only, those who received a life skills curriculum and community service activities; (b) Program & Mentoring, those who received the same services but were also assigned a mentor; and (c) Control Group, those who received no intervention. Surveys were conducted at baseline, at the end of the school year (7–8 months after baseline), and again in 6 months after the program terminated. The author reported that attrition was minimal; more than 90% of the participants completed the posttest and the 6-month follow-up. A number of statistically significant differences at posttest were observed between the Program & Mentoring condition and the Program Only condition, suggesting that mentoring was the crucial intervention component. However, effect size calculations, generally ranging from a quarter to a third of a standard deviation, were indicative of modest program effects. It was reported that restriction of range due to very positive pretest scores was "challenging," and this constraint may have depressed measured program effects to some extent. Furthermore, at the 6-month follow-up, even these modest effect sizes were not found. The authors attributed this finding to the decay of program effects. The process data revealed, however, that mentors and youth were often together for only 6 to 8 months and that dosage was low, sometimes only 45 minutes to an hour each week. Previous researchers

(Grossman, 1999; Rhodes, 2002) have suggested this is not sufficient time to see long-lasting relationships and enduring effects.

Of the studies described in this section, only Aseltine et al. (2000) reported effect sizes as well as the results of significance testing. Because statistical significance testing is bound by the sample size and statistical significance testing alone does not provide an adequate assessment of the magnitude of program effects, effect sizes should routinely be presented so that the meaningfulness of a result can be better interpreted, as should estimates of the effect size that could have been detected given the size of the sample and other study parameters (DuBois, this volume).

As with the original Across Ages study described above, the initial selection of schools in the Aseltine et al. (2000) study was purposive rather than random, followed by random assignment of classes to experimental and control groups. Attrition was reported as minimal, but more than 25% of the youth in the mentor condition were dropped from the analysis because they did not receive the minimum level of exposure (or dosage), defined as at least 2 months of mentoring and more than five mentor contacts. Minimum exposure to the Program Only condition was defined as having attended as least one lesson each week of the 10-week curriculum; 15% of this group was dropped from the analysis. The authors reported the program effects to be short-lived, and power analyses showed the decay of program effects over time was not merely due to the smaller sample size in the 6-month follow-up. However, it was not clear whether other possible effects of differential dosage or attrition were examined in the data analysis. Also, the intervention stage lasted only 7 to 8 months. It is generally thought that interventions must be grounded in stable, long-term relationships and cultural values to have lasting success (Family Planning Council, 2003). This caveat may be especially relevant in attempting to measure program effects several months after the program is completed. No process data were presented, except to say that students, teachers, and parents liked the program and responded to it. Therefore, the possible influences of history (i.e., events specific to particular schools or classes) and diffusion of program effects from experimental to control students are unknown.

Another intergenerational mentoring program, the Abuelas y Jovenes Project, was administered and evaluated by the Family Planning Council (2003), in conjunction with Congreso des Latinos Unidos, Inc., and Temple University's Center for Intergenerational Learning. The project targeted pregnant and parenting females in Philadelphia, Pennsylvania, aged 18 or younger who were TANF (Temporary Assistance for Needy Families) recipients or TANF-eligible. The goal of the project was to test the efficacy of program-initiated mentoring relationships between elder mentors (*abuelas,* Spanish for grandmothers) and low-income adolescent mothers (*jovenes,* Spanish for granddaughters) against traditional case management services. Participants were randomly assigned to one of three groups: (a) Control Group, those who received standard services available to all pregnant teens in Philadelphia, $n = 62$; (b) Case Management Only, those who received one visit a month from professional cases managers and telephone contact as needed, $n = 83$; and (c) Case Management & Mentoring, those who received traditional case management plus two visits a month from an older adult mentor trained and supervised by staff from the Center for Intergenerational Learning, $n = 83$. The program used the Across Ages model and lasted for 24 months, during which participants provided self-report data at 6-month intervals on five behaviors: (a) use of alcohol, tobacco, and marijuana; (b) educational attainment; (c) repeat pregnancy and births; (d) parenting and communication skills; and (e) number of months on TANF. Although almost half of the 228 adolescents who took the baseline survey dropped out by the 24-month follow-up, no differential attrition effects across groups were found on any of the outcome measures or demographics except for race. African American youth were more likely to complete the follow-up surveys than any other ethnic group. Positive changes occurred in only two of the five target behaviors. At the 24-month follow-up, adolescents in the Case Management & Mentoring group, based on self-report and school records, were more likely to have remained in school, and those in the Case Management Only group reduced their reported parenting stress compared with the two other groups.

Even though relatively long, the 24-month intervention period may not have been an adequate dose either in duration or intensity. The process evaluation revealed that funding constraints, combined with a need to serve a large number of teens, resulted in each mentor being matched with four to five teens, which did not permit mentors adequate time to dedicate to each relationship, despite the 24-month intervention period. The difficulty of reaching the adolescents over the phone or in person and the many complications of their lives resulted in fewer services provided. Given the low dosage, on average 46 hours per participant, even 24 months may not have been enough to solidify the bond. The challenges for the Abuelas y Jovenes project, too few mentors for too many teens and inadequate time and structure for relationship development, are not uncommon for many mentoring programs, regardless of the age of the mentor.

Another program that employed the Across Ages model and curriculum, Project Youth Connect (PYC), was conducted over a 3-year period from 1998 to 2002 and was designed to delay and prevent the onset of ATOD use in high-risk youth. In this sequential three-cohort, quasi-experimental study, a program group ($n = 109$) and a control group ($n = 112$) were posttested at three 8-month intervals. Over time, the treatment group showed relatively little statistically significant improvement on 17 measures compared with the control group (Center for Substance Abuse Prevention, 2002). Within the treatment group, however, the duration of the relationship and the strength of the bond (as assessed by a mentee scale developed by a committee comprised of PYC grantees) were correlated positively with favorable outcomes. This suggests that within-group variation in relationship quality may have confounded the between-group comparisons. Another potential factor contributing to the lack of positive outcomes in this study, as well as other intergenerational mentoring evaluations described in this report, was the absence of well-established, reliable, and valid instruments to measure outcomes (see DuBois & Silverthorn, this volume; Grossman, this volume).

PRACTICE

In this section, we describe several intergenerational mentoring programs. Most took place in the community, even in the case of Across Ages, which drew the youth participants from entire classrooms located in neighborhood schools. There appear to be some basic practices that are common across programs and that may be somewhat different from practices that target younger mentors in the mentoring role. These are presented below.

Older Adult Participants

Findings from research focusing on six intergenerational mentoring initiatives were reviewed in the preceding section of this chapter. In each of these programs, adults aged 55 and older were recruited and trained as mentors. The mentors, who ranged in age from 55 to 83, came from a variety of backgrounds. Most were retired from full-time employment, but approximately half worked part-time. Many held blue-collar, construction, or service jobs during their years of paid employment, and some had been teachers, social workers, or nurses. Unlike other types of mentoring programs, there is no indication in published accounts of mentors coming from corporate settings. Rather, the orientation of older mentors to the work world in these programs appears to have been geared toward social service, industry, or self-employment. They typically were asked to spend between 2 and 4 hours per week in face-to-face contact with their protégés and to engage in a variety of activities, depending on the age, developmental, and social issues of the youth. The young people involved were all identified as "high risk" because of growing up in poverty, family disorganization, low academic achievement, and frequent school suspensions.

Finding good mentors requires persistence, resourcefulness, and networking. No one strategy employed in any of the initiatives examined in this chapter yielded a significant number of qualified mentors. In Freedman's (1988) study, mentors were recruited from connections made with foster grandparents, labor unions, and other community volunteers. Other projects have targeted retirees groups, including teachers, telephone workers, and nurses associations; civic groups such as Kiwanis and Rotary Clubs; faith-based institutions; fraternal organizations; and the American Association of Retired Persons (AARP). Recruitment strategies included personal presentations and print, electronic, and broadcast media. Mentors who had rewarding experiences often recruited friends or relatives.

Increasingly, researchers have recognized the importance of time and consistency to the development of the mentor-protégé bond (Taylor, LoSciuto, Fox, Hilbert, & Sonkowsky, 1999; Rhodes, 2002). Youth who are able to see their mentors on a regular basis for more than a hour a week appear to show the greatest improvements in some areas, especially school-related behavior. Many older adults have more free time and schedule flexibility, commodities that are relatively scarce among younger people due to work and family obligations. It should not be assumed that all older adults have copious amounts of time, given that many also are working part-time and are heavily involved in family or community activities. What they do possess, however, is the flexibility to identify priorities and allocate time for activities in which they want to be engaged. In our experience, the relationships that appear to be most effective are those for whom mentoring is the primary activity, where the older mentor is able to put in consistent time, often as much as 2 to 3 hours a week. Relationships in which the mentors are overcommitted and have more sporadic contact are the ones that suffer.

All of the programs had a rigorous screening process and followed steps outlined by the Nonprofit Risk Management Center and the best practices developed by MENTOR/National Mentoring Partnership. The Across Ages project required completion of the preservice training as an additional screening mechanism.

All programs had some type of preservice training, ranging from 3 to 12 hours. Training content included identifying program goals, expectations, and parameters; understanding the developmental and social issues of youth; discussing some strategies for working effectively with the youth and their families; goal setting; and increasing knowledge of agency and community resources. All programs also held regular in-service meetings for mentors to learn new skills and share their experiences in working with the protégés.

Older Mentors and Youth

All programs held some type of orientation for the youth. In some cases, protégés did no more than learn about the program and what was required in terms of time and obligation (Freedman, 1988, 1991). In others, extensive preparation was provided regarding the program goals, the role of a mentor, the youth's responsibility in the mentoring relationship, and an exploration of stereotypes and prejudices about working with older adults (Taylor & Bressler, 2000).

For the most part, matching was an intentional activity. For example, in projects that were focused on academic skills, a mentor and protégé ended up together because the youth needed help in a particular subject and the mentor was there specifically to tutor in that subject. Across Ages structured a series of workshops and activities that helped adults and youth get to know one another prior to matching, thus allowing for more spontaneous matches based on mutual affection and interests. In one program, Abuelas y Jovenes, mentors and teens were matched based on geographic proximity, often without having met, and this proved to be a challenge in facilitating relationships, which took far longer to solidify than programs engaging in planned activities in a supervised setting (Family and Planning Council, 2003).

All programs had some mechanism for monitoring the progress of relationships, specifically the in-service meetings. Staff on the Across Ages and Abuelas y Jovenes projects made weekly or biweekly phone calls to mentors between meetings. These projects also required monthly logs from mentors identifying the activities conducted with the protégés and the kinds of issues they discussed. Program staff also talked with youth on a regular basis to learn about the relationships from their perspective.

The level of family involvement was clearly tied to the population of youth being mentored. Obviously, in programs involving minors, families had to sign consent in order for their children to participate, but this did not always guarantee that families were supportive or enthusiastic. Family events were a regular activity of Across Ages. Other programs involved families only in orientation sessions and providing updates and feedback to parents/caregivers regarding the progress made by the youth.

Challenges in Recruiting Older Mentors

Despite the proliferation of older, healthier people in the general population, recruiting mentors, especially men, in large numbers is still difficult. A recent study conducted by AARP (Prisuta, 2003) suggests a general trend in the United States toward declining volunteerism among older adults. Men and women are retiring later, either because they can't afford to retire or because they are working in very satisfying jobs and often do not want to retire, thus reducing the numbers of people who have the time to volunteer. In addition, greater numbers of women, who have traditionally done most of the volunteering, are working. Men also represent a special challenge because they are less likely to have volunteered as younger adults. People who have not done any volunteering in their younger years are not as likely to start once they get older and retire (Prisuta, 2003). Another factor may be older men's perception of some volunteer opportunities as a "woman's activity." In focus groups conducted to assess the attitudes toward civic engagement and volunteerism among older baby boomers (50–59 years of age), men appeared to be reluctant to volunteer in activities where women were overrepresented (Bressler, Henkin, Jackson, & Montalvo, 2004). All of the intergenerational mentoring programs studied had far more female mentors than male. Declining civic engagement in the general population has serious implications for the mentoring field in general and is not limited to the older adult population.

FUTURE DIRECTIONS

Synthesis

Older adults in the United States are living longer than ever, and they are healthier and better educated than previous generations. As they move into middle and late life, the need to be generative expands beyond care within primary familial relationships and encompasses the larger community, its culture, and its institutions. Generativity theory suggests that older adults are at a developmental stage especially appropriate for mentoring youth, because this type of activity offers the opportunity to provide care and guidance to the next generation, which also validates their own life experience. Theoretically, factors that could contribute to successful intergenerational mentoring relationships include the parallel nature of the developmental tasks associated with adolescence and later life, shared societal status as a result of ageism, and the life experience of the mentor as a model of survival in the midst of adversity. Cultural factors relating to race and ethnicity also may theoretically influence the availability, quality, and effectiveness of mentoring relationships between older adults and youth, with these dimensions enhanced in cultures where older adults have traditionally played a central and respected role in the community. The findings of empirical studies of intergenerational mentoring offer some promise about the potential of programs that utilize older adults, although there is still a great deal to be learned. Studies of programs where intergenerational mentoring is embedded in other program services have dominated the current research.

Recommendations for Research

1. *Mentoring as the single intervention.* To date, there have been no studies that examined the effect of intergenerational mentoring by itself, although LoSciuto et al. (1996) designed the evaluation of the Across Ages program to determine whether program effects were greater for program youth with mentors than program youth who were not mentored. Therefore, randomized control group designs that focus on the efficacy of intergenerational mentoring alone are recommended, assuming the program's mission permits this focus. An alternative is factorial designs that allow assessment of the independent and interactive effects of two or more independent variables, such as mentoring and curriculum. Program dosage in the form of mentoring hours and the strength of the

mentor-protégé bond should be examined in conjunction with the analysis of program outcomes to determine to what extent the form of the relationship may affect the program's effectiveness.

2. *Investigate distinctive characteristics and contributions of older mentors.* As noted, very little research has been conducted specifically on older adults as mentors. Previous studies have emphasized the importance of mutual empathy and trust as prerequisite to a strong mentor-protégé relationship (Rhodes, 2002; Styles & Morrow, 1992) and the importance of time and consistency in developing these connections (Sipes, 1996), both characteristics of generative action, which emerges most strongly in midlife and older adults (Keyes & Ryff, 1998). It is unknown, however, to what extent age and experience contribute to an enhanced capacity for empathy and how the developmental stage of the mentor might affect the relationship between the mentor and protégé. In addition, theories focusing on skill development, social networks, and cultural competence (Blechman, 1992; Vygotsky, 1978; Zippay, 1995), which have been identified as potential explanations for why mentoring may contribute to youth development, need to be explored specifically in the context of intergenerational mentoring. For example, do mentors by virtue of age and experience have denser social networks and therefore greater capacity to expose protégés to people and experiences that can be helpful to their development? Is an older adult who has survived adversity more able to help a protégé navigate in the larger world as well as the home community?

3. *Examine ethnicity and culture as moderators of outcomes.* Cultural factors that seem to facilitate mentor-protégé relationships in African American, Latino, or even European American families may not hold true in other cultures. If we assume, for example, that generativity, associated with middle and late life, is an influence in intergenerational mentoring, what is the nature and content of the mentoring relationship between a protégé and a young "elder," which might be the case for American Indian youth involved in intergenerational mentoring. It may be that for this population, bicultural competence is a critically important component of the mentor-protégé bond, and the degree of bicultural competence may not be a function of age. Research in this area might help us understand whether the influence of knowledge and experience can still be applied if the culture accepts mentors in this role even though they may be 25 or 30 years old. Another question might be whether Asian families would be more receptive to a child's involvement in mentoring if the mentor were older, or if cultural norms, which discourage help seeking outside the family, preclude any participation by Asian youth.

4. *Investigate role of parents/caregivers.* None of the intergenerational programs examined involved parents in activities other than orientations and family events, but as seen in the Across Ages program, parental support appeared to have a positive effect on the mentor-protégé relationship. Future research should begin to identify the attitudes and beliefs of parents regarding their child's participation in mentoring programs and the degree to which parents can support or thwart the relationship with the mentor. For example, experience has demonstrated that when parents feel threatened by their child's developing relationship with a nonfamilial adult, they sometimes attempt to sabotage the relationship. If parents appear to feel less threatened by the presence of an older adult, it may be that older mentors are especially well suited to help strengthen the parent-child relationship because parents do not feel the rivalry they might experience with someone closer in age.

5. *Investigate role of marginalization.* In some qualitative studies, youth perception of a shared "marginalized" status with their mentors seemed to facilitate a connection (Freedman, 1988, 1991). This finding poses two interesting questions that could be addressed by future research. First, to what extent is an older mentor's effectiveness with a youth at risk facilitated when the mentor shares aspects of the youth's background social status? Second, is this type of effect moderated by the age of the mentor because older mentors who have encountered marginalization have more experience in overcoming obstacles than those of similar background who are

younger? Finally, future research may do well to assess the degree to which protégés view their mentors as wiser as a result of their marginalization and adversity and the degree to which this wisdom is useful to the protégés.

Recommendations for Practice

1. *Develop age-sensitive recruiting strategies.* Although recruiting large numbers of mentors for programs is a challenge regardless of the age of the mentors, there appear to be considerations that may be specific to older adults. First, program developers must be aware of ageism as a barrier to recruiting older adults, who need to feel they will be valued and accepted by the host organization and not considered peripheral to the project. Second, recruitment materials and messages need to be group specific. Factors that should be considered are age, culture, education, socioeconomic status, and prior work of the adults being targeted. Recruitment materials, such as flyers, brochures, and public service announcements, should be focused on using language and creating recruitment messages that capture the energy and skills of a population that wants to continue working in some capacity. Materials should be culturally appropriate. Messages aimed at the African American faith community, which emphasize scripture, will be different from those targeting American Indian elders, which emphasize spiritual connections to the land and ancestors.

2. *Provide structured training.* Older mentors and protégés need the opportunity to learn about one another, to appreciate their commonalties as well as their differences, and to perceive their relationships as being mutually beneficial. Programs that provide structured training and activities engaging both sets of participants together in finding these common bonds are more likely to be successful breaking down stereotypes and enhancing communication, essential for facilitating a strong mentor-protégé connection and ultimately helping ensure the development of sustained mutually enjoyable and beneficial relationships.

3. *Promote cultural sensitivity within programs.* In studies of ethnic-specific mental health services (Takeuchi, Sue, & Yeh, 1995),

the results indicated that ethnic clients who attended ethnic-specific programs had lower dropout rates and stayed in programs longer than those using mainstream services. Although the intergenerational mentoring models described in this report served different ethnic groups, none was designed specifically for any particular population. As we have noted, however, older adults from the same cultural background as their protégés may be especially effective in helping youth understand the dominant culture while maintaining a presence in the community of origin (Blechman, 1992). Practitioners will need to identify or develop appropriate recruitment materials and training workshops for youth, families, and mentors. Evaluation tools and instruments must be selected that are sensitive to cultural nuances.

References

Aseltine, R. H. J., Dupre, M., & Lamlein, P. (2000). Mentoring as a drug prevention strategy: An evaluation of Across Ages. *Adolescent & Family Health, 1,* 11–20.

Barresi, C. M. (1987). Ethnic aging and the life course. In D. E. Gelfand & C. M. Barresi (Eds.), *Ethnic dimensions of aging* (pp. 18–34). New York: Springer.

Blechman, E. A. (1992). Mentors for high-risk minority youth: From effective communication to bicultural competence. *Journal of Clinical Child Psychology, 21,* 60–169.

Bressler, J., Henkin N., Jackson S., & Montalvo, M. (2004). *Understanding what older adults and baby boomers want from volunteer experiences.* Paper presented at the Gerontological Society of America Annual Scientific Meeting, Washington, DC.

Burton, L. M., & Dilworth-Anderson, P. (1991). The intergenerational family roles of aged Black Americans. *Marriage & Family Review, 16,* 311–330.

Campbell, D. T., & Stanley, J. C. (1966). *Experimental and quasi-experimental designs for research.* Skokie, IL: Rand McNally.

Center for Substance Abuse Prevention. (2002). *Project Youth Connect Final Report: U.S. D.H.H.S.* (CSAP/SAMHSA). Unpublished report, Rockville, MD.

Center on an Aging Society. (2003). *Child and adolescent mental health services: Whose responsibility is it to ensure care?* Washington, DC: Georgetown University.

Cornman, J., & Kingson, E. R. (1999). What is a social compact? How would we know one if we saw it? Yes, John, there is a social compact. Generations, 22(4), 10–14.

DuBois, D. L., Holloway, B. E., Valentine, J. C., & Cooper, H. (2002). Effectiveness of mentoring programs for youth: A meta-analytic review. *American Journal of Community Psychology, 30,* 157–197.

Erikson, E. H. (1968). *Identity, youth, and crisis.* New York: Norton.

Erikson, E. H., Erikson, J. M., & Kivnick, H. Q. (1986). *Vital involvement in old age.* New York: Norton.

Family Planning Council. (2003). *Abuelas y Jovenes Final Report: Center for Substance Abuse Prevention.* Unpublished report, U.S. Department of Health and Human Services, Washington, DC.

Freedman, M. (1988). *Partners in growth: Elder mentors and at risk youth.* Philadelphia: Public/Private Ventures.

Freedman, M. (1991). *The kindness of strangers: Reflections on the mentoring movement.* Philadelphia: Public/Private Ventures.

Freedman, M. (1999). *Prime time: How baby boomers will revolutionize retirement and transform America.* New York: Public Affairs.

Greim, J. L. (1992). *Adult/youth relationships pilot project.* Philadelphia: Public/Private Ventures.

Grossman, J. B. (Ed.). (1999). *Contemporary issues in mentoring.* Philadelphia: Public/Private Ventures.

Hirsch, B. J., Mickus, M., & Boerger, R. (2002). Ties to influential adults among black and white adolescents: Culture, social class, and family networks. *American Journal of Community Psychology, 30,* 289–303.

Jones-Saumty, D. (2002). *Review of Across Ages for the American Indian population.* Unpublished report, Center for Substance Abuse Prevention, Rockville, MD.

Keyes, C. L. M., & Ryff, C. D. (1998). Generativity in adult lives: Social structural contours and quality of life consequences. In D. P. McAdams & E. de St. Aubin (Eds.), *Generativity and adult development: How and why we care for the next generation* (pp. 227–263). Washington, DC: American Psychological Association.

Kuehne, V. S. (2003). The state of our art: Intergenerational program research and evaluation: Part Two. *Journal of Intergenerational Relationships, 1*(2), 79–94.

LoSciuto, L., Rajala, A. K., Townsend, T. N., & Taylor, A. S. (1996). An outcome evaluation of Across Ages: An intergenerational mentoring approach to drug prevention. *Journal of Adolescent Research, 11,* 116–129.

McAdams, D., & de St. Aubin, E. (1998). *Generativity and adult development: How and why we care for the next generation.* Washington, DC: American Psychological Association.

McLearn, K. T., Colasanto, D., & Schoen, C. (1998). *Mentoring makes a difference: Findings From the Commonwealth Fund 1998 Survey of Adults Mentoring Young People.* New York: The Commonwealth Fund. Available at http://www.ecs.org/html/Document.asp?chouseid=2843

Newman, S., Ward, C., Smith, T., Wilson, J., & McCrea, J. (1997). *Intergenerational programs: Past, present, and future.* Washington, DC: Taylor & Francis.

Philip, K., Shucksmith, J., & King, C. (2004). *Sharing a laugh? A qualitative study of mentoring interventions with young people.* Layerthorpe, York, UK: Joseph Rowntree Foundation/York Publishing Services.

Prisuta, R. (2003). Enhanced volunteerism among aging baby boomers. In *Working paper for baby boomers and retirement: Impact on civic engagement.* Cambridge, MA: Harvard-MetLife Foundation Initiative on Retirement and Civic Engagement.

Putnam, R. D. (2000). *Bowling alone: The collapse and revival of American community.* New York: Simon & Schuster.

Reich, R. B. (1999). Broken faith: Why we need to renew the social compact. *Generations, 22*(4), 19–24.

Rhodes, J. E. (2002). *Stand by me: The risks and rewards of mentoring today's youth.* Cambridge, MA/London: Harvard University Press.

Scales, P. C. (2003). *Other people's kids: Social expectations and American adults' involvement with children and adolescents.* New York: Kluwer Academic/Plenum.

Sheldon, K. M., & Kasser, T. (2001). Getting older, getting better? Personal strivings and personality development across the life-course. *Developmental Psychology, 37,* 491–501.

Sipes, C. (1996). *Mentoring: A synthesis of P/PV's research: 1988–1995.* Philadelphia: Public/Private Ventures.

Styles, M., & Morrow, K. V. (1992). *Understanding how youth and older adults form relationships: A study of four Linking Lifetime programs.* Philadelphia: Public/Private Ventures.

Takeuchi, D. T., Sue, S., & Yeh, M. (1995). Return rates and outcomes from ethnicity-specific mental health programs in Los Angeles, *American Journal of Public Health, 85,* 638–643.

Taylor, A. S., & Bressler, J. (2000). *Mentoring across generations: Partnerships for positive youth development.* New York: Kluwer Academic/Plenum.

Taylor, A. S., LoSciuto, L., Fox, M., Hilbert, S. M., & Sonkowsky, M. (1999). The mentoring factor: Evaluation of the Across Ages' intergenerational approach to drug abuse prevention. *Child & Youth Services, 20*(1/2), 77–99.

Vaillant, G. E. (2002). *Aging well: Surprising guides to a happier life.* Boston: Little, Brown.

VanderVen, K. (1999). Intergenerational theory: The missing element in today's intergenerational programs. *Child & Youth Services, 20*(1/2), 33–47.

Vygotsky, L. S. (1978). *Mind in society.* Cambridge, MA: Harvard University Press.

Weinstein-Shr, G., & Henkin, N. (1991). Continuity and change: Intergenerational relations in southeast Asian families. *Marriage and Family Review, 16,* 351–363.

Zippay, A. (1995). Expanding employment skills and social networks among teen mothers: Case study of a mentor program. *Child & Adolescent Social Work Journal, 12,* 51–69.

20

E-Mentoring

Hugh Miller and Mark Griffiths

Introduction

By overviewing the mentoring literature, a number of generalizations can be confidently made. The definitions and functions of mentors take many different forms, the effectiveness of formal mentoring programs is mixed, and there appears to be a number of factors that enhance the potential for successful mentoring experience. This chapter discusses e-mentoring; that is, mentoring conducted at least partly by means of electronic communication, such as through e-mail, chat rooms, and so on. Although we will use the term *e-mentoring* throughout this chapter, there are many interchangeable descriptions of this process, including telementoring, virtual mentoring, as well as e-mentoring. Similarly to other forms of mentoring that have a range of aims (e.g., to provide models, acculturate, support, sponsor, educate), e-mentoring can be used to support a broad range of intervention goals.

E-mentoring has been defined in a number of slightly different ways. O'Neill, Wagner, and Gomez (1996) defined it as the "use of e-mail or computer conferencing systems to support a mentoring relationship when a face-to-face relationship would be impractical" (p. 39). Alternatively, Single and Muller (2001) described it as,

[A] relationship that is established between a more senior individual (mentor) and a lesser skilled or experienced individual (protégé) primarily using electronic communications, and that is intended to grow the skills, knowledge, confidence, and cultural understanding of the protégé to help him or her succeed, while also assisting in the development of the mentor. (p. 108)

Finally, Bierema and Merriam (2002) have defined it as "a computer mediated, mutually beneficial relationship between a mentor and a protégé which provides learning, advising, encouraging, promoting, and modeling, that is often boundaryless, egalitarian, and qualitatively different than face-to-face mentoring" (p. 212).

Bierema and Merriam (2002) made the point that e-mentoring has two elements that distinguish it from traditional mentoring: the boundless configuration and the egalitarian quality of the exchange. Although there has been much work on the effectiveness of non-electronic mentoring, less is understood about the dynamics, contexts, or results of e-mentoring (Bierema & Merriam, 2002). In the chapter, we give an overview of the kinds of e-mentoring programs reported in the literature and visible on the World Wide Web. We discuss the factors that have been associated with successful and unsuccessful programs, give details of the few empirical evaluations of these programs, and highlight the most promising practices.

There is a wide range of e-mentoring approaches. Many programs have no face-to-face contact, but others combine traditional mentoring programs with some element of electronic communication. Bierema and Merriam (2002), for example, explored how computer-mediated communication (CMC) might be incorporated both formally and informally into the mentoring process. It is clear that many types of CMC, including e-mail, listservs, chat rooms, and computer conferencing, have the potential to facilitate the mentoring process.

There is a range of participants and objectives across e-mentoring programs. There are programs intended to support young people both with and without identified problems or disadvantages. Sometimes the electronic component is used to supplement other contacts between mentors and mentees, and often the demographic profile of mentor volunteers is similar to that in other mentoring programs. In other cases, electronic communication allows some programs to use mentors who would not otherwise be available to their mentees, either because of distance or because of status differences. Digital Heroes (2003), a program set up by *People* magazine and AOL Time Warner to use "the power of the Internet to pair prominent individuals with teens from under-served communities in online mentoring relationships," is an example of one such program.

The potential population of e-mentors is large. In a telephone interview study of 2,000 adults in May 2002 led by O'Connor (2002) for the AOL Time Warner Foundation, the research team attempted to determine how much youth mentoring was taking place in the United States and what the potential for growth in this area was. Results showed that 11% of the sample had formally mentored a young person in the previous 12 months in a variety of settings (school-based programs, Sunday school/religious activities, in the workplace, youth programs, etc.). None appeared to have taken place over the Internet. However, in terms of those who said they would seriously consider being mentors, 86% had access to the Internet. O'Neill and Harris (2000) pointed out that a consistent finding in surveys of potential volunteers is that

the likelihood of volunteering increases with education and household income: both factors are also associated with increased access to electronic communications. This suggests a large pool of possible e-mentors. O'Neill and Harris give an estimate of more than 2 million for the United States and Canada combined.

Although there are many e-mentoring programs currently in operation, most of the programs that have had any detailed evaluation information are in the school support area. These programs are what we what we will call *telementoring*, which emphasizes the instrumental more than the developmental form of e-mentoring. Telementoring is used to achieve a curricular goal, whereas e-mentoring tends to focus more on youth development more broadly. One of the earliest examples of telementoring began in 1994 and was funded by the National Science Foundation (see the final report by Bennett, Hupert, Tsikalas, Meade, & Honey, 1998). Two of the largest (and most notable) telementoring programs are MentorNet (Single & Muller, 2001), which links women undergraduates with female science, technology, and engineering professionals, and the International Telementor Program (2004), which also matches students with industry professionals. In its first 3 years, the International Telementor Program mentored over 11,000 students from nine countries, and the MentorNet program has mentored 7,000 students since its inception in 1997 (Kasprisin, Single, Single, & Muller, 2003).

An approach that is widely used in teaching and to support learning in schools is *curriculum-based e-mentoring* or *curriculum-based telementoring,* in which children from K–12 schools are put in touch with an "outside expert" who can provide intellectual resources, support, and guidance on school-based projects. A number of corporations (e.g., Hewlett Packard) work with schools on entrepreneurial projects by pairing adult mentors with students via e-mail. This form of mentoring is usually one-to-many, though some accounts report one-to-one support patterns growing out of the program (Harris, Rotenberg, & O'Brysan, 1997). Although the primary justification for choosing mentors is their expertise in a topic area or subject, these programs often reflect the hope that contact with the mentor also will provide other elements common to individual face-to-face mentoring, such as providing intellectual guidance and an accessible role model. The "experts" may be educators (e.g., professors) or highly skilled professionals, but the role can also be filled by local volunteers.

Another common form of e-mentoring is when older students participate in electronic classrooms, in which they communicate with each other and with various instructors by e-mail, computer conferences, and chat rooms (e.g., Salmon, 2000). A faculty member or other educational professional takes the role of e-moderator, whose job is to make sure interactions progress smoothly. The title "e-moderator," is used to convey that the adult's role is as a moderator of discussion; nevertheless, many aspects of the role (e.g., acculturation, building confidence, and modeling effective behavior) overlap with conventional definitions of mentoring. Other chapters in this handbook have set out a range of factors that promote effective mentoring. We will consider how these factors can be applied in e-mentoring programs. However, the change of modality from face-to-face to electronic communication seems to affect the applicability of these factors. We will consider some of what is known about the way CMC affects human and mentoring interactions and discuss how that might be relevant to planning e-mentoring programs.

THEORY

The most thorough recent review of the mentoring literature was carried out by DuBois, Holloway, Valentine, and Cooper (2002), who reviewed the evaluations of 55 youth mentoring programs. No single program feature or characteristic was responsible for positive outcomes of the programs, although several practices emerged as moderators of effect size (e.g., ongoing training for mentors, structured activities for mentors and youth, as well as shared expectations for frequency of contact, mechanisms for support and involvement of parents, and monitoring of overall program implementation).

There is little empirical information in the e-mentoring literature about moderators of change, that is, about factors that affect outcomes differently across populations or practices. Research on traditional youth mentoring and theories used to explain the effectiveness of mentoring (for example, DuBois, Neville, Parra, & Pugh-Lilley, 2002) has suggested that the positive results of mentoring result from establishing a relationship with a significant adult, which, in turn, provides social support and leads to increased psychological or behavioral competence. Little of the literature on e-mentoring takes such theory into account: Much of the focus is on issues involved with setting up and sustaining a program and on general assessment of formative outcomes (e.g., attendance). Accordingly, this section of the chapter will introduce factors in CMC that might be important mediators or moderators in the development of relationships and skills involved in mentoring.

Awareness of how online communication works is important to understanding the power and pitfalls of e-mentoring. A weakness that Cravens (2003) identified in her review of e-mentoring, carried out in 2001, was that few coordinators had experience with working with people online. Communication by e-mail is very different from most other forms of interaction. E-mail is primarily text based and relatively fast, with participants often geographically distributed. E-mail is asynchronous (i.e., communication and response can come at quite different times); and e-mail messages do not have to follow each other sequentially. It lacks the full spectrum of visual and aural information that we are dependent upon (often unconsciously) in face-to-face situations.

Earlier studies (e.g., Sanchez & Harris, 1996; Bennett et al., 1998) have emphasized the problems caused by limited e-mail access, especially in school-based mentoring. This is likely to become less of a problem with time as Internet access, both inside and outside the home, becomes more ubiquitous and cheaper, though it may remain an important issue outside North America and Northern Europe.

There are also differing expectations between different users. Experts in Internet communication are proficient in using applications like e-mail frequently and easily. Young students and some teachers may use such media infrequently and have much less accessibility to it in general. Weekly access may be the norm for such groups. Lack of time (or difficulty in making time) appears to be one of the main barriers to effective online communication. For instance, Harris, O'Brysan, and Rotenberg (1996) found that a major problem in an online mentoring program's success was the differing expectations between mentors and mentees related to turnaround time and interaction frequency. Both of these are related to access and familiarity with electronic communication. The importance of matched expectations for interaction frequency echoes what DuBois, Holloway, et al. (2002) found in nonelectronic mentoring.

The possibility of establishing contact between mentors and mentees at different geographical locations, and to some extent at any time of week or day, will help establish relationships and also allow mentees to receive support from mentors who might not otherwise be available to them. Ease of communication, support for the technical aspects of the program, and shared expectations about frequency of communication will moderate both establishing high-quality relationships and receiving support. Effective management of the communication aspects of e-mentoring programs is likely to enable the interactions to continue over a longer time, another factor that has been found to be related to effectiveness in nonelectronic mentoring.

In the related field of online counseling, Psychologist Stuart Tentoni claimed that "Internet therapy is an oxymoron (because) psychotherapy is based upon both verbal and nonverbal communication" (Segall, 2000, p. 40). However, Griffiths (2001) has argued that online relationships can be just as real and intense as those in the offline world, and there should be little surprise that psychologists and educators are beginning to establish online therapeutic relationships. This argument also holds for e-mentoring.

There are several differences between communication on the Internet and face-to-face communication. For instance, research has consistently shown that the Internet has a disinhibiting effect on users and reduces social desirability effects (Joinson, 1998). This may lead to increased levels of honesty and self-disclosure, and self-disclosure is held to be beneficial in developing relationships (Altman & Taylor,

1973). Furthermore, because the Internet is not a face-to-face environment, it is perceived by many users to be anonymous and nonthreatening. It may therefore be more appealing to "socially unskilled" individuals who may not have sought help if the self-help group was only offline and in person. McKenna, Green, and Gleason (2002) have suggested it may even be easier to form relationships on the Internet than face-to-face. Self-disclosure may be less threatening on the Internet than in person, perhaps partly because "gating features" (factors that might inhibit interaction because the communicator might feel awkward about them or the audience might find them off-putting, such as unattractiveness, shyness, or anxiety) are not visible on the Internet. In the context of mentoring, obvious differences in factors like age, accent, income, and status might also become gating features, and it is likely that the inhibitory effects of these factors would be reduced in CMC.

Despite the lack of empirical evidence, all of these seem reasons as to why the Internet may be a good medium for most forms of helping. In relation to models of counseling (for example, DuBois, Neville, et al., 2002), the disinhibiting effect of electronic communication and the reduced significance of factors that present barriers to communication may facilitate the development of relationships between youth and significant adults in cases where these gating factors are likely to be inhibiting in face-to-face relationships. In addition, CMC carries a very restricted amount of information compared with face-to-face interaction. This is usually presented as a disadvantage (as in the quote from Tentoni, above), and it might be expected that CMC will be experienced as being more limited and less satisfactory than face-to-face, so it might be more difficult to establish trust and rapport over electronic links than in everyday meetings. For instance, Bos, Olson, Gergle, Olson, and Wright (2002) found that in experimental groups playing a social dilemma game, it was more difficult to establish trust using text chat on the computer than in any of the other communications channels used (i.e., face-to-face, video, and audio). Trust was highest in those groups that met face-to-face. Furthermore, Kraut, Patterson, Lundmark, Mukhopadhyay, and Scherlis (1998) found that more frequent Internet users were more likely to be lonely and depressed than less frequent users in their sample of Internet users in Pittsburgh households, perhaps because the contact with others they maintained over the Internet was less satisfying than that achieved in real life.

However, other studies suggest either that CMC is not very different from other everyday communication or that the reduced information content of CMC might have advantages in making connections with others. Kraut, Keisler, and colleagues (2002) reported a follow-up study on their original sample, together with a new, more controlled study, in which recent purchasers of a new computer were compared with recent purchasers of a new television. The latter survey used 406 respondents from 216 Pittsburgh households, who completed surveys assessing frequency of Internet use, social support, size of social circles, time spent interacting with family members, extraversion, anomie, community involvement, closeness to family and friends, and well-being. Kraut et al. (2002) claimed that the "Internet paradox" of increased communication leading to greater loneliness had disappeared, and in the second study, Internet use was overall associated with increased social involvement and well-being. They did note that this effect was greatest for extroverts and those with more social support. For introverts and those with less social support in their sample, increased loneliness and decreased community involvement were both associated with increased Internet use, but they pointed out that that these "rich get richer" effects are not very surprising.

Kraut et al. (2002) suggested that one explanation for the change in the more recent study compared with the Kraut et al. (1998) study, referred to above, is that the Internet has become a more hospitable place than when their first study started in 1995. That is, because more people are now connected to the Internet and these people are more familiar with e-mail and messaging systems, it is now much easier to make social contact with family and friends over the Internet than when the research started. Also, there is now more useful, everyday information available over the Internet. Kraut et al. (2002) suggested that these changes made it

easier for their participants to integrate their online and offline lives than had been the case for the participants in the original study. In addition, there may be a moderating effect of X on Y that interacts with sociability and social support: Potential mentees who have lower social support (and so might have most to gain from establishing a mentoring relationship) might have noticeably more difficulty in establishing relationships electronically than those who are more social.

In contrast to Bos et al. (2002), Jarvenpaa and Leidner (1998) found that it was possible to maintain or develop trust among working groups on the Internet. They also identified aspects of groups' behavior that were associated with increased trust, including agreed expectation of frequency of interaction, social (i.e., non-task) communication, expression of enthusiasm for the group and the task, and substantial and timely responses to others' contributions. Similarly, Parks and Floyd (1996) reported that the development of personal relationships, as shown by their respondents reporting that they had formed new friendships with people that they had "met" for the first time through an Internet newsgroup, was associated with the duration and frequency of postings. The point is not that through CMC, individuals are unable to convey relational and personal information, but that it may take longer to do so. Rafaeli and Sudweeks (1997) suggested that what they called "interactive" communication in newsgroups helps these groups function well. Interactive communications reflect what has happened in a series of messages, rather than a one-off response to a single posting. They were found to be more humorous, contain more self-disclosure, display a higher preference for agreement and contain many more first-person plural pronouns than other messages. Training of potential mentors to encourage them to communicate in this manner may have a moderating effect on the development of relationships in e-mentoring.

There are two aspects of CMC that might disadvantage mentees, however. It may be that the extroverted and those with strong social networks get more out of Internet use than the introverted and less well connected (Kraut et al., 2002)—and since all the computer-based communication being discussed here involves writing and reading, a good standard of literacy, and preferably fluency and skill in writing, is a distinct advantage.

In summary, it seems that trust and building relationships in CMC, such as e-mentoring, are associated with a number of distinct variables. These are (a) agreement between the parties about frequency of communication, (b) appropriately frequent and full communication, (c) social as well as task-based communication, (d) some level of self-disclosure, and (e) interactive rather than purely reactive communications. We will discuss in the next section how these factors might relate to what is known about successful and unsuccessful e-mentoring programs.

Research

One of the problems with the growing literature on e-mentoring is that there is little in the way of formal evaluation, and many writings appear to be informal or reflective (e.g., Price & Chen, 2003; Witte, & Wolfe, 2003). Furthermore, what evaluation research there is has concentrated on processes within e-mentoring programs and the participants' feelings of satisfaction and involvement, rather than on longer-term outcomes, like effects on grades, antisocial behavior, or employment. For e-mentoring, there is no information on critical factors (i.e., moderators or mediators) that have emerged in recent research on traditional youth mentoring, such as how social support from extrafamilial adults might affect psychological or behavioral competence (DuBois, Neville, et al., 2002) or how mentoring might impact quality or parental and peer relationships and sense of self-worth (Rhodes, Grossman, & Resch, 2000).

Areas worth researching, based on the points made in the previous section, are whether CMC does have a disinhibiting effect that enhances self-disclosure and whether its relative anonymity reduces gating effects in developing mentoring relationships. A systematic examination of whether the factors associated with developing trust in working groups cited by Jarvenpaa and Leidner (1998) also foster trusting relationships in mentoring would be useful: agreed

frequency of interaction, enthusiasm, nontask communication, and substantial and timely responses to communication. It will be seen that these factors are often mentioned as being important in nonsystematic accounts.

Although the particular mechanisms and affordances of electronic communication influence how e-mentoring programs can best work, we feel that e-mentoring has much to learn from research on more traditional mentoring processes. Research in e-mentoring that parallels face-to-face mentoring research on the effect of factors like ongoing training, structured activities for mentors and mentees, monitoring of the overall program, and some consideration of parental involvement (which has hardly been considered at all in e-mentoring) would be valuable. Cravens (2003) identified the lack of awareness of traditional mentoring programs by those running e-mentoring programs and of the way these programs were evaluated as weaknesses of most of the programs she identified. Furthermore, many of the reports of e-mentoring programs take the form of thoughtful but informal evaluations of "what worked and what didn't," often with little systematic quantitative evaluation of output, and very rarely with comparison of mentored and nonmentored groups. The few quantitative studies that have empirically investigated factors that affect e-mentoring are examined in more detail below.

In a study of mentors and mentees expectations of the mentoring role and how these were linked to satisfaction, O'Neill (2001) reported a factor analytic study of 112 students' ratings of 10 telementoring functions in a database-centered school academic mentoring program, using Knowledge Forum. Knowledge Forum is a database with text, graphics, and links that students can access and add to, to reflect their understanding of the subjects they are studying. The analysis identified two main factors in the students' ratings. O'Neill labeled these "inquiry jumpstart" and "prodding partner." Inquiry jumpstart involved the mentors being helpful by giving guidance and information to get the project going. On the other hand, being a prodding partner was when mentors took a more demanding role by asking questions, reviewing, and offering challenges. O'Neill and Harris (2000), reporting on the same data, stated that both roles were seen as valuable by both mentors and mentees. Students' reported desire for inquiry jumpstart matched mentors' desires to provide this same function, as measured by the desirability ratings that the two groups gave to this function. However, mentors were significantly more desirous to fulfill the prodding partner role than were the students to have such a partner. This is a potential area of mismatched expectations between mentors and students about the most appropriate way of conducting an e-mentoring relationship.

O'Neill and Harris (2000) noted that both students and mentors used the fact that the database allowed all participants to view all other participants' contributions to observe other mentoring interactions in order to develop their mentoring/being mentored skills, and they suggested that this may be a more fruitful source of useful examples than preprepared "training" cases. O'Neill (2001) reported that students who read most of their own mentors' notes and those of other mentors were more likely to rate the success of their relationships with their mentors lower than those who read less widely in the database. He suggested that dissatisfaction might drive students to explore others' contributions and exchanges more widely, and also that wide exploration might alert students to other mentors whom they might regard as doing a more rewarding job than their own mentors.

Kasprisin et al. (2003) reported one of the very few studies examining e-mentoring efficacy. They incorporated a model of training using case studies to develop problem-solving skills and to allow participants to identify potential outcomes and benefits of the program in an attempt to improve e-mentoring outcomes. To do this, they developed a series of Web-based training modules for both mentors and protégés on the MentorNet program. Four hundred students were randomly selected from more than 2,500 undergraduate applicants for the program and split into two groups, matched for full-time and part-time, upper and lower division, age, and traditional or returning student status. The experimental group was required to complete the training program, while the sessions were optional for the control group. Those in the experimental group showed slightly but not significantly improved outcomes

for involvement and satisfaction. They exchanged e-mails with their mentors about 50% more frequently than students who had not undergone mandatory training (a mean of about six per month, as opposed to about four for the controls; this difference was significant at the $p < 0.5$ level). For all participants, there were positive correlations of 0.34 between involvement rate and satisfaction and 0.27 between involvement and "value" (based on questions about whether the participants felt the program had affected their self-confidence and their attitudes to employment). Both of these results are significant at the $p < 0.1$ level.

Others at all levels of schooling have used e-mail to supplement face-to-face telementoring meetings on specific educational projects, such as the writing process (Duin, Lammers, Mason, & Graves, 1994) and learning about books (Lesene, 1997). For example, Stephenson (1997) designed a program to reduce attrition rates in introductory computer programming classes by using e-mail contact between struggling students and computer science mentors. The e-mail contact was in the form of encouragement rather than formal tutoring, but afterward, the students' grades were higher and attrition rate from the programming classes was much lower compared with other classes.

PRACTICE

Mentoring for Support

Mentoring of youth via the Internet appears to be becoming increasingly popular in the United States. However, there has been very little written about it from an academic perspective. Two substantial reports have been written by Bennett et al. (1998) and Cravens (2003).

Bennett et al. (1998) comprehensively overviewed their 3-year experimental project to develop Internet-based e-mentoring environments that linked high school girls on science and technology courses with practicing (female) professionals for ongoing guidance and support. They stressed the importance of the attention and care that needs to be taken when building and maintaining a sense of community among online participants who had never met face-to-face. The report examined a number of areas, including strategies and issues surrounding participant recruitment, establishment of effective access, mentor-student matching, managing participant expectations, facilitation techniques for working online, and the pros and cons of informal discussions.

The project began by developing a number of online communication formats and resources to support different participating groups. These included one-to-one mentoring relationships, peer lounges, discussion forums, online resource materials, and guides for preparation and implementation of e-mentoring.

Prospective mentors were attracted to the program in part because the program targeted girls. Although many suggested they liked the mode of interaction because it was an ideal way for them to mentor given their hectic and inflexible work schedules, the most prevalent problem at the initial stages was the girls' limited e-mail access in the schools. There were limited numbers of computers and limited time after classes when students could get online, and many students had online access only for the duration of their taught classes. For some, this led to the premature ending of the mentoring relationship after only a semester.

Pilot work by the authors had already demonstrated that many participants, both mentors and mentees, did not know what to expect from a mentoring relationship and that most had a complete lack of experience with developing and sustaining online relationships. It was important to get mentors to recognize that the students varied greatly from each other and from their mentors in terms of life experiences. The provision of online training and orientation introduced participants to many common pitfalls of online communication prior to the online mentoring process.

Greater emphasis was placed on training mentors than students for a number of reasons. Mentors were the adults in the relationships and were thus expected to carry the primary responsibility for initiating and sustaining the relationships. Students were less willing to participate in extended training for a variety of reasons, such as their access to e-mail was limited, they were likely to see e-mentoring as an assignment

rather than a necessity, and it was not something they thought that they needed to prepare for.

Over the 3-year period, the matching protocols changed from interview-based matching for small groups (Year 1) to matching based on choices made by teachers and students, based on "mentor profiles" that gave details of mentors' backgrounds and interests (Year 2), to matching done by project staff based on preferences for career fields and/or hobbies students expressed in Web-based applications (Year 3). The reason for the shift was due mainly to the time and labor-intensive nature of the earlier matching protocols. By Year 3 of the project, three quarters reported that their matches were satisfactory using this preference-based matching.

The researchers identified several factors they felt contributed to satisfactory online mentoring relationships for both mentors and students. These include knowing about the mentors' backgrounds, interests, and hobbies and the mentors' use of humor and lightheartedness. There were also a number of very specific strategies that appeared to be critical in the facilitation of online relationships. Students seemed to need to want to feel valued and listened to. Successful mentors gave attention to the students' personal details, and they gave direct affirmations of support or conveyed their agreement with views the students expressed. Personal information from the mentors, presented in the e-mails, helped students come to view their mentors as more than just an e-mail address or text on the screen.

Bennett et al. (1998) went on to highlight some of the key facilitation skills needed to promote active dialogue. These included responding to affective as well as pragmatic issues, validating and highlighting issues raised by participants, offering options for further investigation, using a conversational tone, and inviting other viewpoints and contributions. Good mentors modeled appropriate communication and expected online participation, responding to problems or conflicts that arose among participants and ensuring that all participants were included in the discussion by directly responding to individuals and calling them by their names. It is noteworthy that several of the behaviors recommended in this study overlap with what Jarvenpaa and Leidner (1998) found important in developing and maintaining trust in the experimental e-mentoring study reported above.

Following her work as director of the Virtual Volunteering Project (VVP) from 1996 to 2001, Cravens (2003) produced an index and summary of all known online mentoring programs. Cravens found that the vast majority of e-mentoring programs she located took place in North America and that most e-mentoring program coordinators were unaware of the 40 other e-mentoring programs based in the continent. Most e-mentoring program coordinators had developed their programs from scratch without researching traditional mentoring programs and had little or no experience working with people online. Given the shortcomings noted by Cravens, she produced a comprehensive set of guidelines that site managers of e-mentoring programs should follow, as set out in the next paragraph. Cravens also provided a list of valuable resources to help in the development of e-mentoring programs developed by the Virtual Volunteering Project.

The VVP has concluded that the role of local site managers is crucial in developing sustainable programs. Site managers (often teachers in school mentoring programs) should help define the goals of the program, review the tools and resources available, guide the matching process, and help prepare both youth and mentors before the project starts. They should then maintain active involvement, monitoring and encouraging exchanges (which requires that they have access to information about e-mail traffic, if not to actual e-mails), and report regularly to the overall project coordinator. This involvement of local site managers enables projects to draw on local expertise and experience in setting up workable programs, and helps ensure that they are nurtured by people thoroughly grounded in the project once they are running.

Cravens concluded that until e-mentoring programs adopt the best practices from face-to-face mentoring more fully, the potential benefits of online relationships between e-mentors and their protégés may not be realized. Furthermore, unless there is collaboration with other programs to share resources and findings, the success of e-mentoring programs will at best be sporadic.

In this chapter, it has been assumed that e-mentoring mainly follows the one-to-one model of face-to-face mentoring, but electronic systems also allow one-to-many, many-to-one, and networked patterns of mentoring (e.g., listservs, chat rooms, and bulletin boards). Such electronic technologies shared by diverse groups of individuals can bring together mentors and novices nationally (or internationally) to discuss shared interests.

Packard (2003) has highlighted that this technology can facilitate mentoring in additional ways beyond supporting dyadic conversations via e-mail. She has discussed the advantages of a networked model of mentoring, as used by MentorNet. This model avoids feminist critiques of one-to-one mentoring as providing ways of replicating existing hierarchical culture, gives access to people with diverse backgrounds and strengths, and allows different aspects of the mentoring role to be spread among different people. These advantages are particularly important to the MentorNet program, which uses e-mail to link female college students in science and engineering to women professionals in industry, a kind of mentoring in which intense personal one-to-one relations between partners in mentoring might not be necessary, because even minimal levels of contact with female professionals can change students' attitudes (Packard & Hudgings, 2002).

Curriculum-Based E-Mentoring With "Experts" in K–12 Schools

Many curriculum-based programs have been running since the early 1990s. Some of the problems of Internet access may be reduced in the future, partly by improvements in students' home Internet access. Even though more sophisticated communication technologies are developed, asymmetries of access and expertise between academics and professionals and the public schools likely will continue to be a problem. For example, Harris et al. (1997) gave an account of Electronic Emissary, an agency that brings together schools and mentors worldwide. They concluded that the asynchronous and instantaneous nature of e-mail communication was a problem because it can give rise to quite different expectations of the pace and timing of interactions between the two parties. They explained that often, tech-savvy professionals with ready access to computers were frustrated by slow, intermittent responses from the schools, and school children had to wait for access to rapidly sent responses. They concluded that there was a critical need for an "online facilitator" to help teachers and students plan their projects with realistic expectations and the best use of limited interaction time.

Specific Program Practices

In the introduction, we listed factors that have been found to be important in nonelectronic mentoring. Here, we review those factors to see which have also emerged as important in the e-mentoring literature. The shortage of objective evidence to support these points suggests that until more information is learned about best practices in e-mentoring, program developers should continue to refer to the best practices in the general mentoring literature regarding length of matches, training, and so on (DuBois, Holloway, et al., 2002). The points from research on conventional mentoring that we listed in the introduction are listed below, followed by a comment on how they might apply to e-mentoring:

• *Frequency of contact and appropriate expectations for frequency.* Most commentators note that matching expectations of how frequently e-mails will be exchanged is important, and it has also been found that participants who exchange more messages are more positive about their programs.

• *Longevity of the relationship.* There are no specific studies of this factor, but it is important to keep relationships going, and the short span of many programs (a year or less) is noted as a particular disadvantage and challenge to sustained relationships.

• *Relationship quality, emotional closeness, and interaction levels.* The quality of the relationship, the emotional closeness between individuals, and high levels of interaction between young people and their mentors are particularly important factors. These three are all related to findings that mentors who introduce social

content into their messages and who are attentive and reactive to mentees' responses are felt to be more rewarding and effective than those who send messages that are strictly "on topic." However, a possible disadvantage to e-mentoring is that it may be difficult to establish close, high-quality relationships through CMC and that there is only a limited range of kinds of interaction that are possible in non-face-to-face mentoring.

• *Structure and planning.* Several studies have commented on the need to train mentors, mentees, and local managers and the importance of managers to support and structure the programs and activities. E-mentoring provides extra challenges in training because there is often a need for technical training. However, monitoring may be easier to manage in systems of electronic exchanges than in traditional mentoring. For instance, it is fairly easy for a system manager to track the frequency of e-mail exchanges or to disseminate suggestions to all or to a selected sample of the participants.

• *Mechanisms for support and involvement of parents.* Mechanisms for parental support are hardly mentioned in the e-mentoring literature, perhaps because up until recently, most e-mentoring has been carried out through out-of-home facilities, such as school computer rooms. As mentees become more likely to use home-based Internet access to contact mentors, parental involvement will become a more significant issue. One positive spin-off of a move from center-based to home-based e-mentoring communication is that it may become easier to enlist parental involvement.

FUTURE DIRECTIONS

Synthesis

E-mentoring has several advantages over traditional face-to-face mentoring, but it also poses unique challenges to relationship development and maintenance. It provides flexibility in pace and scheduling. It also transcends physical and geographical boundaries and provides access to individuals who may have previously been unable to access mentoring services. Because symbols of status are often unidentified in electronic communication, e-mentoring can be egalitarian and democratic, with students being more comfortable in their own homes or educational environments, and there may be decreased feelings of intimidation and/or discomfort in new environments. It offers easy access to supportive information and resource experts, so that information is just a "link" away, and has flexible communication methods (e.g., single, multiple, and simultaneous methods, such as e-mail, listservs, Usenet, newsgroups, threaded discussions, and/or chat rooms).

E-mentoring also provides many challenges. Price and Chen (2003) have noted that participants must have access to the Internet and have the basic skills to use the software, equipment, and the Internet. They also point out that e-mentoring programs can vary because of differences in participation motivation, involvement, and personal characteristics, which may make it difficult to maintain continuous interactions and reflective influences through the duration of the program. Also, e-mentoring programs may be difficult to maintain because they require coordination and management (both technical and human), facilitation and planning, and implementation and evaluation.

Much of the work we have reported demonstrates that technology-supported mentoring can complement and extend what is achieved by face-to-face mentoring. However, it is unresolved as to whether in-person experience can ever be fully substituted by technology (Kealy & Mullen, 2003). Furthermore, Kealy and Mullen have made some very astute observations. Technology is constantly changing in ways that are sometimes surprising and unpredictable. They pointed out that when new technologies appear, they often look to the past to define themselves (e.g., the invention of the car being described as a "horseless carriage"). Kealy and Mullen have asserted than instead of viewing e-mentoring with regard to its predecessor (i.e., face-to-face mentoring), perhaps it should be understood on the basis of its unique qualities. Maybe e-mentoring and traditional mentoring should not be compared at all. Traditional mentoring is unlikely ever to be replaced. However, new technologies may provide a useful adjunct to the mentoring boundaries.

Recommendations for Research

1. *Use a rigorous methodology in research.* Little of the overviewed research on e-mentoring has included control groups, random or matched selection of participants, or quantified outcome measures. Therefore, higher standards in future research will need to be achieved if the field is to advance in its awareness of best practices in e-mentoring.

2. *Carry out research on outcomes.* Most of the literature on e-mentoring so far has, understandably, concentrated on setting up and maintaining programs so that the programs support a reasonable level of interaction and satisfaction. The research should now focus on outcomes, like academic success, behavior, and relationships outside the program.

3. *Research different training/orientation schemes.* Despite the need for outcome research, more intensive process and implementation studies also should be conducted. The nature of interaction in e-mentoring could lend itself to giving participants a variety of kinds of preparatory or concurrent training schemes. To better understand what types of training contribute most to relationship development, e-mentoring research also should be conducted on these issues of program fidelity. Program or training schemes that appear most promising and worthy of study include O'Neill and Harris's (2000) "finding out by observing others' interactions" approach, in contrast with MentorNet's more structured training (Bennett et al., 1998).

4. *Take account of factors that have emerged as significant in CMC research.* Knowledge of CMC research as well as study of factors revealed in traditional mentoring research could stimulate questions and guide hypotheses for future e-mentoring research. Ideally, such research would mainly be into process, rather than outcomes, but could be used to support aspects of process that are known to influence outcomes from research on nonelectronic mentoring. For example, the effect of CMC on self-disclosure, and thus the development of relationships with significant adults, and also whether the characteristics of individuals who don't seem to benefit socially and emotionally

from Internet use (Kraut et al., 2002) are also counterindicators for e-mentoring.

Recommendations for Practice

1. *Use guidance from existing schemes and other areas of mentoring.* There is now a large body of practical experience that can be drawn on in planning and maintaining a scheme (e.g., Cravens, 2003). Similarly, although e-mentoring is a new approach, principles and theories that have been developed to guide practice in other areas of mentoring may be relevant and useful, for example, parental involvement and the importance of structured activities for mentors and mentees.

2. *Involve local managers/monitors.* Local managers are essential to get the system set up and working, both technically and interpersonally, and to keep track of what is going on in the communications between mentors and mentees. Beyond the need to screen for appropriate communication content, participants may not have fully developed CMC skills, both technically and interpersonally, and a local manager or monitor can make sure that things are working smoothly.

3. *Make sure expectations are explicit, realistic, and matched between participants.* Availability of technology and time may be very different between the partners, which may lead to misunderstandings of what is possible or acceptable. Clarifying realistic basic levels of communication will help avoid these. Specifically, as has been mentioned several times, matching expectations for frequency and extent of e-mail exchanges seems vital.

4. *Consider making full use of the technology.* E-mentoring gives opportunities for many models of mentoring other than one-to-one and different kinds of interaction other than linear back-and-forth messages. Fluid movement back and forth between one-to-many, one-to-one, and many-to-one communication might be valuable, as is the possibility of mentors contacting and learning from other mentors, and mentees doing the same with their peers. Structures that allow this kind of interaction are worth exploring, but only if adequate management and support are available to maintain systems that are more complex, both technically and socially.

REFERENCES

Altman, I., & Taylor, D. A. (1973). *Social penetration: The development of interpersonal relationships.* New York: Holt, Rinehart & Winston.

Bennett, D., Hupert, N., Tsikalas, K., Meade, T., & Honey, M. (1998). *Critical issues in the design and implementation of telementoring environments.* Centre for Children and Technology. Retrieved November 20, 2003, from http://www.edc.org/CCT/admin/publications/report/09_1998.pdf

Bierema, L. L., & Merriam, S. B. (2002). E-mentoring: Using computer mediated communication to enhance the mentoring process. *Innovative Higher Education, 26,* 211–227.

Bos, N., Olson, J., Gergle, D., Olson, G., & Wright, Z. (2002, April 20–25). *Effects of four computer-mediated communication channels on trust development.* Paper presented at the SIGCHI Conference on Human Factors and Computing Systems: Changing Our World, Changing Ourselves, Minneapolis, MN.

Cravens, J. (2003). Online mentoring: Programs and suggested practices as of February 2001. *Journal of Technology in Human Services, 21*(1/2), 85–109.

Digital Heroes. (2003). *The Digital Heroes campaign.* Retrieved April 20, 2003, from http://www.digitalheroes.org/dhc

DuBois, D. L., Holloway, B., Valentine, J., & Cooper, H. (2002). Effectiveness of mentoring programs for youth: A meta-analytic review. *American Journal of Community Psychology, 30,* 157–197.

DuBois, D. L., Neville, H. A., Parra, G. R., & Pugh-Lilly, A. O. (2002). Testing a new model of mentoring. In G. G. Noam (Ed. in chief) & J. E. Rhodes (Ed.), *A critical view of youth mentoring (New Directions for Youth Development: Theory, Research, and Practice, No. 93,* pp. 21–57). San Francisco: Jossey-Bass.

Duin, A. H., Lammers, E., Mason, L. D., & Graves, M. F. (1994). Responding to ninth grade students via telecommunications: College mentor strategies and developments over time. *Research in Teaching of English, 28*(2), 117–153.

Griffiths, M. D. (2001). Sex on the Internet: Observations and implications for sex addiction. *Journal of Sex Research, 38,* 333–342.

Harris, J., O'Brysan, E., & Rotenberg, L. (1996). Practical lessons in telementoring. *Learning and Leading With Technology, 24*(2), 53–57.

Harris, J., Rotenberg, L., & O'Brysan, E. (1997). *Electronic emissary: Results from the electronic emissary project: Telementoring lessons and examples.* Retrieved November 20, 2003, from http://www.tcet.unt.edu/pubs/em/em01.pdf

International Telementor Program. (2004). Retrieved April 20, 2003, from http://www.telementor.org

Jarvenpaa, S. L., & Leidner, D. E. (1998). Communication and trust in global virtual teams. *Journal of Computer Mediated Communication, 3*(4). Retrieved November 20, 2003, from http://www.ascusc.org/jcmc/vol3/issue4/jarvenpaa.html

Joinson, A. (1998). Causes and implications of disinhibited behavior on the Internet. In J. Gackenback (Ed.), *Psychology and the Internet: Intrapersonal, interpersonal, and transpersonal implications* (pp. 43–60). New York: Academic Press.

Kasprisin, C. A., Single, P. B., Single, R. M., & Muller, C. B. (2003). Building a better bridge: Testing e-training to improve e-mentoring programmes in higher education. *Mentoring and Tutoring, 11,* 67–78.

Kealy, W. A., & Mullen, C. A. (2003). Epilogue: Unresolved questions about mentoring and technology. *Mentoring and Tutoring, 11,* 119–120.

Kraut, R. E., Keisler, S., Boneva, B., Cummings, J., Hegleson, V., & Crawford, A. (2002). Internet paradox revisited. *Journal of Social Issues, 58*(1), 49–74.

Kraut, R. E., Patterson, M., Lundmark, V., Mukhopadhyay, T., & Scherlis, B. (1998). Internet paradox: A social technology that reduces social involvement and psychological well-being? *American Psychologist, 53,* 1017–1032.

Lesene, T. (1997). Reaching reluctant readers: The student teacher on-line mentoring project. *The ALAN Review, 24,* 31–35.

McKenna, K. Y. A., Green, A. S., & Gleason, M. E. J. (2002). Relationship formation on the Internet: What's the big attraction? *Journal of Social Issues, 58*(1), 9–31.

O'Connor, R. (2002). *Mentoring In America.* Pathfinder Research/AOL Time Warner Foundation. Retrieved July 7, 2004, from http://mentoring.web.aol.com/common/one_report/national_poll_report_final.pdf

O'Neill, D. K. (2001, April 10–14). *Building social capital in a knowledge-building community: Telementoring as a catalyst.* Paper presented to the Annual Meeting of the American Educational Research Association. Seattle, WA. Retrieved November 20, 2003, from http://www.sfu.ca/~koneill/

O'Neill, D. K., & Harris, J. (2000, April). *Is everybody happy? Bridging the perspectives and developmental needs of participants in telementoring programs.* Paper presented at the Annual Meeting of the American Educational Research Association, New Orleans, LA. Retrieved November 20, 2003, from http://www.sfu.ca/~koneill/

O'Neill, D. K., Wagner, R., & Gomez, L. M. (1996). Online mentors: Experimenting in science class. *Educational Leadership, 54*(3), 39–42.

Packard, B. W. (2003). Web-based mentoring: Challenging traditional models to increase women's access. *Mentoring and Tutoring, 11,* 53–65.

Packard, B. W., & Hudgings, J. H. (2002). Expanding college women's perceptions of physicists' lives and work through Interactions with a physics careers website. *Journal of College Science Teaching, 32*(3), 164–170.

Parks, M. R., & Floyd, K. (1996). Making friends in cyberspace. *Journal of Computer Mediated Communication, 1*(4). Retrieved July 5, 2004, from http://www.ascusc.org/jcmc/vol1/issue4/vol1no4.html

Price, M. A., & Chen, H.-H. (2003). Promises and challenges: Exploring a collaborative telementoring programme in a preservice teacher education programme. *Mentoring and Tutoring, 11,* 105–117.

Rafaeli, S., & Sudweeks, F. (1997). Networked interactivity. *Journal of Computer Mediated Communication, 2*(4). Retrieved November 20, 2003, from http://www.asusc.org/jcmc/vol2/issue4/rafaeli.sudweeks.html

Rhodes, J. E., Grossman, J., & Resch, N. (2000). Agents of change: Pathways through which mentoring relationships influence adolescents' academic adjustment. *Child Development, 71,* 1662–1671.

Salmon, G. (2000). *E-moderating: The key to teaching and learning online.* London: Kogan Page.

Sanchez, B., & Harris, J. (1996). Online mentoring, a success story. *Learning and Leading With Technology, 23*(8), 57–60.

Segall, R. (2000). Online shrinks: The inside story. *Psychology Today, 32*(3), 38–43.

Single, P. B., & Muller, C. B. (2001). When e-mail and mentoring unite: The implementation of a nationwide electronic mentoring program. In Linda K. Stromei (Ed.), *Creating mentoring and coaching programs.* Alexandria, VA: American Society for Training and Development. Retrieved November 20, 2003, from http://www.uvm.edu/~ pbsingle/2001_ADTD_chpt.pdf

Stephenson, S. D. (1997). Distance mentoring. *Journal of Educational Technology Systems, 26,* 181–186.

Witte, M. M., & Wolf, S. (2003). Infusing mentoring and technology within graduate courses: Reflections in practice. *Mentoring and Tutoring, 11,* 95–103.

21

Integration of Mentoring With Other Programs and Services

Gabriel P. Kuperminc, James G. Emshoff,
Michele M. Reiner, Laura A. Secrest,
Phyllis Holditch Niolon, and Jennifer D. Foster

Introduction

At the bimonthly "rap" session for Cool Girls,
Inc., mentors, Nicole learned that the Girls Club
after-school program was covering a module on
Health, Wellness, and Nutrition as part of its life
skills curriculum. During a phone conversation a
few days later, her protégé, Monique, proudly told
Nicole that she was learning about computerized
spreadsheets through the Cool Tech program.
Nicole and Monique decided it would be fun to
plan a healthy dinner so that Monique could show
what she was learning. They listed the ingredients
they would need and prepared a budget using
spreadsheet software in Nicole's office. That
weekend, they went shopping for groceries and
spent the rest of the day together preparing and
enjoying a delicious and healthy feast.

Recent years have seen a proliferation of programs such as Cool Girls, Inc., that incorporate
mentoring into comprehensive programs and
services designed to promote academic and vocational development, increase social and behavioral competencies, and reduce risk behavior
(Rhodes, Grossman, & Roffman, 2002). Such
programs, often described under the rubric of
positive youth development, reflect a philosoph-
ical shift from efforts to reduce the incidence of
single identified problems in development (e.g.,
delinquency, substance abuse) toward strategies
aimed at increasing opportunities and supports
that will leave young people fully prepared for
the challenges they will face as adults (Pittman,
Diversi, & Ferber, 2002). But what does it mean
to be fully prepared? Many programs have
developed multipronged strategies designed to
address a holistic view of development, attending to its cognitive, psychological, and social
dimensions. Supportive relationships with adults
are often seen as adding value to traditional curricula designed to foster positive outcomes.

Write-up of this work was supported by the W. T. Grant Foundation's W. T. Grant Scholars Program. Special
thanks go to the participants, parents, and staff at Cool Girls, Inc.

In this chapter, we examine issues of theory, research, and practice that relate to youth mentoring within the context of multicomponent programs and services. We begin with a theoretical consideration of mechanisms through which mentoring combined with other programmatic activities may contribute to positive youth development. We next review research on programs and services that include mentoring as (a) part of a multicomponent youth development intervention or (b) a primary vehicle for delivery of or affording access to other services. To ensure at least minimal integration, we consider only programs that involve youth in at least one program component in addition to mentoring. Finally, drawing on our experience in implementing and evaluating Cool Girls (Cool Girls, Inc., n.d.), we outline focal implementation issues particular to programs that integrate mentoring with other services and programs.

THEORY

The growth of youth mentoring interventions is linked to the evolution of primary prevention and, more recently, the field of positive youth development (Albee & Gullotta, 1997; Cicchetti, Rappaport, Sandler, & Weissberg, 2000). This work has brought together practitioners and scholars across multiple disciplines to focus attention on understanding and promoting positive development through empirical study of protective and risk factors as well as program implementation and evaluation. We begin this section by delineating a typology of activities that are expected to contribute to program goals, including outcomes focused on interpersonal relatedness, self-definition, and prevention/promotion (see Table 21.1). We then use this typology to guide our discussion of possible mechanisms through which mentoring may combine with other programs and services to influence outcomes in multicomponent programs.

Activities and Processes of Multicomponent Programs

Programs can take person-centered approaches to work directly with youth- or environment-centered approaches that attempt to change key developmental settings (e.g., home environment or school climate) (Durlak & Wells, 1997). Activities involving youth participants usually take the form of didactic instruction (e.g., classroom-based skills-training curricula), experiential learning (e.g., community service-learning), or relationship building (e.g., support groups, mentoring). Such activities may be directed toward affecting developmental processes (e.g., self-efficacy, intrinsic motivation, capacity for intimacy) or prevention/promotion outcomes (e.g., risk behavior, school performance).

Larson (2000) has advocated a role for developmental science to articulate the processes underlying the link between programmatic activities and intended outcomes. Such theoretical work is needed if we are to move beyond identifying what works toward questions of why and how programs may enhance young people's developmental trajectories. Whereas Larson focused on the potential of youth programming to create opportunities for youth initiative (defined in terms of high levels of both motivation and engagement, combined with goal seeking over time), we offer a theoretical perspective that also attends to relational developmental processes central to mentoring (DuBois, Neville, Parra, & Pugh-Lilly, 2002; Rhodes, 2002).

Interpersonal relatedness and self-definition have been identified as two primary dimensions of psychological and social development that contribute to positive outcomes and protect against maladjustment (Kuperminc, Blatt, Shahar, Henrich, & Leadbeater, 2004). Self-definition involves developing a well-differentiated, integrated, realistic, and essentially positive sense of self. Interpersonal relatedness involves developing intimate, mutually satisfying, reciprocal interpersonal relationships. Blatt and Blass (1995) also have shown how these dimensions correspond with Erikson's (1963) life span theory of human development. For example, the stage of trust versus mistrust focuses primarily on issues of relatedness, whereas the subsequent stage of autonomy versus shame and doubt incorporates previous experiences but focuses primarily on self-definition. Thus, relatedness and self-definition can be seen as mutually reinforcing processes, such that growth in one

Table 21.1   Conceptual Framework for Linking Common Youth Development Program Activities to Developmental Processes and Prevention/Competence Promotion Outcomes

Program Activities	Developmental Processes and Prevention/Promotion Outcomes
Didactic Activities	*Prevention/Competence Promotion Outcomes*
Life skills training	Substance use and attitudes
Social skills training	Aggression/delinquent behavior
Direct instruction	Risky sexual activity
Remedial education	School performance and engagement
	Civic engagement
Experiential Activities	Demonstrated social competence
Leadership training	
Job placement/training	*Self-Definition*
Recreational activities	Self-control/emotion regulation
Community service	Self-concept (efficacy and self-worth)
Cultural activities	Orientation toward the future
Relational Activities	*Relatedness and Social Connections*
Peer counseling	Communication
Counseling	Intimacy
Family services	Trust
Adult mentoring	Providing and receiving social support
Peer mentoring	Sense of belonging

SOURCE: List of activities adapted from Roth & Brooks-Gunn (2003).

dimension portends opportunities for gains in the other (Allen, Moore, & Kuperminc, 1997). Research consistently has indicated that despite important gender- and culture-linked variations, both relatedness and self-definition contribute to improved psychological, social, and behavioral functioning (Kuperminc et al., 2004; Leadbeater, Kuperminc, Blatt, & Hertzog, 1999).

Processes linked to self-definition include initiative (Larson, 2003), autonomy and self-regulation (Allen et al., 1997; Connell, 1990), and perceived self-efficacy (Bandura, 1980). Relatedness processes involve appraisals of the self as worthy and capable of affection and feelings of acceptance, support, and nurturance from important others (Allen et al., 1997; Connell, 1990). In the parlance of youth development, self-definition and interpersonal relatedness stand as important outcomes in their

own right (National Research Council and Institute of Medicine, 2002) but, as will be discussed, also can be viewed as important mediating or moderating processes that contribute to prevention/promotion outcomes.

Reviews of the effectiveness of youth development programs have sought to clarify definitions, compile evidence regarding effectiveness, and articulate the "active ingredients" associated with successful youth outcomes (Catalano, Berglund, Ryan, Lonczak, & Hawkins, 1998; National Research Council and Institute of Medicine, 2002; Roth, Brooks-Gunn, Murray, & Foster, 1998). Roth et al. (1998) described the youth development framework as including (a) components that provide youth with opportunities for challenging and relevant instruction, training, and new roles/responsibilities; (b) emotional, motivational, and strategic supports;

and (c) a focus on increasing competencies and internal assets. Despite somewhat different frameworks, the reviews reached similar conclusions: (a) Programs incorporating more elements of the youth development framework seemed to show more positive outcomes; (b) longer-term programs appeared to be most effective; and (c) with specific relevance to mentoring, caring adult-adolescent relationships were critical. Unfortunately, the preceding reviews offer only limited information about the unique contributions of mentoring or other components because they focused on overall effects of complex programs.

Mechanisms

Evidence is accumulating about strategies known to be effective in reducing risk behaviors among youth (e.g., Albee & Gullotta, 1997; Weissberg, Kumpfer, & Seligman, 2003). With their sights set on addressing a broader range of developmental outcomes, many youth programs seem to be infusing mentoring or mentoring-like components into their activities (Roth & Brooks-Gunn, 2003). However, there has been little articulation of the role that mentoring is expected to play in such programs. To facilitate a stronger theoretical foundation, we propose three mechanisms through which mentoring in combination with other programs and services might contribute to processes of relatedness and self-definition and prevention/promotion: differential, mediated, and moderated effects (see Figure 21.1). We consider quality of implementation and integration of program

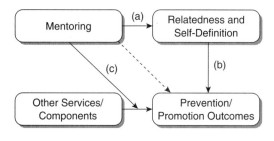

Figure 21.1   Hypothesized Mechanisms Through Which Mentoring May Influence Youth Development Outcomes in Multicomponent Interventions

components as additional factors likely to influence program effectiveness. We do not view these mechanisms as mutually exclusive; rather, we expect that multiple mechanisms can be operative.

Differential Effects

A first possibility is that mentoring may serve to broaden the range of processes and outcomes that are affected by programs (see Path a in Figure 21.1). In particular, whereas program components emphasizing didactic instruction or experiential activities may have stronger effects on specific prevention/promotion outcomes, the inclusion of a mentoring component may lead to important and direct improvements for young people in the areas of self-definition and interpersonal relatedness. Skills training, for example, can provide youngsters with alternate means of resolving everyday conflicts, but interactions with mentors may have greater potential for reinforcing young people's sense of self-worth and feelings that what they do matters to an important other.

Mediated Effects

Of further theoretical significance is the potential for improvements in self-definition and relatedness that accrue from mentoring within a larger, multicomponent program to then contribute to prevention/promotion outcomes (see Path b). Consistent with recent research, which has found only modest direct effects of mentoring interventions across a range of outcomes relevant to prevention/promotion (DuBois, Holloway, et al., 2002), we recognize that as part of a multicomponent program, unique direct effects of mentoring on outcomes such as academic adjustment and risk behavior may be limited. Still, having a mentor may make a noteworthy contribution to competence promotion and risk reduction indirectly through improvements in self-definition and interpersonal relatedness. This type of mechanism would be consistent with recent research indicating that mentoring relationships contribute to academic and behavioral adjustment indirectly through their more immediate consequences for self-esteem and relational processes (e.g., quality of the youth's relationship with parents) (DuBois, Neville, et al., 2002; Rhodes, Grossman, & Resch, 2000; Rhodes et al., 2002).

Moderated Effects

Finally, a mentoring component could moderate the effectiveness of other components and services in ways that enhance overall program impact on prevention/promotion outcomes (see Path c). There are several reasons this might occur. First, supportive mentoring relationships may bridge local patterns of language and behavior among youth and the more formal atmosphere of human service settings in ways that enhance the impact of services provided in those settings (Blechman, 1992). Second, interactions with a mentor may provide a safe and effective context for practice and reinforcement of skills learned through a didactic curriculum. Third, mentors and protégés may participate together in other activities or services (e.g., working together on a community service project), thus potentially enhancing their effectiveness through guidance and support provided by the mentor. Finally, a positive relationship with a mentor also may encourage youth to remain engaged in other areas of a program as well as provide an incentive for youth to remain active in the program over an extended period of time. An additional consideration is that characteristics of participating youth and mentors (e.g., age, gender, ethnicity, attachment styles) may further moderate the effectiveness of mentoring in combination with other efforts. For example, youth from low-income communities might be especially likely to benefit from highly structured apprenticeship programs in which mentors are able to provide both emotional support and job training.

Quality of Program Implementation and Extent of Integration of Program Components

In sum, there is a theoretical basis for expecting that mentoring can contribute to realizing the goals of positive youth development programs through each of the three preceding types of mechanisms. The ability to realize such effects, however, may rest on the extent to which

programs are able both (a) to manage the logistical demands of running multiple program components (Stoil & Hill, 1996) and (b) to integrate mentoring with other program activities effectively. In efforts to balance limited resources with a desire to provide comprehensive youth programming, for example, agencies may choose to reduce the intensity or duration of the mentoring component or fail to provide opportunities for information sharing between program components. Such decisions could weaken the impact of mentoring on youth outcomes.

RESEARCH

Multifaceted programs typically include an eclectic mix of components, and there is little standardization in the outcomes examined across evaluations. Moreover, in addition to formal mentoring components, programs may use alternative terms (e.g., youth associate; Cowen et al., 1996) to describe mentoring or related activities or may recognize that informal mentoring relationships often arise in the context of program implementation (e.g., Rappaport, 2002). We focused our review on programs that included a formal component in which one (or more) young person was matched with an adult in an ongoing relationship intended to provide the youth with guidance, instruction, and encouragement (see Rhodes et al., 2002). The term *mentor* appeared in most program descriptions, although we did not require use of the term for inclusion in the review. Thus, our criteria were more inclusive than those used in the DuBois, Holloway, et al. (2002) meta-analysis. Whereas DuBois et al. found that multicomponent programs that included mentoring were not more effective than stand-alone mentoring programs, the analysis focused only on overall program effects and did not examine the range of theoretical mechanisms or developmental outcomes considered in this review.

We searched existing reviews of evaluations of youth development programs (Catalano et al., 1998; National Research Council and Institute of Medicine, 2002; Roth et al., 1998) and mentoring programs (DuBois, Holloway, et al., 2002) as well as Internet sites of various federal government agencies (e.g., U.S. Department of

Education, Office of Juvenile Justice and Delinquency Prevention) to identify multifaceted youth programs that included mentoring. We found 30 programs that were sufficiently well described to enable some interpretation of the role of mentoring. Our review revealed two predominant modes of incorporating mentoring within overall program structures.

By far the most common was composed of programs in which mentoring was one of multiple program components (22 programs). There was considerable diversity within those programs. For example, mentoring may be made available to all program participants as one of several universal or targeted prevention strategies (e.g., LoSciuto, Hilbert, Fox, Porcellini, & Lanphear, 1996) or as an intensive "booster" strategy for special needs youth (e.g., Dumas, Prinz, Smith, & Laughlin, 1999). In some cases, eligibility for being matched with a mentor occurs after participating in other program components for a period of time (e.g., Emshoff et al., 2003). It was not always possible to infer from program descriptions the extent to which mentoring was integrated with other program components; however, in several cases, the mentors participated regularly in other program activities with their protégés (e.g., Emshoff et al., 2003; LoSciuto et al., 1996) or employed structured activities designed to reinforce overall program goals (e.g., Cavell & Hughes, 2000; Center for Human Resources, 1995; Felner & Adan, 1988; Short et al., 1995).

The second mode of incorporating mentoring (eight programs) included mentoring as the primary vehicle through which skills training or other program components were offered (e.g., King, Vidourek, Davis, & McClellan, 2002) or mentoring as the point of entry for accessing services and maximizing service utilization (e.g., Bettencourt, Hodges, Huba, & Pickett, 1998). Table 21.2 summarizes program descriptions and evaluation findings for the 16 programs with evaluations that used a quasi-experimental or experimental design.

Overview of Evaluated Programs

As shown in Table 21.2, programs varied widely in characteristics of the target population (e.g., age, gender, risk status), as did the

evaluations in the outcomes assessed. Whereas all of the evaluations assessed prevention/promotion outcomes, fewer examined relatedness and self-definition as outcomes, moderators, or mediators. Notably, when evaluations of multicomponent programs provided data only for prevention/promotion outcomes, overall program effects were not consistently positive. Evaluations that provided data on a broader range of outcomes tended to show positive effects in the domains of self-definition and interpersonal relatedness and some positive effects in prevention/promotion. This observation points to the possibility that the inclusion of a mentoring component may have its strongest direct effects focused on relatedness and self-definition and suggests the need for further research to examine possible mediating or moderating effects of those processes on prevention/promotion outcomes. Interestingly, all of the programs in which mentoring was the primary component showed positive effects both on prevention/promotion outcomes and (when measured) relatedness and self-definition. Because integration of mentoring with other services is in some sense the defining feature of such programs, this observation lends some support to the idea that the extent of integration may be an important moderator of program effectiveness.

Evidence of Differential and Moderated Effects

Unfortunately, for our purposes, most of the evaluations were of the "black box" variety (Posovac & Carey, 2003) in that they provide outcome data but fail to allow fine-grained analysis of specific contributions of mentoring to overall program effects (see also Roth et al., 1998). Here, we briefly review findings from evaluations that were designed so as to allow insight into possible differential (i.e., Path a in Figure 21.1) or moderating (i.e., Path c) effects of mentoring when combined with other programs and services (we found no examples of studies examining mediated effects, Path b). The three programs reviewed include (a) Across Ages, (b) the Stress Management and Alcohol Awareness Program (SMAAP), and (c) Prime Time. All three are examples of programs in

(Text continues on page 325)

Table 21.2 Findings of Evaluations of Youth Development Programs (YDP) Integrating a Mentoring Component

Program	Description	Evaluation Design	Selected Findings*
Mentoring as one component of a YDP			
Across Ages Aseltine, Dupre, & Lamlein (2000)	*Goal:* Drug prevention *Setting:* School, community *Target:* High-risk (ages 9–13) *Components:* Adult mentors (age 55+); community service; life skills class/social competence training; family activities	Experimental pre/posttest 1. No intervention control ($n = 138$) (CG) 2. Community service + Life skills curriculum ($n = 135$) (PG) 3. Mentoring + Community service + Life skills curriculum ($n = 85$) (MG)	*Self-Definition* • Self-control (MG > PG, CG), school bonding (MG > PG, CG), self-confidence (MG > PG) *Relatedness* • Family bonding (MG > PG), cooperation (MG > CG), positive attitudes toward elderly (MG, PG > CG), positive attitudes toward helping others (MG > PG, CG) *Prevention/Promotion* • School absences (MG < CG), alcohol use (MG, PG < C G), positive attitudes toward drug use (MG <P G, CG), problem behaviors (MG < CG)
Building Positive Relationships Westhues, Clarke, Watton, & St. Claire-Smith (2001)	*Goal:* Relationship skills *Setting:* Not specified *Target:* At-risk girls (Grades 3–12) *Components:* Group component for girls already in Big Sisters; focus on empathy, relationships, problem solving and self-advocacy	Quasi-experimental pre/posttest 1. Comparison group: Big Sister only ($n = 19$) 2. Program group: Group + Big Sister ($n = 24$)	*Self-Definition* • Self-esteem, self-confidence *Relatedness* • Communication, increased respect for parents *Prevention/Promotion* • School attendance, aggression and fighting
CASASTART (Striving Together to Achieve Rewarding Tomorrows) Harrell, Cavanagh, & Sridharan (1998)	*Goal:* Reduce drug exposure, criminal activity *Setting:* Youth in high-risk environments *Target:* Not specified *Components:* community-enhanced policing/enforcement; case management; juvenile justice intervention; family services; after-school, summer activities; education services; mentoring; incentives	Quasi-experimental pre/posttest 1. No intervention nonmatched control group ($n = 333$) 2. No intervention control group of matched youth and neighborhoods ($n = 203$) 3. Intervention group ($n = 338$)	*Prevention/Promotion* At posttest: • Past month drug use, lifetime gateway drug, any drug use 1-year follow-up: • Past month use, past year use, lifetime use of gateway strong drugs, past year violent crimes, past month and lifetime drug sales

* When describing findings from the program that allowed examination of the effects of mentoring separately from the effects of the rest of the program (Across Ages), we indicated how the findings applied to the mentoring + program groups, the program-only groups, and the control or comparison group. For all other programs, findings reflect positive program findings according to each program's specific evaluation design.

Program	Description	Evaluation Design	Selected Findings*
Colorado Longitudinal Youth Study (CLYS) Blechman, Maurice, Buecker, & Helberg, 2000)	*Goal:* Resilience in juvenile offenders *Setting:* Not specified *Target:* Minors charged with nonviolent misdemeanors *Components:* Juvenile diversion; skills training; mentoring	Multicohort longitudinal natural groups design 1. Juvenile diversion only (JD: *n* = 137) 2. Juvenile diversion + Skills training (ST; *n* = 55) 3. Juvenile diversion + Mentoring (M; *n* = 45)	*Prevention/Promotion* • Arrested within 2 years: ST < M, JD • In 2 propensity blocking quintiles: time until first rearrest: ST > M, JD
Cool Girls Emshoff et al. (2003)	*Goal:* Academic and decision-making skills, health/wellness/nutrition, and awareness of life opportunities *Setting:* School, community *Target:* Lower-income urban girls *Components:* After-school curriculum, tutorial; field trips; life skills programming; 1:1 mentor for eligible participants	Quasi-experimental pre/posttest, program group separated into dosage groups 1. No intervention comparison group (*n* = 27) 2. Moderate attending Cool Girls (*n* = 18) 3. High-attending Cool Girls (*n* = 40) 4. Cool Girls with mentors (*n* = 14)	*Prevention/Promotion* Program effects (high attenders vs. comparison): • Behavioral conduct, extracurricular activities, exposure to cultural resources, grades • Mentored vs. mentor eligible • Behavioral conduct
Early Risers August, Realmuto, Hektner, & Bloomquist (2001)	*Goal:* Academic, social competence, behavioral self-regulation, parent involvement *Setting:* School, family *Target:* Low-middle income, aggressive/ disruptive kindergarten students *Components:* Summer school program; teacher consultation; mentoring; social skills groups; parent education; family support	Experimental, longitudinal pre/posttest design (10 schools randomly assigned) 1. No intervention control schools (*n* = 121 children) 2. Early Risers program schools (*n* = 124 children)	*Prevention/Promotion* • Academic competence, behavioral self-regulation and social competence (for severely aggressive children)
Prime Time Cavell & Hughes (2000)	*Goal:* Delinquency prevention *Setting:* School, home *Target:* Aggressive 2nd- and 3rd-grade children *Components:* Weekly therapeutic mentoring; school-based problem-solving skills-training groups; home and school consultation	Experimental pre/posttest 1. "Standard mentoring" control (*n* = 29) 2. Therapeutic mentoring + Problem-solving skills-training + Home and school consultation (*n* = 31)	*Self-Definition* • Self-competence *Relatedness* • Positive view of mentors *Prevention/Promotion* • Parent- and teacher-rated aggression

(Continued)

Table 21.2 (Continued)

Program	Description	Evaluation Design	Selected Findings*
Quantum Opportunities Center for Human Resources (1995)	*Goal:* Education, service, life skills *Setting:* Not specified *Target:* Economically disadvantaged 9–12th graders *Components:* 1:1 mentoring; educational, service, life development activities; financial incentives for college/career goals (4-year program)	Experimental pre/post design 1. No intervention control ($n = 125$) 2. Intervention group ($n = 250$)	*Self-Definition* • Consider lives a success, hopeful about the future *Relatedness* • Participation in community service *Prevention/Promotion* • High school graduation, pursuit of secondary education, decreased high school dropout, honor or award in past year, decreased teenage parenthood
SMAAP (Stress Management & Alcohol Awareness Program) Short et al. (1995)	*Goal:* Coping, self-esteem, social competence, lowered alcohol expectancies *Setting:* School, neighborhood *Target:* Grades 4–6 *Components:* 8-week school-based curriculum; individual personal trainers (mentors) for some sites (met 3–4 hours/week for 8 weeks)	Experimental pre/posttest design using delayed treatment cohorts as control groups 1. Group program alone (PG) (8 schools) Cohort 1 ($n = 63$); Cohort 2 ($n = 60$); Cohort 3 ($n = 58$) 2. Group program + Personal trainer/Mentor (MG) (5 schools) Cohort 1 ($n = 30$); Cohort 2 ($n = 29$); Cohort 3 ($n = 31$)	In 30 comparisons between the program-only group and the Program + Mentor group (Cohorts 1 and 2), only two were significant (and the findings were in favor of the program only group); therefore, all analyses and the findings presented below represent comparisons of the combined program groups to the delayed treatment controls *Relatedness* • Increased social-support coping *Prevention/Promotion* • Increased knowledge about use and effects of alcohol, emotion-focused coping
STEP (School Transitional Environment Project) Felner & Adan (1988)	*Goal:* Ease school transition, coping skills *Setting:* School *Target:* High-risk students entering middle and high school transitions	Quasi-experimental pre/posttest design with matched control group 1. No intervention control ($n = 113$) 2. Intervention group ($n = 59$)	*Self-Definition* • Self-concept *Relatedness* • Perception of teachers as supportive

Program	Description	Evaluation Design	Selected Findings*
	Components: Reorganize school environment (maintain peer group throughout day); trained homeroom teachers serve as school liaison; 1:1/group mentor and guidance counselor for students		Prevention/Promotion • Academic performance, school absenteeism and school dropout, alternative school placement, perceived school environment
Mentoring as a primary component of a YDP			
Adolescent Diversion Project Davidson & Redner (1988)	Goal: Delinquency prevention Setting: Youth's natural environment Target: Teen offenders Components: Intensive mentoring focused on developing relationships, behavioral contracting, child advocacy, and provision of community resources	Experimental design (2-year follow-up) 1. No intervention (release to parents) control 2. No intervention typical court-processing control 3. Attention-placebo 4. Intervention group: Mentoring + Child advocacy + Community resources	Prevention/Promotion • Recidivism at 2-year follow-up
The Buddy System O'Donnell, Lydgate, & Fo (1979)	Goal: Delinquency-reduction Setting: Community Target: Delinquent youth (ages 10–17) Components: Non-professional adults mentors ("buddies") supervised by graduate students implemented intervention	Experimental wait-list control group 1. No intervention control (n = 218) 2. Intervention group (n = 335)	Prevention/Promotion • Lower arrest rate at 2-year follow-up for youth with prior arrest for major offense • Higher arrest rate at 2-year follow-up for youth with no prior arrest for major offense
Healthy Kids King, Vidourek, Davis, & McClellan (2002)	Goal: Relationships, self-esteem, grades, and goal setting Setting: Not specified Target: At-risk 4th graders Components: Intensive mentoring with focus on relationship building, self-esteem, goal setting, and academic assistance	Quasi-experimental pre/posttest design 1. No intervention control (children not identified as being at risk) (n = 251) 2. Mentored group (at-risk children) (n = 28)	Self-Definition • School connectedness, depressive symptoms, feeling safe at school Relatedness • Family connectedness, communication with parents/guardians, peer connectedness

(Continued)

Table 21.2 (Continued)

Program	Description	Evaluation Design	Selected Findings*
Primary Mental Health Project (PMHP) Cowen, Hightower, Pedro-Carroll, Work, Wyman, & Haffey (1996)	*Goal:* Social/emotional, academic functioning *Setting:* Elementary schools *Target:* Children with mild-moderate school adjustment problems *Components:* Assessment; goal setting and monitoring; individual or group interaction with a mentor; consultation between home, school and mentor	Quasi-experimental pre/posttest design with 2-year follow-up 1. No intervention matched control group from same schools ($n = 61$) 2. Intervention group ($n = 61$)	*Prevention/Promotion* • Improved grades, fewer physical fights with peers in last month, decreased bullying in past month *Relatedness* • Teacher-reported shy-anxious behavior *Prevention/Promotion* • Social/emotional/academic competencies. Adaptive assertiveness • Adjustment problems, trait anxiety
Project RAISE McPartland & Nettles (1991)	*Goal:* Self-esteem, school behavior/ progress, risk behavior *Setting:* School *Target:* At-risk middle and high school students *Components:* School advocates; mentoring for some students; after-school activities and field trips	Quasi-experimental pre/posttest design 1. No intervention comparison ($n = 7,292$) 2. Program group ($n = 314$)	*Prevention/Promotion* • School absences, grades in English courses
Woodrock Youth Development Project LoSciuto, Hilbert, Fox, Porcellini, & Lanphear (1999)	*Goal:* Competence enhancement, drug prevention *Setting:* School, community, and home *Target:* At-risk children and teens ages 6–14 *Components:* After-school program, tutoring, attention and support provided by mentors; wilderness camp with family and mentors	Experimental pre/posttest design 1. No intervention comparison ($n = 474$) 2. Intervention group ($n = 244$)	*Relatedness* • Race relations, decreased ethnocentrism *Prevention/Promotion* • School attendance, lower levels of lifetime drug use, less drug use during past month

which mentoring was one of multiple program components.

Across Ages, an intergenerational mentoring program for middle school students, includes a community service component and a life skills curriculum (LoSciuto et al., 1999; Taylor, LoSciuto, Fox, Hilbert, & Sonkowsky, 1999; see Taylor, LoSciuto, & Porcellini, this volume). In an initial evaluation, 562 middle school students were assigned randomly to the full intervention ($N = 180$), a community service/life skills curriculum group ($N = 193$), or a control group ($N = 189$). With specific relevance to effects attributable to mentoring, the full intervention group reported marginally higher levels of well-being and lower levels of substance use at program completion than the service/curriculum group. Aseltine, Dupre, and Lamlein's (2000) more recent evaluation using the same design and comparison groups found attitudinal and behavioral improvements at the end of the school year for the full curriculum group relative to the service/curriculum-only group (see Table 21.2). However, all of these gains had disappeared by 6-month follow-up. By offering evidence of differential effects of mentoring (i.e., Path a in Figure 21.1), these evaluations provide preliminary support for the idea that mentoring coupled with community service and a life skills curriculum is more beneficial than a less intensive intervention that does not include mentoring. Such effects may, however, be achieved only in the short term while program components are still operational.

The ability to detect differential effects might also be limited by insufficient duration or intensity of the mentoring component. For example, the primary component of SMAAP was an eight-session curriculum for fourth- through sixth-grade children of problem drinkers (Short et al., 1995). The curriculum included didactic material, demonstration and practice of social skills, and homework assignments. In 5 of the 13 participating schools, the researchers were able to match children with "personal trainers," trained undergraduate college students who were randomly assigned to one child. The personal trainer met with the assigned child for 3 to 4 hours per week for 8 weeks, usually in the child's neighborhood, and sought to reinforce the skills taught during school-based lessons,

increase the child's sense of self-worth, and provide a positive adult role model. Despite a high degree of integration between the curriculum and mentoring components and positive overall program effects, only two comparisons (out of 30 tests) between versions of the program that included, versus did not include, personal trainers reached significance; and both favored the curriculum-only group. It may be that the duration of the personal trainer component was too brief for a true mentoring relationship to have formed and for effects to have emerged.

Prime Time works with teacher-identified aggressive second- and third-grade children and provides "therapeutic mentoring," problem-solving skills training, and consultation with parents and teachers. Cavell and Hughes (2000) assigned 62 children randomly to either the full intervention or a "standard mentoring" control condition. Prime Time mentors were trained undergraduate psychology or education students enrolled in a field experiences course. They met for at least 1 hour each week with their protégés over the course of 16 months, completed log sheets after each contact, and received regular supervision. Control mentors, also undergraduate students, were expected to meet weekly with their protégés but received minimal training and no ongoing supervision. Outcome assessments revealed small gains for participants in both conditions in parent- and in teacher-rated behavior. Prime Time children rated relationship quality with their mentors more highly than did controls, and relationship quality moderated the association between treatment condition and parent-rated aggression. Specifically, Prime Time participants who reported high-quality relationships with their mentors showed greater reductions in aggression than those who reported lower-quality relationships and controls. These findings offer preliminary evidence of a moderating effect (i.e., Path c in Figure 21.1) of quality of mentoring on prevention/promotion outcomes. However, there also was some evidence of iatrogenic effects, such that Prime Time children were more likely than controls to endorse attitudes supporting positive consequences of aggression, perhaps resulting from the group context in which the problem-solving skills-training component of the program was delivered (see Dishion, McCord, & Poulin, 1999).

Cumulatively, the findings suggest that benefits of combining mentoring with other intensive program components may be conditional on the quality of the mentoring provided and the need to attend to potential unintended negative consequences that may arise from youth participation in other components either independently or in interaction with mentoring relationships.

In addition to the evidence of differential and moderated effects noted in the previous paragraphs, there is some evidence of moderating effects in the sense that the consequences of combining mentoring and other program components may differ depending on the characteristics of the youth. Blechman, Maurice, Buecker, and Helberg (2000), for example, found that mentoring was more costly and less effective in reducing recidivism than skills training for youth in the juvenile justice system; however, those authors did not test mentoring in combination with skills training. On the other hand, delinquent youth with arrests for major offenses experienced fewer subsequent arrests than youth with no arrests for major offenses when they participated in a program in which mentors (referred to as "buddies") used behavioral contingencies to improve behavior (O'Donnell, Lydgate, & Fo, 1979). It may be that behaviorally disordered youth can benefit from highly structured and behaviorally focused training carried out in conjunction with mentoring (see also Davidson & Redner, 1988).

Summary

There is encouraging, but by no means definitive, evidence that mentoring offers added value when implemented in combination with other programs and services. We offer this conclusion cautiously in light of both methodological limitations of available research and substantive concerns. Specifically, because few research designs have compared conditions that do and do not include mentoring and few designs have gathered data on a broad range of potential moderators, mediators, and outcomes, it is not possible to test competing hypotheses about the role that mentoring may play within complex programs. In addition, the available evidence suggests that beneficial effects of

integrating mentoring with other programs and services may be conditional on quality of and programmatic support for (e.g., training) the mentoring relationships involved and on tailoring program components to the needs and backgrounds of youth participants.

PRACTICE

In this section, we focus on implications for practice that are unique to programs seeking to integrate mentoring into multicomponent programs and services. There is a growing literature, based in both empirical research and practical experience, that documents principles of effective mentoring practice (e.g., DuBois, Holloway, et al., 2002; MENTOR/National Mentoring Partnership, 2003), and we would argue that those principles are applicable to effective implementation of the mentoring component of multifaceted programming. For example, expectations for amount of contact and minimum duration of mentoring relationships likely hold similar relevance for both specialized mentoring and multicomponent programs. The presence of other programs and services offered in conjunction with mentoring also may offer unique opportunities and challenges.

Rhodes et al. (2002) have reported that the rapid growth of site-based mentoring programs situated in schools, workplaces, community agencies, and religious settings has resulted in the establishment of increasingly structured programs that require less time commitment and planning on the part of mentors. Multicomponent programs are often site based, and a consequence of this may be that the mentoring components of such programs are less powerful than many stand-alone mentoring programs. Compared with field-based programs such as Big Brothers Big Sisters, site-based mentoring programs (especially those offered within multicomponent programs) may have reduced expectations for duration and intensity of mentoring relationships (Karcher, Kuperminc, Portwood, Sipe, & Taylor, 2004). Yet through our experience in implementing and evaluating Cool Girls, we believe that mentoring can add value to multicomponent programming (and vice versa), particularly in the context of careful planning and a commitment to maintaining high-quality programming across components. We raise three challenges and issues to which we believe practitioners should attend: (a) balancing breadth versus depth; (b) synergy: being part of something larger versus getting lost in the shuffle; and (c) gauging the timing and sequencing of mentor-protégé matches. These observations draw mainly from experience, but wherever possible, we link our discussion to relevant research and theory.

Balancing Breadth Versus Depth

As noted previously, a common conclusion drawn by reviewers of the youth development literature is that the most effective programs address multiple contexts of young people's lives and incorporate multiple elements of the youth development frameworks. However, some research suggests that running a complex mix of programmatic activities can reduce effectiveness and strain the resources of community-based agencies (Stoil & Hill, 1996). Thus, balancing breadth versus depth is a major challenge for multifaceted youth programming.

With support from the Edna McConnell Clark Foundation, Cool Girls, Inc., has recently undergone a labor-intensive process involving staff, board members, and evaluators to redefine and refocus programmatic goals and link those goals to a comprehensive business plan that will allow the program to grow and improve in a systematic manner consistent with its agreed upon mission and philosophy. One aspect of this process involved articulating the core program components and elaborating a theory of change through which program activities are seen as contributing to program goals. Articulating a theory of change (often in the form of a logic model) enables programs to examine underlying assumptions and link intended short- and long-term outcomes to program activities (Kellogg Foundation, 2001). The further step of linking program planning to resources (i.e., business planning) forces programs to make difficult decisions about their ability to maintain quality given current resources and to identify and plan for future resource needs. Through this process, Cool Girls, Inc., affirmed its commitment to high-quality mentoring (Cool Sisters) as

a core element of its programming, along with academic enrichment (Cool Scholars) and the after-school Girls Club.

The experience of Cool Girls, Inc., illustrates the importance of careful planning that avoids a "kitchen sink" approach to service provision. Identifying the core elements helps program staff to focus their efforts on ensuring that all participants are exposed to the program as intended, while encouraging participation in supplementary offerings whenever possible (e.g., the Cool Tech computer technology and the Cool Biz entrepreneurship programs). Such clarity about core versus supplementary components also provided much needed guidance for the development, implementation, and ongoing refinement of an evaluation plan as an integral part of the cycle of planning, implementing, reflecting, and improving the program over time.

Synergy: Being Part of Something Larger Versus Getting Lost in the Shuffle

Planning alone cannot ensure that things will go smoothly or that program components will work synergistically. In its early days, Cool Girls, Inc., operated at a single site with a small staff and a few volunteers, all with a shared sense of purpose. Mentors tended to be involved as volunteers in other program components. The inevitable division of labor that occurred as the program grew to serve a larger number of girls at multiple sites and added new program components brought about a somewhat less familial program climate. The synergy that at one time seemed to come naturally now requires ongoing planning, reflection, and organizational resources. Monthly "Cool Sister Rap" sessions are one strategy currently used to keep mentors connected to the overall program. These sessions are structured to provide support and reassurance to mentors in addition to providing updates on other program activities and sharing of experiences. Currently, the staff is also planning an electronic newsletter including information about program events as a means of "marketing" the overall program to mentors. Other strategies to promote synergy include requiring prospective mentors to spend time at after-school sites prior to being matched and to require current mentors to make periodic visits to program sites and participate with their protégés in special events.

Mentors associated with Cool Girls, Inc., report that they enjoy having a role within a larger program. Similarly, program staff appreciate the mentors' role as "on-the-ground proponents" of what the program is trying to accomplish through its multifaceted offerings. As illustrated by the opening vignette, mentors need a general understanding of the program and ongoing opportunities for discussion as background to planning relevant, innovative, and fun activities to share with their protégés. However, strategies for ensuring synergy require a great deal of energy on the part both of mentors and program staff. This is not a trivial matter given that busy schedules may limit the ability of program staff to balance responsibility for multiple program components and keep mentors informed. Leaving the responsibility of program integration to mentors, who themselves are busy people, may lead to dissatisfaction with the program and possibly to early termination of mentor-protégé relationships.

Gauging the Timing and Sequencing of Mentor-Protégé Matches

A third set of challenges unique to multifaceted programs involves logistical issues regarding the role mentors play in the overall functioning of programs. As noted previously, in most cases, mentoring is a component of programs that offer multiple programs and services, but in some cases, mentors are the primary agents of direct service delivery (e.g., mentors provide a structured skills-training intervention) or the point of access to other services (e.g., mentors provide information and referrals to health care settings).

Among multicomponent programs, the timing of the mentor-protégé match and, more broadly, the sequencing of mentoring in relation to other program components may have important implications for successful implementation of both the mentoring component and of other components. For example, because of its popularity, some programs might use the promise of matching children with adult mentors as a "hook" to capture the interest of potential

participants. This was in part the strategy implemented by Prime Time (T. Cavell, personal communication, October 15, 2003). The designers of Prime Time also predicted that allowing time for relationships to form between mentors and protégés would have the benefit of "priming" identified aggressive children to be more open than they might otherwise have been to participating in skills training and other intervention efforts aimed at reducing aggression. Cool Girls employs the opposite strategy, advancing the notion that requiring 1 year of participation in its after-school tutoring and life skills programs provides an opportunity for program staff to get to know children and families well enough to assist in improving the quality of matches. Indeed, program records indicate that Cool Girls matches typically last 3.5 years, compared with the much shorter duration of matches reported by most traditional standalone mentoring programs (Rhodes, 2002). Given that there is no research to support one strategy over another, it may be most important for practitioners to articulate a clear rationale for the chosen approach.

FUTURE DIRECTIONS

Synthesis

In this chapter, we have outlined a theoretical framework identifying possible mechanisms through which mentoring (a relational strategy) may operate in conjunction with didactic and experiential strategies undertaken by many programs to affect outcomes related to the broadly defined goals of youth development programs. These goals focus on promoting the development of self-definition and interpersonal relatedness in addition to prevention and competence promotion. Leading researchers are calling for research that can inform theory and practice on what makes for positive mentoring relationships (DuBois, Holloway, et al., 2002; Rhodes, 2002). Consideration of mentoring as a part of multifaceted programs and services adds to the complexity of this task, raising questions about how mentoring and other program components contribute to developmental outcomes for youth participants and about how to maximize synergy across components. Available evidence suggests that the integration of mentoring with other programs and services holds promise as an approach to positive youth development. However, research has not kept pace with the rapid development of such programs. Although we identified a substantial number of programs that attempt to integrate mentoring with other programs and services, there was little consistency in program designs or in outcomes assessed. Most studies focused on overall program effects, and few designs provided insight into the role of mentoring in combination with other programs.

Recommendations for Research

1. *Use of designs, analyses, and measures necessary to investigate effects of mentoring in combination with other program components.* In order to be able to test differential effects of mentoring, experimental or quasi-experimental designs are needed in which multiple versions of a program can be compared. For example, research can build on the designs employed in the evaluations of Across Ages and SMAAP to test program effects with and without a mentoring component. Research designs might also examine variation in other program elements, such as intensity or duration of the mentoring component, or variations in strategies for integrating program components.

Furthermore, evaluations should include measures of change not only in prevention/promotion outcomes but also in processes of relatedness and self-definition. Expanding the range of measurement can enhance the ability to detect differential effects across a broader range of outcomes and enable examination of mediated effects. Inclusion of measures sensitive to the mentoring process and its integration with other program components (e.g., extent of joint attendance at program events/activities and perceived quality of relationship) is needed to examine mechanisms through which mentoring might moderate effects of other program components.

2. *Use of existing data.* A first step toward more sophisticated field experiments may be to conduct further analyses of existing data. For example, studies that take advantage of "naturally occurring" variations in implementation across program sites (Center for Human Resources, 1995) or in individual participants' exposure to various program components (August, Hektner, Egan, Realmuto, & Bloomquist, 2002) would allow examination of how mentoring and/or other program components may contribute to overall program effects. Although vulnerable to internal validity threats, such studies offer the ability to move beyond tests of program efficacy in highly controlled conditions to tests of program effectiveness in the real world (August et al., 2002), particularly if they incorporate statistical controls for preprogram group differences (Blechman et al., 2000).

Process and outcome data from the national evaluation of JUMP (Juvenile Mentoring Program) provide another avenue for using existing data to build theory (Office of Juvenile Justice and Delinquency Prevention, 1998). The database offers descriptive data on prevailing practices in how mentoring is combined with other services across nearly 200 funded programs. If developed systematically and maintained over time, such databases can allow examination of links between program outcomes and variation across multiple program designs (e.g., specialized mentoring versus mentoring paired with didactic classroom-based curricula or community service), variations in implementation (e.g., expectations of frequency of mentor-protégé contact, integrated training and supervision of volunteers and staff serving various roles), and variations in characteristics of the populations served.

3. *Process-oriented research.* In addition to outcome studies, there is a need for in-depth research involving qualitative and observational methodologies. Roth and Brooks-Gunn (2003) have called for creating sophisticated and sensitive observational measures similar to ones that have been validated for research on early childhood education environments. Also, formative research is needed to define the important parameters of program integration. Qualitative research might take the form of multiple case study designs focused on gathering information about different strategies that have been undertaken in efforts to increase the ability of program

components to work together. Once dimensions of program integration have been identified, quantitative methods, such as meta-analysis or large-scale multisite or multiprogram studies, might also be used to examine integration as a moderator of program effects.

With specific relevance to mentoring in the context of multicomponent programs, priorities for future research include (a) a focus on organizational and community capacity to provide high-quality multifaceted programming, (b) attention to program contexts and target population characteristics that facilitate or impede effective use of mentoring, and (c) a focus on conditions that maximize synergy between mentoring and other program components to promote positive youth development.

Recommendations for Practice

1. *Use of existing knowledge and best practices.* Given the dearth of process-oriented research that can provide concrete guidance to program planners and practitioners, we recommend drawing on the existing knowledge base and best practices for stand-alone mentoring programs and comprehensive youth development programs (e.g., MENTOR/National Mentoring Partnership, 2003). We have used our experiences in implementing and evaluating Cool Girls to explore challenges that similar organizations are likely to confront in their own development.

2. *Development of logic models and ongoing evaluation.* We strongly recommend that programs develop a logic model and commit to ongoing evaluation. Our experience has been that these processes are often viewed initially as threatening, but often lead to outcomes that are highly valued by practitioners and researchers alike, including greater clarity about program goals, more informed decision making, and improved program functioning. Although they require some commitment of program resources, these processes need not cost a great deal of money or require expertise in sophisticated research methodology. Increasingly, funding agencies are requiring that programs undergo systematic planning and evaluation,

and many offer technical assistance (e.g., Kellogg Foundation, 2001). In addition, several user-friendly resources are available free of charge via the Internet and can provide useful guidance.

We believe that the theoretical framework offered in this chapter can guide further investigation of process and outcome data that are already being collected. This work, in turn, can help both to refine theory and to contribute to more sophisticated research that will illuminate the role of mentoring in comprehensive efforts to promote positive youth development.

REFERENCES

Albee, G. W., & Gullotta, T. P. (1997). *Primary prevention works.* Thousand Oaks, CA: Sage.

Allen, J. P., Moore, C. W., & Kuperminc, G. P. (1997). Developmental approaches to understanding adolescent deviance. In S. S. Luthar, J. A. Burack, D. Cicchetti, & J. Weisz (Eds.), *Developmental psychopathology: Perspectives on risk and disorder* (pp. 548–567). Cambridge, UK: Cambridge University Press.

Aseltine, R. H., Dupre, M., & Lamlein, P. (2000). Mentoring as a drug prevention strategy: An evaluation of Across Ages. *Adolescent and Family Health, 1,* 11–20.

August, G. J., Hektner, J. M., Egan, E. A., Realmuto, G. M., & Bloomquist, M. L. (2002). The Early Risers longitudinal prevention trial: Examination of 3-year outcomes in aggressive children with intent-to-treat and as-intended analyses. *Psychology of Addictive Behaviors, 16,* S27–S39.

August, G. J., Realmuto, G. M., Hektner, J. M., & Bloomquist, M. L. (2001). An integrated components preventive intervention for aggressive elementary school children: The Early Risers program. *Journal of Consulting and Clinical Psychology, 69,* 614–626.

Bandura, A. (1980). Gauging the relationship between self-efficacy judgment and action. *Cognitive Therapy and Research, 4,* 263–268.

Bettencourt, T., Hodges, A., Huba, G. J., & Pickett, G. (1998). Bay Area Positives: A model of a youth based approach to HIV/AIDS services. *Journal of Adolescent Health, 23S,* 28–36.

Blatt, S. J., & Blass, R. B. (1995). Relatedness and self-definition: A dialectical model of personality development. In G. G. Noam & K. Fischer (Eds.), *Development and vulnerability in relationships* (pp. 309–338). Hillsdale, NJ: Erlbaum.

Blechman, E. A. (1992). Mentors for high risk minority youth: From effective communication to bicultural competence. *Journal of Clinical Child Psychology, 21,* 160–169.

Blechman, E. A., Maurice, A., Buecker, & Helberg, K. C. (2000). Can mentoring or skill training reduce recidivism? Observational study with propensity analysis. *Prevention Science, 1,* 139–155.

Catalano, R. F., Berglund, M. L., Ryan, J. A. M., Lonczak, H. S., & Hawkins, J. D. (1998). *Positive youth development in the United States: Research findings on evaluations of youth development programs.* Washington, DC: U.S. Department of Health and Human Services. Retrieved September 26, 2004, from http://aspe.hhs.gov/hsp/PositiveYouthDev99/

Cavell, T. A., & Hughes, J. N. (2000). Secondary prevention as context for assessing change processes in aggressive children. *Journal of School Psychology, 38,* 199–235.

Center for Human Resources. (1995). *Quantum Opportunities Program: A brief on the QOP pilot program.* Waltham, MA: Brandeis University, Heller Graduate School.

Cicchetti, D., Rappaport, J., Sandler, I., & Weissberg, R. P. (Eds.). (2000). *The promotion of wellness in children and adolescents.* Washington, DC: CWLA Press.

Connell, J. P. (1990). Context, self, and action: A motivational analysis of self-system processes across the lifespan. In D. Cicchetti & M. Beeghly (Eds.), *The self in transition: Infancy to childhood* (pp. 61–97). Chicago: University of Chicago Press.

Cool Girls, Inc. (n.d.). Welcome to Cool Girls, Inc. Retrieved January 30, 2004, from http://www.thecoolgirls.org/index.asp

Cowen, E. L., Hightower, A. D., Pedro-Carroll, J., Work, W. C., Wyman, P. A., & Haffey, W. C. (1996). *School based prevention for at-risk children: The Primary Mental Health Project.* Washington, DC: American Psychological Association.

Davidson, W. S., & Redner, R. (1988). The prevention of juvenile delinquency: Diversion from the juvenile justice system. In R. H. Price, E. L. Cowen, R. P. Lorion, & J. Ramos-McKay (Eds.), *Fourteen ounces of prevention: Theory, research, and prevention* (pp. 123–137). New York: Pergamon Press.

Dishion, T. J., McCord, J., & Poulin, F. (1999). When interventions harm: Peer groups and problem behavior. *American Psychologist, 54,* 755–764.

DuBois, D. L., Holloway, B. E., Valentine, J. C., & Cooper, H. (2002). Effectiveness of mentoring programs for youth: A meta-analytic review. *American Journal of Community Psychology, 30,* 157–198.

DuBois, D. L., Neville, H. A., Parra, G. R., & Pugh-Lilly, A. O. (2002). Testing a new model of mentoring. In G. G. Noam (Ed. in chief) & J. E. Rhodes (Ed.), *A critical view of youth mentoring (New Directions for Youth Development: Theory, Research, and Practice, No. 93,* pp. 21–57). San Francisco: Jossey-Bass.

Dumas, J. E., Prinz, R. J., Smith, E. P., & Laughlin, J. (1999). The Early Alliance prevention trial: An integrated set of interventions to promote competence and reduce risk for conduct disorder, substance abuse and school failure. *Clinical Child and Family Psychology Review, 2,* 37–53.

Durlak, J. A., & Wells, A. M. (1997). Primary prevention mental health programs for children and adolescents. *American Journal of Community Psychology, 25,* 115–152.

Emshoff, J., Kuperminc, G., Foster, J., Niolon, P., Broomfield, K., Secrest, L., et al. (2003, February). *Program evaluation of Cool Girls, Inc.: Data from the 2001–02 school year.* Atlanta: Georgia State University.

Erikson, E. (1963). *Childhood and society* (2nd ed.). New York: Norton.

Felner, R. D., & Adan, A. M. (1988). The School Transitional Environment Project: An ecological intervention and evaluation. In R. H. Price, E. L. Cowen, R. P. Lorion, & J. Ramos-McKay (Eds.). *Fourteen ounces of prevention: Theory, research, and prevention* (pp. 111–122). New York: Pergamon Press.

Harrell, A., Cavanagh, S., & Sridharan, S. (1988). *Impact of the Children At Risk Program: Comprehensive final report II.* Washington, DC: The Urban Institute.

Karcher, M. J., Kuperminc, G. P., Portwood, S. G., Sipe, C. L., & Taylor, A. S. (2004). *Mentoring* programs: *A typology to inform program development, research, and evaluation.* Manuscript submitted for publication.

Kellogg Foundation. (2001). *Logic model development guide.* Battle Creek, MI: Author.

King, K. A., Vidourek, R. A., Davis, B., & McClellan, W. (2002). Increasing self-esteem and school connectedness through a multidimensional mentoring program. *Journal of School Health, 72,* 294–299.

Kuperminc, G. P., Blatt, S. J., & Leadbeater, B. J. (1997). Relatedness, self-definition, and early adolescent adjustment. *Cognitive Therapy and Research, 21,* 310–320.

Kuperminc, G. P., Blatt, S. J., Shahar, G., Henrich, C., & Leadbeater, B. J. (2004). Cultural equivalence and cultural variance in longitudinal associations of young adolescent self-definition, interpersonal relatedness to psychological and school adjustment. *Journal of Youth and Adolescence, 33,* 13–31.

Larson, R. (2000). Toward a psychology of positive youth development. *American Psychologist, 55,* 170–183.

Leadbeater, B., Kuperminc, G., Blatt, S., & Hertzog, C. (1999). A multivariate model of gender differences in adolescents' internalizing and externalizing problems. *Developmental Psychology, 35,* 1268–1282.

LoSciuto, L., Hilbert, S. M., Fox, M. M., Porcellini, L., & Lanphear, A. (1996). A two-year evaluation of the Woodrock Youth Development Project. *Journal of Early Adolescence, 19,* 488–507.

McPartland, J. M., & Nettles, S. M. (1991). Using community adults as advocates or mentors for at-risk middle school students: A two-year evaluation of Project RAISE. *American Journal of Education, 12,* 568–586.

MENTOR/National Mentoring Partnership. (2003). *Elements of effective practice* (2nd ed.). Alexandria, VA: Author.

National Research Council and Institute of Medicine. (2002). (J. Eccles & J. Appleton Gootman, Eds.), *Community programs to promote youth development.* Committee on Community-Level Programs for Youth. Washington, DC: National Academy Press.

O'Donnell, C. R., Lydgate, T., & Fo, W. S. (1979). The Buddy System: Review and follow-up. *Child Behavior Therapy, 1,* 161–169.

Office of Juvenile Justice and Delinquency Prevention (1998, December). *1998 Report to Congress: Juvenile Mentoring Program (JUMP).* Washington, DC: U.S. Department of Justice, Office of Justice Programs, Office of Juvenile Justice and Delinquency Prevention. Retrieved September, 26, 2004, from http://www.ojjdp.ncjrs.org/jump/

Pittman, K., Diversi, M., & Ferber, T. (2002). Social policy supports for adolescence in the twenty-first century: Framing questions. *Journal of Research on Adolescence, 12,* 149–158.

Posovac, E. J., & Carey, R. G. (2003). *Program evaluation: Methods and case studies* (6th ed.). Upper Saddle River, NJ: Prentice Hall.

Rappaport, N. (2002). Can advising lead to meaningful relationships? In G. G. Noam (Ed. in chief) & J. E. Rhodes (Ed.), *A critical view of youth mentoring* (*New Directions for Youth Development: Theory, Research, and Practice, No. 93,* pp. 109–126). San Francisco: Jossey-Bass.

Rhodes, J. E. (2002). *Stand by me: The risks and rewards of mentoring today's youth.* Cambridge, MA: Harvard University Press.

Rhodes, J. E., Grossman, J. B., & Resch, N. L. (2000). Agents of change: Pathways through which mentoring relationships influence adolescents' academic adjustment. *Child Development, 71,* 1662–1671.

Rhodes, J. E., Grossman, J. B., & Roffman, J. (2002). The rhetoric and reality of youth mentoring. In G. G. Noam (Ed. in chief) & J. E. Rhodes (Ed.), *A critical view of youth mentoring* (*New Directions for Youth Development: Theory, Research, and Practice, No. 93,* pp. 9–20). San Francisco: Jossey-Bass.

Roth, J., & Brooks-Gunn, J. (2003). What exactly is a youth development program? Answers from research and practice. *Applied Developmental Science, 7,* 94–111.

Roth, J., Brooks-Gunn, J., Murray, L., & Foster, W. (1998). Promoting healthy adolescents: Synthesis of youth development program evaluations. *Journal of Research on Adolescence, 8,* 423–459.

Short, J. L., Roosa, M. W., Sandler, I. N., Ayers, T. S., Gensheimer, L. K., Braver, S. L., & Tein, J. Y. (1995). Evaluation of a preventive intervention for a self-selected subpopulation of children. *American Journal of Community Psychology, 23,* 223–247.

Stoil, M. J., & Hill, G. (1996). *Preventing substance abuse: Interventions that work.* New York: Plenum Press.

Taylor, A., LoSciuto, L., Fox, M., Hilbert, S. M., & Sonkowsky, M. (1999). The mentoring factor: Evaluation of the Across Ages' intergenerational approach to drug abuse prevention. *Child & Youth Services, 20*(1–2), 77–99.

Weissberg, R. P., Kumpfer, K. L., & Seligman, M. E. P. (2003). Prevention that works for children and youth: An introduction. *American Psychologist, 58,* 425–432.

Westhues, A., Clarke, L., Watton, J., & St. Claire-Smith, S. (2001). Building positive relationships: An evaluation of process and outcomes in a Big Sister program. *The Journal of Primary Prevention, 21,* 477–493.

PART VI

CONTEXTS OF MENTORING

22

SCHOOLS

SHARON G. PORTWOOD AND PENNY M. AYERS

INTRODUCTION

Across a variety of settings, unrelated individuals regularly engage in one-to-one relationships in which one, as mentor, supports, teaches, counsels, and assists the other. The presence of a mentor in the life of a young person is widely believed not only to support healthy growth and development but also to serve as a protective factor against many of the risks facing today's youth (Office of Juvenile Justice and Delinquency Prevention, 1998). Within the school environment, natural mentoring relationships may arise between students and adults (e.g., teachers, counselors, coaches). In addition, formal mentoring programs have gained in popularity as a promising form of intervention for children and youth (Freedman, 1988). To date, however, there is relatively little evaluation research demonstrating positive outcomes as a result of school-based mentoring.

Despite the shortage of sound scientific evidence on their effectiveness, school-based mentoring programs have proliferated. In the Commonwealth Fund 1998 Survey of Adults Mentoring Young People, two thirds of mentors participating in formal programs indicated that the program was sponsored by a school, college, or university (McLearn, Colasanto, & Schoen, 1998). Of the approximately 45% of mentoring programs that are site based, more than 70% are located in schools (Rhodes, 2002). Moreover,

outside of family members, teachers are the group most frequently identified as mentors by youth (DuBois & Silverthorn, in press). Accordingly, there is a critical need for additional knowledge on school-based mentoring.

Overview of School-Based Mentoring Programs

In contrast with community-based mentoring, in which the mentor and mentee meet at a place and time of their choosing, school-based mentoring takes places on school grounds, typically during regular school hours for 1 hour each week. Overall, school-based programs tend to be more structured than community-based programs; they are characterized by regularly scheduled meeting times; and typically, more activities are dictated by the program. More specifically, school-based mentoring programs are more likely than community-based programs to focus on activities intended to improve students' academic performance. Although mentors in school-based programs engage in social activities (e.g., talking and playing games), they may focus on assisting students with their homework and/or other academic-related activities (e.g., reading). In fact, mentees are often selected for participation based on their lack of school success. Therefore, compared with community-based programs, school-based programs serve more youth who are having problems in school and/or who have been held back in school (Herrera, Sipe, & McClanahan, 2000).

A Brief History of School-Based Mentoring

Historically, schools offered some form of remediation only after children had failed academically. However, by the 1980s, there was growing recognition that these compensatory programs were, at best, only marginally successful in alleviating academic failure and school dropout. This prompted interest in the development of primary prevention programs that could provide more personal support to children and youth (Ellis, Small-McGinley, & Hart, 1998). Between 1983 and 1988, a large number of reports addressing education, health, and poverty issues related to children and families highlighted the need for schools to develop collaborative arrangements with community service agencies to provide school-based services, particularly for children deemed to be "at risk" (Dryfoos, 1991). More recently, there has been a growing consensus that schools should be centers for a wide range of social, psychological, and health services for children and families. At the same time, mentoring has been promoted as a prevention and/or positive youth development strategy through popular national initiatives, such as America's Promise, and federal legislation, including Title IV-B of the Social Security Act (1935, as amended). However, while federal legislation purports to encourage mentoring, other legislative directives, most notably the Leave No Child Behind Act of 2001, have put increased demands on schools to demonstrate satisfactory academic outcomes through improved student performance on standardized tests. The resulting pressure on schools has resulted in often severe reductions in the resources (e.g., money and time) directed to nonacademic programs, even those programs, such as mentoring, that may contribute to academic success either directly or indirectly.

Opportunities and Challenges

Given that those targeted by primary prevention programs spend a substantial portion of their time in school, schools represent a natural context in which to establish mentoring relationships for children and youth. There are also a number of ways in which mentoring programs can benefit from the structure and resources of the school environment. Since meetings between mentors and mentees occur at school, more supervision by professionally trained adults is available. Because of this enhanced supervision, school-based programs can be more flexible in regard to mentor selection (e.g., mentor age is not a critical factor). Both programs and mentors can further benefit from easy access to students, teachers, and other school staff. For example, school-based mentors have regular contact with teachers, who can keep them informed of their student's specific needs.

Mentoring programs also bring new resources to the school. One potential advantage of school-based mentoring is that mentors are linked not only to individual children but also to the school environment. Adults are available to contribute their knowledge and support to both children and adults in the schools; teachers, in particular, may benefit from having mentors' additional help in the classroom (Herrera, 1999). At the broader level, successful school-based mentoring programs may establish social support within the school by bringing in caring adults from the surrounding community (Solomon, Watson, Battistich, Schaps, & Delucchi, 1996).

A major advantage of school-based programs is that they tend to cost about half as much per youth than other programs, even when the value of in-kind contributions from the school are considered (Rhodes, 2002). Since they are more likely to receive in-kind contributions such as staff support, office space, and telephones, school-based programs simply do not have the overhead costs associated with most community-based programs. Herrera et al. (2000) found that the average annual cost per mentee in school-based programs was $567, compared with $1,369 in community-based programs. At least one initiative (viz YouthFriends, see Portwood et al., 2001) has reported even lower costs, with the average school district (serving 332 students) incurring a total district cost of $28,000, representing $84 per student and $211 per volunteer.

Mentoring programs may be integrated into or reflect success toward the school's philosophy of helping children; however, in turn, school rules can constrain whether and how a relationship forms (Sipe & Roder, 1999). For example, since formal school-based mentoring occurs within the framework of the academic year, initial volunteer commitments are for 9 months rather than a full year. While this reduced time commitment may serve as a benefit in terms of mentor recruitment, it poses a potential threat to program effectiveness. Given that mentors and mentees in school-based programs typically spend less time together than do their counterparts in community-based programs (Herrera et al., 2000), the degree of mentoring that students receive may not be sufficient, either in terms of intensity or duration, to have a positive effect. In fact, in a meta-analysis of 55 evaluations of mentoring programs, school-based programs had consistently smaller effect sizes than were associated with programs in other settings (e.g., community, workplace) (DuBois, Holloway, Valentine, & Cooper, 2002). Given that frequency of contact, feelings of emotional closeness between mentee and mentor, and longevity of relationship were all associated with stronger program effects, the critical question arises as to whether school-based programs, which operate within the constraints of both the academic calendar and the school day, can be effective.

THEORY

Mentoring in the School Environment

Like all mentoring programs, school-based programs are founded on the premise that children and youth can benefit from the presence of a caring adult in their lives. Rhodes (2002) proposed that mentors influence the development of their mentees in three ways: "by enhancing social skills and emotional well-being; by improving cognitive skills through dialogue and listening; and by serving as a role model and advocate" (p. 35). Identifying problem areas and role modeling prosocial behavior by the mentor may lead to enhanced academic and social competence and personal character

for the mentee. Moreover, developmental (i.e., social-emotional and cognitive) growth serves as one mediator by which improved interpersonal relationships beyond the match may occur. For example, by talking about and modeling prosocial ways to handle conflict, mentors may help mentees to improve their relationships with parents and peers. These improved relationships may, in turn, contribute to other positive outcomes, including academic performance and behavior. In fact, Rhodes, Grossman, and Resch (2000) found support for a model in which the effects of mentoring on global self-worth, school value, and grades, rather than being direct, were mediated through increased quality of mentees' parental relationships and scholastic competence.

Mentors also can serve as role models for mentees by modeling appropriate behavior and engaging in discussions about prosocial ways to resolve various problems. Consistent with Rhodes's (2002) observations, social learning theory suggests that mentors' ability to model and to provide instruction on appropriate behaviors in one of the settings in which positive change is desired (e.g., the school) could prove particularly beneficial. Similarly, mentors may promote competence in areas that are relevant to their own backgrounds. For example, teachers who serve as mentors may be especially effective in promoting academic competencies given their background in education.

Compared with other types of mentoring programs, school-based mentoring may have the added advantage of enhancing school connectedness. Relationships with others and bonds with social institutions, such as schools, can help buffer the effects of stressful life events and to promote normal adjustment (Hawkins, Catalano, & Miller, 1992). Thus, promoting school connectedness is beneficial not only for children who are *not* doing well but also for those who *are* doing well or "good enough" (Karcher, Davis, & Powell, 2002). Developmentally, mentoring can promote social bonding and a sense of belonging that will, in turn, help youth to develop stronger connectedness to self, others, and society (Karcher, 2005). In the context of the school environment, such a sense of connectedness can benefit children both academically and socially.

Characteristics of School-Based Mentoring Relationships

It is believed that successful mentoring relationships are influenced by both individual and relationship factors. For example, the extent to which trust and empathy develop within the context of a mentoring relationship may be moderated by the child's developmental stage (Rhodes, 2002). Since children who are securely attached to adults more easily learn trust, competence, self-management, and prosocial behaviors (Brendtro & Long, 1995; Ellis et al., 1998), it follows that early interventions that foster close relationships with adults should produce the greatest impact. In fact, research indicates that younger children may be more receptive to mentoring than are older youth (Herrera et al., 2000). Older children may be even more resistant to school-based mentoring. For example, privacy may become an issue as children grow older, and this issue may impede the development of relationships with new adults (Herrera, 1999). Moreover, the frequency, intensity, and duration of mentors' and mentees' exposure to each other all contribute to establishing a context sufficient to support the development of a close personal relationship. Initiating mentoring when children are younger, as well as providing extended opportunities for mentor-mentee meetings, may address such potential obstacles, but research has not yet addressed these issues.

RESEARCH

As noted, there is relatively little research on school-based mentoring, and much of the research that is available is merely descriptive in nature. Moreover, existing empirical studies have often suffered from methodological flaws (e.g., lack of a control group), and few have been peer reviewed. Nonetheless, some valuable insights can be gleaned from a review of the current research specific to school-based mentoring.

Characteristics of Mentor-Mentee Relationships

Based on research on community-based mentoring, the quality of the relationship between the mentor and mentee appears to be one key element in producing positive outcomes. Until an emotional bond has been established, none of the positive changes associated with mentoring may occur (DuBois, Neville, Parra, & Pugh-Lilly, 2002). Moreover, ineffective relationships may produce neutral and even negative outcomes (Roberts, Liabø, Lucas, DuBois, & Sheldon, 2004). In a survey of 323 mentors from 35 school-based mentoring programs, eight factors were identified as important to developing positive mentoring relationships in school-based programs: engaging in social activities, engaging in academic activities, hours per month spent together, how decisions are made about how mentors and youth spend their time, similarity of interests between mentor and mentee, prematch orientation and training, postmatch training and support (from program staff), and age of the mentee. School-based mentors reported a more positive and supportive relationship when they engaged in social activities, and engaging in social activities was the strongest predictor of a positive relationship between a mentor and mentee (Herrera et al., 2000).

Although the length and intensity of the mentoring relationship have been identified as crucial components to effecting positive outcomes in community-based mentoring (DuBois, Holloway, et al., 2002; Rhodes, 2002), little is known about the required "dosage" for school-based mentoring. Given that mentoring relationships are tied not only to the school day (which can limit the time of individual meetings) but also to the academic calendar (which limits the frequency of contact and often leads to relationships being suspended over the summer and holidays), school-based mentoring initiatives are particularly challenged in regard to dosage. For example, Aseltine, Dupre, and Lamlein (2000) found that the benefits of an intergenerational mentoring program based in a school did not continue beyond the school year. School-based mentoring relationships also tend to be less intensive than in community settings, with mentors spending about half as much time with their mentees as their community counterparts (6 hours/month vs. 12 hours/month; Herrera et al., 2000).

The school setting itself may constrain the intensity and scope of meetings. Mentors' ability to foster a comfortable and safe environment for disclosure by their mentees may be inhibited by the parameters of a class schedule, and there may be limits to what some students will feel comfortable revealing on school premises. Moreover, school-based mentors' tendency and accompanying pressure from teachers, administrators, and/or parents to focus on academics may discourage them from engaging in the kinds of social activities that might most help them build close bonds. That significantly more community-based mentors felt "very close" to their protégés than did school-based and work-based mentors (45% compared with 32%) lends substance to this possibility. However, to date, no research has systematically examined the effects of academic versus social activities on the outcomes resulting from school-based mentoring.

Program Evaluation

Much of what we know about school-based mentoring comes from the evaluation of formal programs. Recent evaluations have reported that well-run mentoring programs can effect positive outcomes for students such as improved school attendance, improved academic performance, reductions in school disciplinary action (Volunteer Florida Foundation, n.d.), better attitudes about school, improved behavior at home and at school, and improved relationships with parents, teachers, and peers (Sipe, 1996). However, other research—typically descriptive studies from the 1990s—also reported that some mentoring programs are not achieving their intended goals (e.g., McPartland & Nettles, 1991; Slicker & Palmer, 1993).

Sample Evaluation Studies

Initial evaluation data from Big Brothers Big Sisters (BBBS), currently the largest mentoring program in the United States, support a positive impact for their school-based programs. BBBS matches follow a traditional school-based program model in which youth are referred by teachers and then meet one-on-one with a volunteer during the school day for 1 hour a week. Volunteers commit for an entire academic year and limit their contact to school property and activities supervised by the school or BBBS. While the mentoring pairs may devote some time to academic work, they typically engage in relationship-building activities. Based on the observations of teachers, parents, and mentors, as well as reports from the students themselves, 64% of students involved in school-based programs through five BBBS agencies during the 1997–1998 and 1998–1999 academic years developed improved attitudes toward school (Curtis & Hansen-Schwoebel, 1999). In addition, 58% received higher grades in social studies, math, and language; 60% improved their relationships with adults; 56% improved their relationships with peers; 55% were better able to express their feelings; 64% exhibited higher levels of self-confidence; and 62% were more trusting of teachers. Results also indicated that participants were less likely to repeat a grade and had fewer unexcused absences. However, these results are limited by the lack of a comparison group. In a separate study of BBBS school-based mentoring, Herrera (1999) concluded that even with the school-based constraints of meeting only 1 hour per week, children could develop strong relationships that, in turn, fostered positive academic and behavior change, including improvements in confidence, grades, social skills, and attendance. While positive, it should be noted that the outcomes in both of these studies were based solely on the perceptions of teachers, parents, and mentors, rather than objective measures of improvement in each of the relevant areas.

YouthFriends is a large and promising school-based mentoring initiative that serves a diverse population of children and youth across the states of Kansas, Missouri, and Michigan. Similar to BBBS school-based programs, children and youth participating in YouthFriends meet with a caring adult in the school environment for approximately 1 hour each week. In an outcome evaluation employing a pretest-posttest control group design, a total of 170 students (81 YouthFriends and 89 comparison students) across five school districts provided data on eight dependent variables: drug and alcohol use, attitudes and beliefs regarding drugs and alcohol, attitudes toward school, academic performance, school connectedness, attitudes toward self, attitudes toward adults, and attitudes toward the future. Data suggested that Youth-Friends was successful in improving students' attitudes and behaviors in regard to school, improving school connectedness, and effecting positive changes in attitudes toward self, adults, and the future. In addition, when YouthFriends students who had low scores at baseline were examined separately, results indicated a statistically significant improvement on community connectedness and goal setting within this group. Analyses of students' academic performance indicated a positive effect for Youth-Friends participants who had lower grades at baseline, although the possibility of regression to the mean could not be ruled out (Portwood, Ayers, Kinnison, Waris, & Wise, in press).

King, Vidourek, Davis, and McClellan (2002) studied the effectiveness of a school-based mentoring program designed to foster self-esteem and positive school, peer, and family connections in an effort to prevent future negative health behaviors. Mentors were asked to meet with students twice weekly for 1 hour each session, devoting time to each of four program components (i.e., self-esteem enhancement, relationship building, goal setting, and academic assistance/tutoring) during each meeting. Of 28 mentored students, 20 (71%) showed academic letter grade improvements from the first quarter. Although mentored students showed significant improvements in self-esteem and connectedness to school, peers, and family from pretest to posttest, when compared with a control group, mentored students demonstrated significant improvement only on the outcomes of school and family connectedness. It should also be noted that the composition, including size and characteristics, of the control group was not reported.

Some school-based mentoring programs have focused on specific at-risk populations. For example, Cavell and Hughes (2000) conducted an experimental evaluation of Prime Time, a program in which trained undergraduate students provided "therapeutic mentoring," which included mentors providing training in problem-solving skills to teacher-identified aggressive children in second and third grades. Compared with 31 children receiving standard mentoring, students paired with Prime Time mentors did show some statistically significant gains in both parent- and teacher-rated behavior, as well as reductions in aggressive behavior

(Cavell & Hughes, 2000). However, any conclusions from these findings must be tempered by the fact that a nonmentored group was not included in the study.

Limitations and Challenges

A review of the existing literature on school-based mentoring programs illustrates several important methodological and practical limitations typical of research and evaluation in the school environment. One of the foremost problems with examining the effectiveness of school-based mentoring is the difficulty with documenting "dosage," or the extent of individual students' involvement with their mentors over the course of the evaluation year. While precise dosage, which also speaks to the critical variables of duration and intensity, would appear to be an essential variable, not only for research and evaluation but also for program record-keeping purposes, many schools have not maintained dosage data. This may be because of concerns about violating policies, procedures, and possibly even state or local laws designed to ensure the privacy and/or confidentiality of student information. However, perhaps due in part to the popularity of school-based mentoring and schools' interest in establishing their programs' effectiveness, there appears to have been a marked shift toward more accurate and open record keeping. Nonetheless, the critical question of what degree of mentoring is required to produce positives outcome remains to be addressed.

Obtaining a sample size sufficient to detect the likely modest effects of school-based mentoring also presents a special challenge to studies of school-based programs. It can be difficult to distribute and to collect parent consent forms for participants, particularly within the time constraints of the school calendar. Institutional review board restrictions at most institutions also limit the ability of researchers to rely on passive, rather than active, consent procedures, even when the intervention programs are sanctioned by the schools. Not only do the resulting small sample sizes limit the power of analyses to detect statistically significant results, but particularly large samples are required when program effects are small, which the existing literature suggests is the case for school-based mentoring programs (DuBois, Holloway, et al., 2002).

Identifying appropriate outcome measures presents additional challenges. The effects of mentoring on some outcomes may be indirect or latent for some time, such that improvements (e.g., in global self-worth) may not be detectable within the academic year. Longitudinal study also is required to determine the extent to which mentoring attenuates some of the negative but developmentally normal behaviors observed in adolescence, including problem behaviors, relationship instability, and feelings of inadequacy (Rhodes, 2002).

Not only are the psychometric properties of many measures associated with mentoring research less than satisfactory, but students have reported difficulty understanding even "standardized" questions (e.g., "double negatives"; Portwood et al., 2001). Difficulties with the reading level of the instruments may be especially pronounced in schools with large numbers of students identified as academically at risk, who are likely to have reading difficulties, thereby potentially limiting such research to older students or younger students with better reading skills. More troubling than students' difficulty in completing the instrument, however, is the limited ability of measures to assess fully the outcomes of interest. The use of a more complete and comprehensive set of measures could help identify and enhance knowledge around key outcomes associated with mentoring more generally and school-based mentoring in particular, such as school connectedness.

In addition to methodological concerns, the practicalities of data collection in schools also present special challenges. In addition to the obvious difficulties of coordinating schedules and minimizing attrition due to student absences on data collection days, many schools restrict access to researchers and evaluators. Increasing pressure for schools to improve students' academic performance may further lead school personnel to avoid allowing research or evaluation activities that interfere with direct classroom instruction. Overlying all of these challenges is the need to maintain strong collaborative working relationships with school personnel, who are critical to the success of any school-based research effort. If successful, such collaborative efforts can be cost-effective and build system capacity to support students and programs (Taylor & Bressler, 2000); however, establishing the foundation for these relationships requires a substantial investment of time.

Key Findings

As a whole, the evaluation literature on school-based mentoring points to school connectedness as a key outcome variable. Research suggests that a high level of school connectedness serves as a protective factor for a number of adverse behaviors (Battistich & Horn, 1997). Adolescents who form a positive affiliation or bond with their schools are more likely than those who fail to form such a bond to engage in a variety of prosocial behaviors and to achieve their full academic potential, and they are also less likely to engage in problem behaviors such as fighting, bullying, truancy, vandalism, and substance use (Simons-Morton, Crum, Haynie, & Saylor, 1999). For example, in one recent study, decreases in school connectedness were associated with declining health status, increasing school nurse visits, cigarette use, and lack of extracurricular involvement (Bonny, Britto, Klostermann, Hornung, & Slap, 2000). Moreover, there appears to be a clear relationship between school failure and negative attitudes toward school (Flores-Fahs, Lorion, & Jakob, 1997). While limited, current research does suggest that school-based mentoring enhances students' school connectedness (Portwood et al., in press; Farruggia et al., 2003; Karcher, 2005; Karcher et al., 2002; King et al., 2002).

PRACTICE

Although limited, current research, along with theory, illuminates several sound guidelines for effective school-based mentoring practice. For those seeking to implement or to manage a mentoring program, the elements of effective practice identified by MENTOR, the National Mentoring Partnership (2003), translate directly to the school setting. More "best practices" can be identified based on the specific program model.

Program/Mentoring Models

Mentoring programs, like mentoring relationships, can take different forms and target different goals and objectives. Typically, school-based programs focus on addressing students' academic needs (Herrera et al., 2000); however, many such programs actually provide tutoring. One essential difference between tutoring and mentoring is that tutoring is task centered, whereas mentoring can be either relationship centered or instrumental (i.e., goal focused) (Morrow & Stiles, 1995). While a tutor and student may develop a personal bond similar to what characterizes a strong mentoring relationship, this is not essential to the primary goal of tutoring (i.e., academic improvement). Likewise, mentors may engage in activities to improve academics, but the primary goal of these matches is to foster personal bonds between the participants.

Although group mentoring is sometimes utilized in school-based programs, one-to-one matches provide an opportunity for mentors to interact with mentees in a way that targets the unique needs of the student. One-to-one matches may provide a better opportunity for a mentor and mentee to establish a close and trusting relationship in which social and behavioral problems can be addressed.

Teachers as Mentors

Teachers might be considered the best potential mentors for many students. Certainly, good educators and good mentors share many of the same qualities in terms of the caring and support they provide to students. Like teachers, mentors are expected to be open to working with their students, aware and responsive to their needs, patient, and committed to their success. Both groups also are expected to serve simultaneously as a guide, an advisor, and a role model to students. In particular, students may view their teachers as role models for learning. Based on these role expectations and teachers' proximity, it is not surprising that students often seek mentoring-type advice from their teachers and establish informal mentoring relationships (Bisland, 2001; DuBois & Silverthorn, in press).

Peer Mentoring in Schools

Cross-age mentoring by peers may offer several advantages to school-based programs that utilize adult mentors, including reduced costs; simplified recruiting, training, and supervision of mentors; and the potential for benefiting both younger (mentee) and older (mentor) youth participating in the program (see Karcher, this volume). Although peer-helping programs have been in practice since the 1960s (Dennison, 2000), peer mentoring programs must be distinguished from what, at present, are more pervasive models of peer tutoring and peer education, which focus on particular tasks rather than the relationship itself. To date, as with adult school-based mentoring, a majority of studies on peer mentoring are descriptive in nature and lack empirical support; others suffer from serious methodological limitations, such as the lack of a control/comparison group. Nonetheless, a few preliminary studies do indicate that mentees (Karcher, 2005; Karcher et al., 2002) and peer mentors (Karcher & Lindwall, 2003) may benefit from these programs.

Identifying Student Participants

Compared with community-based models, which often rely solely on parents to initiate the process, school-based programs can engage more adults (e.g., teachers, counselors) in the referral process. Programs may also encourage voluntary participation or self-referral. As a result, school-based programs tend to reach a broader range of children and youth than may other mentoring programs.

Recruiting Mentors: Who to Target and How

Mentor recruitment strategies vary, but may include word of mouth, presentations at community events, press releases in local and community newspapers or organizational newsletters, and paid advertisements (Jucovy, 2000). Targeting institutions and businesses may provide access to a more diverse group of volunteers (see Stukas & Tanti, this volume). In addition, corporations may provide release time for program participation, and adopt-a-school programs may be appealing at the institutional level (Herrera, 1999).

Overall, school-based programs seem to appeal to a broader range of potential mentors than do community-based programs. Whereas the overwhelming majority of mentors in community-based programs are between the ages of 22 and 49, school-based programs attract mentors that are equally divided among three age groups: age 21 and younger, age 22 to 49, and age 50 and older (Jucovy, 2000). School-based programs also appear to be able to recruit more male and minority volunteers (Herrera, 1999). The broad appeal of school-based mentoring programs may be attributable to the fact that they require less of a time commitment than community-based programs. Compared with community-based programs, which typically require a commitment of 3 to 5 hours per week, school-based programs may ask mentors to commit as little as 1 hour per week and thus provide an alternative for those who could otherwise not volunteer. In fact, school-based mentors tend to be professionals with limited time to devote to volunteering (Herrera, 1999).

The structure of school-based programs also addresses many of the safety and ethical concerns that potential volunteers have cited as barriers to community-based mentoring. In response to concerns expressed by some volunteers about the neighborhoods where their mentees live, school-based programs allow meetings to occur within the safety of the school environment. The added supervision available through school-based programs may be particularly appealing to male volunteers who fear the risk of false accusations when working with youth. Moreover, some school-based mentors indicate that they appreciated the greater distance from the home life of their mentees, such as less involvement with the youth's family, which helped mentors focus on their relationships as distinct from the often overwhelming problems in children's homes (Herrera, 1999).

While "best practices" dictate that all school-based volunteers must submit an application, participate in an interview process, go through a criminal background check, and submit personal and employer references (Herrera, 1999), overall, they are subject to fewer requirements than are community-based volunteers. For example, volunteers in community-based programs must have a valid driver's license and insurance and are screened by the Department of Motor Vehicles. A visit to the mentor's home is also a routine part of the screening process for community-based programs and, in some, a psychological inventory is conducted on all volunteers. The reduced complexity of the screening process, along with the cost and time involved, again makes school-based programs more appealing to many volunteers. In fact, in one study, the percentage of volunteers who inquired into the program and actually went on to be matched with mentees was significantly higher in school-based compared with community-based programs (Curtis & Hansen-Schwoebel, 1999).

Institutional and Program Support

Developing institutional support is crucial to the success of any school-based mentoring (Jucovy, 2000). Systems and schools will vary not only in how open they are to outside intervention (Herrera, 1999) but also in their enthusiasm for school-based mentoring in particular. Thus, it is important to assess at the outset whether a school is not only receptive to but also prepared and committed to implementing and sustaining a mentoring program. Considering the perspectives of all stakeholders in the process (e.g., district administrators, principals, teachers, counselors, school staff, parents, students) is important in this determination. For example, the school principal's support will encourage teacher, parent, and student participation. The principal may also be instrumental in procuring on-site office space, equipment, and staff support, which add to the cost-effectiveness of school-based mentoring programs.

Generating interest and enthusiasm on the part of teachers, counselors, and parents can help identify students most in need of a mentor, whether to facilitate social, emotional, or academic growth and improvement. For example, teachers can communicate with mentors in terms of students' individual needs. Both teachers and counselors can communicate with parents about the specific activities in which their children may engage, as well as their children's progress throughout mentoring relationships. It is also helpful for school-based programs to appoint a building liaison, whose job it is to recruit mentors, to match mentors and students, and to orient new mentors to the school and school staff. Involving all school staff may be beneficial.

Clearly, students play a critical role in program success. For example, when children view having a mentor as a "perk" that is perceived positively by classmates, this, in turn, may create a more receptive environment for social and behavioral change and reduce peer rejection (Herrera, 1999).

Formal school-based mentoring programs may also draw on a variety of supports outside the school environment. Established program models (e.g., YouthFriends, BBBS, Communities in Schools, Teammates) are increasingly available for replication and may offer a number of advantages, including technical assistance and support in the areas of marketing and volunteer recruitment, screening, and training.

FUTURE DIRECTIONS

Synthesis

Overall, school-based mentoring holds promise for reaching new and larger populations of both mentees and mentors. School-based programs offer a number of advantages from an operational standpoint, including relatively low cost, which is linked to their ability to draw on the resources and structure provided by schools. In turn, mentoring programs may provide additional resources and benefits to participating schools, particularly through additional adults' contributing to the school environment. However, the structure of schools may limit contact between mentors and mentees and impede the formation of the strong relationships associated with positive outcomes for children and youth.

Recommendations for Research

1. *Additional outcomes research on school-based mentoring is needed.* While some initial evaluation results are promising, sound scientific research addressing the effectiveness of school-based mentoring is needed. Methodological limitations, such as small sample sizes and lack of control groups, should be addressed to ensure that the results of future studies are valid and can be generalized across programs.

2. *Future research should focus on outcomes relevant to school-based mentoring.* There is a need to assess student mentees' outcomes more fully and with greater precision. Additional research should focus on outcomes, such as school connectedness, for which current data indicate consistent effects that may be unique to school-based mentoring. While improvements in academic performance will continue to be of great interest, future research must recognize the potential for moderating and/or mediating variables that explain or affect the relationship between school-based mentoring and outcomes. For example, the contributions made by individual characteristics of the mentee (e.g., gender, age) and baseline scores (in areas such as academic performance) to outcomes need to be explored more fully.

3. *Future research and evaluation of school-based mentoring programs must be sensitive to the issue of dosage.* Perhaps the foremost question in regard to school-based mentoring is whether the structural limitations on frequency and duration of contact impede effectiveness. Critical questions remain as to how mentors and mentees can establish the strong bonds necessary to ensure positive outcomes. Future research should also address how to sustain the effects of school-based mentoring.

4. *Research is needed into the characteristics of schools (e.g., school climate, school culture) that impact the success of school-based mentoring.* Although support from institutions and individuals is critical to the success of school-based programs, no empirical research has yet investigated characteristics that make a particular school a good site for program implementation. Such information could greatly benefit practitioners as they seek to implement and to sustain programs.

Recommendations for Practice

1. *School-based mentoring programs should adhere to established guidelines for best practices in mentoring.* Much of what is known about effective mentoring programs

more generally appears applicable to schools. Of particular importance are three features that have been identified as essential to the success of community-based mentoring programs: screening, orientation and training, and support and supervision. When one or more of these program features were absent, mentoring relationships were less likely to be sustained and thus less likely to have an opportunity to effect positive outcomes (Sipe, 1988). These are likely to be equally important in school-based mentoring.

2. *Ensuring school support is vital.* Schools must make a commitment both (a) to provide the resources necessary to implement and to maintain programs and (b) to obtain the empirically sound evaluation data needed to provide the basis for ensuring the effectiveness of these programs. The pressure on accountability for overall program effectiveness should not influence programs to overlook the need for careful research and evaluation.

REFERENCES

Aseltine, R. H. J., Dupre, M., & Lamlein, P. (2000). Mentoring as a drug prevention strategy: An evaluation of Across Ages. *Adolescent & Family Health, 1,* 11–20.

Battistich, V., & Horn, A. (1997). The relationship between students' sense of their school as a community and their involvement in problem behaviors. *American Journal of Public Health, 87,* 1997–2004.

Bisland, A. (2001). Mentoring: An educational alternative for gifted students. *Gifted Child Today Magazine, 64,* 22–25.

Bonny, A. E., Britto, M. T., Klostermann, B. K., Hornung, R. W., & Slap, G. B. (2000). School disconnectedness: Identifying adolescents at risk. *Pediatrics, 106,* 1017–1021.

Brendtro, L., & Long, N. (1995). Breaking the cycle of conflict. *Educational Leadership, 50*(4), 3.

Cavell, T. A., & Hughes, J. N. (2000). Secondary prevention as context for assessing change processes in aggressive children. *Journal of School Psychology, 38,* 199–235.

Curtis, T., & Hansen-Schwoebel, K. (1999). *Evaluation summary of five pilot programs.* Philadelphia: Big Brothers Big Sisters of America.

Dennison, S. (2000). A win-win peer mentoring and tutoring program: A collaborative model. *The Journal of Primary Prevention, 20,* 161–174.

Dryfoos, J. G. (1991). School-based social and health services for at-risk students. *Urban Education, 26,* 118–137.

DuBois, D. L., Holloway, B. E., Valentine, J. C., & Cooper, H. (2002). Effectiveness of mentoring programs for youth: A meta-analytic review. *American Journal of Community Psychology, 30,* 157–198.

DuBois, D. L., Neville, H. A., Parra, G. R., & Pugh-Lilly, A. O. (2002). Testing a new model of mentoring. In G. G. Noam (Ed. in chief) & J. E. Rhodes (Ed.), *A critical view of youth mentoring (New Directions for Youth Development: Theory, Research, and Practice, No. 93,* pp. 21–57). San Francisco: Jossey-Bass.

DuBois, D. L., & Silverthorn, N. (in press). Characteristics of natural mentoring relationships and adolescent adjustment: Evidence from a national study. *The Journal of Primary Prevention.*

Ellis, J., Small-McGinley, J., & Hart, S. (1998). Mentor-supported literacy development in elementary schools. *The Alberta Journal of Educational Research, 44*(2), 149–162.

Farruggia, S. P., Chang, E., Gil-Trejo, L., Heckhausen, J., Greenberger, E., & Chen, C. (2003, April). *The role of very important non-parental adults in adolescent school connectedness, academic achievement, and educational aspirations and expectations.* Paper presented at the Meeting of the Society for Research in Child Development, Tampa, FL.

Flores-Fahs, P., Lorion, R., & Jakob, D. (1997). Impact of home-school liaisons on the reduction of risk factors for ATOD use among preadolescents. *Journal of Community Psychology, 25,* 487–503.

Freedman, M. (1988). *Partners in growth: Elder mentors and at-risk youth.* Philadelphia: Public/Private Ventures.

Hawkins, J. D., Catalano, R. F., & Miller, J. Y. (1992). Risk and protective factors for alcohol and other drug problems in adolescence and early adulthood: Implications for substance abuse prevention. *Psychological Bulletin, 112,* 64–105.

Herrera, C. (1999). *School-based mentoring: A first look into its potential.* Philadelphia: Public/Private Ventures.

Herrera, C., Sipe, C. L., & McClanahan, W. S. (2000). *Mentoring school-age children: Relationship development in community-based and school-based programs*. Philadelphia: Public/Private Ventures. (Published in collaboration with MENTOR/ National Mentoring Partnership, Alexandria, VA)

Jucovy, L. (2000). *The ABC's of school-based mentoring*. Philadelphia: Public/Private Ventures.

Karcher, M. J. (2005). The effects of school-based developmental mentoring and high school mentors' attendance on their younger mentees' self-esteem, social skills, and connectedness. *Psychology in the Schools, 42,* 65–78.

Karcher, M. J., Davis, C., & Powell, B. (2002). The effects of developmental mentoring on connectedness and academic achievement. *The School Community Journal, 12*(2), 35–50.

Karcher, M. J., & Lindwall, J. (2003). Social interest, connectedness, and challenging experiences: What makes high school mentors persist? *Journal of Individual Psychology, 59,* 293 315.

King, K. A., Vidourek, R. A., Davis, B., & McClellan, W. (2002). Increasing self-esteem and school connectedness through a multidimensional mentoring program. *Journal of School Health, 72,* 294–299.

Leave No Child Behind Act, 20 U.S.C. § 6301 (2001).

McLearn, K. T., Colasanto, D., & Schoen, C. (1998). *Mentoring makes a difference: Findings From the Commonwealth Fund 1998 Survey of Adults Mentoring Young People.* New York: The Commonwealth Fund. Available at http://www.ecs .org/html/Document.asp?chouseid=2843

McPartland, J. M., & Nettles, S. M. (1991). Using community adults as advocates of mentors for at-risk middle school students: A two-year evaluation of Project RAISE. *American Journal of Education, 177,* 568–586.

MENTOR/National Mentoring Partnership. (2003). *Elements of effective practice* (2nd ed.). Alexandria, VA: Author.

Morrow, K. V., & Styles, M. B. (1995). *Building relationships with youth in program settings: A study of Big Brothers/Big Sisters.* Philadelphia: Public/Private Ventures.

Office of Juvenile Justice and Delinquency Prevention. (1998, December). *Juvenile Mentoring Program (JUMP): 1998 Report to Congress.* Washington, DC: U.S. Department of Justice, Office of Justice Programs, Office of Juvenile Justice and Delinquency Prevention. Available at http://www.ojjdp.ncjrs.org/jump/

Portwood, S. G., Ayers, P. M., Kinnison, K. E., Waris, R. G., & Wise, D. L. (in press). YouthFriends: Outcomes for a school-based mentoring program. *The Journal of Primary Prevention.*

Portwood, S. G., Ayers, P. M., Wise, D. L., Booth, K. M., Parker, L. C., & Smith, M. L. (2001). *YouthFriends: Results of the 2000–2001 Annual Survey.* Kansas City, MO: Authors.

Rhodes, J. E. (2002). *Stand by me: The risks and rewards of mentoring today's youth.* Cambridge, MA: Harvard University Press.

Rhodes, J. E., Grossman, J. B., & Resch, N. L. (2000). Agents of change: Pathways through which mentoring relationships influence adolescents' academic adjustment. *Child Development, 71,* 1662–1671.

Roberts, H., Liabø, K., Lucas, P., DuBois, D., & Sheldon, T. A. (2004). Mentoring to reduce antisocial behaviour in childhood. *British Medical Journal, 328,* 512–514.

Simons-Morton, B. G., Crump, A. D., Haynie, D. L., & Saylor, K. E. (1999). Student-school bonding and adolescent problem behavior. *Health Education Research, 14,* 99–107.

Sipe, C. (1996). *Mentoring: A synthesis of P/PV's research: 1988–1995.* Philadelphia: Public/Private Ventures.

Sipe, C. L. (1998). Mentoring adolescents: What have we learned. In J. B. Grossman (Ed.), *Contemporary issues in mentoring* (pp. 10–23). Philadelphia: Public/Private Ventures.

Sipe, C. L., & Roder, A. E. (1999). *Mentoring school-age children: A classification of programs.* Philadelphia: Public/Private Ventures. (Published in collaboration with MENTOR/National Mentoring Partnership, Alexandria, VA)

Slicker, E. K., & Palmer, D. J. (1993). Mentoring at-risk high school students: Evaluation of a school-based program. *The School Counselor, 40,* 327–334.

Solomon, D., Watson, M., Battistich, V., Schaps, E., & Delucchi, K. (1996). Creating classrooms that students experience as communities. *American Journal of Community Psychology, 24,* 719–748.

Taylor, A. S., & Bressler, J. (2000). *Mentoring across generations: Partnerships for positive youth development.* New York: Kluwer Academic/ Plenum.

Title IV-B of the Social Security Act, 42 U.S.C. §§601-687 (1935, as amended: Child Welfare).

Volunteer Florida Foundation. (n.d). *Final reportyear two: Mentoring in Florida school year 2001–2002.* Governor's Mentoring Initiative. Retrieved February 10, 2004, from http://www .flamentoring.org

23

WORK AND SERVICE-LEARNING

MARY AGNES HAMILTON AND STEPHEN F. HAMILTON

INTRODUCTION

Paid employment, unpaid internships, and service-learning are common experiences for youth that also can be contexts for mentoring. This chapter proposes a theoretical framework for understanding the possible benefits of work and service programs that incorporate formal mentoring relationships as well as naturally occurring mentoring ties that may arise between youth and adults engaged in work and service. A review of the empirical literature on mentoring of youth in work and service will establish what is known. A case study will illustrate selected dimensions of the proposed theoretical framework, as well as gaps needing further clarification. A synthesis will substantiate recommendations for future research and practice.

Scope and Significance

Work and service are normative experiences for youth. Including informal jobs like babysitting and lawn mowing, 69% of youth work for pay at some time during the year when they are age 15; by age 18, 91% work (U.S. Department of Labor, 2003a, p. 3). Poor and minority youth are less likely than White Anglo youth to be employed while in high school. In 1996–1998, 27.8% White youth aged 15 to 17 were employed during the school year, compared with 12.8% of Black youth and 14.6% of Hispanic youth (U.S. Department of Labor, 2000, p. 40, Table 4.1). The types of jobs held by disadvantaged youth also tend to be less desirable and more hazardous (National Research Council and Institute of Medicine [NRC/IOM], 1998, pp. 49–50).

In 1999, 52% of students in Grades 6 through 12 participated in community service (Wirt et al., 2001, Table 16.1). The Current Population Survey found that 29.5% of teenagers had volunteered for an organization in the year ending in September 2003 (U.S. Department of Labor, 2003b, p. 1). Volunteering in an organization is not identical to service-learning, and this survey did not count all service-learning, but the finding does indicate a fairly high level of involvement. Teenagers' volunteering rates are not reported separately by race, but for all age groups, 30.6% of Whites, 20.0% of Blacks, and 15.7% of Hispanics were counted as volunteers (Table A, p. 2). According to counts that admittedly depend both on varying definitions and on inadequate

Krista Beiswenger assisted with the development of the case study in this chapter and Bridget O'Brien with its data collection.

reporting mechanisms, the number of high school students participating in service-learning programs increased from 81,000 in 1984 to nearly 3 million in 1997 (Shumer & Cook, 1999). Indeed, rising rates of community service are one of the bright spots in the usually dreary statistics on youth (Putnam, 2000).

Definitions

In this chapter, we reserve *work* for paid employment but include both formal (e.g., regular hours as a retail clerk) and informal (e.g., episodic babysitting or lawn mowing) arrangements. *Service-learning* refers to activities that combine specific educational purposes with the aim of benefiting others (see National Service-Learning Clearinghouse, n.d., for a selection of definitions). Experiences may vary in the relative weight placed on education and on service. Service-learning excludes, however, community service activities that may be quite worthy as civic exercises but have little or no educational content—picking up roadside trash is the standard example. Our principal focus is on high school students. Most paid jobs are unavailable to youth under 16, and the employment possibilities of youth under 14 are strictly limited. Voluntary service-learning provides more opportunities for younger youth, but even in unpaid activities, high-school-aged youth have a wider range of choices and more serious responsibilities.

THEORY

What makes work and service promising contexts for mentoring? How may mentors enhance the developmental impact of these experiences? The ecology of human development, social learning theory, and social influence processes provide a theoretical framework for answering these questions. Before examining these theories, we first define the term *mentor* as we use it and suggest a broader definition of mentoring than may be found elsewhere in the handbook chapters. What we take to be the standard definition of a *mentor,* posited as the ideal by most mentoring programs, gives the mentor a quasi-parental role: a person who cares about a

youth, has a long-term commitment, and engages in a wide range of activities with the youth during which he or she teaches and advises the youth about a wide range of topics (see Bronfenbrenner's definition, cited by S. F. Hamilton & M. A. Hamilton, 2004, p. 396, and the "functional roles" of a mentor—what a mentor does—cited by S. F. Hamilton & Darling, 1996, pp. 201–208). We define *mentoring* as something that can be done by multiple people concurrently, not just by a single quasi-parental figure; its scope and duration may vary from one mentor to another (Hamilton & Hamilton, pp. 397–398).

Our observations and interviews with youth and adults in work-based learning programs have revealed a wide range of mentoring roles and relationships (Cornell Youth and Work Program, 2002a, 2002b). At the quasi-parental end, we have found workplace mentors who became so attached to their apprentices that they had them come live with their families to escape conflicts with parents. Another mentor attended parent-teacher conferences in the place of her apprentice's alcoholic mother. At the other end are adults whose mentoring is limited strictly to teaching job-related knowledge and skills. These relationships end with the work day. In some programs, no single person is designated as a mentor, or the person designated formally as such is not the only one who teaches and advises the youth. For example, an auto repair technician given responsibility for mentoring an intern in the Automotive Youth Educational Systems (AYES) program described a form of shared mentoring. He assigned his intern to work with another technician for 2 weeks to learn about air-conditioning, a form of shared mentoring.

Mentors who act almost like parents literally can be lifesavers. However, we do not wish to undervalue the more limited teaching and advising that other adults provide. Their levels of mentoring may be quite sufficient to promote outcomes such as career direction, future employment, degree completion, civic engagement, and personal and social competence. In addition, youth apprentices and interns who need quasi-parental mentors may be able to find such mentors elsewhere, outside the work environment.

The Ecology of Human Development

Bronfenbrenner's (1979) ecological conception of human development identified roles, relationships, and activities as key elements of a developmental context (p. 22). The developmental potential of workplaces and service-learning, and specifically of mentoring in the context of working together to accomplish shared goals, is suggested by his Hypothesis 46: "The development of the child is enhanced through her increased involvement, from childhood on, in responsible, task-oriented activities outside the home that bring her into contact with adults other than her parents" (p. 242).

Bioecological Perspective

In an updated "bioecological" perspective, Bronfenbrenner and Morris (1998) developed the same idea in terms of "proximal processes," which "are posited as the primary engines of development" (p. 996). Proximal processes occur where people interact face-to-face. Mentors in workplaces and service-learning engage with their apprentices or protégés in proximal processes that entail teaching and learning and that persist over time. Bronfenbrenner and Morris went on to outline how development may be affected by the characteristics of the people engaged in proximal processes, implying for our purposes that the characteristics of both the mentor and youth can affect the outcome of the relationship. For example, some adults are more nurturing than others; some youth are more curious and more outgoing than others. Based on this theory, caring and competent mentors are likely to be most effective, especially when their apprentices or protégés are committed, attentive, and diligent.

Learning and Development

Translating some of Bronfenbrenner's (1979, pp. 60, 163) hypotheses into mentoring terms, we would expect learning and development to be enhanced when a youth engages in progressively more complex activities and experiences greater reciprocity with a mentor and deeper emotional attachment to him or her, and when the balance of power between the two progressively shifts toward the youth. A powerful work or service experience would build on a youth's experiences in previous settings, make connections to them, and provide a "balance of challenge and supports." It then may generate a new "developmental trajectory" that carries over into new settings in the future, such as college, career, and adult civic action (p. 288).

Third Parties

Extrapolating from other portions of Bronfenbrenner's (1979, p. 77) theory suggests that a mentoring relationship is affected by the support or antagonism to the relationship that emanates from each member's dyadic relationships with third parties. These parties might include parents, teachers, and the mentors' workplace supervisors, coworkers, and family members.

Mesosystems

Bronfenbrenner's (1979) hypotheses about mesosystems, or the system of microsystems or settings in which a person participates, included the expectation that development is enhanced (a) when a youth participates in multiple settings in which role demands are compatible (p. 212) but different, especially in their cultural or subcultural characteristics (p. 213); (b) when there is two-way communication between settings (p. 216); (c) when some dyads function in more than one setting ("transcontextual dyads," p. 214); and/or (d) when other "supportive links" exist between settings (p. 215). The optimal degree of consistency or variation between settings is posited to depend on the youth's previous experience and sense of competence. The relationship may be curvilinear such that a youth who is developmentally advanced may benefit more from being in a new setting that has no links to old ones (p. 215).

This conception may help account for differences in the effects of mentoring in the workplace or service context. An apprentice, intern, or service protégé whose parents are supportive will have a different experience than one whose parents are disengaged. A young person who arrives with a strong sense of purpose and direction, based on temperament and previous experiences, may be able to take advantage of work and service-learning opportunities more quickly than one who is unfocused and lacks confidence.

Social Learning Theory

Mentors in workplace and service-learning contexts theoretically can model both specific technical (i.e., task-related) behavior and more general personal and social behavior. Bandura's (1986) social learning or social cognitive theory defined "models" as teachers (intentional or unintentional) and "observers" as learners. This theory emphasizes the active role of the learner and the cognitive process that mediates between observation and performance:

> In observational learning of complex novel actions, persons who simply observe the modeled patterns learn little, whereas those who cognitively transform [observed] actions to memorable symbolic codes achieve superior learning and retention of modeled activities. (p. 14)

Modeling

Modeling in Bandura's (1986) terms includes "physical demonstration, pictorial representation, or verbal description" (p. 70). For him, even reading printed instructions, then, is a case of observational learning. "Abstract modeling" is Bandura's term for the way in which someone can teach general rules for thinking and acting:

> Through the process of abstract modeling, observers extract the rules underlying specific performances for generating behavior that goes beyond what they have seen or heard. In abstract modeling, judgmental skills and generalizable rules are being learned by observation. (p. 100)

Bandura (1986) repeatedly emphasized the view that enactive learning or learning by trial and error is inefficient. He argued that learning by doing is most effective when it is guided by someone who already knows. That person then is able to demonstrate, to explain—to "think out loud" about what is being demonstrated and to pass judgment on the learner's performance.

We refer to these functions as aspects of mentor teaching behavior: demonstrating, explaining how, explaining why, and monitoring (M. A. Hamilton & S. F. Hamilton, 2002). Theoretically, workplace and service-learning contexts are likely to be highly conducive to these functions, thus enhancing their potential as contexts for effective mentoring.

Bandura (1986) treated the learner's thoughts and actions as central to the learning process. People are posited to learn not only from the immediate consequences of their actions but also by observing the consequences of others' actions (vicarious learning) and by creating mental models of how things work that enable them to predict consequences that they have neither seen nor experienced personally. Mentoring as modeling, in this view, entails far more than simply being a role model and suggests modeling behaviors that may be regularly observed in workplace and service-learning contexts.

Elaborating on the learner's actions, Bandura (1986) proposed four subfunctions that govern observational learning: attentional processes, retention processes, production processes, and motivational processes (pp. 51–69, 86–92). When the observer/protégé fails to carry out any of these subfunctions, inadequate learning results. The learner may not pay sufficient attention to the mentor (model) or may not retain what the mentor did and said. In the second two, the learner might fail to act on the mentor's lesson, possibly because incentives to do so were insufficient.

Protégé–Mentor–Environment Interaction

Like Bronfenbrenner (1979), Bandura (1986) incorporated into his theory characteristics of the learner, of the teacher, and of the environment. Bandura (1977) viewed behavior as involving a three-way mutual interaction among the model, the observer, and the environment, rather than a bidirectional interaction between person and environment (pp. 9–10). Hence, the apprentice's, intern's, or protégé's interest, willingness to learn, and active search for competence theoretically are as important as the mentor's skill and dedication. A mentor cannot succeed without a youth's active collaboration. In addition, we would claim that a role model cannot be assigned to a youth. A youth must have sufficient liking and respect for an adult to wish to be like him or her before that adult becomes a role model.

Social Influence Processes

According to Kelman (1974), people may accept social influence (persuasion, modeling, etc.) by means of three processes. *Compliance* is a relatively superficial acceptance of influence. A person acts consistently with the influence but without any strong internal commitment. "Means control" (rewards and punishments) is the mechanism through which compliance is achieved. The second process is *identification:* response to influence on the basis of the influencing agent's "attractiveness." The motivation is to be as much like the influencing agent as possible. This process is closest to Bandura's (1986) modeling. Kelman called the third process *internalization,* meaning acceptance not just of the behavior but also of the underlying values and principles that motivate it. "Credibility" of the influencing agent is critical to internalization. Kelman argued that all three processes function simultaneously in various influences and influencing agents. Considering workplace mentoring, one youth, for example, might wear steel-toed shoes on the manufacturing line because his mentor explained to him that this is required dress, purely to avoid the slight risk of getting a formal reprimand (i.e., compliance). With such a limited understanding of the rule, based solely on compliance, this youth might be more likely to take the risk of wearing more fashionable shoes without steel toes. Another youth may think of himself as a responsible employee and incorporate obeying all rules into his definition of responsible workmanship (i.e., identification) as taught by his mentor. Internalization is at work if the youth obeys the shoe rule out of an understanding that risky behaviors endanger not only himself, but others and the company, and holds the conviction that by taking specified precautions, he is operating for the good of all. Mentors may use any one or all three processes to influence the behaviors of the same youth.

Although each of these social processes has a place in mentoring in workplace and service-learning contexts and all might appropriately be used in combination, we view compliance-based mentoring as likely to be rather limited in its impact, while identification and internalization-based mentoring are most likely to yield adaptive learning, that is, learning that can be applied in new situations and transformed as conditions change (Bandura's, 1986, "abstract modeling").

Hypotheses About Mentoring in the Contexts of Work and Service

The preceding theoretical formulations have several theoretical implications for mentoring, especially but not solely in the contexts of work and service. We extract some of the major implications in the form of hypotheses. Each numbered subsection contains several hypotheses that are stated broadly enough to be considered propositions or expectations. Specific research projects would have to refine them, but they suggest some promising directions.

Hypothesis 1 (H1): Goal-Directed Activity

Especially for high-school-aged youth, mentoring will be more powerful when it occurs in the context of joint goal-directed (instrumental) activity, particularly in workplace and service contexts, than when it is in a more purely social context.

H2: High-Quality Work and Service Activities

Work and service activities with the following characteristics will be associated with more effective mentoring: novel or challenging, increasingly complex over time, based on and representative of generalizable principles, and entailing exposure to people and cultural practices that are new and different.

H3: Characteristics of Mentoring Relationships

Mentoring relationships, particularly in workplace and service contexts, will have stronger positive effects on youth when they endure over extended periods of time, are reciprocal, involve deepening emotional ties, are supported by third parties, extend beyond a single setting, and entail two-way communication across settings, especially with the youth's school and family.

H4: Mentor Teaching Behaviors

Mentors, particularly in workplace and service contexts, will be more effective when they provide a balance of challenge and support, progressively give the youth greater autonomy and power, use a variety of teaching behaviors, teach principles as well as practices, rely more on identification and internalization than on compliance, and engage others in teaching or mentoring the youth for whom they are responsible.

H5: Protégé Learning Behaviors

Youth will gain more from mentoring, again particularly in workplace and service contexts, when they are motivated by opportunities to learn new skills through new experiences and relationships and thereby gain confidence and competence in their new roles, attend to their mentors, act on what they are learning, increasingly take initiative and responsibility for their own learning, and think about what they have learned and relate it to their previous learning and future plans.

In summary, Bronfenbrenner's, Bandura's, and Kelman's theoretical conceptions imply that the impact of mentoring in workplaces and service-learning on the learning and development of youth is mediated or moderated by the (H1) goal directedness and (H2) high quality of the *activities*, (H3) the characteristics of the *mentoring relationships*, and the *teaching and learning behaviors* of the (H4) adults and (H5) youth involved, respectively.

RESEARCH

Most research on mentoring has not addressed work and service-learning, and most research on those experiences has not addressed mentoring. However, we will look carefully at findings from research on work and service-learning that relate outcomes of these experiences to specific features that include or imply mentoring. This will allow us to examine and refine the five hypotheses we have stated about ways in which mentoring mediates and moderates those outcomes.

Goal-Directed Activity

The first hypothesis about the importance of goal-directed activity in mentoring within workplace and service-learning contexts finds support in the meta-analysis conducted by DuBois, Holloway, Valentine, and Cooper (2002, Table II, pp. 173–176), which found evidence of relatively stronger effects both for mentoring programs that were located in workplaces and for those that provided structured activities for youth and mentors. Theoretically, as noted previously, work and service-learning can be optimal contexts for mentoring older youth (S. F. Hamilton & M. A. Hamilton, 2004). Both give youth adultlike roles in which they are responsible for producing something of value to others (i.e., *goal-directed activity*). Compared with youths' roles as student and family member, the roles of worker, apprentice, intern, and volunteer are more active and entail more obligations. Responsibilities may become more challenging and complex over time. Theoretically, workplaces and service-learning programs can be "mentor-rich environments" (Freedman, 1993), meaning places where young people and adults can naturally develop relationships around common interests and activities; some of these relationships will involve mentoring. In a nationally representative survey of young adults asked to name one mentor since age 14, 10% named an employer or coworker (DuBois & Silverthorn, in press; see also Mortimer, 2003). We have adduced suggestive evidence for the proposition that mentoring for high-school-aged youth is more attractive and efficacious when it is instrumental and less social than is the case for school-aged children, meaning that the relationship develops around shared goals and actions more than purely social interaction (S. F. Hamilton & M. A. Hamilton, 1992; see also Darling, Hamilton, & Niego, 1994; Darling, Hamilton, & Shaver, 2003). (However, emotional support appears to be important for at-risk youth such as teen mothers. See Klaw & Rhodes, 1995; Rhodes, Contreras, & Mangelsdorf,

354 • CONTEXTS OF MENTORING

1994; Sullivan, 1996.) To our knowledge, this proposition has not been directly tested by empirical research.

High-Quality Work and Service Activities

Reviewing the findings of research on the effects of service-learning, Stukas, Clary, and Snyder (1999) found evidence of positive effects in several domains and a few negative effects, findings that are in accord with other reviews (e.g., Billig, 2000; Eyler & Giles, 1999; Eyler, Giles, & Gray, 1999). Mortimer (2003) has provided the most comprehensive assessment of the effects of high school students' work experience. A key theme in both reviews is that quality matters; that is, positive effects are associated with specific characteristics of the experiences (see also M. A. Hamilton & S. F. Hamilton, 1997, 2004). Research testing this hypothesis with specific reference to mentoring in workplace and service contexts is lacking. However, the findings of the above reviews do converge with the finding of DuBois et al. (2002) that mentoring programs that put into place more "best practices" have stronger effect sizes.

Intensity and Regularity

Mortimer (2003), based both on her own 10-year study of 1,000 high school students (761 at wave 10) and on her synthesis of the literature, has argued that the nature and quality of work determine its impact on youth. She concluded that critical aspects of work for youth include its intensity and regularity. She defined high-intensity work as 20 or more hours per week and low-intensity work as anything less. Regular workers were employed more than 18 months during high school, excluding summers (the median for the sample).

As reported below, there is evidence that youth employment can have many positive effects. Possible negative consequences first reported by Greenberger and Steinberg (1986) appear to have resulted almost exclusively from work of high intensity. Multiple studies have established an association between high-intensity employment and greater substance use

(Mortimer, 2003, pp. 161–163, NRC/IOM, 1998, pp. 133–134). However, these negative effects are not evident among youth employed for fewer hours, nor are they strong or enduring; intensive workers also are more likely than others to engage in delinquent behavior (Mortimer, pp. 161–163).

Type of Service

Stukas et al. (1999) concluded in their review that service-learning varies widely and, correspondingly, has varying effects. S. F. Hamilton (1980) distinguished between service as an individual in an established organization and participating in a group activity designed and led by youth. Voluntary versus required service is another critical dimension, with voluntary service generally viewed as preferable (Stukas et al., pp. 6–7). Metz, McLellan, and Youniss (2003, pp. 195–198) have distinguished "social cause service" (e.g., mounting a campaign to clean up a river) from "standard service" (e.g., tutoring) and found that the former has far more potential to foster civic development, as indexed by concern for social issues and by plans to engage in "social cause" civic activities and service in the future. Only high-quality programs produce convincing evidence of increased commitment to civic engagement and social responsibility (Stukas et al., pp. 6–8). Commitment to civic engagement is indicated both when participants view their voluntary action as enacting their values and when it strengthens participants' intentions to continue to volunteer and their sense of social responsibility.

Connecting Work Experience to School

The impact of employment on school performance has been a controversial issue in research on youth work experience. Some studies (notably Greenberger & Steinberg, 1986) have found that working more than 20 hours per week is associated with lower school grades. However, using better controls for differences that preceded employment, Mortimer (2003) concluded that "the empirical evidence does not support the contention that working in adolescence detracts from educational engagement, number of hours spent doing homework, or academic achievement in high school" (p. 178). Following her subjects after high school graduation, Mortimer (p. 185) found that "steady" workers (those who work regularly but at low intensity, less than 20 hours per week) were more likely to earn a BA 7 years after high school graduation (p. 191) than those whose work patterns were different or who did not work. Intriguingly, "low promise" youth (indexed by ninth-grade GPA, motivation to do schoolwork, academic self-esteem, and educational plans) (pp. 188–189) with a "steady" work pattern were 12 times more likely to earn a BA than low-promise youth who were "more invested" in work (23% vs. 3%) (p. 203).

Eighth graders from three Florida schools rated as having "significant academic and disciplinary problems" participated in a study on the effects of mentoring in the workplace (Rollin, Kaiser-Ulrey, Potts, & Creason, 2003). The teacher-coordinator at each school selected treatment students from eligible applicants, and a comparison group was created from a random sample of remaining applicants. Youth in the treatment group reported to their work sites up to 2 hours a day, 4 days per week and could earn a bonus up to $500, working from 65 to 243 hours in "clerical work, counseling, supervising physical activities, food service, animal care, and customer service" (p. 409). An adult in each work site was designated as a mentor. Six indicators of school behavior known to be related to violence were assessed for the year prior to the mentoring program and the year of the program: unexcused absences, number and days of in-school and out-of-school suspensions, and number of disciplinary infractions on school property. Youth in the treatment groups in all three schools improved significantly more than comparison youth in number of days of out-of-school suspensions and numbers of infractions. Treatment youth in one school improved more than comparison youth in number of in-school suspensions and in the remaining two schools in number of out-of-school suspensions. The authors concluded that the program's impact on school behaviors indicates the beneficial effects of mentoring in the workplace for early teens.

The Rollin et al. (2003) study had a relatively robust design, though it was not a true experiment because the treatment groups were not randomly selected. The outcomes are encouraging, though not all measures showed significant differences in all schools. Moreover, some differences resulted from larger negative trends among the comparison group rather than actual improvements in the treatment group. No information was given either about what the mentors and teacher-coordinators did or about connections between the school curriculum and the work activities.

Linnehan (2003) surveyed attitudes about school relevance, self-esteem, and work of 90 Philadelphia high school youth interested in participating in a work program with a mentor prework and postwork experience during one academic year. Fifteen youth had formal mentoring relationships through a school-to-work program; 24 youth had informal spontaneous mentor relationships in youth jobs they found themselves; 23 were employed with no reported mentor relationship; and 28 did not find any work. The 39 students with a mentor had "significantly higher levels of self-esteem at the end of the school year than those who did not work" and "believed more strongly in the relevance of school" to work (p. 50). No differences were found between youth with formal and informal mentors. The finding that "students who reported higher levels of mentor satisfaction believed more strongly in the relevance of school to work than students who either worked without a mentor or those who did not work" (p. 50) suggests that the quality of the mentoring relationship is important.

The recommendations with which Stukas et al. (1999, pp. 10–14) concluded their review emphasize the importance of integrating service-learning with school and community. McLellan and Youniss (2003) found evidence that when required service was integrated closely with the school curriculum, the structure, notably the presence of a coordinator who actively encouraged reflection, engaged students cognitively and emotionally more than programs without such a structure. No evidence of a general effect on grades has been reported in research on service-learning; the evidence suggests that the strongest potential for positive effects on grades come from service that is closely related to courses (Stukas et al., pp. 4–6). Findings do suggest, however, that service can improve student behavior and attendance (Stukas et al., p. 9).

Support for Efficacy and Mattering

Both work and service are exemplars of support for efficacy and mattering, emphasized by the NRC/IOM (2003, pp. 103–106) as a feature of positive developmental settings. Young people tend to be more engaged in activities that they define as important, in part because adults define them as important. Employed girls had higher reported self-efficacy when they believed they were well paid and that their jobs enabled them to help others (Mortimer, 2003, pp. 157–158). Their perceived self-efficacy was lower when they felt powerless at work. Service-learning experiences that give youth greater autonomy and self-direction and that entail greater responsibility, choice, and independence appear to be most beneficial. Respectful youth-adult relationships and tasks that fit with youth needs also appear to be critical (Stukas et al., 1999, pp. 4, 8).

Opportunities for Skill Building

Providing opportunities for skill building (NRC/IOM, 2003, pp. 106–110) is also epitomized by work and service, whose novelty and challenge provide both opportunity and motivation to learn new skills. Young workers who learn new skills on the job reported increased efficacy and reduced depression (Mortimer, 2003, pp. 157–158, 160). Mortimer's subjects who reported they had more chances to learn at work while in high school were more likely to perceive the jobs they held 7 years after graduation as related to their career goals (pp. 192–193). Apparently, working at challenging jobs is an effective form of career exploration.

Characteristics of Mentoring Relationships

Call and Mortimer (2001, p. 127) found evidence that in some work environments, youth gained support from adult supervisors and from peers that moderated the negative impact of stresses coming from their families. Using data from the third wave of the Youth Development

Study, when most subjects were in Grade 11, Mortimer (2003, p. 66) reported that 71% of youth with jobs said their supervisors were almost always or often "willing to listen to problems and help find solutions," and 38% reported feeling "extremely or quite close to their supervisors." These data suggest that workplaces are places where many, but not all, youth can find adult mentoring. Stukas et al. (1999, p. 14) concluded similarly that attending to relationships—among students, between students and teachers, and between students and their adult site supervisors—is one of the most promising approaches to improving the quality of service-learning. Although they did not use the term, mentoring is implied.

Mentor Teaching Behaviors

The only study we know of that directly and explicitly examined what workplace mentors do is the Cornell Mentoring Youth at Work Study (M. A. Hamilton & S. F. Hamilton, 2002; M. A. Hamilton, S. F. Hamilton, & Vermeylen, 2002). In Phase 1, the preexperiment, we interviewed 62 workplace mentors and 61 of their high school interns or apprentices to find out what mentors teach and how they teach it. Results affirmed a previously developed conceptual framework based on teaching goals—which we categorized as technical, personal, and social competence—and on teaching methods—including demonstrating, explaining how, explaining why, monitoring, reflective questioning, and problem solving. The latter two methods, which we named "challenging" teaching behaviors, and which theory and research predict would be most powerful, were much less likely to be described in the interviews than the first four, which were virtually "universal."

In Phase 2 of the study, we conducted a field experiment by geographically pairing eight sites determined to have high-quality work-based learning programs, then randomly selecting one of each pair of sites to receive two 4-hour mentor training sessions 6 to 8 weeks apart emphasizing the use of reflective questioning and problem solving. We used both the experienced mentors' testimony from Phase 1 and our conceptual framework to design a training program (Cornell Youth and Work Program, 2002c) for novice mentors for the purpose of helping them adopt the goals and the teaching behaviors of expert mentors. Our goal was to accelerate the acquisition of expertise among novice mentors; however, after the first training we discovered that about half of the mentors had 1 or more years of experience! The post-only design included up to four telephone interviews to assess the impact of the training program comparing trained and untrained mentors. We interviewed 89 mentors, retaining those who did not attend the training; 54 youth identified by the mentors were interviewed once. Our open-ended interview started with a list of the most important things taught (mentor) or learned (youth). The remainder of the interview focused on mentor and youth stories about key incidents when learning or teaching occurred. Interviews were coded along two dimensions—goals or competencies and teaching behaviors.

Data analysis continues, but the training appeared to increase the use and consistency of questioning by novice mentors in the treatment sites and the consistency of questioning across interviews by experienced mentors in the treatment sites. Experienced mentors in the training sites, but not novice mentors, appeared to increase their use of problem solving. Interviews with youth at all eight sites supported the findings based on mentor interviews (M. A. Hamilton et al., 2002). These findings are consistent with the finding of DuBois et al. (2002), that "ongoing training" is associated with increased estimated effect size in evaluations of mentoring programs (overall, not only those distinguished as work-based or service-based).

Protégé Learning Behaviors

The importance of reflection is a constant theme in research and theory on service-learning; it enhances the learning opportunities in service (McLellan & Youniss, 2003). Reflection is related to what Bandura (1986, p. 102) called "conceptual learning," not only observing, but thinking about what has been observed and integrating it into a conceptual whole. Stukas et al. (1999, p. 6) concluded that understanding is enhanced by guided reflection on the experience. We view reflection as something a mentor can elicit and as a key component of work and

service when they are intentionally structured for learning (M. A. Hamilton & S. F. Hamilton, 2002). Unfortunately, however, no studies have examined whether reflection enhances the benefits of mentoring received by youth in workplace or service contexts. There also has apparently been no investigation of the contribution of other protégé factors (e.g., previous experiences and relationships) that we noted previously as theoretically having the potential to enhance effects of mentoring within employment and service-learning.

PRACTICE

To explore what effective mentoring in workplace and service-learning looks like in practice, we provide a case drawn from our study described above (M. A. Hamilton et al., 2002). The program with which this case was affiliated is referred to as "work-based learning," but because it sponsors unpaid internships and this one was in a service setting, it also can be considered service-learning, nicely illustrating our point that the two contexts can be quite similar.

As Roger (pseudonym) thinks about going to medical school, he explores dentistry as a possible career option in an 8-hour-a-week internship during his senior year in high school. In his dental office, his mentor, Larry (pseudonym), engages him in *work and service* activities that match all the characteristics hypothesized to be associated with effective mentoring in these contexts.

Mentor Teaching Behaviors

Larry wants to see Roger succeed in any career he chooses. Larry talks to Roger about *how to get along* with dental hygienists and why this is important, explaining that sometimes there might be a conflict with a hygienist who has a different philosophy or way of doing things, "You both just have to compromise . . . for the good of the overall practice." Note that this appeal is based on internalization, in Kelman's (1974) terms.

Larry explains *how to communicate* more effectively with patients. "I try to teach him how to sit down and speak and look at the patient and talk to them eye to eye. . . . He just has a gift, and as far as medicine and working with people, he'd be excellent." But Larry is also critical and challenges Roger's behavior:

> Sometimes he's a little too friendly. . . . Some people are apprehensive and shy, they don't want to talk and they don't open up and they just want to get it over. . . . I told him he's got to be humble and not just talky. . . . Look at the patients and feel them out and if they're not responding to your openness, maybe it's best to quit talking a bit. . . . That's a fine line in learning.

Goal-Directed Activity and Characteristics of Mentoring Relationships

During his third interview, Larry describes two extraordinary *experiences with patients* Roger had had that day. First, a middle-aged patient returned to get his bridge, following the previous week's "big marathon treatment" of "four appointments in one appointment." This man

> Was really embarrassed all his life. When he'd talk, he'd hold his hands over his mouth and he was very timid and shy and I know it was because he was self-conscious of his teeth. I extracted six teeth and did a preparation for a bridge and I did it all in one appointment because the guy drove 600 miles to get this done. . . . I put that bridge in today. And to see the look on that guy's face! . . . I said go in there and thank him [lab technician]. He went in there and started crying and said he changed his life. And it was moving for me. And I made sure my laboratory technician who really did the hard work got a compliment. Made him feel good. . . . That doesn't happen every day, but you know [Roger] got to see that and it was neat.

Larry illustrates how a mentor can foster a youth's *internalization* of values when he asks Roger to make a delivery to an elderly housebound lady, hoping his protégé will realize that caring about people is part of the job:

> And then I made [Roger] do something interesting today also. I had a lady that's 96 years old. Her teeth are worn out and I've done everything I can. She can't wear her teeth any more. . . . And anyway I relined her teeth again today and I did it for free and I had [Roger] take them to her house, do a house call and give the teeth to her. He went with [another assistant] in fact and actually the lady was pretty happy with them, which surprised me. . . . I wanted him to see what it is like to make a house call; to go to somebody's house and see that you can do that. Not everyone has a car and can drive to the office. And that's all part of it. And if you care and you do things like that for people, you don't have to advertise . . . that's how you build a practice . . . by caring. . . .

By sharing stories with Roger about how he has achieved happiness and contentment in his career by helping others, Larry models his sense of intrinsic motivation through his work as a dentist so that Roger will come to *identify this value as part of the profession:*

> I'll tell you something else we talked about and it did really change my life. . . . I mean it was just one of the neatest experiences and I feel guilty every day living in America now after seeing . . . how they live and the pain and suffering they go through, and to go down there [to Latin America] and be able to do dental care the best you could out in the bush was really a neat thing, and to see people walk, you know, 80 miles to get a damn tooth pulled because it's been hurting for months and months, and they'll let you do it without anesthetic just because they want to get rid of the pain. And people waiting by the hundreds all day for 2 days just to let you look at them, and how tolerant the people were and how much they suffer in their day-to-day life. I talked to [Roger] about that too, and that's still fresh in my mind.

Protégé Learning Behaviors

Roger's testimony indicates that his mentor has helped him stay focused by emphasizing *goal-setting and limit-setting:*

> [Larry] said a lot of things about learning how to say no, learning how to control yourself to do something; that you see your long-term goal and to reach that you need to make certain. . . . You

have to be personally committed to many things instead of trying to do a realm of things.

In response to a question about what Roger thought would be the most helpful part of this internship in his next step in life, he replies:

> I really think knowing that I have to have a very profound sense of *personal sacrifice* and goal-setting is very key to any kind of success. Giving up your own personal time and that you have to have a *work ethic* to get these things done and accomplished and, and placed in the order that they need to be.

In Roger's case, this lesson is not a new one. His mentor *reinforced and validated the values he had learned from his family:*

> Yeah, that's, that's really odd because *my family* is who I see as being worker-type people and seeing that other people have this is great. 'Cause I've been told, "Why do you kill yourself so hard?" It's just, I can connect with them, that kind of people. I get to see others who do the same as me, which is nice.

Both Larry and Roger make it clear that what Roger brings to the internship is also important: an outgoing interpersonal style, a commitment to helping others rooted in religion, curiosity about the medical profession, and a strong work ethic.

Summary

Consistent with the hypotheses about effective mentoring in workplace and service contexts, Larry offers both challenge and support, uses different teaching methods, conveys principles as well as practices, and gives Roger increasing responsibility. Larry teaches Roger technical skills that enable him to assist in the office, but he explicitly emphasizes what we refer to as "personal and social competence," underscoring the importance of being able to communicate effectively with coworkers and patients, discussing his plans for the future, especially college, and discussing in depth the moral commitments that guide his life and work and reinforce those held by his family.

FUTURE DIRECTIONS

Synthesis

Applying the ecology of human development, social learning theory, and social influence processes to mentoring in work and service-learning, we generated five hypotheses. Little research on these experiences has directly addressed mentoring, but some of it supports inferences about the influence of mentoring. Despite the limitations of the sources cited, we feel confident in asserting that the presence of a mentor is likely to enhance the positive effects of work and service by contributing to goal-directed activity and the high quality of the activities, establishing mentoring relationships, using challenging and universal teaching behaviors, and creating opportunities that promote youth learning behaviors. Mentors assume a critical role in promoting positive youth development through work and service.

H1. Goal-Directed Activity

The evidence that mentoring of high-school-aged youth is most efficacious in the context of goal-directed activity is only suggestive, but this hypothesis is supported by research indicating that youth find mentors in workplaces and that these mentors have relatively strong effects.

H2. High-Quality Work and Service Activities

A clear finding from research on work and service-learning is that quality matters. Positive effects on youth are associated with indicators of high-quality programs and experiences. Mentors are able to influence these indicators; therefore, although mentoring in these contexts has not been extensively studied, we believe it is reasonable to expect that mentoring is an important part of a high-quality program in these. Theoretically, a workplace mentor can help a youth avoid overcommitment to work and keep school and other commitments in balance, thereby optimizing work's positive effects. Work and service experiences have more positive effects when they give youth a sense of efficacy and mattering. The opportunity to learn new skills has been shown to support efficacy and career directedness. Work experience that is connected to school appears to be entirely beneficial. The type of service performed in service-learning programs has an impact; working for a cause is more likely to affect commitment to civic engagement than is volunteering in an agency.

H3. Characteristics of Mentoring Relationships

Theory predicts that the characteristics of mentoring relationships are important in both contexts. However, little empirical research has examined how mentors and youth relate.

H4. Mentor Teaching Behaviors

The Cornell Mentoring Youth at Work study (M. A. Hamilton et al., 2002) examined how mentors teach youth in workplaces. Training appeared to give a jump-start to questioning behaviors of novice mentors and to promote problem-solving behaviors by experienced mentors.

H5. Protégé Learning Behaviors

Reflection on service-learning experience is the best-studied component of protégés' learning behavior, and the data confirm its importance. Mentors in workplaces and service-learning contexts and classroom teachers can encourage such reflection.

Our major recommendations for future research are implied by the theoretically derived hypotheses that have been the focus of this chapter and from the gap evident between them and available research. Likewise, our recommendations for practice reflect those approaches that appear most clearly to be important for effective mentoring in workplace and service contexts in view of available theory and research.

Recommendations for Research

1. *Compare mentoring effects related to types of goal-directed activities.* Future researchers should compare the effects of mentoring in varied workplaces and service-learning programs, as well as in other contexts. Of particular interest is the presence or absence of goal-directed/ instrumental activity as a setting characteristic

that may mediate the impact of mentoring relationships across different work and service environments.

2. *Conduct experimental research to test causal relations.* Future research should experimentally train and supervise workplace and service mentors. An experiment should attempt to control or at least monitor the types of work and service activities, the qualities of the relationships, and the mentors' teaching behaviors. This design would test what theory predicts and research suggests make mentoring in work and service-learning more powerful experiences.

3. *Examine interactions longitudinally among people, processes, and activities.* Both in studies specifically designed for the purpose and in conjunction with studies for other purposes, those investigating mentoring in workplace and service contexts should systematically monitor what mentors and youth do, how mentoring relationships develop over time, how third parties affect mentoring, mentor teaching behaviors, and youth learning behaviors.

Recommendations for Practice

1. *Build community-wide mentoring in work and service-learning contexts.* Our fundamental recommendation is that communities strive to create community-wide mentoring systems, building social capital by linking youth with mentors in work and service-learning. This entails moving beyond individual programs to building on the entire range of opportunities for mentoring and trying to ensure that those opportunities are made available to all youth. Youth should take leading roles in such an initiative, alongside adults. The following points elaborate on this recommendation.

2. *Enhance mentoring in work and service-learning programs for youth.* Both formal and informal or spontaneous mentoring should be made an explicit component of work and service-learning programs. Employment and service will become rich opportunities for youth development when employers and educators commit resources to creating learning environments for youth. For example, mentoring could become a formally recognized and rewarded job

responsibility of adults who teach and advise youth in their workplace.

3. *Train workplace and service mentors both as teachers and advisors of youth.* Mentor training should be available to both novice and experienced mentors in workplace and service settings to promote youth development by using not only the universal teaching behaviors (demonstrating, explaining how and why, and monitoring), but the more challenging teaching behaviors as well.

4. *Provide third-party support to both mentors and youth.* In addition to training mentors in workplace and service contexts, there should be support for both mentors and youth, possibly provided by a third-party coordinator located in a school or community agency. Such a person or office can provide direct support and refer mentors and youth to additional services through schools, employers, or community organizations.

5. *Progressively adapt mentoring behaviors to meet youth needs.* Each mentoring program in a workplace or service-learning context should consciously design, implement, evaluate, and adapt mentoring to seek the optimal balance of challenge and support for youth served by the program. Evaluation data should be used to adjust and modify the type of mentoring over time. As mentors move beyond showing and telling, they should increase opportunities among youth for reflection, problem solving, and decision making. Youth should be allowed the greatest degree of autonomy and control that is consistent with both their ability and the achievement of organizational goals. Efforts to provide these opportunities for progressively greater youth autonomy should be continuously assessed.

REFERENCES

Bandura, A. (1977). *Social learning theory.* Englewood Cliffs, NJ: Prentice Hall.

Bandura, A. (1986). *Social foundations of thought and action: A social cognitive theory.* Englewood Cliffs, NJ: Prentice Hall.

Billig, S. H. (2000). Research on K–12 school-based service learning: The evidence builds. *Phi Delta Kappan, 81,* 658–664.

Bronfenbrenner, U. (1979). *The ecology of human development: Experiments by nature and design.* Cambridge, MA: Harvard University Press.

Bronfenbrenner, U., & Morris, P. (1998). The ecology of developmental processes. In W. Damon (Series Ed.) & R. M. Lerner (Vol. Ed.), *Handbook of child psychology: Vol. 1. Theoretical models of human development* (5th ed., pp. 993–1028). New York: Wiley.

Call, K. T., & Mortimer, J. T. (2001). *Arenas of comfort in adolescence: A study of adjustment in context.* Mahwah, NJ: Erlbaum.

Cornell Youth and Work Program. (2002a). *Boundaries guide.* Retrieved June 27, 2004, from http://www.human.cornell.edu/youthwork/mentoring/g_boundaries.html

Cornell Youth and Work Program. (2002b). *Boundaries to the mentoring relationship.* Retrieved June 27, 2004, from http://www.human.cornell.edu/youthwork/mentoring/ta_boundaries.html

Cornell Youth and Work Program. (2002c). *Training tools.* Retrieved June 30, 2004, from http://www.human.cornell.edu/youthwork/mentoring/training.html

Darling, N., Hamilton, S. F., & Niego, S. (1994). Adolescents' relations with adults outside the family. In R. Montemayor, G. R. Adams, & T. P. Gulotta (Eds.), *Advances in adolescent development: Vol. 6. Personal relationships during adolescence* (pp. 216–235). Newbury Park, CA: Sage.

Darling, N., Hamilton, S. F., & Shaver, K. H. (2003). Relationships outside the family: Unrelated adults. In G. R. Adams & M. D. Beronsky (Eds.), *Blackwell handbook of adolescence* (pp. 349–370). Malden, MA: Blackwell.

DuBois, D. L., Holloway, B. E., Valentine, J. C., & Cooper, H. (2002). Effectiveness of mentoring programs for youth: A meta-analytic review. *American Journal of Community Psychology, 30,* 157–197.

DuBois, D. L., & Silverthorn, N. (in press). Characteristics of natural mentoring relationships and adolescent adjustment: Evidence from a national study. *Journal of Primary Prevention.*

Eyler, J., & Giles, D. E. (1999). *Where's the learning in service-learning?* San Francisco: Jossey-Bass.

Eyler, J., Giles, D. E., Jr., & Gray, C. J. (1999). *At a glance: What we know about the effects of service-learning on students, faculty, institutions and communities, 1993–1999.* Unpublished manuscript, Vanderbilt University, Nashville, TN.

Freedman, M. (1993). *The kindness of strangers: Reflections on the mentoring movement.* San Francisco: Jossey-Bass.

Greenberger, E., & Steinberg, L. (1986). *When teenagers work: The psychological and social costs of adolescent employment.* New York: Basic Books.

Hamilton, M. A., & Hamilton, S. F. (1997). *Learning well at work: Choices for quality.* Washington, DC: U.S. Government Printing Office.

Hamilton, M. A., & Hamilton, S. F. (2002). Why mentoring in the workplace works. In G. G. Noam (Ed. in chief) & J. E. Rhodes (Ed.), *A critical view of youth mentoring* (*New Directions for Youth Development: Theory, Research, and Practice, No. 93,* pp. 59–89). San Francisco: Jossey-Bass.

Hamilton, M. A., & Hamilton, S. F. (2004). Designing work and service for learning. In S. F. Hamilton & M. A. Hamilton (Eds.), *The youth development handbook: Coming of age in American communities* (pp. 147–169). Thousand Oaks, CA: Sage.

Hamilton, M. A., Hamilton, S. F., & Vermeylen, F. M. (2002, April). *Training workplace mentors to use challenging teaching behaviors.* Paper presented at the American Educational Research Association, AERA Annual Meeting, New Orleans, LA.

Hamilton, S. F. (1980). Experiential learning programs for youth. *American Journal of Education, 88,* 170–215.

Hamilton, S. F., & Darling, N. (1996). Mentors in adolescents' lives. In K. Hurrelmann & S. F. Hamilton (Eds.), *Social problems and social contexts in adolescence: Perspectives across boundaries* (pp. 199–218). New York: Aldine de Gruyter.

Hamilton, S. F., & Hamilton, M. A. (1992). Mentoring programs: Promise and paradox. *Phi Delta Kappan, 73,* 546–550.

Hamilton, S. F., & Hamilton, M. A. (2004). Contexts for mentoring: Adolescent-adult relationships in workplaces and communities. In R. M. Lerner & L. Steinberg (Eds.), *Handbook of adolescent psychology* (pp. 395–428). New York: Wiley.

Kelman, H. C. (1974). Further thoughts on the processes of compliance, identification, and internalization. In J. T. Tedeschi (Ed.), *Perspectives on social power* (pp. 125–171). Chicago: Aldine.

Klaw, E. L., & Rhodes, J. E. (1995). Mentor relationships and the career development of pregnant and parenting African American teenagers. *Psychology of Women Quarterly, 19,* 551–562.

Linnehan, F. (2003). A longitudinal study of work-based, adult—youth mentoring. *Journal of Vocational Behavior, 63,* 40–54.

McLellan, J. A., & Youniss, J. (2003). Two systems of youth service: Determinants of voluntary and required youth community service. *Journal of Youth and Adolescence, 32,* 47–58.

Metz, E., McLellan, J., & Youniss, J. (2003). Types of voluntary service and adolescents' civic development. *Journal of Adolescent Research, 18,* 188–202.

Mortimer, J. T. (2003). *Working and growing up in America.* Cambridge, MA: Harvard University Press.

National Research Council and Institute of Medicine. (1998). *Protecting youth at work: Health, safety, and development of working children and adolescents in the United States.* Washington, DC: National Academy Press.

National Research Council and Institute of Medicine. (2002). (J. Eccles & J. Appleton Gootman, Eds.), *Community programs to promote youth development.* Committee on Community-Level Programs for Youth. Washington, DC: National Academy Press.

National Service-Learning Clearinghouse. (n.d.). Service-learning is . . . . Retrieved May 19, 2004, from http://www.servicelearning.org/article/archive/35/

Putnam, R. D. (2000). *Bowling alone: The collapse and revival of American community.* New York: Simon & Schuster.

Rhodes, J. E., Contreras, J. M., & Mangelsdorf, S. C. (1994). Natural mentor relationships among Latina adolescent mothers: Psychological adjustment, moderating processes, and the role of early parental acceptance. *American Journal of Community Psychology, 22,* 211–227.

Rollin, S. A., Kaiser-Ulrey, C., Potts, I., & Creason, A. H. (2003). A school-based violence prevention model for at-risk eighth grade youth. *Psychology in the Schools, 40,* 403–416.

Shumer, R., & Cook, C. C. (1999). *The status of service-learning: A report on service and service-learning in high schools between 1984 and 1997.* Retrieved June 10, 2004, from http://www.servicelearning.org/res/mono/status.htm

Stukas, A. A., Jr., Clary, E. G., & Snyder, M. (1999). Service learning: Who benefits and why. *Social Policy Report, 13*(4), 1–19.

Sullivan, A. M. (1996). From mentor to muse: Recasting the role of women in relationship with urban adolescent girls. In B. J. R. Leadbeater & N. Way (Eds.), *Urban girls: Resisting stereotypes, creating identities* (pp. 226–249). New York: New York University Press.

U.S. Department of Labor, Bureau of Labor Statistics. (2000). Trends in youth employment: Data from the current population survey. In *Report on the youth labor force* (chap. 4, pp. 30–51, revised November 2000). Washington, DC: Author. Retrieved June 10, 2004, from http://www .bls.gov/opub/rylf/pdf/chapter4.pdf

U.S. Department of Labor, Bureau of Labor Statistics. (2003a). *Employment experience of youths during the school year and summer* (News release USDL Pub. No. 03-40, January 31). Washington, DC: Author. Retrieved June 28, 2004, from http:// www.bls.gov/nls/nlsy97r4.pdf

U.S. Department of Labor, Bureau of Labor Statistics. (2003b). *Volunteering in the United States, 2003* (News release USDL Pub. No. 03-888, December 17). Washington, DC: Author. Retrieved June 10, 2004, from http://www.bls .gov/news.release/volun.nr0.htm

Wirt, J., Choy, S., Gerald, D., Provasnik, S., Rooney, P., Watanabe, S., et al. (2001). *The condition of education, 2001*. Washington, DC: U.S. Department of Education, National Center for Education Statistics. Retrieved June 10, 2004, from http://www.nces.ed.gov/pubsearch/pubsinfo .asp?pubid=2001072

24

AFTER-SCHOOL PROGRAMS

BARTON J. HIRSCH AND VIVIAN WONG

INTRODUCTION

As national interest has been drawn to interventions for youth that can both enhance development and prevent problems, after-school centers have gained increased prominence as a site for program delivery. After-school programs serve a wide range of youth across income levels, in all sections of the country, and in rural as well as urban areas, though much recent policy attention has focused on low-income, urban youth. After-school programs take place on weekdays, after the end of the school day. Programs that are offered during weekends or the summer would not be considered to be after school. Some programs specialize in a particular area (e.g., academic tutoring), whereas others offer activities across multiple domains. Some after-school sites are based exclusively in the local community, and others are part of national organizations such as Boys & Girls Clubs, the Ys, or Scouts.

National after-school programs have been in existence for more than 100 years. The 40 largest national youth organizations, which provide many after-school services, serve approximately 40 million youth. School-based sites are numerous and growing. The 21st Century

Community Learning Centers, the major federally funded after-school program, involves 7,500 schools in more than 1,400 school districts and communities nationwide.

There has been a certain stability in the activities offered at after-school sites over the course of the 20th century and continuing into the present day. As Halpern (2003) noted:

> The basic activity structure that emerged early on among after-school programs changed little over the decades, with clubs and classes, arts and crafts and table games, indoor or outdoor physical activity, cultural activity, and occasional field trips. Participation in the visual and expressive arts has been a constant. Specific emphases have risen or fallen. Pre-vocational activities such as metalwork declined over time. Yesterday's radio clubs have been replaced by today's computer clubs. Academic concerns emerged in the 1960s, and since then most programs have included homework time, perhaps some tutoring and/or reading time. (p. 4)

Under President Clinton, funding for after-school programs increased substantially, to $1 billion in fiscal year 2002. However, the Bush administration used preliminary findings from

Preparation of this chapter was facilitated in part by an award to the first author from the William T. Grant Foundation.

the evaluation of the 21st Century Community Learning Centers (Dynarski et al., 2003), which pointed to limited effects, as justification for proposing a major cutback. The budget fight has brought increased political visibility to these programs, which may well persist for some time in the future.

After-school programs have long emphasized the value of relationships that are formed between youth and staff at their sites. There are good reasons to assert that these ties may have unique strengths and mentoring potential. Relationships between youth and staff in after-school centers develop out of shared activities and reflect choices made by each person, rather than the decision of a coordinator in a formal mentoring program who may have limited familiarity with either the mentee or mentor. After-school program staff, furthermore, often are of the same race and socioeconomic background as youth. These areas of similarity may provide them with a hands-on familiarity with the life circumstances and cultural milieu of youth that is frequently missing in formal, stand-alone mentoring programs (cf. Freedman, 1993).

Mentoring ties have been postulated to play a major role in after-school program effectiveness. Illustratively, the evaluation of the Quantum Opportunities Program, cited by a National Research Council/Institute of Medicine (NRC/IOM, 2002) report as an exemplary intervention, concluded that "if young people are connected with caring adults for sustained periods of time, year-round, positive results do emerge" (Hahn, Levitt, & Aaron, 1994, p. 16). Unfortunately, the evaluation did not assess youth-staff ties in any detail, so it was not possible to substantiate the claim of a causal connection between the relational tie and youth outcomes.

Indeed, despite their evident potential as contexts for mentoring, there has been very little attention paid in the literature on after-school programs to theory and research on mentoring. This is unfortunate. Findings from the mentoring literature may help clarify the conditions under which after-school programs are effective and point to new practices that could enhance the impact of after-school programs. This could include having after-school sites host formal mentoring programs that might complement mentoring efforts by after-school staff.

In this chapter, we begin by proposing a theoretical framework for understanding the determinants and effects of mentoring relationships in after-school programs. This framework is based on both the mentoring literature and the literature on effective youth programs. We then examine research relevant to mentoring within after-school sites based on this framework and highlight areas in which little research has been conducted. Prevailing trends in after-school practices and recent innovations that bear on mentoring are then discussed. The chapter concludes with an outline of recommended future directions for both research and practice.

THEORY

Our proposed framework for understanding mentoring in after-school centers draws on theory and research in mentoring and on youth programs more generally. Theory can play a useful role in guiding our understanding and in suggesting areas for program development. The specificity and strength of a theory, in our view, is related in part to the underlying empirical base. Good prior work exists in the mentoring and youth program areas, but it is limited. For example, much of the research in mentoring is limited to studies of Big Brothers Big Sisters. In the youth program area, it is possible to identify programs with demonstrated success in randomized or quasi-experimental trials, yet the research provides little understanding of the effective ingredients of these programs.

In this chapter, we draw primarily on four sources: a recent integrative review of theory and research on youth programs by the NRC/IOM (2002); an integrative analysis of the mentoring literature by Rhodes (2002); a meta-analysis of the effectiveness of mentoring programs by DuBois, Holloway, Valentine, and Cooper (2002); and the decades-long research program of Public/Private Ventures (see summary by Sipe, 1996). The proposed framework should help organize and guide research on mentoring in after-school programs, but because of its limited empirical base, it should be viewed as quite preliminary.

The initial, simplest formulation of the framework is presented in Figure 24.1. The

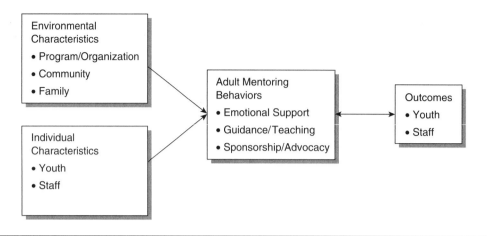

Figure 24.1   Initial Framework for Investigating Mentoring Relationships in After-School Programs

framework is simplified in that it does not depict moderating influences (though we assume that they exist) and does not identify all possible bidirectional effects. It also organizes sets of variables (e.g., environmental characteristics) that likely will need to be differentiated.

As befits a chapter on mentoring within a type of organization, the framework draws attention to the contexts of mentoring relationships. These ties do not exist in a vacuum. They draw upon and are in part determined by both individual and environmental characteristics. There are a wide range of such characteristics that are of potential relevance; this chapter focuses on those that appear to have greatest applicability to after-school settings. Similarly, in considering dimensions of mentoring ties themselves, our focus is on identifying those that are sufficiently broad to capture salient features of ties across a wide range of after-school settings.

It should be noted that the components identified under each category are not meant to be exhaustive. They are provided as examples of important domains but are only a subset of those that ultimately will need to be considered.

Adult Mentoring Behavior

The heart of our concern is what goes on in the relationship between youth and concerned adults in after-school centers. We focus specifically on potential mentoring behaviors of adult staff persons. Three overarching facets of their behavior are highlighted for consideration in the framework. The first, *emotional support,* involves behaviors that may affect the emotional dimensions of ties with youth. Important considerations in this regard may include the adult's capacity to empathize with the youth (Rhodes, 2002) and to be able to have fun with and be a friend to the youth (Sipe, 1996). These factors may enable the youth to respect and open up to the adult, facilitating mental health and an enhanced receptivity to the adult's involvement in the youth's life and goal-directed activities. The second facet, *guidance or teaching,* is assumed to occur both directly via instruction and indirectly via role modeling. These behaviors may facilitate cognitive development (Rhodes, 2002) as well as task accomplishment (NRC/IOM, 2002; Rogoff, 1990). The third facet, *sponsorship or advocacy,* involves behaviors in which the adult serves as a sponsor or advocate for the youth. These efforts may provide the youth with important connections (social capital) to significant adults who can help the youth to obtain positions or experiences that promote their development (Hamilton & Hamilton, 2004). For example, given that many jobs are found through personal social network contacts (Granovetter, 1995), an adult mentor may be able to help an adolescent mentee obtain an internship or summer job that could provide valuable work experience and information regarding possible future careers.

Determinants of Mentoring Behavior: Individual Characteristics and Environmental Characteristics

It is essential for both theory and practice to understand the factors that lead to variations in mentoring behavior. The most fundamental distinction at this level is between individual and environmental factors. By "individual," we refer to characteristics of youth and staff involved in after-school settings. By "environmental," we refer to characteristics of any of a range of potentially important contexts both in and outside of after-school centers.

With regard to *individual characteristics,* we assume that those of both youth and staff are important. Gender generally has been presumed to have important effects on relational styles. Young people's developmental needs for a certain type of mentoring are likely to vary by age as well, and the adult's age may well have implications for the ease with which they are able to establish rapport with the mentee. Similarly, initial rapport, at a minimum, may well be influenced by whether the pair is similar in ethnicity or race and whether the adult is familiar with the youth's background (including social class and neighborhood characteristics, among others). A variety of other personality and social factors of each individual may influence the development of the relationship, such as attachment history, mental health, social skills and attitudes, and whether the adult is oriented toward the youth's strengths rather than problems (NRC/IOM, 2002; Rhodes, 2002). Finally, the frequency with which the youth attends the after-school center and interacts with the mentor can be critical, as longer-term relationships appear especially valuable to youth (Rhodes, 2002). After-school centers vary substantially in youth participation; at some sites, the modal youth attends 5 days per week for several years (e.g., Hirsch, 2005), whereas other sites report modal attendance of only 1 day per week for a few weeks or months (Dynarski et al., 2003).

Turning to *environmental characteristics,* a variety of program and organizational characteristics may impact mentoring ties that develop in after-school settings. Theoretically, important variables in this domain would include the content and range of activities, the extent to which the organizational climate is oriented toward task accomplishment or relationship development, program attractiveness to youth, staff training and supervision, opportunities for youth autonomy and skill development, funding, staff-to-youth ratio, and parental involvement (DuBois et al., 2002; NRC/IOM, 2002; Sipe, 1996).

Organizational features of after-school centers may result in several distinctive elements of mentoring in these settings, compared with stand-alone mentoring programs. Given that after-school activities tend to be group oriented rather than one-on-one, mentoring may more often occur in a peer group context. Such mentoring may involve more complex social processes. As youth are frequently involved with multiple after-school staff, there is the potential for mentoring relationships to evolve with several staff in an extended family type of model (Ferguson, 1994). In addition, given that staff and youth are often simultaneously engaged in varied program activities and that a formal, one-on-one mentoring program may also be hosted by the site, there is the potential for synergy and cross-fertilization (sharing information and implementing complementary interventions), as well as conflict (giving incompatible advice), among these different domains.

With respect of other environmental domains, the youth's family and community each may influence both the quality of mentoring relationships based at after-school programs and the activities that are engaged in within these ties. The extent to which the youth's family is involved with the after-school program and develops communication channels and an alliance with the mentor could help the mentor (DuBois et al., 2002); at the same time, tension between the family and mentor could lead to decreased mentor effectiveness. At a community level, it would not be surprising to find that predominant local concerns, such as violence and gangs, are a topic of discussion and guidance in mentoring relationships at after-school programs.

Outcomes

Among youth, both academic and nonacademic outcomes have been viewed as important indicators of the effectiveness of after-school programs (NRC/IOM, 2002). Academic outcomes include school completion, grades, scores on standardized tests, attendance, and homework completion. Nonacademic outcomes include prosocial values, employment, mental health, identity and competence development, peer relationships, drug or alcohol use, and other indices of development. Mentoring behaviors of staff, as well as ties with mentors through formal programs, in after-school centers could impact youth outcomes in these areas via several mechanisms (cf. Rhodes, 2002). In brief, emotional support may help youth manage emotions that otherwise might be overwhelming, allowing them to focus on accomplishing the types of academic or psychosocial tasks that are a frequent focus of after-school programs. Guidance and teaching can promote effective problem solving, provide interpretive frameworks that reduce uncertainty, enhance positive motivation, and deter youth from pursuing problem behaviors. Advocacy and sponsorship can provide admittance into growth-enhancing opportunities, connection with other mentors, and negotiation of less undesirable sanctions upon problematic behavior.

Turning to adults, it is also important to consider how mentoring relationships formed with youth in after-school settings affect the adults involved. Sarason (1972), for example, has long argued that the ability of staff in human service institutions to be effective will reflect in part their own job satisfaction. Staff in after-school settings who do not find their involvement with youth to be rewarding or grow less interested over time are unlikely to be sufficiently motivated to do good work with their young charges. On the positive side, work on the helper-therapy principle (Riessman, 1965) suggests that after-school staff may benefit in important ways from the act of mentoring. Gains in self-concept and self-efficacy, for example, could fuel increased commitment on the part of the adult to mentoring activities. Successful mentoring relationships also may increase or maintain job satisfaction, leading to less job turnover (a major issue at after-school programs), thus making possible longer-lasting ties between staff and youth. These considerations also may bear on adults who volunteer their services as mentors in after-school centers.

RESEARCH

As noted, there has not been a great deal of research on mentoring in after-school settings. The findings that we consider are from investigations that include a focus on mentoring dimensions of youth-staff relationships, although in only one study (Hirsch, 2005) is the term *mentoring* used as a central organizing concept. Methodologically, most of this work involves qualitative analyses; quantitative studies are especially scarce. The presentation of research findings is organized in terms of our theoretical framework.

Mentoring Behavior

Four qualitative studies capture the diverse range of mentoring behavior by staff that can be found in after-school programs. Larson, Hansen, and Walker (in press) focused on an agriculturally oriented after-school program that is a local affiliate of a national organization. The high school students were involved in planning a 2-day summer camp for younger children. The research involved multiple observations and interviews (with youth and staff) over several months. Analyses of the qualitative data indicated that the two adult leaders provided mentoring that focused on enabling the high school youth to plan and implement the camp successfully. The adults were observed to do this by supporting the goals and directions set forth by youth; fostering a culture of input from the youth; asking questions, but letting youth provide the answers; monitoring the development of the planning and intervening when appropriate; creating intermediate structures (e.g., short-term goals) that offered challenges consonant with youth skill and experience; and stretching youth to take on new roles and identities. These behaviors reflect the guidance and sponsorship dimensions of mentoring identified in our theoretical framework.

McLaughlin, Irby, and Langman (1994) conducted a study of more than 60 community-based after-school programs in three geographically diverse cities judged to be successful by youth participants. The programs reviewed had a wide range of foci, including a Girl Scout troop, a theatre performance group, a tumbling (athletic) program, and academic tutoring. Ethnographic data indicated that staff in these programs communicated empathy for the life circumstances of youth, created programs that developed and displayed youth's strengths, instructed youth in relevant skills, helped youth cope with stressful life circumstances, and served as role models. As McLaughlin et al. (1994) noted, at one point or other, staff served as "youth employment counselors, school advisors, bankers, babysitters, advocates, and more" (p. 100). These relationships tapped all three dimensions of mentoring behavior in the proposed framework: emotional support, guidance and teaching, and sponsorship/advocacy. The staff thus appeared to provide a wider range of mentoring than those in the agricultural after-school program.

An unpublished study of the New York City Beacons, widely regarded as an especially promising after-school program, highlighted an array of staff mentoring behavior (Warren, Feist, & Nevárez, 2002). Data were gathered through both interviews and observations. Staff were found to monitor youth behavior in multiple domains (personal, school, and home life); set high expectations for behavior and academic achievement; provide homework assistance; diffuse peer conflict; and create an atmosphere of mutual respect and trust. The program thus seems especially strong in terms of fostering staff mentoring behaviors relating to guidance and emotional support.

Hirsch (2005) is the only investigation to explicitly link after-school program findings with the mentoring literature. This research was conducted over a 4-year period with six urban Boys & Girls Clubs serving predominantly minority early adolescents. Data were obtained via ethnographic observation, questionnaires, and youth and staff interviews; most data were qualitative, although some quantitative data were obtained as well. The ethnography revealed that many staff were drawn to narrative modes of mentoring with groups of youth, wherein they would tell stories of their prior life experiences, often involving events with club youth, that transmitted the fundamental culture, values, and beliefs of the club regarding the outside world. The narratives would employ both the vocabulary and rhetorical strategies common to vernacular African American discourse.

A series of analyses compared youth reports of club staff behavior with behavior of close kin and school adults. Both academic and nonacademic issues were likely to be discussed with club staff, whereas kin focused almost entirely on nonacademics and school ties focused also entirely on academics (Hirsch, 2005). In addition to addressing varied nonacademic concerns, staff engaged in a host of fun activities with youth in both club and nonclub settings.

Hirsch (2005) was especially concerned with staff behaviors that helped youth develop positive identities. Mentoring in this area was found to involve a diverse array of activities, including those oriented toward fostering youth initiative, socializing youth to positive identities, providing opportunities for youth skill development, providing performance feedback, providing emotional support, promoting code switching, serving as positive role models, and socializing values and behavioral norms of peer friendship groups. These behaviors reflect all three overarching dimensions of adult mentoring behavior in our proposed framework.

Determinants of Mentoring Behavior

Regarding individual characteristics, findings from the qualitative studies cited previously suggest that staff attitudes played an important role in determining their relationships with youth. Staff mentors were characterized by strong beliefs in the potential of youth; they saw youth as resources to be developed rather than problems to be solved (Hirsch, 2005; McLaughlin et al., 1994). In addition, staff perceived as exemplary had a sense of efficacy, believing in their ability to make a difference in the lives of the young people in their programs (McLaughlin et al., 1994). The similarity in background between many staff and youth were noted as well (Hirsch, 2005; McLaughlin et al., 1994). Staff often had lived in that very community, or a similar one, and thus had knowledge and empathy for the issues confronting those youth. In addition, they were often of the same race as the youth, which may well have facilitated rapport and empathy. Shared background extended to appreciating aspects of youth culture. Many staff communicated a sympathetic familiarity with this culture, which gave them credibility with youth. This credibility provided the basis for drawing youth into programs and for providing wide-ranging mentoring (Hirsch, 2005).

Individual characteristics of youth appear salient in some instances but not in others. For example, adolescent gender did not moderate the association between the quality of youth-staff relationships and self-esteem (Pagano, 2000). However, to implement a gender equity initiative at the six Boys & Girls Clubs that were studied, female staff provided girls with sponsorship, protection, role modeling, and skill training of a sort that did not appear to be provided to boys (Hirsch, 2005). Thus, individual characteristics (in this instance, youth and staff gender) interacted with an environmental factor (gender equity initiative) to shape the content of the mentoring behaviors that occurred in a particular set of relationships (adult female staff mentoring girls).

Individual characteristics also may help explain divergent findings on mentoring behavior across studies. Larson et al. (in press), it may be recalled, detailed how staff provided task-oriented guidance to youth planning an agricultural summer camp experience for younger children. Hirsch (2005), on the other hand, drew attention to how staff at inner-city Boys & Girls Clubs functioned as role models, addressed a wide range of life concerns, and made use of culturally distinct linguistic styles to communicate. One factor that differentiates the two samples is the age of the youth. The agricultural program enrolled high school youth, whereas the Boys & Girls Clubs membership was composed primarily of younger adolescents. It is possible that the older youth were more drawn to a specific program activity and were more likely to have the cognitive skills to appreciate and utilize some of the more challenging staff interventions.

At the same time, in terms of environmental characteristics, there were important between-site program/organizational differences that may have had important implications for the types of mentoring behaviors that were observed across studies. The agricultural after-school program focused on accomplishing a specific task, and the mentoring that was provided was designed to facilitate task accomplishment (Larson et al., in press). The staff did not appear to have core goals beyond the program itself. Although much mentoring in the Boys & Girls Clubs did occur during specific program activities, the programs themselves were much less structured, and if they had specific tasks to accomplish, they were not as ambitious as in the agricultural program. At the same time, the club mentors had much broader mentoring goals, which involved teaching lessons about life that ranged widely across education, family ties, sexuality, violence, and so on (Hirsch, 2005). Thus, the task versus process orientation and differences in goals between the sites may well have led to differences in mentoring behavior.

If one compares only the Larson et al. (in press) and Hirsch (2005) studies, it is difficult to tease out any further which of those program differences contributed most to differences in mentoring behavior. The McLaughlin et al. (1994) research, though, provided additional comparison programs that help us do this. Several of the programs described by McLaughlin et al. had specific tasks that needed to be accomplished. For example, there was a theatre group, which put on a play for community audiences, and a tumbling group, which put on athletic performances. In each program, staff provided guidance to enable youth to be successful in completing relevant tasks and projects; it was quite important that youth do a good job. In this manner, these programs are similar to the program studied by Larson et al. and different from the after-school sites studied by Hirsch. However, in contrast to the agricultural group but like the inner-city clubs, the mentors for the theatre and tumbling groups were broadly concerned with youth and provided wide-ranging mentoring across varied life domains. The McLaughlin et al. mentors addressed issues that were as personal and sensitive as those addressed by the club mentors. These additional comparisons suggest that it is not task orientation per se that necessarily leads to differences in mentoring behavior among after-school program staff. Rather, the broader visions and goals of each program appear to be important as well.

Differences in the communities served by these various programs also may have had an important role. The Boys & Girls Clubs tumbling program and theatre group served youth from low-income, predominantly minority communities. Given the high level of violence in these communities, violence was a major staff focus, with staff involved in providing guidance and emotional support, defusing potential confrontations, and in some instances even providing transportation to avoid potential interactions with gangs. In a similar vein, there was a clear press to help youth construct positive identities that needed to be framed in contrast to negative community options. Although identity construction often involves the juxtaposition of positive and negative identities (Markus & Nurius, 1986), this process seems likely to be accentuated under these environmental circumstances. This concern with promoting positive engagements in the context of avoiding negative possibilities in the community may well have contributed to the wider-ranging mentoring. There is no indication that youth in the agricultural group lived in communities that had similar risks.

The theoretical framework presented earlier in the chapter noted several distinctive features of after-school centers that could impact mentoring behavior, such as the prevalence of group-oriented activities, presence of multiple adult staff, youth-staff interactions in a wide range of activities, and the presence of a formal mentoring program on site. Some of these characteristics are described in published reports. For example, Hirsch (2005) has presented in some detail an episode of mentoring that was directed at a group of young people. The mentor clearly sought to socialize the norms of the peer group above and beyond changing the behavior of any one member of the group. The ways in which this mentor emphasized the history, goals, and values of the group are probably different than what would have been said in a one-on-one exchange. In this manner, mentoring behavior was adapted to an important characteristic of the after-school site (i.e., youth congregated in groups, and staff interactions with youth often took place in a group context). At present, however, there are insufficient data to permit a clear analysis of how these program/organizational characteristics may be associated with mentoring in after-school programs.

In a similar vein, the theoretical framework included the potential for family characteristics that would influence mentoring. Youth often are attracted to after-school programs by the presence of siblings or cousins (Loder & Hirsch, 2003). However, none of the studies reviewed reports findings directly related to the influence of family variables on mentoring behavior.

Mentoring Behavior and Outcomes

Drawing on data collected by the Hirsch research group, Pagano (2000) analyzed the linkage between the youth-staff relationship and youth outcomes. This is the principal quantitative study of mentoring within after-school programs and the only study that reports quantitative linkages between mentoring behavior and a youth outcome. The mentoring measure assessed the youth's perception of the mentor as providing trust and appreciation, which taps primarily what we have labeled in this chapter as emotional support. The mentor was defined as the staff member (adult) with whom the youth reported the closest tie. The outcome measure was youth self-esteem. Regression analyses controlled for a variety of personal and environmental factors that could influence self-esteem (i.e., parental marital status, family socioeconomic status, neighborhood poverty rate, parental education, nonclub extracurricular activity, number of days in attendance at club per week, youth reports of the closeness of youth-parent ties).

In cross-sectional analyses of these data collected from 114 youth in four Boys & Girls Clubs, Pagano (2000) found that stronger perceived youth-staff relationships were associated with higher levels of self-esteem among youth in all neighborhoods. However, the youth reports of the level of neighborhood safety moderated the linkage between the perceived quality of the youth-staff relationship and youth self-esteem, such that the association was significantly stronger among youth living in neighborhoods perceived as least safe. There was no corresponding moderating finding for the youth's relationship with their closest kin or school tie. On the basis of follow-up, qualitative interviews, Hirsch (2005) concluded that the moderating finding among club adults was probably due both to the greater proximity of club staff to incidents of potential violence and to their greater perceived effectiveness in controlling confrontations that in other settings would likely escalate into violence.

We are not aware of any studies that investigate whether mentoring behavior in an after-school program is linked with any outcome for the adult staff or mentor. From accounts provided of after-school staff in several of the studies previously cited, it appears highly likely that staff derived intrinsic satisfaction from mentoring efforts, but there are apparently no qualitative or quantitative analyses that address this issue directly.

PRACTICE

In this section, we consider prevailing trends in practice relevant to mentoring of youth in after-school centers as well as recent innovations. Because there is very little written on mentoring in after-school programs from a practice orientation, we devote some attention to other program practices that are likely to provide expanded opportunities for mentoring.

All (or almost all) after-school programs have adult staff. However, it is not the case that having staff on-site translates into high-quality mentoring or, indeed, any mentoring at all. There are some after-school programs where the adults remain off by themselves, behind a desk, in a back room, available to intercede if needed but for the most part unengaged with young people. There are large numbers of school-based after-school programs that are designed to be staffed by teachers but have great difficulty recruiting teachers for this additional work. To address this reluctance, many such sites employ teachers for only limited hours and sometimes place them on-site for a period of only a few weeks at any one time (Dynarski et al., 2003). It is difficult to imagine that many mentoring relationships develop in circumstances where teachers are so weakly motivated and contact is so haphazard.

It is clear that in the after-school centers that were examined in the research reviewed, much mentoring did take place. These types of programs recognize the value of relationships that youth form with staff. Their staff are likely to believe that such ties are an important factor contributing to youth retention in the program. Their leadership may well suggest that the relationship is what is most likely to "make a difference" in helping young people. In short, there is considerable recognition of the value of mentoring. Yet even in these types of programs, mentoring does not typically appear to be the subject of reflexive practice. Conversations about how to mentor effectively, in our experience, are rare in either informal or formal (e.g., staff meetings) contexts. Mentoring is rarely, if ever, the focus of staff workshops, other staff training sessions, or supervision. Ways to improve or enhance staff mentoring receive little attention.

One emerging direction in after-school interventions that does directly relate to mentoring involves the incorporation of a stand-alone mentoring program into activities offered on-site. Some of these emphasize academic tutoring, whereas others range more broadly. These stand-alone programs follow the typical mentoring format of utilizing one-to-one contacts. This type of relational context supplements the kind of mentoring that appears to typically characterize after-school programs. From published reports (e.g., Hirsch, 2005), most such mentoring appears to take place primarily in group contexts. The provision of both group and one-on-one mentoring has the potential for powerful synergies. At present, however, it is our impression that there generally is little communication between the stand-alone mentors and the rest of the after-school staff, so that any integration of efforts or synergies occurs, if at all, by happenstance rather than by design. In terms of the proposed theoretical framework, there is insufficient utilization of environmental characteristics that could provide resources for enhancing mentoring behaviors.

Some new initiatives in academically oriented after-school programs also provide potentially powerful contexts for mentoring. These include initiatives in which there is an emphasis on project-based learning activities utilizing technology, such as computer clubhouses (Resnick, Rusk, & Cooke, 1998). Project-based learning involves the completion of a task in which small teams of youth work with an adult to investigate a question that has relevance in their lives. Employed initially in reform-driven science, mathematics, and social studies classrooms (Stephen, Gallagher, & Workman, 1993), use of project-based learning is also being explored in after-school settings. Computer clubhouse projects have involved, for example, a group of fourth-grade girls who used programmable-brick technology to construct a "city of the future" that included working elevators, buses, and a tour guide (Resnick et al., 1998). These types of activities have engaged young people as active participants, provided opportunities for creative problem solving, and facilitated personal connections to knowledge (Resnick et al., 1998). Many of these activities may promote subject matter learning as well, an ever-increasing concern at the policy level, while also providing a vehicle for young people to have fun and be creative.

The collaborative, dynamic nature of project-based learning at computer clubhouses may enable adults to serve several different mentoring roles (Resnick et al., 1998). Adult staff while involved in project-based learning activities in after-school settings may support youth interests by fashioning environments where youth feel safe to experiment with new ideas, take risks, and follow new directions; they may give guidance; they may serve as role models of adults struggling with problems that need to be solved; and they may connect youth electronically with communities that exist beyond the clubhouse. In terms of our theoretical framework, these types of programs appear to offer excellent opportunities to provide mentoring in the domains of guidance and teaching and of sponsorship and advocacy. They also further illustrate an avenue through which practices focusing on the environmental characteristics of after-school centers may have the potential to facilitate mentoring behaviors by staff in such areas.

FUTURE DIRECTIONS

Synthesis

Research in the area of mentoring in after-school programs is still in its infancy. The available evidence, however, indicates that considerable mentoring by staff does take place in many after-school programs. Indeed, the breadth of life concerns addressed, particularly in programs that serve low-income communities, makes these sites especially promising locations for mentoring. Moreover, organizational features of many after-school sites, such as the presence of multiple staff and prevalence of staff interaction with youth peer groups, present unique opportunities for enhanced mentoring. Although most after-school programs appear to recognize the value of youth-staff relationships, at present, there has not been a great deal of intentional planning to maximize the mentoring potential. A great deal more focused attention from both the research and practice communities on mentoring relationships in these programs seems warranted and is likely to have considerable payoff. Our analysis in this chapter leads us to recommend several priorities for future research and practice.

Recommendations for Research

1. *Research on mentoring in after-school programs should be undertaken using a wide variety of methods.* At present, most research on mentoring in after-school programs has been qualitative. Such studies are important and should continue. It also clearly will be important to conduct quantitative investigations, both to address issues best suited to this approach and to garner the support of those segments of the research and policy community that privilege quantitative findings. The theoretical framework proposed in this chapter suggests several research issues that could be investigated utilizing varied methodologies. Two sets of issues that we see as particularly important to address are the focus of our remaining recommendations in the area of research.

2. *The impact of mentoring relationships in after-school programs on youth outcomes, especially across environmental settings, should be examined.* Research is needed to elucidate the immediate effects of mentoring within a particular after-school activity, the transfer of gains to other domains in that after-school environment, and transfers beyond the after-school center. This research will need to involve longitudinal designs.

3. *The impact of program/organizational characteristics on mentoring in after-school settings should be studied and could lead to important theoretical and pragmatic insights.* Several theoretically important features of after-school programs and organizations may have an important influence on mentoring in these contexts. These include the vision, goals, and intensity of specific activities in which mentoring interactions are embedded, as well as the presence in some after-school centers of more formalized mentoring programs involving outside volunteers. In doing so, it is important to control for the influence of other persons and environmental factors that may affect mentoring experiences and their linkages with outcomes as specified in our proposed framework. Moreover, because after-school programs and organizations are not static, we need to account for fluctuations in these domains.

Recommendations for Practice

1. *Support for effective mentoring relationships should be an administrative priority in after-school programs.* After-school program leaders need to articulate a vision that explicitly highlights the value of mentoring. Training and supervision need to be provided to staff to realize more fully the potential for effective mentoring in after-school centers.

2. *Structured programs in after-school centers should focus on how to maximize the potential for mentoring.* The potential for relationship development should be as much of a concern as is the coverage of curricular content within structured programs that are implemented in after-school centers. Program design should draw on natural mentoring styles that characterize local communities (Hirsch, 2005). This priority tells those who focus on after-school programs to pay more attention to encouraging the development of mentoring relationships within specific program activities.

3. *Programs should be developed to extend the natural range of staff mentoring.* Relationships do not develop in a vacuum. Programs that address sensitive topics or that focus on developing particular youth skills are needed to prod staff to provide mentoring in domains that they would not address on their own. This priority tells those who focus on mentoring that developing programs in a wide array of areas can help achieve mentoring goals.

After-school centers are promising sites for mentoring youth. We hope to see a future edition of this handbook in which a follow-up chapter reviews many new studies and exciting new developments in theory and practice.

REFERENCES

DuBois, D. L., Holloway, B. E., Valentine, J. C., & Cooper, H. (2002). Effectiveness of mentoring programs for youth: A meta-analytic review. *American Journal of Community Psychology, 30,* 157–197.

Dynarski, M., Pistorino, C., Moore, M., Silva, T., Mullens, J., Deke, J., et al. (2003). *When schools stay open late: The national evaluation of the 21st-Century Community Learning Centers program.* Washington, DC: U.S. Department of Education.

Ferguson, R. (1994). How professionals in community-based programs perceive and respond to the needs of black male youth. In R. Mincy (Ed.), *Nurturing black males* (pp. 59–98). Washington, DC: Urban Institute Press.

Freedman, M. (1993). *The kindness of strangers.* San Francisco: Jossey-Bass.

Granovetter, M. (1995). *Getting a job: A study of contacts and careers* (2nd ed.). Chicago: University of Chicago Press.

Hahn, A., Leavitt, T., & Aaron, P. (1994). *Evaluation of the Quantum Opportunities Program (QOP): Did the program work?* Waltham, MA: Brandeis University, Heller Graduate School.

Halpern, R. (2003). *Making play work: The promise of after-school programs for low-income children.* New York: Teachers College Press.

Hamilton, S. F., & Hamilton, M. A. (2004). Contexts for mentoring: Adolescent-adult relationships in workplaces and communities. In R. M. Lerner & L. Steinberg (Eds.), *Handbook of adolescent psychology* (pp. 395–428). New York: Wiley.

Hirsch, B. J. (2005). *A place to call home: After-school programs for urban youth.* Washington, DC: American Psychological Association and New York: Teachers College Press.

Larson, R., Hansen, D., & Walker, K. (in press). Everybody's gotta give: Development of initiative and teamwork within a youth program. In J. Mahoney, J. Eccles, & R. Larson (Eds.), *Organized activities as contexts of development: Extracurricular activities, after-school and community programs.* Hillsdale, NJ: Erlbaum.

Loder, T., & Hirsch, B. J. (2003). Inner city youth development organizations: The salience of peer ties among early adolescent girls. *Applied Developmental Science, 7,* 2–12.

Markus, H., & Nurius, P. (1986). Possible selves. *American Psychologist, 41,* 954–969.

McLaughlin, M., Irby, M., & Langman, J. (1994). *Urban sanctuaries: Neighborhood organizations in the lives and futures of inner city youth.* San Francisco: Jossey-Bass.

National Research Council and Institute of Medicine. (2002). (J. Eccles & J. Appleton Gootman, Eds.), *Community programs to promote youth development.* Committee on Community-Level Programs for Youth. Washington, DC: National Academy Press.

Pagano, M. (2000). *Non-parental social support and the well-being of low-income, minority youth.* Unpublished doctoral dissertation, Northwestern University, Evanston, IL.

Resnick, M., Rusk, N., & Cooke, S. (1998). The Computer Clubhouse: Technological fluency in the inner city. In D. Schon, B. Sanyal, & W. Mitchell (Eds.), *High technology and low-income communities* (pp. 263–286). Cambridge: MIT Press.

Rhodes, J. (2002). *Stand by me: The risks and rewards of mentoring today's youth.* Cambridge, MA: Harvard University Press.

Riessman, F. (1965). The "helper-therapy" principle. *Social Work, 10,* 27–32.

Rogoff, B. (1990). *Apprenticeship in thinking: Cognitive development in social context.* New York: Oxford University Press.

Sarason, S. (1972). *The creation of settings and the future societies.* San Francisco: Jossey-Bass.

Sipe, C. (1996). *Mentoring: A synthesis of P/PV's research: 1988–1995.* Philadelphia: Public/Private Ventures.

Stepien, W. J., Gallagher, S. A., & Workman, D. (1993). Problem-based learning for traditional and interdisciplinary classrooms. *Journal for the Education of the Gifted, 16,* 338–357.

Warren, C., Feist, M., & Navárez, N. (2002). *A place to grow: Evaluation of the New York City Beacons, Final report.* New York: Academy for Educational Development.

25

FAITH-BASED ORGANIZATIONS

KENNETH I. MATON, MARIANO R. STO. DOMINGO,
AND JACQUELINE KING

INTRODUCTION

Faith-based organizations have a long and rich history of community outreach to help individuals in need, including youth (Billingsley, 1992; Cnaan, 2002). The distinctive potential of faith-based organizations as a national resource to provide volunteer help and services to the local community is one of the factors underpinning President Bush's faith-based social policy initiative enacted in 2001. This resulted in the establishment of a White House Office of Faith-Based and Community Initiatives (Executive Order No. 13199, 2001) and of related centers in seven executive branch departments (e.g., Department of Health and Human Services; Executive Order No. 13198, 2001; Executive Order No. 13280, 2002). Related to the focus of the current chapter, faith-based mentoring programs are explicitly listed as one of the possibilities for funding in the federal Mentoring for Success Act (2001).

The domain of "faith-based mentoring" is not clearly defined in the research or practice literature to date. In this chapter, we focus primarily on formal mentoring programs, given their increasing salience in the practice and policy arenas. A faith-based mentoring program is one in which mentors are members of a religious congregation and the mentoring program

is sponsored either by the religious congregation or a faith-based nonprofit organization (Garringer, 2003a, 2003b). The primary purpose of the mentoring relationship is to contribute to the mentee's psychosocial development. We explicitly exclude from the domain of faith-based mentoring programs formal adult-youth relationships focused primarily on religious socialization (e.g., Sunday school, Bible study), group activity (e.g., youth group, youth choir, sports team), or specific-skill development (e.g., tutoring).

Second, and only briefly given space limitations, we consider informal, "natural" mentoring relationships through which adults extend support and guidance to youth in their congregations. Such relationships can develop as a result of sustained interactions between congregational youth and congregational adults (e.g., Sunday school teachers, youth group leaders, youth choir director, parents of congregational friends, ministers) in diverse formal and informal faith-based contexts (Smith, 2003). In the current chapter, when the focus is placed on such relationships, usually following more extensive discussion of formal mentoring programs, the term *natural faith-based mentoring* is used; when the more general term *faith-based mentoring* is used, the ensuing discussion focuses on formal mentoring programs (though the discussion may prove relevant to varying extents to natural mentoring relationships as well).

The prevalence of formal faith-based program mentoring is unclear. A 1998 survey of 1,504 adults mentoring young people found 31% of the mentors involved in formal mentoring programs taking part in programs sponsored by local churches (McLearn, Colasanto, & Schoen, 1998). This was second only to 33% sponsored by a school, college, or university. A 2002 national survey indicated that 24% of the mentors involved in formal mentoring programs mentored in a Sunday school/religious activity program, second only to school-based programs (28%) (AOL Time Warner Foundation, 2002). In both surveys, however, it was unclear to what extent respondents were indicating involvement in religious socialization activities (e.g., teaching a Sunday school class or leading a religious youth group) versus involvement in a mentoring program per se. Interestingly, 12% of the U.S. Office of Juvenile Justice and Delinquency Prevention Office awards for the Juvenile Mentoring Program (JUMP) were to faith-based initiatives (Clarke, Forbush, & Henderson, 2003). More generally, no data are available concerning the percentage of faith-based programs focused on youth in the larger community versus those focused on youth within the sponsoring congregation.

Finally, concerning natural mentoring relationships, a recent study based on a nationally representative sample of 18- to 26-year-olds found that among the approximately three quarters of respondents who reported having a mentor since the age of 14, 5% nominated a minister/priest/rabbi as their primary mentor (DuBois & Silverthorn, in press). It is not known, however, among the other nonparental adults nominated (e.g., friends' parents), what additional percentage may have been members of the youth's congregation and serving as faith-based natural mentors.

Congregations represent important contexts for mentoring programs for several reasons. First, given the large number of Americans who belong to churches, synagogues, and mosques, an extremely large pool of potential mentors exists in the congregational context (Rhodes, 2002). Second, the religious mission of many congregations includes a strong commitment to local communities, including at-risk youth (Ammerman, 2001; Chaves, 1999; Cnaan, 2002; Cohen & Jaeger, 1998). Third, in many minority and inner-city neighborhoods, local congregations appear to have a unique credibility and access to local families and youth that secular organizations appear to lack (Dionne & DiIulio, 2000). Fourth, there is special potential for religious and social support for mentors in the faith-based context, which is noteworthy given the special challenges involved in mentoring at-risk youth (Branch, 2002; Jucovy, 2003). Finally, faith-based mentoring relationships provide a potential for spiritual and religious development of mentees, which may be important given the literature indicating a significant link between religion and positive outcomes for youth (e.g., Johnson, Tompkins, & Webb, 2002; Regnerus, Smith, & Fritsch, 2002; Smith & Faris, 2002).

On the other hand, there are a comparable set of distinct challenges that face the development and viability of faith-based mentoring programs. First, there may be tension between the religious mission of congregations and the beliefs and needs of mentees. Second, there may be a mistrust of religion by key individuals in the larger community who are stakeholders in mentoring programs (e.g., parents, educators, potential funders). Third, congregations, especially those of small or medium size, may have limited organizational capacity to effectively implement and sustain a mentoring program (Hartmann, 2003). Finally, if a program receives funding from the government, potential constitutional issues concerning the separation of church and state arise (Branch, 2002).

Given the increased emphasis in recent years on the importance of mentoring as a strategic intervention to help youth in need in our nation (e.g., Fulop, 2003) and given the potential of faith-based organizations to contribute positively to pressing community needs, a review of research and practice related to faith-based mentoring programs is timely. In the first portion of this chapter, the theoretical underpinnings of faith-based mentoring are examined. Next, extant research on the nature and impact of mentoring in the faith-based context are reviewed. The subsequent section addresses what we know to date about the practice of faith-based mentoring programs, including program development and operation. Finally, the chapter concludes with recommendations for future research and practice relating to the mentoring of youth in the faith-based arena.

THEORY

Religion as a meaning system is an important component of American society, influencing individuals, communities, and the society as a whole in varied ways (Maton, Dodgen, Sto. Domingo, & Larson, in press). Below, pathways through which faith-based mentoring programs may positively influence both individual youth and the larger community are considered. Although relatively little research has examined many of the theoretical pathways depicted, the model presented can provide a framework for future research in this area. Some of the constructs discussed are specific to the faith-based domain; others relate to universal processes described in the broader mentoring literature that can be expected to apply to faith-based mentoring as well.

Pathways of Influence on Individual Youth

Figure 25.1 depicts a set of pathways through which faith-based mentoring programs could theoretically enhance individual youth outcomes. Constructs at the congregational, program, mentor, mentor-mentee relationship, and mentee levels are included.

Congregational Mission, Support, and Capacity

Three potentially important constructs at the level of the congregation are faith-based organizational beliefs and mission, faith-based organizational support system, and faith-based organizational capacity (see Figure 25.1). *Faith-based organizational beliefs and mission* refers to the theology and goals of a congregation, including the extent and nature of congregational priorities related to reaching out to those in need. *Faith-based organizational support*

system refers to the structure and nature of tangible, social, emotional, and spiritual support provided by the congregation to its members. *Faith-based organizational capacity* encompasses the problem-solving capability, leadership, economic and human resources, and member skills within the congregation that allow it to accomplish its primary goals (Pargament & Maton, 2000).

Congregational mission, support system, and capacity are important in part because they may provide distinctive strengths and distinct challenges for mentoring initiatives situated in faith-based versus other contexts. For example, faith-based organizations in inner-city locales may, generally speaking, share a mission of serving those most in need in their communities, provide congregation-wide support to those engaged in such ministry work, and possess a willing pool of potential volunteers. To the extent this is the case, faith-based mentoring may have a distinctive potential to generate successful mentoring initiatives, in contrast to mentoring based in other inner-city contexts.

Although faith-based organizations as a group may differ from non-faith-based organizations on the above constructs, widespread variation likely exists among faith-based organizations on each construct as well. For example, there are important variations in faith-based mission across religions, religious denominations, and individual congregations (Ammerman, 2001; Becker, 1999; Pargament & Maton, 2000). Of special importance for faith-based mentoring programs is the extent to which a congregation's mission focuses on community outreach to those in need. In congregations in which there is a strong focus on community outreach ministry, a critical mass of mentors is more likely to be generated, and mentors' personal and spiritual commitment to the mentoring relationship may be especially strong (Figure 25.1, Pathway a). Interestingly, Loconte and Fantuzzo (2002) report that some congregation-initiated mentoring programs require as many as 4 to 10 years of commitment.

Congregations also vary in their levels of cohesiveness and social support (e.g., Pargament, Silverman, Johnson, Echemendia, & Snyder, 1983). In faith-based organizations with high levels of cohesiveness, the congregational support

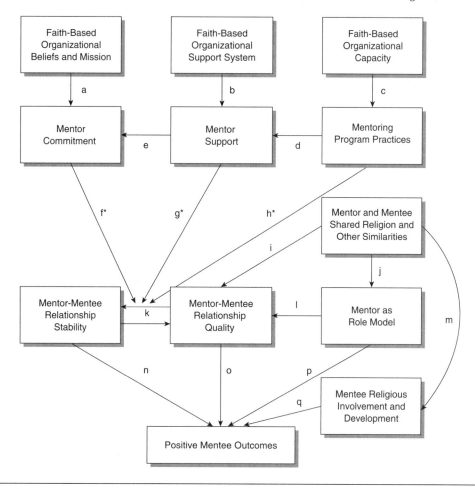

Figure 25.1 Set of Pathways Through Which Faith-Based Mentoring Programs Could Enhance Individual Youth Outcomes

*Each of these pathways leads directly to both mentor-mentee relationship quality and mentor-mentee relationship stability, but to avoid overwhelming the reader with too many arrows, only one arrow was used for each. Thus, mentor commitment, mentor support, and mentoring program practices should not be construed as moderating the link between mentor-mentee relationship quality and stability.

of a ministry such as faith-based mentoring and the support among mentors are likely to be greater (Pathway b). The emotional, tangible, and spiritual support received may contribute importantly by helping the mentor to cope with difficulties that arise in the mentoring relationship and by increasing the mentor's commitment to stay involved over the longer term.

Furthermore, congregations differ in organizational capacity. In part, this may relate to the size of the congregation and the social, economic, and occupational status of its membership. Generally speaking, congregations with greater organizational capacity can be expected

to develop and sustain higher-quality mentoring program practices (Pathway c).

Mentoring Program Practices

Mentoring program practices, as described in the general mentoring literature, include mentor recruitment, mentor screening and training, mentor-mentee matching, and mentor supervision (DuBois, Holloway, Valentine, & Cooper, 2002; MENTOR/National Mentoring Partnership, 2003). The presence of effective mentor supervision, for example, can be expected to directly contribute to levels of support provided to the mentor (Pathway d). Mentor supervision, along with careful recruitment and matching and in-depth training, can generally be expected to enhance mentor-mentor relationship stability and relationship quality (Pathway h).

Mentor Commitment and Support

Given the challenges of working with at-risk youth over extended periods of time, mentor commitment and support appear to be important facets of effective mentoring. Mentor commitment is manifest in the amount of time mentors devote to the mentoring process. Mentor support encompasses the provision of instructional materials, information, emotional support, and constructive feedback. Effective support provided to a mentor can be expected to enhance mentor commitment (Pathway e). Mentor support and mentor commitment are seen as directly contributing to mentor-mentee relationship stability and quality (Pathways f and g).

Mentor and Mentee Shared Religion and Other Similarities

Mentor and mentee shared religion and other similarities such as ethnicity and geographic locale can be expected to contribute to the quality of mentoring relationships in the faith-based context (Pathway i). Theoretically, similarity between mentor and mentee on one or more of these dimensions has the potential to enhance the ease and quality of mentor-mentee communication, facilitate participation in activities of common interest, and, more generally, enhance relationship building (Aronson, Wilson, & Akert, 1998). Sharing key characteristics in common may also enhance the likelihood that a mentor is viewed by a mentee as a valued role model (Pathway j; Aronson et al., 1998). Furthermore, shared religious beliefs and denominational affiliation, and especially shared congregational membership, may enhance the mentee's religious development and involvement (Pathway m). This influence might result from direct mentor encouragement, from mentor-mentee shared involvement in social and religious activities, or indirectly through the mentor being viewed as a positive religious or spiritual role model.

Mentor-Mentee Relationship Stability and Quality

Relationship stability refers both to the frequency of meetings and to the overall length of the relationship. Relationship quality encompasses levels of closeness, trust, support, and caring between mentor and mentee. Enhanced relationship quality likely will enhance relationship stability, and vice versa (Pathway k). Research from the youth mentoring literature indicates that mentor-mentee relationship stability and quality are important contributors to positive mentee outcomes (Pathways n and o; DuBois et al., 2002; Grossman, 1998; Parra, DuBois, Neville, Pugh-Lilly, & Povinelli, 2002). Longer-term, stable relationships with faith-based mentors, as with non-faith-based mentors, may help anchor a youth whose other relationships and social environments may be unstable and turbulent. An enduring tie with a mentor also may allow sufficient trust to develop for positive interpersonal influence to occur. The emotional support from a caring adult provided in a strong, high-quality mentor-mentee relationship may help youth cope with difficult life circumstances, enhance self-esteem, and instill hope for the future.

Mentor as Role Model

To the extent the mentor is viewed by the mentee as having attributes he or she values and respects, the potential for the mentor to serve as an important role model is present. For religious mentees, congregational mentors have the potential to serve as role models of the religious adults they aspire to be, perhaps especially if the mentor is regularly viewed by the mentee carrying out valued roles and activities in the congregation and in the larger community. More generally, in inner-city communities with a shortage of viable adult role models, adults from local congregations may be especially well situated to serve as role models. When the mentor serves as a role model, the quality of the mentor-mentee relationship should be enhanced (Pathway l). Furthermore, viable, positive role models can provide multiple positive influences to mentees, including values and behavioral and moral direction (see Rhodes, 2002, for a detailed discussion), directly resulting in positive youth outcomes (Pathway p).

Mentee Religious Involvement and Development

Religious involvement encompasses attendance at worship services, participation in religious education, and involvement in varied congregation-sponsored social, recreational, and volunteer activities (e.g., youth groups, choir, sports teams). Religious development encompasses enhancement and deepening of religious beliefs and understanding, spiritual experience, and moral convictions. Enhanced mentee religious involvement as a consequence of a mentoring relationship may result in positive psychosocial outcomes, a pathway of influence perhaps distinctive to faith-based mentoring (Pathway q). A large body of research has linked youth religious belief and involvement to positive youth behavioral outcomes, including lower levels of substance abuse, teenage pregnancy, academic failure, and delinquency (e.g., Evans et al., 1996; Johnson et al., 2002; Regnerus et al., 2002).

Smith (2003) has described three specific pathways (not included in Figure 25.1) through which religious involvement and development may promote positive youth outcomes: strengthened moral order, learned competencies, and enhanced social and organizational ties. A strengthened moral order is one way in which youth may develop normative directives that guide their choices and foster self-control. The learning of new cognitive, affective, and behavioral competencies can enhance the success and adjustment of youth in varied domains. These competencies include beliefs and practices that can help youth cope with the stress of difficult situations, to process intense emotions, and to resolve interpersonal conflicts, thereby enhancing well-being and life capacity. Finally, enhanced social and organizational ties provide youth with more meaningful, prosocial relationships with peers and adults through varied involvements in the faith-based context, including both religious (e.g., worship, religious education, Bible study) and social (recreational and cultural)

activities. These relationships and involvements can buffer youth from negative peer and other influences (Irwin, 2002).

Positive Mentee Outcomes

The research literature describes a range of positive mentee outcomes that can emerge from youth mentoring relationships (cf. DuBois et al., 2002; Rhodes, 2002). These include lower levels of substance abuse, teenage pregnancy, academic failure and delinquency, and higher levels of self-esteem and well-being. As described above, positive mentee outcomes are expected to result from mentor-mentee relationships characterized by high levels of stability and quality, those in which the mentor serves as a valued role model and those that contribute to the mentee's religious involvement and development.

Natural Mentoring Relationships

Although the preceding model was developed with an explicit focus on formal, faith-based mentoring programs, many of the proposed pathways may prove relevant for natural mentoring relationships in the faith-based arena as well. For example, congregations whose mission includes a primary focus on congregational community and those with strong support systems may be especially conducive to the development of high-quality natural mentoring relationships. On the other hand, some of the constructs in the model, such as organizational capacity, may be less important for the development of natural mentoring relationships than of formal mentoring programs. In addition, natural mentoring may be more likely than formal mentoring to influence positive youth outcomes as part of a convergent, synergistic process—that is, due to the mutual, reinforcing influence from and among multiple natural mentors in the congregation, such as parents, congregational friends' parents, extended family, and spiritual modeling. Taken together, this network of influences has the potential to reinforce positive behavior norms, academic engagement, and religious and spiritual development (Coleman, 1988; Oman & Thoresen, 2003; Regnerus, 2003; Smith, 2003).

The Potential for
Community-Wide Influence

Taken as a whole, faith-based organizations in a community represent an important pool of potential mentors for youth in need. In any community, there are a large number of congregations; in urban settings in particular, faith-based organizations may represent the primary source of institutional social and human capital (Foley, McCarthy, & Chaves, 2001). Furthermore, the outreach mission of many faith-based organizations, perhaps especially urban and minority congregations, is focused on local community needs, including those of youth (Billingsley, 1992; Dionne & DiIulio, 2000). If a critical mass of congregations and of congregation mentors are effectively mobilized in community-wide mentoring initiatives, there may be the possibility of community-wide influence.

However, given the many stressors and challenges facing urban youth, it is likely that community-wide influence will necessitate a broad array of interventions, including but not limited to mentoring. Faith-based mentoring programs that are embedded within comprehensive, multicomponent programs and faith-based organizations that are involved in a variety of ways and levels in meeting the needs of at-risk youth likely are necessary for a broader, community-wide influence to be generated.

RESEARCH

A literature search revealed little empirical research related to faith-based mentoring programs. Surprisingly, not a single published study was found that systematically examined the outcomes of faith-based mentoring or related pathways of influence. Several published articles document but do not evaluate specific mentoring program efforts (e.g., Irwin, 2002). Unpublished technical reports provide preliminary evidence related to program impact or implementation, but research design limitations in each case preclude drawing conclusions about program effectiveness.

Public/Private Ventures (P/PV) obtained outcome-related data as part of a study of the Amachi Project (Jucovy, 2003). The goal of Amachi is to provide one-to-one relationships to children 5 to 18 years old growing up without parents in Philadelphia; the parents either are currently incarcerated or were incarcerated in the past. Big Brothers Big Sisters (BBBS) and P/PV collaborated on the initiative. Mentors were recruited from 42 inner-city congregations. BBBS surveyed 189 mentors who had been meeting with their mentees 1 year; the children's caregivers were surveyed as well. The vast majority of the mentors (93%) and caregivers (82%) reported that youth self-confidence had improved. Three fifths of the mentors (61%) and caregivers (60%) indicated that youth had an improved "sense of the future." In addition, a majority of mentors and caregivers (percentages not reported) reported that the youth improved academically and behaviorally. Finally, 62% of the matches were reported to have lasted a year or longer. Jucovy indicated that the reports of both perceived outcomes and mentoring relationship length compared favorably with data from other BBBS samples. However, these other samples contained somewhat older children and thus do not serve as a viable standard of comparison. Moreover, given the reliance on retrospective reports of change as well as the absence of a viable comparison group, these data cannot be taken as compelling evidence of program impact (see Grossman, this volume).

Kinship of Greater Minneapolis is an interdenominational Christian organization that sponsors a community-based mentoring program for youth ages 5 to 15 (Garringer, 2003a). The majority of the mentors are church members. As part of an internal evaluation, Kinship sent 390 surveys to parents, mentors, and children. Of these, 46 parents, 66 mentors, and 26 children responded (35% return rate). Perceptions of increased responsibility were reported by 45% of the parents, 61% of the children, and 26% of the mentors. Similarly, increased respect for others was indicated by 45% of the parents, 61% of the children, and 23% of the mentors. Improved social skills were reported by 65% of the parents, 70% of the children, and 23% of the mentors. A perceived increase in optimism was reported by 72% of the parents, 74% of the children, and 61% of the mentors. Overall, 96% of the parents who returned surveys indicated that they and their families had benefited from Kinship. The absence of a comparison sample and pretest data, however, again precludes drawing conclusions about program impact.

Clarke et al. (2003) reported findings from an evaluation of the St. John Baptist Church mentoring program. This program focused on African American students from "working poor" families in a suburban county who were doing poorly in school. African American male mentors were matched with youth and made a 1-year minimum commitment. Partnerships with local schools, government, and businesses also were developed. In the evaluation, the average mentor tenure was found to be 4.5 years. An improvement in GPA for the youth of approximately one half a letter grade also was reported over the duration of the mentoring relationship, but statistical significance was not assessed. Furthermore, outcome data from a comparison sample were not obtained.

Project RAISE recruited two congregational and five noncongregational sponsors (three businesses, one college, one fraternal group), each of whom made a 7-year commitment to provide mentors to 60 at-risk Baltimore youth who were entering sixth grade (Maton & Harris-Kojetin, 1998). The project was sponsored by the Baltimore Mentoring Institute and funded by a local foundation. The primary goal was to enhance high school graduation rates. Mentoring was a key component of the multicomponent program; other components included in-school support and after-school activities. A survey administered to mentors and mentees during the fifth year of the program indicated that students involved with mentors from the two sponsoring churches were significantly more likely than students from the other five sites to have a long-term relationship with a mentor (25.9 months vs. 8.9 months) and to report positive effects from mentoring. Furthermore, the high school graduation rate of youth served by the two faith-based sponsors (52.6%) was significantly higher than that of youth served by the five non-faith-based sponsors (30.6%). However, somewhat different mentee selection processes across sites as well as variations in implementation of the mentoring component limit the conclusions to be drawn from the research.

Finally, P/PV's descriptive process evaluation of its national initiative on faith-based and juvenile justice partnerships revealed both the potential and the challenges of faith-based mentoring initiatives (Hartmann, 2003). On the one hand, the process evaluation revealed the potential of small urban churches to partner with each other and with the juvenile justice system in various communities around the country. On the other hand, it revealed the inability of a number of the faith-based sites to mobilize a sufficient number of congregational volunteers to mentor high-risk youth. Fear of involvement with youth involved in the juvenile justice system, as well as the belief that some in the congregation may not have felt connected with the goals of the initiative, have been offered as possible reasons for the inability to mobilize sufficient numbers of volunteers (Hartmann, 2003).

Concerning natural mentoring relationships, not a single published study was found that systematically examined nonparental, adult-child relationships in the congregational context. Thus, the nature, extent, and impact of such relationships on youth outcomes are unknown. The most relevant literature located were qualitative studies of African American youth that depicted the importance to youth of congregational support and encouragement related to their academic striving and successful achievement (Hrabowski, Maton, & Greif, 1998; Sanders, 1995); these studies, however, did not distinguish perceptions of overall congregational support and encouragement from that received from specific individuals in the congregation—that is, natural mentors.

Given the limited amount of research to date on faith-based mentoring and the major design limitations of the research that does exist, only preliminary observations may be drawn at this time about the impact, mechanisms of influence, and future potential of mentoring in the faith-based arena. Especially noteworthy in several cases are findings that suggest faith-based mentoring programs have the potential for fostering long-term relationships. These findings may be viewed as potentially significant given that research has linked relationship duration (i.e., 1 year or longer) to positive youth outcomes (Grossman & Rhodes, 2002). Although these findings are promising, firm conclusions about the success of faith-based mentoring may not be drawn. Systematic empirical research in this area clearly represents a major priority to inform theory, public policy, and practice.

PRACTICE

Although empirical data are lacking, the appearance of increasing numbers of descriptive reports on faith-based mentoring program initiatives in the mid-1990s and early 2000s suggests an increase in the practice of faith-based mentoring in recent years. These descriptive accounts provide an initial basis for examining the practice of faith-based mentoring, although it should be kept in mind that available descriptions may not be broadly representative of faith-based mentoring practice in the field. The descriptive reports reviewed reveal that faith-based mentoring programs develop through different pathways, take on varied forms, exist in a variety of settings, and involve a diversity of elements, some of which appear distinctive to the religion context. These initiatives also face varied challenges, several of which again may be unique to mentoring in the faith-related arena.

Development, Forms, and Settings

Most faith-based programs reviewed operate through partnerships, either with one or more secular organizations or with other congregations. Congregations most often establish partnerships with schools (e.g., Kennedy, 1997), the juvenile justice system (e.g., Hartmann, 2003), or neighborhood organizations (e.g., Garringer, 2003b). Some also establish relationships with local or regional mentoring centers. Furthermore, in some cases, several congregations have linked together to develop church-mentoring resource networks (United Way of Southeastern Pennsylvania's Volunteer Centers/Philadelphia One-to-One, 1994).

Secular organizations and institutions aid congregations in program management, mentor recruitment, and mentor training, among other functions, thus enhancing organizational capacity. Collaboration has been initiated in some cases when the congregations have actively sought partners who can help them effectively

achieve the goals of their mentoring ministries (Garringer, 2003b). Alternatively, other faith-based mentoring programs have been initiated externally, by various groups who seek partnerships with faith-based organizations. These groups range from local government and local community agencies (Baltimore Rising, 2002) to universities (Clarke et al., 2003) and private foundations (Hartmann, 2003; Jucovy, 2003).

Some externally initiated mentoring projects seek to recruit individual congregations to participate as partners in large-scale initiatives along with other community organizations (Project RAISE; Maton & Harris-Kojetin, 1998). The congregations are expected to recruit mentors from their own membership and become sponsors. Such is the case, for example, with programs that serve youth who have committed felony offenses (King County District Attorney's Office, 2001) or who are children of prisoners (Jucovy, 2003). In other cases, the focus is on recruiting individual volunteers from a set of churches, but the individual congregations do not become actual sponsors (Loconte & Fantuzzo, 2002). That is, they do not provide financial or staff support or develop an overall sense of ownership of the mentoring program.

Although most faith-related mentoring programs target youth in the external community ("outreach"), a number of the smaller programs reviewed focus instead on youth who are members of the congregation ("inreach") (Irwin, 2002). This type of program is initiated by church leaders who realize their own young members face many challenges in coping with their environment (Garringer, 2003b). Mentors are largely adults from the congregation, and mentees are children of adult members. This approach should maximize the potential for enhanced religious involvement and development of the mentee and perhaps enhance collaboration between formal mentors and both parents and natural mentors.

Faith-based mentoring may occur as one component of a larger program or as part of a larger set of services that congregations offer at-risk youth (Garringer, 2003b; Maton & Harris-Kojetin, 1998). Alternatively, it may exist as a stand-alone mentoring program (Jucovy, 2003). In terms of funding, some faith-based mentoring programs receive external funding from federal, state, or other community sources, whereas others receive no external funding (Clarke et al., 2003). When the source of funding for congregation-initiated or congregation-sponsored mentoring programs is the government, concerns related to the separation of church and state may arise, such as whether funding is indirectly supporting religious activities (Kennedy, 1997).

Key Program Elements

Faith-based mentoring, as with other types of mentoring, seems likely to require the inclusion of key program elements to enhance program effectiveness (DuBois et al., 2002; MENTOR/National Mentoring Partnership, 2003). These may include, for example, well-planned and carefully implemented recruitment, screening, matching, and supervision procedures—such procedures can be expected to enhance the development of high-quality and sustainable mentor-youth relationships (Garringer, 2003a). In both the Amachi Project and the St. John's Baptist Church mentoring program, key program practices seemed evident. In both programs, emphasis was placed on matching, screening, and ongoing training of program participants (Clarke et al., 2003; Jucovy, 2003).

A practice that appears to be common to many faith-based mentoring programs is the active endorsement and possible involvement of the congregational leadership (e.g., pastor, priest, rabbi, or other valued religious leaders) in the effort to recruit volunteers from the faith community (Garringer, 2003a). The "blessing" of the head of the congregation and other church leaders may greatly enhance the legitimacy of the program to potential volunteers and help ensure the support of the congregation as a whole in terms of the use of facilities, financial backing, and overt program promotion. Because many programs become collaborative efforts between faith and secular communities, strong leadership that is able to bridge the two communities also may be critical (Jucovy, 2003).

Another potentially key institutional practice evident in the description of several faith-based mentoring programs is the establishment of a clear link between the mission of the congregation and that of the mentoring program. This

may facilitate the recruitment of volunteers naturally looking for the relevance of mentoring to their faith (Garringer, 2003a). Still another potentially important strategic element evident in existing programs is making the mentoring program visible to the entire faith community, to help ensure support. This may include integrating relevant activities into the ongoing rituals of the congregation, such as when a recognition program for mentees, mentors, and parents (or guardians) is incorporated regularly into church worship services (Garringer, 2003b).

Differences in Program Philosophy and Focus

Mentoring programs, including faith-based ones, may differ in important aspects of program philosophy and focus (Branch, 2002). Programs that follow a "programmatic theory" focus on the specific services, for example, academic enrichment and career awareness, that they view as critical to making a difference in the lives of the youth served (e.g., the St. John's Baptist Church mentoring program). Thus, the staff may limit the specific activities that mentors can involve their mentees in to those specified by the program (Branch, 2002). On the other hand, programs that adhere to a more "relational" approach to mentoring seek to avoid overspecification of activities and allow the mentors and mentees to interact with and build relationships in self-initiated ways (e.g., Amachi Project and Kinship of Greater Minneapolis; Aoki et al., 2000; Jucovy, 2003; Keller, this volume).

Importantly, these differences in program philosophy and operationalization have potential implications for "how much religion" or faith-related practices mentors introduce into the mentoring process (Garringer, 2003a). These practices may include the use of prayer, attendance at church activities and Bible study, and the incorporation of religious text, concepts, and/or music into program activities (e.g., Kennedy, 1997). In the Public/Private Venture demonstration study, most of the eight sites surveyed used prayer (the most prevalent), music, and references to the Bible, although none of the programs required participants to join church or attend religious celebrations (Branch, 2002).

However, it was reported that mentors at most of the sites occasionally invited their mentees to their respective churches. The same study reported that programs exhibited fewer of these faith-based practices when secular partners in faith-based mentoring programs took the lead role in a partnership, when activities took place in a neutral setting rather than in a house of worship, and when programs emphasized the uniform delivery of traditional content (e.g., GED instruction).

Challenges

Several challenges regarding the practice of faith-based mentoring have been identified (e.g., Branch, 2002; Hartmann, 2003, Jucovy, 2003). One challenge that appears unique to these programs relates to the separation of church and state, including possible concerns about prose-lytization (Maton et al., in press). This can serve as a barrier to recruiting participants from families who are not religious or who have different religious affiliations than the sponsoring congregation. Perhaps in response to this issue, some faith-based organizations have attempted to create a mentoring atmosphere that is religion neutral (Garringer, 2003a), careful not to promote any religious belief or to make religion an explicit part of program activities (Garringer, 2003b). Interestingly, in the P/PV study mentioned earlier, where prayer between mentor and mentee was commonplace in many sites, mentors reportedly viewed this practice as an expression of their own personal faith rather than an attempt to proselytize. There were no reports of efforts to pressure participants to join religious organizations or to engage in any faith-based practices (Branch, 2002).

Another unique challenge concerns congregations that lack the necessary program infrastructure for screening, training, matching, and supervising mentors. This may especially be the case in smaller or moderate-sized congregations. Unlike school or work-based mentoring settings that may have in their pool of employees staff who are knowledgeable in testing, research, training, and supervising, faith-based organizations may not have access to individuals with such expertise. One likely result of the lack of proper screening and matching is the creation of "bad" matches that can lead to early cessation of mentor-mentee relationships (Branch, 2002). In response to this challenge, some faith-based mentoring initiatives have collaborated with secular mentoring organizations to implement procedures such as screening to ensure that volunteers have the personal attributes necessary to successfully carry out long-term relationships with the mentees (Garringer, 2003a; National Mentoring Center, 2003). As the faith-based mentoring field develops, such collaborative partnerships appear likely to grow in importance.

FUTURE DIRECTIONS

Synthesis

Although faith-based mentoring appears to be growing in magnitude and visibility, scant attention to date has been directed to research or to practice development in this area. The multilevel theoretical model elaborated in this paper details several pathways through which faith-based mentoring programs could have a significant impact on youth outcomes. Our review of the empirical literature, however, revealed very little research on faith-based mentoring. Furthermore, the extant research on faith-based mentoring suffers from research design limitations that preclude the drawing of conclusions about program impact, and no research was found that examined the effects of natural mentoring relationships in the faith-based arena. Our review of existing practices in faith-based mentoring suggests that programs are diverse, encompassing many variations in form, focus, and levels of partnership. These variations have direct relevance to several pathways in the proposed theoretical framework (e.g., organizational capacity) and thus could potentially have important implications for program effectiveness.

Recommendations for Research

Given the dearth of systematic, empirical research on faith-based mentoring, there is a great need for research in a large number of areas. Four priority areas are described as follows.

1. *Prevalence of faith-based mentoring programs, relationships, and practices.* One priority for future research is to systematically examine the prevalence of faith-based mentoring programs, relationships, and practices. Concerning different forms of faith-based mentoring, there is a need to establish the relative prevalence of (a) programs that focus on youth within a congregation ("inreach") versus those that focus on youth in the larger community ("outreach"), (b) programs that include some religious focus versus those whose activities are devoid of any religious focus, (c) those that are initiated by faith-based organizations versus those that are initiated externally (i.e., by groups in the larger community), (d) those that involve partnerships with community groups versus those that do not, and (e) natural mentoring relationships with varying congregational adults. Research similarly should examine the extent to which recommended "best practices" in mentoring are used in programs, as well as the extent of variation in faith-based mentoring programs and relationships across different religions, different denominations within religions, different cultural groups, different geographic locales (urban, suburban, rural), different types of faith-based sites (e.g., congregations versus religious nonprofits), and different-sized congregations. Information about the prevalence of faith-based mentoring programs, relationships, and practices will greatly enhance our understanding of the extent of current activities and potentially suggest directions for future research, action, and policy efforts.

2. *Summative (outcome) evaluation research.* A second, critical focus for future research should be examination of the effectiveness of faith-based mentoring. To date, there does not appear to be any systematic research focused explicitly on this question. Thus, it is not clear whether faith-based mentoring is similar to or different from non-faith-based mentoring in terms of the nature and extent of impact and, furthermore, whether there is variation in outcomes across different types of faith-based mentoring and in association with the degree of utilization of recommended "best practices" in mentoring. Ideally, outcome research should be designed in collaboration with faith-based organizations. It also should involve researchers who have experience in the religious arena to help ensure that investigations are sensitive to distinctive issues related to outcome, process, design, and measurement in the faith-based context.

3. *Theory-building research.* Theory-building research is needed to examine the mechanisms of influence involved in faith-based mentoring. The framework described in this chapter depicts a set of pathways through which faith-based mentoring may enhance individual youth outcomes (see Figure 25.1) and thus represents one promising focus for future research. Several further concerns not addressed in the framework are equally deserving of attention. First, whereas the framework focused exclusively on mediational influences (i.e., processes through which faith-based mentoring may influence youth outcomes), moderational influences (i.e., factors that may influence the strength and/or direction of how faith-based mentoring affects youth) are a further important concern. To take one example, shared mentor-mentee religion may be especially important for youth who are more religious and thus have a greater influence on the quality of the mentoring relationship for such youth. Second, the proposed framework includes several potential constructs specific to the faith-based context, at the organizational, relational, and individual levels of analysis. Larger, external influences on faith-based organizations, such as governmental funding and varied types of partnerships, warrant investigation as well. These types of factors may have both short-term and longer-term influences, expected or unexpected, on faith-based organizations and mentoring programs. Third, it should be recognized that the nature and influence of moderating and mediating variables may differ depending on the specific form of faith-based mentoring. This therefore represents an additional important concern for future investigation. Finally, theory-building research is needed to help establish the extent to which current best practice guidelines in the secular domain generalize to the faith-based arena, as well as the nature of specific practices that may be uniquely suited to the faith-based domain.

4. *Natural mentors and community-wide influence.* Research on faith-based mentoring to

date has been limited to formal programs and their influence on the specific youth served. The lack of attention to the potential influence of natural mentors on youth in the faith-based arena is a significant omission. The scope of future research should be expanded to examine the ongoing roles of adult congregational members as natural mentors, including both their direct influence on congregational youth and their indirect influence through parents and siblings (Maton & Wells, 1995). The nature and extent of natural mentoring in the faith-based context, and its influence over time; similarities and differences from formal mentoring in the extent of influence and theoretical pathways involved (i.e., Figure 25.1); and evaluations of interventions to enhance the impact of natural mentoring all represent important questions that should be addressed.

The lack of investigation of community-wide influences is a further limitation. In particular, as noted earlier, there is a potential for the mobilization of faith-based organizations as part of larger community-wide prevention and promotion initiatives, including faith-based mentoring as one of multiple components. Research should examine the conditions under which such efforts are feasible, their impact on prevalence rates of youth problems in the community and on the quality of family- and neighborhood-level support for youth, and how faith-based mentoring can best be incorporated within community-wide efforts aiming to make a difference in the lives of youth and the environments that affect them (Maton, 2005).

Recommendations for Practice

1. *Follow current best practice guidelines.* In the absence of practice guidelines derived from research on faith-based programs, it is recommended that programs in the faith-based arena follow best practice guidelines developed for the mentoring field more generally (DuBois et al., 2002; MENTOR/National Mentoring Partnership, 2003). These guidelines are based on research that affirms the importance of accountability and responsibility in meeting the needs of young people. They highlight operations such as recruitment, screening, training, and supervision as potentially critical

determinants of the success of mentoring programs and thus provide a promising foundation for the development of effective mentoring programs in the faith-based arena. Program developers should keep in mind, however, the potential limitations of generalizing from guidelines that are not designed with specific reference to mentoring in faith-based contexts. Some practices may generalize only with judicious modification, and other important practices simply may not be represented in the more general guidelines.

2. *Develop partnerships to enhance organizational capacity and potential community impact.* The development of partnerships on the part of congregations represents a promising strategy for enhancing organizational capacity and the community impact of faith-based mentoring. Both secular and faith-based partnerships may prove useful in this regard and should be pursued. Such partnerships may be particularly important for small- and moderate-sized congregations that lack the organizational resources and capacity to oversee a sustained mentoring program. Faith-based organizations to date have partnered mostly with schools (Noell, 1997) and the juvenile justice system (Hartmann, 2003). In addition to these domains, partnerships with youth centers, health programs, and various other neighborhood-based organizations that service youth also should be instituted.

3. *Monitor religiously focused aspects of programs.* When faith-based mentoring programs in the community encompass explicit religious elements, potential issues arise related to the separation of church and state and unwarranted religious influence (Maton et al., in press). It is important to develop guidelines in this area—until this occurs, religious components of faith-based programs should be carefully monitored. Furthermore, when uncertain, programs should err on the side of limiting explicitly religious program components.

4. *Integrate faith-based mentoring into comprehensive prevention and promotion programs.* Mentoring programs, although important, by themselves have limited potential to make a major, sustained difference in the lives of youth

facing multiple family, school, and community risk factors. Thus, it is recommended that whenever feasible, faith-based mentoring initiatives be integrated into larger-scale, community-wide, and comprehensive prevention and intervention programs. Such efforts will have the greatest likelihood of making a difference in the lives of youth, families, and communities most in need.

REFERENCES

Ammerman, N. T. (2001). *Doing good in American communities: Congregations and service organizations working together.* Hartford, CT: Hartford Institute for Religion Research.

Aoki, W. T., Engert, P. A., Turk, A. A., Wilson, R. Chen, J., & Latu, E. (2000). Mentoring and the discipleship of adolescents. *Journal of Psychology and Christianity, 19,* 377–385.

AOL Time Warner Foundation. (2002). *Mentoring in America 2002.* New York: Author.

Aronson, E., Wilson, T., & Akert, R. (1998). *Social psychology.* Boston: Addison-Wesley.

Baltimore Rising: Mayor O'Malley's Youth Violence Reduction Initiative. (2001). Retrieved June 13, 2003, from http://www.ci.baltimore.md.us/government/mocyf/

Becker, B. E. (1999). *Congregations in conflict: Cultural models of local religious life.* Cambridge, UK: Cambridge University Press.

Billingsley, A. (1992). *Climbing Jacob's ladder: The enduring legacy of African-American families.* New York: Simon & Schuster.

Branch, A. Y. (2002). *Faith and action: Implementation of the national faith-based initiative for high-risk youth.* Philadelphia: Public/Private Ventures. Retrieved May 30, 2003, from http://www.ppv.org/ppv/publications/assets/23_publication.pdf

Chaves, M. (1999, Spring). Religious organizations and welfare reform: Who will take advantage of *"Charitable Choice"?* (Nonprofit Sector Research Fund Working Paper Series). Washington, DC: The Aspen Institute.

Clarke, S., Forbush, J., & Henderson, J. (2003, April). *Faith-based mentoring: A preventive strategy for at-risk youth.* Paper presented at the 14th National Conference on Child Abuse and Neglect. Retrieved May 30, 2003, from http://www.itiincorporated.com/Assets/pdf%20files/04-03_FB_Mentoring-StLouis.pdf

Cnaan, R. (2002, Winter). Religion, congregations and community: The Philadelphia Story. *Greater Philadelphia Regional Review, 28–31.*

Cohen, D., & Jaeger, R. A. (1998). *Sacred places at risk: New evidence on how endangered older churches and synagogues serve communities.* Philadelphia: Partners for Sacred Places.

Coleman, J. (1988). Social capital in the creation of human capital. *American Journal of Sociology, 94*(Suppl.), S95–S120.

Dionne, E. J., Jr., & DiIulio, J. J., Jr. (Eds.). (2000). *What's God got to do with the American experiment?* Washington, DC: Brookings Institution Press.

DuBois, D. L., Holloway, B. E., Valentine, J. C., & Cooper, H. (2002). Effectiveness of mentoring programs for youth: A meta-analytic review. *American Journal of Community Psychology, 30,* 157–197.

DuBois, D. L., & Silverthorn, N. (in press). Natural mentoring relationships and adolescent health: Evidence from a national study. *American Journal of Public Health.*

Evans, D., Cullen, F., Burton, V., Dunnaway, G., Payne, G., & Kethineni, S. (1996). Religion, social bonds, and delinquency. *Deviant Behavior, 17,* 43–70.

Exec. Order No. 13198, 66 Fed. Reg. 8495–8498 (2001).

Exec. Order No. 13199, 66 Fed. Reg. 8499–8500 (2001).

Exec. Order No. 13280, 67 Fed. Reg. 77145 (2002).

Foley, M. W., McCarthy, J. D., & Chaves, M. (2001). Social capital, religious institutions, and poor communities. In S. Saegert, J. P. Thompson, & M. R. Warren (Eds.), *Social capital and poor communities* (pp. 215–245). New York: Russell Sage Foundation.

Fulop, M. (2003, Summer). The mosaic of faith-based mentoring. *National Mentoring Center Bulletin,* Issue 12, 1–2.

Garringer, M. (2003a, Summer). Making a difference in the spirit of Kinship. *National Mentoring Center Bulletin,* Issue 12, 3–4, 13–14.

Garringer, M. (2003b, Summer). The work of a saint. *National Mentoring Center Bulletin,* Issue 12, 3–4, 7–12.

Grossman, J. (Ed.). (1998). *Contemporary issues in mentoring.* Philadelphia: Public/Private Ventures.

Grossman, J. B., & Rhodes, J. E. (2002). The test of time: Predictors and effects of duration in youth mentoring programs. *American Journal of Community Psychology, 30,* 199–206.

Hartmann, T. A. (2003). *Moving beyond the walls: Faith and justice partnerships working for high-risk youth.* Philadelphia: Public/Private Ventures. Retrieved September 26, 2004, from http://www.ppv.org/ppv/publications/assets/22_publication.pdf

Hrabowski, F. H., Maton, K. I., & Greif, G. (1998). *Beating the odds: Raising academically successful African American males.* New York: Oxford University Press.

Irwin, D. D. (2002). Alternatives to delinquency in Harlem: A study of faith-based community mentoring. *The Justice Professional, 15,* 29–36.

Johnson, B., Tompkins, R. B., & Webb, D. (2002). *Objective hope: Assessing the effectiveness of faith-based organizations: A review of the literature.* University of Pennsylvania, Center for Research on Religion and Urban Civil Society. Retrieved May 30, 2003, from http://www.man hattan institute.org/crrucs_objective_hope.pdf

Jucovy, L. (2003). *Mentoring children of prisoners in Philadelphia.* Philadelphia: Public/Private Ventures. Retrieved September 26, 2004, from http://www.ppv.org/ppv/publications/assets/21_publication.pdf

Kennedy, T. A. (1997). *Project Starfish: A church and community based public school mentoring program.* Unpublished doctoral dissertation, Drew University, Madison, NJ.

King County District Attorney's Office. (2001). *Youth and congregations in partnership.* Retrieved May 12, 2003, from http://www.brooklynda.org/Text%20version/YCP.htm

Loconte, J., & Fantuzzo, L. (2002). *Churches, charity, and children: How religious organizations are reaching America's at-risk kids.* University of Pennsylvania, Center for Research on Religion and Urban Civil Society. Retrieved May 30, 2003, from http://www.independentsector.org/PDFs/srf03/loconte_joseph.pdf

Maton, K. I. (2005). The social transformation of environments and the promotion of resilience in children. In R. D. Peters, B. Leadbeater, & R. J. McMahon (Eds.), *Resilience in children, families, and communities: Linking context to intervention and policy* (pp. 119–135). New York: Kluwer Academic Press.

Maton, K. I., Dodgen, D. D., Sto. Domingo, M. R., & Larson, D. B. (in press). Religion as a meaning system: Policy implications for the new millennium. *Journal of Social Issues.*

Maton, K. I., & Harris-Kojetin, B. (1998). *Final evaluation of Project RAISE.* Unpublished report, Psychology Department, University of Maryland, Baltimore.

Maton, K. I., & Wells, E. A. (1995). Religion as a community resource for well-being: Prevention, healing, and empowerment pathways. *Journal of Social Issues, 51*(2), 177–193.

McLearn, K. T., Colasanto, D., & Schoen, C. (1998). *Mentoring makes a difference: Findings From the Commonwealth Fund 1998 Survey of Adults Mentoring Young People.* New York: The Commonwealth Fund. Available at http://www.ecs.org/html/Document.asp?chouseid=2843

MENTOR/National Mentoring Partnership. (2003). *Elements of effective practice* (2nd ed.). Alexandria, VA: Author.

Mentoring for Success Act, 147 Cong. H.R. 1497 (2001).

National Mentoring Center. (2003, Summer). A faith-based initiative continues to grow: The NMC checks in with Public/Private Ventures about its recent efforts. *National Mentoring Center Bulletin,* Issue 12, 15–16, 19.

Noell, A. (1997). *Developing an ecumenical ministry to African-American males.* Unpublished doctoral dissertation, Drew University, Madison, NJ.

Oman, D., & Thoresen, C. E. (2003). Spiritual modeling: A key to spiritual and religious growth. *The International Journal for the Psychology of Religion, 13,* 149–165.

Pargament, K. I., & Maton, K. I. (2000). Religion in American life: A community psychology perspective. In J. Rappaport & E. Seidman (Eds.), *Handbook of community psychology* (pp. 495– 522). New York: Kluwer Academic/Plenum.

Pargament, K. I., Silverman, W., Johnson, S., Echemendia, R., & Snyder, S. (1983). The psychosocial climate of religious congregations. *American Journal of Community Psychology, 11,* 351–381.

Parra, G. R., DuBois, D. L., Neville, H. A., Pugh-Lilly, A. O., & Povinelli, N. (2002). Mentoring relationships for youth: Investigation of a process-oriented model. *Journal of Community Psychology, 30,* 367–388.

Regnerus, M. D. (2003). Religion and positive adolescent outcomes: A review of research and theory. *Review of Religious Research, 44,* 394–413.

Regnerus, M., Smith, C., & Fritsch, M. (2002). *Religion in the lives of American adolescents: A review of the literature* (National Study of Youth and Religion, Research Report No. 3). Chapel Hill: University of North Carolina.

Rhodes, J. E. (2002). *Stand by me: The risks and rewards of mentoring today's youth.* Cambridge, MA: Harvard University Press.

Sanders, M. G. (1995). *Breaking the cycle of reproduction: The effect of communities, families, and schools on the academic achievement of African-American youth.* Unpublished doctoral dissertation, Stanford University, Stanford, CA.

Smith, C. (2003). Theorizing religious effects among American adolescents. *Journal of the Scientific Study of Religion, 42,* 17–30.

Smith, C., & Faris, R. (2002). *Religion and American adolescent delinquency, risk behaviors and constructive social behavior* (National Study of Youth and Religion, Research Report No. 2). Chapel Hill: University of North Carolina.

United Way of Southeastern Pennsylvania's Volunteer Centers/Philadelphia One-to-One. (1994). *Church-based mentoring: A program manual for mentoring ministries.* Philadelphia: Author.

26

INTERNATIONAL: THE U.K. AND EUROPE

KRISTIN LIABØ, PATRICIA LUCAS, AND HELEN ROBERTS

INTRODUCTION

Mentoring is becoming established as a pan-European intervention. We know of mentoring programs in 20 countries across Europe: Bulgaria, Croatia, Czech Republic, Denmark, Estonia, France, Germany, Ireland, Latvia, Lithuania, Montenegro, the Netherlands, Poland, Romania, Russia, Serbia, the Slovak Republic, Sweden, Switzerland, and the United Kingdom. This expansion is happening rapidly, and it is timely to consider what direction mentoring in Europe is taking, how this fits with existing theory and research on mentoring, and what would support its development.

This chapter provides an analysis of mentoring theory, research, and practice in the United Kingdom and continental Europe. Key questions are: Is mentoring carried out differently in Europe than elsewhere? What role do cultural differences in Europe play in delivering mentoring? And, most important, what do we know about the research on mentoring and its potential to produce change for children and young people living in Europe today? Given the current state of knowledge, it may not be possible to provide unambiguous answers to these questions. We see this chapter as a step toward increasing the knowledge base in this area and as a call for further culture-specific research into mentoring in Europe. Although our focus is on planned mentoring programs, we also consider research on natural mentoring ties where relevant (Philip & Hendry, 1996). We further acknowledge that in Europe, the concept of mentoring will carry different meanings across national cultures. Our views are inevitably influenced by our U.K./Scandinavian backgrounds and the mentoring practices we have encountered there.

THEORY

Background Theories to Mentoring Programs in the United Kingdom and Continental Europe

Most European mentoring programs refer to resilience theories to explain how this intervention will bring about change in young people.

The authors would like to thank project managers, coordinators, and staff of Big Brothers Big Sisters in Czech Republic, Estonia, Germany, Lithuania, Netherlands, Ireland, Poland, Serbia, and the United Kingdom, and Mentor Sweden, for their helpful responses to our queries.

The importance of a significant adult is described as crucial to providing guidance in making choices in a risk-filled society, as well as being a good role model outside the immediate family: "A positive adult role is essential for a child's successful development and realization of his/her potential" (Big Brothers Big Sisters [BBBS] Serbia, 2002, p. 1), and "One of the most important factors for well-being in youth is good relations with adults" (Mentor Sverige, 2004, para. 1; K. L. translation). One striking finding across Europe is the similarity in the process and perceived impact of mentoring. All programs refer to the value of having an adult to trust, independent of professional contacts such as teachers and social workers. Guidance, role modeling, listening, and caring by the mentor are expected to elicit positive change in the young person's behavior and self-esteem (BBBS Serbia, 2002; Condren, Tully, Slattery, Mudge, & Gorman, 2000; Mentor Sverige, 2004; Tarling, Burrows, & Clarke, 2001). The assumption that an adult role model will help young people is rarely challenged, although some practice guidelines express caution in expecting too much (Benioff, 1997; Skinner & Fleming, 1999).

Theories Developed in Other Cultural Contexts

The emphasis on role modeling and a "significant adult" found in the United Kingdom and European mentoring programs can be traced back to theories of resilience underpinning U.S. mentoring. Werner and Smith found that resilient children often had at least one significant adult in their lives apart from the immediate family (Werner & Smith, 1982). Although valuable as an observational study of naturally occurring phenomena, this research demonstrates neither the effectiveness of planned intervention, the specific processes within effective mentoring relationships, nor the social contexts in which they occur (Rhodes, 2002; Colley, 2003).

From the United States, Rhodes (2002; see also Rhodes, this volume) has argued that when mutual trust and empathy are created in a relationship, this enhances the young person's social-emotional and cognitive development.

More specifically, the theory outlines three mediating processes in a successful mentoring relationship: social and emotional development, improving cognitive skills through meaningful conversation, and role modeling and advocacy. For the mentoring process to improve parent, peer, or other close relationships, all these aspects need to be present. The relationship and its effectiveness, furthermore, may be influenced by a range of contextual factors, which may operate as obstacles or facilitators for improving outcomes for the mentee (Rhodes, 2002). For example, through meaningful conversation about career options, the young person may start thinking about schoolwork and plans for the future and consequently be more motivated academically.

Also highly relevant, but rarely mentioned in European mentoring reports, is attachment theory. Attachment theory addresses how the relationship with a primary caregiver can shape the young child's emerging views or "working models" of self, others, and self in relation to others (Bowlby, 1997). In common with the views of Erikson (1968), attachment theory as applied to later stages of development acknowledges the importance of supportive relationships with other significant individuals (such as mentors) and the potential benefits young people may gain from developing trust and a positive sense of self through actions and talk in these relationships (Dallos & Compley-Ross, 2003). Attachment theory, furthermore, may help explain the damage a broken or failed mentoring match may cause if a young person has a history of insecure attachment relationships.

The preceding theoretical frameworks refer to processes that have been indicated to have considerable cross-cultural relevance and therefore may be important to the development of effective mentoring initiatives in the United Kingdom and continental Europe. We now turn to look more closely at how culture-specific theories may enhance mentoring's potential.

The Importance of Developing Theories Sensitive to Local Cultures

As shown in the previous section, recent mentoring developments in Europe may have much to learn from theories that have influenced the development of mentoring programs elsewhere. Research indicates that mentoring programs implemented with strong adherence to theory are more likely to succeed (DuBois, Holloway, Valentine, & Cooper, 2002). Europe as a continent includes multiple cultures and ethnicities. We assume that every new mentoring program will need to make practical arrangements to make the scheme work locally, but suggest that a theoretical background sensitive to European culture will be important.

Bourdieu's (1973) concept of cultural capital has influenced some U.K. studies on mentoring. Cultural capital may be understood as a person's measure of knowledge and control over his or her immediate social context (Philip, 2003). Mentoring may be seen as an encouragement to young people to look for support outside their own communities rather than enabling local communities to support young people themselves, assuming a deficit model of their own community (Bennetts, 2003; Colley, 2003; Odih, 2002; Philip & Hendry, 2000; Piper & Piper, 1999). The authors referred to are concerned that current forms of planned mentoring tend to ignore important aspects of user-focused service delivery, as well as the impact from the wider society on young people's behavior and sense of agency. Unlocking a young person's potential depends not only on a relationship between two people, but the position young people, their class, and their ethnic groups hold in society. Colley (2003) observed that the employment focus of the mentoring program in the United Kingdom that she studied failed to acknowledge other developments in the young people, such as setting up a home of their own or being a resource in the gray labor market (babysitting). These were important changes for the young people but did not fit with the program's expectations of what employment should entail.

The concern that mentoring lacks attention to the wider context in which young people act and make their choices may reflect the importance of collectivist theories and viewpoints in Europe, compared to a more individualist tradition in the United States. Philip (2003) suggested that the individualistic focus of many mentoring programs is particularly at odds with youth work in the United Kingdom, which has traditionally worked at both group and individual levels. The idea of integrated, multicomponent interventions for youth has enjoyed increased support over the past few years, and mentoring on its own has been seen to lack important aspects of this approach. For this reason, it may be that mentoring projects linked to other initiatives, such as parent training, are particularly pertinent to European circumstances.

One important consideration for mentoring projects in Europe is whether there is a local culture of volunteering or charitable involvement. A survey of volunteering work in 10 European countries found that although volunteering has played an important role in the development of democratic societies across Europe, the type of activity in which people are engaged varies between countries. For example, volunteering activity within sports and recreation seem to be more frequent in Sweden, Germany, the Netherlands, and Ireland than in Great Britain. Voluntary engagement in health and social services, on the other hand, seems to be higher in Great Britain than in, for example, Sweden and Slovakia (Davis Smith, 1996; Gaskin & Davis Smith, 1995). Likewise, in former communist countries, volunteering may not be seen as a positive activity, but rather as a relic of past obligatory work demanded by former state systems (Tosner, 2001).

The position of children's rights in a culture may also affect the impact of different approaches to mentoring. Building participation models into a project, such as having young people on the appointment board for mentoring coordinators, could contribute to a project's success in one place, while being viewed as unacceptable elsewhere. Economic inequalities may also impact a relationship (Colley, 2003; Philip, Shucksmith, & King, 2004). Colley (2003) found that although the mentors meant well, they struggled with judgmental attitudes about their mentees' lives. "Far more needs to be done to challenge mentors to consider the implications of their beliefs about disaffection, and to confront stereotype images of disaffected youth" (Colley, 2001, p. 14). Young people interviewed by Philip and colleagues (2004) said that they found it easier to establish relationships with mentors with backgrounds similar to theirs. Parental and professional expectations regarding the development and learning of young children can vary between European countries (Ojala, 2000), and it may be that this is the same for planned mentoring.

Mentoring programs implemented in the United Kingdom and continental Europe need to consider carefully the preceding sets of concerns relating to cultural sensitivity at the service-planning stage in order to attract volunteers, to gain credibility in the local culture, and to develop effective, theory-based practices in important areas of programs such as training and supervision. It is clear that theories taking European traditions and cultural contexts into account are urgently needed to inform mentoring practice in the area.

RESEARCH

To provide advice and guidance for future mentoring programs in Europe, we need to examine the extent to which mentoring has been shown to be effective in Europe and what factors specific to Europe are likely to influence both the process and the outcomes of mentoring programs. A large meta-analysis of studies conducted in the United States has looked at a range of modifiers on the effectiveness of mentoring, such as program features, goals, and activities (DuBois et al., 2002). The diversity of cultures in the United Kingdom and continental Europe, local volunteering traditions, and features of relationships, programs, communities, and youth are all potentially important moderators in this context. The following section examines the extent and quality of current research evidence on planned mentoring in Europe and considers what conclusions may be drawn on the basis of this literature.

Search Strategy

By making explicit our search strategy and the methods by which we obtained unpublished and non-English-language publications, we hope that the scope and limitations of this review are apparent. In the face of a plethora of possible terms and databases, a decision was made to focus largely on U.K. databases. This method is best understood as a way of mapping the metaphorical and literal geography of the literature, rather than a search strategy suitable for a systematic review, and incorporates other work carried out by our team (Lucas & Liabø, 2003; Roberts, Liabø, Lucas, DuBois, & Sheldon, 2004).

Keywords

Search terms were *mentor* and *buddy*. Searches were age limited, up to and including 29 years of age. Studies retrieved were screened to identify research papers. All evaluations of youth mentoring programs with adult volunteers carried out anywhere in geographical Europe were included.

Databases

Seven databases were searched: ChildData (provided by the U.K. charity The National Children's Bureau), SIGLE (European-wide, gray literature database from the British Library), Index to theses (British database of dissertations), ASSIA (Applied Social Science Index and Abstracts), BEI (British Education Index), PsychINFO (U.S. database that includes studies in languages other than English), and CAREDATA (Developed by the U.K. National Institute for Social Work).

Additional methods were used to locate unpublished and European-wide literature. The Internet search engine Google was used to identify unpublished work. The home page of the European Commission was searched for European Union (EU) mentoring initiatives. All European programs of BBBS were contacted for evaluations and asked about any changes they might have made to adjust programs to local circumstances. Scandinavian Internet search engines Kvasir (Norway) and Eniro (Denmark and Sweden) were used.

Does Mentoring Promote Change?

The intention of the search was to retrieve research studies and other writings on planned youth mentoring in the United Kingdom and continental Europe. The methodological quality of the effectiveness evaluations was considered across two dimensions: allocation of a comparison group and outcome assessment (see Grossman, this volume, for details). With regard to outcome assessment, we chose to include only studies that examined change over the period of the intervention. Data therefore had to be presented before and after (pre and post) the mentoring period. With regard to comparison groups, we placed more weight in our review on those studies that compared change in an unmentored group to change in a mentored intervention group.

With further regard to outcome assessment, special consideration was given to the source or informant. Self-report is often used to assess attitudes or behaviors, and it relies on the frankness of replies. In a scheme such as mentoring, which relies on interpersonal support, it may be difficult for adults or young people to offer replies that they could see as "letting down" their partners. This may mean that at the end of such an intervention, participants are less likely to admit to an undesirable behavior, without actually having changed that behavior (Lucas & Liabø, 2003). If we want to know whether mentoring changes, for example, school attendance, school records rather than personal reports are likely to provide the best assessment (see chapters by Grossman as well as DuBois and Silverthorn, this volume, for further discussion of issues relating to measurement of outcomes in mentoring program evaluations).

Fourteen studies found in our searches addressed the issue of whether mentoring changed mentees' behavior (Appiah, 2001; Clayden & Stein, 2002; Golden, 2000; Hall, 2003; Lucas & Liabø, 2003; Miller, 1998; NOP World Social & Political, n.d.; Pitts, 2000; Sharp et al., 2003; Sharp, Kendall, Bharbra, Schagen, & Duff, 2001; Sims & Golden, 1999; St. James-Roberts & Samlal Singh, 2001; Tarling et al., 2001; Teterski, 2002).

The studies looked at mentoring impact on functioning at school, academic skills, behavior, social skills, self-esteem, offending, and employability. None of the 12 primary research studies examined any negative impact mentoring may have had on the young people or looked systematically at moderators for successful/unsuccessful relationships. All studies concluded that mentoring had been an overall positive intervention, but the methodological quality of the studies weakens these conclusions.

Two of the publications were reviews of mentoring literature (Hall, 2003; Lucas & Liabø, 2003). Of the 12 primary research studies, 4 used a comparison group (Miller, 1998; Sharp et al., 2003; Sharp et al., 2001; St. James Roberts & Samlal Singh, 2001). None of them used random allocation (the most robust design). Two of the studies evaluated the same intervention at different times with different children, but using the same control group twice over. All four studies made some attempt at measuring change by standardized means, such as skills test at baseline and after the mentoring relationship had ended. Four more studies used data collected before and after mentoring, without a comparison group (Golden, 2000; Pitts, 2000; Sims & Golden, 1999; Tarling et al., 2001).

We excluded four studies reporting on the effectiveness of mentoring. The reporting of two evaluations (Appiah, 2001; NOP World Social & Political, n.d.) makes it difficult to determine whether their data were collected at baseline and after or whether mentees were asked to reflect retrospectively about the effects they perceived mentoring to have had on their situations. One study (Clayden & Stein, 2002) looked at the baseline situation for one sample of young people about to be mentored and outcomes for another sample that had been mentored for 6 to 12 months. One of the studies was from outside the United Kingdom (Teterski, 2002), but the report in English was limited and did not sufficiently describe methods used.

Research Reviews

The two overviews of research on mentoring were both published in the United Kingdom. Their search strategies were comprehensive but fell short of a formal systematic review. Both reviews paid attention to the rigor of the studies included. Hall (2003) found that there was a poor evidence base for mentoring in the United Kingdom and that claims of impact were unfounded. Based on the literature reviewed, he recommended that mentoring programs be properly integrated into the larger organizational context and linked to other services, given that the studies found linking to other agencies and having a mentor coordinator were important factors of well-run programs. Other studies reviewed by Hall (2003) found that there would sometimes be a mismatch between the values/aims of the mentor and mentee and that mentors were often untrained. Some studies reported that different aspects of the mentor's role were unclear, for example, whether the mentor was supposed to act on behalf of the mentee, the mentor organization, or another authority.

The other review was written by authors of this chapter looking at effectiveness studies on mentoring for youth at-risk of or already exhibiting antisocial behavior, including U.S. programs. Based on U.S. findings that mentoring may have detrimental effects on some subgroups of young people, the overall conclusion was that caution is needed when implementing programs and that careful evaluation is critical (Lucas & Liabø, 2003; Roberts et al., 2004).

Before/After (Pre-Post) Studies With Comparison Group

The four studies that included a comparison group (Miller, 1998; Sharp et al., 2003; Sharp et al., 2001; St. James-Roberts & Samlal Singh, 2001) are summarized in Table 26.1.

Before looking at the findings of these studies, it may be worth noting how much these projects varied in focus. Miller (1998) looked at the impact of mentoring on exam results in a comprehensive school. The mentoring was a mix of one-to-one relationships and small-group sessions held at the school or the mentor's workplace. Sharp et al. (2001) and Sharp et al. (2003) evaluated an initiative called "Playing for Success," aimed at raising motivation for schoolwork and academic achievement by providing after-school support. Mentoring played a smaller role in this scheme and was delivered to groups by students from local colleges. It is not clear whether "mentors" developed relationships with particular children or were simply available during the scheme to those who needed support. As noted by Kuperminc and colleagues in this volume, mentoring is often embedded in multicomponent programs such as those described above, and this can make it difficult to determine to what extent mentoring (or other program content) may be driving the

results. In project CHANCE, evaluated by St. James-Roberts & Samlal Singh (2001), adult mentors met with the children on a one-to-one basis, for 2 to 4 hours each week, doing activities such as cooking or going to the zoo. The aim of the project was to improve the mentees' behavior, academic records, and school attendance. The mentoring was part of a wider project offering parent support and peer schemes, but evaluated separately.

Two of the studies tested for and did not find a significant difference overall between the mentored and the nonmentored students (Sharp et al., 2001; St. James-Roberts & Samlal Singh, 2001). The second analysis by Sharp et al. (2003) created a model of expected improvement and used this rather than control group data for comparison. This showed a significant change in numeracy scores for all children in the intervention group and in literacy for one group of children.

Miller (1998) reported that overall, there was a statistically significant difference between mentored and nonmentored students. The mentored girls improved their performance in GCSE exams (national exams taken at age 16), by an average 0.39 score "points" compared with the matched peer group. These score points were calculated as the difference between the predicted GCSE results (based on the results in standardized test) and the actual GCSE exam scores. The boys on average all achieved lower than predicted grades in GCSEs, but the mentored boys demonstrated a smaller decline than the comparison group. It is not clear from the study whether these findings were statistically significant, and the author emphasizes that the overall findings mask wide differences between the schools.

Before/After Studies Without Comparison Group

Four studies looked at data from the young people involved before the mentoring relationship began and again later, but did not use a comparison group (Golden, 2000; Pitts, 2000; Sims & Golden, 1999; Tarling et al., 2001). All studies reported that mentoring improved the young people's behavior and attitudes, but the study quality was variable and outcomes were

Table 26.1 Before and After Studies With a Comparison Group

Study	Length of Study	Key Results	Comments
Miller (1998) Study of mentoring to raise school exam results. Case studies of schools and before-after data collected on 90 mentees and 93 matched comparison students not mentored. *n* = 183	1 year	Authors reported a positive difference in exam results for mentored students across schools compared with those not mentored, but vast differences between individual schools. Some mentored children did worse than the comparison students.	Mentored students were selected because they were "promising but underachieving." The control group was selected by mentoring coordinators to be similar to the mentored group in terms of gender balance, range of ethnicity, levels of ability, and range of GCSE subjects. The control group students were not involved in other attainment-raising interventions. Very small changes were detected, and it was difficult to establish from the study report when results were significant and when they were not.
Sharp et al. (2001, 2003) Two studies of a larger program with a mentoring component. The two evaluations collected before/after data on two samples of children attending the scheme at different times (2,095 and 1,132 children) compared with the same control group of 349 children who did not attend (in the same time frame as the first group). *n* = 3576	The evaluation ran over 1 year. The average length of the programs was 10 weeks. The tests were carried out before and after participation in the program.	Overall participating students did not significantly improve study skills and knowledge during the course of the program compared with those who did not participate (Sharp et al., 2001), but were reported to show positive changes in numeracy scores and in literacy (for a subgroup of children) when utilizing a model of expected improvement rather than control group data for comparison (Sharp et al., 2003).	The peer comparison group, made up of children from the same schools as those attending the program, was too small to conduct a meaningful comparison. It may be that the selection was biased, as we do not know why the control group children were not selected to attend the program. In the later analysis (2003), the authors try to make up for differences between control and intervention group by creating a model of expected improvement and using this in the comparison rather than data from the control group. Mentoring played a small part in the overall program, and we do not know the impact made by mentoring on its own.

Study	Length of Study	Key Results	Comments
St. James-Roberts et al. (2001) Before/after study comparing 25 mentored children with a matched comparison group of 25. *n* = 50	The overall project ran for 3 years, but the mentoring evaluation measured change between screening for inclusion of the program and by completion of mentoring relationships (average length 11.5 months).	There were no measurable differences between mentored and nonmentored children on any of the outcomes assessed: behavior (Goodman's Strengths and Difficulties Questionnaire); school attendance and exclusions; reading age; teacher report; national assessments in English, math, and science.	The comparison group was not randomized, but carefully matched to the mentored children in terms of age, ethnicity, gender, geographical area, and scores on the Strengths and Difficulties Questionnaire.

based mainly on self-report. Most important, the reporting did not provide sufficient detail on how data were collected and what questions were asked. Only Tarling et al. (2001) reported the use of standardized tests to measure change, but results were available for only 9 of the 80 young people participating in the project. They did not find any significant changes as a result of the mentoring, although some of the young people did improve their behavior at school (Tarling et al., 2001). Only one of the studies reported a statistically significant change as a result of the mentoring. Golden (2000) found gains on measures of self-esteem and confidence as well as mentees' attitudes to education and work.

Young People's Views on Mentoring

All 14 studies provided positive reports from young people, parents, teachers and mentors, in terms of both how mentoring was perceived to have helped the young person change and how mentoring had been a good experience in itself. It is important to acknowledge that although these views are important, they do not indicate change as a result of the program. For example, authors may simply be reporting positive comments made to them while collecting data, while those who were unhappy said

nothing. It is noteworthy, furthermore, that there were few reports from young people or mentors who dropped out of a program. When evaluating a service, we need to know why people chose not to engage, as there may be lessons to learn for other mentoring programs.

Qualitative Research

Six studies were found that had carried out in-depth qualitative investigations into planned mentoring schemes (Bennetts, 2003; Colley, 2003; Dallos & Compley-Ross, 2003; Philip & Hendry, 1996; Philip et al., 2004; St. James-Roberts & Samlal Singh, 2001).

Colley (2003) interviewed young people, mentors, and coordinators at an employment mentoring program, exploring their different perceptions and expectations of mentoring and how the relationships evolved over one year. Findings suggest that the strict boundaries of the scheme may have compromised the potential for some of the relationships to develop. The sole focus of this scheme was to introduce young people to paid work, which may have ignored some of the important stages in relationship building (see Keller, this volume). Only one of the relationships she looked at succeeded in helping the mentee into work. Colley (2003) concluded that mentoring was beneficial, but not in the ways imagined by organizers:

> Although many of those around them . . . were losing faith in the mentoring process, the young people involved expressed far more positive views. They directed their efforts to making the most of mentoring for social inclusion, while setting their own terms within their mentor relationships. (p. 162)

Philip and Hendry (1996) and Bennetts (2003) studied naturally occurring mentoring relationships in order to inform the development of planned mentoring schemes. Bennetts observed how naturally occurring relationships are usually retrospectively named by mentees or youth as mentoring when individuals are appreciated and honored for what they have done. Philip and Hendry (1996) investigated young people's perceptions of mentoring as they make the transition to adulthood. They spoke with 150 adolescents aged 13 to 18 and found that varying forms of mentoring relationships were significant for the young people. It was important from the perspective of youth that the relationship was negotiable and built on trust and empathy.

In a later study, Philip et al. (2004) spoke with mentees in three planned mentoring schemes. It was clear that the young people drew on support from a range of people within and outside the project, not just their mentors. Young people spoke about difficulties associated with ending the relationship, a finding that parallels issues explored in the U.S. literature regarding the benefits of longer-lasting relationships and the potential harm of relationship breakdown (Grossman & Rhodes, 2002). Philip et al. (2004) also found that all participants in the mentoring schemes found the relationship between trust and confidentiality to be a complex issue. It appears that some mentors did not fully understand the implications of U.K. child protection practice and failed to take into account confidentiality policies. Once again, this finding accords with U.S. work concluding that better training of mentors is associated with greater effect (DuBois et al., 2002). This observation is also important when considering exporting study findings or mentoring programs from one country context to another. In the United Kingdom, those working with children or young people,

whether volunteers or professionals, will normally have protocols in place for child protection under the terms of which adults will report disclosures of abuse made by children to the appropriate authorities. It is usually seen as good practice to tell the young people that this will be the case. Most young people interviewed by Philip et al. (2004) insisted that respecting their confidentiality was crucial for a trusting relationship to develop.

Dallos and Compley-Ross (2003) found that mentees valued qualities, such as advice and direction from their mentors, which had not been emphasized in the mentor training. Trust was established when mentors were generous with their time and attention. The authors describe the process followed by this development as one of "cognitive dissonance," leading young people to first question why mentors would bother spending time with them, and then conclude that if someone could be bothered time after time, perhaps they themselves were not so bad after all. The young people in this study worried whether the relationship would continue after the 2-year period of the scheme. Once again, this work supports the view that length and quality of relationship are of key importance to outcomes and to the mentee's perception of relationship strength (Colley, 2003; Grossman & Rhodes, 2002).

St. James-Roberts and Samlal Singh (2001) used mixed methods to evaluate Project CHANCE. The project drew on theories of cognitive change, and the mentoring focused on creating solutions to individual problems, addressing and changing problem behavior and thereby redirecting development. Core elements of the relationship included teaching life skills, promoting active learning, and providing opportunities for the children to experience personal mastery. The researchers found that in practice, there were large variations in the mentors' approaches. Some were goal focused, whereas others made little preparation in advance of the meetings with the child. Many mentors expressed concern about the boundaries of their role, and some found themselves faced with significant problems in their mentees' lives, such as parental mental health problems or violence in the home toward the children. The researchers concluded,

Children who have behavior problems do commonly have multiple difficulties, including family and special educational needs. . . . In principle these are worthy targets for a solution-focused intervention, but it is less clear whether they are realistic goals for mentors. (St. James-Roberts et al., 2001, p. 20)

PRACTICE

Mentoring practices in the United Kingdom and continental Europe vary just as much as mentoring definitions, programs, and outcomes. In this section, we first consider the status of evidence-based implementation practices in the United Kingdom and continental Europe. We then provide an overview of several categories of mentoring programs identified in our search of the United Kingdom and European literature, followed by a discussion of issues involved in developing mentoring programs in the United Kingdom and continental Europe.

Evidence-Based Implementation Practices

A U.S. meta-analysis of evaluations of mentoring programs for young people looked at the relationship between program effect and program features (DuBois et al., 2002). The researchers found that mentoring schemes that were grounded in theory-based best practices showed evidence of stronger positive effects on youth outcomes than those that did not. Features of good practice included monitoring of implementation, use of mentors with a helping role in their profession, ongoing training, structured activities, and parent support.

These aspects of mentoring have received attention in U.K. programs. For example, projects for young offenders have emphasized the importance of parent support to avoid parents feeling threatened by the mentor's role or being suspicious of what happens during the meetings (Benioff, 1997; London Borough of Hillingdon, 2001). We did not identify any programs explicitly using research findings to support such initiatives, but practice experience seems to play an important part, and a range of good practice guidelines are available, some of which are

based on in-house evaluations (Benioff, 1997; Golden & Sims, 1997; Sims, Jamison, Golden, & Lines, 2000).

U.K. programs have emphasized the importance of a "matching procedure," where the young people are asked what qualities they would value in a mentor, as well as pairing similar interests (Benioff, 1997; Clayden & Stein, 2002). Supervision and support groups for mentors have been recommended in project evaluations and good practice guidelines (Benioff, 1997; Save the Children U.K., 2002; Sims et al., 2000), but none of these features appeared to make a significant difference to the success of the programs evaluated by DuBois et al. (2002).

In Eastern Europe, the Czech center HESTIA (The National Volunteer Centre), which runs mentoring programs as well as other volunteer projects, has emphasized the importance of paying attention to local contexts (Tosner, 2001). Traditionally, volunteering in the Czech Republic has been identified with obligatory work in the old political system; hence, it has negative connotations. It was thought that a public recruitment campaign might scare off potential volunteers because of this history. Instead, this mentoring scheme relied on targeted recruitment from visits to local schools. This example illustrates the need for mentoring program implementation practices widely regarded as effective in the United States to be adapted to fit different European contexts.

European Mentoring Programs

Given the multiplicity of aims and objectives identified in the United Kingdom and European mentoring programs, it may be helpful to categorize programs accordingly. The typology presented below is based on research studies and practice descriptions retrieved from our literature search described previously. Program descriptions have been organized primarily according to their aims and objectives. The setting (where the mentoring is carried out), mentors' and mentees' backgrounds, and program intensity (e.g., length of relationship) were also considered. Four main types of mentoring were identified as being used in the United Kingdom and continental Europe: mentoring for crime prevention, mentoring for career guidance, community mentoring, and cross-age mentoring. (For a more detailed classification of mentoring programs from primarily the U.S. literature, see the chapter by Sipe, in this volume.)

Mentoring for Crime Prevention

Mentoring used in crime prevention is mainly delivered one-to-one, with high intensity and as part of an intervention package (Benioff, 1997; Employment Support Unit, 2000; St. James-Roberts & Samlal Singh, 2001; Tarling et al., 2001). This type of program usually aims to get mentees "back on track" in education or employment and help them become integrated into mainstream society by introducing them to activities that replace the offending. This type of mentoring program has been used extensively in the United Kingdom. A related project was set up in Denmark but with a high level of intensity, in which the mentors were paid to be with the young people on a full-time basis. The mentors were given mobile phones to increase their availability, and their brief was to be with the mentees to help with work, education, and/or other obligations. Mentors were recruited from a range of professions and had mainly the same ethnic backgrounds and genders as the mentees (Pedersen, 1999).

Mentoring for Career Guidance

Career guidance mentoring may be delivered in groups, one-to-one, or via e-mail (e-mentoring, telementoring) (Appiah, 2001; European Commission, 2000; Golden & Sims, 1997; Hugill, 2000; Miller, 1998; Sharp et al., 2003; Sharp et al., 2001). These programs often are organized within the school or a career center. The mentor may be a professional employed by the institution (Reid, 2002) or a volunteer. The typical aims are to improve the educational attainment and achievement and employability of young people or to support young people in transition between schools or education and employment. Mentoring in career guidance is normally at a low level of intensity, with meetings every second week or once a month, and the relationship between mentor and mentee resembles that between a tutor and a student (Miller, 2002). Career guidance mentoring has

been used extensively in the United Kingdom and other EU countries within the framework of the European Social Fund.

In Germany, money from the European Commission has been used to set up TeleMentoring, a project for unemployed young people aged 16 to 24, with the aim of providing vocationally oriented support. The projects offer free Internet access and support from social welfare staff, while volunteers from local businesses act as e-mentors (European Commission, 2000).

Community Mentoring

Community mentoring facilitates one-to-one relationships between adults and young people in the community (Børns Voksenvenner, 2003; Condren et al., 2000). These programs aim to achieve a range of outcomes but often place particular emphasis on self-esteem and integration in the community. Programs present contact with an adult role model as having a preventive effect, helping young people keep away from crime, drug use, and other negative influences. Some of these schemes are less concerned with specific outcomes of mentoring and more with providing adult contact for young people and children perceived to be deprived of this as a result of their social circumstances (Nijnatten, 1997). This type of mentoring is emerging as a popular intervention for integrating youth refugees and asylum seekers into the mainstream community (Save the Children U.K., 2002) and for supporting young people leaving local authority care (Clayden & Stein, 2002; McBriar, Noade, & Ringland, 2001). Community mentoring has been used widely across Europe (BBBS International, 2004a; Gränzer, 2003).

Communications with United Kingdom and European community-based programs in the BBBS network indicate that only minor changes were made to the U.S. version before implementation. It appears, however, that cross-gender matches may be more common in the United Kingdom and continental Europe than in the United States. BBBS Serbia and Netherlands, for example, both identified greater allowance for cross-gender matches as the main change they had made to adapt to local circumstances. When asked why, a representative from one program indicated that some parents (mothers) of mentored children had specifically asked for a male mentor because of lack of contact with the father (BBBS Netherlands, personal communication, October 22, 2003). Difficulties with recruiting enough male mentors have forced some projects to match female mentors with male mentees (BBBS Ireland, personal communication, October 22, 2003; St. James-Roberts & Samlal Singh, 2001; Tarling et al., 2001).

Cross-Age Mentoring

This type of mentoring is delivered by older adults, one-to-one or in groups (Granville, 2000; see also Taylor et al., this volume). These programs may resemble those in any of the preceding categories but have the added objective of developing bonds between generations. Cross-age mentoring has become popular in Germany, possibly due to the country's pension crisis and aging population (Gränzer, 2003).

Developing Mentoring Programs in Europe

There are many resources available in Europe to assist in the process of developing a mentoring program for young people. Two pan-European networks have been established in the last year. Information on the European Network of Children and Youth Mentoring Organisations (ENCYMO) is available online (ENCYMO, 2004). A European network of BBBS was set up in late 2003 (BBBS International, 2003), but the main source of BBBS mentoring material is still BBBS International (BBBS International, 2004b). Mentor International is another useful resource (The Mentor Foundation, 2004). In the United Kingdom, the Youth Justice Board provides comprehensive Web-based information on setting up, running, and evaluating a project (Youth Justice Board, 2004). The U.K. National Mentoring Network has published findings from their evaluation, looking at key considerations in running a mentoring program (Sims et al., 2000).

Many of the issues involved in developing a mentoring program are addressed extensively elsewhere in this volume (see in particular the chapter by Weinberger), and lessons from the United States are likely to be important in developing effective mentoring programs in

Europe. Equally important in our view is the need to consider local circumstances carefully. Increased communication and collaboration across borders as seen in the abovementioned initiatives may facilitate this.

FUTURE DIRECTIONS

Synthesis

A number of theoretical approaches have been developed to explore the ways in which mentoring relationships may operate to promote positive youth development. To date, however, the most elaborated of these (e.g., Rhodes, 2002) have received little attention in either mentoring research or practice in the United Kingdom and continental Europe. In looking at the 20 countries where mentoring programs are delivered, we found effectiveness studies of mentoring in just one, the United Kingdom. These evaluations were small scale and methodologically flawed. Few qualitative studies were found that provided an in-depth exploration of experiences of mentors, mentees, parents, and professionals. The six studies included here are a promising start, but again, these were all from the United Kingdom. Despite the growing practice of mentoring in the United Kingdom and continental Europe, the absence of rigorous effectiveness studies and strong qualitative research means that we cannot determine whether mentoring programs implemented in these countries affect the behavior or achievements of young people, the extent to which mentoring is valued by all parties, or when or how approaches implemented in the United States may need to be modified to fit different European contexts.

Recommendations for Research

1. *Randomized controlled trials to establish the effect of mentoring programs in the United Kingdom and continental Europe.* We need to establish whether mentoring programs in Europe have the potential to elicit positive change in youth (and prevent negative changes), and a randomized controlled trial is the best method for addressing this question. Objective

measures such as police records and grades need to be used when measuring outcomes. While for practical purposes, a trial carried out in one area might be most feasible, opportunities for trials to be coordinated across countries need to be explored, and funding structures within the European Commission might facilitate such a project. Theories and practices developed in the United States have influenced mentoring practices in the United Kingdom and continental Europe. High-quality research is needed to test the relevance of these to local practices here.

For us to know more about the processes and workings of mentor relationships, we need to examine important moderators that influence outcomes for mentored young people. For example, are mentoring programs best delivered as stand-alone projects or as part of more comprehensive schemes? What is the effect of parents being involved or supported alongside the young person? How often should mentor and mentee meet? Which children will benefit most from being mentored? We have been unable to identify a European study so far that has been able to answer these types of questions with a sufficiently robust design.

2. *High-quality, in-depth qualitative studies looking at the mentoring process in the United Kingdom and continental Europe.* We need to establish the extent to which young people and volunteers appreciate the mentoring relationship, and why. In Eastern Europe, where nonpolitical volunteering is a relatively new concept, experiences of being a volunteer mentor as well as a mentee may be particularly relevant to both policymakers and the general public. Given that cross-gender matches appear to be more common in the United Kingdom and continental Europe than in the United States, this aspect of European mentoring merits further investigation, and comparison with similar studies in the United States, to establish whether there are any lessons to be learned across cultures.

3. *Attention to harmful as well as beneficial effects from mentoring.* European research to date has focused mainly on the benefits of planned mentoring schemes. A more balanced examination of effects that includes consideration of harm will serve the needs of young people and mentors and increase the credibility of mentoring initiatives.

Unsuccessful matches, implementation problems, and mentor dedication need to be analyzed, along with follow-up of young people and mentors who drop out of programs.

Recommendations for Practice

1. *Improved systems for audit and evaluation.* It is recommended that ongoing audit and evaluation of implementation and delivery be practiced by mentoring programs in the United Kingdom and continental Europe. Evaluation is becoming a key aspect of service delivery in the United Kingdom, and there may be potential for sharing evaluation experiences across European borders. For in-house evaluations to effectively inform practice, rigorous methods (whether qualitative or quantitative) need to be employed. Attention to less positive aspects of a scheme is as important as showing the positive sides of planned mentoring.

2. *Closer adherence to evidence-based mentoring practice and theories.* Research from the United States (DuBois et al., 2002) has indicated that the most effective mentoring programs are those carried out with close adherence to theory-based practices and guidelines. European mentoring programs are likely to benefit from developing a stronger theoretical framework for their practice. Learning from and adapting U.S. expertise in this area (DuBois et al., 2002; Rhodes, 2002) would be a good start in this direction.

3. *Increased focus on local circumstances.* Much has been learned from mentoring programs in the United States, and the knowledge exchange needs to continue. However, we Europeans need to develop our own position when designing and implementing programs and examine the extent to which local adaptation is required. Existing theory and research reviewed in this chapter would provide a good starting point for considering what revisions may be most appropriate and beneficial.

References

Appiah, L. (2001). *Mentoring: school-business links.* London: Runnymede Trust.

Benioff, S. (1997). *A second chance. Developing mentoring and education projects for young people.* London: Commission for Racial Equality.

Bennetts, C. (2003). Mentoring youth: Trend and tradition. *British Journal of Guidance and Counselling, 31,* 63–76.

Big Brothers Big Sisters International. (2003, November). *BBBS European Network created at Prague meeting.* Retrieved April 15, 2004, from http://www.bbbsi.org/

Big Brothers Big Sisters International. (2004a). *Countries.* Retrieved April 15, 2004, from http://www.bbbsi.org/c_map.htm

Big Brothers Big Sisters International. (2004b). *What we do.* Retrieved April 15, 2004, from http://www.bbbsi.org/wwa_index.htm

Big Brothers Big Sisters Serbia. (2002). *Programme of psychosocial support and help to the minority groups and children with special needs. "Big Brothers-Big Sisters."* Belgrade, Serbia: Author.

Børns Voksenvenner. (2003). *Idéen.* Retrieved April 15, 2004, from http://www.voksenven.dk/

Bourdieu, P. (1973). Cultural reproduction and social reproduction. In R. Brown (Ed.), *Knowledge, education and cultural change* (pp. 71–113). London: Tavistock.

Bowlby, J. (1997). *Attachment and loss.* London: Pimlico.

Clayden, A., & Stein, M. (2002). *Mentoring for care leavers: Evaluation report.* York, UK: University of York Social Work Research and Development Unit.

Colley, H. (2001, Summer). An ABC of mentor's talk about disaffected youth: Alternative lifestyles, benefit dependency, or complete dunces? *Youth & Policy, 72,* 1–15.

Colley, H. (2003). *Mentoring for social inclusion. A critical approach to nurturing successful mentoring relations.* London: Routledge Falmer.

Condren, D., Tully, R., Slattery, M., Mudge, P., & Gorman, N. O. (2000). *Community mentoring. A strategy to raise the self-esteem of young people at risk of failure in education.* Nenagh Tipperary, UK: Mol an Óige.

Dallos, R., & Compley-Ross, P. (2003). *Young people's experience of mentoring.* Unpublished manuscript.

Davis Smith, J. (1996). Volunteering in Europe. *Social Work in Europe, 3*(1), 19–24.

DuBois, D. L., Holloway, B. E., Valentine, J. C., & Cooper, H. (2002). Effectiveness of mentoring programs for youth: A meta-analytic review.

American Journal of Community Psychology, 30, 157–197.

Employment Support Unit. (2000). *INTEGRA: Working with ex-offenders.* Birmingham, UK: Employment Support Unit.

ENCYMO. (2004). *European Network of Children and Youth Mentoring Organisations siteplan.* Retrieved April 15, 2004, from http://www.enymo.homestead.com/pageensiteplan.html

Erikson, E. H. (1968). *Identity: Youth and crisis.* New York: Norton.

European Commission. (2000). *The European Social Fund 1994–1999. Success stories Germany.* Retrieved April 15, 2004, from http://europa.eu.int/comm/employment_social/esf2000/ms/success_stories/d-13-en.pdf and http://www.telementoring-nrw.de/

Gaskin, K., & Davis Smith, J. (1995). *A new civic Europe? A study of the extent and role of volunteering.* London: The Volunteer Centre U.K.

Golden, S. (2000). *The impact and outcomes of mentoring.* Slough, UK: National Foundation for Educational Research.

Golden, S., & Sims, D. (1997). *Review of industrial mentoring in schools.* Slough, UK: National Foundation for Educational Research.

Granville, G. (2000). *Understanding the experience of older volunteers in intergenerational school-based projects.* Stoke on Trent, UK: The Beth Johnson Foundation.

Gränzer, R. (2003). *Mentoring in Europe.* Retrieved April 15, 2004, from http://www.enymo.homestead.com/pageendocumentsonmentoring.html

Grossman, J. B., & Rhodes, J. E. (2002). The test of time: Predictors and effects of duration in youth mentoring programs. *American Journal of Community Psychology, 30,* 199–206.

Hall, J. C. (2003). *Mentoring and young people. A literature review.* Glasgow, UK: SCRE Centre.

Hugill, K. (2000). Is e-mentoring effective? In A. Miller (Ed.), *Perspectives on mentoring. The report on the Ninth National Mentoring Conference 2000.* Manchester, UK: Salford Business Education Partnership.

London Borough of Hillingdon. (2001). *Mentoring. A guide for parents and careers. Stepping Forward Project.* Retrieved April 15, 2004, from http://www.hillingdon.gov.uk/social/yot/mentoring.php

Lucas, P., & Liabø, K. (2003, April). *One-to-one non-directive mentoring programmes have not been shown to improve behaviour in young people involved in offending or other anti-social activities.* Retrieved April 15, 2004, from http://www.whatworksforchildren.org.uk/nugget_summaries.htm

McBriar, N., Noade, L., & Ringland, B. (2001). First evaluation of the Down Lisburn Trust befriending scheme for young people leaving care. *Child Care in Practice, 7,* 164–174.

The Mentor Foundation. (2004). Homepage. Retrieved April 15, 2004, from http://www.mentorfoundation.org/

Mentor Sverige. (2004). *Mentorskapsprogrammet* [The Mentorship Programme]. Retrieved April 15, 2004, from http://www.mentorsverige.se/templates/Page____1891.asp

Miller, A. (1998). *Business and community mentoring in schools.* Norwich, UK: Department for Education and Employment.

Miller, A. (2002). *Mentoring students and young people: A handbook of effective practice.* London: Kogan Page.

NOP World Social & Political. (n.d.). Retrieved April 15, 2004, from http://www.nop.co.uk/news/PDF/mentoring_survey_FF.pdf

Odih, P. (2002). Mentors and role models: Masculinity and the educational "underachievement" of young Afro-Caribbean males. *Race, Ethnicity, and Education, 5,* 91–105.

Ojala, M. (2000). Parent and teacher expectations for developing young children: A cross-cultural comparison between Ireland and Finland. *European Early Childhood Education Research Journal, 8*(2), 39–61.

Pedersen, K. E. (1999). *Drop afmagden—skab kontakten til usædvanlige unge. Teori og metode i projektarbejde med de mest marginaliserde unge* [Drop the powerlessness—make contact with disaffected youth. Theory and methodology in project work with the most marginalized youth]. Copenhagen, Denmark: Ministry of Social Affairs.

Philip, K. (2003). Youth mentoring: The American dream comes to the UK? *British Journal of Guidance and Counselling, 31,* 101–112.

Philip, K., & Hendry, L. B. (1996). Young people and mentoring—towards a typology? *Journal of Adolescence, 19,* 189–201.

Philip, K., & Hendry, L. B. (2000). Making sense of mentoring or mentoring making sense? Reflections on the mentoring process by adult mentors with young people. *Journal of Community and Applied Social Psychology, 10,* 211–223.

Philip, K., Shucksmith, J., & King, C. (2004). *Sharing a laugh? A qualitative study of mentoring interventions with young people.* York, UK: Joseph Rowntree Foundation.

Piper, H., & Piper, J. (1999). "Disaffected" young people: problems for mentoring. *Mentoring and Tutoring, 7,* 121–130.

Pitts, J. (2000, April–October). Youth justice. *Research Matters, 9,* 56–60.

Reid, K. (2002). Mentoring with disaffected pupils. *Mentoring and Tutoring, 10,* 153–169.

Rhodes, J. E. (2002). *Stand by me: The risks and rewards of mentoring today's youth.* Cambridge, MA: Harvard University Press.

Roberts, H., Liabø, K., Lucas, P., DuBois, D. L., & Sheldon, T. (2004). Mentoring to reduce antisocial behaviour in childhood. *British Medical Journal, 328,* 512–514.

Save the Children U.K. (2002). *Young refugees. Setting up mentoring schemes for young refugees in the U.K.* Retrieved April 15, 2004, from http://www.savethechildren.org.uk/temp/scuk/cache/cmsattach/47_youngref3.pdf

Sharp, C., Blackmore, J., Kendall, L., Greene, K., Keys, W., Macauley, A., et al. (2003). *Playing for success. An evaluation of the fourth year.* Slough, UK: National Foundation for Educational Research.

Sharp, C., Kendall, L., Bharbra, S., Schagen, I., & Duff, J. (2001). *Playing for success: An evaluation of the second year.* Nottingham, UK: Department for Education and Skills.

Sims, D., & Golden, S. (1999). *Evaluation of the National Mentoring Network Bursary Programme 1998–1999.* Slough, UK: National Foundation for Educational Research.

Sims, D., Jamison, J., Golden, S., & Lines, A. (2000). *Running a mentoring programme: Key considerations.* Retrieved April 15, 2004, from http://www.nmn.org.uk/uploads/media/p_key.pdf

Skinner, A., & Fleming, J. (1999). *Quality framework for mentoring with socially excluded young people: Executive summary.* Retrieved April 15, 2004, from http://www.nmn.org.uk/uploads/media/qual_frame.pdf

St. James-Roberts, I., & Samlal Singh, C. (2001). *Can mentors help primary school children with behaviour problems? Final report of the Thomas Coram Research Unit between March 1997 and*

2000. London: Home Office Research, Development, and Statistics Directorate.

Tarling, R., Burrows, J., & Clarke, A. (2001). *Dalston Youth Project Part II (11–14). An evaluation.* London: Home Office Research, Development, and Statistics Directorate.

Teterski, S. V. (2002). *Results of experimental research of the program "Big Brothers/Big Sisters" realization in Russia (1999–2000).* Retrieved April 15, 2004, from http://www.bbbsi.org/proven_model/RussianResearchSummary.doc

Tosner, J. (2001). *Program "PET P": The implementation and evaluation of the program PET P in the Czech Republic.* Retrieved April 15, 2004, from http://www.hest.cz/5p_e.shtml

van Nijnatten, C. (1997). Children in front of the bars. *International Journal of Offender Therapy and Comparative Criminology, 41,* 45–52.

Werner, E. E., & Smith, R. S. (1982). *Vulnerable but invincible: A study of resilient children.* New York: McGraw-Hill.

Youth Justice Board. (2004). *Mentoring.* Retrieved April 15, 2004, from http://www.youth-justice-board.gov.uk/PractitionersPortal/PreventionAndInterventions/Mentoring/

27

INTERNATIONAL: AUSTRALIA AND NEW ZEALAND

IAN M. EVANS, ANNA JORY, AND NARELLE DAWSON

INTRODUCTION

This chapter provides an overview of youth mentoring programs in two closely related English-speaking countries—Australia and New Zealand. Both have histories of colonial settlement, with significant but different populations of indigenous people. Both are oriented toward social policies from the United Kingdom but are increasingly influenced by the popular cultures of the United States. Nevertheless, their unique mores, their values regarding family, self-reliance, and social equity, and the nature of their educational and social services all shape the way in which borrowed mentoring programs are interpreted and embraced.

A purpose of this chapter is to illustrate both the imitative and the innovative features of youth mentoring in our region, which is an area generally referred to as *Australasia*—a term encompassing Australia, New Zealand, and islands of the southwestern Pacific. Thus, indigenous methodologies are also examined in the context of efforts to assess mentoring outcomes. The implications for the future of mentoring in Australasia are suggested, as well as possible lessons for mentoring practices in other countries.

In this first section, we introduce the historical and cultural forces that shaped the two

nations. Today, these provide a context for social and educational services within which mentoring relationships are found. We next explain the way such services for children and youth are organized and the conditions that place young people at risk.

Geopolitical and Societal Conditions

Australia and New Zealand were colonized by British settlers in the 19th century and are thus predominantly European. Most institutions are based on British precedents, such as English common law and the Westminster parliamentary model. Although there are commercial and professional ties, the two countries have separate currencies, speak with different accents, and have unique physical geographies, flora, and fauna. There exists a good-natured rivalry that becomes intensely competitive in the sporting arena.

Australia has a vast land mass, equal in area to the 48 contiguous United States, although most European settlement has occurred around the coastal regions, as seen in the development of dynamic, cosmopolitan cities such as Sydney and Melbourne. With urbanization, however, have come problems of child homelessness, runaways, prostitution, and drug addiction. The total population of some 20 million has grown increasingly diverse with recent periods of immigration from continental Europe and Asia.

The indigenous Aboriginal and Torres Strait Islander people, currently numbering about 400,000, were nomadic, hunter-gatherer communities with strong spiritual connection to the land. Aboriginals were persecuted by the settlers. The policy in the first half of the 20th century of forcibly removing Aboriginal children from their parents, either to dormitories or to foster homes, still has negative ramifications, both for family cohesion and the idea of any nonfamily involvements—such as mentoring. Various agencies, such as the Australian Council of Social Services, have issued statements of apology and commitment to the "stolen generation." In 1992, the High Court's Mabo decision recognized the legality of native land title (Rowse, 1993). Any real economic benefits have yet to be seen. Although Aboriginal people still maintain their languages and traditions, especially in art and social custom, they experience overcrowded housing, poor health, and poverty (Loff & Cordner, 2000).

New Zealand's history and geography are very different. The most significant early settlement occurred between 900 and 1300 A.D. with the migration of Polynesians from the central Pacific. These Maori people represent a collectivist society, with elaborate skills in fishing, farming, and creative arts. When British colonists arrived, they seized land by force, but there was no overall conquest of Maori, who were formidable warriors. In 1840 at Waitangi, tribal chiefs signed a treaty with the British Crown, which granted Maori British citizenship but also guaranteed certain partnership rights and autonomous ownership of natural resources.

The Treaty of Waitangi needs to be highlighted because it profoundly affects the provision of youth services and the way in which mentoring programs should be implemented biculturally. Although its principles were violated repeatedly, the treaty has managed to survive as a constitutional document. It has served as the basis upon which recent governments have negotiated the return of illegally seized tribal lands. There has been a parallel renaissance of Maori cultural identity, as seen by developments such as the emergence of Maori

language preschools, separate health services managed by Maori professionals, and an increasing influence of Maori social values and academic leadership. At the same time, New Zealand is also becoming more culturally diverse. For example, the city of Auckland, with over a quarter of the country's 4 million inhabitants, has the largest concentration of Pacific peoples in the world, and there has been an influx of Asian migrants from Hong Kong, Taiwan, and Korea.

Wide economic disparities between rich and poor have recently emerged in New Zealand that impinge on the communities and the lives of children and youth. Their detrimental effects are felt especially hard, as there is little tradition of corporate philanthropy, such as in the United States, which often supports mentoring and other programmatic interventions. Market-driven fiscal policies of the 1990s emphasized individualism and have undermined the shared responsibilities for caregiving across families and generations (Kelsey, 2002). Between 20% and 30% of New Zealand children now live in poor households; a third of all New Zealand families are one-parent families; and a quarter of all children born into two-parent households have experienced separation or divorce by the age of 9 (Fergusson, Horwood, & Shannon, 1984).

Educational, Social, and Health Services

Education

The public education system is derived from the British model: Pupils wear school uniforms and specialize in their subject areas early. High schools tend to lack flexibility in accommodating diverse student interests and abilities. Bullying is a common problem, and troublesome behavior is too often dealt with by suspensions and expulsions. On the positive side, however, firearms, other weapons, and physical assaults against teachers are rare. In New Zealand, the government provides subsidies to schools in low-income communities. However, parents are expected to make donations, which if not forthcoming can result in pupils being excluded from extracurricular activities. Many schools feel underfunded and are drawn to mentoring programs as a low-cost addition to available services. To make ends meet, they encourage enrollment of fee-paying international students from Asia, without recognizing that such pupils, unaccompanied by parents, might be in special need of mentoring relationships.

Successful school completion, a goal of many mentoring programs, has only recently become recognized as a significant protective factor against further social problems such as suicide and delinquency (Fergusson, Beautrais, & Horwood, 2003). For this reason, there is increasing alarm in Australasia over the much greater proportions of Maori (35%) and Aboriginal (33%) children who drop out or leave school at the legal age of 16 without any qualifications (Department for Community Development, 2004; Durie, 2001). With the push toward high-tech industries, traditional unskilled jobs are harder to come by, so government-financed apprenticeships with formal mentors have been reintroduced to encourage young people into worthwhile trades.

Social Services

There is a well-developed network of mainstream churches providing programs in alcohol counseling, family support, parenting, and domestic violence prevention. These organizations have been particularly proactive in establishing mentoring programs. At the government level, Australia is a federal system, and each state has autonomous social welfare agencies, whereas in New Zealand, two civil services dominate the social lives of children: One manages all social welfare (including a special benefit for youth not able to live at home), and the other has responsibility to manage all care and protection functions, as well as young offenders (Curtis, Ronan, Heiblum, Reid, & Harris, 2002). There is a tradition of community-based policing with officers specially trained in youth work. Juvenile courts in both countries have been influenced by theories of restorative justice. In New Zealand, young offenders and their families are obliged to participate in a Family Group Conference, where the impact of the offense on the victim is discussed and apologies called for. It is hoped that by understanding the implications of their offenses and by the

families accepting increased responsibility, reoffending will be reduced.

Health

This is the third domain for which mentoring is especially relevant. In both countries, the health system is public: General practitioner visits are low cost, and free for children younger than 6 or anyone on welfare. Hospitals are sophisticated, and all major medical treatments are available. There are acute psychiatric wards for children with outpatient treatment provided by child and adolescent community mental health clinics. Birth control and sexual health services are easily accessible, despite which teen pregnancy and abortion rates are high (Heaven, 1994). These and other health needs are related predominantly to lifestyle and poverty. For example, severe chronic diarrhea, caused by inadequate sanitation and changes in eating habits, is now endemic in Aboriginal children, as is petrol (gas) sniffing (Hunter, 1990).

New Zealand and Australia have high suicide rates at the younger ages that were escalating until recently. Young Maori males completed suicide at a rate of 40 per 100,000, compared with 26 per 100,000 for non-Maori males. In Queensland, Australia, Aboriginal males die by suicide at a rate four times that of all young people in Queensland: 139 per 100,000 (DeLeo & Evans, 2002). Since 1998, these rates have decreased. It is widely believed that colonization, with its detrimental effects on cultural identity and kin-based rural communities, is responsible for these social disparities. Maori leaders are demanding fewer stop-gap remedies and greater control over their own programs, according to the Treaty principles of partnership and participation. As one Maori researcher has argued: "One thing is certain—mainstream approaches do not work" (Lawson-Te Aho, 1998, p. 6).

Implications

Despite favorable climates and outdoor opportunities, high standards of living, passion for and achievement in sports, and the availability of successful role models in popular media, the arts, and science, young people "down under" experience concerns and challenges similar to those of the other Western industrialized nations. Economic disparities and loss of cultural identity (for both indigenous and European/immigrant groups) are repeatedly identified as the root cause of difficulties faced by youth that place them at risk. To see whether formal and natural mentoring can play some sort of role in mitigating negative influences and how it might best do so, we next examine broad theoretical concepts relevant to mentoring relationships in Australasia.

THEORY

While mentoring programs have spread enthusiastically, a coherent rationale has never been formulated. There is only one conceptually driven paper available (Evans & Ave, 2000) that emphasizes the need to consider local values and cultural traditions when devising program principles. In this section, therefore, we consider those values and assumptions that seem implicitly to be shaping mentoring in Australasia or that we believe should be guiding its design and evaluation.

Local Values Regarding the Nature of Support

It is difficult to define the major cultural and social values in Australia and New Zealand without engaging in broad generalizations and stereotyping. Nevertheless, there are underlying assumptions about how support for others should be conceptualized. Those in the dominant European culture pride themselves on their ingenuity and the ability to solve practical problems with few resources. "Mateship"—being able to rely on your friends—is highly valued, as is self-reliance, which means fixing things yourself in your backyard shed rather than depending on charity (King, 1991). Indeed, historically, the sparse population and large distances have resulted in communities providing close cooperation and support, so that the idea of a stranger being involved with a young family member is distinctly unusual.

Compatible with the emphasis on local community support but contrasting with the rugged

independence ideal is the powerful influence exerted by the collectivism of the indigenous cultures. Recognition of accomplishment is typically afforded to the group, and individual boasting is frowned upon—in the words of a Maori proverb, "It is not up to the kumara (sweet potato) to say how sweet it is." *Mana* (respect) is bestowed, never claimed, and individuals who think of themselves as important or successful—"tall poppies"—are unpopular and need to be cut down to size. Theoretically, therefore, feeling connected to one's cultural group should be a more significant outcome of mentoring than raising self-esteem. A related fundamental value is that of ensuring a "fair go": that people have equal chances. There is strong disdain for snobbery or class distinctions, and customs such as not tipping derive from the assumption that the server is no lesser an individual than the served. Differential power relationships, often implicit in traditional "assigned" or program-based mentoring, tend to be viewed unfavorably.

Adopting Overseas Models

Given this apparent lack of fit between cultural values and formal mentoring, why has programmatic mentoring become established? Partly because Australasia was so cut off before the days of jet travel and the Internet, both countries still tend to be rather imitative. Originally mirroring "Mother" Britain, today they are influenced by the dominant American culture through movies and television but also via articles in scientific journals and professional visits. For instance, in 1999, the Dusseldorp Skills Forum in Australia arranged a study tour of eight U.S. mentoring programs so as to remedy the "lack of information, resources and the relative inexperience in mentoring in Australia" (Tobin, 2000, p. 2). There is a problem with all these sources of transmission of ideas. Often, it is the procedures that are copied rather than the principles and concepts, limiting the degree to which programs can be developed to meet unique local needs.

The unpretentious and self-effacing nature of the two societies makes them quite prone to import programs uncritically. Overseas initiatives are introduced as "a highly successful program from the U.S.A.," with no actual evidence of success being offered. In Australia, for example, Big Brothers Big Sisters of Australia has been operating since 1982, accepting young people aged 7 to 17 who are socially isolated and in need of additional adult support. The focus is on deflecting negative behaviors before they become destructive and is based strictly on the original American model. Even their promotional material contains references to non-Australian concepts and words, such as "cookies." By using the U.S.-franchised materials, however, they are able to claim that they have the most thorough training and supervision procedures of any volunteer organization in Australia. No Australian effectiveness research has been published.

Rhetoric and Implicit Causal Assumptions

A review of more than 200 different mentoring programs in Australia (MacCallum & Beltman, 1999) pointed to the diversity of approaches that had been introduced, but argued that all projects contain three essential components: (a) role modeling, (b) social and emotional support, and (c) direct assistance with academic learning and life skills (p. 93). These elements closely match the conceptual model presented by DuBois, Neville, Parra, and Pugh-Lilly (2002), which proposes that the pathway from program participation to improvement in emotional or behavioral problems is through (a) a significant adult relationship leading to (b) social support that (c) enhances specific psychological or behavioral competencies.

Two specific program examples can be given to provide additional insight into how the dominant discourse around mentoring is quite generic and lacking in cultural specificity. Both assert that mentoring has the direct result of reducing negative social behavior by raising self-esteem and providing direction. The Allsorts Mentoring Program for "disadvantaged young people" aims, above all, for the mentees to "believe in themselves" (Mentoring Australia, 2003). In New Zealand, the Challenge for Change Mentoring Project links 10- to 13-year-old children with adult mentors over a 20-week period. It has the advantage of being a collaboration between the police,

local protection agencies, and schools. It states that mentoring is "a strategic approach to reducing the incidence of youth issues such as truancy, drug and alcohol abuse or offending. This can be achieved by addressing underlying causes such as low self esteem, a lack of positive direction and limited life skills" (Peters, 2000, Section 4).

Implicit Cultural Assumptions Regarding Relationships

Assumptions in Maori culture are potentially quite different. Traditionally, and still true today, Maori children were brought up with multiple parenting carried out by extended family members and sometimes formalized through a style of adoption by aunts and uncles or grandparents, who impart life skills, family history, and tribal custom (Te Whaiti, McCarthy, & Durie, 1997). As one Maori commentator remarked,

> Mentoring occurs naturally as elders pass information, and in almost all instances is voluntary. . . . We *instinctively* show others how we do things, playing the role of mentor, sitting alongside them, and concentrating on finding the best possible avenue for them to become successful. (Geere-Watson, 2002, p. 13)

U.S. theories of youth mentoring (e.g., Rhodes, this volume) have come to emphasize that the effects of mentoring relationship will be mediated by existing parental and peer relationships. In our indigenous cultures, these can be hypothesized to extend to a much larger family context. New Zealand research has confirmed that it is the quality of the attachment to a family member that is more important for children's psychological well-being than specific family structures (Raja & Stanton, 1992). Similarly, DuBois, Neville, et al. (2002) have demonstrated that mentoring is most influential when youth view their mentors as significant to their lives. Harvey and Evans (2003) have begun to explore the competencies of New Zealand teachers who are most likely to establish relationships that their students report to be emotionally meaningful. Key influences appear to be teachers' basic beliefs about the value of children—described by one teacher as "celebrating our children"—as well as the perceived level of positive involvement in the school by the local community.

Summary

Conceptually, we see that formal, volunteer youth mentoring in Australia and New Zealand is very much a foreign import that has not evolved from local extended family structures or community traditions. The types of social problems and needs for which youth mentoring has become a popular prevention approach in the United States and elsewhere certainly exist and may be getting more severe in Australasia. There is an indication, however, that these exacerbating conditions are influenced by culturally specific economic conditions and social policies that need to be addressed in addition to the strategies typified by mentoring programs in the United States. Institutions such as schools and government departments could focus their attention on policies that encourage positive engagement by young people (see also Kuperminc et al., this volume), designed and controlled by the relevant ethnic and cultural groups. Evans and Ave (2000) argued that the specific values and customs of this region would best support such efforts at community-level change, allowing the development of contexts that are rich in natural mentors.

RESEARCH

The research challenge with respect to youth mentoring in Australia and New Zealand comes about partly because there is no agreed upon vision for how our unique cultural and social conditions might shape mentoring programs best. What little empirical research there is has focused almost entirely on attempts to establish the effectiveness of replications of U.S. programs. Nor is there an agenda for determining what kinds of youth needs mentoring might address most meaningfully. This is an important issue given the findings of an American meta-analytic review that environmental risk and disadvantage define the youth for whom participation in mentoring programs is most likely to be of benefit (DuBois, Holloway, et al.,

2002). For example, in our evaluation of six government-funded mentoring programs in New Zealand, we emphasized that the stated purpose of the overall initiative, to reduce youth crime, was far too optimistic an outcome on which to base an evaluation of effectiveness (Ave et al., 1999).

Outcome and Process Considerations

The lack of a comprehensive conceptual model of youth mentoring that includes important elements of unique national needs, indigenous natural mentoring, and cultural concerns, has meant that most programs have evolved in an ad hoc fashion and without an evaluation model built into their designs. An example of this is provided by Project K in New Zealand, perhaps the most sophisticated and widely implemented mentoring effort in the country, involving over 300 students who are "not reaching their potential" in 24 schools. "K" stands for *koru*, the Maori word for the unfolding fern frond and a national symbol of new life. Selection into the program is by means of scores on the Coopersmith Self-Esteem Inventory, and the same instrument also is used to measure change in self-esteem as a result of mentoring. In one study, self-esteem increased significantly compared with a comparison group (Project K, 2002). Staying in school was another statistically significant favorable outcome for mentored youth, with 83% of a sample of 76 participants still in school 14 months later, compared with 67% of control students (Project K, 2002).

In Australia, data have been gathered systematically on a few programs. Sports Challenge International provides groups of students with instruction from elite athletes and has shown improvements over approximately 1 year in self-concept (Delaney & Woods, 1998), although no comparison group was studied. Positive self-reported outcomes also have been identified by the School-to-Work-Plans program emphasizing postschool work (MacCallum & Beltman, 1999). Ward (2004) evaluated a mentoring program for young offenders at high risk for juvenile crime. One third of the original group failed to complete the program and dropped out. Compared with this group, who might be considered treatment failures, those who remained engaged with their mentors showed a reduction in offending and an increased completion of court orders. Based on reports from caseworkers in the juvenile justice system, those who completed the program showed improvements in drug use, living conditions, involvement in education, and other risk variables compared with their status prior to entering the program. Milne, Delaney, Johansson, and Merlene (2002) also reported some positive outcomes for adult mentoring of "entrenched" juvenile offenders but found that only about 20% of the eligible youth were interested in having a mentor. Targeted youngsters who fail to participate or drop out need to be seen as program failures.

A community-based program in Dunedin, New Zealand, has focused on youth who are chronically truant from school (Milne, Chalmers, Waldie, Darling, & Poulton, 2002). The intervention involved several components in addition to mentoring: facilitating school attendance, supporting families, and encouraging sporting, cultural, and work activities. The youth who were assigned mentors were involved in crime, had poor school records, and showed evidence of addictive or violent behavior. The overall program outcomes generally were favorable, with school attendance, drug use, and conflicts at home all showing significant improvement from pre- to postintervention. The mentored group did not demonstrate larger gains than nonmentored youth who participated in the broader program, although this finding is confounded by the different risk levels presented by those selected for mentoring. The mentored teens did improve significantly on a measure of family conflict, which is consistent with the aforementioned model proposed by Rhodes.

Methodological Issues

In most reviews of the Australasian literature, it has been noted with concern that initiatives have been declared successful in the absence of any hard evidence of meaningful outcomes. However, it is widely accepted among the programs themselves that measuring outcomes is of considerable importance, particularly for formative evaluation purposes, and that comparison or control groups are important. We would add that Australasian studies should focus more on tangible gains than on changes in self-report questionnaires that have not been standardized on local youth. A few programs have recognized the need for specific, objective outcomes, especially as some (e.g., Milne et al., 2002) found students' satisfaction with mentoring to be high despite their self-reported improvements in functioning not correlating with any improvement in targeted outcomes such as truancy and grades. Change in attitudes can be measured directly by discourse analysis. For instance, Handley (1994) has described an Australian wilderness program in which participant disequilibrium is maintained through minimal direct intervention by mentors. He has quantified the shifts in attitude by recording the participants' discourse, noting their vocabulary starting to contain more positive and rational self-statements.

We acknowledge the necessity of experimental methods for demonstrating to some audiences that any observed benefits are due to the program and not other factors (see Grossman, this volume). Yet we are doubtful of the value of trying to force programs to fit into only one model of research. The randomized controlled trial is not seen as the gold standard for knowledge acquisition by many indigenous scholars, compared with case studies and other qualitative, action research models (Smith, 1999). It is dangerous to stereotype such preferences, however. For example, in discussing a new Maori-led initiative for mentoring Maori students, one commentator argued that conventional Western research methods are deficit oriented and maintain unequal power relations by the dominant ethnic group (He Ara Tika, 2001). At the launch of this same program, however, the Minister of Maori Affairs, Parakura Horomia, stated, "We need to know what's working and what isn't, and any improvements that need to be made. The programme will track key student data such as participation, retention, and achievement" (Ministry of Education, 2002, p. 1).

An example of a participatory action research model has been provided by Herbert (2001). This particular intervention involved very-high-risk young Maori women and was set in the researcher's own traditional *marae* (meeting house), with its unique customs and protocols. The mentors were respected older women from the same community, many of them grandmothers, who blended traditional activities, such as weaving, into the formal modeling of positive parenting skills, the goal of the program. The researcher had first to obtain consent to conduct the project from leading elders, discuss with them what the desired outcomes for mentees in this community might look like, and then set out agreements as to what would happen to the information and how it would be disseminated in a way that would not disadvantage the participants. Only then could Herbert document improvements by written tests of these young people's knowledge and understanding of child development, and observed changes in how they related to their toddlers.

Projects done to or for indigenous people and minorities, however well intended, can perpetuate power imbalances and impose ideas about social relationships that are not commensurate with the values and customs of those involved. The ethical question is whether at the start of the project the people themselves see that the potential outcomes truly will be for the benefit of the participants. Consistent with the bicultural treaty that mandated a partnership, indigenous concepts need to be given the same weight in planning and implementation as outside ideals of research method. This is one of the valuable lessons from our region that may find acceptance in other cultural contexts where power imbalances are so pervasive that they are not as easily recognized.

Adjunctive Factors

The limited research on mentoring in Australia and New Zealand falls into two categories: (a) enthusiastic descriptions of the value of mentoring, citing common sense but little that would stand up to scrutiny in the social science literature or (b) empirical work relevant to the amelioration of social/emotional problems of young people but which does not consider directly the social context. From the relevant Australasian literature, we will describe two studies that reveal the potential of embedding mentoring within a much clearer, research-driven understanding of factors affecting youth.

Teachers may serve as some of the primary natural mentors in the lives of Australasian young people, and dropping out of school is a critical event that places youth at risk for exacerbating or generating problems (Evans & Ave, 2000). Thus, knowing what factors prevent school dropout, should, in principle, provide useful target areas for more systemically focused mentoring efforts. Zubrick et al.'s (1995) study of factors correlating with the well-being of Australian youth suggested two critical protective factors: a sense of being cared about and a sense of connectedness, especially to family and school. Marjoribanks (2002), in a longitudinal study of Australian adolescents' likelihood of staying in school, found that over and above social class and ethnic variables, important predictors were school environment (e.g., teachers are able to communicate with students), employment aspirations, and coming from a family that discussed future careers, books, and cultural events.

Marjoribanks (2002) also found that Asian Australian children were more likely to stay in school than other ethnic groups. However, such generalizations need to be tempered by an understanding of migrant family circumstances. In both New Zealand and Australia, a common pattern of Asian migration is that of "astronaut families," in which the family is settled in the new country and the father returns to the home country to continue working. Professional families who migrate and do try to stay together may face significant difficulties with lack of commensurate qualifications and discrimination. In these contexts, family tensions increase parents' desire for their teenagers to study hard and succeed in school. The teens themselves, however, model the less studious behavior of their new Caucasian friends (Aye, Guerin, Evans, & Ho, 2000). Generic mentoring programs that do not appreciate such family dynamics may be less likely to succeed.

Another source of empirical information that would seem critical in program design is to recognize that children do not exist in a vacuum (Rhodes, this volume). Teenagers have preexisting networks of adult and peer support. It is possible that a contrived mentoring relationship is less necessary than having the opportunity to discuss problems with friends as they arise. Jackson (2002) studied New Zealand teenagers' willingness to seek help with emotionally distressing experiences. Boys reported greater reluctance to seek help with embarrassing emotional issues, and fathers, in turn, were not perceived as empathic listeners. For both genders, friends were considered the best source of support on account of the assured level of trust and confidentiality.

PRACTICE

Although practical mentoring programs in both Australia and New Zealand contain many worthwhile elements, we have not yet encountered any that explicitly incorporate unique conceptual elements related to cultural conditions or research-based knowledge of family, community, and social influences specific to the two countries. Some of the following aspects of practice, however, do come close to at least accommodating culture-specific knowledge. (Unless otherwise stated, details of these programs may be found in MacCallum & Beltman, 1999, or Peters, 2000.)

Issues Relating to Choice of Mentors

Despite minimal corporate philanthropy, it appears that funding for and employee support of mentoring programs from large companies is slowly becoming more common in Australia, especially from multinationals that are likely to be influenced by U.S. precedents. BP International, for example, uses their own employees to provide tutoring in science for high school students. IBM offers high school girls hands-on experience in engineering and technology to encourage young women to follow careers in information technology. After being exposed to female role models during a technology camp, the students' mentoring relationships are maintained with these volunteer IBM employees through e-mail. In New Zealand, however, programs still report very low levels of success in recruiting mentors from the corporate sector. Because of recent publicity over sexual abuse, men have proved difficult to recruit for programs serving boys from father-absent households, such as Man Alive in Auckland.

University students are relatively easy to enroll as mentors; however, they tend to make short-term commitments and are, of course, not dispersed among the smaller agricultural communities that are characteristic of low-population-density countries like New Zealand and Australia. A history of programs starting and then folding has generated distrust in small communities with high percentages of indigenous people. Programs in our part of the world, therefore, seek stable individuals, living in the community being served, who have experience with young people and are not deterred too easily by initial difficulties or problems. To meet these criteria, one of Australia's largest mentoring programs, the Learning Assistance Program, operating in more than 1,000 schools with 10,000 volunteers, relies on parents of current or former pupils.

Other practical issues arise in indigenous communities with strong extended family and tribal loyalties. Maori providers have reported (see Ave et al., 1999) that it is possible to identify potential mentors who are prepared to act in this role for the young people of their own *whanau* (extended family) or *iwi* (tribe), but they are reluctant to commit to general mentoring or to sign agreements and fill in forms. There is a strong cultural tradition that the young person's whanau needs to judge the suitability of the mentor, rather than for program staff to recommend a match. To overcome these difficulties, the providers were able to adopt a more collective, team approach in which a group of students undertook leadership development programs alongside a group of adults who could act as mentors, a strategy designed to promote mentor-rich environments. In Australia, the Community Development Employment Project is run by and for indigenous Australians, providing, among other activities, mentoring for families and individuals at risk for petrol sniffing. Of note is that the mentors are paid modest wages, as high-need communities rarely can afford the luxury of volunteer mentors. The Australian Department of Education, Science, and Training has created the Indigenous Ambassadors' Program in which high-profile leaders in sport and entertainment visit schools, encourage children, and increase community acceptability of government educational initiatives.

Targeting Youth Needs and Systems

Most youth mentoring in Australasia is still school based, involving partnerships between schools and the corporate sector or with community service organizations, such as Rotary. This typically results in the focus being related to enhancing academic achievement and keeping youth in school; for example, the Australian government's indigenous education strategy starts with an effort to increase attendance rates, with mentoring projects relying on the leadership and skills of indigenous elders. Even when the overall goals are educational, Australasian programs seem to struggle with the issue of whom and what to target, with the consensus now largely being a focus on prevention of further problems in youth identified as being at risk. In our survey of six specially funded prevention programs in New Zealand, 49% of the mentees were already exhibiting conduct problems at school; 18% were reported as being in need of care and protection; 17% had truancy problems; and 15% were receiving mental health care (Ave et al., 1999). Once young people are already exhibiting more seriously problematic behavior, it is likely that mentoring, especially on its own, may be too little too late (DuBois, Holloway, et al., 2002).

If true primary prevention is a goal for mentoring programs, how, in the absence of current problems, does one identify risk and measure meaningful change, at the same time avoiding labeling or stigmatizing youth and families? Some programs in our part of the world have addressed these questions by recognizing that there are demographic, environmental, and family factors placing young people at risk, even if no identifiable individual problems have yet emerged. Examples of an inclusive focus can be seen in the initiative titled "Just Us Youth," in which it was appreciated that all children who have a parent in prison face inevitable social and emotional hurdles (Ave et al., 1999). An Australian initiative to involve fathers in social and family services has emphasized the need for specific strategies to ensure male participation (Fletcher, Silberberg, & Baxter, 2001). In another program, it was argued that the entire youth population was at risk, because for that particular rural region, basic literacy and attendance statistics at local schools were discouraging and there were no youth-oriented community activities. But as all the children needed support, it required more

resources than were available to one mentoring program (Ave et al., 1999).

In New Zealand, there have been limited attempts to intervene at the neighborhood level and to facilitate the involvement of mentor-rich, natural groups (Hungerford et al., 1999). Three low-income, high-crime neighborhoods were identified, and each was required to use their special grant funding to undertake four activities: (a) establish a club for all 7- to 13-year-olds in the area, (b) rejuvenate neighborhood support groups, (c) conduct safety audits, and (d) strengthen community activities. The youth clubs were well attended, encouraging homework completion as well as recreation. The beautification of the neighborhoods was apparent; various solutions, such as traffic speed deterrents, were introduced to improve safety; and residents reported a greater sense of safety as well as community. At the time the initial evaluation was completed, the program had not been in place long enough to ascertain whether it had achieved the primary goal of reducing youth antisocial behavior.

Activities and Resources

Not all youth mentoring programs in Australasia have targeted only youth considered at risk; many are designed to enhance positive attributes in young people rather than reduce or prevent negative ones. There are mentoring activities that encourage students to develop business ventures and entrepreneurial activities. A useful focus is on learning more about careers and work by being paired with a successful mentor in a novel occupation. Moving from school to the world of work is an important transition point that mentors can help negotiate. In Australia, with its great distances and isolated schools, these sorts of developments are seen as particularly promising.

American best practice research (DuBois, Holloway, et al., 2002) indicates that structured activities engaged in during mentor/mentee interactions have a specific role in developing new skills and competencies. On account of Australia and New Zealand's unspoiled and remote landscapes, wilderness experiences are a popular feature of mentor-oriented activities. One Australian project involving youth from indigenous and nonindigenous backgrounds uses athletes and elders to follow and explore the history and culture of a trail used by the Koori people for more than 18,000 years (Bataluk Cultural Trail, 2004). One of New Zealand's living legends is Sir Edmund Hilary, who first climbed Mount Everest, and the outdoor center that bears his name organizes many mentored youth activities. Young people in Australasia can be characterized as risk takers, challenged by physical danger. Engaging in extended overseas travel is the norm. These cultural attributes could provide the basis for the types of novel activities that can most appropriately be facilitated by mentoring relationships with young volunteers.

All local surveys of youth mentoring programs that we identified raised the issue of sustained funding as a chronic problem. A partial solution to this shortage emerges from the more creative use of entitlement funds from the government. For example, in New Zealand, the Independent Youth Benefit, which is granted to many at-risk youngsters, has been tied to a mentoring plan in which clerical welfare staff were able to provide basic counseling and support to adolescent beneficiaries. They were successful in using the financial clout of a state agency to encourage young people back into secondary education, training, or employment (Evans, Wilson, Hansson, & Hungerford, 1997).

FUTURE DIRECTIONS

Synthesis

Mentoring children and youth is a burgeoning activity that has yet to find its own unique voice in Australia and New Zealand. Our two societies are culturally very different from those of Europe or America. Differential power relationships as implicated in traditional mentoring relationships are viewed unfavorably. Social equality and a "fair go" (equal chances) are highly valued. For the indigenous populations particularly, our analysis suggests there is a need to avoid mentoring as a charitable activity or as a way of mitigating social problems that are a function of long-standing historical injustices. It would be preferable for the principles of

mentoring to be incorporated into more general systemic social action policies that are derived from good social science. There is an urgent need for continued homegrown research that will help define the intrinsic social and community supports in this culture and the forces that threaten them.

Mentoring as a strategy to remediate youth problems has a number of disadvantages that are more easily identified in countries where the concept is still new. The emphasis on volunteerism appeals to government agencies eager to see low-cost solutions to complex social problems. Schools in Australia and New Zealand welcome programs, even those that have never been locally evaluated, because they are perceived as bringing in free resources. However, a more careful examination of community-wide support for schools, of school climates that promote natural peer support, and of teachers as natural mentors could encourage initiatives that focus more on the development of more natural mentoring relationships, as well as a reliance on the status of respected elders in our indigenous communities. Such contextual grounding of adult involvement in the lives of young people might better complement the collectivist kin-based traditions of the indigenous populations of New Zealand and Australia. Just as minority groups in a bicultural system will strongly defend their right to develop their own programs, so the majority European populations may need to think about how their own values of equality and independence can be translated into mentoring activities that de-emphasize the role of the mentor as the superior or more successful adult.

Recommendations for Research

1. *Research should investigate the role of local community structures in supporting natural mentoring relationships.* Small nations such as Australia and New Zealand need to be cautious about borrowing the *form* of overseas mentoring programs and concentrate on replicating their *function* for enhancing meaningful relationships. Communities that can be documented as mentor rich should be compared with those that are not, in order to discover the systemic ingredients of supportive, engaging social structures.

2. *The international literature should be critically reviewed in order to guide mentoring programs down under.* There is no need for social scientists in Australia and New Zealand to replicate the quality research that is being conducted overseas. If cultural differences are recognized, it should be possible to generalize the principles from American research. Guidelines might be developed for social validation of recommendations from the international research literature.

3. *Local program evaluation strategies should reflect indigenous concepts of evidence and knowledge.* Ensuring evidence-based practice for mentoring in Australasia is going to require careful monitoring and evaluation of local programs with attention to indigenous concepts of knowledge. Indigenous practices regarding meaningful evidence will have to be incorporated in any evaluation plan, which should benefit from the use of collaborative approaches and qualitative methods such as discourse analysis.

Recommendations for Practice

1. *Mentoring programs need to be integrated with other systemic initiatives.* Australia's and New Zealand's economic and social policies have direct and rapid influence on their citizens' way of life. Social policies around topics such as welfare, education, and public health need to be able to integrate mentoring concepts so that mentoring is not seen as some sort of add-on program or cheap solution to complex needs.

2. *Insights from a bicultural society such as New Zealand should be considered with respect to how they can inform mentoring practice in societies such as the United States and Europe.* New Zealand, and to some extent Australia, can make a significant contribution to understanding how mentoring programs can be tailored and successfully adopted by minority groups elsewhere. Because of the focus on power sharing, New Zealand researchers have had to take seriously issues such as the acceptability of program concepts, equalizing power relationships to ensure community engagement, and the

design of outcome measures judged to be meaningful by the affected groups. These could be useful lessons for dominant groups in multicultural societies worldwide.

References

Ave, K., Evans, I. M., Hamerton, H., Melville, L., Moeke-Pickering, T., & Robertson, N. (1999). *The Mentoring for Children/Youth At Risk Demonstration Project: Final evaluation report.* Psychology Department, University of Waikato, Hamilton, New Zealand.

Aye, A., Guerin, B., Evans, I., & Ho, E. (2000, August). *Autonomy and parental monitoring in Asian households with the father absent or present.* Paper presented at the conference of the New Zealand Psychological Society, Hamilton, New Zealand.

Bataluk Cultural Trail. (2004). Youth leadership program. Retrieved May 10, 2004, from http://www.ramahyuck.org

Curtis, N. M., Ronan, K. R., Heiblum, N., Reid, M., & Harris, J. (2002). Antisocial behaviours in New Zealand youth: Prevalence, interventions, and promising new directions. *New Zealand Journal of Psychology, 31,* 53–58.

Delaney, K., & Woods, G. (1998). *Evaluation of the Sports Challenge Program.* Perth, Australia: Delaney, Woods, & Associates.

DeLeo, D., & Evans, R. (2002). *Suicide in Queensland, 1996–1998: Mortality rates and related data.* Brisbane, Australia: Australian Institute for Suicide Research and Prevention.

Department for Community Development. (2004). *A profile of young Aboriginal people.* Perth, Australia: Government of Western Australia, Department for Community Development. Retrieved May 10, 2004, from http://www.dotu.wa.gove.au/facts/youth_facts2

DuBois, D. L., Holloway, B. E., Valentine, J. C., & Cooper, H. (2002). Effectiveness of mentoring programs for youth: A meta-analytic review. *American Journal of Community Psychology, 30,* 157–197.

DuBois, D. L., Neville, H. A., Parra, G. R., & Pugh-Lilly, A. O. (2002). Testing a new model of mentoring. In G. G. Noam (Ed. in chief) & J. E. Rhodes (Ed.), *A critical view of youth mentoring (New Directions for Youth Development: Theory, Research, and Practice, No. 93,* pp. 21–57). San Francisco: Jossey-Bass.

Durie, M. (2001). *Mauri ora: The dynamics of Maori health*. Auckland, New Zealand: Oxford University Press.

Evans, I. M., & Ave, K. T. (2000). Mentoring children and youth: Principles, issues, and policy implications for community programmes in New Zealand. *New Zealand Journal of Psychology, 29*, 41–49.

Evans, I. M., Wilson, N. J., Hansson, G., & Hungerford, R. (1997). Positive and negative behaviours of independent, adolescent youth participating in a community support programme. *New Zealand Journal of Psychology, 26*, 29–35.

Fergusson, D. M., Beautrais, A. L., & Horwood, L. J. (2003). Vulnerability and resiliency to suicidal behaviours in young people. *Psychological Medicine, 33*, 61–73.

Fergusson, D. M., Horwood, L. J., & Shannon, F. T. (1984). A proportional hazards model of family breakdown. *Journal of Marriage and the Family, 46*, 539–549.

Fletcher, R., Silberberg, S., & Baxter, R. (2001). *Fathers' access to family-related services*. Unpublished report, The Family Action Centre, The University of Newcastle, Australia.

Geere-Watson, K. (2002). *Mentoring*. Unpublished report, New Zealand Federation of Voluntary Welfare Organisations, Wellington, New Zealand.

Handley, R. (1994). *Out of the bush into the wilderness: Tensions and change*. In M. Tainsh, & J. Izards (Eds.), *Widening horizons: New challenges, directions, and achievements* (pp. 25–33). Hawthorn, Australia: Australian Council for Educational Research.

Harvey, S., & Evans, I. M. (2003). Understanding the emotional environment of the classroom. In D. Fraser & R. Openshaw (Eds.), *Informing our practice* (pp. 182–195). Palmerston North, New Zealand: Kanuka Grove Press.

He Ara Tika. (2001). *On the right track: He Ara Tika*. Retrieved April 28, 2003, from http://mentoring.unitecnology.ac.nz

Heaven, P. C. L. (1994). *Contemporary adolescence: A social psychological approach*. Melbourne, Australia: Macmillan.

Herbert, A. M. L. (2001). *Whanau whakapakari: A Maori-centred approach to child rearing and parent-training programmes*. Unpublished doctoral thesis, University of Waikato, Hamilton, New Zealand.

Hungerford, R., Hutchings, L., Robertson, N., Evans, I., Hamerton, H., & Moeke-Pickering, T. (1999). *"Safer streets" neighbourhood based youth at-risk demonstration project: Final evaluation report*. Psychology Department, University of Waikato, Hamilton, New Zealand.

Hunter, E. (1990). Using a socio-historical frame to analyse Aboriginal self-destructive behaviour. *Australian and New Zealand Journal of Psychiatry, 24*, 191–198.

Jackson, Y. (2002). Mentoring for delinquent children: An outcome study with young adolescent children. *Journal of Youth and Adolescence, 31*, 155–122.

Kelsey, J. (2002). *At the crossroads*. Wellington, New Zealand: Bridget Williams Books.

King, M. (1991). *Pakeha: The quest for identity in New Zealand*. Auckland, New Zealand: Penguin Books.

Lawson-Te Aho, K. (1998). *A review of evidence: A background document to support Kia Piki Te Ora O Te Taitamariki*. Wellington, New Zealand: Te Puni Kokiri.

Loff, B., & Cordner, S. (2000). UN condemns Australia over Aborigines. *Lancet, 356*, 1011.

MacCallum, J., & Beltman, S. (1999). *International Year of Older Persons mentoring research project*. Canberra, Australia: Department of Education, Training, & Youth Affairs.

Marjoribanks, K. (2002). *Family and school capital: Towards a context theory of students' school outcomes*. Dordrecht, Germany: Kluwer Academic.

Mentoring Australia. (2003). Official Web site of National Mentoring Association of Australia, Inc. Retrieved September 30, 2004, from http://www.dsf.org.au/mentor/

Milne, B. J., Chalmers, S., Waldie, K. E., Darling, H., & Poulton, R. (2002). Effectiveness of a community-based truancy intervention: A pilot study. *New Zealand Journal of Educational Studies, 37*, 191–203.

Milne, C., Delaney, M., Johansson, K., & Merlene, M. (2002). *Mentoring for young offenders: Final report of the One2One pilot mentoring project*. Unpublished report for the Crime Prevention Division, NSW Attorney General's Department, Sydney, Australia.

Ministry of Education, New Zealand. (2002). *Speech by Associate Minister of Education, Parakura Horomia, at the launch of He Ara Tika*. Retrieved May 3, 2004, from http://www.scoop.co.nz

Peters, J. (2000). *Models of mentoring: Report prepared for the Ministry of Education*. Retrieved April 25,

2004, from http://www.schools.unitecnology.ac.nz

Project K. (2002). *Reaching our goals: Annual report.* Auckland, New Zealand: Author.

Raja, N. S., & Stanton, W. (1992). Perceived attachment to parents and peers and psychological well-being in adolescence. *Journal of Youth and Adolescence, 21,* 471–485.

Rowse, T. (1993). *After Mabo: Interpreting indigenous traditions.* Carlton, Victoria: Melbourne University Press.

Smith, L. T. (1999). *Decolonising methodologies: Research and indigenous peoples.* Dunedin, New Zealand: University of Otago Press.

Te Whaiti, P., McCarthy, M., & Durie, A. (Eds.). (1997). *Mai i rangiatea: Maori well-being and development.* Auckland, New Zealand: University of Auckland Press.

Ward, R. C. (2004). *An evaluation of the mentoring program within the Juvenile Justice System of Western Australia.* Unpublished doctoral thesis, School of Psychology, Murdoch University, Perth, Australia.

Tobin, L. (2000). *What makes a great mentoring program? Highlights of USA study tour, November 1999.* Unpublished report, Dusseldorp Skills Forum, Sydney, Australia.

Zubrick, S. R., Silburn, S. R., Garton, A., Burton, P., Dalby, R., Carlton, J., et al. (1995). *Western Australian Child Health Survey: Developing health and well-being in the nineties.* Perth: Australian Bureau of Statistics.

PART VII

SPECIAL POPULATIONS

28

Talented and Gifted Youth

Carolyn M. Callahan and Robin M. Kyburg

Introduction

Any discussion about the mentoring of gifted and talented youth by adults is predicated on the premise that these youth are unique in their cognitive, educational, social, and emotional developmental needs. The most widely accepted definitions of *giftedness* reflect some version of the following definition taken from federal legislation:

> The term "gifted and talented students" means children and youth who give evidence of high performance capability in areas such as intellectual, creative, artistic, or leadership capacity, or in specific academic fields, and who require services or activities not ordinarily provided by the school in order to fully develop such capabilities. (Pub. L. 100–297, Section 4103. Definitions, 1978)

Estimates of the prevalence of gifted youth were at 3% to 5% of the K–12 school population in the first federal study of gifted and talented students in the United States (U.S. Department of Health, Education and Welfare, 1972). Some authors estimate the pool of potentially gifted youth as high as 10% to 25% percent of the population (Renzulli & Reis, 1985).

Within the more general population of gifted youth, and of particular importance in the study of mentoring gifted students, is the very select and narrow subpopulation labeled *prodigies*. Prodigies are defined by researchers as children age 10 or younger who already are performing at an adult professional's level of skill in a cognitively complex area such as chess, music, or mathematics (Feldman, 1979, 1991).

Within the literature on gifted youth, mentors have been described as supporting gifted and talented youth development in areas ranging from (a) career development to (b) learning about the commitment to a discipline to (c) personal adjustment issues. Nash, Haensly, Rodgers, and Wright (1993) have categorized the functions of mentors of the gifted as role modeling, nurturing creativity, providing career exploration opportunities, providing content-based enrichment in an area of special interest of the youth, and aiding in personal growth, particularly in self-awareness. Others have emphasized the importance of the mentor relationship for inculcating youth into the traditions of a discipline (Boston, 1976; Feldman, 1991) and, of special note, for enhancing the creative productivity of youth (Edlind & Haensly, 1985; Goertzel, Goertzel, & Goertzel, 1978).

As in the broader mentoring literature, a further important distinction is made between mentoring that evolves from formal, structured programs and that which may occur through ties established more informally through extracurricular activities and other outside-of-school aspects of the gifted or talented youth's day-to-day life. Typically, the extraschool or extracurricular mentor relationships are sought out and established by parents of the gifted who are prodigies or talented individuals who exhibit other extremely precocious potential. The mentor's purpose is to help the student develop particular skills and advanced performance expertise in areas not served at exceptional levels within the school environment and sometimes in talent areas not served at all in school settings. Parents of prodigies and other gifted youth will seek out mentors for their children outside of the school setting, and sometimes even outside the local community. As the individual's progress accelerates, this form of mentoring relationship becomes essential, providing instruction in expert skills of the discipline and arranging performance opportunities. As a rule, parents of talented youth in areas such as music, dance, or artistic performance and performance in athletics (swimming, track and field, tennis, etc.) would seek out such mentors, although these mentorships may also be sought in academic areas such as mathematics.

One clear attribute of formal mentoring for gifted and talented youth that distinguishes it from traditional educational options outside the regular classroom, such as an independent study or internship, is the expectation that there will be a relationship between the mentor and protégé that extends beyond specific learning goals. Independent study relies only on a set of goals and related activities to be carried out by the students with oversight by the adult. In an internship, the student is expected to perform prearranged tasks to a stated level of proficiency, demonstrating growth through a sequence of increasing levels of expertise. In internship situations, students are generally assigned a supervisor within an organization or an institution. The expectation of long-term commitments and enduring relationships are absent from both internship and independent-study assignments (Zorman, 1993). While internship arrangements may, in fact, result in relationships between students and supervisors that evolve into mentoring relationships, the experience is not designed to realize that goal.

With these considerations as background, in the sections that follow, we first discuss relevant theoretical perspectives and their implications for identifying factors that may influence the effectiveness of mentoring relationships and programs for gifted and talented youth. We then review extant research literature, followed by a discussion of practice issues relating to mentoring of this special population of youth. Finally, we conclude with suggestions for future research and practice.

THEORY

In the gifted and talented education field, no specific theory directs or supports programs of mentoring for gifted and talented youth. As an alternative, one can examine how the themes of a general theoretical mentoring model, such as the one proposed by Rhodes (2002), might act as a guiding framework with respect to the particular needs of gifted and talented youth. Rhodes theorized that mentoring works via three avenues: improving cognitive skills, enhancing social skills and emotional well-being, and serving as a role model and advocate. In the sections that follow, such "pathways of mentoring influence" (p. 36) will be examined in the context of the unique needs of gifted and talented youth (e.g., providing instructional and skill development opportunities, special challenges of social and emotional adjustment, role modeling and advocating the fulfillment of talent potential). Mentors as teachers and special populations of gifted students will also be discussed.

Reasons for Providing Mentors for the Gifted

Instructional and Skill Development Opportunity

The underlying rationale for providing either school mentoring or extracurricular mentoring for gifted students is recognition of their unique intellectual, social, and affective needs. When given an appropriately stimulating environment, gifted students perform at more advanced levels than their peers. The earliest writings on the importance of mentoring relationships for the gifted suggested the need to create interactions and activities rooted in experiential learning in order to provide such an environment (Boston, 1976). Others have stressed the importance of mentoring relationships for providing activities that are inquiry related and incorporate the necessary opportunities to develop higher-level thinking skills as applied in actual disciplines (Burns & Reis, 1991; Gray & Gray, 1988).

Shore, Cornell, Robinson, and Ward (1991) concluded that there is strong research support for the benefits of career education for the gifted. While not a traditional academic discipline, it comprises a knowledge base critical for gifted youth. Like all students, they need to develop understanding of why people work and the benefits of working, but at a unique, high level of performance. Hence, relationships based on congruent interests and talents for career exploration have been the basis of many mentoring programs for the gifted. Young, gifted individuals who clearly exhibit talents in areas that are unique and not part of the usual school experience can use mentor programs for exposure to careers that extend beyond those that might be presented to and discussed with the general population. Furthermore, gifted youth who exhibit many different areas of strength may be helped through the exploration of multiple interests to help evaluate each one and make informed decisions about areas of potential career development. Cross (1998) also pointed out that mentors may provide models for learning about pathways to the fulfillment of talent potential.

However, Shore et al. (1991) also noted that the gifted need to understand the lifestyles associated with the kinds of work that talented individuals do. As an extension of that understanding, they need to examine the potentially challenging moral or ethical issues in their careers, and they need to become aware of the impact high aspirations, intense focus, and dedication may exert on their lives, which leads to concern about the affective development of gifted youth.

Social and Emotional Adjustment and Support

The literature on gifted and talented youth extends the focus of mentoring to the importance of mentoring in other areas of the social and emotional adjustment of gifted youth. Gifted students may not recognize or accept the importance of their talents both because of the ridicule that they may experience from classmates and because of insufficient knowledge on the part of educators about how to affirm students' evolving expertise, particularly when it surpasses their own (Edlind & Haensly, 1985). Not only might the establishment of the mentoring relationship provide an opportunity for affirming the abilities of the student, a mentor can provide a message that the youth's talents should be developed to the fullest (Batten & Rogers, 1993) and that pursuing high-level performance goals can be both socially and emotionally satisfying, both directly and by providing a model.

Because gifted youth are often faced with confirming evidence that they are "different" from other young people, they may worry about not fitting in or being successful socially with peers. This may exacerbate already significant adolescent developmental challenges of identity formation and achieving autonomy from family and friends, which often relies on building bonds among like peers. Eccles et al. (1993) have theorized that youth development is directly affected by the fit between the developmental stage and available environmental opportunities. Although this theory did not derive from research specifically related to gifted and talented youth, it could be that feeling "misplaced" might be even more pronounced in the gifted population, particularly where opportunities for talent development to elite levels are likely to be sparse. For example, acceleration of gifted students, such as by early entrance to college or grade skipping, in order to accommodate their advanced cognitive developmental needs, may result in a mismatch between the social and emotional developmental stage of the learner and his or her school environment. Such learners may be in positions where they face decisions about college, about majors, or even graduate school at an unusually early age, and in these cases, mentoring may be an especially important means for exploring gifted individuals' commitments to pursue a discipline. Mentors also may help the gifted negotiate "major transitions in academic life, from high school to college, from college to graduate school, and from school to work" (Grybek, 1997, p. 116). When the school/educational options are not available, fit between intellectual developmental stage and the environment can be lacking, and the mentor may provide the stimulation that is necessary for satisfaction with that aspect of development.

Gardner (1993) noted that the creative individual's highly developed sensitivity may lead to more critical evaluations of self and others, a refusal to accept authority, and boredom with routine tasks. In these cases, the mentor can provide a model of adjustment, demonstrating the necessary skills to negotiate the complex interpersonal relationships and social interactions that are associated with high-performance capabilities.

Social and emotional adjustment and support are most likely to occur within the context of effective mentoring relationships resulting from close emotional bonds, what Rhodes (2002) has termed the "active ingredient" (p. 36) between mentor and protégé. To promote the development of such deep personal connections within the gifted and talented population, it may be particularly important to carefully match mentor and protégé. Such bonds are more likely to develop and become sustaining and empathic when mentors are familiar with the gifted protégé's skills and characteristics and the types of processes and experiences required for fulfillment of talent potential (Arnold & Subotnik, 1995). Carefully matching mentor to gifted protégé—particularly on attitudes, values, and lifestyles—is a critical step in establishing a close, mentoring relationship, according to several experts on gifted youth (Pleiss & Feldhusen, 1995; Shandley, 1989). Common interests and approaches to problem solving, personality, stage of development of the youth, and the race and gender of the mentor may be other criteria to consider when pairing mentor to gifted protégé.

Role Models and Advocates
of Talent Development

Rhodes (2002) suggested mentors act as role models when they "exemplify the sorts of knowledge, skills, and behavior that protégés one day hope to acquire" (p. 45). For gifted and talented

youth, we might expect the most effective role models to have experienced similar personal challenges associated with the development of exceptional levels of performance. Gifted females, for example, might best be mentored by professional women, who have experienced similar biases and other barriers to successful talent development and who can model the "lifestyles, modes of thinking, professional practices, costs, and advantages associated with high-level achievement in a particular domain" (Arnold & Subotnik, 1995, p. 120). The greater a gifted youth's "distance from the mainstream" in terms of the typical professional (e.g., females in mathematics, African Americans in mainstream science), the greater the need for role models who share gender, experiential background, values, and attitudes (Arnold & Subotnik, 1995). African American mentors may provide role models with whom minority students can identify and offer critical vocational guidance and advice (Ford & Harris, 1999).

Wright and Borland (1992) theorized that early mentor relationships may be critical to the educational success of poor minority students. They hypothesized that older adolescent academically gifted students from the same circumstances and culture might serve effectively as mentors to younger gifted children. They posit that interactions with

> An indisputable living example of an intelligent young person who has achieved academic success in spite of the odds . . . can mitigate the effects of an absent adult or the negative role model offered as typical of urban minority culture by the media. (Wright & Borland, 1992, p. 125)

Bandura's social learning theory would support this hypothesis in that it suggests that individuals learn by observing the behaviors of others and the outcomes of those behaviors (Cole & Cole, 1996). Further theoretical support for the emphasis on the importance of shared experiential background of mentor and protégé might be found in Rogoff's (2003) basic conception that human development occurs via participation in the sociocultural activities of one's community. Wright and Borland (1992) found that the mentors guided the younger protégés through the classroom, showing them the "tricks of the trade" (p. 125). It may be that the close, empathic bond between mentor and protégé Rhodes (2002) characterized as essential to effective mentoring relationships is activated in these relationships and acts as a conduit for the creation and acceptance of appropriate challenges to the learner's emerging cognitive capacities.

Of critical importance during this process may be the capacity of the mentor to act as a role model so that the protégé can gradually expand his or her own self-awareness as an evolving professional in the discipline (Daloz, 1986). Daloz further argued that as the gifted protégé matures, so too should the nature of the empathic bond between the mentor and the protégé. That is, she hypothesized an effective mentoring relationship evolves from hierarchical dependency to a mutual and reciprocal connection between two independent colleagues, as evidenced by their emerging respect for each other's diverging areas of expertise.

Both Gardner (1993) and Bloom (1985) have examined the role of mentoring in the development of prodigies and other gifted individuals judged to be successful. In an extensive analysis of qualitative case study data of 150 individuals who attained high levels of accomplishment in a variety of fields by the age of 35, Bloom and his colleagues (Bloom, 1985) concluded that optimal cultivation of talent requires different mentors at different stages of development. For example, the first or initial mentors of young, talented students should emphasize making the study interesting, playful, and engaging. In contrast, as the student matures into middle childhood, mentors should provide instruction with stress on precision and accuracy, while at the same time providing encouragement and the support required to develop a commitment to the field. Finally, the adolescent may need help to identify and develop a personal style as well as receive targeted coaching to achieve peak performance.

Mentors as Teachers

Many authors who advocate mentors for gifted students or who describe mentoring that apparently has influenced gifted students have focused on the teaching role of the relationship (e.g., Bisland, 2001; Lupkowski, Assouline, & Stanley, 1990). However, even within the role identified as teaching, levels in the formality of the relationships vary considerably. Simply modeling learning skills daily in order to encourage lifelong learning has been labeled mentoring by some (e.g., Davalos & Haensly, 1997); others have described intensive, prescriptive instruction or tutoring only (Lupkowski et al., 1990). Most literature on mentoring of gifted and talented youth, however, would view the role of mentor as much more complex, even when associated with the teaching function.

Rhodes's (2002) theoretical model, for example, suggests that "meaningful conversation and cognitive challenge" (p. 44) may be among the functions a mentor provides. Among the population of gifted and talented youth, clearly selection of mentors of sufficiently higher levels of expertise to provide such meaningful challenge may be critical. Protégés who exhibit unusually advanced talents in areas such as musical performance or composition, moreover, may need teachers who not only have advanced skills in the discipline but also have skill in developing advanced levels of performance, features of talent development models that are often beyond what is available at school. Such teachers often are or become mentors.

Special Populations of Gifted Students

Three other subpopulations of gifted students need special attention in this discussion: gifted females, gifted from minority populations and/or high poverty environments, and gifted underachievers. Arnold and Subotnik (1995) argued that the more consonant a protégé's gender, social class, ethnicity, experiential background, values, and attitudes are with those of the mentor, the more likely the protégé will relate to the mentor, and the more likely the mentor will be confident in his or her ability to help the young person. Indeed, these populations have received particular attention in the gifted mentoring literature because of the general lack of opportunities afforded for models of excellence. Mentors have been argued to be critical persons in the development of talent in gifted females, for example, because of the need to increase women's confidence in their ability to engage in opportunities to explore and pursue otherwise male-dominated fields (Packard & Nguyen, 2003). In addition, Schwiebert, Deck, Bradshaw, Scott, and Harper (1999) noted the "burden of sexual innuendo that may accompany cross-gender mentorships and discourage the full development of the relationship particularly between a young female and adult male" (p. 243). Shaughnessy and Neeley (1991) noted that social pressures and concerns about appearances also may inhibit older men from serving as mentors for young women, further restricting availability of mentors for gifted young women.

Establishing mentoring relationships for gifted youth from ethnic minority, English-as-second-language learners, and lower socioeconomic class families also has been posited to be a critical factor influencing the development of their potential (Gray, 1983; Wright & Borland, 1992). Black students in general face greater difficulty in achieving a positive racial identity than do White students (Ford & Harris, 1999). Being identified as gifted may exacerbate this difficulty because gifted Black youth also may face the dilemma of choosing between academic success and social acceptance. What Fordham and Ogbu (1986) described as the "burden of acting White" may be even more pronounced for gifted students of color. They hypothesized that due to ambivalence regarding the worth of academic achievement, affective dissonance, and social pressures, many Black students who are academically able do not put forth the necessary effort and perseverance in their schoolwork, and consequently do poorly in school.

The combined challenges of finding mentors for minority students and females makes finding mentors for young minority gifted women even more problematic. And when minorities and/or young women also are from low socioeconomic environments, they may have significantly fewer opportunities for exposure to highly successful role models (Ford & Harris, 1999). Cumulatively, these theoretical considerations suggest that mentoring relationships and programs could have greater impact on gifted and talented youth from the traditionally underserved populations of gifted students described above.

RESEARCH

The limited empirical literature on the role that mentoring has played in the lives of gifted individuals relies primarily on post hoc analyses of biographical data, case study analyses, or retrospective questionnaire data. Controlled evaluations of the effects of mentoring programs for the gifted have been rare. Nonetheless, extant studies have in some instances reported findings that suggest the influence that mentoring relationships and programs may have on gifted and talented youth and the processes through which different types of influence may occur.

Effects of Mentor Relationships

Pleiss and Feldhusen (1995) reported that gifted youth involved in mentoring perceived that these mentoring relationships were beneficial in the further development of their interests and motivation and said that they learned about the lifestyles of specific careers as well as the specific roles, functions, activities, and goals of individuals who are accomplished in those careers. Similarly, interview and questionnaire data from Arnold's (1995) 14-year longitudinal study of valedictorians and salutatorians suggested that mentors help students understand the role of a professional in the field, learn about conducting research in the field, become socialized in the field, and develop self-efficacy. The 103 respondents to Beck's (1989) survey of mentored gifted students who had participated in an 18-week high school mentoring program revealed significant differences in student perceptions of their opportunities and benefits. The questionnaire probed the effects of both the classroom phase of the program and the mentorship phase of the program. According to Beck's results, the mentorship phase,

> Was significantly more effective in helping participants take risks, develop talents, learn about advanced subject matter, work independently, utilize technical skills, utilize research skills, investigate job routines and responsibilities, find out about career entrance requirements, examine lifestyles and characteristics of professionals, see how professionals interact, and make contacts and network. (p. 24)

In case studies of prodigies, Feldman (1991) documented that the mentoring role is much more than simple and somber skill transfer. As Feldman watched a mentor work with a student as they carefully chose paper, ruled neat staffs on paper, arranged pages, and selected the perfect pen and ink for writing scores, he observed,

> I had the sense of a craft being passed on from one generation to another, in a way that can never be done by reading a book or simply observing. This aspect of the composer's craft was treated with the same care and love as the more musical and technical aspects of the domain. (p. 138)

Effects of Mentoring on Special Populations of Gifted Youth

Gifted Females

The potential for positive effects of mentoring for gifted females have been suggested in several studies (e.g., Arnold, 1995; Beck, 1989; Kaufmann, Harrel, Milam, Woolverton, & Miller, 1986; Kerr, 1991; Reilly, 1994/1995). Arnold (1995) conducted a 14-year longitudinal investigation exploring the postsecondary educational and career achievement of academically talented students. A cohort of 46 women, recognized as valedictorians and from varied socioeconomic backgrounds, were interviewed at least six times following high school graduation. Analysis of the interviews revealed that women who were motivated to pursue careers in science, a less traditional field for women, associated their career decisions with mentoring experiences that afforded them opportunities to observe "graduate students and department faculty *doing* science and leading their lives" (Arnold, 1995, p. 121). Arnold concluded, "For women, however, personal sponsorship into testing opportunities was necessary for high career aspirations. Role models, guides, and sponsors all connected women to nonacademic opportunities where their success and enjoyment of professional challenge made career futures seem real" (p. 125).

Similarly, Packard and Nguyen (2003) examined the stability and change of the science-career-related decisions of women who participated in an intensive summer science- and math-related academic program during adolescence. Forty-one ethnically and socioeconomically diverse participants in their last year in high school or first year in college were asked in interviews to reflect upon factors contributing to their decisions to continue in science, mathematics, engineering, or technology (SMET) or to change career paths. Among women who chose to pursue and remain in SMET careers, mentors were reported to play a key role in their decisions to continue in those careers.

Kerr's (1994) in-depth qualitative case study of eminent women, whom she chose based on their achievement of high honors and recognition and a judgment that they "seem[ed] to have fulfilled their own dreams and goals" (p. xii), led her to conclude that mentors were an important factor among the confluence of factors influencing gifted females' career choices and success. Reilly and Welch (1994/1995), reporting on a survey of 33 female and 28 male gifted students who had completed a high school mentoring program, found that three times as many women as men reported that they had made focused career decisions as a result of their mentoring experience. In a related finding, significantly more females in Beck's (1989) study of gifted high school students claimed that mentor relationships contributed to helping them examine ways to integrate career and family. The female mentors were perceived as contributing more to helping students take risks and work independently.

Kaufmann et al. (1986) examined survey data taken from a sample of 255 adults 10 to 15 years after they had been awarded the distinction of being Presidential Scholars in high school. They found that the female Presidential Scholars who reported having mentors also reported earning salaries equal to those of males, while chi-square analyses of the overall sample of Presidential Scholars ($N = 604$) revealed that females reported earning significantly less than the males.

Even though all of these studies lend support to the theory that mentoring relationships assist in the development of talent among gifted youth, they all are flawed in their reliance on post hoc, self-report data, and there is little consensus upon a formal definition of *mentor* or a precise depiction of *mentoring relationship*.

A lack of carefully controlled, experimental studies including pre- and postmeasures precludes true comparisons between groups of gifted youth with or without mentors.

Students From Minority Groups and/or Low Socioeconomic Backgrounds

Arellano and Padilla (1996) found in a sample of 30 Latino undergraduate students enrolled in a highly selective university (73% identified as gifted in elementary school) that these students perceived mentors to have been of great importance to them in setting and achieving academic goals. The sample was divided into three groups based upon parents' possession of "cultural capital" (years of schooling, access to resources, and information networks). Students whose parents possessed less "cultural capital" identified the importance of mentors in helping them access information that they would not have otherwise obtained. In a similar vein, Rodriguez (1986), in comparing traditional counseling with mentor relationships among college students from lower socioeconomic groups, concluded that mentoring relationships can assist students in social and academic integration in the college community and in increasing student commitment to achievement in college. On a survey of 100 Chicanas who obtained doctorates, mentoring was identified as the second most significant factor affecting their success (Achor & Morales, 1990).

Underachieving Gifted

In an in-depth comparative case study analysis of three gifted adolescent males, interviews by Hébert and Olenchack (2000) with the subjects, their teachers, school counselors, advisors, and other professionals significant in their educational placements, and formal and informal document review, documented the positive effects of mentors on reversing underachievement. Specific characteristics of the relationship identified as contributing positively to the protégés' improved school behaviors and academic achievement included social and emotional support and advocacy that supplemented the more direct instructor/student relationship. In addition, the mentors worked with the young men to

help them identify barriers to developing their creative productivity and helped them develop and test strategies for overcoming those barriers.

Functions of the Mentor in Late-Adolescent/Adult Gifted Individuals

The analysis of survey data from Presidential Scholars 10 to 15 years after their high school graduation (Kaufmann et al., 1986) identified three categories of functions filled by mentors. The first, role model, encompassed being an exemplar, enhancing job-related or professional skills, and transmitting professional value and attitudes and was identified as an influence by 61% of the sample. The role model function was followed closely by support and encouragement (i.e., providing either professional or personal support), endorsed by 58% of the sample. The last category, professional socialization and advancement, endorsed by 13% of the sample, included functions such as providing opportunities for increased visibility and career opportunities; teaching the protégé to play the game; defending, protecting, or advocating for the protégé; or introducing the protégé to influential people. Whereas the literature on other populations suggests that professional socialization is valuable, the Presidential Scholars reported fewer benefits from such functions. Rather, they placed far greater significance on the transmission of attitudes and values such as passion for the discipline or profession.

Potential Detrimental Effects of Mentoring

Although most literature emphasizes the potential positive outcomes of mentoring for gifted individuals, there are indications from retrospective studies of eminent individuals (e.g., Gardner, 1993; Simonton, 2000) and case studies of prodigies (Feldman, 1991) that the inappropriate matching of mentors or inappropriate behaviors of mentors may have detrimental effects on the protégé. For example, Simonton (2000) noted that if the mentors are "past their prime, and thus . . . less receptive to new ideas" (p. 117), they may stifle the creativity of gifted youth as they try to mold them in images of themselves. He further cautioned that when the underlying motivations of the mentors are focused on creating clones of themselves in their students, the effect may be injurious by limiting the development of the students' unique talents. Gardner (1993) concluded that a mentor who demands mastery at too advanced a level and too early also may discourage the student from pursuing a particular talent. For these reasons, Simonton recommended that it may be advantageous to highly able students to be given the opportunity to experience multiple mentors.

Finally, several authors (e.g., Grybek, 1997; Levinson, 1978; Pleiss & Feldhusen, 1995; Torrance, 1984) have addressed the dangers of inappropriate termination of the mentor relationship. Because gifted students may be isolated from peers due to the differences in performance levels, they may develop especially strong attachments to mentors and thus become distressed when the mentoring relationship ends prematurely (Grybek, 1997).

PRACTICE

In establishing a mentoring program or arrangement for gifted youth, it is important to carefully consider the following factors: structural components of the mentorship, specific goals of the mentorship, the types of mentoring program or arrangement, the selection of mentors and protégés, the training and supervision of mentors, the evaluation of the mentorship, and, finally, the transition from or termination of the mentoring experience.

Guidelines for Establishing Mentoring Programs or Individual Arrangements for Gifted Youth

Reports of mentor programs abound, and many describe programs distinctly for gifted youth. However, there is little consensus about what constitutes "best practices" in mentoring programs for gifted youth, and, as noted, virtually no rigorous experimental research to inform such determinations exists. Nevertheless, certain commonalities across programs and the limited case study data suggest a number of promising elements among successful mentoring programs and give direction to recommended best practices.

Due to the complexity inherent in all human relationships, mentor associations may lead to harm unless careful attention is paid to the match of mentor to protégé and the careful evaluation of subsequent interactions. Expectations regarding the roles and behavior of the participants need to be clearly communicated and agreed upon, and the nature of the commitment in terms of time and energy needs to be clearly understood (Bisland, 2001). Because the intellectual maturity of gifted students may not be in alignment with their social and affective needs and skills, adults involved should exercise special care to ensure that these factors are considered (Grybek, 1997). For example, mentors should not expect gifted youth to possess the social or emotional maturity to undertake the sophisticated level of personal decisions that might be assumed based on their advanced cognitive developmental levels.

Structural Components

Essential first steps in the establishment of any mentoring program or relationship include agreement on definitions of key terms and the general organizational outline of the program or arrangement. Specific guidelines regarding the kind of mentoring to be provided; who will participate in the program; procedures for matching mentors and protégés; the duration of the mentoring relationships; how goals, roles, work schedules, and responsibilities will be specified, distributed, and adhered to; and, finally, how the experience or program is to be evaluated, terminated, and/or even celebrated need to be articulated. Once a specific outline of a program or arrangement has been established, a program coordinator can set about its implementation.

Specific Goals

Whereas structural components of the arrangement form the backdrop for the progression of the interpersonal relationship that ensues, general goals of the mentoring relationship provide a road map for enhancing the development of the gifted individual. Matching the cognitive, social, and emotional developmental levels of the gifted youth to the ability of the mentor to guide the gifted individual is of critical importance and may lie at the heart of the relationship's success. Indeed, Pleiss and Feldhusen (1995) noted that "the effective mentor engages the child in planned activities that are carefully timed to meet his or her developmental needs and provides opportunities for the protégé to reflect on and assimilate the experiences" (p. 160).

One step in fulfilling these goals is assessing skill or talent level. When interests are as yet unfocused, or in cases where highly gifted students display a multitude of talents, mentoring arrangements may be most effective when they concentrate on exploration, nurturing creativity, and affording the gifted learner exposure to a wide range of possible career options and pathways. Gardner (1993) suggested that in the early years of talent exploration, the mentor should serve as a guide and resource. At the point when talents and aspirations become more specifically defined, the gifted individual will profit most from a mentoring arrangement in which the goal centers on building up proficiency in content knowledge and mastery of requisite skills (Gardner, 1993). Finally, once a student has reached a level of mastery, an intense, interpersonal mentoring relationship with a career professional regarded as a leader in the area(s) of shared interest is required.

Another step toward fulfilling the goal of successfully matching protégés with mentors may involve appreciating the social developmental needs of gifted youth. Whereas cognitively, it may be appropriate for a young protégé to be engaging in, for example, top-level research in a physics laboratory with colleagues many years her senior, socially, she may be inept as a participant in her older fellow researchers' extracurricular activities. Inappropriate matches, even with the most well-intentioned mentors, may be detrimental if the mentor is unaware of the simultaneously divergent sets of developmental needs the youth may have. Some young, gifted students, however, with highly advanced levels of maturity may relish the opportunity to work independently, in which case, older, more detached mentors who make no unwarranted assumptions about age-appropriate behavior for the protégé might approach the protégé effectively based purely on the basis of intellectual level rather than preconceived notions of age-related behavior (Ellingson, Haeger, & Feldhusen, 1986; Timpson & Jones, 1989). While this may work to the advantage of the learner's intellectual stimulation, caution is nevertheless warranted in terms of setting unrealistic expectations of concomitant social developmental levels of the protégé.

Providing mentoring opportunities for gifted students is fraught with challenges stemming from the uniqueness of the population and commonly held assumptions about these students' needs. Unique to some gifted and talented students, for example, is the unevenness of their development. As mentioned above, this unevenness across domains of development poses additional challenges when determining the goals of a mentoring arrangement. A 13-year-old gifted female may be a math whiz whose cognitive needs can be met in a PhD program, whereas in school, she may still need peers of her own age to facilitate appropriate social development, and at home, she may need extra support from parents more like that needed by other adolescents. Gardner (1993) emphasized the need for emotional support as well as technical support for the highly gifted student and suggested that mentors who have an intuitive sense of the protégé's affective needs are most effective. This affirms the importance of ensuring that the gifted receive both appropriate challenges in their areas of talent as well as license to still behave in age-appropriate ways. The recognition that a range of abilities, social development, and emotional needs are likely to present simultaneously has led a number of authors to suggest that multiple mentors may offer the best way of meeting the unique needs of gifted students (Chan, 2000; Clasen & Hanson, 1987; Gardner, 1993; Zorman, 1993).

Types of Mentor Programs or Mentoring Arrangements

A variety of mentor programs or mentoring arrangements can serve the differing goals and needs of gifted youth, each having its own inherent advantages and disadvantages. Mentor programs within a school setting tend to be more formal in nature and are established to meet the needs of larger numbers of gifted students. They necessitate an infrastructure that can be costly in terms of the time and resources necessary to set up and maintain. In contrast, individual mentoring arrangements can be implemented as the need arises and hence are easier to tailor to an individual's needs at a given time.

Double mentoring (two persons simultaneously acting as mentors) is an option for gifted youth requiring both cognitive and affective support beyond what a single mentor is able to provide (Clasen & Hanson, 1987). Sometimes this involves a discipline mentor who provides expertise in the area of interest and a coordinator/teacher mentor who organizes details of the mentoring relationship, supplementing the relationship as necessary with added affective support for the student and training in communication or library research skills (Clasen & Hanson, 1987). Similarly, multiple mentors (a succession of different mentors) may be necessary to ensure that talented youth encounter appropriate mentors well equipped to cultivate the current foci and levels of performance at each stage in the development of their talents. As capacities increase or alter, it may be necessary to change mentors to ensure continued challenge and growth (Simonton, 2000). Multiple mentors also may enrich the mentoring experience for the gifted learner by providing advice from several perspectives. An additional advantage of multiple mentors may be a greater willingness to offer services if the time and energy required can be spread among several mentors. This may be an especially important consideration for mentors in high demand because of their relative scarcity, such as may be the case for mentors from traditionally underserved populations: females in male-dominated specialties, ethnic minorities, or low socioeconomic status backgrounds (Schwiebert, 2000). Multiple mentoring and double mentoring have the possible disadvantage that the intense, complex personal relationship thought to be a major a conduit of the benefits such relationships provide may be less likely to develop.

Other configurations of the mentoring relationships for gifted youth include peer or step-ahead mentoring based upon the principle that mentoring fosters growth in areas of interest in both members of the dyad, enabling each to benefit from the mentoring relationship (Chan, 2000). This form of mentoring may be particularly significant for gifted students because they often have difficulty finding intellectual peers among age peers. Intellectual peers sharing similar challenges, interests, and motivations not necessarily shared by chronological peers may provide for greater acceptance of the reality of being "different." Shared experiences may be conducive to the formation of "empathic bonding," a factor hypothesized to be an important element in mentoring effectiveness in models such as the one proposed by Rhodes (2002). In this configuration, the mentor shares the same background as the gifted student and thus assumes a position with which the protégé can immediately identify. Such mentoring arrangements need to be set within frameworks that include explicit expectations for behavior, carefully monitored to ensure mentors receive supervision and guide the protégé responsibly (Wright & Borland, 1992).

Innovative types of mentor programs or arrangements available to gifted students have evolved due to technological advances, including e-mentoring, in which mentor and youth communication occurs via e-mail, exchanges of sound or image files, or even video conferencing (see Miller & Griffiths, this volume). Because of difficulties in matching the level of sophistication and interests of the gifted student with suitable adults in the community, particularly in rural areas, e-mentoring for gifted learners enlarges and diversifies the pool of potential mentor beyond those in geographic proximity (Bisland, 2001; Chan, 2000). Theoretically, this service delivery mode may be particularly useful in the early, exploratory stages of mentoring, when gifted students may benefit from exposure to diverse mentors (Bloom, 1985). However, without direct face-to-face interaction, e-mentoring is limited in extent and depth of personal relationships that may develop.

Selection for Participation in Mentoring Programs

In most mentoring programs, selection and matching of mentors and protégés is carried out by program staff, generally on the basis of shared interest in a particular discipline or occupation. Although details on matching mentors with protégés are left unspecified in much of the literature on mentoring for gifted students, due to their unique needs, it may be particularly important to match members of the dyad not only in terms of interests and abilities but also in terms of learning styles (Chan, 2000), similar attitudes, values, cognitive styles, and lifestyles (Pleiss & Feldhusen, 1995; Shandley, 1989; Zorman, 1993). Whether a student is self-selecting or is referred by teachers or parents, it is important to identify the student's specific needs and to ascertain whether a student really wants or will profit from a mentor (Berger, 1990).

Mentor Training and Guidance

Given the intensely personal nature of the empathic bond that theoretically may develop between the mentor and the protégé (see "Theory"), initial training for potential mentors may be critical—especially in the unique characteristics of gifted youth. Furthermore, ongoing guidance and support can help the mentor understand and respond appropriately to the unique and varying needs of highly vulnerable, gifted youth. Guidance can help the mentor maintain focus on supporting the gifted youth's progress toward attaining the highest possible level of expertise. Such progress may even require that the student change mentors. Support may also be needed to help mentors avoid imposing their own ambitions inappropriately upon the young, gifted protégés (Simonton, 2000). This may be particularly important in cross-gender matches involving gifted female protégés. In these cases, it may be particularly important that mentors be made aware of the initial power imbalance inherent in these relationships so that they can move toward equity, to avoid perpetuating the stereotype of women as dependent and powerless (Hollinger, 1991).

Evaluation of Mentor Relationships

Formative and summative evaluation is especially important in programs for mentoring of gifted and talented youth. Vygotsky (1934/1987) theorized that instruction be directed not so much toward already mature functions and skills of the learner, but more toward maturing functions—the zone of proximal development.

Because change and cognitive development may be rapid in the gifted population, formative and summative evaluation can be critical to ensure mentoring activities actually address areas of cognitive, affective, and social development in appropriately challenging ways. Formative evaluation provides a "reading" of the youth's progress to date, which can then be used to inform subsequent mentoring activities. As a specific example, Chan (2000) described a program that includes three evaluation components. Two are formative: (a) ongoing reflective journals kept by both the mentor and the protégé and (b) ongoing feedback from teachers, parents, and the program coordinator. A third, more formal and summative evaluation uses standardized measures focusing on areas of academic performance, motivations and attitudes toward school, self-esteem, and confidence. Summative evaluation should assist in overall design and program improvement.

Planning for and Monitoring Transitions and Terminations

Highly developed emotional sensitivities and ability of gifted youth may lead to a tendency to form especially strong empathic bonds with mentors and can make transitions to new mentors and/or terminations of mentoring arrangements especially challenging. Formal, school-based mentor relationships tend to be restricted to a set length of time and to be marked by some form of celebration at the end of the program. In these cases, termination of the mentoring relationship is often less problematic, as its closure is a foregone conclusion. In more intense mentoring relationships often extending for much longer periods of time, however, the termination process can be much more complicated and may warrant special consideration and sensitivity. As a result, coordinators can play a vital role during this transition period by providing guidance to all concerned: heightening awareness to the ambivalence of ending a deep, interpersonal relationship. Some experts have noted that termination of a mentoring arrangement may even entail a period of mourning and a sense of loss (e.g., Bisland, 2001; Grybek, 1997; Levinson, 1978; Torrance, 1984).

FUTURE DIRECTIONS

Synthesis

Mentors have served gifted individuals as long as anyone has tracked the development of talent. Theoretically, advanced ability and intense commitment to the discipline or performance area suggest a need for exposure to adults with similar talent and dedication to the same field and for opportunities to observe and absorb the ways professionals behave in the discipline. Research addressing the effectiveness of these arrangements is severely limited both in scope and in quality. Available data suggest only very tentative conclusions about the effects of mentoring relationships and programs for gifted and talented youth, or how and under what conditions successful mentorships evolve. Consequently, although numerous potential practices can be outlined that are theoretically consistent with the needs of this population, their implications for program effectiveness and youth outcomes are unknown. With these caveats in mind, several directions can be highlighted as priorities for future research and practice relating to the mentoring of gifted and talented youth.

Recommendations for Research

1. *Conduct carefully designed experimental interventions with populations of gifted youth that are clearly defined and documented.* Within the experimental designs, researchers should examine the effects of differing mentor relationship goals and interventions and differing types and lengths of mentorships across varying cognitive levels, talents, developmental stages, and social and emotional characteristics of gifted youth. Such experimental designs should allow for comparisons among those groups and for the investigation of the influences of matching mentor to protégé on the basis of gender, ethnicity, socioeconomic status, interests, learning styles, and personality type.

2. *Construct and validate measures of mentoring relationship processes and outcomes for the gifted youth.* Relying on survey reports of satisfaction as measures of the success of the processes in mentoring relationships for gifted

and talented youth is not sufficient. Rather, carefully developed self-esteem measures examining the full range of possible dimensions, such as emotional and social adjustment and self-perception, would provide more meaningful data. Furthermore, available cognitive outcome measures of achievement designed for the average population may be inadequate for gifted youth due to ceiling effects. It is important to consider other outcome measures, such as enrollment in advanced-placement courses or college courses, production of advanced-level products or engagement in advanced-level performance, heightened career awareness and goals, improved sense of self-efficacy, or other measures based on the stated outcome goals and population served.

3. *Investigate effects of mentoring relationships and programs for specific populations of gifted youth.* Because there are now more minorities and women in professional roles, for example, experimental research programs should capitalize on this development and study the effects of gender and racial matching.

4. *Base future research on a sound theoretical model.* All of the aforementioned recommendations are limited in effectiveness unless researchers identify or develop a viable model for studying the mentoring of gifted youth. Creation of the most informative experimental study will evolve from the testing of models, whether they are developed for the general population (e.g., that of Rhodes) or built on the specific characteristics of gifted youth, such models would greatly enhance the development of effective research programs.

Recommendations for Practice

1. *Build a program around strong leadership and qualified mentors who understand the unique needs of gifted and talented youth.* Provide training in interpersonal skills as necessary to ensure that mentors are empathic to and informed about the unique developmental challenges of gifted youth. Particularly in the case of highly gifted youth, the mentor may profit from strategies to avoid feeling personally threatened by the young person's burgeoning talent. A strong mentorship coordinator can provide

orientation, training, guidance, and support for participants, with a formative and summative evaluation integral to the continued development of the program.

2. *Build flexibility into programs.* Mentor relationships should be dynamic, allowing for latitude and flexibility. The length of the relationship, frequency of meeting, and roles that the mentor and protégé play are examples of program elements to be determined based on the unique cognitive abilities, social, and affective needs of individual gifted youth. If possible, time and space dimensions of mentor relationships should be left open-ended so that the relationship can become established and mature naturally. The use of multiple mentors should be considered, particularly in the case of prodigious youth whose range of needs are unlikely to be met by one individual alone. Journaling by both mentor and protégé may provide a valuable source of formative evidence used to make adjustments to the mentoring arrangements.

3. *Encourage natural or quasi-natural (self-selected) mentoring pairs.* Protégés should be allowed to self-select into mentoring programs and collaborate in the selection of their mentors. An integral part of development is the gradual increase in the amount of direction a gifted learner exercises over career choices and pathways. One way a mentoring program may assist is by providing increasing autonomy in selecting mentors. Another important strategy to forge effective mentoring relationships may be to employ a wide range of matching criteria. Similarity among attributes such as approaches to problem solving, values, cognitive styles, and attitudes may be more suitable criteria, particularly among gifted youth, than other more traditionally used factors, such as ethnicity and gender.

4. *Plan the end of mentoring relationships carefully.* Many gifted youth are highly emotionally astute in nature, an attribute that may lead some to form especially deep empathic bonds with their mentors. For this reason, it may be particularly important for this population to plan for the end of the mentoring relationship carefully and to anticipate a celebratory reaction

to the progress made—but also possibly, a sense of loss as a result of leaving behind a cherished relationship.

REFERENCES

Achor, S., & Morales, A. (1990). Chicanas holding doctoral degrees: Social reproduction and cultural ecological approaches. *Anthropology & Education Quarterly, 21,* 269–287.

Arellano, A. R., & Padilla, A. M. (1996). Academic invulnerability among a select group of Latino university students. *Hispanic Journal of Behavioral Sciences, 18,* 485–508.

Arnold, K. D. (1995). *Lives of promise.* San Francisco: Jossey-Bass.

Arnold, K. D., & Subotnik, R. F. (1995). Mentoring the gifted: A differentiated model. *Educational Horizons, 73*(3), 118–123.

Batten, J., & Rogers, J. (1993). Response to "Mentoring: Extending learning for gifted students." In C. J. Maker (Ed.), *Critical issues in gifted education: Programs for the gifted in regular classrooms* (pp. 331–341). Austin, TX: PRO-ED.

Beck, L. (1989). Mentorships: Benefits and effects on career development. *Gifted Child Quarterly, 33*(1), 22–28.

Berger, S. L. (1990). *Mentor relationships and gifted learners.* Reston, VA: Council for Exceptional Children. (ERIC Document Reproduction Service No. ED321491)

Bisland, A. (2001). Mentoring: An educational Alternative for gifted students. *Gifted Child Today, 24*(4), 22–25, 64–65.

Bloom, B. S. (Ed.). (1985). *Developing talent in young people.* New York: Ballantine Books.

Boston, B. O. (1976). *The sorcerer's apprentice: A case study in the role of the mentor.* Reston, VA: Council for Exceptional Children. (ERIC Document Reproduction Service No. ED126671)

Burns, D. E., & Reis, S. M. (1991). Developing a thinking skills component in the gifted education program. *Roeper Review, 14,* 72–79.

Chan, D. W. (2000). The development of mentorship programs at the Chinese University of Hong Kong. *Roeper Review, 23,* 85–88.

Clasen, D. R., & Hanson, M. (1987). Double mentoring: A process for facilitating mentorships for gifted students. *Roeper Review, 10,* 107–110.

Cole, M., & Cole, S. R. (1996). *The development of children.* New York: W. H. Freeman.

Cross, T. (1998). Working on behalf of gifted students. *Gifted Child Today, 21*(3), 21–22.

Daloz, L. A. (1986). *Effective teaching and mentoring.* San Francisco: Jossey-Bass.

Davalos, R. A., & Haensly, P. A. (1997). After the dust has settled: Youth reflect on their high school mentored research experience. *Roeper Review, 19,* 204–207.

Eccles, J. S., Midgley, C., Wigfield, A., Buchanan, C. M., Reuman, D., Flanagan, C., et al. (1993). Development during adolescence: The impact of stage-environment fit on young adolescents' experiences in schools and in families. *American Psychologist, 48,* 90–101.

Edlind, E. P., & Haensly, P. A. (1985). Gifts of mentorships. *Gifted Child Quarterly, 29,* 55–60.

Ellingson, M. K., Haeger, W. W., & Feldhusen, J. F. (1986). The Purdue mentor program. *Gifted Child Today, 9*(2), 2–5.

Feldman, D. H. (1979). The mysterious case of extreme giftedness. In A. H. Passow (Ed.), *The gifted and talented: Their education and development: The seventy-eighth yearbook of the National Society for the Study of Education* (pp. 335–351). Chicago: University of Chicago Press.

Feldman, D. H. (1991). *Nature's gambit: Child prodigies and the development of human potential.* New York: Teachers College Press.

Ford, D. Y., & Harris, J. J. (1999). *Multicultural gifted education.* New York: Teachers College Press.

Fordham, S., & Ogbu, J. U. (1986). Black students' school success: Coping with the "burden of 'acting White.'" *The Urban Review, 18*(3), 176–206.

Gardner, H. (1993). *Creating minds.* New York: Basic Books.

Goertzel, M., Goertzel, V., & Goertzel, T. (1978). *300 eminent personalities.* San Francisco: Jossey-Bass.

Gray, M. M., & Gray, W. A. (1988). Mentor-assisted enrichment projects: A proven way of carrying out Type III triad projects and of promoting higher-level thinking in GTC student-protégés. In M. M. Gray & W. A. Gray (Eds.), *Proceedings of the First International Mentoring Conference* (Vol. 1, pp. 1–8). Vancouver, BC: International Association for Mentoring.

Gray, W. A. (1983). *Challenging the gifted and talented through mentor-assisted enrichment projects* (Fastback No. 189). Bloomington, IN: Phi Delta Kappa Educational Foundation.

Grybek, D. D. (1997). Mentoring the gifted and talented. *Preventing School Failure, 41,* 115–118.

Hébert, T. P., & Olenchak, F. R. (2000). Mentors for gifted underachieving males: Developing potential and realizing promise. *Gifted Child Quarterly, 44*(3), 196–207.

Hollinger, C. L. (1991). Career choices for gifted adolescents: Overcoming stereotypes. In M. Bireley & J. Genshaft (Ed.), *Understanding the gifted adolescent—educational, developmental, and multicultural issues* (pp. 201–214). New York: Teachers College Press.

Kaufmann, F. A., Harrel, G., Milam, C. P., Woolverton, N., & Miller, J. (1986). The nature, role, and influence of mentors in the lives of gifted adults. *Journal of Counseling and Development, 64,* 576–578.

Kerr, B. A. (1991). Educating gifted girls. In N. Colangelo & G. A. Davis (Ed.), *Handbook of gifted education* (pp. 402–415). Boston: Allyn & Bacon.

Kerr, B. A. (1994). *Smart girls: A new psychology of girls, women and giftedness.* Scottsdale, AZ: Gifted Psychology Press.

Levinson, D. (1978). *The seasons of a man's life.* New York: Knopf.

Lupkowski, A. E., Assouline, S. G., & Stanley, J. C. (1990). Applying a mentor model for young mathematically talented students. *Gifted Child Today, 13*(2), 15–17.

Nash, W. R., Haensly, P. A., Rodgers, V. J. S., & Wright, N. L. (1993). Mentoring: Extending learning for gifted students. In C. J. Maker (Ed.), *Critical issues in gifted education: Programs for the gifted in regular classrooms* (Vol. 3, pp. 313–330). Austin, TX: PRO-ED.

Packard, B. W., & Nguyen, D. (2003). Science career-related possible selves of adolescent girls: A longitudinal study. *Journal of Career Development, 29,* 251–263.

Pleiss, M. K., & Feldhusen, J. F. (1995). Mentors, role models, and heroes in the lives of gifted children. *Educational Psychologist, 30,* 159–169.

Reilly, J. M., & Welch, D. B. (1994/1995). Mentoring gifted young women: A call to action. *Journal of Secondary Gifted Education, 6,* 120–128.

Renzulli, J. S., & Reis, S. N. (1985). *The schoolwide enrichment model: A comprehensive plan for educational excellence.* Mansfield Center, CT: Creative Learning Press.

Rhodes, J. B. (2002). *Stand by me: The risks and rewards of mentoring today's youth.* Cambridge, MA: Harvard University Press.

Rodriguez, R. (1986). Effects of two counseling approaches on institutional integration and persistence of high risk college students (Doctoral dissertation, Fordham Graduate School of Education, 1986). *Dissertation Abstracts International-A, 47/05,* 1625.

Rogoff, B. (2003). *The cultural nature of human development.* Oxford, UK: Oxford University Press.

Schwiebert, V. L. (2000). *Mentoring: Creating connected, empowered relationships.* Alexandria, VA: American Counseling Association.

Schwiebert, V. L., Deck, M. D., Bradshaw, M. L., Scott, P., & Harper, M. (1999). Women as mentors. *Journal of Humanistic Counseling, Education and Development, 37,* 241–252.

Shandley, T. C. (1989). The use of mentors for leadership development. *NASPA Journal, 27*(1), 59–66.

Shaughnessy, M. F., & Neely, R. (1991). Mentoring gifted children and prodigies: Personological concerns. *Gifted Education International, 7,* 129–132.

Shore, B. M., Cornell, D. G., Robinson, A., & Ward, V. S. (1991). *Recommended practices in gifted education: A critical analysis.* New York: Teachers College Press.

Simonton, D. K. (2000). Genius and giftedness: Same or different? In K. A. Heller, F. J. Mönks, R. J. Sternberg, & R. F. Subotnik (Ed.), *International handbook of giftedness and talent* (pp. 111–122). Amsterdam: Elsevier.

Timpson, W. M., & Jones, C. (1989). The naïve expert and the gifted child. *Gifted Child Today, 12*(1), 22–23.

Torrance, E. P. (1984). *Mentor relationships: How they aid creative achievement, endure, change, and die.* Buffalo, NY: Bearly.

U.S. Department of Health, Education and Welfare. (1972). *Education of the gifted and talented.* Washington, DC: Author.

Vygotsky, L. S. (1934/1987). The development of scientific concepts in childhood. In R. W. Rieber & A. S. Carton (Eds.), *Problems of general psychology: Vol. 1. Collected works of L. S. Vygotsky* (pp. 167–241). New York: Plenum Press.

Wright, L., & Borland, J. H. (1992). A special friend: Adolescent mentors for young economically disadvantaged, potentially gifted students. *Roeper Review, 14,* 124–129.

Zorman, R. (1993). Mentoring and role modeling programs for the gifted. In K. A. Heller, F. J. Mönks, & A. H. Passow (Ed.), *International handbook of research and development of giftedness and talent* (pp. 727–741). Oxford, UK: Pergamon Press.

29

ACADEMICALLY AT-RISK STUDENTS

SIMON LAROSE AND GEORGE M. TARABULSY

INTRODUCTION

A mentoring relationship typically is defined as a sustained relationship between an individual with experience (the mentor) and an individual with less experience (the protégé) in which the mentor provides the protégé with different types of support. Such relationships recently have been proposed as a key element in the development of preventive intervention strategies devoted to academically at-risk students (AARS). Since the inception of the well-known, community-based Big Brothers Big Sisters (BBBS) program in 1904, many formal mentoring programs have been developed to address the needs of socially and emotionally at-risk populations. More recently, mentoring programs have been implemented in North American schools to better reach the AARS population. In such programs, AARS typically are paired with volunteer teachers, older students, or adults from the community who, while not necessarily part of the student's school, have knowledge of the school structure and system. Mentors and AARS engage mainly in academic activities (e.g., doing homework) for approximately 1 hour every week for less than

1 year (Herrera, Sipe, & McClanahan, 2000). The growing interest of school administrations and teachers for mentoring AARS has often pushed researchers to study mentoring processes and effectiveness within school contexts. However, it is important to underline at the outset of this chapter that successful mentoring of AARS need not be exclusively limited to programs based in the school setting.

The relevance of extending mentoring to the AARS population is based on the assumption that AARS and mentors may establish significant relationships that have the potential to (a) improve cognitive and socioemotional development, (b) enhance AARS school behaviors, and (c) prevent school maladjustment, failure, and dropout among AARS. In this chapter, we discuss this assumption with respect to contemporary theory and research on mentoring among AARS. We begin by making a critical review of the available theoretical frameworks on youth mentoring and discuss their relevance and applicability. An explanatory model that is based on sociomotivational theory (Connell & Wellborn, 1991) is described, as are practical applications of this model. We then review the

This chapter was supported by grants from Fonds Québecois de la Recherche sur la Société et la Culture and from the Social Humanities Research Council to the first author.

empirical literature on mentoring of AARS. In the third section, practices specific to mentoring AARS are discussed in the context of available theory and research. We conclude by raising important questions that require consideration in future intervention and research. We begin by describing the salient characteristics of AARS.

AARS are defined in this chapter as youth who have already experienced failure or poor grades for a significant portion of their academic histories. Students with poor grades in a given school level (e.g., high school) but that are sufficient to give them access to higher levels of schooling (e.g., college) also may be considered in this group because of their risk for failure in their future studies. Although gifted students sometimes are qualified as academically at risk, they are not included in our definition (for a discussion of mentoring gifted students, see Callahan & Kyburg, this volume). Of course, students can be academically at risk for several reasons: developmental problems, such as cognitive delays, attention deficit and hyperactivity disorders, aggressiveness, and nonnormative developmental circumstances such as parental abuse and negligence, adolescent parenthood, and chronic poverty. In this chapter, however, we focus on students considered to be at high risk academically but who are not characterized by chronic individual problems and who are not exposed to contexts that may be considered to put them at high psychosocial risk (given the high proportion of separation and divorce in the population, single parenthood will be considered as a normative context in this chapter). Therefore, the group of students that we refer to is somewhat distinct from those examined in the other chapters of this section of the *Handbook* and can be distinguished mainly on the basis of academic concerns.

An understanding of the AARS population requires a solid knowledge of the cognitive, emotional, and behavioral correlates of failure or low academic achievement. These specific characteristics often are the target of mentoring intervention for such students. Characteristics of AARS that may form the foci of the mentoring process include the following:

1. Low levels of perceived school competence and erroneous attributions and beliefs regarding the conditions required for school success (Harter, 1999)

2. Negative representations of school in general and of teachers in particular (Pianta, Stuhlman, & Hamre, 2002)

3. Extrinsic motivation in relation to school, as well as external attributions for both school- and career-based decisions (Deci & Ryan, 1985)

4. Lack of interest in school-based and extracurricular activities in general (Tinto, 1993)

5. Difficulty seeking help from teachers and peers when exposed to failure (Richman, Rosenfeld, & Bowen, 1998)

6. Problems with time management, attention in class, and preparation for examinations (Larose & Roy, 1995)

7. Poor coping skills with respect to school expectations and transitions (Eccles & Midgley, 1989)

Mentoring intended for AARS must account for these student characteristics. Moreover, as will be described in the following section, changes in these characteristics should constitute the major mechanisms by which palpable effects of mentoring relationships are detected, whether mentoring programs are conducted in an institutional setting (e.g., school) or a community-based setting.

THEORY

One of the gaps in the mentoring literature that limits our understanding of mentoring processes, outcomes, and intervention among the AARS population is the absence of theoretical models that help integrate empirical findings and transfer these findings to mentoring practices. To our knowledge, only two models of mentoring have been proposed, neither of which was developed specifically for the AARS population. We first review these models with relevance to their implications for mentoring of AARS. Then, we present a theoretical model of mentoring specific to the AARS population.

General Models

The first model (Parra, DuBois, Neville, Pugh-Lilly, & Povinelli, 2002) focuses on interpersonal mechanisms (relationship experiences and relationship closeness) and mentor characteristics (e.g., mentor efficacy beliefs and mentor training) in accounting for the perceived benefits of mentoring. This model suggests that initial mentor training combined with certain sociodemographic characteristics of mentors and protégés (e.g., age, gender, ethnic origin) exert an impact on mentors' beliefs as to their ability to establish helpful mentoring relationships. These personal beliefs about a mentor's efficacy are viewed as predicting the frequency and quality of meetings with mentoring protégés, which are in themselves linked to protégés' perceptions of the benefits of the mentoring relationship. The model also stipulates that the effect of mentor-protégé meetings on perceived benefits are mediated by various indicators of the quality of the mentoring experience for youth as well as by relationship closeness. Thus, more frequent and regular mentor-protégé meetings facilitate the development of more positive and significant mentoring relationships. These relationships, in turn, lead to more positive impressions of the helpfulness of the mentoring relationship on the part of the protégé and mentor, as well as to greater relationship longevity.

This model presents several positive characteristics. First, it proposes that an important relational process operates in the development of beliefs of mentors and youth regarding the benefits of mentoring relationships in which they are involved. Second, the model proposes specific characteristics and experiences of mentors that help them to be more effective (training/support and mentor efficacy beliefs). Finally, the model has been subjected to empirical validation (Parra et al., 2002).

Despite these positive elements, the model nevertheless is perceived as presenting several limitations with respect to informing and understanding conditions that might account or influence the effectiveness of mentoring relationships for AARS. First, the model is relatively silent regarding the characteristics of the AARS that help make the mentoring relationship more effective. No mention is made of the moderating impact of previous relational and academic experiences, attachment style, and attitudes about social support or the need for mentoring. Moreover, the model makes no predictions concerning possible changes in cognitive, emotional, or behavioral characteristics of the AARS likely to be influenced by the mentoring process. Second, the model makes very little reference to the specific actions and behaviors of the mentor perceived as being effective in the mentoring process. Beyond the mentor's efficacy beliefs, what are the specific behaviors that mentors should manifest in the course of their mentoring relationships with the AARS? How might such behaviors be associated with the development of AARS? Finally, it may be pertinent to add that an effective mentoring model for AARS should be able to make specific, targeted predictions regarding changes in academic behavior and achievement and not constrain outcomes to the protégé's perceptions of the usefulness of the mentoring relationship. In all likelihood, there may be many students who perceive the relationship as helpful but who, nevertheless, remain academically at risk.

A second model (Rhodes, 2002; see also Rhodes, this volume) emphasizes the role of mutuality, trust, and empathy as the main ingredients of effective mentoring relationships for youth. It stipulates that these relational dimensions affect youth adjustment outcomes through three processes: social-emotional development, cognitive development, and role modeling and identification. This model also proposes a mediating role of improved close relationships. Specifically, it is suggested that the effects of the mentoring relationship on the protégé's personal development positively influence other relationships (e.g., with parents, peers, teachers) that have a reciprocal, positive effect on the mentoring relationship. In addition, this model emphasizes the moderating role of personal, interpersonal and ecological factors. The effectiveness of the mentoring relationship is considered to be dependent on the socioemotional history of both the mentor and the protégé, their social competence, the duration of the mentoring relationship and the time at which the effectiveness of the relationship is evaluated, and ecological factors such as the age and gender of the protégé and the quality of parent-protégé relationships.

This model provides an important set of guidelines about the pathways of mentoring influence and the conditions under which mentoring could optimally affects AARS adjustment. Contrary to the model presented by Parra et al. (2002), the model is quite explicit about the processes of change and the kinds of changes expected in the behavior of the youth involved in a mentoring relationship, as well as the potential impact of the youth on the quality of the mentoring relationship. However, similarly to Parra's model, Rhodes's model is relatively silent regarding the actions and behaviors of mentors that are believed to underlie positive change in AARS behavior. This criticism is not specific to the models proposed by either Parra and colleagues or by Rhodes, but rather characterizes much of the research on mentoring relationships in which much emphasis for mentoring outcomes is placed on the "bond" that develops between the mentor and the student. In this regard, the results of some studies have suggested that mentoring AARS is not necessarily less effective when mentors do not maintain strong positive emotional bonds with youth (Darling, Hamilton, & Niego, 1994; DuBois, Holloway, Valentine, & Cooper, 2002). If mentoring is structured and centered on the acquisition of concrete skills that AARS want, the affective quality of the relationships with mentors may be less critical than the instrumental function. In this perspective, it is necessary for models of the effectiveness of mentoring relationships for AARS to consider the positive behaviors and concrete actions taken by mentors that lead to positive student outcomes, and not to view successful mentoring as being driven solely by the bonding that takes place in the mentoring relationship.

A second limitation that we perceive in Rhodes's (2002) model vis-à-vis its use with AARS is that little is said regarding the role of schools on the effectiveness of mentoring relationships. This limitation can be explained in that the model was developed to serve as a guide for studies of community-based mentoring relationships (e.g., BBBS), where specific contexts may vary widely and may not necessarily be intended for the specific challenges of AARS.

An important index of the effectiveness of mentoring for AARS lies in its ability to modify or take into account the school characteristics in such a way as to favor student interest, motivation, self-esteem, and success, not solely the quality of the mentoring relationship. Theoretically, mentoring programs for AARS often may be unsuccessful because of (a) volunteer mentors presenting personal values opposite to those of the mentoring approach, (b) the relative absence of male mentors (a possible difficulty in the context of the overrepresentation of male students experiencing academic difficulties), or (c) a lack of recognition of mentoring initiatives by the school setting or a lack of infrastructure support (Herrera et al., 2000). Mentoring programs, whether they take place in a school- or community-based context, should not function in isolation of other school-based resources. Program and school administrators, mentors, teachers, student associations, and any other social agents involved in the implementation of mentoring programs all have roles to play in elaborating, establishing, and maintaining mentoring programs (for further discussion, see Portwood & Ayers, this volume). In the following section, we propose a new model inspired by a sociomotivational perspective of academic success (Connell & Wellborn, 1991) in an attempt to address some of the difficulties mentioned above.

Sociomotivational Model of Mentoring

The model we propose is illustrated in Figure 29.1. It identifies feelings of competence, relatedness, and autonomy that emerge through mentoring as the main mediators of change for AARS. According to this model, the degree to which a mentoring intervention positively impacts school adjustment and academic achievement of AARS depends on improvements in feelings of competence, relatedness, and autonomy in connection with the mentor. Feelings of *competence* may be defined as positive beliefs and expectations regarding the ability of AARS to reach academic objectives. Feelings of *relatedness* include the development of a secure attachment between the AARS and the mentor that can help establish supportive relationships with school members (teachers and peers).

Characteristics of
Mentoring
Interventions

Students' Cognitive
and Emotional
Processes

Students'
School Behavior
Processes

Academic
Outcomes

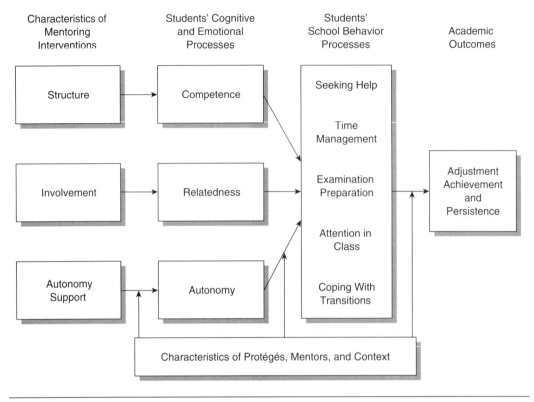

Figure 29.1   The Mentoring Sociomotivational Model

Feelings of *autonomy* include AARS intrinsic motivation regarding personal and academic choices. From the sociomotivational perspective (Connell & Wellborn, 1991), these three categories of feelings (competence, relatedness, autonomy) influence school adjustment and academic achievement through their relation to school behaviors. As such, they are considered as proximal mediators of mentoring relationships, whereas school behaviors (e.g., learning skills) are viewed as distal mediators.

Changes in these three types of feelings are effected directly through interactions between the mentor and the AARS. According to the model, three aspects of the mentor behavior that are critical in the development and consolidation of these feelings are structure, involvement, and autonomy support. *Structure* concerns the extent to which mentors provide the guidance and information necessary for the AARS to be internally motivated. This includes clearly stating expectations the mentor has for the AARS and the importance of these expectations, as

well as the consequences of meeting versus not meeting these expectations.

Involvement refers to the mentor's provision of emotional resources to the AARS. Involvement can take on various forms, such as spending enough time with the AARS, being interested in and attentive to the AARS, being helpful in the regulation of certain negative emotions (especially those related to stressful, academic circumstances), being helpful in changing certain negative representations of the school environment (e.g., perceptions of teacher support), and helping the AARS to mobilize support resources when in need (parents, teachers, peers, etc.). To show such involvement, it is assumed that mentors must be intrinsically motivated, perceive themselves as being competent in their role as a mentor, and possess sufficient counseling experience, ability, or both.

Autonomy support in the model can be defined as the affirmation of the AARS as a unique, active, and volitional individual by the mentor. It entails acknowledgment of the perspective and feelings of AARS, encouragement toward independent thinking and problem solving, and the provision of opportunities to make choices and hold age-appropriate responsibilities.

The sociomotivational model we propose stipulates that the presence of structure, involvement, and autonomy support is also important at the program and institutional levels. Clear, functional guidelines between the different levels of mentoring administration (structure), institutional valuing of mentoring programs (involvement), and the place given to personal decision making at different levels (autonomy support) are all viewed as dimensions of the overall context that are favorable for the successful mentoring of AARS.

Finally, within the sociomotivational model, it is postulated that the challenge of attaining mentoring objectives may vary as a function of AARS, mentor, or contextual characteristics. For example, the level of risk to which students are exposed to, the difficulty for AARS to seek help from others, the values and efficacy beliefs of mentors, and the financial support provided by schools or other sources of funding (government, churches, community organizations) to mentoring programs all may be linked to the effectiveness of mentoring programs, specifically the program's ability to affect cognitions, emotions, and behaviors of AARS and, indirectly, their adaptation, academic achievement, and perseverance.

We believe this model also may serve as a framework for understanding the development of natural mentoring relationships that may develop between AARS and members of the school setting, such as teachers. For example, according to this model, teachers who are secure and able to engage in emotional relationships (involvement), who establish clear rules and who provide clear contingencies in their interpersonal relations (structure), and who encourage students' perspectives and points of view (autonomy support) will more naturally become informal mentors with AARS.

RESEARCH

Theoretical models of mentoring, especially the sociomotivational model that we propose, raise a number of specific hypotheses concerning mechanisms of change by which AARS become less at risk. In the following section, we assess the empirical support for three important hypotheses that emerge from these models, as they have been addressed in the scientific literature.

Opportunities to Improve Cognitive and Emotional Development

The first major hypothesis stipulates that mentoring should lead to improved cognitive and socioemotional development for AARS. There have been a number of experimental, quasi-experimental, and correlational studies conducted among AARS that have shown that mentoring relationships (or perceived security in mentoring, as described in certain studies) can lead to significant changes in a number of cognitive and emotional outcome variables. Mentoring relationships improve attitudes toward school, academic confidence, self-concept, attitudes toward helping, feelings of school connectedness, representations of parental and teacher relationships, and perceptions of support from significant adults outside mentoring relationships (DuBois, Neville, Parra, & Pugh-Lilly, 2002; Jekielek, Moore, & Hair, 2002; Karcher, 2005; Karcher, Davis, & Powell, 2002; Larose, Bernier, & Soucy, in press; Rhodes, Grossman, & Resch, 2000; Slicker & Palmer, 1993). However, very few researchers have tested whether these improvements mediate the impact of mentoring on school adjustment and academic achievement. This question is an important one because two out of three theoretical models (Rhodes, 2002; the sociomotivational model) presume that the impact of mentoring on adjustment and achievement is mediated by cognitive and emotional changes among AARS. Three studies constitute exceptions to this generalization. The first study showed that the effects of a mentoring relationship, within the context of a BBBS program, include an improvement in grades, a reduction in voluntary school absences (i.e., skipping school) that were mediated by improved parental representations, and perceived academic competence (Rhodes et al., 2000). The second study revealed a mediating effect for perceived connectedness to parents in the explanation of changes in spelling achievement by elementary school students who were mentored by high school students (Karcher et al., 2002). Finally, the third study showed that BBBS mentoring relationships buffer behavioral and emotional problems through their effects on perceptions of social support from significant adults outside mentoring relationships (DuBois, Neville, et al., 2002).

These three studies are helpful in understanding the basic processes by which mentoring relationships can have positive effects. However, two of these studies (Karcher et al., 2002; Rhodes et al., 2000) comprise only two data points where the assessment of the mediating variables was conducted at the same time as outcome variables. This design creates the possibility that it is the changes in outcome variables (school adjustment and academic adjustment) that exert an impact on the hypothesized mediator variables (academic competence and parental connectedness), rather than vice versa. In this situation, changes in the hypothesized mediating variables may, in effect, be rather distal effects of the mentoring process, rather than an actual mechanism by which the relationship exerts its impact. This limitation in design highlights the pertinence of assessing the impact of mentoring relationships in longitudinal designs composed of at least three data points and, ideally, four (preintervention, during the intervention, postintervention, follow-up), allowing for the assessment of potential mediators prior to that of outcome variables. This type of design would allow for a clearer distinction between mediator and outcome variables, as demonstrated in the study conducted by DuBois, Neville, et al. (2002), who addressed the mediating impact of perceived support from significant adults prior to documenting changes in emotional and behavioral problems.

Opportunities to Change and Learn New Behavioral Strategies

The second hypothesis derived from theory postulates that the mentoring process provides students with the opportunity to change and learn new behavioral strategies. The results of several studies indicate that mentoring relationships may have a significant impact on the school

behaviors of AARS. Using quasi-experimental or experimental designs, participation in mentoring relationships has been found to be linked to higher attendance in class (but not sufficient to neutralize academic risk), fewer voluntary absences from school, lower aggressiveness, greater levels of social competence, greater vocational skills, greater participation in college preparatory activities, and an overall greater likelihood of taking part in higher education (Barton-Arwood, Jolivette, & Massey, 2000; Grossman, 1998; Jekielek et al., 2002; Soucy & Larose, 2000; Tierney, Grossman, & Resch, 1995). Correlational studies further reveal that perceived security to mentors and mentor attendance to the programs were found to be associated to greater rule compliance (as opposed to acting out) and ability to complete schoolwork (Karcher, 2005; Soucy & Larose, 2000).

Despite these results, however, we have not been able to find any studies that have tested for the role of school behaviors in mediating the impact of mentoring relationships on the school adjustment and academic achievement of AARS. Moreover, few studies have assessed students' behaviors with external observations, revealing an important limitation to many assessments of impact reported in the mentoring literature. Within the current state of knowledge on mentoring relationships, it is possible to affirm that mentoring relationships may affect the perceptions and representations of AARS and that some of these cognitive and emotional factors may mediate the impact of mentoring on school adjustment and academic achievement. However, because the assessments of these later outcome variables often are a result of the self-reports of the AARS themselves, subject to their perceptions and biases, it is possible that these changes reflect subjective, personal assessments, rather than actual behavioral changes. This difficulty is all the more important because several studies have failed to show positive effects for mentoring relationships on school achievement when this latter is based on institutional criteria (Jekielek et al., 2002). It is therefore critical for evaluations of mentoring programs of AARS to include external behavioral assessments in the pre- and posttest data points, as well as at follow-up. As proposed in the model described previously, behaviors such as seeking help from teachers and peers when academic problems occur, asking questions and showing high attention in class, exam preparation, time management, and coping with transition all may serve to mediate the influence of mentoring on academic adjustment and achievement for AARS.

It is also pertinent to underscore that different mechanisms may be operating in mentoring relationships for AARS as a function of mentor and student age, gender, and ethnic origin, as well as the status of mentors (community adult, teacher, peer), the type of mentoring (one-on-one vs. group), and the contexts of mentoring. For example, Herrera and colleagues (2000) have established that volunteer adult mentors in community-based programs have more contact with parents, while mentors in school-based programs have more contact with teachers. Consequently, it is possible that changes in the representations of relationships with teachers, rather than relationships with parents, play a more important role in explaining the impact of school-based programs on the academic situation of AARS.

Other differences may emerge as a function of the kind of program in which AARS are involved. It is conceivable, and perhaps likely, that increased help-seeking from peers to solve academic problems may operate mostly within peer mentoring programs, whereas increased help-seeking from teachers may be the major behavioral change when AARS are paired with teachers or when mentors have considerable contact with their protégés' teachers. Thus, the study of influential processes within mentoring programs for AARS and an understanding of the mediating factors that are involved must necessarily be viewed of as a function of the objectives and methods unique to each specific program.

A final comment is necessary prior to considering the third hypothesis of mentoring programs. Rhodes's model stipulates that mentoring relationships improve relationships with parents, peers, and other significant adults such as teachers. This hypothesis, however, has not been rigorously examined. Some studies have examined the impact of mentoring on outcomes such as relationships with parents (Rhodes et al., 2000), support network of friends (Fishman,

Stelk, & Clark, 1997), and relationships with teachers (Larose et al., in press), but always through the use of self-reports completed by the students. As a result, we do not have truly reliable evidence that mentoring brings about objective changes in the relationships between AARS and the significant agents in their environment. We consider this relative lack of knowledge to be an important weakness in the study of mentoring programs for AARS.

Optimal Context for Mentoring

The third hypothesis derived from sociomotivational and Rhodes's theories described previously stipules that the effects of mentoring on AARS personal and academic development are modulated by both internal and external factors. Special attention has been paid in research to the characteristics of the AARS targeted by specific programs (e.g., level and kind of risk), the characteristics of the mentors (e.g., perceived self-efficacy), and characteristics of the context (e.g., monitoring of mentoring activities) that may potentially moderate the impact of the mentoring relationship for AARS.

With respect to the characteristics of the students targeted by mentoring programs, DuBois, Holloway, and colleagues (2002) have found stronger effects for mentoring when AARS had more favorable life circumstances and better social and psychological functioning at the onset. Other studies paint a similar picture. Among academically at-risk college students, those who show secure attachment relationships to their parents are more likely to develop positive relationships with mentors at school and draw benefits from college mentoring programs than those who express less secure relationships (Larose et al., in press; Soucy & Larose, 2000). On the other hand, stronger impacts of mentoring were found for youth with initially low or moderate achievement levels compared with youth with initially high achievement levels (Grossman & Johnson, 2002), which might, however, reflect a ceiling effect.

With respect to the characteristics of mentors, DuBois, Holloway, and colleagues (2002) have reported evidence of more positive effects on AARS adjustment for programs when mentors have backgrounds in helping professions, such as teachers. Mentors' efficacy beliefs also were found to predict a greater number of mentor/youth meetings as well as more positive experiences in the relationship that, in turn, predict greater perceived benefits from mentoring (Parra et al., 2002). Mentors' motivations for self-enhancement (i.e., the degree to which the mentors were participating in order to grow personally and to have a positive, developmental experience) were found to predict mentors' perceptions of relationship quality above and beyond what was predicted by the student's academic and behavioral risk status, parental involvement, and program quality (Karcher, Nakkula, & Harris, in press). In addition, mentors' income and marital status were found to predict length of mentoring relationships with longer duration for matches involving nonmarried and higher-income mentors (Grossman & Rhodes, 2002). Finally, mentors having interests in common with their AARS protégés were seen as more efficient in establishing close relationships and in initiating significant intervention (Herrera et al., 2000). Otherwise, although mentoring programs devoted to AARS are more attractive for female mentors than for male mentors (Herrera et al., 2000), there is no evidence that mentor gender moderates the impact of intervention.

Other studies have indicated more positive effects for mentoring when the relational style of the mentor is opposite to that of the AARS (Bernier, Larose, & Soucy, 2005). In a longitudinal study on the role of mentoring on AARS adjustment to college, findings indicated that mentors who valued the bonding side of interpersonal relationships appeared to have greater success in improving the academic standing of AARS when the latter exhibited dismissing attachment representations, whereas mentors who placed greater value on the development of student autonomy appeared to have a greater impact when matched with AARS who showed insecure-preoccupied representations of attachment (Bernier et al., 2005). Such results suggest that mentors are more effective when they provide the AARS with a challenging relational stance that is not in line with that of the AARS.

DuBois and colleagues also have found, with respect to school-based programs, that a certain number of contextual characteristics may play a role in program effectiveness (DuBois, Holloway, & colleagues, 2002). These factors include ongoing, structured training for mentors, monitoring of the implementation of programs, and the involvement of parental involvement and support. It is conceivable that such factors may well cross over into community-based programs as moderating variables as well. In addition, it has been found that programs viewed as effective allow for more extended contact between mentors and AARS (i.e., more than 3 hours per month over 1 year), engage AARS in social and academic activities, provide mentors with significant pre-mentoring training in counseling, and structure interactions in such a way as to favor the development of AARS autonomy in decision making (Herrera et al., 2000).

PRACTICE

In this section, we examine certain practices that often are found in mentoring programs for AARS and critically address their potential effectiveness with respect to the theoretical and empirical considerations described in the preceding sections.

Screening Academically at-Risk Students

Screening for AARS commonly involves focusing on academic achievement with little regard for other student characteristics, much as if this population was homogeneous. There is much research, however, confirming, as noted at the outset of this chapter, that AARS are not homogeneous (Eccles & Midgley, 1989; Pianta et al., 2002). Some students experience failure because of what can be considered as temporary difficulties, such as those experienced following a school transition, whereas others may be struggling with more chronic problems, such as learning disabilities, difficult temperament, or negative attachment or family experiences. These different AARS may not require the same amount or type of mentoring help. In addition, the support provided to these different types of AARS may not require the same kinds of skills and experience on the part of mentors. In support of this idea is a finding by McLearn, Colasanto, and Schoen (1998) indicating that mentors do not feel very effective in addressing chronic problems, such as those emerging from difficult family contexts. This situation may be exacerbated by programs where mentors are volunteers who do not always have the clinical training to deal with certain kinds of problems.

In addition to the problems that the heterogeneity of AARS poses for the screening of students, this issue is not often taken into consideration in the development of mentoring programs. AARS who possess varying characteristics and needs, requiring different kinds of prevention work, often are grouped together within the same program. To counter those problems, one mentoring program establishes a psychometric profile for each AARS prior to the student entering the program and makes this profile available to mentors to help them tailor the intervention plan (see Larose & Roy, 1993). Initiatives such as these may help improve the effectiveness of mentoring relationships because they allow for the adaptation of the intervention to the specific needs of students. It is therefore pertinent for practitioners to appropriately assess the personal, social, and academic characteristics of the AARS that take part in mentoring programs in order to understand and adapt program services to this specific population.

Mentor Screening

In light of current theoretical and empirical knowledge regarding the characteristics of mentors that contribute to the success of mentoring for AARS, we believe that it is necessary to improve mentor selection processes. Theoretically, the ideal mentor should have solid knowledge regarding the personal and interpersonal characteristics of AARS; be competent in basic counselling skills, such as capacity for empathy and ability to listen and provide instrumental, vocational, and autonomy support; have strong personal motivation and perception of self-efficacy; feel secure in ongoing interpersonal relationships; have enough time available (as may be allowed by the school); and be a model to the student on both personal and vocational levels. Within the school setting, selecting psychology teachers to fill mentoring roles in areas

of interest to AARS seems to be a promising strategy (Soucy & Larose, 2000). Moreover, certain programs describe selection interviews that focus on the abilities of potential mentors (Herrera et al., 2000). Such strategies may increase the likelihood that AARS are exposed to motivated and competent mentors. In addition, screening procedures provide a way of ensuring high levels of involvement on the part of mentors. Screening will be helpful to the degree that it is not used exclusively to control the selection of mentors (e.g., checking for the possibility of criminal background or deviance), but also keeps track of the different abilities of the mentors involved in a given program.

Mentor Training

Despite accumulating evidence regarding the importance of mentor training in the effectiveness of school-based programs, few programs actually invest in more than minimal training. Thus, although a large majority of school-based mentoring programs in one survey were found to provide training (90%), 45% reported that training was limited to no more than 2 hours (Sipe & Roder, 1999). Furthermore, training rarely concerns the transmission of data and theory-driven information. The reviewed theory and research provides insight into the ways that mentor training may be improved for AARS. This literature suggests that the training of mentors should be articulated around a theoretically and empirically sound model and that this model should guide training prior to and during the implementation of the mentoring program. It also suggests that training should aim at consolidating mentors' knowledge of AARS and of school characteristics that provide the context for students' risk status (organization, culture), emphasize mentors' motivation and perceived efficacy, and provide clear support strategies for both mentors and the protégés. Using as a guide the sociomotivational perspective, which portrays structure, involvement, and support for autonomy as being the engines of student motivation and academic achievement, may provide a useful starting point for such training models.

An example of structure in training mentors would be to teach them to use mentor-protégé contracts, in which rules, the roles of the mentor and protégé, and their shared and distinct short- and medium-term objectives for their working relationship are described. The mentor's involvement in this kind of relationship may be encouraged during training by the teaching of communication skills relevant for AARS: the ways to suggest, reformulate, and reinforce student behaviors; to offer reflections or coping strategies; ask open-ended questions; deal with silence during conversation; clarify issues; and use persuasion skills. Finally, the following aspects of mentor practice should be taught, as they are likely to support autonomy in AARS: offering a variety of academic and social activities, giving responsibilities, allowing students to make certain decisions regarding the inner workings of the mentoring relationship and some of the activities in which the dyad engages, supporting personal objectives (e.g., making friends) that are sometimes different from institutional objectives (e.g., academic perseverance; especially if the mentoring program is taking place in a school setting), and using a style of interaction that favors the use of metacognitive strategies by the student.

Institutional Involvement

The sociomotivational model we propose stipulates that the presence of structure, involvement, and autonomy support is also important at the program and institutional levels, especially for the AARS population, regardless of the context where the program is set, in the school or in the community. Studies suggest that mentoring programs achieve greater success when a trusting relationship (involvement) exists between school administrators and officials, on the one hand, and program supervisors and mentors, on the other (e.g., Grossman, 1998). The involvement of administrators and a good degree of agreement between agents at different levels are critical in maintaining enthusiasm and motivation on the level of the mentoring staff. This is especially important with regard to AARS, because this clientele often reports little academic motivation and may elicit a lack of interest and motivation on the part of mentors and other agents with whom they interact. Good mentoring programs also distinguish themselves on the basis of the quality of their methods (structure).

Those that have appropriate mentor screening practices that do not exclusively focus on issues of monitoring and safety for AARS, that offer prematch and ongoing training and screen AARS in a manner that allows for the identification of the level and kind of risk they are exposed to, and that identify a resource person who is responsible for monitoring program implementation are all recognized as having a greater chance of influencing AARS adjustment. It is also well established that the presence of democratic relations between school administration and program supervisors and mentors empowers individuals within the mentoring program (autonomy) and provides better chances for successful outcomes (Herrera et al., 2000).

FUTURE DIRECTIONS

Synthesis

Despite the apparent benefits of mentoring programs for AARS and of the relative simplicity of this type of prevention program, it is critical that these programs be subjected to the same theoretical and empirical examinations as other intervention initiatives. In the present chapter, we have attempted to provide a critical review of mentoring models that have been subjected to preliminary empirical validation. Often, this evaluation has been preexperimental in nature. In response to the limits of these models for AARS, we have described a sociomotivational model of mentoring that proposes that the effects of mentoring on AARS adjustment, achievement, and persistence are most clearly manifested in its structure, in the involvement of mentors, and in the action aiming to support individual autonomy. This model has served as a reference point for evaluating empirical studies of mentoring for AARS. There appears to be some evidence that structured mentoring programs that provide for a firm relational involvement on the part of the mentor, respecting the autonomy of the AARS, serve to improve certain aspects of AARS well-being. We found strong evidence that mentoring improves academic and social perceptions of AARS, moderate evidence that mentoring positively impacts

AARS school behavioral strategies, and little evidence that mentoring actually improves academic achievement and persistence. We further consider that taking into account the individual characteristics of AARS in terms of screening and intervention practices and, subsequently, paying greater attention to the selection and training of mentors may meaningfully contribute to the overall organization and effectiveness of mentoring programs for this population.

Recommendations for Research

1. *Assess student autonomy.* In line with the sociomotivational model and with the empirical review, we believe that the study of the impact of mentoring on AARS will benefit from the inclusion of measures of student autonomy. To date, some studies have assessed perceptions of competence (e.g., self-concept) and relatedness (e.g., connectedness to parents, peers, and school) as mechanisms that may help explain the impact of mentoring on AARS. Autonomy, as a construct, has not been studied despite the fact that this aspect has been identified as an important predictor of school perseverance and academic achievement (Deci & Ryan, 1985). We perceive this gap in research as significant in light of the often stated goal of mentoring programs for AARS to render protégés more autonomous. This objective is coherent with the developmental goals identified by the authors of several programs dedicated to AARS (Karcher et al., 2002). However, evaluating the autonomy of AARS is not an easy task. It is critical to account for the personal goals of each protégé (which may vary from student to student) and the degree to which these goals are achieved following exposure to a mentoring program. In this regard, the use of qualitative interviews may be helpful in effectively accomplishing this task.

2. *Assess mentor behaviors.* Future research will benefit from a closer examination of the specific behaviors of mentors of AARS. To date, program evaluations have focused on measuring the impact of mentoring for AARS by comparing exposed students to nonexposed students or have examined the frequency or duration of contacts between mentors and AARS. Relatively few studies have attempted to qualify the

exposition by describing mentor behaviors for AARS. Accurate descriptions would allow for a better understanding of the dyadic processes that lead to improved AARS functioning. Within the context of the sociomotivational model, research may focus on breaking down and assessing mentor behaviors for AARS in the areas of structure, involvement, and autonomy support.

3. *Assess ecological factors.* Mentoring may improve relationships between the AARS and teachers, peers, and parents. However, few rigorous assessments of these relational changes in the ecological context of AARS have been conducted so far. Studies should be conducted to address this limitation. In doing so, assessments should focus on observations of change or on perceptions of change from informants other than students, such as parents, teachers, other adults, and peers.

4. *Strengthen evaluation methodologies.* In appropriately addressing the cognitive, emotional, and behavioral mechanisms influenced by mentoring relationships for AARS, it is imperative that longitudinal studies be carried out that include prementoring assessments, assessments during AARS involvement in the mentoring program, and postmentoring and follow-up assessments. It is essential, furthermore, that randomized experimental and/or rigorous quasi-experimental designs (e.g., matched comparison groups) be used to clearly establish the benefits of mentoring programs for AARS. Finally, studies should increase their reliance on informants other than the AARS (e.g., school records, teachers, peers, and parents) and, ideally, include observational measures.

Recommendations for Practice

1. *Assessment of mentors and protégés.* The work we have reviewed strongly suggests the need for mentoring programs to screen AARS to appropriately understand the kind and level of risk to which they are exposed. The use of screening inventories that target learning skills, coping strategies, social and vocational aspirations, and student access to environmental resources (e.g., parental, peer, or teacher support) may be helpful in this regard. Such information could be used to help mentors tailor their

intervention approach. As well, the use of screening or interview techniques with potential mentors is also recommended to ensure the quality of mentors to which AARS are exposed, help in matching mentors with protégés, and identify mentor training needs.

2. *Provide mentor training.* Research on mentoring of AARS in school settings underscores the need for training of mentors. Training of mentors for AARS that is theoretically and empirically driven likely would emphasize the following: (a) helping mentors gain an accurate understanding of AARS and of the cognitive, emotional, and behavioral aspects of the mentoring process in influencing school adjustment and academic achievement for this population; (b) strengthening mentors' perceived competence, especially efficacy beliefs for handling the challenges associated with mentoring AARS; and (c) emphasizing the importance of the dimensions of mentoring AARS linked to the structure, involvement, and autonomy support characteristics of the mentoring relationship.

3. *Provide staff training.* A sociomotivational perspective on mentoring also may be helpful in training staff of mentoring programs for AARS. This type of training should focus on (a) improving the coordination, supervision, and reinforcement of the different people involved in a given mentoring program (involvement); (b) structuring the different components of mentoring (mentor and protégé screening, mentor training, pairing process, mentoring activities) through the establishment of clear rules (structure); and (c) establishing methods of communication that allow all personnel involved (administrators, principals, teachers, mentors, and protégés) to express opinions, communicate ideas, or otherwise have contact with all other members of program personnel (i.e., providing autonomy support).

REFERENCES

Barton-Arwood, S., Jolivette, K., & Massey, N. G. (2000). Mentoring with elementary-age students. *Intervention in School and Clinic, 36*(1), 36–39.

Bernier, A., Larose, S., & Soucy, N. (2005). Academic mentoring in college: The interactive role of student's and mentor's interpersonal dispositions. *Research in Higher Education, 46,* 29–51.

Connell, J. P., & Wellborn, J. G. (1991). Competence, autonomy, and relatedness: A motivational analysis of self-system processes. In M. R. Gunnar & L. A. Sroufe (Eds.), *Self-processes and development* (pp. 43–77). Hillsdale, NJ: Erlbaum.

Darling, N., Hamilton, S. F., & Niego, S. (1994). Adolescents' relations with adults outside the family. In R. Montemayor, G. R. Adams, & T. P. Gullotta (Eds.), *Personal relationships during adolescence* (pp. 216–235). Thousand Oaks, CA: Sage.

Deci, E. L., & Ryan, R. M. (1985). *Intrinsic motivation and self-determination in human behavior.* New York: Plenum Press.

DuBois, D. L., Holloway, B. E., Valentine, J. C., & Cooper, H. (2002). Effectiveness of mentoring programs for youth: A meta-analytic review. *American Journal of Community Psychology, 30,* 157–197.

DuBois, D. L., Neville, H. A., Parra, G. R., & Pugh-Lilly, A. O. (2002). Testing a new model of mentoring. In G. G. Noam (Ed. in chief) & J. E. Rhodes (Ed.), *A critical view of youth mentoring* (*New Directions for Youth Development: Theory, Research, and Practice, No. 93,* pp. 21–57). San Francisco: Jossey-Bass.

Eccles, J. S., & Midgley, C. (1989). Stage/environment fit: Developmentally appropriate classrooms for early adolescents. In R. E. Ames & C. Ames (Eds.), *Research on motivation in education* (Vol. 3, pp. 139–186). San Diego, CA: Academic Press.

Fishman, R., Stelk, W., & Clark, H. B. (1997). The MENTOR school assistance program. *Preventing School Failure, 41,* 128–130.

Grossman, J. B. (Ed.). (1998). *Contemporary issues in mentoring.* Philadelphia: Public/Private Ventures. Retrieved June 12, 2004, from http://www.ppv.org/ppv/publications/publications.asp?search_id=7

Grossman, J. B., & Johnson, A. (2002). Assessing the effectiveness of mentoring programs. *The Prevention Researcher, 9,* 8–11.

Grossman, J. B., & Rhodes, J. E. (2002). The test of time: Predictors and effects of duration in youth mentoring programs. *American Journal of Community Psychology, 30,* 199–219.

Harter, S. (1999). *The construction of the self.* New York: Guilford Press.

Herrera, C., Sipe, C., & McClanahan, W. S. (2000). *Mentoring school-age children: Relationship development in community-based and school-based programs.* Philadelphia: Public/Private Ventures. (Published in collaboration with MENTOR/National Mentoring Partnership, Alexandria, VA)

Jekielek, S., Moore, K. A., & Hair, E. C. (2002). *Mentoring programs and youth development.* Washington, DC: Child Trends.

Karcher, M. J. (2005). The effects of school-based developmental mentoring and mentors' attendance on mentees' self-esteem, behavior, and connectedness. *Psychology in the Schools, 42,* 65–78.

Karcher, M. J., Davis, C., & Powell, B. (2002). Developmental mentoring in the schools: Testing connectedness as a mediating variable in the promotion of academic achievement. *The School Community Journal, 12*(2), 36–52.

Karcher, M. J., Nakkula, M. J., & Harris, J. (in press). Developmental mentoring match characteristics: Correspondence between mentors' and protégés' assessments of relationship quality. *Journal of Primary Prevention.*

Larose, S., Bernier, A., & Soucy, N. (in press). Attachment as a moderator of the effect of security in mentoring on subsequent perceptions of mentoring and relationship quality with college teachers. *Journal of Social and Personal Relationships.*

Larose, S., & Roy, R. (1993). *Le programme d'intégration aux études collégiales: Problématique, dépistage, intervention et évaluation.* Rapport de recherche [The program for integration to college: Issues, tracking, intervention, and assessment. Research report]. Ste-Foy, Canada: Cegep de Ste-Foy.

Larose, S., & Roy, R. (1995). Test of Reactions and Adaptation in College (TRAC): A new measure of learning propensity for college students. *Journal of Educational Psychology, 87,* 296–306.

McLearn, K. T., Colasanto, D., & Schoen, C. (1998). *Mentoring makes a difference: Findings From the Commonwealth Fund 1998 Survey of Adults Mentoring Young People.* New York: The Commonwealth Fund. Available at http://www.ecs.org/html/Document.asp?chouseid=2843

Parra, G. R., DuBois, D. L., Neville, H. A., Pugh-Lilly, A. O., & Povinelli, N. (2002). Mentoring relationships for youth: Investigation of a process-oriented model. *Journal of Community Psychology, 30,* 367–388.

Pianta, R. C., Stuhlman, M. W., & Hamre, B. K. (2002). How schools can do better: Fostering stronger connections between teachers and students. In G. G. Noam (Ed. in chief) & J. E. Rhodes (Ed.), *A critical view of youth mentoring* (*New Directions for Youth Development: Theory, Research, and Practice, No. 93,* pp. 91–107). San Francisco: Jossey-Bass.

Rhodes, J. E. (2002). *Stand by me: The risks and rewards of mentoring today's youth.* Cambridge, MA: Harvard University Press.

Rhodes, J. E., Grossman, J. B., & Resch, N. L. (2000). Agents of change: Pathways through which mentoring relationships influence adolescents' academic adjustment. *Child Development, 71,* 1662–1671.

Richman, J. M., Rosenfeld, L. B., & Bowen, G. L. (1998). Social support for adolescents at risk of school failure. *Social Work, 43,* 309–323.

Sipe, C. L., & Roder, A. E. (1999). *Mentoring school-age children: A classification of programs.* Philadelphia: Public/Private Ventures. (Published in collaboration with MENTOR/National Mentoring Partnership, Alexandria, VA)

Slicker, E. K., & Palmer, D. J. (1993). Mentoring at-risk high school students: Evaluation of a school-based program. *The School Counselor, 40,* 327–334.

Soucy, N., & Larose, S. (2000). Attachment and control in family and mentoring contexts as determinants of adolescent adjustment at college. *Journal of Family Psychology, 14,* 125–143.

Tierney, J. P., Grossman, J. B., & Resch, N. L. (1995). *Making a difference: An impact study of Big Brothers/Big Sisters.* Philadelphia: Public/Private Ventures.

Tinto, V. (1993). *Leaving college: Rethinking the causes and cures of student attrition.* Chicago: University of Chicago Press.

30

JUVENILE OFFENDERS

ELAINE A. BLECHMAN AND JEDEDIAH M. BOPP

INTRODUCTION

In 2001, U.S. law enforcement agencies made 2.3 million arrests of juveniles under the age of 18, and according to the FBI, juveniles accounted for 17% of all arrests and 15% of all violent crimes (Snyder, 2003). Frequency of arrests as a juvenile infers continued offending as an adult and adverse life outcomes including homelessness, substance abuse, and mental illness (Draine, Salzer, Culhane, & Hadley, 2002). Each juvenile offender who becomes a career criminal costs society $1.7 to $2.3 million and costs victims additional unknown amounts (Cohen, 1998).

An examination of 162 youth who were transferred to and sentenced in adult court during 1999 found that youth receiving adult probation or boot camp were 1.74 to 2.29 times more likely to reoffend in the following 2 years than were youth receiving substantially less expensive community-based juvenile sanctions (Mason, Chapman, Chang, & Simons, 2003). California's juvenile prison system costs a total of $6 billion a year, or $80,000 per youth, and yields a recidivism rate approaching 90% (Broder, 2004).

The poor results of detention outside the community have heightened interest in community-based interventions for juvenile offenders such as mentoring. Since 1996, the Office of Juvenile Justice and Delinquency Prevention has invested over $40,000,000 in Juvenile Mentoring Programs, or JUMPs (White, Mertinko, & Van Orden, 2002). JUMPs are community-based programs that match at-risk youth with volunteer adult mentors in one-to-one relationships. A series of reports compiled by a technical assistance contractor to JUMP grantees mention the need to prevent juvenile offender recidivism and describe program-reported improvements in behavior of mentees (Mertinko & Forbush, 2003; Novotney, Mertinko, Lange, & Baker, 2000; White, Mertinko, & Van Orden, 2002). Yet JUMP research funding has yielded no scientifically robust observational or experimental evaluations of the impact of mentoring on juvenile offenders' recidivism.

In 2004, the U.S. Congress announced that funds for youth mentoring (including mentoring of juvenile offenders) would increase about 4 times, from $27.4 million in 2003 to $100 million in 2004 (Consolidated Appropriations Act, 2004). Federal funding for child mental

Portions of this chapter were presented at the National Research Summit on Mentoring, Kansas City, MO, October 2003.

health and social services will remain about the same, $98.5 million in 2003, $98.4 million in 2004 (Consolidated Appropriations Resolution, 2003; Consolidated Appropriations Act, 2004). Increased funding will double funds available for care of youth with special needs, with approximately half of the funds supporting paraprofessional mentors and the remaining half supporting mental health professionals. Our purpose is to shed light on justifications for such policy and funding decisions. We consider, in turn, theory and scientific evidence. We end with public policy recommendations for research and practice in mentoring of juvenile offenders.

THEORY

When John Bowlby (1944) described the weak attachment bonds of 44 persistent juvenile thieves, he inspired contemporary social-control theories of juvenile delinquency, beginning with Travis Hirschi's social control theory (1969). In Hirschi's social control theory, delinquency results when connections to society are so weak that the individual weighs the personal benefits and costs of delinquent acts without consideration for the impact on others. In this theory, susceptibility to social control depends upon (a) attachment to parents, peers, teachers, religious leaders, and community members; (b) commitment to investments in conventional behavior, such as reputation, education, family, and wealth; (c) involvement in conventional activities; and (d) belief in conventional values.

In Gottfredson and Hirschi's general theory of crime (1990), early childhood parental supervision and discipline presumably establish a self-control trait and related susceptibility to social control. In this theory, the insufficient self-control of juvenile offenders motivates their delinquent acts.

In Sampson and Laub's age-graded theory of informal social control (1993), social bonds that are established across the life span increase susceptibility to informal social control and reduce propensity for criminal offenses. This theory asserts that adolescents form strong attachments to parents who offer consistent discipline and adequate supervision.

Host Provocation Theory

Host provocation (HP) theory joins a stress-diathesis and a social control hypothesis. First, HP theory posits that when an at-risk youth, with many personal diatheses or challenges (e.g., a history of abuse and behavior problems) is exposed to many antisocial stressors or provocations (e.g., drugs and alcohol, deviant peers, and violent mass media), a delinquency offense is a very likely result (Blechman, Fishman, Fishman, & Lewis, 2004; Blechman & Stoolmiller, 2003; Stoolmiller & Blechman, 2003). Second, HP theory posits that extensive exposure to antisocial provocations is prima facie evidence of insufficient social control, whether it is because the youth lacks internal self-regulatory capacity or because parents and other socialization agents exercise insufficient external control.

Blechman proposed HP theory because social control theories of delinquency insufficiently consider the interactions of diverse individual differences (e.g., abuse, behavior problems, and cognitive disabilities) and environmental stimuli (e.g., drugs and alcohol, violent mass media) in the onset, maintenance, and desistance of juvenile delinquency.

In HP theory, illustrated in Figure 30.1, youth burdened with many life challenges (e.g., abuse, behavior problems, cognitive disabilities, depression, difficult temperament) are more resistant to external social controls (e.g., parent supervision, prosocial activities), slower to acquire internal controls (e.g., attachment bonds, emotion regulation, moral judgment), and are ever more willing *hosts* for the antisocial provocations that drive delinquency (e.g., deviant peers, alcohol and drugs, violent mass media) than their less challenged peers. The greater a youth's exposure to antisocial provocations, the greater the youth's chances of an officially recorded critical event, such as a first or repeated police arrest.

In HP theory, no one factor (e.g., internal controls alone) or one manifestation of any factor (e.g., attachment bonds alone) represents the prime gateway to delinquency. Instead, numerous manifestations of life challenges, internal controls, and external controls are recognized as jointly influencing exposure to antisocial provocations and delinquency.

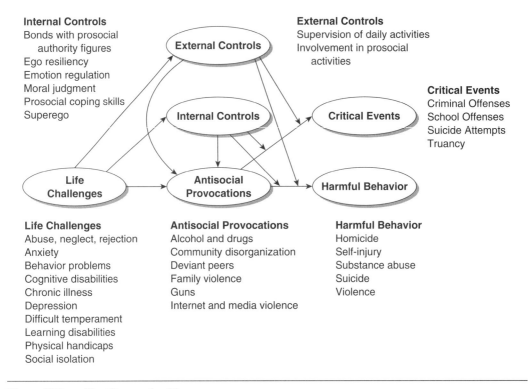

Internal Controls
Bonds with prosocial
 authority figures
Ego resiliency
Emotion regulation
Moral judgment
Prosocial coping skills
Superego

External Controls
Supervision of daily activities
Involvement in prosocial
 activities

Critical Events
Criminal Offenses
School Offenses
Suicide Attempts
Truancy

Life Challenges
Abuse, neglect, rejection
Anxiety
Behavior problems
Cognitive disabilities
Chronic illness
Depression
Difficult temperament
Learning disabilities
Physical handicaps
Social isolation

Antisocial Provocations
Alcohol and drugs
Community disorganization
Deviant peers
Family violence
Guns
Internet and media violence

Harmful Behavior
Homicide
Self-injury
Substance abuse
Suicide
Violence

Figure 30.1   Host Provocation Theory

In HP theory, life challenges (e.g., a history of abuse or behavior problems) are presumed to be enduring. However, HP theory also presumes that changes in internal and external controls and in antisocial provocation exposure may occur at any time, with predictable effects on recidivism. A first-time juvenile offender who is diverted from adjudication by the district attorney's office under conditions that increase supervision and monitoring and decrease exposure to deviant peers is less likely to reoffend than a first-time offender who is sent to a detention facility where frequent exposure to deviant peers occurs.

A future test that explicitly pits HP theory against a competing explanation is required. Meanwhile, empirical findings do support several premises of HP theory. First, consistent with HP theory, studies have found that juvenile offenders face disproportionate numbers of life challenges, including abuse (Smith, 1988), behavior problems (Broidy et al., 2003), cognitive and learning disabilities (e.g., Kataoka et al., 2001), co-occurring mental and personality disorders (e.g., Fago, 2003), depression (e.g., Wiesner, 2003), trauma (Baer & Maschi, 2003), and social isolation (Maegiste, 1992).

Second, consistent with HP theory, studies have found weaker external controls among juvenile offenders. Compared with nondelinquent peers, they receive less effective parent supervision and social support (e.g., Flannery, Williams, & Vazsonyi, 1999) and spend less time in prosocial activities (Brownfield, & Sorenson, 1993). These findings may reflect the difficulties involved in parenting juvenile offenders (Hillian & Reitsma-Street, 2003), given that successful monitoring of adolescents depends more upon teens' spontaneous and trusting disclosures than on parents' intrusive tracking and surveillance efforts (Kerr & Stattin, 2000).

Third, consistent with HP theory, studies have found that juvenile offenders evidence poorer internal controls than their nondelinquent peers, including less mature impulse control (White et al., 1994) and ego development (Novy, Gaa, Frankiewicz, Liberman, & Amerikaner, 1992).

Fourth, consistent with HP theory, studies have found that juvenile offenders are more often and intensively exposed to antisocial provocations, including family dysfunction (Burton, Foy, Bwanausi, Johnson, & Moore, 1994), deviant peers (e.g., Wiesner & Capaldi, 2003), drugs and alcohol (Winters, Weller, & Meland, 1993), and family violence (e.g., Crimmins, Cleary, Brownstein, Spunt, & Warley, 2000) than nondelinquents. Moreover, exposure to antisocial provocations such as deviant peers and illicit substances increases with each arrest and incarceration (e.g., Benda, Toombs, & Peacock, 2003).

Theory and Juvenile Offender Mentoring

HP theory suggests that mentoring may prevent recidivism in at least three ways: (a) increase external controls by helping parents and teachers with supervision; (b) strengthen internal controls by promoting attachment bonds, self-regulation, and prosocial values; and (c) reduce exposure to antisocial provocations, such as deviant peers, drugs and alcohol, and violent mass media, through immersion in competing, prosocial activities.

RESEARCH

In this section, we review the results of research relevant to the impact of mentoring on juvenile offenders. We restricted our review to studies that measured outcome via officially recorded delinquency or criminal offense rates. Officially recorded offenses have several advantages in outcome measurement. First, offense rates represent more objective (albeit still imperfect) information than responses to rating scales or questionnaires. Second, offense rates are easily compared across studies, while variations across studies in psychological measures obstruct cross-study comparisons. Third, changes in offense rates can be monetized in terms of dollars expended on adjudication and detention of offenders, while changes in scores on psychological measures are not easily monetized. Fourth, offense rates can be collected for many decades for all youth participants in an intervention, while psychological measures cannot be repeatedly administered over time to all original respondents (e.g., parents, youth). Finally, most adults, not just behavioral scientists, can comprehend the value of a reduction in offense rates. The value of an improved score on a psychological measure is not so obvious.

Our research review has three parts. First, we consider five peer-reviewed studies that evaluate the impact of a mentoring or mentoring-like intervention on postintervention delinquency or criminal offense rates. Next, given the small number of such studies, we consider a meta-analysis of studies evaluating the impact of various interventions, including mentoring, on postintervention offense rates. Finally, we consider the results of a report from the Washington State Institute for Public Policy on the benefits and costs of prevention and early intervention programs for youth (Aos, Lieb, Mayfield, Miller, & Pennucci, 2004).

Evaluations of Impact of Mentoring on Offense Rates

The availability of only five studies evaluating the impact of mentoring on postintervention offense rates limited our review in several ways. First, we felt compelled to include studies with obvious methodological flaws that might compromise internal validity. Second, we felt compelled to include any study including a face valid mentoring or mentoring-like intervention. In other words, we chose to include studies that included programs that while not specifically referred to as "mentoring programs" had mentoring-like qualities.

The Cambridge-Somerville Youth Study (CSYS) provides the most extensive information currently available about the long-term impact of mentoring on offense rates. Between 1935 and 1939, the CSYS recruited boys below age 12 from a low-income, high-crime area. Boys were matched on age, family environment, and delinquency-prone histories and then randomized to either an untreated control or to an experimental mentoring condition. In the experimental condition, "a social worker . . . tried to build a close personal relationship with the boy and assist both the boy and his family in a number of ways" (McCord, 1992, p. 198). At the program's end in 1945, boys in the mentoring condition had been visited, on average, two times a month for 5.5 years. When the men were about 47 years old, three objectively defined adverse outcomes were measured: conviction of an FBI index crime; death before age 35; and alcoholic, schizophrenic, or manic-depressive diagnosis. The mentoring group fared significantly worse than the untreated control on all outcomes. No added benefit was associated with more frequent or longer-lasting help or better rapport (McCord, 1992).

In 1979, O'Donnell, Lydgate, and Fo reported the results of a 3-year experiment with the Buddy System. The authors describe this as a community-based program that trained indigenous nonprofessionals as behavior change agents (see also Fo & O'Donnell, 1974, 1975). Participants were 10- to 17-year-olds who were referred for behavior and academic problems and randomly assigned to the experimental Buddy System ($n = 335$) or a no-treatment control condition ($n = 218$). The authors reported that the impact of the Buddy System on recidivism in the 3 years following program entry depended on whether or not youth had been arrested for a major offence in the year prior to participation in the study. Youth who had been arrested the year before program entry and subsequently participated in the Buddy System had a lower arrest rate within 3 years after entry. Youth who had never been arrested, not been arrested during the year before entry, or had been arrested for only minor offenses showed a higher arrest rate within 3 years after entry. The authors reported that the higher recidivism rate occurred chiefly among youth who had spent more than 1 year in the Buddy System. The authors' interpretation was that the peer network effect created by the Buddy System reduced recidivism among some juvenile offenders and instigated the onset of offending among nonoffenders.

In 1987, Davidson, Redner, Blakely, Mitchell, and Emshoff reported the results of a longitudinal experiment involving 213 juvenile offenders who were randomly assigned to one of four experimental treatment conditions (action, action family, action court, relationship), to an attention placebo condition, or to a treatment-as-usual control condition. In action,

action family, and relationship conditions, a youth was paired with a college student for 18 weeks of supervised one-on-one treatment. In the action court condition, youth were paired with a juvenile court officer. The three action conditions focused on advocacy and behavioral contracting, and the relationship condition focused on interpersonal relationship skills. Systematic manipulation checks indicated a high degree of integrity in the different treatment conditions. Results indicated no significant differential effects on self-reported delinquency. However, all treatment conditions involving a specific intervention model located outside the formal juvenile justice system produced lower recidivism rates than the attention-placebo condition, the treatment-as-usual control condition, or the action court condition located within the juvenile justice system.

In 2000, Blechman, Maurice, Buecker, and Helberg presented a comparative cost-benefit analysis of juvenile diversion alone, juvenile diversion and skill training, and juvenile diversion and mentoring. Using Rosenbaum and Rubin's (1983) propensity analysis methodology, they compared juvenile offenders' recidivism following nonrandom assignment with juvenile diversion (JD, $n = 137$) to JD plus skill training (ST, $n = 55$) or to JD plus mentoring (MEN, $n = 45$). In JD, youth met with juvenile court officers. In ST, youth attended anger management classes led by paraprofessional youth workers. In MEN, youth met with volunteer adult mentors. Intake characteristics that distinguished intervention groups were used to calculate assignment propensity scores. After propensity score blocking balanced intake characteristics, ST proved more cost-effective than MEN, achieving a 14% relative reduction in recidivism at a savings of $33,600 per 100 youth. In ST, 37% were rearrested 2 years or more after intake, compared with 51% in MEN and 46% in JD. In two of five propensity subclasses, time to first rearrest was longer in ST ($M = 767$ days) than in MEN ($M = 638$ days) or JD ($M = 619$ days). They found that ST saves $33,600 per 100 youth when compared with MEN, due to the increased rate of recidivism in MEN. ST provided the greatest return on investment calculated solely in terms of short-term program costs; this return would have been much greater had the long-term costs of recidivism to the community and to victims been included in the analysis.

In 2001, Dembo, Ramirez-Garnica, and colleagues reported the results of a study of the impact of Family Empowerment Intervention (FEI) on 3-year postintervention recidivism of 303 juvenile offenders. FEI, a systems-oriented intervention delivered in-home by well-trained paraprofessionals, was developed at the Hillsborough County, Florida, Juvenile Assessment Center by Dembo and his colleagues (Dembo, Dudell, Livingston, & Schmeidler, 2001). Juvenile offenders (and their families) who were diverted from juvenile court adjudication at the Hillsborough Center were randomly assigned either to FEI or to an Extended Services Intervention (ESI) for 10 weeks. FEI families received three 1-hour, home-based meetings per week from a clinician-trained paraprofessional. ESI families received monthly phone contacts and, if indicated, referral information. Compared with youth who did not complete FEI, youth who completed FEI evidenced marginally statistically significant lower rates of officially recorded new charges and new arrests. In a subsequent report (Dembo, Schmeidler, & Wothke, 2003), FEI completers reported less delinquent activity over the 36-month postintervention follow-up than other study participants. Further analyses showed that "implementing the FEI for 3,600 diversion cases would save the Hillsborough County juvenile justice system $4.7 million in cumulative direct costs over a three-year period" (Dembo & Schmeidler, 2002, p. 160).

Meta-Analysis of Interventions With Juvenile Offenders

In 1992, Lipsey presented the results of a meta-analysis of 443 evaluations of about 23 different interventions with juvenile offenders. Lipsey found that (a) there was less posttreatment evidence of delinquency in experimental than in control groups, (b) better-controlled studies yielded slightly larger mean effect sizes equivalent to a 20% decrease in recidivism, and (c) more structured treatments (e.g., skill-oriented) seemed more effective than less structured approaches (e.g., counseling).

WSIPP Report on Prevention and Early Intervention Programs

In 2004, the Washington State Institute for Public Policy (WSIPP) issued a report about the benefits and costs of prevention and early intervention programs (Aos et al., 2004). The WSIPP report involved a comparative cost-benefit analysis of programs for at-risk youth that measured seven outcomes: crime, substance abuse, educational achievement, teen pregnancy, suicide attempts, child abuse or neglect, and domestic violence. Mentoring programs for youth without justice system involvement were relatively ineffective, with a net benefit per youth from Big Brothers Big Sisters of $48 and a net cost per youth from Quantum Opportunities of –$15,022. However, investments in effective programs for juvenile offenders had the highest net benefit, ranging from $1,900 per youth for diversion programs with services to $31,200 per youth for dialectical behavior therapy. Mentoring programs in the juvenile justice system had a midrange benefit of $16,700 per youth.

The WSIPP report concludes with this lesson learned:

> In our formal evaluation of Washington's effort at implementing research-proven programs for juvenile offenders, one important lesson was learned. The programs work and they produce more benefits than costs—but only when implemented rigorously with close attention to quality control and adherence to the original design of the program. Without quality control, the programs do not work. This lesson is so central that we think it should be part of any legislative direction to implement a state local reimbursement arrangement or, for that matter, any attempt by the state to implement research-based programs in the state system. (Aos et al., 2004, p. 9)

The WSIPP report was published after we finished writing this chapter. This was our first exposure to the mentoring programs for juvenile offenders evaluated in the report. We quickly revised the chapter to refer to the report's important results. We did not have the time to obtain and explore the methods and results of each of these studies (see Yates, this volume, for a discussion of methodological issues associated with the WSIPP report). The following suggestions are derived solely from the WSIPP report.

Delinquency and Criminal Offense Outcomes

The studies we reviewed suggest these outcomes:

1. Unstructured mentoring by social workers yielded higher recidivism rates and other adverse outcomes than no intervention at all (McCord, 1992).

2. Mentoring by trained paraprofessionals was somewhat effective in reducing recidivism among recently arrested youth, while encouraging recidivism among others (O'Donnell et al., 1979). When mentoring by trained paraprofessionals involved youth alone or youth and family, it was significantly more effective in reducing recidivism than an attention-placebo, justice system treatment as usual or mentoring by a juvenile court officer (Davidson, Redner, Blakely, Mitchell, & Emshoff 1987).

3. Skills training was significantly more effective in reducing recidivism than unstructured counseling (Lipsey, 1992) and significantly more cost-effective in reducing recidivism than unstructured mentoring (Blechman et al., 2000).

4. Mentoring by trained paraprofessionals who delivered an in-home family systems intervention was significantly more cost-effective in reducing recidivism than monthly phone contacts (Dembo & Schmeidler, 2002).

5. Mentoring of juvenile offenders in the juvenile justice system (vs. regular juvenile court processing) resulted in a benefit of $16,700 per youth (Aos et al., 2004).

Theory and Outcomes

We can at best speculate about how HP theory might account for the findings of the studies we reviewed:

1. An intervention may increase subsequent offenses through greater exposure to other deviant peers in mentor-sponsored group activities (McCord, 1992).

2. An intervention may reduce subsequent offenses through more effective external controls imposed on participants by parents and teachers and mentors embedded in the justice system (Aos et al., 2004; Davidson et al., 1987; Dembo & Schmeidler, 2002).

3. An intervention may reduce subsequent offenses through more effective internal controls (e.g., attachment bonds, self-regulation, and prosocial values) (Blechman et al., 2000; Davidson et al., 1987).

4. An intervention may reduce subsequent offenses through more structured activities and less exposure to antisocial provocations (Lipsey, 1992).

FUTURE DIRECTIONS

Synthesis

Future U.S. government allocations to the care of youth with special needs, including juvenile offenders, budget about equal amounts for mentoring by paraprofessionals and for mental health services delivered by professionals. Nevertheless, there is no evidence that unstructured mentoring contributes to a reduction in delinquency or criminal offenses. In fact, the limited available evidence suggests that compared with professionally delivered or supervised alternatives, unstructured mentoring is significantly less cost-effective in reducing recidivism.

To date, federal funding for mentoring programs has not contributed to our scientific knowledge about outcomes for juvenile offenders or underlying mechanisms of change. Higher levels of future federal funding for mentoring service delivery programs are likely. How these mentoring programs will be evaluated is much less clear. And so we offer recommendations for research and practice that a thoughtful program administrator can implement within a service delivery budget and without additional research funds.

Recommendations for Research

Here are two research recommendations that any mentoring program administrator can implement without a large research budget and with great benefit to the delivery of mentoring services.

1. *In the course of delivery of mentoring services, conduct a well-designed observational study evaluating the officially recorded offense rate outcomes attributable to juvenile offender mentoring.*

2. *In the course of delivery of mentoring services, collect process data about mentoring dosage that will illuminate mechanisms responsible for mentoring outcomes.*

Here is our rationale for these research recommendations.

Conventional wisdom to the contrary, we believe that a true experiment employing random assignment is not the best way to advance the field. Random assignment (the hallmark of a true experiment) is impractical for most juvenile offender mentoring programs. The lack of juvenile offender mentoring research appears directly attributable to pressures for random assignment and countervailing difficulties in achieving random assignment. If a court has sent a juvenile offender to a mentoring agency, the agency cannot very well randomize the youth to receive or not receive mentoring. Randomization to a waiting-list control is not particularly ethical because the best time to begin intervention with a young offender is during the crisis surrounding an arrest. Moreover, the information resulting from a waiting-list control is of little value because it sheds no light on the relative long-term, postintervention impact of mentoring on recidivism.

The purpose of random assignment is to equalize preexisting characteristics of subjects in experimental, control, and comparison conditions so that results (e.g., recidivism rates) can be attributed solely to the intervention condition rather than to preexisting differences (e.g., number of prior arrests). With small numbers of protégés per condition, random assignment is unlikely to equalize preexisting differences across conditions (Cohen, 1992). Following random assignment, it is always advisable to identify any preexisting differences between conditions and to employ statistical techniques (such as propensity scoring; Blechman et al., 2000) that compare between-condition recidivism outcomes while controlling for preexisting differences. A failure to control for preexisting

between-condition differences poses a threat to internal validity of results and the hazard of a Type I experimental error (Basskin, 2003; Wilcox & Keselman, 2003). Results may, for example, be the product of favorable preexisting differences rather than the experimental mentoring condition itself. Investigators may mistakenly conclude that mentoring is responsible for lower recidivism rates, ignoring the influence of favorable preexisting characteristics.

Random assignment cannot equalize protégés on between-condition intervention integrity and strength differences. The integrity of mentoring (the mentor follows program guidelines and fulfills scheduled commitments to the protégé) and the strength of mentoring (the participation of the protégé in scheduled commitments with the mentor) usually vary from one protégé to another within an experimental mentoring condition. In addition, the frequency of professionally delivered educational, medical, mental health, and social services usually vary from one protégé to another. We expect pretreatment characteristics (e.g., highly motivated and committed parents) to be correlated with the integrity and strength of mentoring and the frequency of professionally delivered services.

An intent-to-treat analysis is the most conservative method of testing differences between an experimental mentoring intervention and a control or comparison condition (Mazumdar et al., 2002). An intent-to-treat analysis would include postintervention recidivism data from all protégés, regardless of mentoring integrity and strength or frequency of professionally delivered services (see, for example, Bradley et al., 2003). An intent-to-treat analysis diminishes chances of finding differences between an experimental mentoring condition and control or comparison conditions. An intent-to-treat analysis can, however, be quite informative. If postintervention recidivism scores among all protégés are equivalent, regardless of the integrity and strength of mentoring or the frequency of professionally delivered services, then we must look to the influence on recidivism of preexisting characteristics.

Consider the possibility that there is a dose-response relationship between mentoring and recidivism (Feaster, Newman, & Rice, 2003; Shapiro et al., 2003). If mentoring has an impact on recidivism, then the impact should vary with mentoring integrity and strength, or, in a word, *dosage*. We should expect a dose-response relationship such that protégés who receive the highest possible, 100% dosage of mentoring evidence the best postintervention recidivism rates; those who get 50% dosage of mentoring evidence middling postintervention recidivism rates; and those who get 0% dosage of mentoring (e.g., those who drop out early from a mentoring intervention) evidence the worst postintervention recidivism rates. We might find a linear relationship between perfectly correlated mentoring dosage and recidivism outcomes. There may be a tipping point, above which a stronger mentoring dosage has no incremental effect on recidivism outcomes. There may be a "just-good-enough" mentoring dosage that yields best recidivism outcomes, while stronger and weaker doses both yield worst recidivism outcomes. Finally, there may be an interaction between preexisting juvenile offender characteristics and optimum mentoring dosages.

A study that randomly assigns juvenile offenders to an experimental mentoring condition or to a nonmentoring control condition can inform us about recidivism outcomes for only youth who get 0% dosage of mentoring (in the nonmentoring control) versus those who get mentoring dosages ranging from 0% to 100%. By randomizing half our potential protégés to the nonmentoring control, we have reduced the sample size for each condition, our statistical power (Cohen, 1992), and our chances for finding a statistically significant difference in postintervention recidivism outcomes between the mentoring and nonmentoring conditions. Uncontrolled variability in mentoring dosages in the mentoring condition further reduces chances of finding between-condition recidivism differences. By employing random assignment, we have reduced our sample size, our capacity to detect small effect sizes (small but real differences between groups), and increased the hazard of Type II error (mistakenly concluding that there is no between-condition difference) (Algina & Keselman, 2003).

Using a well-designed observational study, program administrators can provide mentoring to all eligible juvenile offenders, avoid certain threats to the internal validity of results, dodge Type I and II errors, and contribute invaluable new knowledge about mentoring dosage-recidivism outcome relationships. An informative observational study would be distinguished by data collection and by data analysis methods.

Data collection would focus on preexisting protégé characteristics, mentoring dosage (integrity and strength), frequency of professionally provided services, and long-term, postintervention recidivism outcomes.

Data analysis would examine recidivism outcomes in relationship to mentoring dosage, while controlling for preexisting characteristics and frequency of professionally provided services.

We envision a first generation of independently conducted observational studies that identify optimal mentoring dosages for effective prevention of recidivism across subsets of juvenile offenders (e.g., early vs. late onset). First-generation juvenile offender mentoring research would establish procedural guidelines for one or more mentoring protocols (e.g., one protocol for early-onset and one for late-onset offenders).

We envision a second generation of cross-site collaboration, in which mentoring programs around the country employ identical data collection methods and identical mentoring protocols. Smaller programs might continue to use observational designs that examine mentoring dose-recidivism response relationships. Larger programs might use experimental designs in which protégés are stratified on preexisting characteristics and randomized to conditions providing different dosage levels of mentoring. Collection of cost input data (total costs of each hour of mentoring a juvenile offender) in all programs would provide the basis for economic analyses, examining which mentoring dosage levels yield the best long-term recidivism rates at the lowest costs. Examination of theoretical mechanisms responsible for recidivism reduction might follow determination of the most cost-effective juvenile offender mentoring protocols.

Recommendations for Practice

For juvenile offenders, unstructured mentoring, disconnected from the juvenile justice system, holds no promise as a comprehensive method of reducing recidivism. Unstructured mentoring may at times increase recidivism. As a means of reducing recidivism, unstructured juvenile offender mentoring is likely to be less cost-effective than professionally delivered evidence-based treatments. Delivery by trained and carefully supervised paraprofessionals may increase the cost-effectiveness of evidence-based treatments. It may be more expensive to recruit mentors and train them as paraprofessionals than to simply recruit applicants for paraprofessional jobs and embed them in the juvenile justice system so that the mentors can be mentored by trained justice system professionals.

These considerations cast doubt on the wisdom of initiatives such as JUMP that direct substantial resources to the support of unstructured mentoring as a means of reducing juvenile offense rates.

Here are two practice recommendations that any mentoring program administrator can implement and evaluate, consistent with our earlier research recommendations:

1. *Include a mentor as a member of an individualized caregiver team for a juvenile offender.*

2. *Use a client-centric information system[1] to guide, coordinate, and evaluate the impact of the caregiver team and of its mentor member.*

Here is our rationale for these practice recommendations.

Mentors might contribute to the cost-effective prevention of juvenile offender recidivism if they participated on individualized caregiver teams (Blechman et al., 2004). For each juvenile offender, this caregiver team integrates all the people involved in a juvenile offender's community care: parents and kin, mentors, educators, health and human service providers, juvenile diversion, probation, and parole officers. Each caregiver team develops and implements a risk reduction plan that distributes and coordinates responsibilities for "24/7" (i.e., around-the-clock) supervision and monitoring among team members. The team's purpose is to prevent new school, delinquency, or criminal offenses for at least 2 years after a prior offense or for the period specified in juvenile diversion, probation, or parole conditions.

Each team accomplishes implements, evaluates, and continuously improves its risk reduction plan via a client-centric Internet mentoring information system. Parents or guardians authorize team members for access to data categories and functions in the youth's mentoring information system account. Some team members contribute to risk reduction by providing educational services, job training, evidence-based interventions, and counseling sessions at schools, clinics, courts, or family residences. Other team members, most notably parents, kin, and mentors, contribute by transporting youth to and from scheduled treatment activities and monitoring and supervising youth at times when no treatment activities are scheduled and during unstructured leisure time. One or more mentors may make significant contributions when a youth's parents and kin are unavailable for transportation, monitoring, supervision, and unstructured leisure activities.

Caregiver team members use a client-centric information system to share information privately and securely, schedule youth and team member activities, confirm youth and team member adherence to scheduled activities, collect information about new youth offenses, push automated alerts about nonadherence and new offenses up supervisory hierarchies, and following nonadherence or new offenses, improve risk reduction plans.

Program administrators use the client-centric information system to automate the collection and reporting of data about protégés' preexisting characteristics; mentoring dosages (integrity and strength); professionally delivered educational, medical, mental health, and social services; long-term postintervention recidivism outcomes; and hourly costs. Research administrators use the mentoring information system to direct the first and second generations of research that we envisioned above.

NOTE

1. The first author, Elaine Blechman, patented the client-centric Caregiver Alliance Toolbox Internet information platform to support the research and

practice recommendations offered in this chapter. More information about the Toolbox is available at http://www.caregiveralliance.com.

REFERENCES

Algina, J., & Keselman, H. J. (2003). Approximate confidence intervals for effect sizes. *Educational & Psychological Measurement, 63,* 537–553.

Aos, S., Lieb, R. Mayfield, M. M., & Pennucci, A. (2004). *Benefits and costs of prevention and early intervention programs for youth.* Olympia: Washington State Institute for Public Policy.

Baer, J., & Maschi, T. (2003). Random acts of delinquency: Trauma and self-destructiveness in juvenile offenders. *Child & Adolescent Social Work Journal, 20,* 85–98.

Basskin, L. (2003). Statistical interpretation can also bias research evidence. *British Medical Journal, 327,* 752.

Benda, B. B., Toombs, N. J., & Peacock, M. (2003). An empirical examination of competing theories in predicting recidivism of adult offenders five years after graduation from boot camp. *Journal of Offender Rehabilitation, 37*(2), 43–75.

Blechman, E. A., Fishman, D., & Fishman, C., & Lewis, J. (2004). *Caregiver alliances for at risk and dangerous youth: Establishing school and agency coordination and accountability.* Champaign, IL: Research Press.

Blechman, E. A., Maurice, A., & Buecker, B. (2000). Can mentoring or skill training reduce recidivism? Observational study with propensity analysis. *Prevention Science, 1,* 139–155.

Blechman, E. A., & Stoolmiller, M. (2003). *The age-crime curve: Confirmed and decomposed into four latent class offender trajectories.* Manuscript in preparation, University of Colorado-Boulder.

Bowlby, J. (1944). Forty-four juvenile thieves: Their characters and home-life. *International Journal of Psycho-Analysis, 25,* 19–53.

Bradley, S. J., Jadaa, D., Brody, J., Landy, S., Tallett, S. E., Watson, W., et al. (2003). Brief psychoeducational parenting program: An evaluation and 1-year follow-up. *Journal of the American Academy of Child & Adolescent Psychiatry, 42,* 1171–1178.

Broder, J. M. (2004, February 15). Dismal California prisons hold juvenile offenders. *New York Times,* p. 12.

Broidy, L. M., Nagin, D. S., Tremblay, R. E., Bates, J. E., Brame, B., Dodge, K. A., et al. (2003). Developmental trajectories of childhood disruptive behaviors and adolescent delinquency: A six-site, cross-national study. *Developmental Psychology, 39,* 222–245.

Brownfield, D., & Sorenson, A. (1993). Self control and juvenile delinquency: Theoretical issues and an empirical assessment of selected elements of a general theory of crime. *Deviant Behavior, 14,* 243–264.

Burton, D., Foy, D., Bwanausi, C., Johnson, J., & Moore, L. (1994). The relationship between traumatic exposure, family dysfunction, and post-traumatic stress symptoms in male juvenile offenders. *Journal of Traumatic Stress, 7,* 83–93.

Cohen, J. (1992). A power primer. *Psychological Bulletin, 112,* 155–159.

Cohen, M. A. (1998). The monetary value of saving a high-risk youth. *Journal of Quantitative Criminology, 14,* 5–33.

Consolidated Appropriations Act (2004) (enacted). H.R. 2673, 108th Cong. Washington, DC: U.S. Government Printing Agency.

Consolidated Appropriations Resolution (2003) (enacted). H.R. Res. 2, 108th Cong. Washington, DC: U.S. Government Printing Agency.

Crimmins, S., Cleary, S., Brownstein, H., Spunt, B., & Warley, R. (2000). Trauma, drugs, and violence among juvenile offenders. *Journal of Psychoactive Drugs, 32,* 43–54.

Davidson, W. S., Redner, R., Blakely, C. H., Mitchell, C. M., & Emshoff, J. G. (1987). Diversion of juvenile offenders: An experimental comparison. *Journal of Consulting & Clinical Psychology, 55,* 68–75.

Dembo, R., Dudell, G., Livingston, S., & Schmeidler, J. (2001). Family Empowerment Intervention: Conceptual foundations and clinical practices. *Journal of Offender Rehabilitation, 33*(1), 1–31.

Dembo, R., Ramirez-Garnica, G., Schmeidler, J., Rollie, M., Livingstone, S., & Hartfield, A. (2001). Long-term impact of a Family Empowerment Intervention on juvenile offender recidivism. *Journal of Offender Rehabilitation, 33*(1), 33–57.

Dembo, R., & Schmeidler, J. (2002). *Family Empowerment Intervention: An innovative service for high-risk youths and their families.* Binghamton, NY: Haworth Press.

Dembo, R., Schmeidler, J., & Wothke, W. (2003). Impact of a family empowerment intervention on delinquent behavior: A latent growth model analysis. *Journal of Offender Rehabilitation, 37*(2), 17–41.

Draine, J., Salzer, M. S., Culhane, D. P., & Hadley, T. R. (2002). Role of social disadvantage in crime, joblessness, and homelessness among persons with serious mental illness. *Psychiatric Services, 53,* 565–573.

Fago, D. P. (2003). Evaluation and treatment of neurodevelopmental deficits in sexually aggressive children and adolescents. *Professional Psychology: Research & Practice, 34,* 248–257.

Feaster, D. J., Newman, F. L., & Rice, C. (2003). Longitudinal analysis when the experimenter does not determine when treatment ends: What is dose-response? *Clinical Psychology & Psychotherapy, 10,* 352–360.

Flannery, D. J., Williams, L. L., & Vazsonyi, A. T. (1999). Who are they with and what are they doing? Delinquent behavior, substance use, and early adolescents' after-school time. *American Journal of Orthopsychiatry, 69,* 247–253.

Fo, W. S., & O'Donnell, C. R. (1974). The Buddy System: Relationship and contingency conditions in a community intervention program for youth with nonprofessionals as behavior change agents. *Journal of Consulting & Clinical Psychology, 42,* 163–169.

Fo, W. S., & O'Donnell, C. R. (1975). The buddy system: Effect of community intervention on delinquent offenses. *Behavior Therapy, 6,* 522–524.

Gottfredson, M., & Hirschi, T. (1990). *A general theory of crime.* Stanford, CA: Stanford University Press.

Hillian, D., & Reitsma-Street, M. (2003). Parents and youth justice. *Canadian Journal of Criminology & Criminal Justice, 45,* 19–41.

Hirschi, T. (1969). *The causes of delinquency.* Berkeley: University of California Press.

Kataoka, S., Zima, B., Dupre, D., Moreno, K., Yang, X., & McCracken, J. (2001). Mental health problems and service use among female juvenile offenders: Their relationship to criminal histories. *Journal of the American Academy of Child and Adolescent Psychiatry, 40,* 549–555.

Kerr, M., & Stattin, H. (2000). What parents know, how they know it, and several forms of adolescent adjustment: Further support for a reinterpretation of monitoring. *Developmental Psychology, 36,* 366–380.

Lipsey, M. W. (1992). Juvenile delinquency treatment: A meta-analytic inquiry into the variability of effects. In T. D. Cook, H. Cooper, D. S. Cordray, H. Hartmann, L. V. Hedges, R. J. Light, T. A. Louis, & F. Mosteller (Eds.), *Meta-analysis for explanation: A casebook* (pp. 83–127). New York: Russell Sage Foundation.

Maegiste, E. (1992). Social isolation and juvenile delinquency in second generation immigrants. *Studia Psychologica, 34,* 153–165.

Mason, C. A., Chapman, D. A., Chang, S., & Simons, J. (2003). Impacting re-arrest rates among youth sentenced in adult court: An epidemiological examination of the Juvenile Sentencing Advocacy Project. *Journal of Clinical Child & Adolescent Psychology, 32,* 205–214.

Mazumdar, S., Houck, P. R., Lui, K. S., Mulsant, B. H., Pollock, B. G., Dew, M. A., et al. (2002). Intent-to-treat analysis for clinical trials: Use of data collected after termination of treatment protocol. *Journal of Psychiatric Research, 36,* 153–164.

McCord, J. (1992). The Cambridge-Somerville Study: A pioneering longitudinal experimental study of delinquency prevention. In J. McCord & R. E. Tremblay (Eds.), *Preventing antisocial behavior: Interventions from birth through adolescence* (pp. 196–206). New York: Guilford Press.

Mertinko, E., & Forbush, J. (2003, April). *Juvenile Mentoring Program (JUMP). Return on investment: Factors impacting the sustainability of JUMP projects.* Potomac, MD: Information Technology International.

Novotney, L. C., Mertinko, E., Lange, J., & Baker, T. K. (2000). *Juvenile Mentoring Program: A progress review.* Washington, DC: U.S. Department of Justice, Office of Justice Programs, Office of Juvenile Justice and Delinquency Prevention. Available at http://www.ojjdp.ncjrs.org/jump/

Novy, D., Gaa, J., Frankiewicz, R., Liberman, D., & Amerikaner, M. (1992). The association between patterns of family function and ego development of the juvenile offender. *Adolescence, 27,* 25–35.

O'Donnell, C. R., Lydgate, T., & Fo, W. S. (1979). The Buddy System: Review and follow-up. *Child Behavior Therapy, 1,* 161–169.

Rosenbaum, P. R., & Rubin, D. B. (1983). The central role of the propensity score in observational studies for causal effects. *Biometrika, 70,* 41–55.

Sampson, R. J., & Laub, J. H. (1993). *Crime in the making: Pathways and turning points through life.* Cambridge, MA: Harvard University Press.

Shapiro, D. A., Barkham, M., Stiles, W. B., Hardy, G. E., Rees, A., Reynolds, S., et al. (2003). Time is of the essence: A selective review of the fall and rise of brief therapy research. *Psychology & Psychotherapy: Theory, Research & Practice, 76,* 211–235.

Smith, W. (1988). Delinquency and abuse among juvenile sexual offenders. *Journal of Interpersonal Violence, 3,* 400–413.

Snyder, H. N. (2003, December). *Juvenile arrests 2001.* Washington, DC: U.S. Department of Justice, Office of Justice Programs, Office of Juvenile Justice and Delinquency Prevention.

Stoolmiller, M., & Blechman, E. A. (2003). *Substance use is a robust predictor of recidivism.* Unpublished manuscript.

White, C., Mertinko, E., & Van Orden, D. (2002, October). *Juvenile Mentoring Program (JUMP). Mentoring—An important strategy for diversion and re-entry programs.* Potomac, MD: Information Technology International.

White, J., Moffitt, T., Caspi, A., Bartusch, D., Needles, D., & Stouthamer-Loeber, M. (1994). Measuring impulsivity and examining its relationship to delinquency. *Journal of Abnormal Psychology, 103,* 192–205.

Wiesner, M. (2003). A longitudinal latent variable analysis of reciprocal relations between depressive symptoms and delinquency during adolescence. *Journal of Abnormal Psychology, 112,* 633–645.

Wiesner, M., & Capaldi, D. M. (2003). Relations of childhood and adolescent factors to offending trajectories of young men. *Journal of Research in Crime & Delinquency, 40,* 231–262.

Wilcox, R. R., & Keselman, H. J. (2003). Modern robust data analysis methods: Measures of central tendency. *Psychological Methods, 8,* 254–274.

Winters, K., Weller, C., & Meland, J. (1993). Extent of drug abuse among juvenile offenders. *Journal of Drug Issues, 23,* 515–524.

31

Pregnant and Parenting Adolescents

Lynn Blinn-Pike

Introduction

Pregnant and parenting adolescents face economic, social, medical, and academic challenges. They often lack the support that they need to overcome difficult circumstances and become healthy and productive citizens and parents. This chapter will focus on how mentoring can provide social support for pregnant and parenting adolescents.

The goal of this first section of the chapter is to provide an overview of the remainder of the chapter and to highlight issues and findings that provide important background for considering theory, research, and practice pertaining to mentoring of pregnant and/or parenting adolescents. In the section that addresses theoretical issues, social support theory and adult development theory, specifically Erikson's theory of generativity, are reviewed as they relate to mentoring pregnant and/or parenting adolescents. The following section considers extant research on mentoring pregnant and/or parenting adolescents. In the subsequent section pertaining to practice, there is a description of a promising one-to-one mentoring program for pregnant and/or parenting adolescents. Finally, in the last section, recommendations are presented to improve research and

practice related to mentoring pregnant and/or parenting adolescents.

Definitions

Several terms used in this chapter require definition. First, for this chapter, the term *mentoring* refers to both informal (naturally occurring) and formal (programmatically arranged) one-to-one relationships between adult females and pregnant and/or parenting adolescents. In both informal and formal relationships, mentors to pregnant and/or parenting adolescents are nonparental figures who develop friendships with them over time and serve as confidants and sources of information (Rhodes, Ebert, & Fischer, 1992).

In formal relationships, mentors are introduced to adolescents through organized programs and are "matched" with the adolescents. Informal relationships include ties with extended family, teachers, neighbors, and other adults that develop through unplanned meetings in locations such as schools, churches, or neighborhoods. Informal mentoring as conceptualized in this chapter also includes mentoring that may occur in the context of a one-to-one relationship that forms between an adult service provider or caseworker and a pregnant or parenting adolescent. For example, paid professional or paraprofessional home nurse visitors may provide mentoring while addressing the programmatic goal of improving the health of the young mother and her baby or preventing child maltreatment. Although not generally defined as mentors, they provide friendship and social support as a result of repeated visits with the young women they serve (Olds, Hill, Robinson, Song, & Little, 2000).

Second, the term *adolescents* refers to females between 10 and 22 years of age. This definition includes early adolescents because recent national studies indicate that 1 out of 5 adolescents has had sex before age 15 (Bruckner & Bearman, 2003; Flanigan, 2003; Terry & Manlove, 2003). Females in their early 20s are included because many of them experience their emerging adulthood while also experiencing pregnancy or parenthood. Many mentoring projects for pregnant and/or parenting adolescents use this broad definition and provide services for young mothers into their mid-20s.

In the past, more attention has been paid to mentoring adolescent mothers than to mentoring adolescent fathers (Rangarazan & Gleason, 1998). Yet increasingly, adolescent fathers are receiving attention and are being included in mentoring programs designed specifically for them (Mazza, 2002; Smith, Buzi, & Weinman, 2002). The focus of this chapter, however, is on mentoring the pregnant adolescent or adolescent mother because most of the available theory, research, and program practices have focused on mothers.

Adolescent Pregnancies and Births

Although pregnancy rates have declined in recent years, a large number of adolescents continue to become pregnant in the United States, and they need the support that can be provided through effective mentoring. The pregnancy rate for adolescents in the United States is approximately 85 per 1,000 females ages 15 to 19 (Singh & Darroch, 2000). This rate increased in the early 1990s to 116 per 1,000 females and then began to decrease in 1996 to the present rate. The pregnancy rate for adolescents ages 18 to 19 (100 per 1,000 females ages 18–19) is higher than the pregnancy rate for those ages

15 to 17 (80 per 1,000 females ages 15–17) (Child Trends, 2003).

Adolescent birthrates also have declined overall in recent years, although there is considerable variation in birthrates among different ethnic groups. The birthrate for adolescents in the United States is approximately 43 births per 1,000 females ages 15 to 19 (Hamilton, Martin, & Sutton, 2003). This rate increased in the early 1990s and then began to decrease in 1996 to the present rate, which is only slightly lower than the rate in 1986 (50 per 1,000). The birthrate for adolescent ages 18 to 19 is higher (73) compared with the birthrate for those 15 to 17 (23) and younger than 15 years (0.7). Currently, approximately 79% of adolescent births in the United States are to unmarried females, and this number has increased since the 1960s (Child Trends, 2003). These trends differ by race/ethnicity, age, and marital status. Before 1994, Black adolescents had the highest adolescent birthrate. However, Hispanics currently have the highest rate. In 2001, the birthrates per 1,000 15- to 19-year-old females for the major racial/ethnic groups were Hispanics (86), Blacks (72), Native Americans (56), non-Hispanic Whites (30), and Asian/Pacific Islanders (20).

The preceding figures and trends can have a direct impact on the size, composition, design, and funding of local mentoring programs serving pregnant and/or parenting adolescents. Depending on the geographic location of the mentoring program, the figures above point out that the pool of pregnant or parenting adolescents from which to recruit mentees will likely be made up predominantly of unmarried, minority females older than 17 years of age. The size of the pool may be decreasing in areas where the adolescent pregnancy rate is declining from its high levels in the mid-1900s. Local, state, and national funding may target the group(s) with the highest pregnancy and/or birthrates, who presently are minorities, particularly Hispanics.

Unique Aspects of Mentoring Pregnant and Parenting Adolescents

It is important to differentiate between pregnant and parenting adolescents because each group presents unique issues related to mentoring.

Pregnant teens are the focus of national debates over issues such as abstinence, sex education, contraception, and abortion. Parenting adolescents are the focus of, and are affected by, the national debates over adolescent issues such as adoption versus keeping babies, marriage, and adequacy of parenthood.

Mentoring programs for pregnant and/or parenting adolescents both face challenges similar to and different from those faced by other youth mentoring programs. Most youth mentoring programs serve higher-risk adolescents with co-occurring goals such as reducing substance use, fostering academic success, securing employment, developing positive interpersonal relationships, and preventing delinquency. Mentoring programs for pregnant and/or parenting adolescents often address these same goals, but they also target some of the unique goals and issues described below.

Pregnant Adolescents

Mentoring pregnant adolescents requires a basic knowledge of obstetrics and pediatrics because much of the mentoring time is spent discussing medical issues surrounding pregnancy, labor and delivery, and preparation for parenthood. The pregnant adolescent may ask her mentor for advice on topics such as prenatal care, preparation for delivery, care of a newborn, breast-feeding, and so on. The following are examples of the kinds of information that it may be important for mentors to know or for mentors to arrange for their mentees to learn through timely referrals to appropriate experts: (a) what will occur at each prenatal visit to the health care provider; (b) what medical complications can occur during pregnancy, labor, and delivery; (c) what drugs are given during pregnancy, labor, and delivery; (d) what are the signs of premature labor; (e) how to prepare for breast-feeding; (f) how to care for a newborn; and (g) how to report child abuse or domestic violence.

Many mentoring programs support mentors in attending prenatal visits and childbirth classes with their pregnant mentees, particularly if the adolescents have no family members or spouses/partners available to fulfill these roles. Depending on the nature of the mentor-adolescent relationship and their comfort levels, the mentor may become the mentee's coach during labor and delivery.

Adolescent Parents

Effectively mentoring an adolescent mother requires that the mentor have a basic knowledge of (a) infant/child care and safety; (b) breast-feeding; (c) infant/child development; (d) parenting; (e) family planning; (f) financial management; (g) nutrition; (h) legal issues surrounding paternity and child support, adoption, and foster care; (i) community resources; and (j) how to report child abuse and domestic violence (Blinn-Pike, Kuschel, McDaniel, Mingus, & Poole-Mutti, 1998).

Pregnant and Parenting Adolescents

Because approximately 25% of adolescent births are to females who have had a previous pregnancy (National Center for Health Statistics, 1997), the pregnant adolescent may already have had one or more children and be caring for them while experiencing her current pregnancy. In this case, the mentor might assist with the care of the older children while also mentoring the pregnant adolescent. In addition, she may become pregnant again while being mentored as an adolescent parent. When mentoring either the pregnant or parenting adolescent, the more children she has, the more complicated the mentoring relationship is likely to be and the more restricted the freedom is likely to be with which the dyad can pursue activities in the community. In addition, with more children, the parenting adolescent can be expected to need more support, and there will be a higher risk that her children will experience poverty, a dysfunctional family, and/or abuse (Zuravin, 1988).

THEORY

Social Support Theory

Pregnant and/or parenting adolescents face uphill struggles related to economics, health, education, interpersonal relationships, family relationships, and future success. Since the early 1980s, social support theory has been the dominant perspective used to explain the impact of having supportive individuals in the lives of pregnant and/or parenting adolescents (MacLeod & Weaver, 2003). Thompson (1995) defined *social support* as the social relationships that provide (or can potentially provide) material and interpersonal resources that are of value to the recipient, such as access to information and services, sharing of tasks and responsibilities, and skill acquisition.

After a brief overview of outcomes generally associated with social support during pregnancy and/or parenting, a more in-depth discussion of social support theory and research relevant specifically to mentoring pregnant and/or parenting adolescents is presented (see Barrera & Bonds, in this volume, for an examination of the more general role of social support in mentoring).

Cohen and Wills (1985) conducted a review of the literature on social support and referred to social support in pregnancy as having a "buffering" effect for individuals already under stress. Findings of numerous studies have indicated that both adolescent and adult women with low social support during pregnancy experience (a) poorer health during pregnancy, (b) later enrollment in prenatal care, (c) more difficult labors, and (d) greater depression (Giblin, Poland, & Sachs, 1987; Jacoby, Gorenflo, Black, Wunderlich, & Eyler, 1999; Renker, 1999; Stevenson, Maton, & Tei, 1999; Webster et al., 2000).

There also is evidence that infants born to mothers with low social support during pregnancy are more likely to display delayed psychomotor skills as infants, have more frequent hospitalizations than other infants, and require more psychiatric services later in life (Sydsjo, 1992). The preceding findings suggest that social support provided by a mentor to a pregnant adolescent may promote positive outcomes for both the mother and her child.

Numerous studies have pointed out that both adolescent and adult mothers with low social support (a) are more likely to experience depression, (b) are at increased risk for child abuse, and (c) show poorer parenting behaviors (Burchinal, Follmer, & Bryant, 1996; Chaffin,

Bonner, & Hill, 2001; Simons, 1996). Theoretically, support from informal or formal mentors may help prevent parenting adolescents from experiencing a range of negative outcomes, including dropping out of school, having repeat pregnancies, having negative postnatal outcomes, using violence with their children, becoming involved with high-risk partners, and receiving long-term public assistance (Cosey & Bechtel, 2001; Oakley, 1988; Sarason, Pierce, & Sarason, 1990; Webster et al., 2000).

To develop a better understanding of the role of social support in the lives of pregnant and/or parenting adolescents, each of the following questions may be useful to consider. First, is the social support provided by mentors to pregnant and/or parenting adolescents best conceptualized as a one-dimensional or multidimensional construct? Second, does social support provided by mentors have stress-buffering effects when provided to pregnant and/or parenting adolescents? Third, is the social support provided through mentoring relationships always good for both the adolescent mother and her child? And fourth, what are the mechanisms by which mentors provide social support to pregnant and/or parenting adolescents? Each of these questions is explored below.

With regard to the first question, numerous researchers dealing with social support in general have identified it as a multidimensional construct involving such differing functions as expressive (emotional), tangible (instrumental), and instructional (informational) support (Heaney & Israel, 2002). These differing functions have been used as a practical heuristic for categorizing and describing the various types of support and services that may be provided by mentors of pregnant and/or parenting adolescents (Blinn-Pike et al., 1998). However, Brown (1986) found that when applied to pregnant women (aged 16–42), a measure of social support yielded one factor or underlying dimension of support that accounted for 48% of the variance in partner support and 61% of variance in "other" support. Evidence of independence for ratings of emotional, material, informational, and appraisal support was lacking. Brown's findings may be due in part to the fact that separate analyses were not conducted for the adolescents and adults in the sample.

Differences in developmental characteristics between pregnant adolescents and adult women could affect the dimensionality of their experiences of social support. It remains to be determined whether social support for pregnant adolescents most closely resembles a one-dimensional or multidimensional construct. If Brown's findings are empirically validated and social support is a unidimensional construct for pregnant and/or parenting adolescents, mentors will have a more generalized impact on their mentees' perceptions of being supported, without differentiating the types of support that are provided.

With regard to the second question, research is mixed on whether the effects of social support on the health and well-being of pregnant and/or parenting adolescents are moderated by their levels of exposure to stressful events or by other factors such as incomplete psychological, cognitive, and physical development (Heaney & Israel, 2002).

The third question, whether social support provided through mentoring is necessarily and uniformly beneficial to the adolescent mother and her child, highlights the potential importance of the adage "Do no harm" when mentoring pregnant and/or parenting adolescents. At times, pregnant and/or parenting adolescents may perceive the members of their support networks, including mentors, both as intrusive and as sources of conflict and disappointment. Oakley (1988), for example, pointed out that for a pregnant woman who is already well supported, the arrival on her doorstep of an extra enthusiastic supporter may actually constitute a stressor. Pregnant and/or parenting adolescents who have adequate support from family and friends may find it stressful to make time for mentors in their lives and experience the mentor's presence as a social strain.

In relevant empirical research, Rhodes and Woods (1995) examined the ways that social support and social strain interacted in the lives of pregnant adolescents attending an alternative school and discussed how experiencing the dual transitions of pregnancy and adolescence can place stress on social relationships. Negative life events and social strain were found to be associated with greater reported symptoms of depression. A significant positive interaction

also was found between cognitive guidance (advice on how to do something or get something) and social strain.

In terms of parenting adolescents, Lewin (1996) reported evidence that significant relationships can provide both support and conflict in the lives of adolescent mothers. What they found to differentiate between feeling supported and feeling conflictual were factors such as the sources of support, the amount of conflicted support, and the presence of a stable adult male in the adolescent mother's childhood. Lewin concluded that, for the most part, conflicted support relationships did not result in more negative outcomes for the mother and baby, but instead that supportiveness and conflict could coexist within the mother's relationships without being harmful. Likewise, Way and Leadbeater (1999) examined family support during the first-year postpartum as a predictor of educational attainment at 6-years postpartum. In this research, higher perceived emotional support from family and residence with the grandmother predicted lower educational achievement for the adolescent mother. To the extent that family members provided support in an intrusive or otherwise counterproductive manner and assumed control over the care of her infant, the adolescent mother may have felt worthless, depressed, and not in control of her life. A sense of learned helplessness (Cemalcilar, Canbeyli, & Sunar, 2003) or the development of an overdependence on family and relatives concerning the care of her infant may have carried over into lack of initiative concerning schoolwork. Such processes further illustrate factors that could compromise the benefits of support provided in mentoring relationships for pregnant and/or parenting adolescents.

The fourth question focuses on the lack of understanding of the process through which mentors and mentoring programs may provide beneficial forms of social support to pregnant and/or parenting adolescents. Examples of supportive activities that can be performed by a mentor of a pregnant adolescent include (a) attending birth education classes together, (b) attending prenatal visits together, (c) helping time the adolescent's labor contractions, and (d) serving as labor and delivery coach.

Examples of supportive activities that can be performed by a mentor of a parenting adolescent are (a) supporting the adolescent in her decision to breast-feed; (b) helping the adolescent prepare a safe environment for a newborn or young child; (c) helping her find resources such as housing, furniture, and baby care items; (d) helping her care for a sick infant or child; and (e) providing transportation for her to attend scheduled postnatal, family planning, and pediatric appointments.

After conducting a mentoring program for pregnant and/or parenting adolescents for 3 years (1994–1997), Blinn-Pike et al. (1998, p. 123) proposed a process-oriented version of social support theory related specifically to mentoring pregnant and/or parenting adolescents called "quasi-parenting." The idea of quasi-parenting as social support emerged from an analysis of detailed weekly narratives that were written by 99 mentors over 6 months of mentoring. Blinn-Pike and colleagues (1998) proposed that assuming quasi-parenting roles is one of the mechanisms through which mentors can be effective with these two populations.

Quasi-parenting was defined as occurring when the mentor and adolescent were comfortable with (a) the mentor providing the adolescent with the types of emotional, instrumental, and/or instructional support that are generally assumed to be the purview of the family; (b) reaching a level of emotional intimacy in which they discuss personal and intimate details of the adolescent's life; and (c) the mentor being involved in the mundane, important, and critical aspects of the adolescent's life.

The criteria used in determining quasi-parenting above is in keeping with what Veiel (1985) suggested when he differentiated between social support provided on an everyday basis, on one hand, and that available in significant or crisis situations, on the other. As a quasi-parent, a mentor might be the individual who assists the pregnant and/or parenting adolescent with everyday chores such as laundry or grocery shopping. The mentor also may be involved in more important events such as helping her plan her wedding and more critical events such as helping her seek counseling about previous or ongoing abuse. These considerations suggest that in addition to the extent to which the pregnant or parenting adolescent is receiving instrumental, emotional, and tangible forms of support in the mentoring relationships, a further significant factor mediating outcomes could be the degree to which the dyad has reached a point in the relationship when they both are receptive to the mentor assuming a quasi-parenting role as evidenced by the three criteria listed earlier.

A further important theoretical issue relevant to each of the four preceding questions is the time frame required for different processes involving social support in the mentoring of pregnant and/or parenting adolescents to emerge. Available research suggests that both the advantages and disadvantages to youth of mentoring relationships are proportional to how long the relationships last (Grossman & Rhodes, 2002). Theoretically, longer-term relationships may be essential for certain processes relating to social support for pregnant and/or parenting adolescents to fully emerge, such as the mentor assuming and being accepted in a quasi-parenting role. Conversely, as more useful and appropriate social support is provided by the mentor, there may be a greater likelihood of the mentor meeting the adolescent's needs in ways that strengthen the relationship and help it endure. The duration of mentoring relationships for pregnant and/or parenting adolescents thus may exhibit important and bidirectional linkages with processes relating to social support.

The Role of Mentors in Mentoring Relationships With Pregnant and/or Parenting Adolescents

Another significant set of theoretical considerations pertains to the characteristics of mentors that may promote the most effective mentoring of pregnant and/or parenting adolescents. Specific questions include the following. What type of individual makes the best mentor for adolescents? What motivates a mentor to want to make a commitment to mentoring a pregnant and/or parenting adolescent? And what predicts which mentors are able to sustain their relationships with these adolescents over time? Greater understanding of these issues could be instrumental in helping identify effective approaches to the tasks of recruiting, assigning (i.e., making "match" decisions), and sustaining mentors in programs for pregnant and/or parenting adolescents. This could include the development of psychometrically sound instruments, with high predictive validity, to use to screen potential mentors for the ability to develop and sustain quality relationships with their assigned adolescents.

Theoretically, the concept of *generativity* may provide a useful framework for considering mentor characteristics that promote effective mentoring of pregnant and/or parenting adolescents. Generativity, or the concern for future generations, is an important concept in adult development theory. In 1950, Erikson introduced the concept of generativity and described it as the seventh stage in the life cycle, loosely associated with middle adulthood. Generativity is the concern for and commitment to promoting the next generation. Through parenting, teaching, and mentoring, generative individuals attempt to benefit youth and promote the welfare of individuals and social systems that will outlive them. Theorists have described generativity as a "need to be needed" that is fulfilled by nurturing, assisting, or being in some other way important to others (Stewart, Franz, & Layton, 1988, p. 56). Erikson believed that bearing and raising children was the prototype for generativity. McAdams and de St. Aubin (1992, p. 29) similarly noted that generative adults often are described as striving to "give birth to" and nurture things, people, and outcomes that may outlive them.

Theoretically, highly generative individuals thus may be drawn to mentoring roles, particularly mentoring pregnant and/or parenting adolescents, because of the opportunity to mentor two generations—both the adolescent mother and her child(ren). Highly generative individuals may be inclined to invest time and effort in mentoring pregnant and/or parenting adolescents, furthermore, because they view this experience as an opportunity to mold or shape both the adolescent and child(ren). Programatically, highly generative individuals thus may be more easily recruited to mentoring programs for pregnant and/or parenting adolescents and, once involved, may be more likely to sustain strong commitments to both their mentees and their mentees' children.

The Loyola Generativity Scale (LGS) is one of the most well-known self-report measures of generativity (McAdams & de St. Aubin, 1992). The LGS includes 20 items that measure generative concern and the belief in the goodness of the human species. Examples of items include, "I try to pass along the knowledge I have gained through my experiences," and "If I were unable to have children of my own, I would like to adopt children." Highly generative individuals, as measured on the LGS, have been shown to (a) be more invested in their children's education (Natagawa, 1991); (b) have larger support networks and networks of friends (Hart, 1997); (c) express greater attachment to and involvement in their communities (Cole & Stewart, 1996); and (d) have greater satisfaction with life, happiness, self-esteem, and goal stability (de St. Aubin & McAdams, 1995). The identified characteristics of highly generative individuals also would be desirable in mentors of pregnant and/or parenting adolescents. These qualities and behaviors thus could be influential in mediating any beneficial effects that are associated with pairing highly generative individuals as mentors for pregnant and/or parenting adolescents.

RESEARCH

To date, there has been only limited research on the impact of mentoring on pregnant and/or parenting adolescents. The following highlighted studies have examined outcomes associated with the presence of natural or informal mentors, as well as formal mentors, in the lives of pregnant and/or parenting adolescents. Natural and formal types of mentors are considered separately in this section. Only studies that utilized a quasi-experimental or experimental design with a comparison or control group are included.

Natural Mentors

Rhodes et al. (1992) examined natural mentors in the social networks of African American adolescent mothers. They found that when 58 adolescent mothers with natural mentors were compared with 71 adolescent mothers without natural mentors, the mentored group reported (a) lower levels of depression; (b) larger support networks, excluding their mentors; (c) greater utilization of social support; and (d) more satisfaction with the natural support they had received. In a second study, Rhodes, Contreras, and Mangelsdorf (1994) similarly found that when 19 Latina adolescent mothers with natural mentors were compared with 35 adolescents without natural mentors, the mentored group reported (a) lower levels of depression, (b) greater satisfaction with their support resources, and (c) recollections of more satisfying childhood relationships with their mothers.

Finally, in a recent longitudinal study, Klaw, Rhodes, and Fitzgerald (2003) studied the role of natural mentors in the lives of pregnant and/or parenting adolescents who were tracked over 2 years. Results indicated that at end of this period, compared with 89 pregnant and/or parenting adolescents who did not identify lasting mentoring relationships, a group of 36 who did report lasting mentoring ties were more likely to have remained in school or graduated. In addition, the young women reporting long-term mentoring relationships reported more emotional attachment to their mentors than to their mothers and that emotional support from their mentors was more important to them than maternal support.

Formal Mentoring Programs

Blinn-Pike and Mingus (1997) conducted the Missouri Volunteer Resource Mothers Program (MVRM) from 1994 to 1997 and followed 75 pregnant adolescents (30 mentored and 45 comparison group). Adolescents in the mentored group were assigned a mentor, a trained volunteer from the community whose job was to provide emotional and instrumental social support through 3 hours of weekly contact. Comparison group adolescents were not assigned a mentor. More detail about the operation of the MVRM program is available in the "Practice" section of this chapter. The mentored group was recruited from social service agencies, local health departments, and schools in three counties in Missouri. The comparison group was recruited from similar sites in three Missouri counties where mentoring was not available for pregnant and/or parenting adolescents. The mentor and comparison counties were matched on size, adolescent pregnancy rate, and urbanicity. There were no significant differences between the two

groups on age, race, average number of months pregnant, number in school, number employed, number living with their parents, or number married. The mentored group reported entering prenatal care slightly later (mean = 2.25 months versus 1.66 months) and reported receiving slightly less public assistance.

Blinn-Pike and Mingus (1997) surveyed both groups on the Parenting Stress Index (PSI) (Abidon, 1990) within 4 weeks of delivering their babies, and when their babies were 1 year old. The PSI measures the adolescent mother's perception of her parental competence, attachment to her infant, depression, social isolation, heath, and maternal role. The results revealed that the mentoring had the greatest impact on the PSI subscale related to social isolation, which measures severe isolation from peers, relatives, and other support systems. At both the postpartum and 12-month assessments, when controlling for initial group differences, the mentored group had significantly lower (better) social isolation scores. In addition, at 1-year postpartum, the results revealed that compared with the nonmentored group, the mentored group (a) had taken their infants to the hospital less often, (b) breast-fed longer, and (c) knew more about infant care and where to obtain social services.

Silfven (1990) used an experimental design to evaluate the effects of a social support (mentoring) intervention on postpartum depression. In this research, 88 pregnant adolescents were assigned randomly to either the mentored group (46) or a control group (42). Adolescents in the mentored group were assigned a mentor, a trained volunteer from the community whose job was to provide emotional and instrumental social support for 3 hours per week. Control group adolescents were not assigned a mentor. All adolescents were assessed in their third trimesters of pregnancy, and at 4-weeks and 3-months postpartum on a series of depression measures. The results showed that there were no differences in rate or severity of depression between the mentored and control subjects at any of the three times.

Both the Blinn-Pike and Mingus and Silfven studies were rare in their longitudinal designs and use of a comparison or control group. However, both evidenced programmatic limitations that impacted the results, such as relatively small sample sizes due to the resource-intensive nature of their mentoring programs and the characteristics of the adolescents, including geographic mobility and emotional and familial instability.

According to Blinn-Pike and Mingus (1997), interviews and focus groups with the mentors and mentees revealed that the 30 adolescents in the mentored group represented only those dyads who had reached the "quasi-parenting" stage of their mentoring relationships and had received mentoring for at least 12-months postpartum. An additional 42 pregnant adolescents enrolled in the MVRM program and did not participate, and 14 received less than 12 months of mentoring. No assessments were made of the levels of generativity of the mentors in the MVRM program. It is not known whether the mentors who remained in their roles for at least 12 months were more generative in their thinking.

Silfven (1990) reported that the lack of significant group differences in depression scores at 3-months postpartum may have been due to the fact that (a) the mentoring began too late in the adolescents' pregnancies, (b) some of the mentor/mentee matches did not start soon enough, (c) some of the mentees needed to be rematched during the intervention period, (d) the mentoring intervention was not intensive enough and needed to be more than 3 hours per week, and (e) postpartum depression should also have been assessed using clinical interviews and the *DSM-IV* criteria for diagnosing major or minor depression.

PRACTICE

Previously in this chapter, it was suggested that (a) there may be significant differences in effective mentoring practices for pregnant versus parenting adolescents; (b) assessing social support, specifically quasi-parenting, may be helpful in understanding the ways in which mentoring can be effective with pregnant and/or parenting adolescents; and (c) more attention needs to be paid to generativity as a possible factor in why mentors are attracted to a mentoring program for pregnant and/or parenting adolescents and why some mentors are more successful than others.

In this section, a promising training model for the development of mentoring programs for pregnant and/or parenting adolescents is described that was designed to be sensitive to each of the preceding concerns.

After directing and evaluating a one-to-one community-based mentoring program for more than 100 pregnant and/or parenting adolescents for 3 years, Blinn-Pike (1997) developed a multifaceted program for assisting other groups in starting mentoring programs for pregnant and/or parenting adolescents. Blinn-Pike's program was developed at the Center on Adolescent Sexuality, Pregnancy, and Parenting (CASPP) at the University of Missouri, Columbia, and was called the Missouri Volunteer Resource Mothers Program (MVRM). The training strategies were aimed at program developers and included opportunities for them to (a) be involved with a listserv, (b) view a Web site, (c) receive on-site technical assistance, and (d) attend an annual conference. In addition, an MVRM training manual and training video were available. On-site consultation on MVRM was provided to program developers in Georgia, Hawaii, Missouri, New Mexico, and New York.

The MVRM training model was based on five programmatic recommendations that stem from the (a) medical focus imposed by working with pregnant and/or parenting adolescents, (b) the potentially controversial nature of any program dealing with adolescent sexuality and parenthood, (c) the goal of moving mentor-mentee relationships toward quasi-parenting through the provision of intensive social support, and (d) the goal of involving highly generative mentors who will remain committed to the program over time. First, it is recommended that the nature and scope of the mentoring program be locally based and context specific. It must reflect local values and attitudes toward adolescent sexuality, pregnancy, and parenting. Second, it is recommended that mentoring staff and mentors be prepared for the adolescents to (a) move frequently; (b) be preoccupied with events in their lives and their interpersonal relationships with their families, babies' fathers, and babies' fathers' families; and (c) be in need of legal, psychological, and medical referrals. More generally, mentoring pregnant and/or parenting adolescents is assumed by the model to require dynamic and fluid processes, because these adolescents frequently are in psychological and physical distress and subject to changing contextual circumstances.

Third, it is recommended that a multifaceted evaluation component be included in the program, including analysis of weekly mentor reports, pre- and posttests with all participants, pretests and posttests with a nonmentored comparison group of pregnant and/or parenting adolescents, and interviews and focus groups with mentors and adolescents. The evaluation data can be used to guide program development, to help secure funding, and to demonstrate that accountability procedures are in place (see the chapters by Grossman and by Coyne, Duffy, & Wandersman, in this volume, for more in-depth information on program evaluation and accountability).

Illustratively, Blinn-Pike and Mingus (1997) content analyzed the weekly contact reports from 30 mentors over the course of the first 6 months of their relationships with pregnant and/or parenting adolescents. It was discovered that what was *not* happening between the mentor and mentee was of significant importance. On a checklist identifying what information the mentor had provided to the mentee, few mentors checked that they had provided information about violence, substance abuse, or cigarette smoking. More popular topics included preparation for labor and delivery, seeking needed parenting resources, and how to parent a newborn. Subsequent interviews with the 30 mentors revealed that they felt uncomfortable and unprepared to discuss the more sensitive topics with their mentees. As a result of this identified and unmet need, additional funding was secured to provide mentors with training on how to talk about sensitive topics with their mentees.

Fourth, it is recommended that program staff seek mentors who espouse generativity themes in their application materials and interviews. Blinn-Pike and Mingus (1997) reported that some of the reasons mentors gave for being involved in the MVRM program that did not represent generativity were (a) to be able to include the experience on their resumes, (b) to fill personal needs for social contact with other women, and (c) to have a volunteer opportunity

where their young children could accompany them.

Fifth, and finally, it is recommended that the program follow a specific and sequential framework. The MVRM framework was developed after observing numerous mentoring programs and reviewing the research literature on successful mentoring programs. As shown in Table 31.1, the framework contains a broad overview of 10 elements that are assumed to be necessary to ensure the effectiveness of a mentoring program for pregnant and/or parenting adolescents. The overview serves as a general introduction to the elements prior to beginning a program. The overview provides an answer to the question, "What will we do if we start a mentoring program for pregnant and/or parenting adolescents?" The elements are outlined in the leftmost column of Table 31.1.

In addition, the MVRM training manual is divided into two more specific sections describing (a) why and how it is important to prepare before starting a mentoring program for pregnant and/or parenting adolescents and (b) a step-by-step strategy for operating the program. These two sections are summarized in the middle and right-most columns of Table 31.1, respectively (see Coyne and colleagues, in this volume, for more in-depth discussion of results-based tools for mentoring program accountability and evaluation).

FUTURE DIRECTIONS

Synthesis

As was pointed out in the descriptions of the studies by Blinn-Pike and Mingus (1997) and Silfven (1990), mentoring programs for pregnant and parenting adolescents are labor- and resource intensive, thereby making it difficult to gather a knowledge base of generalizable results. Large sample sizes and experimental evaluation designs are rare. In addition, although social support theory has been valuable in understanding adolescent outcomes derived from mentoring relationships, there has been no theoretical foundation from this literature on which to make programmatic decisions in relation to mentoring pregnant and/or parenting adolescents.

Table 31.1   Framework for Mentoring Programs for Pregnant and/or Parenting Adolescents

Overview	*Preparation Before You Start*	*Step-by-Step Strategies for Conducting a Program*
Assess compatibility with local culture and values.	1. Begin with a vision.	1. Form a coalition.
Assess commitment of staff, organization, and community.	2. Clarify stakeholders' commitments.	2. Set program goals and objectives.
Develop clear goals and objectives that can function within a larger context of existing services that support adolescents.	3. Assess program feasibility.	3. Secure funding.
Conduct a small-scale pilot program.	4. Become knowledgeable about adolescent development.	4. Recruit mentors.
Orient both prospective mentors and adolescents to their new roles.	5. Address program risk factors and confidentiality issues.	5. Recruit adolescents.
Focus on being dyad driven, and addressing the needs of both the mentors and adolescents.	6. Master the framework for successful youth mentoring programs.	6. Orient and train mentors.
Carefully select and match dyads in the best interests of both individuals and the program.	7. Evaluate preprogram planning process.	7. Orient adolescents.
Monitor the relationships between mentors and adolescents, sometimes as often as once a week.		8. Match mentors and adolescents.
Conduct ongoing training for mentors as well as for nonmentoring staff and volunteers.		9. Organize and conduct regular group meetings.
Conduct both process and outcome evaluation as an integral part of the overall program from the beginning.		10. Evaluate each step.

SOURCE: Blinn-Pike (1997).

Despite the limitations described above, a promising framework for program development may begin to emerge by addressing the constructs of quasi-parenting and generativity. Identifying dyads that have achieved quasi-parenting relationships may assist with understanding the characteristics of successful and enduring mentoring relationships. The concept of generativity from adult development theory appears to hold significant promise for answering important questions concerning who makes the best mentors for pregnant and/or parenting adolescents.

Recommendations for Research

1. *Investigate mentoring of pregnant and/or parenting adolescents within the framework of social support theory.* Four questions were discussed earlier in this chapter about social support and mentoring pregnant and/or parenting adolescents: (a) dimensionality of support,

(b) stress-buffering effects of support, (c) possible negative effects of support, and (d) mechanisms by which mentoring is provided. At present, there is a need for systematic investigation of each of these questions. One priority in this area should be to conduct research that examines the comparative benefits of mentors who do and do not assume quasi-parenting roles with pregnant and/or parenting adolescents. To assess when a mentoring relationship reaches a quasi-parenting stage, mentors and adolescents can be asked to keep records of their activities together. These can then be content analyzed for evidence of meeting the quasi-parenting criteria described previously in this chapter.

The suggested mentor "contact form" contained in the MVRM manual asks the mentor to check items from three lists (activities carried out together during the contact, problems discussed, and services or referrals provided), record the length and location of the contact, and add any notes that are important for the program staff to be aware of related to the adolescent and/or their relationship. When this is completed on a regular basis (including telephone contact) and analyzed by the program staff, it is a useful tool with which to chart their movement toward the three criteria of a quasi-parenting relationship.

2. *Investigate the role of generativity in mentoring of pregnant and/or parenting adolescents.* The concept of generativity holds promise for increasing understanding of mentor characteristics that promote effective mentoring of pregnant and/or parenting adolescents and, by implication, for the development of screening tools to use to recruit and retain effective mentors. As a first step in addressing this possibility, research should be conducted to investigate several questions. Specifically, compared with mentors who are low on generativity, are highly generative mentors more likely to (a) sustain mentoring relationships over time; (b) develop enriching, educational, and supportive relationships with adolescents; (c) develop positive attachments to pregnant and/or parenting adolescents; or (d) assume quasi-parenting roles with pregnant and/or parenting adolescents? Ideally, these questions could be examined by administering an instrument assessing generativity, such as the LGS, to mentors within studies of

pregnant and parenting adolescents that are longitudinal and experimental or quasi-experimental in design.

3. *Conduct rigorous evaluations of formal mentoring programs of pregnant and/or parenting adolescents.* Given the paucity of data addressing the effectiveness of formal mentoring programs of pregnant and/or parenting adolescents and the mixed results of studies that have been conducted, there is also a pressing need for further investigations of this nature. Adolescent outcome indicators in these studies could include, for example, educational outcomes, birth outcomes, health status during pregnancy, and mental health and be complemented by infant outcome indicators such as birth weights, gestational ages at birth, APGAR scores, and achievement of developmental milestones.

4. *Conduct rigorous examinations of the similarities and differences in mentoring processes and program practices that are most effective for pregnant versus parenting adolescents.* Program developers will benefit from recognizing that mentoring pregnant adolescents is qualitatively different from mentoring adolescent parents. The former is focused more on medical issues and preparation for labor and delivery. The latter is focused more on parenting skills and knowledge, as well as achieving educational, social, and financial goals. In addition, the complexity of mentoring adolescents who are both parents and pregnant needs to be addressed. Likewise, the complexity of operating a mentoring program that includes both pregnant and parenting adolescents needs to be addressed.

5. *Investigate how to effectively mentor adolescent fathers.* Finally, as recognition grows of the potential importance of providing mentoring opportunities to adolescent fathers, research should be conducted to keep pace with and inform these trends. The issues raised in preceding recommendations provide a useful starting point for a research agenda in this area.

Recommendations for Practice

1. *Clearly define program goals and philosophy.* The conflictual and sometimes hostile feelings that exist about adolescent sexual and reproductive issues at the local, state, and national

levels cannot be ignored within mentoring programs for pregnant and/or parenting adolescents. Prospective mentors may worry that their values will be challenged and their relationships with their mentees will be damaged if their mentees choose to have abortions or to place their babies for adoption. It is recommended that program developers write a statement for mentors and community stakeholders stating the mentoring project's philosophy related to abstinence, sex education, adolescent contraceptive use, family planning, abortion, adoption, and so forth. This will prevent miscommunication with stakeholders and assist potential mentors in deciding whether they want to be become involved based on the match between their views on these issues and the philosophy of the program.

2. *Develop and disseminate recommended program practices.* The MENTOR/National Mentoring Partnership (2003) has published a second edition of their guide titled *Elements of Effective Practice.* This publication contains the latest views on effective mentoring practices, many of which have received empirical support (DuBois, Holloway, Valentine, & Cooper, 2002). The topics covered include program design and planning, management, operations, and evaluation. However, the unique practices that are necessary when mentoring pregnant and/or parenting adolescents, and that have been discussed in this chapter, are not covered. A further recommendation is that a publication dealing with recommended elements of practice in mentoring pregnant and/or parenting adolescents be written and widely disseminated. There are mentoring programs for pregnant and/or parenting adolescents that have used the MENTOR/National Mentoring Partnership and the MVRM models, but these programs have not received widespread attention. A nomination and selection process could be used to determine which strategies from such programs should be included as recommended practices. A comprehensive description of programs for mentoring of pregnant and/or parenting adolescents with the strongest empirical support to date could be included as well, thereby increasing awareness of the designs, cultural adaptations, and evaluation findings of some of the most promising programs for this population.

REFERENCES

Abidon, R. R. (1990). *Parenting Stress Index* (3rd ed.). Charlottesville, VA: Pediatric Psychology Press.

Blinn-Pike, L. (1997). *Missouri Volunteer Resource Mothers training manual.* University of Missouri: Columbia.

Blinn-Pike, L., Kuschel, D., McDaniel, A., Mingus, S., & Poole-Mutti, M. (1998). The process of mentoring pregnant adolescents: An exploratory study. *Family Relations, 47,* 119–127.

Blinn-Pike, L., & Mingus, S. (1997). *Missouri Volunteer Resource Mothers Project: Research report.* Final report submitted to the Missouri Children's Trust Fund, Jefferson City, MO.

Brown, M. A. (1986). Social support during pregnancy: A unidimensional or multidimensional construct? *Nursing Research, 35,* 1–4.

Bruckner, H., & Bearman, P. (2003). Dating behavior and sexual activity of young adolescents: Analyses of the National Longitudinal Study of Adolescent Health. In A. B. Brown & C. Flanigan (Eds.), *14 and younger: The sexual behavior of young adolescents* (pp. 31–57). Washington, DC: National Campaign to Prevent Teen Pregnancy.

Burchinal M. R., Follmer, A., & Bryant, D. M. (1996). The relations of maternal social support and family structure with maternal responsiveness and child outcomes among African American families. *Developmental Psychology, 32,* 1073–1083.

Cemalcilar, Z., Canbeyli, R., & Sunar, D. (2003). Learned helplessness, therapy, and personality traits: An experimental study. *Journal of Social Psychology, 143,* 65–81.

Chaffin, M., Bonner, B. L., & Hill, R. F. (2001). Family preservation and family support programs: Child maltreatment outcomes across client risk levels and program types. *Child Abuse and Neglect, 25,* 1269–1289.

Child Trends. (2003). *Teen births.* Retrieved September 10, 2003, from http://www.childtrends databank.org

Cohen, S., & Wills, T. A. (1985). Stress, social support and the buffering hypothesis. *Psychological Bulletin, 98,* 310–357.

Cole, E. R., & Stewart, A. J. (1996). Meanings of political participation among Black and White women: Political identity and social responsibility.

Journal of Personality and Social Psychology, 71, 130–140.

Cosey, E. J., & Bechtel, G. A. (2001). Family support and prenatal care among unmarried African American teenage primiparas. *Journal of Community Health Nursing, 18,* 107–115.

de St. Aubin, E., & McAdams, D. P. (1995). The relations of generative concern and generative action to personality traits, satisfaction/happiness with life and ego development. *Journal of Adult Development, 2,* 99–112.

DuBois, D. L., Holloway, B. E., Valentine, J. C., & Cooper, H. (2002). Effectiveness of mentoring programs for youth: A meta-analytic review. *American Journal of Community Psychology, 30,* 157–197.

Erikson, E. H. (1950). *Childhood and society.* New York: Norton.

Flanigan, C. (2003). Sexual activity among girls under age 15: Findings from the National Survey of Family Growth. In A. B. Brown & C. Flanigan (Eds.), *14 and younger: The sexual behavior of young adolescents* (pp. 57–65). Washington, DC: National Campaign to Prevent Teen Pregnancy.

Giblin, P. T., Poland, M. L., & Sachs, B. A. (1987). Effects of social supports on attitudes and health behaviors of pregnant adolescents. *Journal of Adolescent Health Care, 8,* 273–279.

Grossman, J. B., & Rhodes, J. E. (2002). The test of time: Predictors and effects of duration in youth mentoring relationships. *American Journal of Community Psychology, 30,* 199–219.

Hamilton, B. E., Martin, J. A., & Sutton, P. D. (2003). Births: Preliminary data for 2002. *National Vital Statistics Reports, 51.* Hyattsville, MD: National Center for Health Statistics.

Hart, H. M. (1997). *Generativity and social interventions among African-American and White adults.* Unpublished doctoral dissertation, Northwestern University, Evanston, IL.

Heaney, C. A., & Israel, B. A. (2002). Social networks and social support. In K. Glanz, B. K. Rimer, & F. M. Lewis (Eds.), *Health behavior and health education* (pp. 185–210). San Francisco: Jossey-Bass.

Jacoby, M., Gorenflo, D., Black, E., Wunderlich, C., & Eyler, A. E. (1999). Rapid repeat pregnancy and experiences of interpersonal violence among low-income adolescents. *American Journal of Preventive Medicine, 16,* 318–321.

Klaw, E. L., Rhodes, J. E., & Fitzgerald, L. F. (2003). Natural mentors in the lives of African American Adolescent Mothers: Tracking relationships over time. *Journal of Youth and Adolescence, 32,* 223–232.

Lewin, A. B. (1996). *Patterns and consequences of conflict in the support relationships of teenage mothers.* Unpublished doctoral dissertation, Rutgers University, New Jersey.

MacLeod, A. J., & Weaver, S. M. (2003). Teenage pregnancy: Attitudes, social support, and adjustment to pregnancy during the antenatal period. *Journal of Reproductive and Infant Psychology, 21,* 49–59.

Mazza, C. (2002). Young dads: The effects of a parenting program on urban African-American adolescent fathers. *Adolescence, 37,* 682–693.

McAdams, D. P., & de St. Aubin, E. (1992). A theory of generativity and its assessment through self-report, behavioral act and narrative themes in autobiography. *Journal of Personality and Social Psychology, 62,* 1003–1015.

MENTOR/National Mentoring Partnership. (2003). *Elements of effective practice* (2nd ed.). Alexandria, VA: Author.

Natagawa, K. (1991). *Explorations into the correlates of public school reform and parental involvement.* Unpublished doctoral dissertation, Northwestern University, Evanston, IL.

National Center for Health Statistics. (1997). *Preliminary data for 1996.* Washington, DC: Author.

Oakley, A. (1988). Is social support good for the health of mothers and babies? *Journal of Reproductive and Infant Psychology, 6,* 3–21.

Olds, D., Hill, P., Robinson, J., Song, N., & Little, C. (2000). Update on home visiting for pregnant women and parents of young children. *Current Problems in Pediatrics, 30,* 107–141.

Rangarazan, A., & Gleason, P. (1998). Young unwed fathers of ADC children: Do they provide support? *Demography, 35,* 175–186.

Renker, P. R. (1999). Physical abuse, social support, self-care and pregnancy outcomes of older adolescents. *Journal of Obstetric, Gynecological and Neonatal Nursing, 28,* 377–388.

Rhodes, J. E., Contreras, J. M., & Mangelsdorf, S. C. (1994). Natural mentor relations among Latina adolescent mothers: Psychological adjustment, moderating processes and the role of early parental acceptance. *American Journal of Community Psychology, 22,* 211–227.

Rhodes, J. E., Ebert, L., & Fischer, K. (1992). Natural mentors: An overlooked resource in the social networks of young, African American mothers. *American Journal of Community Psychology, 20,* 445–461.

Rhodes, J. E., & Woods, M. (1995). Comfort and conflict in the relationships of pregnant, minority adolescents: Social support as a moderator of social strain. *Journal of Community Psychology, 23,* 74–84.

Sarason, B. R., Pierce, G. R., & Sarason, I. G. (1990). Social support: The sense of acceptance and the role of relationships. In B. R. Sarason, G. R. Pierce, & I. G. Sarason (Eds.), *Social support: An interfactional view* (pp. 95–128). New York: Wiley.

Silfven, S. T. (1990). *Postpartum depression in unwed teenage mothers* (Doctoral dissertation, University of Wisconsin, 1997). *Dissertation Abstracts International, 52-B,* 1738. (UMI No. 9111361)

Simons, R. L. (1996). The impact of marital and social network support on quality of parenting. In G. R. Pierce & B. R. Sarason (Eds.), *Handbook of social support and the family* (pp. 269–287). New York: Plenum Press.

Singh, S., & Darroch, J. E. (2000). Adolescent pregnancy and childbearing: Levels and trends in developed countries. *Family Planning Perspectives, 32,* 14–23.

Smith, P. B., Buzi, R. S., & Weinman, M. L. (2002). Programs for young fathers: Essential components and evaluation issues. *North American Journal of Psychology, 4,* 81–92.

Stevenson, W., Maton, K., & Tei, D. M. (1999). Social support, relationship quality, and well-being among pregnant adolescents. *Journal of Adolescence, 22,* 109–121.

Stewart, A. J., Franz, E., & Layton, L. (1988). The changing self: Using personal documents to study lives. *Journal of Personality, 56,* 41–74.

Sydsjo, G. (1992). Prevalence and significance of social and psychological risk factors during pregnancy. *International Journal of Technological Assessment in Health Care, 8*(Suppl. 1), 123–128.

Terry, E., & Manlove, J. (2003). Dating and sexual experiences among middle school youth: Analyses of the NLSY97. In A. B. Brown & C. Flanigan (Eds.), *14 and younger: The sexual behavior of young adolescents* (pp. 17–31). Washington, DC: National Campaign to Prevent Teen Pregnancy.

Thompson, R. A. (1995). *Preventing child maltreatment through social support.* Thousand Oaks, CA: Sage.

Veiel, H. O. F. (1985). Dimensions of social support: A conceptual framework for research. *Social Psychiatry, 20,* 156–162.

Way, N., & Leadbeater, B. (1999). Pathways toward educational achievement among African American and Puerto Rican adolescent mothers: Reexamining the role of social support from families. *Development and Psychopathology, 11,* 349–364.

Webster, B. A., Linnane, J. W., Dibley, L. M., Hinson, J. K., Starrenburg, S. E., & Roberts, J. A. (2000). Measuring social support in pregnancy: Can it be simple and meaningful? *Birth, 27,* 97–103.

Zuravin, S. J. (1988). Fertility patterns: Their relationship to child physical abuse and child neglect. *Journal of Marriage and the Family, 50,* 983–993.

32

ABUSED AND NEGLECTED YOUTH

PRESTON A. BRITNER AND LISA KRAIMER-RICKABY

INTRODUCTION

Children and adolescents who have experienced maltreatment and, in many cases, out-of-home placements are becoming an increasingly important population to serve and support. During the past decade, mentoring programs have been expanded to include these youth in greater numbers. Based on findings reported in their meta-analysis of mentoring program effects, DuBois, Holloway, Valentine, and Cooper (2002) suggested that youth from backgrounds of greater social and economic risk (defined broadly) both have the most to gain and tend to benefit the most from youth mentoring, especially when best practices are employed and strong relationships are formed. Yet despite some optimism that mentoring has the potential to benefit many maltreated youth by helping them build trusting relationships with caring adults (Rhodes, 2002), program planners must be even more diligent in their efforts to protect against further abuse or rejection with this special population.

This chapter presents the current state of theory and research supporting mentoring initiatives for abused and neglected youth. We propose several unique but important practices drawn from these literatures to help program developers and government agencies more effectively use mentoring as a support mechanism for maltreated youth. We conclude with some specific recommendations for practice and evaluation. As background for our discussion, the remainder of this introduction provides a brief overview of maltreated youth and issues pertinent to this population.

Populations

In 2001, 3 million referrals were made to child protective service agencies in the United States regarding the welfare of approximately 5 million children (U.S. Department of Health & Human Services [DHHS], 2003). Approximately 903,000 children were found to be victims of maltreatment (i.e., psychological or emotional abuse, physical abuse, sexual abuse, and/or neglect; U.S. DHHS, 2003). Compounding the nature of this social problem, the perpetrators usually are the parent or parents (84% in 2001; U.S. DHHS, 2003). Abuse by parents can damage the faith youth have in others and sense of security more severely than had the perpetrators been unfamiliar adults (Rohner & Britner, 2002). Aggravating this sense of insecurity, many abused and neglected children wind up in out-of-home placements (i.e., state custody, including foster care, group homes, and other residential placements). On any given day, about 542,000 children are living in foster care in the United States (U.S. DHHS, 2003). In response to this large population of youth within the child welfare system, mentoring programs designed specifically for maltreated youth (and/or those in foster care) are in operation in several states.

Even when mentoring programs are not specifically targeted to them, abused and neglected youth can be found among the ranks of youth regularly involved in mentoring programs. According to the 1998 Commonwealth Fund Survey, approximately 10% of the protégés in the national sample of mentoring programs had been physically or sexually abused (McLearn, Colasanto, & Schoen, 1998). Abused and neglected youth also have been included in studies of mentoring program effectiveness (e.g., Grossman & Rhodes, 2002).

Historical Background and Current Developments

Increasingly, the child welfare system encounters children who are medically fragile, behaviorally demanding, and/or in need of mental health services (Redding, Fried, & Britner, 2000). According to Halfon, Mendonca, and Berkowitz (1995), the vast majority of children in foster care display emotional or developmental problems. These youth are at greater risk for unintended pregnancy and childbearing, educational underachievement and dropout, and substance abuse (Hafton, English, Allen, & DeWoody, 1994). As they "age out" of the system, abused and neglected youth typically experience high rates of unemployment, homelessness, unintended pregnancy, substance abuse, and costly adult forms of dependency, such as welfare and social services utilization, psychiatric commitment, and incarceration (Courtney, Piliavin, Grogan-Kaylor, & Nast, 2001; Hafton et al., 1994; Mech, Pryde, & Rycraft, 1995).

Although these data paint a bleak picture, there have been some bright spots on the policy landscape. The John F. Chafee Foster Care Independence Program legislation of 1999 provides health care coverage to former foster children until age 21 and has doubled the funding for independent living programs for youth in state custody, including mentoring, life skills, housing, and college tuition assistance programs. In fact, much of the formal mentoring that occurs with maltreated youth takes place when the youth are in state custody (Britner, 2003). Sometimes mentoring is viewed as an option only after the child is in a stable placement, while in other instances of "foster care drift" (i.e., a series of removals and/or returns to the family), a mentor may be assigned to attempt to represent a rare "constant" in a youth's life. In addition to the vulnerability of these youth, the increased fiscal accountability resulting from the use of public funds for mentoring underscores the need to increase understanding of the impact of this type intervention for maltreated youth, including the processes through which it may be able to contribute to their gains in critical areas such as social, cognitive, and independent living skills.

Opportunities and Challenges

Enthusiasm for the possible benefits of mentoring also must be tempered by concerns about the risks of failed mentoring relationships. The potential that has been indicated for mentoring programs and relationships to sometimes have negative effects on some youth appears to be heightened for youth who enter programs with significant personal vulnerabilities such as may stem from experiences of maltreatment (e.g., Grossman & Rhodes, 2002). Maltreated youth, furthermore, may be especially susceptible to adverse impact of experiences such as the termination of a mentoring relationship because of painful losses, trauma, separations, and/or rejection they already have experienced in their lives (Rhodes, 2002).

THEORY

Several theoretical models of the processes of youth mentoring seem particularly useful as frameworks for guiding research on mentoring programs and relationships for abused and neglected youth. Other theories point to techniques and cautions that are unique to this population.

Established Mentoring Frameworks

Rhodes's Model

The model of youth mentoring proposed by Rhodes (Rhodes, 2002; Rhodes, this volume) suggests that there is a crucial step to mentoring in which mentor and protégé form an emotional bond. Theoretically, only then can the mentor influence the protégé's developmental outcomes by (a) enhancing social skills and emotional well-being, (b) improving cognitive skills through dialogue, and (c) serving as a role model and advocate for the youth. Several aspects of Rhodes's (2002) model are of particular importance for the present discussion. First, Rhodes proposed within her model several factors that may moderate the impact of youth mentoring. Several of these factors reflect domains in which enduring and pronounced deficits are evident for abused and neglected youth, such as interpersonal history and social competencies. For example, a maltreated youth's past experiences of rejection by parents or other close adults and/or the presence of antisocial behaviors may make it more difficult for him or her to form a social bond with a mentor.

Other moderators proposed by Rhodes may be inherently linked to some degree with the categorical status of maltreatment. For instance, relationship duration commonly may be truncated due to mobility associated with foster care placements for this population. In sum, maltreated youth, as a population, are highlighted by this model as having characteristics and experiences that theoretically would be expected to make it notably more difficult for mentoring relationships or programs to achieve positive effects.

A second feature of Rhodes's (2002) model that merits highlighting is the manner in which the impact of the mentor-protégé relationship is expected to be mediated (at least in part) through improvements that occur via mentoring in the youth's parental, peer, and other close relationships. Given the nature and quality of their prior relationships, this type of mediational pathway may be constrained for abused and neglected youth in at least two ways. First, some of the other individuals with whom these youth have significant relationships (e.g., parents) may be inherently limited in their capacities to enter into more favorable relationships with them. Second, maltreated youth by virtue of their interpersonal histories may be less open to investing effort in attempts at change or growth in their relationships. There may be more obstacles in the path to positive outcomes of mentoring for maltreated youth.

Despite the preceding considerations, Rhodes's (2002) model also points toward the potential for certain processes that could facilitate *significant* effects of mentoring for this population. Of particular note is the potential moderating role of the youth's ecological circumstances. It could be that in the absence of family connections and consistent external support (e.g., due to multiple foster placements), the life circumstances of maltreated youth are often such that the introduction of a mentor may represent a notably more salient and potentially influential positive source of change in a youth's social resources and self-esteem than is the case for most youth outside of this population.

The lack of family data on maltreated youth who are engaged in mentoring programs limits our ability to test many of the mediational paths suggested in Rhodes's (2002) model of how mentoring works. Do close relationships with important others (including mentors) protect against familial risks or help individuals repair insecure "working models" of close relationships? What would be the effects of a mentor when the child-parent relationship is marked by abuse and/or neglect? These important questions remain unanswered.

Self-Esteem

Supportive mentoring relationships have been theorized to be vital to fostering self-esteem, thereby contributing to resilience in high-risk youth, including youth living in foster care (Yancey, 1998). DuBois, Neville, Parra, and Pugh-Lilly (2002) have presented a structural model in which mentoring that results in the development of a significant bond between youth and mentor widens youth perceptions of their social support networks, which, in turn, bolsters youth resources, including self-esteem. Maltreated youth would seem particularly likely to be in need of "updated" working models (Bowlby, 1969) of both how they see themselves and how they think they are perceived by others, as key foundations for a positive self-concept. Mentors may be able to help meet this need.

Broader Theories and Their Relevance

There are several theoretical orientations from outside of the core mentoring literature that may be useful in guiding investigations and evaluations of mentoring for abused and neglected youth.

Acceptance-Rejection Theory

Parental acceptance-rejection (PAR) theory is "a theory of socialization that attempts to explain and predict major antecedents, correlates, and consequence of parental acceptance and rejection the world over" (Rohner, 1986, p. 14). The theory posits the importance of close relationships in a variety of outcome areas. Parental rejection has been implicated in an array of developmental, behavioral, and psychological problems among children, adolescents, and adults. Parental rejection has, for instance, been associated with different forms of psychopathology (including depression), behavior problems, psychological adjustment problems, substance abuse, attachment disorders, academic problems, and troubled personal relationships (Rohner & Britner, 2002). Conversely, parental acceptance has been associated with an array of positive outcomes, such as the development of prosocial behavior (e.g., generosity, empathy, and helpfulness) in children, positive peer relationships in adolescence, and overall psychological well-being in adulthood, including a sense of happiness, life satisfaction, and low psychological distress (Rohner & Britner, 2002).

PAR theory may be useful as a framework for examining how the perceptions that maltreated youth have of rejection or acceptance in their relationships with their mentors could contribute to social, behavioral, and interpersonal outcomes. Given their difficult interpersonal histories noted previously, abused and neglected youth may perceive themselves as experiencing rejection in mentoring relationships in response to behaviors (e.g., missed meetings) that may do relatively little to shake the security of other youth (Rhodes, 2002). Assessments grounded in Bowlby's (1969) attachment theory are now being used in process and outcome evaluations of mentoring programs (e.g., Westhues, Clarke, Watton, & St. Claire-Smith, 2001). PAR theory may also provide a useful framework for conceptualization and measurement of mentoring processes, relationship disruption, youth perceptions of rejection, and youth functioning.

Social Exchange Theory

Social exchange theory is based on the concept of social economics and thus posits that human interactions are transactions in which the aim is to maximize one's rewards and minimize one's costs (e.g., Sabatelli & Sheehan, 1993). The theory has been used to explain what compels or motivates individuals to volunteer and sacrifice their time in order to assist others for no apparent tangible rewards. When used as a theoretical basis for understanding volunteer participation and motivation, a social exchange differs from an economical exchange in that whereas there is a general expectation of some future reward or return, the exact nature of the reward is not stipulated in advance. According to social exchange theory, relationships continue only when rewards outweigh costs (Sabatelli & Sheehan, 1993).

Applied to the mentoring of maltreated youth, it is noteworthy that these youth may be prone to receive relatively high costs compared to rewards when presented with the opportunity to form a relationship with a mentor. Some maltreated youth—especially those with histories of rejection—may push hard to "test" mentors to see whether they are committed to the relationship and whether they will "stick around for awhile." Likewise, other youth may simply be reluctant to engage or invest in relationships given few experiences in their past that would suggest a high potential for positive payoffs. Theoretically, these possibilities suggest that perceived costs and rewards of investing in mentoring relationships could be important in mediating outcomes for youth from backgrounds of maltreatment by affecting factors such as the strength and quality of the ties that they form with mentors and the likelihood of early termination due to relationship difficulties.

RESEARCH

Although several of these theories reviewed in the preceding section have been used to guide research on youth mentoring, few have been applied to the study of abused and neglected youth specifically. Indeed, overall, there is a dearth of research on mentoring that is focused directly on this special population. In this section, we review the findings of this literature and consider limitations of the research that has been conducted to date.

Current Research Findings

Mentoring programs are well received as support services and have been found to produce positive effects (Tierney, Grossman, & Resch, 1995). Yet "virtually no research has examined the efficacy of mentoring programs with foster youth" (Rhodes, Haight, & Briggs, 1999, p. 186) or youth with maltreatment histories. There are no published studies to date on mediating or moderating processes in mentoring relationships with abused, neglected, or foster youth such as those suggested by the theories reviewed in this chapter. There are relevant studies of mentoring in both naturally occurring and formal settings pertinent to this population, and each are considered separately in the sections that follow.

Naturally Occurring Mentors

Research has suggested that resilient youth, regardless of their temperament, physical attractiveness, or intelligence, have at least one person in their lives who accepts them unconditionally (Werner, 1993). In a study by Beier, Rosenfeld, Spitalny, Zansky, and Bontempo (2000), youth with self-identified, naturally occurring adult mentors were about 50% less likely than those without mentors to have ever carried a weapon, used an illicit drug over the past 30 days, smoked more than five cigarettes daily, and had sex with more than one partner over the past 6 months. It is unclear, however, to what degree these findings would apply directly to abused and neglected youth. Their convenience sample of 294 youth seeking routine outpatient medical care was diverse, but it was not a sample at particular risk for abuse and neglect.

Studies on naturally occurring mentors for abused and neglected youth are, at this point, mostly confined to anecdotal and survey data. In the 1998 Commonwealth Fund Survey, mentors, most of whom were not involved in formal mentoring programs, reported that they felt they had "helped [the maltreated youth with whom they worked] a lot" in 55% of the relevant cases (McLearn et al., 1998). Although this phone survey is useful in providing some estimation of the scope of the problem of maltreatment, it is limited in many ways (e.g., simple, self-report data from mentors only).

Formal Mentors

Turning to formal mentoring programs, we find some examples of mentoring research that directly address abused and neglected youth and youth in foster care. Grossman and Rhodes (2002) examined data from 487 mentored youth and 472 control youth in the Public/Private Ventures impact study of urban Big Brothers Big Sisters programs, in which youth were assessed at baseline and at 18-month follow-up. Within the mentored group, youth who had experienced emotional, sexual, or physical abuse were more likely than other youth (risk ratio of 1.53, $p < .05$) to have had their mentor relationships end prematurely. These findings are consistent with theory discussed previously suggesting that maltreated youth may be more susceptible to early termination of their mentoring relationships in formal programs and, relatedly, less likely to experience the same degree of benefits from such ties as other youth. In this sample, relationships that terminated in under a year failed to show positive impacts evident for longer-term relationships; youth in relationships that lasted less than 6 months showed deficits relative to matched controls (i.e., youth with no mentors; Grossman & Rhodes, 2002).

Using the same data set as Grossman and Rhodes (2002), Rhodes et al. (1999) studied 90 mentored foster youth (78 in relative care, 12 in nonrelative care) in comparison to control foster youth. Relative to controls, at the 18-month follow-up, there was evidence of improvements in self-esteem and prosocial support from friends (e.g., "Would your friends agree to do you a favor if you asked?"), whereas declines on these outcomes were apparent for those without mentors. This study is useful because of its longitudinal, experimental design. The findings are limited, however, by the small sample size and by scant information about the maltreatment and placement histories of the foster youth, and thus provide no examination of the potential role of such histories moderating outcomes within this population as suggested by theory (Rhodes, 2002). Findings for other outcomes assessed in the larger program of research, such as substance use risks, attitudes, and behaviors, were not reported for foster versus nonfoster youth. Nonetheless, overall, this research does provide support for theory discussed previously suggesting that gains in social support received in other relationships and self-esteem may be important proximal outcomes of positive mentoring relationships for youth from backgrounds of maltreatment (DuBois, Neville, et al., 2002; Rhodes, 2002).

For the past decade, the Connecticut Department of Children and Families (DCF) has funded and developed One-on-One Mentoring programs as part of a comprehensive youth development program for youth in state custody. In the first step of an ongoing longitudinal evaluation of this program, preliminary findings for the first 143 participants are available based on cross-sectional measurements of youth on a waiting list for mentors (controls), those currently involved in mentoring relationships, and those for whom a mentoring relationship had ended within the first 6 months (Britner & Kraimer-Rickaby, 2002). Youth with disrupted matches reported higher rates of delinquent externalizing behaviors but not anxious/withdrawn internalizing behaviors, as assessed by youth self-report subscales, than did youth in intact matches or in the control group (waiting list). There were no differences between the groups with respect to youth self-assessments of self-esteem, social support, and intrapersonal and interpersonal assets.

Some of the problems staff reported about matches that had ended included poor or inconsistent contact between mentor and protégé and mentors who did not "feel a connection" to their protégés, observations that are consistent with theory highlighting these aspects of relationships as barriers to positive outcomes for mentoring among maltreated youth (Parra, DuBois, Neville, Pugh-Lilly, & Povinelli, 2002). Some of the strengths noted for intact matches included their more consistent/stable contact and that the mentors and protégés reported enjoying each other's company to a greater degree (Britner & Kraimer-Rickaby, 2002). Future results from the longitudinal study will provide more information about changes in the youth and the mentoring relationships over time.

Need for Longitudinal Study

We do not have adequate data to evaluate what best practices or factors (e.g., DuBois, Holloway, et al., 2002) influence the effectiveness of mentoring with abused and neglected youth. Process and outcome evaluations must address positive and (unintended) negative consequences of mentoring. Researchers should examine an array of outcomes, including the possibility of enhanced connections to peers, families, schools, communities, and vocations as a result of mentoring. These improved relationships may serve as mediators between mentoring and positive youth development outcomes, as outlined by Rhodes (2002). Rhodes also notes, however, the possibility of mixed messages and competing loyalties when parents/guardians and mentors set different examples for youth. This may be particularly salient for maltreated children and youth in state care, for whom multiple "support services" are in place.

Social exchange theory may be useful in understanding how potential mentors weigh the perceived costs and benefits of investing in a mentoring relationship over time, at the stages of volunteering, completing training, match, and maintaining the mentoring relationship. However, this theory has yet to be applied to the study of mentors of abused and neglected youth, who may be initially resistant to a relationship but may also stand to benefit the most from a sustained, caring relationship. PAR theory's framework and measures may also help in the study of mentoring processes, relationship disruption, youth perceptions of rejection, and youth functioning over time in the mentoring relationship.

PRACTICE

In this section, we describe program delivery models for mentoring of abused and neglected youth, discuss some of the practice issues that are specific to working with this special population, and provide some guidance for establishing performance standards for minimum components to the practice of mentoring abused and neglected youth.

Program Delivery Models

Most programs are one-on-one, state-sponsored programs, perhaps due to protective concerns and custody issues for youth (Britner, 2003). Some formal programs targeting abused and neglected youth are beginning to employ some elements of recently emerging program models, such as e-mentoring. For example, the Orphan Foundation of America (OFA) recently was established by the National E-Mentoring Institute to meet the technical assistance and mentoring program development needs of agencies specializing in fostering transition and permanency for foster youth. E-mentoring may encourage interactions beyond those possible in face-to-face meetings. Youth in state custody, in particular, may benefit from e-mentoring as a means to keep in contact with a mentor following a move across different placements or between placements and home. For older foster youth who are attending college or aging out of care, e-mentoring may allow their contact to continue when in-person activities are no longer convenient or as routine.

Although mentoring programs specifically designed for foster youth exist in at least six U.S. states, no programs have yet published process or outcome evaluation results. One promising model is the Kempe Fostering Healthy Futures program, a research-based, prevention program for preadolescent children in foster care. Foster children receive an intensive prevention curriculum aimed at reducing adolescent risk behaviors, attend a 30-week therapeutic skills group, and get frequent mentoring and advocacy from graduate students in social work (H. Taussig, personal communication, October 14, 2003). The program is comprehensive, intensive, and nicely grounded in the use of mentoring best practices (e.g., MENTOR/National Mentoring Partnership, 2003); it is also more clinically oriented than many other models. It is in its early stages of implementation, and no data are yet available.

Tailoring Mentoring Practices to the Population of Abused and Neglected Youth

What makes mentoring work? Elements of effective practice proposed by leading policy and advocacy organizations in the mentoring field, such as the MENTOR/National Mentoring Partnership (2003) as well as those suggested by research (e.g., DuBois, Holloway, et al., 2002) should be applicable in the design, implementation, and evaluation of mentoring programs for maltreated youth. However, some accommodations in the practices within formal mentoring programs may be necessary. In particular, given the potentially adverse consequences of yet another failed relationship and greater susceptibility to this occurring when abused and neglected youth are the focus of mentoring efforts, it may be particularly important that mentoring programs that serve these youth have a solid infrastructure that fosters the development of enduring, effective mentoring relationships (Sipe, 1996). As explained in the following sections, creation of this type of infrastructure may necessitate effective practices tailored to the needs of maltreated youth in the areas of recruitment and screening, orientation and training, ongoing support and retention, and termination policy. Given the limitations of the research to date on mentoring abused and neglected youth, the practice recommendations in this section are informed by theory but lack empirical justification.

Recruitment and Screening

During recruitment, programs may find it beneficial to provide potential mentors with realistic expectations and risks/benefits of working with foster youth. As with all programs, mentors must be screened for safety and pass background checks, and screening must be used to be as certain as possible that further abuse at the hands of the mentor does not occur. Practices that may be particularly significant for abused and neglected protégés relate to the psychological needs and degree of stability of the youth's home life. Youth should be assessed for the kind of serious psychological or behavioral difficulties that might more appropriately require professional assistance given the noteworthy potential for such problems stemming from their histories of abuse and neglect. Furthermore, it may be advisable for youth who are not in a stable placement not to be referred until stability in the home, group home, or foster care has been established (Britner, 2003).

It can be particularly difficult to recruit mentors for maltreated youth. Hirsch, Mickus, and Boerger (2002) suggest that "attention to potential natural mentors in the youth's social network, and among staff of youth development organizations" (p. 302) may prove more fruitful than trying to recruit formal mentors for at-risk youth. The advantages of natural mentors may be especially potent when such ties are formed with staff who have prior experience working with maltreated youth. Such adults not only will have already been screened and trained and be somewhat more prepared for the difficult early phases of the relationship, but they may also be more likely to have greater contact with the youth over time.

Orientation and Training

Given theory and research highlighting the potentially unique challenges and issues associated with mentoring abused and neglected youth, mentors in training for these youth should be provided with an informational orientation that is tailored to this population. Topics of relevance might include information on the workings of the child welfare system, research on correlates of maltreatment and foster care, and relevant findings from attachment and PAR theory research.

Prematch and postmatch training may be critical for the development of positive mentoring relationships. Program staff, mentors, and foster parents all routinely request more—not less—training and detailed information about youth case histories in order to prepare themselves to help youth succeed (Redding et al., 2000). Training topics might include the common goals and needs of maltreated youth, trust issues, life skills, anger management, attachment, crisis intervention, boundaries, and cultural awareness (see Britner, 2003).

In accordance with theory and research reviewed previously, mentors should be prepared for a period of initial distrust and limit testing by protégés and be provided with training specifically geared to helping them to address challenges in this area. More generally, given the range of other factors pertaining to both maltreated youth and their life circumstances that may theoretically present significant barriers to effective mentoring this population, high-quality training may need to be provided both at the outset of relationships and on an ongoing basis throughout their development at levels that exceed those typical of most programs for youth without this type of vulnerability. Training geared specifically toward issues highlighted as important for this population based on available theory and research, furthermore, may be essential for establishing among mentors an adequate sense of self-efficacy for building and sustaining rewarding relationships with maltreated youth (Parra et al., 2002).

Ongoing Support and Retention

According to Rhodes (2002), an important component to developing a relationship is continuity in meeting and a shared motivation by both the youth and the mentor to remain responsive to the development of the relationship. Although mentor recognition is a common practice in mentoring programs (Weinberger, this volume), periodic formal recognition of mentors and youth may be an especially important part of retention efforts. From the perspective of social exchange theory, ongoing praise and support may be vital for retaining mentors as a way of offsetting the emotional costs of working with youth with whom it may be more difficult to establish a strong and consistent positive connection. Extrapolating further from this theoretical perspective, it may be useful for mentors to be reminded both of their value to the program as well as the extent to which other mentors to such youth also face difficulties establishing or maintaining a relationship.

Integration of Multiple Interventions

Mentoring for most special populations occurs in conjunction with other programs. In many cases, there is a need for greater integration of services in order to eliminate "support overload" or redundant or conflicting messages from multiple adult authority figures (e.g., social workers, caregivers, parents, foster parents, mentors). We also need to study the overlapping protocols and samples within larger child welfare systems in order to begin to disentangle risks, services, and outcomes related to mentoring abused and neglected youth.

Termination Policy

There are some unavoidable systemic issues that may cause a match to terminate (e.g., youth moving from placement, youth voluntarily leaving the system, caseworker turnover). In some cases, volunteers may decide to end the match due to time management issues and scheduling conflicts. Program staff report that many mentors who choose to end a match do so because of a perceived lack of interest on the part of the youth. The mentor also may have a difficult time understanding the youth's ideas about the nature of the relationship (Britner & Kraimer-Rickaby, 2002). These are particularly salient issues when dealing with youth who have experienced maltreatment, as many of these youth have histories of inconsistent contact with adults and peers due to the transient nature of child welfare and foster care services.

FUTURE DIRECTIONS

Synthesis

Theories from both within and outside the mentoring literature suggest that youth who have experienced abuse or neglect have the potential to benefit from mentoring relationships and programs. These theories are equally clear in highlighting a range of potential barriers to effective mentoring of this population as well the potential for unintended harmful effects when relationships fail and programs are not adequately designed to address their needs. Unfortunately, to date, very little empirical research has been conducted to assess the effectiveness of mentoring relationships or programs for youth who have experienced abuse and neglect. The few existing studies suggest positive effects for high-quality mentoring relationships

that persist, but the potential for negative effects for those relationships that end prematurely. Consistent with their histories, which often are characterized by violence, trauma, and rejection, both theory and available findings thus underscore the need for practitioners to be especially vigilant to unintended (negative) effects and the risks associated with failed mentoring relationships among youth who have backgrounds of maltreatment. The importance of a solid program infrastructure and sufficient mentor training and support cannot be understated, furthermore, given both the vulnerability of abused and neglected youth to perceive rejection more easily than other youth and the emotional costs and challenges that mentors can experience when working with this population.

Recommendations for Research

1. *Test theoretical models of mentoring with abused and neglected youth.* Researchers should test the same theoretical models examined in the broader mentoring literature to identify the extent to which processes and outcomes proposed in these models apply to this population. Ideally, this research should take into account the heterogeneity among youth who have experienced maltreatment by testing for differences across potential moderators such as type and severity of abuse or neglect. Studies of potential differences across program-sponsored and more naturally developing mentoring ties are also clearly merited.

2. *Investigate theoretically relevant mediators and moderators unique to abused and neglected youth.* Available theory suggests a range of potentially important mediating and moderating processes that could have distinctive importance for youth with backgrounds of abuse and neglect. Illustratively, what is the effect of a mentor when the child-parent relationship is marked by severe abuse and/or neglect? How is the mentoring process influenced by a youth's multiple foster care placements? Are the perceived costs and benefits of investing in a mentoring relationship, as suggested by social exchange theory, important in moderating outcomes of mentoring program involvement for this population? These remain

unanswered questions and important areas for investigation.

3. *Conduct rigorous evaluations of mentoring interventions for abused and neglected youth.* We need to design and conduct rigorous evaluations of the efficacy of mentoring programs for abused and neglected youth. These evaluations should be experimental or quasi-experimental in design and should address the efficacy of both general mentoring programs for participating youth with backgrounds of abuse or neglect and programs that are targeted specifically to this population. There is a need for repeated and multiple measures from multiple respondents, and systematic tracking and evaluation. Focused research is especially needed to evaluate the intended benefits and to identify any unintended impacts of mentoring. Heeding the 5th-century B.C. charge of Hippocrates, research should test that, first, we are doing no harm as we seek to do good in the lives of these youth.

Recommendations for Practice

1. *Emphasize recruitment, screening, and training of high-quality mentors.* Every attempt must be made to recruit and screen effectively, and then train and prepare each high-quality mentor extensively for the possibility that it may be difficult to start up a relationship with his or her protégé. These steps are important for all mentoring, but perhaps more so with a population of maltreated youth who may have experienced extensive trauma, rejection, and instability.

2. *Provide mentors information and ongoing training.* Extensive information about the youth should be shared with—not withheld from—mentors. Ongoing support for the mentor, in the form of information, resources, trainings, and staff interest and availability, is likely to be critical well beyond the period of the initial match for relationships in which the youth has a background of experiences of abuse or neglect. Frequent contact is vital so that youth do not perceive rejection.

3. *Integrate mentoring within the network of other services.* Mentoring for most special

populations occurs in conjunction with other programs. In many cases, there is a need for greater integration of services in order to eliminate "support overload" or redundant or conflicting messages for the youth from multiple adult authority figures (e.g., social workers, caregivers, parents, foster parents, mentors).

4. *Reward mentors.* The development and implementation of program policies and practices should continually consider the factors that motivate individuals to volunteer—and stay active—throughout their involvement with the program. Praise, support, and periodic recognition may help keep mentors motivated and engaged in their work with abused and neglected youth, even if the initial attempts at relationship formation are more challenging due to the youth's interpersonal history.

REFERENCES

Beier, S., Rosenfeld, W. D., Spitalny, K. C., Zansky, S. M., & Bontempo, A. N. (2000). The potential role of an adult mentor in influencing high-risk behaviors in adolescents. *Archives of Pediatric and Adolescent Medicine, 154,* 327–331.

Bowlby, J. (1969). *Attachment and loss: Vol. I. Attachment.* New York: Basic Books.

Britner, P. A. (2003). *Final report: Independent living programs* (Report prepared for the Director of Youth Services, State of Connecticut Department of Children and Families). Storrs: University of Connecticut.

Britner, P. A., & Kraimer-Rickaby, L. (2002, July). *One-on-one mentoring with maltreated youth in out-of-home placements.* Paper presented at the 14th International Congress on Child Abuse and Neglect, Denver, CO.

Courtney, M. E., Piliavin, I. P., Grogan-Kaylor, A., & Nast, A. (2001). Foster youth transitions to adulthood: A longitudinal view of youth leaving foster care. *Child Welfare, 80,* 685–718.

DuBois, D. L., Holloway, B. E., Valentine, J. C., & Cooper, H. (2002). Effectiveness of mentoring programs for youth: A meta-analytic review. *American Journal of Community Psychology, 30,* 157–197.

DuBois, D. L., Neville, H. A., Parra, G. R., & Pugh-Lilly, A. O. (2002). Testing a new model of mentoring. In G. G. Noam (Ed. in chief) & J. E. Rhodes (Ed.), *A critical view of youth mentoring* (*New Directions for Youth Development: Theory, Research, and Practice, No. 93*, pp. 21–57). San Francisco: Jossey-Bass.

Grossman, J. B., & Rhodes, J. E. (2002). The test of time: Predictors and effects of duration in youth mentoring relationships. *American Journal of Community Psychology, 30,* 199–219.

Hafton, N., English, A., Allen, M., & DeWoody, M. (1994). National health care reform, Medicaid, and children in foster care. *Child Welfare, 73,* 99–115.

Halfon, N., Mendonca, A., & Berkowitz, G. (1995). Health status of children in foster care: The experience of the center for the vulnerable child. *Archives of Pediatric and Adolescent Medicine, 149,* 386–392.

Hirsch, B. J., Mickus, M., & Boerger, R. (2002). Ties to influential adults among Black and White adolescents: Culture, social class, and family networks. *American Journal of Community Psychology, 30,* 289–303.

John F. Chafee Foster Care Independence Program, 42 USC § 677 (1999). (Title I of Foster Care Independence Act, Pub. L. 106–169, 113 Stat. 1828).

McLearn, K. T., Colasanto, D., & Schoen, C. (1998). *Mentoring makes a difference: Findings From the Commonwealth Fund 1998 Survey of Adults Mentoring Young People.* New York: The Commonwealth Fund. Available at http://www.ecs .org/html/Document.asp?chouseid=2843

Mech, E. V., Pryde, J. A., & Rycraft, J. R. (1995). Mentors for adolescents in foster care. *Child and Adolescent Social Work Journal, 12,* 317–328.

MENTOR/National Mentoring Partnership. (2003). *Elements of effective practice* (2nd ed.). Alexandria, VA: Author.

Parra, G. R., DuBois, D. L., Neville, H. A., Pugh-Lilly, A. O., & Povinelli, N. (2002). Mentoring relationships for youth: Investigation of a process-oriented model. *Journal of Community Psychology, 30,* 367–388.

Redding, R. E., Fried, C., & Britner, P. A. (2000). Predictors of placement outcomes in treatment foster care: Implications for foster parent selection and service delivery. *Journal of Child and Family Studies, 9,* 425–447.

Rhodes, J. E. (2002). *Stand by me: The risks and rewards of mentoring today's youth.* Cambridge, MA: Harvard University Press.

Rhodes, J., Haight, W. L., & Briggs, E. C. (1999). The influence of mentoring on the peer relationships of foster youth in relative and nonrelative care. *Journal of Research on Adolescence, 9,* 185–201.

Rohner, R. P. (1986). *The warmth dimension: Foundations of parental acceptance-rejection theory.* Newbury Park, CA: Sage.

Rohner, R. P., & Britner, P. A. (2002). Worldwide mental health correlates of parental acceptance-rejection: Review of cross-cultural and intracultural evidence. *Cross-Cultural Research: The Journal of Comparative Social Science, 36,* 16–47.

Sabatelli, R. M., & Sheehan, C. L. (1993). Exchange and resource theories. In P. G. Boss, W. J. Doherty, R. LaRossa, W. R. Schumm, & S. K. Steinmetz (Eds.), *Sourcebook of family theories and methods: A contextual approach* (pp. 395–411). New York: Plenum Press.

Sipe, C. (1996). *Mentoring: A synthesis of PP/PV's research: 1988–1995.* Philadelphia: Public/Private Ventures.

Tierney, J. P., Grossman, J. B., & Resch, N. L. (1995). *Making a difference: An impact study of Big Brothers/Big Sisters.* Philadelphia: Public/Private Ventures.

U.S. Department of Health & Human Services (DHHS). (2003). *National clearinghouse on child abuse and neglect information: Statistics.* Retrieved October 1, 2003, from http://nccanch. acf.hhs.gov/

Werner, E. (1993). Risk, resilience and recovery: Perspectives from the Kauai longitudinal study. *Development and Psychopathology, 5,* 503–515.

Westhues, A., Clarke, L., Watton, J., & St. Claire-Smith, S. (2001). Building positive relationships: An evaluation of process and outcomes in a Big Sister program. *The Journal of Primary Prevention, 21,* 477–493.

Yancey, A. K. (1998). Building positive self-image in adolescents in foster care: The use of role models in an interactive group approach. *Adolescence, 33,* 253–267.

33

YOUTH WITH DISABILITIES

KATHERINE E. MCDONALD, FABRICIO E. BALCAZAR,
AND CHRISTOPHER B. KEYS

INTRODUCTION

Approximately 5,690,000 school-aged children in the United States have some form of physical, emotional, and/or cognitive impairment that limits one or more of their major life activities (U.S. Department of Education, 2002). Youth with disabilities constitute 10% of all people under the age of 21 in the United States (Asch, Rousso, & Jefferies, 2001). They regularly encounter the personal and social consequences of membership in a stigmatized minority group (Charlton, 1998; Fine & Asch, 1988) and the challenges of having an impairment. Youth with disabilities frequently experience high levels of social and physical exclusion. They often grow up in families without other people with disabilities, and well-meaning family members may be more concerned with protecting them from harm than encouraging them toward independence (Rousso & Wehmeyer, 2001). In fact, the more severe the disability, the less likely the youth is to engage in age-appropriate activities with peers (Odom, McConnell, & McEvoy, 1992).

As a result of this segregation and other factors that limit their prospects for community integration and personal fulfillment, youth with disabilities are at risk for poor developmental outcomes. Consequently youth with disabilities are less well equipped with the emotional, social, and cognitive resources necessary to achieve positive life outcomes. For example, few youth with disabilities pursue postsecondary education, and as adults, many face unemployment or underemployment and low levels of engagement with their communities (Charlton, 1998; Newman, 1992; Wagner, 1992; Wagner, Blackorby, Cameto, Hebbeler, & Newman, 1993).

The at-risk status of youth with disabilities, coupled with findings indicating that other at-risk youth have benefited significantly from having caring adults in their lives (Rhodes, 2002), has led researchers and practitioners to consider mentoring programs as one way of promoting positive development among this population. Unfortunately, for a number of reasons, few mentoring programs have made an active attempt to include young disabled people (Rousso, 2001, p. 341). Program staff may believe that they are not properly trained to meet the needs of disabled youth. Staff may assume that youth with disabilities cannot participate or fear that, if disabled youth attend, nondisabled youth will leave the program. Youth with disabilities may also face problems with the inaccessibility of program settings, activities, or transportation, as well as overprotective parents (Froschl, Rousso, & Rubin, 2001). In addition, there are few mentoring programs designed specifically for youth with disabilities.

In this chapter, we first consider theoretical concerns related to mentoring youth with disabilities. We examine the construct of disability as well as dimensions of mentoring relationships (program-sponsored or naturally occurring) and programs that may be of particular importance to youth with disabilities. We then review research on mentoring programs for youth with disabilities according to the age of the mentees. Next, we consider issues of practice, focusing in particular on those that appear promising but have not yet received rigorous evaluation. Finally, we synthesize material from the preceding sections and offer recommendations for future research and practice.

THEORY

Conceptualizations of disability and their corresponding definitions have varied over the years. Traditional frameworks of disability emphasize the medical nature of disability and focus on individual-centered deficits and impairments. Newer paradigms depart from a medical framing of disability by defining it primarily as a social issue. Here, the focus is on the relationship between the disability and the environment; relevant elements of the environment are stressed as primary determinants of the experience of having a disability. Under this socioecological model, disability is redefined as a function of the person in context. The disability experience is now viewed as the gap between what a person is capable of and the demands of his or her environment. Herein, disability is not inherent to an individual, but is instead located in the interaction between the individual and his or her environment. In this paradigm of disability, *impairment* is used to refer to the biological basis of disability, whereas *disability* is reserved to describe the individual-environment interactions that create the disability experience (Brand & Pope, 1997; Nagi, 1991; Pledger, 2003; Rioux, 1997).

As we seek to understand the experience of disability, it is useful to consider factors that may contribute to the at-risk status of youth with disabilities. In particular, it is important to consider the socially created disadvantages that may accrue among persons with impairments as well as contextual barriers that can limit their community integration (Rousso & Wehmeyer, 2001). This social perspective refocuses our attention away from the traditional assumptions of individual dysfunction and pathology toward a view that is sensitive to the manner in which adverse consequences of disability often are created through social and/or physical structures that discriminate against people with impairments (Pledger, 2003; Rioux, 1997).

This socioecological conceptualization of disability stresses that youth with disabilities regularly confront both the social implications of having a stigmatizing condition as well as the functional limitations that arise from decreased mobility, cognitive processing or aptitude, and/or emotional stability. Furthermore, it emphasizes that specific experiences linked to disability status can be amplified or mitigated by contextual elements, including the specific type of disability, gender, race/ethnicity, and/or socioeconomic status of the youth (Block, Balcazar, & Keys, 2002; Newman, 1992; Rousso & Wehmeyer, 2001; Wagner, 1992; Wagner et al., 1993).

Emerging conceptual models in disability studies help us understand processes that may lead to poor adulthood outcomes for people with disabilities. Many disability scholars argue in this regard that an important role is played by the pervasive assumptions of the pathology, incompetence, and helplessness of people with disabilities (Fine & Asch, 1988). Assumptions of disease and incapacity can both dehumanize youth with disabilities and engender feelings of inferiority and hopelessness about the future (Charlton, 1998; Froschl et al., 2001; Rousso, 2001). Experiences of assumed incapacity may affect youth adversely at school, in their communities, and with their families and, in the long run, contribute to poor adulthood outcomes. Common experiences include exclusion from neighborhood schools and youth-specific programs, as well as a lack of exposure to appropriate adult role models with disabilities (Froschl et al., 2001; Wagner et al., 1993). The absence of adult role models with disabilities is of particular theoretical relevance because most youth with disabilities are raised by nondisabled parents (Charlton, 1998; Rousso, 2001).

With this socioecological view of disability, we can consider theoretical concerns most relevant to mentoring relationships and programs for youth with disabilities. In general, these factors can be dichotomized as program elements that seek to engage youth with disabilities and "plug into" their lives and elements that seek to motivate youth with disabilities and activate their interest in positive development. Elements that plug into youth's lives include mentoring programs that have a developmentally appropriate focus, are accessible, and involve early intervention, family members, and multiple intervention components. Elements that activate youth with disabilities include assuming a competence-based approach, promoting the youth's control, engaging successful mentors with disabilities, and focusing on the youth's interests and goal attainment. With respect to program elements that plug into the life circumstances of youth with disabilities, implementing programs that are developmentally appropriate is critical. Both the form of the relationship encouraged and the goals of the mentoring relationship must respond to the developmental age of the youth. Second, program accessibility may be a key dimension of successfully mentoring youth with disabilities. Program accessibility refers to a competence-based philosophy that youth can participate given proper social and physical conditions. Accessibility includes designing the program so that youth with disabilities can participate (e.g., accessible transport, materials, and activities and adequate supports), establishing appropriate goals, and including disability awareness training for mentors as needed so that youth with disabilities can fully engage in the mentoring relationship. For example, e-mentoring (i.e., mentoring via the Internet) may hold significant potential to be well adapted to youth who face physical barriers (e.g., living in rural locations and challenges with accessibility of transport or buildings) to connecting with mentors. Similarly, a personal care attendant may be necessary for a youth with quadriplegia to assist with her bodily functions so that she can attend activities; plainly written instructions may make an activity understandable to a youth with an intellectual disability; and asking that mentors use fragrance-free products may make an environment accessible for a youth with multiple chemical sensitivities. Beyond ensuring equal access, mentoring programs that affirmatively recruit, welcome, engage, and support youth with disabilities are likely to have a more positive impact.

Focusing on early intervention, families, and multiple program components may also help mentoring programs plug into the lives of youth with disabilities. Attention to early intervention may serve these youth particularly well. Early intervention can promote positive development before multiple disadvantages have accrued and before a path toward negative life outcomes has further advanced. Such an approach would include, for example, addressing positive aspects of disability from an early age rather than after a youth's problems with self-concept have compounded. Second, because youth with disabilities mature within families in which they are often the only person with a disability, the more mentoring programs can reach out to include family members, the more effective they may be. Exposure to mentors with disabilities may help families understand disability better and see, for the first time, evidence of a child's strengths and possibilities for his or her future. As a result, the youth's social environment may improve, thus bolstering positive effects across settings. Last, one clear directive of socioecological model of disability is the possibility that mentoring alone may be able to address only certain experiences linked to having a disability. To fully address the needs of youth with disabilities, it may be imperative to consider additional forms of intervention/service provision, such as skill building (e.g., teaching youth how to recruit help) (Balcazar, Keys, & Garate, 1995).

It is also critical that mentoring programs activate the interest of youth with disabilities. To do so, approaches that are strengths based, accord control to mentee and work toward their goal attainment, engage mentors with disabilities, and focus on the interests of youth may be particularly useful. A competence-based approach to mentoring assumes youth can successfully engage in relationships, derive benefit from them, and plays to their strengths. Mentoring by definition involves relationship (DuBois, Neville, Parra, & Pugh-Lilly, 2002; Rhodes, 2002); relationships by definition involve power dynamics (Charlton, 1998). People with disabilities, historically, have had relatively little control over their lives. As such, since the helping relationships inherent to mentoring can take a variety of forms, we must be vigilant to these constructs as we consider mentoring these youth. Although some helping relationships further disempower marginalized groups by reinforcing their powerlessness, other helping relationships can empower members of these groups by promoting their competence, abilities, and influence (Epse-Sherwindt & Kerlin, 1990; Tucker & Johnson, 1989). Thus, empowerment theory (Zimmerman, 1995) also plays a potentially important role in understanding how some mentoring relationships can lead youth to grow and mature while others may reinforce dependency. A natural correlate of this process is the construct of self-determination (Wehmeyer, 2002). Self-determination involves addressing the knowledge, skills, and attitudes that students with disabilities need to take more control over and responsibility for their lives. Preparing youth to lead self-determined lives is especially important as youth mature into adults. In part, fostering self-determination through mentoring includes helping youth set and work toward goals.

The final constructs important to activating youth with disabilities involve using mentors with disabilities and focusing on the interests of youth. Since few youth with disabilities have contact with successful adults with disabilities, in fostering such relationships, mentoring programs can fulfill a unique need in the lives of these youth and go a long way in addressing their social isolation. Engaging mentors with disabilities similar to their mentees may serve particularly well to help youth identify with mentors (Rhodes, 2002), perceive positive aspects of disability, and begin to envision successful life outcomes for themselves. A final directive of the socioecological framework of disability highlights that much previous research and practices have, in fact, been highly irrelevant to the lived experience of disability (e.g., a focus on medical concerns rather than social concerns). In line with this consideration is that programs must be sensitive to the variety of interests and unique perspectives of youth with disabilities that stem from the experience of many social identities, not merely a disability-specific identity.

To summarize, conceptualizations of disability as a socioecological process point to the multiple unique dimensions of mentoring youth with disabilities that may be relevant to fostering benefits for these youth. We have identified nine factors that may have particular value for increasing the likelihood of success in mentoring children and youth with disabilities. Four of these factors engage youth with program elements that plug into their lives and their life contexts: having a developmentally appropriate focus, fostering program accessibility, intervening early, and incorporating families. An additional five factors seek to motivate youth by activating their interest: taking a competence-based perspective, promoting participant influence on and control of mentoring activities and life situations, focusing on goal attainment, engaging successful individuals with similar disabilities, and making the program relevant to the lives and interests of youth.

RESEARCH

We searched relevant databases and reference lists for manuscripts on mentoring programs and/or naturally occurring relationships involving youth with disabilities with a mean age equal to or less than 19. We limited our definition of mentoring to a relationship with one mentor. The searches yielded 14 empirical investigations of mentoring programs for youth with disabilities but none specifically addressing naturally occurring mentoring relationships. Of the 14 studies, 10 were peer-reviewed, published empirical studies and 3 were ERIC project reports and/or briefings. The final study was an unpublished manuscript.

Given the small body of extant research on this topic, it becomes critical to note the research designs and their corresponding rigor as we evaluate the validity of and support for researchers' conclusions. In terms of research design, one study used an experimental (i.e., randomized) design. Three studies used a quasi-experimental, pre/post design with matched comparison groups; a fourth used a similar design but with posttests only. The findings of these studies thus begin to address issues of program impact. Of the other 9 studies, several of which relied heavily on qualitative methodologies, 3 used a single-group design with either pre/post assessments or multiple assessments during the course of the program, and 6 used a posttest-only, single-group design. Due to multiple threats to internal validity, these studies are inherently limited in their ability to address issues of program impact (see Grossman, this volume). However, their findings do provide insights into specific processes that may be important to focus on as potential facilitators of relationship and program effectiveness for youth with disabilities.

We use their age to structure the review of research because program goals and formulations varied greatly depending on the age of mentees. Following consideration of specific studies pertaining to preschool, elementary and middle school, and high school youth, both methodological and substantive issues relating to these studies and their findings are discussed.

Preschool Children

At the preschool stage of development, family involvement and early intervention are of particular interest. Watkins and colleagues (1998) investigated the usefulness of having adult deaf mentors share their language (American Sign Language [ASL]), culture, and knowledge of deafness with young deaf children (aged 0–5) and their parents. During home visits across an average of 17.6 months, deaf mentors worked on communication and language skills and exposed families to Deaf culture. Families also received parent advisor home visits. The evaluation centered on the capacity of the program to promote children's ASL language and communication, interfamilial communication, and positive parental attitudes about deafness. Participating children ($n = 18$) and a matched comparison group of children ($n = 18$) from a different state who received parent advisor home visits only were tested on language skills every 6 months. Child–parent interactions were videotaped regularly, and parents' attitudes were assessed at completion of the program. Results were encouraging: Relative to comparison group children, mentored children demonstrated quicker and greater gains in language communication skills. The parents of mentored children, furthermore, demonstrated greater comfort in interacting using both ASL and signed English relative to parents of control group children. They also expressed perceptions more consistent with contemporary values of Deaf culture and community. Consistent with theoretical considerations discussed previously, the use of mentors with disabilities, early intervention, and the inclusion of the parents may have served to address the children's social isolation and to promote positive perspectives on disability.

Shepard-Tew and Forgione (1999) recruited middle school students with learning disabilities to help preschool children ($n = 29$) overcome physical and emotional challenges believed to inhibit their engagement in an arts program. Unfortunately, the researchers measured a very limited number of outcomes, thus failing to make it possible to ascertain the efficacy of this model, particularly with respect to its impact on mentees. Using posttraining, prementoring questionnaires, the researchers found that mentors expressed a high degree of comfort with the task ahead of them and behaved appropriately at the arts festival. They also found that with the support of mentors, the preschoolers were able to participate in the arts program. The researchers did not investigate additional effects of the program on mentees. This program points to the potential benefits of early intervention and accessibility considerations.

Elementary and Middle School Youth

Five studies were conducted with elementary and/or middle school youth. These studies point to the potential benefits of making programs age appropriate, involving families, using mentors with disabilities, and fostering youth self-determination. In a qualitative study rich with potential constructs of interest, Todis, Powers, Irvin, and Singer (1996) examined the experiences of three youth who participated in a mentoring program designed to promote the competence and independence among children with physical disabilities. Each youth was matched with a successful adult who had a similar physical disability. Pairs were expected to complete community-based activities in specified domains (e.g., visit to mentor's home, engage in recreational activities) but were given control over the details of these activities and two additional ones. Each pair completed a variety of activities that primarily followed the interests of the mentee over a period of approximately 6 months. Interviews and field observations yielded a complex picture of elements of the mentor-mentee relationship that may have promoted or thwarted the goals of the project. Generalized behavioral changes were observed for only one of the three mentees. One participant appeared to be too young and immature to benefit significantly from the relationship. He demonstrated behavioral changes toward greater independence in the company of his mentor, but these changes did not transfer to his interactions with others. There was, however, evidence that his parent gained beneficial knowledge including accessibility-focused home remodeling ideas, disability-specific knowledge and culture, and new perspectives of her son. The other participant to fail to exhibit noteworthy change already demonstrated a substantial degree of independence and self-competence at the outset of the study. It appeared that the mentoring relationship was not able to facilitate or advance this youth's stated interests in mastering the finer points of social integration. The remaining mentee evidenced gains in skills and confidence (e.g., taking greater initiative) that were noted by her family and readily apparent in how she conducted herself. She also appeared to become more vocal and integrated into her family. Her relationship with her mentor was characterized by the least amount of mentor control. Although this study may not greatly contribute to generalizable knowledge about the impact of mentoring youth with disabilities, it makes important contributions in identifying processes and conditions under which programs may be more effective. These theoretical considerations include elements of control, inclusion of the youth's family, and the reminder that mentoring may not be able to affect the needs of all youth.

Shedding further light on potential factors relevant to mentoring youth with disabilities, four additional studies have been done with this age group and deserve attention with respect to evaluation design and findings. Noll (1997) used a single-group, posttest design and observational data to conduct a process evaluation of a program using cross-age (ninth graders), nondisabled peers as mentors to promote the social and academic success of seventh graders

(n not reported). Findings suggested that mentees experienced less social rejection and more classroom acceptable behavior. Similarly, Muscott, O'Brien, and College (1999) recruited nondisabled high school and college students to promote character education among elementary school students with serious emotional disturbances and learning disabilities. Based on observations and interviews with 24 youth, they concluded that mentees had learned skills that would help them to make friends, work more effectively in groups, and be more engaged citizen-leaders. Because of the absence of a comparison group and pretest data, however, these conclusions must be regarded as speculative. Also in a school setting, Buckner (1993) sought to improve the social and academic success of middle school students with leaning disabilities ($n = 18$) by pairing them with same-age mentor/ tutors and an adult professional. Using a single-group, pre/post test design, findings indicated improvements in academics, attendance, and self-esteem. Last, using the same design as Buckner, Packer (1994) matched hearing buddies to mainstreamed elementary children with hearing disabilities and found that their rates of interactions with nondisabled peers increased for participants in the program.

High School Youth

Seven mentoring studies targeted high school students with disabilities. One notable contribution of this set of studies is their emphasis on goal attainment and connections to adults with disabilities. Powers, Sowers, and Stevens (1995) used a randomized posttest-only design to evaluate an intervention to promote perceived self-efficacy and knowledge of the community among adolescents with physical disabilities. For 6 months, adult mentors and adolescent mentees who had similar physical disabilities met twice a month to pursue natural activities selected together. Mentors were expected to model strategies for managing assistance that would be relevant to the youth as well as to focus on issues related to accessibility, such as housing adaptations and agency services. Following completion of the program, although there were no group differences with respect to general self-efficacy, mentored youth ($n = 5$) did report higher levels of disability-specific self-efficacy relative to the control group ($n = 5$). Based on survey responses, mentored youth also demonstrated greater knowledge related to overcoming barriers to community participation than the nonmentored youth. Reports of parents, furthermore, suggested that only mentored children showed gains in community knowledge and self-confidence. Findings from interviews with participating youth and their parents were consistent with these results. On the one hand, there was potential for reports to be biased positively by knowledge of the youth's participation in the program. On the other, this is to our knowledge the only published study of youth with disabilities to use a randomized group design. Therefore, inferences regarding program impact are made with cautious confidence.

Welkowitz and Fox (2000) used small groups of disabled and nondisabled youth facilitated by an adult to promote the self-concept and school success of high school students with emotional-behavioral disabilities. Pre- and posttest qualitative and quantitative assessments of more than 100 youth in two schools revealed greater improvements in absenteeism and disciplinary referrals for mentored youth relative to nonmentored youth, as well as slightly greater improvements in relational skills as measured by a variety of surveys.

Rousso (2001) evaluated a community-based project that sought to strengthen the educational, vocational, and social aspirations of adolescent girls with physical and sensory disabilities. Most notably, this program demonstrated innovative ways to activate the interest of participating youth by making program content relevant. It also highlighted the utility of mentors with disabilities and a goal-focused approach. To develop the mentoring program, two conferences were held in which each party discussed what they would like to learn and share. Project staff also addressed the topic of giving and receiving help. Mentors, who were accomplished women with disabilities, were asked to serve as positive role models in order to help mentees develop constructive, realistic aspirations. Pairs interacted in a variety of ways to meet their needs (e.g., addressing inaccessible environments) and interests, including conversations over the telephone and outings.

Relationships were expected to last 1 to 2 years, with meetings occurring every 4 to 6 weeks. However, less than one half of the pairs met beyond a few months. In a process-oriented evaluation, staff conducted direct observations, participants completed feedback forms, and mentees answered questionnaires and participated in interviews. In their questionnaires and interview responses, most of the mentees reported being inspired by their mentors. They indicated that they had begun to take steps toward greater independence, including taking public transportation, arranging for their own transit, and expanding their goals. They also noted that their relationships with their mentors helped facilitate moving out of their parents' homes. Additional findings from the evaluation suggest that while access to a mentor may assist adolescent girls with positive visions for their futures, a mentor does not necessarily help the girl develop the skills required to realize that vision (e.g., self-advocacy, problem solving). Consequently, the researchers recommended that a skills development component be added so that girls could implement their visions; such a component was later added to the project (Rousso, 2001).

Moccia, Schumaker, Hazel, Vernon, and Deshler (1989) evaluated a project designed to facilitate the transition into adulthood of 32 high school students with learning disabilities. Their research highlights the utility of goal-focused mentoring. Nondisabled adults from the community were expected to work regularly with mentees for about a year to help the mentee complete high school and become engaged in satisfying adult pursuits. Mentees met with their mentors and project staff to set specific goals related to, for example, education, careers, and independent living and to develop the subgoals and tasks that would be implemented to achieve their major goals (e.g., outlining tasks necessary to obtain an associate's degree by a specified date). Outcomes were assessed through the systematic tracking of participants and a non-mentored matched comparison group. After the program, mentored youth were significantly more likely to have graduated from high school and were more satisfied with their high school experiences. Mentored youth also were more likely to have enrolled in higher education and, although they earned less money than the nonmentored group, were more satisfied with their jobs. Mentored youth, furthermore, were able to identify their aspirations with greater specificity.

West, Targett, Steininger, and Anglin (2001) took a similar approach to promote the acquisition of competitive employment among adolescents with disabilities ($n = 43$). Their work demonstrates the importance of program elements above and beyond mentoring. Adult mentors without disabilities at employment sites were one component of the program. The researchers were pleased that participants obtained employment that had social integration opportunities greater than is typical of entry-level jobs as measured by an index created for the study. However, the researchers also noted that mentees had higher turnover rates than they anticipated but which were not unusually high given the age and experience level of participants.

Last, a group of researchers (Ryerson-Espino et al., 2003; Taylor-Ritzler et al., 2001) examined the effectiveness of combining social skills training with case management (who served in a mentoring capacity) to support the transition to adulthood for ethnic minority high school students with disabilities from low-income communities. Their approach was goal driven and focused on empowering the students to take control of setting and achieving their goals. This model was evaluated using both a single-group, pre/post test design and a matched comparison group, pre/post test design, with data on outcome measures obtained from skill development exercises and goal attainment logs. Results from both studies indicate the intervention's success. Participating youth developed mentoring relationships primarily with case managers but in some cases with community members, thereby increasing networks of available instrumental support, and used a wider variety of self-help strategies. Furthermore, participants addressed challenges more successfully and attained more of their employment and independent living goals.

Conclusions

The 14 studies reviewed employed a variety of methodological approaches to investigate mentoring programs and relationships for youth with disabilities. The studies evaluated programs designed to use mentoring relationships to help youth with disabilities overcome obstacles, achieve their goals, participate in community life, improve existing skills, and/or develop new competencies. Overall, findings provide preliminary evidence of the benefits of mentoring for youth with disabilities. At the same time, in accordance with a broad socioecological view of factors affecting the outcomes of this population, the modest magnitude of the effects suggested by data also implies that the mentoring experience may be best regarded as only one of many contextual factors with the potential to exert a significant influence on the complex development of youth with disabilities. However, until more rigorous comparative data are collected that replicate these initial results, these conclusions remain tentative.

Impact of Mentoring Programs

As a result of more scientifically sound research methods and/or similar findings emerging across multiple studies, the following results can be considered to have relatively greater support. It should be noted, however, that in no instances can empirical support be considered definitive in view of limitations in both the scope and quality of existing studies. First, there is evidence that providing mentors to preschool, elementary, and middle school youth with disabilities may be able to promote gains in communication skills (Muscott et al., 1999; Noll, 1997; Watkins et al., 1998). Second, it appears that mentors may be able to assist high school youth with disabilities to attain more positive outcomes following transitions. Research in this regard provides initial evidence that mentoring programs can promote gains in mentees' rates of high school graduation, school attendance, and attainment of employment following graduation (Ryerson-Espino et al., 2003; Taylor-Ritzler et al., 2001; West et al., 2001). Mentors also may be able to increase mentees' level of satisfaction with their high school experiences and jobs, despite having obtained jobs with lower pay than their nonmentored peers (Moccia et al., 1989). Third, there is evidence that mentoring can help school-aged youth with disabilities expand and better articulate their aspirations. Mentoring also seems to inspire their self-confidence and promote skills related to disability-specific issues, such as independent living and mobility (Powers et al., 1995; Rousso, 2001; Ryerson-Espino et al., 2003; Taylor-Ritzler et al., 2001; Todis et al., 1996). Finally, results suggest that benefits of mentoring extend beyond mentees themselves to their families. These include more positive parental attitudes toward the disability status of their children, greater awareness of how to promote the independence of a child with a disability, and improved family communication (Todis et al., 1996; Watkins et al., 1998).

Other possibilities have received tentative but less clear empirical support. For preschool, elementary, and middle school children with disabilities, these include some evidence of the potential for mentoring to increase their levels of participation in community-based programs (Shepard-Tew, 1999) and improve their in-class behavior (Noll, 1997). Mentoring also may help children and youth with disabilities establish friendships, work with others, and experience less rejection from nondisabled peers (Muscott et al., 1999; Noll, 1997). Mentoring also may help high school youth secure work that has significant potential for social integration (West et al., 2001). Furthermore, serving as mentors may allow youth with disabilities to gain confidence in their ability to help (Shepard-Tew, 1999).

Facilitating Factors

Although not yet systematically investigated, several elements of programs and relationships are highlighted by extant research (particularly qualitative studies) as potentially important facilitators of positive outcomes for youth with disabilities. Consistent with theoretical considerations discussed previously, some findings have suggested that both a low level of control exhibited by the mentor and the ability of the mentor to build trust through listening to the mentee may be important in helping the mentee engage in and derive benefit from the relationship (Rousso, 2001; Todis et al., 1996). Other findings have suggested that engaging youth in an enjoyable program is important for boosting participation and motivating mentees (Muscott et al., 1999). Other results have pointed toward

an emphasis on skill development that is appropriate to the mentee's skill and maturity level (Rousso, 2001; Ryerson-Espino et al., 2003; Taylor-Ritzler et al., 2001; Todis et al., 1996), having mentors with whom youth could identify (i.e., those who have similar disabilities; Powers et al., 1995; Rousso, 2001; Todis et al., 1996), parent involvement (Todis et al., 1996; Watkins et al., 1998), and establishing clear goals for the mentoring relationship (Ryerson-Espino et al., 2003; Taylor-Ritzler et al., 2001) as factors allowing youth to benefit more from the mentoring relationship. Although based on very limited empirical data, it is noteworthy again that these possibilities parallel dimensions of mentoring programs and relationships for youth with disabilities that were noted previously to be potentially important in mediating outcomes from a theoretical perspective. Future research is needed to examine the utility of these hypothesized factors in facilitating the effectiveness of mentoring programs.

PRACTICE

Knowledge gained through research on mentoring youth with disabilities can and should be used to inform practice. At the same time, examining practices not yet evaluated can help identify frontiers of innovation. Given the early state of development of mentoring research concerning youth with disabilities, attending to these practice frontiers may be especially useful. Our focus continues to be on planned mentoring programs since, as with the research studies, we found no accounts of efforts to promote natural mentoring relationships for youth with disabilities, an important shortcoming in the extant literature. In this regard, for the programs considered in this section, we examine the types of youth with disabilities that are targeted for mentoring programs, characteristics of the mentors, program goals, and the ways in which program practices both are consistent with and may go beyond proposed "best practices" for mentoring programs. The reader is reminded that although mentoring programs have exploded in popularity, there has been no active effort reported to date to engage youth with disabilities in general mentoring programs

(Rousso, 2001). Accordingly, our focus remains on programs specific to youth with disabilities.

Targeted Youth

Most research evaluates programs directed at youth with physical or learning disabilities. In comparison, other mentoring programs for which evaluation data do not yet appear to be available have addressed a broader range of disabilities. One prominent example is Best Buddies. Best Buddies is an international organization that provides one-to-one friendships to people, including youth, with intellectual/ developmental disabilities (I/DD) (Best Buddies International, 2004). Their focus on these youth highlights that theoretical considerations concerning mentoring youth with disabilities do not exclude people with I/DD. In fact, these youth too might benefit from mentoring.

Mentor Characteristics

One promising direction within practice is programs that are created by people with disabilities who recognize the need for youth to learn information relevant to their lives. A group of students with learning disabilities in a program designed to promote their self-advocacy felt so positively about the benefits they derived from it that they went on to mentor younger students with learning disabilities in order to impart their emerging expertise (Pocock et al., 2002). This approach has great potential given theoretical considerations that mentees benefit from identifying with a successful disabled mentor and that the relevance may increase as it is peer driven. Yet peer mentoring has not been widely used or evaluated for these youth.

Program Goals

In general, programs described in the literature but not yet evaluated seem to have a strong emphasis on positive development. Consistent with a strengths-based approach, they focus less on deficits in youth with disabilities (e.g., social skills) than do many evaluated programs. One of the most widely disseminated transition-focused programs, High School/ High-Tech (2003), focuses on promoting careers in science and technology for youth with disabilities. Another program, Mentors, Inc.: Arts & Disability Mentoring (n.d.), aims to support youth with disabilities in their pursuit of professions in the arts industry by connecting youth with art professionals. Started in 1999 by the American Association of People with Disabilities, there is also a National Disability Mentoring Day cosponsored by the U.S. Department of Labor Office of Disability Employment Policy. The day is set aside to profile the National Disability Employment Awareness Month. It seeks to enable youth to learn more about jobs and how to prepare for them. Each of these programs assumes that youth with disabilities can have successful, diverse, and exciting lives and encourages them to participate in a variety of career paths.

Best Practices

The mentoring field in general has benefited from the availability of recommendations for effective practice. Critical elements include well-designed, -planned, -managed, -operated, and -evaluated programs (MENTOR/National Mentoring Partnership, 2003). Key dimensions of effective mentoring practice suggested by research include careful screening, orientation, and training of mentors; providing ongoing supervision of and support for the mentoring relationship; and providing opportunities for parent involvement (DuBois, Holloway, Valentine, & Cooper, 2002). It is clear that many of the programs for youth with disabilities are responsive to these guidelines. Unfortunately, we have not yet fully considered how this set of best practices should and can be adapted to youth with disabilities. Program accessibility is clearly a necessary consideration. One particularly promising direction of best practices that addresses accessibility is programs that use e-mentoring (e.g., DO-IT: Disabilities, Opportunities, Internetworking, and Technology, 2004). E-mentoring may be particularly well suited to reach youth challenged to connect with others due to inaccessible or unavailable transportation or who live in rural areas.

In sum, mentoring is gradually becoming more available to youth with disabilities often excluded from programs targeted at youth without disabilities. As this growth takes place, greater innovation is occurring and thus, we hope, strengthening the likelihood of mentoring programs' abilities to promote the positive development and full societal inclusion of youth with disabilities. As they offer practice-related innovations, mentoring programs for youth with disabilities are offering a host of untested material ripe for evaluation.

FUTURE DIRECTIONS

Synthesis

Mentoring programs directed toward youth with disabilities are growing. Theoretically, there is a basis to expect that mentoring relationships can be beneficial for youth with disabilities. However, the realization of such benefits may depend on a range of factors related to engaging youth by plugging into their lives and motivating them by activating their interests. While extant research has indicated some of the areas of success (e.g., the attainment of communication and social skills, disability-related knowledge and perceived self-efficacy, greater independence, and more favorable transition outcomes) and limitations (e.g., general self-efficacy, advanced social skills) of mentoring for youth with disabilities, we currently know relatively little about the efficacy of elements hypothesized to be crucial to the effectiveness of mentoring relationships or programs for youth with disabilities. Nor has research systematically assessed the impact of potentially important moderators. Programs' abilities to plug into the lives of youth with disabilities (e.g., having developmentally appropriate foci and integrating families) and to activate the interest of these youth (e.g., involve mentors with disabilities and foster self-determination) may determine their effectiveness. Unfortunately, most research to date lacks sufficient rigor or precision to adequately address these hypotheses. From this review, we have identified practice and research-related recommendations intended to foster the continued growth of this area. Recommendations for youth identified in other chapters may bear relevance to youth with disabilities and should be considered as well.

Recommendations for Research

1. *Conduct more qualitative research.* There is a significant need for more qualitative research on mentoring youth with disabilities. This type of investigation is needed to increase awareness and understanding of those aspects of mentoring programs and relationships unique to the experiences and needs of this population that may facilitate or thwart deriving meaningful benefits. Illustratively, qualitative research could prove valuable as a means of illuminating processes relating to issues of control in the mentoring relationships of youth with disabilities, which we have highlighted throughout this chapter as an important theoretical concern. An important aspect qualitative research should examine is naturally occurring mentoring relationships among youth with disabilities. Qualitative methods may be particularly useful in initially elucidating the important elements of these relationships. Although these ties and their formation have received little study to date, naturally occurring mentoring has the potential to inform the planning of future mentoring programs for youth with disabilities.

2. *Broaden sensitivity to sociocultural factors.* Research should attend to dimensions of human diversity that may moderate (by either promoting or impeding) the efficacy of particular approaches to mentoring youth with disabilities. Expanding dimensions of sociocultural variables above and beyond disability, such as gender, socioeconomic status, ethnicity, and sexual orientation, will likely assist us in our understanding of how to successfully structure mentoring programs for a variety of youth with disabilities. There is also a need for attention in research to youth who have a wider variety of disability types and more extensive forms of disabilities, who often may be overlooked as potential beneficiaries of mentoring relationships. In fact, extant research has not yet addressed the role of the severity of the disability—a factor with many important implications for program development and implementation. In addition, whether as researchers or collaborators, people who experience disability themselves should be involved in the design, implementation, and interpretation of research in this area. A participatory approach can be expected to have the

added benefit of promoting a more complete understanding of the complex issues involved in mentoring relationships for youth with disabilities (see Jason et al., 2004).

3. *Investigate untested theory, emerging constructs, and innovative practices specific to youth with disabilities.* Research focused on the further development of key theoretical constructs and related intervention strategies that may have specific relevance to youth with disabilities is sorely needed. We have identified a host of variables that may significantly affect the success of mentoring relationships and programs for this population and thus are promising candidates for investigation. These include issues related to the disability status of the mentor, the degree to which relationships are oriented toward youth empowerment, and the integration of the family into program design. The wide range of current programs that reflect innovative practices yet have not been the subject of investigation represent another promising direction. Studies should also attempt to understand how to promote long-term mentee–mentor relationships and examine the long-term effects of the mentoring experience. Finally, there clearly is a need to systematically examine the utility of best practices from the general mentoring literature and, in doing so, to explore the relative efficacy of adaptations to these practices that are tailored specifically to mentoring youth with disabilities.

4. *Conduct rigorous evaluations of mentoring programs for youth with disabilities.* To strengthen the knowledge base regarding the impact of mentoring programs for youth with disabilities, priority should be given to conducting well-controlled evaluations of programs. Ideally, these should be controlled experiments using random assignment to mentoring conditions. In the absence of true experiments, a priority should be placed on the use of strong quasi-experimental designs such as those that include preassessment and postassessment and a carefully matched comparison group. For evaluations to be informative regarding both outcomes and mediating processes, measures that capture theoretically relevant dimensions of the mentoring relationship should be used. In some cases, relevant measures exist but have

received little or no use. These include, for example, procedures that are available to assess goal attainment in the context of mentoring relationships (Garate-Serafini, Balcazar, Weitlauf, & Keys, 2001).

Recommendations for Practice

1. *Be responsive to evidence for effective mentoring practices.* As research from mentoring programs targeted at youth expands, programs should strive to adopt practices that are consistent with the best available evidence. Some constructs for which there is emerging evidence include involving parents in the program and providing access to successful role models with disabilities. As another example, theory and some research suggest that programs should employ practices that promote the development of relationships in which mentors encourage the self-competence of youth with disabilities and allow them to exercise choices.

2. *Expand emphasis on sociocultural diversity.* Programs should seek to target a wide variety of mentees and mentors. Active engagement of youth and mentors with a variety of forms of disability, particularly those more stigmatized, will expand the group who benefit from mentoring programs. Similarly, more programs not targeted at youth with disabilities should reach out to these youth and make their programs accessible and relevant. Finally, this recommendation demands that we not define youth with disabilities uniquely by their disability status. These youth also have experiences, interests, and concerns, linked to their gender, ethnicity, age, socioeconomic background, sexual orientation, hobbies, and abilities.

3. *Consider additional program components.* Given the realities of youth with disabilities, it may be unrealistic to assume that a mentor alone can address the variety of needs faced by these youth. These experiences place youth with disabilities at risk in a variety of ways. Attention to a wider variety of interventions and/or program components may increase the efficacy of the mentoring relationship and better serve the needs of this population of youth.

REFERENCES

Asch, A., Rousso, H., & Jefferies, T. (2001). Beyond pedestals: The lives of girls and women. In H. Rousso & M. Wehmeyer (Eds.), *Double jeopardy: Addressing gender equity in special education* (pp. 337–360). Albany: State University of New York Press.

Balcazar, F., Keys, C., & Garate, J. (1995). Learning to recruit assistance to attain transition goals: A program for adjudicated youth with disabilities. *Remedial and Special Education, 16,* 237–246.

Best Buddies International. (2004). Retrieved May 22, 2003, from http://www.bestbuddies.org/home.asp

Block, P., Balcazar, F., & Keys, C. (2002). Race, poverty and disability: Three strikes and you are out! Or are you? *Social Policy, 33*(1), 34–38.

Brandt, E., & Pope, A. M. (1997). *Enabling America: Assessing the role of rehabilitation science and engineering.* Washington, DC: National Academies Press.

Buckner, A. (1993). *Mediating at-risk factors among seventh and eighth grade students with specific learning disabilities using a holistically based model.* Doctoral dissertation, Nova University, Florida. (ERIC Document Reproduction Service No. 368122)

Charlton, J. (1998). *Nothing about us without us: Disability oppression and empowerment.* Berkeley: University of California Press.

DO-IT: Disabilities, Opportunities, Internetworking, and Technology. (2004, May 26). Retrieved June 16, 2003, from http://www.washington.edu/doit/

DuBois, D. L., Holloway, B. E., Valentine, J. C., & Cooper, H. (2002). Effectiveness of mentoring programs for youth: A meta-analytic review. *American Journal of Community Psychology, 30,* 157–197.

DuBois, D. L., Neville, H. A., Parra, G. R., & Pugh-Lilly, A. O. (2002). Testing a new model of mentoring. In G. G. Noam (Ed. in chief) & J. E. Rhodes (Ed.), *A critical view of youth mentoring (New Directions for Youth Development: Theory, Research, and Practice, No. 93,* pp. 21–57). San Francisco: Jossey-Bass.

Epse-Sherwindt, M., & Kerlin, S. (1990). Early intervention with parents with mental retardation: do we empower or do we impair? *Infants and Young Children, 2,* 21–28.

Fine, M., & Asch, A. (1988). *Women with disabilities: Essays in psychology, culture, and politics.* Philadelphia: Temple University Press.

Froschl, M., Rousso, H., & Rubin, E. (2001). Nothing to do after school: More of an issue for girls. In H. Rousso & M. Wehmeyer (Eds.), *Double jeopardy: Addressing gender equity in special education* (pp. 313–336). Albany: State University of New York Press.

Garate-Serafini, T., Balcazar, F., Weitlauf, J., & Keys, C. (2001). School-based mentoring programs for minority youth: Program components and evaluation strategies. In R. Majors (Ed.), *Educating our Black children: New directions and radical approaches* (pp. 214–257). London: Routledge.

High School/High-Tech. (2003). Retrieved May 22, 2003, from http://www.high-school-high-tech.com/pubs/19_47_228.CFM

Jason, L., Keys, C., Suarez-Balcazar, Y., Taylor, R., Davis, M., Durlak, J. A., & Isenberg, D. H. (Eds.). (2004). *Participatory community research: Theories and methods in action.* Washington, DC: American Psychological Association.

MENTOR/National Mentoring Partnership. (2003). *Elements of effective practice* (2nd ed.). Alexandria, VA: Author.

Mentors, Inc.: Arts & Disability Mentoring. (n.d.). Retrieved July 5, 2003, from http://mentorsinc.org/Links/LinksMain.cfm

Moccia, R., Schumaker, J., Hazel, S., Vernon, D., & Deshler, D. (1989). A mentor program for facilitating the life transitions of individuals who have handicapping conditions. *Reading, Writing, and Learning Disabilities, 5,* 177–195.

Muscott, H., O'Brien, S., & College, R. (1999). Teaching character education to students with behavioral and learning disabilities through mentoring relationships. *Education and Treatment of Children, 22,* 373–390.

Nagi, S. (1991). Disability concepts revisited: Implications for prevention. In A. Pope & A. Tarlov (Eds.), *Disability in America: Toward a national agenda for prevention* (pp. 309–372). Washington, DC: National Academies Press.

Newman, L. (1992). *Hispanic secondary school students with disabilities: How are they doing?* The National Longitudinal Transition Study of Special Education Students, prepared for presentation at the Hispanic Research Issues Special Interest Group of the American

Educational Research Association Annual Meeting, San Francisco. Menlo Park, CA: SRI International.

Noll, V. (1997). Cross-age mentoring program for social skills development. *The School Counselor, 44,* 239–242.

Odom, S., McConnell, S., & McEvoy, M. (1992). Peer-related social competence and its significance for young children with disabilities. In S. L. Odom, S. R. McConnell, & M. A. McEvoy (Eds.), *Social competence of young children with disabilities* (pp. 3–36). Baltimore: Paul H. Brookes.

Packer, B. (1994). *Promoting successful mainstream experiences for hearing-impaired elementary students through in-service training, peer, mentoring, and pragmatics groups.* Doctoral dissertation, Nova University, Florida. (ERIC Document Reproduction Service No. 372548)

Pledger, C. (2003). Discourse on disability and rehabilitation issue: Opportunity for psychology. *American Psychologist, 58,* 279–284.

Pocock, A., Lambros, S., Karvonen, M., Test, D., Algozzine, B., Wood, W., & Martin, J. (2002). Successful strategies for promoting self-advocacy among students with LD: The lead group. *Intervention in School and Clinic, 37,* 209–216.

Powers, L., Sowers, J., & Stevens, T. (1995). An exploratory, randomized study of the impact of mentoring in the self-efficacy and community-based knowledge of adolescents with severe physical challenges. *Journal of Rehabilitation, 61*(1), 33–41.

Rhodes, J. E. (2002). *Stand by me: The risks and rewards of mentoring today's youth.* Cambridge, MA: Harvard University Press.

Rioux, M. (1997). Disability: The place of judgment in a world of fact. *Journal of Intellectual Disability Research, 41,* 102–111.

Rousso, H. (2001). What do Frida Kahlo, Wilma Mankiller, and Harriet Tubman have in common? Providing role models for girls with (and without) disabilities. In H. Rousso & M. Wehmeyer (Eds.), *Double jeopardy: Addressing gender equity in special education* (pp. 337–360). Albany: State University of New York Press.

Rousso, H., & Wehmeyer, M. (Eds.). (2001). *Double jeopardy: Addressing gender equity in special education.* Albany: State University of New York Press.

Ryerson-Espino, S., Ritzler, T., Keys, C., Balcazar, F., Garate-Serafini, T., & Hayes, E. (2003). *An exploration of employment transition goal pursuing and helping processes among ethnic minority youth with disabilities.* Unpublished manuscript, University of Illinois at Chicago.

Shepard-Tew, D., & Forgione, J. (1999). A collaborative mentor-training program for learning-disabled middle-grade students. *Educational Forum, 64,* 75–81.

Taylor-Ritzler, T., Balcazar, F., Keys, C., Hayes, E., Garate-Serafini, T., & Ryerson Espino, S. (2001). Promoting attainment of transition-related goals among low-income ethnic minority students with disabilities. *Career Development for Exceptional Individuals, 24*(2), 147–167.

Todis, B., Powers, L., Irvin, L., & Singer, G. (1996). A qualitative study of a mentor intervention with children who have multiple disabilities. In L. Powers, G. Singer, & J. Sowers (Eds.), *On the road to autonomy: Promoting self-competence for children and youth with disabilities* (pp. 237–254). Baltimore: Paul H. Brookes.

Tucker, M., & Johnson, O. (1989). Competence promoting vs. competence inhibiting social support for mentally retarded mothers. *Human Organization, 48,* 95–107.

U.S. Department of Education. (2001). *Twenty-third annual report to Congress on the implementation of the Individuals with Disabilities Education Act.* Jessup, MD: Education Publications Center.

Wagner, M. (1992). *Being female—a secondary disability? Gender differences in the transition experience of young people with disabilities.* Menlo Park, CA: SRI International.

Wagner, M., Blackorby, J., Cameto, R., Hebbeler, K., & Newman, L. (1993). *The transition experiences of young people with disabilities: A summary of findings from the National Longitudinal Transition Study of Special Education Students.* Menlo Park, CA: SRI International.

Watkins, S., Pittman, P., & Walden, B. (1998). The Deaf Mentor Experimental Project for young children who are deaf and their families. *American Annals of the Deaf, 143,* 29–34.

Wehmeyer, M. (2002). *Self-determination and the education of students with disabilities.* (ERIC Digest ED470036)

Welkowitz, J., & Fox, W. (2000). *A model mentor/advisor program supporting secondary youth with emotional and behavioral challenges and their families within rural Vermont. Vermont University, Burlington, Center on Disability and Community Inclusion.* (ERIC Document Reproduction Service No. 462787)

West, M., Targett, P., Steininger, G., & Anglin, N. (2001). Project Corporate Support (CORPS): A model demonstration project on workplace supports. *Journal of Vocational Rehabilitation, 16,* 111–118.

Zimmerman, M. (1995). Psychological empowerment: Issues and illustrations. *American Journal of Community Psychology, 23,* 581–599.

PART VIII

POLICY ISSUES

34

YOUTH MENTORING AND PUBLIC POLICY

INTRODUCTION

For the past 15 years, mentoring has been the single most publicly talked about, written about, and broadly popular social intervention in America to improve the lives of disadvantaged youth. It now appears as an approved activity in many pieces of public social legislation, from the 1996 Welfare Reform Act to the Workforce Investment Act of 1998. Foundation officials say that mentoring now appears in almost all human service funding proposals, whether requested or not.

Our highest elected officials love it. In 1997, then President Clinton, former Presidents Bush and Ford, and former First Lady Nancy Reagan joined General Colin Powell in Philadelphia, along with thousands of citizens representing communities across America, to celebrate volunteerism and to propose five essential "nutrients" key to disadvantaged youth: Mentoring was first on the list. And in his 2003 State of the Union message, President Bush proposed nearly half a billion dollars for two new mentoring initiatives. Sitting in the seat next to the first lady was Philadelphia's Democratic Mayor John Street, whose city the president had recently visited twice—specifically to spend time at Philadelphia's innovative mentoring program

for children of prisoners. The list could go on and would include the inclusion of the message of mentoring in many TV shows—a purposeful inclusion inspired by one wealthy philanthropist's belief in the power of the mass media to affect volunteering.

All this during an era when skepticism about the effectiveness and utility of social programs was increasing, and included many Democrats; when long-standing social programs that seemed like permanent fixtures, such as Aid to Families With Dependent Children (AFDC) and Head Start, were ended or challenged; and when the language of social welfare was being replaced by that of personal responsibility.

How did mentoring fare so well in these times? Is mentoring now a durable part of American social policy? If so—is this unalloyed good news? I will address each of these questions in the present chapter and conclude with recommendations for both research and practice in the area of youth mentoring.

HOW IT HAPPENED

Social policy trends, like trends in any part of life, are not totally explainable by rational analysis and orderly chains of logic. But it is also not entirely mysterious as to why mentoring should have such sustained popularity.

First, *mentoring makes sense to most people,* regardless of their politics. Young beings need support and guidance from older beings—we all know that instinctively. Watch a few nature shows on the Discovery Channel and you see how universal the need is; it applies to bears, foxes, birds, and whales as well as humans. Read a little science on mammalian development and you find that the more complex a young being's brains, the more adult support and guidance needed; ergo, little humans need a lot of help from bigger humans. Common sense and science wholeheartedly agree.

And many people—again, regardless of their politics—can remember the importance to them of a nonfamily adult in their lives, how that person helped them think clearly on a hard issue or set them on a learning or work path that has made a great positive difference in their lives. So besides the backing of common sense and science, mentoring stirs up in many adults very personal, meaningful, and positive memories.

Mentoring also offers to some people a comfort from the fear of ungoverned little humans growing up into unruly adults, wreaking havoc on everything around them. Though I have not taken a scientific survey, my experience is that except for a few ideologues, most adults, perhaps especially those with children, would take a view of raw human nature that has at least as much of Hobbes as of Rousseau. Just recently, I heard a report on National Public Radio of 225 Chihuahuas in California that had been set free as pups, turned feral, and were roaming in bands, frightening hikers. If unparented, Chihuahuas can group together and inspire fear in adult humans. . . .

Second, *mentoring fits neatly with dominant American cultural values.* That mentoring makes sense—intuitively, experientially, and scientifically—may to some not seem so distinctive: After all, doesn't meeting any number of youthful needs (e.g., housing, health, education) make sense?

But mentoring's strength is not only that the need it represents—adult support and guidance—seems somehow more basic than other needs but also that it can be met in ways that do not grate against dominant cultural values. Most Americans are not for "big government" (a Democratic president, Bill Clinton, announced that the era of big government was over); are for volunteerism and the "personal touch" versus the paid professional in helping people; and prefer to think most individual issues can be resolved by willpower and determination, with a minimum of outside help, rather than by the provision of comprehensive services. Agree or not, right or wrong, these are rock-solid elements of the American value system. That America "works," is so dominant in the world, and attracts immigrants from all other nations is for most the confirming evidence of that value system.

Most social programs scrape like fingernails on a blackboard against one or more of these values. Talk of the need for "comprehensive" or "long-term" services not only runs counter to these values—to many, it seems to undercut their development!

Mentoring does no grating against these basic values. It seems in fact to affirm them: some help from a kindly adult, a volunteer at that, no government bureaucracy needed; and the result is that the youth marches into his or her future on a mainstream path, transformed. The specter of dependency is not present. Thus, mentoring has never had the uphill struggle that most social programs face in gaining support; rather, it has only picked up speed and momentum, like a downhill racer.

Third, *mentoring has results.* In an era in which social programs are increasingly called on to prove their worth with hard numbers, mentoring seems golden. P/PV's 1995 impact study of the Big Brothers Big Sisters (BBBS) program, using a random-assignment methodology, produced evidence that mentoring had positive impacts on a range of important elements in a youth's life, from initiating drug use to attending school to fighting in the schoolyard (Tierney, Grossman, & Resch, 1995). Big Brothers Big Sisters of America (BBBSA) has used the impact study and its findings very effectively in its marketing, helping them almost triple in size over the 9 years since the results came out. In a political atmosphere where the prevailing sentiment is that most social programs are either ineffective or if effective, not impressively effective, mentoring stands out.

Much as mentoring's commonsense appeal benefits from its consistency with American cultural values, so does the perception of its evaluation findings benefit from that consistency. For though the impact findings are real and impressive, in fact they apply to the 18 months after mentoring began—that was as long as comparative follow-up work could extend, as no one wanted to deny the control group the possibility of a mentor longer than that. Thus, we have no scientific evidence that mentoring "turns lives around"; its long-term transformational impact is, scientifically speaking, not known. The truth is that a number of social programs that have been rigorously evaluated also produce positive impacts for a modest time period. But none affirm common sense and basic American values as much as mentoring, and thus mentoring's documented good results, albeit more short term than transformational, are widely accepted as ultimate proof of its value.

Fourth, *mentoring has BBBS as its exemplar.* Ideas abound for helping young people. Many get tried; some have their brief moment in the sun; most come and go in fairly brief cycles. There are many reasons for this revolving-door nature of American social policy, and one in particular is very relevant to the staying power of mentoring: America is a land of institutions and brand names more than it is a land of ideas. Its competitive, free-market economic system drives this orientation and makes most Americans fleetingly interested in ideologies and ideas, and enduringly interested in the institutions and brand names that represent them. Though it is easy to criticize this orientation as anti-intellectual and shallow, it is equally easy to spot its strength: Americans are inclined to pay more attention to the concrete manifestations of ideas—to the *accountability* of ideas—than to their mental images.

BBBSA is one of America's most recognized, most respected nonprofit institutions. It was privately initiated, organized, governed, and grown to a national federation; it uses volunteers; it only does mentoring. It fits perfectly with American values, and it is well-known. Mentoring as a social program idea benefits enormously from the existence of BBBSA: It gives it not only respect and credibility, but staying power.

Fifth, *mentoring's costs are not high.* At an estimated $1,000 to 1,500 per year per mentor (Fountain & Arbreton, 1999), mentoring's costs fall in the range of most after-school and summer programming and are much less than intensive remedial programming and more comprehensive service programs. In addition, mentoring's costs, which mainly go toward the selection, training, and ongoing support of mentors, have been supported in the evaluation literature as critical to the effective functioning of volunteer mentors (DuBois, Holloway, Valentine, & Cooper, 2002). In short, mentoring has a significant number of important assets that help explain why it has become such a popular social intervention—and why its popularity has endured.

But why now? Mentoring and BBBS have been around for a long time—as a formal program, for almost a century (see Baker & Maguire, this volume). Why the surge in growth and popularity in the last decade of the 20th century and early years of this one?

It's difficult to address issues of "historical period" confidently when the one you're living in is part of the issue. But there are several factors that no doubt play important roles. One is simply a sense of discouragement that many feel—Republicans and Democrats, conservatives and liberals—that so few social programs generate substantial and positive results. That discouragement prompted a lot of searching for new ideas, or for ideas to revitalize. The notion of a more straightforward and humanized social intervention, after several decades of interventions focused on "services," was, in retrospect, simply waiting to happen.

Second, the private sector actively promoted the idea. The Commonwealth Foundation was aggressively spreading the word of mentoring's virtues and effects by the late 1980s. Early in the 1990s, several individual philanthropists, most notably Ray Chambers and Geoff Boisi, began to promote mentoring in high-profile ways that the social policy sector rarely attempts or is comfortable with. The 1997 Presidents' Summit was one result; the formation of a national mentoring advocacy organization, The One to One Partnership, Inc. (now referred to as MENTOR/National Mentoring Partnership) was another; use of the popular media was another.

Furthermore, the 1997 Presidents' Summit was formed to build upon the work of organizations such as the Points of Light Foundation, United Way of America, Communities in Schools, and MENTOR. In fact, mentoring (caring adults in the lives of young people) was considered the cornerstone of America's Promise, the organization that emerged out of the Presidents' Summit. So, in short, mentoring had champions, who bred other champions, across all sectors.

By 1995, the evidence of mentoring's effectiveness was out—and was picked up and used by the already growing champions. As noted, by 2003, BBBS was almost triple the size it had been less than a decade previously. It had been roughly the same size for the preceding two decades.

Third, America's politics—almost always conservative about social policy except for brief periods in the 1930s and 1960 to 1970s—returned to conservatism in the 1980s and 1990s. Though the 1990s were dominated by a Democratic president, a flush economy, and a healthy federal budget, there were few new social policy initiatives of any size or significance. A Democratic president declared the end of "the era of big government"; a Democratic Secretary of Labor (Robert Reich) did not pursue additional funding for youth programs because there was so little evidence of their effectiveness. An intervention based on volunteers, like mentoring, was appealing simply because it was politically feasible. Some of its supporters were enthusiastic; some were lukewarm, resigned to it because so little else was feasible; together, they made its growth possible.

Is Mentoring Now Established Social Policy?

You might think, after the foregoing discussion, that the answer to the question of whether mentoring is now established social policy would be a resounding "yes." But the answer is more complicated than that, despite mentoring's popularity, press, results, and growth.

Part of the complication has little to do with mentoring and more to do with the complex political structure of the United States. If, for example, our standard of "established social policy" is a major act of Congress, funded sufficiently to meet the needs of a substantial share of those who need it, mentoring is not established social policy.

But of course few things are, by that standard. Social Security is; Head Start almost is; Job Corps is not; nor is the recent Leave No Child Behind Act (2001) legislation—as most social policy legislation is not. If we take away the "substantial share" requirement, we get more "established" social policy, but we also get more emptiness: Consider the legislation of several decades ago calling for full employment. . . .

Mentoring has neither a major act of Congress nor an allocation of federal funds for mentoring in the various departments sufficient to provide mentors to more than a modest share of those youth who might need mentors. So it is not "established federal policy."

On the other hand, mentoring has enjoyed the leadership of Congressman Tom Osborne of Nebraska, who, in 2002, spearheaded the creation and funding of a new federal grant program dedicated exclusively to mentoring. Just 2 years later, this program was slated for a major increase, along with a mentoring program for children of prisoners, as part of the Bush administration's proposal to expand the reach of mentoring. In addition, mentoring is now promoted or permitted in a wide range of federal legislation, over a wide range of federal departments. There are special mentoring initiatives located in the Justice, Education, and Health and Human Services Departments, and the Workforce Investment Act (1998), administered by the Labor Department, encourages mentoring generally, while the Labor Department's major initiative on prisoner reentry specifically emphasizes it.

Thus, mentoring has made numerous inroads into federal policy in every federal department that deals with youth. It has the support of all major political and business leaders—and the public. Thus, it could be said to be "beginning" to be federal social policy, and the extent to which those beginnings flourish (or wither) is, simply, unknown. But the foundations are strong.

So strong that even in an era of serious budget deficits and very limited interest in social policy by the dominant Republican Party—an era in which discretionary social programs are likely to be one of the first lines of attack for reduction—mentoring's foothold is probably as firm as a social program could hope for. You can read the 2003 and 2004 State of the Union messages as an indication that it may be one of those rare social interventions that get promoted and increased as others are being criticized and cut.

In addition, assessing whether a particular idea is "established social policy" solely or primarily through the lens of major federal legislation is a narrow view in several respects. Certainly, federal funds are indispensable to any social policy if it is to achieve significant size. But there are ways to use federal funds that do not involve major legislation: earmarks; special initiatives within federal departments; and an emphasis, encouragement, or allowance of a particular practice (like mentoring) within other pieces of legislation. Mentoring has achieved all of these "other" ways of using federal monies. In total, their actual use amounts to probably no more than $250 million of federal funds, which at a $1,000 per mentor per year cost would fund 250,000 mentors. But that is triple the size of the entire BBBS program in America in 1995, which provides some idea of how recent the growth in mentoring, and in public funding for it, is. For until recently, mentoring was supported primarily through private funds.

How large that private funding is, is difficult to say with precision. That it, like public funding, has been growing, seems clear, considering that new mentoring programs have sprung up like wildflowers in a wet spring over the past decade, well before the recent increase in federal monies. A 1997 survey indicated that almost 40% of the mentoring programs surveyed were less than 5 years old (Sipe & Roder, 1999). Most of those are small, and unlike BBBSA, it is difficult to know much about their size, effectiveness, or funding source. My conservative estimate is that in aggregate, they equal the size of BBBSA and are heavily financed by private funds, usually individual philanthropists, small foundations, or United Ways. Thus, they represent perhaps $250 million in private funds, which along with

BBBSA's private funding of $200 million amounts to close to $500 million in private funding.

No thorough survey has been done of state and local government funding of mentoring, using state and local tax revenues. We do know that some states, New York and California are major examples, have established statewide mentoring initiatives, using state resources. So have some localities. Though it is impossible at this point to make an accurate guess on the aggregate state and local resources being used, it does seem likely that when you add all public and private finances being directed to formal mentoring programs, they put mentoring in the billion-dollar range.

Is that large? Certainly, not by federal standards, where billion-dollar programs are numerous. But as funds directed to one very particular and defined kind of intervention, it joins a less numerous class. As funds directed to a particular kind of intervention with robust, positive results—even if not quite so strong as its advocates claim—it joins an even more exclusive club.

But more important than the total funds for mentoring's potential to become a vital element of American social policy is the depth and variety of its sources. Ron Haskins, formerly majority staff director of House Ways and Means Committee during the first Bush administration and now a senior fellow at The Brookings Institution, has created, based on his legislative experience, an interesting pictorial of the various factors that influence the durability of legislation (Haskins, 2003). Though he does not claim exactness or invariability for the share of influence he ascribes to each factor, two broad features stand out: One is the variety of influences; the second is the power of inertia that a "policy continent"—the aggregate of institutions and influential individuals that have a stake in a particular policy—can exert. Change is not easy in our form of government. Once something is in, with a lot of people and institutions behind it, it's hard to get out. Being so consistent with dominant values and having some hard evidence of impact, as mentoring is and does, must add something to that staying power.

Haskins is talking about federal legislation only, but it does not seem much of a leap to see his first broad feature—variety of influences—as a critical feature for the sustainability of any particular social policy at all levels of government. In a representative form of government with a complex, competing set of institutions, sectors, and individuals that can have influence, the broader the support for a particular intervention as policy, the better its chances to become policy, stay policy, and grow.

Thus, mentoring, though relatively new to the public social policy agenda and neither established nor large on that agenda, would appear to have a strong foothold. The very fact that it came to public policy with such strong and varied support from private institutions and individuals makes it likely that its presence on that agenda will not be fleeting.

IS MENTORING AS SOCIAL POLICY A GOOD THING?

It is not hard to make the argument that mentoring's emergence into the world of public social policy and funding is an unalloyed good. The substantive bottom line is clearly positive, for even if mentoring is not quite as effective and transformational as its advocates claim, it certainly has hard evidence that it does in fact improve the lives, behavior, and performance of many youth—and 30 years of social experimentation have not produced a wide range of options to choose from that can make that claim. Who can be against something that has evidence of effectiveness?

It also would appear to have a broader social value. The decline in confidence in the capacity of social programs to make a real difference in the lives of youth has steadily grown over the past 30 years. The erosion has been particularly deep concerning policies for adolescents and has even made many who generally favor strong public social policy turn their support and efforts almost exclusively to young children—leaving little political capital for social initiatives to help youth in the 8- to 17-year age range. Some speak openly, some whisper, but agreement has grown: The 8 to 17 age range may be too late.

There are several solid grounds on which to decry this "go younger" trend, but it is foolish to

dismiss it as totally irresponsible or to claim it is entirely political. Certainly, it is consistent with the conservative trend in American politics, but the skepticism about the effectiveness of social policies for youth also embraces much of the center of American politics, and some of the left of center. That leaves very little. Skepticism has spread this far in good part because there is substantial evidence to support it—and much less evidence to counter it. The recent study of after-school programming—the latest billion-dollar-plus federal social policy initiative—has added yet another arrow to the quiver of skepticism (Dynarski et al., 2003).

Surely, having a concrete policy initiative like mentoring, which works for adolescents, is an essential step to the rebuilding of confidence in public social policy. For how can moral advocacy secure anything beyond rhetorical agreement, heartfelt sympathy, and window dressing funding if here is no confidence that much of anything can in fact be accomplished?

Mentoring would also appear to be a direct (if insufficient) response to another broad trend in American life: the reduction of adults in the lives of youth. Both parents working, the prevalence of one-parent families, the growth of a distinct youth culture, the reduction of local funding for school-based after-school programs, legal and practical reasons why employees in public systems (teachers, correctional officials, etc.) are discouraged from befriending youth—these factors have all converged to make declining adult presence in youthful lives a major social transformation. Mentoring at best only dents this transformation, but it is hard to see that as an argument against it.

In short, the above three reasons present a powerful rationale for applauding the appearance of mentoring, if not breathing a healthy sigh of relief that something has taken root that actually helps young people and that has broad support across the political spectrum.

Case closed? If only it were so simple. There are, in fact, several important critiques and some real resistance to mentoring as mainstream social policy. On analysis, some seem weak—and some very thoughtful. Few are voiced publicly or loudly because mentoring is popular, is successful, and has the three strong rationales outlined above. I have presented the concerns below and tried to assess their substantive and political importance.

The Zero-Sum Game

Many individuals and institutions involved in social policy see it as a sector with no significant prospects for expansion: If one aspect of policy gets bigger, another will get smaller. Those who grew up in the 1960s and 1970s may have believed that such expansion was inevitable or have seen its achievement as simply a function of politics, but in retrospect, those views seem optimistic and naive.

For the past 25 years, America's basically centrist values vis-à-vis the role of the public sector on social welfare issues have asserted themselves. The profusion of legislation in the 1960s and early 1970s to address social issues now seems less an inevitable social trend than an artifact of an unusual set of historical circumstances, shaped primarily by America's success in World War II and the climax of the civil rights movement.

This reassertion of dominant values was most vividly apparent in the 1990s, when a Democratic president in a booming economy with a massive federal budget surplus could not move forward major "progressive" social legislation, nor really made much effort to do so. To say that the Republican-controlled House and Senate blocked such movement is only to say that the American political system on balance did not support such movement—much as it also did not support any major "regressive" movement on social policy, as the brief flash of Newt Gingrich and the Contract With America movement showed.

The political system instead reflected well the preference of the culture for a centrist, practical conservatism on social issues. The Democratic Party itself reflected that centrism; its leadership was proud to "change welfare as we know it" (read: remove entitlements and their incentives for dependency) and be the ones to proclaim the end of the era of Big Government.

Does this mean the end of public social policy? Hardly. Centrism does not imply total destruction of or lack of opportunity in social policy; it does imply caution and limits rather than unbridled enthusiasm.

The most powerful and durable manifestation of centrism is the outcomes movement, which in the 1990s spread like wildfire throughout the social policy world, in both the public and philanthropic sectors. Put most simply, that movement said: Don't just tug at my heartstrings; prove that your social policy accomplishes something. The fact that this proof has not come easily has played a strong role in the growing suspicion that maybe many social problems are simply not "solvable" by social policy.

That suspicion and the evidence that backs it has a political consequence: It generates declining interest in the body politic generally in continuing to try to create social policy that will solve those problems, and generates fuel for those who never wanted to try in the first place.

Passion of a few for not trying at all, and less interest from many in the prospects of trying, add up to an emerging political decision that moves social policy another notch down on the priority list of uses for public policy and taxpayer money. And given that only a small minority of Americans ever had the desire for America to become like a Northern European social welfare state, the politics of social policy for young people begins to look more like a series of occasional arguments than a sustained and serious effort.

In this view of the current state of American politics, the success of mentoring becomes less a building block—hey, things *do* work; have hope, voters, we should keep at these issues!—than a growing piece of a diminishing pie. For many voters, discovering that mentoring works is a satisfying end to this somewhat depressing process of finding solutions to tough human and social problems.

Furthermore, mentoring's success may hasten the pie's shrinkage. For mentoring is something volunteers do, and what they do is very limited: They develop a relationship. If that's all it takes, some social conservatives would (and do) say, what is all this talk about social change and comprehensive services? What's the public sector need to do except provide a little cash for expansion of mentoring; the major work and the major money are all private.

These conclusions play very well to the interests and beliefs of a small but very vocal and politically powerful group of American leaders and institutions; they also are very seductive to a larger group of Americans who would like to believe these kids can be helped and if it can be done simply, privately, and without much burden on the taxpayer's wallet, all the better.

Is the "zero-sum/declining sum" critique of mentoring accurate? More accurate than the "building optimism for social policy through success" argument? I think that both these positions are accurate, in the sense that both are in play. We are currently in some version of a zero-sum game, with mentoring absorbing a larger share of the resources. But also we do need to have success, not just moral claims, to increase interest and the size of the pie.

How this all resolves itself—which analysis turns out right—is less a matter of cultural values or historical trend and more a matter of *who uses mentoring the most effectively as an advocacy tool.* Centrism, even a conservative centrism, does not inherently deny growth or possibility for new initiatives in social policy: It simply makes them hard to get. The pie can grow—if a convincing case can be made not only that it should, but that it will produce outcomes.

One thing seems likely: To deny or undercut mentoring's importance is not a sound strategy for the future of public social policy for youth. Mentoring simply has too much going for it: It is a social initiative with broad appeal, which gives hope that adolescence is not too late to intervene. Mentoring needs to be built on—used as a foundation stone—to advocate successfully for other social initiatives.

Mentoring's greatest usefulness, far beyond its value as a program, is its affirmation of the value and role of nonfamily adults in children's lives and in their healthy development. Focusing on mentoring only as a program can easily play into the zero/declining-sum game because mentoring's advocates, in their zeal to expand, will undercut the importance of other initiatives—that's what competition is all about. Seeing mentoring too broadly—as affirming the role of adults—only plunks mentoring into the thicket of family policy issues (e.g., shouldn't we promote more family in kids' lives, rather than mentors?). That can go many ways.

No, mentoring is a practical response to the immobilizing "Does it take a village or just parents to raise a child?" debate. The answer is, as usual, in-between: It takes parents and some caring strangers. Mentors are strangers; so are coaches, teachers, police, juvenile guards, and so on. Formal mentoring programs formalize and demystify what that means and how to do it. But it's just one way. Kids need more—in today's world, as many as they can get. Mentoring is the headline on what needs to be done in every institution that deals with young people. Practice will vary, because roles vary, but youth need more nonfamily adults making intentionally positive contributions to their sense of importance, usefulness, and integrity. Strangers have a lot to do with both success and character.

The Limits on Scale

Though mentoring seems straightforward—a caring relationship—that simplicity is deceptive, and that deceptiveness has profound consequences for the number of volunteers that mentoring can expect. For one, not all adults are adept at developing relationships with a young stranger (even in BBBS, with its careful selection and training, about one in four just don't do that good a job; Tierney et al., 1995). Second, only a modest percentage of adults want to (Scales, 2003).

Getting volunteers always has been a challenge for mentoring agencies. When P/PV did its study in the early 1990s, most sites in the study had long waiting lists, and it was not unusual for a youth to wait 18 months to get a mentor.

But the more serious limit on the number of volunteers available is neither competence nor desire, but what mentoring asks of its volunteers. This is no monthly visit to the playground, or weekend helping rebuild the barn. It's once a week, several hours a week, for 52 weeks—that's what the research to date tells us it takes to get results (Grossman & Rhodes, 2002; Tierney et al., 1995). A little multiplication delivers the sobering message that a mentor is committing more than 100 hours a year—that's almost 3 standard workweeks!

How many adults, even the most competent and caring, will volunteer to do that? Of course, better effort on the part of mentoring agencies will unearth more volunteers—but most new volunteers go to replace retiring ones. It is difficult to substantially increase the number of volunteers willing to put in the time mentioned above (see Stukas & Tanti, this volume).

So unlike most social policies, "going to scale" is not primarily a function of financial resources. Beyond a certain point, you simply can't "buy" volunteers.

When you hear that Americans are the hardest-working people on the planet—averaging, for example, *9 weeks a year* more work than the Germans—you can imagine why adding 3 weeks of mentoring would be a challenge. An AOL Time Warner poll conducted in 2002 found, however, that of those adults who do not currently volunteer as mentors, 42% (or 54 million adults) would seriously consider mentoring if they had a variety of supports (AOL Time Warner Foundation, 2002). These include a choice of mentoring options, depending upon schedule and interests, access to expert help, orientation and training before mentoring, release time and encouragement from employer, and flexibility in where the mentoring takes place.

Mentoring organizations have been responsive to the challenges and the opportunities. Some BBBS localities—Boston is a notable example—have brought in business consultants, streamlined their process, and sunk more resources into recruitment in order to find out truly what the natural limits on scale are. Smart effort will move that limit well beyond the current number. Some corporations and mentoring providers, Goldman Sachs and LA Team Mentoring, for instance, have incorporated more flexible, volunteer-friendly approaches such as bringing young people to the workplace for mentoring sessions and teaming up two or more adults to mentor one or more children.

Advocates estimate that about 15 million youth need mentors (MENTOR/National Mentoring Partnership, n.d.). It seems a safe bet that whatever the natural limit on volunteers willing to serve as mentors in formal programs such as BBBS is, it's substantially short of that.

That mentoring can never address the full scope of need is not a criticism, but simply a fact; it is a natural limitation of any social initiative based on volunteering. Its importance lies not in that it invalidates mentoring or that it should reduce efforts and resources to take mentoring to its fullest scale, whatever that is, for social initiatives with evidence of effectiveness are not legion. Its importance is that it should be realized and stated for the fact that it is.

The tendency to embrace simple solutions and to become exhausted by tough social problems are ordinary human traits, which if allowed to flourish become serious social and moral failings of the larger society. Mentoring's advocates have the tough responsibility of not overselling their product; it is a discipline achieved only by remaining aware of and stating that volunteer mentoring is an important but limited programmatic solution. If mentoring's critics will not encourage it reaching its maximum scale—and mentoring's advocates will not acknowledge that the maximum will still fall way short of need—they both may contribute to the "diminishing sum" process noted earlier.

Quality Control

The most confounding factor regarding tracking and assessing the scale issue over the coming years is knowing what we mean by mentoring and what we expect of it—that is, the issue of quality control. A significant part of mentoring's appeal as a public policy initiative worthy of taxpayer support is the belief generated by the 1995 impact study that mentoring produces changes in youth behavior vis-à-vis drug use, violence, and school performance. Our current state of knowledge says it takes the volunteer time and effort noted above to achieve that.

But the current strategy emphasized by BBBSA and many of its local affiliates is to recruit volunteers to mentor children at their schools, usually over lunch, for 1 to 1.5 hours per week. This does make recruitment easier and accounts for a substantial share of the growth of BBBSA over the past 5 years. It also raises the question of whether such modifications to mentoring's basic and proven model will produce the same impressive results. If they don't, does mentoring still make sense as a public policy initiative?

BBBSA has agreed to have another impact study to resolve the question of school-based mentoring's impact. And BBBSA leaders note that this modification is not intended to reduce the involvement of mentors with youth—only to get more volunteers by not scaring them off with a huge time commitment and the challenge of each week figuring out what to do and where to go. What they expect is that most adults, once they get involved with a young person, will not put a 1-hour-a-week time clock on their involvement. They may be right, and there is no doubt they're right to try out and test new approaches to upping the limit on scale. But it is critical to know, given the resources being committed.

And what about the issue of quality control in non-BBBSA programs, which account, by best estimate, for the majority of all current mentors? The quality control problem is not peculiar to mentoring; it is the *bête-noir* of all social initiatives that achieve popularity and scale. Our decentralized political system and romance with "local uniqueness" make it very difficult to replicate initial impact. Head Start is a relevant example, because it too had early evidence of impact and achieved rapid popularity and growth; its growth has been plagued by lack of rigor and quality control.

Should the quality control issue—both its generic nature and mentoring's early swerve from the "proven model"—be enough to dampen enthusiasm for mentoring as a social policy fixture with a steady tap into the taxpayers' pockets?

The answer is a clear "no." Quality control of large-scale social policy initiatives is, as noted above, largely an artifact of our political system and culture, often exacerbated by the inadequate capacity of public bureaucracies to train, monitor, and control. Mentoring is a rare social policy initiative in that it comes to the taxpayer with a private, nationwide organization, BBBSA, already in place. A second, more recent private organization, MENTOR/National Mentoring Partnership, not only advocates mentoring but actively promotes quality standards. Thus, the capacity and potential for quality control and transparency of action are at a higher level from the outset than the vast majority of social policy initiatives. In fact, each of the 3,700 programs in MENTOR's volunteer referral system agrees to adhere to the *Elements of Effective Practice* (MENTOR/National Mentoring Partnership, 2003) and can get help to do so from the network of State Mentoring Partnerships (MENTOR/National Mentoring Partnership, 2004).

Though BBBSA isn't and will never be the only organization doing mentoring, its "market share" is substantial (if you're from the for-profit world, it's awesome). MENTOR/National Mentoring Partnership's influence is extensive with other mentoring initiatives. Thus, the potential for widespread quality programming is high. The recent adoption of school-based mentoring by BBBSA is a good example. Conceptualized and introduced in 1983 by Dr. Susan Weinberger (the Norwalk Public Schools Mentoring Program) and by the New York City Board of Education (the New York City Mentoring Program), school-based mentoring has been seen as a promising form of mentoring for many years. BBBSA capitalized on school-based mentoring's potential to serve more young people, and because of BBBSA's visibility and leadership, it was not a hidden change or, as in Head Start, the invisible blooming of a thousand wildflowers. It was planned, made public, and is in the process of being evaluated for impact. Under our system, with its inherent bias toward chaos rather than control, you can't do much better.

The Mentees

Perhaps the most challenging critique of mentoring as a programmatic intervention is that its mentees are not the youth who are likely to be the biggest problems to themselves, their families, their friends, their communities, and the society at large (viz, taxpayers). Analyzing this critique demands care, for it is not true that mentoring as commonly practiced purposefully goes out to enroll youth who don't need much help. In fact, mentoring's traditional practice of enrolling youth whose single parent or guardian says they need a mentor, and its new variation, school-based mentoring, which enrolls youth whose teachers say they could benefit from a mentor, get about as intimate a judgment of need as you could ask for—certainly more likely to be accurate than eligibility based on race or income, professional interviews, or Rorschach tests.

No, mentoring's limit on the youth it enrolls is not that the youth it usually gets can't benefit from mentoring; it's that the youth it usually doesn't get have the bigger problems. Mentoring's strengths, based on experience and data, are generally in the 8-through 13-year age range, and concentrated in the years 9 through 11. They are youth with a responsible parent or a teacher who finds them sympathetic.

Youth who are older; who don't have a parent caring, knowledgeable, or insightful enough, or a teacher who finds them sympathetic; who are on the streets or in homeless shelters; who are in foster care or a juvenile institution—these youth do not get volunteer mentors in the course of ordinary mentoring programs. Yet their "at risk-ness" is clearly magnitudes higher than the 10-year-olds who now make up the majority of mentees.

At first blush, it seems unlikely that these higher-risk youth will get mentors: How many adult volunteers will take on such a challenge? In fact, the emerging evidence is mixed. Rigorous attempts to resolve this ambiguity represent one of mentoring's most promising opportunities, for the more likely its mentees are, without mentors, to become problems, the more valuable its services are; the more important (and justifiable) it becomes as public social policy; and the less important it is to have huge numbers of volunteers. The better you can target, the smaller the numbers get.

P/PV's recent multisite, high-risk older youth demonstration, which focused in part on securing mentors for older youth who had already had brushes with the criminal justice system, had very modest success in securing volunteer mentors. Given a choice on how to use their time and good intentions, few volunteers chose to work with older youth (Bauldry & Hartmann, 2004).

On the other hand, the WAY program of Children's Village, a residential treatment facility for very troubled foster care youth, has been successful in getting volunteer mentors for these youth as they are leaving foster care. Careful analysis of efforts such as the two above may tell us whether strategy, effort, personnel, or happenstance made the difference—and whether the success appears replicable.

For younger youth without the support of a referring parent, the record is also mixed. The Amachi initiative, which provides mentors for youth with children in prison, has in its initial

stages been remarkably successful in getting volunteer mentors by targeting faith organizations and congregations (Jucovy, 2003). In Philadelphia, Amachi's demonstration city, more than 500 volunteers came forward in the first year. That is clearly a success by the standard of traditional mentoring, though it also reflects the conclusion of the earlier discussion: It is way short of the number of youth with parents in prison, which in Philadelphia alone is more than 20,000 youth.

But Amachi's success, however modest, indicates the appeal to policymakers of focusing mentoring on a group of youth with significant prospects of troubled lives: President Bush announced it in his 2003 State of the Union as a major policy initiative, and currently Amachi is being implemented in more than 50 new jurisdictions, with federal support.

On the other hand, an initiative begun in the early 1990s in Portland, Oregon, called Friends of the Children (FoCh) (Friends of the Children, 2002), which targets first graders who are already exhibiting troubling behaviors in the classroom and whose families range from unsupportive to dysfunctional, tried but finally gave up on providing mentors through volunteers and instead hires and pays their Friends. Some of the difficulty in recruitment may have been FoCh's blunt message: These kids need help and support, lots of it, and they're going to need it for a long time. No seduction here.

But the decision that volunteers were not sufficient was not made without trying, and it certainly was not tinged by ideology: The program's founder is not biased toward professional social services, nor does he hope for a social welfare state. Given that in its initial years, he paid for the program out of his own pocket, he had many reasons to prefer volunteers.

FoCh appears to target a higher-risk group than Amachi and proposes a more demanding program; it is no surprise that volunteers were judged insufficient. But Amachi youth are not all cherubs, and certainly their "situation" is bound to chill some volunteers. Amachi, by recruiting exclusively through churches, is betting both that faith volunteers will take on tougher kids and, equally important, that their congregations will support the individual volunteers and supplement what they do, thus emulating a family setting in density and duration (see Maton, Sto. Domingo, & King, this volume). Again, it will be critical to look more closely at the issues posed by the very different approaches of Amachi and FoCh and see whether volunteering is indeed a viable strategy for addressing older and higher-risk youth groups.

In short, innovative approaches to targeting and recruitment may both increase mentoring's value to social policy and take some pressure off the numbers of mentors required to ensure that youth at serious risk of a life of problems are served. Or they may not; we just don't know yet. These issues are mentoring's "frontier."

Insufficient Content

Another substantive critique is simply that mentoring is not enough. In this view, mentoring's results are not likely to hold up as a youth ages; it won't be transformational, because an at-risk youth needs more, at more times of his or her life, than a mentor provides.

Like the previous critiques, this one does not lend itself to a clean answer. On the one hand, mentoring does not provide all or even most things that every youth needs. But then, no social intervention does, or ever will. Nor do most families. Nor, I think, is this sort of perfection worth pursuing—it only diverts us from what is possible.

Nor does mentoring provide enough to ensure even a fair chance that each youth's assets and talents are built on. Only a lucky minority in life get that, and we have yet to figure out how to duplicate it through social policy with consistency, at any scale. But this is worth striving for. And no doubt, some form of mentoring will be a part of it.

The question for social intervention policy is: Does mentoring provide enough input to help avoid some problems, achieve some successes, and leave some personal attributes that together provide a stronger foundation for the challenges and decisions that this youth will likely face? Only evaluations will answer that series of questions definitively; the findings to date are promising. But it is on this issue that I think

mentoring's critics undervalue it. For many youth who are already behind in life, with only modest support and few prospects, neither services and opportunities (the liberal approach) nor punishment and/or appeals to determination and resolve (the conservative approach) touches the chords that make humans keep moving forward when they are in difficult circumstances and have little to fall back on. Both the standard conservative and standard liberal approach assume enough emotional connectedness in reserve to counter those inevitable moments when services aren't sufficient, opportunities aren't what they seemed, determination just falters, or punishment doesn't deter. What young people need at moments like that is something much more personal: faith; or another person we don't want to let down, who has confidence in us; or best of all, both.

The need for these "other factors" is especially acute for many disadvantaged youth. For though we all love to tell youth that "you can be anything you want"—and love to celebrate those exceptional individuals who have done just that—in fact, most youth, like most of us, don't believe it. Most youth with a strike or two against them especially don't believe it. They know that whatever they get out of life will be a struggle and will most likely have limits. When that is your view on life, and when it is rooted in experience, disappointment and setbacks are wearying, not inspirational pebbles on some inevitable path to the top. Willpower alone waivers; plans seem futile; services seem abstract.

The desire to pick yourself up and go on demands a deeper touch. A nonfamily friend who cares may do the trick. The very lack of family ties is what makes this possible for some youth; the caring and confidence are more trustworthy, unaffected by history (see Rhodes, this volume).

Thus, mentoring often may not be enough to achieve certain goals; it also often may be the indispensable element to ensure that the bottom doesn't fall out for youth attempting to achieve those goals, to ensure that hope and effort are maintained. Maintenance of hope and effort through difficult times do build character, confidence, and resilience. That is the stuff that makes, step-by-step, for transformation.

Change, Not Charity

This critique harks back to the earlier discussion of "zero/declining sum," with a slight twist: that at its core, mentoring is a charitable act, a kindness to a stranger, improvement in the life of people one at a time—whereas what we need is social change, where change comes to larger groups of individuals all at once and, at the same time, positions future generations better. Mentoring as social policy, under this critique, is diversionary at best, reactionary at worst. Even if it is effective and does build confidence in social policy, it remains diversionary and/or reactionary because what it builds confidence in is the capacity of individuals to help individuals; it blunts the fundamental need for broader social change.

It is hard to see how any responsible citizen could be against a social change that would suddenly improve the lives of large numbers of youth. Thus, I pay careful attention to this critique.

But the strength of this critique seems primarily at the ideological and rhetorical level. Unless we can set forth what social change we're talking about in concrete terms and make the case equally concrete as to how mentoring gets in the way, it's difficult to see why we shouldn't help individuals when we know how to do it, and when it's politically feasible to do so. Putting aside individuals for the sake of highly conceptual ideas of a greater good has been a common practice throughout human history in every corner of the globe; it's hard to find good examples where the promise has been delivered, and easy to find examples where it has not. But we should always be open to broader changes with widespread benefits, so long as they can be concretely articulated and examples brought forth.

The notion of helping individuals is too easily maligned by rhetoric. That such help, even out of charity, has become regressive to many in the social policy world seems more the product of frustration than of clear-minded strategy.

FUTURE DIRECTIONS

Reviewing the pros and cons of the above issues leads me to conclude that on balance, the advance of mentoring into the realm of public policy and public funding has been a very positive phenomenon, substantively and strategically. It has injected the importance of adult–youth relationships, and in particular nonfamily relationships, into almost every major policy initiative that deals with youth—an important counter to the highly technocratic and/or highly political approaches that have dominated so many policy initiatives and that miss the simply human factor at the core of most individual improvement.

Mentoring is also something about which there is broad agreement that it works. Though I don't dismiss lightly the "zero/declining sum" and "change not charity" critiques, I think that both underestimate the widespread sense that little or nothing works has played in getting social policy to the low esteem in which it's held today. I think both also underestimate the durability of the outcomes movement; it is too consistent with a centrist-practical political culture to be dislodged for long by the fervor of big ideas, whether from the left or right. We should use its traction, not resist it.

However, despite all its benefits, I am not convinced that mentoring as a program initiative should have its own policy domain or its own major legislation. In my estimation it is better for the long-term effectiveness of social policy if mentoring and its broader idea of the critical importance of nonfamily relationships are as policy (a) injected in appropriate forms into the various existing legislation and policy domains relating to youth and (b) highlighted or tested as special initiatives to demonstrate new uses or emphases for mentoring, be they targeting children of prisoners or homeless families, assisting the transition from foster care, guiding the transition into work and careers, reducing the extreme isolation of juvenile facilities, or working with very young children who are exhibiting poor behaviors in the classroom. It is with these highest-risk youth that the human factor exemplified by mentoring is most missing and needed, and it is with those youth and the institutions with whom they interact that its lessons most need to be injected and integrated. The recent report from *The White House Task Force for Disadvantaged Youth* (2003) underscored this view.

Efforts to aggregate mentoring into, say, a "Million Mentors" piece of legislation, as some have suggested, would in my judgment shift the balance among the pros and cons laid out above under the various critiques, away from mentoring's strengths:

- It would make quality control more difficult, in the rush for numbers and funding.
- It would remove incentives to target underserved, high-risk youth, again, to get numbers and money.
- It would play to the sense that "we've found the answer," which is just too convenient and easy to do in a political world so fixated on sound bites and media strategy.
- It would narrow mentoring's importance to that of a program, when its ultimate importance lies more in the imaginative and flexible use of its lessons in all institutions that deal with youth.

In sum, mentoring's emergence over the last decade from the world of private philanthropy into that of public policy and funding has been important and beneficial. But the usual next step—consolidating its various gains into major social policy legislation—is not in my judgment the best next step. Infiltration, not consolidation, is where mentoring's greatest usefulness lies in the years ahead.

In the following, I've outlined recommendations in the areas of research and practice that I believe will help the field of mentoring to actualize its potential in a manner consistent with this vision.

Recommendations for Research

1. *Evaluate the impact of mentoring's newest forms.* School-based mentoring is the largest of these; BBBSA has already agreed to an impact study. Group mentoring may be a contradiction in terms, but it is growing and needs evaluation. Career mentoring for older youth is even less developed but needs investigation. We need to ensure that mentoring's new forms are worthy of the resources they are getting.

2. *Assess the effectiveness of various approaches to securing volunteers.* If mentoring were a business with a hard bottom line, you can be sure that the value and costs of different approaches to securing volunteers would by now have been thoroughly assessed. We need to do so.

Recommendations for Practice

1. *Extend mentoring to higher-risk youth.* The WAY and Amachi programs mentioned earlier indicate great potential for extending mentoring to higher-risk youth; other attempts have been less fruitful. With so many youth in juvenile facilities, homeless shelters, and other friendless institutions, it is irresponsible not to mount serious efforts to do so.

2. *Inject the lessons of mentoring into the training of all professions that work with youth.* Mentoring's broadest impact will come not by expanding it as a discrete program, but by having its lessons influence the practices of all institutions and employees who work with youth. The young bear on the Discovery Channel did not know the lineage, clan, or reputation of the older bear who took him in; he just needed an older bear who cared. . . .

REFERENCES

AOL Time Warner Foundation. (2002). *Mentoring in America 2002.* New York: Author. Retrieved July 20, 2004, from http://mentoring.web.aol.com/common/one_report/national_poll_report_final.pdf

Bauldry, S., & Hartmann, T. (2004). *The promise and challenge of mentoring high-risk youth.* Philadelphia: Public/Private Ventures.

DuBois, D. L., Holloway, B. E., Valentine, J. C., & Cooper, H. (2002). Effectiveness of mentoring programs for youth: A meta-analytical review. *American Journal of Community Psychology, 30,* 157–197.

Dynarski, M., Moore, M., Mullens, J., Gleason, P., James-Burdumy, S., Rosenberg, L., et al. (2003). *When schools stay open late: The national evaluation of the 21st Century Community Learning Centers Program, first year findings.* Washington, DC: U.S. Department of Education.

Fountain, D. L., & Arbreton, A. (1999). The cost of mentoring. In J. B. Grossman (Ed.), *Contemporary issues in mentoring* (pp. 48–65). Philadelphia: Public/Private Ventures.

Friends of the Children. (2002). Retrieved June 1, 2004, from http://www.friendsofthechildren.com/

Grossman, J. B., & Rhodes, J. E. (2002). The test of time: Predictors and effects of duration in youth mentoring relationships. *American Journal of Community Psychology, 30,* 199–219.

Haskins, R. (2003, December). *Does research influence policy?* Presentation to W. T. Grant Foundation Board of Trustees meeting, New York City.

Jucovy, L. (2003). *Amachi: Mentoring children of prisoners in Philadelphia.* Philadelphia: Public/Private Ventures.

Leave No Child Behind Act, 20 U.S.C. § 6301 (2001).

MENTOR/National Mentoring Partnership. (n.d.). Retrieved June 1, 2004, from http://mentoring.web.aol.com/about_us/what_we_do.adp

MENTOR/National Mentoring Partnership. (2003). *Elements of effective practice* (2nd ed.). Alexandria, VA: Author.

MENTOR/National Mentoring Partnership. (2004). *State Mentoring Partnerships.* Retrieved July 21, 2004, from http://www.mentoring.org/state_partnerships/state_local_profiles.adp?Entry=home

Scales, P. C. (2003). *Other people's kids: Social expectations and American adults' involvement with children and adolescents.* New York: Kluwer Academic/Plenum.

Sipe, C. L., & Roder, A. E. (1999). *Mentoring school-age children: A classification of programs.* Philadelphia: Public/Private Ventures. (Published in collaboration with MENTOR/National Mentoring Partnership, Alexandria, VA)

Tierney, J. P., Grossman, J. B., & Resch, N. L. (1995). *Making a difference: An impact study of Big Brothers/Big Sisters.* Philadelphia: Public/Private Ventures.

Welfare Reform Act—Personal Responsibility and Work Opportunity Reconciliation Act, 42 U.S.C. § 1305 (1996).

The White House Task Force for Disadvantaged Youth: Final Report. (2003). Retrieved October 1, 2004, from http://www.ncfy.com/disadvantaged/FinalReport.pdf

Workforce Investment Act, Section 504 of the Rehabilitation Act, 29 U.S.C. § 794d (1998).

35

COST-BENEFIT AND COST-EFFECTIVENESS ANALYSES

BRIAN T. YATES

INTRODUCTION

We can and should measure the costs, benefits, cost-effectiveness, and cost-benefit of youth mentoring! It is likely that we and our youth will benefit from it. It can be more complex, and more time-consuming, than research that measures only the effectiveness and benefits of youth mentoring. It seems possible, however, that the higher costs of research that measures, analyzes, and reports costs, benefits, cost-effectiveness, and cost-benefit—in addition to effectiveness—may reveal that mentoring is less costly than alternative approaches to helping youth and may be comparable or superior in its benefits, cost-effectiveness, and cost-benefits. Thus, it is possible that the higher costs of cost-inclusive research could be justified by higher benefits to mentoring (e.g., by increased dissemination of mentoring approaches and by increased funding). A complete and scientific reporting of the complete costs of mentoring would be of value, in its own right, of course. Finally, within the wide variety of mentoring programs that currently exist, cost-inclusive research could reveal whether one approach to mentoring is significantly more cost-effective or than others, in general and for specific types of mentors and mentees.

This chapter provides a framework for assembling descriptive and inferential research on elements of cost-effectiveness and cost-benefit analyses of youth mentoring. Definitions, and a series of simple tables, are given for assembling and disseminating findings of research on costs, benefits, cost-benefit, effectiveness, and cost-effectiveness of youth mentoring. References for guidelines on cost-effectiveness, cost-benefit, and other cost-inclusive analyses are provided as well. First, however, a general overview of the relevance of the preceding topics to mentoring is provided.

Heard in the field . . .

Mentoring not only is a great joy to me in my old age, but it keeps me out of trouble and it only takes a few hours out of my day! (A retired mechanic, a mentor)

Mentoring is wonderful when it works, but is it worth it? It takes so much time and energy, from all concerned, and it doesn't always turn out the way anyone hoped. (A critical observer of mentoring)

What if we could show people not only how wonderful mentoring can be, but how much less expensive it is than rearrests, jail, income support, or treatment for substance abuse? (A professional advocate for mentoring)

Oh, Herbert—of course it's nice that you try to help that boy downtown, but what about us? What about our kids, and our bills? Don't they deserve some of your time and attention? (A mentor's spouse)

We sure enjoyed being Big Brothers and Big Sisters in college. But enough's enough! Now it's time to pay back those school loans and make some money so we can buy a house and raise some kids of our own. (A couple who just graduated from college)

I wish we could accept more applications for mentors, but I am totally backlogged this month! What with the background checks, the individual interviews, and running those training sessions—I just wish I had some time to be a mentor myself again these days! (A harried mentoring program manager)

Each of these brief, hypothetical scenarios illustrates the importance of considering costs as well as effectiveness and benefits of youth mentoring (see also Murray, 1991; Tierney & Grossman, 2000). Each also provides a different perspective on the trade-offs between the costs of mentoring and its effectiveness and benefits, that is, on the cost-effectiveness and cost-benefit of mentoring.

Mentoring Outcomes: Effectiveness, Benefits

Mentoring has discernible, often positive outcomes. Mentoring can be effective. Youth who are mentored may be less likely to engage in substance abuse or criminal activities and may live better lives and contribute more to society (cf. DuBois, Holloway, Valentine, & Cooper, 2002). Mentoring also can have measurable monetary benefits. Youth who have been mentored may require fewer services from social and health service providers and may be more likely to work, pay taxes, and become parents (and mentors to future youth). However, mentoring does not always succeed. Research on the outcomes of mentoring tries to understand both why mentoring sometimes succeeds beyond the wildest expectations of all involved, and why it sometimes fails despite the best efforts of all those involved.

Mentoring Costs: Briefly . . .

What is certain is that mentoring takes time, effort, energy, and at least some money. These are only some of the costs of mentoring. Mentors devote many hours to working with their mentees. As noted at the start of this chapter, that can take time from work that the mentor could do to increase his or her own earnings. In school-based mentoring, for example, more time can be spent traveling to and from the mentee's school, residence, or workplace than actually meeting with the child. Other forms of mentoring may require little or no travel time of mentors. Additional time may be spent training to be a mentor and in supervision sessions to maintain and improve mentoring. These are hours from which the mentee may benefit greatly, but which both mentees and mentors could have spent in other activities. For some mentors, and for some mentees, these other activities could have produced income and therefore have *opportunity costs* to both the mentor and mentee. In addition, although the time and energy of the mentor are obvious necessities for mentoring to occur, so are the time and energy of those who operate "behind the scenes" to match mentors with mentees and to provide support for development and continuance of these relationships.

So is it worth it? That depends on the perspective used when asking the question and on how one defines and measures three things: (a) *costs* or the resources required for mentoring, (b) *effectiveness* or the nonmonetary gains produced by mentoring, and (c) *benefits* or the monetary outcomes. There are several ways, furthermore, to compare costs and effectiveness (in *cost-effectiveness analysis*), and costs and benefits (in *cost-benefit analysis*). Finally, it may be worthwhile to include in these analyses information about what goes on in the program (i.e., the specific activities that make up the program) and with the mentees (i.e., what is supposed to change in their hearts and minds), and not just its costs compared to its effectiveness and benefits. This chapter provides an orientation to these different ways of understanding how mentoring outcomes can be related to mentoring costs.

THEORY

Although quantitative, scientifically based analyses of cost-effectiveness and cost-benefit originated in evaluation of weapons systems and in centralized government decision making, respectively, both also have a relatively long history in human services (e.g., Carter & Newman, 1976; Newman & Sorensen, 1985; Weisbrod, 1983), and it is still common to read and hear "cost-effective" or "cost-beneficial" applied to a human service such as mentoring without any actual data being reported on cost-effectiveness or cost-benefit measures. It also is still common to confuse cost-effectiveness analysis with cost-benefit analysis. There often are misunderstandings about distinctions between costs and benefits, and between costs and undesired outcomes. The following definitions are widely accepted by experts in cost-effectiveness and cost-benefit analyses (e.g., Gold, Siegel, Russell, & Weinstein, 1996; Levin & McEwan, 2001; Nas, 1996; Thompson, 1980). By eliminating some widespread misconceptualizations of what these analyses do, these definitions should reduce confusion in the mentoring field about how to measure costs and benefits and how to conduct cost-effectiveness and cost-benefit analyses—as well as possibly diminish concerns about the desirability of cost-effectiveness analysis and cost-benefit analysis due to fears about what they include or exclude. Figure 35.1 diagrams differences among cost-effectiveness, cost-benefit analysis, cost-outcome analysis, and cost-procedure-process-outcome analysis, each of which is described in more detail.

Costs are the value of the amounts and types of resources combined to provide a human service, particularly the value of providers' and administrators' time as well as the value of space, equipment, supplies, and other resources needed to implement the service (cf. Levin & McEwan, 2001; Yates, 1996). These resources include, but need not be limited to, those that can be valued in terms of money. Social skills and tolerance for hassle are, arguably, necessary for mentors to bring to the mentoring relationship.

Social skills are not "spent" as time and space are, but without them, it may be difficult or impossible for mentoring to occur. Tolerance for hassle may be expended, depending on how much hassle has been encountered in one's day prior to mentoring. These resources also need to be present for the procedure of mentoring to occur. Occasionally in the mentoring literature, "costs" have been measured, but these are rarely the value of the resources used in mentoring. More often, "costs" have been referred to as subjectively rated outcomes that are negative (e.g., Ragins & Scandura, 1999), such as possible loss of identification with a parent. Defining costs as outcomes sets the stage for confusion: What, then, are we to call the price of resources consumed in mentoring? At least for cost-effectiveness and cost-benefit analyses, "cost" refers to the value of resources used in an activity such as mentoring, as recommended by Gold et al. (1996) and others. Negative outcomes should not be called "costs" from this perspective, but rather should be referred to as unanticipated or undesired outcomes.

Effectiveness is what a service accomplishes—its outcomes—measured in the units in which those outcomes occur (e.g., academic performance as grades, employment as hours or days worked, depression lifted as change on a psychological measure of depression).

Benefits are outcomes of a service that can be measured in monetary units such as dollars. Some outcomes occur in monetary units, such as health care services no longer needed as a result of a program (a *cost-savings* benefit) or income due to part-time employment (a *direct* benefit). Other outcomes can be transformed into monetary units (e.g., the monetary value of a drug-free day or an arrest or incarceration avoided). It is possible to measure benefits in subjective terms (e.g., Ragins & Scandura, 1994), but such indices are more correctly referred to as measures of effectiveness (see Gold et al., 1996).

Level of Specificity and Analysis

With respect to mentoring, costs, effectiveness, and benefits have the potential to be measured and compared at multiple levels of specificity, including (a) the individual youth,

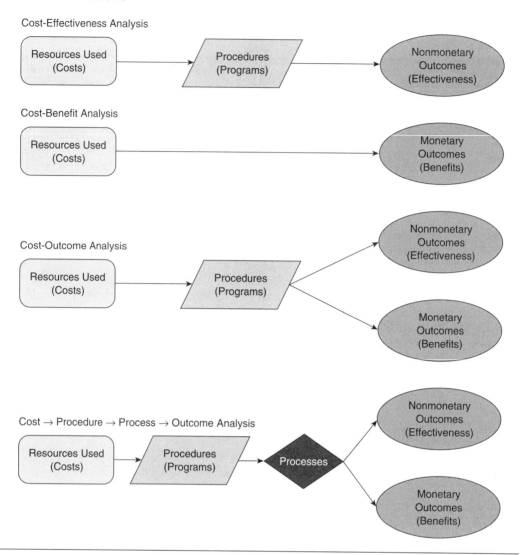

Figure 35.1   Differences Between Cost-Effectiveness Analysis, Cost-Benefit Analysis, Cost-Outcome
Analysis, and Cost → Procedure → Process → Outcome Analysis

(b) the set of youth with whom a mentor is working, (c) youth receiving different types of mentoring, and (d) youth being mentored in one or more programs. Consider, for example, a hypothetical mentoring program serving a large metropolitan city. Costs, effects, and benefits could be measured (a) for any given youth in the program after he or she receives mentoring, (b) for groups of youth served by specific mentors (assuming that the program allows for this), (c) for youth receiving different, specific types of mentoring, and (d) for all youth mentored by a particular program. Costs, effectiveness, and

benefits usually can be measured at an individual level and aggregated to find the average or total cost, effectiveness, and benefits, such as for a group of youth, mentor, or a program. Often too, costs, benefits, and sometimes even effectiveness can be measured at a more general group, program, or community level and then broken down or *disaggregated.* For example, the average cost of mentoring per youth seen in a program could be calculated by dividing total program expenditures for a year by the number of youth seen during the year. The overall effectiveness of a program could be measured in part by the number or proportion of youth who recede to criminal activity within 12 months. Intermediate levels of measurement and analysis also may be available for cost as well as effectiveness. Measurement of costs (and effectiveness and benefits) at the level of *individual* youth allows quantitative, statistical analyses to test apparent differences among mentors, groups of youth, programs, communities, and approaches to human services.

Cost-Effectiveness Analysis (CEA)

Cost-effectiveness describes the relationship between costs and *non*monetary outcomes (i.e., effectiveness) that are produced by a human service program or almost any other effort (see Figure 35.1). Applied to mentoring, cost-effectiveness can be expressed as ratios of cost to effectiveness or effectiveness to cost, at the level of the individual youth, mentor, program, or geographic area. Cost-effectiveness relationships also can be understood readily with graphs of effectiveness against cost. Relationships shown by these graphs may be quantified by statistical regression analyses, often ones that cast outcomes as logarithmic functions of costs (cf. Siegert & Yates, 1980). Cost-effectiveness measures can be understood and compared at individual, group, program, and community levels. *Cost-effectiveness analysis* (CEA) would involve comparing cost-effectiveness relationships for different mentors, groups of youth, programs, intervention approaches, or community areas. Some cost-effectiveness analyses compare ratios statistically; others use upper and lower estimates of costs and effectiveness, such as for different mentors, groups of youth, or programs, to see whether costs or effectiveness overlap. Graphs and tables can be used to contrast cost-effectiveness relationships for different mentors, different youth, different types of mentoring, or different programs. For more information, see Gold et al. (1996), Levin and McEwan (2001), and Yates (1980b, 1996).

Cost-Benefit Analysis (CBA)

Cost-benefit is, in the present context, the relationship between costs and benefits that is produced by a human service program.

Cost-benefit relationships can be expressed as ratios of benefits over costs, as the difference between benefits and costs *(net benefit)* and as the time required for a program to pay for itself *(time to return on investment)*. Cost-benefit relationships also can be understood easily with graphs of benefits against costs (Gold et al., 1996), adding a third dimension of time to show how investment in human services now may yield benefits that accumulate to pay back those investments severalfold over subsequent years. Costs and benefits are measured in the same units, so they can be combined in ways that costs and effectiveness cannot (because costs and effectiveness are measured in different units). *Cost-benefit analysis* (CBA), applied to mentoring, could entail the comparison of cost-benefit relationships for different mentors, groups of youth, programs, or approaches. Indices of cost-benefit relationships can be compared using the same techniques as noted previously for cost-effectiveness relationships. Different programs or procedures need not be contrasted for cost-benefit analysis to be meaningful: Even a single program or service procedure can be judged to be cost-beneficial if the sum of the benefits measured are greater than the sum of the costs measured.

Cost-Utility Analysis and Cost-Procedure-Process-Outcome Analysis

There are a variety of other types of cost-related analyses used by program evaluators, including *cost-utility analysis* (CUA; Gold et al., 1996; Levin & McEwan, 2001) and *cost → procedure → process → outcome analysis* (CPPOA; Yates, 1996). CUA is similar to cost-effectiveness analysis but selects a measure for outcomes that although not monetary, is general enough to be compared for a wide range of programs. An example: years of life saved by a program. Because years of life saved can vary in quality, depending on the severity of the individual's condition, these years of life are adjusted for quality using standardized rules. The result is Quality-Adjusted Life Years (QALYs; see Gold et al., 1996).

An often-noted problem with CEA and CBA is that these analyses seem to ignore what "goes on" between "costs in" and "outcomes out."

MENTORING Resources

→

MENTORING Procedures

→

YOUTH Processes

→

Outcomes

MENTORING Resources

<u>YOUTH</u>
- Time
- Transportation
- Child care
- Communications

<u>MENTORS</u>
- Time
- Transportation time and transportation expenses
- Paperwork time
- Child care
- Communications

<u>MENTORING MANAGEMENT RESOURCES</u>
- Time
- Time preparing materials
- Copying
- Space
- Food
- Advertising
- Child care
- Transportation
- Postage
- Consultants, advisors

<u>FAMILY INVOLVEMENT</u>

MENTORING Procedures

<u>SOCIAL CONTACTS</u>
- Sharing a meal
- Choosing & pursuing activities together

<u>ATHLETIC ACTIVITIES</u>
- Participation
- Watching professionals
- e.g., soccer, baseball, football, tennis, karate, volleyball, ping-pong

<u>EXPOSURE TO NOVEL EXPERIENCES</u>
- Backwoods hiking
- Visit museums
- Eat at fancy restaurants
- Attend the ballet
- Go to opera

<u>OUTINGS FOR ADULTHOOD</u>
- Visit rental properties
- Identify adult education resources
- Job training and placement

<u>OTHER</u>
- Scrapbooking

YOUTH Processes

<u>SOCIAL</u>
- Successful bonding
- Acquisition of key social skills, addition to existing skills
- Improved verbal skills

<u>PSYCHOLOGICAL</u>
- Improved long-term memory for emotions, feelings
- Reduced anxiety
- Increased self-efficacy expectancies

<u>NEUROPSYCHOLOGICAL</u>
- Oxytocin levels improved
- Cortisol levels decreased

Outcomes

<u>SHORT-TERM OUTCOMES</u>
- School attendance
- Reading skills
- Grades
- Problem-solving skills
- Academic
- Interpersonal
- Competency feelings in school
- Quality of relationships with
  ○ Friends
  ○ Family
- Family support
- Client (youth) satisfaction
- Value judgments

<u>LONG-TERM OUTCOMES</u>
- Continuation of the above
- Initiate smoking, alcohol use at later ages
- Less initiation, continuance of drugs
- Reduced use of health, mental health services
- Reduced early pregnancy, STDs, HIV

Figure 35.2   Cost → Procedure → Process → Outcome Analysis (CPPOA) for Youth Mentoring

SOURCE: Adapted from Vance (2002).

Applied to mentoring, critics might point out that simply saying that one program is not as cost-effective or cost-beneficial as another really does not add much value or understanding (other than possibly deciding to not continue or fund the less cost-effective or cost-beneficial program). Most researchers, including most analysts of cost-effectiveness and cost-benefit, want to understand what was responsible for the superior cost-effectiveness or cost-benefit, so they can improve the design of a mentoring program in terms of these criteria and so they can help other programs be similarly cost-effective and cost-beneficial. CPPOA offers several ways of doing this.

As illustrated in Figure 35.1, CPPOA collects information on what happens in the program *(procedures)* and in the individual *(processes; see* Prochaska et al., 1994) from the time that resources are used to implement program activities to the time that discernible, measurable *outcomes* occur. CPPOA may be particularly useful when trying to understand why human services sometimes do not work despite their considerable cost (Taxman & Yates, 2001; Yates, 1980a, 1997). Manuals and advanced methodological texts provide further details regarding application of CPPOA to social work and other fields of research as well (Yates, 1999; Yates, Delany, & Lockwood Dillard, 2001).

For example, Kissel found that a 3-year program for preventing substance abuse actually increased willingness to use, and use of, gateway drugs by fourth graders (Kissel, as cited in Yates, 2002). A simple CEA or CBA would just divide negative effectiveness or negative benefits by the cost of the program and stop there. However, because CPPOA measures and analyzes both observable program procedures and internal client processes, in addition to costs and outcomes (whether effectiveness or benefits), it illuminated the reasons the program was iatrogenic. Kissel found that even though program procedures had been designed to increase the psychosocial processes of communication with parents, positive feelings about school, and social responsibility, those procedures actually had no statistically significant effect on communication with parents or feelings about school—and actually decreased students' social responsibility significantly (Yates, 2002).

Kissel also found that decreased social responsibility was significantly related to increased willingness to use, and actual use of, gateway drugs. Kissel's CPPOA went further, examining the significance of specific relationships between each prevention program procedure, each measured process within the students, and each outcome. Only one program procedure—student small groups—had any significant impact on any psychosocial process. Although this procedure was implemented frequently, the more that students participated in student small groups, the more their social responsibility decreased and the more they were willing to use gateway drugs and actually used them. This unintended, deleterious effect was even more severe for girls than for boys. The procedure of student small groups may or may not have been implemented as specified by program planners (i.e., at high fidelity), but the more important finding of Kissel was that she identified the psychosocial mechanism responsible for the deleterious outcomes—plus the apparent cause for its use (its low cost). Simply measuring the adherence of a program procedure as implemented to that same procedure as planned (e.g., percentage of topics addressed in group) probably would not have revealed why the procedure failed to produce the desired outcomes.

A similar example of using CPPOA to improve a youth mentoring program would begin by detailing the specific resources used to implement those particular program procedures that were designed to change the psychological, social, and even biological processes that lead to targeted nonmonetary and monetary outcomes. This CPPOA model of a youth mentoring program is only beginning to be developed, as detailed toward the end of this chapter (see Figure 35.2 in particular). After data are collected on each of the cost, procedure, process, and outcome variables specified in the model for a number of youth before, during, and after participating in the program, the program CPPOA model can be analyzed or "solved" using *operations research* methods such as linear programming. Linear programming solves the CPPOA model to find the least expensive way to achieve outcomes, or the maximum effectiveness or benefits possible within budget constraints (see Yates, 1980a, 1997).

RESEARCH

Mentoring is often described in the professional literature as a cost-effective or cost-beneficial alternative to other programs. However, the actual cost-effectiveness and cost-benefit of mentoring are seldom measured quantitatively and are even more rarely analyzed statistically. Even scientifically reliable and validated descriptions of costs of mentoring services remain rare in the professional literature. Cost-effectiveness and cost-benefit analyses remain scarce in mentoring, with apparently only two instances of such analyses thus far in the literature (Blechman, Maurice, Buecker, & Helberg, 2000; Grise, Watters, Baker, Ferguson, & Fisher, 2004). In the sections that follow, the methodologies and findings of the few relevant studies of the costs, benefits, cost-effectiveness, and cost-benefit of mentoring are presented and used as points of illustration in articulating general guidelines to facilitate measurement and analyses of costs, cost-effectiveness, and cost-benefit in youth mentoring.

Perspectives on Costs and Benefits

When collecting data on mentoring, it is important to acknowledge and measure costs as well as outcomes from the perspectives of youth, mentors, friends and family of youth, program managers, and the community. The use of multiple informants and data sources for assessing program effects from different perspectives is discussed at length by Grossman in this volume. In terms of costs, paid and volunteer mentors may be thought of as costing less than paid staff, or even nothing, from the perspective of community representatives and funders, as in Grise et al. (2004). However, unpaid and underpaid staff of some programs may spend considerable time recruiting, conducting background checks, matching, training, assigning, and monitoring mentors. These staff can routinely record and report this time, and the value (cost) of these activities can be estimated from what those persons would have been paid in their best alternative employment for their levels of education and experience (see Yates, Haven, & Thoresen, 1979). A comprehensive reporting of time spent in support activities not only shows the true amount and value of resources used in mentoring but also allows complete replication of mentoring programs in other communities. Programs can view collection and reporting of the value of volunteered and donated resources as showing their ability to mobilize community resources and the "savings" they create by using volunteered and donated resources (Yates et al., 2004).

Examining differences in perspectives on costs and benefits can aid understanding of why mentors mentor. For instance, why do mentors work so hard for so little? One answer is that from their perspective, they actually work hard for a great deal. Mentors may receive benefits that typically exceed the costs of time not spent working or with family and friends, transportation to and from mentees' locations, and incidental expenses such as supplies and admission to museums or parks. It is important to list and measure these benefits, for all to see. Understanding mentors' perceptions of costs and benefits may help understand why some people mentor while others do not (Ragins & Sandura, 1999).

Mentors can be thought of as a particular type of volunteer. It has been recognized for some time that the benefits received by volunteers (e.g., training, education, personal insight, gratification from helping others, a "paying back" of what they received from their own mentors) probably equal or exceed the costs borne by volunteers (e.g., earnings foregone due to time spent volunteering rather than working, transportation expenses paid by volunteers, challenges and pain of recalling one's own youth and mistakes). For example, Yates (1980a) found that benefits exceeded costs for both an academic institution and the nearby community when students volunteered for paraprofessional training at a local residential program for predelinquent adolescents. A traditional view of social exchange is that benefits can exceed costs in a social interaction for only a subset of participants, with the other participants experiencing more costs than benefits. Traditionally, then, there are always "losers" and "winners." When benefits and costs are measured from the perspective of each party in the interaction, however, costs can diminish and benefits can increase so that all parties perceive their benefits to exceed their costs, and all are "winners" (Yates, 1980a).

Different perspectives can result in different findings for costs, benefits, and even effectiveness, and thus different findings of cost-effectiveness and cost-benefit analyses. For example, the start of this chapter included a quote from a couple that had enjoyed mentoring while in college, but now found that the opportunity cost of the time they would have to spend mentoring had increased (due to their increasing earning power) and their need for money had increased, while the benefits of mentoring to them had (apparently) not increased.

Framework for Collecting Cost, Effectiveness, and Benefit Data

Table 35.1 provides a framework for collecting data on both costs and outcomes from the perspectives of different interest groups. Nonmonetary outcomes (effects) and monetary outcomes (benefits), such as cost-savings and income, are included. Filling in the "blanks" (cells) of this sort of table can move us far along the path to concrete analyses of the cost-effectiveness and cost-benefit of mentoring.

Collecting Data on Costs (Resources Used for Mentoring)

Research has begun to isolate the contributions of specific components and types of mentoring (e.g., Heard, 1990; Tierney & Grossman, 1995, 2000; cf. DuBois, Holloway, et al., 2002). Describing the costs of implementing specific, common components of mentoring may help us improve the cost-effectiveness and cost-benefit of mentoring by using those elements of mentoring that are most effective, most beneficial, and least costly (cf. Yates, 1999, 2000). Costs of alternative components, or alternative ways of implementing the same component, also could be productive foci for research on costs.

Table 35.2 provides a framework for assembling these data in a detailed manner that can be used to understand why different mentoring procedures may differ in costs. The table asks that data on costs be listed as would findings on any other variable, with means and variances. Some studies incorporated into this table reported both averages and ranges, which provide some

Table 35.1 Alternative Perspectives on Costs, Effectiveness, and Benefits

To begin cost-effectiveness and cost-benefit analyses, fill in the cells with lists and then measure with numbers

Alternative Perspectives on Costs, Effects, Benefits	*Costs (Resources Consumed Because Mentors Are Involved)*	*Outcomes*		
		Effects (Nonmonetary Outcomes of Mentoring)	*Benefits (Monetary Outcomes of Mentoring)*	
			Cost-Savings (e.g., ER visits avoided)	*Direct (e.g., youth income)*
Mentors				
Program managers				
Youth (client youth)				
Youth family				
Competing programs				
Community members				
Funders				
Others				

Table 35.2 A Framework for Assembling Research Findings on the Costs of Components of Mentoring

Mentoring Components (Some based on Sipe, 1998)	Cost (Mean, Variance) for Each Type of Resource Used in Mentoring*				Researcher, Citation
	Total	Time	Space & Transportation	Other	
Screening					
Orientation and training					
Support and supervision					
Traditional one-on-one mentoring, in the community	Approximately $1,000 per youth mentored per year (range: $24 to $2,447 per youth mentored)				Public/Private Ventures (P/PV) impact study of Big Brothers Big Sisters mentoring (Tierney & Grossman, 1995)
	Approximately $1,000 per youth per year (median: $685; range: $12 to $1,900) (mean: $2,289, including volunteered and donated resources; median: $1,533)				(Tierney & Grossman, 1995)
	$1,030 per youth per year (in comparison cited below)				(Fountain & Arbreton, 1998)
Group mentoring	$408 per youth per year or $13.25 per contact hour per youth (as opposed to $1,030 per youth per year or $25.75 per contact hour per youth for one-on-one mentoring, in a direct comparison)				(Fountain & Arbreton, 1998)
School-based mentoring program	$566 per youth per school year (range: $19 to $2,875)				Public/Private Ventures (P/PV) impact study of 16 schools (Tierney & Grossman, 1995)
	Approximately $1,500 per youth per year				(Sponsor-A-Scholar; Johnson, 1998)
Hospital youth mentoring programs	$2,500 to $3,000 per youth ($1,000 to $10,000)				(Harwood, Bazron, Eldridge, & Junior, 1998)
Unspecified type of mentoring	$2,070, average cost per youth				Kids-in-the-Middle, Oregon (personal communication, D. Vought, Citizens for Safe Schools, Klamath Falls, OR, March 2004)

*The following columns should, ideally, extend through all subsequent rows, for a detailed reporting of costs. Unfortunately, only total cost per youth was found in the research literature to date.

measure of both central tendency and dispersion of the distribution of cost findings. The major types of resources that contribute to costs in most human services are the time of providers (cf. Fountain & Arbreton, 1998; Yates, 1980a), which for mentoring would include the time of mentors and mentor supervisors, as well as the time of mentees and possibly their parents. Other substantial resources used in some mentoring efforts include space and transportation. These types of costs are listed in the middle columns of Table 35.2. Even more detailed breakdowns of resource types are possible. Fountain and Arbreton (1998), for example, list the number of full-time equivalents (FTEs) of different types of staff (i.e., mentors, professional staff, managers, support staff) who worked or volunteered in the mentoring programs they surveyed.

Different types of mentoring, which can be viewed as different potential components of mentoring programs, are listed in the rows of Table 35.2. The first three components are (a) screening, (b) orientation and training, and (c) support and supervision, taken from Sipe's (1998) analysis of mentoring programs. These components seem to be widely accepted as important for most mentoring programs (Grossman, 1998), but specific costs for them were not found in the research literature to date. These are only samples of the many different mentoring procedures that could be listed here, of course. Specific costs were found for several different types of mentoring, which are listed following Sipe's components. These typically are findings from just one study, however. Just as with effectiveness findings, little confidence can be placed in findings from a single study. Findings on costs need to be replicated by different investigators using different methods before they can be used to make decisions about which type of mentoring to use and to make predictions about the likely costs of that mentoring.

Table 35.2 also reports preliminary cost findings that are available at mentoring Web sites (e.g., National Mentoring Center, 2004) but not in the professional, peer-reviewed literature. The findings cited in the initial rows of cost figures are assumed to be per year; that information was not provided, but is in line with other mentoring figures that are annual (e.g., Fountain & Arbreton, 1998). These findings can be regarded as only preliminary, because most do not seem to have been validated using traditional social science procedures and typically reflect a limited range of perspectives—all of which limit generalizability and applicability. Also, careful reading of the cost reports indicates that many do not collect data on the costs actually paid, but only on the costs budgeted. To the degree that expenditures do not match budgets, these costs may under- or overestimate the actual costs of mentoring. Moreover, without

specification in these reports of the types of resources that composed the cost, it is difficult to assess the comprehensiveness of the estimates provided (and hence their accuracy) or to understand why mentoring cost as much as it did. The costing perspectives adopted typically are those of the program (total budget, divided by total youth mentored). Rarely are volunteered and donated resources measured and valued (see, however, Fountain & Arbreton, 1998). Also, the estimates pertain to only a limited range of mentoring program models, all implemented within the United States. They therefore may not generalize to other program models (e.g., e-mentoring) and to mentoring in other countries.

Additional useful information to have in reports of costs are the types and amounts of time, space, transportation, and other specific resources that made a specific mentoring procedure possible—as well as the current monetary value of those resources. This information could include the amount of volunteered time and donated resources used, which could allow a comprehensive understanding of what it takes to operate a mentoring program. In a comprehensive survey of mentoring program costs, Fountain and Arbreton (1998) found that the monetary value of volunteered and donated resources (which they term "off-budget" costs) slightly exceeded the costs actually paid by the program for staff, space, and other resources (p. 55). This can be interpreted to imply that the cost of mentoring programs, defined comprehensively from a societal perspective, is a bit more than double the cost reported for mentoring programs based on their budgets or their expenditures.

Collecting Data on Effectiveness and Benefits

Effectiveness

Most research related to youth mentoring has, to date, focused on the effectiveness of mentoring using nonmonetary measures of mentoring outcomes (e.g., DuBois, Holloway, et al., 2002; Kluger, Alexander, & Curtis, 2000). These findings can be assembled in the manner suggested by Table 35.3. Different measures

Table 35.3   A Framework for Assembling Research Findings on the Nonmonetary Outcomes or Effectiveness of Components of Mentoring

| Mentoring Components | *Nonmonetary Measure (Mean, Variance) of* Effectiveness *for Each Type of Outcome Examined in Research Cited (any number of measures may be used in the literature!)* | | | |
	Effectiveness Measure 1	*Effectiveness Measure* m	*Effect Size*	*Researcher, Citation*
Screening				
Orientation and training				
Support and supervision				
Mentor matching (one-to-one), 12-month				
Traditional one-on-one mentoring, in the community				
Group mentoring				
School-based mentoring program				
Mentoring + Juvenile Diversion versus Skill Training + Juvenile Diversion	Recidivism (rearrest) was higher for Mentoring + Juvenile Diversion (37% versus 51%)			Blechman et al. (2000)
Overall mentoring			$d = .14$ (95% confidence interval: .10 to .18)	DuBois, Holloway, et al. (2002)

may generate different findings; all can be incorporated, however, in a table similar to Table 35.3 but with more columns. A final set of columns can be added for summary measures and measures that can be compared across studies and combined, such as effect sizes. There is considerable variability in findings of effectiveness, as there is in findings of cost. Some mentoring programs are not effective (Sipe, 1996); some generally effective programs can be iatrogenic for some youth under particular conditions (Grossman & Rhodes, 1999).

Research on effectiveness can result in cost-effectiveness analyses only if costs are measured for the same youth for whom effectiveness is measured. Given the large number of studies that have been conducted on the nonmonetary outcomes of mentoring of different sorts and the amount of space required to represent these studies adequately in this table, only a few studies have been included to illustrate this part of CPPOA as applied to mentoring. The preceding section on costs provides a framework for adapting to mentoring research

Table 35.4   A Framework for Assembling Research Findings on the Monetary Outcomes or Benefits of Components of Mentoring

	Monetary Measure or Benefit (Mean, Variance)			
Mentoring Components	*Direct Benefits (e.g., income increased for youth)*	*Benefits (cost-savings, e.g., reduced use of physical or behavioral health services by youth)*	*Benefits for Mentors (e.g., reduced use of physical or behavioral health services)*	*Researcher, Citation*
Screening				
Orientation and training				
Support and supervision				
Mentor matching (one to one), 12-month				
Traditional one-on-one mentoring, in the community				
Group mentoring				
School-based mentoring program				
Overall mentoring				
Mentor matching (one-to-one), 12-month				

the detailed guidelines for measuring costs in research studies that are provided by Levin and McEwan (2001) and Yates (1996, 1999). Describing the typical effects of youth mentoring on outcomes using measures that are the same for different programs is necessary to make cost-effectiveness analysis possible. Meta-analyses of effect sizes have been performed for the effectiveness of mentoring (see DuBois, Holloway, et al., 2002), but similar meta-analyses cannot yet be conducted for costs, benefits, cost-effectiveness indices, and cost-benefit indices until substantial research literature becomes available.

Benefits

To make cost-benefit analysis possible, research needs to add outcome variables that reflect the monetary outcomes actually produced by mentoring. Monetary outcomes of mentoring could include both cost-savings (e.g., in reduced health service and criminal justice costs) and income increments (e.g., for youth part-time employment or youth operating small businesses). Each of these potential benefits can be measured in short-term follow-ups of a year or two and can be estimated for the youth's future adulthood (see Yates, 2002). For example, the value of each year of incarceration avoided for a youth as a result of a program could include both the cost of incarceration to taxpayers and any income the youth might have earned during that period. Table 35.4 provides a framework for collecting data on these and related outcomes. However, very few entries based on extant published quantitative research can be made at this time.

Assembling Data and Findings on Cost-Effectiveness and Cost-Benefit

Cost-effectiveness analysis requires that costs be related to effectiveness in a meaningful manner. Ideally, this requires measuring costs and effectiveness for the same individual youth and calculating indices of cost-effectiveness, such as the ratio of cost to effectiveness, for each youth. The same goes for cost-benefit analyses: Data on costs and benefits are, ideally, assembled for each individual youth, and then are contrasted in ratios or difference scores or other indices, again, for each individual youth. By collecting and combining data on costs and outcomes at the individual level, possible relationships between the cost of a program and its outcomes are preserved. For example, more time may be spent on some youth than others, but those youth also may experience better outcomes. If outcomes for individual youth are divided by an average cost or if average outcomes for youth are divided by average costs for youth, much meaningful information is abandoned.

To describe the cost-effectiveness or cost-benefit of a mentor, the indices of cost-effectiveness or cost-benefit would be averaged across all youth served by a mentoring program. In addition, cumulative cost-benefit for the mentoring program can be calculated by summing the net benefit for each youth in the program. Findings from these studies can be assembled in frameworks such as Table 35.4. For example, Blechman et al. (2000) reported that relative to one form of mentoring plus juvenile diversion, skill training plus juvenile diversion was more effective in reducing rearrests (51% versus 37% rearrested) and less expensive (by $336 per youth). Blechman et al. did not assign youth randomly to these conditions but used *propensity analysis,* a statistical method of adjusting scores to take into account differences between groups prior to assignment to their conditions.

Some investigators have reported cost-benefit analyses that assemble information on outcomes from uncontrolled studies and that draw cost information from other sources (e.g., Grise et al., 2004). Although convincing at first glance, this sort of study is considerably more convincing when cost data are assembled for

each individual youth being mentored and when more traditional research controls (e.g., random assignment or propensity analysis) are used to assess outcomes. Without convincing data on outcomes, these sorts of studies become primarily comparisons of costs. And while the costs of mentors may be less expensive than that of professionals, true cost-benefit and cost-effectiveness analyses ask whether this lower cost produced similar, better, or worse outcomes. One could, for example, note that while the costs of mentoring may well be less than those of professional therapists, the effectiveness of professional therapists has been found to be substantially better than the effectiveness of mentors. If the effect size for mentoring is on the order of .14 to .19, it is substantially less than the effect size of psychotherapy, reported by numerous researchers as exceeding .80 (e.g., Lipsey & Wilson, 1993; Smith & Glass, 1977).

Combining information on costs and outcomes in a more useful manner than described above, in the form of cost-effectiveness and cost-benefit indices calculated for each individual who was mentored, can provide a firmer foundation for reviews that integrate research and policy. Washington State has been one of the leaders in this effort, for youth in particular, and has completed a detailed cost-benefit analysis of mentoring programs (see Aos, Lieb, Mayfield, Miller, & Pennucci, 2004). These analyses found only a small net benefit for Big Brothers Big Sisters programs (a net benefit of $48 per youth after an investment of $4,010 per youth), based on analysis of data from Public/Private Venture's well-known evaluation of this program (see Grossman, 1998), and a negative net benefit for one other program classified under the category of mentoring. Cost-benefit estimates also were reported for three other programs under the category of juvenile offender programs in the report, which were directed toward youth already involved in the juvenile justice system. For these programs, higher, positive estimates of net benefit were reported, on average $16,672 across three programs.

It is unfortunate that more cost and benefit data were not available for more mentoring programs. Moreover, from what is shown in the report of Aos et al. (2004), it seems possible that the costs and benefits reported were measured in different manners by different researchers. These benefits (and possibly the costs) then were empirically adjusted by Aos et al. to reflect the varying validity of research designs and settings used by different researchers. Aos et al. also seem to have accepted the total cost reported for use in cost-benefit analysis. Although they offer strong qualifications for their findings in the text of their document, it is easy for decision makers to ignore these words and to focus on numbers in tables ranking programs according to their reported net benefit and benefit/cost ratios.

Strong advocacy and use of cost-benefit findings are, for this author, simultaneously exhilarating and terrifying. I have called for such analyses in my professional workshops and articles since the late 1970s. However, given the nascent state of empirical research in the costs, benefits, effectiveness, cost-benefit, and cost-effectiveness in mentoring, dramatic publication of cost-benefit findings may render premature and potentially destructive judgments about which programs to fund and which not to support. This could terminate programs that have greater benefits than have been measured, while perpetuating programs that may not have measured their costs as comprehensively as did other programs.

Of course, when costs and benefits are measured and analyzed in similar manners for competing programs, the best must win and the worst must not be funded any longer. It seems unlikely, however, that research on costs, benefits, and effectiveness of mentoring has evolved to that mature state. It is only beginning; it is only now starting to emerge from foundation and government-funded reports into the realm of critical, peer-reviewed publications in the social sciences. Programs that report benefits and costs comprehensively and that are shown to generate benefits that exceed by severalfold their costs do deserve funding. If, however, programs that have not yet reported benefits and costs comprehensively are judged on the data available, they may be prevented from showing how cost-beneficial they are.

For valid comparisons of the costs, benefits, cost-benefit, and cost-effectiveness of alternative programs that will truly invest the people's money for maximum return, it seems essential that those costs and benefits be measured with similar measures administered in similar ways. If some programs report costs from different perspectives than are used by other programs, excluding or including different costs, or using different rates for valuing volunteer time, comparisons of the costs of those programs will be invalid and could be misleading. For example, one program might include costs of conducting background checks on potential mentors and of training and supervising those mentors, whereas another program might exclude some or all of those costs even though they did conduct background checks and train and supervise mentors. Also, one program might value the costs of volunteers' time at nothing or at the minimum wage, while another program might include costs of volunteers' time using the wage the volunteer could have earned given their levels of education and experience—and include time spent getting to and from meetings with mentees as well as time spent meeting with them!

It is possible that programs trying to report costs in a complete, comprehensive, and scientific manner may appear more costly than other programs. To encourage complete reporting of costs, programs might list the different categories of costs and related activities that they are and are not reporting, as is advocated and described in this chapter, along with the rates that may have been used to monetize apparently "free" resources. If programs are to be compared on their costs, they should be compared on measures that are reported by each program. (Programs not using a particular resource would simply report "zero" for that item or activity.) Simply comparing the total cost of programs can yield erroneous conclusions.

Furthermore, if some programs report outcomes such as effectiveness or benefits using different perspectives, including some benefits that are not measured or reported by other programs, comparisons of the benefits of those programs will be invalid and could be misleading as well. Ideally, all possible benefits would be measured for all programs. The basic categories are finite (e.g., reduced use of criminal justice, health, and mental health services, increased income), and, again, the rates paid for

Table 35.5   Assembling Cost-Effectiveness and Cost-Benefit Analyses Research on Mentoring

Mentoring Components	Cost-Effectiveness or Cost-Benefit Measure (Mean, Variance)			Researcher, Citation
	Cost-Effectiveness	Cost-Benefit	Other (e.g., cost utility)	
Mentor matching (one-to-one), 12-month				
Site-based vs. nonsite mentoring				
Mentoring in inner-city vs. affluent communities				
Other components of youth mentoring				
Overall				
Mentoring + Juvenile Diversion versus Skill Training + Juvenile Diversion	14% relative increase in recidivism for Mentoring + Juvenile Diversion at a cost of $336 per youth			Blechman et al. (2000)

those services can be reported. In practice, many programs devote their measurement efforts to assessing the benefits they hope to be greatest, which may inadvertently cause them to omit major benefits from their findings. If programs are to be compared in terms of their benefits, they should be compared on those measures that are reported by every program. Comparing programs according to the summed total of benefits when some programs report only one or two of several possible categories of benefits could shortchange some programs that simply did not measure major benefits.

Finally, if analyses subtract costs from benefits, or divide benefits by costs, for different programs when those costs and benefits are measured from different perspectives, excluding or including different costs and benefits, those comparisons will be invalid and can mislead decision makers. Working with the "Garbage In, Garbage Out" (GIGO) concept common in computer programming, given the dependence of cost-benefit analyses on high-quality and complete data on both costs and benefits, even some "garbage in" can yield considerable (and potentially misleading) "garbage out." Put another way, a cost-benefit analysis is only as good as its weakest measure of costs or benefits.

Toward Understanding Cost-Effectiveness and Cost-Benefit

Collecting data on the cost, effectiveness, and benefits of youth mentoring programs are important initial steps in conducting cost-effectiveness and cost-benefit analyses of youth mentoring. Computing indices of cost-effectiveness and cost-benefit are critical steps in describing how well youth mentoring works relative to the value of resources consumed to mentor youth. Compiling these measures of cost, effectiveness, benefits, cost-effectiveness, and cost-benefit for different components or types of mentoring starts us on the road to improving cost-effectiveness and cost-benefit.

However, rather than simply comparing costs and other variables and choosing the components of mentoring with the best cost-effectiveness or cost-benefit findings, it can be helpful to understand why some components or types of mentoring work better than others. As noted earlier, this is what CPPOA does. Applied to mentoring, CPPOA can be used to assemble research on the relationship between specific activities of mentoring and changes in youth social functioning, youth psychological processes, and even elements of youth neurological functioning.

Researchers such as DuBois, Neville, Parra, and Pugh-Lilly (2002) and Grossman and Rhodes (1999) have conducted analyses to isolate the key mentoring procedures that change internal youth processes that, in turn, yield the outcomes desired. Vance (2002) cites an array of studies that support development of detailed CPPOA models of youth mentoring. Using the work of Vance, which focused specifically on mentoring and similar programs for youth with severe emotional and behavioral disorders, Figure 35.2 depicts the resources, procedures, processes, and outcomes for a CPPOA model that illustrates a more detailed, complete, and potentially more useful picture of mentoring than is provided by CEA or CBA alone. These short- and long-term outcomes (listed in the right-most column in Figure 35.2) are produced by social, psychological, and biological processes listed in the adjacent column, according to both theory and research findings reviewed by Vance (2002). For example, the short-term goals of school attendance, grades, problem-solving skills, and quality of relationships and the long-term goals of no or delayed use of alcohol and tobacco and delayed initiation of sex are achieved by social bonding, reduced anxiety, increased self-efficacy, and improved memory for emotional states, and improved neuropsychological states.

In turn, these social, psychological, and neuropsychological processes are achieved by mentoring. In this particular model, mentoring activities can be viewed at a more specific level, as an artful integration of social contacts such as sharing a meal, participation in athletic activities, exposure to novel experiences, and outings. These activities are possible only if both youth and mentors devote their time to mentoring activities. Often additional resources, including those listed in the left-most column of Figure 35.2, are needed for mentoring to occur.

FUTURE DIRECTIONS

Synthesis

Understanding the relative costs and effects or benefits of youth mentoring is critically important to the field's further scientific development and to its ability to sustain its current foothold as a highly popular and well-supported mode of intervention for youth. As has been discussed in this chapter, progress will be more likely when those working in youth mentoring acquire a more complete understanding of terms such as *cost, benefit, cost-effectiveness,* and *cost-benefit* and see how youth mentoring can be supported and improved through *cost-effectiveness analysis, cost-benefit analysis,* and *cost → procedure → process → outcome analysis* (CPPOA). In the near future, the very existence of mentoring programs for youth may depend on inclusion of data on costs and benefits, as well as effectiveness, in our research. For instance, in 2003, the Washington State legislature asked the Washington State Institute for Public Policy,

> Is there credible scientific evidence that for each dollar a legislature spends on "research-based" prevention or early intervention programs for youth, more than a dollar's worth of benefits will be generated? If so, what are the policy options that offer taxpayers the best return on their dollar? (Aos et al., 2004, p. 1)

To date, little relevant research on these issues has been conducted in youth mentoring, and most of what has been done has limitations due to the way in which costs and benefits were measured and how cost-effectiveness and cost-benefits were analyzed. Future research needs to improve on this track record in each of the areas described below before we can make informed judgments about whether different approaches to mentoring of youth are the best use of the limited funds and limited volunteer resources available in the community. Specific strategies are recommended below for how those working in applied contexts can approach assessments of costs, benefits, and cost-effectiveness and cost-benefits of mentoring.

Recommendations for Research

1. *Develop logic models to structure hypothesized causal linkages between resources, procedures, processes, and outcomes.* Use network diagrams such as Figure 35.2 to hypothesize clear relationships between (a) attainment of specific outcomes that are caused by modifications of (b) particular psychological, social, or even biological mechanisms (processes) within the individual youth, which are themselves caused by (c) specific methods of mentoring (procedures); also note each type of (d) resource needed to conduct those outcome-related methods of mentoring and the amount of each type of resource needed. These CPPOA linkages should not show all outcomes as determined by all processes, all procedures, and all resources, but should specify which mentoring outcomes are determined by which biospsychosocial processes, which are, in turn, fostered by which mentoring procedures which are made possible by which particular combination of resources. Parts of the logic model can be based on theory, such as which outcomes are connected to which biopsychosocial processes. Other parts of these logic models can be based on clinical knowledge, such as which mentoring procedures will best change which biopsychosocial processes for the mentors and mentees of the community. Additional parts of these logic models can be based on practical knowledge of administrators and managers, for example, regarding how to mobilize volunteers and donated resources to implement mentoring procedures that promise to have the biggest impact on processes and, eventually, on outcomes.

2. *Measure and analyze costs comprehensively.* Cost measurement should go beyond dividing budgets by the number of youth mentored. Incorporate into mentoring research the assessment of the many specific resources used in youth mentoring. Measure the amounts of each type of resource used, whether the resource was obtained with money or was volunteered or donated. These should include, but not necessarily be limited to, personnel (direct and administrative), space, transportation, liability insurance, and equipment and materials costs.

3. *Measure and analyze benefits, not just effectiveness.* The impacts of youth mentoring may include changes in use of health and other human services by youth and others and changes in criminal justice services received by youth and others. Measuring these outcomes is important because mentoring may reduce expenditures for health and other human services and for criminal justice services or may increase availability of those services for others who need them. In addition, income of youth and others may change as a result of mentoring and needs to be added to changes in health and other service expenditures to reflect the monetary benefits of youth mentoring.

4. *Use cost-effectiveness and cost-benefit analyses of youth mentoring to discover how to help the most youth as much as possible for the least necessary amount of time, energy, and money.* We need to go beyond the findings of how much different forms of mentoring cost, and include information on how beneficial, cost-beneficial, and cost-effective these different forms of mentoring are. We also can compare the costs, effectiveness, and benefits of mentoring with other means of helping youth.

5. *Rather than conducting "cost studies" that are separate from other research, integrate the measurement, analysis, and systematic improvement of costs, benefits, cost-effectiveness, and cost-benefits into traditional research on effectiveness.* The research called for in the preceding recommendations should be integrated into a comprehensive approach to research in youth mentoring. To do this in a manner that fosters systematic application of theory, research findings, and understanding of what needs to be changed in youth and how, use CPPOA to generate data for use in operations research that maximizes effectiveness or benefits within budget constraints (see Yates, 1980b).

Recommendations for Practice

1. *Incorporate into youth mentoring programs the measurement, monitoring, analysis, and reporting of data on costs and benefits, cost-benefits, and cost-effectiveness.* To make this possible, in terms of resources required of programs and program staff and directors, implement the following recommendations as well.

2. *Provide ongoing opportunities for practitioners and policymakers to learn about cost-effectiveness and cost-benefit analyses.* Policymakers need basic grounding in cost-effectiveness and cost-benefit analyses. They need to develop an understanding of how to conduct and how to interpret and use cost-effectiveness and cost-benefit analyses. The necessary training might be provided via brief, interactive workshops and selected readings. Program directors could collect some cost and benefit data on their own and could build into their proposals for funding more detailed collection and monitoring of cost, benefit, cost-benefit, and cost-effectiveness data for different mentors, approaches to mentoring, and different types of mentees.

3. *Increase funding for collection of cost and benefit data and for analyzing the cost-effectiveness and cost-benefit of youth mentoring.* The cost-effectiveness and cost-benefit of youth mentoring cannot be assumed. Youth mentoring cannot, at present, be said to be so cost-beneficial or cost-effective according to peer-reviewed research that it can simply be offered without measuring and regularly monitoring its effectiveness, benefits, or costs. At the very least, funds should be allocated to systematically evaluate and optimize the cost-effectiveness and cost-benefit of youth mentoring while it is being offered.

4. *Implement federal-level initiatives for controlled, theory-based research as well as rigorous clinical trials, and evaluate the impact on costs as well as outcomes of implementing evidence-based practices.* Requests for proposals (RFPs) and requests for contracts (RFCs) should explicitly encourage inclusion of collection and analysis of data on costs, monetary benefits, cost-effectiveness, and cost-benefit in all research, evaluation, and program implementation in youth mentoring.

5. *Persuade journal editors, editors of other professional publications, and developers of professional conferences to encourage and solicit manuscripts that report findings on costs, benefits, cost-effectiveness, and cost-benefits of youth mentoring.* Costs and related topics need official emphasis, given the current emphasis on outcomes in training and publication guidelines. They also need to go through peer review prior to publication.

6. *Incorporate cost-effectiveness and cost-benefit training into graduate program requirements.* Education in methods of collecting and analyzing data on costs, benefits, cost-effectiveness, and cost-benefits is needed for graduate students as well as program directors and professional researchers. This is especially critical in disciplines most likely to conduct research on mentoring, such as psychology, sociology, education, and social work.

REFERENCES

Aos, S., Lieb, R., Mayfield, J., Miller, M., & Pennucci, A. (2004). *Benefits and costs of prevention and early intervention programs for youth* (Report to the Washington State Legislature). Olympia: Washington State Institute for Public Policy. Retrieved July 18, 2004, from http://www.wsipp.wa.gov/

Blechman, E., Maurice, A., Buecker, B., & Helberg, C. (2000). Can mentoring or skill training reduce recidivism? Observational study with propensity analysis. *Prevention Science, 1,* 139–155.

Carter, D. E., & Newman, F. L. (1976). *A client-oriented system of mental health service delivery and program management: A workbook and guide* (DHEW Pub. No. ADM 76–307). Rockville, MD: National Institute of Mental Health.

DuBois, D. L., Holloway, B. E., Valentine, J. C., & Cooper, H. (2002). Effectiveness of mentoring programs for youth: A meta-analytic review. *American Journal of Community Psychology, 30,* 157–197.

DuBois, D. L., Neville, H. A., Parra, G. R., & Pugh-Lilly, A. O. (2002). Testing a new model of mentoring. In G. G. Noam (Ed. in chief) & J. E. Rhodes (Ed.), *A critical view of youth mentoring (New Directions for Youth Development: Theory,*

Research, and Practice, No. 93, pp. 21–57). San Francisco: Jossey-Bass.

Fountain, D. L., & Arbreton, A. (1998). The cost of mentoring. In J. B. Grossman (Ed.), *Contemporary issues in mentoring* (pp. 48–65). Philadelphia: Public/Private Ventures.

Gold, M. R., Siegel, J. E., Russell, L. B., & Weinstein, M. C. (Eds.). (1996). *Cost-effectiveness in health and medicine.* New York: Oxford University Press.

Grise, P., Watters, K., Baker, K., Ferguson, K., & Fisher, T. H. (2004). *Mentoring evaluation study, school year 2001–2002: Second year Section VII: Cost-benefits.* Tallahassee: Florida State University, Department of Communications.

Grossman, J. B. (1998). The practice, quality, and cost of mentoring. In J. B. Grossman (Ed.), *Contemporary issues in mentoring* (pp. 5–11). Philadelphia: Public/Private Ventures.

Grossman, J. B., & Rhodes, J. E. (1999). *The test of time: Predictors and the effects of duration in youth mentoring relationships.* Philadelphia: Public/Private Ventures.

Harwood, H., Bazron, B., Eldridge, G., & Junior, N. (1998). *The impacts on hospitals of youth mentoring projects: The Commonwealth Fund's hospital youth mentoring project.* Fairfax, VA: The Lewin Group.

Heard, C. A. (1990). The preliminary development of the Probation Mentor Home Program: A community-based model. *Federal Probation, 54*(4), 51–56.

Johnson, A. W. (1998). *An evaluation of the long-term impacts of the Sponsor-A-Scholar Program on student performance: Final report to The Commonwealth.* Princeton, NJ: Mathematica Policy Research.

Kluger, M. P., Alexander, G., & Curtis, P. A. (Eds.). (2000). *What works in child welfare.* Washington, DC: Child Welfare League of America.

Levin, H. M., & McEwan, P. J. (2001). *Cost-effectiveness analysis* (2nd ed.). Thousand Oaks, CA: Sage.

Lipsey, M. W., & Wilson, D. B. (1993). The efficacy of psychological, educational, and behavioral treatment: Confirmation from meta-analysis. *American Psychologist, 48,* 1182–1209.

Murray, M. (1991). *Beyond the myths and magic of mentoring: How to facilitate an effective mentoring program.* San Francisco: Jossey-Bass.

Nas, T. F. (1996). *Cost-benefit analysis: Theory and application.* Thousand Oaks, CA: Sage.

National Mentoring Center. (2004). What is the average cost of running a mentoring program? Retrieved June 8, 2004, from http://www.nwrel.org/mentoring/faq_cost.html

Newman, F. L., & Sorensen, J. E. (1985). *Integrated clinical and fiscal management in mental health: A guidebook.* Norwood, NJ: Ablex.

Prochaska, J. O., Velicer, W. F., Rossi, J. S., Goldstein, M. G., Marcus, B. H., Rakowski, W., et al. (1994). Stages of change and decisional balance for 12 problem behaviors. *Health Psychology, 13,* 39–46.

Ragins, B. R., & Scandura, T. A. (1994). Gender differences in expected outcomes of mentoring relationships. *Academy of Management Journal, 37,* 957–971.

Ragins, B. S., & Scandura, T. A. (1999). Burden or blessing? Expected costs and benefits of being a mentor. *Journal of Organizational Behavior, 20,* 493–509.

Siegert, F. A., & Yates, B. T. (1980). Cost-effectiveness of individual in-office, individual in-home, and group delivery systems for behavioral child-management. *Evaluation and the Health Professions, 3,* 123–152.

Sipe, C. L. (1996). *Mentoring: A synthesis of P/PV's research: 1988–1995.* Philadelphia: Public/Private Ventures.

Sipe, C. L. (1998). Mentoring adolescents: What have we learned? In J. B. Grossman (Ed.), *Contemporary issues in mentoring* (pp. 10–23). Philadelphia: Public/Private Ventures.

Smith, M. L., & Glass, G. V. (1977). Meta-analysis of psychotherapy outcome studies. *American Psychologist, 32,* 752–760.

Taxman, F. S., & Yates, B. T. (2001). Quantitative exploration of Pandora's box of treatment and supervision: What goes on between costs in and outcomes out. In B. C. Welsh & D. P. Farrington (Eds.), *Costs and benefits of preventing crime* (pp. 51–84). Boulder, CO: Westview Press.

Thompson, M. S. (1980). *Benefit-cost analysis for program evaluation.* Beverly Hills, CA: Sage.

Tierney, J. P., & Grossman, J. B. (1995). *Making a difference. An impact study of Big Brothers/Big Sisters.* Philadelphia: Public/Private Ventures.

Tierney, J., & Grossman, J. B. (2000). What works in promoting positive youth development: Mentoring. In P. M. Kluger & G. Alexander (Eds.), *What works in child welfare* (pp. 323–328). Washington, DC: Child Welfare League of America.

Vance, J. E. (2002). Mentoring to facilitate resiliency in high-risk youth. In B. J. Burns & K. Hoagwood (Eds.), *Community treatment for youth: Evidence-based interventions for severe emotional and behavioral disorders* (pp. 139–153). New York: Oxford Press.

Weisbrod, B. A. (1983). A guide to benefit-cost analysis, as seen through a controlled experiment in treating the mentally ill. *Journal of Health Politics, Policy, and Law, 8,* 808–845.

Yates, B. T. (1980a). Benefits and costs of community-academia interaction in a paraprofessional training course. *Teaching of Psychology, 7,* 8–12.

Yates, B. T. (1980b). *Improving effectiveness and reducing costs in mental health.* Springfield, IL: Charles C Thomas.

Yates, B. T. (1996). *Analyzing costs, procedures, processes, and outcomes in human services.* Thousand Oaks, CA: Sage.

Yates, B. T. (1997). Formative evaluation of costs, cost-effectiveness, and cost-benefit: Toward cost → procedure → process → outcome analysis. In L. Bickman & D. Rog (Eds.), *Handbook of applied social research methods* (pp. 285–314). Thousand Oaks, CA: Sage.

Yates, B. T. (1999). *Measuring and improving cost, cost-effectiveness, and cost-benefit for substance abuse treatment programs* (Pub. No. 99–4518). Rockville, MD: National Institute on Drug Abuse/NIH. Retrieved October 3, 2004, from http://165.112.78.61/IMPCOST/IMPCOSTIndex.html

Yates, B. T. (2000). Cost-benefit analysis and cost-effectiveness analysis. In A. Kazdin (Ed.), *Encyclopedia of psychology.* Washington, DC: American Psychological Association.

Yates, B. T. (2002). Roles for psychological procedures, and psychological processes, in cost-offset research: Cost → procedure → process → outcome analysis. In N. A. Cummings, W. T. O'Donohue, & K. E. Ferguson (Eds.), *The impact of medical cost offset on practice and research: Making it work for you* (pp. 91–123). Reno, NV: Context Press.

Yates, B. T., Campbell, J., Jones, K., Mannix, D., Freed, M. C., & Johnson, M. (2004, February 9). *Costs of consumer-operated services: Delivery systems, use of volunteered resources, and program models interact to determine cost per visit and per consumer.* Paper presented at the annual meeting of the National Association of State Mental Health Program Directors, Arlington, VA.

Yates, B. T., Delany, P. J., & Lockwood Dillard, D. (2001). Using cost → procedure → process → outcome analysis to improve social work practice. In B. A. Thyer (Ed.), *Handbook of social work research* (pp. 207–238). Thousand Oaks, CA: Sage.

Yates, B. T., Haven, W. G., & Thoresen, C. E. (1979). Cost-effectiveness analysis at Learning House: How much change for how much money? In J. S. Stumphauzer (Ed.), *Progress in behavior therapy with delinquents* (pp. 186–222). Springfield, IL: Charles C Thomas.

36

MENTORING FOR RESULTS

Accountability at the Individual, Program, Community, and Policy Levels

SHAWN M. COYNE, JENNIFER L. DUFFY,
AND ABRAHAM WANDERSMAN

INTRODUCTION

Mentoring programs have great potential to contribute to positive youth development, yet that potential is not always realized. In this chapter, we look at the concept and role of accountability within the context of mentoring programs. We begin this chapter by briefly discussing the role mentoring programs play in positive youth development and the evidence to date on the effectiveness of mentoring programs. Next, we describe how accountability tools may be able to be used to increase the effectiveness of mentoring interventions and describe two such tools: the Getting to Outcomes system and the Caregiver Alliance. The potential for using such tools at multiple levels of analysis (the individual level, program level, community level, and policy level) is highlighted. Finally, future directions in research and practice are discussed.

Youth and young adults face a variety of risks, including drug abuse, teen pregnancy, school failure, and involvement with the juvenile justice system. The prevention field has developed many interventions to try to prevent these problems (Nation et al., 2003). In a National Academy of Sciences report (National Research Council and Institute of Medicine [NRC/IOM], 2002), Eccles and Appleton Gootman acknowledge that the prevention of such problems is important, but they place such prevention programs within the broader framework of youth development. Beyond the prevention of problems, positive youth development allows youth to "engage with caring adults inside and outside their families, develop a sense of security and personal identity, and learn rules of behavior, expectations, values, morals, and skills needed to move into healthy and productive adulthood" (NRC/IOM, 2002, p. 3; see also the chapter by Kuperminc & colleagues, this volume).

Eccles and Appleton Gootman (NRC/IOM, 2002) identify a number of characteristics of settings that help promote positive development, including physical and psychological safety, an appropriate level of structure, supportive relationships, opportunities to belong, positive social norms, support for efficacy, skill-building opportunities, and integration with efforts in the family, school, and community. Mentoring programs clearly strive to provide youth with supportive relationships and have the potential to meet many of the setting characteristics. However, the research to date on mentoring shows that that potential is not always met.

With the publicity received by programs such as Big Brothers Big Sisters, mentoring has become a strategy many organizations turn to as positive youth development and intervention/ prevention strategies are considered (Wandersman et al., 2004). This strategy has been shown to be successful (e.g., Tierney, Grossman, & Resch, 1995). Yet when evaluators dig deeper into the research, it becomes apparent that many mentoring programs have not demonstrated positive outcomes (DuBois, Holloway, Valentine, & Cooper, 2002). The lack of success in some programs does not lead to the conclusion that mentoring programs should be discontinued or avoided in planning. Instead, these mixed results lead to additional questions about when a mentoring program is likely to achieve success and when it is not.

In a meta-analysis of evaluations of mentoring programs, DuBois et al. (2002) were able to identify certain elements that were associated with more successful programs. Their findings revealed that although, on average, programs when evaluated have yielded only modest effect sizes, there were several features of the programs that predicted greater effect sizes. These features included utilization of greater numbers of theory-based and empirically based best practices and the development of strong relationships between mentors and youth. It is noteworthy, too, that the importance of developing strong relationships between mentors and youth has been underscored by a growing body of empirical literature. These studies have pointed toward a range of specific factors that appear to be critical components of effective relationships, including a bond of mutuality and trust, a regularly occurring pattern of contact sustained over a significant period of time, meaningful conversation, role modeling, and advocacy (see Rhodes, this volume).

More generally, Nation et al. (2003) conducted a review of reviews to examine the principles that contribute to effective prevention programs. They identified nine principles that fall in the categories of program characteristics, matching a program with a target population, and implementation and evaluation. Specifically, these principles are comprehensiveness, variety of teaching methods, sufficient dosage, theory-driven approaches, positive relationships, appropriate timing, sociocultural relevance, outcome evaluation, and training for staff. Some of these principles can be found in the features identified as being characteristics of successful mentoring programs, such as use of theory-driven practices, establishing positive relationships, provision of training to mentors, and dosage (i.e., frequency of mentor-youth interaction and duration of relationship) (DuBois et al., 2002). These and the other principles identified by Nation et al. (2003) provide implementers of mentoring programs with another set of guidelines for planning interventions and assessing their potential effectiveness.

ACCOUNTABILITY TOOLS

Understanding what elements may be necessary to achieve a successful mentoring program, however, is only half of the recipe. Program planners also must determine the best means for implementing these ingredients in order to achieve their goals. Selection of implementation strategies is a crucial step. The field of community psychology has provided some examples of accountability tools and toolboxes that programs can use for this very purpose. An accountability tool is a particular strategy or activity employed to achieve some level of accountability. A toolbox is a collection of tools packaged in an overall strategy or structure that an agency can utilize to guide its program and to build accountability. Ideally, accountability tools and toolboxes should help an organization to build capacity and should provide quality assistance for the program implementers (Wandersman & Florin, 2003). More than just needing information about possible programs, an organization needs help in understanding its own needs and capacities, in defining goals and targets, in strategically and effectively planning for implementation, and in assessing implementation success. Toolboxes are designed to go through this process with the organization in a step-by-step process. The toolbox may help the organization make better decisions regarding selecting programs that match its needs and capacities. It then may help the organization in making implementation decisions and in conducting follow-up to assess success.

Getting to Outcomes

Getting to Outcomes (GTO) is an accountability toolbox that uses 10 accountability questions to guide program development and evaluation (Wandersman, Imm, Chinman, & Kaftarian, 2000). The Getting to Outcomes 2004 workbook/toolbox is a RAND Corporation document and is available free for download (Chinman, Imm, & Wandersman, 2004). The GTO toolbox includes step-by-step instructions for how to address each of the accountability questions, detailed explanations of the concepts related to each of the questions, programming tools for use at the various planning stages, and concrete examples of how one program worked through each stage of the GTO process.

Although the questions can be used at any stage in the life cycle of a program (e.g., preprogram, middle of the program), they are presented in Table 36.1 in chronological order for a project that is about to start. Each question involves a number of self-assessment steps. The answers to each question lead to the next question. With careful consideration of each question and its answers, an organization should significantly increase the likelihood that it will achieve desired outcomes and demonstrate that it is acting with accountability.

As noted in the table, the questions begin with an examination of needs and resources, goals, and targets (Questions 1 and 2). GTO then moves to selecting appropriate intervention programs and successful implementation (Questions 3–6). The later questions of GTO consider program evaluation, means of improvement, and sustainability (Questions 7–10). Using the GTO strategy does not require the development of a brand-new program framework. Rather, GTO can be used within existing program frameworks, as a tool to operationalize

Table 36.1 The 10 Accountability Questions of Getting to Outcomes (GTO) and How to Answer Them

The Accountability Questions	Literatures for Answering the Question
What are the needs and resources in your organization/school/community/state?	Needs assessment; resource assessment
What are the goals, target population, and desired outcomes (objectives) for your school/community/state?	Goal setting
How does the intervention incorporate knowledge of science and best practice in this area?	Science and best practices
How does the intervention fit with other programs already being offered?	Collaboration; cultural competence
What capacities do you need to put this intervention into place with quality?	Capacity building
How will this intervention be carried out?	Planning
How will the quality of implementation be assessed?	Process evaluation
How well did the intervention work?	Outcome and impact evaluation
How will continuous quality improvement strategies be incorporated?	Total quality management; continuous quality improvement
If the intervention (or components) is successful, how will the intervention be sustained?	Sustainability and institutionalization

the established framework in a user-friendly way. For example, MENTOR/National Mentoring Partnership provides a good framework for developing a mentoring program, found in their *Elements of Effective Practice* (MENTOR/National Mentoring Partnership, 2003). This framework includes (a) program design and planning, (b) program management, (c) program operations, and (d) program evaluation. These components fit well within the GTO Questions 2, 4, 6, 7, 8, and 9. Table 36.2 provides an illustration of how GTO can be used within the *Elements of Effective Practice* framework. Matching GTO to MENTOR's guidelines enhances their framework with a structured, comprehensive toolbox to systematically work through their framework, add additional components, and implement effectively. This integration of the two frameworks illustrates the solution proposed by Wandersman and Florin (2003) for promoting more effective interventions: (a) building capacity of community organizations (the GTO system helps build the capacity of organizations to perform the essential strategies needed to achieve outcomes) and (b) providing quality technical assistance (MENTOR can provide quality technical assistance to organizations offering mentoring).

Table 36.2   The 10 Accountability Questions of Getting to Outcomes (GTO) Matched to the MENTOR/National Mentoring Partnership Elements of Effective Practice

The Accountability Questions	MENTOR/National Mentoring Partnership Elements of Effective Practice
What are the needs and resources in your organization/school/community/state?	
What are the goals, target population, and desired outcomes (objectives) for your school/community/state?	1. (a) Program design and planning: Design the parameters for the program (target population, desired outcomes)
How does the intervention incorporate knowledge of science and best practice in this area?	
How does the intervention fit with other programs already being offered?	
What capacities do you need to put this intervention into place with quality?	
How will this intervention be carried out?	1. (b) Program design and planning: Plan how the program will be managed 3. Program operations: Ensure strong, everyday operations
How will the quality of implementation be assessed?	2. Program management: Ensure the program is well managed
How well did the intervention work?	4. Program evaluation: Ensure program quality and effectiveness
How will continuous quality improvement strategies be incorporated?	4. Program evaluation: Ensure program quality and effectiveness
If the intervention (or components) is successful, how will the intervention be sustained?	

The GTO strategy was developed with a focus on results-based accountability. Not only is accountability becoming a typical requirement of funders, but many intervention organizations also are coming to recognize its value. Rather than a simple assessment of success of the program, GTO provides a means to assess success, examine weaknesses, and plan for corrective action. The GTO system is designed with an emphasis on Continuous Quality Improvement (CQI) to allow community organizations to achieve success and to command some control over their programs' destiny. GTO goes one step further than CQI by considering how to sustain a program, an often neglected element of programming.

In addition to its accountability focus, it is equally important to note that the GTO strategy is a knowledge-based system. A knowledge-based system creates a customized tool that provides the community organization with a pool of relevant knowledge and tools for effective intervention strategies. Thus, the organization is able to make decisions not only from an educated standpoint, but from a background of information that is tailored to their field. This knowledge-based system provides a list of evidence-based intervention strategies that provides information on program elements, program goals, and program requirements in order for a community organization to determine the best match for its unique situation. The combination of an accountability focus and a knowledge-based focus begins to deal with the problem of the gap that exists between science and practice. Wandersman and Florin (2003) and Wandersman (2003) have argued that the gap between science and practice will be best resolved with a community-centered approach. Rather than "only" providing a toolbox of evidence-based interventions and suggestions for implementation, the GTO approach thus begins with a focus on the community (or school or neighborhood) that is the context of the intervention. The first GTO question asks what the current needs are and what the potential resources are. After these questions, GTO then provides guidance, in the form of its steps and questions, as to how to select and apply the most appropriate program for the community. Building on this strategy, the GTO developers

have designed a Web-based GTO system called "interactive GTO," or iGTO. The iGTO system adds the strengths of Web technology to the original GTO program (Zhang & Wandersman, 2002). iGTO provides accessibility to the database for a multisite intervention program, has multiple links to helpful information, and provides the opportunity to keep more current data as multiple users can input their data from wherever they are located.

Caregiver Alliance

A second toolbox is the Caregiver Alliance (described also in the chapter by Blechman & Bopp, in this volume). This toolbox is based on a conceptual approach of utilizing caregiver teams. Each team incorporates the multiple people and components involved in a youth's care. This may include mentors, educators, health care workers, parents, and judicial system workers, among others. The Caregiver Alliance is an Internet information system designed for information sharing and treatment coordination of clients (Blechman, Fishman, Fishman, & Lewis, in press). The information can be shared and viewed by individual team members, based on what pieces of information the parents have granted access for each team member. This toolbox aims to remedy the difficulties found when clients are involved in multiple organizations or agencies. The program also could help create reports and aid in program evaluation. Most important, the system is designed to allow care providers to gain a holistic view of the client and the client's needs. This approach could be particularly useful to mentoring programs as an aid in identifying and targeting needs of individual youth and in matching appropriate mentors to those needs.

Integrative Use of Toolboxes

As the GTO and Caregiver Alliance examples demonstrate, accountability toolboxes can vary widely, from strategies that organize community resources to strategies that structure the planning, selection, implementation, and assessment of interventions for specific clients. However, both toolboxes have a common focus on promoting accountability by increasing communication across stakeholders and on spurring program planners to identify and address problems and to increase quality. Expanding on the advantages of both toolboxes, one also can imagine utilizing them in an integrative manner within one program. GTO could be used by a community-planning group to strategize program planning and implementation. It also could be used for evaluation purposes. Building on the strengths of a well-designed and well-implemented program, the Caregiver Alliance could provide additional tools for program user or staff member implementation, such as coordinating multiple components of the program and incorporating the target population into the strategy and structure of the intervention plan. The combination of both of these toolboxes would allow a program to focus strategic efforts on success at both the program level and the individual level. A more detailed discussion of how these two toolboxes could be combined can be found later in this chapter in the discussion of community-level accountability (see "Applying Accountability Strategies at Multiple Levels" section).

A general model for understanding how toolboxes such as GTO and the Caregiver Alliance can be incorporated into process and outcome improvement efforts for mentoring programs within the broader context of community programming was proposed by Wandersman et al. (2004; see Figure 36.1). When considering community program implementation, it is useful to start by assessing the abilities of community organizations to plan, implement, and maintain mentoring programs with the purpose of positive youth development. Each community organization has a capacity (in terms of skills and motivation) related to the goals of successful mentoring programs. The skills and motivation can be categorized at two levels: the individual level (individual staff and volunteers involved in a program) and the organizational or program level. This can be thought of as a two-by-two matrix, with motivation and skill along one axis and the program and its individuals along the other (see Box 1 in Figure 36.1). Conceptualizing a community organization this way allows an understanding of the problem many organizations face: Not every organization/program has sufficient skills and motivation to effectively

implement their programs (Wandersman & Florin, 2003; Wandersman et al., 2000).

Skills and motivation are important aspects of the capacity of an organization to implement a program. However, resources exist that can build on or enhance a community organization's skills and motivation (see Box 2 in Figure 36.1). These resources can be conceptualized as structured guides and toolboxes that guide an organization along the path of skill development and program implementation. This is precisely where GTO and the Caregiver Alliance have a particularly important role to assume in the process of program development. Other toolboxes also exist either in manual or software form (e.g., MENTOR's *Elements of Effective Practice*). Resources also can be conceptualized as umbrella agencies that provide guidance, experience, and research-based suggestions (e.g., MENTOR/National Mentoring Partnership). Although these resources are useful in and of themselves, they gain strength when they incorporate best practices and research-driven programs (see Box 3, Figure 36.1).

The resources inform the practice of the organizations and enhance their motivation and skills; in turn, the organizations inform the resources of practical issues that need consideration and areas in need of research. According to the model, this interactive relationship can have a positive impact on the program implementation (see Box 4, Figure 36.1). This will directly affect the outcomes of the program, including those relating to positive youth development and staff capacity (see Box 6, Figure 36.1).

Linking all of these previously noted components from Figure 36.1 together is the important element of evaluation (see Box 5, Figure 36.1). Evaluation can interact with the community organization and its programs at two points. An evaluation designed to help shape a program to perform more effectively constitutes a formative evaluation (Rossi, Freeman, & Lipsey, 1999). An evaluation of the outcomes makes up a summative evaluation. Information from an evaluation is delivered back to the community organization. When evaluative feedback is considered and incorporated, it should create a feedback loop that impacts the matrix of skill and motivation found in the first box.

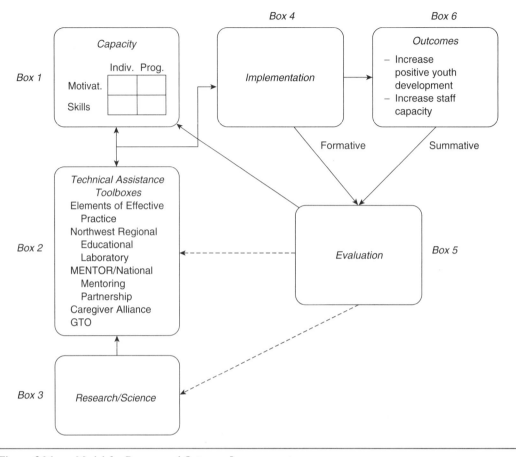

Figure 36.1   Model for Process and Outcome Improvement

However, evaluation has an additional function as well. Evaluation feedback shared with resources and research/science bodies can help shape a research agenda to be oriented toward the needs of the community organizations. For example, an evaluation that concludes that organizations need improved matching of mentors to mentees to achieve better outcomes could cause resources to respond by providing greater guidance in this area. In addition, research/science bodies could respond to this type of information by conducting research on the question of how best to approach the issue of matching mentors and mentees. Figure 36.1 purposely shows a dotted line between evaluation and these bodies. It is very common for an evaluation report to be addressed only to the providers. Thus, these other bodies rarely see this information, despite its benefits. A consideration of evaluation is an appropriate introduction to the topic of applying accountability concepts at multiple levels of analysis.

APPLYING ACCOUNTABILITY STRATEGIES AT MULTIPLE LEVELS

When considering an intervention, there are multiple levels of analysis that can be examined, including the individual level, the program level, the community level, and the policy level. The accountability strategies discussed above are most frequently applied in developing and determining the effectiveness of programs, but these strategies are not limited to use only at the program level of analysis. Accountability tools can be used at any of these levels to explore important questions related to the quality of mentoring. A summary of the strategies to be discussed at each level can be found in Table 36.3.

Table 36.3 Summary of Levels of Accountability for Mentoring Programs and the Matching Strategies

Level	Accountability Strategies
Individual	GTO Needs assessment Caregiver Alliance BBBSA Mentor Report on the Match P/PV Youth Survey
Program	GTO Program evaluation (formative and summative) BBBSA Mentor Report on the Match P/PV Youth Survey
Community	GTO Caregiver Alliance
Policy	Interaction and coordinated planning between funder, mentor program planners, and evaluators GTO

GTO: Getting to Outcomes
BBBSA: Big Brothers Big Sisters of America
P/PV: Public/Private Ventures

Individual Level

At its most basic level, mentoring is an intervention that relies on the development of a relationship between individuals. As noted, characteristics of mentor/mentee relationships, including amount of contact, length of relationship, and feelings of closeness, have been found to be related to positive outcomes for mentees. However, although some mentor/mentee pairs develop close, long-lasting relationships with relatively little additional support, many do not. The likelihood of developing a relationship that contributes to positive outcomes may be increased with the use of accountability-focused tools and strategies.

Many of the accountability questions from the GTO system described in the preceding section can be applied to the development of individual mentor/mentee relationships. The available needs and resources of the child or youth being mentored can be assessed, individual-level goals for the outcomes of mentoring can be linked to those needs and resources; evidence-based strategies about what to do in the mentoring relationship can be identified; and a plan for achieving those goals can be determined. In addition, process evaluation questions (such as whether the mentor and mentee are spending the anticipated amount of time together and whether they report satisfaction with the relationship) and outcome evaluation questions (such as whether the mentee is showing increased social competence) are important for monitoring the mentoring process so that problems can be identified and addressed. Then, ideas for CQI in the mentoring relationship and sustainability should be considered.

Information to support these processes can be drawn from a number of resources. Mentoring program staff members are often well positioned for gathering information about mentee strengths and areas for improvement. Some programs already incorporate information about mentee needs and resources into the process of matching mentees to mentors. In addition, staff members of many organizations collect some information about the frequency of contact between the mentor and mentee, how the relationship is developing, any problems identified, and outcomes. However, depending on the size of the programs and the number of staff members available, staff may not be able to closely monitor the development and progress of all the mentoring relationships they supervise. This set of circumstances provides an excellent opening for utilization of a toolbox such as the Caregiver Alliance described previously. The database foundation of this toolbox and its ability to be accessed by multiple users directly address some of the challenges faced by mentoring programs in trying to monitor, evaluate, and improve relationships and outcomes at the individual level.

Mentors generally have much more contact with the youth they are mentoring than do program staff members, and in addition, they typically have only a single mentoring relationship on which to focus. This makes mentors excellent resources for learning about the evolving needs of the youth they are mentoring. Simple tools can be used to collect information from mentors on the needs and progress of young people with whom they are working. One such tool is the "Mentor Report on the Match" form developed by Big Brothers Big Sisters of America (BBBSA, 2001). Mentors can use this tool to rate changes in the behaviors of the child or youth they are mentoring related to the three main outcomes of importance identified by BBBSA: confidence, competence, and caring. This instrument is brief and easy to use and could be completed by mentors on an ongoing basis. At least one chapter of BBBSA, Big Brothers Big Sisters of Northcentral Wisconsin, has designed a Web-based version of the form so that mentors can easily complete it from any location with Internet access. Furthermore, mentors are not limited to providing information to program staff about the progress of the young people with whom they are working. They also can use tools such as the Mentor Report to identify the needs of their mentees and to develop plans to address these needs, either alone or with assistance from program staff and other resources. For example, when completing the Mentor Report, a mentor might become aware that his or her mentee is having difficulty completing school assignments and his or her grades are starting to fall. In response to this observation, the mentor might talk with the mentee specifically about these difficulties and work with him or her to develop a plan to make sure assignments are completed.

Another valuable source of information on the mentoring relationship is the young person being mentored. The Youth Survey was developed by Public/Private Ventures (P/PV) to help programs monitor the quality of individual mentoring matches and monitor program effectiveness (P/PV, 2002). Youth respond to questions about three qualities of their mentoring relationships: satisfaction, emotional engagement, and the extent to which the relationship is youth centered. This brief tool has the potential to yield important insight into the relationship between the youth and his or her mentor, and if used often, it may help program staff to identify problems early and intervene to help improve the relationship (see also Nakkula & Harris, this volume, for a review of measures of mentoring relationship quality).

Program Level

Typically, mentoring practitioners and researchers are interested in looking beyond the results for individual participants and examining the overall effectiveness of mentoring programs. Program evaluation is necessary to determine the effectiveness of the program and to promote program accountability. Program evaluation can take place at multiple times and for more than a single purpose. As noted, summative evaluation looks at program outcomes. Formative evaluation examines the processes of carrying out the program and provides an assessment of how well it was implemented. As indicated by the model described previously (see Figure 36.1), evaluation can play a key role in connecting all components of planning a mentoring program, though it is not always used in this way.

While evaluation is an important component of accountability, evaluation alone is not the only way to increase the effectiveness of mentoring programs. As discussed, accountability strategies such as GTO can be useful tools for helping organizations build the capacity to evaluate and increase program effectiveness. Each of the 10 steps of GTO shown in Table 36.1 may be applied at the program level to mentoring programs. As noted, a program can use GTO at any stage of the development process. Those programs in the early stages of development can begin with the earliest GTO steps by assessing the needs and resources available to them, determining program goals, and identifying best practices that fit with the context in which the intervention takes place. Programs already up and running are likely to find it most useful to begin with later steps of the GTO process, such as those relating to process and outcome evaluation (Questions 7 and 8). However, the accountability process does not end with such evaluations. Rather, this information regarding both areas in which the program is successful and those in which there are problems can be used as part of a CQI process to make the changes necessary to address existing problems (Question 9) and to plan for sustaining those program components that are successful (Question 10). In addition, this process may lead programs back to the beginning of the GTO cycle, as they can begin to assess the current needs of the community and the population with which they are working as they plan for the next implementation and determine what changes could be made in the program to better meet those needs. Theoretically, when agencies return to the beginning of the GTO cycle, they should arrive with enhanced capability and skills.

When conducting evaluations of mentoring programs, data pertaining to individual mentor/mentee relationships (such as that collected using tools like the BBBSA Mentor Report on the Match and the P/PV Youth Survey described previously) may be aggregated and used to help assess whether the program is meeting the needs of the young people involved (i.e., for summative evaluation) and may provide useful information about what other services are needed to better meet those needs (i.e., for formative evaluation). For example, if the P/PV Youth Survey reveals that youth participating in a mentoring program do not perceive their relationships with their mentors to be youth centered and are not emotionally engaged, program staff may seek to remedy this situation by gathering more information about problems from youth and mentors and by providing training and support to remedy the identified problems. In addition, such aggregated information could potentially be used to look at some of the most immediate (or proximal) outcomes of mentoring programs, though

such information would not be sufficient for a full summative evaluation (see Grossman, this volume, for a discussion of evaluating program impact).

Community Level

Community-level accountability is important for the promotion of positive youth development. Just as Bronfenbrenner (1979) conceptualized in his model of human development, all program and individual work takes place within a context, which includes a local community. Ecological models such as this suggest that to be most effective, any program needs to fit within the current community needs and resources. The program will benefit from community cohesiveness, and it may be possible to rely on community coordination to build the program. However, these benefits will not be realized if there is no accountability at the community level. The first questions in the GTO process target the available resources and needs specifically (Questions 1–2). The GTO toolbox also can be used for developing means to build community infrastructure and coordination. By assessing community accountability and making the community, however it is defined, answerable to its development and support roles, stronger programs will be built that may lead to better outcomes.

The relationship between a mentoring program and the community is important. A mentoring program can be planned and implemented without consideration of and coordination with the community. However, if the community agrees that positive youth development is a priority, it can assess the needs of the community and mobilize and coordinate resources to meet priority community needs. For example, does the community have activities and resources that a mentor could take advantage of to build his or her mentor/mentee relationship? Does the community have existing organizations that could be coordinated to provide a pool of volunteers for the program or a pool of clients in need? On a more basic level, does the community have the organization to create these resources and then to coordinate them? For example, a mentoring program set in a community that has a park recreation program, a community education program, and a museum with programs for children will have more resources for a mentor to utilize. Also, a community that has existing organizations such as a Junior League, a Rotary Club, or an environmental club (such as a local Sierra Club) is more able to support a mentoring program and its need for a pool of adults to volunteer. Furthermore, a community that has both these types of resources and a means to coordinate them so that they may help each other will experience smoother program operation and increased likelihood of success. Once a community examines and addresses these issues, all programs that take place within it will have greater ease in development and should have greater success.

Community accountability can be considered in a second manner as well. Undoubtedly, most have heard a horror story of a child who "fell through the cracks" or "got lost in the system" and didn't receive appropriate care. Often times, this care was available, but due to multiple errors, the appropriate services were not accessed. Community accountability can begin to address this. On a very basic level, a tool such as the Caregiver Alliance can see that community agencies work together to create cohesive case management that ensures that the client receives all appropriate services. From a mentoring perspective, community accountability can be used to coordinate services to see that a mentee receives specifically what he or she needs and to help the mentor play a role in this. Furthermore, in a mentoring relationship, particularly those provided to youth, the mentor is often a volunteer. Volunteers arrive to the program with the same goals as the program developers but may not have the same background knowledge. Employing a community accountability strategy can help volunteers to be aware of what opportunities they can bring to mentoring relationships. The Caregiver Alliance provides an excellent example of how this strategy can be utilized. For example, a program using the Caregiver Alliance toolbox will provide a new mentor, who may want to be helpful but may not know how, with a list of coordinating agencies that also are involved in the program and a list of recommended activities. For example, this tool can be used to link mentors with educational programs, social service

providers, health care providers, and recreational programs that may be helpful to their mentees.

Mentoring programs can exist without community commitment, cohesiveness, organization, or coordination, but the likelihood of achieving desired outcomes will decrease. This discussion and the examples provided address the purpose of and need for community accountability in youth mentoring. Furthermore, the examples provide suggestions for toolboxes that will facilitate this kind of accountability.

Policy Level

A final level of accountability to be considered is policy-level accountability. This involves incorporating the viewpoints of all stakeholders to improve the process, including the funder and evaluator as well as program planners and implementers. The usual program planning process generally has minimal interaction between these stakeholders. The funder provides money without getting involved in planning; the program implementers plan with little outside input; and the evaluator provides a report at an end point to the implementers. This could be conceptualized as three circles that touch each other but do not overlap (see Figure 36.2A). An alternative way to think about this interaction is to overlap the involvement. Imagine a funder getting involved in the planning process to understand what and how funding is needed. Imagine an evaluator getting involved in the beginning, middle, and end of a program to help shape the process as well as to help scrutinize it. Finally, imagine the evaluation report being a document that all three bodies can benefit and learn from. This perspective uses those same three circles in our conceptualization but clearly has them overlapped (see Figure 36.2B). This increased function overlap allows each body to understand the other's needs. Then, each is better able to assist the functions of the other's; this should lead to greater outcomes. This overlapping model is explicitly described elsewhere (see Crusto & Wandersman, 2004; Fetterman, Kaftarian, & Wandersman, 1996; Wandersman, 2003; Yost & Wandersman, 2000).

Taking this approach to combine program planning, funding, and evaluating helps make

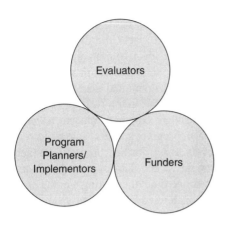

Figure 36.2A   Model of Traditional Stakeholder
                   Relationships for Programming

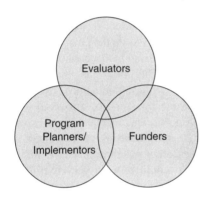

Figure 36.2B   Model of Improved Stakeholder
                   Relationships for Programming

each of the three bodies accountable not just to each other (typically the implementer is the only one accountable—to the funder) but also allows each body to be accountable to the project and its goals. With this approach, each will clearly understand the needs required to have successful outcomes. Each then can coordinate their activities to aid the other bodies.

In considering mentoring programs specifically, program planners, funders, and evaluators could coordinate to discuss what youth outcomes are needed and why. For example, do they want to see an overall decrease in youth delinquency, a decrease in substance use by youth, an increase in positive community contributions by youth, or some combination of these? Understanding this should lead to an understanding of not only how the program

should be shaped but also what type of funding will be required to accomplish the goals and what the evaluators should include in the evaluation plan. For example, if the funder and program planners are interested only in measuring decreases in negative activity, such as delinquency and substance use, then individual interviews or questionnaires focused on learning about positive contributions by youth will not be necessary. Furthermore, if this is the case, the evaluators can work with program planners to build interventions focused on substance use and delinquency into the program and to ensure that the interventions and any outcomes are measurable. Empowerment evaluation offers principles and practices that can help programs reach results (Wandersman et al., 2005). Wandersman et al. (2005) have provided the following definition of this approach to evaluation:

> *Empowerment Evaluation:* An evaluation approach that aims to increase the probability of achieving program success by: (a) providing program stakeholders with tools for assessing the planning, implementation, and self-evaluation of their program, and (b) mainstreaming evaluation as part of the planning and management of the program/organization. (p. 2)

Empowerment evaluation expands the purpose, roles, and potential settings of evaluation beyond that of traditional evaluation approaches. Very often, program planners design interventions with vague definitions of success, which makes evaluation difficult; an empowerment evaluation can increase communication between these bodies and help prevent this. This type of three-way discussion also can increase awareness of the importance of evaluation, which may help ensure that there is appropriate funding for this portion of the project.

A toolbox such as GTO can be used to facilitate this interaction of stakeholders. Defining the goal as an active interaction and cooperation between stakeholders, the 10 accountability questions can be used to develop a process that builds this kind of interaction and then assesses the success of the goal. For example, the three bodies can begin by asking themselves what their needs and resources are in building this collaborative interaction (Question 1). Next, they can ask what their goals and desired outcomes are in their interaction (Question 2). Is there a collection of best practices to support this type of relationship (Question 3)? This provides another illustration of how GTO could be used at multiple levels for multiple purposes within the context of youth mentoring initiatives. In fact, toolboxes such as GTO can be used in more than one place for a single intervention project. For example, GTO could be used to foster policy-level accountability for youth development and used separately to enhance program-level accountability for a mentoring program, while the Caregiver Alliance was used at the same time to promote individual-level accountability for both the mentoring program and other services promoting positive youth development.

FUTURE DIRECTIONS

Synthesis

Research in the field of mentoring has identified a number of elements that are correlated with successful programs (DuBois et al., 2002). In addition, research outside the field of mentoring has identified elements of effective prevention programs, which overlap with the elements identified for mentoring (Nation et al., 2003). To increase the effectiveness of mentoring programs, planners need to be aware of these elements and know how to implement them. Accountability tools can help guide the implementation process. These tools are designed to help an organization build capacity and should provide quality assistance (Wandersman & Florin, 2003). Although two such toolboxes were discussed in depth here, other effective toolboxes also can be sought.

Toolboxes are a means of building accountability into a program. Accountability often is conceptualized as a unidimensional activity; nonetheless, it can be considered at multiple levels. These include the individual, program, community, and policy levels. Each level of accountability provides different potential types of benefits, and thus theoretically, each can be applied to mentoring programs to enhance their outcomes. Specifically, activities at the differing levels can be used in efforts to monitor and increase the success of individual mentoring participants, to assess the overall success at a programmatic level, to evaluate the readiness of a community to support a mentoring program, and to establish mutual accountability among the funder, the mentoring program implementers, and the program evaluators to help ensure long-term program success. Taking accountability levels a step further, program planners also can employ accountability strategies at multiple levels at one time, thus taking a broad and holistic approach to ensuring success.

Recommendations for Research

1. *Conduct research on current toolboxes to define and identify how they are useful in applications to youth mentoring.* When mentoring programs are conducted within a context of accountability, how do their outcomes differ from ones not conducted in that context? Which levels of accountability hold the most potential to impact on mentoring outcomes? Although some of these questions can be answered within the frameworks of experimental or quasi-experimental design, a meta-analysis of accountability data from mentoring programs that have used relevant tools also could provide very useful information. This same type of analysis could be used to look at the results of accountability at different levels.

2. *Study the process and effectiveness of employing multiple levels of accountability.* There is little, if any, systematic study of mentoring programs that has successfully incorporated all levels of accountability. A model of how this can be accomplished would be immensely helpful to future program implementers. Even more helpful would be a model that integrates all four levels of accountability into one structure. Incorporation of toolboxes might aid this process, so a model that demonstrates this as well would be useful. These models can then be used to guide the development of research studies that examine the impact of each of the four levels of accountability and the impact of the various combinations.

3. *Conduct empirical investigations of toolboxes, as well as develop new toolboxes, to help promote accountability at all levels*

for mentoring. Although two well-developed toolboxes have been described here, experimental or quasi-experimental research on their effectiveness would be highly useful. Furthermore, the development and subsequent research of additional new toolboxes could provide more options to mentoring programs and help ensure positive outcomes.

Recommendations for Practice

1. *Use toolboxes to address accountability issues in program planning, implementation, and evaluation.* As program planners and implementers move forward to develop positive youth development programs, specifically mentoring programs, we encourage active consideration of the accountability issues discussed in this chapter when planning and implementing programs. Toolboxes such as those described in this chapter, supplemented by frameworks and guidelines specific to the field of mentoring (e.g., *Elements of Effective Practice*), should be taken advantage of by programs to facilitate this process. Planning and implementation are essential parts of developing a successful program, and both planning and implementation may be strengthened significantly through the adoption of an accountability perspective and appropriate follow-through with relevant tools and resources. Program planners could challenge themselves to incorporate one toolbox into their existing structure within the next 2 to 3 years. They should then plan to enhance their accountability through CQI use of the toolbox.

2. *Ask and answer the full range of accountability questions.* Program planners need to ask themselves where their accountability lies. Do they have individual accountability? Program accountability? They also need to ask about the breadth of their accountability. More than just responsibility for outcomes, accountability includes appropriate match between the needs and characteristics of the community and the program, fidelity of program implementation, evaluation planning, and attention to overall program structure. Although consideration of questions relevant to all of these concerns may seem to make the task of program planning

much larger, it makes the task of ensuring successful outcomes much easier. If program planners don't currently address all levels of accountability, they should attempt to add at least one level or to increase the breadth of their accountability within the next year.

REFERENCES

Big Brothers Big Sisters of America (BBBSA). (2001). *Mentor Report on the Match.* Philadelphia: Author. Retrieved June 13, 2004, from http://www.bbbsmc.org/poereport.php?mentor

Blechman, E. A., Fishman, C. A., Fishman, D. B., & Lewis, J. E. (in press). *Caregiver alliances for at-risk and dangerous youth: Establishing school and agency coordination and accountability.* Champaign, IL: Research Press.

Bronfenbrenner, U. (1979). *The ecology of human development: Experiments by nature and design.* Cambridge, MA: Harvard University Press.

Chinman, M., Imm, P., & Wandersman, A. (2004). *Getting to Outcomes 2004: Promoting accountability through methods and tools for planning, implementation, and evaluation.* Santa Monica, CA: RAND Corporation Technical Report. Retrieved October 3, 2004, from http://www.rand.org/publications/TR/TR101/

Crusto, C., & Wandersman, A. (2004). Setting the stage for accountability and program evaluation in community-oriented grantmaking. In A. Roberts & K. Yeager (Eds.), *Desk reference on evidence-based practice research in healthcare and human services* (pp. 162–177). New York: Oxford University Press.

DuBois, D. L., Holloway, B. E., Valentine, J. C., & Cooper, H. (2002). Effectiveness of mentoring programs for youth: A meta-analytic review. *American Journal of Community Psychology, 30,* 157–197.

Fetterman, D., Kaftarian, S., & Wandersman, A. (Eds.). (1996). *Empowerment evaluation: Knowledge and tools for self-assessment and accountability.* Thousand Oaks, CA: Sage.

MENTOR/National Mentoring Partnership. (2003). *Elements of effective practice* (2nd ed.). Alexandria, VA: Author.

Nation, M., Crusto, C., Wandersman, A., Kumpfer, K. L., Seybolt, D., Morressey-Kane, E., et al.

(2003). What works in prevention: Principles of effective prevention programs. *American Psychologist, 58,* 449–456.

National Research Council and Institute of Medicine (NRC/IOM). (2002). (J. Eccles & J. Appleton Gootman, Eds.), *Community programs to promote youth development.* Committee on Community-Level Programs for Youth. Washington, DC: National Academy Press.

Public/Private Ventures (P/PV). (2002). *Measuring the quality of mentor-youth relationships: A tool for mentoring programs.* Portland, OR: Northwest Regional Educational Laboratory.

Rossi, P. H., Freeman, H. E., & Lipsey, M. W. (1999). *Evaluation: A systematic approach* (6th ed.). Thousand Oaks, CA: Sage.

Tierney, J. P., Grossman, J. B., & Resch, N. L. (1995). *Making a difference: An impact study of Big Brothers/Big Sisters.* Philadelphia: Public/Private Ventures.

Wandersman, A. (2003). Community science: Bridging the gap between science and practice with community-centered models. *American Journal of Community Psychology, 31,* 227–242.

Wandersman, A., Clary, E. G., Forbush, J., Weinberger, S. G., Coyne, S. M., & Duffy, J. L. (2004). *Community organizing and advocacy: Increasing the quality and quantity of mentoring programs in the community.* Manuscript submitted for publication.

Wandersman, A., & Florin, P. (2003). Community interventions and effective prevention. *American Psychologist, 58,* 441–448.

Wandersman, A., Imm, P., Chinman, M., & Kaftarian, S. (2000). Getting to outcomes: A results-based approach to accountability. *Evaluation and Program Planning, 23,* 389–395.

Wandersman, A., Snell-Johns, J., Lentz, B., Fetterman, D., Keener, D., Livet, M., et al. (2005). The principles of empowerment evaluation. In D. Fetterman & A. Wandersman (Eds.), *Empowerment evaluation principles in practice* (pp. 27–41). New York: Guilford Press.

Yost, J., & Wandersman, A. (2000). Results-oriented grantmaking. In W. K. Kellogg Foundation (Ed.), *Empowerment evaluation and foundations: A matter of perspectives* (pp. 1–19). Battle Creek, MI: W. K. Kellogg Foundation.

Zhang, X., & Wandersman, A. (2002). A Web-based IT approach for outcomes in prevention. Small Business Technology Transfer Grant (NIDA R41 DA014890–01A1).

AUTHOR INDEX

570 • HANDBOOK OF YOUTH MENTORING

SUBJECT INDEX

ABOUT THE EDITORS

David L. DuBois, PhD, is an Associate Professor in the Division of Community Health Sciences within the School of Public Health at the University of Illinois at Chicago. He received his doctorate in clinical-community psychology from the University of Illinois at Urbana-Champaign. He has authored numerous peer-reviewed studies of youth mentoring, including a meta-analytic review of the literature on the effectiveness of youth mentoring programs. In 2003, he co-chaired the National Research Summit on Mentoring. Along with Jean Rhodes, he then coauthored the National Research Agenda for Youth Mentoring that emerged from the Summit. Currently, he is conducting research on youth mentoring with funding from the National Institute of Mental Health and the William T. Grant Foundation. He serves as a consultant to local, state, and national mentoring organizations and has been a mentor himself in a Big Brothers Big Sisters program.

Michael J. Karcher, EdD, PhD, is an Associate Professor of Education and Human Development at the University of Texas at San Antonio. He received a doctorate in human development and psychology from Harvard University and a doctorate in counseling psychology from the University of Texas at Austin. He conducts research on school-based and cross-age peer mentoring as well as on adolescent connectedness and pair counseling. He currently conducts the Study of Mentoring in the Learning Environment (SMILE), which is a 3-year research project funded by the William T. Grant Foundation to examine the effects of school-based mentoring.

ABOUT THE CONTRIBUTORS

Penny M. Ayers is currently a doctoral student in the Interdisciplinary PhD Program at University of Missouri–Kansas City. Her degree combines the disciplines of psychology and sociology with an emphasis on criminology and criminal justice, particularly as these subjects pertain to juveniles. Her research focuses on evaluating community- and school-based programs. She has presented her research nationally and has coauthored several articles related to mentoring and program evaluation. She consults with the Jackson County Family Court on special programs for system-involved girls, and as Project Coordinator for the KC Metro Child Traumatic Stress Program, she is responsible for the project's daily operations.

David B. Baker is Director of the Archives of the History of American Psychology and Professor of Psychology at The University of Akron. He received his PhD in counseling psychology from Texas A&M University in 1988. He has taught the history of psychology at the undergraduate and graduate level for the past 15 years, and in 1995 was named Professor of the Year by the Texas Psychological Association Division of Students in Psychology. He became the director of the Archives of the History of American Psychology in 1999. Recognized as the largest archival collection of its kind, its mission is to acquire, preserve, and make available primary source material in the history of psychology. In addition to his administrative and teaching duties, he maintains an active program of research and writing on the rise of professional psychology in 20th-century America.

Fabricio E. Balcazar, PhD, is an Associate Professor in the Department of Disability and Human Development and the Department of Psychology at the University of Illinois at Chicago. He received his doctorate in developmental and child psychology from the University of Kansas. He has conducted research on the development and evaluation of systematic approaches for promoting the empowerment of minorities and underserved populations. His research includes approaches for promoting empowerment in vocational rehabilitation service delivery, school-to-work transitions, mentoring in dropout prevention, improvement of the rehabilitation outcomes of individuals with violence-induced spinal cord injuries using peer mentors, and strategies to increase the effectiveness of consumer advocacy organizations of people with disabilities.

Manuel Barrera, Jr., is Professor of Psychology at Arizona State University and Adjunct Senior Research Scientist at Oregon Research Institute (Eugene, Oregon). He received his PhD in clinical psychology from the University of Oregon. He has conducted research on the measurement of social support, its factor structure, and its relations to stress and psychological distress for adolescents and adults. Currently, he is interested in social support interventions that are designed to treat and prevent chronic illness.

Diana E. Behrendt currently is pursuing her master's degree at the Institute for Policy Studies at Johns Hopkins University. Her research interests include adult transition, risk behavior prevention, and reproductive health issues.

Jeffrey B. Bingenheimer, MPH, is a doctoral student in the Health Behavior and Health Education department in the School of Public Health at the University of Michigan. His current research deals with the impact of social, economic, and political conditions on the population dynamics of infectious diseases.

Elaine A. Blechman, PhD, received her doctorate in clinical and social psychology from UCLA in 1971. She is Professor of Psychology at the University of Colorado at Boulder. She has published seven books and more than 100 scientific papers and chapters about coping, competence, and resilience promotion among at-risk youth and women. She has developed and evaluated family, school, and peer-group interventions for at-risk youth, with an emphasis on juvenile offenders. Her latest book, *Caregiver Alliances for At Risk and Dangerous Youth: Establishing School and Agency Coordination and Accountability,* overcomes legal, scientific, and technological barriers to cost-effective community care of youth who pose a danger to self or others. She patented the Caregiver Alliance Toolbox information platform and is evaluating its benefits in operating virtual caregiver teams and fostering cross-agency coordination of services for children with special health care needs, special-ed students, juvenile offenders, substance abusers, and truants.

Lynn Blinn-Pike, PhD, is Professor in Human Development and Family Studies at Mississippi State University. She received her doctorate from Ohio State University. Her research interests include adolescent sexuality, pregnancy and parenting, along with research methods and program evaluation. She has been the principal investigator and evaluator on several national adolescent pregnancy prevention and HIV projects. Her current research interests involve examining the relationship between early gambling behavior and early sexual activity in adolescent males.

G. Anne Bogat, PhD, is Professor and Director of Clinical Training at Michigan State University. She received her doctorate in 1982 in clinical-community psychology from DePaul University, Chicago, Illinois. Her research interests include mentoring, social support, and family violence. In 2002, she coedited, with Jean Rhodes, a special issue of *American Journal of Community Psychology* on youth mentoring. Recent work focuses on the longitudinal assessment of risk and resilience factors for women and children living in households with partner abuse. Her work has appeared in journals related to community psychology, domestic violence, and child development.

Darya D. Bonds is a Postdoctoral Fellow at the Prevention Research Center at Arizona State University. She obtained an MA and PhD in developmental psychology from the University of Notre Dame. Her primary research interests include the effects of social support, interparental conflict, and parenting practices on child adjustment.

Jedediah M. Bopp is research assistant to Elaine Blechman, PhD, at the University of Colorado at Boulder. His current interests include juvenile delinquency and psychopathology, and coordinating care in rural areas. He plans to pursue a doctoral degree in clinical psychology in the future.

Preston A. Britner, PhD, is an Associate Professor in the School of Family Studies at the University of Connecticut. He earned his PhD in developmental psychology at the University of Virginia. He is the editor of *The Journal of Primary Prevention* and serves on the editorial boards of *Child Abuse & Neglect* and the *Journal of Child & Family*

Studies. He was recognized as a 2003–2004 Teaching Fellow, the highest teaching honor at the University of Connecticut. He coauthored *Preventing Child Abuse and Neglect Through Parent Education* and has published in the areas of attachment relationships, child care, foster care, mentoring, and social policy and law affecting families.

Carolyn M. Callahan, PhD, a Professor in the Curry School of Education, University of Virginia, is also Associate Director of the National Research Center on the Gifted and Talented. She received her doctorate from the University of Connecticut. She teaches courses in the area of education of the gifted and is executive director of the Summer Enrichment Program. She has authored more than 125 articles, 25 book chapters, and monographs on the topics of creativity, the identification of gifted students, program evaluation, and the issues faced by gifted females. She received recognition as Outstanding Faculty Member in the Commonwealth of Virginia and was awarded the Distinguished Scholar Award from the National Association for Gifted Children and The Certificate of Merit from the Association for the Gifted.

Timothy A. Cavell, PhD, received his doctorate in clinical psychology from Louisiana State University. He is currently Professor and Director of Clinical Training at the University of Arkansas. His research focuses on parent- and mentor-based interventions for high-risk children and the prevention of delinquency and adolescent substance abuse. His work has been funded by the National Institute on Drug Abuse, the William C. Hogg Foundation, and the Texas Higher Education Coordinating Board. He has published more than 40 articles and chapters, as well as a book, *Working With Parents of Aggressive Children: A Practitioner's Guide* (2000), published by the American Psychological Association. He is a member of the American Psychological Association, the Society for Research in Child Development, the Association for the Advancement of Behavior Therapy, and the Society for Prevention Research.

Yarí Colón is currently a doctoral student in the Clinical-Community Psychology program at DePaul University in Chicago, Illinois. Her research focuses on the educational experiences of Latino adolescents. She is conducting her master's thesis on the roles of acculturation status and the economic value of education in students' academic performance. She also works as a research assistant on a project examining the role of natural mentoring relationships in Latino adolescents' academic achievement as well as during their transition from high school.

Shawn M. Coyne is a graduate student in the Clinical-Community Psychology program at the University of South Carolina. She has worked on the evaluation consulting/research team with Dr. Wandersman for a year and has presented at the American Evaluators' Association on the topic. She has jointly written two papers published in *The Community Psychologist* on the benefits of combining clinical and community psychology. In addition, she has jointly submitted an article on community organizing and advocacy as it relates to increasing the quality and quantity of mentoring programs.

Nancy Darling, PhD, is an Associate Professor of Psychology at Bard College. She received her doctorate in human development and family studies from Cornell University. Her research focuses on how adolescents influence and are influenced by relationships with parents, peers, and unrelated adults and how these different social spheres interact to change the course of individual development. During the last several years, her work has taken on two complimentary foci: adolescent socialization and the development of romantic relationships. The former work includes cross-cultural studies of the negotiation of adolescent autonomy in Chile, Italy, the Philippines, and the

United States. The latter work includes observational studies of adolescents' and adults' interactions with romantic partners.

Narelle Dawson, MSocSci, PGDipPsych(Clin), is a Consultant Clinical Psychologist responsible for mental health needs at Parentline Advocacy Services. Her clinical qualifications were earned at the University of Waikato. Currently, she also is working in partnership with the Australian Institute for Suicide Research and Prevention to design, monitor, and evaluate the National Suicide Prevention Strategy in Fiji. She has 23 years' experience in treating trauma following conflict, sexual abuse, and homicide within families and is an Australian by birth, a registered teacher, a pilot, and a mother of four daughters. She is completing a doctoral thesis at Massey University, investigating the outcomes for at-risk and suicidal youth on government welfare benefits.

Jennifer L. Duffy is a graduate student in the Clinical-Community Psychology program at the University of South Carolina. Some of her research interests include program evaluation, violence prevention, and positive youth development. She is a member of the evaluation consulting/research team at the University of South Carolina, and she has jointly submitted an article on community organizing and advocacy as it relates to increasing the quality and quantity of mentoring programs.

James G. Emshoff, PhD, is an Associate Professor of Psychology and Director of the Community Psychology Program at Georgia State University. He also founded and serves as Director of Research at EMSTAR Research, Inc., an evaluation and organizational services firm. He has received many honors, including the American Medical Association Substance Abuse Prevention Award. He has conducted evaluation research focused on substance abuse, violence, HIV/AIDS, child abuse, community collaboratives, mentoring, delinquency, and health promotion programs at the local, state, and national levels and provides technical assistance in prevention and evaluation to many organizations. He received his doctorate from Michigan State University.

Ian M. Evans, PhD, is Head of the School of Psychology at Massey University, where he teaches a graduate course on ethics in psychological practice. He earned his doctorate from the University of London. Before moving to New Zealand in 1995, he was Professor and Director of Clinical Training at SUNY–Binghamton, where he was involved in dropout prevention research in rural schools; see Evans, I. M. Cicchelli, T. Cohen, M. & Shapiro N. (Eds.). (1995). *Staying in school: Partnerships for educational change.* Baltimore, MD: Brookes. He has served as president of the New Zealand Psychological Society and is a fellow of the Royal Society of New Zealand.

Jennifer D. Foster, PhD, is a Postdoctoral Fellow at the University of Miami Child Protection Team. She received her doctorate in clinical-community psychology from Georgia State University and completed her clinical internship at the University of Miami Mailman Center for Child Development. Her research and clinical interests are in mentoring and youth development programs, and the impact of community and domestic violence and child abuse on children, families, and communities, particularly with recent immigrants. Recent publications have focused on youth development programs and the impact of community violence on urban adolescents.

Mark Griffiths, PhD, is Professor of Gambling Studies at the Nottingham Trent University. He received his doctorate in psychology from The University of Exeter (U.K.) and is internationally known for his work into gambling and gaming addictions. He has won three international awards for his gambling research but also researches into technological addictions and the psychology of the Internet. He has published more than 120 refereed research papers, 2 books, numerous book chapters and more than 350 other articles.

Jean Baldwin Grossman, PhD, is both Senior Vice President for Research at Public/Private Ventures and on the faculty of Princeton University's Woodrow Wilson School. She has coauthored several publications on mentoring including, *Making a Difference: An Impact Study of Big Brothers Big Sisters, Contemporary Issues in Mentoring,* and a series of academic papers with Jean Rhodes and her colleagues. She has spent her career evaluating social programs of all kinds. She currently is working on evaluating other mentoring programs and after-school initiatives. She received her PhD in economics from the Massachusetts Institute of Technology.

Mary Agnes Hamilton is a Senior Research Associate in Human Development at Cornell University and Director of the Cornell Youth and Work Program in the Family Life Development Center. Her research and program development focus on understanding and enhancing the quality of learning environments in the community, mentoring relationships between nonrelated adults and youth, youth involvement, and the transition to adulthood. She seeks to advance educational opportunities and challenges to enable all youth to gain character and competence. Her MAT is from Duke, CAT is from Harvard, and PhD is from Cornell.

Stephen F. Hamilton is Associate Provost for Outreach and Professor of Human Development at Cornell University and Codirector of the Family Life Development Center. He earned an EdD from Harvard in 1975. His research in adolescent development and education investigates the interaction of school, community, and work during the transition from adolescence to adulthood. It also grounds program and policy development, especially related to education, employment, and citizenship. His book, *Apprenticeship for Adulthood: Preparing Youth for the Future,* helped guide the School-to-Work Opportunities Act of 1994. He actively supports the work of educators, youth workers, and citizens engaged in community youth development.

John T. Harris is the President of Applied Research Consulting, a Virginia-based independent consulting firm specializing in program evaluation and instrument construction to support youth development programming. His research focuses on youth mentoring and violence prevention/social skills education. He has coauthored several surveys, including the Match Characteristics Questionnaire, the Youth Mentoring Survey, the Self-Reported Assessment of Behavior and Social Skills, and the Across Time Orientation Measure. He received his master's degree in human development and psychology from the Harvard Graduate School of Education.

Barton J. Hirsch, PhD, is Professor of Human Development and Social Policy at Northwestern University, where he also is on the faculty of the Institute for Policy Research and the Northwestern University/University of Chicago Joint Center for Policy Research. He received his doctorate from the University of Oregon. His research examines contexts of adolescent development, including parents, extended families, friendships, peer groups, school, and neighborhood settings. Over the past several years, he has been studying urban boys and girls clubs. His book on the initial phase of that research, *A Place to Call Home: After-School Programs for Urban Youth,* will be published by the American Psychological Association in 2005.

Anna Jory, MA, is a graduate student in the clinical training program at Massey University. She is a qualified teacher and has had extensive experience as an elementary school teacher. She earned her master's degree from Massey University. Her master's thesis research project investigated the use of cognitive-behavioral therapy principles in the treatment of drug addiction and substance abuse in teenagers. She is currently an intern at the Psychology Clinic at Massey University.

Thomas E. Keller, PhD, is an Assistant Professor in the School of Social Service Administration at the University of Chicago and a Faculty Associate with the Chapin Hall Center for Children. His current research, funded by The Spencer Foundation and the National Institute of Mental Health, focuses on the development and influence of youth mentoring relationships in Big Brothers Big Sisters school-based and community-based programs. Prior to earning his doctorate in social welfare at the University of Washington, he worked for several years with a Big Brothers Big Sisters affiliate in Seattle as a case manager, supervisor, and program director.

Christopher B. Keys, PhD, is Professor and Chair of the Psychology Department at DePaul University and Professor Emeritus at the University of Illinois at Chicago. He received his doctorate from the University of Cincinnati. He is past chair of the Council of Community Psychology Program Directors, past president of the Society for Community Research and Action, and is a fellow of the American Psychological Association and the Society for Community Research and Action. He is interested in research, theory, and action concerning the empowerment of people with disabilities and their families through education, advocacy, and social change. His most recent book is a coedited volume on participatory community research methods published by the American Psychological Association.

Jacqueline King is a student in the Human Services Psychology PhD Program of the University of Maryland Baltimore County, where she is a Meyerhoff Research Fellow. She received her master's degree in experimental psychology from Towson University, where she was awarded the 2002 Outstanding Psychology Graduate Student Award. Her research focuses on community mentoring programs, youth mentoring relationships, and intergroup relations evaluation. Her planned dissertation research will focus on an evaluation of My Sister's Circle, a mentoring program for at-risk Baltimore city girls entering middle school. The results of her master's thesis, *In-Group and Out-Group Evaluation by African American and European American College Students,* was presented at the Eastern Psychological Association Conference in April 2003.

Lisa Kraimer-Rickaby, MA, is a PhD candidate in the School of Family Studies at the University of Connecticut. She has been involved with a study of foster youth, state-sponsored, independent living services, including a One-on-One Mentoring program for youth in state custody in Connecticut.

Gabriel P. Kuperminc, PhD, is an Associate Professor in Community and Developmental Psychology at Georgia State University. His doctoral dissertation from the University of Virginia was recognized by the American Psychological Association, Division 27 Dissertation Award. He received postdoctoral training at Yale University. His major research interests are in the intersection of ethnicity and culture with adolescent development, social competence, and school- and community-based interventions to promote youth development. Recent publications have focused on cultural variations in developmental processes among ethnic minority and immigrant youth, risk and protective factors affecting adolescents' psychological adjustment, and youth development programs.

Robin M. Kyburg, MA, is a doctoral student in Educational Psychology with an Emphasis in Gifted Education at the University of Virginia. She was a social studies teacher in Grades 7–12 before moving to Europe, where her professional experiences were predominantly focused on serving as a specialist tutor of culturally and ethnically diverse children with learning disabilities in a variety of educational settings and subjects. Presently, she works as a research assistant at the National Research Center on the Gifted and Talented, focusing on the qualitative analysis in an ongoing research project on the Advanced Placement and International Baccalaureate programs, and as a continuing education instructor for Project LOGgED ON.

Simon Larose, PhD, is Professor of Educational Psychology at Université Laval (Québec City, Canada) and member of the Psychosocial Maladaptation Research Unit. He received his doctorate in psychology from Université Laval. His main fields of research and teaching are adolescent and young adult development, attachment, mentoring, school transitions, and academic adjustment. Between 1996 and 2002, he conducted an important study on the role of attachment in adolescent adjustment to mentoring relationships and to college. This research was aimed at gaining a better understanding of the antecedents, mechanisms, and outcomes of college-based mentoring. His current research program is concerned with understanding the mechanisms of school persistence in late adolescence and young adulthood.

Kristin Liabø is a Research Fellow in the Child Health Research and Policy Unit at City University, London. She earned an MSc degree from the London School of Economics and Political Science. She is currently working on the project *What Works for Children?* which looks at levers and barriers for implementing research in practice. Recent publications include briefing papers on effective interventions for the U.K. children's think tank, the National Children's Bureau, an article on mentoring in the *British Medical Journal,* and two pieces on evidence in *Archives of Disease in Childhood.* She is cowriting a chapter about using research in practice, to be published in an edited collection by the U.K. Health Development Agency.

Belle Liang, PhD, is an Assistant Professor of Psychology at Boston College and a licensed clinical psychologist. She received her degree in clinical psychology from Michigan State University in 1994. Her research focuses on developmental and cross-cultural perspectives of clinical and community intervention, especially mentoring relationships and programs with ethnic minorities and adolescents. She has also developed measures of mentoring qualities for use with diverse adults and youth.

Leonard LoSciuto, PhD, is the Director of the Institute for Survey Research at Temple University. He received his doctorate in 1966 from Purdue University. He is also Professor of Psychology at Temple University, teaching graduate and undergraduate courses in social psychology, statistics, research methods, and consumer behavior. His major research areas are survey research methodology, attitude and opinion measurement, and program evaluation. Within this methodological focus, he is especially interested in youth drug abuse research, including prevention program evaluation and consumption patterns. Numerous federal agencies have supported his work over the years, including various components of the National Institutes of Health, Substance Abuse and Mental Health Services Administration, Environmental Protection Agency, and National Science Foundation.

Patricia Lucas, PhD, worked on mentoring while a Research Officer in the Child Health Research and Policy Unit at City University, London. She is currently a lecturer in early childhood at the School for Policy Studies, University of Bristol, U.K. She is currently conducting a systematic review of infant size and growth, combining reviews of lay views and life course outcomes. She is also working with Australian colleagues on a systematic review of the effectiveness of nutrition interventions to reduce health inequalities. Her most recent publications are a series of effectiveness summaries for social care practitioners, including one-on-one mentoring, and a journal article on sleep strategies for children with Down's syndrome.

Colleen P. Maguire received her master's degree in psychology in 2002, and she is currently working on her doctorate degree in the Collaborative Program in Counseling Psychology at the University of Akron. She is also the current co-chair for the Student Affiliate Group of the Society of Counseling Psychology. Her primary research interests are in the scholarship of teaching, counselor supervision, professional issues, mentoring, and the interface of health and employment.

Kenneth I. Maton is Professor of Psychology and director of the Community-Social Psychology PhD Program in Human Services Psychology at University of Maryland, Baltimore County. He received his doctorate from the University of Illinois at Urbana-Champaign. His research focuses on empowering community settings, minority youth achievement, and the community psychology of religion. Specific mentoring-related research projects include an evaluation of Project RAISE, which included a faith-based mentoring component for at-risk youth, and a longitudinal evaluation of the Meyerhoff Scholars Program, a multifaceted academic support program for minority college students. His most recent book (coedited) is *Investing in Children, Youth, Families, and Communities: Strengths-Based Research and Policy* (publisher: American Psychological Association, 2003). He is past president of the Society for Community Research and Action (Community Psychology Division of the American Psychological Association) and serves on the editorial boards of *American Journal of Community Psychology, Analysis of Social Issues and Public Policy,* and *Journal of Community Psychology.*

Katherine E. McDonald, MA, is a doctoral candidate in Community & Prevention Research in the Department of Psychology at the University of Illinois at Chicago. Her research examines the socioecological experience of disability through the lenses of young adults who belong to multiple marginalized groups. She is interested in using research to promote the full community integration and empowerment of people with disabilities. Her most recent publications include reflections on how the processes of academic conferences reflect the strengths and struggles of participatory community research.

Hugh Miller, PhD, is Principal Lecturer in Psychology at Nottingham Trent University, U.K., where his main teaching and research interest is in how people develop and present identities on the Internet, and more generally in individuals' interaction with the material world, especially how we adjust socially to deal with new technologies. His first degree was in physiology and psychology from Oxford, and he received his doctorate in cognitive psychology from the University of Nottingham, some considerable time ago.

Michael J. Nakkula is the Marie and Max Kargman Assistant Professor of Human Development and Urban Education at the Harvard Graduate School of Education, where he serves as the codirector of the Risk and Prevention master's program. His research and writing focuses on developmental approaches to facilitating psychosocial and academic growth, including mentoring and social skills/conflict resolution programming. He is the primary author of the book, *Matters of Interpretation: Reciprocal Transformation in Therapeutic and Developmental Relationships With Youth* (1998). He received his doctorate in counseling and consulting psychology from the Harvard Graduate School of Education.

Phyllis Holditch Niolon, MA, is a doctoral student in Community Psychology at Georgia State University. She received her master's in psychology from Georgia State

University and her undergraduate degree from the University of Virginia. Her major research interests center on adolescent development and violence against women, and she has focused her thesis and dissertation work on adolescent dating aggression. Her most recent publication was a review of youth development programs involving volunteering and community service, and she is currently working on several publications of her research on adolescent dating aggression.

Lorraine Porcellini is the Study Direction/Sampling Coordinator at Temple University's Institute for Survey Research (ISR) and is chiefly responsible for the day-to-day functioning of the Sampling Department. She acts as liaison to all ISR departments to coordinate the sampling-based activities of members of each project team and to provide statistical support. Since 1985, she has been involved in a variety of projects in the fields of health, family functioning, drug and alcohol use, intrafamily violence, and program evaluation. Her primary professional activities include program evaluation design, implementation, and analysis; the development and implementation of sampling design and data collection procedures; and the calculation of noncompliance estimates, survey weights, and sampling errors.

Sharon G. Portwood, Associate Professor of Psychology at the University of Missouri–Kansas City, received her JD from the University of Texas School of Law in 1985. She received her PhD in psychology from the University of Virginia in 1996. She is the author of numerous articles and book chapters covering a range of topics, including law and policy responses to crimes committed by and against children, and mentoring. Her work has been presented both nationally and internationally. She has served as a consultant to state and not-for-profit agencies in regard to needs assessment and program development, implementation, and evaluation.

Michele M. Reiner, MSW, is Executive Director of Cool Girls, Inc. She is a graduate of Duke University and earned a master's degree in social work from Columbia University. Her professional career has focused on youth development and civic engagement, including work with the Atlanta Outward Bound Center and CityCares. She also has presented at numerous national and international conferences on topics such as: "Volunteering: A Bridge to Understanding Diversity," "Service Learning," and "Volunteering in the 21st Century."

Jean E. Rhodes, PhD, is a Professor of Psychology at the University of Massachusetts, Boston. She received her doctorate in clinical/community psychology from DePaul University. She has conducted a wide array of research studies that demonstrate both the impact of mentoring programs and the way in which programs can be structured to best serve youth. Her recent book, *Stand by Me: The Risks and Rewards of Mentoring Today's Youth* (Harvard University Press, 2002) provides a synthesis of the research on mentoring. She is author of a research column for the National Mentoring Partnership's Web site, www.mentoring.org. Rhodes is a fellow in the American Psychological Association and the Society for Research and Community Action, and a member of the John D. and Catherine T. MacArthur Foundation Research Network on Transitions to Adulthood.

Helen Roberts has been Professor of Child Health at City University since 2001, where she heads the Child Health Research and Policy Unit. Before that, she was Head of R&D with the U.K. children's charity Barnardo's. She works on inequalities in child health, evidence-based care for children, the gap between what we know and what we do, and methods of consulting children effectively. Her most recent book is *What Works for Children?* with Di McNeish and Tony Newman, published in 2002 by Open

University Books, and she is writing a book on systematic reviews with Mark Petticrew. She has a master's in industrial sociology with anthropology from the Université d'Aix-Marseille, France, and a DPhil from the University of Sussex.

Bernadette Sánchez is currently an Assistant Professor of Psychology at DePaul University in Chicago, Illinois. She received her PhD from the Community and Prevention Research program at the University of Illinois at Chicago. Her research has focused on the natural mentoring relationships and educational experiences of urban ethnic minority youth, particularly Latino adolescents. Bernadette has recently been examining the role of natural mentors in assisting youth in their transition from high school.

Laura A. Secrest, MS, is a doctoral student in Clinical Psychology at Georgia State University. She received her master's in psychology from Texas A&M University and began a predoctoral clinical internship at Saint John's Child and Family Development Center in Santa Monica, California, in September 2004. Her research interests include the impact of parenting and mentoring relationships on youth development and violence against women. Her most recent publication was an examination of the investigator-community collaboration in the development and implementation of a family-based HIV prevention program.

Naida Silverthorn, PhD, is a Research Coordinator at the Health Research and Policy Centers at the University of Illinois at Chicago as well as a Lecturer at Northeastern Illinois University. She completed her doctorate in clinical psychology from the University of Ottawa and worked in clinical practice with youth and families until accepting a postdoctoral research fellowship with Dr. David DuBois at the University of Illinois at Chicago in 2002. Her research interests are in the areas of adolescent self-esteem, positive youth development, and mentoring.

Cynthia L. Sipe, PhD, is an independent consultant who works with nonprofit youth organizations and school districts to evaluate programs and reform efforts. She earned her doctorate in sociology from Indiana University. She has conducted extensive research on mentoring programs, authoring or coauthoring several reports. Through her affiliation with Youth Development Strategies, Inc. (www.YDSI.org), a national nonprofit research, evaluation, and technical assistance organization that helps communities improve long-term outcomes for their youth, she assists program operators to assess the quality and effectiveness of their programs and improve service delivery to youth participants.

Anne-Marie Smith, PhD, received her doctoral degree in clinical psychology from Texas A&M University. She interned at the Morrison Center for Youth and Families in Portland, Oregon. She completed her postdoctoral studies with the Oregon Youth Authority working with juvenile offenders. Her clinical interests lie in the areas of forensic evaluations, adolescent and adult psychopathology, delinquency interventions, program development, and multicultural issues. She has research interests in the area of juvenile delinquency and mentoring interventions for youth. She is currently a clinical/forensic psychologist at the Oregon State Hospital and is a member of the American Psychological Association.

Renée Spencer, EdD, LICSW, is an Assistant Professor at the Boston University School of Social Work. She received her master's in social work from the University of Texas at Austin and her doctorate in human development and psychology from the Harvard Graduate School of Education. Her research focuses on youth mentoring relationships, adolescent development, and gender. Recent publications include "Growth-Promoting Relationships Between Youth and Adults: A Focus Group Study," to be published in *Families in Society,* and "Someone to Watch Over Me: Mentoring Programs in the After-School Lives of Children and Adolescents," with Jean Rhodes, in *Organized Activities as Contexts of Development: Extracurricular Activities, After School, and Community Programs,* edited by J. L. Mahoney, J. Eccles, and R. Larson (2005).

Mariano R. Sto. Domingo is currently a student in the Human Services Psychology PhD Program in Community Social Psychology at the University of Maryland, Baltimore County. He is a faculty member on study leave from the Department of Psychology, University of the Philippines. He earned his master's degrees in international relations and social psychology from the International University of Japan and University of the Philippines, respectively. He was also an exchange student at the Johns Hopkins University School of Advanced International Studies in Washington, DC. He is past vice president of the Pambansang Samahan sa Sikolohiyang Pilipino (National Association for Philippine Psychology).

Arthur A. Stukas, PhD, is a Lecturer in Social Psychology in the School of Psychological Science at La Trobe University, in Melbourne, Australia. He received his doctorate from the University of Minnesota. His research interests focus on the personal and situational factors that underlie value-expression and goal-directed behavior, including such varied behaviors as volunteerism and community involvement, organ and tissue donation, principled stands against prejudice, and active disconfirmation of erroneous interpersonal expectations. He recently coedited (with Michelle Dunlap) an issue of the *Journal of Social Issues* on "Community Involvement: Theoretical Approaches and Educational Initiatives."

Chris Tanti is a PhD candidate in the School of Psychological Science at La Trobe University, in Melbourne, Australia. Originally trained as an occupational therapist, she has worked with children and adolescents in a variety of intellectual disability services and mental health services. Her current research interests include adolescent development and psychopathology, the formation of identity during childhood and adolescence, and adolescent peer group behavior. Her PhD research is investigating the development of social identity in adolescence.

George M. Tarabulsy is a graduate of Université Laval (PhD) and McGill University (MA) and currently is Professor in the School of Psychology at Université Laval (Quebec City, Canada). He is also research fellow with the Québec Fund for Cultural and Social Research and member of the Psychosocial Maladaptation Research Unit. His research interests focus on the connections between socioemotional and cognitive development in populations at high psychosocial risk, and on the development of effective family and community-based intervention strategies. His recent work has focused on parent-child attachment relationships as mediators of the association between psychosocial risk and the development of adaptation.

Andrea S. Taylor, PhD, is the Director of Youth Development and Family Support at Temple University's Center for Intergenerational Learning. She received her doctorate from Temple University. She is the developer of Across Ages, an intergenerational mentoring program designated as an evidence-based model and listed in the National Registry of Effective Program Practices. Her work in recent years has been supported by SAMHSA and the DOE and has focused on intergenerational mentoring as an approach to positive youth development and the prevention of school failure, substance abuse, and early or repeat teen pregnancies. She is also a Senior Research Associate at Temple University's Institute for Survey Research and is involved in projects addressing issues of civic engagement across the life span, especially older adults. She provides consultation, training, and technical assistance in intergenerational mentoring and substance abuse prevention to private, nonprofit organizations, universities, school districts, federal, and state agencies.

Gary Walker is president of Public Private Ventures (P/PV), a national nonprofit organization whose mission is to improve the effectiveness of social policies and programs, especially in the areas of at-risk youth and workforce development. P/PV does research and evaluation work in both these areas. He also serves on the boards of directors of the William T. Grant Foundation and the Hasbro Foundation, and on the Aspen Institute's Roundtable on Community Change. He speaks and writes frequently on social policy issues, including *The Policy Climate for Early Adolescent Initiatives* (2001, Philadelphia: P/PV). He received his law degree from Yale Law School.

Abraham Wandersman, PhD, is a Professor of Psychology at the University of South Carolina–Columbia. He received his PhD from Cornell University in the following areas of specialization: social psychology, environmental psychology, and social organization and change. He performs research and program evaluation on citizen participation in community organizations and coalitions and on interagency collaboration. He is a coauthor of *Prevention Plus III,* a coeditor of *Empowerment Evaluation: Knowledge and Tools for Self Assessment and Accountability,* and author of many other books and articles. In 1998, he received the Myrdal Award for Evaluation Practice from the American Evaluation Association. In 2000, he was elected President of Division 27 of the American Psychological Association (Community Psychology), the Society for Community Research and Action. In 2004, he coauthored the RAND publication of *Getting To Outcomes–2004: Promoting Accountability Through Methods and Tools for Planning, Implementation, and Evaluation.*

Susan G. Weinberger, Ed.D, is the founder and President of the Mentor Consulting Group based in Norwalk, Connecticut. She was a pioneer in developing school-based mentoring in the early 1980s and served as Director of the Norwalk Mentor Program for 12 years. Her model has been replicated in 45 states, Bermuda, and Canada. Susan is chair, Public Policy Council, MENTOR/National Mentoring Partnership. She consults to the Office of Juvenile Justice and Delinquency Prevention Programs, Department of Labor, Housing and Urban Development, Center for Substance Abuse Prevention, Big Brothers Big Sisters of Canada, and Governor's Prevention Partnership in Connecticut. Her publications include the *My Mentor & Me* series, *Guidebook to Mentoring, Manual for Mentors,* and *Strengthening Native Community Commitment through Mentoring.* She received her doctorate from the University of Bridgeport, College of Business and Public Management.

Vivian Wong is a doctoral student in Human Development and Social Policy at Northwestern University. Her research interests include the role of after-school programs on adolescent development and determinants of relationship quality among unmarried, cohabiting parents. Prior to coming to Northwestern University, she administered ScienceQuest, an after-school program funded by the National Science Foundation. As policy researcher for the Sexuality Information Education Council of the United States (SIECUS), Wong examined how federally funded abstinence education programs were implemented in classroom and after-school contexts.

Brian T. Yates, PhD, is a tenured Full Professor in the Department of Psychology at American University in Washington, DC, where he began as an Assistant Professor in 1976, following receipt of his PhD in psychology from Stanford University. He has published 5 books and 53 articles and book chapters. Most of his publications apply cost-effectiveness or cost-benefit analysis to the systematic evaluation and improvement of mental health and other human services. His manual for helping substance abuse treatments measure, report, and improve cost, cost-effectiveness, and cost-benefit was published in 1999 by the National Institute on Drug Abuse.

Marc A. Zimmerman, PhD, is Professor of Health Behavior and Health Education in the School of Public Health, Psychology, and the Combined Program in Education and Psychology at the University of Michigan. He received his doctorate in psychology from the University of Illinois at Urbana-Champaign. He is director of the Prevention Research Center of Michigan and the Youth Violence Prevention Center and principal investigator for the Flint Adolescent Study, a longitudinal study designed to investigate adolescent assets and resources. His primary research interests include the application and development of empowerment theory and the study of adolescent health and resiliency.